Africa South of the Sahara
LANGUAGE FAMILIES

TROPIC OF CANCER

Arabic

Tuareg

Tubu

Arabic

Wolof

Fulani

Songhai

Hausa Kanuri

Kordofanian

Bambara

Mossi
Gur

Sara

Amharic

Somali

Fon

Akan Ewe Yoruba

Gbaya

Oromo

Igbo

Efik

Sango

Tigrinya

Ewando

Mongo

Luo

Fang

Ganda

Maasai

Gikuyu

EQUATOR

Lingala

Kinyarwanda
Kirundi

Kongo

Luba

Swahili

Chokwe

Bemba

Mbundu

Chichewa

!Kung

Shona

Nama

Sotho

Nguni

Malagasy

LANGUAGES

NILO-SAHARAN

AFRO-ASIATIC

NIGER-KORDOFANIAN
(Including BANTU)

KHOISAN

MALAYO-POLYNESIAN

0°   20°   40°

ENCYCLOPEDIA OF
AFRICA
SOUTH OF THE SAHARA

ENCYCLOPEDIA OF
AFRICA
SOUTH OF THE SAHARA

JOHN MIDDLETON
EDITOR IN CHIEF

J. F. ADE. AJAYI
GORAN HYDEN
JOSEPH C. MILLER
WILLIAM A. SHACK
MICHAEL WATTS
EDITORIAL BOARD

VOLUME 3

CHARLES SCRIBNER'S SONS

Macmillan Library Reference USA
SIMON & SCHUSTER MACMILLAN
NEW YORK

SIMON & SCHUSTER AND PRENTICE HALL INTERNATIONAL
LONDON   MEXICO CITY   NEW DELHI   SINGAPORE   SYDNEY   TORONTO

Copyright © 1997 Charles Scribner's Sons

An imprint of Simon & Schuster Macmillan
1633 Broadway
New York, NY 10019

Library of Congress Cataloging-in-Publication Data

Encyclopedia of Africa south of the Sahara / John Middleton, editor in chief.
    p. cm.
    Includes bibliographical references and index.
    ISBN 0-684-80466-2 (set : alk. paper). — ISBN 0-684-80467-0 (v. 1
: alk. paper). — ISBN 0-684-80468-9 (v. 2 : alk. paper). —
ISBN 0-684-80469-7 (v. 3 : alk. paper). — ISBN 0-684-80470-0
(v. 4 : alk. paper).
    1. Africa, Sub-Saharan—Encyclopedias. I. Middleton, John, 1921–
    .
DT351.E53   1997
967'.003—dc21   97-31364
                                                           CIP

15 14 13 12 11 10 9 8 7 6 5 4 3 2 1

PRINTED IN THE UNITED STATES OF AMERICA

ENCYCLOPEDIA OF
AFRICA
SOUTH OF THE SAHARA

USING THE ENCYCLOPEDIA

THIS ENCYCLOPEDIA contains 3 introductory essays, 878 separate articles, and 3 appendixes. Many subjects are clustered together in *composite entries*, which may comprise articles on several regions, periods, or genres. Thus, "Literature" embraces sixteen separate articles on the various language groups, while "Travel and Exploration" has five parts in chronological order.

THE COUNTRIES OF MODERN AFRICA each receive extensive treatment. For most nations, the composite consists of (1) Geography and Economy, with map and statistical table; (2) History and Government; and (3) Peoples and Cultures. In some cases, comparable coverage is compressed into a single entry. All country entries focus on the post-independence era. Earlier regional and colonial history may be explored under such headings as "Southern Africa" or "Colonial Policies and Practice: British (etc.)," as indicated in the cross-references. There is also a long master narrative under "History of Africa."

CROSS-REFERENCES. *See also* references following an entry call attention to related articles of particular or more general relevance. Cross-referencing is selective: obvious sources of information (such as most country, city, and ethnic-group entries) are not listed. For full cross-referencing consult the index.

ETHNIC GROUPS are treated selectively in some seventy-three brief entries. A fuller list of African peoples, with concordance of their multiple ethnolinguistic names, appears in Appendix C. The cultures and histories of the larger groups may be pursued in the relevant regional and national entries.

BIOGRAPHIES are limited to reasonably well-documented historical figures, supplemented by a selection of living persons. Emphasis has been placed on indigenous Africans rather than colonial figures. Further biographical information may be accessed through the index.

MEASUREMENTS generally appear in metric form, following African usage. English measures are occasionally provided for convenience. Following are approximate English equivalents for the most common metric units:

$$1 \text{ centimeter} = 0.39 \text{ inches}$$
$$1 \text{ kilometer} = 0.62 \text{ miles}$$
$$1 \text{ hectare} = 2.5 \text{ acres}$$
$$1 \text{ square kilometer} = 0.39 \text{ square miles}$$
$$1 \text{ kilogram} = 2.2 \text{ pounds}$$
$$1 \text{ liter} = 2.1 \text{ pints}$$

SCHOLARSHIP is cited in customized bibliographies following most articles and is surveyed broadly under "Research and Knowledge" for African contributions to learning and in Appendix A for the state of African studies outside Africa.

ENCYCLOPEDIA OF AFRICA SOUTH OF THE SAHARA

LITERATURE–RÉUNION

LITERATURE

*[The **Overview** is followed by articles on these African literatures: **Afrikaans, Ethiopic, Hausa, Islamic Literature** (in a variety of languages), **Somali, Southern African Languages, Swahili,** and **Yoruba.** There follow treatments of **Anglophone Literature** in Western, Eastern, and South Africa and of **Francophone** and **Lusophone Literature.** The section concludes with an article on **Women Writers.** Of related interest is the very next entry, **Literature and Verbal Arts.**]*

OVERVIEW OF LITERATURE IN AFRICAN LANGUAGES

The outburst of African creative writing in European languages in the twentieth century has tended to deflect attention from the fact that black Africa has been producing written works for many centuries. Few people, however cultured, are aware that the writing technique was put to literary uses in seventh-century Ethiopia, that is, about the time English literature was arising in Anglo-Saxon Northumbria.

Ethiopia

During the first millennium B.C.E., migrants and invaders from the kingdom of Saba (Sheba), in southern Arabia, brought their Semitic script to the kingdom of Aksum in northern Ethiopia. This was used only for epigraphic inscriptions until the fourth century, when Aksum was converted to Christianity by Alexandrian monks who translated the Bible from the Greek into the local language, Geʿez. No early manuscripts survive, but it is known that by the late seventh century the whole Bible was available in Geʿez.

In the following centuries, the center of power shifted southward to the kingdom of Shoa (Shewa), whose language was Amharic. By 1200 C.E., Geʿez was no longer spoken, but it remained the cultural tongue of the realm. In fact, what is known as the golden age of Geʿez literature took place in the fourteenth and fifteenth centuries. The reign of Amda Tseyon I (1314–1344) witnessed the emergence of original Ethiopian writing, both religious and secular; it included legendary history and prose chronicles as well as saints' lives and the qenè, a form of metaphorical devotional poetry.

A first attempt also was made to produce literary writing in the vernacular, Amharic, as the rulers encouraged the composition and diffusion of praise poems known as "imperial songs." This was a short-lived experiment, and Geʿez remained the language of liturgy and culture, the only one to be written, until the end of the nineteenth century.

The early growth of Amharic literature was a by-product of the determination of Emperor Menilek II (1844–1913) and his successor, Haile Sellassie (1892–1975), to modernize the country, to promote the development of an educated elite, and to unify the polyethnic, multilingual population as resistance to Western imperialism. After a period that lasted until the Italian conquest (1936), the liberation of Ethiopia (1941) ushered in the flowering of Amharic drama and prose fiction while a few younger authors began to write in English.

Islam

Arabic-Islamic influence was the second element in the spread of written literature in sub-Saharan Africa. Although it took widely divergent forms in the eastern and western parts of the continent, its genesis was characterized at first by the introduction of the Arabic script and the prevalence of religious inspiration.

At an early date, close relations with Arabia and Persia had created a hybrid culture with its own language, Swahili, along the coast of the Indian Ocean. We do not know when the Arabic script began to be used to transcribe this Bantu tongue; the oldest preserved manuscripts date to the eighteenth century. They comprise a vast amount of devotional and narrative poetry; the bulk of the

Aksumite funerary inscription from Melazo.
Modern Ethiopic writing derives from this script.
COURTESY J. LEELANT

latter is made up of *tendi*, long epics focusing mainly on biblical episodes and incidents in the life of the Prophet.

At the beginning of the nineteenth century, political disputes between the local rulers and those of Oman fostered the appearance of secular writing in the form of political-polemical poetry. Further diversification appeared in the late nineteenth century after Protestant missionaries had introduced the roman script, and the German and British conquests had provided new subject matter. Christian themes and episodes in the colonial wars were treated in the *tendi* tradition; oral folktales were committed to writing and modern-type fiction, poetry, and drama were inaugurated. Since independence, writers in Tanzania have produced a vast amount of writing in Swahili, now the official language of the country, whereas most writers in Uganda and especially Kenya have turned to English.

The process was different in west Africa, whose commercial and cultural contacts were chiefly with Morocco and Egypt. From the middle of the eleventh century, Muslims conquered the Sahelian empires of Ghana, Mali, and Songhai, spreading the Arabic language and script. Timbuktu became an important center of Islamic learning, where the written art flourished from the fifteenth to the seventeenth century in the form of historical chronicles and treatises dealing with Muslim theology, law, science, and medicine.

After a period of decay, an Islamic revival and the need to propagate the reform movement impelled its leaders increasingly to use vernacular languages written in the Arabic script. This signaled the beginning of literary writing in Fulani and Hausa in present-day northern Nigeria and, somewhat later, Wolof in Senegal. This mainly religious trend declined during the twentieth century under the impact of the colonial educational system: only the Hausa have maintained a steady flow of creative writing, mostly in the roman script.

Europe

European colonization spread the writing skill throughout sub-Saharan Africa. During a humanitarian prologue at the end of the eighteenth century, Western-type literacy was initiated in Sierra Leone and Liberia under the aegis of antislavery movements led by Protestant churches; their primary purpose was to propagate Christianity. In all areas under British administration, education was in the hands of Protestant missionaries who set out to make the Scriptures available in the vernacular languages. In the course of the nineteenth century, many African languages thus acquired a written form, English hymns and such edifying tales as *The Pilgrim's Progress* were translated and printed on local missionary presses, and gifted converts were encouraged to compose hymns and fiction of their own. Among the Muslim Hausa and Swahili, the Roman script began to supersede Arabic in the transcription of vernaculars. By the end of the century, there was an embryonic corpus of indigenous literary works in several African languages: Hausa, Igbo, and Yoruba in Nigeria; Xhosa, Sotho, and Zulu in southern Africa; Swahili in east Africa. Each of these now possesses a genuine literary history.

Later in the nineteenth century, colonial administrators became aware of the need for a literate African elite. Literature bureaus were set up in most British-controlled territories, often providing a decisive impetus for vernacular literature. In South Africa, one of the paradoxical results of apartheid was that the Bantu Education Act of 1953 fostered the quantitative growth of the written output while at the same time ensuring a distinct lowering in its quality. As the twentieth century neared its end, most of the countries that had been part of the British Empire had produced a substantive body of creative writing in both the vernaculars and English.

History followed a different course in areas ruled by the Romance language–speaking nations, chiefly France and Portugal but also Spain and Italy. Here, written use of the vernaculars was effectively prevented in the name of a concept of assimilation that viewed the European languages as the only medium capable of ensuring the educated elite's access to "civilization." Despite many African leaders' advocacy of "authenticity" since independence, there is little indication that this situation is likely to change in the foreseeable future. If some creative writing is produced in Wolof and in Malagasy, that is due to Islamic influence in Senegal and to British influence prior to the French conquest of Madagascar (now Malagasy Republic) in 1896. And the peculiar international status of the Congo (now Zaire) in the early days of Belgian colonization allowed a written literature to emerge in the Kongo language.

BIBLIOGRAPHY

Andrzejewski, B. W., S. Pilaszewicz, and W. Tyloch, eds. *Literatures in African Languages: Theoretical Issues and Sample Surveys.* Cambridge, 1985.

Gérard, Albert S. *Four African Literatures: Xhosa, Sotho, Zulu, Amharic.* Berkeley, 1971.

———. *African-Language Literatures: An Introduction to the Literary History of Sub-Saharan Africa.* Washington, D.C., 1981.

———. *Contexts of African Literature.* Amsterdam, 1990.

ALBERT S. GÉRARD

See also **Language Use; Languages and History; Publishing; Writing Systems.**

AFRIKAANS

For two centuries after the first arrival of Dutch colonists in 1652, a new creolized language, widely spoken but largely unwritten, developed in the double isolation of Africa from Europe and of the hinterland from Cape Town. The main impulse for its development was the attempt of indigenous peoples and imported slaves to speak the language of their Dutch masters. From the time of permanent British occupation (1806), Afrikaans was marginalized and featured in English and Dutch writings largely for comic effect. In 1875 a group of white "patriots" in the Cape Province began to promote written Afrikaans to foster national consciousness. Much of the early work was crude and derivative, yet in the poetry of Eugène Marais (1871–1936) and Frederick Louis Leipoldt (1880–1947) there is an assertion of individual talent inspired by the local scene and, in the case of Marais, by African orature.

By the 1930s a new generation of poets, comprising notably Nicolaas Petrus van Wyk Louw (1906–1970) and Elisabeth Eybers (1915–), advanced the liberation of the individual consciousness in an aggressive aestheticism still inspired by European models. Gradually, a postcolonial and predominantly white identity was announced by Diederik Johannes Opperman (1914–1985) and, ironically, by a naturalized foreigner, Peter Blum (1925–1990).

Drama and fiction oscillated between uneasy romanticism (Christiaan Maurits van den Heever, 1902–1957) and shallow naturalism (Jochem van Bruggen, 1881–1957), rising only rarely to a grasp of moral issues (Jan van Melle, 1887–1953). After the Second World War, fiction turned more toward the experience of the urbanized individual, and with Jan Sebastian Rabie (b. 1920) leading the renewal, novelists like Etienne Leroux (1922–1989), André Brink (b. 1935), and Chris Barnard (b. 1939); the dramatist Bartho Smit (1924–1986); and the exiled poet Breyten Breytenbach (b. 1939) opened Afrikaans literature to foreign influences ranging from existentialism to Zen. This precipitated a collision with the conservative establishment.

In the 1970s, following skirmishes with censorship that had won them the support of a large young readership, these writers, as well as John Miles (b. 1938), began to focus more uncompromisingly on the South African experience in the mounting struggle against apartheid. The literature also became more diversified, and several female writers rose to prominence (Elsa Joubert, b. 1922; Wilma Stockenström, b. 1933; Antjie Krog, b. 1952).

With the gradual dismantling of apartheid from 1990, writers have begun to move beyond the constraints of politics to revisit history (Brink;

Joubert; Karel Schoeman, b. 1939), redefine genres (Koos Prinsloo, 1957–1995), and explore feminism (Jeanne Goosen, b. 1940) or forms of postmodernism (Etienne van Heerden, b. 1954). And the almost exclusively white literature in which a Coloured poet like Adam Small (b. 1936) was a rarity is now restored to voices previously silenced (e.g., Abraham Phillips, b. 1945).

BIBLIOGRAPHY

Coetzee, Ampie. "Literature and Crisis: One Hundred Years of Afrikaans Literature and Afrikaner Nationalism." In *Rendering Things Visible: Essays on South African Literary Culture,* edited by Martin Trump. Athens, Ohio, 1990.

Kannemeyer, J. C. *Geskiedenis van die Afrikaanse Literatuur.* 2 vols. Pretoria, 1978–1983.

ANDRÉ BRINK

See also **Afrikaner Republics; Cape Dutch Settlements; Language Use.**

ETHIOPIC

Ethiopic literature is basically religious. It is written in the Ge'ez language, which has served the country, especially the Ethiopian Orthodox Church, since the introduction of Christianity in the fourth century. Ge'ez would have disappeared long ago, like many other extinct Ethiopic languages, had it not been for the Christian religion. Although Ethiopia is a country of many languages, until the nineteenth century the local literature flourished almost exclusively in Ge'ez. A literary language, Ge'ez is no longer spoken, but no one is sure when it ceased to be a spoken language—it may have been in the tenth century.

Characteristics of Ethiopic Literature

The content of Ethiopic literature is basically religious because even the royal chronicles, intended to be records of the national events that took place at and around the mobile royal court, have religious meaning. Historical incidents (glorious victories, suppression of revolts, disgraceful defeats) happen not because the king or any agent makes them happen but because God, using the agent, wants them to happen.

A considerable part of the literature consists of translations that came mostly from Coptic (Christian) Arabic. From its beginning in the fourth century to the middle of the twentieth, the Ethiopian Orthodox Church was closely related to the Coptic Church of Alexandria. Until 1951, the spiritual head of the church, the metropolitan (*abun*), was a Copt (Egyptian). Knowledge from and about the Christian world came to Ethiopia via the Coptic Church and Ethiopian monasteries in Egypt and Palestine. But by using the Ge'ez language and locally composed liturgical materials, as well as music by native musicians, the Ethiopian Orthodox Church has preserved its cultural independence throughout its history.

Contribution of Ethiopic Literature

Ge'ez literature has preserved a relatively high number of apocryphal, especially inter-Testamental, works no longer extant in other languages. Biblical scholars and church historians believe that even though such works are excluded from the biblical canon in the West, their contribution to the understanding of Christianity is uniquely significant. The Book of Enoch (*Henok*), the Book of Jubilees (*Kufale*), the Ascension of Isaiah (*'Irgete Isayiyyas*), and the Synodicon (*Sinodos*) are considered to be the most important of these works.

Ethiopians' interest in writing down the hagiographic stories (*gedl,* "contending" with the evil spirit) of their saints produced a class of literature of great value for the study of the social and political history of the Horn of Africa. The "contendings" include reports of clashes between the spiritual and political leaders on questions of national significance, and between Christianity and African religions.

The Aksumite Period: Fourth to Tenth Centuries

The literature of the Aksumite period is, primarily, from foreign sources. The very first books the new church received from the Mediterranean world through the Greek language include the Gospel of St. Matthew (some believe the Gospel of John) and the Psalter. These must have been followed by the other Gospels and the remaining books of the Bible. Scholars are more or less certain that the *Physiologus,* a collection of fables; the *Regulae Pachomii,* the monastic rules of Pachomius, the Egyptian monk who started communal Christian monastic life in the fourth century; the *Oerilos,* a collection of Christological treatises by early church fathers; the Ascension of Isaiah; *The Paralipomena of Baruch;* and *The Shepherd of Hermas* were translated into Ge'ez during this period.

The coming to Ethiopia of the Pachomian rules during this period indicates that Ethiopian Christianity was shaped by monastic principles from the beginning. Some scholars suggest that the translation of the *Oerilos* into Ge'ez so early must have been inspired by the need to defend the young church from heresies of the time, especially the Christological formula adopted at the Council of Chalcedon (451), defining the mode of the union of the divine and human natures in Christ.

This period is most noted for St. Yared's laying the foundation of the Ethiopian hymnody. His composition of hymns in honor of God and the saints form the nucleus of the *diggwa*, the church's antiphonary. Yared is credited not only with the composition of the first hymns of the *diggwa*, which has grown huge in the course of time, but also with supplying three types of melodies for them.

The Early Solomonic Dynasty: 1270–1434

No work of any significance from the decline of Aksum in the tenth century to the rise of the so-called Solomonic dynasty in 1270 has come to light, even though a spiritually dynamic dynasty, the Zagwe, ruled during part of the period (1137–1270). In stark contrast, the times of Yikunno Amlak (who established or restored the Solomonic dynasty in 1270) and his descendants was highly conducive to the flourishing of literature.

Metropolitan Selama II (1348–1388) brought with him from Egypt a significant collection of religious books used by the Coptic Church. These, which included Arabic versions of some rituals and a number of hagiographical accounts of the desert fathers and of the Diocletian martyrs, were translated into Ge'ez at the metropolitan's palace and at the monasteries of Hayq Istifanos in Amhara (modern Welo) and Debre Libanos in Shewa.

One of the first works to appear during this period was the *Kibre negest* (Glory of the Kings, written in 1314/1322), a legend by means of which the Solomonic dynasty of Ethiopia acquired its legitimacy. According to the legend, Makidda (the Queen of Sheba or the South—"Ethiopia," I Kings 10:1–13, and Matthew 12:42) visited Jerusalem to admire the king's wisdom, converted to Judaism, and bore a son to Solomon. When the son, Menilek I, reached maturity, he visited his father. On his return to Sheba, Solomon sent with him priests and people of the law to help him set up a "Jewish" state. His mother abdicated in favor of Menilek, who brought back the Ark of the Covenant, which he and his new entourage had stolen.

Ethiopians give this story and the fact that the Jews have rejected Christ, whereas Ethiopians have accepted him as the expected Messiah, as strong proofs that they have replaced the Old Israel as the new chosen people of God. Indeed, the faithful practice circumcision, observe the dietary rules (on what is kosher), and honor Saturday as the Sabbath, all as prescribed in the Jewish scriptures of the Old Testament.

The *Kibre negest* was widely known in Ethiopia as far back as the sixth century; and the claim of the translator(s) of this work from Arabic into Ge'ez that it was suppressed during the non-Solomonic Zagwe Dynasty is plausible. But the puzzle—why the work, which serves a non-Arabic cultural milieu, was originally composed in Arabic—has not been resolved. Its Ge'ez version appeared only during the reign of Amde Siyon (1314–1344). Was there a time in the history of Ethiopia when Ethiopian scholars—at least in Egypt and Palestine—used Arabic as their written language? If that was the case, at least some of the works translated from Arabic that are almost exclusively of interest to Ethiopia may have been composed by Ethiopians.

It was also probably during this period that the synaxary of the Coptic Church was translated from Christian Arabic into Ge'ez. The work is a collection of short biographies of the saints of the universal church (until 451) with notices for the feasts and fasts of the year. Historically valuable biographies of Ethiopian saints were later inserted in the collection. The stories are read in church on the days the saints and the feasts are commemorated. Some scholars believe that the present Coptic synaxary is a retrotranslation from Ge'ez.

During the reign of Emperor Dawit (David) I (1381–1411), a collection of about thirty-three miracles of Mary were translated into Ge'ez. The stories, originally in Arabic, came from the Mediterranean world, especially France, Spain, Egypt, Byzantium, and Syria.

Two prominent men of literature, Abba Giyorgis of Gasicha or Segla (in modern Welo) and another scholar, whose name and region we do not know, belong to this period. Both wrote theological treatises in the form of sermons to be read when celebrating the major feasts of the church. *The Book of the Mystery (Mesihafe mistir)* and *The Interpretation of Divinity (Fikkare melekot)*, expositions of Orthodox Christology and refutations of heresies; *The Book of Hours (Mesihafe se'atat)*, for the twenty-four hours of the day; *The Lord Reigneth (Egzi'abher negse)*, a collection of hymns to the saints; and *The Harp of Praise (Arganone widdase)*, praises of Mary, were written by Abba Giyorgis. The anonymous author calls himself Ritu'a Haymanot, "the Man of the Orthodox Faith," a nom de plume that is also the

Page from the *Kibre Hemamat*, a Lenten prayer
book, written in Ge'ez approximately six
hundred years ago. THE NATIONAL LIBRARY OF
ETHIOPIA

title of his collection of sermons. Ritu'a Haymanot's
theological doctrine that no Christian will go to
hell is interesting and controversial.

The Period of Zara Ya'iqob: 1434–1468

No single author of traditional Ethiopian literature is known to have produced as much as Zara
Ya'iqob did. His extraordinary devotion to the Virgin and his determination to keep the church and
his empire united drove him to become a prolific
writer. First, he substantially increased his father's
collection of the miracles of Mary (*Te'ammire Mar-
yam*) by importing more stories and composing
new ones.

Zara Ya'iqob's strong devotion to Mary and his
firm view on the meaning of the Trinity had created schism (rather than unity) in the church. His
other teachings—(1) that God has an image (a form
that looks human) and (2) that the Trinity is like
three suns with one light, as opposed to one sun
with three attributes (disk, light, and heat, repre-

senting the Father, the Son, and the Holy Spirit,
respectively)—were strongly resisted by the theologians of the time. They especially refused to define the image of God, "whom no man has ever
seen" (John 1:18).

The treatises that the emperor wrote (in the form
of homilies and exhortations) include *The Book of
Light (Mesihafe birhan)*, the light being Christ, whose
knowledge reveals that Saturday is the Sabbath
and magic is evil; *The Book of the Nativity (Mesihafe
milad)*, condemning those who deny the incarnation of God; *The Sword of the Trinity (Seyfe sillase)*
and *The Epistle of Humanity (Tomare tisbi't)*, both
against the practice of magic; *The Glorification of the
Beloved (Sibhate fiqur)*, a special prayer to Jesus for
the time of tribulation; *The Lord Reigneth (Egzi'abher
negse)*, hymns for the commemoration of the saints;
The Revelation of the Miracle (Ra'iye te'ammir), on
Christian baptism, the virginity of Mary, almsgiv-
ing, and the harmony of the canonical books; and
homilies about the angels to be read on the days
dedicated to them.

The translation of the account of the Arab conquest of Egypt by John, bishop of Nikiu, *Yohannis
medebbir* (ca. 690), now preserved only in Ge'ez,
must have taken place at the end of this period
(1602). Historians say that this unique Ethiopic
source has made it possible for them to write a
history of the Arab conquest of Egypt.

The civil wars of the sixteenth century and the
assault of the Muslims from the east on the Christians and their institutions, followed by the Oromo
(Galla) migration into the interior of Ethiopia, not
only brought a suspension of literary activity but
also did great damage to what had been achieved.
Manuscripts buried at that time for their protection
are still occasionally recovered as farmers plow the
land. Moving the state's capital from Shewa to
Gonder for safety in the late sixteenth century provided a better chance for resuming literary activity.

The Gonderite Period: 1607–1755

Ethiopians are great lovers of poetry. The hymns
of the *diggwa* (the antiphonary) and the two collections titled *Egzi'aber negse (The Lord Reigneth)* are
all poetic. In the course of time, the synaxary entries
and the hundreds of miracles of Mary have each
been supplied, at their conclusions, with a hymn
of about five rhyming lines. A special class of poems
called *qinie* is used primarily to praise God and the
saint of the day during a church service. They have
to be new hymns designed for the occasion and
composed by one of the clergy on that day or the
day before. This means that almost every day, in

each major church, an individual *qinie* poem is sung—freshly composed for that particular day, following Psalms 96:1 and 98:1, "O Sing unto the Lord a new song." A *qinie* poem cannot be used more than once. Some scholars have published collections of the most memorable ones. Although the practice is very old, *qinie* gained popularity only during the Gonderite period of 1607–1755, and since then has been used to eulogize heroes and flatter authorities.

Starting at a time still unknown, the composition of special poetic hymns called *melkiʿ,* to greet and praise the glorious and miraculous parts of the body of a saint (of angels as well as of humans), has greatly enriched Geʿez literature. This genre reached its peak during the Gonderite period.

The several collections of chants—*Mezmur* (for the seasons), *Zimmare* (for the Mass), *Mewasiʾt* (for the commemoration of the dead), *Miʿraf* (for the Psalter)—are most probably contributions of scholars of the Gonderite era. The most recent collection in the series is the *Ziq,* which incorporates new verses of litanies (composed at the various churches of the city of Gonder) and stanzas from the *melkiʿ* and from other sources.

It was probably during this period that the book of civil and canon laws, the *Fitha negest* (Laws of the Kings), was translated from Arabic. Canon law had, of course, been known in Ethiopia since the translation of the Synodicon (*Sinodos*) into Geʿez before the fifteenth century. The *Fitha negest* was the law of the land until the twentieth century, when it was replaced by a new constitution (1931, revised in 1955) and a modern civil and criminal code.

Modern Period

When the central power in Gonder weakened in the mid-eighteenth century, Geʿez literary activity declined with it. Regional governors, the *mesafint,* assumed from the central government so much more power than was rightfully theirs that historians have compared the condition of the Ethiopian state of that period with that of Israel during the era of the Judges, and have called the period by its Geʿez equivalent, *Zemene mesafint* (1775–1855). No literary creation of national significance, other than the royal chronicles, can be attributed to this era. There were compelling needs at this time to replace Geʿez as a literary language with a popularly understood one. This threat to Geʿez came from Amharic, used by Catholic missionaries who saw the advantage of employing such a vernacular to capture the minds of the faithful. Amharic,

which was (and still is) widely used as a national means of communication, or lingua franca, gradually became the principal tool for literary production as well. Amharic literature, perhaps the most extensive in any African language, deserves a special treatment.

The themes treated by the first authors in Amharic were, predictably, controversial theology and Christian ethics. This was soon followed, interestingly, by a criticism of tradition as an impediment to progress. Today, the themes of Amharic literature are not much different from those of the West: love, social and political problems, and death—with little or no concern for life after death, which was the preoccupation of Geʿez literature. The combat against colonialism and its influence on the African mentality, dominant themes elsewhere in Africa, do not preoccupy Ethiopian writers.

The traditional style of composing poems is being replaced by that of the West. Young writers are increasingly strangers to traditional learning, which is steadily being displaced by Western education. The influence of English expression on Amharic has produced virtually an independent Amharic dialect. The circulation of a work written in this "dialect" has to be limited to a relatively small sector of the otherwise large literate population of the country.

It is probably worth noting that the Amharic literature in the diaspora, especially in the United States, has reached a comparatively respectable level. Several types of Amharic computer software programs created by engineers of Ethiopian nationality have greatly facilitated its growth. This development should not be surprising. The political exiles and refugees who have been forced to leave Ethiopia by the hundreds of thousands (some say in the millions) since 1974 belong to the county's educated class—readers and writers of ideas dealing with contemporary issues. Nostalgia for Ethiopian life, hardships suffered by refugees, and current political issues are the themes of the Amharic literature produced on non-Amharic soils. However, because the succeeding generations will inevitably assume the local cultures, this literature's future does not seem very bright.

BIBLIOGRAPHY

Note: CSCO = Corpus Scriptorum Christianorum Orientalium.

Bezold, Carl, ed. and trans. *Kebra Nagast: Die Herrlichkeit der Könige.* Munich, 1909.
Budge, Ernest A. W., trans. *The Queen of Sheba and Her Only Son Menyelek: A Complete Translation of the Kebra Nagast.* London, 1922.

Cerulli, Enrico. *Il libro etiopico dei Miracoli di Maria e le sue fonti nelle letterature del medio evo latino.* Rome, 1943.

———. *La letteratura etiopica.* Florence, 1968.

Conti Rossini, Carlo, and Lanfranco Ricci, eds. and trans. *Il Libro della Luce del Negus Zarʾa Yāʿqob (Maṣḥafa Berhān).* CSCO 250 and 251, Scriptores Aethiopici 47 and 48. Louvain, 1964–1965. CSCO 261 and 262, Scriptores Aethiopici 51 and 52. Louvain, 1965.

Getatchew Haile. "Religious Controversies and the Growth of Ethiopic Literature in the Fourteenth and Fifteenth Centuries." *Oriens christianus* 65 (1981): 102–136.

———. *The Mariology of Emperor Zarʾa Yaʿəqob of Ethiopia: Texts and Translations.* Orientalia Christiana Analecta 242. Rome, 1992.

Kane, Thomas L. *Ethiopian Literature in Amharic.* Wiesbaden, 1975.

Molvaer, Reidulf. *Tradition and Change in Ethiopia: Social and Cultural Life as Reflected in Amharic Fictional Literature ca. 1930–1974.* Leiden, 1980.

Ricci, Lanfranco. "Letterature dell'Etiopia." In *Storia delle letterature d'Oriente,* edited by Oscar Botto. Vol. 1. Milan, 1969.

Ullendorff, Edward. *Ethiopia and the Bible.* London, 1968.

Wendt, Kurt, ed. and trans. *Das Maṣḥafa Milād (Liber Nativitatis) und Maṣḥafa Sellāsē (Liber Trinitatis) des Kaisers Zarʾa Yāʿqob.* CSCO 221 and 222, Scriptores Aethiopici 41 and 42. Louvain, 1962. CSCO 235 and 236, Scriptores Aethiopici 43 and 44. Louvain, 1963.

Yacob Beyene, ed. and trans. *Giyorgis di Sagla: Il libro del Mistero (Maṣḥafa Mesṭir).* CSCO 515 and 516, Scriptores Aethiopici 89 and 90. Louvain, 1990.

GETATCHEW HAILE

See also **Christianity; Ethiopian Orthodox Church; Writing Systems.**

HAUSA

Praise-song, extolling the values of traditional leadership in terms of descent, piety, military achievement, administrative expertise, and generosity, was an integral part of aristocratic court life in Hausa city-states both after the Islamic jihad of 1804 and before. Among ordinary people praise-song and epithetic declamation were particularly associated with farming activities and with boxers, wrestlers, and hunters. Praise of a patron was closely linked to vilification of that patron's rivals. The twentieth century has seen both famous court singers such as Narambada, Jankidi, and Saʾidu Faru, who use drum ensembles and a male chorus, and the rise of freelance popular singers, such as Mamman Shata and Dan Maraya, who both praise patrons and address current social and political issues (e.g., drug abuse, prostitution, unemploy-

ment). A wide variety of instruments are used in the accompaniment of song: drums, bowed fiddles, plucked lutes, and others.

The Islamic jihad of 1804 saw a flowering of Hausa religious poetry alongside writing in Arabic and Fulani. The military campaign by the followers of Shehu Uthman dan Fodio was accompanied by a battle for the hearts and minds of the people. In this effort, the *shehu* used Hausa poetry, written in the Arabic script (*ajami*) by members of his family, including his scholar daughter, Nana Asmaʾu. Poetry in Hausa, setting out the precepts of Islam and attacking non-Islamic practices, circulated in manuscript form among the Islamic literati and was committed to memory by itinerant reciters who then traveled among Hausa communities, reciting such devotional literature. The didacticism of this religious poetry has lived on in the more secular poetry of the twentieth century. Modern Nigerian poets such as Akilu Aliyu, Mudi Sipikin, Muʾazu Hadeja, and Saʾadu Zungur (also a radical political figure) have addressed a wide range of topical, political, and social issues (e.g., independence, civil war, Northern identity, education, political parties). Such poetry conforms to strict rhyme schemes creating regular stanzas, it displays rhythmic patterns which conform in many instances to Arabic meters, and it is intoned publicly without musical accompaniment. A continuing issue in the discussion of Hausa literature is the nature of the relationship between the oral song and the written poetry traditions, a relationship in which much cross-influence has taken place over the years.

Imaginative prose writing in Hausa dates very specifically from a colonial writing competition in 1933 that was designed to produce roman-script materials for pleasurable reading in schools and for adults in education. As a result of the competition, five novelettes were published by the Gaskiya Corporation, the sole publisher in Northern Nigeria until the 1970s. The stories drew extensively upon the oral-tale tradition and were, in the main, episodic with a quest or journey theme in which the hero (or heroes) endures hardship before finally returning home triumphant. A mixture of fantasy and reality was characteristic of a number of these stories and their successors over a period of forty years. In the 1980s, novels broke with the picaresque tradition and displayed a social realism that portrays, for example, the rise of a rapacious entrepreneurial class in Nigeria as a result of the oil boom of the 1970s and early 1980s, and malpractice

Excerpt from the nineteenth-century Hausa poem *Milkin Audu* praising the life and works of Shehu 'Uthman dan Fodio. From Mervyn Hiskett, *A History of Hausa Islamic Verse* (London, 1975). REPRODUCED BY PERMISSION OF THE AUTHOR

and oppression during elections. S. I. Katsina, in his novels *Turmin Danya* (1982) and *Tura Ta Kai Bango* (1983), exemplifies this new trend.

BIBLIOGRAPHY

Baldi, Sergio. *Systematic Hausa Bibliography.* 1977.

Boyd, Jean. *The Caliph's Sister.* London, 1989.

Furniss, Graham. *Poetry, Prose, and Popular Culture in Hausa.* Edinburgh, 1996.

Hiskett, Mervyn. *A History of Hausa Islamic Verse.* London, 1975.

Pilaszewicz, Stanislaw. "Literature in the Hausa language." In *Literatures in African Languages: Theoretical Issues and Sample Surveys,* edited by B. W. Andrzejewski, S. Pilaszewicz, and W. Tyloch. Cambridge, 1985.

Skinner, Neil. *Anthology of Hausa Literature in Translation.* Zaria, Nigeria, 1980.

GRAHAM FURNISS

See also **Asma'u, Nana; Oral Culture and Oral Tradition.**

ISLAMIC LITERATURE

Islamic literature is that realm of verbal arts which reflects Islamic ethos and cultures, whether or not it deals explicitly with Islamic precepts or has been directly inspired by Islamic doctrine. Despite the many images of Islam prevalent in different parts of the continent, there is a core of common beliefs, similar institutional patterns, and shared values which have helped to forge an Islamic culture and literature that is also uniquely African.

The greater part of this literature is in African, and especially in Afro-Islamic, languages ranging from Afar, Somali, Swahili, and Nubi in eastern Africa, to Fufulde, Hausa, Wolof, and Mandingo in western Africa. Afro-Islamic languages are indigenous tongues of predominantly Muslim communities which have absorbed a significant proportion of Islamic idiom. Arabic, the language of Islamic ritual and Qur'anic revelation, has also served as a literary medium in Sudan and in the western African regions of Hausaland, Senegal, and the Gambia, and in the old Mali and Songhai empires. More recently, Islamic literature has also appeared in Western languages, particularly in French and English.

Much of the Islamic literature has tended to be written. Islam regards the written word with tremendous veneration. The advent of the religion and Qur'anic literacy, therefore, inspired the emergence of African versions of the Arabic script which came to be used in the construction of a new creative literature in local languages. The inception of European colonial rule led to the marginalization of these local varieties of the Arabic script and, in some cases, to their eventual replacement with the Latin script.

Despite the primacy accorded to the written word in Islam, however, the oral tradition has proved highly resilient and has remained the dominant mode in some literatures, especially those in Somali and Mandingo languages. But even in these cases, pre-Islamic myths and beliefs were in many instances replaced with new ones that have given oral literature in Muslim Africa a peculiarly Islamic imprint. This, for example, is clearly demonstrated in the works of Amadou Hampate Ba (b. 1901) of Mali and Abdillahi Suldaan (1920–1973) of Somalia.

In form and substance, the Islamic heritage has perhaps been most influential in the poetic genre and least influential in the area of drama; prose fiction occupies a position between these two. The bulk of Islamic literature has, in fact, been in verse, and its literary masterpieces have been overwhelmingly poetic. Some of the most prominent poets, from Sheikh Husayn al-Zahra (1833–1894) of the Sudan to Sheikh Muhammad Abdulle Hassan (1856–1921) of Somalia, from Sayyid Abdallah bin Ali bin Nassir (1735–1810) of Kenya to Sheikh 'Uthman dan Fodio (1754–1817) of Nigeria, have come from the leading ranks of Muslim scholars and clergy. Much of this poetry has been composed in local languages and comprises didactic and homiletic verse in a prosodic style which is strongly reminiscent of the Arabo-Islamic *qasida.*

This classical, poetic dimension of Islamic literature has been concerned with a wide range of themes, including the life histories of prophets and other prominent Muslim figures; odes to the Prophet Muhammad, Muslim saints, and martyrs; Islamic mysticism and philosophy; the transitory and illusory nature of this world; religious, social, and political admonition; and Islamic duties and principles of Islamic conduct and morality. Some of these poems, like the Swahili *Hamziyya* of Sayyid Aidarus bin Athman bin Ali (1705–1775), are direct translations from Arabic sources.

Islamic literature in prose exists in Arabic, indigenous African languages, and Western languages. The bulk of this literature is in the form of novels and novelettes, but it includes the short stories of al-Tayyib Zaruq (b. 1935) in Arabic, Saida Hagi-Dirie Herzi (b. 1955) and Abdulrazak Gurnah (b. 1948) in English, Aliyu Makarfi in Hausa, Ahmed Mgeni (b. 1938) in Swahili, and others. A small proportion of the prose fiction in non-Western languages, like some of the Hausa and Swahili novelettes of Umaru Dembo (b. 1945) and Shaaban Robert (1909–1962), respectively, compare with the narratives of *The Thousand and One Nights* in their use of fantasy. Much of the prose literature that is Islamic in content, however, also tends toward some form of realism.

The thematic substance of this prose literature is quite varied, ranging from marriage in a changing society to tyranny and the class struggle. Furthermore, the writers differ substantially in their ideological orientation toward Islam. Some are strongly empathetic and reverent toward it: Cheikh Hamidou Kane (b. 1928), Camara Laye (1928–1980), and Aminata Sow Fall (b. 1941), writing in French; Jabiru Abdillahi, writing in Hausa; and Mohamed Said Abdalla (b. 1918), writing in Swahili, probably be-

long to this category. Some are irreverent and stand as reformists of various shades, including French-language writers Mariama Ba (1929–1981) and Birago Diop (b. 1906), Somali novelist Shire Jamaac Axmed, Swahili novelist Said Ahmed Mohamed (b. 1947), and Arabic novelist Tayeb Salih (b. 1929). And others, like English-language novelist Nuruddin Farah (b. 1945), coming from a Western liberal perspective, and French-language novelist Ousmane Sembène (b. 1923), coming from a Marxist perspective, can be described as cultural apostates. What gives this literature its common Islamic thrust, then, is merely the Islamic sociocultural background against which it is constituted.

In drama the heritage of Islam is virtually negligible. Islamic culture is featured in some of the Hausa plays of Shu'aibu Makarfi (b. 1918), the Somali plays of Ahmed Farah Ali (b. 1947), and the Swahili plays of Ebrahim Hussein (b. 1943), and others. Also, plays staged by students and theater groups in both eastern and western Africa have had an Islamic content. But, in general, the Islamic impact on African drama has been weak, both in form and in substance.

Despite many similarities, the regional Islamic literatures of eastern Africa, on the one hand, and western Africa, on the other, show an interesting contrast. Because of its proximity to the Arabian Peninsula and the long-term influx of Arab immigrants, Islam in eastern Africa has retained a strong Arab character. In western Africa, however, the religion became more indigenized since its foundations were laid, mainly by gradual contact with Berbers rather than with Arabs. As a result, while the Islamic literature of eastern Africa is pervaded with cultural Arabisms, a good section of the literature of western Africa projects an interplay of tensions and accommodations between the legacy of Islam and more indigenous traditions.

BIBLIOGRAPHY

Andrzejewski, B. W., Stanislaw Pilaszewicz, and Witold Tyloch, eds. *Literatures in African Languages: Theoretical Issues and Sample Surveys.* New York, 1985.

Gérard, Albert. *African Language Literatures.* Washington, D.C., 1981.

Harrow, Kenneth W., ed. *Faces of Islam in African Literature.* Portsmouth, N.H., 1991.

Kritzeck, James, ed. *Anthology of Islamic Literature: From the Rise of Islam to Modern Times.* New York, 1964.

ALAMIN MAZRUI

See also **Camara Laye; Islam; Sembène Ousmane; 'Uthman dan Fodio.**

SOMALI

For centuries, oral literature, especially poetry, has been the dominant form of cultural representation in Somalia. The absence of an alphabet for Somali precluded the development of a written tradition. In 1972, President Mohammed Siad Barre announced the adoption of a modified version of the Latin script for the writing of the Somali language. The first few years afterward were characterized by an unstructured output of creative works.

Later, a sophisticated experimentalist group of fiction writers emerged. The writings of this group created a bridge between the oral and the written forms. For example, characters in the novels of this group are described by their physical appearance and by the kind of clothes they wear. The narrator also describes the character via the ambience. This technique has affinities with traditional Somali narrative.

The two best-known writers of this group are Faarax M. J. Cawl (1937–1991) and Xuseen Sh. Axmed Kaddare (b. 1942). Cawl's *Aqoondarro waa u nacab jacayl* (1974; *Ignorance Is the Enemy of Love*, 1982) is a fictionalization of the dervish wars against British colonialism. The story also dramatizes the importance of mastering the three R's.

Kaddare's *Waasuge Iyo Warsame* (n.d.; Waasuge and Warsame; *Waasuge e Warsame*, 1990) is about a journey to Mogadishu by two old men. The "and" linking the two names of the title heroes alludes to a contradiction between Waasuge (a peasant) and Warsame (a pastoralist). Thus, the reader is introduced to a fictional world marked by counterpoints.

The experimentalists are complemented by another group whose novels further test the limits of the genre. Nuruddin Farah (b. 1945) and Maxamed Daahir Afrax (b. 1952) are the two best-known of this group. In "Tolow waa talee, ma . . ." (1973–1974), Farah, whose novels in English have internationalized the Somali situation, experiments with stream-of-consciousness writing. The story, a fictionalized account of the military coup that brought Barre to power, was serialized in *Xiddigta Oktoobar* (October Star). Soon after, the regime's censorship board ordered the serialization to cease. Farah then published the story in English, under the title *A Naked Needle* (1976).

Maxamed Daahir Afrax's second novel, *Maana Faay* (1981; repr. 1993), is the story of the eponymous heroine's painful love, complicated by corruption and greed. Serialization of the novel in the government daily was discontinued by the censors.

Ironically, the writing and publishing of novels in the Somali language increased during the civil war. By some accounts, more than three hundred novels were published in the period. This was the result of (1) the emergence of a new breed of entrepreneurs engaged in desk-top publishing and (2) the absence of censorship. Among the most promising young writers in Somali today are Awees Hussein Shiino, whose novel *Dayaxmadoobaad* (1991; Lunar Eclipse) apocalyptically treats the ravages of the civil war, and Fartuun Mohamed Kusow, perhaps one of the best female novelists on the Somali literary scene.

Written poetry and drama lag behind prose fiction in Somali. There are, however, a few published volumes of poetry, starting with *Geeddiga Wadaay!* (1973; Lead the Trek), by Cabdi Muxumad Amiin (b. 1935), which extols the initial accomplishments of the military regime, and ending with *Hal-Karaan* (1993), by Maxamed Ibraahim Warsame Hadraawi (b. 1943), a collection of his poems from 1970 to 1990.

All in all, both prose writers and poets have succeeded in transforming the linguistic aspect of Somali in such a way that development of the written form and the discussion of new themes are possible.

BIBLIOGRAPHY

Ahmed, Ali Jimale. *Daybreak Is Near . . . : Literature, Clans, and the Nation-State in Somalia*. Lawrenceville, N.J., 1996.

Andrzejewski, B. W. "Somali Literature." In *Literatures in African Languages*, edited by B. W. Andrzejewski, Stanislaw Pilaszewicz, and Witold Tyloch. Cambridge, 1985.

Banti, Giorgio. "Letteratura." In *Aspetti dell'espressione artistica in Somalia*, edited by Annarita Puglielli. Rome, 1987.

ALI JIMALE AHMED

SOUTH AFRICAN LANGUAGES

Oral Literature

The Nguni (Zulu, Xhosa, Swati) and Sotho (Sesotho, Tswana, North Sotho) languages have a rich oral literary tradition, the major genres of which are praise poetry (in Zulu and Xhosa, *izibongo*; in Sotho, *lithoko*) and oral narrative (in Zulu, *izinganekwane*; in Xhosa, *iintsomi*; in Sotho, *litsomo*). Other oral forms include proverbs and riddles. D. K. Rycroft, an ethnomusicologist and linguist, describes praise poems as "a cumulative series of praise names applying to a single referent; though those of prominent people and royalty are interspersed with concise narrative passages or comments, having been repeatedly expanded and polished by official bards in the course of time" (p. 11). A typical praise stanza first employs a praise name personifying a quality of the king and then links it to an action employing the same quality in verb form, as in the following praise of the Emperor Shaka, collected by James Stuart and included in *Izibongo: Zulu Praise Poems,* edited by Trevor Cope (1968):

> UDlungwana KaNdaba!
> UDlungwana woMbelebele,
> Odlung' emanxulumeni,
> Kwaze kwas' amanxulum' esibikelana.

> Dlungwana [Rager] son of Ndaba!
> Rager of the Mbelebele brigade,
> Who raged among the large homesteads
> So that until dawn the dwellings were being
>   destroyed

(p. 89)

The art and tradition of praising both in public and in private continue into the present; a professional praiser performed at the installation ceremony for President Nelson Mandela in 1994. The largest collection of Zulu *izibongo* was recorded and transcribed by James Stuart in the 1920s. These nineteenth-century royal praises, together with a collection edited by C. L. S. Nyembezi in 1958, are the source material for such later editions as Trevor Cope's *Izibongo* and Rycroft and A. B. Ngcobo's meticulous *Praises of Dingana* (1988). Liz Gunner and Mafika Gwala added an important collection in 1991 that includes contemporary praises of political leaders and of ordinary people including some humorous praises of and by women, and some touching praises that children have composed for themselves. Royal Xhosa *izibongo* have been collected by Walter B. Rubusana as *Zemk'inkomo magwalandini* (The Cattle Are Departing, You Cowards!, 1906), and by Henry M. Ndawo (1925) and D. L. P. Yali-Manisi (1952). Harold Scheub's collection (1975) includes praises by Xhosa commoners, and Jeff Opland's study (1983) emphasizes the complexity of the poetic tradition in Xhosa. Sotho *lithoko* have been collected by M. Damane and P. B. Sanders (1974), and Daniel Kunene (1971) analyzes their structure.

Scheub describes the oral narrative as moving outward from the familiar to the unfamiliar and from conflict to resolution. In the course of that movement transformations occur, and the listener's emotions are engaged through symbolizing processes and the patterning of images. Two of the most famous performers of extended narrative were Lydia umkaSetemba (Uskebe Ngubane), whose nineteenth-century Zulu narrative *Umxakaza-wakogingqwayo* was reconstructed from notes by Henry Callaway (1868), and Nongenile Masithathu Zenani, a Gcaleka performer whose narrative, performed in 1975, took almost a month to complete, according to Scheub. Popular themes in Zulu and Xhosa oral narrative are human encounters with the sharp-witted amoral trickster (in Zulu, *uchakijana;* in Xhosa, *uhlakanyana*) or with the dull-witted cannibalistic *amazimu* (Zulu: ogres, sing. *izimu*). *Uchakijana's* victims accept him in whatever human guise he assumes and are generally unaware of his true identity to the end. The *amazimu,* on the other hand, seem to be simultaneously both human and ogre, and the humans they encounter use their knowledge of an *izimu's* weaknesses in planning their escape, which is generally successful. In narratives involving animals, a particular human quality is associated with each character: the chameleon is untrustworthy, the rock rabbit lazy, and so on. Sotho *litsomo* have been collected by E. Jacottet, and by B. Tlali and O. Chevrier. Zulu *izinganekwane* were collected by Callaway, V. Dube, W. Bleek, and B. Vilakazi; and Noverino Canonici produced an analysis of the form in 1993. Xhosa *iintsomi* have been collected by G. Theal, H. Ndawo, and H. Scheub.

Early Literature

Protestant missionary work in southern Africa in the nineteenth century laid the foundation for literature in African languages. Missionary linguists first created orthographies and then documented the languages for their own study. Then followed the construction of printing presses and the translation of the Bible and religious materials, thereby "fixing" a particular dialect as the literary standard. The early converts (in Zulu, *amakholwa*) were intimately involved in the translation work and composed hymns and prayers of their own, the earliest known being a hymn of praise in Xhosa "UloThixo omkhulu ngosezulwini" (He the Great God, High in Heaven), written in 1820 by Ntsikana, a convert and preacher and the first of many great writers of Xhosa hymns. A collection of hymns by Isaiah Shembe (c. 1868–1935), a Zulu prophet and founder of the church iBandla lamaNazaretha (The Church of the Nazarites), was published in 1940, though some of the hymns were composed early in the century. The earliest text in Zulu appeared in 1901 and was an account by three of Bishop John Colenso's first converts of a journey to the court of King Mphande in 1859. Early Sotho articles on folklore were published in the newspaper *Leselinyana la Lesotho* (Little Light of Lesotho) founded in 1864 by Rev. A. Mabille of the Paris Evangelical Society. In 1893 Azariele Sekese published some of his articles as *Mekhoa ea Basotho le maele le litsomo* (Customs of the Basotho, with Sayings and Proverbs), which became the first published literary work. The first collection of Venda folklore with German translation was of *Midzimu ya Malombo* by C. Endemann, published in 1927. Several Xhosa-language journals and newspapers were founded and flourished for short periods in the nineteenth century, and *Imvo Zabantsundu*, founded in 1884 by D. T. Javabu, is still in publication, as is *Ilanga lase Natal*, the Zulu-language newspaper founded in 1904 by J. L. Dube. This first period in vernacular literature was marked in Zulu by writers such as Magema Fuze, P. Lamula, and Titus Z. Masondo, who documented Zulu history and traditions as seen through the new lens of Christianity. Motenda, Mudau, and Dzivhani produced historical accounts of the Venda people.

Emergence of the Novel

The translation of English-language works of fiction into Zulu, Xhosa, and Sesotho led to the beginnings of imaginative written genres in these languages. John Bunyan's *The Pilgrim's Progress* was particularly influential, its theme echoing struggles the Christians were themselves experiencing, and its allegorical form and character-typing echoing the format of the traditional *iintsomi*. Novels integrating the two themes of challenge of the Christian life and the importance of tradition emerged in all three languages with characters fulfilling single and specific functions. In Sesotho the best-known writer of this period is Thomas Mofolo (1877–1948), who wrote *Moeti oa Bochabela* (The Traveller to the East, 1907), *Pitseng* (1910), and *Chaka* (1925), a historical novel tracing the life of the Emperor Shaka. In Xhosa, Samuel Mqhayi wrote *Ityala lamawele* (1914) and *UDon Jade* (1929); J. J. R. Jolobe wrote *Elundeni loThukela* (On the Rim of the Thukela Valley, 1958), and A. C. Jordan wrote *Ingqumbo yeminyanya* (The Wrath of the Ancestors, 1940). In Zulu, James Gumbi wrote *Baba ngixolele* (Father, Forgive Me, 1965); Benedict Vilakazi wrote *Noma nini* (No Matter How Long, 1935) and *Nje nempela* (Just So, 1933); and J. M. Zama wrote *Nigabe ngani?* (On What Do You Pride Yourselves? 1948). In Venda in the 1950s T. N. Maumela published *Elelwani*, E. S. Madima wrote *A si ene*, W. M. Ma-

kumu wrote *Nyabele Muthia-Vivho,* and W. M. D. Phopho published a historical novel entitled *Phusu-phusu dza Dzimauli,* which traced the history of the Rammbuda clan.

Literature After 1960

By the 1960s novelists were producing powerful works on the theme of isolation and self-destruction and the need to reinterpret tradition to meet the needs of urban life. In these novels Christianity remains a strong element, though it is seen as too permissive in its Western form to replace the network of rights and obligations that hold traditional society together. Protest against the increasingly oppressive political forces is muted. An early exponent of this genre in Xhosa was Guybon Sinxo, who wrote *UNomsa* (1922), *Umfundisi waseMthuqwasi* (The Priest of Mthuqwasi, 1927), and *Umzali Wolahlêko* (The Prodigal Parent, 1933). Representative of the period in Zulu were R. R. R. Dhlomo's *Indlela yababi* (The Path of the Evil Ones, 1946), C. L. S. Nyembezi's *Mntanami! Mntanami!* (My Child! My Child!, 1950) and *Inkinsela yaseMgungundlovu* (The Big Man from Pietermaritzburg, 1961), James Gumbi's *Waysezofika ekhaya* (He Was About to Go Home, 1968), Kenneth Bhengu's *Ubogawula ubheka* (Look Before You Leap, 1968), and O. E. H. Nxumalo's *Ngisinga empumalanga* (I Look to the East, 1969). Works in Sesotho include S. P. Lekeba's *Gauta e Ntjhapile* (Johannesburg Has Ensnared Me, 1961), H. M. Lethoba's *Kgunou le Maria* (Kgunou and Maria, 1962), and A. T. Maboee's *Menyepetsi ya maswabi* (Tears of Grief, 1962).

Poetry

Literary poetry began to appear in the Xhosa journals in the mid-nineteenth century. Nyembezi called Samuel Mqhayi the father of Xhosa poetry, and James Jolobe is recognized as the finest Xhosa poet. Their work presented the suffering of the Xhosa people and evoked happier times, when society was ordered by traditional rights and obligations. Jolobe's greatest poem, "Ingqawule," collected in *The Xhosa Ntsomi* by Harold Scheub (1975), tells the story of the great cattle-killing of 1857 following the prophecy of the young woman Nongqawuse. Widespread starvation followed:

Abhonga ebhongile amaxhaka eenkomo
Lawolel' ixhalanga lashiyela impethu

The oxen bellowed, and fell one by one.
Vultures gathered, and left portions for maggots.

Yamphlophe imimango ngamathambo esizwe
Ingamawakawaka idini lempazamo.

The ridges were white with the bones of the
   nation,
The foolish sacrifice was in the thousands.
(quoted in Andrzejewski et al., pp. 567f)

Zulu literary poets of this period include P. My-
eni, whose *Hayani maZulu* (Sing Out, Zulu People,
1969), is a reworking of *izibongo* in literary form;
D. B. Z. Ntuli, who wrote *Amagwevu* (Body Blows,
1969); M. J. Makhaye, author of *Isoka lakwaZulu*
(The Young Bachelor from Zululand, 1972); and
O. E. H. Nxumalo, whose poetry includes contemporary political material, as in *Ikhwezi* (The Morning Star, 1965). In the 1960s M. E. R. Mathivha published a poetic drama entitled *Mabalanganye* (1963).

Effects of Apartheid

The promotion of Nguni, Sotho, and Venda literatures by missionaries in the nineteenth and early
twentieth centuries led to a vibrant literary culture
that was reinforced through vernacular education
policies in the mission schools. Elementary school
textbooks contained history and folktales written
by well-respected authors such as C. L. S. Nyembezi, and high school libraries were stocked with
novels and poetic anthologies. During the four decades of apartheid following World War II, the
strength of these vernacular literary traditions and
of the presses that promoted them, many now controlled by government sympathizers, became a tool
in the grand design to foster ethnic loyalties in
order to subvert black solidarity. Strict censorship
of all materials produced in African languages prevented the overt development of protest literature
under conditions where it would naturally have
flourished. At the same time, the Bantu Education
Act of 1953 moved school syllabi for black children
away from academic goals and toward competence
in trades and manual occupations, while maintaining the emphasis on vernacular education. Those
who wished to be published in African languages
had severe restrictions placed on them and were
simultaneously encouraged to write novellas for
high school readers that avoided all reference to
current political conditions. Some writers abandoned African languages and joined the large community already writing in European languages in
order to find publishers abroad and to reach a
larger audience.

The new South African constitution, enacted into
law in 1997, recognizes nine African languages as
official, in addition to Afrikaans and English. The
impact of this, together with the many other radical
changes made in South Africa at this time on literature in African languages in the twenty-first century, will be far-reaching.

BIBLIOGRAPHY

Andrzejewski, B. W., S. Pilaszewicz, and W. Tyloch, eds.
  *Literatures in African Languages: Theoretical Issues and
  Sample Surveys.* Cambridge, 1985.
Canonici, Noverino N. *The Zulu Folktale Tradition.* Dur-
  ban, 1993.
Cope, Trevor, ed. *Izibongo: Zulu Praise Poems.* Collected
  by James Stuart; translated by Daniel Malcolm. Ox-
  ford, 1968.
Gérard, Albert S. *Four African Literatures: Xhosa, Sotho,
  Zulu, Amharic.* Berkeley and Los Angeles, 1971.
Gunner, Liz, and Mafika Gwala, eds. *Musho! Zulu
  Popular Praises.* East Lansing, Mich., 1991.
Kunene, Daniel P. *Heroic Poetry of the Basotho.* Oxford,
  1971.
Mathivha, M. E. R. *History of Venda Literature.*
————. "An Outline History of the Development of
  Venda as a Written Language." In *Essays on Literature
  and Language: Presented to Prof. T. M. H. Endemann by
  His Colleagues.* Turfloop, 1973.
Rycroft, D. K., and A. B. Ngcobo, eds. *The Praises of
  Dingana.* Pietermaritzburg, 1988.
Scheub, Harold. *The Xhosa Ntsomi.* Oxford, 1975.

SANDRA SANNEH

See also **Apartheid; Language Use: Language
  Choice in Writing;** and individual ethnic
  groups.

SWAHILI

Inhabitants of the east African coast, the Swahili
owe the evolution of their identity, language, and
literature to several cultural streams, mainly the
Bantu, the Arabian, and the Islamic. While stories,
animal fables, and historical tales are abundant,
poetry has been the major literary medium, taking
such prosodic forms as the *utenzi, shairi, wimbo,* and
tumbuizo. The earliest extant poems are attributed
to the legendary poet-warrior-hero Fumo Liyongo,
believed to have lived more than a millennium ago.
The technical virtuosity of Liyongo's style suggests
that the art of Swahili poetry was already very
highly developed well before his time, while close
examination of poems composed in later centuries
indicates that their formal properties are derived
mainly from the two forms that Liyongo used.

Many traditional compositions that have come
down in manuscript form have a religious bias
because manuscript preparation was done mainly
by Islamic shaikhs. Notable among these compositions are *Al-Inkishafi, Dura mandhuma,* and *Hamziyya.*

Most Swahili verse is secular, however, covering all aspects of life. Such verse is transmitted orally and rarely preserved in print. Muyaka bin Haji al-Ghassany (fl. 1766–1840) is the first Swahili poet whose work was reliably collected and transcribed (in the 1880s). His poetry is predominantly secular. Mbarak Ali Hinawy's quotations from the verses of Suud Said al-Maamiry (fl. 1810–1878) and Muhamad Ahmad al-Mambassy (fl. 1856–1890) in his own *Al Akida and Fort Jesus Mombasa* (1950) illustrate the varied uses of verse forms in the transmission of messages in times of political conflict.

The inception of British colonial rule led to new developments in Swahili literature and to its popularization beyond the confines of Swahili ethnicity. Many English books, such as *Treasure Island, King Solomon's Mines,* and *Gulliver's Travels* were translated into Swahili. Such colonial efforts interacted with local narrative traditions to give rise to the Swahili novel, whose best-known pioneer was Shaaban Robert (1909–1962). Over the years the Swahili novel has become more realistic, as in the writings of Euphrase Kezilahabi (b. 1944), Said Ahmed Mohamed (b. 1945), Katama Mkangi (b. 1944), and Mohamed Suleman Mohamed (b. 1945).

The short story is a less developed form; it continues to show great affinity with the Swahili *ngano* from the oral tradition. The potential of the short story in Swahili has been demonstrated by writers like Ahmed Mgeni (b. 1938) and Mugyabuso Mulokozi (b. 1950).

Swahili drama began either with entertaining stage performances inspired by the cinema or, in more serious forms, under the influence of Western plays that were included in the academic curriculum. Leading playwrights like Ebrahim N. Hussein (b. 1943), Penina Mlama (b. 1948), and Chacha Nyaigotti-Chacha (b. 1952) are all products of this educational experience. In poetry, the little there is of Western impact has been in the form of experimentation with free and abstract verse. The main proponents of this fledgling trend have included Euphrase Kezilahabi, Mugyabuso Mulokozi, and Alamin Mazrui (b. 1948).

Much of twentieth-century Swahili literature has been a response to the colonial experience and its continuing aftermath. Nationalistic reactions of various kinds and the clash between the rural and urban experience have tended to preoccupy many Swahili writers. In Tanzania, the Zanzibar

Fragment of the *Utenzi wa Isa,* a Swahili epic poem. FROM JAN KNAPPERT, *EPIC POETRY IN SWAHILI AND OTHER AFRICAN LANGUAGES* (LEIDEN, 1983)

revolution of 1964 and the Arusha Declaration of 1967 have also contributed to thematic developments. Translations from other literary traditions—ranging from Shakespeare's *Merchant of Venice* to Wole Soyinka's *The Trials of Brother Jero*—have become more common in recent years.

BIBLIOGRAPHY

Bertoncini, Elene Zúbková. *Outline of Swahili Literature: Prose Fiction and Drama.* Leiden, 1989.
Gérard, Albert S. "East Africa: Swahili." Chapter 5 in *African Language Literatures: An Introduction to the Literary History of Sub-Saharan Africa.* Harlow, Essex, 1981.
Shariff, Ibrahim Noor. *Tungo Zetu.* Trenton, N.J., 1988.

IBRAHIM NOOR SHARIFF

See also **Languages and History; Theater.**

YORUBA

Among the Yoruba of southwestern Nigeria, many genres of traditional oral literature still survive: *ijala,* hunters' chants; *iwi egungun,* masquerade chants; *rara,* a social chant form; *sango-pipe,* praise chants for the god of thunder; *ifa,* divination poetry; and some children's poetry; all are enjoyed in their traditional modes, especially in the rural areas and on radio and television. Important social ceremonies are not complete without a local poet performing *ewi* (poetry) in a modernized chanting mode. Popular contemporary Yoruba poets Olanrewaju Adepoju and Tubosun Oladapo use *ewi* to express social commentary.

Written literature in Yoruba started about 1817, when missionaries began collecting Yoruba words in order to produce a written form of the language. Mrs. Hannah Kilham collected and published Yoruba vocabularies in 1828. The first collection of poems was published in 1848. Yoruba newspapers, which began publication in 1859, started serializing creative writings; the serialized works led eventually to the first Yoruba novel, *Itan Emi Segilola* (1928). The great pioneer of original Yoruba poetry was J. S. Sowande (Sobo Arobiodu).

Daniel O. Fagunwa (1910–1963), the pioneer novelist, set the pace in fantasy with five novels springing essentially from the Yoruba oral tradition. A few other novelists imitated his style, but soon the call for realistic novels inspired writers like Isaac O. Delano, Joseph Folohan Odunjo, Adebayo Faleti, Afolabi Olabimtan, Kola Akinlade, Oladejo Okediji, and Akinwumi Isola, who have produced novels based on contemporary life. Today, about 120 Yoruba novels have been published or are in press.

There are two currents of Yoruba drama today: the traveling theater tradition, in which groups perform their unscripted plays with popular appeal, and the literary drama, which exists in published forms and is also occasionally performed. Traveling theaters derive their methods and style from the traditional *alarinjo* masqueraders, who traveled about with a large repertoire of short social satires. There are about 115 traveling theaters, but only a few are active. Popular theater leaders include Hubert Ogunde, Moses Olaiya, Oyin Adejobi, and Isola Ogunsola. Today, however, films and television have lured all of them from the proscenium stage.

BIBLIOGRAPHY

Ogunsina, Bisi. *The Development of the Yoruba Novel.* Ibadan, Nigeria, 1992.
Olatunji, Olatunde. *Features of Yoruba Oral Poetry.* Ibadan, Nigeria, 1984.

AKINWUMI ISOLA

See also **Oral Culture and Oral Tradition.**

ANGLOPHONE LITERATURE IN WESTERN AFRICA

Anglophone western African literature is a byproduct of nineteenth-century Christian missionaries' campaigns to win converts to their religion in that part of the world. Their need for local collaborators as catechists and, later, ordained priests prompted them to establish schools to produce such helpers, and in the process to devise alphabets for reducing the local languages to writing.

While it is customary to cite as pioneering African literature the early writings of certain expatriated Africans, like the 1789 life story of Olaudah Equiano (Gustavus Vassa), who was abducted into slavery from the eastern part of present-day Nigeria, the history of writing in anglophone western Africa properly begins in the twentieth century. Together with literatures from elsewhere in Africa, especially those in non-African languages, it constitutes a record of the impact that five centuries of European activities have had on Africa and the lives and institutions of Africans.

Fiction

The first published work of anglophone fiction was *Ethiopia Unbound: Studies in Race Emancipation,* by Joseph Ephraim Casely-Hayford, a politician and

"My name is Akara-Ogun, Compound-of-Spells." Illustration by Bruce
Onabrakpeya from D. O. Fagunwa, *Forest of a Thousand Demons* (New York:
Random House, 1982). REPRODUCED WITH PERMISSION. PHOTO COURTESY OF THE
LIBRARY OF CONGRESS.

freedom activist of the Gold Coast (now Ghana). Published in 1911, the work is essentially a justification of African cultures in the face of European derogation and a championship of Africans' legitimate place in history. The informing culture is the Fante, with which the author was most familiar; the "Ethiopia" in the title served as a synecdoche for all of Africa. Several decades were to elapse before the appearance of another significant work of fiction, this time by another Gold Coast writer, R. E. Obeng. His *Eighteenpence* (1941) explores the judicial systems in his country during the colonial period.

In 1952 Amos Tutuola's *The Palm-Wine Drinkard and His Dead Palm-Wine Tapster in the Deads' Town* took the reading public by storm and launched one of the most unusual literary careers in the history of African letters. It is the tale of a palm-wine addict who travels to the town of the dead in an attempt to bring his dead tapster back among the living, so he can continue providing the palm wine the hero cannot live without. In this episodic saga, the hero encounters numerous frightful and weird creatures who guarantee that his quest will be arduous and suspenseful and an occasional helper who offers him some respite from his trials. Because the author chose to write in English despite his limited education, the language of the work is what Dylan Thomas described as "young English." With Thomas's enthusiastic endorsement, what he described as the "brief, thronged, grisly and bewitching story, or series of stories" proved hugely popular with European and American readers especially, who mistook the unconventional English for bold experimentation. By contrast, in Africa it attracted a mixed or downright hostile reception from most readers, who believed that Tutuola's poor command of English, and his apparent acceptance by Western critics as exemplary of the best Africa could produce, reflected badly on them. Worried about what they considered the embarrassing conception of Africans the white world might derive from Tutuola's flawed style and sensational, spirit-infested plots, early African critics directed intense criticism at him and his writing. Tutuola nonetheless followed his initial success with eight more novels and two collections of short stories, but his appeal for Western readers has proved ephemeral at best.

Tutuola's success encouraged other, better educated west Africans to take up writing. When Chinua Achebe, one of the first students of the University College, Ibadan (now the University of Ibadan), published *Things Fall Apart* in 1958, he quickly displaced Tutuola as western Africa's most celebrated anglophone novelist. Set around the moment of initial contact between the British and Africans in an Igbo (Ibo) community, it was the first in a series of five novels in which the author chronicles the conflicted history of Nigeria, from before the arrival of the Europeans to the postcolonial era of military coups and dictatorial rule. Achebe has asserted that his major motivation was the necessity he perceived to correct the unflattering portrayal of the African that he had encountered in his reading of such colonial works as Joyce Cary's *Mister Johnson* (1939) and Joseph Conrad's *Heart of Darkness* (1899).

In 1960, the year that saw the emergence of several new African nations, *The African*, by Gambia-born William Conton, appeared in print. Conton's novel documents the exploits of Kisimi Kamara, the first premier of an imaginary, newly independent west African state, who single-handedly forces an end to South Africa's apartheid regime. As wishful as it was improbable, the novel nonetheless testified to the belief west Africans had of their unlimited possibilities at that point in history to reshape their world for the better. Such euphoria and optimism quickly yielded to disappointment and pessimism in the face of massive official corruption and misgovernment and the attendant civil strife. Among the eloquent records of the new mood are Ghanaian Ayi Kwei Armah's *The Beautyful Ones Are Not Yet Born, a Novel* (1968), and his compatriot Kofi Awoonor's *This Earth, My Brother* (1971). The first is an indictment of the corrupt politics of the Kwame Nkrumah years, while the second focuses on its devastating impact on individual lives. In four more novels, the last being *The Healers* (1978), Armah broadened his scope to chastise the fatuousness of Western (specifically American) societies, European and Arab predatory escapades in Africa, and Africans' complicity in their own victimization and exploitation.

While most writers in this early period were drawn to the political problems of the newly independent states, others kept their focus on individuals coping with such things as the tyranny of tradition. For example, the Nigerian Flora Nwapa in *Efuru* (1966) and *Idu* (1970) wrote of the lives of women and the challenges inherent in juggling their roles as women, mothers, spouses, and individuals. Another example is Ghanaian Ama Ata Aidoo, especially in her short stories collected in *No Sweetness Here* (1970).

Since the management of English was such an important factor in the reception and valuation of Tutuola's work (and, by extension, in the development of anglophone fiction in general), Gabriel Okara's *The Voice* (1964) deserves mention as a highly acclaimed and successful experimentation with English. The novel, the only one by the Nigerian author, is the story of Okolo, whose search for the enigmatic "it" gets him into trouble with the powers in his community. Its appeal derives mainly from the poetic effects the author achieves by imposing Ijo syntax on the English language and by transliterating the idioms of the Nigerian language into English.

In fiction as in other genres, Nigeria has by dint of sheer population size dominated the anglophone western African literary scene. Not surprisingly, therefore, the major crisis in the country's postcolonial history, the 1966–1970 Biafran war, has been one of the dominant subjects of the western African anglophone novel. Examples are *The Combat* (1972), by Kole Omotoso; *The Last Duty* (1976), by Isidore Okpewho; *Forty-Eight Guns for the General* (1976), by Eddie Iroh; *Destination Biafra* (1982), by Buchi Emecheta; and *Heroes* (1986), by Festus Iyayi.

Long after the ending of the war, the social strife that has become a permanent feature of life in the country has continued to engage the attention of writers, many of whom propose socialist alternatives to the successive (and successively discredited) regimes, both civilian and military. Femi Osofisan's *Kolera Kolej* (1975) is representative; it attacks the social problems of his country by contriving the story of a unique but also corrupt and ineffectual solution to a cholera epidemic on a university campus.

Ben Okri, another Nigerian novelist, has also dramatized the loss of meaning and the lack of security that characterize the times, but he has done so in a style that recalls (to many critics) magical realism, in works such as *The Famished Road* (1991) and *Songs of Enchantment* (1993), both novels, and the collection of short stories, *Stars of the New Curfew* (1988). Included in the collection are stories like "Worlds That Flourish" and "What the Tapster Saw," stories in which Okri has reworked materials that Tutuola had earlier made familiar to readers, but in such a way as to show their possibilities in the hands of a master artist. Usually mentioned in the same breath with Okri, because of the similarity of their styles, is the Sierra Leonean Syl Cheney-Coker, whose nonrealistic *The Last Harmattan of*

Alusine Dunbar (1990) spans centuries of social and political intrigue in western Africa.

Poetry

Early western African anglophone poetry until the 1950s, like that of the Ghanaian Gladys Casely-Hayford (daughter of the aforementioned Ephraim) and Nigerian Dennis Osadebey, is unremarkable largely because of its supine embrace of imposed Western manners and sensibilities. Olumbe Bassir's *An Anthology of West African Verse* (1957) included a disproportionately large number of entries from francophone western Africa in English translation, a testimony to the vigorous impetus poetry derived from the Negritude movement in the francophone areas. The generation of English-language poets who succeeded the Casely-Hayfords and Osadebeys, poets trained in the local universities, expressed some disdain for the cultural narcissism of negritude but nonetheless shared the same experiences and motivations as those that explain the content and tenor of Achebe's fiction.

The Gambian poet Lenrie Peters's first collection, *Poems*, was published in 1964, and his fourth, *Selected Poetry*, appeared in 1981. Throughout, he has kept his focus on the discontinuities between past and present. Kofi Awoonor of Ghana also began his writing career in 1964, with the publication of *Rediscovery*. Since then he has published four other volumes, the latest being *Until the Morning After* (1987). Evident in all his poetry is his respect for tradition and his deep commitment to the sustaining influence of the past.

One of the most celebrated of anglophone poets is the Nigerian Christopher Okigbo, whose only collection, *Labyrinths; with Path of Thunder* (1971), was published posthumously after he lost his life fighting for Biafra in the Nigerian civil war. The poems in it are, collectively, the homage of a returning prodigal to his nurturing "mother Idoto," a figure representing traditional Africanness. The 1986 Nobel laureate, Nigerian Wole Soyinka, published *Idanre and Other Poems* in 1967; he has followed with several other collections, including a volume in 1988 titled *Mandela's Earth and Other Poems*. His versatility and range discourage any encapsulated characterization of his poetry beyond the observation that it is informed (as is his work in general) as much by conversance with tradition as by erudition in non-African letters.

The younger generation of anglophone western African poets include Kofi Anyidoho of Ghana (*A*

Harvest of Our Dreams, 1984, and *Earthchild,* 1985); the Nigerians Tanure Ojaide (*The Blood of Peace,* 1991), Ken Saro-Wiwa (*Songs in a Time of War,* 1985), who was hanged in 1995 by the Nigerian military dictator Sani Abacha for his environmental activism, and Niyi Osundare (*The Eye of the Earth,* 1986), who won the 1991 Noma Award for Publishing in Africa for *Waiting Laughters* (1990). Also deserving of mention are Syl Cheney-Coker (*The Graveyard Also Has Teeth,* 1980), and Ghanaian Abena P. A. Busia (*Testimonies of Exile,* 1990).

Drama

In the 1960s and 1970s, some anglophone western African theater scholars (and a few non-Africans) devoted considerable effort to proving that modern African theater (especially modern Nigerian and, even more specifically, modern Yoruba theater) evolved organically out of traditional religious and festival rituals. The effort ignored the quite obvious and well-documented evidence of the decisively seminal dramatic performances of the Western and Westernized elite communities (European and African) in local cities toward the end of the nineteenth century, the subsequent derivative performances in missionary schools, and later in the breakaway African churches that came into existence when deteriorating race relations between Europeans and Africans in the newly constituted colonies resulted in the segregation of the races. What is undeniable, in any case, is that the new drama was the product of the educated African elite.

Among the pioneers were the Ghanaian Joe de Graft, whose *Sons and Daughters* appeared in 1964, and the Sierra Leonean R. Sarif Easmon, who published *Dear Parent and Ogre* in 1964. Both dealt with generational conflicts between parents and their children. Ama Ata Aidoo's *The Dilemma of a Ghost* (1965) explored the difficulties inherent in intercultural marriages (here between a Ghanaian man and an African American woman), while her *Anowa* (1970) posits the troublesome proposition that African men alone were culpable for the African part in the slave trade, the women being implacably opposed to the traffic. Her compatriot Efua Sutherland was long a commanding figure in the development of Ghanaian drama as a writer, promoter of others' works, and the driving force in the construction of the National Theater. She wrote several plays for Ghana radio, including *The Marriage of Anansewa* (1975), an exploration of marriage through the medium of traditional storytelling;

Foriwa (1967), in which two women lead their people toward a better society; and *Edufa* (1967), the story of a man's attempt to deliver his wife to a death meant for him.

Discussion of anglophone western African theater is inevitably dominated by Wole Soyinka, undoubtedly the most successful dramatist on the continent. His first major play was *The Swamp Dwellers* (1963), written in 1957. It tells an enigmatic story of poverty, betrayal, and desertion of the home hearth in the Nigerian delta area. Other early plays like *The Lion and the Jewel* (1962), *The Strong Breed* (1963), and the satirical *The Trials of Brother Jero* (1963) deal with social and religious themes, but the most famous (or notorious) of his early works was *A Dance of the Forests* (1963), originally commissioned for the occasion of Nigeria's independence in 1960. Rather than offering a celebrative piece to a people basking in the euphoria and promise of newly won freedom, it treated the newborn nation to a debunking of all notions of a glorious past and a pessimistic (but prophetic) declaration that the future will be every bit as ignominious as its past had been.

As the political situation deteriorated in the country, and especially after his traumatic experiences during the civil war, Soyinka's plays became increasingly bitter and caustic; for example *Madmen and Specialists* (1971) depicts the country's leaders as demented and treats its audience to a dose of cannibalism. Perhaps his most successful play internationally has been *Death and the King's Horseman* (1975), in which he dramatizes the fateful consequences of official British interference in traditional rituals they had no means of understanding.

Another notable Nigerian dramatist is Ola Rotimi, who characteristically exploits traditional materials and rituals in plays such as *The Gods Are Not to Blame* (1971), *Kurunmi* (1971), *Ovonramwen Nogbaisi* (1974), and *If . . . : A Tragedy of the Ruled* (1983). Rotimi is sometimes criticized for his close adherence to classical Greek tragic models, in which regard he takes after John Pepper Clark-Bekederemo, whose *Song of a Goat* (1961) unequivocally declared its Greek affinities. One of the most exciting dramatists to emerge after the civil war is Femi Osofisan, whose Brechtian (often musical) theater champions the common cause in socialistic terms. His plays include *The Chattering and the Song* (1977), described by a critic as the most revolutionary play ever written in Nigeria, *Once Upon Four Robbers* (1980), and *Morountodun* (1982).

Other Works

In addition to creative works, anglophone western African writers have produced significant essays on a variety of subjects. For example, Kwame Nkrumah, the founding president of Ghana, wrote several political and philosophical treatises, the last of which was *Neo-Colonialism: The Last Stage of Imperialism* (1965). Also, the Nigerian politician Chief Obafemi Awolowo published his *The People's Republic* in 1968, and Wole Soyinka issued the first installment of his autobiography, *Ake: The Years of Childhood,* in 1981. He has since produced two sequels.

BIBLIOGRAPHY

Amuta, Chidi. *The Theory of African Literature: Implications for Practical Criticism.* London, 1989.

Bruner, Charlotte, ed. *The Heinemann Book of African Women's Writing.* London, 1993.

Gérard, Albert S. *European-Language Writing in Sub-Saharan Africa.* 2 vols. Budapest, 1986.

JanMohamed, Abdul R. *Manichean Aesthetics: The Politics of Literature in Colonial Africa.* Amherst, Mass., 1983.

Larson, Charles R. *The Emergence of African Fiction.* Rev. ed. Bloomington, Ind., 1972.

Obiechina, Emmanuel. *Culture, Tradition, and Society in the West African Novel.* African Studies Series, no. 14. New York, 1975.

Ogungbesan, Kolawole, ed. *New West African Literature.* London, 1979.

Owomoyela, Oyekan, ed. *A History of Twentieth-Century African Literatures.* Lincoln, Nebr., 1993.

Roscoe, Adrian A. *Mother Is Gold: A Study in West African Literature.* Cambridge, 1971.

Taiwo, Oladele. *An Introduction to West African Literature.* London, 1967.

OYEKAN OWOMOYELA

See also **Achebe, Chinua; Awolowo, Obafemi; Casely-Hayford, J. E.; Equiano, Olaudah; Language Use; Popular Culture; Soyinka, Wole; Theater.**

ANGLOPHONE LITERATURE IN EASTERN AFRICA

Eastern African literature comprises the literary traditions, as well as the works that have contributed to the literary traditions, of Kenya, Somalia, Tanzania, and Uganda. Eastern Africa's most internationally well-known writers are novelists Ngugi wa Thiong'o and Nuruddin Farah and the poet Okot p'Bitek. Ngugi wa Thiong'o's novels, particularly *A Grain of Wheat* (1967) and *Petals of Blood* (1977) are the most widely read works of eastern African literature. Nuruddin Farah's novels, particularly *Maps* (1986) and those in the three-volume series, Variations on the Theme of an African Dictatorship (1979–1983), have received international critical acclaim. Okot p'Bitek's book-length satiric poems have delighted a wide range of audiences. Many readers in eastern Africa are also familiar with the poetry of Shaaban Robert, Muyaka bin Haji, Abdilatif Abdalla, Taban lo Liyong, Siti binti Sa'id, and Sayyid Muhammad 'Abdallah Hasan. Meja Mwangi, Austin Bukenya, Euphrase Kezilahabi, and Said Ahmed Mohamed are novelists whose works are read by many eastern Africans. Eastern Africa's two best-known plays are *Ngaahika Ndeenda* (1977) (*I Will Marry When I Want,* 1982), written by Ngugi wa Thiong'o and Ngugi wa Mirii, and *The Trial of Dedan Kimathi* (1976), written by Ngugi wa Thiong'o and Micere Mugo. The plays of Ebrahim Hussein, Francis D. Imbuga, Penina Muhando, Jay Kitsao, Chacha Nyaigotti-Chacha, and Alamin Mazrui are also familiar to many east Africans.

English and KiSwahili are the two most widely used literary languages in eastern Africa, although many other east African languages have also been used for literary composition. Most of east Africa's writers, including Ngugi wa Thiong'o, Nuruddin Farah, and Okot p'Bitek, have published in two or more languages. Many contemporary east African writers have published works in English, and these works are often considered to be part of what is referred to as anglophone African literature. These works written in English, while certainly a part of English language literary traditions including anglophone African literature generally, have also been informed by east African language literary traditions. Of these, the oldest written tradition is that of Swahili. Literary works in KiSwahili were written in manuscript form beginning in the mid-eighteenth century, if not earlier. Nearly all of the extant manuscripts from the eighteenth and nineteenth centuries are manuscripts of poems, and most of these are religious poems. The two best-known are Sayyid Abdallah bin Ali bin Nassir's *Inkishafi* (*Al-Inkishafi: Catechism of a Soul,* 1977) and Mwana Kupona's "Utendi wa Mwana Kupona." Moral and ethical concerns were central to these poems and have continued to be of importance to east African literary traditions. Mwana Kupona's poem in particular has influenced a wide range of contemporary poets including Abdilatif Abdalla and Said Ahmed Mohamed. Islamic and, more recently, Christian religious imagery, symbolism, and language continue to be central to understanding the works of many east African writers, even the works of those who write from explicitly progressive perspectives (such as Abdilatif Abdalla) and those who critique religious belief from a Marxist point of view (such as Ngugi wa Thiong'o).

During the colonial era in eastern Africa a wide range of works that challenged, criticized, and urged resistance to colonialism and imperialism were composed in east African languages, often by political activists. Such works included the early-nineteenth-century KiSwahili poetry of Muyaka bin Haji of Mombasa, who opposed control of the eastern African coast by the Anglo-Omani sultanate of Seyyid Said, and the poetry of Zahidi Mngumi of Lamu, who debated with Muyaka as well as with fellow Lamu poets concerning efforts by the Mazrui rulers of Mombasa to control the Lamu Archipelago. Another example is Kibabina's poem about resistance to Omani rule in Siyu. In a narrative poem, Hemedi Abdulla el-Buhriy documented the Abushiri resistance to the German conquest of what later became Tanganyika. Abdul Karim bin Jamaliddini used the same poetic form to provide an account of the Maji Maji resistance to German colonial rule. Sayyid Muhammad 'Abdallah Hasan led the primary resistance to British rule of Somalia and his poetry was central to his political campaigns. Swahili poets beginning in the 1920s published poetry in the newspaper *Mambo Leo*. These poems were written on a wide range of subjects, and a number of poems on political topics were published, often in coded form. Political poetry in English and KiSwahili is still published in a wide range of newspapers and magazines.

Poetry was not the only genre in which opposition to colonialism was articulated by east African writers. Perhaps the most influential work published during the middle years of colonialism in eastern Africa was Jomo Kenyatta's 1938 *Facing Mount Kenya*, an ethnography of the Gikuyu as well as a strongly stated critique of colonialism. Kenyatta also edited a newspaper in Gikuyu. Another prolific writer of the early colonial period was Apolo Kagwa, who between 1893 and 1905 wrote five books in Luganda on Baganda history and culture. Kagwa's works included *Basekabaka be Buganda* (*The Kings of Buganda*, 1971) and *Ekitabo kye Empisa za Baganda* (*The Customs of the Baganda*, 1934).

In 1952 songs in opposition to colonial rule were composed and collected by Gakaara wa Wanjau and Stanley Mathenge, and Kinuthia wa Mugia, among others. These songs were published in Gikuyu by Gakaara wa Wanjau, Kinuthia wa Mugia, and Henry Muoria, all of whom were imprisoned or forced into exile because of these and other political publications. In 1984 Gakaara wa Wanjau won the Noma Award for Publishing in Africa for his prison diary, *Mwandiki wa Mau Mau Ithaamirio-ini* (*Mau Mau Writer in Detention*, 1988).

Throughout the 1950s poets who supported the Tanganyika African National Union (TANU) exchanged and published poems that called for political independence and an end to colonial rule. Shaaban Robert is the best known of this group of poets and his most famous poem is "Kiswahili," a poem that advocates the use of Swahili as a liberating language. Saadan Kandoro, one of the founding members of TANU, Mathias Mnyampala, and Amri Abedi, the first African mayor of Dar es Salaam, were all active poets during this time. Although better known for his forceful and often witty essays and speeches, Julius Nyerere, who subsequently became the first president of Tanzania, was also a TANU poet who exchanged poetry with his contemporaries.

Since independence, eastern African writing in opposition to neocolonialism and postindependence government policies and practices has often been inspired by the earlier works of the colonial resistance period. This inspiration is particularly evident in Abdilatif Abdalla's collection of poetry *Sauti ya Dhiki* (1973), and in Ngugi wa Thiong'o's novels written in Gikuyu, *Caitaani Mutharaba-ini* (1980) (*Devil on the Cross*, 1982) and *Matigari ma Njiruungi* (1986) (*Matigari*, 1987), and in his last novel written in English, *Petals of Blood* (1977). The impact of earlier colonial resistance writing is also evident in Ebrahim Hussein's play *Kinjeketile* (1969) and in Said Ahmed Mohamed's poetry in *'Sikata tamaa* (1980). Many eastern African writers have written novels that present eastern African perspectives on colonial history. The best-known of these are Ngugi wa Thiong'o's *A Grain of Wheat* (1967), *Weep Not, Child* (1964), and *The River Between* (1965). Other historical novels include Meja Mwangi's *Carcase for Hounds* (1974) and Samuel Kahiga's *Dedan Kimathi: The Real Story* (1990). Plays based on colonial-era events include Ngugi wa Thiong'o and Micere Mugo's *The Trial of Dedan Kimathi* (1976), Ebrahim Hussein's *Kinjeketile*, and Kenneth Watene's *Dedan Kimathi* (1974).

Contemporary writers, like their predecessors, have also often been activist writers and have been persecuted for their writing. Abdilatif Abdalla wrote *Sauti ya Dhiki* (1973) while he was imprisoned for having written a Kenya People's Union pamphlet, and Abdilatif and Ngugi wa Thiong'o have worked together through the United Movement for Democracy in Kenya and other organizations to document and draw attention to human rights struggles in Kenya. Ngugi wa Thiong'o wrote *Caitaani Mutharaba ini* (1980) (*Devil on the Cross*, 1983), his first novel in Gikuyu, while imprisoned (without charge but presumably for coauthoring *Ngaahika Ndeenda*). He has documented his prison experiences in *Detained: A Writer's Prison Diary* (1981). Persecuted east African activist writers have also included, among many others, Byron Kawadwa, a Ugandan playwright who was murdered by agents of Idi Amin; Nuruddin Farah, who was forced into exile and sentenced to death in absentia by Somalia's former dictator Mohammed Siyad Barre; Gakaara wa Wanjau, who was imprisoned by both the colonial and postindependence governments of Kenya; journalist and novelist Wahome Mutahi; and politician and novelist Koigi wa Wamwere, who in 1995 was sentenced to four years in prison and six strokes of the cane on charges that human rights groups have documented were fabricated by the government of Daniel arap Moi in Kenya. A number of prison diaries and novels with prison settings have been published by eastern Africans. These include Wahome Mutahi's *Three Days on the Cross* (1991), Ngugi wa Thiong'o's *Detained* (1981), Koigi wa Wamwere's *Conscience on Trial* (1988), J. M. Kariuki's *Mau Mau Detainee* (1963), and Gakaara wa Wanjau's *Mwandiki wa Mau Mau Ithaamirio-ini* (1983) (*Mau Mau Author in Detention*, 1988).

Just before and after independence a number of east African writers began to publish works in English. The best-known English-language works by east African writers that were published during this period were Ngugi wa Thiong'o's novels *The River Between, Weep Not, Child,* and *A Grain of Wheat* and Okot p'Bitek's two satirical poems *Song of Lawino* (1966) and *Song of Ocol* (1970). Taban lo Liyong's first volume of poetry, *Frantz Fanon's Uneven Ribs,* was published in 1971 and his volume of criticism, *The Last Word,* appeared in 1969. Nuruddin Farah's *From a Crooked Rib* (1970) was published toward the end of this period in 1970. Two Tanzanian novelists also wrote novels in English shortly after independence. Gabriel Ruhum-bika's *Village in Uhuru* was published in 1969 and Peter K. Palangyo's *Dying in the Sun* was published in 1968. Three east African novelists who have continued to write in English are Nuruddin Farah (*From a Crooked Rib,* 1970; *A Naked Needle,* 1976; *Sweet and Sour Milk,* 1979; *Sardines,* 1981; *Close Sesame,* 1983; *Maps,* 1986; and *Gifts,* 1992); Meja Mwangi (*Carcase for Hounds,* 1974; *Going Down River Road,* 1976; and *Cockroach Dance,* 1979); and Abdulrazak R. Gurnah (*Paradise,* 1994).

One of the major literary events in eastern Africa during the early years of independence was the founding of *Transition,* a journal of literary and social commentary, by Rajat Neogy at Makerere University. *Transition* is one of Africa's oldest and most influential journals. It was subsequently edited by Wole Soyinka in Accra, Ghana, and is now edited by Soyinka, Kwame Anthony Appiah, and Henry Louis Gates and published by Duke University in North Carolina.

In the early 1960s and 1970s Kenya, Tanzania, and Uganda were part of what was the East African Community, and at the University of Nairobi Ngugi wa Thiong'o, Okot p'Bitek, and Taban lo Liyong were among those who pressured for curricular revisions that would emphasize works by African writers, oral literature, and works in east African languages. Similar debates took place at Makerere and the University of Dar es Salaam. During this period KiSwahili departments were established at the University of Nairobi and the University of Dar es Salaam. As a result of these curricular revisions and a widely shared commitment to Swahili and Swahili literature, the 1970s and 1980s generation of university-educated Kenyan and Tanzanian writers has produced works written almost exclusively in KiSwahili. The best-known of this group of writers are playwright Ebrahim Hussein, novelist and poet Said Ahmed Mohamed, novelist E. Kezilahabi, and playwright and poet Alamin Mazrui. The orientation of their works is progressive, generally explicitly socialist, and often highly critical of neocolonialism and of east African government policies and political culture, particularly those of the Moi government in Kenya. Notable among these works are Ebrahim Hussein's play *Kwenye Ukingo wa Thim* (1988), which uses a highly publicized and politicized inheritance case in Kenya as the basis for a complex drama that explores issues of ethnicity, class, and gender, and Said Ahmed Mohamed's novel *Kiza katika Nuru* (1988), which considers the patriarchal and class bases of neocolonial corruption.

The most stylistically elegant and finely crafted works of east African literature share a clear progressive and internationally informed political orientation as well as commitments to the literatures, languages, and historical experience of east Africans. For example, Ngugi wa Thiong'o's *Petals of Blood* is a socialist realist novel in which the social and political upheavals in the imaginary community of Ilmorog model the colonial and neocolonial history of Kenya and other postcolonial conditions in Africa and elsewhere. His *Matigari ma ungi* is a prose poem in resistance to neocolonialism that uses the languages, images, proverbs, and mythologies of east African and other historically relevant resistance literatures. Ngugi wa Thiong'o's works are informed by Marxist and Pan-Africanist perspectives, as are numerous other east African novels and plays, including Alamin Mazrui's *Kilio cha Haki* (1981), Penina Muhando's *Pambo* (1975), and Said Ahmed Mohamed's *Kiza katika Nuru* (1988). Nuruddin Farah's works share Ngugi's Pan-Africanist perspective, but also incorporate feminist viewpoints and problematize notions of national, ethnic, linguistic, and gender identity. His three novels with the series title Variations on the Theme of an African Dictatorship (*Sweet and Sour Milk*, *Sardines*, and *Close Sesame*) each comment on Siyad Barre's regime in Somalia as well as upon other dictatorships and forms of tyranny. *Sardines* considers dictatorship as patriarchy and patriarchal social structures and behavior as dictatorial. Farah's *Maps* questions notions of national, ethnic, and gender identity and boundaries and comments upon the intermixture of political and personal struggles in efforts to establish viable personal and political identities.

A number of east African writers have also written literary criticism. Ngugi wa Thiong'o's *Moving the Centre* (1993) and *Decolonising the Mind: The Politics of Language in African Literature* (1986) are the two most influential of these critical works. In *Decolonizing the Mind*, Ngugi issued his well-known "Farewell to English," a statement of his decision to write thereafter exclusively in Gikuyu and Ki-Swahili. This statement remains controversial among African writers and critics of African literature. Among east African writers and critics, there are few who would question the decision to write in KiSwahili, the national language of Kenya and Tanzania and the language of choice for most Kenyan and Tanzanian writers. There are some, however, who do not agree with Ngugi's argument that it is important also to contribute to literature

in additional African languages. They express the concern that by writing in Gikuyu rather than Ki-Swahili, Ngugi might be undermining the status of KiSwahili as the primary language of eastern Africa.

Another important contribution made to literary theory by eastern Africans has been the concept of "orature" as articulated by Pio Zirimu and Austin Bukenya, used to distinguish spoken compositions from those composed in written form. East African study of orature has been particularly informed by their work as evidenced both in the body of research that has been produced and in the importance of orature in east African literature curricula. One of the most notable east African studies of orature is Wanjiku Mukabi Kabira's *The Oral Artist* (1983), a study of the oral narrative performances of Kabebe, an artist from Kiambu, Kenya.

Categories of genre distinctions such as oral and written, popular and literary, poetry and song, which may be useful in the study of other literatures, are often less relevant to the study of east African literatures. For example, poets who composed and exchanged poetry within the *gicaandi* genre of Gikuyu poetry did so using an ideographic system of symbols that encapsulated poetic images. These symbols were painted on a particular type of gourd. Poets who composed *gicaandi* poetry did so with reference to their gourds during competitive exchanges with other poets. The winner of a *gicaandi* contest won his rival's *gicaandi* gourd/codebook. *Gicaandi* poetry itself was not written, but its poetic images were. Another example is that of Siti binti Sa'id's popular songs of the 1920s and 1930s. These songs were studied as poetry in the literary biography of Siti binti Sa'id written by the eminent poet Shaaban Robert. A number of works produced in one medium have often been transferred to other media. For example, the political songs written and published by Gakaara wa Wanjau, Kinuthia wa Mugia, and Henry Muoria in the early 1950s were translated and included in *Thunder from the Mountains* (1980) by editor Maina wa Kinyatti. These songs have more recently been reissued on cassette tapes by Joseph Kamaru and Irungu wa Kario. The songs have also been used by Ngugi wa Thiong'o in his plays and novels.

In 1977 the Kamiriithu Community Educational and Cultural Centre north of Nairobi staged in Gikuyu the play *Ngaahika Ndeenda* (published in 1980), by Ngugi wa Thiong'o and Ngugi wa Mirii, which harshly criticized the government. The theater was bulldozed, Ngugi wa Thiong'o was jailed without trial for a year, and the two authors were exiled. They had criticized the government before, so the fact that the play was performed in Gikuyu seems to have been the decisive factor for the authorities. Nevertheless, production and publication of the play has had a continuing impact on theater in eastern Africa. This impact is demonstrated by continued restagings of productions of *Ngaahika Ndeenda*, which often come up against government censorship, and by the current popularity of nightclub plays in Gikuyu, as well as by the many forceful political plays in KiSwahili and the often socially and politically relevant drama produced for school drama festivals. Ngugi wa Mirii now lives in Zimbabwe, where his work in community action theater is supported by the government. He has also organized community theater workshops on drug-related issues in the United States and Canada.

By writing in KiSwahili and other east African languages, Kenyan writers in particular have often been able to have their works read and studied even if these works are highly critical of the government. For example, Abdilatif Abdalla's prison poetry in *Sauti ya Dhiki* (1973) was highly critical of then-president Jomo Kenyatta and of Kenyatta's ruling party, yet this work was awarded the Kenyatta Prize in Literature and was assigned reading in Kenyan secondary schools during the last years of Kenyatta's life, even though the author had been forced into exile. Similarly, while Alamin Mazrui was in prison, his play *Kilio cha Haki* (1981) (a drama that depicts government cooperation with a multinational corporation in breaking up a strike led by a dynamic female labor leader) was required reading in Kenyan secondary schools. However, in other cases works in east African languages have been suppressed. Ngugi wa Thiong'o's *Matigari ma Njiruungi* is not available in the original Gikuyu edition, but is available in eastern Africa in English translation.

BIBLIOGRAPHY

Gérard, Albert S., ed. *European-Language Writing in Sub-Saharan Africa*. Budapest, 1986.

Kaggia, Bildad. *Roots of Freedom, 1921–1963*. Nairobi, Kenya, 1975.

Lindfors, Bernth, ed. *Mazungumzo: Interviews with East African Writers, Publishers, Editors, and Scholars*. Athens, Ohio, 1980.

Mutiso, G. C. M. *Socio-Political Thought in African Literature: Weusi?* London, 1974.

Samatar, Said S. *Oral Poetry and Somali Nationalism: The Case of Sayyid 'Abdille Hasan*. Cambridge, 1982.

Sicherman, Carol. *Ngugi wa Thiong'o: The Making of a Rebel*. New York, 1990.

ANN BIERSTEKER

See also **Education; Human Rights; Kagwa, Apolo; Kenyatta, Jomo; Language Use; Ngugi wa Thiong'o; Oral Culture and Oral Tradition; Shaaban Robert.**

ANGLOPHONE LITERATURE IN SOUTHERN AFRICA

Anglophone writing in southern Africa is more commonly—and rather cumbersomely—known as English-language writing, or writing by English-speakers. This description is understood also to have meant writing exclusively by Whites or those of European extraction. In the first surveys of this literature—by Ian D. Colvin in his introduction to Sidney Mendelssohn's *South African Bibliography* (1910) and by Manfred Nathan in his book-length *South African Literature* (1925)—this is entirely the case. However, since World War II the meaning of anglophone writing has shifted to indicate writers and performers of all colors who choose to write in English rather than in other languages of the region. In contemporary southern Africa, more practicing writers are of African than of European ancestry.

The term "southern Africa" needs some clarification because there is no working geopolitical region to which it corresponds. Roughly, "southern Africa" refers to South Africa; Namibia (formerly German South-West Africa); Lesotho (formerly Basutoland); Swaziland; Botswana (formerly Bechuanaland); Zimbabwe (formerly Southern Rhodesia); Zambia (formerly Northern Rhodesia); and Malawi (formerly Nyasaland), although these last two are sometimes classified as central African. This cluster of countries, in which British colonialism was a common formative experience, is flanked by Angola and Mozambique of the lusophone sphere of influence. Alternatively, all these countries, South Africa excepted, until 1994 formed the "front-line" states of the Southern African Development Coordinating Conference (SADCC), an association founded in 1980 to reduce economic dependence on South Africa which, at that time, was driven by apartheid policies.

The first English-language descriptions of southern Africa date back to explorers like Sir Francis Drake, who rounded the Cape of Good Hope in the 1570s. The seaward view of the subcontinent was known to Shakespeare, and John Donne worked a reference to Table Mountain into one of his poems, "Progress of the Soul" (1601). In 1634 Thomas Herbert wrote *Some Yeares Travaile into Afrique*, which first familiarized European readers with the inland aboriginal inhabitants, the San and Khoi peoples, then known as Bushmen. Daniel Defoe in *Captain Singleton* (1720) and Jonathan Swift in *Gulliver's Travels* (1726) had their characters make use of the facilities of the Dutch-sponsored entrepôt at Cape Town, the base for ever more penetrating and well-recorded expeditions.

The Cape was first occupied by the British in 1795, and in 1806 their rule became entrenched. The classic pattern of nineteenth-century colonization was applied: from 1820 in the Eastern Cape and from 1824 in Natal. Then hunters and missionaries moved into the interior, followed by transport-riders and administrators. David Livingstone (1813–1873), from his base near Mafeking, on the border of the Kalahari Desert, caught the popular imagination by opening up the "Dark Continent," contributing to the "scramble" for Africa by other colonial powers. By the end of the Victorian period, the imperial strategist Cecil Rhodes could talk of having started a railway line from the Cape that was destined almost to reach Cairo.

Early surveys of South African poetry, like that of Sir T. Herbert Warren in *The Cambridge History of English Literature* (1917), consider the Scottish romantic, Thomas Pringle (1789–1834) as the father of South African English verse. Rudyard Kipling is quoted there as saying: "it's a case of there's Pringle, and there's Pringle, and after that one must hunt the local papers" (p. 373). Pringle, the Cape's most influential man of letters, founded the first national library and the first literary review (*The South African Journal*, 1824) and championed the freedom of the press. "Afar in the Desert," his rhapsodic poem about belonging yet feeling alien in the wilderness of the hinterland, is indeed where English literature begins to inscribe Africa from personal experience. Settler mores and the plantation culture with which he clashed forced him to assume a liberal stance, particularly against the slavery system. His *Narrative of a Residence in South Africa* (1835) chronicles this battle of the individual conscience against the illiberal state-in-formation, a stance that may be said to characterize much of the output of the next century and a half.

In the *London Mercury* (1929), under the heading "South African Literature," Francis Brett Young drew a distinction between the copious documentary scribblers of the frontier press and the popular theater of his day, nominating Olive Schreiner (1855–1920) as the pioneer of "literary art" in Africa. In particular he mentioned her *Story of an African Farm*, first published in London in 1883 to huge and enduring acclaim. As Elaine Showalter remarks in her introduction to a 1993 reprint of the novel, "instead of civilized ladies and gentlemen discussing courtship over tea, it told the story of passionate dreamers arguing about the oppression of women and children, the meaning of life, the battle between good and evil, and the existence of God."

Young correctly places *The Story of an African Farm*, a problematic, contradictory text, at the head of a tradition of realist fiction. From the fringe of the British Empire, writers kept writing back to Britain with challenging and subtle social insight. Sarah Gertrude Millin (1889–1968) followed with *God's Step-children* (1924) and Pauline Smith (1882–1959) with her collection of short stories, *The Little Karoo* (1925).

A parallel tradition of adventure romance began at the same time with the publication of H. Rider Haggard's *King Solomon's Mines* (1885). Rather than the domestic site dealt with by the realist mode, this kind of fiction takes as its natural material the he-man's urge toward expansion and the inevitable conquest of the weak by warfare. *Jock of the Bushveld* (1907), by J. Percy Fitzpatrick (1862–1931), remains the most popular account of the preindustrial days of gold diggers and bushwhackers. The British-Zulu wars of 1879 and the so-called Boer War of 1899–1902 against the Afrikaner republics of the Transvaal and the Orange Free State were widely chronicled in this branch of the literature, which persists to the present in the works of writers like Laurens van der Post (1906–1996) and Wilbur Smith (b. 1933).

With the election of a Liberal government in Britain in 1906, the formation of the Union of South Africa in 1910 was assured (the land eventually acquired dominion status). In *The New Countries*, an anthology edited by Hector Bolitho in 1929, work from Australia, Canada, and New Zealand was included alongside South African pieces—notably by William Plomer (1903–1973), whose novel *Turbott Wolfe* (1925) had shockingly advocated "mixed race" marriages. The categorization of South African English work as part of Commonwealth literature continued even after South Africa was expelled from the Commonwealth in 1961—William H. New's *Among Worlds: An Introduction to Modern Commonwealth and South African Fiction*

(1975) is an example. In 1994, with the overthrow of the apartheid regime, South Africa returned to the Commonwealth.

The first Black African literary figure of note in South Africa is Sol T. Plaatje (1877–1932). His historical novel, *Mhudi*, subtitled *An Epic of South African Native Life a Hundred Years Ago,* was largely written in 1917 but first published—by the missionary Lovedale Press—in 1930. However, only when it was reprinted in the Heinemann African Writers Series (1978) could it be said to have made any lasting impact. "When I first read this beautiful book," Bessie Head wrote then, "I was absolutely in despair. I needed to copy the whole book out by hand so as to keep it with me" (quoted from the jacket). Written as an attempt to preserve vanishing Black versions of southern African history in order to serve the Africanizers of the future, *Mhudi* is now considered a model of resistance to European acculturation.

Among the first attempts at a South African cultural-national initiative was the movement begun in Natal around the satirical journal, *Voorslag,* edited mainly by the poet Roy Campbell (1901–1957). *Voorslag* (1926–1927) gave rise to equally short-lived and embattled efforts: *The Sjambok* of Stephen Black (1880–1931) in Johannesburg in 1929 and *The Touleier* of Herman Charles Bosman (1905–1951), also in Johannesburg (1930). Since then, intermittent journals advocating that South African work be directly presented to South African readers have appeared more reliably; *Contrast,* founded in Cape Town in 1960, remains active in the 1990s. From the 1920s, book publishing has developed into a sophisticated industry as well.

The parallel development of Afrikaans-language culture, given a boost by the accession to power of the Nationalist government in 1948, also has acted as a stimulus, although during the deep apartheid period, English-language work assumed an increasingly oppositional position beginning in the 1960s. The famous novel published the year the Afrikaner nationalists took over, *Cry, the Beloved Country,* by Alan Paton (1903–1988)—still the most read South African work—has come to be taken as the typical protest novel, written against segregatory practices.

In a survey like "The Color of South African Literature" by Martin Tucker (in his *Africa in Modern Literature,* 1967), writers like Doris Lessing (b. 1919) are featured. Although her early work was exclusively about Rhodesia, she is still classified by Tucker as a South African writer. The same often

applies to Thomas Mofolo (1877–1948), whose *Chaka* (originally written in Sesotho in 1925), when it first appeared in an English translation in 1931, made a great impact, especially on the Negritude writers elsewhere in Africa. Today he would be more usefully classified as the father of Lesotho literature. Both Lessing and Mofolo have, in effect, founded autonomous literatures.

In 1970, at a Modern Language Association conference on British Commonwealth literature, it became clear that as a result of purges and the censorship system of apartheid, southern African literature had really been split into two (the second part being a diaspora of those driven into exile). The school of urban journalists that formed around *Drum* and other magazines—for example, Can Themba (1924–1969), Lewis Nkosi (b. 1935), and Nat Nakasa (1937–1965)—was disbanded and banned. Many great works were now written overseas in the form of autobiographical testimony— two are *Tell Freedom* (1954), by Peter Abrahams (b. 1919), and *Down Second Avenue* (1959), by Ezekiel (now Es'kia) Mphahlele (b. 1919). A figure like Dennis Brutus (b. 1924) took to poetry as the basis of his campaign against racial discrimination. By 1974, in his chapter "South Africa" (in Bruce King's collection, *Literatures of the World in English*), John Povey could remark that the gulf between South African expatriates and those at home was absolute.

With the Chimurenga (War of Liberation) declared in the future Zimbabwe, Lessing was prohibited entry. Writers crucial to the formation of a rapidly expanding Zimbabwean literature were active: Dambudzo Marechera (1955–1986) is the prime example, his novella *The House of Hunger* (1978) being a key work about the displacements of young blacks in the ghetto environment. Another is Shimmer Chinodya (b. 1957), whose panoramic *Harvest of Thorns* (1989) is a near-perfect account of Zimbabwe's transition to independence.

A collection like Colin and O-lan Style's *Mambo Book of Zimbabwean Verse in English* (1986) is an admirable summary of what is now the independent and independent-minded, largely black enterprise of ZimLit. In 1992, when Lessing published her *African Laughter: Four Visits to Zimbabwe*—part history, part cultural commentary, and part reminiscence—she stated her position as one of the major figures of the new literatures in English vis-à-vis the burgeoning land of her youth.

The same may not be said of Zambia, to the north, where restrictive government procedures have retarded literary growth. The National Educational Company in Lusaka has published a few plays, notably by Kabwe Kasoma (b. 1933), and some poetry collections. The autobiography of former President Kenneth Kaunda (b. 1924), *Zambia Shall Be Free* (1962), remains in print. An early novel promoting unity in the land is *The Tongue of the Dumb* (1971), by Dominic Mulaisho (b. 1933).

The first novel about independent Zambia, *Quills of Desire,* by Binwell Sinyangwe (b. 1956), was not published until 1993, by Baobab Books in neighboring Zimbabwe. There, thanks to enlightened publishing policies, together with the technically advanced annual book fair, an alternative to the publishing industry in South Africa is being formed.

Swaziland, by contrast, is a nonstarter: in *A New Reader's Guide to African Literature* (1983), edited by Hans M. Zell, Carol Bundy, and Virginia Coulon, only one work by a writer of Swazi origin is recorded. Only one poem from there—by Oswald Basize Dube (b. 1957), a praise poem in honor of King Sobhuza II—has been included in a regional collection, *The Penguin Book of Southern African Verse* (1989).

Malawi, on the other hand, despite the persecution of intellectuals under the rule of President Hastings Banda, has produced a powerful group of poets, most of them associated with the writers' workshop at Chancellor College in Zomba. These include David Rubardiri (b. 1930), Felix Mnthali (b. 1933), Jack Mapanje (b. 1944), and Frank Chipasula (b. 1949), the latter being the editor of the influential anthology *When My Brothers Come Home: Poems from Central and Southern Africa* (1985). In 1967, a rediscovery akin to that of Plaatje in South Africa occurred when George Simeon Mwase's classic account of the Chilembwe Rising of 1915, *Strike a Blow and Die,* was first published.

A work of similar impact—since it records African history in the making, from the inside point of view—is *A Bewitched Crossroads* (1984). It is about the origins of Botswana, the country of adoption of Bessie Head (1937–1986), who alone has made Botswanan literature, beginning with her novel *When Rain Clouds Gather* (1968). By the time of her short-story collection *The Collector of Treasures* (1977), she was hailed as one of Africa's trendsetting women writers. She did not live to see her home country, South Africa, free of apartheid and was never permitted to return to it.

In South Africa in the 1980s, despite the severance of cultural ties with the rest of the region, several major careers continued undiminished, as if challenged to excel by the very bleakness of the situation. One is that of Nadine Gordimer. Born in 1923, she began publishing stories in 1937; in 1991 she was awarded the Nobel Prize for literature, primarily in recognition of her tireless struggle against censorship. As a founder of the Congress of South African Writers, she has ensured the unfettered publication of many younger figures, particularly through the journal *Staffrider*. Another novelist with a sustained and equally distinguished output is J. M. Coetzee (b. 1940).

Another noteworthy career is Athol Fugard's (b. 1932). By 1958 he was writing and directing the plays that would make him one of the most produced dramatists in the English-speaking theater. The techniques used in his collaborative texts—for example, *Sizwe Bansi Is Dead* (1974), devised with his performers—have stimulated much other African drama and numerous imitations.

With the election of the first nonracial majority government in South Africa in 1994, southern Africa may for the first time become integrated as a literary whole.

BIBLIOGRAPHY

Alvarez-Pereyre, Jacques. *The Poetry of Commitment in South Africa.* London, 1984.

Barnett, Ursula A. *A Vision of Order: A Study of Black South African Literature in English (1914–1980).* Amherst, Mass., 1983.

Chapman, Michael, ed. *Soweto Poetry.* Johannesburg, 1982.

Chapman, Michael, Colin Gardner, and Es'kia Mphahlele, eds. *Perspectives on South African English Literature.* Johannesburg, 1992.

Coetzee, J. M. *White Writing: On the Culture of Letters in South Africa.* New Haven, Conn. 1988.

Driver, Dorothy. "South African Literature: In English." In *Encyclopedia of World Literature in the Twentieth Century.* Edited by Leonard S. Klein. New York, 1984.

Gérard, Albert S., ed. *European-Language Writing in Sub-Saharan Africa.* 2 vols. Budapest, 1986.

Gray, Stephen. *Southern African Literature: An Introduction.* New York, 1979.

———. "South African Poetry: In English." In *The New Princeton Encyclopedia of Poetry and Poetics.* Edited by Alex Preminger and T. V. F. Brogan. Princeton, 1993.

Gray, Stephen, ed. *The Penguin Book of Southern African Stories.* London, 1985.

Haarhoff, Dorian. *The Wild South-West: Frontier Myths and Metaphors in Literature Set in Namibia (1760–1988).* Johannesburg, 1991.

Mphahlele, Ezekiel. *The African Image.* Rev. ed. New York, 1974.

Smith, M. van Wyk. *Drummer Hodge: The Poetry of the Anglo-Boer War, 1899–1902.* Oxford, 1978.

———. *Grounds of Contest: A Survey of South African English Literature.* Cape Town, 1990.

Veit-Wild, Flora. *Teachers, Preachers, Non-Believers: A Social History of Zimbabwean Literature.* London, 1992.

Watts, Jane. *Black Writers from South Africa: Towards a Discourse of Liberation.* Houndmills, U.K., 1989.

STEPHEN GRAY

See also **Gordimer, Nadine; Human Rights; Kaunda, Kenneth; Language Use; Plaatje, Sol; Publishing.**

FRANCOPHONE LITERATURE IN WESTERN AFRICA

Whatever else the twentieth century will be remembered for, one of its most memorable achievements will be the independence of the African continent and the renaissance and recognition of its invaluable artistic contribution to human creativity. For the first time the voice of the black continent is heard around the world, even though it is through the written languages of the colonizers.

Although the French were on the Senegalese coast as early as the seventeenth century, African writing in French appeared later than in English. Speculations as to the reasons for this tardiness are varied and somewhat inconclusive. A possible explanation lies in the different colonialist strategies: British indirect rule allowed more intellectual freedom to the natives than did the direct and assimilating rule of France's "civilizing mission." Another possible reason could be found in the very different attitudes toward language and writing promoted by the Anglo-Saxon missionaries and their Catholic counterparts mostly present in French territories. Whatever the reasons, Robert Cornevin states in his *Littératures d'Afrique noire de langue française* (1976; Black African Literatures in French) that the first native writing in French was Léopold Panet's (c. 1819–1859) account of the traveling mission that the French undertook from Senegal to Morocco. His chronicle was first published in *La revue coloniale* (Colonial Review) in 1850. As for the first fictional writing, Robert W. July dates it to a 1920 children's book titled *Les trois volontés de Malic* (Malic's Three Wishes), written by a Senegalese schoolteacher, Ahmadou Mapaté Diagne. Ironically, the African francophone novel entered the literary stage with *Batouala, véritable roman nègre*

(1921; Batouala, a True Black Novel), written by René Maran, from Martinique. *Batouala*, which won the prestigious Prix Goncourt, is set in central Africa and depicts the hard reality of native life under colonial rule. It provoked a scandal and repressive measures against the author by the colonial authorities. Thus, notwithstanding its genuine literary merits, it became a best-seller in France, and Léopold Senghor hailed the work as the father of the black novel. After this remarkable beginning a few novels were published in Paris: *Force-bonté* (1926; Strength and Kindness), by Bakary Diallo; *Karim* (1935) and *Mirages de Paris* (1937; Mirages of Paris), by Ousmane Socé; *L'esclave* (1929; The Slave) by Félix Couchoro; *Doguicimi* (1938), by Paul Hazoumé. These novels are not without literary value and present an interesting variety of inspiration, but they do share a common acceptance of colonialism, a viewpoint that would soon be brought into question by the Negritude movement.

Negritude has been much discussed, much praised, and much maligned. The limits of this essay do not allow an in-depth rendition of the movement, but I will attempt an overview of this watershed moment in the history of francophone black literature. Negritude germinated in the French West Indies but came into flower in Paris in the 1930s with *La revue du monde noir* (Review of the Black World), created by Dr. Sajous and two sisters, Paulette and Andrée Nardal. This review propagated the ideas of the American Negro Renaissance, which considerably influenced the French-speaking elite. The review ceased publication after six issues. However, the seeds of revolt and self-awareness had been sown, and in 1932, a group of West Indians published the inflammatory *Légitime défense* (Self-Defense), which was censored immediately. This new review denounced, among other things, the alienation of the Antilles bourgeoisie, its shameless imitation of French culture, and its betrayal of its own race and cultural heritage. It went further than mere criticism, pledging to change the situation by fighting for the black race on all fronts.

Revolutionary ideas, whether political, social, or artistic, were not foreign to the post–World War I Parisian intelligentsia. The surrealist movement had already had an impact on the artistic world, and on poetry in particular. *L'art nègre* had been discovered at the beginning of the century and had influenced cubism; Africa entered the mainstream of modern art well before the Exposition des Arts Décoratifs of 1925 and the Exposition

Coloniale of 1931 had revealed it to the general public. In 1921, Blaise Cendrars had published his *Anthologie nègre* (Negro Anthology) glorifying the diversity of African languages and the cultures that they expressed. Paris was then the intellectual mecca of the Western world and the perfect terrain for new ideas. In 1934, a small review, *L'étudiant noir* (The Black Student) appeared, founded by three black students who were to become very famous: Léopold Sédar Senghor from Senegal, Aimé Césaire from Martinique, and Léon Damas from French Guiana. It was they who elaborated the notion of Negritude. The word itself was coined by Césaire in 1939, in *Cahier d'un retour au pays natal* (Return to My Native Land), but it was Senghor who became and remained its most eloquent and controversial theoretician. For him, Negritude was "the cultural heritage, the values and most of all the genius of the Negro-African civilization." It must be emphasized that Negritude is the offspring of French colonialism and its assimilating policies, and thus was later scorned, ridiculed, and attacked by many anglophone African writers, in particular the Nigerian playwright and Nobel Prize winner Wole Soyinka and the South African novelist and critic Ezekiel Mphahlele. Although Soyinka toned down his famous "the tiger has no need to proclaim its tigritude," and in his study *Myth, Literature, and the African World* (1976) stated that Negritude should not be "underestimated or belittled," he sees it mostly as the problem of a small African elite in search of identity in the metropolis of France. Mphahlele views it as a romantic vision of the continent.

World War II interrupted the publication of *L'étudiant noir*, but in 1947 there appeared, simultaneously in Paris and in Dakar, the review *Présence africaine* (African Presence), founded by Alioune Diop and a group of young writers. This review was sponsored by such personalities as André Gide, Jean-Paul Sartre, Emmanuel Mounier, Michael Leiris, Senghor, Césaire, Richard Wright, and others. With *Présence africaine* the black world had a strong voice, a forum from which to speak and to be heard by the world. By that time the triumvirate of Negritude was already well known for its literary output, and by the 1950s Césaire, Senghor, and Damas had each published several collections of poems. Senghor's *Anthologie de la nouvelle poésie nègre et malgache de langue française* (1948; Anthology of the New Black and Malagasy Poetry in French) brought attention to a wide array of promising young poets, and Negritude poetry constitutes

without a doubt the finest corpus of poetry of modern Africa. In the subsequent years few poets have risen to that level of excellence, the exception being Tchicaya U Tam'si, who in the 1950s published three remarkable volumes of poetry: *Le mauvais sang* (1955; Bad Blood), *Feu de brousse* (1957; Bush Fire), and *Triche-coeur* (1958; Cheating Heart), followed by *Épitomé* (1962; Epitome) and *Le ventre* (1964; The Belly). His difficult and complex poetry expresses the anguish of the African experience in often raw, violent, and striking images.

In the 1950s there appeared what could be called the "new wave" of the African novel. Following in the footsteps of the pioneers of Negritude, this new generation of African francophone writers is fully conscious of their political and cultural predicament as subjects of a colonial power whose "civilizing mission" had been seriously questioned by the economic and moral bankruptcy brought on by World War II. They no longer accept the colonial paternalistic ideology and see themselves as the victims of an abusive power from which they dream of freeing themselves. Through its fiction this preindependence generation would proceed to put colonialism on trial and would expose, often with bitter irony, the arrogance and misery colonialism brought to the continent. Three novelists from Cameroon published, with amazing unity, a devastating portrait of colonialism. In *Le pauvre Christ de Bomba* (1956; The Poor Christ of Bomba) and *Le roi miraculé* (1958; The "Miraculated" King) Mongo Beti depicts ironically but with a certain sympathy the misguided foolishness and naïveté of the missionaries who never understood that to the natives they were simply another group of white men imposing their will. In *Cette Afrique-là* (1955; This Particular Africa), Jean Ikellé-Matiba compares German and French colonialism and conveys the message that this colonized Africa will soon no longer exist. Ferdinand Oyono, in *Une vie de boy* (1956; A Boy's Life) and *Le vieux nègre et la médaille* (1956; The Old Negro and the Medal) gives a very sarcastic and often bitter portrait of colonial power and its brutality.

Along with the denunciation of colonialism, this new generation of writers expresses the identity crisis which they are experiencing and which brought on Negritude. The novel would become a principal medium by which to explore this lost identity. In *Mission terminée* (1957; Mission to Kala), Mongo Beti's protagonist Jean Medza is painfully aware that he belongs to a lost generation forced to live in a world not intended for him. This existential anguish of the cultural hybrid who is the product of two irreconcilable worlds is debated on the philosophical level in Cheikh Hamidou Kane's moving novel *L'aventure ambiguë* (1961; The Ambiguous Adventure). The young protagonist, Samba Diallo, member of the noble family of the Diallobés, is torn between the Islamic teaching of his spiritual master, Thierno, and the teaching of the rational and godless French school. This internal conflict that the young man cannot resolve provokes many interesting debates between diverse characters. It is Samba's aunt, "the most royal lady," who most eloquently expresses his dilemma when she breaks the traditional silence of women to address the people, advising them to send their children to the French school so they will "learn to forget them." She understands that the only way to survive and to resist those "who came and won even though they were in the wrong" is to beat them at their own game, and that means a Western education.

This theme of the importance of education is a leitmotif of the African novel, be it in French or in English. Getting the white man's knowledge is perceived as the only road to freedom. In the 1970s women writers saw the school as the road to emancipation. Kane's novel could also be classified as a bildungsroman because it describes the coming of age of a young African. The same could be said of Mongo Beti's *Mission terminée,* where the young Medza, educated in the French school, has become so Westernized that he has to learn about Africa by going to the bush, where he discovers the lost paradise of childhood with his cousin Zambo and the boys and girls of the village of Kala.

In the same vein, yet with a totally different viewpoint, is Camara Laye's coming-of-age novel *L'enfant noir* (1953; The Dark Child). Although the novel takes place in colonial times, the white man is absent from the book. His presence is felt only indirectly through the presence of the school. Through the story of his childhood Laye is trying to recapture and to understand the ever-changing forces of Africa. Primarily a poetic and subjective vision of the motherland, *L'enfant noir* nonetheless contains an element of sociological account of life in a Guinean village, which greatly contributed to its immediate success. As an idyllic portrait of Malinke culture, it sounded a false note in the ironic and bitter African fiction of the 1950s, which at the time was concerned primarily with the struggle for independence and the psychological trauma of colonialism. Although the book was a great success with the French public, Laye was much criticized by African intellectuals. They saw in his text an inconceivable indifference to the drama of colonialism and interpreted his lack of anguish as a lack of commitment. In his celebrated and unfair critique, published in *Présence africaine* in 1954, Mongo Beti expressed his disappointment and dismay at the "monstrous absence of vision and depth in the Guinean's book." He compared *L'enfant noir* with Richard Wright's *Black Boy* and drew the obvious although erroneous conclusion that Laye presented an idyllic and therefore false image of Africa, deliberately closing his eyes to unpleasant reality.

This commitment to reality and political involvement marks the African novel since the 1950s and will carry it into the twenty-first century. No one embodies this mission better than the great social novelist of the francophone novel, Sembène Ousmane of Senegal (known in the West as Ousmane Sembène). Autodidact and Marxist, Sembène published his first novel, *Le docker noir* (The Black Docker), in 1956; it was soon followed by many others, such as *O pays, mon beau peuple!* (1957; O Country, My Beautiful People), *Les bouts de bois de Dieu* (1960; God's Bits of Wood), *L'harmattan* (1964; The Harmattan), *Vehi-ciosane; ou, Blanche-genèse, suivi du Mandat* (1965; Vehi-ciosane; or, White-Genesis, followed by The Money-Order), *Xala* (1973), and *Le dernier de l'empire* (1981; The Last One of the Empire). In contrast with his contemporaries of the post-Negritude era, Sembène does not dwell on the angst of being a cultural hybrid, nor does he waste much ink on the evil of colonialism. As a Marxist, he is resolutely turned toward the future of Senegal and the continent. This future of course means independence from the French, but also a critical appraisal of traditional mores such as the subjection of women and the negative influence of religion, be it Islam or ancestral beliefs.

Since the 1950s, Sembène has been convinced that the future of Senegal belongs to its people and that only they can bring about changes; they must take matters into their own hands rather than relying on outsiders. This call to communal action is what links his entire body of work from his novels to his cinema. His literary masterpiece remains *Les bouts de bois de Dieu,* a social epic based on the great strike which paralyzed the Dakar-Niger railway from 10 October 1947 to 19 March 1948. This novel can be viewed as part of the grand tradition of *littérature engagée,* in the spirit of Émile Zola's *Germinal* and André Malraux's *Man's Fate.* Sembène creates an unforgettable cast of

31

characters, including women as prominent players and indispensable partners in the success of the fight. Although the social and political context is that of colonial rule, he is very careful not to fall into the conflict of colonizer versus colonized but, rather, to view the situation as a class struggle and elevate the debate to the eternal and international conflict of the haves versus the have-nots. For the union men in charge of the strike, the owners of the railroad do not represent France but simply a class, whereas Sembène's railroad workers are brothers to Zola's mine workers because they all belong to the same class: the proletariat. Differences of culture and race are dismissed as irrelevant to the conflict; the negotiations take place among equals, among men who disagree; and what is expected is justice, not paternalistic kindness. In fact, the leitmotif running throughout the text is the song of a blind destitute woman: "Happy the man who can fight without hatred."

Clearly, Sembène's strikers, men and women alike, have never suffered from what Ngugi wa Thiong'o calls a "colonized mind." They know that oppression is not a permanent and inevitable condition but a moment of history. Shortly after independence, Sembène's novels were quick to reflect the disenchantment that was rapidly setting in and the fact that, for the poor, things had not changed. This denunciation of the greed of the African ruling class and its shameless collaboration with the former colonial masters is still the main topic of the African novel. Sembène's political and social preoccupations reflect those of his contemporaries; he decries the corrosive effect that money has on the moral fiber of his society and recognizes the necessary emancipation of women and their equal participation in the building of the nation.

Finally, Sembène resolved for himself, at least partially, the thorny issue of language that had anguished many African writers since the 1950s. This problem of writing in the language of the colonialist is an ongoing, complex question in African letters. One of the related issues is that of communication. Who reads African novels? Mostly the educated elite and Westerners. To alleviate this problem, Sembène decided to make movies in Wolof, the main language of Senegal. In 1963 he directed his first film, *Borrom Sarrett*. Today he is equally known and respected as a writer and as a filmmaker.

As previously stated, many of Sembène's concerns are found also in the fiction of most postindependence novelists writing in either English or French. The writer remains for the most part politically engagé and feels committed to be the witness of his or her time. The originality of the francophone novel, therefore, lies not in its subject matter but in its aesthetics. One trend of this new aesthetics is the manipulation and dislocation of time, which is no longer linear; the other is the incorporation of the oral tradition as subtext to the main narrative. A few examples will suffice to illustrate this evolution of francophone creative writing. The first writer who comes to mind is Ahmadou Kourouma, whose two novels are stylistic landmarks of francophone fiction. His first novel, *Les soleils des indépendances* (1968; The Suns of Independence), recounts the downfall of Fama, Malinke prince of Horodugu, disillusioned by the disappointments of independence. In his second novel, *Monnè, outrages et défis* (1990; *Monnew: A Novel*, 1993), Kourouma rewrites a hundred years of Malinke history through the commentaries and perspectives of the protagonists.

What characterizes the two texts is an evershifting viewpoint that gives the reader a wide range of interpretation. This fluidity of the story line and the unreliability of the narrator correspond to the unreliability of the language of the text, since in this case the French can be seen or read as nothing more than a transliteration of the Malinke. A case in point is *Monnè*, which has no equivalent in French, and the author tells us that *outrages et défis* (outrage and defiance) are just approximations of the original meaning. Furthermore, the French has taken a Malinke rhythm which moves the reader from proverbs to anecdotes in the extraordinary world of the author's imagination. All this makes two remarkable and very enjoyable texts in which the French language itself has turned African.

Similarly, *L'étrange destin de Wangrin* (1973; The Strange Destiny of Wangrin), Amadou Hampaté Bâ's magnificent only novel, is thoroughly anchored in ancestral thinking and more particularly in the epic of the Bambara. According to the author/ narrator, it tells the true adventures of Wandrin, a native interpreter during the colonial period. This so-called veracity of subject could classify the text as testimonial literature. But Bâ refuses to abide wholeheartedly by the Western canon. His text, which he does not label a novel, although it may certainly be considered as such, can also be viewed as a rereading and in part a rewriting of the Bambara epic. The protagonist moves in the same spatial area as that of the epic, the region of Segu in

Mali, but the temporal space has changed. And all of the actions of the modern hero are echoed in the epic, and thus the ancient oral text infuses the written one. The interpreter, a lovable rogue whose vocation allows him to be a professional liar and get away with it, meets his downfall when he ceases to follow the dictates of ancestral wisdom. It is the moral intrusion of the past into the present which gives its tragic depth to an otherwise highly comical text.

This reclaiming of "orature" as a literary tradition is continued by the next generation of writers, whose work literally burst on the literary scene in the 1980s. However, this return to the sources of ancestral creativity does not mean a nostalgic glorification of the past. On the contrary, this next generation of francophone writers is thematically anchored in the unbearable neocolonial present and the bitter failure of independence. This bleak reality is expressed through the stylistic device of oral literature, resulting, among other things, in a subversion of "le français de France" (the French from France), producing the same deliberate Africanization of the language practiced by Kourouma. The straightforward political commitment of the previous generation is now expanded to style as a form of protest as well as the coming of age of a genuine African literary tradition.

The most prominent example of this new style is Sony Labou Tansi, who died of AIDS in 1995. His first novel, *La vie et demie* (Life and a Half), was published in 1979; it was followed by *L'état honteux* (1981; The Shameful State), *L'anté-peuple* (1983; The Antipeople), and *Les sept solitudes de Lorsa Lopez* (1985; The Seven Solitudes of Lorsa Lopez). From his first novel onward, Labou Tansi placed himself in the literary tradition of the Congo by paying homage to his predecessors Sylvain Bemba, Henri Lopes, and Tchicaya U Tam'si. He created a distinctive style using such traditional devices as repetition of images, chiseled one-liners that could be considered modern proverbs, and burlesque genealogies of "providential guides of the nation." Also striking is the violence of his imagery describing the horrors of totalitarian regimes in bloody and often eschatological metaphors. Labou Tansi creates a disturbing universe on the brink of madness that is saved from the abyss by the energy of life-giving laughter, "le rire vital." The plots of his novels are reduced to a basic idea propelled by the evocative violence of the language.

Labou Tansi's legacy can be found particularly in the work of two women novelists: Calixthe Bey-ala and Werewere Liking. Beyala's violent and erotic images denounce the sordidness of the urban life of the poor and its effects on the young, particularly women and children. Her first two novels, *C'est le soleil qui m'a brûlée* (1987; The Sun Hath Looked Upon Me) and *Tu t'appelleras Tanga* (1988; Your Name Shall Be Tanga), established her as an original and somewhat scandalous writer due to the violence of her style, all the more striking in a woman writer. Beyala's strident, caustic, and haunting metaphors re-create with words the nightmare and despair of the urban slums. Her repetitive rhythm infuses her texts with an incantative quality. Werewere Liking, a multifaceted artist, poet, playwright, and painter, Africanizes the novel and transforms it into a hybrid genre rich with poetry, ancient rituals, and myths. Many of her texts are called *roman-chant* (novel-chant), in which the plot is totally subordinated to a poetic temporality where the protagonists are types more than individuals. However, like her contemporaries, her subject matter remains anchored in the malaise besieging African societies.

Finally, in keeping with this *nouvelle écriture*, or new writing, which is so significant in the francophone novel of the 1980s and 1990s, Aminata Sow Fall's fifth novel, *Le jujubier du patriarche* (1993; The Jujub Tree of the Patriarch), marks a definite stylistic break with her previous writing as she, too, digs into the oral literature of the past to speak of the present.

In conclusion, it is evident that the francophone novel is alive and well. I concur with the African critic Jonathan Ngaté, who feels that the francophone novel has now established a literary tradition of its own. The future will surely bring a decontinentalization of the African novel in favor of national literatures, as each nation creates its own specific genius out of the arbitrary absurdity of the colonial borders.

BIBLIOGRAPHY

Anozie, Sunday Ogbonna. *Sociologie du roman africain: Réalisme, structure et détermination dans le roman ouest-africain.* Paris, 1970.

Blair, Dorothy. *African Literature in French.* Cambridge, 1976.

Erickson, John D. *Nommo: African Fiction in French South of the Sahara.* York, S.C., 1979.

Irele, Abiola. "The Negritude Debate." In *European Language Writing in Sub-Saharan Africa,* edited by Albert S. Gérard. Vol. 1. Budapest, 1986.

Joppa, Francis Anani. *L'engagement des écrivains africains noirs de langue française: Du témoignage au dépassement.* Sherbrooke, Québec, 1982.

July, Robert William. *The Origins of Modern African Thought: Its Development in West Africa During the Nineteenth and Twentieth Centuries.* New York, 1968.

Kane, Mohamadou. *Roman africain et traditions.* Dakar, Senegal, 1982.

Kesteloot, Lilyan. *Les écrivains noirs de langue française: Naissance d'une littérature.* 3d ed. Brussels, 1965.

Makouta-M'boukou, Jean-Pierre. *Introduction à l'étude du roman négro-africain de langue française: Problèmes culturels et littéraires.* Abidjan, Côte d'Ivoire, 1980.

Miller, Christophe L. *Blank Darkness: Africanist Discourse in French.* Chicago, 1985.

Mouralis, Bernard. *Littérature et développement: Essai sur le statut, la fonction et la représentation de la littérature négro-africaine d'expression française.* Paris, 1984.

Ngaté, Jonathan. *Francophone African Fiction: Reading a Literary Tradition.* Trenton, N.J., 1988.

Senghor, Léopold S. *Liberté.* Volume 1, *Négritude et humanisme.* Paris, 1964.

Soyinka, Wole. *Myth, Literature, and the African World.* Cambridge, 1979.

SONIA LEE

See also **Diop, Alioune; Language Use; Negritude; Ngugi wa Thiong'o; Sembène Ousmane; Senghor, Léopold Sédar; Soyinka, Wole.**

FRANCOPHONE LITERATURE IN CENTRAL AFRICA

The colonial legacy is very much alive in the geographical configuration of today's Africa, as well as in many aspects of Africa's contemporary culture, including languages and literatures. The presence of French as an official language in central Africa—Gabon, the Central African Republic, the Congo, Zaire, Rwanda, and Burundi—stands as a manifest legacy of colonization.

The cultural policy in the French colonies was one of cultural assimilation, carried out mainly through the educational system. In school the Africans learned and mastered the French language and were introduced to the culture of the colonizer. The Belgian policy was similar to that of France. References and cultural models were the same: the cultural history of the French-speaking region of Belgium (Wallonie) taught in the Belgian Congo's schools was, with few exceptions, the same. Like other former French colonies, after its independence, the Congo maintained French as the major European language, coexisting with several major African languages with the status of national languages. Thus, a context of multilingualism and cultural assimilation through the French or the Belgian educational system enabled the development of a modern African literature in French. In her groundbreaking book, *Les Écrivains noirs de langue française: Naissance d'une littérature* (1963), the Belgian-born scholar Lilyan Kesteloot chronicles the birth and the first manifestations of francophone literature, inaugurated by intellectuals from the former French colonies and the French Caribbean. This literature developed brilliantly, particularly in west African countries such as Senegal, Cameroon, Guinea, and Côte d'Ivoire. Only after 1960, the year of its independence, was such development possible in Zaire, the former Belgian colony; it was only then that its cultural isolation from the other francophone African countries ended.

The Central African Republic

From the perspective of literary history, the Central African Republic is particularly interesting: it is here that the West Indian writer from Martinique, René Maran, was sent as a colonial administrator and worked for many years. His controversial Goncourt Prize–winning novel, *Batouala,* and some of his other works, like *Djouma, chien de brousse* and *Le Livre de la brousse,* drew upon this experience. *Batouala* is particularly important as the first manifestation of a critique by a black person of colonial methodology and is often considered the precursor of the francophone novel.

The first manifestations of central African writing in French can be found in the journal *Liaison,* founded in 1950 as a cultural journal of French equatorial Africa. Although it was a creation of the colonial administration, the journal was a forum where African intellectuals could voice their opinions on social and cultural matters and publish a variety of literary texts. At a more local level, the Catholic journal *La Voix de l'Ubangui* was instrumental in promoting and publishing literature in French by Africans. Having had almost no presence outside the country, the literary production and reputation of the Central African Republic are still emerging, compared with other countries in west and central Africa, where former French or Belgian colonies have produced a good number of well-established, nationally and internationally known writers. The publication of a special issue of the journal *Notre Librairie* (April–May 1987) dedicated to literature of the Central African Republic brought attention to the emergence of a central African literature in French. Before that, Jean-Dominique Penel's *Anthologie de la poésie centrafricaine,* printed in 1983 by the French Cultural Center in Bangui, brought together many local poets' writings and made them available to a public who would not otherwise have had the opportunity to discover their poetry.

The dominant themes of the existing central African literature are not very different from those elsewhere in Africa: the encounter between Africa and the West and its consequences, the conflict or the blending of tradition and modernity, the opposition between the village and the urban environment. They reflect the transformation of African society and the individual's quest to find an identity and a way of life in the new context. There is also a desire to preserve or to adapt tradition, through using folk material or including historical events and characters in the written work.

The young central African literature is represented by poetry, theater, and fiction. Most plays, even when they have been performed for the local public, remain unpublished. The novel, as elsewhere in Africa, appears to be the more practiced and the more published genre. Some novelists are gaining visibility within the country, and their works have been published in Africa as well as in France: Cyriaque Robert Yavoucko's novel *Crépuscule et défi* (1979); Pierre Sammy-Mackfoy's *L'Odyssée de Mongou* (1978, 1983); Étienne Goyémidé's *Le Silence de la forêt* (1984) and *Le Dernier Survivant de la caravane* (1985); Gabriel Danzi's *Un soleil au bout de la nuit* (1984). Pierre Makombo Bamboté remains unquestionably the dominant figure of central African literature. Two major collections of his poetry, *La Poésie est dans l'histoire* (1960) and *Chant funèbre pour un héros d'Afrique* (1962), were followed by other collections of poetry and short stories as well as two novels: *La Randonnée de Daba* (1966) and *Princesse Mandapu* (1972), the novel that put him in the spotlight of African literature. Bamboté's *Coup d'état nègre* (1985) concerns the events and the political climate under the dictatorial regime of Jean-Bedel Bokassa, as does a novel by Thierry Jacques Gallo, *N'Garaba maison des morts: Un prisonnier sous Bokassa* (1988).

Gabon

In terms of intellectual life, literature, and the conditions of reading, writing, and publishing, the situation in Gabon is similar to that of many African countries. During the colonial period, the journal *Liaison* provided an opportunity to the aspiring writers in equatorial Africa to publish their works in its pages. The publication of an *Anthologie de la littérature gabonaise* (1976) by the Ministry of Education and of a special issue of the journal *Notre*

Librairie (April–June 1991) raised awareness about Gabonese writers by presenting their works to the public. As elsewhere in Africa, the first manifestations of a new literature were inspired by traditional oral literature, and very often new works in French are rewritings of the oral literature, in an attempt to recapture and preserve the tradition by communicating it in a modern context. The major figure in this genre is André Raponda Walker, the Gabonese Catholic priest who collected the folk material and published it as *Contes gabonais* (1953). The new literature in French is represented by works of poetry, theater, and fiction. For the most part, the young authors' reputations do not extend beyond the national borders of Gabon. Authors are very much concerned with the national past, as well as the social and cultural situation of their immediate environment. There has been almost no poetry published, and the majority of the plays are performed without being published. The recurrent themes in fiction are a social critique of colonization, but also of local practices and beliefs such as witchcraft; a critique of modern society embodied by the urban environment and portrayed as inhuman; a questioning of some practices related to family and marriage; the revalorization of the African past; and a quest for identity.

Along with Raponda Walker, Vincent de Paul Nyonda belongs to an older generation. He has published a dramatic play, *La Mort de Guykafi* (1981), and a comedy, *Deux albinos à la MPassa* (1971), reenacting in a parodic mode the arrival of the nineteenth-century French explorer Pierre-Paul Savorgnan de Brazza. Young authors include Angèle Ntyugwetondo Rawiri, the major female writer in the country, who has published three novels: *Elonga* (1980), *G'amèrakano* (1983), and *Fureurs et cris de femmes* (1980). The first two offer a general social critique: love of money and physical beauty instead of moral and social qualities; they also denounce witchcraft as a manifestation of human envy, jealously, and malice. The third novel focuses on the condition of African women caught between tradition and modernity. Interestingly, Ntyugwetondo's representation of modernity for African women reproduces the dichotomy used in works by African male writers such as Cyprian Ekwensi's popular novel *Jagua Nana* (1961), in which modernity is embedded in the context of the city, a place of corruption and degradation for women.

Maurice Okumba-Nkoghe has published collections of poetry, *Paroles vives* (1979) and *Le Soleil de la misère* (1980). He also has written fiction: *Siana* (1982), an autobiographical novel, and *La Mouche et la glue* (1984), a novel of destiny, love, death, and rebellion against the father. The rebellion against the paternal authority symbolizes the daughter's will to break with a tradition that dictates a woman's choice of a husband. *Au bout du silence* (1985) by Laurent Owondo is a novel that recounts, through the use of symbolism, the spiritual itinerary of the hero and his psychological development. From a strictly aesthetic standpoint, Okumba-Nkoghe and Owondo emerge as the most accomplished writers of a Gabonese literature still in the process of formation.

Zaire

In the Belgian Congo (present-day Zaire), the birth of African writing in French, as elsewhere in sub-Saharan Africa, took its inspiration from oral literature, and the works were published in local journals. As the Zairian critic Mukala Kadima-Nzuji shows in his book *La Littérature zaïroise de langue française, 1945–1965* (1984), the journal *La Voix du Congolais* (1945–1959) was instrumental in the promotion of African writing. Although created and controlled by the colonial administration, the journal provided the Congolese *évolués* with a forum where they could express their views on the social and cultural problems of their society. At the same time, pieces of oral traditional literature and literary works in French, mainly poems by Africans, also were published. Literary contests organized by the journal were a stimulant for literary creativity. Antoine-Roger Bolamba is considered a pioneer with *Esanzo: Chants pour mon pays* (1955), a collection of poems inspired by the oral tradition of the author's ethnic group, in which the lyric mode veils a political revendication embedded in images of blood and fire. Before Bolamba, Paul Lomami-Tshibamba was a pioneer with his novel *Ngando* (1948), much celebrated at the time of its publication and awarded the Prix Littéraire de la Foire Coloniale de Bruxelles in 1948. The novel, like his later short stories *La Récompense de la cruauté* (1972) and *N'Gobila* (1972), is presented in terms of magic realism and embodies a symbolic dimension. One might add Philippe Lisembé Élebé as a bridge between generations, with his volume of poetry, *Orphée rebelle* (1972), and with plays such as *Simon Kimbangu; ou, Le Messie noir* (1972) and *Chant de la terre, chant de l'eau* (1973), a dramatic adaptation of the Haitian writer Jacques Roumain's acclaimed novel *Gouverneurs de la rosée*.

In the late 1960s, and particularly during the 1970s, a generation of writers appeared who were trained in literature and were in contact with the literary production of other black writers and the literary currents that produced them, including the negritude movement. A renewed interest in and enthusiasm for literature accompanied the emergence of this new crop of writers. Although of varying aesthetic value and published modestly as duplicated booklets, their poems translate the idealistic and generous intentions of the young poets and their desire to not only write about social and cultural matters but also to create works of art. Among the literary groups (for example, the Union des Écrivains Zaïrois) and poetic movements (for example, concretism), the Pléiade du Congo was a "literary circle" that sought to bring together young poets to share and discuss their works. This period of creative effervescence saw the rise of poets like Philippe Masegabio (*Somme première*, 1968); Gabriel Sumaïli (*Aux flancs de l'équateur*, 1966; *Testaments*, 1971); Mukala Kadima-Nzuji (*Les Ressacs*, 1969; *Préludes à la terre*, 1971; *Redire les mots anciens*, 1977). These three collections of verses attest Kadima-Nzuji's poetic evolution. His poetry is one of controlled emotions celebrating telluric forces—earth, water—but also love. Although Mukadi Tshiakatumba Matala has published only one collection of verses, *Réveil dans un nid de flammes* (1969), his poetry is of a remarkable quality, embedded in intense lyricism and metaphors of love and revolt, suffering and death. Another young poet, Tshinday Lukumbi, published *Marche, pays des espoirs* (1968). Madiya (Clémentine) Faïk-Nzuji emerged as a talented poet and the leading female poet with several collections of poetry: *Murmures* (1968); *Kasala* (1969); *Le Temps des amants* (1969), a vivid poetic celebration of love and sexual fulfillment; and *Lianes* (1971). Valentin Mudimbe, with *Déchirures* (1971), *Entretailles précédé de Fulgurances d'une lézarde* (1973), and *Les Fuseaux parfois* (1974), presents a poetry of philosophical reflection that attenuates the violence of rebellion, suffering, destruction, and death.

The Editions du Mont Noir, founded by Valentin Mudimbe in 1971, wanted to promote a high quality Zairian literature. The publishing house was very selective and has identified some of the most talented poets of the country: Kadima-Nzuji, Faïk-Nzuji, Mudimbe, Sumaïli, and young talents such as Elisabeth Francesca Mueya, Olivier Musangi, and François Mayengo.

In theater, 1970 inaugurated a period of creativity and innovation. In Zaire at this time, as in other African countries, many plays were written and performed without being published. Theater is probably the most popular genre because it is accessible to the public. The themes are very much related to the conditions of life and the current problems of Zaire's society: quest for the past, loss of traditions, social and moral disintegration, corruption, and social critique. Mikanza Mobiem's acclaimed plays *Pas de feu pour les antilopes* (1970) and *Procès à Makala* (1976) were very successful in Kinshasa in the 1970s. Other plays, such as Pius Nkashama Ngandu's *La Délivrance d'Ilunga* (1977) and Bikisi Tandundu's *Quand les Afriques s'affrontent* (1984), represent a "literary theater" that is not necessarily to be performed.

In fiction, Mudimbe, today in exile in the United States, has emerged as a major novelist and scholar, renowned for his literary work as well as for his scholarly production. He has received international recognition and literary prizes, and his novels have been translated into Portuguese, English, German, and Dutch. Mudimbe's novels are intensely introspective; his characters, internally tortured or divided. Like many African writings, these novels deal with the problems of contemporary Africa: crisis of identity as well as a spiritual and psychological journey in *Entre les eaux* (1973), *Shaba deux: Les Carnets de Mère Marie-Gertrude* (1989), and *L'Écart* (1979); with moral and political degradation in the spheres of political power in *Le Bel Immonde* (1976); with the quest for or the rewriting of African history in *L'Écart*. It is particularly in the formal innovations and in a highly sophisticated language and style that Mudimbe manifests his profound originality and his contribution to African letters.

Zamenga Batukezanga situates himself apart from most of the writers in Zaire and represents what might be called popular culture. His novels, written in the language of everyday life, are very popular: *Les Hauts et les bas* (1971), *Bandoki* (1973), *Souvenirs du village* (1972), *Terre des ancêtres* (1974), *Carte postale* (1974), and *Mille kilomètres à pieds* (1979) are among his first works in an ongoing production of short novels dealing with the meeting of tradition and modernity, urban life and social critique. In the short novel *Giambatista Vico; ou, Le Viol du discours africain* (1975), Mbwil a Mpaang Ngal deals with cultural alienation and promotes a revalorization of orality. This first work is continued by another short novel, *L'Errance* (1979), and more recently by *Une saison de symphonie* (1994).

In the new wave of Zairian writers of the 1980s and 1990s, the most prolific is Pius Nkashama Ngandu, today exiled in France. His production includes literary criticism and creative genres: poetry, theater, and especially novels. After a short story "La Mûlatresse Anna," he began his career as a novelist with *Le Fils de la tribu* (1983), followed by novels that include *Le Pacte de sang* (1984), the most accomplished of his novels; *Les Étoiles écrasées* (1988); the voluminous *Un jour de grand soleil sur les montagnes d'Ethiopie* (1991); and *Yakouta* (1995). Ngandu's novels, sometimes poignant and often written in poetic language, are dominated by the theme of loss, exile, pain, and death inflicted by a dominant power that crushes and destroys individuals physically and psychologically. Mpoyi Buatu entered the realm of letters with his novel *La Reproduction* (1986). Kamanda Kama appears to be a promising author who produces novels of a philosophical orientation in which solitude and anguish pervade: *Les Myriades des temps vécus* (1992), *Lointaines sont les rives du destin* (1994), and *Quêtes initiatiques* (1996?). Another emerging writer is Djungu Simba, whose novel *Cité quinze* (1988) depicts the deterioration of urban life, which creates a marginalized and forgotten proletariat.

The Congo

The Congo has produced a good number of writers. Between 1950 and 1960, the journal *Liaison* served as a forum for the intellectual elite and civil servants of the central African French colonies and for young literary talents. Locally published anthologies mention numerous young writers who are still learning the craft. Among those who will reach literary prominence are Guy Menga, Sylvain Bemba, and Jean Malonga; the last is noted for two novels, *Coeur d'Aryenne* (1954) and *La Légende de M'Pfoumou Ma Mazono* (1954). Guy Menga inaugurated his literary career with two successful comedies, *La Marmite de Koka-Mbala* (1969) and *L'Oracle* (1969), which became very popular in the country. His narratives include *La Palabre stérile* (1968) and the hilarious picaresque tale *Les Aventures de Moni-Mambou* (1971). Jean-Baptiste Tati-Loutard's poetry unfolds like a metaphysical meditation, reflecting with serenity human suffering, love, and death. His poems, collected in *Normes du temps* (1974) and *Poèmes de la mer* (1968), have the fluid rhythm and beauty of the sea. Théophile Obenga, better known for his work in Egyptology and African history, made a literary interlude with *Stèles pour l'avenir* (1978), a long poem in four movements that culminates in jubilation, in contrast with the melancholic and pessimistic tone of the beginning.

Gérard Félix Tchicaya U Tam'si (1931–1989) is one of Africa's major writers. His literary presence dominates several decades of African literary production, starting with collections of extremely well crafted meditative poems: *Le Mauvais Sang* (1955), *Feu de brousse* (1957), *A Triche-coeur* (1958), *Epitomé* (1962), *Le Ventre* (1964), *L'Arc musical* (1970), and *Le Pain ou la cendre* (1977). In the 1980s Tchicaya, now an established and internationally recognized author, turned to theater and to fiction. If Tchicaya's poetry is rather surrealistic and hermetic with religious overtones, his plays *Le Zulu* (1977), *Le Destin glorieux du Maréchal Nnikon Nniku* (1979), and *Le Bal de N'dinga* (1988) are comic and satiric representations of African political power and the disintegration of the people's hopes and expectations. His novels confront the African past and present with a nostalgic social criticism and bitterness in the trilogy *Les Cancrelats* (1980), *Les Méduses ou les orties de mer* (1982), and *Les Phalènes* (1984), and in his final novel, *Ces fruits si doux de l'arbre à pain* (1987). If *La Main sèche* (1980) contains an essential oneiric dimension, Tchicaya's last novel, in its critique of the justice system, appeals to the reader's moral concerns.

Emmanuel Dongala's first and acclaimed novel, *Un Fusil dans la main, un poème dans la poche* (1973), is the odyssey of an Afro-American romantic revolutionary in Africa. It was followed by a novel with epic overtones, *Le Feu des origines* (1987). Henri Lopes started his literary career with short stories and short novels: *Tribaliques* (1971) and *Sans tamtam* (1977) cast a pessimistic and critical gaze on the Congo's social and political practices while *La Nouvelle romance* (1976) calls for women's emancipation. During the last decade, Lopès has become a prominent Congolese novelist with *Pleurer-Rire* (1982), which, in a humorous and satiric mode, presents a critique of African dictatorial regimes, denouncing their excesses, abuses, and violation of human rights. In *Chercheur d'Afrique* (1990), Lopès adopts a parodic tone to veil the mulatto character's anxiety about origin and identity. *Sur l'autre rive* (1992) reenacts and at the same time subverts the transatlantic slave migration through the story of an African woman who voluntarily migrates to the Antilles and assumes a new name, anxious to find a new identity and to erase Africa from her memory.

The most remarkable of the youngest generation of Congolese writers is doubtless Sony Labou Tansi (1947–1995), a prolific and multifaceted author who produced fiction as well as poetry and drama. At times provocative, humorous, or sarcastic, his novels constitute a dramatic contestation of power and repression. The novels *La Vie et demie* (1979), *L'Anté-peuple* (1983), *L'État honteux* (1981), *Les Sept Solitudes de Lorsa Lopez* (1985), and *Les Yeux du volcan* (1988), embedded in baroque and magic realism, emphasize literary and political similarities with Latin American writings, and excess, incongruity, and despair. Labou Tansi influenced the staging and performance of plays by creating the Rocado Zulu Theater at the time he was producing his own plays *Conscience de tracteur* (1979), *Je soussigné cardiaque* (1981), and *Moi, veuve de l'empire* (1987).

Rwanda and Burundi

Unlike most African countries, where there are several national African languages, Rwanda and Burundi, like Tanzania, have only one national African language. Creative writing in French is almost nonexistent, and the emergence of a local literature in French has yet to happen. The few literary attempts are limited to single works by (in Zambia) the novelist Sowerio Naigiziki in the 1950s and the poets Migambi Mutabaraka and Cyprien Rugamba, and (in Burundi) the novelist Ndayizigamiye Kayoya. The voluminous and epic oeuvre of Alexis Kagame, a Catholic priest from Rwanda, constitutes a major literary monument and manifests Kagame's literary presence. His two masterpieces, *La Divine Pastorale* (1952) and *La Naissance de l'univers* (1955), first written in Kinyaruanda and then translated into French, find their inspiration in the oral tradition of Rwanda as well as in the Catholic theology in which Kagame was trained.

Conclusion

Without forsaking the specificity of their artistic projects, African writers tackle issues relevant to their societies. Their work thus embodies African gazes and voices, a vision from within. It echoes the aspirations, the fears, and the hopes of the peoples of sub-Saharan Africa.

At the linguistic level, using French for their own purposes, African writers have appropriated the colonial language for themselves, adopting and adapting it, playing with it, and sometimes recreating it. Through linguistic interference from African languages, the use of the African oral tradition, and references to the past and the present, they bear testimony to an important moment in African history: the cultural contact between Africa and Europe.

African writers practice a multiplicity of literary genres, each adapted accordingly. In poetry and fiction, they blend their own creativity with the legacy of the oral tradition, re-creating indigenous literary and artistic forms and, at the same time, internalizing and reinventing literary techniques from the West. In doing so, they have given birth to a new, dynamic, and rich body of works that, in their diversity, reflect the African writer's own situation as a multicultural subject of contemporary times.

BIBLIOGRAPHY

Blair, Dorothy. *African Literature in French.* Cambridge, 1976.

Brambilla, Cristina, ed. *Letterature dell'Africa.* Bologna, 1994.

Chemain, Roger, and Arlette Chemain-Degrange. *Panorama critique de la littérature congolaise contemporaine.* Paris, 1979.

Dabla, Sewanou. *Nouvelles écritures africaines.* Paris, 1986.

Gérard, Albert S., ed. *European-Language Writing in Sub-Saharan Africa.* 2 vols. Budapest, 1986.

Kadima-Nzuji, Mukala. *La Littérature zaïroise de langue française, 1945–1965.* Paris, 1984.

Kesteloot, Lilyan. *Black Writers in French.* Translated by Ellen C. Kennedy. Philadelphia, 1974.

Kom, Ambroise. *Dictionnaire des oeuvres littéraires nègro-africaines de langue française des origines à 1978.* Sherbrooke, 1983.

Malanda, Ange Séverin. *Henri Lopès et l'impératif romanesque.* Paris, 1987.

Mouralis, Bernard. *V. Y. Mudimbe; ou, Le Discours, l'écart et l'écriture.* Dakar, 1988.

Ngandu, Pius Nkashama. *Les Années littéraires en Afrique, 1987–1992.* Paris, 1994.

Nkashama, Pius Ngandu. *Dictionnaire des oeuvres littéraires africaines de langue française.* Ivry-sur-Seine, 1994.

Notre Librairie. No. 63 (January–March 1982), on Zaire; no. 105 (April–June 1991), on Gabon; no. 97 (April–May 1987), on the Central African Republic; nos. 92–93 (March–May 1988), on the Congo.

Quaghebeur, Marc, and Emile Van Balberghe, eds. *Papier blanc, encre noire: Cent ans de culture francophone en Afrique centrale.* 2 vols. Brussels, 1992.

ELISABETH MUDIMBE-BOYI

See also **Bokassa, Jean-Bedel; Colonial Policies and Practice; Kagame, Alexis; Negritude; Oral Culture and Oral Tradition.**

LUSOPHONE LITERATURE

Modern lusophone literature from Africa began largely in the mid-twentieth century. On the Cape Verde island of São Vicente, a literary movement emerged as early as the 1930s in the city of Mindelo, where *Claridade,* an arts and letters journal, was founded in 1936.

Jorge Barbosa, Osvaldo Alcântara (pseudonym of Baltasar Lopes da Silva), and Manuel Lopes formed a trio of Cape Verdean poets who cultivated nativistic verse with a creole ethos. Baltasar Lopes's *Chiquinho* (1947), Manuel Lopes's *Chuva braba* (1956; Torrential Rain), and António Aurélio Gonçalves's *Pródiga* (1956; The Prodigal Daughter) are neorealist novels based on such themes as drought, wanderlust, and emigration.

Later Cape Verdean writers, while acknowledging the *Claridade* generation's breakthroughs, took issue with its general lack of social activism. Thus Ovídio Martins, in his poem "Anti-Evasão" (Anti-Escapism), and Onésimo Silveira, in "Um poema diferente" (A Different Poem), both written in the 1960s, asserted their generation's resolve to come to grips with the archipelago's social ills and economic woes. Engagé writers also stressed the islands' Africanness in contrast to the claim by some of their *Claridade* elders that Cape Verde's hybrid culture was more European than African.

Meanwhile, in 1951 Angola's Luanda-based New Intellectuals launched *Mensagem* (Message), a landmark literary journal. Viriato da Cruz edited *Mensagem,* the short existence of which (two issues in two years) can be attributed to the colonial authorities' displeasure with the journal's militant tone. Cruz, himself a poet, joined with other black, white, and *mestiço* (mixed-race) writers to produce works of cultural revindication and social protest. Among the socially conscious writers were António Jacinto, Aires de Almeida Santos, António Cardoso, Mário António (Fernandes de Oliveira), Costa Andrade, and Arnaldo Santos. Not a few of these writers paid for their political activism with long prison terms.

By the 1960s the Lisbon-based Casa dos Estudiantes do Império (House of Students from the Empire), established in the 1940s, was a gathering place for militant students from the colonies and their Portuguese collaborators. Anticolonialist activities and the publication of small volumes of socially conscious poetry and short stories led, in 1965, to the house's closing. One of the house's illustrious members was Agostinho Neto, a celebrated poet who, in 1975, became independent Angola's first president. Neto wrote most of his poems while serving time as a political prisoner; his collected verse, translated into English, appears in the volume *Sacred Hope* (1974).

José Luandino Vieira also fell victim to repression; in fact, he wrote at least four of his collections of stories and one novel while a political prisoner. Vieira was born in rural Portugal but raised from infancy in Luanda. Although of European extraction, Luandino excels as a chronicler of the language and customs of Luanda's African and *mestiço* shantytowns. *Luuanda: Short Stories of Angola* (1980), the English translation of Luandino's best-known work, published originally in 1964, appeared in the prestigious Heinemann African Writers Series.

By the late 1940s there was considerable literary activity in Mozambique, Portugal's East African colony. In the 1950s and early 1960s poems of defiance and racial identification appeared in the cities of Lourenço Marques (now Maputo) and Beira. During this phase José Craveirinha literally transformed the language of Mozambican poetry. Craveirinha, whose first major collection of poetry is called *Chigubo* (1964), the name of a Ronga dance, was joined in this transformation of poetic discourse by Noémia de Sousa, who, although she has no book to her credit, became Mozambique's first significant female writer of color.

Mozambican prose fiction began to appear as early as the 1920s. It was, however, Luís Bernardo Honwana, from a prominent family of Ronga ethnicity, who transformed Mozambican prose fiction with *Nós matámos o Cão-Tinhoso* (1964; *We Killed Mangy-Dog and Other Mozambique Stories,* 1969), the English translation being the first lusophone African work to appear in the Heinemann African Writers Series.

From the nineteenth century until independence, most of the best-known writers from the tiny two-island colony of São Tomé e Príncipe spent much, if not all, of their adult lives in Portugal. In 1883 Caetano da Costa Alegre, São Tomé's first significant poet, arrived in Portugal at the age of nineteen, and there he wrote his romantic poems, some with poignant references to the vicissitudes of being black in a white world.

Francisco José Tenreiro was born on São Tomé Island to an African mother and a Portuguese father, who took his young son to live in Lisbon. Tenreiro visited the island of his birth, and he dedicated much of his intellectual and artistic energy to São Tomé, but he lived out his short life in Portugal. There he collaborated with Mário Pinto de Andrade, the Angolan intellectual and literary critic, to publish, in 1953, the first anthology of lusophone African poetry. Moreover, Tenreiro's posthumous *Coração em África* (1964; With My

Heart in Africa) established his reputation as the Portuguese language's premier negritude poet.

Three other significant poets who lived and wrote in Portugal are Maria Manuela Margarido, from Príncipe, and Alda Espírito Santo and Tomás Medeiros, from São Tomé. Of the three only Espírito Santo took up residence on the islands after independence.

Because the former Portuguese Guinea, located between Senegal and the Republic of Guinea, was for centuries little more than an entrepôt, the colony generally lacked the institutional infrastructure to give rise to an autochthonous urban middle class. Thus, a characteristic literature only emerged in Guinea-Bissau after independence.

In the transition to the postcolonial present, writers and critics in the five lusophone countries have sought to redefine the cultural past and fix the epistemological boundaries of their respective national literatures. Authenticity is at best an elusive quality with respect to cultural expression. However, when lusophone literary movements emerged during colonial times, the test of acceptability, if not authenticity, was often a given work's nativistic essentialism and the author's perceived commitment to the concepts and images of political and cultural nationalism. Moreover, while applying a rather circumscribed definition of authenticity, the tendency was to include anyone and everyone whose work, regardless of artistic value, followed the prescribed ideology. As independence euphoria waned, however, in each of the five lusophone countries the definition of a so-called authentic body of writing began to become more open-ended. With respect to inclusiveness, by the 1980s the trend was to welcome writers, both past and present and without regard for ideology, into the fold of lusophone African writers. Indeed, writers by this time were more likely to be judged on their craft and artistry than on their political commitment or how overtly their works expressed a given national or ethnic ethos.

In the 1980s and 1990s the literary scene became influenced in part by *lusofonia,* which can be defined as a kind of pan-Lusitanianism, with all that this implies with respect to language, neocolonialism, and transnationalist integration. Nevertheless, some experienced and promising writers and their works have begun to constitute a literary canon in the lusophone countries of Africa. Moreover, a number of Lusophone works have gained acceptance as part of the literary corpus of the wider Portuguese-speaking world.

Among established Cape Verdean poets and works are Corsino Fortes, *Árore e tambor* (1986; Tree and Drum); Oswaldo Osório, *Clar(a)idade assombrada* (1987; Overshadowed Clarity); Arménio Vieira, *Poemas, 1971–1979* (1981); Vera Duarte, *Amanhã amadrugada* (1993; Tomorrow's Dawning); and José Luís Hopffer C. Almada, *À Sombra do sol* (1990; In the Shadow of the Sun).

A prolific contemporary Cape Verdean novelist is Henrique Teixeira de Sousa. Since 1978 Sousa has published four novels, including *Xaguate* (1987; The Xaguate Hotel). And Manuel Veiga, a linguist as well as a writer, gained notoriety with *Oju d'agu* (1987; The Wellspring), an important, if controversial, creole-language novel. Some have claimed that by adapting the international linguistic alphabet to Cape Verdean creole, Veiga made his novel virtually unreadable, even by native speakers of the vernacular.

One of the most readable novels to appear since independence is *O testamento do sr. Napumoceno da Silva Araújo* (1989; The Last Will and Testament of Mr. Napumoceno da Silva Araújo), by Germano Almeida, a prolific writer with four novels to his credit. A rather curious, albeit engaging, novel of the postcolonial period is Arménio Vieira's *O Eleito do sol* (1989; The Sun's Chosen One), an allegorical satire of present-day Cape Verdean politics set in ancient Egypt.

Foremost among those Angolan poets who established themselves before and continued to produce after independence are Manuel Rui, Arlindo Barbeitos, Ruy Duarte de Carvalho, and David Mestre. Some of the promising poets to appear since independence are Paula Tavares, E. Bonavena, José Luís Mendonça, Rui Augusto, Ana de Santana, and Lopito Feijóo.

Three of contemporary Angola's most compelling novels are *O Ministro* (1990; The Minister), by Uanhenga Xitu; *A geração da utopia* (1992; The Generation From Utopia), by Pepetela; and *Crónica de um mujimbo* (1989; Chronicle of a Rumor), by Manuel Rui. All three are, in fact, the authors of a number of well-received works of postindependence short stories and novels. Also worthy of mention is *A conjura* (1989; The Conspiracy), a prize-winning historical novel by José E. Agualusa.

In the 1980s and 1990s Mozambique saw the emergence of several signficant poets. Luís Patraquim, author of *Monção* (1980; Monsoon), is José Craveirinha's direct heir. Other young poets with a keen sense of craft and the power of language are Juvenal Bucuane, Hélder Muteia, Armando Artur, and Eduardo White.

As for Mozambican fiction, Mia Couto, of Portuguese extraction, and Ungulani Ba Ka Khosa, a member of the Tsonga ethnic group, burst on the scene with the former's *Vozes anoitecidas* (1986; Voices Made Night, 1990) and the latter's *Ualalapi* (1987).

From São Tomé and Príncipe we can identify about ten postindependence poets with a sense of craft. They include Francisco Costa Alegre, Frederico G. dos Anjos, and Conceição Lima. And Anjos, with his *Bandeira para um cadáver* (1984; Flag for a Cadaver), is also one of a very few fiction writers in postcolonial São Tomé. The most popular of contemporary São Tomean works of fiction is, however, *Rosa do Riboque e outros contos* (1985; Rosa From Riboque and Other Stories), by Albertino Bragança.

In Guinea-Bissau, after a flurry between the immediate postindependence years and 1980, literary activity declined, in part because of the political climate. With the return of stability there was a resurgence starting in about 1982, which is the year of the publication of *Não posso adiar a palavra* (I Can No Longer Postpone the Word), by Hélder Proença, arguably the best of Guinea-Bissau's contemporary poets. The founding of a writers' association in 1986 is another indication of the resurgence. Another important publication, in a sparse literary landscape, is *Antologia poética da Guiné-Bissau* (1990; Anthology of Poetry from Guinea-Bissau), a volume that includes works by Proença as well as thirteen other contemporary poets.

A major breakthrough occurred with the publication of *A escola* (1993; The School), four short stories by Domingas Samy. Not only is this the first postcolonial fiction by a citizen of Guinea-Bissau, it is the first such work by a Guinean woman. Another landmark publication is *Eterna paixão*, by Abdulai Sila; his is the first novel ever by a native-born Guinean. He subsequently published two other novels.

Sila is also a co-founder of Grupo de Expressão Cultural (GREC; Cultural Expression Group) and its journal *Tcholona* (Vanguard). Moreover, Sila is the founder and owner of *Ku Si Mon* (With Their Own Hands), Guinea-Bissau's first independent publishing house.

The government-run Instituto Nacional de Estudos e Pesquisa (INEP; National Institute of Studies and Research), which previously published only in the area of the social sciences, established a literature series. One of the first publications in that series is *Kebur: Barkafon di poesia na kriol* (1996; Harvest: An Anthology of Poetry in Creole). The appearance of this anthology gives evidence of the rising legitimacy of creole as a language of "serious" literature. And Tony Tcheka (pseudonym of António Soares Lopes Júnior), one of Guinea-Bissau's most recent revelations, further contributes to this legitimation with *Noites de insónia na terra adormecida* (1996; Sleepless Nights in the Slumbering Land), a collection of poetry in both Portuguese and creole.

Lusophone literature is still in its formative stage. But there is no doubt that lusophone Africa's Portuguese- and creole-language writers, drawing on a rich heritage, will continue to be extraordinarily compelling, both quantitatively and qualitatively.

BIBLIOGRAPHY

Burness, Don, ed. and trans. *A Horse of White Clouds: Poems from Lusophone Africa.* Foreword by Chinua Achebe. Athens, Ohio, 1989.

Butler, Phyllis Reisman. "Writing a National Literature: The Case of José Luandino Vieira." In *Toward Socio-Criticism: Selected Proceedings of the Conference "Luso-Brazilian Literatures: A Socio-Critical Approach."* Edited by Roberto Reis. Tempe, Ariz., 1991.

Ellen, Maria M., ed. *Across the Atlantic: An Anthology of Cape Verdean Literature.* North Dartmouth, Mass., 1988.

Hamilton, Russell G. *Voices from an Empire: A History of Afro-Portuguese Literature.* Minneapolis, 1975.

———. "Lusofonia, Africa, and Matters of Languages and Letters." *Callaloo* 14, no. 2 (1991): 324–335.

———. "Portuguese-Language Literature." In *A History of Twentieth-Century African Literatures,* edited by Oyekan Owomoyela. Lincoln, Nebr., 1993.

Moser, Gerald M. *Changing Africa: The First Literary Generation of Independent Cape Verde.* Philadelphia, 1992.

Moser, Gerald M., and Manuel Ferreira. *A New Bibliography of the Lusophone Literatures of Africa.* London, 1993.

Wolfers, Michael, ed. and trans. *Poems from Angola.* London, 1979.

RUSSELL G. HAMILTON

See also **Neto, Agostinho.**

WOMEN WRITERS

In Africa, one could safely say that women's writing came on the wings of freedom. With the exception of South Africa and the Portuguese colonies, most African countries had liberated themselves from colonialism by the late 1950s or early 1960s. A decade later, women writers started to appear all over the continent, bringing the African woman's point of view into the public sphere for the first time, thus breaking the ancestral custom which barred women from public speaking. For African women, writing came as a double liberation, first from the oppression of colonialism and second from the patriarchal imposition of silence.

As writers in European languages, African women belong to a relatively new literary tradition, born for the most part of colonialism and engaged in the reaction against it after World War II. The late 1950s was a watershed period for African letters, with the appearance of such young male novelists as Mongo Beti, Camara Laye, Cheikh H. Kane, Chinua Achebe, and Ngugi wa Thiong'o. Brought up under colonialism, these young writers came of age with independence and thus simultaneously became the witnesses of their liberation and the creators of a new African literature.

As for women writers, very few wrote during the colonial period, and those who did were anglophone. These include Adelaide Casely-Hayford (1868–1959) from Sierra Leone and her daughter Gladys May Casely-Hayford or Aquah Laluah (1904–1959); Mabel Dove-Danquah (b. 1910) from the Gold Coast (Ghana); and Caroline Ntseliseng Klaketla (b. 1918), who was the first woman from Lesotho, South Africa, to be published. African women's writing became formally and globally recognized with the Nigerian novelist Flora Nwapa's first novel, *Efuru*, published in 1966 by Heinemann in London. Thirty years later, African women writers constituted an ever-increasing literary presence on the continent. In sub-Saharan Africa at the close of the twentieth century, women's writing was entering its second generation. The literary corpus is as wide as it is varied, counting many novelists, poets, essayists, and playwrights. Although a fair amount of poetry, songs, and plays are written in various African vernaculars, the bulk of the corpus is in European languages and more precisely in French and English (the lusophone women's production was still very small in the mid-1990s).

This essay considers those female novelists writing in French and English who are of African descent, which means that the work of Nobel prize winner Nadine Gordimer will not be discussed here. The rationale behind inclusion is not a question of race but rather of history and analytical coherence. Black African women writers, regardless of their specific cultures and languages, share a major historical experience: the trauma of a colonial past. Furthermore, they are linked by a commonality of traditions and customs that can be found in many African societies, such as polygamy;

the importance of motherhood; gender-defined field and household tasks, which are basically the same all over the continent; as well as the major role women have always played in commerce and storytelling. To these common experiences one must add the joint heritage of oral literature, or "orature," defined by the Ugandan literacy critic Pio Zirimu as any unwritten creativity. Although these unwritten texts vary with each African culture, epic and initiation poems, songs, folktales, and proverbs are found all over the continent. The oral literature of Africa represents an enormous literary corpus that is as much an integral part of the contemporary African writer's inspiration and influence as the Western literary canon learned in European schools. This rich and diverse common background gives to the African woman's writing a remarkable coherence of vision in spite of the cultural differences.

In contemporary African societies, plagued by economic and social difficulties, women and the family constitute the cornerstone of the social stability upon which the future of the continent will be built. Keenly aware of this fact, African women writers are casting a cold eye on their respective societies and use their fictional worlds to denounce ancestral misogyny and the many injustices which are and have always been inflicted against women. In their criticisms of certain traditional mores such as polygamy, forced marriages, and limited access to education, they exhibit what the West would interpret as a feminist attitude. And yet, most female novelists refuse the label "feminist" as another Western ideological frame into which they must fit. They distance themselves from an ideology that was elaborated for a world which bears very little resemblance to their own. African women's demands for equality and the abandonment of certain traditions no longer valid are not to be viewed as strictly gender related, but rather as comprising their participation in the larger goal of nation building. For example, as a rule African women have the right to vote, but in many instances they do not have access to education. In contemporary Africa, the state came into existence before the nation, and African women writers envision their liberation in the context of a nation in the making, which implies deep social change as well as political will.

The Writers and Their Audience

But who are these women who, going against the traditional grain, feel that the time has come for

them to speak up? Are they the modern avatar of the griots so prominent in traditional west Africa, or that of the ancestral storytellers? This filiation, proposed by many critics, is in fact quite problematic. For if it holds, the female griots or praise singers, in contrast to their present or past male counterparts, never sing the history of the group or the royal genealogy. As praise singers, they can be at the disposal of a single, notable individual. They often perfom traditional songs at weddings or festivities. In fact, their role is defined by centuries of practice, and the range of their creativity remains in their performance and vocal quality. The same can be said of the storyteller, whose role is to teach her audience, mostly women and children, the wisdom of the clan, the tales being as a rule didactic in intent. If, according to Chinua Achebe, the modern writer is to be the teacher of his or her people, the message of the written text differs radically from the oral one. Contemporary African writers in general, but female writers in particular, do not praise the tradition, nor do they wish to maintain the status quo—quite to the contrary. The written word of women weaves subversive tales: texts that are no longer the new performance of an old story but a creation born of the writer's imaginary world, a private universe spun from the experiences and emotions of an individual often in conflict with her own culture. It may be that the solitude essential to writing—especially writing in a foreign language—inevitably distances the writer from her social context.

So who are these women writers? They are, for the most part, Western educated and the product of some of the best French and British schools. They write in a language which is not theirs, the language of the former colonialist. This plight of the African writers sentenced to create a whole literature in an imposed language was the object of passionate discussion among the male writers of the first generation. The debate is still open and is revisited periodically. Interestingly, women writers show very little anguish in regard to the language question. They see French or English as a tool which gives them access to self-expression, a means "to break the silence," to quote Calixthe Beyala. This desire to be heard publicly, to be present, to have a voice and to give a voice to the silent majority of women, is an end in itself. Like the Senegalese writer Nafissatou Diallo (b. 1941), who feels that she did not write just to tell a story but to break the taboos that prevent women from publicly lifting the veil from their private thoughts, the

African woman writer, willingly or not, speaks not only for herself but often serves as the spokesperson for the women of her society. Conscious of this grave responsibility, the Nigerian critic and poet Molara Ogundipe-Leslie (b. 1949) considers that the African women writer has a triple obligation: as a woman, as a writer, and as a Third World citizen. Not all women writers espouse this ontology, but as a rule they agree, even if they feel burdened by it, that when they speak their voice is plural.

But for whom do they write? For the Western public, which has easy access to the books that are mostly published in Europe, although publishing houses are present here and there in Africa. In an interview given to the *New York Times,* the Nigerian novelist Buchi Emecheta (b. 1944) said that it was time for Africa to tell its own story in its own terms. Tsitsi Dangarembga (b. 1959), a poet, playwright, and novelist from Zimbabwe, said she wanted to write because she realized that she was absent from the books that she read. As for the African public, only the educated segment of the population is literate, and this means fewer women than men read. And yet, Africans show an ever-increasing interest in their literature and, according to the Senegalese novelist Aminata Sow Fall, those who are unable to read manage to have books read to them. The immense success of Mariama Bâ's first novel, *Une si longue lettre* (1979; published in English as *So Long a Letter* in 1981), underscores this point. This novel marks a turning point in the history of the African novel in that for the first time, the narrative voice is that of the female protagonist telling her own story. The emergence of this first-person narration, the overwhelming presence of this fictional "I," was revolutionary in the literary context of the time. In contrast to the autobiographical first person much in favor in Western women's writing, which represents only the narrator-author, the fictional "I" of Mariama Bâ's heroine is collective. It represents the voice of the Senegalese woman, telling her society and the world that she exists as an individual, that she is suffering from societal injustices, and that from now on she will decide how to live her life. The novel became a best-seller whose success is yet to be equaled, thus indicating the need that women had to read their own story: for the first time they had a voice.

Writing About Themselves

What do African women write about? Before answering this question in some detail, it must be

Mariama Bâ. © GEORGE HALLETT

noted that in spite of the enormous cultural diversity which characterizes the African continent, the cohesiveness of women writers' preoccupations comes as a remarkable yet not so surprising finding. After all, most African states are experiencing the same postindependence socioeconomic difficulties, which greatly affect the welfare of women and children, particularly in the urban areas. Furthermore, the status of women, which stems from traditional rural customs in effect all over the continent since time immemorial, is confronted everywhere with the forces of change brought on by women's access to education and their newly established rights as citizens.

Women write about themselves; from the 1970s onward, a fair amount of autobiographies were published in conjunction with the appearance of the feminine novel. In francophone Africa, Nafissatou Diallo led the way with her autobiography, *De Tilène au plateau: Une enfance dakaroise* (1975; published in English as *A Dakar Childhood* in 1982), followed in 1983 by the remarkable *Le baobab fou* (*The Abandoned Baobab: The Autobiography of a Senegalese Woman*, 1991) by Ken Bugul (Marietou M'Baye) and by Andrée Blouin's *My Country, Africa: Autobiography of the Black Pasionaria* which, oddly enough, was written in English with the help of an American woman. According to the African critic Irène Assiba d'Almeida, these three texts share a common goal, that of autobiography as a means for self-discovery. A similar claim could be made for the works of anglophone writers such as Charity Waciuma's *Daughter of Mumbi* (1969), Noni (Nontando) Jabavu's autobiographical novel *Drawn in Colour: African Contrasts* (1960), and Sekai Nzenza's *Zimbabwean Woman: My Own Story* (1988). These autobiographies read as a personal rendition of their authors' lives, but they can also be understood as feminine anthropological testimonies, valuable for the Western and African reader alike.

Women also write about themselves in their fiction, which represents the main corpus of their literary production. The fictional writing of African women can be analyzed along three main axes or thematic fields of creative inquiry: the world of women; women in the world; and the world according to women.

The world of women refers to the gendered psychic space into which women are born and in which they find themselves locked, fulfilling the role that society has allocated them in the name of biology. Consequently, in female fiction the first role to be revisited is that of motherhood. The maternal image so prominently explored by male writers of the first generation, and particularly in francophone fiction, in which the mother often symbolizes Africa in its ancestral glory, is demystified in women's fiction. Here, mothers and mothers-in-law usually occupy secondary roles. Their rigid attitudes anchored in the past are seen as a negative force burdening the young generation, which they often beat into compliance through emotional blackmail.

In traditional thinking, maternity and sterility, like a Janus mask, represent the two faces of the African woman's destiny. Women writers reject this concept, which reduces woman to her biology and promotes motherhood to the rank of an institution. Rather, they portray motherhood as a choice and not an obligation; they insist that being a mother is not tantamount to being a woman. Buchi Emecheta, in her famous novel *The Joys of Motherhood* (1979), whose title is borrowed from Flora Nwapa's *Efuru*, enlarges the doubt expressed by Nwapa as to the validity of a woman's wanting children above all else, even though motherhood does not always lead to fulfillment. Emecheta, with the piercing irony reflected in her novel's title, denounces vigorously what the American poet Adrienne Rich calls "the institutionalization of motherhood." This is not to imply that women writers are opposed to motherhood. Simply, they view the act of bearing children as a reality and not a fatality—a reality which in contemporary Africa is not without tragic overtones in view of the economic difficulties affecting many rural areas. In today's world, children are no longer automatically a blessing. Calixthe Beyala in her novel *Tu t'appelleras Tanga* (1988; published in English as *Your Name Shall Be Tanga* in 1996) denounces the plight of children who populate the streets of big-city slums, often abused by their parents who brought them into a world where they are no longer a gift or a sign of wealth.

As for sterility, it is still regarded among many in today's Africa as a woman's ultimate tragedy. Women writers dedramatize this subject in pointing out that contrary to traditional thinking, a barren woman is still a woman. Sterility must not be lived as a humiliation and an existential crisis. Barren women do not deserve the disdain of society. In many novels, the sterile heroine is persecuted by her husband's family as well as her own. In order to conceive, she is portrayed as willing to go to any extreme, consulting local medicine men and ingesting any available potions, driving herself to the edge of despair and even madness, as in Flora Nwapa's short story "The Child Thief," Aminata Maiga Ka's novel *La voie du salut, suivi de Le miroir de la vie* (The Path to Salvation, followed by The Mirror of Life, 1985), Ntyugwetondo Rawiri's novel *Fureurs et cris de femmes* (Women's Cries and Fury, 1989), and the aforementioned *Joys of Motherhood*. Through this obsession with motherhood and the tragedy that sterility represents for women, female writers question traditional societal values, where a woman achieves status only through her children and her husband.

On Men

So what are women writers' views of marriage and of husbands? As a rule they are very negative. Polygamy, the customary matrimonial regime of Africa, is not viewed kindly in African letters. Male writers have unanimously denounced it as an injustice toward women as well as an economic disaster in today's world economy. Women writers, while agreeing with these arguments, add to their criticism of polygamy another dimension which reflects their priorities. They consider polygamy as an obstacle to the well-being of the couple, since it prevents closeness and trust. They affirm the desirability of monogamy, not as a panacea against the difficulties of marriage and as the promise of instant happiness, but as a mark of respect. Women want to enter the matrimonial bond as equal partners and not as one of many. Furthermore, women writers equate polygamy with a reactionary male mentality detrimental to a healthy interaction between the sexes. To them it is a deterrent to the progress of modern society.

It is in fact male mentality that is at the forefront of the novelists' preoccupation and the subject of their most virulent criticism. Heroes are a scarce commodity in women's writing. Rather, the contemporary African male is put on trial as the source of the majority of African women's problems. This negative portrait of the male, who strives to maintain the social status quo because it is to his advantage, highlights the malaise of a contemporary Africa torn between two worlds. The depiction goes beyond the usual dichotomy of tradition versus modernity so often analyzed by the critics. Rather, it is a question of social power and of generation. The mores of the past corresponded to the reality of agrarian patriarchal societies, where time and wealth had different meaning from that of the modern world and where women were for the most part a commodity belonging to the group. Throughout their fictional work, women writers delineate clearly the profound differences which exist among women according to their generation. Older women reject change because somehow it devalues their lives and their suffering. Many African males cling to the patriarchal order because it gives them a sense of power and an identity no longer easily found in their changing society. Younger heroines, often the author's spokesperson, entertain the belief that the future of the continent will not be realized without its women, whose survival lies in the death of the old masculine mentality. This metaphorical execution is at the core of Tsitsi Dangarembga's novel *Nervous Conditions* (1989), whose heroine begins her narrative by stating, "I was not sorry when my brother died." The death of the brother symbolizes the end of male domination, the end of the patriarchal order. His demise was her only opportunity to further her education in that she was able to take his place. Had he lived, she would have had to stay in the village and the story would never have been told: a story of escape as she calls it; escape from woman's ancestral fate. In *C'est le soleil qui m'a brûlée* (1987; published in English as *The Sun Hath Looked Upon Me*, 1996), Calixthe Beyala also equates the liberation of woman with the symbolic death of the traditional male. Another provocative example of feminine affirmation in opposition to the patriarchal order is Werewere Liking's *Elle sera de jaspe et de corail* (It will be of Jasper and Coral, 1983) subtitled *Journal of a Misovire*. "Misovire" is a neologism invented by the author to offset the word "misogyny," but with a positive twist—the word refers not to a man hater but to a woman who has not yet found a man worthy of her admiration. Contrary to the categorical flat semantic of the word "misogyny," "misovire" connotes many possible interpretations, even a hopeful one (after all, the man may exist), but more importantly offers an opening on the future of gender relationships. This hope for a better understanding between the sexes, not only at the private level but as fundamental to a new social order, is the raison d'être of women writers' criticism of the patriarchy.

Defining the New African Woman

Entertaining the dream of a better future for themselves and their societies, women writers are creating the blueprint of the new African woman. Women's writing counts many heroines who, confronted with the difficulties of life, are forced to reconsider their lives and resolve to escape their predicament entirely by themselves. In so doing, they achieve a new consciousness of who they are and more importantly who they want to be. This redefinition of the self, more common in an urban context, does not mean a simple refusal to conform to societal norms but the difficult task of discovering one's own specificity and the strength to move forward. The paradigm for this newly found self-awareness is Mariama Bâ's protagonist, Ramatoulaye, heroine of *Une si longue lettre*. In this epistolary novel, dedicated to all women and men of goodwill, the recently widowed Ramatoulaye writes a long letter to her childhood friend Aîssatou, who is now living in the United States. Ramatoulaye's writing starts as a therapeutic exercise in which she pours her heart out, telling her friend of her husband's betrayal after twenty years of marriage, his taking of a second wife the age of their oldest daughter, and his subsequent death, leaving her with nothing but debts to care for their twelve children. Ramatoulaye, who is a teacher, came of age with independence. Free, educated, idealistic, and young, she and her husband participated in the genesis of a nation. Because they shared the same enthusiasm and the same ideals, her husband's betrayal is more than the failing of the flesh, but a breach of faith. A devout Muslim, Ramatoulaye accepted the second wife, even though her children wanted her to divorce. Aîssatou herself had left her husband when, intimidated by his mother, he took a second wife. Ramatoulaye, however, looking at herself in the mirror, realizes that at her age and in her circumstances she has no option but to stay married. Forced to fend for herself because of her husband's death, she slowly emerges as an "I" instead of a "we." The power of words leads her toward a new equilibrium and a discovery of her true self. Through the act of writing she discovers her voice and finds the courage to speak up "after thirty years of silence." Ramatoulaye's life story resonated with many women, which explains the novel's extraordinary reception in Senegal and the fact that it is now a classic of African letters. But the great appeal of the text resides not in its reflection of the life drama lived by so many but in the vitality of Ramatoulaye, a woman among many who became a heroine and a role model in spite of herself. Becoming aware of who she is, she refuses to slip back into what she must be in order to conform to societal and family expectations. She no longer exists only to please others but also to please herself. She has learned to say no; she has become an individual, a creator of her own destiny. She is also a writer, telling her own story from her point of view, in her own words. Ramatoulaye's story could easily have been a third-person narrative, but through her heroine's writing Bâ introduces the important theme of women's self-generated creativity.

To write is to mark one's place in history; it is to go from being a mere player to being a creator. Women's writing testifies to the reality of women's lives, thus making daily existence into an art form. The woman writer as modern storyteller is not reinforcing the group's cultural identity, but instead reexamining it with a dry eye and an unflinching desire for change. Many African women novelists equate the creative act of writing to maternity. A novel is like a child, "a brain-child" to quote Buchi Emecheta's heroine, Adah, protagonist of *Second-Class Citizen* (1974), who feels that a book is a special offspring because it involves only one progenitor; it is a totally free endeavor, therefore it is the supreme creation. This metaphor of the book as a child seems a natural concept for women whose cultures value them primarily as mothers. To bear a child or write a book constitutes a social act, a contribution to society. Writing, like children, guarantees the immortality of the group, but for women it is also the gateway to equality. The written word implies education; the thirst for knowledge is an overwhelming theme of African female fiction. Very few fictional heroines have second thoughts about the fact that going to school means a Western education. As already mentioned, women writers are a product of Western education, even if they did their schooling in Africa, and in their work they equate education with liberation. They do not subscribe to the cultural angst which tormented some male writers, as evidenced in such works as Mongo Beti's *Mission terminée* (1957; published in English as *Mission to Kala*, 1969), Isidore Okpewho's *Song of Lawino* (1966), Cheikh H. Kane's *L'aventure ambigue* (1961; published in English as *The Ambiguous Adventure*), and others who saw Western education as what N'gugi wa Thiongo called another form of colonization. Although they may agree that Western schools constitute a threat to indigenous cultures and traditional mores, as far as they are concerned the benefit outweighs the risk. Tsitsi Dangarembga's *Nervous Conditions* presents a particular interest in this subject, since the cultural alienation of its protagonist, Nyasha, leads this character to self-destruction. Nyasha's rejection of the West is antithetical to her cousin Tambu's embracing of Western education, although the latter knows full well that there is a price to be paid for her actions. The difference between the two girls stems from their socioeconomic backgrounds. Nyasha comes from the well-to-do branch of the family; Tambu is a poor relation from the bush where she was raised in poverty. She cannot afford to have an existential crisis; but once educated she will empathize with her cousin's plight and write about it, to pay homage to her suffering and their differences. In this text, the author reexamines a common theme of African literature, the city versus the country, and it is evident that her heroine entertains no nostalgia about life in the bush. For her the village is not a lost childhood paradise as it is sometimes portrayed in male fiction, but a harsh place where harsh demands are made of women. Tambu's sentiments echo those of many young African women, fictional or otherwise. The city, in spite of its many pitfalls, provides the hope of a better life, but most of all the possibility of education.

Attacking Social and Political Ills

The vision that women writers have of their world is that it must change to accommodate women's aspirations to live as equal partners with their men, to be educated, and to control their own bodies. As artists and as women, they are most eager to be instrumental in bringing on that change.

As women in the world and citizens of free states, African women writers, like their male counterparts, denounce the social and political abuses of their respective countries. African literature being a literature "engagée," women novelists no doubt echo Werewere Liking's "misovire," asking herself "will my writing be useful?" Consequently, in their work they address some of the most problematic issues plaguing African societies today. Among the societal issues they engage are witchcraft, infanticide, the corrupting power of money, and prostitution.

It will suffice in the limited scope of this essay to give an overview of women writers' viewpoints on the power of money and the social and political ills that it generates in African societies. This troubling reality is a major theme of the postindependence novel. It is worth noting that female novelists in their denunciation of the overall immorality of their respective societies do not only accuse the elite in power but point out that the average citizen, man or woman, bears some responsibility for the moral decay of the state. In putting their compatriots on trial, it would seem that women writers are trying to energize the silent majority into a more active role in redressing of the moral drift. For example, in *La grève des bàttu* (1979; published in English as *The Beggars' Strike, or, The Dregs of Society,* 1986) Aminata Sow Fall revisits the theme of corruption already explored in Ousmane Sembène's novel *Xala* (1973). Although both authors denounce the same problem in the same context—corruption in the city of Dakar—they view the situation quite differently. Sembène condemns corruption in the name of a Marxist orthodoxy, while Fall deplores it in the name of failing moral convictions. This ethical preoccupation has been at the forefront of women's writing from the beginning. In Senegal, Fall has been a constant critic of the unconditional valorization of money, fed in part by the taste for ostentation. In Nigeria and Ghana, respectively, Flora Nwapa and Ama Ata Aidoo deplore throughout their work the nefarious influence of money. The second generation of writers, among them Calixthe Beyala, Ntyugwentondo Rawiri, Werewere Liking, Veronique Tadjo, Tanella Boni, and Buchi

Emecheta denounce such corruption even more aggressively.

The most troubling manifestation of the corrupting power of money remains female prostitution, rampant in late-twentieth-century African urban centers. The character of the young prostitute occupies an important place in African letters in general. For the male novelists, she is often a positive protagonist, examples being the heroine, Penda, in Sembène's *Les bouts de bois de Dieu* (1960; published in English as *God's Bits of Wood,* 1962), the eponymous Jagua Nana of Ekwensi, and Wanda in Ngugi's *Petals of Blood* (1977). The image of the prostitute with the heart of gold and the right political convictions remains a masculine myth. In women's writing, the character of the prostitute is never romanticized, and prostitution is viewed as a totally negative activity provoked and maintained by a disastrous socioeconomic climate. In women's fiction, prostitution mirrors a pathetic and sordid reality: the young woman who sells herself to a rich man, or "big man," as he is often ironically labeled by the novelists, for an easier life, a good job, or a diploma. The young woman who exercises what Nigerian women call "bottom power" is in the process of becoming a banality. The obsession of the writers with this deplorable state of affairs manifests itself in the brutality of their denunciation. Their verdict is clear; appalling poverty often caused by political corruption and mismanagement gives birth to moral decay.

Among the numerous examples of the moral tragedy of prostitution to be found in women's writing, some situations recur like haunting leitmotivs. One of them describes the mother as a procurer of johns for her own daughter, as in Ntyugwentondon Rawiri's *G'amérakano—Au carrefour* (At the Crossing, 1988), Flora Nwapa's short story "The Delinquent Adults," Calixthe Beyala's *Tu t'appelleras Tanga,* and others. The other situation that recurs in stories about prostitution involves the young woman as a willing participant. Often characters are shown as becoming the mistress of a rich man in order to better their material condition, as in Ama Ata Aidoo's short story "Two Sisters." In this narrative, Mercy is a typist who lives with her sister Connie, who is married and expecting a child. Mercy wants more than what she can afford with her salary and she finds "a big man" willing to satisfy her needs. Her sister, who disapproves, will end up accepting gifts from the man and justifying her moral abdication. Here again, the writer levels an ironic and chilling gaze on the complacency of the protagonists, who represent all levels of society and who participate in destroying its moral fiber. Sometimes the desired outcome of prostitution is other than money—in Buchi Emecheta's *Double Yoke* (1990), a young student sells herself to an important professor in order to get a good grade.

As for political and ideological conflicts, the fictional universe of women writers closely reflects the malaise of a continent where the political structure is still in the making and neocolonialism is a major but often anonymous player. As for the underprivileged women and children, they are cast adrift in political turmoil over which they have no control: they must submit in order to survive. Their struggle, usually absent from history books, is immortalized in the fictional universe of female novelists. One of the most dramatic postindependence conflicts was that of Nigeria: the secession of the eastern region of Biafra and the civil war that followed. This war, which lasted from 1967 to 1970, could not but mark the psyche of Nigerian novelists. Flora Nwapa and Buchi Emecheta, the two most famous women writers of the country, bore witness in their fiction, in very different ways, to the violence and senselessness of the conflict. Flora Nwapa, in a collection of short stories *Wives at War* (1980) and a novel *Women Are Different* (1986), depicts the ordeal for the average woman and family trying to survive. Neither ideology nor political arguments are held by the protagonists, who are indifferent to the political circumstances of the conflict gripping their homeland. In fact, in the novel, in order to feed her five children the heroine opens a bakery, an opportunity offered by the war, and manages to get rich. After the war her success is attributed by others to wrongdoing. No negative judgment is passed on the protagonist by the author, but rather an admiring homage is paid to her courage and ingenuity. We feel the author's sympathy for this woman, who in the midst of a situation she does not understand, does what women have done since time immemorial—takes care of her own as best she can.

Buchi Emecheta, in her historical novel *Destination Biafra* (1982), differs greatly from Nwapa in the portrait that she gives of the conflict. She was not in Nigeria during the war but being an Igbo (Ibo), she felt the urgency to testify for the women and children who were killed mercilessly during the conflict. She dedicates her book to them. In contrast to Nwapa's heroine, Emecheta's heroine is a young educated woman who belongs to the Nigerian elite. Like Nwapa, she empathizes with the ordi-

nary folk who are helpless victims of a conflict they do not understand; however, her heroine understands very well the political interests and the corruption of those in power, which keep the conflict alive. This awareness gives to the text an urgency, a moral outrage, and an accusative tone absent from Nwapa's text.

The struggle against apartheid and the government which sustained it since 1948 constitutes the major theme of black South African literature. As is often the case, women have played an important though overlooked role in the struggle: their weapons were patience and silence, their struggle quiet and without glory, keeping as best as possible the family together and the dream of freedom alive. For years women waited for their men to come back: from the mine, from jail, from forced labor, while facing alone the brutality and chicanery of the police. South African women writers such as Lauretta Ngcobo and Miriam Tlali have drawn a very fine portrait of the African woman's ordeal and survival against all odds. Miriam Tlali, first woman writer of Soweto, in such works as *Muriel at Metropolitan* (1975) and *Amandla* (1980)—both novels were censured by the government—and her collections of short stories, *Mittloti* (1985) and *Soweto Stories* (1989), exposes every facet of women's lives: not only their difficulties with the apartheid regime but the sexism they must face from their own communities. The author provides insight into the daily lives of the common people, their failures and small victories. In her fiction she takes a strong stand against injustice, regardless of who is inflicting it, and refuses to be silent about the brutality of men toward women or the sexual attraction between the races, which occurred in spite of the antimiscegenation law. Her fictional characters are infused with the energy drawn from moral courage and the clarity of vision of those who have little to lose.

Alienation

As mentioned earlier, women's writing reflects the moral anomie besieging African societies. The alienation of the protagonists underlines the disintegration of the social and moral fiber particularly evident in the large urban centers. Metaphorically, this malaise is often equated with madness, and the alienated character is portrayed as suffering from a mental breakdown. There are many mad women in women's fiction, and the cause of their illness is always man-made, which constitutes a breach with traditional thinking, in which madness is as a rule linked with the other world, the world of spirits off-limits to ordinary human intervention. But in the imaginary universe of women novelists, human responsibility is at the core of the madness or depression of the heroine and can therefore be redressed. It is a question of societal will, thus highlighting the moral dimension of women's writing. The multiple causes of the protagonist's mental alienation, be they political, social, or affective, are directly connected to their environment.

With the exception of the South African novelist Bessie Head, political alienation appears mostly in the fiction of the second generation of women writers. Their protagonists express their anger and frustration through uncommon behavior, which is interpreted as provocation by the political power, itself the cause of the characters' subversive behavior. In *Tu t'appelleras Tanga*, Calixthe Beyala depicts the social and political alienation of two women who, refusing to accept the intolerable behavior of the state, find themselves in prison, subjected to a terrible repression. Their protestation will not be heard except by the reader, so the text itself, written in a lapidary and provocative style, vindicates the ordeal of the protagonists. The writer in her function as witness enshrines for posterity the futile and gallant gestures of the unsung heroine. This impassioned and useless refusal to submit characterizes Tsitsi Dangarembga's heroine, Nyasha, in

Bessie Head. © GEORGE HALLETT

Nervous Conditions. Her cousin, narrator of the text and helpless witness to Nyasha's descent into madness, which in her case takes the form of anorexia, records the ordeal. Nyasha suffers from an acute identity crisis due in part to the fact that she spent a great part of her childhood in England; upon her return she felt like a foreigner in her own land. But what makes her suffering even more unbearable is the colonized attitude of her father. Unaware of his lost identity, since he is more Westernized than the British masters of his land, he cannot comprehend his daughter's drama. Unable to accept the unfairness of history which has made her into a cultural hybrid, Nyasha lashes out at herself in a self-destructive rage.

As for the social and affective reasons that cause the heroine's profound alienation, they often stem from deeply rooted social mores, such as the importance of ethnicity in traditional society, still operative, or from the opposite, the disintegration of traditional values. Interestingly, Senegalese women writers, critics and witnesses of their society, have throughout their work underlined the disastrous consequences of these issues. For example, in many novels, the fate of the foreign wife takes on a tragic cast. She finds herself totally isolated and rejected by her in-laws, who often condone the misbehavior of the husband at the expense of common decency. In Mariama Bâ's *Une si longue lettre* and *Un chant écarlate* (1981; published in English as *Scarlet Song,* 1986), the foreign wives, respectively from Côte d'Ivoire and from France, become ill with unhappiness and grief. In fact, in the second novel, the French wife sinks into total madness and kills her child, who was never accepted by the Senegalese family because of his mixed parentage. Bâ's novel is not a warning against mixed marriages but rather an accusation against her society of being closed-minded and keeping alive traditional mores that no longer have any meaning. Even more dramatic is the problem of infanticide fairly common in African urban centers. To kill one's child in a culture where maternity is an end in itself can be seen as a form of madness, as it can only be the result of total despair and complete alienation from one's society. Senegalese novelists concerned by this new social drama have, through their fiction, attracted the attention of the public to the fact that these young women are not monsters but desperate young country girls working as maids in the city, who because of their loneliness and naiveté are easily seduced and abandoned by irresponsible young men. These young males are themselves drifting alone in the city, accountable to no one. When the girls realize that they are pregnant and alone, they do not know where and to whom to turn. Shame prevents them from returning to the village, and the indifference and callousness of their employers prevent them from asking for help. Aminata Maiga Ka in *Le miroir de la vie*, Aminata Sow Fall in *L'appel des arènes* (The Call of the Wrestling Fields, 1982), and Mariama Ndoye in her short story "Yadikône or the Second Birth," from her collection *De vous à moi* (Between You and Me, 1990) depict the ordeal of these girls, and in doing so put Senegalese society on trial, particularly the members of the upper class, who treat the poor as if they were born only to serve. This traditional attitude stems from the caste system still in place and the cause of many social conflicts. It is evident that women novelists, like their male counterparts, see themselves as teachers of their people and hope to serve as catalysts for social change.

So what is the world according to women writers? It is neither a utopia nor an unattainable dream, but a tangible world where the pursuit of happiness is a legitimate endeavor. Let us remember that happiness as a social concept is a relatively new idea. It appears in Europe in the eighteenth century at a time of great sociopolitical upheaval. It coincides with the desire of people to become citizens, to be in charge of their destiny in a democratic world, not without parallel in modern Africa. In the context of African letters, happiness in women's writing is associated with the hope and dream of a better future at both the social and personal levels. In other words, happiness is a projection, not yet a reality, but sometimes it can act as a buffer against the harsh demands of big-city slums so forcefully described in Calixthe Beyala's novels. In *Tu t'appelleras Tanga*, the heroine dreams of the perfect man and a "little house in the meadow" like the one she has seen in Hollywood movies. Meanwhile, she decides to alter the terrible present and "kidnap happiness" in order to give it to an abandoned street kid by acting as his caring mother, the one he never had. In Zaynab Alkali's *The Stillborn* (1984), the female protagonist, Li, concludes that even though some dreams are stillborn, others will come to life and succeed if the dreamer is strong enough. She goes back to the city to find her husband, with whom she will share her dream. Finally, Ramatoulaye, the heroine of Mariama Bâ's *Une si longue lettre*, ends her long letter with the word "happiness." She says that she will keep on looking for it, and that it will have the face of a man.

It is not fitting to draw any firm conclusions about African women's writing, since by the mid-1990s it had barely begun, albeit promisingly. This essay is meant to serve as a window opened on a rich landscape, a map to guide a curious reader through a continent led by the imagination of its women.

BIBLIOGRAPHY

Andrade, Susan Z. "Rewriting History, Motherhood, and Rebellion: Naming an African Woman's Literary Tradition." *Research in African Literatures* 21, no. 1 (1990): 91–110.

Borgomano, Madeleine. *Voix et visages des femmes dans les livres écrits par les femmes en Afrique francophone.* Abidjan, Nigeria, 1989.

Brière, Éloise, Beatrice Rangira-Gallimore, and Marie-Noelle Vibert, eds. "Nouvelles écritures féminines." *Notre librairie*, nos. 117–118 (1994).

Bruner, Charlotte H., ed. *Unwinding Threads: Writing by Women in Africa.* London, 1983.

Busby, Margaret, ed. *Daughters of Africa: An International Anthology of Words and Writings by Women of African Descent from the Ancient Egyptian to the Present.* New York, 1992.

D'Almeida, Irene Assiba. *Francophone African Women Writers: Destroying the Emptiness of Silence.* Gainesville, Fla., 1994.

Davies, Carole B., and Anne A. Graves, eds. *Ngambika: Studies of Women in African Literature.* Trenton, N.J., 1986.

Guyonneau, Christine H. "Francophone Women Writers from Sub-Saharan Africa." *Callaloo* 24 (1985): 453–478.

Lee, Sonia. *Les romancières du continent noir.* Paris, 1994.

Mudimbe-Boyi, Elizabeth, ed. "Post-colonial Women's Writing." *L'esprit créateur* 33, no. 2 (1993).

———. "Anglophone and Francophone Women's Writing." *Callaloo* 16, no. 1 (1993).

Thiam, Awa. *La parole aux négresses.* Paris, 1978.

SONIA LEE

See also **Achebe, Chinua; Beti, Mongo; Gender; Gordimer, Nadine; Language Use; Publishing.**

LITERATURE AND VERBAL ARTS. What is literature? Consideration of this question within the context of sub-Saharan Africa forces one to think about issues of history and sociology as well as aesthetics. "Literature" is a socially determined category. The pitfall of using this term in an African context comes from an assumption that is built into the word: the idea that literature is necessarily written. In Africa, the boundaries between written and oral traditions are porous; the two inform and feed off one another. Twentieth-century African literatures have taken as one of their principal tasks the preservation and re-invention of epics, tales, and proverbs that were previously transmitted from mouth to ear. Because of the intimacy between these two traditions, problems of terminology arise: "literature" seems to refer exclusively to what is written; "oral literature" sounds like a contradiction in terms, so some scholars have coined the word "orature" to refer to texts that are spoken. But in order to view all of these written and oral forms together, a more general term such as "verbal arts" must be used. This has the advantage of grouping together all aesthetic and narrative uses of language, regardless of their means of representation. Then it becomes possible to analyze and compare specific texts (either oral or written) and traditions.

To characterize the verbal arts of sub-Saharan Africa as a whole would be nearly as difficult as, say, describing all the literatures of Asia. The degree of cultural diversity in sub-Saharan Africa is too great to allow for reliable generalities about all its verbal arts. That diversity is often underestimated by outside observers. To make a comparison: British literature and Russian literature may have many elements in common, but the extent to which they are seen as part of one "European" literature is usually overshadowed by the perception of their linguistic, historical, and philosophical differences. In contrast, the literatures of Senegal and Angola, two countries separated by a greater distance than Great Britain and Russia, are far more likely to be grouped together and labeled "African." Removed from each other geographically and historically, colonized by different powers, Senegal and Angola nonetheless share cultural traits; but any comparison between them does not necessarily flow from a general "Africanness" that can be universally applied. It is at the level of greater specificity that reliable observations can be made.

What, then, can be said about the verbal arts of sub-Saharan Africa as a whole? Two phenomena are nearly universal and may serve as useful signposts: a relation to orality and a history of colonialism, and consequently a persistent question about language choice.

Orality and Its Transcriptions

Studying oral traditions in Africa raises questions about perspective and representation. While oral art forms remain lively in many parts of Africa, they are generally perceived to be endangered by forces of modernization. From the time of early colonization, preservation of these forms has been an active concern among Europeans and Africans alike; but preservation has usually meant conversion to writing. Orality in its true form is immediate. It is specific to a time, a place, a language, and a social structure. Wider dissemination entails recourse to a medium that alters the original text. In the great Mande tradition of western Africa, orature is the province of a hereditary caste of bards called *jeli* (known in English as griots) who serve as ambassadors, go-betweens, court jesters, musicians, and historians. But the day when large numbers of griots could make their living by performance alone is past. Some have abandoned the verbal and musical arts altogether; some, interestingly, have adapted to the modern world by embracing analogous lines of work, as hired document finders or as private detectives.

Most notably for our purposes here, traditional griots memorize and perform epic texts such as the famous *Sunjata,* the story of the hero who founded the Mali Empire in the thirteenth century. This text, like many oral texts, is reinvented each time it is performed; while certain elements remain constant, much variation is allowed, and flattery of the particular audience is expected and remunerated. As the most prestigious of all Mande texts, *Sunjata* is sponsored and performed regularly; it also has been transformed into many different forms of written literature. Two widely circulated books, originally written in French, come from this oral epic: Djibril Tamsir Niane's *Soundjata, ou l'épopée mandingue* (*Sundiata: An Epic of Old Mali*) and Camara Laye's novelistic *Le Maître de la parole* (*The Guardian of the Word*). These texts represent one paradigm of modern African literature: the written text is a re-creation of an oral text. In both cases a griot's performance was recorded, transcribed, and translated into a European language, using narrative devices (such as chapters) associated with literature in that language, then published and distributed to hundreds of thousands of readers throughout the world. While the music, the verse form, and the cultural immediacy of the original performance have been sacrificed in this transition, wide readability and influence have been gained. For better or for worse, this has been the path by which many elements of specific African cultures have become known to a wider world.

It should not be presumed, however, that this process is simply one of Westernization. The adaptation of oral epics, proverbs, and traditions in European languages permits broader circulation of these materials within Africa as well as outside it. Thus, the story of the Zulu leader and emperor,

Chaka, told in the Sesotho-language novel *Chaka,* by Thomas Mofolo (written around 1909, published in 1925), was translated into English (in 1931 and 1981) and then into German, French, Italian, and eventually Swahili. It thereby gained African readers in other regions, including some writers who created texts based on the same story: Léopold Sédar Senghor of Senegal wrote a long poem called "Chaka" in 1956, dedicated to "the Bantu martyrs of South Africa"; the Malian author Seydou Kouyaté Badian created a play in 1962, *La Mort de Chaka* (The Death of Chaka); the above-mentioned Niane wrote a play about Chaka in 1971; versions have been written by Fwanyanga Mulikita, Abdou Anta Ka, and others. Together, these texts reflect a common, pan-African body of thought on the tragedies of leadership. The process of committing this story to writing and then translating it into a European language contributed to the construction of a multicultural African hero known throughout the continent and beyond.

A similar process has taken proverbs and tales from individual language groups and made them available in translation to many others. In French, Ousmane Socé Diop's *Contes et légendes d'Afrique noire* (1938) and Birago Diop's *Les Contes d'Amadou Koumba* (1947; *Tales of Amadou Koumba,* 1966) reworked oral traditions but followed a precedent set by an early French governor of Senegal, Baron Jacques-François Roger, who in 1828 published a volume of "Senegalese fables" in French verse. In English, Amos Tutuola's novel *The Palm-Wine Drinkard* (1952) was based on oral materials and used a creolized form of English that had wide appeal in the West; Ghanaian writer Kofi Awoonor's poetry is said to be heavily influenced by the Ewe dirge. In Portuguese, a missionary named Carlos Estermann collected traditional poetry, fables, and riddles in a three-volume ethnography of southwestern Angola in 1956; in the 1960s, Angolan writers produced altered, stylized traditional tales. The debt of modern, written literatures in Africa to orality is far too vast to be cataloged. The rhythm, the diction, and the sensibility of oral traditions infuse written African literatures across the continent.

Colonialism and Language

The pattern of dissemination described above, whereby use of a European language facilitates intra- and intercontinental communication, is the direct result of colonialism. The British, the French, the Belgians, and the Portuguese, in the process of establishing rule over virtually all of sub-Saharan Africa, set up their respective languages as necessary means of communication within and among their colonies. For colonized peoples, these European languages became prerequisite to advancement in the colonial system. The contrast is often drawn between the British and French styles of colonizing, which were associated with different attitudes toward African languages. The British model, indirect rule, encouraged use of African languages by colonial officials and expected African cultures to remain largely intact even as they were subjected to foreign control. The French ideal was the assimilation of Africans to a French notion of "civilization" through learning the French language and emulating French ways; in fact, the right to become French in any real sense was limited to a tiny elite. (Assimilation was also the official policy in the Portuguese colonies.)

These two broad policies flowed from deep philosophical and cultural characteristics of Britain and France, and as the colonizing powers remade Africa in their own image, they implanted long-lasting practices and attitudes toward language use. The more pluralistic British view allowed for some development of African-language literacy through official literature bureaus, school competitions, and other programs. (In addition, missionaries were often the first to put African languages in written form; it was a missionary press that made it possible for Thomas Mofolo to publish in Sesotho.) The French system encouraged the use of French exclusively and punished students who dared to speak their own language in the schoolyard. Material support was not channeled by the French toward the development of African-language literacies.

The style of African literature in English and French was affected by these different approaches, as the first two African best-sellers illustrate: in British Nigeria, Tutuola's *The Palm-Wine Drinkard* was written in a creolized English that some thought was just "bad grammar"; simultaneously, Camara Laye from French Guinea created *L'Enfant noir* in a French that bore no trace of African influence. It was not until 1968 that a francophone novel (Ahmadou Kourouma's *Les Soleils des indépendances*) would dare to Africanize French. Since independence, more African-language literature has been produced in former British colonies than in former French colonies, which have remained closely tied to France politically and linguistically. Writing and publishing in African languages are far more advanced in Kenya and Nigeria than they are in Senegal or Côte d'Ivoire.

A debate over language choice has preoccupied African literary circles since independence.

The most fundamental shortcoming of European-language literacy in Africa has been its confinement to a small elite. In most African countries, only a tenth or so of the population is literate in the European language that the government and the literary culture use (although there are wide variations; within a nation, the literacy rate in cities may be much higher than in rural areas). Thus, the pattern of dissemination described above, whereby elements from local cultures become known throughout Africa and the world by virtue of transcription and translation, must be seen as broad but shallow. If many more Africans can read a text in French or English than a text in Wolof, it is still only a small, socially privileged percentage of Africans who benefit from European-language literacy.

The arguments against continuing use of European languages are ideologically compelling, while those in favor are practical and realistic. In 1963 Obiajunwa Wali, writing in the eastern African journal *Transition*, asserted that "African literature as now understood and practiced [that is, in European languages] is merely a minor appendage in the mainstream of European literature. . . . Any true African literature must be written in African languages." This argument is made in terms of cultural nationalism: in order to be truly independent, Africans must decolonize their minds; this can be done only by discarding the tools of European thought and using African languages in their place. The Kenyan writer Ngugi wa Thiong'o renewed this argument in the 1980s, announcing that he would abandon English and write exclusively in Gikuyu.

But the ironies and limitations associated with the recourse to African languages are visible in Ngugi's position. Works that he writes in Gikuyu are translated into English and other languages; the English version dominates the market, inside Africa and outside. The desire to be read by large numbers of readers imposes the use of a European language on African writers, even those who are concerned with cultural autonomy. A philosophy of defiant resignation runs through the francophone countries: the Congolese poet Tchicaya U Tam'si stated, "If the French language colonizes me, I'll colonize it right back" (quoted in Christopher L. Miller, *Theories of Africans*, p. 188). Reverse colonization of a language means creolization and Africanization; it is visible in the style of Kourouma, Sony Labou Tansi (Congo), Williams Sassine (Guinea), and others; these francophone writers join a longer-established anglophone-tradition of Africanization. An Afro-Portuguese literary language has evolved in Angola, Mozambique, and Cape Verde.

Making do with European languages—and making them do things they have not done elsewhere—may best describe the condition of most literature produced in Africa today. The majority of what is written in Africa, for literary and for more mundane purposes, uses a European language. But the diversity of African literatures includes certain long-established written traditions, like the Amharic one in Ethiopia, as well as flourishing postcolonial literatures in Yoruba, Hausa, Swahili, and other languages. In addition, the Islamic tradition has exerted an influence in many parts of the continent for centuries, bringing Arabic literacy for religious purposes, providing script for African languages, and affecting the creation of poetry.

BIBLIOGRAPHY

Badian Kouyaté, Seydou. *La Mort de Chaka*. Paris, 1972.

Blair, Dorothy. *African Literature in French*. Cambridge, 1976.

Camara Laye. *L'Enfant noir*. Paris, 1953. Translated into English by James Kirkup and Ernest Jones as *The Dark Child*. New York, 1954.

———. *Le Maître de la parole*. Paris, 1978. Translated into English by James Kirkup as *The Guardian of the Word*. New York, 1984.

Camara, Sory. *Gens de la parole: Essai sur la condition et le rôle social des griots dans la société Malinké*. Paris, 1976.

Hamilton, Russell G. *Voices from an Empire: A History of Afro-Portuguese Literature*. Minneapolis, 1975.

Klein, Leonard S., ed. *African Literatures in the 20th Century*. New York, 1986.

Miller, Christopher L. *Theories of Africans*. Chicago, 1990.

Mofolo, Thomas. *Chaka*. Translated by Daniel P. Kunene. London, 1981.

Ngugi wa Thiong'o. *Decolonising the Mind*. London, 1986.

Niane, Djibril Tamsir. *Soundjata, ou l'épopée mandingue*. Paris, 1960. Translated into English by G. D. Pickett as *Sundiata: An Epic of Old Mali*. London, 1965.

Owomoyela, Oyekan, ed. *A History of Twentieth-Century African Literatures*. Lincoln, Nebr., 1993.

Roger, Baron Jacques-François. *Fables sénégalaises*. Paris, 1828.

Senghor, Léopold Sédar. *Poèmes*. Paris, 1984.

Wali, Obiajunwa. "The Dead End of African Literature?" *Transition* 3, no. 10 (1963): 13–14.

CHRISTOPHER L. MILLER

See also **Camara Laye; Epics and Epic Poetry; Language Use; Mande; Ngugi wa Thiong'o; Oral Culture and Oral Tradition; Popular Culture; Publishing; Senghor, Léopold Sédar; Theater.**

LIVINGSTONE, DAVID (b. 1813; d. 1873), medical doctor, missionary, and explorer in southern Africa. Of Scottish working-class origins, Livingstone became an icon for his own times as well as for later generations. His importance lies, first, in his impact on popular and official European thinking about missionary work, the abolition of the slave trade, and other matters of African policy; much unofficial and official activity was stimulated during and after his lifetime. Second—although he

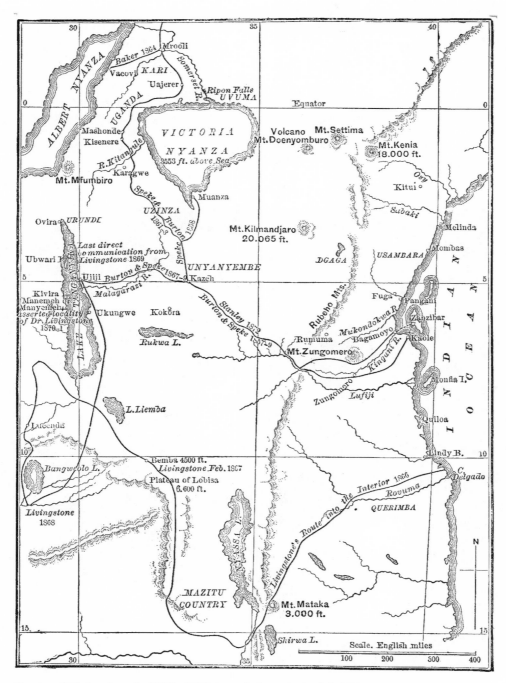

Route of Livingstone's 1865–1873 travels in equatorial Africa. NORTH WIND PICTURE ARCHIVES

was wrong about the source of the Nile—he was a great practical geographer and field scientist. Third, refusing to accept stereotypes of either servility or barbarism, albeit with some ambivalence, he championed Africans as potential full members of modern civilization. Fourth, in voluminous notebooks, journals, and letters he gathered an enormous amount of information on the natural condition of Africa and the lives of its peoples, much of which he published in three major works: *Missionary Travels and Researches in South Africa* (1857); *Narrative of an Expedition to the Zambesi and Its Tributaries, and of the Discovery of the Lakes Sherwa and Nyassa, 1858–1864* (1865); and the posthumous *Last Journals of David Livingstone in Central Africa, from 1865 to His Death* (1874).

From 1841 to 1857, Livingstone was employed by the London Missionary Society and initially worked mainly among the Tswana peoples. But from 1849 he showed an increasing desire to travel into unexplored areas in order to find new fields for missionary work, preparing the way by his own geographical exploration. Thus, longer-term goals became more important to him than immediate conversions to Christianity in one place; Livingstone came to believe that missionary work embraced secular objects such as the promotion of trade as well as religious evangelism. He discovered Lake Ngami in 1849 and then, from 1853 to 1856, made one of the greatest exploratory journeys ever, from Linyanti to Luanda and then eastward across the continent to the mouth of the Zambezi River. Despite the success in locating Lake Malawi in 1859, Livingstone proved a rather poor leader of the official British Government Zambesi Expedition of 1858–1864, which tried to introduce "legitimate" trade as an alternative to the slave trade by finding raw materials for export to Britain.

The Qur'anic school founded by Ahmadu Lobbo. FROM *D'HOMME À HOMME: HAMPATÉ BÂ.* REALIZED BY JEAN CASENAVE.

From 1865 to 1873, he explored and reported on the slave trade mainly in present-day Zambia and Tanzania, refused to be "rescued" by the journalist Henry Morton Stanley in 1871, and resumed his search for the Nile in what were really the headwaters of the Zaire River. In this wrongheaded search, he drove himself to death near Lake Bangweulu. His African porters carried his body to the coast, whence it was transported back to Britain for burial in Westminster Abbey.

BIBLIOGRAPHY

Among hundreds of biographies, Tim Jeal's *Livingstone* (1973) is perhaps the most acceptable of the modern ones, although there is little understanding of Africa. This understanding is supplied by the anthropologist Isaac Schapera in his excellent editions of various Livingstone papers from the pre-1856 period, notably *The African Journal, 1853–1856,* 2 vols. (1963). For a guide to Livingstone materials, see Gary W. Clendennen and Ian C. Cunningham, eds., *David Livingstone: A Catalogue of Documents* (1979).

ROY C. BRIDGES

See also **Christianity; Colonial Policies and Practice; Stanley, Henry Morton; Travel and Exploration.**

LOBBO, AHMADU (Ahmad b. Muhammad b. Abi Bakr b. Saʿid Lobbo; b. 1775; d. 1845), a Fulani (Fulbe) Muslim reformist leader who founded a Muslim state in the Masina region of present-day Mali. Although his own scholarly career was apparently undistinguished, Ahmad Lobbo rose to prominence as a critic of what he considered to be the laxity of Islamic practice and the poor quality of Islamic scholarship that prevailed in the Masina, and especially in Jenne, the major regional center of religious learning. His preachings assumed a broader political significance when he denounced the repressions that Muslims were forced to endure from non-Muslims, both Fulani clan leaders (*ardoʾen*) and the Bambara rulers of the neighboring kingdom of Segu. His ideas and actions were strongly influenced by ʿUthman dan Fodio, whose reformist preachings in Hausaland had led to a successful jihad. As tensions grew in the Masina, Ahmad attracted an increasing number of partisans to his cause, and in 1818 his Muslim community won a major battle against a non-Muslim coalition of Fulani and Bambara. Subsequent military successes led to the establishment of a Muslim state, ruled by Ahmadu Lobbo as commander of the faithful (*amir al-muʾminin*) and a council of forty

learned scholars. This new state, the *dina*, became one of the most highly centralized Muslim states ever to appear in western Africa.

BIBLIOGRAPHY

Bâ, Amadou Hampaté, and J. Daget. *L'empire peul du Macina.* Paris, 1962.

Brown, William A. "The Caliphate of Hamdullahi ca. 1818–1864: A Study in African History and Tradition." Ph.D. diss., University of Wisconsin, 1969.

LOUIS BRENNER

See also **Islam; ʿUthman dan Fodio.**

LOBENGULA (b. 1836? d. 1894), last ruler of the Ndebele kingdom in what is now Zimbabwe. Lobengula inherited a kingdom in disarray and spent much of his reign trying to strike a balance between rebellious Ndebele factions and European and settler demands. Lobengula's father, Mzilikazi, a fearsome fighter who founded the kingdom after splitting with Shaka Zulu in the 1820s, died in 1868, but two years passed before Lobengula won the civil war and acceded to the throne. At the same time European prospectors were clamoring for land and mineral rights following the discovery of gold on the edge of his domain (1867).

Lobengula, last ruler of the Ndebele. From David Carnegie, *Among the Matabele* (London, 1894).
COURTESY SOUTH AFRICAN LIBRARY, CAPE TOWN

Lobengula ruled Matabeleland, the southwestern portion of the land between the Zambezi and Limpopo Rivers. South African settlers and prospectors wanted the area for their own. Lobengula was never as strong as his father in dispensing with internal and external threats. In the face of external demands he made a few agreements on farming and mining rights and signed an agreement in 1888 stating he would have territorial negotiations only with the British.

Cecil Rhodes, who thought Matabeleland contained the next big gold reef, formed the British South Africa Company in 1889 and was granted a concession in the southwestern part of the country. The company's 1890 expedition found very little in the way of mineral wealth and faced big losses. After an Ndebele attack on an outpost of the company in 1893, the company decided to retaliate harshly despite Lobengula's repeated requests for peace. As Rhodes's adviser Dr. Leander Jameson noted, "Getting Matabeleland open would give us a tremendous lift in shares and everything else." An army made up of the company's police force, settler irregulars, and off-duty imperial regiments attacked Bulawayo in 1893 and razed it. Lobengula died of smallpox while retreating.

BIBLIOGRAPHY

Bhebe, Ngwabi. *Lobengula of Zimbabwe*. London, 1977.
Oliver, Roland, ed. *Cambridge History of Africa*. Volume 6. Cambridge, 1994.

THOMAS F. McDOW

See also **Concessionary Companies.**

LOCAL GOVERNMENT. *See* **Community Development and Local Government.**

LOMÉ. The capital and main port of Togo, Lomé was founded in the late eighteenth century on the site of an Ewe settlement. The city's name was derived from a local word meaning "little market." Lomé was selected as the colonial capital of German Togoland in 1897, and during German colonial rule much of the city's infrastructure was built. Located in the southwest corner of the country, Lomé is linked by rail to Palimé in the northwest, to Sokodé in the north, and to Anecho along the coast in the east; cash crops are transported by rail to Lome's port, from which they are exported. Cocoa, coffee, palm products, and cotton account for two-thirds of Togo's export earnings.

Lomé's industrial sector is essentially of postindependence origins. Limestone and phosphate exports and tourism contributed to its commercial expansion in the 1970s. Massive infrastructural building, a liberal investment code, and extensive smuggling across the Ghanaian border by Lomé's entrepreneurial marketwomen contributed to the city's growth. An economic collapse in the 1980s, however, led to drastic economic restructuring that continued into the 1990s. Structural adjustment policies have been accompanied by paralyzing strikes and riots. In 1993, one-third of Lomé's estimated 600,000 people fled to Ghana during the political violence and social tumult following the economic collapse.

KATHARYN CALDERA

LOZI. The Lozi (Barotse, Barozi) are the largest ethnic group of the Zambezi River plain in western Zambia. Subgroups include the Kwanda, Makoma, Mbowe, Mishhulundu, Muenyi, and Mwanga. The Lozi language is derived from the Sotho dialect of Kololo. There are about 400,000 Lozi in Zambia and 50,000 in Zaire.

The Lozi are descendants of the Luyi. In the 1830s the Luyi, led by King Mulambwa, were conquered by the Kololo, led by King Sekeletu. The Kololo ruled the Luyi until 1864, when the Lozi, as they were now called, led by King Lewanika, defeated the Kololo.

The Lozi are cattle herders, while cultivated plants account for 40 percent of their food supply. In the past all cattle belonged to the king, and the people paid tribute to be able to use the cattle. They are excellent smiths and also construct immense canoes used to ferry cattle across the Zambezi. Their villages are small and compact, consisting of a few circular huts surrounded by a fence.

There is a highly stratified sociopolitical system, with a divine monarch (*linabi*) at the top, then his chief councillor (*nyambela*), the princes and princesses, then commoners and slaves. The heir of a family is chosen by the father. Descent is reckoned patrilineally. Labor is divided according to gender. Women were not allowed to raise cattle or do field labor. Marriage is decided between fathers with the payment of a bride wealth. Nonsororal polygyny is practiced. Traditional Lozi religious belief included a High God, many categories of spirits, and ancestors. The Lozi are known for their skill in making and playing many different kinds of drums, such as the *manbas, kangomhbro,* and *zanza*.

By 1965 the Lozi had come under the rule of the Zambian national government. Although local, minor disputes can still be handled by village leaders, the original highly stratified society has lost much of its effectiveness.

BIBLIOGRAPHY

Encyclopedia of World Cultures. Volume 9, *Africa and the Middle East.* Edited by John Middleton and Amal Rassam. Boston, 1995.

Gluckman, Max. *Essays on the Lozi Land and Royal Property.* Livingston, Northern Rhodesia, 1943.

———. *The Judicial Process Among the Barotse of Northern Rhodesia.* Manchester, U.K., 1955.

GARY THOULOUIS

LUANDA. The city of Luanda was founded in 1575 by Paulo Dias de Novais of Portugal. The city's name derives from the word *loanda,* meaning "tax" or "duty," referring to the cowrie shells which were used to pay dues to the king of Kongo. Although the early colonial settlement drew its political organization and cultural identification from Portugal, much of its social organization and economic resources were drawn from the local Mbundu. Over the centuries Luanda developed a distinctive Creole culture which reflected the lifestyle and interests of its Afro-Portuguese population. Luanda became the administrative center of the Portuguese colony in 1627 and was a major outlet for slave traffic to Brazil. In the mid-seventeenth century the American demand for slaves escalated, and until 1850, when Brazil abolished the slave trade, Luanda thrived on commerce in slaves.

Luanda is the political base of the Movimento Popular de Libertação de Angola (MPLA) and has been the administrative capital of Angola since independence in 1975, the year civil war erupted. In the years since the war began, the highway network linking Luanda to provincial capitals has been mined, and some two hundred bridges have been destroyed or damaged. In 1992 all rail service from Luanda to the interior was halted. Luanda's manufacturing sector—oil refining, cement production, vehicle assembly, and metalworking—functioned below capacity or not at all.

In the 1920s the city's *baixa* district was transformed into a European-style business center. The Africans living there were removed to shantytowns which came to be known as *musseques,* a Kimbundu word referring to the red-clay fields in which manioc is grown. Since the mid-1970s the *musseques*

have grown rapidly, their numbers swollen by refugees fleeing the fighting in the countryside. In 1995 an estimated 2.25 million people lived in Luanda, about 70 to 80 percent in the *musseques,* overwhelming urban infrastructure and services such as water and food supply, sanitation, schools, and health facilities.

BIBLIOGRAPHY

Amaral, Ilídio de. *Luanda: Estudo de geografia urbana.* Lisbon, 1968.

Monteiro, Ramiro Ladeiro. "From Extended to Residual Family: Aspects of Social Change in the *Musseques* of Luanda." In *Social Change in Angola,* edited by Franz-Wilhelm Heimer. Munich, 1973.

Vieira, José Luandino. *Luuanda.* Translated by Tamara L. Bender with Donna S. Hill. Exeter, N.H., 1980.

KATHARYN CALDERA

LUBA. Comprising one of the largest ethnic groups in the Shaba district, the Luba of southern Zaire number an estimated 1.1 million. They share their name with other, smaller and culturally and linguistically distinct groups who live elsewhere in the region—particularly, the Luba-Hemba to the east and the Western Luba. Their language, Kiluba, belongs to the Central Bantu language family. They are a patrilineal people, hierarchically ordered into chiefdoms that are the remnants of the once powerful Luba Kingdom. Founded by the eighteenth century, the kingdom collapsed around 1900.

It appears that the Luba have long occupied their current territory—archaeological evidence suggests a continuity of cultural tradition in the region dating back to as early as the eighth century. Local tradition holds that the origin of the kingdom itself was due in part to the arrival of a hunter from the east, who married the daughters of a local ruler, and went back to his homeland with his new wives. From one of these unions came a son. When the son came of age and became a possible threat to his father's rule, he fled to the land of his mother in order to escape death at his father's hands. Upon his return to his mother's people, he killed his maternal uncle and became the first king.

Regardless of origin-tales, it is clear that by the early 1800s the Luba Kingdom was already a power in the region, with a large and formidable army at the service of the king (*mulopwe*), whose court was established at what is now the town of Kabongo.

Outside of the capital, the remainder of the Luba territory was organized into semiautonomous chiefdoms that paid tribute to the capital. During the period of the kingdom's ascendancy, Luba influence on the cultural practices of peoples throughout the region was pronounced, due in part to the kingdom's strong role in long-distance trade. In the mid- and late 1800s, the incursion of slave traders from Angola and invasions by peoples from Tanzania armed with European firearms weakened the kingdom. Belgian colonizers arrived in the region around 1900 and divided the kingdom into two administrative units, effectively causing the collapse of the kingship. The hierarchical organization of localized chiefdoms, however, remains in place.

Luba villages are organized around lineages: a small village generally contains only the members of a single patriline; larger villages may contain more than one lineage section, but within a single section only one patrilineal group will be represented. Ideally, marriage is patrilocal—that is, a man brings his wife (who is a member of a different patrilineage) to live in the community of his father. Traditionally, polygyny was the ideal, although monogamy was usual for the average man and has become even more common with increasing Christian conversion. Households provide separate dwellings for the husband and wife, young children of both sexes living in the mother's house.

Luba are well represented in urban centers. Rural Luba are primarily slash-and-burn agriculturalists. Staples grown are cassava and maize. Fishing and hunting are also important elements of the Luba rural economy. During the 1800s, the wealth of the Luba Kingdom was based on trade, and important commodities included salt, smelted iron, woven raffia-cloth, copper, and fish.

BIBLIOGRAPHY

Petit, Pierre. "The Sacred Kaolin and the Bowl-Bearers (Luba of Shaba)." In *Objects-Signs of Africa*, edited by Luc de Heusch. Turvuren, Belgium, 1995.

Reefe, Thomas Q. *The Rainbow and the Kings: A History of the Luba Empire to 1891*. Berkeley, 1981.

NANCY E. GRATTON

LUBUMBASHI. Known as Elisabethville during the Belgian colonial occupation, Lubumbashi derives its name from the Luba Kingdom—currently the Luba are one of the two largest ethnic groups in Zaire—which dominated the Shaba region in southern Zaire from the fifteenth to nineteenth centuries. Lubumbashi is currently the second largest industrial center in Zaire, a result of its proximity to the extraordinarily rich deposits of copper and cobalt in southern Shaba. Open-pit and underground mines, as well as refineries and smelters, are found throughout the city. Mining has been the cornerstone of the city since 1906, when the Union Minière du Haut-Katanga was formed as a joint endeavor of the Société Générale de Belgique and British Tanganyika Concessions, Ltd., to extract copper and other minerals from Lubumbashi and surrounding areas. In 1967, it began operating as the government-owned GEOMINES, later renamed GECAMINES, the Générale des Carrières et des Mines, and is the largest corporation in Zaire, providing half of the nation's total revenues and two-thirds of its foreign exchange. The twentieth-century history of Lubumbashi is inseparable from the company, which has effectively acted as a state within a state and which thoroughly dominates the economic affairs of the city. The production of copper has declined steadily, and the mines are expected to produce primarily zinc by the end of the 1990s.

Lubumbashi also serves as a manufacturing center for tobacco products, textiles, shoes, metalwork, palm oil, and food processing. The city was the capital of the secessionist state of Katanga from 1961 to 1963. In May 1990, students were murdered on the campus of the University of Lubumbashi in what appeared to be a government-ordered killing. The exact population and ethnic composition of the city are difficult to determine with any accuracy, but it is safe to assume that in the late 1990s Lubumbashi has over one million inhabitants.

MICHAEL WATTS

See also **Minerals and Metals.**

LUGARD, FREDERICK JOHN DEALTRY (Lord Lugard of Abinger; b. 1858; d. 1945), British colonial administrator. Born in India to missionary parents, Lugard served in the British army in India from 1879 to 1886. During the late 1880s and through the 1890s he led expeditions in central, east, and west Africa, most notably intervening in Buganda to end civil war and bring the territory under British rule. During these years, in which he was in close contact with Africans in precolonial societies, Lugard developed his basic concepts: the need for

European, preferably British, rule to develop good government in the disturbed and frequently warring societies of Africa, and to end slavery and slave trading.

From 1900 to 1906, Lugard served as the first high commissioner of the protectorate of Northern Nigeria. In the Muslim emirates of this region, he created the administrative system that came to be known as "indirect rule," in which traditional authorities retained considerable control of local affairs. This became the pattern for most of British colonial Africa in the next thirty years. Direct taxation was introduced, the proceeds being divided between local and central administrations.

Lugard next gained new experience as governor of Hong Kong from 1907 to 1912. He then returned to Africa as governor-general of Northern and Southern Nigeria from 1912 to 1919, with the task of unifying the two colonies. In a period dominated by the First World War, his attempts to extend indirect rule to the loosely organized societies of the south were only partially successful, and he failed to establish an efficient central adminis-

tration on which to build a democratic and united Nigeria.

After retiring in 1919, Lugard worked unceasingly on matters pertaining to Africa. In 1922, his influential text on colonial administration, *The Dual Mandate in British Tropical Africa,* was published; he was British representative on the League of Nations Permanent Mandates Commission from 1923 to 1936 and served on the League's committees on slavery and the International Labour Organization's committee on native labor; he was the first chairman of the International Institute of African Languages and Cultures; he campaigned on issues such as opposition to the transfer of power to European settlers in Kenya and opposition to the Italian invasion of Ethiopia. His work was always *for* Africans, but it was rarely *with* Africans. He was a man of his time: while he accepted that the independence of African peoples was the aim of colonial rule, he considered that his task was to protect Africans from exploitation rather than to prepare them for that independence.

BIBLIOGRAPHY

Flint, John E. "Frederick Lugard: The Making of an Autocrat." In *African Proconsuls: European Governors in Africa,* edited by L. H. Gann and Peter Duignan. New York, 1978.

Perham, Margery. *Lugard.* 2 vols. London, 1956–1960.

MARY BULL

See also **Colonial Policies and Practice.**

Captain F.J.D. Lugard, shortly after his appointment as High Commissioner for Northern Nigeria. THE BODLEIAN LIBRARY, OXFORD, MS. BRIT. EMP. S. 99N; JFB33 C400

LUMUMBA, PATRICE EMERY (b. 1925; d. 1961), political leader and the first prime minister of independent Zaire. Born in Katako Kombe in the Sankuru district of the Kasai province of the Belgian Congo, Lumumba obtained his primary education at both Catholic and Protestant mission schools. Despite his limited formal education, he found work as a clerk, first in Kindu and then in the post office in Stanleyville (now Kisangani). Through voracious reading and taking courses by correspondence with European professors, he improved both his formal education and his standing in various biracial sociocultural organizations in Stanleyville. He founded and chaired the Post Office Workers Society (Amicale des Postiers), cofounded the Belgo-Congolese Union, and became the general secretary of the Association of Native Public Servants. One of the first *évolués,* a colonial status attained by the educated indigenous elite through *immatriculation* (a juridical act of assimilation of

Patrice Lumumba at a 1960 press conference, just prior to Zairian independence. AP/WIDE WORLD

agitation, the 1960 Brussels Round Table to discuss the Congo's independence. He emerged as the most important leader of the independence movement because of his views, oratorical skills, and ability to form coalitions with groups from all the provinces of the country. His party obtained a relatively sweeping victory in the 1960 general elections. Despite opposition from Belgium, Lumumba became prime minister and led the country to independence on 30 June 1960.

As prime minister, Lumumba immediately faced a series of crises: army and mutiny secessions by Katanga and Kasai provinces—and consequent Belgian and United Nations interventions—and Colonel Joseph Mobutu's coup. Provoked by domestic anti-Lumumba forces and external powers, including Belgium, these crises led to Lumumba's arrest and murder in Elisabethville (now Lubumbashi) on 12 February 1961.

Lumumba's legacy and importance lie in his staunch anti-imperialism, Pan-Africanism (e.g., an accord with Kwame Nkrumah to form a union of Ghana and Zaire), antiracist and antitribalist nationalism, and uncompromising commitment to the unity of the country and the nonviolent liberation of colonized people.

BIBLIOGRAPHY

Kanza, Thomas. *The Rise and Fall of Patrice Lumumba: Conflict in the Congo.* Boston, 1979.
Patrice Lumumba. Panaf Great Lives series. London, 1973.
Sangmpam, S. N. *Pseudocapitalism and the Overpoliticized State: Reconciling Politics and Anthropology in Zaire.* Aldershot, U.K., 1994.

S. N. SANGMPAM

See also **Mobutu, Sese Seko; Pan-African and Regional Organizations.**

European culture), Lumumba wrote, in 1956, *Congo, My Country* (published posthumously), in which he expounded his views of the future of the colonial society. After serving a jail term for a seemingly concocted charge of embezzlement of post office funds, he moved to Léopoldville (now Kinshasa), where he became a successful sales manager for the Bracongo brewery.

In 1958, Lumumba founded Mouvement National Congolais (MNC; Congolese National Movement), which differed from other parties in its broad nationalist and Pan-African appeals. Shifting from his earlier support for independence within a Belgo-Congolese union, Lumumba called for immediate and total independence. He attended the Accra (Ghana) first All-African People's Conference in 1958 and, after serving a jail term for political

LUNDA (Aluund). Over 1.5 million people living in Angola, Zaire, and Zambia consider themselves to be Lunda. The name today encompasses hundreds of individually named local groups that have in common a perceived link to the Lunda Empire that flourished between the sixteenth and nineteenth centuries in what is now Zaire. This early empire arose through its ability to control trade between the interior and both the Atlantic and Indian Ocean coasts. Centralized, stratified, and possessed of a strong army, the empire was capable of controlling trade, monopolizing the provisioning of caravans from the coasts, and exacting tariffs on the trading parties that passed through their territory. The Lunda Empire was broken up by the colonial powers of England, Portugal, and Belgium, which divided Lunda territory among themselves and brought an end to caravan trade in the region.

The precolonial economy of the Lunda Kingdom was based on controlling the long-distance trade of the region, but at the local level subsistence agriculture was important. The staple crop was cassava, supplemented by crops grown in part to provision the caravans passing through the region. Lunda crafts, particularly copper and iron smithing, pottery and basket making, weaving, and wood sculpture, were all important prior to the start of the colonial period. Ivory, honey, wax, and slaves were also traded. While Lunda participation in trade was forcibly disrupted during the colonial period, Lunda now participate extensively in interregional trade, exchanging food products for manufactured commodities.

Lunda society retains much of the stratification that characterized its precolonial organization. Lineages are ranked, and titles are inherited matrilineally. Within a lineage, stratification is based on age grade, and the age-based hierarchy cross-cuts the stratification by lineage. Lineage-based authority, however, is frequently undercut by the authority assumed by national governments. Still, at the level of the village the role of a chief or other local leader is respected.

BIBLIOGRAPHY

Bustin, Edouard. *Lunda Under Belgian Rule: The Politics of Ethnicity.* Cambridge, Mass., 1975.

Heusch, Luc de. *The Drunken King; or, The Origin of the State.* Translated and Annotated by Roy Willis. Bloomington, Ind., 1982.

McCulloch, Merran. *The Southern Lunda and Related Peoples (Northern Rhodesia, Belgian Congo, Angola).* London, 1951.

NANCY E. GRATTON

LUO. The Luo-speaking population predominates in a roughly sickle-shaped territory along the eastern side of the Lake Victoria (Nyanza) basin in Kenya, starting from just southeast of the Kenya-Uganda border and extending into the northern Mara region of Tanzania. Luo in Kenya have been estimated to number about 2.6 million (1997); over three-fourths of this population live in Nyanza Province, whose largest city is Kisumu. Tanzanian censuses have not distinguished ethnolinguistic groups since 1957, when Luo in that nation were estimated at just below 100,000. Tracing descent from ancestors who gradually migrated south from the Bahr al-Ghazal region of the Nile in present-day southern Sudan, Luo appear to have settled the lake basin for about five centuries. Luo have been known by other names, including JoLuo, JoLwoo, JoRamogi, and Nilotic Kavirondo (distinguished from Bantu Kavirondo or Luhya). Now, however, the people are known almost universally as Luo or JoLuo, *jo-* being the plural prefix; the origin of the name "Luo" is obscure.

The Luo language, DhoLuo, is currently classed in the southern subgroup of western Nilotic tongues, being akin to Padhola, Acoli, Lango, and related tongues in Uganda (the term "Lwoo" is sometimes applied to all these peoples and some others in present-day Sudan, as well as to Luo in Kenya and Tanzania). Most peoples neighboring the Kenyan Luo homeland (clockwise from northwest, Luhya, Nandi, Kipsigis, Gusii, Maasai, Suba, Kuria, and Jita) speak languages only distantly or not related to Luo. As second languages, many Luo speak Swahili or English; Luo are known throughout east Africa for proficiency in the latter. A small percentage, mostly male, know Luhya, Gusii, or other tongues of neighboring groups. Luo have largely assimilated Suba from a Bantu tongue. The various dialects of Luo within Kenya are mutually intelligible to a high degree.

The present Luo country, flattest and driest by Lake Victoria, turns hillier and more fertile to the north and east, rising to about 1,500 meters above sea level. Rural population densities can exceed 500 per square kilometer in the hills, very high by east African standards. Though remains of pre–twentieth century, circular stone-fortified settlements (*gundni bur,* sing. *gunda bur*) dot the Luo country, rural-dwelling Luo now live mainly in scattered multi- or single-house homesteads (*mier,* sing. *dala*) with fields surrounding them, stretching downhill, or scattered in fragments. Most Luo towns grew around marketplaces in the twentieth century. Important Luo-speaking communities are found in Nairobi, Mombasa, Kampala, and other east African cities, where some grew around early-twentieth-century railroad-worker enclaves. Many inhabitants of these neighborhoods remain socially, economically, and spiritually attached to homes back in the Lake Victoria basin and migrate back and forth.

The rural Luo-speaking population lives mainly by hoe and, since the 1920s, by animal-plow farming, supplemented by herding, fishing, and important labor migration and remittances. White maize (corn) overtook sorghum and finger millet as the main and favorite staple in the late twentieth century. Luo also grow root and leaf crops, as well as industrial cash crops that now include (from lowland to highland) cotton, groundnuts, tobacco, sugarcane, and coffee. Luo keep cattle, sheep and goats, donkeys, and fowl; of these cattle are supremely important culturally, being used for bridewealth (marriage payments from groom and his kin to bride's kin), ceremonial sacrifice, and much else. Specialized fishers use launch and canoe, and dragged or floated nets, or set traps in streams. Women now do more farm and house work than men; men and boys do more animal tending. In monetary and commercial terms, the Luo-dominated area of Kenya is less advantaged than the neighboring upland area of Gusii, enjoying less fertile soils, less regular rainfall, and a less developed economic infrastructure. Luo are noted for an economic ethos favoring cattle accumulation and economic redistribution among kin and neighbors, though there are many exceptions.

Luo society is well known for its patrilineages and clans that divide and subdivide over generations. While these kin groups (contrary to some theories about modernization) have grown more pronounced and important over the twentieth century, Luo also rely on ties through women, through unrelated friends, and through many kinds of voluntary associations. As patrilineages are exogamous and postmarital residence generally virilocal (bride moves to husband's home) the movement of women around the Luo country creates political bonds and homogenizes Luo culture to a degree. Elder men receive much public respect; land and cattle are inherited patrilineally (though women do most of the farmwork); and a fourth to a third of rural Luo homesteads are polygynous. (Patriliny, polygyny, and the payment of bridewealth tend to reinforce each other.) Luo age-grading is much less pronounced than that of their Nandi, Maasai, and Kuria neighbors; it now occurs mainly through schooling. Luo do not ordinarily circumcise or scarify males or females, but until the mid-twentieth century the bottom incisor and canine teeth of both were conventionally extracted in youth as an initiation and ethnic marking. Along other lines, Luo informally stratify society locally into land patrons (*weg lowo,* sing. *wuon lowo,* literally, owners or masters of the land) and land clients (*jodak,* sing. *jadak*), who are often their affinal kin. Many cultural rules relate to the importance of maintaining proper sequence and recognizing seniority. Breaches are perceived as inviting mystically rooted affliction and require purification. Funerals and postmortem ceremonies (*tero buru*) are important public gatherings, and the custom of placing graves inside family homesteads anchors land claims.

Politically, Luo were multicentered before British colonial rule, with clan federations (*ogendini,* sing. *oganda*), sometimes called tribes, under male leaders called *ruodhi* (sing. *ruoth*). Luo responses to colonialism were very mixed, partly as a result of coercive and discriminatory agricultural policies that forced them to plant some crops but denied them others. Since Kenya's independence in 1963, Luo have risen as high as vice president (Oginga Odinga) and several cabinet posts (Tom Mboya and Robert Ouko were internationally celebrated but martyred Luo leaders). Luo have tended to favor opposition movements, as Gikuyu-speakers until the late 1970s and members of Kalenjin groups thereafter have dominated Kenya's independent government and economy. Urban Luo welfare associations are commonly based on older lineage and clan models.

The Luo-speaking public faces important health challenges, some stemming from seasonal or chronic malnutrition. Common ailments include malaria, childhood diarrheal diseases, perinatal gynecological illnesses, marasmus, schistosomiasis, and in the late twentieth century, acquired immunodeficiency syndrome (AIDS). Luo continue to address such problems with a diverse, flexible, and experimental mix of local healing (including herbal medicine and faith healing) and introduced medical practices.

Religion and education have been important channels for Luo energy and talent, partly as a result of mission schooling. Catholic and Protestant Christianity have blanketed the region since the establishment of the first missions in the early years of the twentieth century; small enclaves of Luo Muslims influenced by Arab and other immigrant traders are also found. The Luo country and neighboring areas are home to one of the greatest proliferations of independent Christian churches in the world, continually dividing and subdividing rather like Luo lineages. The Maria Legio and the Roho Maler (Holy Spirit) are the two most popular sets of independent Luo churches; other noted movements have included the Mumbo millenarian (or revitalization) movement of Luo and Gusii in the early twentieth century. Christianity has by no means eradicated indigenous religion. In the attention to a high deity; to ancestors and spirits; to witchcraft, divination, and healing; and to ethics in general, local and Christian religious faiths have interthreaded in complex mutual influence. Religion, healing, and divination afford some women important social and economic opportunities.

Intellectually and numerically, Luo-speakers have dominated many departments in the University of Nairobi and other east African universities, partly because of their comparative strength in the English language. Novelists, poets, and playwrights issuing from the Luo population (such as Grace Ogot, Asenath Bole Odaga, and, from the neighboring Ugandan Padhola population, Okot p'Bitek) have tended to make their names by transcribing, translating, and elaborating a rich Luo stock of oral stories. Many others have made their mark in journalism. Of Luo-speakers traveling and living outside Africa, a large number have gained their opportunities through academic or other intellectual channels.

BIBLIOGRAPHY

Crazzolara, J. P. *The Lwoo.* Verona, 1950.

DuPré, Carole E. *The Luo of Kenya: An Annotated Bibliography.* Washington, D.C., 1968.

Evans-Pritchard, E. E. "Luo Tribes and Clans." In *The Position of Women in Primitive Societies and Other Essays in Social Anthropology,* edited by E. E. Evans-Pritchard. Repr. New York, 1965.

Ocholla-Ayayo, A. B. C. *Traditional Ideology and Ethics Among the Southern Luo.* Uppsala, 1976.

Ogot, Bethwell A. *History of the Southern Luo.* Volume 1, *Migration and Settlement, 1500–1900.* Nairobi, 1967.

Shipton, Parker. *Bitter Money: Cultural Economy and Some African Meanings of Forbidden Commodities.* American Ethnological Society Monograph 1. Washington, D.C., 1989.

Southall, Aidan. "Lineage Formation Among the Luo." International African Institute Memorandum 26. London, 1952.

Sytek, William. *Luo of Kenya.* New Haven, 1972.

Whisson, Michael. *Change and Challenge: A Study of the Social and Economic Changes Among the Kenya Luo.* Nairobi, 1964.

PARKER SHIPTON

See also **Mboya, Tom; Odinga, Oginga.**

LUSAKA. The Zambian capital of Lusaka was once known as a meeting place for those challenging European rule in southern Africa. During the colonial period Lusaka was the hub of campaigns against British colonialism, and in the 1970s and 1980s it was the headquarters of the African National Congress and other liberation movements fighting the white-dominated regimes in South Africa, Zimbabwe, and Mozambique. This is an ironic identity for a city built as a British colonial capital and intended to remind the African population of European superiority. In the 1930s the city and its large Government House were planned by a student of the renowned colonial architect Sir Herbert Baker (famous for his work in South African cities as well as New Delhi) at a time when there were more than one hundred Africans for every European in the colony. The architecture and plan of Lusaka were meant to demonstrate European dominance and to "be the outward and visible sign at all times of the dignity of the Crown."

Cecil Rhodes's British South Africa Company took control of the area that included Lusaka in the 1890s, hoping to find mineral wealth and a source of labor for the mines farther south. In the 1920s copper was discovered in the northwest part of what, in 1924, became the British protectorate of Northern Rhodesia (present day Zambia). The capital of Northern Rhodesia was Livingstone, but Lusaka was built up in the 1930s and became the capital in 1935. Lusaka was more centrally located, and the British considered its altitude and climate healthier than Livingstone's.

In the colonial period "the outward and visible sign" of the colonial capital did not quell notions of African independence. The Federation of African Societies met in Lusaka in 1948 to found the Northern Rhodesia African Congress, a group that agitated for African rights. Lusaka was also the center point of a 1960 civil disobedience campaign aimed at undermining the Central African Confederation, a politico-economic consolidation of Northern Rhodesia, Southern Rhodesia, and Nyasaland set up in 1953. The disobedience campaign led to the breakup of the confederation in 1963 and to Zambia's independence in 1964.

Lusaka grew immensely after independence, gaining 148,000 people between 1963 and 1969, an increase of over 75 percent. Because of the rapid increase in population in Lusaka, Kenneth Kaunda's government tried to shift growth away from the capital and encourage settlement in Kafue, to

Lusaka cityscape. IAN MURPHY/TONY STONE WORLDWIDE

the west. Even with these efforts, Lusaka's population was more than 800,000 in 1988.

The plain around Lusaka is home to two major ethnic groups, the Nyanja and the Soli, and supports ranches and farms. The city is multiethnic and produces cement, textiles, and shoes, and processes food. The town is roughly separated into the new section, which houses the government offices, and the old town, which is along the rail line. Railways are an important mode of transportation in Zambia: Lusaka is linked by lines to Livingstone, the Copper Belt, and Tanzania. In the 1970s, with Chinese assistance, Tanzania and Zambia built the Tan-Zam Railroad connecting Kapiri Mposhi (on the Zambia–Copper Belt line) with Dar es Salaam in order to give Zambia an outlet to an independent African country.

Lusaka's role as an anticolonial, frontline capital dwindled after African-led governments took power in Mozambique in 1975, Zimbabwe in 1980, and South Africa in 1994. In the 1990s the challenges that faced the city were internal: environmental, economic, and demographic. Lusaka's population continued to increase even though the region was drought-ridden and had an inflation rate of as much as 500 percent in the first years of the decade.

BIBLIOGRAPHY

Fage, J. D., and Roland Oliver, eds. *The Cambridge History of Africa.* Volume 7. Edited by A. D. Roberts. Cambridge, 1986.

Griffiths, Ieuan Ll., *The Atlas of African History.* 2d ed. London, 1994.

THOMAS F. McDOW

LUTULI, ALBERT JOHN MAVUMBI (1898–1967), president of the African National Congress (ANC) of South Africa between 1952 and 1967. Born in Salisbury, Southern Rhodesia (later Zimbabwe), Lutuli grew up in Groutville, Natal, South Africa. The son of a preacher, he taught in a primary school before becoming an instructor at Adams College

Albert John Lutuli in 1961, on the announcement that he had been awarded the Nobel Peace Prize. ARCHIVE PHOTOS/LONDON DAILY EXPRESS

in Natal, in 1921. Elected as chief of the Abase-maklolweni Zulu in 1935, he returned to Groutville to administer local justice and organize peasant cane growers.

Lutuli joined the ANC in 1945. In 1952 he was deposed from his chieftancy and elected ANC president, both consequences of his contribution to the ANC's Defiance Campaign. With Lutuli at its head, the ANC completed its transformation from an assembly of notables into a popular movement. Confined to Groutville by government banning orders most of the time, Lutuli was unable to play an assertive part in ANC campaigns, and he was not involved in the decision to initiate sabotage operations in 1961. His importance lay in his moral stature. Less patrician than any of his predecessors in the ANC leadership, Lutuli was a figure who commanded widespread loyalty. He was awarded the Nobel Peace Prize for 1960. At the time of his death, Lutuli's nonviolence and "middle of the road" socialism seemed to be eclipsed by the more radical programs of exiled guerrillas. His gentle vision embodies an African liberal tradition which remains relevant.

BIBLIOGRAPHY

Callan, E. *Albert John Luthuli and the South African Race Conflict.* Kalamazoo, Mich., 1965.
Gordimer, Nadine. "Chief Luthuli." *Atlantic Monthly* 203, no. 4 (1959): 34–39.
Lutuli, Albert. *Let My People Go.* New York, 1962.
Pillay, Gerald J. *Voices of Liberation.* Volume 1, *Albert Lutuli.* Pretoria, 1993.

THOMAS LODGE

See also **Apartheid.**

M

MAASAI. The best-known name of the Maa-speaking peoples of the Rift Valley region of eastern Africa is Maasai. They have or have had a pastoral economy, technology, culture, and society and are today threatened with the destruction of their way of life by local governments, development agencies, and tourism to an extent greater than most other African peoples. A Maasai saying has it that "Fools do not understand cattle," historically a sadly true remark that applies particularly to the plight of the Maasai. There are over 250,000 Maasai in Kenya and Tanzania.

Maasai are usually characterized as cattle herders who grow little grain, depending for it upon their agricultural neighbors. However, some Maasai are agriculturalists, and they intermarry and have close ties also with Bantu-speaking Gikuyu and Kalenjin farmers, and with Okiek hunter-gatherers. These classifications of forms of production are largely stereotypes, however; the various Maasai groups have also been traders, and today some are town dwellers. The notion of "pure" Maasai is largely an invention of outside observers, mostly travel writers, journalists, and photographers looking for peoples who may be romanticized as "untouched" by Western culture, especially for the local tourist industry.

The Maa-speaking peoples include the pastoralist Maasai proper of the Rift Valley, comprising some dozen groups or sections that include the Matapato, Purko, Loitokitok, Uas Nkishu, Kisongo, and others; the Samburu and Ariaal in the far north of Kenya; the Chamus (Njemps) of the Baringo region; and the Parakuyo (Baraguru) of eastern Tanzania. There are also the agricultural Maasai groups, often known as the Kwavi and the Arusha, of Tanzania.

All these groups may be considered Maasai. The main defining criteria include speaking a Maa language; at least traditionally being cattle herders; sharing many cultural details in clothing, bead decoration, and the like; possessing a range of complex age systems; exhibiting a lack of centralized political leadership but with great authority given to the ritual functionaries generally known as "prophets"; and formerly possessing an effective military organization for raiding and warfare. In general, the Maasai have shown an unwillingness to accept the trappings of Western culture arising from a fierce pride in their traditional way of life.

BIBLIOGRAPHY

Spear, Thomas, and Richard Waller, eds. *Being Maasai: Ethnicity and Identity in East Africa.* London, 1993.

Spencer, Paul. *The Samburu: A Study of Gerontocracy in a Nomadic Tribe.* London, 1965.

———. *The Maasai of Matapato: A Study of Rituals of Rebellion.* Manchester, 1988.

JOHN MIDDLETON

See also **Ethnicity and Identity; Production Systems.**

MACAULAY, HERBERT SAMUEL HEELAS (b. 1864; d. 1946), Nigerian political leader, considered the father of Nigerian nationalism. Born to the Reverend Thomas and Abigail Macaulay, daughter of Bishop Samuel Ajayi Crowther, Macaulay received his early education in Lagos. In 1890 he became the first Nigerian to win a colonial government scholarship to study abroad, pursuing a degree in civil engineering at Plymouth, England. He later became a government surveyor in charge of Crown grants. In this position he had a close experience of colonial administration. He resigned in 1899 to set up his own engineering business and to engage in political protest.

On 30 August 1910, Macaulay convened the inaugural meeting of the Lagos branch of the Anti-Slavery and Aborigines Rights Protection Society. His profession brought him in close contact with the traditional rulers who were regarded as custodians of communal land. Through his newspaper, the *Lagos Daily News,* he championed the land and political rights of Nigerians. In 1923, he founded the first political party in Nigeria, the Nigerian National Democratic Party (NNDP), to achieve his political goals.

In 1944 Macaulay was elected the first president of the National Council of Nigeria and the Cameroons (NCNC). He died on the eve of a country-wide NCNC tour at the age of eighty-two.

BIBLIOGRAPHY

Coleman, James S. *Nigeria: Background to Nationalism.* Berkeley and Los Angeles, 1971.
Uwechue, R. *Makers of Modern Africa.* London, 1981.

OLUTAYO ADESINA

MACAULAY, THOMAS BABINGTON (b. 1826; d. 1879), Anglican clergyman and school administrator. Macaulay was born at Kissy, Sierra Leone, the son of liberated slaves from Yorubaland.

Macaulay was educated in Sierra Leone at Kissy Local Primary School, the Church Missionary Society (CMS) Grammar School and Fourah Bay College, and the Islington College, London, where he graduated in 1848. In 1852, he was sent to the Yoruba CMS Mission, where he worked at Igbein and Owu in Abeokuta. He was ordained in 1854 and married Abigail Crowther, daughter of Bishop Samuel Ajayi Crowther.

The dispute between the emigrants from Sierra Leone and Rev. Henry Townsend on Anglican political influence at Abeokuta led to a face-off between the Crowthers, Macaulay, and Townsend. Townsend posted Macaulay first to Owu and thereafter transferred him out of Abeokuta. Eventually, Macaulay pleaded, with the support of Reverend Crowther, that he be allowed to start a grammar school in Lagos. This was accepted and the CMS Grammar School, Lagos, was founded by Macaulay in December 1859.

Macaulay was the principal of CMS Grammar School in Lagos from 1859 until his death. He was the father of seven children including Herbert Macaulay, considered the father of modern Nigerian nationalism.

BIBLIOGRAPHY

Ajayi, J. F. Ade. *Christian Missions in Nigeria, 1841–1891: The Making of a New Elite.* London, 1965.
Kopytoff, Jean H. *A Preface to Modern Nigeria: The "Sierra Leonians" in Yoruba, 1830–1890.* Madison, Wis. 1965.

OLATUNJI OJO

MACAULAY, ZACHARY (b. 1768; d. 1838), abolitionist, entrepreneur, governor of Sierra Leone, father of Thomas Babington (Lord) Macaulay. Zachary Macaulay was a plantation overseer in Jamaica (1784–1792), where he learned

Zachary Macaulay. CHURCH MISSIONARY SOCIETY, LONDON

management and developed a hatred for the slave trade and slavery. He was sent by the Sierra Leone Company to Freetown, first to serve as a councillor (1792–1794), then as acting governor (1794–1795) and governor (1796–1799). He was acting governor when in 1794 French Jacobins invaded and destroyed the nascent colony, and he embarked on the process of rebuilding it. A firm, courageous, and caring ruler, when returning to Britain in 1799 he took with him to be educated there twenty-one African boys and four African girls from Sierra Leone. Macaulay became a member of the famous Evangelical Clapham sect and through it was active in the abolitionist movement, the British and Foreign Bible Society, the Church Missionary Society, and the National Society for the Education of the Poor (promoters of Andrew Bell's teaching method, which was widely adopted in Sierra Leone). He was secretary to the Sierra Leone Company and honorary secretary to the African Institution, which replaced the Sierra Leone Company when Sierra Leone became a Crown colony in 1808. He founded the firm of Macaulay & Babington through which he traded in Sierra Leone. His reputation explains the popularity of Macaulay as a surname adopted by liberated Africans in the colony.

BIBLIOGRAPHY

Booth, Charles. *Zachary Macaulay: His Part in the Movement for the Abolition of the Slave Trade and of Slavery.* London, 1934.

Groves, C. P. *The Planting of Christianity in Africa.* Volume 1, *To 1840.* London, 1948.

Kup, A. P. *Sierra Leone: A Concise History.* Newton Abbot, England, 1975.

J. F. ADE. AJAYI

See also **Christianity.**

MACHEL, SAMORA MOISES (b. 1933; d. 1986), anticolonial military strategist and president of the Republic of Mozambique. After primary schooling in the Portuguese colonial system, Machel became a hospital nurse in the colonial capital of Lourenço Marques (Maputo), and he early embraced anticolonial activism, having been inspired by the African spirit of the times and, more directly, by the example of Eduardo Mondlane in 1949 and later. After the formation of Frente de Libertação de Moçambique (FRELIMO) at Dar es Salaam (in Tanganyika, about to become Tanzania) during 1962, Machel joined Mondlane and others and volunteered for

Samora Machel, 1986. CORBIS-BETTMANN

military training under FRELIMO. FRELIMO secured training for volunteers in Algeria (independent from France in 1962) and then, in handfuls, sent them into northern Mozambique. There they shaped a military strategy that soon began to have success. In 1969, after Mondlane's assassination, Machel took over the FRELIMO leadership and proved a capable military strategist as well as an inspired leader. His clinching success in these roles came in 1974–1975, when his forces contained and then outflanked the Portuguese army in central Mozambique. The country won independence in 1975, and Machel was elected president. His later years were spent in launching the new republic while defending it from banditries sent into Mozambique from Rhodesia and South Africa. He was killed in 1986 in an aircraft crash in circumstances strongly indicative of external sabotage. Consistently effective as a man of action rather than an ideologist, he achieved widespread admiration, at home and abroad, as a wise unifier of the diverse strands of opinion gathered in the independence movement which he led to victory.

BIBLIOGRAPHY

Christie, Iain. *Machel of Mozambique.* Harare, Zimbabwe, 1988.

Munslow, Barry, ed. *Samora Machel, an African Revolutionary: Selected Speeches and Writings.* London, 1985.

BASIL DAVIDSON

See also **Colonial Policies and Practices; Mondlane, Eduardo Chivambo.**

MADAGASCAR

[The complex story of this almost continent-sized island warrants special treatment. **Early Settlement** *addresses the prehistoric era. The modern kingdom, colony, and nation-state are treated in* **Geography and Economy** *and* **History and Government** *(*1750–1895 *and* **Since 1895**). *Additional articles treat the island's* **Peoples and Cultures** *and its* **Religious Systems.***]*

EARLY SETTLEMENT

The early settlement of Madagascar remains enigmatic and controversial. The Malagasy people have ancestral roots in many lands bordering the Indian Ocean, yet when, how, and why their ancestors arrived is still unclear. Adding to the mystery is that Madagascar, the fourth-largest island in the world, was apparently one of the last great islands to be settled. Over the less than two millennia of human occupation, the Malagasy have forged a fundamental unity of language and culture. At the same time, however, populations in different regions have developed distinctive political, social, and ethnic identities.

In Madagascar today, there is a shared common language. Malagasy, however, displays much regional variation in phonology and vocabulary. It is usually described as having twenty or more dialects, each associated with a particular ethnic group or region. The languages most closely related to Malagasy are of the Austronesian family and are found in interior Borneo. However, Malagasy has also been greatly altered by influence from one or more Bantu languages. Some believe this situation was the product of early Indonesian residence on the coast of Africa, but others argue that it happened through the interaction of two languages on Madagascar itself.

The diversity of physical appearance among the Malagasy stands in contrast to their linguistic unity. To the earliest European observers, some populations appeared to be "Malay"; others, "African." Some scholars believe that the Malagasy are primarily the descendants of light-skinned Malays and dark-skinned Melanesians. Others see African origins as predominant. Still others note that oral histories point to "Arab" or "Persian" origins.

While for some authors, African populations initially settled the island, and were joined later by Asian immigrants, others argue for the reverse; further, many believe that the original settlers were the descendants of a population of Afro-Indonesians originally formed in communities on the eastern coast of Africa.

Limited genetic research indicates that modern Malagasy gene frequencies reflect major contributions from both Indonesia and East Africa. African and Asian genes are not, however, uniformly mixed—some local populations are more Asian in origin, and others are more African. However, there is much local diversity in ancestry and appearance in all regions, whether in the "Asian" highlands or along the "African" coasts. Finally, it seems likely that immigrants from other areas around the Indian Ocean—such as the Persian Gulf and India—have contributed to the Malagasy ancestry.

There is no evidence of human arrival on Madagascar before the beginning of the first millennium C.E. No Stone Age archaeological sites have been discovered, and even the earliest known settlers brought iron tools. In addition, recent paleoecological research documenting the history of vegetation gives no evidence of human impact more than 1,900 years old, although it becomes unmistakable by the fourteenth century. Madagascar's giant lemurs, elephant birds, and pygmy hippos, whose extinction is usually connected with human settlement, may have survived in some areas until the twelfth century.

The first traces of human activity appear along the southwest coast. The evidence is limited to extinct pygmy hippopotamus bones that bear the marks of butchery with metal tools. These bones, recovered in the early twentieth century, have radiocarbon ages of the first to fourth centuries C.E.; however, there are no associated artifacts. At the northern extreme of the island, the deepest archaeological layers in a rock shelter near the coast have radiocarbon dates of the fifth and eighth centuries.

The site of the oldest known continuous occupation on Madagascar is on the east coast islet of Nosy Mangabe; it dates to the eighth century, which is also the age of the oldest known sites on the Comoros Islands. About eighty kilometers south of Nosy Mangabe, a village and a string of small hamlets along the Mananara River valley date to the late eighth through the twelfth centuries. These sites have yielded earthenware ceramics, iron slag, and traces of the manufacture of chlorite schist (soapstone) vessels. In addition, Nosy Mangabe has yielded sherds of ninth–tenth century Near Eastern pottery, and at one Mananara site, what appears to be a necklace with beads of silver, gold, carnelian, and glass has been found.

Between the tenth and the mid-fourteenth centuries there were settlements at nearly all well-studied areas of Madagascar's coasts. Near the end of this period, the earliest known occupations of the interior were established. During this period we have good evidence for nearly all of the hallmarks of traditional Malagasy ecological adaptations: rice farming; cattle, sheep, and goat herding; and marine fishing. As today, economic activities varied according to the local environmental condition. In the arid south, for example, the eleventh-century site of Andranosoa was clearly a village of fairly specialized herders. In terms of settlements, this was a period of great diversity. Sites ranged from small farming hamlets to the urban trading center of Mahilaka on the northwest coast, which had a wall enclosing seventy hectares of masonry residences, at least one mosque, workshop areas, and an inner precinct. Mahilaka's 5,000 to 10,000 residents imported Near Eastern and Far Eastern ceramics that also have been found at coastal trading communities of the east African coast. Mahilaka probably served as a trading center where island products such as tortoiseshell, chlorite schist, gold, crystal quartz, and possibly wood, tree gum, and iron were exchanged for ceramics, glass vessels, trade beads, and possibly cloth.

The earthenware ceramics of the coastal sites are probably regional variations of a common tradition, although the earliest earthenware of the central highlands are stylistically distinctive and their origins are unclear. The coastal ceramics, particularly in the north, bear strong resemblance to the ceramics of contemporary settlements on the Comoros Islands, and in some aspects they resemble contemporary ceramics of East African coastal communities. On the other hand, there is no clear evidence of direct contact between any of these communities and the eastern Indian Ocean.

In the subsequent centuries leading up to the European arrival in the sixteenth century, Mahilaka was succeeded by a series of trading centers along the north and northeast coasts, none as large as it had been. In other regions, settlements often took the form of five to ten villages surrounding a regional center of perhaps 1,000 residents. All of these centers contained concentrations of trade goods, which suggests that they may also have known a concentration of wealth and political authority.

Soon after the Europeans' arrival, there was a series of dramatic changes across the island. The slave trade and the import of guns led to increasing levels of military conflict, population relocations, and reorganizations of political power. In the Imerina region of the central highlands, there was a swift increase in population density, with concurrent increases in political complexity. Along the northwest and east coasts, there were increases in political complexity, though these are not well documented archaeologically. In some areas, however, the basic patterns established in the fourteenth and fifteenth centuries continued with little evident change.

BIBLIOGRAPHY

Deschamps, Hubert. *Histoire de Madagascar.* 3d ed. Paris, 1965.

Dewar, Robert E. "Extinctions in Madagascar: The Loss of the Subfossil Fauna." In *Quaternary Extinctions,* edited by Paul Martin and Richard Klein. Tucson, Ariz., 1984.

Dewar, Robert E., and Henry T. Wright. "The Culture History of Madagascar." *Journal of World Prehistory* 7 (1993): 417–466.

Kottak, Conrad. *The Past in the Present: History, Ecology, and Cultural Variation in Highland Madagascar.* Ann Arbor, 1980.

Vérin, Pierre. *The History of Civilisation in North Madagascar.* Translated by David Smith. Rotterdam, 1986.

———. *Madagascar.* 2d ed. Paris, 1990.

ROBERT E. DEWAR

GEOGRAPHY AND ECONOMY

The Mozambique Channel, which is 390 kilometers wide, separates Madagascar from the coast of eastern Africa. It is possible that Madagascar was once connected to southern Africa and India; together they would have formed the continent known to theory as Gondwana Land. With an area of 587,044 square kilometers, Madagascar is the fourth largest island in the world. Long and thin, it stretches over a distance of 1,600 kilometers from Cape Bobaomby in the north to Cape Vohimena in the south; its width does not exceed 580 kilometers.

Climate

Trade winds blow throughout the year. Those from the southeast meet the monsoon from the northwest during the warm season from December to May, which is followed by the southerly movement

The Republic of Madagascar

Population: 13,126,600 (1994 est.)

Area: 587,044 sq. km (226,658 sq. mi.)

Official language: Malagasy

Languages: French, Malagasy

National currency: Franc Malgache

Principal religions: Traditional 52%, Christian 41% (split nearly evenly between Roman Catholic and Protestant), Muslim 7%

Capital: Antananarivo (estimated pop. 833,000 in 1988)

Other urban centers: Mahajanga, Toamasina, Fianarantsoa, Antseranana, Toliary, Antsirabe, Tolagnaro

Annual rainfall: Varies from 3,000 to 5,000 mm (120–190 in.) on the east coast to 510 mm (20 in.) in the southwest

Principal geographical features:

Rivers: Sambirano, Betsiboka, Ikopa, Tsiribihina, Mangoky, Onilahy, Menarandra, Mandrare, Mananara, Mananjary, Mangoro, Maningory, Fiherenana

Lakes: Alaotra, Ihotry, Itasy, Tsiazompaniry, Mantasoa, Kikony

Islands: Nossi-Bé, Sainte-Marie

Economy:

GNP per capita: US$240 (1995)

Principal products and exports:

Agricultural: coffee, cloves, vanilla, sugar, tobacco, flowers, fish, prawns, lobster, rice, maize, cassava, banana, sweet potato, cotton, livestock

Manufacturing: food processing, chemical fertilizer, soap, radios, cement, vehicle assembly, tobacco processing, textiles, leather, wood and paper products, petroleum refining

Mining: chromium ore, graphite, mica, bauxite, copper, nickel, some gold

Government: Independence from France, 1960. Constitution adopted in 1959, enacted 1960. New constitution adopted in 1975, replaced in 1992. Multiparty democracy. Under 1992 constitution, the president is elected by universal suffrage for 5-year-term, limited to 2 terms. Bicameral national legislature consists of the 138-member Assemblée Nationale, elected by universal suffrage according to proportional representation, and the Senate, one-third of which is filled by appointment. The president appoints the prime minister from candidates selected by the Assemblée Nationale. For purposes of local government there are 6 provinces, headed by Secretary of State delegates; 18 prefectures; 92 subprefects; and 705 cantons, headed by cantonal chiefs.

Heads of state since independence:

1960–1972: President Philibert Tsiranana

1972–1975: Prime Minister Major General Gabriel Ramanantsoa

Feb. 1975: Colonel Richard Ratsimandrava

Feb.–June 1975: General Gilles Andriamahazo

1975–1993: President Didier Ratsiraka

1993–1996: President Albert Zafy

1996–1997: Interim president Norbert Ratsirahonana

1997–: President Didier Ratsiraka

Armed Forces: Voluntary enlistment

Army: 20,000

Navy: 500

Air Force: 500

Paramilitary: 7,500

Transportation:

Rail: 1,095 km (679 mi.), railways are state owned.

Ports: Toamasina, Mahajanga

Roads: 49,555 km (30,724 mi.), 11% paved

National Airline: Air Madagascar

Airports: Ivato at Antananarivo for international flights. There are 211 airfields throughout the country.

Media: 5 daily newspapers, including *Midi Madagascar,* 24 periodicals. Strong book publishing industry.

Television (since 1967) and radio provided through Radiodiffusion Nationale Malgache.

Literacy and Education:

Total literacy rate: 80% (1990 est.) Education is free, universal, and compulsory for ages 6–13.

Postsecondary education provided at Université d'Antananarivo, Université de Fianarantsoa, Université de Toamasina, Imadefolk-Institut Malgache des Arts Dramatiques et Folkloriques, Institut National des Sciences Comptables et de l'Administration.

of the Intertropical Convergence Zone (ICZ). One side of this mountainous island is exposed to the winds and has an annual rainfall between 3,000 and 5,000 millimeters. On the other side the winds are less moist, even relatively dry, due to the foehn. Because of its topography and orography—its highest peak is 2,882 meters—the country is known for the extreme variety of its climate. The east is warm and humid, the south has vast tracts of semidesert, the west is warm and dry, and the high central area has a cool climate. Climatic change in Madagascar is so sudden that one can go from a warm and humid area to a cool and dry one in just a few tens of kilometers. Violent cyclones occur between January and April.

The quantity and type of vegetation depend on the local rainfall. The great rain forest now exists only on the eastern slopes and in the extreme northwest. The west is filled with savannas dominated by the baobab tree (*Andasonia*) in the south and by satrana palms (*Medemia*) in the north. In the central highlands there are still a few areas of forest that are protected from destruction because they are sacred, and there are gallery forests in river valleys. The hills are covered with sparse steppe vegetation (*Hyparrhenia* and *Aristida*), and reforestation programs have returned eucalyptus and pine trees to the area since the beginning of the twentieth century. The south has thorny xerophytes (*Didierea* and *Alluaudia*).

Geology

Madagascar's crystalline insular shelf, composed of granite and gneiss, is broken in several places by magma intrusions. In the central highlands, erosion has created a countryside of bare hills, called *tanety*, dotted with huge gullies called *lavaka* and swampy lowlands now used for rice farming. Large flat areas, known as *tampoketsa*, tend to have a bauxite or ferrous shell that is evidence of severe past erosion.

This crystalline base extends westward under a series of sedimentary strata from the northwest (Mahajanga [Majunga] Basin) to the west (Morondava Basin), and in a fringing reef along the east coast. In the calcareous parts of these sedimentary strata there are cuestas and rough karstic regions. Erosion has fashioned spectacular sights in several places: ruinlike shapes in the Isalo massif, needles of rock in Tsingy of Bemaraha, and vast grottoes in Ankarana at Ambilobe.

Sand dunes dominate the landscape of the extreme south. The three series of dunes—tatsimian,

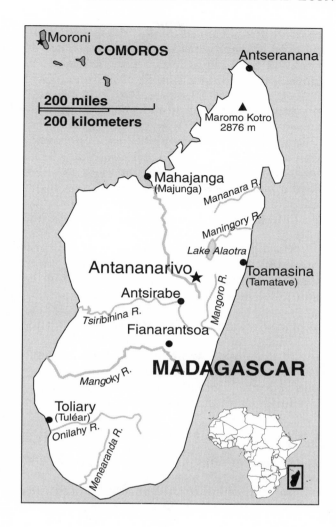

karimbolian, and flandrian—can be differentiated by their degree of redness, which is caused by age. The red tatsimian sands contrast sharply with the more recent, white flandrian dunes. The flandrian dunes make magnificent beaches that are protected by coral reefs.

Population and Cities

Madagascar has a population of about 14 million, unevenly distributed, but with an average density of 20 people per square kilometer. This population has a growth rate of 3 percent per year, a life expectancy of 57 years, and a GNP of U.S. $240 per person.

The eastern and central areas, especially between Antananarivo and Fianarantsoa, are densely populated, and the west and south are sparsely populated (two or three people per square kilometer). Some parts of the west have nearly no population at all. The majority of Malagasy people (80 percent) live in rural areas; the capital, Antananarivo, and its suburbs have 10 percent of the population, and the balance live in provincial and regional towns.

Toamasina, capital of the eastern province and the most important port of Madagascar, is connected to Antananarivo by railway. Toliary and Tolagnaro are the two great cities of the southwest. Fianarantsoa, in Betsileo territory, is the capital of the south. Mahajanga is an important port for coastal trade where even large ships can moor safely. It is not as significant a port as Toamasina, but the establishment of new industries there is important.

Antseranana, in the extreme north, was the last city to become a provincial capital. It has never been a commercial center because it lacks a connection to the interior, but has compensated for this by specializing in two economic activities unique in Madagascar: naval dockyards and saltworks.

These are the administrative and economic centers of Madagascar. With the exception of Antananarivo, their activities are determined by their location and the local agricultural, fishing, or mining potential. The occupations of the inhabitants vary accordingly.

The Economy

In the eastern forested regions, the people first cleared the land by means of the ancient practice of *tavy*, an itinerant method of cultivation that requires burned land. On this hastily prepared soil, they planted rice, manioc, and bananas. On sloping land, this practice caused massive deforestation. Had the government not protected the remaining forest, rain would have eroded the soil completely in just a few years. As it is, the soil lacks the fertility to produce an acceptable yield. Although the people understand its negative effects, they continue to practice *tavy* because the alternatives require an investment, albeit minimal, that they cannot afford.

The east has always produced valuable crops: vanilla, coffee, cloves, pepper, and various fruits. In the past they were cultivated by foreign colonizers, but now they are grown by small national producers who suffer greatly from the worldwide instability of agricultural prices. In addition, frequent cyclones disrupt the economy of the region.

In the central highlands, rice farming is a tradition. Gravity-fed irrigation of carefully arranged rice fields, with as many as eighty levels of terraces, employs a hydraulic system that has not changed over time.

In sharp contrast to the laborious farming methods of the central highlands are those of the vast marshy plains such as those of Lake Alaotra and of the Betsiboka River, known as the rice granaries of Madagascar. Their average yield is similar to that of the plain of Betsimitatatra. These marshes were drained by the first kings of Antananarivo in the eighteenth century.

In the midwest and west, vast open spaces allow those who raise zebu (*Bos indicus*) to have large herds, but this commerce is sometimes limited by the affectionate tie that can arise between the zebu raiser and his herd. Zebu are as numerous as people and have always represented a natural wealth to be exploited.

The Tandroy herders (originally from the south) have created a network of *rabatteurs* throughout the island. They walk hundreds of kilometers to bring livestock to market. The most important livestock markets are Tsiroanomandidy, about 100 kilometers west of Antananarivo, and Ambalavao, which is 50 kilometers south of Fianarantsoa.

The floodplains of the river deltas in the west have extremely fertile soil, called *baiboho*. Agriculture in these areas is mechanized, and the crops vary according to national and global market conditions. When cotton promised more profit than the cape pea, cotton was grown. More recently tobacco, after a difficult period, became profitable. In the northeast the crop is sugarcane, which is grown along with other export crops such as cocoa and the perfume plant ylang-ylang.

On any island one would expect to find an active fishing culture. In fact, only the Vezu of the southwest coast are true fisherfolk, able to venture onto the high seas. Other inhabitants of the island practice occasional subsistence fishing.

The south has always been the least favored area of Madagascar because of its semiarid climate. In spite of its sparse vegetation, the south is a significant area for the raising of cattle and goats. During the dry season (July to September) the livestock must be moved constantly in search of pasturage and water.

The difference in living conditions between the cities and the country is a serious problem. The state has attempted to solve it though a policy of decentralization. However, the globalization of the economy has placed great strains on Madagascar. It must now find industries that can ameliorate its economic disparities. The most important problem is assuring the survival of a population of which the majority lives below the poverty line. Since the enactment of the structural adjustment program that the international financial institutions demanded, a multitude of informal businesses have appeared, and these ensure the survival of many families.

In the long term, capital investment aimed at developing industrial fishing, mining, and food crops, among others, will surely improve the standard of living. The most significant trend is the growth of the tourist industry, which is based on the fauna and flora of Madagascar.

BIBLIOGRAPHY

Cowell, Maureen. *Madagascar: Politics, Economics, and Society.* London, 1971.

Heseltine, Nigel. *Madagascar.* London, 1971.

Jolly, Alison, Philippe Oberle, and Roland Albignac, eds. *Madagascar.* Oxford, 1984.

Vindard, G. R., and R. Battistini, eds. *Biogeography and Ecology in Madagascar.* The Hague, 1976.

See also **Agriculture; Antananarivo; Climate; Development; Economic History; Geography and the Study of Africa.**

HISTORY AND GOVERNMENT:
FROM 1750 TO 1895

From the beginning of the sixteenth century to the first half of the eighteenth century, regional populations on Madagascar spread out within their own territories. The years 1750–1895, by contrast, were a period of national integration, although this process by which the Malagasy people become politically unified often met with resistance.

The Kingdom of Madagascar (1817–1895) arose from a combination of two factors: first, the Merina Kingdom's desire to expand to the sea; second, the project of a "Pax Britannia" in the southwest Indian Ocean and the determination of Sir Robert Farquhar, the British governor of Mauritius, to oppose French territorial claims. This Kingdom of Madagascar, created and defended by force of arms, was taken over by an oligarchy which sought to increase its wealth; national cohesion was damaged as a result. Thus, the work of unification ended with a certain degree of hostility among various Malagasy populations.

By the middle of the eighteenth century, the island of Madagascar was in a virtual state of anarchy. On the east coast, the death of Merina's king, Ratsimilaho, in 1750 marked the end of the dream of unity. When Queen Andriamasinavalona divided the kingdom among his four sons, the so-called Merina anarchy of the eighteenth century ensued. To the west, the Boina Kingdom reached its greatest expansion, but destabilizing forces and struggles for the throne were already evident.

The final third of the eighteenth century and the first decade of the nineteenth century were marked by two great figures. The last great sovereign of Boina, Queen Ravahiny (r. 1770–1808), brought order to its territories, suppressed revolts in Ambongo and in the north, and developed trade. Andrianampoinimerina (r. c. 1783–1810) reunified and expanded Imerina (the land of the Merina people), fostering friendly relations with Ravahiny.

The Merina were surrounded by warlike neighbors (Sakalava, Sihanaka, Bezanozano) who enslaved them, raided their herds, and destroyed their harvests. In order to fight against chronic famines the Merina had embarked upon the tremendous undertaking of irrigated agriculture, and had constructed an entire network of canals in an effort to increase rice production. The distribution of water for swamp drainage and rice irrigation required the people to work hard and cooperate. Poor harvests and the fear of enemy raids helped create and maintain the environment of insecurity in which the people lived. This shared insecurity strengthened group cohesion. Thus, by the end of the eighteenth century, the Merina peasantry was ready to accept a king capable of commanding the people's respect and of bringing about the discipline and solidarity needed for survival.

Andrianampoinimerina met these expectations. His wars, within and outside of Imerina, were undertaken in order to guarantee the security of his kingdom, thus satisfying the peasantry. Yet these wars also aimed to fulfill the wishes of the tradespeople, who sought control of the ports and the creation of a vast market where they could ply their trade without disruption. As a result, what his subjects desired most dovetailed with the king's dream of unity.

The newly unified Merina kingdom annexed Betsileo, gazed greedily upon the Sakalava territories, and set out to bring the entire island under its control. During his short reign, Radama I (1810–1828) asserted the dominance of the Merina over the other Malagasy peoples, with the exception of those in the south and in Ambongo. He succeeded in creating a unified state, the Kingdom of Madagascar. In this he was assisted by the English, by a divided opposition, and perhaps as much by his desire to unify the island as by the greed that motivated his richest subjects. His kingdom was recognized by foreign powers. Radama managed to create a state, but not yet a nation. This latter task would fall to his successors.

Beginning with the reign of Queen Ranavalona I (1828–1861), the heads of the most important Hova clans, Tsimahafotsy and Tsimiamboholahy, who were already the heads of the army, seized political power and took over trade. The Andriana—members and associates of the royal family—were ousted from the government; the queen became nothing more than a useful tool in the hands of the Hova—a middle class ranked below the nobility and above the slaves. Thus, the middle class was able to pursue a political agenda similar to that of Radama, but toward a wholly different end.

Unfortunately, this nascent Hova oligarchy did everything possible to increase its wealth and preserve its privileges, even at the price of impoverishing the general population. Defending the state amounted to maintaining the privileges of the most powerful and continuing the injustices and divisions that were detrimental to the cohesion of Malagasy society. Wishing to ward off any possible danger, the oligarchy supported nationalism as a way of channeling the fury of the Malagasy people, who were oppressed in Imerina as well as elsewhere, and turning that fury against foreign imperialism, which the oligarchy perceived as its own enemy.

The great officers and ministers of the capital, as well as the governors of the provinces and the great merchant families of Antananarivo, competed with the foreign households of Tamatave (later Toamasina) and Majunga (later Mahajanga) for a trade monopoly. The former carved out several properties, particularly on the east coast, and tended vast herds of cattle. Thus there was a takeover of economic life as well as political life. Certain positions, called Andriambaventy, were granted to obedient non-Merina servants of the Merina cause; except in such cases, however, the high offices within the administration and at the top of the hierarchy of honors were inaccessible to non-Merina. The oligarchy sought to dominate rather than to unite the different populations of the island. Due to their politics, members of the oligarchy were viewed as foreigners by those outside its province of origin.

Radama II (1861–1863), who rapidly introduced Western ways without considering all of their ramifications, was assassinated in 1863. His brother, the prime minister, Rainivoninahitriniony, was ousted in 1864. Afterward, Rainilaiarivony guided the destiny of the Kingdom of Madagascar. Husband of the three previous queens (Rasoherina, Ranavalona II, and Ranavalona III), and simultaneously holding the positions of prime minister and commander in chief of the royal army, he held the actual power, guiding his country for more than thirty years. A worthy representative of the men enriched through commerce or the military, Rainilaiarivony devoted all his energy to reorganizing and modernizing the army, an indispensible tool for pacifying the conquered regions and defending the kingdom. The subjugated provinces continued to be exploited, but not as severely as in the first half of the century. The prime minister, some of his close colleagues, and governors of the provinces, such as Rainandriamampandry in Tamatave, considered it necessary to gain the trust of the non-Merina populations. In addition, with varying degrees of success, they pursued something close to a politics of assimilation.

Ranavalona I had fought against the acceptance of Protestant Christianity. Beginning in 1869, however, when Ranavalona II and Rainilaiarivony converted, it became the official religion. The degree to which people adhered to it varied across regions. The adherents were generally those who received a full-time education, who were numerous in Imerina and few elsewhere. The development of Christianity and education thus widened the gap separating the Merina from other populations on the island—a gap that grew out of conquest, political domination, and economic exploitation. Furthermore, as a result of inefficiency and abuse, the centralized administration put even more distance between the oligarchy and the various subjugated populations.

Despite the shortcomings of the oligarchy, the modern state established by Radama I, who freely chose the Western model of the nation-state, contributed greatly to the political unification of Madagascar. His efforts were built upon by Rainilaiarivony, who avoided the excesses of Ranavalona I and the careless reforms of Radama II. Unification did not succeed because of the selfishness of the oligarchy and the intrigues of the French colonialists, who ceaselessly urged their government to conquer the island.

BIBLIOGRAPHY

Covell, Maureen. *Historical Dictionary of Madagascar.* Lanham, Md., 1995.

Delivré, Alain. *L'histoire des rois d'Imerina.* Paris, 1974.

Esoavelomandroso, Manassé. *La province maritime orientale du "Royaume de Madagascar."* Antananarivo, Madagascar, 1979.

Raison-Jourde, Françoise. *Les souverains de Madagascar.* Paris, 1983.

MANASSÉ ESOAVELOMANDROSO

See also **Andrianampoinimerina; Radama I; Ranavalona, Mada.**

HISTORY AND GOVERNMENT: SINCE 1895

The history of Madagascar in the century preceding colonization by the French was characterized by consolidation of the kingdom of Madagascar under Merina rule (the Merina is the largest and most dominant of the Malagasy ethnic groups) and by negotiations with Great Britain and France that ultimately resulted in the country's subjugation. Around 1797 the Merina kingdom, divided among four warring kings, was reunited under King Andrianampoinimerina (r. 1787–1810). His son, Radama I (1810–1828), conquered much of Madagascar, except the south and part of the west. The British, who had colonized nearby Mauritius and who hoped to prevent the French, who had colonized Réunion, from occupying Madagascar, titled Radama "king of Madagascar." While he encouraged the London Missionary Society to Christianize the people, his wife and successor, Queen Ranavalona I (r. 1828–1861), reversed his welcome of the Europeans. An absolute monarch ruling from the Malagasy capital of Antananarivo, she was interested in European education but quarreled with both Great Britain and France and in 1845 closed the island's ports to trade (reopening them in 1853). Radama II, her son, reopened the island to European religious and commercial influence but was assassinated in 1863. He was followed in power by Rainilaiarivony, prime minister and the husband of three successive queens (Rasoherina [r. 1863–1868], Ranavalona II [1868–1883], and Ranavalona III [r. 1883–1897]). He and Ranavalona II were converted to Protestantism in 1869. They fostered close ties to Great Britain and tried to unify and modernize the state along European lines.

However, during this period the French were manipulating events to gain a strong foothold on the island. They used the Lambert Charter, concluded by Radama II with Lambert, a French adventurer, but annulled by the Antananarivo regime through payment of indemnities, as well as the kingdom's conversion to Protestantism, as a provocative repudiation of French claims. Matters became more ominous when France asserted the right for all French nationals to own land on the island and claimed the land in the northwest, the area covered by the Lambert Charter, for France and illegally removed the queen's flags. The Madagascar government sought redress from both England and the United States but to no avail. The Franco-Malagasy war of 1883–1885 left Madagascar independent, and the nation resisted the French attempt in 1885 to impose protectorate status. In 1890 France and Britain signed a treaty by which Britain would recognize a French Madagascar protectorate, while France gave recognition of Britain's Zanzibar protectorate. The French forces landed in May 1895 and overwhelmed the Malagasy troops; by October the French had concluded an agreement with Queen Ranavalona III and Madagascar became a protectorate. In October 1896 the Menalamba (Red Shawl) rebellion by the Merina oligarchy began; the French, through General J. S. Galliéni, in 1897 put down the insurrection, deposed and deported the queen, and so brought the kingdom to an end.

From Colonization to Independence

The French regime immediately quelled several additional rebellions (1898 in the northwest and 1904 in the southeast) and instituted policies abusive to all but white settlers. The 1904 rebellion took over a year to subdue. It occurred in a period of enactment of repressive measures, including forced labor, summary execution, and imposition of taxes. From 1896 to 1905 General Galliéni was in control, first as military commander, then as governor-general. He extended privileges to French settlers. During his rule and that of his successors, the French language was made compulsory in the schools. Railroads and motor roads were built. Cities were modernized and ports built up. Three-quarters of all Malagasy trade was with France, with Madagascar's exports being agricultural products and industrial raw materials.

In the 1920s several nationalist organizations took root. The first, organized by the Merina and led by Protestant ministers, was the Union Chrétienne des Jeunes Gens (YMCA), banned in October 1906. The Merina then organized a secret society, Vy Vato Sakelika (VVS; Iron and Stone), which was outlawed in 1915. Started at the medical school in the capital, this organization won the support of intellectuals, civil servants, and others there.

During this time the French settlers proposed their own government, which took the form of a Consultative Assembly. Delegations on financial and economic matters were supportive of the settler interests and deaf to those of the indigenous Malagasy. Also given the right to similar delegations, the Malagasy found these to be completely ineffectual.

Anticolonial feelings were strengthened by Malagasy participation in World War I in the French cause, which led them to expect a better life and to bitterly resist forced labor. Jean Ralaimongo emerged as a symbol of resistance, remaining in France after the war to argue that the Malagasy should receive French citizenship and that Madagascar should become a French department.

The French failed to respond, fostering nationalist sentiments and a demonstration on 19 May 1929 in the capital. Although the French imprisoned the leaders, by 1936 events in France leading to the election of the Popular Front resulted in a diminishment of French colonial abuses. The 1930s saw the lifting of the trade union ban, provision for freedom of the press, cessation of the forced labor system, admittance of more Malagasy to French citizenship, reprieve of detention sentences, and the return to Madagascar of the remains of Queen Ranavalona III.

Malagasy participation in World War II helped spark the struggle for independence. The Malagasy witnessed the defeat of the pro-Vichy administrators in Antananarivo, which bolstered morale. Further, they had suffered deprivations during the war. In 1944 the Brazzaville Conference allowed for representation from the French colonies in Parliament. Madagascar sent four elected representatives, two of whom, Jean Ravoahangy and Jean Raseta, were indigenous Malagasy. In France they positioned themselves to advocate Malagasy independence. Meanwhile, in 1946 the first political party in Madagascar, the Mouvement Démocratique pour la Rénovation Malgache (MDRM), was established, with Raseta as president. In the same year, Madagascar became an overseas territory of the French republic, with all Malagasy becoming French citizens.

The deprivations of the peasants, the awareness among Malagasy intellectuals of nationalistic movements around the world, and the retrograde effect of resistance to change by the white settlers and civil servants erupted in violence in the pivotal Malagasy Revolt, which began on 29 March 1947. While the number of French and other non-Malagasy dead may have reached several hundred, a conservative estimate of 90,000 Malagasy died in violent reprisals; the revolt leaders were executed and Ravoahangy and Raseta, along with the famous poet Jacques Rabemananjara, were exiled to France. The strength of the MDRM was broken. The date the revolt broke out is celebrated every year as a symbol of Malagasy nationalism and independence; sufferings incurred by the people fomented hatred between the ruled and rulers.

Several factors contributed to the momentum for independence in the early 1950s. The French released from prison several revolt leaders, and Catholic bishops signed a statement demanding independence. Trade unions had always continued in existence. The leadership of Philibert Tsiranana, who would be Madagascar's president from 1960 to 1972, emerged during this time. Of a humble peasant background, a school teacher and founder of the Parti Social Démocrate (PSD), he became a delegate to the French parliament. Meanwhile, the French Socialist government in 1956 issued the *loi cadre*, which gave internal self-government to overseas territories. In 1958 Madagascar, following Tsiranana's direction rather than that of the Merina-dominated political party, voted to become a self-governing republic within the French community, rather than for complete independence without relation to France. A 1959 constitution provided for universal suffrage, a president, and two legislative bodies: the National Assembly and the Senate. On 26 June 1960 Madagascar regained its independence.

The Post-Independence Era

President Tsiranana adopted a socialist policy and continued very close relations with France. He had been in France during the 1947 revolt and suppression, returning to Madagascar only in 1950, and therefore had not experienced the upheavals of that period. The exiled MDRM leaders, Ravoahangy and Rabemananjara, joined his government; only Raseta desisted. Tsiranana developed relationships with anticommunist countries and set as his goal alleviation of the deprivations of the Malagasy peasantry. He was a founding father of the Organization of African Unity (OAU) and yet tarnished his reputation by trading with apartheid South Africa. Tsiranana was reelected president twice (1965, 1972) by, according to official estimates, 99.9 percent of the votes cast.

The close relations with France, in particular the French control of the economy, hampered

Tsiranana's government in providing economic opportunities needed by both the peasantry and the better-educated Merina. In the economic sector, major positions were given to Europeans, and the level of corruption was high. Since education had been given priority by the government, young people in the country desired better opportunities and became restive, leading to a student movement of April–May 1972. Tsiranana was, however, able to support the interests of the Merina and at the same time foster relations with other groups afraid of the resurgence of Merina dominance on the island. After a bout of ill health and treatment in France in 1970, Tsiranana's political strength had declined. Strikes and rebellions erupted due to several factors: the deportation by Tsiranana of an opposition political figure; criticism of Tsiranana's reliance on France and South Africa; and a growing mass refusal to pay taxes. When the police quelled discontent and shot over four hundred demonstrators, matters worsened. Opposition parties refused to take part in the general and presidential elections, charging control of the election by the president's PSD party. When General Richard Ratsimandrava, commander of the gendarmerie, and General Gabriel Ramanantsoa, commander of the army, did not intervene on his behalf, Tsiranana requested the latter to head a new government.

Prime Minister Ramanantsoa (1972–1975), a Merina, made a number of changes in Malagasy policy. Although having studied at the École Spéciale Militaire and risen to lieutenant-colonel in the Defense Ministry in Paris, Ramanantsoa negotiated with France to close all French bases in Madagascar, withdraw all foreign troops, and relinquish all French public property. He sought closer ties with African countries and with the OAU. He restored order in the country by releasing political detainees and reformed the economy by instituting austerity measures and abolishing the hated head and cattle taxes. He acted against corruption, increased legal holidays, and reformed the civil service. French teachers and civil servants were replaced with those of Malagasy origin, and the government began a study of local dialects toward the development of a common Malagasy language.

As of 1974 opposition political parties became more active, and a coup was attempted in December. In February 1975 Ramanantsoa's former interior minister, Colonel Richard Ratsimandrava, took over the governmental power surrendered to him by Ramanantsoa. Ratsimandrava had been a revolutionary advocate of village communities and direct involvement of the population in local government and had thus represented opposition to Ramanantsoa's bourgeois oligarchical government. He was, however, assassinated six days later. A trial of military officers and political leaders followed, with Didier Ratsiraka, who had been uninvolved in the earlier conflicts, appointed by the Military Directorate to power.

Lieutenant Commander Ratsiraka (president, 1975–1993) had served as foreign minister under Ramanantsoa and fostered Ramanantsoa's policy of breaking with South Africa and pursuing involvement with the OAU. A leftist politician leading a military regime, his program included the goals to "feed, house, clothe, teach and transport the population" and also to affirm Malagasy language and history. The president's party was the Avant-Garde de la Révolution Socialiste Malgache (AREMA). In 1977 the "Malagasy Revolution" fostered by AREMA continued to spread through elections and debates at all community levels. Until 1979 the economy improved, and development projects were initiated; agriculture was a priority. Ratsiraka reformed the army and politics and followed a policy of nationalization of banks, insurance companies, and cinemas.

When the economy began to worsen, however, structural adjustment programs were initiated in conformity with International Monetary Fund (IMF) guidelines; while these brought some benefits, for example to the rice market, over the next several years they contributed to unemployment and hardship, food price increases, and food shortages. In 1983 the president's AREMA party won close to 65 percent of the vote and 84 percent of the legislative seats. President Ratsiraka attempted unsuccessfully during this period to create a one-party state. In 1989 he was reelected by 61.64 percent of votes cast. Although lawlessness and criminal activity festered, the president increased freedom of the press and allowed the formation of new parties. Criticism of the government by churches and other groups and support for constitutional change were expressed. During this period the political leadership of Albert Zafy, who was to become Madagascar's next president, emerged. A doctor and academician, Zafy founded the Union Nationale pour le Développement et la Démocratie (UNDD) in 1990. Later that year he was elected president of the opposition grouping of parties, the Comité des Forces Vives (CFV). Unrest in the country escalated in 1991. Following a July call for a general strike, a mass pro-democracy assembly of four hundred thousand near the presidential palace was subjected to police fire on 10 August, with many demonstrators killed. In this demonstration, Zafy was injured.

Zafy continued to oppose Ratsiraka by advocating small- and medium-scale enterprises and set up a rival government. This period then saw a power-sharing compromise with the government and polarizarion between pro-democracy (opposition group) advocates and federalism (pro-Ratsiraka) advocates. But on 19 August 1992 Madagascar approved a new constitution, which provided for a two-chamber parliament to be elected by proportional representation and which limited the president to two terms in office. In federal elections held on 25 November, Zafy was elected president by 45 percent of the vote (Ratsiraka bringing in 29 percent) according to official results. With no one receiving a majority of the votes, a second round of elections between the two frontrunners was held on 10 February 1993; the results were Zafy 66.74 percent, and Ratsiraka 33.26 percent. Albert Zafy became president on 27 March 1993.

Parliamentary elections for 138 seats were held on 16 June, with backers of President Zafy winning 74 of the 134 seats for which results were announced. A new civilian, democratic government was now in power in Madagascar. In 1995 the presidential system, and Zafy's position, were affirmed by a referendum that allowed for the prime minister's appointment and dismissal by the president rather than by parliament. In February 1997 Ratsiraka was reelected president.

Madagascar entered the late 1990s with the security of the democratic government no longer in question. Its challenges were the lifting of poverty, social and economic development, negotiation or repayment of foreign debt, and utilization and protection of the island's remaining—and in many respects unique—natural resources.

BIBLIOGRAPHY

Allen, Philip M. *Madagascar: Conflicts of Authority in the Great Island.* Boulder, Colo., 1995.

Covell, Maureen. *Madagascar: Politics, Economics, and Society.* New York, 1987.

Ellis, Stephen. *The Rising of the Red Shawls: A Revolt in Madagascar, 1895–1899.* New York, 1985.

Feeley-Harnik, Gillian. *A Green Estate: Restoring Independence in Madagascar.* Washington, D.C., 1991.

Gow, Bonar A. *Madagascar and the Protestant Impact: The Work of the British Missions, 1818–95.* New York, 1979.

Kent, Raymond K. *From Madagascar to the Malagasy Republic.* New York, 1962. Repr. 1976.

Kottak, Conrad P., et al., ed. *Madagascar: Society and History.* Durham, N.C., 1986.

Rajoelina, Patrick. *Quarante années de la vie politique de Madagascar, 1947–1987.* Paris, 1988.

Thompson, Virginia, and Richard Adloff. *The Malagasy Republic: Madagascar Today.* Stanford, 1965.

NANCY G. WRIGHT

See also **Andrianampoinimerina; Antananarivo; Colonial Policies and Practice; Decolonization; Ethnicity and Identity; Literature; Pan-African and Regional Organizations; Political Systems; Postcolonial State; Radama I; Ranavalona, Mada; Trades Unions and Associations; World War II.**

PEOPLES AND CULTURES

Madagascar is a large island, more like a small continent, which lies in the Indian Ocean just off the coast of southern Africa. Although the precise ethnic makeup of the island's 12,092,157 inhabitants (1993 census) has been subject to lengthy scholarly debate, it is now accepted that the people of Madagascar originated in both Indonesia and Africa, settling the island in successive waves somewhere between 400 and 900 C.E. The inhabitants of Madagascar speak Malagasy, an Austronesian language which most closely resembles Manjaan, spoken in southern Borneo. Widely shared cultural traits reveal a blend of African and southeast Asian influences including complex beliefs linking the living and the dead, elaborate mortuary practice, rice cultivation, cattle herding, and rectangularly shaped houses that are carefully oriented to cardinal points endowed with political and ritual significance. Common underlying cultural traits have evolved in response to diverse geographical locales and historical forces, making the island's peoples a study in variations on shared cultural themes.

Ethnic Groups

Under the *politique de races* instituted during the French colonial period, the peoples of Madagascar were divided into different groups according to their customs, so as to facilitate the colonial administration. Each group was to be governed by local officials who, it was hoped, would act as links between the inhabitants and the colonial administration. The result of this division and codification, which produced essentialized ethnicities from what were in fact fluid political groupings, endures today, and the census for Madagascar lists twenty official ethnic groups. These include, in descending order of numerical importance, the Merina, Betsimisaraka, Betsileo, Tsimihety, Sakalava, Antandroy, Antaisaka, Tanala, Antaimoro, Bara, Sihanaka, Antanosy, Mahafaly, Antaifasy, Makoa, Bezanozano, Antankarana, and Antambahoaka. Malagasy themselves, however, create communities of belonging rooted in kinship, shared locality and customs, submission to a precolonial polity, and the adoption of common historical narratives, although the relative importance of these mechanisms in the creation of communities varies from group to group. The worth of using ethnicity, then, as a basis for categorizing the Malagasy population is questionable, and it seems more useful to examine the precise political and historical structures through which local communities have formed.

Numbering roughly three million, the Merina of the central highlands of Madagascar comprise one-fourth of the island's population. Grouped into several microkingdoms during the eighteenth century, the inhabitants were gradually drawn together in a single polity under the rule of Andrianampoinimerina (r. c. 1783–1810). Formerly a word used to designate the geographical area, the word "Merina" appears to have first been used to indicate allegiance to King Andrianampoinimerina. The Merina were thus originally a geographical and political grouping that was later ethnicized.

Contemporary Merina are highly literate and Christian. While the majority of people continue to earn their living through working irrigated rice land, many have left the countryside to work as administrators, traders, and teachers or have emigrated to France. Traditional Merina society is divided into endogamous descent groups, each of which is associated with a particular ancestral territory and a family tomb. The population is further divided according to different ranks: about one-third are considered noble (*andriana*), one-third are commoners (*hova*), and one-third are descendants of former slaves (*mainty-andevo*) brought to Imerina during the slave trade in the nineteenth century. Although manumission was granted under the French in 1896, the freeman-slave distinction remains important and has been translated into inequalities in contemporary economic status. A central rite expressive of ethnic identity, and shared by rural and urban Merina alike, is the *famadihana*, a ceremony of reburial, in which corpses are periodically exhumed and rewrapped in new shrouds.

A similar example of allegiance to a common polity, combined with common customs and shared locality, in the production of local groupings is provided by the Antaisaka of the southeast. Numbering only 400,000, and inhabiting the southeastern corner of the island, the Antaisaka practice wet rice cultivation and inhabit small villages numbering from 200 to 3,000 people. Within villages, groups are typically divided into named patrilineages, the localized fragments of more dispersed clans. The Antaisaka migrate throughout Madagascar in search of wage labor, either to the coastal city of Toamasina (Tamatave), where many work as pushcart (*pousse-pousse*) drivers, or to the plantation areas of the northwest. Officially designated an ethnic group under the colonial *politique de races*, the Antaisaka appear in fact to be made up of diverse family groupings who came to the region from different areas. As in other parts of the island, earlier arrivals (*zokintany-tompontany*) were held to have special ritual and political powers, for example, the right to sacrifice cattle, to sow the season's first rice, or to wear certain items of clothing for display. Latecomers were accepted into the realm only if they recognized the ritual and political powers of the ruler and adopted certain customs. Political formations were thus premised on a system of ritual agency whereby a domain formed around a ruler held to have legitimacy by his subjects.

Second largest of Madagascar's so-called ethnic groups, the Betsimisaraka inhabit the central east coast, from Mananjary in the north to Vohémar in the south. Depending on whether they inhabit the coast or the littoral plateau, Betsimisaraka farm rice either in lakes or using slash-and-burn methods on hillsides. Local political groupings are small, organized at the level of independent families, formed around a male elder. The Anglican and Catholic churches have gained converts, particularly around major towns like Toamasina, Mahanoro, and Fenoarivo; however, ancestor worship has not diminished in importance, and in some areas Christian proselytization appears to have had little effect. Following colonial conquest, Betsimisaraka were forced to inhabit villages comprising more than one ancestry. However, the ideal of independent households, each controlling its own affairs under the direction of a male elder, remains strong. During the eighteenth century, a number of families to the north banded together to gain control of the slave trade and formed an alliance which they called the Betsimisaraka, a name which means "those who will not be rendered asunder." The alliance lasted little more than a generation and only operated in the northermost portion of

Antandroy Tomb. Detail of a fresco showing the capture of a crocodile.
© NUNDSANY ET PÉRENNOU

Betsimisaraka territory. However, following the Merina conquest of the east coast in 1817, the name was used to denote the east coast as an administrative division of the Merina empire. The use of the name "Betsimisaraka" to refer to the peoples of the central east coast was continued under the French. In the late twentieth century, however, it is arguably the common narrative of Merina domination and local resistance, in conjunction with other bases for solidarity such as kinship and locality, that are central to the shaping of local identity.

Fifth largest of Madagascar's peoples, and numbering around 700,000, the Sakalava inhabit the west coast of the island, between the Onilahy River in the south and the island of Nosy Be to the north. Traditionally, "Sakalava" was the name given to the various monarchies founded by the Maroseranâ dynasty as they conquered their way north, absorbing autochthonous peoples along the west coast. The region was formerly comprised of two kingdoms, Menabe to the south and Boina to the north. "Sakalava" refers to those inhabitants, divided into independent clans, who express their willing submission to the power of monarchy through their participation in ritualized work. Contemporary Sakalava continue to recognize the spiritual and political efficacy of dead kings, embodied in sacred relics, who appear in rites of spirit possession (tromba), a central religious ceremony constitutive of Sakalava identity. Sakalava peasants work as farmers and cattle herders, and relatively few have converted to Christianity. In addition, communities of fisherpeople, called Vezo, also inhabit the west coast. Despite official classification as Sakalava, Vezo do not recognize the Sakalava monarchy; community identity is derived from their livelihood and occupation of a particular coastal locale.

In addition to Malagasy, groups of Chinese, Indo-Pakistanis, and Comoreans also inhabit Madagascar. First brought to Madagascar in order to build the railroad which runs between Antananarivo and Toamasina, the Chinese have settled mainly on the east coast, where they work as small traders and middlemen between Malagasy producers and larger companies. The Indo-Pakistanis, numbering around 20,000, also work as traders, and have settled mainly on the west coast. While the Chinese have intermarried and remain on friendly terms with the local population, the Indo-Pakistani community remains largely insulated and has, particularly in times of economic scarcity, been subject to attacks and riots.

Merina Versus *Côtier*

Perhaps the most salient division in Madagascar—which like the "ethnic" groupings is clearly the result of historical events and political interests—is that between Merina and *côtier* ("coastal peoples"), a term actually denoting groups other than the Merina, many of whom were forcibly incorporated into the Merina kingdom. Under the Anglo-Merina treaty of 1817, the Merina king Radama I (r. c. 1820–1828) forged a pact with General Robert Farquhar, the British governor-general to Mauritius, in which it was agreed that in exchange for stopping the slave trade to the neighboring Mascarene Islands, Britain would provide Radama with military and technical expertise. The superior firepower enabled Merina to gain at least nominal control over two-thirds of the island. The division between the Merina and the coastal peoples was reinforced subsequently by the French. Despite early French efforts to portray themselves as liberators of the coastal peoples from Merina domination, the French policy of *la politique de races* proved too expensive to maintain in practice, and French administrators fell back on bureaucratic structures put in place by the Merina. This meant that more resources, particularly schools and health care, were created in and around Antananarivo, the historic capital of the Merina peoples. Merina elites, often associated with old families who controlled slaves, land, and trade during the nineteenth century, have been able to maintain their privileged status through increased access to education, and political and economic opportunities in contemporary Madagascar. Although there is a growing coastal elite, and the first president of the Malagasy Republic, Philibert Tsiranana (1960–1972), as well as President Didier Ratsiraka (1975–1992; 1996–) are of coastal origin, Merina continue to fill the majority of positions in the state bureaucracies, schools, and professions. The division of Merina versus *côtier*, though further complicated by divisions of class and political alliance, remains a delicate issue, one that is easily capitalized on by political groups seeking to capture local constituents.

National Identity

Awareness and expression of Malagasy national identity has fluctuated and changed form according

The Great Zoma Market of Antananarivo. PHOTO © GERALD CUBITT

to particular historic and economic conjunctures. A sense of national unity first emerged during the nineteenth century as Malagasy responded to increasing attempts by European powers to meddle in the island's affairs. In 1817 the British recognized the Merina king Radama I as "king of Madagascar" (as opposed to simply king of Imerina) and the "Merina nation." The island was further integrated under French rule, which standardized the language and currency, and organized all of the Malagasy peoples in a single political and administrative structure. Following French conquest in 1895, the national movement within Madagascar was linked with local attempts to regain the sovereign rights recognized in the Anglo-Merina treaty of 1817. This ethnic nationalism had a religious dimension, as the Merina queen Ranavalona II had converted to Protestantism in 1869. Under French rule, the national movement became closely allied with the Protestant church in opposition to French Catholicism. Beginning with the anticolonial rebellion of 1947, and extending throughout the period of independence, the basis of national identity broadened to include the coastal peoples and a variety of Christian sects.

The impulse toward division which is latent in the historic division of Merina versus *côtier* and occasionally activated during moments of political crisis is offset by the fact that Madagascar remains a nation whose boundaries are geographically, not politically, imposed. In addition, people share a common standardized language, although here too the traces of old inequities remain, as it is the Merina dialect which is in fact defined as official Malagasy. Unity constructed out of the diversity of different peoples is espoused in official rhetoric and on public occasions like the official celebration of independence, held on 26 June. The socialist revolution of 1975, when industries were nationalized and the language of schooling was switched from French to Malagasy, a decision that was reversed in 1992, marks the high point of Malagasy nationalism. Since the late 1980s, increasing foreign debt has led to a serious deterioration of the state infrastructure and repeated devaluation of the Malagasy franc. As roads deteriorate and travel becomes more difficult, many rural communities seem to have only sporadic contact with the state, while some seem to exist outside the bounds of state control or national consciousness altogether.

BIBLIOGRAPHY

Gérard Althabe, *Oppression et libération dans l'imaginaire: Les communautés villageoises de la côte orientale de Mada-

gascar*, Paris 1967, analyzes the role of spirit possession in Northern Betsimisaraka reactions to the changes of the neocolonial period; Rita Astuti, " 'The Vezo Are Not a Kind of People'; Identity, Difference, and 'Ethnicity' Among a Fishing People of Western Madagascar," *American Ethnologist* 22, no. 3 (1995): 464–482, challenges the relevance of "ethnicity" as a basis for determining communities of belonging in Madagascar and suggests that local groupings be thought of as constructed through practice and locality; Maurice Bloch, *Placing the Dead: Tombs, Ancestral Villages, and Kinship Organization in Madagascar*, New York, 1991, discusses the Merina kingship system, specifically the role of tombs and the ritual of the *famadihana* in the creation of descent groups; Jennifer Cole, "The Necessity of Forgetting: Ancestral and Colonial Memories in East Madagascar," Ph.D. diss., University of California, Berkeley, 1996, analyzes the role of Merina and French colonial conquest in conjunction with local ancestral connections in the formation of contemporary Betsimisaraka identity; Conrad Phillip Kottak et al., eds., *Madagascar: Society and History*, Durham, N.C., 1986, offers a range of articles addressing cultural variation among a variety of Malagasy groups. Gillian Feeley-Harnik, *A Green Estate: Restoring Independence in Madagascar*, Washington, D.C., provides a comprehensive ethnography of the Sakalava of the Analalava region, particularly the role of the reburial of the Sakalava king in the construction of the Sakalava polity; Françoise Raison-Jourde, ed., *Les souverains de Madagascar: L'histoire royale et ses resurgences contemporaines*, Paris, 1983, contains a wide variety of articles by distinguished Malagachisants discussing the role of royalty from the precolonial period in the formation of contemporary political ideologies; Lesley Sharp, *The Possessed and the Dispossed: Spirits, Identity, and Power in a Malagasy Migrant Town*, Berkeley, 1993, studies spirit possession in a multiethnic town.

JENNIFER COLE

See also **Colonial Policies and Practice; Death, Mourning, and Ancestors; Ethnicity and Identity; Language Families; Literature; Nationalism; Slave Trade.**

RELIGIOUS SYSTEMS

Madagascar presents unique challenges for the historical and contemporary study of religious systems in their social, political, and ecological complexity. This entry outlines some of the major contributions of Malagasy studies to scholarship on death, burial, ancestry, and spirit mediumship; the political economy and ecology of religious experience; the social construction of history; the nature of memory and forgetting; and the historical linguistics of Malagasy cosmologies.

In addition to the diverse Malagasy "ways of the ancestors" (*fomban-drazana*), honored throughout the island, Madagascar's peoples have also adopted religious faiths introduced by traders, missionaries, and new immigrants to the island, beginning with Islam as early as the twelfth century C.E. Between 9 and 15 percent of Malagasy, residing mainly in the northern and western provinces of Antseranana and Mahajanga, now identify themselves as Muslims, most of them Sunni, but some Shia, including Bhora and other Indian Shiites called Karana. Christian missions were established from the sixteenth century onward. Some 45 percent of Malagasy are now Christians, about evenly divided between Catholicism and Protestantism. Hindus (Banians) and Buddhists (Sinoa), descendants of immigrants from Gujarat and south China in the late nineteenth and early twentieth centuries, comprise about 1 percent of the population.

The Ways of the Ancestors

Whether or not they identify with an established religion, Malagasy throughout the island recognize through ritual what they consider to be the interdependence of living and ancestral people. Explorers' accounts from the eighteenth century onward document the veneration of Malagasy people for ancestors, their own and those of others. According to the evolutionary theories of the nineteenth century, "ancestor worship" was a decidedly lesser form of polytheistic religion, to be abandoned upon conversion to a monotheistic faith. Ethnographic and historical research in Madagascar, as in Africa, has since shown this assumption to be false. Respect for ancestors derives from ontological convictions about the changing social-somatic nature of persons as they are created and reformed through interpersonal relations extending through life into death and ancestry, conceived as the riverine "spring" or arboreal "root" of future life. The common phrase "ancestral custom" (*fomban-drazama*) refers especially to rituals of burial, childbirth, circumcision, naming, and others effecting the creation and transformation of persons through interpersonal relations between the dead and living.

Although nineteenth-century missionaries tried to forbid Malagasy practices involving ancestors, like the invocation of ancestors at funerals, or spirit possession, Françoise Raison-Jourde shows how highlanders had integrated Christianity into ancestral custom well before the colonial era. The nationalization of missions after independence, together with doctrinal changes (for example, Vatican II), has contributed to the vitality of contemporary religious life. Some churches have grown by specializing in the exorcism of spirits, whereas others have developed new integrated forms of religious worship. *Le prince charmant* (Jacques Lombard and Michèle Fieloux, 1989) is a powerful video documentary of the personal, as well as social, dimensions of religious pluralism in southwestern Madagascar told through the life story of a Malagasy woman, raised as a Catholic, who became the medium of a Sakalava royal ancestor from the colonial period and is now recognized as a great healer.

Religion and Historical Consciousness

Malagasy have been writing about "the ways of the ancestors," their historical origins, and their practices of medicine, divination, astrology, and geomancy since Arabic script was first adopted to make "great writings" (*sorabe*) in southeastern Madagascar beginning in the fifteenth century, followed by Roman orthography in the early 1820s. Raombana, a Merina nobleman who wrote a nine-thousand-page *History, Annals, and Journal* of Imerina in English in 1845–1854, including information from his archaeological research on Merina tombs, expresses the intensity of Malagasy interest in "the ways of the ancestors" past and present. Raombana's written history coexisted with numerous oral narratives in the highlands and on the coasts. Furthermore, Malagasy historical consciousness is expressed in many other forms in ritual and in material culture, particularly houses and tombs, ranging from the micro-histories of praise-names to the living historical pageantry embodied in spirit mediums, to popular literature, and to personal taboos.

Numerous scholars have documented the grander size and substantiality of tombs compared to ordinary houses. One of the most important social processes achieved through burial services is the occasion for kin who have moved away in the course of "searching" their living to rejoin around one or more ancestral tombs. Tombs also constitute generative relations among people who thereby become kin by gathering around the ancestral tombs.

Except for some memorials for individuals whose bodies could not be returned to their homelands (for example, soldiers killed in European wars), most Malagasy tombs contain more than one forebear and are created out of descendants' combined resources, carefully calculated and including their labor, which is interpreted as ancestral "service." The impoverishment that the living will endure to assure their own burial as remembered ancestors is well documented. One of the most important purposes of the regional or hometown associations formed by migrants in towns throughout Madagascar is to provide for the funerals of their members, especially the cost of returning the deceased's bones to his or her selected burial place.

The salience of burials and reburials in Malagasy religious practices, together with population decline during the colonial period, suggested to some scholars that Madagascar was a "civilization of death." Subsequent research shows to the contrary that Malagasy have used "ancestral practices" to keep alive their historical consciousness of themselves as sovereign peoples in the face of efforts to subordinate them—such as harsh labor practices or the deadly military reprisals following the rebellion of 1947–1948, in which an estimated 100,000 people died. Raombana wrote her history during the reign of the Merina queen Ranavalona I (r. 1828–1861), who repeatedly had to force French and English diplomats, merchants, and missionaries to respect Malagasy ancestral ways and the political autonomy with which they were associated. Yet the ancestral ways of Merina royalty, critical to the creation of a Merina state in the nineteenth century, were themselves the historical outcome of repeated efforts to appropriate the ancestral practices of other Malagasy, thereby redefining them as "commoners" or "slaves" by comparison to "nobles." At least one other "kind" of people emerged during this same period from refusing the subordination entailed in conforming to royal mourning practices. One of the striking historical ironies of the colonial and postcolonial periods is the widespread adoption of royal "ancestral custom" in popular protests throughout Madagascar against French colonial officials and the Malagasy elites who succeeded them and also in everyday negotiations for access to resources like land or labor.

Debates among scholars of Madagascar over the capacity of ritual to constitute ideologies of enduring social order show that the most striking social-historical dimension of Malagasy religious practices, especially repeated burials (which occur in relation to spirit possession), is their dialectical character, expressed in the very diversity of the materials involved. Malagasy cosmologies of personhood emphasize continuity between life, death, and future life. Yet death, like life or ancestry, is not simply a state of being, but the outcome of relations among people, which are inescapably moral relations. In the most absolute terms, ancestry in Madagascar was and is defined by contrast to slavery, which, although no longer legal, still represents the ultimate condition of non-being: "lost" in relation to land and "without kin" in relation to labor and other critical sources of support. In contrast to birth, where interpersonal unity is required to "stand up" a new human being, a good death is a contradiction in terms. People do not die by themselves; they must be made dead in some way, whether by killing, or more commonly by the myriad forms of social subordination and effacement that Malagasy see as little murders. In the words of a Betsileo funeral oration, "the dead are wrapped in remembering (*fahatsiarovana*)," literally the "making not separate" of awareness of relationships that brought them to this pass.

Thus Malagasy rituals, particularly those involving the social creation and transformation of persons and groups, provoke intense historical awareness and renewed debate about intractable moral issues. Through the unwrapping and reburial involved in spirit possession, these speculations about morality and legitimacy may be projected onto a regional or national or even international scale. Scholars working from various theoretical perspectives now seek to explain how gender complementarity and difference interact with other dimensions of personhood in reproducing or transforming social systems of hierarchy or equality, given the social heterogeneity of Malagasy communities, and important regional and historical differences in ideas and practices concerning gender, sexuality, siblingship, and marriage, as well as political, economic, and ecological practices.

Although Malagasy rites of social identity, hierarchy, and equality are very diverse, they commonly involve the representation of people and social-historical processes through environmental imagery, notably trees, stones, earth, water, and fire. The controversy that has long surrounded the unique fauna and flora of the island—ranging from its nineteenth-century reputation as the home of the "man-eating tree" to current debates about conservation—should be examined not only in relation to Madagascar's current position in world trade networks but also in relation to such organic metaphors of political relations.

BIBLIOGRAPHY

Astuti, Rita. *People of the Sea: Identity and Descent Among the Vezo of Madagascar.* Cambridge, 1995.

Blanchy, Sophie. *Karana et Banians: Les communautés commerçantes d'origine indienne à Madagascar.* Paris, 1995.

Bloch, Maurice. *From Blessing to Violence: History and Ideology in the Circumcision Ritual of the Merina of Madagascar.* Cambridge, 1986.

Decary, Raymond. *La mort et les coutumes funéraires à Madagascar.* Paris, 1962.

Delivré, Alain. *L'histoire des rois d'Imerina: Interprétation d'une tradition orale.* Paris, 1974.

Domenichini, Jean-Pierre, Jean Poirier, and Daniel Raherisoanjato, eds. *Ny razana tsy mba maty: Cultures traditionelles malgaches.* Antananarivo, Madagascar, 1984.

Feeley-Harnik, Gillian. *A Green Estate: Restoring Independence in Madagascar.* Washington, D.C., 1991.

Graeber, David. "Dancing with Corpses Reconsidered: An Interpretation of *Famadihana* (in Arivonimamo, Madagascar)." *American Ethnologist* 22 (1995): 258–278.

Grandidier, Alfred, and Guillaume Grandidier. *Collection des ouvrages anciens concernant Madagascar.* 9 vols. Paris, 1903–1920.

Kottak, Conrad P. *The Past in the Present: History, Ecology, and Social Organisation in Highland Madagascar.* Ann Arbor, 1980.

Kottak, Conrad P., Jean-Aimé Rakotoarisoa, Aidan Southall, and Pierre Vérin, eds. *Madagascar: Society and History.* Durham, N.C., 1986.

Meriot, C., and Jean-Aimé Rakotoarisoa, eds. *Les ancêtres et la société à Madagascar.* Bordeaux, 1985.

Ottino, Paul. *L'étrangère intime: Essai d'anthropologie de la civilisation de l'ancien Madagascar.* Paris, 1986.

Raison-Jourde, Françoise. *Bible et pouvoir à Madagascar au XIXe siècle: Invention d'une identité chrétienne et construction de l'état (1780–1880).* Paris, 1991.

Raison-Jourde, Françoise, ed. *Les souverains de Madagascar: L'histoire royale et ses résurgences contemporaines.* Paris, 1983.

Ravololomanga, Bode. *Être femme et mère à Madagascar (Tanala d'Ifanadiana).* Paris, 1993.

Sharp, Lesley A. *The Possessed and the Dispossessed: Spirits, Identity, and Power in a Madagascar Migrant Town.* Berkeley, 1993.

Vérin, Pierre. *Madagascar.* Paris, 1990.

GILLIAN FEELEY-HARNIK

See also **Christianity; Myth and Cosmology; Religion and Ritual.**

MÃE AURÉLIA CORREIA. *See* Correia, Mãe Aurélia.

MAGHILI, MUHAMMAD IBN ABD AL-KARIM AL- (d. 1504), scholar and activist of Tlemcen in western Algeria. After early study in Tlemcen, al-Maghili took up residence in Tamantit, the chief town of the central Saharan oasis of Tuwat. There he conducted a vigorous campaign against what he saw as the unwarranted privileges of the Jewish community in their capacity as a protected or tolerated community within the Islamic body politic. In particular, al-Maghili argued that it was unlawful for them to maintain a synagogue. Although opposed by the local *qadi* (judge), he obtained legal opinions (*fatwas*) from North African scholars, some of whom gave strong support to his stance. He led an attack on the Jewish community and destroyed their synagogue, causing many of them to leave Tamantit for good. Subsequently, al-Maghili spent some years in western Africa, where he was well received by the sultan of Kano (in what is now Nigeria), Muhammad Rumfa (r. c. 1463–1499), and the ruler of the Songhai empire, Askiya al-Hajj Muhammad (Abi Bakr; r. 1493–1528), whose capital was at Gao (in what is now Mali). For both of these rulers al-Maghili wrote treatises of advice on Islamic rulership, and his replies to the *askiya*'s questions became an authoritative text for later Muslim revolutionaries, such as 'Uthman dan Fodio (1754–1817), as he sought to establish a state in what is now Nigeria.

BIBLIOGRAPHY

Hunwick, John, ed. and trans. *Sharī'a in Songhay: The Replies of al-Maghili to the Questions of Askia al-Hajj Muhammed.* London, 1985.

JOHN O. HUNWICK

See also **Islam.**

MAHDIYYA. The Mahdist Revolution (1882–1885) and the Mahdist state (1885–1898) in the Nilotic Sudan were known as the Mahdiyya. Muhammad Ahmad ibn 'Abd Allah (1844–1885), a Sudanese holy man, proclaimed himself to be the Mahdi (the divinely guided one, or messiah) in March 1881 and declared a jihad against the Egyptian colonial regime. The Mahdists won a series of victories, culminating in January 1885 in the capture of the colonial capital, Khartoum, and the death of General Charles Gordon, who had been sent by the British to evacuate the Egyptian garrisons.

The Mahdi died five months after the fall of Khartoum and was succeeded as ruler of the new state, with a new capital at Omdurman, by 'Abdullahi ibn Muhammad, the Khalifa (successor).

Despite several revolts, of which that of Abu Jummayza in 1888–1889 was the most serious, a severe famine in the winter of 1888–1889, and major conflict with Ethiopia, culminating in the battle of al-Qallabat and the death of the Ethiopian ruler, John II (March 1889), the Mahdist State survived under the Khalifa's authoritarian rule. The Khalifa ruled by using a combination of his own kinsmen from the Ta'aisha, a tribe of cattle nomads; slave troops inherited from the previous colonial regime; colonial functionaries, such as printers, boatmen, and scribes; and a small group of educated Sudanese from the Nile Valley peoples. Toward the end of his rule, the Khalifa consciously adopted a policy of trying to conciliate the various ethnic groups that made up the state. However, southern Sudan, which had been part of the colonial state, was effectively abandoned.

The end came when the British government of Lord Salisbury decided in 1896 to undertake the "reconquest" of Sudan, ostensibly on behalf of Egypt, which had been occupied by Britain in 1882. The reasons for this decision had nothing to do with Sudan, but much to do with European politics. The Mahdist state was destroyed at the battle of Karari (outside Omdurman) in September 1898 and the Khalifa hunted down and killed the following year (November 1899).

The Mahdist movement reemerged as a quasi-political movement under the Mahdi's posthumous son, Sir Sayyid 'Abd al-Rahman al-Mahdi (d. 1959), who was encouraged by the British colonial administration as a counterweight to Egyptian influence. His movement, the Ansar (the helpers), evolved into a political party, the Umma (Community), whose head in the late twentieth century was Sadiq al-Mahdi, a great-grandson of the Mahdi.

BIBLIOGRAPHY

Holt, P. M. *The Mahdist State in the Sudan, 1881–1898.* 2d ed. Oxford, 1970.

R. S. O'FAHEY

See also **Colonialism and Imperialism; Islam.**

Man reading the Qur'an at shrine of the Mahdi.
ABBAS/MAGNUM PHOTOS

MAHERERO, SAMUEL (b. 1854?; d. 1923), chief of Okahandja and later paramount chief of the Herero of Namibia between 1894 and his exiled death in Botswana. He was the son of Maherero Tjamuaha, the first Herero chief of Okahandja, whom he succeeded as chief in 1891. Named Uereani at birth, he was baptized as Samuel in 1868 by Rhenish missionaries, from whom he received his missionary schooling. Samuel's elder brother and missionary protégé Wilhelm (Uaita) was originally intended to succeed his father as chief, but Wilhelm was killed in a battle against the Nama in 1880. Following the death of his father in 1890, Samuel Maherero cooperated with incoming German colonialists. Through the sale of confiscated lands, he was able to mobilize German support in overthrowing and subduing rival Herero chiefs. In the aftermath of the rinderpest epizootic, Maherero retained his power and influence through the sale of land and the supply of labor to the German colonial administration and the South African gold mines. In 1904, following a series of misunderstandings and the self-fulfilling war prophecies of white settlers, Maherero led the Herero in a war against Imperial Germany. After a string of battles, Maherero and his followers were driven into the

Omaheke region of the Kalahari Desert. Many of the Herero died of hunger and thirst as they struggled to reach water and the safety of the Bechuanaland Protectorate (present-day Botswana), where Maherero and a handful of his followers were granted sanctuary. After a short sojourn in Bechuanaland, Maherero crossed over into South Africa, where in exchange for supplying labor to the gold mines of the Rand, he and his followers were permitted to live on a farm near Groenfontein in the northern Transvaal. Prohibited from returning to the land of his birth and from buying land in South Africa, Maherero returned to the town of Serowe in Bechuanaland in 1921, where he died of stomach cancer. His body was taken by rail to Okahandja and buried next to the graves of his father and grandfather.

JAN BART GEWALD

MAJI MAJI. The Maji Maji Rebellion took place between 1905 and 1907 in German East Africa, centered on the areas of the Rufiji delta and the southern highlands. It is recalled as one of the most important events in the history of the entire region, even though militarily it failed.

The rebellion was by some twenty small ethnic groups of southeastern Tanganyika (present-day Tanzania). Hitherto known as distinct and often-quarrelling "tribal" groups, they united against German rule. They had suffered long disruption by the Ngoni conquests and the slave trade, and the ending of slavery in 1897 had led to many disturbances in former systems of ethnicity and stratification. In addition, the German administration's enforcement of cotton growing, its increasingly stringent demands for taxes and compulsory labor, and the replacement of indigenous local clan and territorial leaders by the more centralized agents of the administration were all resented by local inhabitants who, divided by "tribal" differences, could not present a common front to the brutal colonial administration. But those brutalities were not unique to southeastern Tanganyika, so more local causes were clearly important.

The many local peoples shared common cultural, linguistic, and religious practices, and they also underwent similar disasters such as famine and drought. Most groups recognized the powers of the renowned center of healing and divination at Kibega on the Rufiji River, where oracular messages from the deity Bokero were interpreted by the custodian of the shrine when in a state of possession. Water (*maji* in Swahili) from the river was distributed for drinking and anointment; it was also held to bring about rain in time of famine as well as fertility of livestock and people.

In 1902 a medium and healer called Kinjikitile established himself at Ngarambe, where he became custodian of a pool in which it was said had appeared a rainbow-colored snake with a black monkey's head. The snake had given Kinjikitile powers of divination and mediumship while from Bokero came his mystical strength. Kinjikitile spread his message that—on his orders—the peoples of the region should band together to fight the Germans and that by drinking the pool's water they would become immune to German bullets. In addition, he proposed that drinking the water partially removed the drinkers from their sectional adherence to the traditional mystical forces of their diverse ancestors. Drinking the water thus was believed to form mystical links of common cult membership among men and women of the different ethnic groups involved. Kinjikitile had local assistants, of whom the most important was named Hongo. Hongo was also the name of the spirit said to have been sent by Bokero to Kinjikitile, who himself became widely known as Bokero.

The year 1904 brought drought. People came from throughout the area to Ngarambe to ask for rain, and Kinjikitile's message spread widely. In July of 1905 the first attacks were made on German positions. Kinjikitile and Hongo were seized and hanged by the Germans in August of the same year. After their deaths the uprising spread and became more serious, until the insurgents were finally defeated in 1907. Besides losing immense numbers of men and women, the initial enthusiasm waned, faith in the powers of the pool at Ngarambe faltered, and the rebels fragmented into their original local ethnic groups, with the sense of common endeavor being lost.

The Maji Maji Rebellion has entered historical memory throughout Tanzania and beyond, a process fostered strongly by President Nyerere of Tanzania, who held it up to his citizens as an event that represented the common purpose and identity of the people of Tanzania.

BIBLIOGRAPHY

Gwassa, G. "Kinjikitile and the Ideology of Maji Maji." In *The Historical Study of African Religion*, edited by T. O. Ranger, and I. N. Kimambo. London, 1972.

Gwassa, G. E., and John Iliffe. *The Records of the Maji Maji.* Nairobi, 1968.

Iliffe, John. "The Organization of the Maji Maji Rebellion." *Journal of African History* 8 (1967).

Wright, Marcia. "Maji Maji: Prophecy and Historiography." In *Revealing Prophets,* edited by D. Anderson and Douglas Johnson. London, 1968.

JOHN MIDDLETON

See also **Kinjikitile.**

MALAGASY REPUBLIC. *See* **Madagascar.**

MALARIA. *See* **Disease.**

MALAWI

Geography

Malawi is, like many countries in sub-Saharan Africa, a wholly colonial creation. Little more than 160 kilometers from east to west at its widest point, it hugs the lake with which its people are historically and economically linked, Lake Malawi, formerly Lake Nyasa. Indeed, its colonial name, Nyasaland, basically means "the land of the lake." A landlocked republic, it lies at the southern end of the East African Rift system and is bordered by Tanzania in the north, Mozambique in the east and south, and Zambia in the northwest. It has an area of 118,484 square kilometers. More than one-fifth of the total area of the country is taken up by the lake (24,208 square kilometers), which is freshwater. Its average elevation is between 750 and 1,300 meters, although there are higher mountain ranges in the north and south. In the north, the Vipya and Nyika plateaus reach more than 2,000 meters in places. South of the lake are the Zomba and Mulanje mountain ranges and the Shire highlands. Mount Mulanje rises to 3,050 meters above sea level and is the highest mountain in central Africa. In general the climate is temperate: the main wet season occurs between November and April, when the average rainfall is between 750 and 1,000 millimeters annually. Somewhat higher rainfall occurs in the more mountainous regions. There is a cool season between May and August (59°F to 64°F on the plateaus, up to 75°F in the Rift Valley), and a brief hot season in September–October.

Malawi enjoys some of the most fertile soils in the region, a feature which has attracted settlement throughout the territory's history. The upper and lower Shire Valley are particularly rich, as is the area north of Lake Chilwa, in the southeast of the country. The Shire Valley in general has played a key role in Malawi's past, not least during the colonial period. The Shire River leaves Lake Malawi at its most southerly point and exits the country at Chiromo after a journey of some 250 miles. The elevated ground between Lilongwe and Kasungu is also fertile, and the good plateau soils of Cholo and Mulanje in the far south and Nkhata Bay on the Lake Malawi shore are today the major tea-producing areas. Much potential is still to be realized, for although more than half of the country's land area is considered arable, much less than this is actually under cultivation. Forest land is found mainly in the north but also stretches into the western and central areas. The country is well watered, and fishing is an important source of income on Lakes Malawi and Chilwa. The lakes and rivers also hold out potential for irrigation and hydroelectric power and are being exploited for this purpose. One of the most densely populated countries in Africa, the population was estimated at around ten million in 1994, but it is extremely unevenly distributed. Almost 90 percent of Malawi's inhabitants live in the southern and central regions; the southern region alone accounts for over 50 percent of the population, while the north has only 12 percent. This distribution is due to both historical and environmental factors.

History

The first Bantu-speaking immigrants may have arrived in the area now known as Malawi some two thousand years ago. However, the "modern" history of the region might be said to begin with the appearance of the "Maravi" or Malawi peoples (thus named in contemporary Portuguese sources) by the fifteenth and sixteenth centuries. This wave of immigration came from the north, probably originating in the Shaba and Luba regions of modern-day Zaire. A number of chiefdoms and kingdoms were established, but three in particular with hereditary titles were dominant up to the eighteenth century. Kalanga sporadically dominated the country to the southwest of Lake Malawi during the sixteenth and seventeenth centuries. Lundu was based along the Shire Valley and was also powerful in the sixteenth and seventeenth centuries, when his kingdom prospered through the ivory trade with the coast; this polity enjoyed considerable military power, twice defeating the Portuguese and conquering territory in modern-day Mozambique. Undi, west of the lake, rose to prominence

The Republic of Malawi

Population: 10,032,600 (1994 official est.)

Area: 118,484 sq. km (45,747 sq. mi.)

Official languages: English and Chichewa

Languages: Chichewa, English, Tonga, Yao, Tumbuka

National currency: Malawi Kwacha

Principal religions: Traditional 53%, Christian 35% (predominantly Anglican and Roman Catholic), Muslim 12%

Capital: Lilongwe (estimated pop. 395,500 in 1994)

Other urban centers: Blantyre, Zomba, Mzuzu

Average annual rainfall: 760–1,010 mm (30–40 in.)

Principal geographical features:

Mountains: Mulanje, Mulanje and Zomba mountain ranges, Dedza, Sapitwa Peak, Nyika Plateau, Vipya Plateau

Rivers: Shire, Lilongwe, Bua, Dwangwa, Kasitu, South Rukuru

Lakes: Malawi (also called Nyasa), Malombe, Chilwa

Economy:

GNP per capita: US$160 (1995)

Principal products and exports:

Agricultural: tobacco, tea, sugar, cotton, rice, groundnuts, maize, sorghum, millet, pulses, fruit, roses, chili peppers, fish

Manufacturing: agricultural product processing, detergent, soap, glycerines, animal feed, shoes, matches, gin, plastic goods, beer, farm implements

Mining: lime, coal; exploitation of bauxite deposits may be feasible in the future.

Government: Independence from Great Britain, 1964. Republican constitution approved in 1966. New constitution, 1995. Multiparty democracy. President elected by direct universal suffrage for 5-year term. 177-seat National Assembly elected for 5-year term by direct universal suffrage. 1995 constitution calls for formation of a senate; however, elections to fill it have not yet taken place. For purposes of local government, the country is divided into 3 regions, 24 districts, and 8 municipalities.

Heads of state since independence:

1964–1966: Prime Minister Hastings Kamuzu Banda

1966–1994: President-for-Life Hastings Kamuzu Banda

1994–: President Bakili Muluzi

Armed forces: President is commander in chief. Enlistment is voluntary.

Army: 10,000

Navy: 200

Air Force: 200

Paramilitary: 1,500

Transportation:

Rail: 789 km (490 mi.), owned by Malawi Railways and its subsidiary, Central African Railway Company

Roads: 12,215 km (7,573 mi.), 25% paved

Lake ports: Chipoka, Bandawe, Karonga

National Airline: Air Malawi

Airports: Kamuzu International Airport in Lilongwe, former international airport at Blantyre, 3 others limited to domestic service

Media: 2 daily newspapers: *Daily Times, Malawi News.* 5 weeklies, 43 periodicals. Radio service provided by Malawi Broadcasting Corporation. No television.

Education and literacy:

Total literacy rate: 41.2%. Schooling is free and about two-thirds of children receive some formal education. Postsecondary education provided by thirteen 2-year teacher-training colleges, Banda College of Agriculture, Malawi Polytechnic, Chancellor College, Kamuzu College of Nursing, Malawi Institute of Education, and University of Malawi.

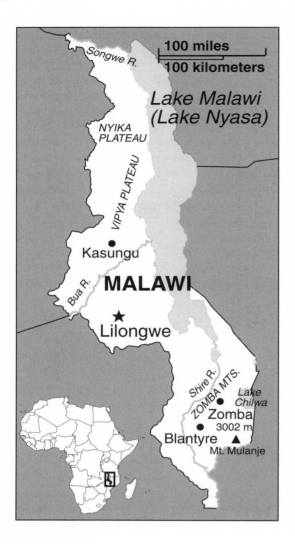

European missionaries were active in the region from the 1850s, beginning with the most celebrated of them all, David Livingstone; they saw as one of their primary tasks the ending of the slave trade in the region. Nyasaland was subsequently closely associated with missionary work, and the mission stations and schools there were among the most famous in Africa. The Free Church of Scotland operated in the Shire Highlands from 1876, and further north from 1881. Although the Dutch Reformed church established itself in 1888, it was the British missionaries who dominated the region and who also played a key role in the founding of a colonial administration. Prominent among these was Dr. Robert Laws, who was instrumental in the foundation of the Livingstonia mission station in northern Nyasaland. While missionary activity flourished, the British South Africa Company (BSAC), which had received its royal charter in 1889, was developing an economic interest in the territory north of the Limpopo. The BSAC, headed by Cecil Rhodes, was convinced that great mineral wealth might be exploited in this large swath of central Africa. The British government was prepared to support the BSAC in order to protect its perceived strategic interests against the encroachments of other European powers. In the case of Nyasaland, the threat came in the form of the Portuguese at Mozambique.

The eastern frontier of the BSAC's influence was represented by Lake Nyasa and the highlands to the south. Just as Dr. Laws was a critical figure in the growth of mission work in the region, so Harry Johnston, the British consul at Mozambique, was responsible for the creation of a colonial infrastructure. Johnston secured a series of treaties with chiefs in the Lake Nyasa region, treaties which (however dubious) formed the basis of the British Central Africa Protectorate, as the territory was initially known. Missionary pressure also contributed to the assumption of Foreign Office control. The Colonial Office took over responsibility in 1904, and the territory was renamed Nyasaland in 1907.

Unlike British colonies to the west and south, Nyasaland was lacking in the mineral resources which had prompted BSAC expansion into the region. As in these other territories, however, large areas of land were alienated to white farmers who settled and developed plantations in the favorable Shire Highlands. Even so, the settler population in Nyasaland never approached the proportions of those in Northern and Southern Rhodesia. Rather,

during the eighteenth century and drew strength from commercial relations with the Portuguese.

Trade with the coast fundamentally altered political relations in the region, insofar as rulers had to rely on their control of commerce rather than tribute as before. Competition for trade became of paramount importance. The older Malawi kingdoms declined in importance after the Yao, west of Lake Malawi, began trading directly with the coast in the eighteenth century. The Yao also invaded southern Malawi in the mid-nineteenth century, pursuing commercial gain. The region was also invaded by the Ngoni from the south in the nineteenth century, further disrupting existing sociopolitical structures. These developments were directly linked to the importance of, first, the ivory trade and, second, the growing demand for slaves at the coast during the nineteenth century.

the gold, diamond, and, later, copper mines of the Rhodesias and South Africa increasingly drew large numbers of workers from Nyasaland to those regions, often for many years at a time. In particular, the Rhodesian Native Labour Bureau began recruiting labor in Nyasaland from 1903 and was later joined by the Witwatersrand Native Labour Association, based in South Africa. The outward flow of migrant labor continued even after the governor of the territory passed legislation restricting the practice in 1911. There were relatively few economic incentives for Africans to remain within the territory; although some African farmers later became pioneers of cash-crop production, notably of tobacco, such activity often had to be carried out on white land where the price for such produce was fixed and Africans had to provide labor in lieu of rent and taxes. Yet the sustained migration of labor further impoverished many rural communities already displaced by land alienation. Notably, Nyasa migrant workers based in Southern Rhodesia later formed the nuclei of nationalist and protest movements of that territory.

Economic conditions for white farmers improved markedly prior to World War I. They turned to the production of cotton and tobacco, and the value of their exports more than doubled between 1905 and 1913 following the extension of a railway link from Blantyre to Port Herald. The growth of the plantation system contributed to the eruption of African armed rebellion in 1915. An African clergyman, John Chilembwe, led an uprising of plantation laborers bonded by their Christian faith; they harbored grievances concerning the impositions of white employers as well as the brutality of African soldiers in the service of the colonial state. The rebellion was brief but intense, failing to gather wide support before being crushed. As with uprisings in other parts of colonial Africa, however, the Chilembwe revolt provided Africans in Nyasaland with a "tradition of resistance" in the latter stages of colonial rule.

As already noted, Nyasa workers in other parts of central Africa contributed to the growth of protest movements throughout the region. Nowhere was this more clearly demonstrated than in the growth of the Jehovah's Witnesses-based Watchtower movement, which originated in northern Nyasaland and took root in the mining compounds of Northern and Southern Rhodesia. The Nyasaland African Congress (NAC), established in 1944, extended its influence into Southern Rhodesia via more than one hundred thousand Nyasa migrant workers in that colony, as well as being the main engine of protest in Nyasaland itself. In particular, the NAC, in common with other African political organizations in the region, protested against the movement toward a Central African Federation. This would join Nyasaland in an administrative block with Northern and Southern Rhodesia. The colonial authorities attempted to calm African fears by offering African politicians a greater stake in government. In 1949, for example, a number of Africans were given seats on the Legislative Council in Zomba, the capital.

The colonial authorities, however, were determined to establish the federation, which duly came into being in 1953. Britain was convinced that such an administrative unit was the best way to secure the long-term economic and political development of the region, while also creating a pluralist and multiracial society. But Africans, in Nyasaland as elsewhere, saw the federation as reinforcing white minority rule and opposed it bitterly. During the 1950s the NAC expanded and protest became increasingly forceful. In particular, there was a sharp increase in rural unrest as a result of government interference in agricultural practice. This was undoubtedly critical to the success of the NAC which, like other such movements, required widespread rural support if it was seriously to challenge colonial rule. Civil disobedience in Nyasaland in 1959 led to widespread arrests and a crackdown on protests; among those incarcerated was the prominent NAC leader, Dr. Hastings Kamuzu Banda. Simultaneously, however, the strength of the opposition led the colonial authorities to reconsider the viability of the federation, and by 1960 colonial governments were forced to concede the necessity of offering enfranchisement to the African majority. In 1961, the newly formed Malawi Congress Party (MCP) under Banda rallied mass support and won a majority of seats in the local assembly. Nyasaland became internally self-governing in January 1963 and won independence as Malawi in July 1964.

Throughout the thirty years of his rule, Banda was synonymous with Malawi itself, and it was difficult to envisage the ship of state without him at its helm. Prime minister from 1964, he became president when Malawi became a republic in 1966. He was life-president of Malawi from 1971, and also held the posts of president of the MCP and minister of external affairs, works and supplies, agriculture, and justice. Charismatic and religious, he was revered by his people for much of his time in office, being regarded as a something of a father figure; the Malawian media often referred to him as Ngwazi, meaning savior or conqueror. An elder of the Church of Scotland, he clearly regarded his role as extending beyond the conventional confines of secular government, issuing decrees on matters such as hairstyles and the length of women's skirts, and strictly censoring books, magazines, and films.

As was characteristic of many other regimes in independent Africa in which the cult of personality flourished, Banda's rule was ruthless with regard to opposition and dissension within government ranks. He acted swiftly against such opposition only a few weeks after the end of colonial rule. A number of government ministers were unhappy with Banda's desire for links with South Africa; they also wanted to Africanize the Malawian bureaucracy and opposed Banda's retention of Europeans in the civil service, police, and armed forces. In September 1964 three such opponents were dismissed from the government and others resigned in protest. Shortly afterward a former colleague of Banda's, Henry Chipembere, led an armed revolt in the south of the country. This had been crushed by early 1965. A similar insurrection led by Yatuta Chisiza was suppressed in 1967, and thereafter Banda's presidency faced no serious challenge until the early 1990s. He was able to consolidate his control of the country, and opponents were either driven into exile, imprisoned (for example, Gwanda Chakuamba in 1981), or killed (Albert Nqumayo, secretary-general of the MCP, in 1977). One potential successor, Dick Matenje, was mysteriously killed in 1983, apparently as a result of a car crash. For many years the government harassed Jehovah's Witnesses who refused to join the MCP, and thousands of Witnesses fled into exile in neighboring countries in 1970, 1972, and again in 1976. A number of opposition groups operated in exile, most prominently the Socialist League of Malawi and the Malawi Freedom Movement.

By the early 1990s, Banda's regime was coming under increasing criticism for alleged human rights abuses, for example from the direction of Amnesty International and the Roman Catholic Church in Malawi. In September 1992 the Alliance for Democracy (AFORD) was formed by opposition politicians, as was another pressure group for political reform, the United Democratic Front (UDF). In October 1992, Banda finally and with great reluctance agreed to a national referendum on the transition to multiparty democracy. The referendum took place in June 1993, and although the opposition was strongly supported in the north and south of the country, the MCP retained its support in the central region. Banda remained in power following an amnesty for political exiles and a cabinet reshuffle. In May 1994, however, a general election saw Banda finally relinquish political office. In the presidential election, Banda won some 34 percent of the vote, but Bakili Muluzi of the UDF won 47 percent and was quickly inaugurated as the country's new head of state. In early 1995 Banda, who was increasingly ill, and several former colleagues in the MCP government, were arrested for their alleged involvement in the killing of opposition politicians in 1983. All the accused, however, were acquitted in December 1995.

Economy

At independence in 1964, Malawi was among the poorest countries in the world. This situation had scarcely improved at the end of the 1990s, as industry failed to develop to any significant degree and the economy continued to be dominated by the plantation system, itself a hangover from the colonial era. Deposits of bauxite exist and may be profitably exploited, but Malawi is otherwise lacking in mineral resources. The industrial development which has occurred has had little impact upon the broad population, which remains firmly rooted in the agricultural sector. Since the 1960s the government has tried to encourage foreign investment through the Malawi Development Corporation. The bulk of industry is located in the south of the country, particularly at Blantyre and Lilongwe, the capital. At Blantyre and nearby Limbe, industries include tanning, footwear, cement, brewing, chemicals and fertilizers, tobacco curing, sawmills, textiles, and groundnut processing. Lilongwe, built during the 1970s largely through South African finance, has an international airport and such industries as tobacco processing, plastics, knitwear, and canning. Tourism is also promoted, particularly in Blantyre; partly to encourage this, and also to spur industrial growth, roads have been upgraded and air traffic developed. The Malawian rail network is confined to the south, from where railways link the major centers with ports on the coast of Mozambique.

Cotton is produced in the Shire Highlands and at several points along the shore of Lake Malawi. Tea and tobacco are the biggest foreign currency earners, tea being produced predominantly in the far south, tobacco around Kasungu, Lilongwe, and along the Shire. Other exports include coffee, groundnuts, rice, and sugar. Over two-thirds of the working population operate in the agricultural sector, either on smallholdings or the plantations producing export crops. During the first two decades of independence, the success of Malawi's agricultural economy was suggested by the fact that agricultural exports accounted for some 95 percent of the country's foreign earnings, while a rapidly growing population seemed to be adequately fed. By the mid-1980s, however, it was clear that heavy economic burdens fell on the poorest farmers who owned little more than an acre of land each. Indicators of deep-rooted rural poverty came in the form of high infant mortality and the prevalence of tuberculosis and malnutrition. This situation was exacerbated by the fact that Malawi in general suffered from a lack of medical and health services, most of which were concentrated in the large towns. It is clear that Banda's "agricultural miracle" was to a considerable extent an illusion, engendered by relative stability and a degree of prosperity for a small minority.

Banda's economic policy was largely characterized by a desire to attract foreign investment and encourage private enterprise. He eschewed any form of African socialism and, controversially, was keen to retain links with the white-dominated economies to the south. South African loans were used to build a new capital at Lilongwe. During the 1970s white businessmen from Rhodesia were also brought in to manage the plantations which produced Malawi's major exports. Most of these plantations were, and continue to be, owned by multinational corporations, others by wealthy Malawians. A similar situation exists within the comparatively much smaller manufacturing sector—for example, the processing plants at Lilongwe and Blantyre. These are concentrated in a very few hands, including, when he was still in office, those of Banda himself.

Peoples and Cultures

Malawi today comprises several major ethnic groups, including the Chewa, Yao, Nyanja, Chipoka, Tonga, Tumbuka, and Ngonde. As noted above, the name "Malawi" is itself derived from the word—sometimes rendered "Maravi"—used to describe the large migrating group which entered the present-day territory during the fifteenth and sixteenth centuries. Although it is misleading to talk about a "Malawi people" in this sense, it is clear that there are broad similarities within the Maravi or Malawi group, not least in terms of lan-

guage—today Chichewa is the most common African language in Malawi—and culture, notably in the masked dance complex. Indeed, Malawi is prominent among east African states through its masked societies, which arguably represent its most conspicuous modern cultural characteristic. Alongside the Makonde and Makua in Mozambique, the Chewa of Malawi are among the most celebrated practitioners of an activity which is both art and, as all art should be, social and historical observation.

The Chewa are the largest single group in Malawi, occupying the central region and areas of the far south. While of the Maravi or Malawi chiefdoms, the Chewa have often been singled out for closer examination by anthropologists and historians alike. Their cultural features—not least the masked dance and the secret society—are shared by several other of the groups mentioned above. The origins of the Nyau dance society among the Malawi kingdoms is unclear; at some point it became a focal point of resistance to invaders, possibly in the fifteenth century. Used as a tool of social and political control, it was known as "the great prayer" and depicted the creation of the world. Above all, however, it is of critical importance as a defining cultural feature of many of the peoples of modern Malawi. Masked dance societies survived despite repeated attempts by missionaries and colonial authorities to suppress them, Europeans regarding them as potentially subversive. Today the masks themselves, and the dances during which they are worn, are used as commentaries depicting both current affairs and past events. Other unifying cultural traits can be traced directly to the power struggles between various chiefdoms in the sixteenth and seventeenth centuries. For example, the religious influence of M'Bona, a rain priest, apparently spread over a large area of southern Malawi only after he was martyred by Lundu, who sought to control the Shire Valley.

In broad terms, the Malawi peoples belong to the closely related group of matrilineal Central Bantu speakers, and it may be argued that the predominance of descent or kinship through the female line is indicative of more expansive cultural semblance among the various peoples. Cultural synthesis is also suggested by certain religious practices and similar modes of thought regarding worship, although of course in recent decades these forms of cultural cohesion have become partially shrouded by the widespread adoption of Christianity and, to a lesser extent, Islam. (Even so, some 19 percent of the population still hold to what are vaguely termed "traditional beliefs.") For example, the worship of deities was mostly conducted through a senior member of the matrilineal group, who was empowered to perform the act of worship through the group's dead ancestors. Moreover, there existed an almost ubiquitous belief in a single creator or "High God," and a clear cultural unity in the practice of propitiating ancestral spirits. Through ceremonies of this kind, emphasis was placed on the cohesion of the kin group. Although in retreat throughout the region, and practiced by dwindling numbers in neighboring Mozambique, accessories such as the lip-plug were at one time common throughout Malawi, as was scarification. Again, these traits emphasize, on a very basic level, some form of cultural homogeneity.

At the same time, however, it is dangerous to overemphasize the conformity of Malawian cultures. This is clearly demonstrated by the attitudes of the various Malawian groups themselves, who in certain circumstances and from different historical perspectives regard each other as quite separate. Peoples and cultures are never, of course, static, and Malawi's history demonstrates this very clearly. As already noted, the invasions of the Yao to the south of the lake in the nineteenth century introduced new cultural complexity to the region, not least because of the very different historical experience of the Yao. The same can be said of the settlement of the Ngoni during the same period, although their cultural distinctiveness has gradually been diluted. When the decisions regarding the creation of official boundaries fell to the European powers in the 1880s and 1890s, little thought was given to cultural or ethnic bonds within the territory, while strategic, economic, and diplomatic considerations were paramount. This situation was not unique to Malawi, as even a cursory glance at the cultural map of Africa shows. It meant that, in a way scarcely envisaged by the European mapmakers, the cultures and peoples of Malawi spread beyond the borders of the territory itself. Thus, the Tumbuka straddle the frontier between Zambia and Malawi; in the north large numbers of Ngonde are in Tanzanian territory; and in the south various groups, including the Mang'anja, are divided between Malawi and Mozambique. Thus, peoples and their cultures are constantly subject to forces for change and adaptation, and there can be little doubt that Malawi, youthful as the country is, and the cultures within its borders, will continue to mutate.

BIBLIOGRAPHY

Alpers, Edward A. *Ivory and Slaves in East Central Africa: Changing Patterns of International Trade to the Later Nineteenth Century.* London, 1975.

Dequin, Horst. *Agricultural Development in Malawi.* 2d ed. Munich, 1970.

Gertzel, Cherry. "East and Central Africa." In *The Cambridge History of Africa.* Volume 8, *From c. 1940 to c. 1975,* edited by Michael Crowder. London, 1984.

Linden, Ian. *Catholics, Peasants, and Chewa Resistance in Nyasaland, 1889–1939.* Berkeley, 1974.

McCracken, John. *Politics and Christianity in Malawi, 1875–1940: The Impact of the Livingstonia Mission in the Northern Province.* Cambridge, 1977.

———. "British Central Africa." In *The Cambridge History of Africa.* Volume 7, *From 1905 to 1940,* edited by A. D. Roberts. London, 1986.

McMaster, C. *Malawi: Foreign Policy and Development.* New York, 1974.

Pachai, Bridglal. *Malawi: The History of the Nation.* London, 1973.

Pachai, Bridglal, ed. *The Early History of Malawi.* Evanston, Ill., 1972.

Pike, John G. *Malawi: A Political and Economic History.* New York, 1968.

Pike, J. G., and G. T. Rimmington. *Malawi: A Geographical Study.* London, 1965.

Shepperson, George, and Thomas Price. *Independent African: John Chilembwe and the Origins, Setting, and Significance of the Nyasaland Native Rising of 1915.* Edinburgh, 1958.

Williams, T. D. *Malawi: The Politics of Despair.* New York, 1978.

RICHARD REID

See also **Banda, Ngwazi Hastings Kamuzu; Boundaries, Colonial and Postcolonial; Chilembwe, John; Colonial Policies and Practice; Ivory Trade; Labor Migration; Livingstone, David; Plantation Economies and Societies; Political Systems; Religion and Ritual; Rhodes, Cecil John; Secret Societies; Slave Trade.**

MALI

GEOGRAPHY AND ECONOMY

During the nearly seventy years that Mali was subject to French colonial rule (1892–1960), its boundaries and its name were altered repeatedly to suit the needs of the colonial administration. The area that roughly corresponds to the Republic of Mali was known initially as the Soudan Français (1892–1902) and then, combined with other French holdings in western Africa, as Sénégambie et Niger (1902–1904); a reconfigured version of the latter entity was named the Haut-Sénégal et Niger (1904–1920). By 1937 Mali had been reestablished as a distinct French colony, called again Soudan Français. Subsequent name changes—the République Soudanaise (1958–1959), the Fédération du Mali (1959–1960), and the République du Mali (which dates from 22 September 1960)—represent political but not territorial regroupings. Mali's border with Burkina Faso was adjusted slightly in December 1986 by the International Court of Justice.

Topography and Climate

Mali is for the most part a vast flatland of Precambrian rock (granite and shale) covered by sandstone and alluvial quartz. Few elevations exceed 500 meters, though there are exceptions; for example, the Adrar des Isforas mountain region, 890 meters at its peak. The northern half of Mali, above 15° north latitude, falls within the semiarid margin of the Sahara Desert, the Sahel, or makes up part of the desert proper. The chief course of relief in this dry landscape is the Niger River, which cuts northeast through the center of the country nearly as far as Timbuktu. There the river begins its gradual curve first east, then southeast toward the country's border. When the Niger rises, as it does annually during the rainy season, it floods a vast expanse of land, known as the inland delta, which lies between Ségou and Timbuktu. When the waters recede from the inland delta they leave behind shallow lakes like Debo. The land that emerges is used for cultivation, but the soil, like that in southern Mali (the other major growing region in the country), presents major problems for agriculture.

Mali is generally hot and dry, but the climate varies significantly from north to south. The northernmost region of the country, within the Sahara, gets very little rain at all and endures temperatures that range on average from 49° to 60° Celsius. The region that falls within the Sahel gets 175–500 millimeters of rain per year; average temperatures range from 27° to 38° Celsius. Rainfall in southern Mali varies as much as 1,000 millimeters, from 500 to 1,500 millimeters per year; average temperatures range from 24° to 35° Celsius. Mali's dry season begins in November with a cool wind, the alize, which drives down temperatures throughout the country. In February the hot, sandy wind, the harmattan, starts to reverse the effects of the alize and gradually, over the course of the next few months, pushes temperatures up to their highest levels.

Monsoon winds initiate the rainy season in late May or early June. Though the rainy season extends through the end of October, most of the rain actually falls in July and August.

Droughts, Transportation, and Power

During 1970–1974 and 1984–1985 Mali suffered two major episodes of drought. The first was largely confined to the sahelian areas inhabited by the nomadic herding peoples the Tuareg and the Moors. Famine was widespread among these peoples and drove an estimated twenty thousand of them to seek refuge in Algeria, Libya, Niger, and Burkina Faso. The drought of 1984–1985 was brief but general throughout the country and particularly severe, draining the Niger to the lowest level ever recorded, so low that one could walk across the riverbed at Bamako. This drought drove more northerners into neighboring countries and also into southern Mali, which left areas around Gao and Timbuktu deserted. The drought had disastrous effects on agriculture in Mali, especially on the production of subsistence crops; until 1990 the country depended on foreign imports and donations of food.

The drought of 1984–1985 affected many other sectors of the economy, too, since Mali relied on its rivers, then as now, to generate power and to provide transportation. Both goods and people travel around the country by means of the Niger, the Senegal, and other rivers because the roads are generally rather poor and the railroad is limited to a single track. (It originates at Koulikoro, passes through Bamako, and continues on through Senegal as far as Dakar; thus, Mali gains access to one of the region's major seaports. Another is reached by the paved road that runs from Bamako to Abidjan in Côte d'Ivoire.) As valuable as it is, river transport is limited by seasonal fluctuations in the depth of the rivers. The seasonal ebb and flow also affects the country's supply of electricity. Eighty percent of Mali's electricity is generated by hydroelectric plants, the largest being the facility at Manantali on the Senegal River, built under the auspices of the Organisation pour la Mise en Valeur du Fleuve Sénégal (OMVS) (Organization of Senegal River States); the plant was opened in 1992 and is expected to reach full capacity by 1998. That same year, Mali's electrical network is to be linked to the Ivoirian national grid.

Key Sectors of the Economy

An increased (if unreliable) supply of electricity will make a difference to Mali's developing

République du Mali (The Republic of Mali)

Population: 9,504,800 (1994 est.)

Area: 1,240,007 sq. km (478,767 sq. mi.)

Official language: French

Languages: Arabic, Bambara, French, Fulani, Malinke

National currency: C.F.A. franc

Principal religions: Muslim 90%, traditional 8%, Christian 1.5% (mostly Protestant)

Capital: Bamako (estimated pop. 600,000 in 1993)

Other urban centers: Mopti, Ségou, Kayes, Gao, Kimparana, Sokola, Araouane, San, Timbuktu

Annual rainfall: varies from 500–1,500 mm (20–60 in.) in south to 175–500 mm (7–20 in.) in sahelian zone to 0–175 mm (0–7 in.) in saharan zone

Principal geographical features:

Mountains: Adrar des Iforas, Timetrine Mountains, Manding Mountains, Bandiagara Plateau, Hombori Mountains

Lakes: Faguibine, Garou, Do, Niangay, Debo, Sélingue, Télé, Oro, Fati, Haribomo, Aougoundou, Kabara, Tanda, and other seasonal lakes

Rivers: Senegal, Niger (Joliba), Bafing, Bakoye, Bani, Baoulé, Bagoé, Falémé, Sankarani

Economy:

GNP per capita: US$250 (1995)

Principal products and exports:

Agricultural: cotton, livestock, fish, groundnuts, sheanuts, millet, sorghum, maize, rice, sugar

Manufacturing: food and beverage processing, textiles, cement, cigarettes, pharmaceuticals, plastics, soap, farm implements

Mining: gold, phosphates, salt, limestone, marble

Government: Independence from France, 1960. Constitution, 1960. New constitution approved 1974, enacted 1979. New constitution approved in 1992. Multiparty democracy. President elected for 5-year term by universal suffrage. 147-member Assemblée Nationale elected for 5-year terms universal suffrage. President appoints prime minister and cabinet. For purposes of local government there are 6 regions divided into 42 cercles (counties).

Heads of state since independence:

1960–1968: President Modibo Keita

1968: Lieutenant Moussa Traoré and Captain Yoro Diakité

1968–1969: Captain Yoro Diakité, acting chairman of Comité Militaire pour la Libération Nationale (CMLN)

1969–1979: Colonel Moussa Traoré, chairman of the CMLN

1979–1991: President Moussa Traoré

1991–1992: Lieutenant Colonel Amadou Toumani Touré, chairman of the Comité de Transition pour le Salut du Peuple

1992–: President Alpha Oumar Konaré

Armed forces:

Army: 6,900

Navy: 50

Air force: 400

Paramilitary: 1,800

Transportation:

Rail: 646 km (401 mi.)

Roads: 18,000 km (11,185 mi.), 8% paved

Airlines: International flights by Air Afrique and privately owned Trans Air Mali; domestic flights by national Mali Tombouctou Air Service, Air Mali

Airports: International facilities at Bamako, 7 domestic airports throughout the country

Media: 2 daily newspapers: *L'Essor-La Voix du Peuple, Bulletin Quotidien de la Chambre de Commerce et d'Industrie du Mali*; 13 other main periodicals. No publishing. Radiodiffusion Nationale du Mali provides radio and 2 hours per week television service.

Literacy and Education:

Total literacy rate: 32% (1990). Education is universal, free, and compulsory from ages 6–15. About one quarter of children receive primary education. Less than 10 percent receive secondary education. Postsecondary education provided by École Nationale d'Administration, École Nationale d'Ingénieurs, École de Médecine et Dentisterie, École Normale Supérieure, Centre Pédagogique Supérieur, Institut Polytechnique Rural de Katibougou. There is no university.

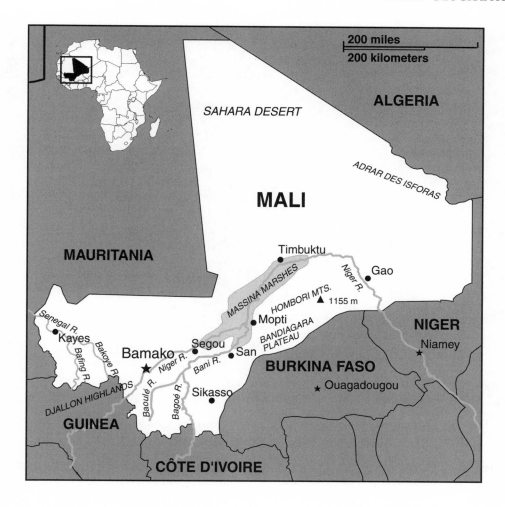

economy. But in the 1990s most economic activity in Mali remains in agriculture and, to a lesser extent, pastoralism and fishing; there is very little industry in the country. Eighty percent of Mali's workforce is employed in agriculture, producing 40 percent of the gross domestic product (GDP). Most farmers just cultivate food crops for their own use—the principal ones being millet and sorghum—and they do so, for the most part, in the traditional manner; few farmers in Mali employ any machinery. But the Malian economy depends heavily on commercial agriculture. The most important cash crop is cotton; it produces about half of Mali's total export earnings. Livestock, including cattle, sheep, and goats, are the second greatest source of foreign earnings; they are exported primarily to Côte d'Ivoire. Some livestock are also raised for subsistence, but only by a very small percentage of the population: the drought of 1984–1985 destroyed an estimated 40–80 percent of all Malian livestock and was particularly devastating to subsistence pastoralism.

Manufacturing and mining in Mali have been quite limited, though both are in the process of expanding in the 1990s. Manufacturing contributes only about 7 percent of GDP and is largely confined to consumer goods for domestic use, especially food. Most manufacturing takes place in Bamako, but there are exceptions: for example, fish are processed at a canning factory in Mopti (the center of the Malian fishing industry); textiles are produced at a large factory in Ségou; rice is processed at several plants in the inland delta. (Domestic and foreign investors seek to turn Mali into a major source of rice for regional export.) Most of Mali's mineral resources have remained unexploited, in part simply because the poverty of the country's infrastructure makes mining a particularly expensive venture. There is prospecting for petroleum, uranium, tungsten, manganese, diamonds, and other

101

Malian family seeking to escape from drought conditions. HARTLEY/PANOS PICTURES

minerals in the 1990s. Salt, which has drawn outsiders to Mali since the Middle Ages, is still mined in the far north, at Taoudenni. Gold mining has attracted the greatest investment, particularly since the early 1990s; gold is expected to become a principal source of foreign earnings.

Economic History and Future Prospects

In the mid-1990s Mali remains one of the poorest countries in the world and indeed in Africa; average annual income per capita amounts to only U.S. $250. Mali's current economic problems have their origins in the socialist policies of Modibo Keita (first president of the Republic of Mali, 1960–1968). The nationalization of the principal sectors of the economy, as well as the huge expansion of the administrative bureaucracy, both of which were initiated during Keita's tenure, proved to be a financial disaster. So too was the decision in 1962 to establish Mali's economic independence from France by withdrawing from the CFA Franc Zone and creating a new national currency (the Mali franc). As the national debt increased from year to year, the government responded by printing money, actually doubling the amount in circulation between

1960 and 1967. The value of the Mali franc was stabilized in 1967 when Mali negotiated readmission to the CFA Franc Zone. The regime of Moussa Traoré (1968–1992) initially adopted most of Keita's economic policies, but beginning in 1970 it also garnered—and came to depend on—substantial aid from France and other Western donors.

In 1981, under pressure from the World Bank, the International Monetary Fund, and other donors, Mali began a long, ongoing process of economic reform, including privatization of the parastatals. The implementation of reform measures was inconsistent through the early 1990s on account of domestic resistance and led to the temporary suspension of foreign aid in 1987–1988 and again, briefly, in 1993–1994. But in the late 1990s Mali's economy seems to be moving in a positive direction. The country has benefited from substantial debt relief, granted in 1990 and 1996. Since the establishment of multiparty democracy in 1992 it has attracted much new foreign investment in private enterprise, notably from the United States. Cash remittances from Malian expatriates have boosted the economy to some extent; totaling U.S.$23 million per year in the late 1990s, such payments may be expected to grow in the future. Actual prosperity remains a long way off for Mali. As the country attempts to modernize its economy, it faces many difficult challenges. Among them are a high rate of population growth—2.5 percent per year—and a largely uneducated population.

BIBLIOGRAPHY

Krings, Thomas. *Agrarwissen bäuerlicher Gruppen in Mali, Westafrika: Standortgerechte Elemente in den Landnutzungssytemen der Senoufo, Bwa, Dogon, und Somono.* Berlin, 1991.

Maharaux, Alin. *L'industrie au Mali.* Paris, 1986.

Roberts, Richard L. *Warriors, Merchants, and Slaves: The State and the Economy in the Middle Niger Valley, 1700–1914.* Stanford, Calif., 1987.

Schreyger, Emil. *L'office du Niger au Mali, 1932–1982.* Wiesbaden, Germany, 1984.

B. MARIE PERINBAM

See also **Bamako; Climate; Development; Drought and Desertification; Hunger and Famine; Minerals and Metals; Niger River; Pan-African and Regional Organizations; Sahara Desert; Timbuktu; Transportation.**

HISTORY AND GOVERNMENT

Early History

The territory of Mali, located at the center of the ancient and medieval states involved in the trans-Saharan trade, was the site of many kingdoms and empires at least as far back as the ninth century C.E. Many modern Malian towns—Gao, Timbuktu, Jenne, Ségou, for example—have their origins in these early civilizations. Such towns attracted Arabs and Berber peoples from the north and black peoples from the southern parts of Africa who together produced complex new cultures in Mali. If Malian towns were famous by the Middle Ages for two particularly valuable commodities—gold and salt—they were also renowned for their intellectual and artistic wealth, including their architecture. Some were major centers of Islamic scholarship, drawing students of the Qur'an from Asia as well as from other parts of Africa.

The three principal early empires in Mali were Ghana, or Wagadu (c. 800–1200); Mali (c. 1100–1700); and Songhai (1335–1591). Ghana, a federation of kingdoms spanning what is now northwestern Mali and adjacent parts of present-day Mauritania, reached its height in the eleventh century. Mali, originally just a small kingdom located at the headwaters of the Upper Niger (at Kangaba),

gradually expanded so that at its apogee in the fourteenth century it included most of the area of modern Mali as well as Senegal, Gambia, and parts of Mauritania. Songhai developed first around Gao, but it too ultimately extended its reach throughout most of the whole of present-day Mali and also into what is now Niger and Burkina Faso. All three empires exploited slavery to an extent previously unknown in western Africa.

We know relatively little about the period between the sixteenth and the eighteenth century in Mali. Kingdoms that originated during this time include Jaara (c. 1500–1900), Kaarta (1633–1854), and Segu (1600–1862). The history of the region begins to be better known from the nineteenth century on, when the theocratic state of Macina as well as the Tukulor Empire flourished. Under the Muslim teacher Cheikou Amadou (1755–1849), Macina, first established in 1400, became an Islamic state in 1810. About forty years later 'Umar ibn Sa'id Tal (1794–1864), a prominent Tukulor scholar from Senegal, embarked upon a series of military campaigns to establish an empire in the western Sudan that would be centered on the teachings of Tijani Sufism. Beginning in 1852, the forces of al-Hajj 'Umar (as he came to be called) conquered a vast territory including Kaarta in 1854 and Macina and Segu in 1862. When the French sought to gain control of Mali, the principal power they had to contend with was the Tukulor Empire of al-Hajj 'Umar.

French Colonial Rule

The French made their earliest contacts with the indigenous peoples of Mali as early as the fifteenth century. But it was only in the nineteenth century (when the British and the Germans were also exploring the Malian territory) that the French, operating out of their settlements in Senegal, began an effort to colonize Mali. In the late 1850s armed conflicts between the French and the Tukulor Empire resulted in a temporary truce, but beginning in 1876 and especially after 1888 the French stepped up their military efforts to dominate the whole of Mali. The indigenous states, including the Tukulor Empire (fragmented after 1864, though nominally ruled by a son of al-Hajj 'Umar, Ahmadou), were relatively fragile and easily crushed by the French army in the early 1890s. Ahmadou was driven from power in 1892, the very year the French declared Mali—that is, the area that constitutes the modern country—a distinct colony to be known as Soudan Français.

This colony was subsequently merged with other French holdings in western Africa to form two other administrative entities (Sénégambie et Niger, 1902–1904, and Haut-Sénégal et Niger, 1904–1920). The name Soudan Français was revived for the Malian territory in 1920, and in 1937 Soudan Français was restored to the status of a separate colony. Life for Africans in Soudan Français was somewhat less oppressive than in other French colonies only because the French found fewer natural resources to exploit there. The French abolished slavery in the region. They did, however, recruit forced labor for some projects, notably the construction of the railroad (still in use) that runs from Koulikoro (in Mali) to Dakar. They pressed Africans into service in the French army. During the two world wars, in fact, Soudan Français furnished the most important contingent of troops from all of Afrique Occidentale Française (AOF): from 1914 to 1918 alone, 49,500 African men, about 20 percent of whom perished in the war.

Demobilized African troops later played a key role in the political struggle for independence, as did workers and a number of intellectuals. African political organizations were not permitted in Soudan Français until just after World War II. But cultural organizations, such as the Arts et Travail society founded in 1937 by Modibo Keita, then a young teacher, later first president of independent Mali, provided cover for some early, clandestine political activity. As early as the 1920s the Tijani leader Hamallah and his followers were a force for organized resistance to French authority, which grew throughout the 1930s and early 1940s. Hamallah's followers eventually found political leadership in the African nationalist party the Rassemblement Démocratique Africain (RDA) and its local subsection, the Union Soudanaise (US), which were born in Bamako in 1946.

Independence and After

Soudan Français achieved independence in stages. Like all the colonies of the AOF it was granted the right to limited self-government in 1956; the degree of its autonomy increased in 1958 when it became a member of the Communauté Française under a new name: the République Soudanaise. The next permutation in its political status was realized in January 1959 when Keita, then head of US-RDA and an elected member of the French government, joined with the Senegalese Léopold Sédar Senghor to unify their two new countries under the name the Fédération du Mali. France granted indepen-

dence to this political entity on 20 June 1960, but the federation dissolved less than two months later. The République du Mali was established shortly thereafter, on 22 September 1960. Modibo Keita, who had been prime minister of the Fédération du Mali, became the president of the new republic.

Together with a legislative assembly of eighty members, Keita governed Mali as a one-party state. The party, the US-RDA, and Keita himself espoused a socialist program of economic restructuring, which, combined with some of Keita's other policies, produced an economic disaster in Mali. The new administration soon severed all of Mali's ties with France. Though it officially adopted a foreign policy of nonalignment, in fact it began to alienate Western countries and develop ties with the Eastern bloc. Domestic opposition to Keita's government was muted. The decision to withdraw Mali from the CFA Franc Zone and create a new national currency (the Mali franc) led to some political protest in Bamako in 1962, but it was quickly suppressed and not repeated. A rebellion launched that same year by the Tuareg people, in northern Mali, was also soon suppressed in a bloody campaign.

Discontent with Keita's government grew throughout the 1960s as Mali's economic crisis deepened. But strong opposition emerged only in 1967, after the government negotiated Mali's reentry into the CFA Franc Zone. The decision to cede a measure of the country's economic autonomy to France divided the members of the US-RDA, with hard-liners openly protesting the change in policy. Keita responded by initiating a radical reorganization of both the party and the government, dissolving the assembly in 1968. A newly formed militant youth group of Keita's supporters began to conduct political purges that extended even to members of the army. When they did, a group of young army officers, led by Lieutenant Moussa Traoré, took over the country in a coup d'état on 19 November 1968. While promising an eventual return to civilian government, Traoré ruled Mali through the army for over a decade.

Crises and Resolutions: 1970–1996

The form of Mali's government changed over the course of Traoré's years in power. Initially, it consisted of a military body called the Comité Militaire pour la Libération Nationale (CMLN), presided over by Traoré as president and Captain Yoro Diakité as "head of government." A new constitution, approved by a referendum in 1974 (and amended in 1981), established the basis for a return to elected government, including a president and a legislature, in 1979. The constitution designated Mali a one-party state, so that when Traoré ran for president in 1979 and 1985 he did so as the uncontested representative of his party, the Union Démocratique du Peuple Malien (UDPM), winning 99 and then 98 percent of the vote. An organized prodemocracy movement only began to coalesce in 1990, when Traoré, then under intense political pressure, allowed for a national discussion of democratic reforms within the framework of the one-party state.

The preceding two decades were years of crisis, beginning with a devastating drought in northern Mali from 1970 to 1974. Initially the government ignored those most affected, the Tuareg and the Moors, thus embittering the Tuareg especially, who had already suffered greatly in the early 1960s (albeit under a different regime). Many Tuareg died during the drought; thousands sought refuge in neighboring countries. A subsequent drought in 1984–1985 impelled more Tuareg to migrate. This drought, while brief, was particularly severe and general throughout the entire country; it compounded Mali's already staggering economic problems, which had only grown since 1968. The government's attempts to impose austerity measures in the 1980s met with considerable political resistance, especially from students and civil servants, whose ability either to find or retain jobs was imperiled. In 1990 a new crisis erupted when the Tuareg, responding to new government provocation, initiated a well-organized, well-armed rebellion.

On 26 March 1991, just days after violent prodemocracy demonstrations in Bamako, members of the army staged another coup, led by Lieutenant-Colonel Amadou Toumani Touré. Touré first installed the military Conseil de Réconciliation Nationale (CRN) to run the country but quickly replaced it with another organization, the Comité de Transition pour le Salut du Peuple (CTSP), designed to make and implement plans for a multiparty democracy. Legislative elections contested by twenty-one parties took place in February and March 1992. Ten parties won seats in the new 129-member national assembly, the majority of seats going to the Alliance pour la Démocratie au Mali (ADEMA), the Comité National d'Initiative Démocratique (CNID), and the revived US-RDA. The ADEMA candidate, Alpha Oumar Konaré, won the presidential elections, which took place in April.

That same month the Tuareg and the CTSP signed a treaty called the National Pact. Though sporadic fighting between the Tuareg and the Malian army continued into 1995, by the spring of 1996 the Tuareg were engaged in voluntary disarmament, and a genuine peace had been established. Mali has hardly been free of political tensions in the years since Konaré's election: opposition politicians have charged that ADEMA has undue influence on the government; both ADEMA and CNID have split, with dissenting members forming new parties; students and others have continued to protest, sometimes violently, the imposition of certain economic reforms. But the new government has actively encouraged the development of democratic institutions, among them a free press, including independent radio stations. It has made itself available in an annual national forum to answer people's questions on the radio. Democracy has attracted new foreign investment in the private sector, which offers the best hope for improvements in the economy and thus for Mali's long-term political stability. Elections are scheduled for 1997.

BIBLIOGRAPHY

Brasseur, Paule. *Bibliographie générale du Mali, 1961–1970.* Dakar, Senegal, 1976.

Conrad, David C., ed. *A State of Intrigue: The Epic of Bamana Segu According to Tayiru Banbera.* Oxford, 1990.

Coquéry-Vidrovitch, Cathérine, and Odile Goerg, eds. *L'Afrique occidentale au temps des Français: Colonisateurs et colonises (c. 1860–1960).* Paris, 1992.

Diarrah, Oumar. *Le Mali de Modibo Keïta.* Paris, 1986.

Diawara, Mamadou. *La graine de la parole: Dimension sociale et politique des traditions orales du royaume de Jaara (Mali) du XVème au milieu du XIXème siècle.* Stuttgart, Germany, 1990.

Gallais, Jean. *Hommes du Sahel: Éspaces-temps et pouvoirs. Le delta intérieur du Niger, 1960–1980.* Paris, 1984.

Konaré, Alpha Oumar, and Adam Ba Konaré. *Grandes dates du Mali.* Bamako, Mali, 1983.

MAMADOU DIAWARA

See also **Drought and Desertification; Hamallah of Nioro; Segu State; Senghor, Léopold Sédar; Slavery and Servile Institutions; Sudanic Empires of Western Africa; Timbuktu.**

PEOPLES AND CULTURES

For more than six hundred years Mali has been at the center of multiple networks of trade and social exchange between the peoples of the southwestern rain-forest zone and those of the Sahel and the Sahara to the north. The Niger River has been critical to the formation of those networks. Flowing north from the Futa Jalon mountain range (in present-day Guinea) through the center of Mali just over the border of the Sahel and then bending south (through Niger and Nigeria), ultimately emptying into the Bight of Benin, the Niger River has functioned for centuries as a principal artery of traffic and long-distance trade—and sometimes warfare. Beginning in medieval times the Niger gave rise to an urban culture, including such cities as Mopti and Segu, the economy of which was originally based on warfare and on trade in slaves, salt, gold, and other goods. Malian cities dating from the premodern period stand in sharp contrast to those like the capital, Bamako, that have achieved their importance since French colonial rule.

The characteristically high mobility of the Malian peoples has created a web of social relations and commercial networks that crisscrosses the country and even transcends the national boundaries. These networks are based on kinship, alliance, and common regional origin. Families are organized hierarchically not only in terms of sex but also age and generation and they are generally patrilineal, patrilocal, and polygynous. Since the late nineteenth century, urbanization and the migration of youth in search of labor have weakened the family's authoritarian structure. Nevertheless, especially in rural areas, authority and control within the family remain in the hands of the eldest male of the senior generation. In contrast, in the regions to the north of Mali, authority within many families of the Tuareg, Moors, and other peoples has been substantially undermined by ecological degradation and concomitant migration, and also by the political crises that made refugees of numerous people beginning in the 1970s.

The family is the principal unit of production in Mali, engaged primarily in subsistence farming. Similar to many other African societies, children participate in the family production starting at an early age: about 54 percent of all Malian children aged 10–14 work full- or part-time. Considering the extremely limited number of job opportunities for people with a school education, many parents, in particular farmers, have little incentive to send their children to school. Therefore, the rate of school enrollment in Mali figures among the lowest of the entire world; in 1993 only 21 percent of the eligible population was actually enrolled in primary or secondary school. Illiteracy in Mali among all people over the age of six was estimated at 81.2 percent in 1988. The government seeks to increase primary school enrollment to as much as 50 percent by the year 2000, but such an increase will likely depend on greatly expanding job opportunities for those who have some education.

Some Malian cultural groups include individuals of three social origins: first, those who are of free or noble birth; second, the descendants of slaves; and third, professionals, called *nyamakala*, who perform specialized services for noble patrons. The *nyamakala* often work as blacksmiths, as specialists in elaborate speech and musical performance, or as leathermakers. What sets them apart is that they are considered to control *nyama*, a powerful, though impure and potentially destructive, force. They have attracted considerable scholarly attention because of their seemingly ambiguous social status: on the one hand, nobles both fear and respect the *nyamakala* because of their power; on the other hand, they hold them in contempt because of their contamination with *nyama*.

Mali is composed of a number of what have often been considered distinct ethnic groups. Each so-called ethnic group does have its own language and particular cultural practices. In any given region, however, the differences between the cultural practices, languages, and economic activities of these "ethnic" groups are often mitigated by networks of commerce and migration that promote cultural and commercial exchange. In the past, when families or individuals moved from one area to another, they integrated themselves into the sociopolitical hierarchy of their new community, where they would acquire a newly fashioned ethnic identity. They often also learned new skills to practice a novel profession, and adopted the predominant language of their new home, sometimes favoring it over their native language. For this reason, a person's family name, clan identity, and place of origin play a greater role in forming his or her identity than that person's "ethnic" or linguistic affiliation.

In addition to migration, another factor that has led to the blurring of ethnic divisions in some regions is the existence of hunter organizations. These associations assimilate people of diverse "ethnic" origins into single, overarching social units. Historically, hunting, associated with magic knowledge and other powers necessary to dominate the forces of wilderness, has been of marginal economic importance though of great symbolic significance. Not surprisingly, then, oral accounts portray the legendary kings of the medieval southern empires as hunter-heroes who relied on supernatural powers to establish and maintain their rule. In contemporary Mali, city dwellers still reminisce about hunter organizations, which have become a dominant symbol of a heroic past.

Despite the integrating effects of trade networks, migration, and hunter organizations that increase the fluidity of ethnic boundaries, it is common both in and outside the country to refer to Malian peoples by ethnic names. Ethnic identity plays a part in contemporary national politics in Mali. Ethnic groups—and also certain cultural practices—are associated with different regions of the country.

Regional Cultural Practices and Ethnic Groups

Since the eleventh century, Malian peoples have been exposed to Islamic influence that originated in northern Africa. During the fifteenth and sixteenth centuries rich merchants and the rulers of the Songhai Empire transformed the northern cities of Timbuktu, Jenne, and Gao, which gradually turned into centers of Islamic erudition. From there, Islamic culture expanded southward as the Songhai Empire extended its control to Segu. Despite its urban roots, in the 1990s Islam is the religion of 85 percent of the total Malian population, rural and urban. However, many Malians combine Islam with traditional religious beliefs and practices. This holds true more often in the south than in the north. The few Christians, primarily Catholic, are mostly Dogon and Bobo and comprise only 1 percent of the total Malian population. Traditional religious practices that are still mostly unaffected by Islam are to be found among the Dogon and the Senufo.

Peoples who speak Mande-related languages native to the country's southern and central regions—approximately 50 percent of the total population—dominate Mali politically. These peoples live in the core areas of the former kingdoms of Ghana, Mali, Segu, and Kaarta and are strongly represented, both locally and nationally, in political and administrative positions. Among them, the Bambara (or Banmana, as they call themselves), who cultivate mainly millet and sorghum in a northward-pointing triangle located between the borders of the Côte d'Ivoire (Ivory Coast) and Mauritania, form the largest group. Their language, Bambara, is the lingua franca of commerce throughout Mali. Together with French, Bambara is used in public administration. Closely related to the Bambara people in language and traditions are the Malinke, agriculturists who are concentrated in the southwest, and the Dyula, who as traders cover Mali's entire southern triangle. The Soninké, who inhabit central Mali, also speak a Mande-related language. They live primarily in the regions of Nioro and Segu and are involved in both agriculture and livestock raising, as well as in national and international trade.

The Dogon, the Bobo, and the Senufo-Minianka live in southwestern Mali. Although their ancestors had once been under the sway of the medieval Mande emperors, they still maintain some traditions and practices that clearly distinguish them from the Mande. Like people from the north, they are underrepresented in political and administrative positions. Nevertheless, they have been well integrated into Mali's cotton export economy since colonial times. Today they benefit from their closeness to Bamako, Mali's capital and economic center, and from an infrastructure in the southern triangle that is more developed than in the north.

In the northeast, the Songhai and the Fulani (or Peule) dominate the Niger Bend. The Songhai, descendants of those people who built the Songhai Empire, grow millet and sorghum and raise livestock. Their traditions have been strongly shaped by Islamic culture, and this clearly distinguishes them from the Mande people to the south. Many of the Fulani were originally nomadic cattle herders who have become sedentary as a result of serious cattle losses during the extended droughts of the 1970s and 1980s. The Fulani are especially numerous in the Mopti, Segu, Sikasso, and Nioro regions where they herd not only their own livestock but also that of other ethnic groups. Another group inhabiting the Niger Bend are the Boza, who are predominantly agriculturists and fishers.

The droughts of the 1970s and 1980s have also seriously impaired the subsistence activities of the Tuareg and the Moors, northern peoples who are made up of both Berber groups and their former slaves captured among the peoples of southern Mali. The Tuareg and the Moors are mainly pastoralists and traders and inhabit the vast areas of the northern Sahel and the Sahara. The lifestyle of the Tuareg, more than that of the Moors, was strongly affected by colonization, which the Tuareg opposed vigorously. Moreover, since independence, these northern peoples have benefited little from the government's investment in infrastructure and, in general, have been denied political participation at the national level. Largely as a consequence of these two disadvantages—which had devastating ramifications for the northern peoples during the droughts—many of the Tuareg and the Moors have opposed the government. Some of them engaged in an armed rebellion during 1990–1993. Many Tuareg and the Moors have cast their opposition specifically as a matter of ethnic conflict between themselves and the southern, Mande-related peoples.

Another consequence of the droughts and of the precarious living conditions in the Sahelian zone has been the migration of young men to work as wage laborers in Bamako and other countries in western Africa, such as Côte d'Ivoire, Ghana, Sierra Leone, and Gabon; some have even migrated to France. Malians have formed large expatriate communities (up to 20 percent of the foreign population of other countries in western Africa) while maintaining strong ties to their families in Mali through letters, radio messages, and cash remissions. In neighborhood groups and on festive occasions, expatriate Malians often preserve and even revive the traditional cultural practices of their home communities. Thus, the high mobility and cultural flexibility that have in the past characterized Malian peoples continue within and beyond the borders of the current nation-state.

BIBLIOGRAPHY

Amselle, Jean-Loup. *Logiques métisses.* Paris, 1990.
Brasseur, Paule. *Bibliographie générale du Mali, 1961–1970.* Dakar, 1976.
Gallais, Jean. *Hommes du Sahel: Éspaces-temps et pouvoirs. Le delta intérieur du Niger, 1960–1980.* Paris, 1984.

DOROTHEA SCHULZ

See also **Niger River; Sudanic Empires of Western Africa.**

MAMI WATA

[Mami Wata is a figure of religious and aesthetic significance in many parts of the continent. This entry is in two parts, describing the quite different versions of the phenomenon in Western Africa and Zaire.]

WESTERN AFRICA

In the pidgin vernaculars of west and central Africa, ''Mami Wata'' is used in various contexts to refer to a female river deity; to differing female river deities as a general term of description; or to

exceptionally beautiful women who are considered to typify the various qualities of Mami Wata. In the twentieth century Mami Wata has developed as an autonomous deity with specific cult and shrine practices.

Mami Wata is generally characterized as a beautiful and seductive river goddess with long flowing hair and fair skin who is capable of bestowing sudden and unexpected good fortune on her devotees or of wreaking terrible personal misfortune, often resulting in madness and abject poverty, on those who incur her displeasure. Sometimes she is depicted with a fish's tail to indicate her connections with the water spirit world. Both men and women enter her cult for a variety of reasons. These can be physical and spiritual sickness, constant dreams that contain images from the water world, or strange and distant behavior that marks the individual as belonging to Mami Wata. Her devotees are sometimes considered to be in a sexual liaison with her in the spirit world—a liaison that Mami Wata jealously maintains with punitive sanctions.

But however this relationship is defined, as a deity Mami Wata is linked with notions of irresistible female sexuality. Her other outstanding characteristic is her embodiment of and identification with modernity in contemporary urban life (even when her shrines are in rural areas). She is represented as fast-living and independent, sometimes with connections to Indian mystic powers. The music played for her in religious ceremonies features modern instruments, such as the harmonica and guitar; and occasionally popular pidgin English lyrics from highlife music are sung to celebrate the behavior of independent urban women—especially in the associations between money and female sexuality. Offerings associated with her can consist of sweet drinks and food, perfume, talcum powder, and all the fineries of the modern urban woman. When possessed, her devotees sometimes smoke cigarettes, further accentuating these contemporary traits.

Mami Wata as a deity appears to have arisen in the early twentieth century in the riverine areas of southern Nigeria and then spread through Nigeria and beyond, particularly to other regions of west Africa. The diffusion of her cult has not been a single, unified process but has changed and been adapted to local circumstances and contexts, taking quite different historical trajectories. For example, the introduction of Mami Wata from the delta region of Nigeria to the Bwa-speaking area of Burkina Faso by a migrant oil worker in the 1970s entailed a complete transformation in the social practices and the artifacts used in association with Mami Wata in its new context. It now appears as a masquerade with tall headdress in a style similar to other Bwa masquerades.

A key factor in the development of the image of Mami Wata has been the influx of prints from Europe and India since the end of the nineteenth century. There has been a vast array of images, including al-Baraq, the winged horse that carried the prophet Muhammad to Jerusalem and back in a single night; the entire pantheon of Hindu gods and goddesses; Rosicrucian and other sects; Western and Eastern film posters; and many other diverse materials. A small insert that is often identified as a representation or "photograph" of Mami Wata is on a widely occurring print found in west and central Africa of a female snake charmer holding aloft a snake. Mami Wata is depicted in half-figure as a beautiful woman with long flowing hair and a fair complexion. The representation is based on an original chromolith printed in Hamburg circa 1885 that was widely copied in both Europe and India and repeatedly distributed in sub-Saharan Africa throughout the twentieth century. This print is used to represent Mami Wata in many shrines in west Africa, but other images are also used, such as prints of gods from the Indian Hindu pantheon. As described by Henry Drewal, this has sometimes led to Mami Wata practices being explicitly linked to Indian mysticism. However, in other localities different elements may be developed. The impact of the snake charmer print is particularly evident in the early Mami Wata wooden carvings found among the Anang and Ibibio peoples of southeastern Nigeria, where the small inset in the print is transformed into a literal rendering as a protrusion on the side of such carvings.

Explanations of the advent of Mami Wata have emphasized her possible development from interactions with overseas visitors, whether in the ships' figureheads associated with visiting European traders or the general encounter with the material goods and social mores of these visitors. However, indigenous religious categories (for example, among the Igbo [Ibo] of southeastern Nigeria, where there is evidence of Mami Wata in the Mbari shrines by the 1920s) often associate white with spiritual purity. And, similarly, associations of flowing hair with female sexuality also preceded these European encounters. The development of Mami Wata as a category has rearticulated and extended these prior associations to accommodate

encounters with foreigners. However, Mami Wata is concerned predominantly with the articulation and expression of African social realities and in particular with social change, which is often exemplified in the emphasis on modern practices and artifacts found at Mami Wata shrines. Mami Wata as religious practice focuses on these local concerns rather than the representation of exotic encounters with visiting foreigners.

Mami Wata has been used as a term of reference for a cluster of variables throughout west and central Africa. Mami Wata as an expression of specific religious practice is found predominantly in west Africa in the form of cults and shrines, whereas in central Africa it is usually restricted to its more generalized associations. In the personification of the female, these focus on the role of women and on relations between the sexes. They have provided an impetus for imagery in the literary, lyrical, and visual mediums of expression. The mysterious and seductive qualities of Mami Wata express many of the characteristics of economically independent urban women who have acquired far more autonomy of action than their rural counterparts. In using the term "Mami Wata," men emphasize the seductive but ambivalent qualities of these urban women. Their high expectations are exemplified in songs such as the 1960s major highlife hit by Victor Uwaifo (from Benin City) about Mami Wata.

In Zaire, images of Mami Wata are prominent in the popular art of bar murals, paintings, and record covers. Johannes Fabian relates these visual images to a strand of popular culture that expresses the tensions between individual social aspirations and political experience in the urban areas. Mami Wata is a visual image that has been used since the 1950s in Zaire and may initially have been linked to the strong presence of west African traders during this period. Its popularity and recurrence in Zairian painting traditions lie in its ambivalence. It can describe the fluidity of social relations and encounters, but it also comments on the vagaries of individual fortune in urban life. The fact that personal success can be attributed to the secret favor of a Mami Wata spirit has the additional implication that the gaining of such material success and social power has been acquired by illegitimate and spiritually harmful social connections. In this context the image of Mami Wata can serve as a powerful indictment of social inequalities in the urban environment. Chéri Samba, a prominent Zairian artist (who has established a reputation in the

Representation of Mami Wata ritual. COURTESY OF THE AUTHOR

ers as women, when performing in a state of possession, through assertive and demonstrative behavior. Similarly, beautiful women encountered briefly are often described as Mami Wata because her devotees are considered to be exceptionally good-looking. The popular and widespread presence of Mami Wata throughout west and central Africa resides in the different ways she can be interpreted and used in her different contexts, but most important, in the way in which she is identified with modern urban lifestyles and experiences.

BIBLIOGRAPHY

Drewal, Henry John. "Mermaids, Mirrors, and Snake Charmers: Igbo Mami Wata Shrines." *African Arts* 21, no. 2 (1988): 38–45.

———. "Performing the Other: Mami Wata Worship in Africa." *The Drama Review* 32, no. 2 (1988): 160–185.

Fabian, Johannes. "Popular Culture in Africa: Findings and Conjectures." *Africa* 48, no. 4 (1978): 315–334.

Salmons, Jill. "Mammy Wata." *African Arts* 10, no. 3 (1977): 8–15.

CHARLES GORE

ZAIRE

One of the most widely known icons in Zaire is the mermaid, called Mami Wata (mammy water) in the west and Mamba Muntu (crocodile person) in the east. Her paintings were hung all along the city houses in the mid-1960s but gradually disappeared in the 1980s. Some artists became famous for producing as many as fifteen paintings a day. The imagery of Mami Wata provides a commentary upon the world from the point of view of the individual. Her paintings are related to the painted portrait (in Zaire, always based upon a photograph), which serves as a declaration of the social legitimacy of the individual. This is visually associated with apocalyptic visions of the end of the world, which in Zaire was popularly expected to occur sometime in the 1980s. Mami Wata tells how to succeed in the world of postcolonial modernity and at the same time is a reminder of the price of such success. The acceptance of Mami Wata in Zaire was matched by social commentary that condemned association with her as immoral because the wealth she provides is not shared. The ambiguity of her image rests upon its fascination, to which is opposed the moral condemnation of any man who has recourse to her. The icon of Mami Wata divides the world into two spheres, the masculine and the feminine, which are strictly distinct but irrevocably linked. The image recalls the

international art markets), and other artists have used this image extensively in their work. It is seen as a popular, progressive image by their patrons.

Many independent churches in west and central Africa have produced a copious literature on the threat of Mami Wata. Her untrammeled sexuality is used to exemplify the seductive dangers of the material world. Furthermore, it epitomizes the ever-present threat of fracture of the bonds of community that these churches are assiduously fostering among their worshipers. This church literature uses the contrast with Mami Wata to define its participants as apart from a secular and unredeemed world in which Mami Wata is ever present. However, in contrast, the image of Mami Wata also presents an autonomous role for women that highlights their individual capabilities rather than through kinship or other affiliation. This makes it a popular image of empowerment for women. For example, in Benin City, female religious devotees of Mami Wata emphasize their autonomous pow-

opposition of these spheres with regard to access to social power, mimicking the opposites of nature and culture, tradition and modernity. In purely Western terms, Mami Wata is a binary representation of the world, in which there are only winners and losers who partake unequally in a finite stock of wealth; it is a very Christian world, where everything has a price.

The Zairian mermaid symbolically reproduces the colonial universe, in which the white woman was kept outside the world of the colonized common people. The artists give her those attributes of her sex that the colonial culture publicly acknowledged, and deprived her of the attributes of a fecund woman. Her abundant breasts are displayed, but her buttocks and genitals are encased in the tail of a fish. Mami Wata stands in opposition to the ''legitimate'' woman, who guarantees the continuity and prosperity of the group and whose representation emphasizes attributes of fertility.

It is difficult to establish a solid link between the image of Mami Wata and the Christian missionary culture. The Marian cult, and the Catholic organization Légion Marie, came to the Belgian Congo relatively late. Before the 1950s, images of the Virgin and explicit references to her as one who interceded between believers and God were rare. As elsewhere, women available to participate in organized parish activities were, for a long time, limited to the towns, where African women did not become numerous until after World War II. The establishment of the Légion Marie appears to coincide with an increase in the number of Christian women and to have shortly preceded the popularity of Mami Wata.

In the Belgian Congo, the white woman was everywhere a powerful and sexual object of desire, strictly reserved for white men. White women were restricted to the colonial urban centers, idle and emphatically protected from contact with black men. Wives of the colonizers did not arrive in the colony in great numbers until the 1950s. Until that time, it was common for a white man to keep his African housekeeper as a mistress. These elements, combined with the Marian cult, explain how the mermaid came to be symbolically represented by a white woman. By extension, the black prostitute has also been portrayed as a quasi mermaid. She too is a feminine object, and also, like Mami Wata, lures rural men to ''modernity.'' Only a ''free woman'' (prostitute) could earn and spend money on her own, to the detriment of the social group.

The idea of a half-woman, half-fish aquatic being combines many elements: precolonial beliefs in aquatic spirits; the partly empirically based conviction that the whites were ghosts who came from beyond the sea (their white skin called to mind the appearance of a drowning victim); and elements of west African folklore. Anglophone west Africans played an important role in the construction of urban society and culture, particularly in western Zaire. Soldiers came first, then educated agents of commercial and industrial companies, and finally sailors. They were the founders of the first dance clubs, introducing European styles, and the first social dance music. They also imported the name Mami Wata. By contrast, in southeastern Zaire, she is called Mamba Muntu (crocodile person), probably referring to the sorcery with which the crocodile (held to embody an aquatic spirit) is associated. It appears that these two symbols of evil, represented in Christianity by the serpent and in precolonial

Mamba Muntu (crocodile person), the eastern version of Mami Wata. FROM THE COLLECTION OF BOGUMIL JEWSIEWICKI

culture by the crocodile, contributed to the development of the image of Mami Wata.

Finally, the popular representation of Mami Wata owes much to colonial imagery, which widely published images of black women in which they were treated as ethnographic and sexual objects. Many postcards, modestly entitled "young woman of _____ tribe," displayed the black woman in the position that later artists adopted for Mami Wata: the bared breasts facing the viewer, the lower part of the body outside of the visual field. Some of these images depicted the nude woman holding a mirror.

All these elements achieve hybrid form in a representation that makes visually explicit the paradigm of access to wealth, power, and modernity. The painting of Mami Wata, which could be purchased in the 1960s for the price of three or four bottles of beer, established the paradigm for social success for all men. In this image a white woman, or perhaps more accurately an honorary white woman since she was not truly white of skin, opened the way through the great gulf that separated blacks from whites, the powerful from those condemned to being exploited, the modern from the traditional, and so on. Since these two worlds could not be merged, the prosperity of an individual's community of origin became the price of his success. A man who benefited from her favors repaid Mami Wata with the lives of his kin.

The mermaid is usually accompanied by a snake and sometimes holds a cup into which the latter dips its tongue. She carries a watch, some jewels, a comb and a mirror, sometimes a book that represents the Bible. Like an Eve, she seduces black men with the promise of knowledge and power in order to free him from sin and damnation. This promise of access to knowledge is underlined by the mirror she carries; it is a widely recognized divination tool in both the non-Christian cults and the syncretic churches. Sometimes Mami Wata wears glasses, initially associated with whites, then with educated people, and perceived as a tool that permits better sight with which to conspire on the side of power.

Since the 1980s Christian imagery, especially images of Christ and scenes from the Old Testament, replaced Mami Wata as an evocative protective force, a promise of divine intercession. In the parlor of the urban home where one once found a Mami Wata, today one sees the religious images that painters mass-produce. Most urban dealers switched from the paintings of Mami Wata, often already taken down from the parlor wall, to the religious images. Today it is often difficult to purchase a religious painting to hang in its place. Owners of these religious images fear nefarious effects in the absence of a protective force.

There have long been rumors that all the powerful men who arose as religious or political leaders, including Mobutu Sese Seko himself, had a Mami Wata. Yet by the end of the 1980s the mermaid had lost her popularity, to be replaced by west African marabouts (Islamic holy men) and numerous secret societies, satanic cults, and eastern cults, all fueled by mysticism. In the 1980s in northeastern Zaire, one often found pictured a Muslim adoring the mermaid as she emerges from the water. The few local Muslims are small traders, probable descendants of the "Arabs" of the nineteenth-century trade, perhaps businessmen from the Levant, called "Lebanese" in Zaire. Their striking economic success and their exclusive relations with politicians and army officers gave rise to the conviction that their power comes from Mami Wata.

In Zairian culture Mami Wata was, and still is, the representation of the relationship between power and the individual male. She speaks with great clarity about the political culture of Mobutu's regime. Success in life, money, women, and power could not come without the arbitrary power of the president or one of the vassals who acted in his name. To attract the attention of one of the powerful, just as to attract the attention of a Mami Wata by stealing her comb or her mirror, might just as well open the doors to prosperity as the doors of hell. Like that of Mami Wata, the generosity of the president was capricious and unpredictable; the least disloyalty, the slightest attempt at automony, became punishable by exclusion from his inner circle.

There is no Mami Wata for women; instead, the successes of market women are attributed to sleeping with the serpent, the Christian symbol of evil, who, after each act of sex, vomits up money. It should be noted that if the image of the mermaid is beautiful, that of *nguma* (the serpent) is ugly. One has the impression that this represents a male point of view that there is a double contradiction. The first is that the woman holds power—represented here by a Christian incarnation of evil—while the woman should only be a mediator between a man and power. The second contradiction is she has money that properly belongs only to a man, since in a colonial society he was the only salaried worker. The black woman should have access to money only through a man, whose power in the city resides in his access to and control over money.

BIBLIOGRAPHY

J. Fabian. *Remembering the Present: Painting and Popular History in Zaire.* Berkeley, 1996.

BOGUMIL JEWSIEWICKI

MANDE. The various peoples who speak Mande languages and dialects are dispersed throughout the region between the upper reaches of the Niger River and the Atlantic coasts of western Africa. Today the Mande speakers amount to over twenty million.

It has been conventional to make a geographical and historical distinction between the nuclear Mande, those living in Mali and the area of the headwaters of the Niger River, and the peripheral Mande, who have migrated from the nuclear area over many centuries to live dispersed through the modern states of Senegal, Gambia, Guinea, Sierra Leone, Liberia, Côte d'Ivoire, and Burkina Faso.

The Mande occupied the present nuclear area by perhaps 5000 to 4000 B.C.E., and it was they who domesticated the sudanic food crops of tropical Africa, most of which have spread throughout the remainder of the world. These include several kinds of millet and sorghum, African rice, many types of beans, groundnut, okra, kola, sesame, tamarind, and probably cotton. With this highly productive agricultural base they established the great medieval empires of the western African savannah and the southern Sahara. The first was Ghana or Wagadu, established perhaps by the fourth century C.E. and flourishing from the ninth to the eleventh centuries. Its people were the ancestors of the present-day ethnic group known as Soninke or Sarakole. The second empire was Mali, peopled by the Malinke, which lasted from the twelfth until the fifteenth century. These empires controlled the trans-Saharan commerce between the gold-producing regions of the forest zone to their south and the states of the Mediterranean which sent salt, textiles, brass, and other commodities in return. After its decline Mali was largely taken over by the smaller states of the Bambara (Bamana) to its south. Soninke, Malinke, and Bambara are still the principal peoples occupying the modern country of Mali and together amount to some five million people.

Besides the Bambara, Malinke, and Soninke, other nuclear Mande groups, most living south and west of Mali itself, include the Boza (or Sorko),

fisher people on the Niger; the Yalunka (or Dialonke), Kagoro, Kasonke, Konyaka, Koranko, Nono, and Soso. The Soninké, Boza, Yalunka, Nono, and Soso have been for many centuries Muslims; the others retain their indigenous faiths. They are generally peasant farmers, recognize patrilineal descent, and live in large villages and small towns. The Soninke, Malinke, and Bambara are highly stratified societies, with hereditary nobilities as the highest rank and endogamous "castes" of hunters and smiths as the lowest. The remaining nuclear Mande are politically uncentralized, with minimal stratification. In former centuries slavery was universal. Most of the Mande peoples are renowned for their aesthetic work in textiles, wood carving, and music and masquerade.

The groups who may generally be classified as peripheral Mande (meaning merely that they do not occupy the central region of Mali and its nearby areas yet speak Mande languages) have over the centuries moved outward from the Upper Niger to the west, southwest, and south, and settled among non-Mande peoples. These movements, mostly peaceful, were mainly to search for new lands for intensive farming of the Sudanic crops that were then unknown to the indigenous occupants. In addition their skills as traders and the social and religious importance of their many literate Muslim lineages gave them high status. They include the Dan, Busansi, Dafi, Beng, Gbande, Guru, Kono, Kpelle, Ligbi, Loko, Mende, Ngere, Samo, Sia, Tienga, Loma, and Vai. Throughout this region the Mande-speaking trading groups known as Dyula (or Wangara) and Dafi built networks of both trade and Islamic learning. There has throughout history been much ethnic intermixture among these groups and between them and their non-Mande neighbors. In all, the peripheral Mande probably number almost ten million people.

BIBLIOGRAPHY

McNaughton, Patrick R. *The Mande Blacksmiths: Knowledge, Power, and Art in West Africa.* Bloomington, Ind., 1988.

JOHN MIDDLETON

See also **Jenne and the Sahara Borderlands; Sudanic Empires of Western Africa.**

MANDELA, NELSON (Nelson Dalibhunga Rolihlahla Mandela; b. 1918), antiapartheid leader and president of South Africa (1994–). Mandela was born to Henry Gadla Mphakanyiswa and Nosekeni Fanny Mandela at Mbhashe in the Umtata district of the Transkei. Though a scion of the Thembu royal house, Henry Gadla was not in line for the succession. Nonetheless, he was a chief, albeit later deposed for insubordination. Fanny Mandela, a devout Methodist, was his third wife, which meant that her son, Nelson, could not inherit the chieftainship. This set the young Mandela on the course of education and urban politics and paved the way for his presidency of South Africa.

After his father's death, the nine-year-old Nelson Mandela, as arranged by his father, traveled to Mqekezweni, where the acting chief of the Ama-Thembu, Jongintaba David Dalindyebo, took charge of his education. He enrolled at the local school and eventually gained admission to Fort Hare College in 1938 but was expelled in 1940 for engaging in a strike action. In 1941 he traveled to Johannesburg, where he took up temporary employment as a policeman at the mines and met Walter Sisulu, who encouraged him to study law. Mandela simultaneously enrolled for a B.A. degree by correspondence, which he obtained in 1942, and went on to study law at Witwatersrand University. Here he was exposed to Indian and white students and to radical, liberal, and Africanist thought. He joined the African National Congress (ANC) and in 1944 founded the ANC Youth League with Walter Sisulu and Oliver Tambo.

In 1948 the Afrikaner National Party came into power and began institutionalizing racism as apartheid. A spate of racist laws were passed in quick succession, among them the Group Areas Act of 1950, which ultimately resulted in the uprooting of millions of Black, Coloured, and Indian people, and the Bantu Education Act of 1953, designed to make sure that Africans remained menial laborers.

The ANC responded by adopting a program of militant action against the Nationalists. With Mandela on its executive committee, the ANC in 1951 organized a national work stoppage in cooperation with the Indian Congress. This was followed in 1952 with the Defiance of Unjust Laws Campaign, in which 8,577 volunteers defied racist laws and were imprisoned. The outbreak of violence and the six-month banning of fifty-two leaders, among them Mandela and the newly elected president-general of the ANC, Albert Luthuli, ended that campaign. Banning orders restricted the rights of movement and association. In 1953 Mandela was served with his second such order, this one for

Nelson Mandela. REUTERS/CORBIS-BETTMANN

two years. A third, five-year, banning order came in 1956.

On 25–26 June 1955 the ANC and other antiapartheid organizations convened the Congress of the People in Kliptown, just outside Johannesburg, at which some three thousand delegates adopted the Freedom Charter as a blueprint for a nonracial, democratic South Africa. Discontent within the ANC over the charter and alleged White and communist influence resulted in a split in 1958 and led to the formation of the Pan-African Congress (PAC) under the leadership of Robert Sobukwe. Meanwhile, the government declared the Freedom Charter a treasonable document and in 1956 brought to trial 156 key figures, among them Mandela and Luthuli. The trial continued until March 1961, when all of the accused against whom charges had not already been dropped were acquitted.

In 1960 a peaceful anti-pass demonstration organized by the PAC resulted in the massacre at Sharpeville, in which police killed 69 protestors and injured 180. Blacks responded with a massive work stoppage; the government retaliated by declaring a state of emergency, banning the ANC and PAC and detaining thousands throughout the country, among them Mandela. After his release, he participated in the organization of a national conference of antiapartheid groupings against the government's intention to leave the British Commonwealth and establish a racist republic. In the campaign which followed the conference, he went underground to facilitate his work and avoid arrest and came to be known as the Black Pimpernel.

In 1961 Mandela, having reached the conclusion that the power of the Nationalists would never be broken through mass civil action alone, initiated Umkhonto we Sizwe (the Spear of the Nation) to organize sabotage against key state installations. December 1961 saw the first bomb blasts in South Africa against apartheid. Mandela left the country secretly and traveled to African nations incognito to raise funds and set up training bases for Umkhonto cadres. He himself underwent military training in Algeria and Tunisia.

Mandela returned to South Africa in July 1962, was arrested in August, and was sentenced in November to five years imprisonment, three for incitement to strike and two for leaving the country without a passport. In June 1964, he was sentenced to life imprisonment for sabotage and attempting to overthrow the state through violent revolution.

Mandela's personal life had seen drastic changes from 1957 to 1960. He and his first wife, Eveline, divorced in 1957. He married Winnie Madikizela in 1958, and by early 1960 they had two daughters. Imprisoned numerous times beginning in the late 1950s and subjected to a long series of bans, Winnie nonetheless persisted in her antiapartheid activities and contributed significantly in keeping her husband in the public eye. (The Mandelas were divorced in 1995. That year, Winnie Mandela was dismissed from her government position amid controversial charges of abuse of power.)

The antiapartheid struggle escalated in 1976 when African youth in the township of Soweto revolted against the enforcement of Afrikaans as a medium of instruction. The revolt spread to other parts of the country and brought out the workers. By 1985 the government was in crisis. In 1988 Mandela's condition of imprisonment improved significantly, and the government began negotiating

with him. The last Afrikaner president, F. W. de Klerk, unbanned the ANC, PAC, and the South African Communist Party and released Mandela in 1990. (The two men shared the Nobel Prize for peace in 1993.) The first nonracial democratic elections followed in 1994, and Mandela was inaugurated as the first democratically elected president of the country.

BIBLIOGRAPHY

Johns, Sheridan, and R. Hunt Davis, Jr., eds. *Mandela, Tambo, and the African National Congress: The Struggle Against Apartheid, 1948–1990, A Documentary Survey.* New York, 1991.
Mandela, Nelson. *No Easy Walk to Freedom.* London, 1988.
———. *Long Walk to Freedom: The Autobiography of Nelson Mandela.* Boston, 1994.
Meer, Fatima. *Higher Than Hope: The Authorized Biography of Nelson Mandela.* New York, 1990.
Vail, John. *Nelson and Winnie Mandela.* New York, 1989.

FATIMA MEER

See also **Apartheid; De Klerk, Frederik Willem.**

MANSA MUSA (fl. early fourteenth century), emperor of Mali (r. ca. 1312–1337), the most famous of the Malinke sovereigns, under whom the empire reached its maximum size. He owes his fame to the pilgrimage he made to the holy places of Islam in 1325.

Ascending the throne after his predecessor, Abobakar II, died in a maritime expedition in the Atlantic Ocean, Mansa Musa endeavored to consolidate the borders of the empire. He was assisted in this by a brilliant general, Saran Mandian.

A prince educated in Arabic, he resumed the tradition followed by Malian sovereigns of making a pilgrimage to Mecca. He prepared painstakingly for the journey and, following tradition, required the towns and provinces to make a contribution. He left Niani with a large retinue, taking with him a great quantity of gold drawn from the treasure accumulated by several generations of sovereigns.

Mansa Musa dazzled the inhabitants and the court of Cairo upon his arrival in 1324. According to an historian of the time, he came on horseback superbly clothed, with over ten thousand subjects of his empire, and distributed gorgeous gifts magnificent to behold. The Malian sovereign and his companions distributed so much gold in Cairo that the price of that precious metal dropped. This added to his fame; several decades after his trip to Cairo, chroniclers were still writing about the splendor and the generosity of the Malians.

Mansa Musa returned home from the holy places with an architect, the famous Ishaq El Teudjin, who constructed for him several buildings. Among these were the Gao mosque; the Djinguereber, which is the well-known Timbuktu mosque; and a palace, named the Madougou, in the same city. In Niani itself the Arab architect built a mosque and a remarkable "audience room," a square room topped by a dome and decorated with arabesques of bright colors. Of these monuments, all built with earthen bricks, none survive except the Djinguereber in Timbuktu.

A patron sovereign, Mansa Musa attracted poets and other people of letters to his court. He built several libraries and supported education in the Qu'ran.

Under his reign Mali reached its greatest size. The empire extended from Teghazza in the Saharan plain in the north to the Guineo-Ivorian forest in the south; from Banjul in the west to Azelik (in present Niger) in the east. At the end of the fourteenth century, a portrait of Mansa Musa holding a large nugget of gold in his hands appeared on the first European maps showing the kingdoms and peoples of Africa.

Despite his fame, however, Mansa Musa is not favorably remembered in Mandinka oral traditions. He is reproached for squandering the gold of the Crown and thus weakening the empire. Yet his work is long lasting. All Malian cities bear his mark. To him are owed their monuments of hard-packed earth spiked with wood, a style so characteristic of Sudanese architecture.

BIBLIOGRAPHY

Levtzion, Nehemia. *Ancient Ghana and Mali*. London, 1973. Repr. New York, 1980.

Mansa Musa represented offering a golden nugget to a Berber trader in a Spanish map of 1375. BIBLIOTHÈQUE NATIONALE DE FRANCE

Ly Tall, Madina. *Contributions de l'histoire de l'empire du Mali (XIIIe–XVIe siècles)*. Paris, 1977.

Niane, Djibril Tamsir. *Recherche sur l'empire du Mali au moyen âge*. Paris, 1975.

DJIBRIL TAMSIR NIANE

See also **Mande Region, History; Oral Culture and Oral Tradition; Sudanic Empires of Western Africa; Timbuktu.**

MAPONDERA, PAITANDO KADUNGURE (d. 1904), Negomos leader and warrior. Mapondera, whose name means "he who vanquishes the stronghold of his enemy," was the son of Gorenjena, a member of the Changamira Rozvi royal family in eastern Rhodesia (now Zimbabwe) and famed ruler and warrior of the Negomos. Mapondera earned the praise name "Hugumu" for his leadership in battles against both European settlers and other Africans who impinged on the Mazoe district. His first distinction came during a struggle against Ndebele invaders, during which he killed their leader, Chiyama Mikomo.

With his reputation and the relative security of his territory against other Africans established, Mapondera concentrated on relations with Portuguese and British merchants who had come into the area in the last quarter of the nineteenth century. In 1891, Mapondera entered into a mineral concession with the Portuguese Selous Exploitation Syndicate, intending to benefit from trade with Europeans without threatening his people's independence. The following year, the British were eager to institute their administration in the area. To this end, they attacked Mapondera's village, captured his half brother, and put him in prison, where he committed suicide. British dominion grew, and inhabitants of the Mazoe were forced to pay taxes to their "sovereigns." Mapondera, disillusioned, began to see Europeans as an enemy.

Publicly denouncing the British Southern Rhodesia Native Commission and encouraging Africans to resist all forms of European authority, Mapondera formulated his belief that blacks must band together to fight colonialists. In 1895, he lead some forty men to ambush European settlements and patrols. The conflict continued to escalate, and Africans from the Mazoe district, as well as the Tete district in Mozambique, conspired to organize forces and to share resources and information regarding the activities of Europeans. Mapondera's guerrilla attacks continued while his movement grew in number, and were successful, to some ex-

tent, in disrupting trade. When two Mozambican leaders, King Muenemutapa Chioco and Makombe Hanga, the Barue monarch, resisted partnership with the Portuguese, Mapondera openly supported them by decrying not only colonialists in Africa but also Africans who made concessions to Europeans. He once said to a Shona chief who disagreed with his idea of unity among African peoples, "You have no excuse now, as we warned you years ago against being friendly with White men in the country. We will kill you when we have killed the White chief."

As Mapondera's contingent grew, Europeans came to regard him as a key enemy. In 1902, the Portuguese occupied his headquarters and conquered his village. Caught crossing from Mozambique into Southern Rhodesia, Mapondera surrendered and was sentenced to seven years' imprisonment. He died in prison as the result of a hunger strike in 1904.

BIBLIOGRAPHY

Mutswairo, Solomon M. *Mapondera, Soldier of Zimbabwe*. Harare, 1983.

SARAH VALDEZ

See also **Colonial Policies and Practice: Southern Africa.**

MAPS AND MAPMAKING. *See* **Cartography.**

MARANKE, JOHN (1912–1963), founder in 1932 of what is now an independent church with an international following, the Apostolic Church of John (or Johane) Maranke (Vapostori or Bapostolo). Maranke was born in the Bondwe area of the Maranke Tribal Trust land of Southern Rhodesia (now Zimbabwe) under the name of Muchabaya Ngomberume. He was a descendant of the royal Sithole lineage on his father's side. His mother was daughter of the Shona chief Maranke, whose clan name he adopted after a dramatic spiritual calling to found the church.

Little accurate information is available about Maranke's childhood. According to local missionaries, Maranke attended the American Methodist mission school under the name of Roston, after which he migrated to the town of Umtali in eastern Zimbabwe as a laborer. Close family and church members, however, dispute Maranke's affiliation with the Methodist mission.

In the official testament of the church, *Humbowo Hutswa we Vapostori* (The New Revelation of the Apostles), John recounts his first spiritual vision, which took place in 1917, when he was five. Over the years, he experienced a series of mysterious illnesses and dreams, culminating in a near-death experience in 1932. On 17 July 1932, John claimed to have seen a sudden flash of lightning and to have heard a booming voice dubbing him John the Baptist, instructing him to preach and seek converts from many nations. John began by proselytizing within his immediate family, converting his older brothers, Conorio (Cornelius) and Anrod, and his uncle, Peter Mupako. The first public sabbath ceremony was held on 20 July 1932 near the Murozi River (dubbed the Jordan) in the Maranke Reserve. Approximately 150 people joined the new group.

Maranke used visionary experiences as the inspiration for establishing the ritual practices and social hierarchy of the church. These practices drew heavily on Old Testament doctrines and showed evidence of influences from Methodist liturgy, Seventh-Day Adventism, and traditional Shona religion. By 1934, the social organization of the group was firmly in place. Maranke, who considered himself to be a *mutumwa,* or holy messenger and reinterpreter of Christian doctrines, devised a Saturday sabbath ceremony (*kerek*) consisting of prophetic readings, preaching, and hymns in Shona, interspersed with songs in various local dialects. Other ritual practices included a Eucharist or Passover celebration (*paseka* or *pendi*), mountain prayer retreats (*masowe*), and healing rituals. Maranke maintained tight control over the group's leadership hierarchy by bestowing the spiritual gifts (*bipedi*) of preaching, baptism, healing, and prophecy, and a series of ranks (*mianza*) at the annual Passover ceremony. He further elaborated this leadership structure following minor internal conflicts in local congregations during the 1940s and 1950s.

Until his death in 1963, John and his immediate relatives controlled the *paseka* and the leadership hierarchy from Bocha, Zimbabwe. John's eldest sons, Abel and Makebo, initiated a traveling *paseka* to neighboring countries in 1957. After John's death, leadership was passed to Abel and Makebo. There was a brief schism resulting in the founding of a spin-off Apostolic group under Simon Mushati, John's maternal cousin.

After Makebo's death in the late 1980s, Abel assumed leadership until his death in 1992. The church expanded rapidly across several African nations, establishing large congregations in Zaire, Zambia, Malawi, Mozambique, and Botswana, and with some European converts within and outside

John Maranke administering the *paseka.* FROM THE COLLECTION OF BENETTA JULES-ROSETTE, COURTESY OF KANGWA WILLIAM

of Africa. The 1992 succession was initially smooth, and leadership was transferred, by spiritual consensus, to Mambo Noah, a ranking healer in the Zimbabwean congregation. For a short period, Clement Sithole, one of Maranke's younger sons who had briefly studied in England, challenged Noah and attempted to reform the church but eventually returned to the fold with his followers. The fundamental leadership structure established by Maranke has demonstrated longevity, and the church continues to grow, with more than 500,000 members across Africa.

BIBLIOGRAPHY

Daneel, M. L. *Old and New in Southern Shona Independent Churches.* Vol. 1, *Background and Rise of the Major Movements.* The Hague, 1971.

Jules-Rosette, Bennetta. *African Apostles: Ritual and Conversion in the Church of John Maranke.* Ithaca, N.Y., 1975.

Maranke, John. *The New Witness of the Apostles.* Translated by J. S. Kusotera. Bocha, Zimbabwe, 1953.

Mariotti, Luciana. *Il millennio in Africa: "L'Apostolic Church of John Maranke."* Rome, 1991.

Mary Aquina, O. P. "The People of the Spirit: An Independent Church in Rhodesia." *Africa* 37 (January 1967): 203–219.

Murphree, Marshall W. *Christianity and the Shona.* London, 1969.

BENNETTA JULES-ROSETTE

MARGAI, MILTON AUGUSTUS STRIERY (b. 1895; d. 1964), prime minister of Sierra Leone (1961–1964). Born to a rural paramount chief of slave descent, he overcame Creole prejudices to become the first "protectorate native" to graduate from the Fourah Bay College in Freetown. He studied medicine in England, becoming the first physician from the protectorate. Margai practiced medicine for twenty-five years in the colonial service, working with secret societies to professionalize midwifery in rural areas. He published books on the subject, gaining wide support with womens' groups and the trust of local chiefs for his efforts. Margai formed the Sierra Leone People's Liberation Party (SLPP) in 1951. He won the elections that year, becoming minister while diffusing ethnic tensions by including Creoles in his administration. Margai's brother, Albert Margai, challenged his careful leadership style, becoming prime minister in 1958. In 1959 Milton Margai was knighted and appointed parliamentary leader the same year. He led an all-party independence delegation to London in 1960 for independence negotiations, prov-

ing to be a conservative pro-British leader. This, combined with the popular support he had garnered, led him to become prime minister in 1961 when independence was granted. Margai remained committed to democracy and encouraged foreign investment until his death. He was succeeded by his brother, Albert Margai.

BIBLIOGRAPHY

Cartwright, John R. *Political Leadership in Sierra Leone.* London, 1978.

RICHARD R. MARCUS

See also **Creoles.**

MARKET SYSTEMS. *See* **Exchange and Market Systems.**

MARRIAGE SYSTEMS. The study of African systems of marriage has always been influenced by the evolution of anthropology as a discipline. Interpretations of marriage practices have been, and continue to be, shaped by the dominant theory of a period.

The diversity of forms that marriage assumes in Africa bars any monolithic interpretation. However, it can be characterized by certain traits, the most striking of which is the transfer of material and symbolic goods that always accompanies a marriage. It can be said that these transfers, called either bride price or bride service, according to circumstances, signify in legal terms the passage of a woman from one group to another, with all concomitant consequences for the social membership of the children resulting from the union.

As elsewhere, marriage in Africa is a matter between familial groups, narrowly or widely extended, as much as between individuals. It lies at the center of a social and symbolic display that invokes ancestors as witnesses to the coming offspring; fixes the relations between the social groups of the new spouses, among which individuals, goods, and symbols will circulate; assigns social membership and social status to offspring; seals an alliance between groups; and, finally, gives rise to a series of rituals that only death will end.

African systems of marriage are well known for the numerous forms they can assume. Beyond the classic polygamy that can be considered the second great constant in Africa, one can find the following types of marriage: (1) levirate (union of a widow with the younger brother of the late husband);

(2) sororate (union of a man with the younger sister of his wife, either while his wife is alive or after her death); (3) union between close blood relatives (union of a man with his niece, first cousin, second cousin, or even half sister or granddaughter); and (4) union with in-laws, relatives whose relationships have been formed by previous marriages (union of a man with his wife's brother's daughter or with the widow of his maternal uncle). One also finds "ghost marriages," often involving two women, designed to mitigate a lack of offspring; two women may marry to counteract a problem resulting from sterility, to maintain the status of a woman of wealth, or to allow queens to retain their dominant position in the social hierarchy. These types of marriages do not all occur within the same society; each culture selects some and forbids others, which suggests that the choice is not random but obeys a logic coherent with the social organization of the culture. The resulting ensemble of marriages forms a matrimonial system specific to the society.

Beyond these general considerations, interpretations begin to diverge, especially when marriage is viewed in the context of other aspects of kinship and society: filiation (descent); lineage; residence; inheritance; the composition and nature of familial groups; economy; and politics. Debates on the subject have occupied African studies for nearly a century, but thanks to them and the diverse theories they have produced, we can now view the matter with some clarity.

The theory of descent groups, elaborated by British anthropologists, has tended to interpret marriage and its judicial and legal aspects, such as rights over children, by the patri-, matri-, or bilinear descent groups by which societies are organized. However, no broad generalizations can be advanced. The theory of alliance advanced by Claude Lévi-Strauss has long stumbled over matrimonial systems that do not present mechanical regularities which can be deduced from uniformly applied rules: although marriages between certain types of cousins are preferred, unions between other types of cousins are not necessarily prohibited, preventing the creation of unidimensional models that would structure society as a whole. Finally, marriages are often accompanied by the payment of bride price, which complicates the idea of the simple exchange of a sister for a wife, as is postulated in Lévi-Strauss's theory.

Patrilineal Societies

The best examples of the societies in which marriage between cousins is preferred are found in central and southern Africa. The Bantu societies of the south, such as the Tswana, Sotho, and Venda, which practice pastoralism and agriculture, are characterized by patrilineal descent. Marriage is sanctioned by a heavy bride price in cattle paid by the close agnatic (i.e., paternally related) kin of the husband to the kin of the fiancée. The preferred marriage is between a man and his mother's brother's daughter, or matrilateral cross-cousin marriage. Another type of favored marriage is between a man and his father's brother's daughter, or patrilateral parallel cousin marriage. In the local social hierarchy, the former type of marriage occurs among the common classes, while the latter—and the union of a man with his brother's daughter or even his half sister—is favored by the elites. In the first case, a permanent relation is created between the two parties to the matrimonial exchange; the transferred cattle circulate from group to group, and the stable relations between them are reproduced with each generation. The transfer of cattle bonds a brother with his sister because her marriage provides the cows that he can give to the brother of his (female) cousin in order to marry her. Their children will reenact similar marriages, which will have the effect of bonding their groups through payments of cattle. In the second case, marriage with the father's brother's daughter offers two advantages: it keeps the animals within the patrilineage and reenforces the political status of the two participating families. The two types of marriage have opposite effects, one leading to the circulation of cattle and women, the other to their retention, but each allows the reproduction of the social and political hierarchy. The Lovedu accomplish the same thing by emphasizing the responsibilities of brother and sister. The sister's marriage and the cattle transfer create for her brother a right to claim her daughter as a wife for his son. This right is also tied to the elevated status of women in this society. The scarcity of cattle, in combination with high bride price, constrains the average man to a single choice: to give his sister in marriage in order to acquire the cattle needed for him to negotiate his own marriage.

Other peoples in southern Africa make different marriage choices. The Tsonga, while maintaining a high bride price, forbid marriage with first and second cousins, as well as with a great many other relatives. Although this would presumably lead to the dispersal of siblings, a brother and sister are in fact bonded together because the marriage of one depends on that of the other: the cattle obtained by the marriage of the sister enables the brother to marry. In this case, only the circulation of bride price bonds groups together, for the network does not allow the same marriage alliances to be reenacted in successive generations. The Zulu also insist on setting a high bride price. The payment of cattle confers rights of paternity over the children, as is manifest in certain types of unions. In a ghost marriage, for example, even after his death a man is still considered to be the father of any children that his widow will have with a male relative of the husband (in the levirate form). Similarly, when an unmarried man dies, another will marry a woman in his name and produce children on his account. Finally, a rich woman of high status may marry another woman, giving cattle for her. Her wife will then have children with a member of the cattle-giving woman's kin group, but the cattle-giver is the socially recognized father.

The Lozi of central Africa, agriculturalists and fishers as well as pastoralists, constantly reshape their villages and mode of residence. Unlike many other patrilineal peoples, they do not have extended descent groups. Like the Tsonga and the Zulu, they forbid marriage with cousins, but their interdictions reach even further, including any type of blood relative (patrilineal, matrilineal, or cognatic). They also forbid sororal polygyny and any type of marriage of a man to a woman of the same descent group as any of his other wives or of his father's or brothers' wives. Dispersion is thus assured, but marriage remains unstable. In the late nineteenth century the bride price was largely symbolic, consisting of hoes, mats, and only one or two head of cattle, before being largely replaced by money in the early twentieth century. Unlike the Tsonga and Zulu, the Lozi did not believe that the payment of bride price allowed the children to be assigned to a social father rather than the biological father, but it did give the husband rights over his wife. Matrimonial interdictions were associated with a biological recognition of paternity. Cognatic and alliance relationships were extended by forming structured networks based on factors other than bride price.

Matrilineal Studies

The rules of marriage and bride price follow a different logic in the matrilineal societies of central Africa, which face different issues regarding the type of marriage, rights of the children, and modes of residence of the married couple. In many cases, one cannot speak of marriage compensation in the sense of bride price, but rather of "bride service,"

made by the son-in-law. This is the case with the Bemba of Zambia, agriculturalists in a poor region. After many years of "service" (working for his wife's kin), a Bemba man is finally allowed to bring his wife and children home, and eventually to marry his wife's sister as well. This arrangement, a sort of trial marriage, is performed after ritual activities and the wife's agreement to follow her husband into his village. He also chooses his place of residence, which may be that of his father, maternal uncle, or father-in-law, depending on the personality and status of the head of the household. The marriages of a brother and sister are not linked by the need to acquire bride-price cattle, but marriage between matri- or patrilateral cousins occurs widely. This offers the couple the advantage of remaining in a familiar village and provides a temporary stability to groups that regularly undergo restructuring. In sum, the reasons for preferring certain types of marriages are opposite to those of heavily patrilinear societies.

The situation is different when the mode of residence tends to be patrilocal, as with the Ila of Zambia or the Kongo of west-central Africa. Kongo children go to live with their maternal uncle at puberty, where they constitute a group of homogenous brothers. Ila children remain explicitly with their father. Bride price for both these groups is high and favors the departure of the wife for her husband's home. Ila marriage between cross cousins, notably with the daughter of the father's sister, counterbalances matrilineal descent and reinforces agnatic authority.

To summarize, the customs relating to cousin marriage and bride price in central and southern Africa follow their own internally consistent logic and, depending on various contexts (kinship, economy, politics), one phenomenon may complement, substitute for, or oppose the other. This is not the case in other parts of Africa, where in certain societies all types of cousin-marriage are allowed, whereas in others, all are forbidden, or where there is an ambiguous relation between matrimonial exchange and bride price.

In western Africa, Fulani pastoralists, whether nomadic or sedentary, apply two criteria to the possibilities of marriage and bride price: consanguinity and proximity. Residential endogamy accompanies consanguinial endogamy, but the importance of bride price paid in cattle varies among the different Fulani societies. There are three most common types of marriages—the union of a man with the father's brother's daughter, the mother's brother's daughter, or the father's sister's daughter. Only one possibility is favored statistically by a given society, and that possibility is contingent upon the extent to which the society is patrilineal or cognatic. Only two societies acknowledge all three types of unions without preference, in addition to that of a man with the mother's sister's daughter. This situation reflects the tension between kin groups: the father seeks a daughter-in-law from his relatives, the mother from hers.

The residency alternative ultimately followed in any given case is completely based on concerns about retaining or restricting the circulation of cattle. As a rule, the more numerous the consanguineous marriages within a society, the lower the bride price, even to the point where none is paid at all. Thus, the relation between the size of the bride price and the marriage of cousins is not the same as that observed in southern Africa. Furthermore, matrimonial strategies are tightly linked to political motivations that alternate between endogamy (marriage with a cross cousin) and exogamy (parallel cousin marriage)—according to whether the lineages of each society are primarily concerned with expansion or consolidation. Historical processes are thus introduced into matrimonial systems. The choice of a particular mate, however, cannot be as easily summarized in terms of simple strategies because it is based on preestablished models of marriage favored according to what is at stake at the particular moment. This point is subject to discussion, and other examples may enrich the debate.

The Asante of Ghana have what is known as a double descent system. In such systems social groups are organized according to the principle of matrifiliation, but the patrilineal line perpetuates itself through several generations in another manner, by the masculine transmission of the spirit (*ntoro*) of the father. Each individual is composed of the blood of his mother and the spirit of his father. Marriage of a man with the daughter of his maternal uncle, a matrilateral cross cousin, is recommended (leading to a de facto residence with the maternal uncle of the man) though seldom carried out between true first cousins, whereas marriage of a man with the father's sister's daughter has been the privilege of the Asante princes since the eighteenth century. It offers the double advantage of producing presumptive heirs belonging at the same time to the royal matrilineage and to the other two or three agnatic lineage groups issuing from the first sovereigns but also from individuals who carry in their blood their mother's lineage and their paternal grandfather's spirit, serving in effect as his reincarnation. Marriage between cousins is not the only type of matrimonial system, and systems representing an opposite tendency occur widely in many societies. Within them, marriage between first and often second cousins is prohibited, but the exchange of sisters, or marriage by exchange, is favored. In the marriage of cousins, the circulation of wives and bride prices among kin groups is replaced by a sort of direct reciprocity—one that is not renewed in future generations. This system is clearly illustrated in Nigeria, where marriage with bride price takes place only when a man has no sister to give in exchange for his bride, and so has none of the rights to progeny, who will belong to his wife's group. Only the exchange of sisters sanctions the affiliation of the children to their father. This is the case with the Tiv, the Mambila, and many others. With the Tiv, the reciprocity of the double marriage must also extend to the number of children they create; if one of the marriages results in more offspring than the other, the surplus is given to the other couple to equilibrate the two lineages. With the Mossi of Burkina Faso, when the reciprocity is not immediately assured, the daughters from the first marriage belong to the chief, who will redistribute them at the appropriate moment, thereby assuring a deferred reciprocity. Thus, the exchange of sisters that is not renewable in the following generation (meaning that it cannot be reproduced by a marriage between cousins) can be seen as opposed to bride price, which is thus nothing more than a remedy for the lack of a sister. Similar substitution can evolve toward a system of marriage by purchase in which the exchange of sisters is preeminent in the ideology, but no longer in the practice, of marriage.

However, even in the simplest models of reciprocity, other means are employed that act against direct exchange. The Tiv, after reequilibrating children between two couples, use the wards for inaugurating new exchanges. The daughters resulting from marriage with a stranger are utilized in this manner. This is a well-known way of circumventing the norm and adding to a personal network of matrimonial alliances. All the same, in matrilinear societies, one expected strategy is to keep for oneself, secure from one's wife's brother, one's own children resulting from secondary marriages with slaves or with patrilinear neighbors who will find it normal that the husband take his wife with him. Marriage by exchange is therefore rarely simple and is often quite complex.

This is also the case with systems of secondary marriage found on the plateau of Jos in Nigeria. It applies at the same time to the multiplicity of marriages, the principle of nondoubling, and the rejection of divorce. Women must achieve marriages with many men from different exogamous groups. When a first marriage takes place within a group, the next ones, which are all secondary marriages, must never occur within the groups required for the preceding unions. Each time two groups exchange their daughters, they cannot do so again, either in primary or secondary marriage. The forced dispersion of these multiple alliances structures the constitutent groups by multiple, but different, bonds. Women, therefore, have many husbands, never divorce (thus, there is no reimbursement of bride price), and change their residence each time they go or return to one of their husbands. Young children follow their mother, then rejoin the group to which they belong, whether it be that of their father or their maternal uncle. This occurs according to the principle of reequilibration of children in marriages of sister exchange or even according to whether the father has "bought back" the child of his brother-in-law; sometimes, the children rejoin one of their mother's other husbands. In sum, these systems organize a complex structure of relations between groups, a multicirculation of women despite direct exchange, and finally a redistribution of children in a manner relatively independent from the principle of descent. It militates against the simple ideology of exchange and descent.

Other systems widely extend the matrimonial interdictions, even to the point of nonrenewable exchange of sisters, accompanied by matrimonial payments. These are the so-called semicomplex systems, in which matrimonial prohibitions are so numerous as to overflow the categories of blood relative and unilineal descent. The Samo of Burkina Faso; the Kako, Gbaya, and Beti of Cameroon; and the Minyanka of Mali, all patrilinear, enact three types of marriage prohibitions: (1) lineage interdictions, including relatives belonging to the patrilineages of an individual's four grandparents; (2) cognatic interdictions, with all cognatic blood relatives for four generations beginning with great-grandparents; and (3) interdictions against doubled alliance in all lines where close blood relatives of the same sex (for a man: father, father's brother, and brother; for a woman, mother, mother's sister,

and sister) are already married. These sanctions apparently lead to the dispersion of marriages, but within the context of communities practicing endogamy the choice of spouse comes closer to the possibilities of marriage once the interdictions cease.

Among the Samo, Françoise Héritier has proved, thanks to the use of an informative treatment of genealogies, that the circulation of women used two models at the same time, that of nonrenewed exchange of sisters and that of consanguineally perpetuated exchange up to the fifth generation, which is to say the marriage between third cousins (between great-great-grandchildren). These systems are independent of unifiliation, for one finds them among both the matrilinear Senufo and the bilinear Gagu of Côte d'Ivoire. The variations in bride price complicate marriage systems to a greater or lesser extent without transforming them radically. On the other hand, the renewal of marriage by direct exchange largely utilizes the possibilities offered by the effects of polygamy, which attributes different marriage prohibitions among half cousins and half siblings and thus permits more rapid returns.

The particularity of African marriage systems is the way in which the simplest rules of alliance are complicated by the use of bride price, polygamy, and the multiple orientation of marriages. To the "mechanical" rules of marriage and individual strategies must be added a veritable matrimonial politics.

Polygamy

Polygamy (or polygyny, inasmuch as it concerns a man's marriages) constitutes another general characteristic of African marriage. Used broadly, it varies from a limited polygamy practiced only by certain members of the community to a general norm, or even to the extended polygamy of chiefs and kings. In all cases, it is a means for the enlargement of the family and a sign of power and prestige of the head of household, while also reinforcing the productive capacity of familial groups. One consequence, from the point of view of matrimonial systems, is always the complication of models of alliance, however simple they may be, each unit being composed of groups of half-siblings whose matrimonial fate will thus be different. Another consequence is the introduction into patrilinear systems of filiation of feminine stock that differentiates and segments the masculine lines. Within the man's place of residence, matricentric households composed of each co-wife and her children constitute the point of departure of all segmentation (and of the resultant social hierarchy). Polygamy, the manifestation of masculine domination, has its other side: it imposes the feminine principle on masculine preeminence and makes it the means of social differentiation between men.

Polygamy is also a means of diversifying alliances in such a manner that if the first marriage can follow the paths indicated by rules and tradition, the others are more the result of choice and individual strategy. The models of African systems of marriage are always complex from this double point of view. By allowing individual choice, polygamy is subject to transformation and adaptation to new conditions while remaining a means of establishing prestige and power. Indirectly, it is tightly linked to divorce, the sole means for women to decide their matrimonial future. In Africa men never divorce on their own initiative, for it involves renouncing all the goods, alliances, and symbols they had invested in their union. Divorce, initiated by wives, is not always a recent phenomenon; often attested traditionally, it testifies to the capacity of women to take the initiative, and many are those who, after a traditional first marriage, make their personal choice. This feminine equivalent to masculine polygamy (polyandry remaining a rare phenomenon, and systems of secondary marriage limited) reflects upon the latter: the divorce of women destabilizes the polygamy of men whose matrimonial life follows a fluctuating course.

The matrimonial systems presented here have undergone transformations as a result of modernity; certain systems have dissolved, while others resist or adapt. The greatest changes have occurred in what one might call the complex "bride price, polygamy, divorce, and separation." The rupture between the city and the country is obvious, but often the generalized monetarization of bride price has profoundly changed its meaning, indeed has changed the entire marriage system. One may detect gerontocracies in which the old, or even the ancestors, as holders of power and goods, have trapped the women, leaving little chance to the young of gathering sufficient money to pay bride price. But on the other hand, in the areas in which there is no lack of work, it is through monetarization that the young liberate themselves from the tutelage of their ancestors by providing them compensation, the fruit of their labor. Still elsewhere, a high bride price testifies to the superior status of the woman, and socioeconomic motivations for marriage assume full importance. On the other hand—among the Zulu, for example—the monetarization of bride price has made women more dependent. These variations in the transformations undergone by bride price are linked to marriage systems in which they have occurred, testifying to their weight with respect to current changes. Polygamy and divorce follow the same type of variations.

The fall of polygamy predicted by theoreticians of modernity is only partial; indeed, the opposite can be observed in some places. The reasons for one situation or the other are sometimes directly opposed. Polygamy may be retained to increase the size of the family or abandoned to have fewer women and children in order to raise the latter in better fashion. The choice of the city dweller may depend on his standard of living. The rich find it hard to resist the prestige and power polygamy offers, especially with women of the elite, who can also be tempted by the advantages provided by such a marriage, even as a second wife. Another common solution is to have a "field woman" and a "city woman," or, among the urban elite, a wife and mistresses. The change of marriage systems in the context of modernity is inaugurated in particular by women who seek by means of divorce or separation a better matrimonial situation than that of "little wife" or mistress. Their strategies are always limited by the question of economic autonomy and attribution of children, who are rarely granted to them except in specific contexts to be found in matricentric households. The accelerating development of African cities, along with their relations with the countryside, are transforming marriage systems more and more by accentuating the individual strategies of men as well as of women at the expense of the strategies of familial groups traditionally subjected to the domination of men, whether they be father, brother, or maternal uncle. It can be asked whether, in parallel with these changes, the meaning and symbolic foundations of African marriage disappear or continue to resist. The recent realization by observers of the women's point of view has clarified women's matrimonial strategy as well as women's relative independence in their conjugal choices. But polygamy, divorce, and multiple marriage reveal, in any case, the ultimate aim of these feminine strategies, that is, to transform the final suitable marriage into a durable alliance.

BIBLIOGRAPHY

Bohannan, L. "Dahomean Marriage: A Revaluation." *Africa* 19 (1949): 273–287.

Clignet, Rémi. *Many Wives, Many Powers.* Evanston, Ill., 1970.

Comaroff, John. *The Meaning of Marriage Payments.* London, 1980.

Dupire, Marguerite. *Organisation sociale des Peuls.* Paris, 1970.

Fortes, Meyer. "Kinship and Marriage Among the Ashanti." In *African Systems of Kinship and Marriage,* edited by A. R. Radcliffe-Brown and Daryll Forde. London, 1950.

Gluckman, Max. "Kinship and Marriage among the Lozi of Northern Rhodesia and the Zulu of the Natal." In *African Systems of Kinship and Marriage,* edited by A. R. Radcliffe-Brown and Daryll Forde. London, 1950.

Goody, Jack, and Stanley Tambiah. *Bridewealth and Dowry.* Cambridge, 1973.

Héritier, Françoise, and Elisabeth Copet-Rougier, eds. *Les complexités de l'alliance.* Volume 1, *Les systèmes semi-complexes.* Paris, 1990. Volume 3, *Économie, politique et fondements symboliques (Afrique).* Paris, 1993.

Heusch, Luc de. *Why Marry Her? Society and Symbolic Structures.* New York, 1981.

Kuper, Adam. *Wives for Cattle: Bridewealth and Marriage in Southern Africa.* Boston, 1982.

Muller, Jean-Claude. *Du bon usage du sexe et du mariage: Structures matrimoniales du haut plateau nigerian.* Paris and Québec, 1982.

Ngubane, Harriet. "Marriage, Affinity, and the Ancestral Realm: Zulu Marriage in Female Perspective." In *Essays on African Marriage in Southern Africa,* edited by Eileen J. Krige and John Comaroff. Cape Town, 1981.

Obbo, C. "The Old and New in East African Elite Marriage." In *Transformation of African Marriage,* edited by D. Parkin and D. Nyamwaya. Manchester, U.K., 1987.

Richards, A. I. "Some Types of Family Structure Amongst the Central Bantu." In *African Systems of Kinship and Marriage,* edited by A. R. Radcliffe-Brown and Daryll Forde. London, 1950.

Smith, M. G. "Secondary Marriage in Northern Nigeria." *Africa* 23 (1953): 298–323.

Tardits, Claude. "Femmes à crédit." In volume 1 of *Échanges et communications: Mélanges offerts à Claude Lévi-Strauss,* compiled by Jean Pouillon and Pierre Maranda. Paris, 1970.

ELISABETH COPET-ROUGIER

See also **Kinship and Descent; Kinship and Marriage.**

MASCARENE ISLANDS. *See* **Mauritius; Réunion; Seychelles.**

MASERU. Maseru is the capital of Lesotho, the only country in the world to have all its frontiers higher than 1,000 meters above sea level. The city began in 1869 as a British police camp set up by the Moho-kare River on the western border of Lesotho to keep watch over Thaba Bosiu—Maseru's mountain fortress and the Lesotho capital which lay just to the east. A year later, the administrative capital was moved to Maseru. The initial population was dominated by the Bamolibeli and remained a fairly constant 15,000. Following Lesotho's independence in 1966 and the reforming of the South African migrant labor laws in the 1970s, many Basotho moved in, attracted by the possibilities of employment with foreign aid agencies. By 1993 the inhabitants of Maseru numbered 180,000—10 percent of the total population of Lesotho. Maseru's economy depends on the income of its migrant labor and the aid industry—arguably the biggest contributor to Maseru's growth. The main languages of Maseru are Sesotho and English.

BIBLIOGRAPHY

Ambrose, David. *Maseru: An Illustrated History.* Morija, Lesotho, 1993.

MARTHA HANNAN

MASKS AND MASQUERADES. Although masking is not universal in Africa, many societies have long and rich traditions of masquerades. In the fourteenth century Ibn Battuta, an Arab geographer, commented upon the use of articulated bird masks in the court of the Mali Empire. In 1738 Francis Moore was one of the first Europeans to give an account of an African masquerade, which he encountered in the Senegambia in west Africa. From the mid nineteenth century through the early decades of the twentieth century many travelers, missionaries, and colonial officials published descriptions of masquerades from diverse regions in Africa. Throughout the twentieth century African masks and the masquerade rituals and ceremonies within which they appear have been the focus of study and exegesis by anthropologists and others.

Throughout Africa masks take many forms and include a variety of carved wooden constructions, as well as those which are made entirely from bark, animal skins, plant fibers, and woven cloth. Masquerades may be owned collectively by communities, lineages, initiation and other voluntary associations, or by individuals. With few exceptions, women are excluded from direct participation in masquerading.

In the late twentieth century masquerades continue to be used by many groups living in west Africa, including the Dogon, Bamana, Mossi, Senufo, Mende, Dan, Yoruba, Igbo (Ibo), Ijaw, Ibibio,

Efik, Idoma, Mambila, and Bamileke. Numerous central African groups, including the Chokwe, Kuba, Luba, Hemba, Teke, and Lega, among many others, also utilize masks. By contrast, masquerades are much less significant among groups living in northern, eastern, and southern Africa, although they are performed by some Berber peoples living in Morocco, as well as by the Makonde in Tanzania and the Chewa in Malawi.

In many societies masquerades are the visible manifestation of spirits. These spirits may be ancestral or powerful bush, forest, or water spirits. Among the Yoruba of southwestern Nigeria, Egungun ritual society masquerades are embodiments of ancestral spirits. Ancestral spirits also appear as important masquerades among the Okpella and the Igala of Nigeria and among the Chokwe of Zaire. Forest and bush spirits among the Senufo and Dan of Côte d'Ivoire and the Igbo of Nigeria are made visible through the vehicle of masquerades. In Ijaw communities in Nigeria, water-spirit masquerades are performed in annual public ceremonies that are intended to honor and propitiate these powerful beings.

In a number of African societies masks were formerly used in a regulatory capacity and played a central role in the governance of the community. Masquerades were used as strategies for social control by warrior associations among the Bamileke in Cameroon and in the Cross River area in Nigeria. Among the Dan of Côte d'Ivoire and the Igala, Idoma, and certain Igbo groups in Nigeria, a masked figure sat in judgment of criminals, levied and collected fines, and presided over cases involving land disputes. Among the Bamana of Mali, the Komo men's association and its masquerade were charged with eradicating witchcraft.

Masks play central roles in chieftaincy rituals. In contemporary rural Malawi, spirit masks of the Chewa Nyau society perform at the installation of village headmen. This modern ritual, which has its origins in precolonial rituals for the installation of divine kings, conjures up images of a heroic past, but also reflects and reconfigures current political realities. In the twentieth century among the Bamileke, regulatory societies have been transformed into prestige titled societies and the distinctive beaded elephant mask has been incorporated into chieftaincy rituals. In Côte d'Ivoire among the Dan, a chief may own several old and important masks. These old masks are no longer used in performance, but are laid beside the chief in ritual contexts as a validation of his political authority. Pecto-

ral and hip masks have been a long-standing part of leadership regalia and are still worn today by the *oba* of Benin and the *attah* of Idah in Nigeria as symbols of political authority.

Masquerades are often material symbols of secret knowledge and serve as ritual separators between various segments of the community, such as men and women, initiated and noninitiated, community members and strangers. Among the Lega of Zaire, for example, different ranks within the Bwami initiation association own and use a variety of masks. Miniature wooden and ivory masks are the property of several of the highest ranks within the association. These masks might either be worn on the body or carried by members during various ceremonies, and function as mnemonic devices alluding to the esoteric knowledge that is the purview of each specific rank. Leaders of the men's Poro association in Liberia and Sierra Leone often own small miniature versions of larger-scale spirit masks to which they have titular rights. These personal masks validate a man's right to sit at Poro counsels and to participate in decision making. They also serve as a means of identification and a validation of authority for itinerant Poro leaders.

Throughout Africa masquerades play a central role in coming-of-age ceremonies. During these rituals, the separate realms of bush and village, living and dead converge. First, the novices are sequestered for a period of time outside of the village, in the bush, the domain of the spirits. During this period, the initiates are symbolically reborn as adults under the watchful eye of masked spirits. Masks are often used to orchestrate the training in esoteric knowledge, and in the closing ceremonies of initiation, spirit masks appear in public ceremonies when the young people are presented to the community as adults. Among the Chokwe, masked spirits control the boy's initiation camp and bar women from entry into the ceremonies. Among the Gola, Bassa, and Vai of Liberia and the Mende, Bullom, and Temne of Sierra Leone, the water-spirit guardian of the women's Sande association takes the form of a masquerade. The spirit presides over the initiation camp, protects young girls during their seclusion, participates in their training, and appears with them during their reentry into the community as adult women.

Death produces a dangerous rupture in the social fabric, and it is carefully managed through a variety of rituals. In the closing phase of many societies' funeral ceremonies, including those of

Dogon dancers, Mali. JASON LAURÉ/IMPACT VISUALS

the Dogon of Mali, the Mossi of Burkina Faso, the Dan of Côte d'Ivoire, and the Chewa of Malawi, masks play an important role. Among the Hemba of Zaire, the final phase of the funeral marks the end of mourning for the bereaved and the return of the village to a normal social life. In the ritual, the *so'o* mask, an allegorical figure of death, is used in two performances. The first performance emphasizes the state of disorder caused by death; the second performance restores order to the village. Among the Kuba and Kuba-related peoples of Zaire, many of the masks that play a critical role in men's initiation appear at the funerals of titled elders. Their use in performance reinforces distinctions in power between titled and nontitled men and between men and women. The masks validate the institution of title-taking and reinforce the authority invested in senior titleholders.

Masks and the performances in which they are used often embody important forms of symbolic classification and the ordering of social experience. Among the Dogon of Mali the towering vertical form of the *sirige* mask represents the multistoried family house, and the graphic motifs engraved and painted on this mask symbolize the history of generations within Dogon communities. The masker's symbolic gestures reenact fundamental episodes of the Dogon creation myth.

In several Berber communities in Morocco, masquerades are performed between the Sunni Muslim feast of sacrifice and the celebration of the New Year. In these masked rituals, characters parody and contest central values, which the Muslim feast of the sacrifice sanctifies.

In Zaire the Teke *kidamu* mask, carved in the shape of a flat disk with clearly articulated bipolar divisions, is symbolically rich. This mask type, first created around 1860, has been continually modified in the twentieth century, reflecting a history of shifting and evolving relationships between two competing segments within the Teke political organization. The mask's primary symbolism and its use in performance express the essential nature of Teke society and highlight relationships Teke have had with their neighbors over the centuries.

In Côte d'Ivoire some Dan spirit masks are defined as entertainers. In Mali, youth-association puppet masquerades, which are performed by

127

Bamana, Bozo, Somono, and Maraka troupes, are defined by the participants as play, although the content of these masquerade performances is often quite serious and explores the nature of society and people's relationship with powerful spirit entities.

Multiple masking traditions may exist parallel to one another in a single society. Moreover, every masquerade tradition has its own history, which may be marked by periodic transformations in the material repertoire (the masks and their costumes), in the context of use, and in the universe of interpretations assigned to them. Spirit masks among the Dan operate in a variety of contexts. Many are central to boys' initiation, while others act as messengers, debt collectors, adjudicators, and entertainers. Throughout its life history an individual Dan mask from any of these contexts might acquire prestige as it ages and subsequently its behavior, role, and interpretation is modified accordingly.

Among the Bamana of Mali the Chiwara men's association performs paired male and female antelope masquerades in annual rites which inaugurate the farming season. The form, iconography, and performance of these paired masquerades embody the virtues that the Bamana associate with farming. Chiwara is the mythical antelope who introduced farming to the Bamana and the pairing of the male and female mythical antelopes recreates the essential conditions for agricultural fertility symbolizing the union of the sun, the male principle, and the earth and water, the female principle. Today, in those Malian communities where the Chiwara men's association is now defunct, these same antelope masquerades are often incorporated into festivals that the community defines as entertainments. The interpretation of the masquerades in their new performance context clearly resonates with meanings emergent in the older context. However, in many multiethnic communities today these same Chiwara masquerades evoke a distinctive Bamana ethnic identity based on participants' sense of a shared history and a group investment in an agricultural life.

Masquerades have undergone repeated transformations over time and new forms and contexts of use are continually emerging in Africa. In Sierra Leone in the 1950s Ode-Lay masked associations, which were multiethnic and urban, grew up in Creole neighborhoods in Freetown as a response to disruptive social change. The inspiration for the Creole Ode-Lay associations, however, is to be found in Yoruba secret societies which were established in Sierra Leone by Yoruba immigrants after 1807. The Ode-Lay masked performances draw heavily upon Yoruba hunters' association and Egungun society rituals. Other key elements have been borrowed from Mende and Limba masking traditions. The Ode-Lay masquerades are militant and during the performances participants perform martial arts games with each other or with members of competing troupes. By the 1970s members of Sierra Leone's ruling party served as patrons for Freetown's various Ode-Lay associations and, as a way of extending their influence and consolidating their authority outside of the capital, they encouraged the establishment of Ode-Lay associations in more rural areas. Elsewhere in Mali, Zaire, Nigeria, and Côte d'Ivoire masquerades have been incorporated into the repertoire of national dance troupes and stand as valued examples of artistic and cultural patrimony. Other masquerades, like those which are still performed today at Dogon funerals, are now occasionally performed for tourists. In Mali the Chiwara antelope mask has been adopted as a national cultural symbol and is used on the masthead of *Jamana*, a Malian cultural publication. The mask is also used as an emblem for Bamako, the capital city.

BIBLIOGRAPHY

Arnoldi, Mary Jo. *Playing with Time: Art and Performance in Central Mali.* Bloomington, Ind., 1995.

Bascom, William. *The Yoruba of Southwestern Nigeria.* New York, 1969.

Bastin, Marie-Louise. "Ritual Masks of the Chokwe." *African Arts* 17, no. 4 (1984): 40ff.

Biebuyck, Daniel. *Lega Culture: Art, Initiation, and Moral Philosophy Among a Central African People.* Berkeley, 1973.

Binkley, David A. "Avatar of Power: Southern Kuba Masquerade Figures in a Funerary Context." *Africa* 57, no. 1 (1987): 75–97.

Blakely, Thomas D., and Pamela A. R. Blakely. "So'o Masks and Hemba Funerary Festival." *African Arts* 21, no. 1 (1987): 30ff.

Borgatti, Jean. "Anogiri: Okpella's Masked Festival Heralds." In *West African Masks and Cultural Systems,* edited by Sidney L. Kasfir. Tervuren, Belgium, 1988.

Dieterlen, Germaine. "Symbolisme du masque en Afrique occidentale." In *Lemasque,* from exposition held at Musée Guimet, December 1959–September 1960 (Paris, 1960): 49–50.

Dupré, Marie-Claude. "Le masque *kidumu* maître d'l'histoire tssayi." In *Art et politiques en Afrique noire/Art and Politics in Black Africa,* edited by Bogumil Jewsiewicki. Ottawa, 1989.

Fischer, Eberhard, and Hans Himmelheber. *The Arts of the Dan in West Africa.* Zurich, 1984.

Geary, Christraud. "Elephants, Ivory, and Chiefs: The Elephant and the Arts of the Cameroon Grassfields." In *Elephant: The Animal and Its Ivory in African Culture,* edited by Doran H. Ross. Los Angeles, 1992. Pp. 229–257.

Griaule, Marcel. *Masques dogons.* Paris, 1938.

Hammoudi, Abdellah. *The Victim and Its Masks: An Essay on Sacrifice and Masquerade in the Maghreb,* translated by Paula Wissing. Chicago, 1993.

Harley, George W. *Masks as Agents of Social Control in Northeast Liberia.* Cambridge, Mass., 1950.

Horton, Robin. "The Kalabari Ekine Society: A Borderland of Religion and Art." *Africa* 33, no. 2 (1963): 94–114.

Ibn Battuta. *Travels in Asia and Africa, 1325–1354,* translated and selected by H. A. R. Gibb. Repr. London, 1984.

Kasfir, Sidney L. "Introduction: Masquerading as a Cultural System." In *West African Masks and Cultural Systems,* edited by Sidney Kasfir. Tervuren, Belgium, 1988.

Kaspin, Deborah. "Chewa Visions and Revision of Power: Transformations of the Nyau Dance in Central Malawi." In *Modernity and its Malcontents: Ritual and Power in Postcolonial Africa,* edited by Jean Comaroff and John Comaroff. Chicago, 1993.

Moore, Francis. *Travels into the Inland Parts of Africa.* London, 1738.

Nunley, John W. *Moving with the Face of the Devil: Art and Politics in Urban West Africa.* Urbana, Ill., 1987.

Sieber, Roy. *Sculpture of Northern Nigeria.* New York, 1961.

Siegmann, William. *Rock of the Ancestors: Liberian Art and Material Culture from the Collections of the Africana Museum.* Suacoco, Liberia, 1977.

Steiner, Christopher, and Jane Guyer, eds. *To Dance the Spirit: Masks of Liberia.* Cambridge, 1986.

Zahan, Dominique. *Sociétés d'initiation bambara, le n'domo, le koré.* Paris, 1960.

———. *Antilopes du soleil: Arts et rites agraires d'Afrique noire.* Vienna, 1980.

MARY JO ARNOLDI

See also **Dance; Festivals, Carnivals, and Rituals of Rebellion; Secret Societies; Symbolism.**

MASSAWA. For centuries the port city of Massawa (Mits'iwa, Mesewa), on the west coast of the Red Sea, has been of historical importance to the Horn of Africa. To merchants, adventurers, explorers, and invading armies, Massawa served as the gateway to ancient Abyssinia, to modern Ethiopia, and, since 1993, to the new nation of Eritrea. After the Suez Canal opened in 1869, the Red Sea became a great highway for ambitious foreign powers seeking to annex Ethiopia and invade the interior by occupying Massawa. The city was under Turkish and occasionally nominal Egyptian rule from the sixteenth century until 1885, when Italian troops landed at Massawa and moved inland, finally linking the interior with the external world of trade and commerce. Though defeated at the battle of Adowa in 1896, Italy retained control over the port city through its colony of Eritrea, which was annexed by Ethiopia in 1952. With the independence of Eritrea, Massawa's governing power changed again. Its economic importance to trade and commerce in the Horn of Africa remains unchanged.

BIBLIOGRAPHY

Pankhurst, Richard. *Economic History of Ethiopia, 1800–1935.* Addis Ababa, 1968.

Talhami, Ghada Hashem. *Suakin and Massawa under Egyptian Rule, 1865–1895.* Washington, D.C., 1979.

WILLIAM A. SHACK

MAT MAKING. *See* **Basketry and Mat Making.**

MATHEMATICS. *See* **Number Systems.**

MATRIARCHY and MATRILINY. *See* **Kinship and Descent; Kinship and Marriage; Marriage Systems.**

MAU MAU. Of an unknown and, to date, an unexplained origin, the term "Mau Mau" is part of a myth that shrouds an intricate part of Kenyan history. "Mau Mau" is variously used, first, to refer to a complex anticolonial, mainly agrarian, guerrilla liberation movement in Kenya during the period 1952–1956. It also refers to the forest guerrillas and civilian supporters of Mau Mau, as well as to the period from 1952 to 1960 when Britain placed Kenya, then a British colony, under martial law and emergency regulations as it implemented military, social, economic, and constitutional counterinsurgency measures. Given currency and international infamy by the British colonial government, "Mau Mau"—and its political, economic, sociocultural, and religious causes and effects—continues to elicit varying interpretations.

From the very beginning, the Kenyan freedom fighters rejected the term "Mau Mau" and referred to the movement by various other names, including "Kiama Kia Muingi" ("the community's party"); "Muhimu," Swahili for "important"; "Kenya Land Freedom Army"; the "African government"; and "the KCA," in reference to the proscribed Kikuyu Central Association (KCA). (An extra-provincial political party, the KCA was established in 1924 among the Gikuyu people in their Central Province homelands and in diaspora in the White Highlands, Nairobi, Nakuru, and Tanganyika. It was a constitutionalist organization advocating security of land tenure, political representation, better wages and working conditions, and social services for Africans and was proscribed in 1940 for fear that it might ally with the enemy during World War II.) Increasingly, however, the freedom fighters referred to themselves as the "Kenya Land and Freedom Army." This name was in keeping with their two prime objectives: the first, to recover the "stolen" White Highlands (covering approximately 7.5 million acres of land in the Rift Valley alienated for European commercial cropping and livestock farming, and comprising 50 percent of the arable land, or 20 percent of the most prime land, in Kenya); the second, to attain the independence of the entire country from British colonialism.

"Mau Mau" was in use as early as 1947; by 1949 the colonial government had publicly associated the term with a clandestine movement. The British attributed to Mau Mau the sporadic but escalating acts of intimidation and violence that were evident among the Gikuyu on their reservations in the Kiambu, Nyeri, and Muranga districts and also those Gikuyu on European settler plantations in the Rift Valley and in urban centers, especially Nakuru, the settler "capital," and Nairobi, the colony's actual capital. The British also associated the movement with the administration of secret oaths that bound their partakers to a pact against the colonial government. In 1950 the government banned Mau Mau. However, neither the movement nor the violence—directed against those, both African and European, who were generally perceived to be hostile to Mau Mau—abated. In fact, the period immediately after the banning of Mau Mau was followed by an intensification of oathing among the Gikuyu in their three reservations and in diaspora. The oath, hitherto a cultural tool of selective inclusion in solidarity with Mau Mau, was now administered indiscriminately to adults and children, binding them in opposition to the colonial government. By 1952, the oath of unity was superseded by the Batuni platoon oath, which anticipated a military confrontation between those who partook in it and the colonial state.

The assassination of Senior Chief Waruhiu, a key government supporter, on 7 October 1952 was the last straw. At that point the colonial government considered it expedient to declare a state of emergency and institute martial law—and justify doing so as an attempt to restore "law and order." The declaration of emergency was preceded by the mass arrest of over 150 key African political and trade union leaders, which prematurely catapulted the liberation movement into the "public" arena and also into the forest domain. After 20 October 1952 the liberation struggle became an open secret, covert in its operations, yet openly discussed, condemned, and pursued by the colonial government among others.

Intensive government surveillance and interrogation led to the imprisonment and detention of thousands of Africans, mostly from the Gikuyu ethnic group, which was perceived to be at the core of the rebellion. In fact, the architects and key supporters of Mau Mau were members of the Gikuyu, the most politically conscious ethnic group in Kenya. There were also a small number of Mau Mau supporters in the Embu, Meru, and Maasai ethnic groups. The level and intensity of support that Mau Mau received varied from region to region: it was a fractured liberation movement. Mau Mau was composed of peasants, urban workers, the unemployed, squatter laborers, World War II veterans, and trade unionists. A negligible number of its supporters were educated. Approximately 5 percent of the freedom fighters were female.

The lifeline of the movement consisted of "civilian" noncombatants who provided diverse material resources, including food, medicine, and ammunition, and intelligence reports. There were male, female, and juvenile noncombatants. Support for Mau Mau was strongest in the Muranga (Fort Hall) and Nyeri Gikuyu reserves and also in the White Highlands among Gikuyu squatter laborers. Kiambu, Nairobi's lucrative kitchen garden and labor reservoir, gave considerably less support to Mau Mau. Urban guerrillas largely operated from Nairobi and Nakuru.

Under the declaration of emergency, thousands of Gikuyu were repatriated from the White Highlands and urban centers to the already overcrowded Gikuyu reservations where conditions were generally difficult, and they were received quite coldly. Rather than succumb to this indignity and suffering, some of the Gikuyu men fled to the Mount Kenya Forest and the Nyandarua range, which border parts of Gikuyu homelands. Here they regrouped, embarked on military training, and waged sporadic guerrilla attacks against colonial installations, including police stations, guard posts, European settler homesteads and livestock in the White Highlands, African loyalists in colonial employ, and those Gikuyu in the reservations who were suspected of anti–Mau Mau activities and sentiments.

The outbreak of the guerrilla war was the culmination of a long period in which Africans had made many frustrated efforts to remedy the extensive agrarian, social, and political grievances that had reduced them to second-class citizens in their own country. The establishment of a European settler economy beginning in the first decade of the twentieth century ultimately alienated 7.5 million acres of land for a mere 4,000 or so European farms. The largest quantity of land was excised from Maasai territory. The Kipsigis, Luyia, Nandi, and Gikuyu also lost land.

Previously, up to the late 1930s, on the pretext of possible infection, Africans were not allowed to grow high-income crops, including coffee and tea, or keep high-grade livestock. These were both restricted to European settlers. The new need to raise money to pay taxes and buy various goods and services—for example, schooling and medical care—resulted in extensive male labor migrancy. The migrants became, among others, agricultural, dock, railway, and junior civil service workers. Consequently the bulk of the local agricultural labor fell on women. Their productive and reproductive labors underwrote the responsibilities of the colonial government. At work, Africans received meager "single" wages that could barely support one worker, not his family. Most occupied the lowest rungs of the civil service, were paid much lower wages than Europeans, got no pensions, and inhabited squalid urban houses. Discontent among Africans was rampant.

The takeover of land entailed the massive transfer, or concentration, or both, of other vital resources and services to the European settler sector; these included labor and agricultural, veterinary, and social services. Thus was created a society highly stratified in terms of race and writhing with the tensions of inequality, which culminated, eventually, in the Mau Mau uprising.

Although they lost less land than other Kenyan ethnic groups, those Gikuyu who occupied land contiguous with the initial European settlements were adversely affected by the appropriations. Hemmed in by new colonial boundaries, the Gikuyu found themselves on the frontier of colonial conflicts and contradictions. Overnight, hundreds of Gikuyu were transformed from landowners to landless squatters. By 1945 there were up to a quarter of a million squatters on settler-owned land.

Mau Mau was thus fueled by legitimate grievances that had been variously articulated by previous political associations. Adding to the grievances was lack of political representation in the Legislative Council, which first met in 1907. Up to 1944, Africans were represented in the council unofficially by Europeans, including European missionaries. Africans created alternative political and welfare institutions such as the East African Association, established in 1919; the Kavirondo Tax-Payers and Welfare Association of 1923; the Kikuyu Central Association (KCA) of 1924; the Kavirondo Central Association of the 1920s; the Taita Hills Association and the Akamba People's Party in 1938; and the Kenya African Union (KAU) of 1944. These organizations were earlier attempts to mediate extensive African grievances in a constitutional, conciliatory, and hence not so confrontational manner.

After being banned in 1940 on the eve of World War II, the KCA went underground, becoming more secretive and militant. This radicalization was equally evident in the KAU. Both parties secretly recruited members through oaths. At the same time the trade union movement also became increasingly radical. In 1947, 1948, 1950, and 1952 there were numerous strikes in different parts of Kenya and in diverse sectors of the economy. The sense of militancy and urgency that developed, especially among younger Kenyans, ultimately was channeled into Mau Mau.

Mau Mau represents a critical turning point in the African political struggle against the colonial regime in Kenya. It was a mosaic of diverse concerns, including the recovery of alienated land, the redress of lack of political representation, betterment of socioeconomic conditions (wages, living conditions, and social services), and political independence, with the major motivations recovery of the "stolen lands" and the achievement of independence. For this reason some scholars have concluded that, despite its overwhelmingly Gikuyu ethnic composition, Mau Mau was the expression of an African nationalism. Put differently, the argument goes, Mau Mau was a case of ethnicity merely serving nationalist concerns. From this perspective, the chief objectives of the movement are more important than its ethnic composition. Other scholars have portrayed Mau Mau as an ethnic movement devoid of any nationalist objectives. These scholars point not only to the ethnic membership of the movement but also to the Gikuyu format of the oaths, prayers, and songs as evidence that Mau Mau was exclusive and not inclusive. Former freedom fighters counter this argument by claiming that the Gikuyu dominated the movement only during a preliminary stage and that it had been hoped, before the British closed in on Mau Mau, that other ethnic groups and their prayer forms, and so on, would also be incorporated into the movement.

The colonial government saw no raison d'être for Mau Mau. It did not acknowledge the economic, social, or political grievances of the African community. A 1960 study commissioned and endorsed by the colonial government concluded that Mau Mau was a mental illness, a psychological breakdown of the primitive Gikuyu caused by their inability to cope with the rapid pace of change introduced by colonialism. The government portrayed Mau Mau as a possibly communistic rebellion and as an atavistic and barbaric organization that tried to coerce its members into resuming the practices of a dark and bestial past. Mau Mau killings and brutal oaths were cited as obvious evidence of dementia and retrogression. At the same time, British counterinsurgency to Mau Mau displayed its own chilling forms of brutality as a warning to prospective or actual supporters of the movement.

The struggle created strife and division between family members, between the rich and poor, and between members of the Gikuyu ethnic group. Mau Mau increasingly superseded conventional domestic arrangements, including the traditional patriarchal power structure; it demanded priority and total loyalty. Among those Gikuyu who opposed Mau Mau were African loyalists in colonial pay and Christians who, in keeping with missionary teaching, saw the movement as a force of darkness versus the Christian force of light. Mau Mau has been termed a civil war between factions of the Gikuyu ethnic group. However, though there were divisions among the Gikuyu, they were not always so neat as that. It was not unusual for Gikuyu individuals to belong to the loyalist troops while secretly supporting the movement. This suggests how complex Mau Mau was. Any attempt to compartmentalize the mental geography of the movement is a treacherous undertaking.

Mau Mau ideology advocated and anticipated the eradication of racist and discriminatory policies in Kenya. Mau Mau espoused the individualist ac-

cumulation of wealth in a capitalist economy; it did not advocate a socialist system based on the nationalization of the key resources of the land. The leaders of Mau Mau did not have a clear sense of exactly which socioeconomic model they wanted to adopt once Kenya attained independence. However, the idea that land should be redistributed among the freedom fighters and other landless people was widely embraced throughout the movement. The socioeconomic changes anticipated by Mau Mau were monumental. But powerful opposition from the colonial government forced the movement to limit its military efforts to a series of fragmented attacks around the country, which precluded its achieving a true revolution.

Pursuing a strategy of overkill, Britain adopted a military solution to a political problem, and Mau Mau was defeated by 1956. The war left at least twelve thousand Africans and about one hundred white people dead. Notwithstanding its military defeat, Mau Mau shocked Britain into recasting its role in Kenya. Constitutional and economic reforms ultimately ushered in African majority rule in 1963 and, with it, the intricate and controversial Africanization of the White Highlands.

BIBLIOGRAPHY

Barnett, Donald L., and Karari Njama. *Mau Mau from Within: Autobiography and Analysis of Kenya's Peasant Revolt.* New York, 1966.

Berman, Bruce, and John Lonsdale. *Unhappy Valley: Conflict in Kenya and Africa.* London, 1992.

Edgerton, Robert. *Mau Mau: An African Crucible.* New York, 1989.

Furedi, Frank. *The Mau Mau War in Perspective.* London, 1989.

Kanogo, Tabitha. *Squatters and the Roots of Mau Mau, 1905–63.* London, 1987.

Maloba, O. Wunyabari. *Mau Mau and Kenya: An Analysis of a Peasant Revolt.* Bloomington, Ind., 1993.

Throup, David. *Economic and Social Origins of Mau Mau, 1945–53.* London, 1988.

TABITHA KANOGO

See also **Colonial Policies and Practice; Gikuyu; Independence Movements; Maasai.**

MAURITANIA

OVERVIEW

Mauritania, on the continent's Atlantic coast, stretches from the Senegal River northward to Morocco and includes about one-third of the Sahara

Desert. Located at the far west of the belt of states that divide arabophone North Africa from sub-Saharan Africa, it shares many of the ethnic tensions and ecological crises common to states along that divide. The northern frontiers encircle the south and west of the Saharan Democratic Republic and form part of Algeria's southwestern boundary. The north shares with the territory of Western Sahara a region of extreme southern Mediterranean climatic patterns. Historically, the area has provided winter pasturage. It also includes the commercial entrepôts of Shinqit/Chianguetti and Wadan/Ouadene and the salt mines at Idjil, which once attracted caravans passing from Morocco to the Western Sudan. Mauritania's eastern frontier with Mali roughly demarcates the Hodh, a region known historically for the caravan staging posts of Tishit, Walata, and Nema, still vibrant economic centers in the late nineteenth century.

Up to 80 percent of Mauritania's population today, as during the past two hundred years, lives in a triangle in the extreme southwest of the country demarcated by the capital, Nouakchott, in the north, the Atlantic coast on the west, and the Senegal River in the south as far east as Kaedi. It is in this area, the administrative regions of Trarza and Brakna, that sufficient spring and fall rainfall traditionally supported nomadic economies based on animal husbandry and raiding. This nomadic population was interdependent with sedentary, riverain agriculturalists farming along the Senegal River. There, during the nineteenth century, the sale of gum arabic harvested in the region provided its first major commercial contact with overseas merchants.

The impact of colonial rule was relatively benign in this territory, which was characterized as the "vide" by administrators. With their administrative capital at St. Louis (in what is now Senegal), the French exerted minimal effort to integrate the territory into their empire once the region was "pacified" and no longer harbored threats to Morocco's southern frontiers.

The usual indices of modernization in Mauritania were exceedingly modest at independence: the country had but a handful of university graduates, a hastily created capital consisting of a few buildings, a few kilometers of paved road, no port facilities, and three *lycées* with fewer than a thousand students.

At independence in 1960, a major effort was launched to develop an industrial sector through the exploitation of rich iron ore deposits, some four hundred miles inland from the northern port city of Nouadhibou, as well as copper deposits at Akjoujt. Revenues from these ventures largely subvented the government's costs during the first decade of the republic. Falling world prices led to the abandonment of copper production in 1976. By the late 1980s iron ore exports had dropped to 40 percent of the government's export earnings and, effectively, only serviced interest on the country's mounting debt. Periodic announcements of oil exploration off the southwest coast have raised hopes for additional mineral revenues for the country.

The traditional livestock economy was largely erased during the sahelian drought years of the 1970s and 1980s, resulting in the sedentarization of 80 to 90 percent of the former nomadic population. Settlements in the southwest and along the "Road of Hope" (the Trans-Mauritanian Highway), built in the 1970s and stretching eastward from Nouakchott to Nema, absorbed much of this population. Nouakchott grew from about 40,000 in the early 1970s to well over 300,000 (some estimates place the population closer to 500,000) by the late 1980s. Villages elsewhere in the country typically grew by a factor of ten during that period. At the same time agricultural production along the river was severely affected by the same drought conditions and, by 1973, fell to one quarter of domestic food needs, where it remained for most of the following two decades.

Despite efforts to expand agricultural production by the Organisation pour la Mise en Valeur de Fleuve Sénégal (OMVS; made up of Mauritania, Senegal, and Mali) Mauritania has been dependent upon external food aid to meet minimal requirements since the mid-1970s. By the early 1980s foreign assistance (about one-third from the Arab world and one-fifth each from Western countries and multilateral agencies) had become a fundamental part of the Mauritanian economy. Since 1983 fishing off the Atlantic coast, among the richest world fisheries, has accounted for the country's main foreign exchange earnings, although external experts worry about the consequences of overharvesting in this relatively uncontrolled sector.

The first elected government, led by Mokhtar Ould Daddah, was unseated by a military coup in 1978, which established the Comité Militaire de Salut National (CMSN, the Military Committee for National Salvation) at a time when the country's daunting domestic economic problems were being compounded by heavy military spending in the

133

République Islamique de Mauritanie (Islamic Republic of Mauritania)

Population: 2,270,000 (1995 est.)

Area: 1,030,700 sq. km (397,953 sq. mi.)

Official languages: Arabic and French

Languages: Arabic, French, Poular, Soninke, Wolof

National currency: Ouguiya

Principal religions: Muslim, nearly 100%

Capital: Nouakchott (estimated pop. 300,000/500,000 in 1988)

Other urban centers: Atar, Zouérate, Kaédi, Nouadhibou, Rosso

Annual rainfall: varies from less than 500 mm (20 in.) in south to less than 100 mm (4 in.) in desert northern half of the country

Principal geographic features:

> *Plateaus:*   Adrar, Tagant, Assaba
>
> *Rivers:*   Senegal, other small seasonal rivers
>
> *Lakes:*   R'Kiz, d'Aleg (seasonal)

Economy:

> *GNP per capita:*   US$460 (1995)

Principal products and exports:

> *Agricultural:*   fish, livestock, gum arabic, rice, millet, sorghum
>
> *Manufacturing:*   petroleum refining, plastics and chemicals production, food and beverage processing, paper manufacturing, textiles, smelting
>
> *Mining:*   iron ore, some gold, gypsum

Government: Independence from France, 1960. Republic proclaimed in 1961. Constitution, 1961. New constitution adopted in 1991. Multiparty Arab and African Islamic republic. President is elected for a renewable 6-year term. Bicameral Assemblée Nationale, with 56-member senate and 79-member lower house, elected for 5-year terms. President appoints prime minister and Council of Ministers. For purposes of local government there are 45 municipal districts and 164 rural districts.

Heads of state since independence:

> 1960–1961: Prime Minister Mokhtar Ould Daddah
>
> 1961–1978: President Mokhtar Ould Daddah
>
> 1978–1979: Lieutenant Colonel Mustapha Ould Mohammed Salek, chairman of the Comité Militaire de Redressement National (CMRN)
>
> 1979: Lieutenant Colonel Mustapha Ould Mohammed Salek, chairman of the Comité Militaire Salut National (CMSN)
>
> 1979–1980: Prime Minister Lieutenant Colonel Mohammed Khouna Ould Haidalla
>
> 1979–1980: Lieutenant Colonel Mohammed Mahmoud Ould Louly, chairman of the CMSN
>
> 1980–1984: Lieutenant Colonel Mohammed Khouna Ould Haidalla, chairman of the CMSN
>
> 1984–: President Colonel Maaouya Ould Sid'Ahmed Taya

Armed forces:

> *Army:*   15,000
>
> *Navy:*   500
>
> *Air force:*   150
>
> *Paramilitary:*   6,000

Transportation:

> *Rail:*   704 km (436 mi.)
>
> *Ports:*   Port Autonome at Nouadhibou, Port de l'Amité at Nouakchott, Bogue, Kaédi, Rosso
>
> *Roads:*   6,490 km (4,024 mi.), 24% paved
>
> *Airline:*   Served by Air Afrique
>
> *Airports:*   International facilities at Nouakchott and Nouadhibou; 23 smaller airports and airstrips throughout the country

Media: Main periodicals: *Ach-Chaab, Al-Bayane, Le Calame, Eveil-Hebdo, Mauritanie Demain, Le Peuple, Journal Officiel.* State-controlled radio and television provide limited service. 2 radio stations, with broadcasts in Arabic, French, Soninke, Tukulor, and Wolof.

Literacy and education:

> *Total literacy rate:*   37.7% (1995 est.). In the past enrollment levels were low. At present about one-third of school age children receive formal education. Postsecondary education is provided by Université de Nouakchott, Institut National des Hautes Études Islamiques, École Nationale d'Administration, Institut Supérieur Scientifique.

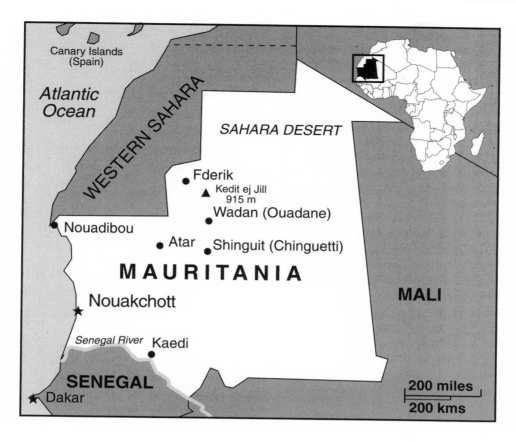

Western Saharan war. By 1979 the CMSN had disengaged itself from the Western Saharan conflict, although politics connected with that arena in the north and long-standing tensions between the Moorish cultural majority and black ethnic groups in the south have led to subsequent reshuffles in the CMSN leadership.

Col. Maaouya Ould Sid'Ahmed Taya was named to the presidency in 1984 and has aggressively sought to contain the influence of a Dakar-based African Liberation Front established in 1983 (and its successors) seeking to unite the black Mauritanian population. A coup attempt in 1987 led to the expulsion of a large number of Tukulor officers and enlisted men from the army, and in the following year reputed Ba'athist opponents of the government were put on trial. Despite these difficulties, the Ould Taya government kept to its plans for elected municipal councils in 1986 and continued gradually toward a return to a degree of civilian rule, albeit with ultimate CMSN authority.

Economic crises in both Senegal and Mauritania, coupled with historic animosity between the riverain population and the Moors triggered a confrontation between these two states in 1989, which led to the expatriation of tens of thousands of the others' nationals from each country and heightened tension along Mauritania's southern frontier.

The 1995 estimated 2.27 million population of Mauritania is divided between arabophone speakers of the Hassaniyya dialect, formerly attached to the nomadic economy, and agriculturalists living along the Senegal River dominated by Halpular and Sarkole-speakers, although Wolof is also a lingua franca for many southwestern riverain peoples. The politically dominant arabophone elites are very self-conscious of their cultural allegiance to the Arab world. Subordinate black African populations include ethnic groups living in the extreme south, lower-class Hassaniyya-speakers (former slaves) who were originally drawn from these southern groups, and immigrants from elsewhere in sub-Saharan Africa whose skilled labor has played a major role in the urban and mining economies. Since independence domestic politics, like external relations, has been very much infused with these divisions.

Mauritania's first president, Mokhtar Ould Daddah (1960–1978), sought to achieve a delicate balance between the Moorish, arabophone political majority and the nascent republic's heavy dependence upon relatively larger numbers of Western-educated, southern (and francophone) African populations. Dating from the 1978 coup the military leadership has steadily privileged the Arabic-speaking population in its domestic and foreign policies. Changes in language policy in the schools (favoring Arabic over French), civil service hires and military promotions, and national media policy have all contributed to a heightened Arab self-definition in Mauritania at the expense of riverain populations and urban, black African technocrats and laborers. The founding (and to date the only unifying) religious ideology that led to the creation of an Islamic Republic of Mauritania has proved of limited value in bridging the cultural, social, and economic divides that have plagued the country since independence.

BIBLIOGRAPHY

Chassey, Francis de. *Mauritanie, 1900–1975: Facteurs économiques, politiques, idéologiques et éducatifs dans la formation d'une société sous-dévelopée.* Paris, 1984.

Gerteiny, Alfred G. *Mauritania.* New York, 1967.

"Mauritania." In *Africa Contemporary Record: Annual Survey and Documents.* 22 vols. New York, 1968–.

Pazzanita, Anthony G. *Historical Dictionary of Mauritania.* 2d ed. Lanham, Md., 1996.

Stewart, Charles C. "North-South Dialectic in Mauritania: An Update." *Maghreb Review* 11, no. 1 (1986): 40–45.

———. "Une interpretation du conflit Mauritano-Sénégalais." In *Mauritanie, entre arabite et africanité.* La Calade, France, 1990.

CHARLES C. STEWART

See also **Arab World, African Relations with; Colonial Policies and Practice; Northern Africa.**

POLITICAL HISTORY

Mokhtar Ould Daddah and the War for the Western Sahara

If many of Mauritania's economic difficulties stem from the droughts of the 1970s and 1980s, many also derive from a critical decision made by the country's first president, Mokhtar Ould Daddah, in November 1975. It was then that Ould Daddah signed the Madrid Agreement, whereby Morocco and Mauritania each laid claim to different portions of the former Spanish colony the Western Sahara—and so provoked a highly destructive guerrilla war with the Saharawi organization the Frente Popular para la Liberación de Saguia el-Hamra y Río de Oro (the Western Sahara), commonly known as the Frente Polisario, or Polisario Front. Armed by Algeria, the Polisario Front waged a devastating campaign all across Mauritania during 1976–1977, even shelling the capital twice. Many of its attacks, focused on the iron ore mines and on the railroads, were designed to cripple the Mauritanian economy—and indeed they were entirely successful in doing so.

Ould Daddah's signing of the Madrid Agreement marked a critical turning point in the history of Mauritania and also in his own political fortunes—it eventually led to his fall from power—but other policies Ould Daddah embraced also had fateful consequences for the republic. One was to frustrate the potential development of multiparty democracy in Mauritania in the years just after independence. By 1964, all preexisting political parties had been subsumed into one official organization, the Parti du Peuple Mauritanien (PPM); the following year the constitution was amended to make all other parties illegal. Other critical policies emerged from Ould Daddah's desire to reorient the country, both politically and culturally, in favor of its Arab majority population: he started a process generally known as "Arabization." In 1966, for example, Ould Daddah decreed that all education beyond the primary level be conducted exclusively in Hassaniya Arabic. He initiated many changes in foreign policy to cultivate the member states of the Arab League and distance Mauritania not only from France but also from other countries in sub-Saharan Africa. By 1973 Mauritania itself had become a member of the Arab League.

Mauritania established a defense pact with Morocco in the spring of 1977, when it was desperately embattled with the Polisario Front. But the combined efforts of the Mauritanian army and Moroccan troops, supported by advisers and matériel from France, were insufficient to turn the tide of the war. It was largely in frustration with continual defeat that the Mauritanian officer corps organized a rebellion and overthrew Ould Daddah on 10 July 1978. The new military government—the Comité Militaire de Redressement National (CMRN), which was soon reformed as the Comité Militaire de Salut National (CMSN)—promised an eventual return to multiparty democracy. But neither the CMRN nor the CMSN had any particular political agenda beyond a single, driving goal: to disengage the country from a ruinous war. The coup, in fact, produced some immediate results: the Polisario Front welcomed the new regime and declared a cease-fire within Mauritania. Peace, however, was not fully established until 5 August 1979, when the CMSN and the Polisario Front signed a formal treaty in Algiers. In the Algiers Agreement Mauritania utterly renounced its claim to territory in the Western Sahara.

CMSN Governments: Ould Haidalla and Ould Taya

Crucial to the successful negotiation of the Algiers Agreement was the new Mauritanian prime minister, Lieutenant Colonel Mohammed Khouna Ould Haidalla, who was himself (like many Mauritanians) a Saharawi. In January 1980, Ould Haidalla assumed total dominance of the CMSN as both head of government and head of state and began to address the country's most pressing problems, including the economic crisis engendered by the war and growing resistance by black Mauritanians to the country's ongoing Arabization. Slavery was outlawed in Mauritania during Ould Haidalla's term in office (on 15 July 1980), but generally his government was distinguished for its actions to restrict the freedom of most Mauritanians: it enforced the harsher provisions of the Islamic legal code, the *Shari'a*, and refused to tolerate political dissent. (Dissenters were both harassed and imprisoned.) A brief experiment in civilian government under Ould Haidalla's ultimate authority, begun on 15 December 1980, ended less than five months later with the resumption of full control by the military. While Ould Haidalla remained in power, an eventual return to multiparty democracy seemed only more and more unlikely.

But Ould Haidalla alienated the CMSN by undertaking a variety of independent and allegedly self-serving initiatives. (He was ultimately charged with an abuse of power for improper dealings with the fishing industry, from which he and his family profited inordinately.) Chief among the sources of tension was Ould Haidalla's close relationship with the Polisario Front and his decision to recognized the SADR government-in-exile in February 1984, which put Mauritania at odds with Morocco. On 12 December 1984, while Ould Haidalla was out of the country, the CMSN quietly removed him from office and replaced him with the leader of this bloodless coup: Colonel Maaouiya Ould Sid'Ahmed Taya.

Ould Taya began at once to implement both political and economic reforms, the latter designed in consultation with the IMF and the World Bank. He released most political dissenters from prison,

granted amnesty to many who had gone into exile, relaxed the implementation of the *Shari'a*, and began a campaign to root out government corruption. (His government formally recognized the SADR but distanced itself from the activities of the Polisario Front.) However in 1986, when civil servants and employees of some of the parastatals protested the imposition of austerity measures, Ould Taya began to reverse his course. He did permit municipal elections to take place in December 1986 and indicated an intention to gradually prepare for a return to elected national government. But the second half of the 1980s in Mauritania was a period of increasing political unrest, and Ould Taya responded by clamping down on groups he perceived to be a threat to his regime. As he did so, Amnesty International and other organizations repeatedly charged his government with human rights violations, including the torture and murder of political prisoners.

Domestic and International Upheavals: 1986–1990

Chief among the groups in conflict with Ould Taya was the Dakar-based Forces de Libération Africaine de Mauritanie (FLAM), established in 1983, which together with newer groups has sought to unite black Mauritanians in a struggle *for* equal rights with the Moors and *against* the Arabization of the country. FLAM's first provocative act in Mauritania was to issue a statement in April 1986, "The Manifesto of the Oppressed Black Mauritanian," which demanded an end to discrimination in education and employment. It also challenged the official claim that blacks constitute a minority of the Mauritanian population. Subsequently thirty prominent black activists were arrested on the charge of subverting "national unity," a development which only served to intensify the building racial tensions in the country. Matters worsened in October 1987, when the government charged fifty-one black Mauritanians (all members of the Tukulor ethnic group, some members of the army officer corps or the presidential guard) with conspiring to effect a coup d'état. Perhaps as many as five hundred Tukulor officers and enlisted men were also simply expelled from the armed forces.

In April 1989 racial conflicts in Mauritania spilled over into an international crisis with Senegal. Trouble began with a disagreement between Senegalese farmers and Mauritanian herdsman over grazing rights in the Senegal River Valley. After Mauritanian solders allegedly shot and killed two of the farmers, rioting erupted first in Dakar, where

Senegalese attacked resident Mauritanians, their homes, and their shops, and then in Nouakchott and Nouadhibou, where Mauritanians retaliated against resident Senegalese. Accounts of the numbers killed in the rioting that took place in Mauritania vary considerably: two hundred to four hundred or more may have been killed; fifty to sixty were apparently killed in Senegal. Tens of thousands of people fled each country, aided by government-sponsored airlifts. The Ould Taya regime evidently took advantage of the crisis not only to repatriate Senegalese but also to force black Mauritanians out of the country. More than 240,000 Mauritanians left the country one way or the other, most ending up in refugee camps in Senegal; approximately 40,000 went into Mali. Meanwhile diplomatic relations between Senegal and Mauritania grew increasingly hostile; they were severed in August 1989. During 1989–1990 the two countries verged on a state of war.

If racial tensions within Mauritania contributed substantially to the country's conflict with Senegal, the reverse, of course, is also true. The forced expulsion of black Mauritanians, particularly, spurred FLAM to increase its political activity, especially in the Senegal River Valley. On 1 May 1990, a new group of black activists, Front Uni pour la Résistance Armée en Mauritanie (FURAM), announced that it would pursue an armed struggle against the government. One week later FLAM declared that it, too, had decided to engage in armed resistance. At the end of 1990 the government alleged that black Mauritanians worked in concert with Senegal on a plan for a coup in November.

Earlier that same year Mauritania became embroiled in two other international crises. The first was the Tuareg rebellion in Mali. The outbreak of civil war propelled thousands of Tuareg refugees into Mauritania, among other countries; Malian troops followed in pursuit of Tuareg guerillas, who they claimed had launched attacks from inside Mauritania. The second crisis followed from the Iraqi invasion of Kuwait.

The Persian Gulf War; Multiparty Democracy

When Saddam Hussein launched the invasion of Kuwait on 2 August 1990, one of the few countries from whom he got support was Mauritania, which thus alienated many of its Arab allies. Mauritania had only recently developed close ties with Iraq, thanks primarily to the efforts of Mauritanian members of the Damascus-based Arab Ba'ath Socialist Party (ABSP). The Mauritanian chapter of the ABSP, founded in 1979 or 1980, had largely been at odds with the government through the 1980s. In October 1982 eleven ABSP members were convicted of plotting to overthrow the government, then headed by Ould Haidalla Ba'athists were arrested under Ould Taya, too, in September 1987 (just before the mass arrests of the Tukulor) and again in July 1988; they were charged with a variety of crimes, among them, acting as Iraqi spies. However, shortly thereafter, Ba'athists—who are all Moors—were able to take advantage of the developing racial crisis in Mauritania to ingratiate themselves into positions of influence. Within months of the 1988 arrests, the status of Mauritanian Ba'athists was transformed, and Mauritania was receiving economic aid as well as military equipment and advisers from Iraq.

But the ABSP and Iraq itself lost ground in Mauritania nearly as quickly as they had gained it: just as soon it became quite clear that Iraq was badly losing the Persian Gulf War. During 1991–1995 the Ba'athists had little part in Mauritanian politics; they did not participate in the multiparty elections that were held in 1992. Ould Taya—yielding finally to pressures from outside as well as inside Mauritania—announced in 1991 that he would permit preparations for those elections to go forward. A new constitution, approved by referendum on 12 July 1991, provided for a National Assembly and a Senate, as well as a president, all to be elected by universal suffrage. Few restrictions were placed on the formation of political parties, the one major exception being that Islamic parties were outlawed. The principal contestants in the 1992 elections were the Parti Républicain, Démocratique et Social (PRDS), whose candidate for president was Ould Taya, and the Union des Forces Démocratiques (UFD), which supported the politically unaffiliated Ahmed Ould Daddah (brother of the former president of the republic). Black Mauritanians generally supported Ould Daddah.

Tensions were high in the months leading up to the elections. Though the government had promised to relax restrictions on the press and on political demonstrations, on occasion it responded to expressions of dissent in the repressive way it always had. On 15 January 1992, FLAM, which had briefly embraced the political process, accused the government of "flagrant irregularities" in voter registration and declared that it would take up arms again. When Ould Taya won the presidency on January 24th, with nearly 63 percent of the vote, the opposition parties charged the government with fraud; protesters rioted in Nouadhibou. Many of the opposition parties, including the UFD, boycotted the elections for the National Assembly and the Senate, held in March and April, respectively. (Only a small proportion of the voters turned out for any phase of the elections.) The upshot was to leave Ould Taya—and his party—very much in control of the new political institutions: 36 of 56 Senate seats and 67 of 79 seats in the Assembly went to members of Ould Taya's PRDS. Ould Taya was sworn in as the elected president of Mauritania on 18 April 1992.

International and Domestic Politics: 1992–1996

The new government soon took steps to put Mauritania on good—or better—terms with its neighbors and also with the various countries it had been at odds with during the Persian Gulf War. It reestablished diplomatic relations with Senegal in 1992 and reopened the border about two weeks later. Many problems persisted, however, among them, the question of how to repatriate and compensate the black Mauritanians who had been deported to Senegal, and also to Mali, during 1989–1990. During 1992–1995 Mauritania and Mali negotiated agreements on the return of the refugees from each of their countries and also on the demarcation of their shared border. Mauritania began to restore its ties with Kuwait and other members of the Arab League beginning in 1993. In 1994–1995 Mauritania helped revive the floundering Union du Maghreb Arabe (UMA), an organization founded in 1989 to facilitate mutual economic support among Mauritania, Libya, Morocco, Algeria, and Tunisia. Though Mauritania has been criticized by Western countries, particularly for failing to fully eradicate slavery, relations with the West, especially France, have improved since the institution of democracy.

The political opposition in Mauritania remains vigorous, though the UFD has been torn by internal conflicts. It changed its name in May 1992 to UFD-Ère Nouvelle, to signify a new beginning for the party, and elected Ahmed Ould Daddah chairman a few weeks later, on 15 June. Subsequently members of the party fell out over the question of whether or not to continue to boycott the political system; some also complained that Ould Daddah had too much personal control over the party. In February 1993 UFD-Ère Nouvelle members under the leadership of a former foreign minister, Hamdi Ould Mouknass, broke away from UFD-Ère Nouvelle to found the Union pour le Progrès et la Démocratie (UPD). To avoid further factionalism, the UFD-Ère Nouvelle announced in July 1993 that it would now participate in electoral politics. It planned to field candidates in the national elections scheduled for 1996 and 1998.

MARGARET A. SABIN

MAURITIUS. An island of volcanic origin in the southwestern Indian ocean, Mauritius is situated 800 kilometers east of Madagascar at 20° south latitude and longitude 57° east. The island, which is largely surrounded by coral reefs, covers 1,865 square kilometers and consists of a plain which rises from the northeast toward the southwest and is broken by gorges, small rivers, and peaks which are the remnants of an ancient volcanic crater. The climate is subtropical but moderated by the southeast trade winds. Annual rainfall varies widely depending upon locale, from more than 5,000 millimeters on the windward slopes of the central plateau to only 900 millimeters on the west coast. The Republic of Mauritius includes the island of Rodrigues (585 kilometers to the east) and the dependencies of Agalega (935 kilometers to the north) and the Cargados Carajos Shoals, or Saint Brandon Islands (370 kilometers to the north-northeast), giving the country a total land area of 2,040 square kilometers.

Cartographic evidence suggests that the first humans to reach Mauritius were Arab seafarers who visited the Mascarene Islands (Mauritius, Réunion, and Rodrigues) sometime before the sixteenth century. The first European visitors were the Portuguese, who reached the island early in the sixteenth century. Mauritius remained uninhabited, however, until 1638, when the Dutch East India Company made the first of several unsuccessful attempts to colonize the island. Abandoned by the Dutch in 1710, the island was colonized in 1721 by a small party of settlers from the neighboring Île de Bourbon (now Réunion) under the auspices of the French Compagnie des Indes. The island, known as Île de France during the period of French rule (1721–1810), served as a naval base from which French interests in India were supported. The island's strategic importance ultimately led to its capture in 1810 by a British expeditionary force, and then to its formal cession to Britain by the Treaty of Paris in 1814. The island, once again named Mauritius, remained a British Crown colony until independence in 1968.

The Republic of Mauritius

Population: 1,111,600 (1994 est.)

Area: 2,040 sq. km (788 sq. mi.)

Official language: English (French also used)

Languages: English, French, Creole, Bhodjpuri, Chinese, Gujerati, Hindi, Telegu, Urdu

National currency: Rupee

Principal religions: Hindu 52.5%, Christian 30.1% (mostly Roman Catholic, some Church of England), Muslim 16.6% (mostly Sunni), Buddhist, Confucian, Ba'hai

Capital: Port Louis (estimated pop. 143,509 in 1993)

Other urban centers: Curepipe, Beau Bassin–Rose Hill, Vacoas-Phoenix, Quatre Bornes, Island of Rodrigues

Annual rainfall: Varies from less than 900 mm (36 in.) on the west coast to 5,000 mm (200 in.) or more in the central region.

Principal geographical features:
> *Mountains:* Moka Range, Grand Port Range, Black River Range
> *Rivers:* Grande Rivière Sud-Est, on Mauritius

Economy:
> *GNP per capita:* US$3,280 (1995)

Principal products and exports:
> *Agricultural:* sugar, tea, tobacco, bananas, tomatoes, groundnuts
> *Manufacturing:* sugar processing, beverage processing, textiles, clothing, electronics
> *Tourism*

Government: Became an independent parliamentary democracy within the British Commonwealth in 1968; became a republic within the Commonwealth in 1992. Multiparty parliamentary democracy. Prime minister is head of government and of the Council of Ministers, which is responsible to the National Assembly. The unicameral National Assembly, elected by universal suffrage, consists of 62 members who serve 5-year terms. The prime minister nominates the president, who serves a 5-year term. For purposes of local government there are 9 administrative districts and urban-rural councils. The island of Rodrigues has considerable autonomy and has 2 elected representatives to the National Assembly and a minister in the Cabinet.

Heads of state since independence:
1968–1982: Prime Minister Sir Seewoosagur Ramgoolam
1982–1995: Prime Minister Sir Anerood Jugnauth
1992: President Sir Veeraswamy Ringadoo
1992–: President Cassam Uteem
1995–: Prime Minister Navin Ramgoolam

Armed forces: The United Kingdom has treaty obligations for defense of Mauritius.
> *Paramilitary:* 1,300

Transportation:
> *Port:* Port Louis
> *Roads:* 1,831 km (1,099 mi.), 93% paved.
> *National Airline:* Air Mauritius
> *Airport:* Sir Seewoosagur Ramgoolam International Airport at Plaisance

Media: 7 daily newspapers in French and English, including *Le Mauricien, The Sun, L'Express.* 2 daily publications in Chinese: *Chinese Daily News* and the *China Times.* 26 weekly, bi-weekly, or monthly newspapers in English and/or French. There is an active book publishing industry. Television (since 1965) and radio are government controlled, provided by Mauritius Broadcasting Corporation.

Literacy and education:
> *Total Adult Literacy rate:* 81.8%. Education is free and compulsory for ages 5–12. Secondary schools are predominantly religious or private; matriculation to them is on a competitive basis and only 50% of students go on. Post-secondary education provided by University of Mauritius, the Mauritius Institute of Education, the Mahatma Gandhi Institute, the Mauritius College of the Air (television and radio), and Institut Africain et Mauricien de Bilinguisme.

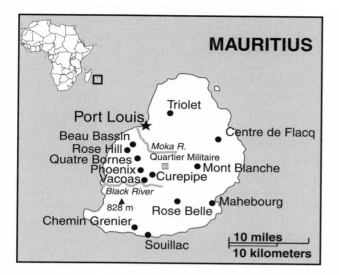

During much of the eighteenth century, the island's economic life remained focused largely upon maritime activities. Although attempts were made to cultivate indigo and spices on a large scale, local agriculture concentrated upon the production of the foodstuffs and naval stores needed by French squadrons and privateers operating in the Indian Ocean. In 1769 Port Louis was opened to free trade by all French nationals; in 1787 this privilege was extended to foreigners, with the result that the island rapidly became an important commerical entrepôt which drew shipping from as far away as northern Europe and the United States. A British blockade during the Napoleonic Wars and the colony's subsequent inclusion into the British Empire, however, undermined the island's position as a commercial center for the western Indian Ocean. As a result, Mauritian colonists turned increasingly to the production of sugar.

Sugarcane was introduced onto the island by the Dutch during the seventeenth century, and was reintroduced by B. F. Mahé de Labourdonnais, the colony's governor from 1735 to 1746. Despite Labourdonnais's support, the sugar industry languished until the first decade of the nineteenth century, when the interruption of French sugar supplies caused by the great slave revolt in Saint Domingue (later Haiti) encouraged planters on the Île de France to begin expanding their production. The abolition in 1825 of the preferential tariff on West Indian sugar entering Great Britain revolutionized the Mauritian sugar industry. The acreage planted in cane increased dramatically and, from the mid-1830s onward, sugar accounted regularly for 85 percent or more of the value of the colony's exports.

Sugar continued to dominate the Mauritian economy until the early 1980s. Unlike many plantation economies in the colonial world, the local sugar industry did not attract much long-term metropolitan investment. The industry's dependence upon the often inadequate resources of domestic capital and the falling world market price of sugar contributed to the subdivision, or *morcellement,* of sugar estates and other properties during the nineteenth century. The *petit morcellement,* which lasted from 1839 to around 1848, saw the creation of a free peasantry from among the colony's population of former apprentices. The *grand morcellement,* which began in the mid-1870s and continued into the 1920s, led to the development of a sizable Indo-Mauritian small-planter class.

Mauritian society and culture is characterized by considerable diversity. The island houses four principal communities—Franco-Mauritian, Creole, Indo-Mauritian, and Sino-Mauritian—which are often further subdivided along class, ethnic, linguisitic, and religious lines. Many Franco-Mauritians trace their ancestry to the merchants, artisans, soldiers, and sailors from France and other European countries who migrated to the colony during the eighteenth century. The origins of the Creole population stem from the local demand for servile labor. An estimated 160,000 slaves were imported into the Mascarenes before 1810, principally from Madagascar, Mozambique, and the Swahili coast, with smaller numbers of slaves arriving from India, Southeast Asia, and West Africa. Inclusion in the British Empire brought an end to the legal slave trade to Mauritius, but another 30,000 or more slaves were introduced illegally into the colony from Madagascar and the East African coast between 1810 and the late 1820s.

This workforce proved, however, to be inadequate to meet the labor needs of the island's rapidly expanding sugar industry after 1825. This fact, coupled with the abolition of slavery in 1835 and the withdrawal of the colony's ex-apprentice population from estate labor at the end of the apprenticeship system in 1839, led to the introduction of indentured laborers from India. More than 451,000 Indian immigrants arrived to work on the colony's sugar estates between 1834 and 1910, two-thirds of whom remained permanently on the island. Approximately 60 percent of these immigrants came from northern India, especially the provinces of Bengal and Bihar, one-third came from the Madras

Presidency in southern India, while the remainder arrived from central and western India via the port of Bombay. In the mid-nineteenth century, small numbers of Chinese immigrants also began to arrive on the island's shores; most of them were Hakka speakers from the province of Hunan.

Mauritius became an independent state within the British Commonwealth on 12 March 1968 under a constitution which provided for a system of multiparty parliamentary government that has continued to the present day. A member of the Organization of African Unity (OAU), Mauritius hosted the OAU's annual conference in 1976. In 1992, Mauritius became a republic, with a president replacing Queen Elizabeth II as head of state. Since the 1970s, the national government has sought to lessen the country's dependence upon sugar by diversifying its economy. To this end, an Export Processing Zone was established in 1971 to encourage the development of export-oriented industries, especially textiles and clothing. Tourism has also been encouraged and has become the most important source of foreign exchange after sugar and textiles.

BIBLIOGRAPHY

Allen, Richard B. "Creoles, Indian Immigrants, and the Restructuring of Society and Economy in Mauritius, 1767–1885." Ph.D. diss., University of Illinois at Urbana-Champaign, 1983.

———. "The Slender, Sweet Thread: Sugar, Capital, and Dependency in Mauritius, 1860–1936." *Journal of Imperial and Commonwealth History* 16 (1987–1988): 77–200.

Bowman, Larry W. *Mauritius: Democracy and Development in the Indian Ocean.* Boulder, Colo., 1991.

Simmons, Adele Smith. *Modern Mauritius: The Politics of Decolonization.* Bloomington, Ind., 1982.

Toussaint, Auguste. *Histories des îles Mascareignes.* Paris, 1972.

RICHARD B. ALLEN

See also **Plantation Economies and Societies; Slave Trade.**

MBOYA, TOM (b. 1930; d. 1969), Kenyan labor and political leader. Thomas Joseph Odhiambo Nienge Mboya was born to a poor Catholic Luo family near Nairobi. He attended mission schools; then, unable to pay for the Cambridge School Certificate course, entered the Kabete Sanitary Inspectors' School near Nairobi.

While working as a sanitary inspector, Mboya was elected secretary of the African Staff Association (1951) and founded the Kenya Local Government Workers Union (1952). After one-third of its leadership was arrested in crackdowns on Africans following the Mau Mau uprising and the British-declared state of emergency, Mboya, age twenty-three, became the general secretary of the Kenya Federation of Labour. Strictly political African organizations were illegal until 1960, so labor organizations were powerful in the 1950s. In addition, union membership grew rapidly as the number of African workers increased and they became more aware of the economic racism in the colony.

Mboya studied industrial relations at Oxford (1955–1956), and in 1957, after his return to Kenya, became one of eight elected Africans on the Legislative Council, where he successfully fought for a new constitution for the colony. Mboya's international prestige grew. He chaired the All-African People's Conference in Ghana (1958) and was awarded an honorary Doctor of Laws degree from Howard University in the United States (1959).

Mboya and Oginga Odinga, both Luo leaders, founded the Kenya African National Union (KANU) in 1960, at a time when many Gikuyu, the primary group involved in the Mau Mau uprising, were in concentration camps or jail, including their leader, Jomo Kenyatta. Kenyatta was elected president of KANU in absentia, and Mboya was elected general secretary. In the preindependence government, KANU formed an alliance with the Kenya African Democractic Union (KADU), and Mboya was minister of labor. After independence (1963), KANU had the majority in Parliament. Kenyatta was prime minister and Mboya was minister of justice and constitutional affairs.

KADU voluntarily dissolved in 1964. Later that year Kenya became a republic with Kenyatta as president and Odinga as vice president. Mboya served as the minister of economic planning and development. He used his post to push the Economic Commission for Africa to establish a Marshall Plan for the continent in order to stop the trend of growth without development.

In response to Kenyatta's steps to centralize power within the government, Vice President Odinga resigned in 1966 and founded the Kenya People's Union (KPU) as a political foil to the ruling party. Odinga's move sharpened ethnic politics and power rivalries. Gikuyu were concerned with keeping power for themselves, especially because Kenyatta was growing old. Mboya, an articulate, ambitious ideologue with broad-based support, was seen as a serious contender. He was assassinated in Nairobi on 5 July 1969; a Gikuyu man was tried and found guilty. Mboya's death shocked the

Tom Mboya (*right*) with Jomo Kenyatta at the Kenya Constitutional Conference in London, 1962. ARCHIVE PHOTOS

country and further polarized Luo and Gikuyu. Later that year Odinga was jailed, the KPU was banned, and Kenya remained a one-party state.

Mboya wrote two books: *Freedom and After* (1963) and *The Challenge of Nationhood* (1970).

BIBLIOGRAPHY

Goldsworthy, David. *Tom Mboya: The Man Kenya Wanted to Forget.* Nairobi, 1982.
Miller, Norman N. *Kenya: The Quest for Prosperity.* Boulder, Colo., 1984.

THOMAS F. MCDOW

See also **Independence Movements; Kenyatta, Jomo; Odinga, Oginga; Trades Unions and Associations.**

MEDICINE. *See* **Disease; Healing; Health Care.**

MENDE. The Mende constitute one of the largest of the Mande groups and are located primarily in Sierra Leone. The Mende language is a member of the Niger-Congo family, the widespread Mande cluster of western Africa. There are approximately 1.4 million Mende in Sierra Leone and a small number in neighboring Liberia.

The Mende came to what is now Sierra Leone from the south in the sixteenth century. Mende society traditionally placed a high value on ability in war. Leadership status was attained through successful conquest of smaller, neighboring groups. Through such military means, by the mid-eighteenth century the Mende had expanded their territory and formed several powerful states with about sixty independent chiefdoms. Their power in the region was augmented by the wealth they accrued through their participation in European trade, including the slave trade. This wealth and strength permitted the Mende to resist colonial control throughout the nineteenth century. In 1898, several Mende leaders refused to pay taxes levied by the British, touching off what came to be known as the House Tax War.

Through their expansion by conquest, the Mende encountered and frequently adopted cultural elements of other peoples of the region. In addition, many Mende groups were converted to Islam, while others were heavily influenced by the evangelization of European Christians. The result has been a highly syncretic cultural blend, but traditional beliefs and practices also have a strong place in Mende society. In particular, the traditional secret societies of *poro* (for men) and *sande* (for women) remain very important. Initiation into these societies is a necessary rite of passage into adulthood.

Mende society is patrilineal. The typical rural Mende village is composed of between 70 and 250 widely dispersed households, each of which is headed by the senior resident male. The economy is largely agricultural, with both staple and cash crops grown. Access to land traditionally depended upon lineage membership. Locally produced crafts include pottery (made by women), and weaving and ironworking (done by men).

BIBLIOGRAPHY

Harris, W. T., and H. Sawyerr. *The Springs of Mende Belief and Conduct.* Freetown, Sierra Leone, 1968.
Little, Kenneth. *The Mende of Sierra Leone: A West African People in Transition.* London, 1969.

GARY THOULOUIS

See also **Religion and Ritual; Secret Societies.**

MENGISTU HAILE MARIAM (b. c. 1942), vice chairman (1974–1977), chairman (1977–1987), Provisional Military Administrative Council; chairman of the council of ministers; president, People's Democratic Republic of Ethiopia (1987–1991). At age fourteen Mengistu joined the juvenile unit of the Ethiopian army, and at eighteen joined the regular army. After graduating from officer training school, he was given his army commission, ultimately rising to the rank of colonel.

Mengistu was a charismatic individual with illusions of grandeur. He was a leading figure in the military coup that overthrew the imperial regime of Haile Sellassie in 1974. Initially he gave the impression of having only the good of the country at heart, but over the first three years of the Ethiopian revolution it became clear that Mengistu had a vision of remaking Ethiopian society and earning the reputation of having delivered Ethiopia from its historic backwardness.

By 1977 Mengistu and his supporters had adopted a Marxist-Leninist ideology and had become clients of the USSR. Over the next thirteen years socialist policies were introduced. Their stated aim was to correct historic injustices based upon the ethnic chauvinism of imperial regimes

Mengitsu Haile Mariam, c. 1990. PA/WIDE WORLD

dominated by the Amhara ethnic group. Mengistu was primarily committed to the maintenance of Ethiopian unity, and he tried to minimize the importance of ethnicity and other particularistic affinities by adopting the Marxist-Leninist approach. In the end he failed, mainly because of his inability to resolve the demand of the province of Eritrea for self-determination and because ethnic opposition emerged against his statist development strategy.

BIBLIOGRAPHY

Giorgis, Dawit Wolde. *Red Tears: War, Famine, and Revolution in Ethiopia.* Trenton, N.J., 1989.
Tekle, Amare. "Mengistu Haile Mariam." In *Political Leaders of Contemporary Africa South of the Sahara: A Biographical Dictionary,* edited by Harvey Glickman. Westport, Conn., 1992.

EDMOND J. KELLER

See also **Postcolonial State.**

MENILEK II (b. 1844; d. 1913), emperor of Ethiopia (1889–1913). Menilek was the son of Haile Malakot

at the court of Téwodros, who held all his potential rivals there, Menilek mastered the intricacies of national government and politics. He escaped to Shewa in 1865, and after Téwodros's death in 1868, he sought the imperial throne, losing out to Yohannes IV (r. 1872–1889). Thereafter, Menilek made Shewa the actual center of Ethiopia's political economy by expanding his holdings south and east. When Yohannes died in battle in March 1889, Menilek became emperor. In May 1889, he signed the infamous Treaty of Wichale (Uccialli), whose mistranslated Article XVII was cited shortly thereafter by Italy when it declared Ethiopia a protectorate.

War ensued, which Ethiopia won at the Battle of Adwa on 1 March 1896. In the following decade, Menilek expanded Ethiopia to its present size by colonizing southern and eastern Ethiopia. He taxed their riches to build communications, especially the Addis Ababa–Djibouti railway, which spurred economic growth and the development of an oligarchy. Addis Ababa became Ethiopia's first modern city and its political center. The emperor suffered a paralytic stroke on 27 October 1909, and his grandson Lij Iyasu (d. 1935), gradually took power in his own right. Menilek lingered comatose until his death during the night of 12–13 December 1913.

BIBLIOGRAPHY

Darkwah, R. H. Kofi. *Shewa, Menelik, and the Ethiopian Empire*, London, 1975.

Marcus, Harold G. *The Life and Times of Menelik II: Ethiopia, 1844–1913.* Oxford, 1975.

Rosenfeld, Chris Prouty. *Empress Taytu and Menilek II: Ethiopia 1883–1910.* London, 1986.

HAROLD G. MARCUS

See also **Téwodros.**

MERINA. *See* **Madagascar.**

MEROË. The city of Meroë, about 200 kilometers (124 mi.) north of Khartoum in modern Sudan, was the residence of the rulers of the ancient state of Kush, which lay along the Nile from a short way south of Aswan in Egypt to at least as far south as the modern town of Sennar on the Blue Nile.

Originally the rulers of this state lived and were buried at Napata farther north. At Napata, close to the sacred hill of Jebel Barkal, the earliest Kushite kings, who conquered Egypt (where they became the pharaohs of the twenty-fifth dynasty), ruled

Menilek II. COURTESY OF ATO KABBADA BOGALA

(r. 1847–1855), heir to King Sahle Sellassie of Shewa (r. 1813–1847). He received a standard church education and was tutored in the military and governmental arts. He respected the progressivism of his grandfather and valued his policy of expansionism to obtain control of southern Ethiopia's resources and trade. Menilek learned the importance of modern weaponry from Téwodros II (r. 1855–1868), who conquered Shewa in 1855–1856. While exiled

from about 750 B.C.E. Retreating from Egypt in the middle of the seventh century B.C.E., at the time of King Tanwetamani, the Kushites developed their own culture and administration, originally heavily influenced by the civilization of pharaonic Egypt.

Perhaps in the sixth century B.C.E., the Kushitic royal residence, and thus the administrative capital of the country, was moved from Napata to Meroë. The date of this move has been much discussed. It is known from excavations that the town of Meroë had been occupied, though perhaps not by royalty, from the eighth century B.C.E. Whenever the kings moved to Meroë, they continued to be buried, under small pyramids, at Nuri, close to Napata. The first royal burials at Meroë were not until about 300 B.C.E., but this does not necessarily imply that the rulers were not living there. The religious importance of Napata, a center of the worship of the god Amon—a part of the heritage derived from long Egyptian occupation of the country prior to 1000 B.C.E.—was the reason for royal burials to continue at Nuri.

The detailed history of Meroë is scarcely known. A chronology can be based on a series of royal burials at Napata and Meroë, where there are pyramid burials of about seventy rulers, stretching from about 750 B.C.E. to the middle of the fourth century C.E. By using a few approximately fixed dates and allocating hypothetical lengths of reign to rulers—many of whose names are known from inscriptions on their pyramids or on objects from the tombs—approximate dates for individual rulers have been calculated.

There were contacts with the Mediterranean world, and during Ptolemaic and Roman times in Egypt this contact was close. Objects of Mediterranean origin appear in Meroitic contexts, including the famous head of the Roman emperor Augustus found at Meroë, thought to have been taken from Aswan in one of the conflicts between Meroë and the Roman garrison of Egypt.

So far as we can tell, Meroitic royalty, at times with ruling queens, was similar to that of Egypt, though details of administrative method and state organization are difficult to discern. The close association of royalty with the gods was similar, and many of the gods depicted on the walls of temples and pyramid chapels were of Egyptian origin. There were also distinctive Meroitic gods, of whom the best known was the lion-headed god Apedemek.

The city of Meroë, which has been studied and partially excavated, was a large and important ur-

ban center—the largest in its time in Africa south of Egypt. It contained elaborate stone-built palaces and temples as well as areas of small mud-brick houses, the dwellings of the common people.

Besides being an administrative and religious center, Meroë was renowned for its industrial activities. It has long been famous for its iron production, and the large mounds of iron slag that mark the site caused it to be considered the place from which the knowledge of iron smelting spread farther into Africa. Though a more cautious view now prevails, Meroë was an important producer of iron, and now that furnaces have been found, it is known that iron was being produced from as early as the fifth century B.C.E. Other products were pottery—showing a range of types in Mediterranean, Egyptian, and indigenous styles—glass, cloth, and precious metals. After Meroë had become the main town of Kush, there was a change in the material culture from the highly Egyptianized art of Napata. Although it still showed Egyptian and Egyptianizing forms, indigenous elements were increasingly used.

The people of Meroë, known from skeletal remains as well as representations in art, were similar to the earlier inhabitants of the region and to the present-day population of the northern Sudan.

The civilization of Meroë was a literate one—early inscriptions were in Egyptian, but by the third century B.C.E. an ingenious writing system, based on the use of twenty-three Egyptian hieroglyphs, was developed, first as hieroglyphs and then in the abbreviated form known as Meroitic cursive. Unfortunately though the phonetic values of the signs are known the numerous texts cannot be translated, and the Meroitic language remains largely unknown.

The end of the Meroitic state came about the middle of the fourth century C.E. The evidence for this lies in the approximate date for the last royal burials and an inscription of the Ethiopian king Aezanes Aksum, which says that he campaigned in the area of Meroitic rule and caused a massive disruption. The finding of fragments of Aksumite inscriptions and an Aksumite coin at Meroë is evidence for an Aksumite presence there.

BIBLIOGRAPHY

Adams, William Y. *Nubia: Corridor to Africa.* Princeton, 1977.
Shinnie, Peter L. *Meroe: A Civilisation of the Sudan.* London, 1967.
———. *Ancient Nubia.* London, 1996.

Shinnie, Peter L., and Rebecca J. Bradley. *The Capital of Kush.* Volume 1, *Meroe Excavations 1965–1972.* Berlin, 1980.

Welsby, Derek. *The Kingdom of Kush.* London, 1996.

PETER L. SHINNIE

See also **Aksum; Archaeology and Prehistory; Egypt; Northern Africa.**

METALLURGY

HISTORY

Metals have been worked in sub-Saharan Africa for more than two millennia. Those who produced these metals and the objects they fashioned have played dominant roles in the history of the subcontinent. African myths of origin often refer to the revolutionary impact of metalworking, and objects of iron, copper, and gold have long been central to political, economic, social, and religious life. So abundantly was Africa endowed with deposits of gold that for centuries it was synonymous with the glittering metal, first to the Arab and Indian Ocean worlds, then to Europe. However, in Africa itself iron has been the primary metal in all spheres of life, from utilitarian to ritual, and in many societies, copper was traditionally more highly esteemed than gold.

Resources and History

Much of Africa south of the Sahara is exposed lateritic crust, that is, low-grade iron. Metallurgists primarily exploited the richer deposits of oxides such as hematite, magnetite, and limonite. Gold, in both alluvial and reef form, occurs much more widely throughout the continent than is generally realized. Copper deposits, in contrast, are relatively scarce in west Africa, with the exception of areas of the southern Sahara in Mauritania and Niger, although they are more plentiful in regions of central and southern Africa. Lead occurs occasionally, especially in association with copper; tin was exploited in a few areas, especially in southern Africa. Despite tenacious Portuguese beliefs to the contrary, little silver is found in Africa, and use of the metal is recent except in the Sahara and Sahel.

During the period from about 500 B.C.E. to 500 C.E., the working of iron and copper spread over the entire subcontinent apparently in tandem; there is no evidence of a sequence from copper to arsenical copper or bronze and finally to iron, as in the Middle East and Europe. The lack of clear routes of diffusion from North Africa, the Arabian Peninsula, or the Indian Ocean has led some scholars to propose that metallurgy may have developed independently in Africa. Technically, however, this would have been difficult. Iron smelting requires precise control of temperature and gases within the furnace, and it is hard to imagine how mastery of these factors would have been achieved without a long period of experimentation with metals that are easier to work, such as copper and its alloys, or without kiln firing of ceramics, which also demands high-temperature pyrotechnology. If metalworking was not invented independently, it may have reached Africa from several resources rather than from a single one.

The diffusion of metalworking throughout the Congo Basin, and into eastern and southern Africa, was long held to be associated with the migration of Bantu agriculturists. More recent archaeology and linguistic reconstructions have undermined this theory except in southern Africa. The technology seems to have spread in complex patterns, and at the same time stone-using hunter-gatherers coexisted with iron-using farmers in many areas. Indeed, until recently, ironworkers frequently continued to use stone tools for rough forging.

The effects of metallurgy may have been gradual rather than revolutionary, but they were undoubtedly profound. Iron tools and weapons increased the efficiency of agriculture, hunting, fishing, and warfare, contributing to the evolution of complex societies characterized by production of surpluses, craft specialization, and social stratification. Iron, copper, and gold all entered circuits of trade. Raw iron and copper and forged objects were traded locally to peoples lacking resources or specialists. With the development of the trans-Saharan trade during the first and early second millennia C.E., copper and brass wares became major imports into west Africa, often exchanged directly for gold. The opening up of maritime routes between Europe and west Africa in the second half of the fifteenth century led to an exponential increase in these imports and, for a brief period, in exports of gold. Eventually iron bars became a staple import from Europe. Africa's mineral wealth, actual and mythical, was a major catalyst for European discovery and eventually for conquest.

Technology

As more and more African sites are surveyed and excavated, the scale of precolonial iron smelting becomes apparent. Whereas some industries produced only enough for local needs, others engaged in intensive production, often over long periods of time. The Middle Senegal Valley, the Bassar region of western Togo, Kano and its environs in northern Nigeria, and the Ndop Plain of Cameroon are thus far the best known of these protoindustrial centers, but areas of Futa Jallon and Yatenga may also have been major producers. Modern geological surveys have shown that virtually all copper deposits in sub-Saharan Africa, except what became known as the Copperbelt (in Zambia), were identified and worked by indigenous metallurgists before the colonial period.

African smelters used an enormous variety of furnace types to produce bloomery iron or raw copper: open bowls, low shaft, high shaft, permanent, impermanent. So far it is impossible to tell whether furnace forms were dictated by the nature of local ores or of the charcoals used almost universally for fuel. A peculiarly African innovation is the tall shaft furnace that relies on natural draft, drawing air in through a number of holes around the base, rather than on bellows; outside of Africa, only a single example is known from Burma. Although inefficient in its use of fuel, such a furnace

Building an iron-smelting furnace, Banjeli, Togo.
CARLYN SALTMAN

avoids the intense labor inputs of bellows operators.

In some areas the same craftsmen smelted and smithed iron and copper. In others, there was a high degree of specialization: not only might smelter and smith be separate, but there might be distinctions between those who forged tools and those who made ornaments of copper, brass, or gold. Further, these occupations were often hereditary, especially in the western Sudan. Smiths and smelters were, however, invariably male. Women and children provided a great deal of the ancillary labor of mining, preparing ores, and making charcoal.

The art of lost-wax casting reached a remarkable level of sophistication throughout west Africa, as far south as the Cameroon Grassfields. This method involves making a model of the object to be cast in wax, then enveloping it in clay. When the wax is melted, metal is run in to take its exact form. Finds from three small sites at Igbo Ukwu in southeastern Nigeria, dated to the eighth to tenth centuries C.E., include bronze pendants, staff heads, and vessels that illustrate the mastery of the technique as well as a virtuoso delight in replicating natural materials in metal. Although the method is an ancient one, African brass casters have their own refinements. Both Akan and Grassfields artists often attach the crucible to the mold in order to reduce the buildup of gases and enable the molten metal to flow more quickly and evenly. Although most lost-wax casting utilizes copper alloys such as bronze and brass because of their lower melting temperature and greater ductility without unwanted gases, some of the classic heads and figures from Ife were cast in pure copper, a rare technical feat.

Cultural Role of Metallurgists and Metals

While much of the literature emphasizes the "otherness" of the African smith, this is most characteristic of west African peoples such as the Mande, among whom smithing is often hereditary and smiths are endogamous, and of pastoral societies such as the Maasai, among whom smiths are looked down on, at least in part because they perform manual labor. Where the craft is not hereditary, aspirants often must pay costly apprenticeship and initiation fees, which tend to restrict access. Smiths also may function as sculptors, diviners, amulet makers, circumcisers, and morticians; their wives often are potters and excisers (those who perform genital excision on girls and young women).

The complex and often ambivalent attitudes expressed toward smiths derive in large measure from the acknowledgment of their power. The rest of society, from farmer and hunter to king and priest, is dependent on the smith's ability to transform inert matter into hoes, spears, emblems of authority and status, and symbols of the spirits—objects that are believed to be endowed with agency. Because he is literally "playing with fire," the metalworker must be a master of ritual knowledge. This is particularly true of smelting, the primary act of transformation: it usually takes place in isolation and involves invocations and offerings to the ancestors, strict observance of sexual and menstrual taboos, and ample use of medicines. Comparable rituals attend the setting up of a new forge or manufacture of a new hammer or anvil.

Because of their evident access to supernatural power, smiths are frequently associated with kingship, especially in central Africa, where they commonly play a major role in royal investiture and in manufacturing elements of regalia. And like chiefs, smiths are often feared as potential sorcerers or witches, because the power they wield can be beneficent or dangerous.

Although beliefs about metalworking show as much cultural variation as the forms of the objects produced, they nevertheless seem to reveal a common core of paradigmatic elements, invoking the human model of gender and age to explain transformative power.

BIBLIOGRAPHY

Célis, Georges. *Eisenhütten in Afrika/Les fonderies africaines du fer.* Frankfurt-am-Main, 1991.

Childs, S. Terry, and David Killick. "Indigenous African Metallurgy: Nature and Culture." *Annual Review of Anthropology* 22 (1993): 317–337.

Cline, Walter. *Mining and Metallurgy in Negro Africa.* Menasha, Wis., 1937.

Échard, Nicole, ed. *Métallurgies africaines: Nouvelles contributions.* Paris, 1983.

Fowler, Ian. "Babungo: A Study of Iron Production, Trade, and Power in a Nineteenth-Century Ndop Plain Chiefdom (Cameroons)." Ph.D. diss., University of London, 1990.

Herbert, Eugenia W. *Iron, Gender, and Power: Rituals of Transformation in African Societies.* Bloomington, Ind., 1993.

Kense, François J. *Traditional African Iron Working.* Calgary, Alberta, 1983.

Maret, Pierre de. "Ceux qui jouent avec le feu: La place du forgeron en Afrique centrale." *Africa* 50 (1980): 263–279.

McNaughton, Patrick. *The Mande Blacksmiths: Knowledge, Power, and Art in West Africa.* Bloomington, Ind., 1988.

EUGENIA W. HERBERT

See also **Archaeology and Prehistory; History of Africa.**

TECHNOLOGY

Origins

Fuel-and-combustion technology is known from all regions of the world. Many studies show that an open wood or charcoal fire can easily attain 1000°C. Such a temperature can fire pottery to a good hardness, anneal copper, and set in motion solid-state reduction of iron oxide. In essence, there is nothing unique about the reduction of copper or iron that would prevent multiple inventions. Indeed, the metallurgist J. E. Rehder stated:

> Copper is very easily melted in a charcoal hearth and a native copper tool or knife inserted for annealing can easily disappear, to be found later as a small ingot in the bottom of the hearth. This would lead to intentionally melting several pieces to make a large one, which is basic metallurgy. Copper oxide adhering to native copper from a local surface deposit would be automatically reduced when the copper was melted, to yield more metal in the hearth than was apparently added. This is a simple and natural origin of smelting. ("Primitive Furnaces and the Development of Metallurgy," *Journal of the Historical Metallurgical Society* 20 [1986], 91)

A contrary view supporting a single origin for the invention of metallurgical technology was advanced by Theodore Wertime:

> One must doubt that the tangible web of discovery, comprehending the art of reducing oxide and then sulfide ores, the recognition of silver, lead, iron, tin, and possibly arsenic and antimony as distinctive new metallic substances, and the technique of alloying tin with bronze could have been spun twice. ("Man's First Encounter with Metallurgy," *Science* 146 [1964], 3649)

Historians of technology usually subscribe to one of these two models of the development of metallurgy. Africanists are likewise divided, with some supporting the diffusionist model and others favoring the independent invention of iron and copper technology. Diffusionists have maintained that metallurgy in Africa must have been introduced from elsewhere, possibly the Near East via North Africa or the Nile corridor, or from the Near East or the Indian subcontinent via the east coast of Africa, for the following reasons. First, there is little archaeological evidence for pyrotechnologies in sub-Saharan Africa predating the beginning of copper and iron production. Second, no archaeological sequence demonstrates development from lithics, to copper, to bronze, and then to iron. Third, no African archaeological sites are contemporary with or predate the beginning of copper and iron production in the Near East.

Those favoring the independent invention of metallurgy have argued that Africa indeed has a pyrotechnological tradition of use of native copper, copper smelting, and iron smelting. They point out that the lack of evidence for prehistoric mining of copper in Africa is a result of the scarcity of copper and not of necessary expertise. They point to a tradition of copperworking in the Old Kingdom of Egypt (c. 2686–2181 B.C.E.), where a crucible furnace for casting bronze, dating to 2300–1900 B.C.E., was recovered within the temple precinct at Kerma. Several copper mines and a smelting site at Akjoujt, Mauritania, date from between the ninth and the third centuries B.C.E. Copper mining and smelting were practiced in the region west of Agadez, Niger, in the early first millennium B.C.E., but native copper was melted before about 2000 B.C.E. Iron smelting at Agadez began by about 500 B.C.E. The reconstructed metallurgical sequence for the Agadez region has been divided into three phases: Cuivre I (c. 2000–1000 B.C.E.), when native copper was melted; Cuivre II (c. 900 B.C.E.), when copper was smelted; and Fer I (c. 500 B.C.E.), when iron smelting began. The evidence for metallurgy in Niger prompted Ronald F. Tylecote to concede, "Clearly we now seem to have some signs of a Copper Age in West Africa" ("Early Copper Slags etc. from the Agadez Region of Niger," *Journal of the Historical Metallurgical Society* 16 [1982], 62).

Copper production and iron production in Africa were roughly contemporaneous. Iron may initially have been produced as a by-product of copper, "since iron ore can be reduced to cast iron in any furnace capable of smelting copper, simply by adding a little less ore and blowing a little harder" (Rehder, 91). The use of iron in Egypt and northwestern Africa between about 1200 and 1000 B.C.E. is widely accepted by archaeologists. The production of iron is known to have been undertaken in these areas in the eighth and ninth centuries B.C.E. Iron smelting furnaces have been carbon 14–dated to the period 1000–500 B.C.E. in Nigeria, Niger, Tanzania, and Rwanda.

The Technology of Copper and Iron in Sub-Saharan Africa

The basic requirements of metallurgy include ore, water, fuel, transport, a reasonable level of furnace technology, and labor. Studies in the thermodynamics of smelting have shown that smelting of iron is much more difficult than of any other metal, including aluminum, copper, gold, lead, silver, and zinc. Because iron oxides are more stable than those of other metals, high temperature and low partial pressure of oxygen are required to reduce it. These conditions are difficult to attain at or near the earth's surface. The separation of copper and iron from their oxides requires carbon monoxide as a reducing agent. Carbon monoxide reacts with the metal oxides to produce carbon dioxide and the metal. It is obtained by burning carbon in a very limited supply of oxygen. The minimum temperature at which the reduction of iron from iron oxides and silicates occurs is about 1100°C.

A successful smelting operation is a delicate balancing act between two opposed requirements. On the one hand, the smelter must maintain a temperature sufficiently high to keep the slag fluid. Furnace temperatures are raised by admitting more air to the furnace, thereby increasing the rate of combustion of the fuel. But too much air will produce more carbon dioxide than can be reduced to carbon monoxide. Without an atmosphere rich in carbon monoxide, metallic iron (and copper) cannot form, and the smelter will be left with only useless slag to show for his efforts.

The invention of kilns and furnaces had two advantages over open fires: they were less smoky, and hence more approachable, and they could attain higher internal temperatures for reducing ores. Although the design of furnaces requires skill, greater skill is required to manage the furnace to produce the metal. These skills are subtle, take a long time to master, and must be maintained by regular use. Widespread use of metals occurred only after metalworkers could consistently obtain furnace temperatures sufficiently high to maintain a fluid slag. This very complex technique is of great interest to archaeometallurgists in Africa and elsewhere.

Many historians of technology are convinced that the use of copper and its alloys preceded that of iron because copper has a lower melting point (1083°C), which makes it easier to smelt and melt. Copper smelting involved cleaning ore to get rid of waste rock. The ore was then preroasted to expel impurities, including antimony, arsenic, and sulfur. Roasting converted copper sulfite to copper oxide, which was reduced through heating in the furnace.

Through experimentation, copper workers invented and mastered the technique for casting copper from its native or smelted state in molds. Using the lost-wax technique permitted the casting of complicated objects such as statuettes, figurines, and jewelry. African casters produced brass by the lost-wax technique as early as 800 C.E., at Igbo Ukwu. Ife casters used copper for bracelets, anklets, rings, collars, ceremonial axes, hoes, and currency from the eleventh century on. The famous Benin brasses were cast in the thirteenth and fourteenth centuries C.E. The object to be cast was first modeled in wax around a small clay core. It was then totally enclosed in clay and baked. The molten wax escaped through orifices that were then plugged. Molten metal was then poured into the mold and the orifices sealed. After the metal set, the clay core was broken and the cast object was removed. Earliest evidence of the lost-wax method is at Ur in Mesopotamia around 3000 B.C.E.

The best-known copper alloy used by African casters was brass, an alloy of copper and zinc. When it contains less than 36 percent zinc, brass is ductile when cold and can be worked into complex shapes without the necessity of frequent annealing. Vast deposits of copper in Katanga, in what is now Zaire, allowed the Katangese to cast *katanza* crosses, which they traded extensively in west and central Africa. These ingots were later refashioned into tools and ornamental weapons, including the Luba throwing knives. The Benin bronzes are technically brasses (true bronze is an alloy of copper and tin). Prehistoric mining and use of tin in Africa were rare. Other African societies known to have used the lost-wax technique are the Dogon of Mali and the Sao of Cameroon.

Both direct and indirect processes of iron smelting were widely used by ancient African smelters. The direct process involves the production of bloomery iron by the cementation process. Bloomery iron is produced in the solid state as a result of smelting iron ore. Pure iron melts at 1537°C, but bloomery iron usually is not heated above 1250°C. The carbon content in bloomery is variable but usually low. High-carbon bloomery steel has properties similar to modern carbon steels. Bloomery iron smelted at 1200°C is usually a spongy mass of iron oxide and iron silicate (or slag) arising from the reaction between ferrous oxide and silica gangue in reducing conditions. It is a soft metal with a tensile strength of about 40,000 pounds per square inch (p.s.i), only slightly more than the strength of pure copper, which is about 32,000 p.s.i. Hardening, through forging, increases the strength of iron to almost 100,000 p.s.i.

The indirect process involves the production of cast iron in a blast furnace and the manufacture of wrought iron and steel from cast iron by decarburization. Cast iron contains between 2 percent and 4.5 percent of alloyed carbon. It exists in two forms, white and gray, so called for the appearance of the surface when it is fractured. In gray iron, most of the carbon exists as graphite, and the silicon content usually exceeds 1 percent. In white carbon, most of the carbon exists as cementite. The production of white cast iron is favored by fast cooling rates and low silicon content. Both cast irons are brittle: gray, because of lack of strength and disposition of the graphite; white, because of the extreme hardness and brittleness of cementite. Cast iron with 4 percent carbon can be melted at 1,150°C, resulting in homogeneous metal with few or no nonmetallic inclusions. This metal is, however, very brittle and impossible to hammer-forge until it is decarburized to wrought iron or steel.

Analysis of metallurgical samples from African industrial sites has documented a variety of smelting and forging techniques. African ironworkers produced high-carbon steel and even cast iron in their bloomeries. They used two methods to decarburize high-carbon steel or cast iron. The first was annealing at the hearth while making the desired object in an oxidizing atmosphere. The second involved consolidating bloom in open crucibles at the hearth. The quality of iron produced and used was quite variable. This is confirmed by the variability in the carbon content of the samples. Both hot forging and cold forging were undertaken. Cold-hammering was evidenced by broken slag inclusions and by the distortion of the microstructure. Cold-forging was probably used in the fine finishing of smaller objects, such as nails and knives. The tool kit was probably simple, including stone hammers, and the artifact may have been held with crude calipers or tongs or even in the hand; with such tools cold-hammering would have been the easiest way to finish small tools. Pressure-welding technology was systematically employed by African forgers to fabricate desired objects. It involves heating individual metal pieces at high temperatures in the forge and then quickly hammering them together. The Luba of the Upemba Depression, in what is now Zaire, are known to have used this technique. The indications of hot-welding of hypoeutectoid steel to eutectoid or hypereutectoid steel reasonably suggest that hot-hammering or welding probably was used to improve the quality of the object forged.

Analysis of iron artifacts from Swahili sites of the east African coast have revealed crucible steel dated to 630–890 C.E. These are the first crucible steel samples known from sub-Saharan Africa. The crucible steel process was adapted in the Near East in the seventh century and in Toledo, Spain, a little later. Islamic scholars, including al-Biruni in the eleventh century and al-Tarsusi in the twelfth century, noted that the crucible steel process was widely used and understood in the Islamic world. The only other known centers for the production of crucible steel before the eighteenth century were in Arabia, south India, Sri Lanka, China, and Spain.

Significance of Metallurgy in Africa

Archaeologists agree that African bloomery smelting and brass casting were technologically sophisticated and technically distinct from European and Asian bloomery processes. First, Peter Schmidt and his collaborators have argued that the preheated blast, an invention of enormous importance to the industrial revolution, was first employed in Africa, possibly as early as the late first millennium B.C.E. Second, Nikolaas van der Merwe has stated that African ironworkers developed a method of making steel (the "African direct steel process") that was distinct from steelmaking developed elsewhere. Third, C. L. Goucher has found that African iron and steel were often of a quality superior to that imported from Europe. Fourth, Nikolaas van der Merwe and D. H. Avery have pointed out that natural-draft smelting furnaces (those that operate without bellows or equivalent devices) are an African invention. Finally, L. M. Diop has claimed that iron smelting may have been independently invented in Africa. David Killick, on the other hand, finds no convincing evidence that African bloomery technology was fundamentally different from that employed elsewhere in Europe; the same mechanisms of ore reduction and of bloom formation and carburization have been observed in both African and non-African bloomery furnaces.

Metal tools had functional advantages over microlithic tools. The possession of iron technology led to prosperity, population increase, migration, and colonization of ecological zones difficult to exploit with stone-tool technology. Metallurgy in sub-Saharan Africa has been associated with population increase or migration from western Africa into southern and eastern Africa. This correlation has relied on the appearance of ironworking, agriculture, and permanent settlements, and in some areas, the first appearance of pottery. Bantu-speaking communities lived in permanent settlements. They were farmers who grew bulrush millet (*Pennisetum americana*) and finger millet (*Eleusine coracana*). They possessed metallurgical technology and raised cattle and sheep or goats.

The migration and population increase made possible by acquisition of metallurgical technology have been heralded as a revolutionary event in the history of Africa because iron permitted more efficient clearing of forests for agricultural land, higher agricultural productivity, and concomitant population increases. By the tenth century C.E., several societies in Africa had begun to develop complex forms of rulership, exploitation of resources, and complex sociopolitical organizations. Throughout this development, ironsmiths and copper casters retained key roles in African societies. Sometimes they were rulers or persons of high status. Even when they were of low status, they retained important ritual, spiritual, magical, or conflict resolution powers.

Conclusion

Our thinking on Africa's contribution to human cultures and its place in the modern world still has contradictions. Because of European colonization of Africa, there has been a common failure to recognize the role of traditional African technologies and to assess their suitability in postcolonial Africa's sustainable development. Although there are many important questions that need to be studied regarding the influence of technology and other elements of traditional knowledge—in agriculture, stockbreeding, and medicine—scholars continue to dwell on origins of technology in Africa. Scholars can begin to provide the much-needed leadership and service to Africa when they move beyond debate over diffusion versus independent invention and undertake in-depth studies to document the unique contributions of Africa to metallurgical technology and other fields.

BIBLIOGRAPHY

Alexander, W., and A. Street. *Metals in the Service of Man.* Harmondsworth, U.K., 1969.

Childs, S. Terry. "Transformations: Iron and Copper Production in Central Africa." In *Recent Trends in Archaeometallurgical Research,* edited by Peter Glumac. Volume 8, MASCA Papers in Science and Archaeology series. Philadelphia, 1991.

Childs, S. Terry, and David Killick. "African Metallurgy: Nature and Culture." *Annual Review of Anthropology* 22 (1993): 317–337.

Cline, Walter Buchanan. *Mining and Metallurgy in Negro Africa.* Menasha, Wis., 1937.

Diop, L. M. "Métallurgie traditionnelle et l'âge de fer en Afrique." *Bulletin IFAN* (Institut Francais d'Afrique Noire), ser. B 30 (1968): 10–37.

Goucher, C. L. "Iron Is Iron 'Til It Rust: Trade and Ecology in the Decline of West African Iron-Smelting." *Journal of African History* 22 (1981), no. 2: 179–190.

Grébénart, Danillo. "Les Métallurgies du cuivre et du fer autour d'Agadez (Niger), dès origins au début de la période médiévale. Vues générales." In *Métallurgies africaines: Nouvelles contributions,* edited by Nicole Échard. Paris, 1983.

Hassan, Ahmad Yusuf al-, and Donald R. Hill. *Islamic Technology.* Cambridge, 1986.

Herbert, Eugenia. *Iron, Gender, and Power.* Bloomington, Ind., 1993.

Killick, David J. "A Comparative Perspective on African Iron-working Technologies." In *The Culture and Technology of African Iron Production,* edited by Peter R. Schmidt. Gainesville, Fla., 1996.

Kusimba, Chapurukha M., David Killick, and Richard G. Creswell. "Indigenous and Imported Metals on Swahili Sites of Kenya." In *Technology and Culture in Africa,* edited by S. Terry Childs. Volume 11, MASCA Papers in Science and Archaeology series. Philadelphia, 1994.

Lebeuf, Jean-Paul. "The Ancient Metallurgy of Copper and Its Alloys in the Region of Lake Chad." In *The Art of Metal in Africa,* edited by Marie-Thérèse Brincard and translated by Evelyn Fischel. New York, 1982.

Maddin, Robert, James D. Muhly, and Tamara S. Wheeler. "How the Iron Age Began." *Scientific American* 237, no. 4 (1977): 122–131.

Merwe, Nikolaas J. van der. "The Advent of Iron in Africa." In *The Coming of the Age of Iron,* edited by Theodore A. Wertime and James D. Muhly. New Haven, Conn., 1980.

Merwe, Nikolaas J. van der, and D. H. Avery. "Science and Magic in African Technology: Traditional Iron Smelting in Malawi." In *The Beginning of the Use of Metals and Alloys,* edited by Robert Maddin. Cambridge, Mass., 1988.

Miller, Duncan, and Nikolaas J. van der Merwe. "Early Metal Working in Sub-Saharan Africa: A Review of Recent Research." *Journal of African History* 35, no. 1 (1994): 1–36.

Needham, Joseph. *The Development of Iron and Steel Technology in China.* Cambridge, 1964.

Okafor, Edwin Eme, and Patricia Phillips. "New ^{14}C Ages from Nsukka, Nigeria, and the Origins of African Metallurgy." *Antiquity* 66, no. 252 (1992): 686–688.

Phillipson, David. *The Later Prehistory of Eastern and Southern Africa.* New York, 1977.

Rostoker, William, and Bennet Bronson. *Pre-Industrial Iron: Its Technology and Ethnology.* Philadelphia, 1990.

Schmidt, Peter, ed. *The Culture and Technology of African Iron Production.* Gainesville, Fla., 1996.

Schmidt, Peter R., and S. Terry Childs. "Ancient African Iron Production." *American Scientist* 83, no. 6 (1995): 525–533.

Taylor, S. J., and C. A. Shell. "Social and Historical Implications of Early Chinese Iron Technology." In *The Beginning of the Use of Metals and Alloys,* edited by Robert Maddin. Cambridge, Mass., 1988.

Tylecote, Ronald F. *A History of Metallurgy.* London, 1976.

CHAPURUKHA M. KUSIMBA

METALS. *See* **Minerals and Metals.**

MFECANE

INTRODUCTION

John Omer-Cooper's classic interpretation of the violent early-nineteenth-century rise of the Zulu nation (a period known as the Mfecane) underlies nearly all standard histories of southern Africa, at least those published through the early 1990s. When Omer-Cooper wrote in the 1960s, historians, particularly in southern Africa, were intent upon adding Africans to a regional historiography then focused almost exclusively on whites and intent upon providing evidence of African "initiative" and accomplishments. Africans' achievements were usually attributed to European influence; left to their own devices, they were often suspected of uncontrollable tendencies toward violence. Shaka, the military leader and then king, who created overwhelmingly successful African armies in what is today Natal (then a region around the lower Mfolozi River inhabited by speakers of the northern Nguni languages) during the second decade of the nineteenth century, owed much of his achievement, in this view, to his brutal, even pathological cruelty.

Omer-Cooper avoided reliance on white inspiration for the rise of the Zulu by emphasizing local circumstances, particularly a hypothesized population growth among the northern Nguni that sparked struggles for survival in increasingly crowded lands, and he expanded Shaka's significance as a leader by emphasizing his political creativity and the strong Zulu state that he left to his successors in nineteenth-century Natal. Omer-Cooper traced parallel processes of state building under other African leaders who emerged at the heads of bands of refugees from Shaka's wars: notably, Sobhuza gathered the people who later became known as Swazi in the region that later became Swaziland, shortly after 1815; after 1818, Zwangendaba led others through the area west of Lake Malawi and eventually founded several so-called Ngoni states as far north as the latitude of Lake Tanganyika; in the same year, Soshangane followed the coastal plains north beyond the mouth of the Limpopo, where he settled his followers as the Gaza state in what subsequently became Mozambique; Mzilikazi was at the head of another group who moved into the modern Transvaal in about 1821 and then, defeated by Dutch Trekboers in 1837, migrated to their permanent home, as Ndebele, in what is now western Zimbabwe; Sebetwane, with followers known as Kololo, moved after 1825 all the way to the upper Zambezi floodplain, today far western Zambia.

A series of other African leaders organized groups of refugees on the fringes of the High Veld (the Orange Free State and the Transvaal until 1994), fought battles—including those at Dithakong and Mbholompo—during the 1820s, and established other communities in and around the area that became the modern Republic of South Africa. All these groups together have subsequently dominated the ethnic geography and politics of the entire southeastern quadrant of Africa. Many of them became centers of resistance against the consolidation of European colonial authority throughout the region during the 1880s and 1890s. In the nationalist-era vision of African history of the 1960s, the state-building achievements of the leaders of these movements and the scale of events that seemed to flow from Shaka's original wars in the 1810s and 1820s in Natal inspired the image of a single, sweeping "Mfecane"—a term variously glossed but often taken to mean a "crushing"—at the start of modern history in the region, a story made by Africans, not whites. This account has recently begun to dissolve into several new narratives of early nineteenth-century history in southern Africa.

JOSEPH C. MILLER

HISTORIOGRAPHY

In 1966 the historian John Omer-Cooper published *The Zulu Aftermath: A Nineteenth-Century Revolution in Bantu Africa.* This study celebrated the achievement of the early nineteenth-century Zulu kingdom in southeast Africa, led by Shaka, an African political and military genius, and argued that its emergence caused massive upheaval among neighboring chiefdoms. Consolidation of the Zulu state in turn set in motion a ripple effect of dislocation and disruption that extended across much of southern Africa. This set of events Omer-Cooper labeled the Mfecane (*lifaqane* and *difaqane* are the equivalent terms written in the Southern Sotho orthographies of Lesotho and South Africa respectively). He drew the term "Mfecane" from a large body of earlier historical writing but infused it with new significance as a time of revolutionary African state building and accorded it major importance, as a source of pride and independence of spirit, in the historical consciousness of the African communities who later came under white rule.

Scholars are in broad agreement that the early nineteenth century was indeed a period of increased violence and social dislocation across much of southern Africa. The reasons for these troubled conditions received renewed attention in the late 1980s, when Julian Cobbing questioned their designation as Mfecane. He suggested that the essence of the term, as it has been used historiographically, lies in the claim, designed to mask the impact of white settlement, that the rise of the Zulu kingdom was their chief cause. Omer-Cooper and Christopher Saunders have challenged this assertion, arguing that in the historiography the term has often been used rather to refer to the disruptive character of these upheavals. Saunders, in particular, has argued that Cobbing's intervention oversimplified a historiography that in fact used the term "Mfecane" in various senses over time and by no means ignored the violence associated with colonialism. More readily accepted than Cobbing's thesis has been John Wright's reassessment downward of the size of the Zulu kingdom and of the extent of Zulu power, both points made in response to Cobbing's rejection of the idea of the Zulu kingdom as the "Mfecane motor."

Where Omer-Cooper and other historians have indeed seen the rise of the Zulu kingdom as the root impulse behind the upheavals, Cobbing has suggested that the causes of these commotions were settler, and even missionary, labor-raiding and slaving expeditions mounted to feed demands for slaves in the Cape Colony, to the south, and through Portuguese Mozambique, to the north. Cobbing has gone on to suggest that the notions of Shaka as a vicious tyrant and of a Zulu-generated "Mfecane" were settler inventions or elements of—as he puts it—an "alibi" dating back to the 1820s and designed to mask not only the settlers' own illegal labor procurement practices but also the subsequent dislocation of local populations from their lands.

Cobbing's hypothesis has prompted considerable reassessment of this period. His suggestion that the upheavals of the time were not, or perhaps not simply, a consequence of the rise of the Zulu kingdom has been widely accepted, as has his insistence on the need to look more closely at the neglected role of slave trading in southern Africa. His more specific claims regarding the early impact of slave trading and the extent of labor raiding, his indictment of missionaries as major agents in those activities, and his assertion that the term "Mfecane" has no meaning among the African communities concerned, have provoked heated controversy.

Elizabeth Eldredge has taken the lead in reexamining the evidence for the timing and dimensions of European slave trading and labor raiding. Cobbing suggested that the Delagoa Bay (modern-day Maputo) slave trade had grown in the course of the eighteenth century to the point at which it became the prime cause of wars during the 1810s, which culminated in the rise of the Zulu kingdom in the 1820s. In contrast, Eldredge's careful periodization of the slave trade has demonstrated that the numbers of slaves taken did not reach significant proportions until the mid-1820s: in other words, *after* the emergence of the Zulu kingdom and the attendant regional destabilization. Likewise, Carolyn Hamilton has shown that vilification of Shaka, which Cobbing characterized as the first act of a colonial conspiracy by dating it within the Zulu king's lifetime, did not occur until *after* the death of Shaka in 1828.

Another area of contention concerned two key battles that Cobbing used to implicate settlers as leading agents of the violence, at Dithakong (1823),

which pitched several highveld groups against one another, and at Mbholompo (1828), where the British engaged Ngurane refugees from the Zulu kingdom. Cobbing argued that from the start government officials and missionaries planned these confrontations as slave raids. Cobbing's critics have conceded that the acquisition of laborers may have been a by-product of the battles, but they have insisted that slaving was not their main purpose. In particular, Cobbing's characterization of the battles as slave raids has been challenged first by Eldredge and Guy Hartley for not taking into account the campaigns waged against slavery by the missionaries concerned, while Jeff Peires has criticized Cobbing for ignoring pertinent African sources that show local initiatives and forces at work in causing the upheavals. Peires has also challenged Cobbing's allegation that the term "Mfecane" was coined by white settlers in search of an alibi and has no root in any African language; he asserts that in Xhosa *imfecane* is derived from the verb *feca*, meaning "to crack, bruise, break down the maize or sweetcorn stalks" and that it appeared in Xhosa-language newspapers as early as 1863.

The debate about the Mfecane has stimulated reassessment of the circumstances and the aggressiveness of European expansionism in early nineteenth-century southern Africa; it has also underscored the need for closer attention to be paid to the sources of conflict in intra-African politics in the region; it has demonstrated the need to link contemporaneous events across a region that was in fact much more integrated than the formerly prevailing segregated histories of "whites" and "blacks" could comprehend; it has drawn attention to the transfrontier activities of groups like the Griqua and Kora, who did not fit neatly into the historical categories of "white" and "black," "settler" and "native" or "African," which for so long dominated this historiography; and finally it has demanded of researchers a new and more critical interrogation of the available sources, both oral and written.

BIBLIOGRAPHY

Cobbing, Julian. "The Mfecane as Alibi: Thoughts on Dithakong and Mbolompo." *Journal of African History* 29, no. 3 (1988): 487–519.

Hamilton, Carolyn, ed. *The Mfecane Aftermath: Reconstructive Debates in Southern African History.* Johannesburg and Pietermaritzburg, 1995.

Omer-Cooper, John. *The Zulu Aftermath: A Nineteenth-Century Revolution in Bantu Africa.* London and Ibadan, 1966. 2d ed., 1969.

CAROLYN HAMILTON

See also **Shaka Zulu; Southern Africa.**

MILITARY GOVERNMENTS AND ARMIES.

Coups d'état and military governments have been major features of African political life since the early 1960s, and since the late 1970s organized armed conflict has become a factor in the domestic and international politics of significant numbers of African states. From 1960 to mid-1994, sub-Saharan Africa experienced seventy-one successful military coups and well over twice that number of failed coup attempts. The successful ones have come in waves of different intensities. From 1960 to 1974 they averaged three a year, with a peak average of 3.7 for the years 1974 to 1980. The next wave, from 1986 to 1994, was barely a ripple, averaging 1.3 a year.

Only a fine and often imperceptible line seems to distinguish coup-prone countries from those that have avoided direct military intervention, and it is far from certain that the recent diminution in frequency of coups represents a trend. In general, the armies most likely to plot and initiate a coup, and to succeed in establishing military rule, tend to be large, to take up more of the gross national product and of total government expenditure, and not to have to share the national territory with troops lent by a major foreign power. They are likely to have factionalized officer corps, with tensions over allocations of benefits among ethnic elites reflected in the factional structure. When one reflects that the two most coup-prone countries are as different as Nigeria and Burkina Faso (six each), one realizes that there is no single pattern of vulnerability.

The diversity of Africa's military regimes matches the diversity of their civilian counterparts. The exceptions, of course, are the growing number of civilian governments actually chosen by and beholden to free electoral choice. One thoughtful typology classifies military regimes into four categories, to each of which can be added a civilian counterpart (see Table 1).

The boundary between civilian and military government can itself be uncertain. Most military governments depend on civilian agents at all but the highest levels, and several military regimes have in appearance civilianized themselves over time. Were Étienne Eyadema's and Mobutu Sese Seko's regimes still military by the early 1990s? When did they begin to take on a more civilian orientation? Jerry Rawlings's rule in Ghana began as a stern military dictatorship but later was transformed into a civilian government chosen in a somewhat fair election. However great or small the difference between civilian and military rule, the wave of democratization that swept Africa in the first half of the 1990s has severely diminished the legitimacy of all forms of authoritarian rule, and that includes all forms of military rule.

The issue of military versus civilian rule in Africa became a factor in the cold war competition of the great powers. In the West, where several influential scholars wrote about the militaries of developing countries as agents of technocratic development, Colonel Mobutu Sese Seko was seen by the United States as far preferable to the civilian radical Patrice Lumumba in the Congo, and General Joseph Ankrah was preferred over Kwame Nkrumah in Ghana. The Soviet Union, beginning with its sales to the Nigerian federal government during the Biafran civil war, found that the trade in arms and military training was one sphere in which it could decisively undercut the West. As the Soviet army increased its foreign policy influence in the 1970s, the Soviet government began looking with particular favor on military regimes, and Soviet scholars began discovering "progressive" virtues in the likes of Bénin's Mathieu Kerekou, Somalia's Siyad Barre, and Ethiopia's Mengistu Haile Mariam. With the end of the cold war, most such illusions and some of the arms trade faded away.

Since the mid-1970s the incidence and scale of armed conflict have increased significantly in sub-Saharan Africa. This both caused and resulted from an increase in military capacity. In the 1960s, most African armies were tiny and hard put to extend their forces beyond national borders. By 1982, however, Ethiopia had a quarter million men under arms and modern tank and air forces. The first, and so far only, successful invasion of one African country by another was accomplished in 1979 when the Tanzanian army defeated the Ugandan army and overthrew Idi Amin. A Somali invasion of Ethiopia failed the same year. The independence of Angola and Mozambique increased the scale of fighting in southern Africa, most notably through the South African Defense Force's raids into those two countries and its support of armed opponents of their governments. Although the new South Africa is at peace with its neighbors, civil strife has continued in Angola.

TABLE 1 Typology of Military and Civilian Regimes in Africa

Regime Type	Military	Civilian
Personal Dictatorship	Amin's Uganda	Touré's Guinea
Radical Leftist	Ngouabi's Congo	Keita's Mali
Managerial Brokerage	Eyadema's Togo	Boigny's Ivory Coast
Holding Operation	Okello's Uganda	Lule's Uganda

SOURCE: Decalo, Samuel. *Coups and Army Rule in Africa.* 1990.

If classic inter-state armed conflict remains rare in Africa, the use of violence has increased domestically with the rise of "politico-military movements," in effect, armed opponents who seek to seize power by the gun. The Frolinat movement in Chad, formed in 1966, was the first of these to make its mark, but Somalia, Rwanda, Liberia, Angola, Mozambique, Ethiopia, and Sudan have all confronted such challenges in the 1990s. Each of these conflicts has its own etiology, but each is helped along by the cold war legacy of readily available arms across the continent, ineffective or abusive rule by civilian and military governments, and economic desperation. Most such movements benefit from the tolerance, if not the complicity, of neighboring regimes. Unlike the coups d'état of the past, which were mostly limited to the capital's administrative center and over by nightfall, the more recent conflicts between governments and politico-military movements usually begin at the periphery, spread across the country, and result in the killing of large numbers of innocent civilians. Ironically, as governments have learned to protect themselves from coups, they have encouraged armed opposition to take a much more virulent form, one which in some cases has caused both state and civil society to disintegrate.

The troubles in Africa and elsewhere in the post–cold war world have given many African armies the opportunity to participate in multilateral peacekeeping operations. Troops from Senegal, Botswana, Nigeria, and Tanzania, among others, have become highly skilled at such tasks. However useful, such use of force to discourage armed conflict must be bolstered by political and economic reform if peace is to prevail.

BIBLIOGRAPHY

Decalo, Samuel. *Coups and Army Rule in Africa.* New Haven, Conn., 1990.

Foltz, William J., and Henry S. Bienen, eds. *Arms and the African: Military Influences on Africa's International Relations.* New Haven, Conn., 1985.

Jenkins, J. C., and A. J. Kposowa. "The Political Origins of African Military Coups: Ethnic Competition, Military Centrality, and the Struggle over the Postcolonial State." *International Studies Quarterly* 36 (1992): 271–292.

Johnson, T. H., Robert O. Slater, and Pat McGowan. "Explaining African Military Coups d'Etat, 1960–1982." *American Political Science Review* 78, no. 3 (1984): 622–640.

WILLIAM J. FOLTZ

See also **Ethnicity and Identity; Genocide, Violence, and Civil Society; Political Systems; Postcolonial State; Warfare.**

MILITARY TECHNOLOGY, HISTORY. Little is known about African armies before about 1200. In the period following 1200, Africa can be divided into several military zones, in each of which a distinct art of war prevailed. One of the first distinctions to be made is between those areas where cavalry was used and those where it was not. The great northern savannas, south of the Sahara and north of the tropical rainforest of western and central Africa, were the one area in Africa where horses could survive well enough to make cavalries possible. For the cavalries of the western savanna, however, mounts proved to be a problem. The largest and fastest horses, imported from the desert regions, could not reproduce well in western Africa, and the local breeds of horses, established for some time, were smaller and not as powerful.

Perhaps because of the problem with mounts, western African cavalries relied on missile tactics rather than shock tactics. Cavalrymen carried javelins or bows, and tactics consisted largely of harrying opponents with these weapons, charging with the saber only when the opponent was broken.

Coastal societies in Senegambia lacked horses but often encountered horsemen along their interior boundaries, ranging from the Serer in modern Senegal, around to modern Sierra Leone, and then in modern Bénin, where a gap in the rain forest allowed cavalries to operate. Perhaps because of the threat of cavalries, armies in these areas were often organized in tight phalanxes and generally fought in close order. Weapons typically were handheld, although archery played a support role. Along the Gold Coast (modern Ghana), even though cavalry was not present, tight formations, typically of professional soldiers using hand-to-hand weapons, with archery only as support, were the norm. Information on this period is lacking for most of the rest of western Africa.

In Angola, armies also were composed entirely of infantry, but with more loosely organized formations than those of western Africa. Archers were used as skirmishers; most tactics were based on hand-to-hand fighting by highly trained, skilled soldiers. In Kongo some soldiers carried defensive arms, typically shields; in Angola there was less use of defensive arms. Instead, soldiers were trained to dodge weapons and fought in loose formations with room between members.

The arrival of Europeans initially had little impact on the tactics of African armies. In Senegambia, Europeans supplied horses, generally of the larger and more powerful sort; these were incorporated into existing armies, for which similar horses had long been imported from the desert. In other societies, Europeans occasionally offered their services as mercenaries during the sixteenth and seventeenth centuries. Although European-made firearms were purchased by African military leaders in the sixteenth and seventeenth centuries, these were treated as just another sort of missile weapon and did little to displace indigenous missile weapons such as bows. In Angola, where significant numbers of European soldiers were engaged in wars of conquest after 1579, the most significant contribution to the local art of war was the use of European soldiers as a sort of heavy infantry. They bore more defensive arms (body armor and helmets) than their African counterparts, but their skill in hand-to-hand fighting, usually with the sword, was valued more than any technical advantages in weapons.

None of the early African armies had highly developed logistical systems. Most armies were accompanied by large bands of porters who carried food and supplies—in Angola, they were often half as numerous as the army itself. Where rivers made transport of foodstuffs possible, they were used; in other cases, armies resupplied through foraging or looting the countryside. Logistical problems tended to limit the maximum size of armies as well as their range.

The development of the flintlock musket and its importation into Africa in large numbers after the early eighteenth century had a profound impact on the conduct of war in many African societies. In areas where cavalry played an important role, such as Senegambia and the savanna interior of the Guinea coast, firearms remained relatively unimportant until well into the nineteenth century. But in coastal societies, firearms were incorporated into the armies, displacing bows almost entirely and, moreover, resulting in tactical changes. On the Gold Coast, the tight formations of the seventeenth century gave way to more open formations in which all combatants carried firearms. Instead of closing on opponents, African generals sought to win the day through musket fire, often maneuvering to avoid close fighting. Formations were loose, and individual units were small and mobile to accommodate these changes. Similar changes took place both in Kongo, where the larger, looser formations equipped with firearms replaced the smaller units and more skillful professional soldiers of earlier times, and in Angola, where the Portuguese-led armies and their African opponents both fought in the same way.

The Kingdom of Dahomey (modern Bénin) had to make different adaptations to accommodate the potential of firearms. Because its soldiers had to fight horsemen of the interior kingdoms, especially Oyo, they could not use loose formations. Instead, they developed tight formations of musketeers and drilled the soldiers to maintain a high rate of firing, including rotation of platoons. Without cavalry support, however, Dahomean units were not always effective against opposing cavalry.

Where cost or transportation factors made it impossible to supply African armies with large numbers of firearms, the older art of war remained, even where cavalry did not play a role. In the eighteenth century, the Lunda of central Africa had good success, even against opponents bearing firearms, with the older tactics of rapid closing for hand-to-hand fighting.

BIBLIOGRAPHY

Law, Robin. *The Horse in African History.* Oxford, 1980.

JOHN K. THORNTON

See also **Warfare.**

MINERALS AND METALS

MINING INDUSTRIES

Mining in the Precolonial Past

The exploitation of minerals found on or under the ground has long been a major aspect of how Africans have learned to master their natural environment. The Iron Age had begun in sub-Saharan Africa by 500 B.C.E., and the use of iron spread rapidly, with an attested site within modern South Africa by the third century C.E. Iron was crucial in the improvement of agricultural tools and weapons. The processes Africans developed, either through invention or imitation, for refining metal were also applied to other mineral substances, such as gold, copper, and tin. Gold from Africa found its way far outside the continent; gold mines located in what became Ghana and Guinea were linked to the Middle East by trade routes over the Sahara, while gold in what is now Zimbabwe provided wealth for the coastal sultanate of Kilwa (in present-day Tanzania) and was shipped across the Indian Ocean. In south-central Ghana, probably the most important African producer of gold, gold dust was used as a form of currency, and gold was fashioned into distinctive and beautiful ornaments.

Mining in the precolonial African context was quite different from the forms that it would take under the impulse of the Industrial Revolution. Although ingenious, African methods of underground mining allowed only relatively shallow access to deposits. Furthermore, there were no means for emptying water out of flooded mines. Mines had to be abandoned when the limited technical means for retrieving ore were reached. Most labor was performed in the dry season, much of it by women, so that it had a subsidiary character to core household accumulation processes. Culturally, the practice of mining was shot through with ritual ceremony and taboos and had a semisacral character; in western Africa, smiths were often a caste set apart from the population at large.

Links to growing Western markets often exhausted African mining activities. Mines ran out of workable ore while imported metal products replaced local raw materials. The fabled gold mines of south-central Africa lured the Portuguese up the Zambezi Valley and onto the central plateau of modern Zimbabwe, but they never succeeded in organizing any effective mineral production. As the slave trade expanded to new levels in the eighteenth century, the Gold Coast (later Ghana) exported slaves instead of gold, and the slave traders purchased men and women with imported gold. Nonetheless, the mining activities of the colonial period depended heavily on the relocation of sites of production that had long been known and worked by Africans. This was true of such major copper sources as Tsumeb in Namibia, Phalaborwa in South Africa, and the extraordinarily rich deposits of the Copperbelt on both sides of the Zaire-Zambia border as well as the gold of Ghana or the tin of the Jos Plateau region of Nigeria.

Mining and the Emergence of Modern South Africa

The development and export of mineral resources played a central part in the development of capitalism in colonial Africa from early days. By contrast to the difficulties inherent in creating new systems of agriculture and the slowness with which modern industry developed, mineral development proceeded successfully and profitably in many colonies. The most successful mineral development of all occurred in what is now South Africa. It began with the exploitation of Namaqualand copper in 1854 and reached a turning point with the discovery of the rich diamond deposits around Kimberley after 1867. Within a few years, Kimberley rivaled Cape Town in size, and unprecedented amounts of capital and labor poured into the diamond fields. In the early years, mining was dominated by small diggers, mainly but not exclusively white. Labor was expensive, and the profits in large part accrued to speculators, illegal diamond buyers, and the purveyors of goods and services to the mining camp population. By 1888, however, a process of amalgamation had been completed and the entire industry became dominated by one firm, De Beers, associated with Cecil Rhodes. Amalgamation allowed for the rational recovery of ore from the ground and the hoarding of diamonds at times of glut. With it went the transformation of the labor force; by the 1880s a reduced number of white skilled workers, who lived in family suburbs, were employed together with black migrants living in closed compounds, under constant surveillance for theft and receiving lowered wages.

Developments from 1886 on the Witwatersrand followed from those in Kimberley in terms of labor control, race relations, and the organization of capital. The gold mines of the Transvaal contained reliable, if not especially rich, shafts of gold-bearing ore at great distances from the ground. With technical difficulties overcome, the field could be developed only through harnessing capital and labor on a larger scale than anywhere else in world mining. The Rand gold mines attracted the majority of all capital invested in Africa up to World War II. Within South Africa the impact was convulsive. A complex series of events relate the discoveries to the political crisis that doomed the Boer republics and led to the formation of the Union of South Africa. The country's urban infrastructure and agriculture had to be transformed to make the mining industry viable. Between 1907 and 1922 a series of major strikes, mainly on the part of white workers, challenged the industry at a time when accident and disease rates were terrifying. In order to obtain a sufficient labor force, the gold mines created a subcontinental recruitment system, with most workers in most of the twentieth century coming from outside the borders of South Africa itself.

Gold mining formed the base of a new era of capitalist accumulation in South Africa. For one thing, the mines spawned the creation of secondary industry in such sectors as metals, timber, and chemicals. For a second, the state succeeded in harnessing the revenues derived from mine taxes to create a modern infrastructure and put resources into other sectors of the economy. The means by which labor was recruited and controlled—settlement in compounds; the pass system, which controlled the free movement of prospective workers; and the deferred forms of payment and down payment systems—were widely imitated not only in other mining industries in the region but also in other sectors of the economy. The once-turbulent white mining community was transformed into a small class of supervisory and skilled labor. It accounted for less than one-tenth of the total, yet at a peak in the early 1970s absorbed two-thirds of the wage bill.

By contrast with Kimberley, the gold mines were never monopolized by a single firm. Instead, from an early date they were dominated by a small number of mining finance houses whose investments interpenetrated to a significant extent. These houses, of which the most important from the 1920s was the Anglo-American Corporation, were increasingly South African in character. When the state fiscal regime, for developmental and security

Premier Diamond Mine near Pretoria, South Africa. COURTESY SOUTH AFRICAN COMMUNICATION SERVICE

reasons, made it difficult for South African investments to go outside the country, mining-based investment flowed into property, agriculture, and industry.

Despite the continued preeminence of gold and diamonds, a major feature of mining in South Africa was coal and base metals—including asbestos, antimony, chrome, tin, copper, and iron ore—from the late nineteenth to the late twentieth centuries. In certain phases, such as the 1960s, good demand for base metals allowed these mining activities to take up the slack in the export economy when the price of gold was such as to lower prices in the South African gold mines.

Colonialism and the Mining Economy

The great economic significance of South African mining to twentieth-century capitalism should not take away from the large-scale development of mining elsewhere in colonial Africa. A second great mining complex in south-central Africa included the Copperbelt of Northern Rhodesia (now Zambia) and Katanga (now Shaba) Province in the Belgian Congo (now Zaire). This set of mines was a major world producer of copper, and those on the Zaire side of the frontier also came to yield uranium and cobalt in important quantities. Elsewhere in the region, copper also proved the salvation of German colonialism in South West Africa (now Namibia) and, from the eve of World War I up to the late twentieth century, the Namibian economy has depended on mineral exports. Southern Rhodesia (now Zimbabwe) never witnessed the development of a "Second Rand," as its conquerors had hoped, but scattered coal, gold, tin, asbestos, chrome, and other deposits were a very important part of its economy. The Belgian Congo was a mineral-rich colony that exported gold, tin, and other ores. In western Africa mining was also a major economic activity. Especially notable were the diamond mines of the Gold Coast and Sierra Leone, the tin mines in Northern Nigeria, the coal mines in eastern Nigeria, and underground gold mining in the Gold Coast. In Tanganyika, commercial gold and diamond mining played an important part in the economy.

Mines sustained many African colonial economies. Nonetheless, in contrast with South Africa, these economies were classics of the enclave type of development excoriated by radical dependency theorists. Investment was confined fairly narrowly to the mining industry, with few linkages beyond the necessary transport and other infrastructural developments. The mine owners remained overwhelmingly based in the metropolitan countries, where profits reverted, and had little stake in African society.

In some cases even tighter controls over mine workers were maintained than in South Africa. However, this was not the general pattern. In the Copperbelt, workers from an early date were encouraged to bring their families to the mining towns. To take an extreme example, in the Nigerian tin-mining camps, employers had little control over the lives of workers, and hiring remained largely in the hands of Nigerian labor contractors. The large workforce was characterized by massive turnover as tens of thousands of short-term migrants arrived during the course of the year. While African workers in such colonies as the Congo and the Gold Coast did increasingly include a significant skilled stratum, the mass of workers did not easily become transformed into an urban proletariat, and the retention of rural roots and affinities was everywhere important.

Mining in Africa since 1960

The early years of independence saw a further increase in mining development in many African countries, typically with single Western investors

giving way to consortia. Examples would include the diamond mines of Botswana, iron-ore mining in Mauritania, bauxite mining in Guinea, and uranium mining in Niger. Often the newly independent African state got a share of ownership in addition to tax revenues from mining operations. In such countries as Tanzania, Ghana, and Nigeria, miner insurgency in the late colonial period had played an important part in a growing challenge to colonial hegemony on which national movements had battened. With independence, the unions' wings were clipped since the new states were responsible for enforcing a profitable order on the mines. A striking feature in the post-colonial era was the growing importance of industrial as opposed to precious minerals, partly linked to the cold war arms buildup.

It was a natural temptation for new states to contemplate nationalization of the mines. The Convention People's Party government of Kwame Nkrumah in Ghana, the United National Independence Party government in Zambia, and Mobutu Sese Seko's regime in Zaire were among those that actually took this step with regard to major mining property. The results proved disastrous. Continued dependence on foreign expertise and management proved inevitable. As mining suffered increasing economic setbacks from the 1970s, it proved very difficult for the state to rein in expenses and maintain equipment. Also, it has not proven very easy for independent African governments to find a discipline in the labor process to replace the harsh controls of the colonial era. With the growing pressure from the World Bank and other Western agencies to impose structural adjustment on state budgets in Africa, the nationalization movement went into reverse, and in the 1990s African governments are in the process of trying to privatize the mines they had taken over.

A key part of the background to this ebb and flow has been the faltering position of mining in the world economy. Change in industrial processes has greatly reduced the once-increasing demand for such metals as copper and iron ore, virtually eliminating new mining developments in Africa since the beginning of the 1980s. Questions about nuclear power have cut back uranium mining. While gold and diamond mining have survived better, they have had an erratic prosperity. Much production today comes from petty entrepreneurs, often evading state controls, who shoulder their own risks. Big international mining houses tend to cold shoulder Africa, preferring to build up their investments in more stable and conservative political environments.

Even South Africa is an important case in point. Since the mid-1980s, a majority of gold miners have joined a militant trade union, a fact linked to the declining share of workers coming from outside the country. Perhaps even more important than the struggles within the industry, the entire national economy suffers from the stagnation in the mining sector. After a remarkable boom in 1979–1982, the price of gold fell dramatically and gold no longer provided a fiscal base for economic activity on the part of the South African state. South Africa has continued to depend on minerals as its core export and must make a difficult adjustment in its trade economy. There and in the majority of African states, the heritage of mining is inseparable from the colonial economy with its characteristic forms of control and extraction. This heritage is increasingly problematic from the point of view of both economic and social development today.

BIBLIOGRAPHY

Crush, Jonathan S., Alan Jeeves, and David Yudelman. *South Africa's Labor Empire: A History of Black Migrancy to the Gold Mines.* Boulder, Colo., 1991.

Ferguson, James. "Mobile Workers, Modernist Narratives: A Critique of the Historiography of Transition on the Zambian Copperbelt." *Journal of Southern African Studies* 16 (1990): 385–412, 603–621.

Freund, Bill. *Capital and Labor in the Nigerian Tin Mines.* Atlantic Highlands, N.J., 1981.

———. "South African Gold Mining in Transformation." In *South Africa's Economic Crisis,* edited by Stephen Gelb. 2d ed. London, 1991.

James, Wilmot G. *Our Precious Metal: African Labour in South Africa's Gold Industry, 1970–1990.* Cape Town, South Africa, 1992.

Lanning, Greg, and Marti Mueller. *Africa Undermined: Mining Companies and the Underdevelopment of Africa.* New York, 1979.

Turrell, Robert Vicat. *Capital and Labour on the Kimberley Diamond Fields, 1871–1890.* New York, 1987.

Van Onselen, Charles. *Chibaro: African Mine Labour in Southern Rhodesia, 1900–1933.* London, 1976.

Yachir, Faysal. *Mining in Africa Today: Strategies and Prospects.* Atlantic Highlands, N.J., 1988.

BILL FREUND

See also **Economic History; Metallurgy; Slave Trade; Trades Unions and Associations.**

RESOURCE DISTRIBUTION

Distribution

Africa is resource rich, but mineral and metal deposits, as well as the benefits from this wealth, are unevenly distributed. Sub-Saharan Africa accounts for 8 percent of the world's total mining production. If petroleum is included, the production value is more than $35 billion. However, only nineteen sub-Saharan countries benefit substantially from mineral wealth, and even those that do have sizable mineral and metal deposits do not always obtain the benefits of these riches.

The basis for Africa's mineral wealth is the geology of sub-Saharan Africa. The foundation of Africa is a core of stable, continental crust composed of Precambrian rocks. This is the craton, composed mainly of granite, gneiss, and greenstones. In terms of mineral and metal deposits, greenstones are the most favorable rocks for gold and other mineral deposits. Such areas include the principal goldfields of Ghana (Ashanti), Ethiopia (Adola), Zimbabwe (Midlands), and the border between Swaziland and South Africa (Barberton Belt). In addition to these known gold deposits, there are undeveloped greenstone belts in Burkina Faso (Boromo, Aribinda, and Dori-Assakan), northwestern Tanzania, and northern Zaire (Kilo, Moto, Nagayu, and Isiro). Minerals and metals are also found in depositional basins. Examples are the goldfields of the Witwatersrand in South Africa, Tarkwa in Ghana, and the Copperbelt that runs through Zambia and Zaire. Mineral and metal deposits are associated with crustal movements which have led to the formation of sedimentary basins. The Karoo sequence, which holds most of Africa's coal, is a large sedimentary deposit located in Mozambique, Malawi, South Africa, Tanzania, and Zimbabwe.

Furthermore, minerals and metal resources are associated with areas where the crust has fragmented, allowing magma to well up and form what are called kimberlite intrusives. These are the source of diamond deposits in Angola, Guinea, Botswana, South Africa, Tanzania, and Zaire. Mineral and metal deposits are also found in areas where the crustal plates are diverging. One such area is the Rift Valley, which runs through eastern Africa. This geological activity has led to the formation of nonmetallic minerals such as kaolin clay, bentonite, pozzolana, and fluorite, as well as of salt lakes, which contain valuable minerals including salt, soda ash, and potash.

Mineral and metal deposits are also associated with volcanic activity, which formed the South African Bushveld Complex and the Great Dyke of Zimbabwe. These areas contain chromium and platinum. Younger volcanic areas contain phosphates (Angola, Uganda, Tanzania), and under

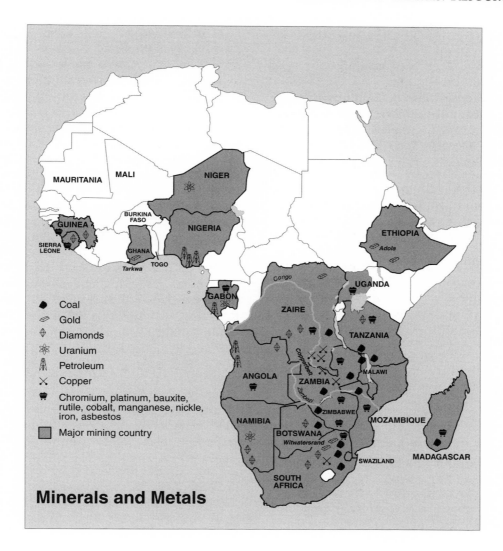

Minerals and Metals

Coal
Gold
Diamonds
Uranium
Petroleum
Copper
Chromium, platinum, bauxite, rutile, cobalt, manganese, nickle, iron, asbestos
Major mining country

some circumstances copper (South Africa), gold, and nickel. Mineral deposits are also created by erosional processes and chemical weathering, as is the case with bauxite in Guinea; rutile in Madagascar, Mozambique, and Sierre Leone; alluvial gold deposits in southern Ethiopia and northern Zaire; and alluvial diamonds in Namibia.

As a result of its geological past, Africa is well endowed in bauxite, copper, cobalt, diamonds, manganese, rutile, uranium, iron, and petroleum. More than half the world's diamonds, platinum, and cobalt are produced in Africa. The world relies on African mines for up to a third of its uranium, manganese, and chromium, and a tenth of its rutile, copper, and bauxite. Africa also supplies some 8 percent of the world's phosphates, 7 percent of its iron ore, and 6 percent of its petroleum.

The distribution of mineral wealth is, however, highly uneven. Nineteen countries benefit from commercial-scale mining, but out of these countries only two, South Africa (gold and diamonds) and Nigeria (petroleum), account for more than half the total mineral production. Five other countries—Zambia (copper and cobalt), Zaire (copper and cobalt), Botswana (diamonds), Angola (petroleum), and Gabon (petroleum, manganese, and uranium)—are major producers of minerals. Some African countries are important because they are world leaders in the production of strategic minerals and metals. Zambia and Zaire produce 69 percent of the world's cobalt and 12 percent of the world's copper. Guinea is the world's second largest bauxite producer; Sierra Leone is the second largest rutile producer; Zimbabwe is the third

163

largest producer of asbestos; Gabon is the third largest manganese producer. Gabon, Namibia, and Niger together produce 24 percent of the world's uranium.

In spite of Africa's mineral wealth, only South Africa has become wealthy as a result of its mineral deposits. This is because most of Africa's mineral wealth is controlled by transnational corporations or parastatal companies. In addition, the majority of minerals and metals are exported as raw ore. While some of this production is exported as finished metals, none of the ore is used to make manufactured products. As a result, the jobs generated by mining are, for the most part, unskilled or semiskilled, and in several areas, notably South Africa, migrant labor is dominant. Another important reason why Africa's mineral wealth has failed to generate real wealth for Africa's nations is that mining operations are enclaves to the rest of the economy. They have strong links to the export market but few links to the local economy. Thus wealth is siphoned off rather than put back into local economies.

History of Exploitation

The history of mineral development in Africa provides clues to the current state of mineral production and the reasons behind the uneven distribution of mineral wealth. Mining has always been an important economic activity in Africa. Gold panned from alluvial deposits and riverbeds was the mainstay of trade in the west African kingdoms of Ghana, Mali, and Songhai. Copper was found in the watersheds of the Congo and Zambezi Rivers in central Africa and mined in Katanga (Shaba) long before the arrival of Europeans. Iron was worked in the ancient civilization of Meroë, which straddled the banks of the upper reaches of the Nile. Ironworking technology spread slowly south, and Africans closely guarded its secrets from Europeans.

Until the middle of the nineteenth century, Africans maintained control over their mineral resources, but this declined as the slave trade caused social upheaval and the presence of Europeans on the continent increased. The discovery of diamonds in South Africa, at Kimberley in 1867, marked the beginnings of the transfer of Africa's mineral wealth to Europeans. Britain annexed the Kimberley area in 1871 from the Griqua ethnic group and the South African Republic. And while the British controlled the production, African miners were the basis of the fortunes made by the likes of Cecil Rhodes, who, along with European financiers, bought up the claims of individual miners and formed mineral giants such as De Beers, which today controls the production and marketing of diamonds throughout the world.

Other mineral discoveries soon followed. Gold was discovered in the Witwatersrand in the 1880s. From the 1880s to the 1930s, prospectors and financiers from Germany, the United States, Belgium, France, South Africa, and Britain established mines throughout the mineral-rich areas of the continent, including Angola, the Belgian Congo (present-day Zaire), Southern Rhodesia (present-day Zimbabwe), Northern Rhodesia (present-day Zambia), Nigeria, and Sierra Leone. Mineral production increased dramatically during the twentieth century, displacing agricultural products, and led to the transformation of trading routes. Prior to mining, trading routes ran across the continent to the Indian Ocean, where traders plied between Arabia, India, and China. But new mining trade routes were designed simply to bring the minerals to waiting ships that took them to Europe and the Americas. Railways were built, but they did not connect centers of population. For instance, the route from the Katanga copper mines in the Belgian Congo ran through Angola, not the Congo, so this railway provided little economic stimulus to the area. The mines operated as enclave economies until the 1960s.

Independence brought a wave of nationalization to Africa, and mines in Zambia, Sierra Leone, Uganda, Ghana, Tanzania, Zaire, Togo, and Mauritania were nationalized following independence. As a result, African mining enterprises are now roughly split between privately owned and state-owned mines. The private mines are owned by transnational corporations, or are jointly owned by private companies and the state. The rest are controlled by parastatal mining companies run by national governments. However, the lock that transnational corporations have historically had on African mineral production means that there are few small-scale mining operations. Technology drives this as well. Mining has become more mechanized and larger-scale. In addition, with marketing and production of key minerals in some cases controlled by a single company, as is the case with De Beers, it is hard for small companies to compete. However, mining does occur on a small, noncommercial scale in more than thirty African countries. Artisanal mining generates an estimated $800 million a year and employs more than 1 million workers.

Africa's share of the world mineral production has slipped since independence. Private companies, wary of political instability and the threat of nationalization, have invested elsewhere, notably Latin America and Asia. As a result, sub-Saharan Africa's share of the world mineral production has fallen since 1960 and is stagnant with a growth rate of 1 to 2 percent a year. The irony behind this decline is that Africa still contains vast mineral wealth, but much of it has not been tapped or investments in new mining projects have been curtailed or halted. For example, new deposits have been discovered but have yet to be developed. These include the Fungerume copper deposits in Zaire and the Adola gold belt in Ethiopia.

As a result of its history, and the way in which its minerals and metals are controlled by a few large companies, Africa's mineral wealth is largely a source of *potential* wealth for much of Africa. Without more refining of ore and the creation of finished products, better linkages to local economies, and indigenous capital for investment in new exploration, Africa's mineral wealth will continue to be unevenly distributed and underdeveloped.

BIBLIOGRAPHY

Cunningham, Simon. *The Copper Industry in Zambia: Foreign Mining Companies in a Developing Country.* New York, 1981.

Labys, Walter C. *The Mineral Trade Potential of Africa's Least Developed Countries.* New York, 1985.

Ogunbadejo, Oye. *The International Politics of Africa's Strategic Minerals.* Westport, Conn., 1985.

Stock, Robert. *Africa South of the Sahara: A Geographical Interpretation.* New York, 1995.

World Bank. *Strategy for African Mining.* World Bank Technical Paper no. 181. Washington, D.C., 1992.

DAVID SMETHURST

See also **Fuel.**

MIRAMBO (b. 1840? d. 1884), military innovator, trade profiteer, and ruler of the Nyamwezi in what is now Tanzania. Legend has it that Mirambo was captured by Ngoni peoples when he was young, and learned from them spear-fighting techniques and political leadership. As a chief, Mirambo used these methods to build his political influence and his own private army. Equipped with firearms and required to undergo vigorous conditioning, this military unit became known as a *rugaruga* and was used later by other Nyamwezi leaders.

Swahili-Arabs dominated the flourishing east African ivory trade from their inland post at Tabora, the link between the expanding ivory frontier and Zanzibar, the major entrepôt of east Africa. In the early nineteenth century various Nyamwezi groups took part in the ivory trade as hunters, porters, and caravan leaders. The Nyamwezi were not centrally organized (there were thirty-one Nyamwezi chiefdoms in 1859), and often the Swahili traders would play groups off against one another. As elephants became more scarce in Nyamwezi areas, it was necessary for expeditions to travel farther and farther to bring back ivory. Mirambo, whose capital, Urambo, was in the vicinity of Tabora, sought to unify the Nyamwezi in order to better organize trade and deal a blow to the Swahili.

With an army of five thousand, Mirambo began a campaign of bringing Nyamwezi groups under his control and disrupting trade between the ivory

Mirambo, in a photograph taken between 1882 and 1884. A. C. UNOMAH

frontier, which was at that time to the west and south of Lake Tanganyika, and Zanzibar. By harassing caravans and making ivory acquisition more difficult, Mirambo and his *rugaruga* caused the price of ivory to rise. Sultan Barghash of Zanzibar sent a large caravan to make peace with Mirambo in 1875, and after negotiations an agreement for a temporary alliance was reached the next year. For the next eight years Mirambo controlled the corridor bounded by Tabora and Lake Tanganyika that stretched from Lake Victoria in the north to Lake Rukwa in the south. Mirambo profited greatly from trade passing through his large sphere of influence by charging tolls, levies, and protection fees, but his empire dissolved shortly after his death in 1884.

BIBLIOGRAPHY

Bennett, Norman Robert. *Mirambo of Tanzania: 1840?– 1884.* New York, 1971.

THOMAS F. McDow

See also **East African Interior.**

MISSIONARIES. *See* **Christianity.**

MOBUTU SESE SEKO (b. 1930; d. 1997), Zairian military leader and president of Zaire. Born Joseph-Désiré Mobutu in Lisala, he attended a succession of schools before his expulsion from junior high school at the age of nineteen due to behavioral problems. He was conscripted into the army in 1950, serving for most of the next six years at the noncommissioned officer school in Kananga and then at army headquarters in Kinshasa. He then became a journalist in Kinshasa. He was sent to the Brussels 1958 World's Fair and spent 1959–1960 in a journalist training program in Brussels.

In the wake of an army mutiny in Congo in July 1960, Mobutu, then allied to the radical nationalist Congolese leader Patrice Lumumba, was named army chief of staff and was able to achieve relative control of the armed forces. On 14 September he initiated his first coup to "neutralize" tensions between Prime Minister Lumumba and President Joseph Kasavubu, appointing an interim government of young university graduates. Enjoying support from Western nations, especially the United States, he participated in Lumumba's removal to Shaba (Katanga), in January 1961, where Lumumba was assassinated.

Mobutu Sese Seko and his wife, Bobi Ladawa, enter their villa on the French Riviera in January 1997. LAURENT REBOURS/AP/WIDE WORLD

On 24 November 1965, Mobutu seized power through the army. In 1967 he created a single political party (Mouvement Populaire de la Révolution) to underpin his personal rule and was elected by plebiscite for seven-year presidential terms in 1970, 1977, and 1984. In his early years of rule, he renamed the nation Zaire (in 1971), recentralized the administration, for a time stabilized the economy, and created the illusion of strong development. Since 1975, however, the country has been in prolonged decline, and the regime became notorious for venality and misrule. Despite legalization of opposition parties in 1990, Mobutu continued to maintain himself in power.

In 1991 he appointed an opponent, Étienne Tshisekedi, prime minister after rioting in Kinshasa, but dismissed him after twelve days. He dissolved the legislature in 1994. In 1996 Mobutu began treatment for prostate cancer. Beginning in September 1996 a revolt led by Laurent Désiré Kabila, head of the Alliance of Democratic Forces for the Liberation of Congo, spread across Zaire from the east. After negotiations with Kabila failed, Mobutu fled Kinshasa in May 1997 for exile, at first in Gabon, as Kabila's forces entered the capital.

BIBLIOGRAPHY

Monheim, Francis. *Mobutu, l'homme seul.* Brussels, 1962.

Young, Crawford, and Thomas Turner. *The Rise and Decline of the Zairian State.* Madison, Wis., 1985.

CRAWFORD YOUNG

See also **Congo Free State; Lumumba, Patrice.**

MODES OF THOUGHT IN AFRICAN PHILOSOPHY.

The African mind has been deeply engaged over the ages by fundamental questions about the world and human experience. This is evident from the rich resources of speculative thought in African oral traditions and, in places, from long-standing written records of philosophical reflection. This entry will be mostly concerned with traditional modes of thought, drawing a methodological distinction between the traditional and the modern phases of African philosophy.

African Philosophy: Modern and Traditional

The characterization of modern African philosophy encounters complex issues and is currently the subject of considerable controversy. The reason for this is simple. Because of the Western colonization of Africa, the philosophical education of modern African scholars has come to be conducted in Western-style institutions. Even deeper inroads have been made into the African psyche by the advent of industrialization and the conversion of great numbers of Africans to foreign religions. Amid the easily visible evidences of the almost inextricable intermingling of African and Western categories of thought, some postindependence African philosophers, motivated by considerations of authenticity, have been cautious of Western admixtures, demanding some connection with the traditional in any thought structures that might merit the designation African philosophy. Others have been more liberal, trusting more to contemporary validity in the evolving tradition than to connection with the traditional as a necessary condition for any exploitation of foreign sources of insight. The height of this kind of liberality is reached by Paulin J. Hountondji's controversial definition of African philosophy in his seminal *African Philosophy: Myth and Reality* (1983) as "literature produced by Africans and dealing with philosophical problems." Not even Hountondji's position, however, implies that African concerns, traditional and contemporary, should not be at the center of modern African philosophy.

No such complications of definition beset the study of African traditional philosophy, though there are secondary issues of approach. Some seem content with more or less narrative interpretations while others insist on a critical and reconstructive agenda. On almost all hands, however, there is the recognition that the relevant traditional bodies of thought are philosophical in the sense that they attempt answers to questions displaying the high abstractness and generality characteristic of philosophy. For example, many of the oral traditions offer ideas on questions of the following kinds: What is the explanation of the order in the cosmos? What is the nature of human personality? What, from an ontological perspective (that is, in terms of the ultimate constituents of human personality), is the significance of death for the human species? Are human beings subject to an overarching destiny and how does such an idea stand with moral responsibility? What is the criterion of goodness for an individual as well as a community? And what is the role of extra-human beings, such as the supreme being and the ancestors, in regard to the basis of morality and its enforcement? The general nature of the answers to these questions depends, not deterministically but still determinately, on the broad characteristics of the cultures involved, in terms, principally, of social ethos and linguistic habits. Detailed generalizations must await particularistic philosophical studies of the multifarious peoples of Africa. But some affinities of philosophical orientation can be discerned among various groups of African peoples, such as the Bantu peoples of eastern and southern Africa and the ethnic populations of west Africa, on account of substantial cultural similarities.

Cosmogony and Ontology

Certain articles of shared belief, indeed, would appear to be almost universal on the continent. Thus, there is nearly everywhere belief in a hierarchy of existents, at the top of which is a supreme being or power postulated to account for the orderliness of phenomena and to hold to ultimate account the not-infrequent moral disorderliness of the human species. Next below the supreme being are a variety of extra-human beings of divers powers and purposes that can be tapped by humans, the next in the hierarchy, if they know how. Below our species come, in a descending order, the world of the lower animals and plants and the realm of inanimate reality. The universality of this picture of the world in Africa is limited only by rare cases, such as the system of the central Luo, who, according to Okot p'Bitek, do not postulate a supreme being at all.

The rest of the scheme, however, remains in place even in that case.

What modes of conceptualization does this worldview evince? The question calls for some prior conceptual unraveling. For example, in what sense is the generally postulated supreme being supposed to account for the cosmos or, more strictly, for the order therein? The wording of this question is chosen advisedly. It is arguable that what puzzles the African mind is the order of phenomena rather than the sheer existence of those phenomena, a notion that may not even be coherent within the indigenous conceptual frameworks. This hypothesis is in close harmony with the strongly empirical strain that runs through much of African cosmogonic thinking.

In terms of detail, the cosmogonies are heterogenous, though in terms of diction they are almost always mythopoeic. The Akan of Ghana are somewhat of an exception to the second part of the last remark, for their cosmogony is given expression in "drum stanzas" (J. B. Danquah's apt phrase) astringent in their verbal economy. Drum stanzas are versified aphorisms rendered on "talking drums." Some of the most profound metaphysical ideas of the Akan, such as the present one, are contained in drum "texts" of this kind, famous for their compressed expression. To compress even more: The Creator created things. What did he create? He created Order, Knowledge, and Death (Danquah, *The Akan Doctrine of God*, 1944). More characteristic is the Yoruba account of what happened "in the beginning." In one famous version the town now known as Ile-Ife was the scene of creation. The supreme being sent an agent with a packet of loose earth to go and spread upon the land, which was just a watery marsh, and solidify it in preparation for human habitation. Being thirsty on the way, the agent drank a good quantity of palm wine and was overtaken by slumber before completing his work, whereupon the supreme being sent another agent to accomplish the task. The intriguing drama of the Yoruba myth is matched by the elaborate symbolism of that of the Dogon: The process of creation takes place in a cosmic egg of two partitions, each containing a pair of twin beings which are "direct emanations and sons of God." Each twin being contains both male and female principles, symbolizing the fundamental role of opposites in all phenomena. As in the Yoruba story, something goes wrong, and the male element in one of the twin beings bursts out prematurely, an aberration that results in the creation of

the earth, with its imperfections. God, of course, intervenes with some rescue work, which defines various details of the cosmogony.

These summaries do not capture the mythopoeic richness of the Yoruba or Dogon accounts of first things, but they do provide a basis for raising a question of philosophical interpretation: Do these accounts espouse a notion of creation out of nothing or one of the introduction of order into a preexistent manifold of indeterminacy? A myth is a metaphor, and its explication ought to reflect the format of the metaphor. By this criterion, the sense in which the supreme being in the Yoruba myth seems to be intended to account for the world is that in which an architect accounts for the form of a building. Whether empirically warranted or not, such an idea of a cosmic architect is, conceptually, more empirically oriented than the idea of a creator ex nihilo. The same would seem to be even more evidently true of the Akan case. The Dogon myth too appears to harbor no ex nihilo intentions. But there is a further dimension. The cosmic egg appears to be an *emanation* of the supreme being, a notion which seems to forestall some of the paradoxes of divine creation even of the purely architectural sort.

How universal is this empirical orientation in cosmogony in Africa? Unanimity is not at hand. Some authors see a doctrine of ex nihilo creation in some African traditional talk of God. Thus E. E. Evans-Pritchard maintains that the Nuer of southern Sudan characterize creation by the use of language that can only mean that God created the world out of nothing. J J. Maquet is positive that the Banyarwanda of Rwanda believe that the world was created by God out of nothing. According to him, they are clear on this because they say that before creation there was nothing. And indeed, even of the Akan, Kwame Gyekye has asserted that their doctrine of origins is one of divine creation out of nothing. The possibility that the various peoples of the vast continent of Africa do not share one mode of cosmogonic reflection cannot, of course, be discounted. But a thorough appraisal of the issue is unlikely without a semantic analysis of the concept of existence in the languages concerned.

In this last connection the observations of Alexis Kagame, a Rwandan philosopher and linguist, about how the concept of existence is rendered in the languages "throughout the Bantu zone" are of the greatest philosophical interest. According to him, the analogue of the verb "to be" in these languages is expressed by either of two roots: *li* and *ba*. But these words by themselves, unlike the English verb "to be," are incomplete and incapable of expressing the notion of existence in any context. One has to add the adverb of place *ho* for this purpose. So that, ignoring idiomatic niceties, the notion of "exists" is expressed by means of either *liho* or *baho*, meaning "is there," "is at that place." Remarkably, the word *ho* has exactly the same function in the rendition of the concept of existence in Akan. Gyekye provides lucid testimony to what he calls the "locative implication" of the Akan expression for "exists." To express the notion the Akan say *wo ho*, where *wo* has the same semantic incapacities as the Bantu *li* or *ba*. Existence, therefore, is essentially spatial in both the Bantu and Akan conceptual frameworks. The ontological implications of this concept of existence for philosophies articulated in these and cognate languages are nothing short of global.

The most immediately relevant implication of the locative conception of existence relates to the notion of absolute nothingness which is involved in the doctrine of creation out of nothing. If to exist is to be at some place, then the notion of there being nothing must become that of there not being anything at some given location or locations. But the notion of location already logically defies absolute nothingness, and a fortiori, renders the conception of creation out of nothing incoherent. Whether this incoherence afflicts the idea of creation out of nothing as it occurs in English and other languages is, of course, a matter for independent inquiry. But in the study of African traditional modes of thought this semantic circumstance is one that may well necessitate important expository revisions.

Another implication of the locative conception of existence affects the ontological nature of the second layer of beings in the outline of the African worldview given earlier on. They were called "extra-human beings." These are postulated beings such as the ancestors and forces or powers such as witchcraft and "the lesser gods" (an imperfect phrase used here for lack of a more economical one). They are often described as spiritual and supernatural, though occasional skeptical riders are heard. Thus Geoffrey Lienhardt, in his conceptually sensitive study of the Dinka of southern Sudan (*Divinity and Experience*, 1961), studiously abstains from the natural-supernatural dichotomy on the grounds that it has implications about the course of nature which are inapplicable to Dinka thought.

Kofi A. Busia also, speaking of Akan thought, notes therein the "apparent absence of any conceptual cleavage between the natural and the supernatural" (*The Challenge of Africa*, 1962). And John Mbiti, for his part, talking of the thought habits of Africans in general, remarks that "no line is drawn between the spiritual and the physical" (*African Religions and Philosophy*, 1990). The last two authors do not always keep to the terms of these observations, but the observations themselves are of the first consequence in the understanding of African worldviews and their contrasts with their Western counterparts.

The key is this: In any language in which a locative understanding of existence is as evidently fundamental to discourse, as it is in many African languages, all classes of admitted entities will naturally be viewed as belonging to one spatiotemporal realm of being. There will, accordingly, be no place for spiritual entities conceived in the Cartesian manner as non-spatial, immaterial substances. If one speaks of spirits in such a locatively oriented conceptual milieu, that will only be intelligible in the usage of the noun "spirit" in which it fails to be semantically cognate to the adjective "spiritual" in its usual Cartesian sense. That non-Cartesian usage, too, is not at all uncommon in Western religious and metaphysical as well as lay discourse. The poltergeists, regular ghosts, angels, and apparitions of all sorts that are spoken of in Western "spiritualist" literature, for example, are spirits in this sense. They are, in fact, conceived in physical imagery though credited with unusual powers, such as of mysteriously appearing in places and disappearing at will and of influencing things at far distances without perceptible contact. This category of alleged beings may, for convenience, be called quasi-material or paraphysical. Clearly, the extra-human beings and powers of the African worldview may also be said to be quasi-material.

A certain circumspection is nonetheless required in making comparisons with Western thought. It is not the fact of accommodating the quasi-material category of entities that distinguishes African from Western thought, since the latter traffics in entities of this sort, as well, of course, as material ones. The real difference is that Western thought—which, like African thought, is not a monolith—contains important belief systems that revolve around the notion of the spiritual in the sense of the nonspatial, while African thought, at least in many instances, does not operate with such a category. This is the basic difference, and it flows from the spatial conception of existence palpably resident in many African languages. But there are also other differences of considerable interest.

For instance, because the extra-human entities are regarded as intrinsic, though not commonplace, parts of the one spatiotemporal order of the cosmos, there is neither a theoretical nor a practical motivation for bifurcating reality into the spheres of nature and supernature. For this reason, African explanations of phenomena can move back and forth from the material to the quasi-material without any ontological qualms. Commonly, the explanation of a puzzling event in the physical environment will appeal to circumstances of physical causation. Only if this fails, as a rule, will recourse be had to quasi-material causes, which often have person-like properties. It is not the case, as is supposed, for example, by Robin Horton in his classic 1967 essay "African Traditional Thought and Western Science" (reprinted in Horton's *Patterns of Thought in Africa and the West*, 1993), that Africans, in their traditional condition, turn to explanations of the second kind because they apprehend order more readily in the human sphere than in the world of inanimate phenomena. Horton's suggestion was that in industrial societies with their complexities and rapid changes, "order, regularity, predictability, simplicity" are seen not in the human sphere (from which they are "lamentably absent") but in inanimate phenomena. For this reason, people feel less at home with persons than with things, and the mind in its search for "explanatory analogies" turns most readily to the inanimate. By contrast: "In the traditional societies of Africa, we find the situation reversed. The human scene is the locus *par excellence* of order, predictability, regularity. In the world of the inanimate, these qualities are far less evident. Here, being less at home with people is unimaginable. And here, the mind in quest of explanatory analogies turns naturally to people and their relations" (p. 215). For Horton, this explains why Africans tend to appeal to person-like entities such as "gods" and "spirits" in their explanations. In whatever way the sense of order may come to the industrialized psyche, it is apparent from the "drum stanza" quoted earlier on that in the case of the Akan, for example, order is thought to be *cosmologically* prior to all else. It cannot, therefore, be that the Akan mind derives its apprehension of order from precedents in the "human scene." Nor should it strain interpretative ingenuity to see that one of the lessons of the Yoruba and Dogon myths of creation, recounted in

severely compressed form above, is that the elements of disorder in the unfolding of cosmic order result from human will.

Human Personality

The notion of quasi-materiality, to which attention has been called, is also important for understanding African conceptions of personhood. Given the present state of philosophical data about the various peoples of Africa, it is not judicious to generalize continentally with too much confidence concerning African concepts of personhood. But from various accounts, the following provisional generalization appears supportable: A person is generally held to consist of two distinct, though not ontologically discontinuous, types of elements. One is material, the other quasi-material. The first is uniformly characterized as the body, but the second is multiple and subtly variegated in description.

The Yoruba, for example, distinguish between the life force, which they call the *èmí*, and the individuality principle, which they call *orí-inú*. The *èmí* is thought of as a life-giving entity which flows directly from God to animate the otherwise inert assemblage of bodily essentials. But life is not just life. For good or ill, there is always a unique direction imparted to life by the combination of character, potentiality, and circumstance. The *orí-inú* is the postulated entity in the makeup of a person which is held to be responsible for this dimension of human life. We may call it, for short, its destiny. With characteristic dramatic vividness, the Yoruba traditional myth of human incarnation tells of the *orí* kneeling down before God to receive the blueprint of its destiny before departure to its earthly abode. (In an alternative scenario, the *orí* proposes and God disposes.) Once brought upon the earth through the intimacy of man and woman, psychophysiological functions assume a cardinal importance in the life of an individual. And to account for these the Yoruba point to the *opolo*, the brain, as the physiological basis of the power of reasoning and to the *okàn*, the heart, as the basis of will and emotion. As far as the basic ontological differentiation of constituents is concerned, though certainly not in terms of detail, this Yoruba analysis of personhood is typical of the notions entertained on the same subject in west Africa by the Mende of Sierra Leone, the Dogon of Mali, and the Akan of Ghana.

In basic essentials a similar conception of human personality is encountered elsewhere in Africa. In his survey of concepts of personhood among the peoples of the Bantu area, which, by his reckoning, "covers roughly one-third of the African continent," Kagame finds a common inventory of the constituents of personhood. First, there is an animating principle that makes a human being a sentient being. This he calls, in translation, the "shadow." (One of the components in the constitution of a person in the Akan conception, by the way, is *sunsum,* which literally means "shadow.") Second, there is what he calls the principle of intelligence, and, third, the heart, which, almost exactly as in the Yoruba case, is the seat of will and emotion and constitutes the mechanism for the integration of the total personality. By E. E. Evans-Pritchard's account in his *Nuer Religion,* the Nuer too resolve the human person into "three component parts, *ring,* flesh, *yiegh,* breath or life, and *tie,* intellect or soul" (p. 144). Of all the groups noted, the Lugbara have the longest inventory of personhood, but each constituent is intriguingly analogous to some item in the previous inventories. John Middleton notes in his *Lugbara Religion* (1960) that the Lugbara conceive a person to consist of *rua* (body), *ava,* (breath), *oriandi* (soul), *endrilendri* (shadow), *adro* (guardian spirit), and *tali* (personality).

The clarification of the ontological status of the postulated components of personhood raises subtle issues. For example, all the authors cited in connection with African ideas of personhood, with the arguable exceptions of Evans-Pritchard and Middleton, speak directly or indirectly of the nonbodily constituents of human beings as spiritual or immaterial. The standpoint of this discussion, on the other hand, is that African modes of thought dispense with sharp ontological dualisms, such as that between the physical and the spiritual or the natural and the supernatural. The issue, of course, is an open one, and is likely to be debated in African philosophy for a considerable time to come.

Immortality and Morality

The foregoing considerations about personhood have implications for African conceptions of immortality. It is safe to say that practically all African societies—though not all traditional Africans, for indigenous skeptics exist—communally entertain beliefs in immortality and cherish expectations of it. Equally universally, the African world of the dead is conceived to be continuous with and analogous to the world of the living, sometimes even reproducing its basic political order. This is generally noted by scholars, but its consequences for the

ontological status of the inhabitants of the postmortem realm are rarely realized. In any event, if the inconsistencies of Cartesian dualism, in which an immaterial, nonspatial soul is supposed to be housed in the space of a material body, are not to be gratuitously attributed to African traditional metaphysics on an even grosser scale, it must be recognized that African conceptions of the beings in question do not fit any Western scheme of the material and the spiritual. Of these departed immortals, the best that might be said, by way of a description, is that they are, to adapt a phrase of Evans-Pritchard's "shadowy replicas of the living."

The immortals just spoken of are, of course, the ancestors. Not only are they in some respects essentially similar to the living, but also they are regarded as being in constant interaction with the living sectors of their lineages, of which, usually, they remain highly venerated members. For most traditional Africans, the ancestors are tireless guardians of the morality and well-being of the living, rewarding virtue and punishing error in their own paraphysical way. It should not, however, be inferred from their impact on the enforcement of morals that they are viewed as the basis of morality in African society. One of the safest generalizations about African ways of thought is that morality is founded therein purely upon the necessity for the reciprocal adjustment of the interests of the individual to the interests of the community. This perspective on ethics is connected with the well-known communalist ethos of African traditional societies. So deep does this emphasis on community run that the very concept of a person includes a requirement of basic communal respectability. Moral thinking in such societies habitually focuses on the imperatives of the harmonization of interests, to which the individual is oriented from early childhood through widely irradiating circles of kinship ties. Moral rightness or wrongness, on this showing, is understood in terms of human interests. But no ethical understanding, of itself, ensures the infallible practice of its precepts. Hence the need for sanctions against deviations from rectitude. It follows that the moral importance of the departed ancestors or the various extra-human powers, or even the supreme being, can only consist in their being regarded as sources of sanctions designed to instill or reinforce the will to virtue. The same applies to the moral role of living elders, parents, and civil authorities.

One corollary of this last point is that it is misleading to suggest, as is so often done, that morality rests on religion in African thought. Insofar as the notion in question involves construing the belief in the ancestors or other extra-human forces and the procedures directed toward them as an integral component of African religion, there would seem to be a deeper issue at stake here in respect of African modes of thought. Since, as already argued, these beings cannot be intelligibly described as supernatural, and since they are not credited in any degree with the cosmic creativity or ultimacy of the supreme being, it is difficult to see how that characterization could be validated from within an African conceptual framework.

More things are spoken of in traditional African philosophy than have been touched upon, but the foregoing should give some sense of its conceptual potential.

BIBLIOGRAPHY

Abraham, Willie E. *The Mind of Africa.* Chicago and London, 1962.

Appiah, Kwame Anthony. *In My Father's House: Africa in the Philosophy of Culture.* New York, 1992.

Evans-Pritchard, E. E. *Nuer Religion.* Oxford, 1956.

Gbadegesin, Segun. *African Philosophy: Traditional Yoruba Philosophy and Contemporary African Realities.* New York, 1991.

Griaule, Marcel, and Germaine Dieterlen. "The Dogon of the French Sudan." In *African Worlds: Studies in the Cosmological Ideas and Social Values of African Peoples,* edited by Cyril Daryll Forde. London, 1954.

Gyekye, Kwame. *An Essay on African Philosophical Thought: The Akan Conceptual Scheme.* Cambridge, 1987; Philadelphia, 1995.

Harris, William T., and Harry Sawyer. *The Springs of Mende Belief and Conduct: A Discussion of the Influence of the Belief in the Supernatural Among the Mende.* Freetown, Sierra Leone, 1968.

Horton, Robin. *Patterns of Thought in Africa and the West: Essays on Magic, Religion, and Science.* Cambridge, 1993.

Kagame, Alexis. "The Empirical Acceptation of Time and the Conception of History in Bantu Thought." In *Cultures and Time,* edited by Louis Gardet et al. Paris, 1976.

———. "The Problem of 'Man' in Bantu Philosophy." *The African Mind: A Journal of Religion and Philosophy in Africa* 1, no. 1 (1989).

Little, Kenneth. "The Mende in Sierra Leone." In *African Worlds: Studies in the Cosmological Ideas and Social Values of African Peoples,* edited by Cyril Daryll Forde. London, 1954.

Maquet, Jacques Jerome Pierre. "The Kingdom of Ruanda." In *African Worlds: Studies in the Cosmological Ideas and Social Values of African Peoples,* edited by Cyril Daryll Forde. London, 1954.

Menkiti, Ifeanyi. "Person and Community in African Traditional Thought." In *African Philosophy: An Intro-*

duction, edited by Richard A. Wright. Lanham, Md., 1984. For a dissenting opinion see Gyekye, "Person and Community in Akan Thought," in *Person and Community: Ghanaian Philosophical Studies,* edited by Kwasi Wiredu and Kwame Gyekye. Washington, D.C., 1992.

O'Donohue, John. "A Bantu Philosophy: An Analysis of Philosophical Thought Among the People of Ruanda, Based on *La philosophie bantu-rwandaise de l'être* (Brussels, 1956) by M. l'Abbe Alexis Kagame." *Journal of African Religion and Philosophy* 2, no. 1 (1991).

p'Bitek, Okot. *African Religions in Western Scholarship.* Nairobi, 1970. Repr. 1979.

———. *Religion of the Central Luo.* Nairobi, 1971. Repr. 1978.

Tempels, Placied. *Bantu Philosophy.* Paris, 1959.

Wiredu, Kwasi. "Morality and Religion in Akan Thought." In *African American Humanism: An Anthology,* edited by Norm R. Allen, Jr. Buffalo, N.Y., 1991.

———. "The Concept of Mind with Particular Reference to the Language and Thought of the Akans." In *Contemporary Philosophy: A New Survey,* volume 5, *African Philosophy,* edited by Guttorm Fløistad. Dordent, Netherlands, 1987.

———. "The African Concept of Personhood." In *African-American Perspectives on Biomedical Ethics,* edited by Harley E. Flack and Edmund D. Pellegrino. Washington, D.C., 1992.

———. "Death and the Afterlife in African Culture." In *Person and Community: Ghanaian Philosophical Studies,* edited by Kwasi Wiredu and Kwame Gyekye. Washington, D.C., 1992.

KWASI WIREDU

See also **Myth and Cosmology; Philosophy and the Study of Africa; Religion.**

MOGADISHU. Mogadishu, the capital of Somalia, was reduced to rubble and depopulated by violent intraclan fighting in the early 1990s after the fall of the government of Siad Barre. The shelling and gun battles destroyed 600-year-old Islamic secular buildings and mosques as well as the city's modern infrastructure.

Founded in the tenth century as an Arab outpost on the Indian Ocean, Mogadishu was the most important town in east Africa by the thirteenth century. At the time it was the primary outlet for the gold trade from Sofala, in southern Africa, and was also the northernmost town in the Swahili trading system. During the fourteenth century the town grew considerably and had a large population of rich merchants and a well-developed court life. The Arab traveler Ibn Battuta visited in the fourteenth century, and a Chinese expedition reached Mogadishu in the 1420s. The old city of

Mogadishu. HUBERTUS KANUS/PHOTO RESEARCHERS, INC.

Mogadishu, called Hammawein or Xamar Weyne, was very beautiful and rivaled such Swahili towns farther down the coast as Lamu, Mombasa, and Zanzibar.

Unlike most east African coastal towns that had to contend with the Portuguese, the city-state of Mogadishu was ruled by its own sultans and remained independent until the middle of the nineteenth century, when it came under the suzerainty of the al-Busaid sultans who ruled Muscat and Zanzibar. The city remained under the sultan of Zanzibar's control until, under heavy British pressure, the sultan leased (and later sold) Mogadishu to the Italians.

The Italians made Mogadishu the capital of Italian Somaliland, a territory that covered most of the southern part of what is now Somalia. After World War II, Italian territory in the Horn of Africa was entrusted to the British, and British trusteeship of Somalia lasted until independence (1960).

Mogadishu is the largest city and major port of independent Somalia, and it grew rapidly. In 1965 the population was 141,000; in 1974, it was over 250,000. Many of Somalia's exports, mostly fruits and animal hides, were exported through Mogadishu, and the city supported meat, fish, and milk processing; soft-drink bottling; textile and cosmetics production; and cotton ginning.

Toward the end of his embattled rule, Siad Barre tried to flush rebels out of Mogadishu by shelling the city for four weeks. More than 50,000 people were killed and as much as 75 percent of the city was left in ruins. When Barre fled the country after his regime collapsed (1991), fighting between rival factions broke out and the city was left with no central authority and dwindling food supplies.

Clan leader Mohammed Farah Aidid launched a three-month attack in November 1991 in an attempt to root supporters of his rival, Ali Mahdi Mohammed, from parts of Mogadishu. The colossal destruction left burned-out buildings and dead bodies scattered throughout the city; 14,000 people were killed, nearly twice as many were injured, and 400,000 people fled to the countryside or abroad. American troops and a United Nations peacekeeping force attempted to bring order to Mogadishu, but to no avail. The rebuilding of the city looked like a daunting task in the mid-1990s. The UN peacekeeping force pulled out in 1994, leaving no peace, no constitution, no government in power, and virtually no infrastructure.

BIBLIOGRAPHY

Samatar, Ahmed I. "The Curse of Allah: Civic Disembowelment and the Collapse of the State in Somalia." In *The Somali Challenge*, edited by Ahmed I. Samatar. Boulder, Colo., 1994.

THOMAS F. MCDOW

MOI, DANIEL ARAP (b. 1924), second president of Kenya. Educated by missionaries at the Kabartonjo Island Mission in the Rift Valley and at the Government African School at Kapsabet, Daniel Torotich arap Moi trained to become a teacher and began his first job in 1945 at the Government African School. There, he rose to the position of headmaster, and later returned as assistant principal. In 1955, Moi was one of the first Africans nominated to the Legislative Council. He left the council in 1960 to become assistant treasurer of the Kenya African National Union (KANU), the major political party. Later that year, he joined the Kenya African Democratic Union (KADU), which had been formed by politicians who feared Gikuyu and Luo domination of KANU. Following the elections of 1961, in which Jomo Kenyatta was elected president in absentia and the way was prepared for Kenyan independence, Moi was appointed minister of education. He entered local government in 1962, where he served for two years.

In 1964, the year following Kenya's official independence, KADU was absorbed into KANU, and Moi served as minister of home affairs in President Kenyatta's cabinet. He was appointed vice president in 1967, and, on Kenyatta's death in 1978, Moi succeeded him as president. He was officially elected to the position a year later. Moi began his reign by launching an anticorruption drive, releasing political prisoners who had been held under his predecessor. By 1981, however, when Kenya hosted the eighteenth summit of the Organization of African Unity (OAU), there was widespread disillusionment with Moi's initial anticorruption campaign, which had been widely relaxed and had been replaced with the familiar heavy hand of governmental power.

Kenya was officially declared a one-party state in 1982. Later that year the air force staged a coup, accusing Moi's government of widespread corruption and brutality. Nairobi shops were looted, and masses of people gathered to celebrate. Moi's forces, however, were swift in defeating resistance, and responded by dissolving the air force and jailing those who had participated in the celebrations. Moi suspended his minister of home and constitutional affairs, the Gikuyu politician Charles Njonjo, accusing him of attempting to overthrow the government.

The Law Society of Kenya, joined by groups from universities and churches, continually spoke out against human rights violations committed by Moi's government. In 1986, the underground group Mwakenya (Union of Patriots for the Liberation of Kenya) emerged while expatriate Kenyans organized to form their own organizations of dissent. These associations came together as the United Movement for Democracy, which emerged under the leadership of Ngugi wa Thiong'o, a Kenyan writer. Initial foreign response to Moi was varied: President Ronald Reagan of the United States criticized Kenya's human-rights record during an official visit Moi made to America in 1987, yet Margaret Thatcher warmly received him in London soon after, giving Kenya an aid package of £50 million.

For the 1988 elections in Kenya, Moi abolished the secret-ballot system of voting and replaced it with a new procedure in which voters were required to line up behind larger-than-life photographs of their chosen candidate. Amid accusations of intimidation and rigging, Moi was reelected unopposed. Popular calls for a multiparty political system and rampant frustration with Moi's policies were exacerbated by the 1990 murder of Minister of Foreign Affairs and International Cooperation Robert Ouko, generally considered to be among the few uncorrupted Kenyan politicians remaining in office. The formation of the Kenyan National Democratic Party was announced in 1991, amid international pressure to democratize and growing internal unrest. Later that year, Moi conceded to the formation of an opposition party, the Foundation for the Restoration of Democracy (FORD). Despite the opponents' persistent charges of voting fraud, Moi was reelected with 36.4 percent of the vote in 1992.

BIBLIOGRAPHY

Karimi, Joseph. *The Kenyatta Succession.* Nairobi, 1980.

SARAH VALDEZ

See also **Independence Movements; Kenyatta, Jomo; Mboya, Tom; Ngugi wa Thiong'o.**

MOMBASA. Mombasa is the largest port in east Africa and Kenya's second largest city. It has been a favorite stop for travelers on the east African coast for centuries. Ibn Battuta passed through in 1331, and Vasco de Gama was there in 1498.

Founded in the eleventh century by Arab traders, Mombasa was favorably located for coastal trade and succeeded Kilwa as the primary Swahili town in the fifteenth century. From the early sixteenth century, and for more than a hundred years, the Portuguese and Omani Arabs vied for control of the town; the massive fort, Fort Jesus, was built by the Portuguese in 1593. The local Mazrui clan captured the fort and the town in the 1740s, challenging Omani rule until the Omani sultan of Zanzibar took the town in 1832. Though Mombasa was under nominal Zanzibari rule until Kenyan independence (1963), British colonial interests predominated after the 1890s.

The British established the capital of their East African Protectorate in Mombasa in 1887. The city was the nexus for the Indian Ocean dhow trade, overland caravans, European explorers, and Indian and Arab businessmen. The completion of a rail line to Lake Victoria in 1902 brought new prosperity to the city, and it began to grow out from the Swahili old town. By 1930, thanks in part to a post–World War I boom, the city had spread to the mainland from the 7.5-square-mile (3 sq. km) island it originally occupied.

Dockworkers' strikes in Mombasa after World War II upset the port economy and were the beginning tremors of a nationalist movement on the coast. After independence in 1963, however, the town grew as up-country traders, especially Gikuyus, arrived to set up businesses. With the dredging of Kilindini harbor, the modern deep-water port on the southwest side of Mombasa Island, the city became the primary port for Kenya, Uganda, Rwanda, and Burundi. In addition to shipbuilding and repair activities around the port, Mombasa is also one of Kenya's primary industrial areas, processing sugar, refining oil, and producing cement and fertilizer.

In the 1950s white settlers from South Africa and Rhodesia began to visit the Kenya coast for vacation, and Mombasa became the center of a growing tourist trade. Tourism exploded in the 1970s, and by the late 1980s hotels and beachfront resorts lined the north and south coasts of city. Each year more than a quarter of a million people arrived to take in the warm sun, beautiful coral, and relaxed atmosphere and to visit the old town, Fort Jesus, and nearby game parks.

More than 640,000 people live in Mombasa (1994 est.), many of them Swahili Muslims. Since the advent of multiparty democracy in Kenya in 1992, Daniel arap Moi's government has refused all attempts to register the Mombasa-based Islamic Party of Kenya (IPK) and has banned its meetings and deported its leader. Though Moi's politics, AIDS, and overdevelopment may threaten tourism, one of the city's most lucrative sectors, Mombasa has thrived as a sailors' town for nearly a thousand years and will continue to be the most important port for east Africa for the foreseeable future.

BIBLIOGRAPHY

Willis, Justin. *Mombasa, the Swahili, and the Making of the Mijikenda.* Oxford, 1993.

THOMAS F. McDOW

See also **East African Coast.**

MONDLANE, EDUARDO CHIVAMBO (b. 1920; d. 1969), Mozambican anticolonial activist. Born in Gaza province, Mozambique, Mondlane was educated in South Africa, in Portugal, and in the United States, where he obtained a bachelor of arts degree and then a doctorate at Northwestern University. After working for a time for the United Nations, Mondlane identified himself completely with the anticolonial cause in Mozambique, accepting that Portuguese imperialist intransigence might well make war unavoidable. "We could continue indefinitely living under a repressive imperial rule, or find a means of using force against Portugal which would be effective enough to hurt Portugal without resulting in our own ruin" (*The Struggle for*

Eduardo Chivambo Mondlane. ADARSH NAYAR, CAMERA PRESS LONDON/ARCHIVE PHOTOS/CAMERA PRESS

Mozambique, p. 125). Having launched his country's independence movement, Frente de Libertação de Moçambique, (FRELIMO) in 1962, Mondlane presided over a gradual enlargement of anticolonial warfare and in 1968 assembled a representative congress, held in Niassa province, at which compromise with the Portuguese empire was rejected. Traveling widely, Mondlane was increasingly accepted as one of the founders of a liberated Africa. In 1969 he was murdered in Dar es Salaam by a parcel bomb of Portuguese or South African provenance. His reputation linked courage with humane tolerance and moderation. But his murder warned prophetically that the mindless terrorism promoted by externally organized banditries, chiefly from racist South Africa, could now prove fatal to the whole project of anticolonial independence.

BIBLIOGRAPHY

Isaacman, Allen, and Barbara Isaacman. *Mozambique: From Colonialism to Revolution, 1900–1982.* Boulder, Colo., 1983.

Mondlane, Eduardo. *The Struggle for Mozambique.* Baltimore, Md., 1969.

Munslow, Barry. *Mozambique: The Revolution and Its Origins.* London and New York, 1983.

BASIL DAVIDSON

See also **Machel, Samora Moises.**

MONEY

[Money can be thought of as having three distinct aspects. It can serve as a medium of exchange, a store of wealth, or a standard of value. Western monies combine all three aspects, but in many cultures, including traditional African cultures, these different aspects are sometimes embodied in different forms of currencies.]

MONEY, CURRENCIES, AND MEANS OF EXCHANGE

The items that made up the money of sub-Saharan Africa in the precolonial period exhibited tremendous variety. The colonial money systems that succeeded the precolonial currencies were by contrast highly uniform. Yet the links between them were closer than might be imagined. Among the most important items used as money in precolonial Africa were the following:

Beads. Certain types of beads were utilized as currency over wide areas, although in general the economies where bead moneys circulated were not the larger and richer ones.

Brass and copper. Brass and copper, usually in the form of wires, rods, or fabricated objects, served as money in many areas, with the wires usually of lesser worth than the other forms. Some of this currency was made in Africa, but a substantial amount was imported from Europe. The famous horseshoe-shaped manillas of west Africa (from Portuguese *manilha*, bracelet) were in this category.

Cloth. Cloth, often woven in strips or sometimes made into mats, served as money. From the eighteenth century, locally made cloth moneys were replaced in some areas by cloth imported by Europeans. The most important import was originally a cloth of Indian provenance, large amounts of which were produced in and around Madras and Pondicherry. Called blue baft by the British because of its indigo dye, and *pièces de guinée* by the French, this cloth became the major money of the Mauritanian trade in gum arabic, where for a time its use was officially encouraged by French colonial officials. Similar cloth was eventually produced in Europe, where low-cost manufacturing techniques resulted in inflation and the eventual abandonment of cloth as money.

Coins. In the precolonial period a variety of coins from overseas saw some use, though the silver coins and even some made from base metals were too valuable for day-to-day purchases. In west Africa, silver dollars, particularly those of Latin American origin, were much used in trade along the coast, while the coins of European countries had some use at major points of trade. Maria Theresa dollars—minted not only by Austria but also by Britain and later Italy—circulated in as much as a third of the continent, mostly in eastern and central Africa.

Cows. Akin to the ancient Roman republic's use of cows as money (hence "pecuniary," from Latin *pecus,* cow), numerous societies, especially in east Africa, utilized cows for monetary purposes.

Gold dust. Gold dust served as money, especially among the Asante in west Africa. Production of gold dust was subject to substantial state control, with the grains carefully weighed by those who used this currency.

Iron. Most often in the form of bars and rods, sometimes ingots, and sometimes fabricated objects such as hoes, knives, spearheads, and axes, iron served as money in a variety of regions. The iron was often imported.

Salt. Salt money was used in many parts of the continent, most commonly in the form of blocks, cakes, cones, or bundles.

Seashells. The "money cowrie" (*Cypraea moneta*), imported from the Maldive Islands of the Indian Ocean, was in wide circulation in west Africa. Originally, Maldive cowries were shipped along the North African coast and across the Sahara by caravan. Later, they came as ballast in the Indiamen sailing home to Europe, and thus were in greater supply and lower in cost than otherwise would have been the case. European merchants transhipped them onward to Africa. Around the middle of the nineteenth century, west African money users became willing to accept a substitute cowrie shell, *Cypraea annulus,* obtained from the east African coast near Zanzibar, so the number of cowries in circulation expanded vastly. *Annulus* already had had considerable circulation in parts of central Africa. In some areas, especially the Congo, another indigenous seashell, the *zimbu,* fished mainly in the region of Luanda (Angola), served a similar purpose. Certain snail shells and cone shells also circulated in some western coastal areas and parts of the Congo.

Slaves. For high-value transactions in all areas, slaves frequently served as money.

Under colonial rule, a process was begun, and rather rapidly accomplished in many areas, wherein the precolonial moneys were first supplemented and then supplanted by colonial currencies. These consisted of silver coins for higher-value transactions, and copper, bronze, and nickel coins for those of lower value. Later, from about the time of World War I, paper notes were introduced into circulation.

For all their variety, Africa's moneys in the precolonial period can be categorized in three respects: official status, substitutability, and source. One comparison that we shall not be using is "primitive" moneys versus "modern" moneys. Such a comparison lacks analytical relevance in the many cases where a so-called primitive money such as the cowrie shell acted reasonably well as a medium of exchange, standard of value, and store of value, just as does any so-called modern money such as a currency note or a check written on a bank account.

A more useful comparison is between the moneys that were informal, that is, nonofficial, not introduced or controlled by governments, and those that were formal, that is, official government currencies. The precolonial moneys of Africa were informal, almost always put into circulation not by governments but by producers, merchants, and traders often organized by lineage and as commercial diaspora. The money supplied by these groups depended on their reaction to money demand. Money came at a price: the opportunity cost of the real resources that went into its production. If it had come at no cost, entrepreneurs would immediately have oversupplied the currency to the point of rendering it worthless for transactions.

Informal moneys served west Africa reasonably well over a period of several centuries, but they possessed two major weaknesses: first, they were high in cost; and second, they offered to entrepreneurs the chances of profit if money-users could be persuaded to accept lower-cost variants. When lower-cost variants were successfully introduced in great quantity, as particularly with the cowrie, inflation resulted.

When the informal moneys were demonetized, there was a great loss of resources tied up in them when their non-monetary use was limited (the cowrie), some loss with brass manillas, and little or no loss with the iron, cloth, gold dust, and foreign silver coin currencies which were returned to commodity use or (in the case of the coins) exported.

Frequently, more than one type of money was in circulation at the same time in the same area. In some of these cases, there were customary fixed equivalencies among the moneys, and a number of examples of Gresham's law ("bad money drives out good") arose when moneys of lower commodity value supplanted moneys of higher value. Indeed, the period of informal moneys was one of considerable instability, with frequent changes in the type of money employed. More often the values floated against one another with exchange rates determined by market forces, so neither overvaluations nor devaluations took place. On occasion production of informal money was restrained by action at the source, as when the Maldive sultans controlled the fishing of cowrie shells, while sometimes local conditions made it very difficult to increase supply, as when political instability and violence in the desert meant that salt had to be convoyed from the Saharan points of production.

With a very few exceptions, such as Asante gold dust, government involvement in the provision of "official" money had to await the colonial period.

With colonial rule, the informal moneys were replaced by the coins, and later paper notes, of the colonial administrations. The process was slower in some areas than in others and indeed has not been fully completed in some border locations, where informal moneys such as the cowrie survive in limited use.

A second means of categorizing the moneys of Africa is by whether they had virtually complete substitutability and a fairly rapid movement between their use as money and their consumption as commodity, with the identity of individual units extinguished by the consumption (cloth made into garments and salt eaten, for example), or whether such substitutability was more difficult and did not extinguish the commodity (cowries, gold and silver coins, colonial paper notes). For example, cowries, gold, and silver were all employed for decoration and display as well as being used for money, but they continued to exist and maintain their monetary value. Cloth and salt are examples of money that moved rather rapidly into end consumption, with a high "throughput" into and finally out of monetary use. The iron and brass currencies appear to fall midway in this spectrum.

A final comparison can be made between the moneys that were imported (cowries, some of the iron, copper, and brass, some of the cloth, gold and silver coins, and the later colonial currencies) and those that were domestically produced. A major distinguishing feature is that the imported moneys all required exports in order to obtain them: in effect, they had to be purchased by means of exporting. In the precolonial period, the major export through which imported moneys were obtained was slaves, though primary product exports (cocoa, cotton, gum arabic, ivory, palm oil, peanuts, and various metals and minerals) also figured in both precolonial and colonial times. Only the coins from overseas were "convertible" in the sense that traders from Europe and the Americas would take them back again in payment for goods. The rest of the imported moneys were blocked; rarely would traders accept them.

Whether precolonial or colonial, the moneys of Africa had more in common than might be generally supposed. They were all "full-bodied" moneys that tied up real resources. As mentioned above, the precolonial commodity currencies were in general put into circulation through private enterprise with their value determined by demand and supply (cost of production and transport). Because the commodity moneys involved an appreciable cost

of transport, there was often a value gradient, with a given quantity of cloth, cowrie, or salt money commanding more goods at locations farther away from these moneys' point of production or importation.

The colonial silver and token coins, and especially paper money, were cheaper to produce, but for Africa they were just as expensive as the precolonial, informal currencies. The cost of the precolonial currencies, imported or domestic, was the real resources given up to acquire them. The cost of colonial money was the same, in that exports were needed to obtain them. Typically, reserves of metropolitan currencies were required as a backing for colonial money, reserves that could only be earned through exports of commodities from Africa. The seigniorage gain that accrued from putting low-cost colonial moneys into circulation at values above their cost of production was in large measure not realized by Africans. Instead, the seigniorage accrued to the metropolitan governments in Europe which managed the colonial moneys. These governments in effect sold money to Africa at a price (in African exports) that was equal to the face value of the currency.

Whether money was precolonial or colonial, for Africans its cost was substantial, and costly it remained until the end of the colonial period. Colonial governments could indeed claim that their money issues brought a greater degree of monetary stability compared to the precolonial currencies. These latter could be overproduced or overimported, with resulting inflation, or could be subject to unpredictable leakages into consumption. (It is also true that the colonial moneys, their quantity dependent on balance of payments surpluses, tended to fluctuate with the international business cycle, with the money supply falling, damagingly, in recession and rising during prosperity.) But whatever benefits of stability were conferred by the colonial moneys could have been achieved equally well and at much lower cost by judicious limits on the expansion of the money supply by the colonial monetary authorities.

One notable aspect of the transition from the precolonial to the colonial moneys was the loss in value when an erstwhile money (unlike salt or metal) could not be used for consumption. For example, the cowrie currency in large part had to be simply abandoned as junk, although many cowries were physically destroyed by the French. Colonial practice for undermining the precolonial currencies usually did not mean their complete prohibition, but instead involved bans on their further importation and requirements that tax payments be made in the colonial money.

Relative constants in Africa's variegated monetary history, both precolonial and colonial, were the tendency for the money supply to grow as the economy expanded, and for more convenient moneys to supersede the less convenient. That meant movement toward moneys that were longer-lasting in durability and less likely to leak into immediate commodity use. It is highly probable that states everywhere, whether indigenous or colonial, found taxation easier when moneys were more formal—and indeed that the increased efficacy of the tax mechanism probably strengthened the states themselves.

BIBLIOGRAPHY

Curtin, Philip D. "Africa and the Wider Monetary World, 1250–1850." In *Precious Metals in the Later Medieval and Early Modern Worlds,* edited by J. F. Richards. Durham, N.C., 1983.

Guyer, Jane I., ed. *Money Matters: Instability, Values, and Social Payments in the Modern History of West African Communities.* Portsmouth, N.H., 1995.

Hogendorn, Jan S., and Henry A. Gemery. "Cash Cropping, Currency Acquisition, and Seigniorage in West Africa: 1923–1950." *African Economic History* 11 (1982): 15–27.

———. "Continuity in West African Monetary History? An Outline of Monetary Development." *African Economic History* 17 (1988): 127–146.

Hogendorn, Jan S., and Marion Johnson. *The Shell Money of the Slave Trade.* Cambridge, 1986.

Hopkins, A. G. "The Currency Revolution in South-West Nigeria in the Late Nineteenth Century." *Journal of the Historical Society of Nigeria* 3, no. 3 (1966): 471–483.

———. "The Creation of a Colonial Monetary System: The Origins of the West African Currency Board." *African Historical Studies* 3, no. 1 (1970): 101–132.

Lovejoy, Paul E. "Interregional Monetary Flows in the Pre-Colonial Trade of Nigeria." *Journal of African History* 15, no. 4 (1974): 563–585.

Ofonagoro, Walter I. "From Traditional to British Currency in Southern Nigeria: Analysis of a Currency Revolution, 1880–1948." *Journal of Economic History* 39, no. 3 (1979): 623–654.

Quiggin, Allison Hingston. *A Survey of Primitive Money: The Beginnings of Currency.* London, 1949.

Webb, James L. A., Jr. "Toward the Comparative Study of Money: A Reconsideration of West African Currencies and Neoclassical Monetary Concepts." *International Journal of African Historical Studies* 15, no. 3 (1982): 455–466.

JAN HOGENDORN

See also **Economic History; Exchange and Market Systems.**

MONEY AND MONETIZATION

Money in one form or another is now used and sought throughout Africa, but its history is uneven, its usefulness sometimes superseded, and its moral implications often debated. On parts of the coasts and near some inland trade routes, cash as minted currency has been familiar for many centuries. In other, less traveled inland areas it came into common use only in the early twentieth century as new European colonial taxation, cash cropping initiatives, and wage labor recruitment sharply increased the needs for and use of cash. But even in most of the latter areas, the idea of money was not new, and other local and regional commodities had long served some of the same purposes.

Money is something valued and capable of circulating indefinitely among its users, but useful only for purposes related to exchange. As a material object, a means of exchange and communication, and a polyvalent symbol, money means different things to different people. What translates as money varies widely by language, and financial concepts like income, investment, and capital may have no convenient translation into some African languages—a sign of deeper cultural differences in economic life. Evidence gathered by direct observation in Africa has qualified and challenged assumptions of economists, social philosophers, and the broader public about money's uses, meanings, and effects on society.

Currencies and Quasi-currencies

Money merges into other categories of things exchanged. Objects that African peoples have used as money or quasi-money (i.e., money with some uses beyond exchange) have included items and substances as diverse as cowrie shells, salt blocks, cloth strips, gold dust, iron bars, copper crosses, glass beads, buttons, company scrip, minted coins and banknotes, checks, and notes and bills of exchange. Money in every African city now includes electronic money: credits and debts without paper, coin, or other material specie. Where and whether animals should be deemed money, for instance in the many eastern African settings where cattle play a crucial part in marriage transfers, is a matter of perennial scholarly debate, but in such contexts and usages they are never merely money. Likewise, cowries have widely served as money but also, in some cultures, have sexual or other

Tanzanian paper currency. ANDREW HILL, HUTCHISON LIBRARY

symbolic connotations and aesthetic values not so quantifiable. The same commodity may oscillate in and out of use as currency as it changes hands or as times change. No part of Africa has not seen some succession of currencies come and go, whether through trade, conquest, or policy reversals, and people throughout Africa have long understood that what counts as money today may not tomorrow.

Money's Features and Functions

Money is a sign of human interdependence, and it suggests trust in, or reliance upon, shared understandings. Money's familiar advantages over other means of exchange are that it can be easily standardized, recognized, counted, transported, divided, and substituted for other money or other things. But some of these same attributes and others, like concealability, make money volatile and contestable in impoverished communities, ones without easy access to banks, or ones not long accustomed to financial calculation. Control over the production and circulation of money is envied or contested most anywhere. African experience qualifies classical Euro-American understandings of money's functions as a store of wealth, medium of exchange, means of payment, standard of value, and unit of account.

Classical assumptions about money's stability of value have proved unreliable in Africa south of the Sahara. Most colonial regimes shifted currencies repeatedly and unpredictably, and some of the European-introduced moneys and quasi-moneys (for instance cowries in places, or metal rods like *mitakos* in the lower Congo in the 1890s) were moreover unusable in commerce with Europeans themselves. Independent but unstable state regimes can tax money's earning or spending, overprint it to dispense patronage at election times, and devaluate or abolish it overnight. Inflation erodes its purchasing power. Paper money kept in homes is susceptible to theft, fire, flooding, and insect damage. Banks and financial institutions' interest rates for savings have generally augmented depositors' money more slowly than animals multiply by breeding, despite the latter's being subject to sudden major losses periodically through droughts, epizootics, or other causes. Money's versatility and liquidity can make it tempting to spend; and its concealability can limit the influence of kin or neighbors on its prudent use. Hence, wherever money is found, people devise ways to limit its uses.

While some theorists of social evolution have supposed that money tends to acquire new positive functions as time passes, changes in policy and political conditions have sometimes made currencies lose functions. Continued three-digit inflation in some settings, as in late twentieth-century Zaire, has reduced money's convenience to the point where, by the 1980s, urbanites there needed "brick" bundles or even sackfuls of banknotes for daily purchases, and many resorted to bartering food, gasoline, and cigarettes and to passing new local currencies instead. Barter does not just recede into history as an economy monetizes. It continually reappears where money becomes scarce, inflation high, or polities unstable.

Migration and monetary remittance, between nations and between continents, play an ever-greater role in African economic life as agricultural ecosystems are threatened, terms of trade worsen, and indebtedness increases. Some communities have lately survived on little else, for instance in the cases of some Somalis' circular migrations to Yemen, Lesothoans' to South Africa, or Mauritanians' to Senegal. Border controls and currency-exchange restrictions hinder movements of people and money. Despite the rise of international electronic banking and the liberalizing of many nations' currencies over the past few decades, many migrants continue preferring to remit money via trusted friends or relatives in cash, for reasons of security, solidarity, or convenience. Meanwhile, people in many parts of Africa choose to save in plural currencies (not always legally) in order to trade across borders and to guard against abrupt devaluation of any one currency.

Liquidity and Illiquidity

Whereas neoclassical economic theory has tended to assume general human preferences for asset liquidity and divisibility, observation on the ground reveals many instances where people try to keep or make large parts of their wealth illiquid and indivisible in order to remove it from their own temptation, while keeping it accessible enough for emergencies. This is particularly so in face-to-face communities where it can be hard for persons with money to refuse requests for sharing, giving, or loan repayment. Commonly, in African communities as elsewhere, concern about gossip, witchcraft, or other social sanctions may underlie such decisions about saving or hoarding, mingling with more strictly economic concerns like inflation.

In many parts of the continent, regardless of access to banks or post office saving facilities, many continue to invent their own means of saving. They devise break-open saving receptacles, join self-help contribution clubs like rotating saving and credit associations, or entrust cash to kin or neighbors—most often, it seems, to persons elder to or more

solvent than themselves—to save for them. As these strategies suggest, a major concern of savers continentwide is not to appear antisocial. Some rural savers prefer holding large banknotes to their equivalent in smaller ones, because they are harder to break up. Others seek to defer collecting wage or crop earnings to let them accumulate. Gold earrings in coastal western Africa allow women to wear their wealth while they save it and defend it from their men; metalsmiths can add gold as a woman ages. Whatever the merits of saving, it is seldom a lesson that richer peoples can teach poorer ones for the first time. To infer from such practices as gifting, bridewealth, or sacrificial ceremonies that large sections of African populations are merely profligate spenders may be to overlook many ways of saving and investing going on in indirect or diversified forms, or for longer-term rewards than are apparent.

Cultural Conditioning of Exchange

Some theorists have supposed that money gradually penetrates all exchanges until nothing remains that cannot be bought and sold. Visiting Tiv in northeastern Nigeria from 1949 to 1953, anthropologist Paul Bohannan observed morally ranked "exchange spheres" as follows. Foods, small animals, raw materials, and tools were freely exchangeable for each other; they made up what he called a subsistence sphere. A second, higher sphere of "prestige" goods included slaves, cattle, cloth, and brass rods. The supreme third sphere consisted of humans other than slaves, particularly women. "Conveyance" within spheres was a morally neutral act, but strong moral values surrounded "conversion" between spheres. Money, made widespread through colonial taxation and cash cropping, provided, in Bohannan's view, a new "common denominator," entering into exchanges in all three spheres and scrambling these together.

But no society's norms permit all things to be bought and sold, and money never penetrates exchange circuits evenly or absolutely. Protected from some kinds of market activity almost anywhere, by moral discouragement or outright legal or spiritual prohibition, are human bodies (or at least certain ones) and their parts or fluids, land where blood has been shed in battle or rites of passage, sacred human-made objects, and religious and scholastic distinctions and offices. Sale, rental, and mortgaging of rural land have been morally, legally, or religiously prohibited in many parts of Africa south of the Sahara (parts of Ghana having long been exceptional in this regard), though legislators and financiers enacting state land-tenure reforms have sought to challenge and change these rules in numerous countries in the past century. Cattle in many herding societies, for instance among Fulani (Fulbe) in the western Sahel, have in the past been deemed properly saleable only in personal or family crises, and such sales widely stigmatized. Just as land or livestock may not be deemed attachable as liens for cash loans, cash may not be considered an adequate or lasting substitute for appropriated or confiscated land or animals. Islamic sacred law (Shari'a) condemns lending and borrowing at interest, while it condones profiting by trade. All these kinds of restrictions on exchange are debated in public and private, and nowhere is there a society whose norms about sales and other exchanges are not sometimes contravened in practice.

Whereas classical and neoclassical economic theory assumes money to be fungible, or readily substitutable for other money, ethnographic findings suggest that in fact, people throughout Africa (and probably all over the world) earmark money derived from particular activities for particular uses. Frequently such designation has symbolic and moral significance. Thus, in many cultures, money from antisocial activities (which might include murder, theft, or gambling), or from sales of commodities symbolically associated with evil or spiritual pollution, is perceived as dangerous to its earner or holder and others related. Such "tainted" money can take many forms: among Mandinko in the Gambia, it can come from selling hot peppers; among Luo in western Kenya, from selling gold, tobacco, or patrimonial land; among Nuer in southern Sudan, from stigmatized domestic service. In some settings such rewards are scrupulously kept out of sacred activities like marriage or funerals, while in others they and the people associated with them are deemed ritually purifiable. Here again, however, people sometimes break their own cultural rules for profit or convenience.

People who share other commodities do not always share money, or vice versa. Foreigners in Africa sometimes express surprise at sharing or hoarding habits within families that differ from their own, though not necessarily in a systematic way. Among Luhya of Kenya or Soninke of the Gambia in recent decades, unmarried adult sons have been expected to surrender cash wages directly to fathers in their homesteads, and in some areas wives to husbands. In these same settings,

however, adults commonly keep locked boxes, partly to conceal and protect cash from their spouses. Patterns like these give the lie to stereotypes of African individualism or kin communalism. Foreign-based employers and crop buyers have sometimes caused cross-cultural misunderstandings by paying only men as "household heads" for work done by women, children, and attached dependents, when it was not assumed among families that the new cash would be shared.

Money always has qualitative as well as quantitative values, and it can be used to symbolize almost anything—good, evil, or neutral. Banknotes and coins carry political symbols: portraits of current rulers; slogans and emblems of state or party; or idealized depictions of dress, monuments, or technological or military power. They daily remind users of nationhood on a continent where nations are dubiously rooted entities of questionable legitimacy in popular thought. The nationalist symbolism belies both the rich local meanings that Africans attach to money and the degree of practical control that foreign and international powers (notably the World Bank and International Monetary Fund, and the French government in the CFA zone) have exerted over fiscal and monetary policy in African countries in recent decades.

Money and Wealth

Money does not always mean wealth, or vice versa. Much of rural Africa prefers to keep its main wealth in other, more useful or aesthetically satisfying forms, whether mineral, vegetable, animal, or human. In some areas a wealthy person is someone who, by careful giving or lending, has accumulated not just money but personal obligations in addition or instead. Nor is an influx of cash always helpful in alleviating poverty. If it rescues parts of a population temporarily from destitution it can at the same time impoverish other, disadvantaged parts or an adjacent population through commodity price inflation, a subtle but major contributor to famines in Africa as elsewhere. Or it may stimulate excessive local borrowing and thus lead to interpersonal debts and misunderstandings (a process fictionalized in Sembène Ousmane's pessimistic 1972 novella of Dakar, *The Money Order*). What is true at the micro level is sometimes true at the macro, too. Cash cropping and the production of new industrial exportables like oil may bring immediate new rewards to a region or nation but also introduce subtle new risks and dependencies, for instance through currency overvaluation that can disrupt domestic food production, as has happened in Nigeria and Cameroon in recent decades.

Across Africa money is perceived as a mixed blessing and never publicly allowed to take over any economy fully. Policies designed to monetize an economy may both help and hurt the people involved. To discern the effects of financial development and philanthropic relief programs from without or within, there is no substitute for direct and patient local observation.

BIBLIOGRAPHY

Bohannan, Paul. "The Impact of Money on an African Subsistence Economy." *Journal of Economic History* 19, no. 4 (1959): 491–503.

Ensminger, Jean. *Making a Market: The Institutional Transformation of an African Society.* Cambridge, 1992.

Guyer, Jane I., ed. *Money Matters: Instability, Values, and Social Payments in the Modern History of West African Communities.* Portsmouth, N.H., 1995.

Hill, Polly. *Studies in Rural Capitalism in West Africa.* Cambridge, 1970.

Hogendorn, Jan, and Marion Johnson. *The Shell Money of the Slave Trade.* New York, 1986.

Hopkins, A. G. *An Economic History of West Africa.* New York, 1973.

Hutchinson, Sharon. *Nuer Dilemmas: Coping with Money, War, and the State.* Berkeley, Calif., 1996.

Meillassoux, Claude. *Maidens, Meal, and Money: Capitalism and the Domestic Community* (translation of *Femmes, greniers, et capitaux*). Cambridge, 1981.

Parkin, David J. *Palms, Wine, and Witnesses: Public Spirit and Private Gain in an African Farming Community.* San Francisco, 1972.

Parry, Jonathan. "On the Moral Perils of Exchange." In *Money and the Morality of Exchange,* edited by J. Parry and M. Bloch. Cambridge, 1989.

Pick, Franz, and René Sédillot. *All the Moneys of the World: A Chronicle of Currency Values.* New York, 1971.

Rivallain, Josette. *Paléo-monnaies africaines.* Paris, 1986.

Rodinson, Maxime. *Islam and Capitalism.* London, 1974.

Seidman, Ann. *Money, Banking, and Public Finance in Africa.* London and Atlantic Highlands, N.J., 1986.

Sembène Ousmane. *The Money-Order, with White Genesis.* Translated by Clive Wake. London, 1972.

Shipton, Parker. *Bitter Money: Cultural Economy and Some African Meanings of Forbidden Commodities.* American Anthropological Association. Washington, D.C., 1989.

PARKER SHIPTON

See also **Debt and Indebtedness; Development; Economic History; Economies, Alternative; Exchange and Market Systems; Land Reform and Resettlement; Production Systems.**

MONGO. The Mongo people live primarily in the Congo Basin of central Zaire. It is likely that they first entered the region around the first century C.E., whereupon those of the early arrivals who settled along the rivers developed fishing-based economies while those who settled inland built up economies based on hunting and root-crop farming. The term refers not only to the Mongo proper—speakers of the Mongo dialect, who number some 220,000—but also to the speakers of the larger Mongo family of related languages. All told, the Mongo-speaking population totals nearly 3.5 million people.

Farming was based upon the swidden, or slash-and-burn method, whereby land was initially cleared of brush and the remaining ground cover burned off to yield an arable area. The ash resulting from the burning of the ground cover was the only fertilizer traditionally used. Such fields were farmed for several years, until the soils no longer provided adequate nutrients to support a reasonable crop. The old fields were then abandoned, and the group would move on to clear new lands and start the process over again. Foraging was, and remains, an important additional element of the livelihood for both groups; the equatorial forest yields palm kernels, wild mushrooms, wild fruits and vegetables, and edible insects. Small game is trapped; larger game—from antelope to elephants—were traditionally hunted by groups of men using bow and arrow and spears. The arrival of the Europeans in central Africa brought new crops, which altered the local Mongo economies. Of particular importance was the Portuguese introduction of the banana, beans, groundnuts, and maize in the sixteenth century.

Mongo communities were traditionally formed of a collection of patrilineal, patrilocal households, each headed by a senior male. Authority over such activities that required village-wide cooperation, such as clearing land for farming or organizing for defense, was in the hands of a council of such senior men. When necessary, inter-village alliances could be formed. In such cases, authority rested in a loose council of elders, prominent male seniors, and ritual specialists.

In Mongo traditional society, women were excluded from positions of authority and had access to land only through a husband or male kin. Although women performed the bulk of the agricultural work, they had no control over the distribution or sale of their crops. Slaves, taken during local raids on neighboring groups, had even less social standing in the community, but were entirely dependent upon the household that sponsored them. Over time, slaves were usually assimilated into the group through marriage.

BIBLIOGRAPHY

Birmingham, David, and Phyllis M. Martin, eds. *History of Central Africa*. Vol. 2. New York, 1983.

Miracle, Marvin. *Agriculture in the Congo Basin: Tradition and Change in African Rural Economies*. Madison, Wis., 1967.

GARY THOULOUIS

MONROVIA. The capital of Liberia, Monrovia is on the coast of west Africa. Founded in 1822 with the arrival of the first boatload of black Americans sent back to Africa by the American Colonization Society in order to solve their perceived problem of the "freed slave," Monrovia was named after the U.S. president James Monroe. The land was bought by the American settlers, later known as Americo-Liberians, from the local De chief, King Peter, and the town quickly grew up on a hilly peninsula at the mouth of the Mesurado River. However, the doubtful legality of this purchase, together with the fact that the settlers regarded the Africans as peons, formed the basis for later conflict.

In 1989, Monrovia was a city of about 3.4 million people. This population included a core of long-established inhabitants and a large number of people who came to the capital during the postwar economic boom based on rubber and iron ore. The new inhabitants included many foreign traders and merchants, as well as rural Liberians. At this time over 80 percent of Monrovians were Christians.

Following the outbreak of civil war in 1989, many Liberians fled to Monrovia. In 1992 the city was ravaged by the National Patriotic Front of Liberia under the leadership of Charles Taylor. The suburbs were mostly destroyed, but the central, old part of the town was successfully defended by the Economic Community of West Africa States Monitoring Group, the United Liberation Movement of Liberia for Democracy, and the Armed Forces of Liberia. In 1996 Monrovia was the site of peace negotiations between the warring factions.

BIBLIOGRAPHY

Brown, George W. *The Economic History of Liberia*. Washington, D.C., 1941.

Fraenkel, Merran. *Tribe and Class in Monrovia*. London, 1964.

Yancy, M. *Historical Lights of Liberia's Yesterday and Today*. New York, 1954.

MARTHA HANNAN

Monrovia, Liberia. SEAN SPRAGUE, IMPACT VISUALS

MONTANE ENVIRONMENTS. *See* Ecosystems.

MOORS IN AFRICA. The name "Moor" derives from the people and country known in Roman times as Mauretania. It comprised the present country of Morocco with the Western Sahara and the coast of the present Republic of Mauritania as far as its capital, Nouakchott. It was a narrow strip along the Atlantic coast, never extending more than 300 miles (483 km) inland. The name has gone through many mutations of meaning over the past twenty-five hundred years, as a result of indiscriminate usage.

A summary of the word's history explains its meaning. The Greek word Μαυροι (Mauroi), the root word of Mauretania and therefore of "Moors," is first attested in a poem by Pindar (d. c. 435 B.C.E.) and in a play by Aeschylus (d. 456 B.C.E.). Neither Mauretania nor Mauroi is mentioned in Herodotus's *Histories,* composed around 439 B.C.E., the earliest known account of the peoples of northern Africa. By common consensus "Mauroi" means dark skinned; it should not be confused with μελας (*melas,* black).

In 27 B.C.E. Emperor Augustus extended the Province of Africa to include Numidia and present-day Tunisia. The rest of Algeria and northern Morocco were nominally independent under a vassal king of Mauretania. In 40 C.E. the last king was assassinated on the orders of Emperor Caligula, and his possessions were made an imperial province. By the third century most of Morocco had ceased to be administered; Emperor Diocletian did not control more than Mauretania Tingitana, the immediate vicinity of Tangier (Tingis), which was administered from Spain. Vandals from Spain controlled the country from 429 until 534, when Belisarius took it for Byzantium.

After the Arabs had conquered Egypt in 640, they made no effort before 670 to penetrate further west than Libya. Northern Africa was not subdued by the caliphate until the end of the century. In 712 a majority Berber army crossed into Spain, seizing the country in what was almost a ceremonial parade. The army continued into France but in 732 turned back south of Poitiers without giving battle, an event that marks the limit of Arab expansion in western Europe.

By 756 the Islamic state of al-Andalus had been constituted in Spain by an Umayyad dynasty of Syrian descent. The incomers, to whom the term "Moors" was now more broadly extended, included not only Berbers from northern Africa but also Syrians, Yemenis, and Jews. For some four hundred years these peoples left monuments that attest a marvelous flowering of civilization unequaled in the Europe of its time. In law and learning, in art and poetry, in religious writing, in architecture, in its supreme expressions in the Mesquita, the Great Mosque of Córdoba, and the Alhambra palaces and the exquisite Generalife in Granada, the Moors reached incomparable heights of taste and elegance, only to collapse politically in the eleventh century.

A further Berber invasion by the Almoravids lasted only half a century. In its turn it was overthrown by a new Berber group, the Almohads, in 1145. Thereafter the Christian kingdoms, first Portugal, and then Spain, slowly eroded Moorish power, culminating in the fall of Granada, and the unification of present Spain in 1492. In the following year all Jews who would not convert to Christianity were expelled, followed by the expulsion of the Moors in 1502.

The term "Moors" slowly penetrated European languages outside the Iberian Peninsula. In French it is first found as *mor* in a work of Chrétien de Troyes in 1175. The spelling Maure occurs first in 1636.

The Moors who were expelled from the kingdom of Granada first migrated to their ancestral homelands. Fez was a particular center of attraction. Many had emigrated before, including Jews of Arab culture; one was Musa ibn Maymun (Mosheh ben Maimon; in English, Maimonides), Saladin's personal physician and confidant and outstanding astronomer, philosopher, and theologian. In art and architecture, Islamic influences persisted in the exuberant styles of architecture in Portugal and Spain.

The relatively narrow original sense of the word "Moor" was extended through usage over time. In Jerusalem in 1480, and there and in Sinai in 1483, a German friar, Felix Faber, draws a clear distinction between those he counts as Moors and those he regards as Saracens. The Moors are from the Iberian Peninsula and northern Africa; the Saracens are Muslims of eastern origin, from the Arabic word *sharq* (east). By the time Vasco da Gama wrote his *Voyages,* he used the term to refer to east African Muslims he encountered after rounding the Cape of Good Hope. His usage was followed by the distinguished head of the Casa da India (the India Office in Lisbon), João de Barros, and thereafter indiscriminately by European writers of all nations. The word "Moor" had been severed from its origins.

BIBLIOGRAPHY

Cornevin, Robert. *Histoire de l'Afrique.* Vol. 1. Paris, 1962.

Freeman-Grenville, G. S. P. *The East African Coast: Select Documents from the First to the Earlier Nineteenth Century.* Oxford, 1962.

————. *The New Atlas of African History.* London, 1991.

————. *Historical Atlas of the Middle East.* New York, 1993.

G. S. P. FREEMAN-GRENVILLE

See also **Arabs; Northern Africa.**

MORTALITY. Before the Pasteurian revolution, sub-Saharan Africa constituted a dangerous environment where little could be done to extend human life. The frailty of human existence is reflected in African beliefs about death. Despite a broad variety of religious practice, most sub-Saharan cosmologies contain a common core of beliefs about the afterlife. Only the deaths of the elderly are seen as unavoidable natural occurrences. Other deaths result from spiritual forces. The Kongo distinguish between this world of human habitation and the land of the dead, a parallel world of night inhabited by the dead and by powerful spirits. They interpret most deaths as resulting from human invocations of spiritual forces. A smaller number of deaths come from spiritual forces which have responded to violations of rules of proper conduct. The Lugbara, while attributing great power to the dead, do not see their world as parallel to that of the living. Recently dead relatives, however, do have the power to ask spirits to send illness to living members of the lineage who have violated rules by proscribed sexual relations or disrespect for elders. Sorcerers can also cause death by invoking spirits or poisoning food.

In addition to these spiritual explanations for death, many groups also have pragmatic mechanisms for dealing with "bad deaths," which directly threaten community survival. During an epidemic, the infected can be shunned or buried without the usual rituals. Sometimes whole villages are relocated to avoid contagion.

Africans are subject to the pathogens of both the temperate Eurasian landmass and the moist tropics. This combination means that death rates are the highest in the world. Mortality levels are high for people of all ages, but especially for infants and children, and childbearing is hazardous for women. Few people survive to old age. The most common causes of death are infectious diseases transmitted through a variety of means. Airborne droplets bring bacteria which produce pulmonary diseases like pneumonia and tuberculosis and viruses such as measles directly from one person to another. Drinking water serves as a medium for the transmission of fecal oral diseases such as bacillary and amoebic dysentery and typhoid fever. Insects convey tropical diseases such as malaria and yellow fever. Although human populations have developed resistance to some pathogens, microscopic populations also mutate to create new menaces to human survival.

Techniques for Extending Life Span

Coherent technologies for extending life expectancy were first developed in temperate countries at the beginning of the twentieth century, when much of sub-Saharan Africa was first coming under colonial rule. Mortality levels fell precipitously and nearly simultaneously in Western Europe, North America, Australia, and New Zealand. Demographers describe these increases in life expectancy as transitions in mortality, epidemiology, and health. The mortality transition refers to the sequence in which the death rate fell differentially by age group: first among adolescents and young adults, then among children, and finally among the elderly. The epidemiologic transition refers to a change in the cause of death from infectious and parasitical to chronic and degenerative diseases. The health transition refers to the increasing role of personal choices relating to cleanliness, food, and substance abuse in reducing mortality.

African mortality patterns did not immediately follow these trends. In fact, mortality levels actually rose in certain areas during the early years of the twentieth century, as a result of colonial administrative and economic policies. In the absence of a public health infrastructure, mortality levels rose in urban areas and at mine sites through the introduction of pathogens from other parts of Africa and from industrial cities in other parts of the world. Epidemics of pneumonia, typhoid fever, tuberculosis, cholera, and plague spread through many parts of the continent. Colonial authorities responded with the resources they could muster locally, but lacked the levels of financing available in the European colonizing powers. Furthermore, the authorities spent disproportionately on expatriates.

Another problem lay in government response to specifically tropical diseases. Empirically, specialists in tropical medicine and hygiene had already discovered measures which could extend the lives of tropical populations, such as the use of quinine for the treatment of malaria. Importing a broad spectrum of preventatives and treatments, however, involved high costs, and procedures commonly used in Europe and North America were only sparingly applied. One of the pioneers of an integrated approach to tropical hygiene was the American physician William C. Gorgas, who recommended in 1914 that techniques developed to protect the lives of workers who dug the Panama Canal could be adapted to South African mine workers.

Between the wars, European colonizers still received the lion's share of available resources. The principal African beneficiaries of these medical advances were those in closest contact with the colonial government and economy—that is, mine workers, employees of colonial governments, and urbanites—a relatively small proportion of the entire population. Among the best-served locales were Dakar; nine towns in what is now Ghana, including Accra; and the copper towns in what are now Zaire and Zambia.

Also dating from this period were systematic campaigns to control particular diseases. Governments initiated spraying programs against the anopheles mosquito and the tsetse fly to reduce infection from malaria and sleeping sickness. They also built regional laboratories for the production of smallpox and yellow fever vaccine for Africans, who were then vaccinated. Private companies built laboratories for more specialized vaccines against typhoid, tetanus, and diphtheria.

The success of these campaigns is hard to measure given the absence of vital registration and reliable, periodic censuses. Even today, most national mortality statistics are based on surveys which are not totally representative of the countries to which they pertain. The United Nations International Children's Emergency Fund (UNICEF) and the World Bank use an indicator which measures the proportion of children who die before their fifth birthday. On this basis, in 1960 roughly 20 percent of sub-Saharan African children died before the age of five, a proportion which had decreased to about 10 percent by 1990. England and France, in comparison, reached the 20 percent threshold about 1900, the 10 percent level about 1930, and in the 1990s are below one percent. African child survival therefore trails that of the two leading former colonial powers by about sixty years.

After the Second World War, two innovations, one of them medical, the other fiscal, contributed to a reduction in mortality levels. The development of cheap and effective broad-spectrum antibiotics, which were distributed through public health clinics and missions, provided caregivers with valuable weapons against pneumonia and tuberculosis. These medical innovations were disseminated through a growing network, thanks to direct grants from colonial governments and the United Nations. Mortality levels, which had approximated those of mid-nineteenth-century Europe, began a steady decline.

Mortality Patterns Since 1960

Following independence, which in territories north of the Zambezi River occurred about 1960, African majority regimes assumed control of health-care delivery, but little changed. Most countries were still dependent on foreign revenue sources; United Nations and single-donor agencies tended to supplant the former colonizers as providers of health care. Until African physicians and nurses could be trained to replace expatriates, moreover, foreign personnel directed the delivery. Indeed, the spatial distribution of resources also persisted, in that urban areas originally built to accommodate colonial rulers continued to receive a disproportionate share of hospitals, clinics, schools, and water-treatment facilities.

Despite these regional disparities, conditions continued to improve, even after a severe economic downturn which began about 1973. The reasons for this continued improvement were both internal and external. A post-independence boom in school attendance trained future generations of parents in private hygiene and recourse to medical services. International agencies established vaccination programs to eliminate childhood diseases such as smallpox, measles, and typhoid fever, and also subsidized water-purification systems to reduce mortality from diarrheal diseases.

Nonetheless, African mortality rates remain among the highest in the world. Part of the explanation lies in the continued importance of infectious diseases as a cause of death, including old scourges such as malaria, for which there is neither effective prevention nor cure, and AIDS, which was first described in 1983. In Europe, by contrast, people survive most infections, ultimately succumbing to the chronic and degenerative diseases of old age. Another factor contributing to continued high levels of mortality is the poverty of health-care facilities in rural areas. Indeed, poverty limits the effectiveness of almost all sub-Saharan health-care facilities. At the end of the twentieth century, untimely death is still very much a part of African life.

BIBLIOGRAPHY

Bockie, Simon. *Death and the Invisible Powers: The World of Kongo Belief.* Bloomington, Ind., 1993.

Bond, George C. "Living with Spirits: Death and Afterlife in African Religions." In *Death and Afterlife: Perspectives of World Religions,* edited by Hiroshi Obayashi. New York, 1992.

Curtin, Philip D. "The End of the 'White Man's Grave'? Nineteenth-Century Mortality in West Africa." *Journal of Interdisciplinary History* 21, no. 1 (1990): 63–88.

Feachem, Richard G., and Dean T. Jamison, eds. *Disease and Mortality in Sub-Saharan Africa.* New York, 1991.

Fetter, Bruce. "Health Care in Twentieth Century Africa: Statistics, Theories, and Policies." *Africa Today* 40, no. 3 (1993): 9–23.

Van de Walle, Étienne, et al. *Mortality and Society in Sub-Saharan Africa.* Oxford, 1992.

BRUCE FETTER

See also **Death, Mourning, and Ancestors; Development; Disease; Healing; Population Data and Surveys; Religion and Ritual; Spirit Possession.**

MOSHOESHOE I (b. 1786; d. 1870), king of the Sotho and founder of the Basotho nation. Moshoeshoe was born Lepoqo in the village of Menkhoaneng. His parents were Mokhachane (Libenyane), a minor Koena chief, and Kholu, daughter of Ntsukunyane, a neighboring Fokeng chief. From an early age, Moshoeshoe aspired to be a great chief. However, he was a very impatient, hot-tempered youth who killed followers for offenses as trivial as slowness in carrying out his orders. He sought advice from Mohlomi, a doctor, sage, and Koena kinsman, on how to become a successful leader. Mohlomi advised Moshoeshoe to be humane and just, to form alliances by marrying into different lineages, and to fight only if peaceful means failed. Mohlomi's advice and Moshoeshoe's own realization that peace, not war, would earn him more followers changed him into a mature, dignified personality. From 1830 to 1870, he was able to grasp and deal with the complex changes resulting from the interaction of black and white populations. His approach to these developments earned him the respect of contemporary African rulers, colonial officials, and European commentators.

Moshoeshoe I. NATAL ARCHIVES, PIETERMARITZBURG

The greatest challenges facing Moshoeshoe during his reign were European settlers' attempts to conquer Basotho and seize their land. Forced by economic and political pressures at home, Britain, the dominant political power in the region, took sides with the settlers. Despite the modernity and sophistication of the British and the settlers' weaponry, Moshoeshoe vanquished an invading British force in 1852, while in two wars in 1858 and 1865 to 1867 the settlers failed to defeat him. Such was his diplomatic skill that by 1868 he was able to pry the British government's loyalty from the settlers' side and bring it firmly onto his side—an act which saved warweary Basotho from total conquest by the settlers. By doing so he achieved his lifelong dream to make an ally of Britain and secure for Basotho the protection of the only superpower then existing. It is therefore not an exaggeration to say that the existence of an independent Lesotho today is a result of his statesmanship.

BIBLIOGRAPHY

Casalis, Eugene. *The Basutos; or, Twenty-Three Years in South Africa.* London, 1861. Repr. Cape Town, 1965.

Ellenberger, D. Fred. *History of the Basuto, Ancient and Modern.* London, 1912.

Sanders, Peter B. "Sekonyela and Moshweshwe: Failure and Success in the Aftermath of Difaqane." *Journal of African History* 10, no. 3 (1969): 439–455.

Thompson, Leonard. *Survival in Two Worlds: Moshoeshoe of Lesotho, 1786–1870.* Oxford, 1975.

MOTLATSI THABANE

MOSSI. The Mossi (Moose) are the most important and largest population group of Burkina Faso, accounting for 48.6 percent of the population. Their language, Mooré, belongs to the Gur group, which is part of the Niger-Congo family. Mooré is widely spoken as the lingua franca of Burkina Faso. The Mossi as an ethnic group originated from very different populations. In the center of the country they merged with Nioniosse, Ninsi, and Gurunsi; in the north with the Dogon and Kurumba; in the south predominantly with the Bisa. Different and competing empires were organized in societies with feudal features until the French colonial period (from 1896) and later independence of the Republic of Upper Volta (1960). Slaves (*yemse*), commoners (*talse*), and nobles (*nakombse*) were ruled by a sovereign (*naaba,* pl. *nanamse*) assisted by a rigidly organized and led administration. Mossi who conquered Timbuktu during the reign of Emperor Mansa Musa of Mali (1312–1337) are mentioned repeatedly in the Arabic sources *Ta'rikh al-fattash* (sixteenth century) and *Ta'rikh as-sudan* (seventeenth century). Historical continuity between these early Mossi who attacked the Mali empire and the later *nakombse* has come under doubt. Oral traditions link the origin of all Mossi dynasties, including the disputed dynasty of Gurma, to Naaba Wedraogo. He is said to be the son of a princess with masculine traits and character from Gambaga, a town and trading center in the Mamprusi region of what is now northern Ghana. His father is said to have been a hunter of Mande origin.

During the fifteenth century, warriors on horseback, wearing chain or cotton armor (characteristic of the middle Sudan), arrived from the south and founded the first Mossi dynasties in a buffer zone between Bisa in the west, Mamprusi in the south, and the Gulmanceba in the east. Initially these rulers did not reside in one place but moved the court from province to province. From this mobile base they or continuously seceding, smaller groups sought to gain control over unconquered new areas. The genesis of all later empires rests thus on the *nakombse* generations, who—often in rivalry—founded empires of different sizes and extents, the most important being Ouagadougou around 1495 and Yatenga around 1540. Genealogical and historical reasons, however, account for the fact that only five of nineteen recent rulers have the right to be called *Rima* (independent sovereign). This means they need not greet anybody but God. The five are Tenkodogo, Gurma, Ouagadougou, Yatenga, and Busuma. Although the *rima* lost many of their privileges during the colonial period and after independence, especially under the revolutionary president Thomas Sankara (1983–1987), they are still regarded with respect, even by politicians (especially before elections).

BIBLIOGRAPHY

Badini, Amadé. *Naître et grandir chez les Moosé traditionnels.* Paris and Ouagadougou, 1994.

Izard, Michel. *Bibliographie générale des Mossi.* Études Voltaiques 12 and 13. Paris and Ouagadougou, 1962.

———. *Gens de pouvoir, gens de la terre: Les Institutions politiques de l'ancien royaume de Yatenga (Bassin de la Volta Blanche).* Cambridge and Paris, 1985.

———. *L'Odyssée du pouvoir. Un Royaume africain: État, société, destin individuel.* Paris, 1992.

Izard, Michel, and J. Ki-Zerbo. "From the Niger to the Volta." In *UNESCO General History of Africa,* vol. 5, *Africa from the Sixteenth to the Nineteenth Century,* edited by B. A. Ogot. Paris, 1992.

Sinner, Eliot P. *The Mossi of the Upper Volta: The Political Development of a Sudanese People.* Stanford, Calif., 1964.

Zahan, Dominique. "The Mossi Kingdoms." In *West African Kingdoms in the Nineteenth Century,* edited by Daryll Forde and P. M. Kaberry. London, 1967.

UTE RITZ-MÜLLER

MOSSI REGION, HISTORY. At present, half the population of Burkina Faso, some four million people, call themselves Moose; in the singular, Moaga. ("Mossi" is the French version of the ethnonym.) The Moose speak Mooré, which is a Gur language.

They constitute by far the largest ethnic group in the White Volta basin, an area estimated at 63,500 square kilometers. This is the result of historical developments by which Moose kingdoms came to dominate the region from the mid-fifteenth century onward. In a long and gradual process of expansion, migrant Moose achieved political rule over autochthones of different ethnic origins. Once incorporated into the Moose kingdoms, the newly conquered peoples came to identify themselves as Moose as well.

According to local oral traditions, the first Moose originated in Gambaga, one of the centers of early Dagomba and Mamprusi kingdoms situated in what is today northern Ghana. Yenenga, the daughter of the Mamprusi king Nedega, is presented as the mother of Ouédraogo, the first Moose king. All Moose kingdoms—in due course over twenty major kingdoms arose in the region—were founded by patrilineal descendants, the so-called *nakombse,* of Ouédraogo. The first kingdoms were established in the south; later the sons of rulers were sent up north to found kingdoms of their own. Tenkodogo, Ouagadougou (Moogo), Yatenga, and Boussouma were among the most important kingdoms.

Michel Izard has dealt extensively with the historiography of the Moose. Historical dates for the events mentioned in the oral traditions can be deduced from an internal comparison of the corpus of traditions and from matching oral with written Arab sources. The current view is that during the seventeenth and eighteenth centuries the political institutions of the Moose kingdoms became very elaborate. Certain institutional innovations can be attributed to specific kings. For example, during the short reign of Naaba Warga (1737–1744) the royal court of Ouagadougou was reorganized into various political offices and distinct groups of servants. A particular marriage practice, the so-called *napogsyure,* was central to the system for recruiting male servants from the villages: after seven to ten years of court service, a young man would receive a wife from the king. The first child from a marriage of this type would be given to the king: a daughter would be given in marriage by the king; a son would do temporary service at the court. This system was crucial to the establishment of lasting political networks, with the king at the center. Characteristically, court officials were never kinsmen of the king. A king would be surrounded by loyal dependents, whereas his patrilineal kinsmen typically would be appointed to village headmanships at a safe distance from the capital.

Conflict and competition between *nakombse* kinsmen triggered the political innovations introduced by Naaba Kango, who ruled over Yatenga for about thirty years in the mid-eighteenth century. The opposition of the princes forced Naaba Kango to go into exile but, with the help of the kingdom of Segu, he regained his throne and reorganized Yatenga. Naaba Kango founded the capital Ouahigouya, the architecture and organization of which were influenced by his experiences in Mali. He nominated non-kinsmen to the newly created position of war chief. Since these political functions were not hereditary, the loyalty of the king's officials was assured.

Political processes were also shaped by the wider regional setting. Trade influenced the Moose kingdoms in two ways. First, some of the kingdoms capitalized on their strategic locations along caravan routes (salt from the Sahara was exchanged for kola nuts from the forest zones in the south). This trade was dominated by Sudanese people as well as by Asante from what is nowadays Ghana. Moose farmers sold them their donkeys, cotton, and grain. To cultivate trade the Moose kings gave protection to one particular group of traders, the Yarse, Muslim traders of Mande origin. This was the case, for instance, in Yatenga, Maane, and Ouagadougou. Second, the slave trade on the coast had its effects on the region, particularly in the eighteenth century: since people could be bought and sold, the courts of Moose kings also included royal captives.

Since the oral traditions focus mainly on the internal history of the royal family, the implications of the political system for "ordinary" Moose are, at times, hard to assess. Despite the elaborate system of government, it should be stressed that political relationships were never rigid, hermetic, or uniform. Moose kingdoms were not homogeneous since they involved people with a wide range of social identities. Groups of people always had options with respect to the political alliances they engaged in. Moreover, the king and his administration did not intervene equally in all spheres of social life. For instance, the political involvement of the government in the economic domain was limited. Land tenure and agriculture, with sorghum and millet the staple crops, were largely the affair of kin groups in the villages. Subjects did not pay taxes to the king on income or property.

One group of "ordinary" Moose stood out in particular: people claiming descent from the original inhabitants of the land, the autochthones. They were called *tengabiise*, children of the earth. In all the Moose kingdoms the distinction between the *nakombse*, strangers by origin, and the autochthones was expressed in an elaborate division of tasks, foremost related to ritual practices. Whereas the *nakombse* ruled the people, the autochthones were in charge of rituals related to the earth, *tenga*. The king and his associates—his wives and sisters, court officials, war chiefs—on the one hand and the earthpriests on the other were all engaged in a complex ritual system, the main aim of which was to ensure good harvests, as well as the welfare of the kingdom as a whole.

BIBLIOGRAPHY

Alexandre, Pierre. *La langue moré.* 2 vols. Dakar, Senegal, 1953.

Dim Delobsom, A. A. *L'empire du mogho-naba: Coutumes des Mossi de la Haute-Volta.* Paris, 1932.

Fage, J. D. "Reflections on the Early History of the Mossi-Dagomba Group of States." In *The Historian in Tropical Africa,* edited by J. Vansina, R. Mauny, and L. V. Thomas. London, 1964.

Hammond, Peter B. *Yatenga: Technology in the Culture of a West African Kingdom.* New York, 1966.

Izard, Françoise. *Bibliographie générale de la Haute Volta, 1956–1965.* Paris and Ouagadougou, Burkina Faso, 1965.

Izard, Michel. *Introduction à l'histoire des royaumes mossi.* 2 vols. Paris and Ouagadougou, Burkina Faso, 1970.

———. "The Peoples and Kingdoms of the Niger Bend and the Volta Basin from the 12th to the 16th Century." In *General History of Africa,* volume 4, *Africa from the Twelfth to the Sixteenth Century,* edited by D. T. Niane. Berkeley, 1984.

———. *Gens du pouvoir, gens de la terre: Les Institutions politiques de l'ancien royaume du Yatenga (Bassin de la Volta Blanche).* Paris, 1985.

———. *L'odyssée du pouvoir: Un Royaume africain: État, société, destin individuel.* Paris, 1992.

Izard, Michel, and Joseph Ki-Zerbo. "From the Niger to the Volta." In *General History of Africa,* volume 5, *Africa from the Sixteenth to the Eighteenth Century,* edited by B. A. Ogot. Berkeley, 1992.

Kawada, Junzo. *Genèse et évolution du système politique des Mosi méridionaux (Haute Volta).* Tokyo, 1979.

Kouanda, A. "Les Yarse: Fonction commerciale, religieuse et légitimité culturelle dans le pays moaga." Ph.D. diss., Université de Paris I, 1984.

Skinner, Elliott P. *The Mossi of the Upper Volta: The Political Development of a Sudanese People.* Stanford, 1964.

SABINE LUNING

MOURNING. *See* **Death, Mourning, and Ancestors.**

MOVEMENTS, POLITICAL. *See* **Independence Movements; Prophetic Movements.**

MOZAMBIQUE

GEOGRAPHY AND ECONOMY

Mozambique is a country totally out of balance and in crisis. Its recent violent history; its vast geographical and climatic contrasts; its mind-boggling ethnic, and thus linguistic and religious, diversity; and its enormous size (e.g., a coastline of 2,300 kilometers [1,430 mi.]) are kept together only by boundaries that were defined during the colonial period. Mozambique is also somberly united by a violent past of thirty years. All conventional indicators of national and international agencies that try to capture Mozambique are deficient, incomplete, most likely insufficient, and often simply unavailable. Definitely, Mozambique is one of the poorest countries, if not the poorest in the world, with the lowest gross national product (GNP) per capita (U.S.$115 in 1995), with an inordinately high rate of development assistance in relationship to its gross domestic product (GDP) (65 percent in 1994), and a virtually nonexistent state apparatus in the areas of general administration, public health, law and order, public education, and public infrastructure. This dismal state of affairs is foremost the result of 450 years of Portuguese colonialism, some thirty years of civil war until 1995, and the preceding ten years of a war of liberation that crippled nearly all sectors of the Mozambican economy and society. Figures vary too greatly for us to know how many people died in the war of liberation or the civil war. An entire generation of young men has been diminished to a few, and countless men, women, and children have been permanently maimed and will continue to be crippled by the millions of indiscriminately broadcast land mines in the countryside. The contemporary social fabric is under economic stress: families torn apart, countless women traumatized by rape as a habitual part of the civil war (mainly by Resistência Nacional Moçambicana [RENAMO] troops), a staggering number of orphans, an untold number of children born out of wedlock, eighteen thousand worker-returnees from former East Germany, thousands of male teenagers and young men who experienced guerrilla warfare all add to the grim picture. In short:

191

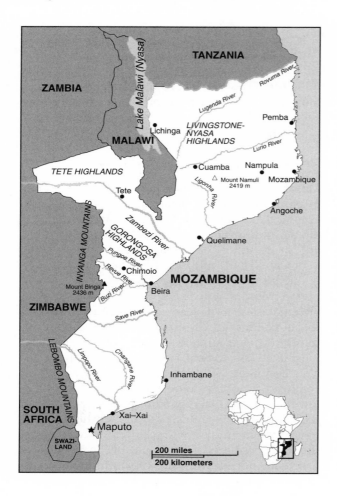

season lasts from November/December to March/April with a precipitation between 1,000 mm and 1,400 mm (about 39 to 55 in.) that can reach some 2,000 mm (nearly 80 in.) in the mountainous regions. South of the Save River the average rainfall is 600 mm to 800 mm (about 23 to 31 in.), with even less rain in the western regions; long spells of drought do occur intermittently. The agroecological zones are defined by the mixture of physical characteristics and population patterns. The possibility of a highly varied and productive agriculture, aside from a very likely high number of still undiscovered mineral reserves, suggests enormous economic potential. Problems of destruction of forest reserves and wildlife resources through indiscriminate logging and as a consequence of the protracted civil war are grim. The consequences of large hydroelectric projects (human displacement, water-borne diseases, and negative downstream effects) affect large bioregions. Most threatened is the vast mangrove vegetation of the coastal areas, an unusually rich source of prawns and shrimp production.

Mozambique is characterized by a twofold transformation process: on the one hand, it has to overcome the transition from a state-centered economy to a market economy and from a civil war economy to a peacetime economy. Thus, all indicators about economic activities are subject to very wide variations and are in constant flux. Some two-thirds to three-quarters of the population is engaged in some form of subsistence production with very little export-oriented agriculture (predominantly cashew nuts). Some 10 percent of the population is engaged in manufacturing and 15 percent in the service industry. The economic activities are concentrated in the coastal belt where more than 50 percent of the population resides.

At present, Mozambique is undergoing another great social transformation. The prospects of it becoming a prosperous nation could be promising indeed. The combination of immense natural resources, availability of arable land, and the emerging civil society are indicators that this war-torn country will finally stabilize. The conflicting parties (FRELIMO [Frente de Libertação de Moçambique] and RENAMO) concluded a peace treaty (1992); free national elections in 1995 gave legitimacy to a new government, though not creatively and wisely used, and made life and commerce safer. Civic organizations are emerging; political parties are in their infancy; and denominational activities of Christian churches and missions, Islamic broth-

a whole society needs to rebuild itself on the social, political, infrastructural, and environmental ruins that were produced over the last centuries.

Mozambique is endowed with abundant land, water, forest, and wildlife resources. Its topography displays three distinct features. (1) The coastal areas, rising to 200 meters (650 ft.) above sea level, cover about 42 percent of the country's land, of which over 50 percent is susceptible to flooding. (2) The middle plateau (between 200 m and 500 m or about 650 and 1,625 ft.) mostly in the northern region extending westward to the Zambezi valley, covers about 29 percent of the area. (3) The upland plateau (500 to 1,000 m or about 1,625 to 3,300 ft.) is mostly situated in the northern part and covers some 25 percent of the nation's space. (4) Highland and mountain areas (1,000 m and above, or about 3,300 ft.) near the Malawi and Zimbabwe border cover 4 percent of the land area.

Climatically the country is divided into two main regions. North of the Save River the rainy

erhoods, and independent African churches are increasing their impact. Foreign donors are intensifying their efforts in the rebuilding of a Mozambican society.

Mozambique's history has largely been formed by neighboring Bantu states in the area of present-day South Africa, Portuguese colonialism, and postcolonial insurgency aided by international destabilizing activities. Vasco da Gama claimed this area for the Portuguese empire in 1498, competing with Arabian merchants who had traded with the coastal populations since the eighth century. Until the establishment of the Estado Novo in 1926, the Portuguese domination never reached far inland, allowing private organizations in the form of concessions (*prazos*) to exploit the interior of the country. Some twenty thousand slaves were shipped, predominantly to Brazil, by these private merchants between the seventeenth and mid-nineteenth centuries. Antonio de Salazar's dictatorial regime in Portugal (1926–1970) modernized colonization and established a mixture of forced labor, enforced agricultural production, and enforced migrant labor to South African mines (to collect remittances), thus allowing the continuation of the Portuguese estate system. After World War II, Portugal further intensified its colonization efforts, channeled international capital to Mozambique (e.g., the Cabora Bassa hydroelectric dam), and increased subsidized Portuguese settlement, thus expelling numerous indigenous occupants from their good agricultural lands.

The FRELIMO, a coalition of three nationalist organizations, in 1962 started its military liberation struggle against Portugal, initially heavily influenced by its first leader, the U.S.-trained sociologist Dr. Eduardo Mondlane. FRELIMO embarked on a revolutionary-socialist model of people's power after its military leader since 1966, Samora Machel, was nominated its president in 1970. FRELIMO's military and international diplomatic campaign made it the choice for the negotiations for independence after the collapse of the regime in Portugal in 1974. Machel, as Mozambique's first president, oversaw the (never successful) transformation of FRELIMO from an underground liberation movement into a Marxist-Leninist party that established close ties to the nations of the Warsaw Pact. Internally, it attempted to transform the Mozambican society into a secular, antitribal political force devoted to a planned economy. The reorganization of the society was marred by enormous internal problems. The mass exodus of the 200,000 Portu-

guese settlers and organized military destabilization by the South African Defense Forces, later in conjunction with RENAMO, drew Mozambique into a protracted, extremely bloody and cruel civil war that lasted until 1992. After Machel's death in 1986, Joaquim Chissano's government hesitantly introduced less controlling policies and started to widen political participation but could not ease the internal turmoil. After decades of destruction and strife, the mythical dimension of FRELIMO as a liberating force diminished to a bleak record.

The contemporary economic and social policies have to contend with some 1.5 million citizens as refugees in neighboring countries, some 3.5 million citizens as refugees within Mozambique, and rapid urbanization around the centers of Maputo, Beira, and Nova Sofala. First initiatives of emerging cooperatives, agribusiness investments (Lonrho), and cooperative endeavors of South African farmers with Mozambican counterparts will likely lead to a stable subsistence production if not surplus food production. Whether the newly elected government with a FRELIMO majority will lead to a sustainable economic growth, it is too early to predict.

BIBLIOGRAPHY

Azevedo, Mario J. *Historical Dictionary of Mozambique.* Metuchen, N.J., 1991.

Isaacman, Allen F., and Barbara Isaacman. *Mozambique: From Colonialism to Revolution, 1900–1982.* Boulder, Colo., and Aldershot, Eng., 1983.

Newitt, M. D. D. *A History of Mozambique.* Bloomington, Ind., 1995.

FRANK HIRTZ

See also **Machel, Samora Moises; Mondlane, Eduardo Chivambo**

HISTORY AND GOVERNMENT

The modern Mozambican state has its roots in a radical nationalist movement which developed in the 1950s. Long before this there had been armed rebellions against the Portuguese colonial authorities, but these were regional rather than national in character. Workers staged strikes and peasants resisted forced labor, but in the first half of the twentieth century a unitary, independent Mozambican state was little more than the dream of a few intellectuals.

Nationalist consciousness and organized resistance on a national scale was slow in developing, mainly as a result of Portuguese repression of political activity and the enormous difficulties of com-

República de Moçambique (The Republic of Mozambique)

Population: 16,653,400 (1994)

Area: 799,384 sq. km (308,642 sq. mi.)

Official language: Portuguese

Languages: Portuguese, Sena, Shona, Makua, Thonga, Shangana, Swahili

National currency: Metical

Principal religions: Traditional 65.6%, Christian 25%, Muslim 10%

Capital: Maputo (est. pop. 1,010,000 in 1987)

Other urban centers: Tete, Beira, Quelimane, Sofala, Inhambane, Mozambique, Nampula, Xai Xai

Annual rainfall: 1,420 mm (55 in.) in center, less in the north and south

Principal geographical features:

Mountains: Livingstone-Nyasa Highlands, Tete Highlands, Gorongosa Highlands, Lebombo Mountains, Mount Namuli, Mount Binga, Serra Zuira, Serra Mecula, Mount Jesi, Mount Mabu, Mount Chiperone

Lakes: Malawi (Nyasa), Cabora Bassa, Chilwa, Amaramba, Chuita, Barride Chicamba Real, Marrangua, Barride de Massingir

Rivers: Zambezi, Messinge, Chiulezi, Lugenda, Lurio, Maracoleta, Luleio, Limpopo, Gorongosa, Changane, Save, Revue, Pungue, Rovuma, Licungo, Buzi, Molocue, Monapo, Messalu, Ligonha

Economy:

GNP per capita: US$115 (1995)

Principal products and exports:

Agricultural: shrimp, fish, cashews, sugar, tea, sisal, cotton, citrus fruits, copra, coconuts, maize, millet, sorghum, cassava, sweet potatoes, groundnuts, beans, rice, livestock

Manufacturing: agricultural product processing, food and beverage processing, cement, textiles, tires, radios, petroleum refining

Mining: tantalite, some gold, mineral sands, titanium, iron ore, nepheline syenite, oil and natural gas

Government: Independence from Portugal, 1975. Constitution, 1975. New constitution approved in 1990. Multiparty parliamentary democracy. President elected for up to 3 consecutive 5-year terms by direct universal suffrage. 250-member Assembleia Nacional elected for 5-year terms by direct universal suffrage. President appoints prime minister and cabinet. The office of prime minister was created in 1986. For purposes of local government there are 10 provinces headed by elected local assemblies, and each province is subdivided into districts.

Heads of state since independence:

1975–1986: President Samora Machel

1986–: President Joaquim Alberto Chissano

Armed Forces: President is commander in chief. Two-year compulsory military service.

Army: 30,000

Navy: 750

Air Force: 4,000

Transportation:

Rail: 3,512 km (2,177 mi.)

Ports: Maputo, Quelimane, Mozambique, Nacala, Beira, Inhambane, Porto Amelia

Roads: 26,095 km (16,179 mi.), 20% paved

National airline: Linhas Aereas de Moçambique

Airports: International facilities at Aeroporto Internacional de Maputo. Other main airports at Beira and Mozambique. Numerous other airports and airstrips along the coast and in the interior.

Media: Two daily newspapers: *Diario de Moçambique, Noticias*. Two weeklies: *Domingo, Tempo*. Numerous other publications. Approximately 30 books are published annually. Radio is nationalized, provided through Radio Mozambique, Radio Pax, Emissora do Aero Clube. Televisão Experimental was established in 1981.

Literacy and Education:

Total literacy rate: 33% (1990). Education is compulsory for 7 years. Since the end of the civil war, the government has placed a strong emphasis on education, particularly primary. Post-secondary education provided at Universidade Eduardo Mondlane, Centro de Estudos Africanos, Instituto de Línguas, Instituto do Desenvolvimento da Educação, Instituto-Ciencias da Saúde, Instituto Nacional de Investigação Agronómica, University Teaching Hospital.

munication in a country with many indigenous languages and few opportunities for travel, contact, and the sharing of ideas. An early pathbreaker was the Nucleus of Secondary Students of Mozambique (NESAM), created in Lourenco Marques in 1949 by a new generation of students who were fluent in Portuguese. One of the founders of NESAM, Eduardo Mondlane, wrote later: "Under cover of social and cultural activities, [it] conducted among the youth a political campaign to spread the idea of national independence and encourage resistance to the cultural subjugation which the Portuguese imposed" (*The Struggle for Mozambique*, 113).

By cementing personal contacts, it established a nationwide network of communications which extended among former members as well as those still in school, and which could be used by a future underground. NESAM was significant not only for its forthright nationalistic stance but also because it produced some of the most important Mozambican political leaders of the second half of the century. They included Mondlane, who would lead the independence war from 1964 until his death in 1969, Joaquim Chissano, who became president of Mozambique in 1986, and Pascoal Mocumbi, Chissano's prime minister.

The students were strongly influenced by nationalist intellectuals such as the poets Marcelino dos Santos, José Craveirinha, and Noémia de Sousa. Then came quite separate attempts to create a nationwide radical nationalist movement by Mozambicans working in neighboring countries. Three main exile groups were formed in the early 1960s in Rhodesia, Malawi and Tanganyika (present-day Tanzania), and Kenya. The groups had a predominantly ethnic or regional base and, being exiled in different countries, offered little hope for the creation of a genuine nationalist front. But when Tanganyika became independent from Britain all three moved their headquarters to Dar es Salaam.

It was there, on 25 June 1962, that they came together to form FRELIMO (Frente de Libertação de Moçambique) with the blessing of Julius Nyerere, the Tanganyikan independence leader. But the rivalry between the groups was bitter, and no one party would accept the leadership of another. The solution was found at the first congress of FRELIMO in September 1962. Eduardo Mondlane was elected president. By now an anthropologist and sociologist, with a Ph.D. from Northwestern University in the United States, he was not associated with any of the exiled parties. He had worked as a research officer in the trusteeship department of the United Nations, preparing background papers on the trust territories of Tanganyika, Cameroon, and South West Africa.

The movement he headed was united in name but not in practice. Mondlane, Joaquim Chissano, Marcelino dos Santos, and other intellectuals soon learned that some of the founders still saw the independence movement from a tribal point of view and did not grasp the implications of a front which embraced all Mozambicans. In addition, some saw the struggle as a war against the whites, a view which Mondlane did not share. Another bone of contention was the form the fight for independence would take. The first congress declared that all means of struggle would be used, which meant that war was coming unless the Portuguese agreed to negotiate independence peacefully. Some of the former exiles were unprepared for anything except the peaceful resistance they had witnessed in eastern Africa and Malawi.

Some of the members of the three former protonationalist groups abandoned FRELIMO and tried to form new groups, but their efforts were largely in vain. As it turned out, all offers of negotiation with the Portuguese government were refused. Soon after the foundation of FRELIMO, thousands of people were arrested in Mozambique because of their alleged support for the movement. In January 1963 Mondlane began sending recruits to Algeria for military training. A second group, including a young man named Samora Machel, who would become the independent Mozambique's first president, went for training later in the year. On 25 September 1964, Mondlane proclaimed the beginning of the armed struggle for national independence. He was not giving the Portuguese a polite warning: the first shots were fired the same day.

The Independence War

FRELIMO's plan was to launch a widespread uprising. Clandestine militants had been sent to seven of the nine provinces, covering the south, center, and north of the country, to mobilize the people for war. Soon, however, this plan began to crumble. Before the end of 1964 guerrilla fronts in the central Tete and Zambezia provinces were forced to close. It had been thought that with the coming of independence in Zambia and Malawi, these countries would become rear bases for fighters in Zambezia and Tete. But this did not happen. Zambian independence was still being consolidated, and President Hastings Banda of Malawi openly collaborated with the Portuguese.

The situation in the south was even worse. The South African and Rhodesian authorities and the British police in Swaziland prevented arms supplies getting through and assisted in catching young Mozambican patriots as they slipped across the border on their way to Tanzania to volunteer for military training. By the end of 1964, fifteen hundred FRELIMO sympathizers had been arrested. By 1965 the war had been confined to the two northern provinces of Cabo Delgado and Niassa, separated from Tanzania by the Ruvuma River. The Cabo Delgado front was a classic people's war. Just before the struggle began, fifteen thousand Mozambicans fled across the Ruvuma to escape the Portuguese repression. When the flight stopped soon thereafter, the people moved into guerrilla-controlled areas. They were no longer forced to produce cash crops and were able to grow food for themselves and the guerrillas. Liberated areas were rapidly established.

Niassa posed far more serious problems for the movement. This province is about the size of England and had then a population of a little more than a quarter of a million. A mobile guerrilla army like FRELIMO needed food supplies from the peasants, but they were few and far between. Nevertheless, the struggle advanced slowly but surely. In 1968 FRELIMO reopened its front in western Tete province, crossing in from a now stronger and more confident Zambia. With its military advance, FRELIMO developed economic policies for its expanding liberated areas. FRELIMO leaders were forbidden to have employees, and rural clinics, schools, and orphanages were established and provided their services for free. Collective crop production became the norm. A socialist orientation was apparent, if not stated.

A massive setback for FRELIMO came in February 1969, when Eduardo Mondlane was assassinated by a book bomb delivered to him at his office in Dar es Salaam. Tanzanian police investigated the case with the help of Interpol and came to the conclusion that the bomb had been sent by the Portuguese secret police, with the help of traitors inside FRELIMO. After a brief internal struggle, Samora Machel, the movement's military commander, was elected president of FRELIMO in 1970. Under his leadership the guerrillas thrust south across the Zambezi, then into the central heartland of Manica and Sofala.

By 1973, many Portuguese officers were tired of fighting what increasingly appeared to be hopeless wars in Mozambique, Angola, and Guinea-Bissau. Plotting began, and on 25 April 1974, the Armed Forces Movement overthrew the fascist government in Lisbon, restoring democracy and paving the way for independence for Portugal's African colonies. On the seventh of September that year, at a ceremony in Lusaka, the new Portuguese government agreed to hand over power to FRELIMO, and a transitional government was set up with Joaquim Chissano. as prime minister. Independence day was set for 25 June 1975. Machel stayed outside Mozambique during the transition, returning in May to make a triumphal tour of the country and to be sworn in as president of the People's Republic of Mozambique on independence day.

FRELIMO came to power on the crest of a wave of popular support so high that a one-party state was inevitable. Single-party governance was nothing new for Mozambicans, who had never had the chance to vote in multiparty elections in the past. They were happy and the international community offered no protest. The new government had support across a broad international spectrum. The Soviet bloc and China, which had provided military hardware and training for the guerrillas, and the Scandinavian countries and Holland, which had given humanitarian assistance, were particularly delighted. The West in general was supportive.

Looking on apprehensively, however, were the white minority regimes of Rhodesia and South Africa. FRELIMO was allied with the liberation movements in their countries, and the fact that Mozambique's first cabinet included people of all races did little to alleviate their anxiety. That anxiety, and the concomitant security threat, were clear enough to the new government in Lourenco Marques, soon to be renamed Maputo. But there were more pressing problems for FRELIMO.

The Mozambicans inherited a bankrupt country. Colonial Mozambique could not feed itself and imported food from South Africa and Rhodesia. There had been a balance of payments deficit every year after 1957. By 1970, exports covered less than half of the cost of imports, and the annual trade deficit had grown to U.S.$50 million. There was an industrial base, with an oil refinery, sugar and cashew processing plants, and textile, chemical, and metal industries. But industry was not integrated and was largely dependent on imported raw materials. The industrial base, as well as agricultural marketing, had been held tightly in Portuguese hands. Virtually all skilled jobs had been reserved for the Portuguese, while the Mozambicans were left with one of the lowest educational levels in the world: 90 percent illiteracy.

With FRELIMO's victory, 90 percent of the two hundred thousand Portuguese had fled in panic, leaving behind half-finished blocks of flats and expensive new machinery not yet installed. Some simply left. Others sabotaged the economy before they went. They killed cattle, disabled machinery, and smuggled capital out of the country. Thus 1975 to 1977 was a period of desperately keeping the economy going, with the aid of workers' committees in the workplace. In rural areas the larger farms were abandoned and the trading network collapsed. Few industries were nationalized as a policy, but the government took over all the abandoned enterprises—mostly small businesses and shops. Run-down larger firms were increasingly "intervened," a process like bankruptcy under which the firm remains officially private but the government appoints the management. By 1980 the state owned the bulk of the economy, but in some areas, such as textiles, agriculture, and banking, the state and private enterprise were competing. During these heady revolutionary days reliable statistics were hard to come by. But it appears that during 1974–1976, Mozambique's total payments balanced for the first time in twenty years. Exports had dropped, but imports had dropped farther because of the industrial collapse and the drop in demand for imported consumer goods after the Portuguese left.

Alongside the economic developments of the period, dramatic political events were taking place. On 3 March 1976, Machel's government closed the border with landlocked Rhodesia, in compliance with United Nations sanctions which the Portuguese had never observed. This ended Rhodesia's use of the Beira and Maputo ports, a serious blow to a landlocked economy. After his border-closure speech, Machel allowed the armed Zimbabwean liberation movement to resume using facilities in western Mozambique. The Zimbabwe African National Union (ZANU) had started to move men and arms over the border in 1972 from FRELIMO's liberated areas, but this had been suspended because of peace moves in the region. Machel's decisions changed the face of southern Africa. The relentless assault on the Rhodesians by ZANU forces operating out of bases in Mozambique played a

major part in the winning of Zimbabwean independence in 1980.

Even before the outset of the conflict the Rhodesians had been involved in the creation of a new force which would wreak havoc in Mozambique: the Mozambique National Resistance (RENAMO). Between 1976 and 1980 RENAMO attacks were pinpricks which caused no serious problems for Mozambique. RENAMO was used by the Rhodesians as a backup for their own operations against Mozambique and ZANU. Ken Flower, head of the Rhodesian Central Intelligence Organization (CIO), explained the origins of RENAMO in an interview three months before his death in July 1987. "I myself went twice to see the Portuguese Prime Minister on that subject in 1971 and 1972 and got only half-hearted acceptance. But still, they allowed us, as it were, to do our own thing. And we in turn [developed] this movement, which we ourselves generated, it is true, but to a certain extent was self-generating, and we called it then the Mozambique Resistance. . . . Certainly, we armed them" (*Conspicuous Destruction*, 17).

It was a low-key operation, but in 1980 the picture changed. Rhodesia was now Zimbabwe, and there was no place for RENAMO on Zimbabwean soil. Ken Flower asked the South Africans to assume sponsorship of RENAMO and they agreed. "We made the arrangements in a few days between making the decision in principle to the actual handover, to effect a transfer to the South Africans" (ibid., 26). Machel's government was either unaware of this development or considered RENAMO an insignificant threat. With Zimbabwe independent and the conflict apparently over, Mozambique turned its attention to the economy. In 1981 the government unveiled a ten-year plan which called for $10 billion in finance for big development projects, including more investment in heavily mechanized state farms which were already buckling under their own weight, becoming a liability rather than a boost to the economy.

While concentrating on the state farming sector the government paid scant attention to the peasants—the majority of the population—who found hardly any consumer goods to buy in rural shops. They stopped producing surpluses and this, coupled with a devastating drought between 1982 and 1984, led to severe economic depression. By the start of the drought, RENAMO had increased its strength from five hundred to a thousand members to eight thousand in just two years and was receiving ample supplies and training from the South

Africans. It was regularly resupplied by air and sea from South Africa to the extent that, according to some military experts, it was better equipped than the Mozambican army. RENAMO carried out a major military onslaught, claiming it was fighting an oppressive regime. A major focus for RENAMO was the fact that FRELIMO had adopted Marxism-Leninism as its ideology at a congress in 1977.

The Peace Process

In 1984 Machel and South African president P. W. Botha signed the Nkomati accord, a nonaggression pact under which South Africa was to end its support for RENAMO and Mozambique was to ban African National Congress guerrillas from using its territory as a base. Most analysts believe that Mozambique stuck to its side of the bargain while South Africa did not. Foreign minister Roeloff (Pik) Botha admitted this in 1985. The war escalated. In 1986 Mozambique suffered another blow. While returning from a summit in Zambia on the nineteenth of October, Machel's plane crashed into a hillside just inside South Africa, killing the president and thirty-four others. There were widespread allegations at the time that the South Africans had lured the plane off course with a phony radio beacon. Joaquim Chissano, foreign minister since independence, took office in November.

By late 1988 it had become clear that there was no military solution to the war. With Chissano's permission, a delegation of Mozambican Catholic and Anglican bishops traveled to Kenya, where they met two senior RENAMO leaders. The churchmen returned to Maputo to tell Chissano that they believed RENAMO too was tired of the war and that peace negotiations were possible. Proximity talks continued until 1990. In that year Chissano unveiled a new, multiparty constitution, and in July the first round of direct negotiations between the government and RENAMO began in Rome. On the thirtieth of November the new constitution came into effect, and the People's Republic of Mozambique became the Republic of Mozambique.

In October 1992 the two sides signed an agreement ending the war. A United Nations peacekeeping force was sent to supervise the peace process, which ended with general and presidential elections in October 1994. FRELIMO won an overall majority in the parliament, the Assembly of the Republic, and Chissano defeated RENAMO leader Afonso Dhlakama in the presidential poll. The United Nations declared the election free and fair.

The total cost of the war to Mozambique is beyond calculation. Tens of thousands were killed in the fighting, and far larger numbers died of the ensuing hunger and disease. One estimate of the total number of the war dead is six hundred thousand. Mozambique was left bankrupt and the government wholly dependent on foreign aid. In March 1996 the Bank of Mozambique said that the country's foreign debt was U.S.$5.4 billion. Shortly before Machel's death in 1986 the government decided to move away from centralized state planning and build a market economy. The following year the World Bank's Structural Adjustment Program was adopted. Implementation was accompanied by widespread privatization, massive currency devaluations, growing unemployment, and the spread of corruption. The transition caused considerable hardship. The guns had fallen silent, but the future was clouded with uncertainty.

BIBLIOGRAPHY

African Contemporary Record. New York, 1981.

Christie, Ian. *Machel of Mozambique.* Harare, Zimbabwe, 1988.

Hall, Margaret. "The Mozambican National Resistance (RENAMO): A Study in the Destruction of an African Country." *Africa* 60 (1990): 40–68.

Human Rights Watch. *Conspicuous Destruction: War, Famine, and the Reform Process in Mozambique.* New York, 1992.

Mondlane, Eduardo. *The Struggle for Mozambique.* 2d ed. London, 1983.

Mozambican Revolution. Dar es Salaam, 1963–1967; *Mozambique Revolution.* Dar es Salaam, 1967–1975 (newspaper published by the FRELIMO Information Department).

Munslow, Berry. *Mozambique: The Revolution and Its Origins.* London, 1983.

IAN CHRISTIE

See also **Colonial Policies and Practice: Portuguese Policies; Machel, Samora Moises; Mondlane, Eduardo Chivambo.**

PEOPLES AND CULTURES

Mozambique is inhabited by approximately 16 million people, the large majority of whom reside in rural areas. The last census to differentiate peoples according to ethnic affiliation was undertaken by the Portuguese colonial administration in 1970 when the total population was half its present size. It identified the Makua-Lomwe ethnic group concentrated in the area north of the Zambezi River as the largest, with 3 million individuals; the

"Thonga," residing in the area south of the Save River, as second largest with 1,850,000; and the Makonde, Yao, "Ngoni," Malawi (or Maravi), Sena, Shona, Chope, and Tonga as other groups of notable size.

Very little ethnographic literature exists on the peoples of Mozambique. The Portuguese colonial administration, in particular under the Salazar regime, was reluctant to host researchers who might grow familiar with indigenous peoples and question colonial policies, as British researchers in neighboring territories sometimes did. Administrators themselves often gathered ethnographic and historical information and were sometimes mandated to produce monographs on the people they governed, but most did so without academic training. Beginning in the late 1950s, the historian António Rita-Ferreira attempted to give order to the Portuguese colonial map of Mozambique with works cataloguing its peoples and cultures. The ethnologist A. Jorge Dias (and his research collaborators), under the direct sponsorship of the Portuguese Overseas Ministry, wrote the only ethnography based upon substantial field research conducted among a Mozambican population in the colonial period.

The work of Dias richly describes the Makonde, an agrarian society centered on the Mueda Plateau near the Rovuma River border with Tanganyika (now Tanzania). In the late 1950s, when Dias studied them, the Makonde traced descent through the mother's line, and young men, upon marriage, took up residence and asserted claims to land in the settlement of their maternal uncles. Scholars, including Dias, however, divided the population of Mozambique into two groupings, with matrilineal peoples occupying the territory north of the Zambezi and patrilineal peoples occupying the territory to the south. The settlements of the Shona people of central Mozambique south of the Zambezi, for example, contrasted sharply with those of the Makonde, consisting of a male lineage head, his wives and children, and their dependents. The authority of a lineage head among the Shona rested in his control over the cattle necessary both for mixed agriculture and for the negotiation of marriages.

Dias theorized that the varied kinship systems found in Mozambique represented historical adaptations accomplished by different communities in response to the possibilities afforded them by their natural environments: patrilineal systems tended to emerge where the soil provided a poor base for agriculture but where controlable levels of tsetse fly made the keeping of cattle possible, requiring warriors to defend the herd; matrilineal systems predominated where tsetse made cattle raising impossible but where soils provided a rich agricultural substrate. The natural environment was by no means determinant of social organization, however. The Swiss missionary Henri Junod speculated that the "Thonga" among whom he lived in the late nineteenth and early twentieth centuries had once been a matrilineal people despite the patrilineal forms of organization he witnessed. Continuing to the present day, in fact, prolonged and intensifying exposure of societies everywhere in Mozambique to the forces of mercantilism and capitalism have encouraged the transformation of local social organization and the shift, more generally, toward economic, political, and social practices congruent with patrilineal kinship.

Nature has been no more determinant of ethnic identities in Mozambique than of kinship systems; notwithstanding the colonial perspective, which took "tribal" groupings as natural categories, ethnicity in Mozambique, as elsewhere in the world, has been the dynamic production of peoples perpetually engaging social forces (both local and foreign) that are as historically fundamental to their "environment" as the landscapes on which they have lived. Scholars now seeking to fill the void in the ethnographic record on Mozambique consequently look to the histories of its peoples for points of departure. Although this academic project was delayed by a postindependence government as suspicious of anthropology as was its colonial predecessor, it now proceeds on the foundation of an historical record generated by historians such as Edward Alpers, Allen Isaacman, Patrick Harries, Leroy Vail, and Landeg White, and the numerous contributors to the three-volume history of Mozambique produced by the history department at the Eduardo Mondlane University in Maputo, all of whom have produced textured "social histories" of the peoples they have studied.

The earliest residents of the territory were most probably nomadic bands of hunter-gatherers, like the San found elsewhere in the southern African region, who shared little in common with any of Mozambique's present-day peoples. According to archaeological evidence, East Bantu migrants began to arrive in the region in small groups around 250 C.E.; over the next century and a half, successive waves of migrants either displaced or absorbed residents (including previous migrants) of the areas they came to occupy, laying the foundations of a shared Bantu heritage reflected in the contemporary African languages of Mozambique. Bantu migrants also brought with them the knowledge of ironworking, allowing the peoples of the region to make tools and to become sedentary farmers. The cultural innovations of these agrarian societies included systems of inheritance, ancestral cults, and the sexual division of labor, and they were able to produce agricultural surpluses and to carry on rudimentary trade with one another.

When Portuguese explorers arrived off the coast of eastern Africa around 1500, they found Swahili, Arab, and Indian merchants already trading there. Small-scale chiefdoms had become concentrated into states of increasing dimensions, which coordinated trade caravans to the coast and levied tariffs on routes passing through their territories. Two principal states flanked the Zambezi River: the *mwene mutapa* controlled the gold trade in the area between the Zambezi and Save Rivers, and the Malawi exercised dominion over the trade in ivory in the area between the Zambezi and Lake Nyasa (today Lake Malawi). Within these states, local chiefs and councils of elders often maintained claims to the lands occupied by their forebears, overseeing their distribution among family members and performing ritual functions to ensure the benevolent oversight of the group's ancestral spirits, but these same chiefs and their peoples were subject to demands for tribute from the larger state.

Portuguese suzerainty over the coast after 1525 led to the greater incorporation of the region into the world economy, where ivory and, later, slaves were in increasing demand. The emergence of the Yao ethnicity along the southeastern margins of Lake Nyasa was closely bound up with their embrace of caravan trade to the coast, which differentiated them from fellow descendants of the Malawi, including the Cewa and Manganja. Where a headman—generally the eldest brother of the sorority group (*mbumba*) around which the settlement was constituted—had once controlled the hunt among these predominantly agricultural peoples, he now took responsibility for organizing the caravan. In the seventeenth century, as detailed in Alper's work, Yao chieftaincies grew in size and strength as they specialized in the overland transport of ivory tusks and slaves gathered by neighboring peoples, and travel to distant lands came to be considered among the Yao as an essential rite of passage into manhood.

In the eighteenth century, Makua chieftaincies closer to the coast gained increasing power by brokering the commerce in slaves to ports in the vicinity of the island of Mozambique, thereby procuring the arms, ammunition, and powder with which they could sponsor more wide-ranging slaving parties in the interior. Dispersed settlements on the periphery of strong chiefdoms often entered into mutual security arrangements with those who would otherwise take them as captives, further augmenting the power of the influential chiefs (*mwenes*) around whom the Makua ethnic identity was constructed, but the small-scale matrilineal origins of these conglomerate communities were reflected in the tradition sustained among them of a strong female councillor to the *mwene* (called an *apwia-mwene*). In addition to producing centralized, militarized chieftaincies with expansive tendencies, the slave trade also created margins around those chieftaincies where fragmented populations moved constantly in search of refuge; from this shared experience, ethnic identities such as that of the Makonde were born.

In the Zambezi River valley, the Portuguese monarchy granted Crown estates (*prazos de coroa*) in the first half of the seventeenth century in an effort to establish a more permanent European presence in the Mozambican interior. As the Portuguese settlers (*prazeiros*) who held these estates attempted to gain hegemony over local sultanates and chieftaincies, however, they formed alliances with local families, through the negotiation of marriages, producing a mixed Afro-Portuguese culture. While continuing to dwell on European-style estates, *prazeiros* had limited access to European institutions such as churches and schools, and as they made more regular use of African languages they became increasingly illiterate. Most eventually adopted African agricultural technologies as well as such local practices as polygamy and the belief in witchcraft.

Ironically, the trade in slaves from which the Portuguese benefited so greatly—as many as one million people were exported from the area by the Portuguese, Arabs, Indians, Africans, and others—ultimately limited Portuguese influence by empowering African slavelords in the northern and central Mozambican interior, including *prazeiros* who asserted their autonomy from the Portuguese governor. In the eighteenth century, Banyan Indian merchants took advantage of Portuguese weakness to establish a stronger presence on the Mozambican coast and even to move into the Makua-speaking interior, where greater Islamization of the population followed.

In southern Mozambique, where the peoples of the region lived in intermediate-sized chieftaincies established in the first half of the second millennium around migrant conquerors from the Sotho- and Shona-speaking areas of the southern African interior, the trade in ivory and slaves was more limited. Dramatic changes would be wrought there, however, by Nguni regiments scattering in the wake of the *mfecane*. Several Nguni regiments moved through southern Mozambique and settled farther north (giving rise, for example, to the Angoni ethnicity found here today), but the most notable group was that of Soshangane, who took up residence in Chaimite near the Save River in southern central Mozambique. At the time of his death in 1858, Soshangane's Gaza empire reached as far north as the Zambezi. The Gaza Nguni referred to those they had conquered as "Tsonga"—meaning slave, or servant—and they appropriated their cattle, conscripted their young men into military service, and gave captured women as brides to members of their growing regiments. While the Nguni invasion introduced pronounced class division into the societies of the southern half of Mozambique, the Nguni system of integrating conquered peoples allowed not only for the absorption of local populations into its ranks but also for the adoption of local cultural practices and languages by the rulers of the empire. As a result, the Shangaan peoples of the Limpopo River valley—originally called so because they had been "subjected to the rule of Soshangane"—eventually came to be considered as assimilated aristocracy (*mabulundlela*) within the ruling houses of the Gaza empire. Closer to Lourenço Marques, smaller chieftaincies consolidated their autonomous identities as Ronga under the protective umbrella afforded them by the Portuguese presence there, just as Tonga peoples in the vicinity of the Portuguese fort at Inhambane had done a century earlier under the threat of Tsonga invasion.

Only in the final decade of the nineteenth century and in the first two decades of the twentieth did the Portuguese succeed in subjecting the societies of the Mozambican interior to colonial overrule. In doing so, they found allies and military conscripts among populations who had resisted the powerful kingdoms which had formed throughout Mozambique, such as the Chopi (Chope) of Inhambane (whose name, meaning "archers" and calling attention to their defensive prowess, was given them by Nguni never capable of completely subduing them). Notwithstanding this "divide and conquer" strategy, Portuguese colonialism did little in comparison with other forms of European colonialism to consolidate "tribal" identities among African populations in Mozambique. While stronger senses of ethnic affiliation did emerge among many of those forced to leave Mozambique to work abroad, Portuguese colonial labor mobilization and taxation through localized "native authorities" (*autoridades gentilicas*), as well as Portuguese oversight of these activities at the level of the administrative post, forestalled the emergence of indigenous power brokers with broad geographical reach in the colonial era. The colonial requirement that religious missions provide education in the Portuguese language in order to encourage the "nationalization" (meaning "luso-fication") and cultural "assimilation" of "native" populations also undermined the further consolidation of strong ethnic identities.

Upon coming to power over an independent Mozambique in 1975, President Samora Machel sought to create a new society in which neither race nor ethnicity would be salient categories (contributing to the new government's hostility toward anthropology, which it considered the "colonial science" of "tribal" peoples). While 90 percent of Portuguese inhabitants left Mozambique, with Machel's blessing some 20,000 remained. A relatively larger number of Asians also continued to live in Mozambique after independence. Because of the potential divisiveness of more than a dozen major language groups within the nation's territorial boundaries, Portuguese was adopted as the official langauge. Machel placed constraints on both Christian and Muslim clerics, and the exercise of political authority and religious ritual founded in kin-based social institutions was made the object of aggressive "anti-obscurantist" government campaigns.

Machel's nation-building agenda, however, generated considerable hostilities in regions where his FRELIMO (Frente de Libertação de Moçambique) party was not well established and alienated "traditional authorities" who, despite having cooperated with the colonial administration, sometimes retained legitimacy among their communities. Historians of Mozambique's sixteen-year-long civil war (1977–1992) trace the roots of the RENAMO (Resistência Nacional de Moçambique) insurgency to Rhodesian and later, South African attempts to destabilize Mozambique. RENAMO did, however, have substantial support among the Ndau subgroup of the Shona peoples in central

Mozambique and among Makua-speaking populations in northern Mozambique. While neither the war nor the elections agreed to in the peace settlement can be accurately characterized as "tribally" determined, RENAMO did achieve electoral victories in 1994 in the populous Mozambican provinces of Sofala, Zambezia, and Nampula, where these groups constitute majorities.

The civil war gave evidence that perceived differences along racial, ethnic, class, religious, generational, and gender lines remain salient among Mozambicans after more than two decades of independent governance. Perhaps more important, however, it gave foundation to an historical experience—albeit one of violence and flight (more than five million sought refuge in Mozambican towns and cities and across borders in neighboring countries)—which, like colonialism and FRELIMO governance before it, was shared by Mozambicans throughout the country. Through such painful experiences, the process of forging a Mozambican nation continues.

BIBLIOGRAPHY

Alpers, Edward A. *Ivory and Slaves: Changing Pattern of International Trade in East Central Africa to the Later Nineteenth Century.* Berkeley, Calif., 1975.

Departamento de História, Universidade Eduardo Mondlane. *História de Moçambique.* 3 vols. 2d ed. Maputo, Mozambique, 1988–1993.

Dias, A. Jorge, Margot Dias, and Manuel Guerreiro. *Os Macondes de Moçambique.* 4 vols. Lisbon, 1964–1970.

Geffray, Christian. *La cause des armes au Mozambique: Anthropologie d'une guerre civile.* Paris, 1990.

———. *Ni père ni mère: Critique de la parenté, le cas Makhuwa.* Paris, 1990.

Harries, Patrick. *Work, Culture, and Identity: Migrant Laborers in Mozambique and South Africa, c. 1860–1910.* Portsmouth, N.H., 1994.

Isaacman, Allen. *Mozambique: The Africanization of a European Institution, the Zambesi Prazos, 1750–1902.* Madison, Wis., 1972.

Junod, Henri Alexandre. *The Life of a South African Tribe.* New York, 1966.

Rita-Ferreira, Antônio. *Agrupamento e caracterização étnica does indígenas de Moçambique.* Lisbon, 1958.

———. *Povos de Moçambique: História e cultura.* Porto, Portugal, 1975.

Smith, Alan Kent. "The Peoples of Southern Mozambique: An Historical Survey." *Journal of African History* 14, no. 4 (1973): 565–580.

Vail, Leroy, and Landeg White. *Capitalism and Colonialism in Mozambique: A Study of Quelimane District.* Minneapolis, 1980.

HENRY WEST

See also **Bantu; Colonial Policies and Practice; East African Coast; Ethnicity and Identity; Machel, Samora Moises; Mfecane; Postcolonial State; Slave Trade; Zambezi River.**

MOZAMBIQUE REGION BEFORE 1950. Mozambique's ancient history remains obscure. The earliest known semipermanent settlement at Matola, in the far south, dates back to 70 C.E. Archaeological evidence indicates that the inhabitants of Matola relied on agriculture and fishing. They also smelted iron and produced pottery. By the ninth century there were large agricultural and trading communities along the Indian Ocean Coast and adjacent to the Zimbabwean highlands. Two centuries later, the Muslim geographer al-Mas'udi reported that the Mozambican port of Sofala was an integral part of the Indian Ocean trading complex.

Before the arrival of the Portuguese in 1498, most Mozambican communities, organized into independent chieftaincies, were governed by land chiefs who enjoyed religious authority. As direct descendants of the founding or conquering lineage, chiefs were the ultimate owners and spiritual guardians of the land; they distributed parcels to their subordinates, received annual taxes in either agricultural produce or labor, and were entitled to the larger tusk of any elephant that died in their territory. The local economies rested on farming. The planting, weeding, and harvesting was done primarily by women, while men felled the trees and cleared the fields. The northern Makua proverb, "A man is the axe; and a woman the hoe," reflected the gendered division of labor. In many areas, cattle keeping, hunting, fishing, mining, and metallurgy were often important secondary activities. Farmers traded surplus agricultural products and other specialized goods within and between villages and, sometimes, across ecological zones.

Muenemutapa, the Malawian Confederation, and the Portuguese

Before the sixteenth century, two powerful state systems dominated central Mozambique. The older and more important kingdom of the Muenemutapa stretched south from the Zambezi River to the Save River and into the highlands of contemporary Zimbabwe. At its apex in the sixteenth century, the Muenemutapa empire, including the outlying provinces of Barue, Manica, Sedanda, and Quiteve was probably the largest and most powerful state in central and southern Africa. Northeast of the Zambezi River was the Malawian Confederation.

Elaborate religious institutions and rituals and a monopoly of foreign trade, primarily in gold and ivory, reinforced the power of the respective royal families.

Swahili merchants trading in the Malawian and Muenemutapa kingdoms were part of an Indian Ocean commercial system linking east Africa with the Middle East and Asia. By the middle of the fifteenth century, they had established commercial and religious sultanates along the Mozambican coast between the northern ports of Angoche and Mozambique and Sofala in the south. In the sixteenth century the Portuguese challenged Swahili control of the coast. By 1525, they had conquered Sofala, occupied Angoche, and established a settlement on Mozambique Island, and over the next century they dislodged Swahili traders from much of the interior. In 1607 Lisbon forced rulers of the Muenemutapa kingdom to cede all the mines

The ramparts of the Fortaleza de São Sebastião, Mozambique Island. Construction of the fort began in 1558. ANDREW BANNISTER/ANTHONY

within their territory and in 1632 defeated the Malawian ruler Muzura. To consolidate its inland position, the Portuguese monarch distributed crown estates, called *prazos da coroa*, to Portuguese settlers in the Zambezi valley, the Sofala hinterland, and on the Querimba Islands.

Portuguese influence began to decline by the middle of the seventeenth century. The sultanate of Angoche revolted, the Barue forced out the estate holders, and the Malawian rulers refused to recognize Lisbon's authority. In 1692 the Muenemutapa and their Rozvi allies drove the Portuguese from the Zimbabwean highlands and the Zambezi interior. To revive the colony's sagging fortunes, in 1752 Lisbon severed Mozambique's ties with Goa and bestowed on it autonomous colonial status. Portugal's political setbacks were matched by its failure to consolidate control over the prosperous interior ivory trade in the north. Indian merchants, based on Mozambique Island and the northern coastal towns, filled this vacuum, developing close commercial ties to Yao and Makua merchants and elephant hunters. By 1750 Indian merchants dominated the major trading networks, and ivory had replaced gold as the principal export commodity.

Effects of the Slave Trade

During the nineteenth century Mozambique became a major slave exporting center. Commerce in slaves began midway through the eighteenth century when the growth of sugar plantations on the Indian Ocean islands of Île de France (Mauritius) and Bourbon (Réunion) created a regional demand for captives. Early in the nineteenth century low prices drew slavers from Brazil, the United States, and the Caribbean islands to the Mozambican coastal ports. Although Lisbon outlawed the slave trade in 1836, slaves continued to be the dominant export commodity throughout the century. In all, it is likely that more than one million Mozambicans were sold as cheap bound labor to plantations of both the new world and Madagascar, Réunion, and São Tomé.

The slave trade had far-reaching economic and social consequences. Armed with guns, often acquired in exchange for captives, African and Portuguese slave raiders destroyed entire communities in the Shire and Zambezi valleys. The violent disruption of much of the rural economy and the export of many of its most productive members intensified the crises of food security and rural impoverishment. Drought, locust plagues, and banditry during the first third of the nineteenth century further disrupted economic life in central and northern Mozambique. The slave trade also increased disparities in wealth and social inequality within many Mozambican societies. A relatively small African merchant class, often allied with the ruling aristocracy, accumulated substantial profits from the sale of slaves. The wealth and power of the northern Yao chiefs Makanjila and Mataka, of the sultanate of Angoche and Quitangonha, and of the racially mixed *prazeiro* warlords Bonga, Kanyemba, and Mataquenha were legendary.

Although the slave trade's effects were far less pronounced in southern Mozambique, local com-

munities were conquered by the Gaza Nguni, who had fled from South Africa. With their superior military technology, they forged a powerful state which, by 1840, extended from the Lourenço Marques hinterland north to the Inhambane coast and inland to the Save River. Under the leadership of Soshangane, they also conquered many Tonga and Chopi chieftaincies and forced the *prazeiros* living on the southern banks of the Zambezi to pay an annual tribute.

The slave trade and the Gaza Nguni expansion undermined Portugal's efforts during the second third of the century to expand its limited coastal holdings. In the north, for example, the colonial army was defeated at Tungue Bay in 1853 and a decade later in Angoche. After the 1884–1885 Berlin Conference, which established the guidelines for the partition of Africa, Portugal intensified efforts to conquer the countryside.

Portuguese Colony

Most African societies took up arms to defend their homelands and way of life, although some, like the Inhambane and Tsonga, cooperated with the Portuguese. While the Gaza Nguni and the Barue initially tried to forestall invasions through negotiation, these diplomatic tactics failed. Many polities, from the Barue to the northern Mozambican sultanates, fought valiantly and scored impressive short-lived victories. Not until the defeat of the northern Makonde in 1917 were the Portuguese finally able to overcome stiff African resistance.

Having imposed its rule, the colonial state faced pressing economic and political problems. It had a growing fiscal deficit and lacked a modern infrastructure and a viable system of administration and law. And Portuguese investors showed little interest in Mozambique.

To create political stability and social control, Lisbon constructed a centralized racially bifurcated colonial order. Three levels of Portuguese administration operated under the auspices of the governor general of Mozambique. At the highest level were the district governors. Each district was further divided into European and non-European areas. By the 1920s fewer than 15,000 Europeans resided in Mozambique, primarily in the capital city of Lourenço Marques and the port town of Beira. The overwhelming majority of Africans, estimated at 3.9 million in 1930, lived in rural districts (*circumscrições*), which were further subdivided into localities (*postos*). Each was governed by a Portuguese official. The administrators had virtually absolute

Mozambique in the Nineteenth Century

SWAHILI MERCHANTS

Zanzibar

Kilwa

Lindi

Makonde

(Present Borders)

Yao

Querimba Islands

Nyasaland

Makua

(Present Borders)

Zambezi River

Shire River

Mossuril
Mozambique

Tete

Angoche

ZIMBABWE HIGHLANDS

Muenemutapa

Areas
of Portuguese
Settlement

(Present Borders)

Beira
Sofala

Save River

Limpopo River

Inhambane

Matola

Lourenço Marques

*Gaza
Nguni*

power over their subjects. They were assisted by African police (*sipais*) and by chiefs (*régulos*) who collected taxes, settled minor disputes, recruited labor, and promoted production of cash crops.

State planners addressed the colony's acute financial problems in two ways. Given the absence of investment capital, they sought to make Mozambique profitable by exploiting "idle" Africans. Tax requirements and vagrancy laws were introduced to induce peasants to work for local planters, European farmers, and industrialists as contract laborers. Because low wages and harsh living and working conditions made this option unattractive, penal labor and *chibalo*, or coerced labor, were instituted to meet the demands of the underfinanced capitalist sector. Local administrators sent *sipais* at night to seize men, and occasionally women, from their homes, for *chibalo* labor. They then distributed the recruits to European employers for a minimum of six months with little or no compensation. Colonial authorities also used *chibalo* laborers to build roads, lay railroad lines, and construct bridges to minimize state expenditures.

Thousands of men, anxious to avoid colonial labor demands, fled across the border to work on the higher-paying mines and plantations of South Africa, continuing a pattern which had begun in the middle of the nineteenth century. To reap financial benefits from this migration, the Portuguese government signed agreements with the South African government and later with the Witwatersrand Native Labour Association (WNLA), the official representative of the South African gold mining industry around the turn of the twentieth century. The agreements specified that a fee of thirteen shillings per Mozambican laborer be paid by mine owners to the colonial government. A similar accord, the Tete Agreement, was signed with Rhodesia in 1913. By 1920 almost 100,000 Mozambican men, primarily from the southern part of the colony, were working in the gold mines, and several thousand from Tete district were employed on Rhodesian farms and in mines.

The other strategy for overcoming the shortage of investment capital was to turn over the direct administration and exploitation of much of central and northern Mozambique to foreign-owned concessionary companies. The three most significant were the British-dominated Moçambique Company, Zambesia Company, and the Niassa Company. Because they were underfinanced they made little effort to comply with their mandate to develop large-scale agricultural and mining projects

and create an infrastructure. Instead, they merely used their police power to extract taxes from Africans living on the land and subleased some of their holdings to European farmers and agricultural companies who subsequently developed the large sugar, tea, and copra estates that dominated central Mozambique.

The Salazar Era

In 1926 a conservative alliance brought down the Republican government in Lisbon. António Salazar, who became the prime minister in 1932, ruled as an ironhanded dictator for more than thirty years, with far-reaching consequences for Mozambique. In 1933 his regime issued decrees ending the quasi-sovereign status linking the colonies and Portugal into a single formal entity. This legislation also enshrined the earlier distinction between Africans (*indígena*) and Europeans (*não indígena*) and stipulated that only the latter enjoyed full rights of citizenship. The small number of Africans who could read and write Portuguese, had rejected "tribal customs," and were gainfully employed in the capitalist economy theoretically enjoyed the same rights. The relatively privileged position of *assimilados* was first explicitly articulated in 1917 legislation. By 1945, less than two thousand Africans had become *assimilados*.

The Salazar regime also adopted a vigorous neo-mercantile strategy under which the human and natural resources of Mozambique, as well as its markets, were exploited to benefit the Portuguese home economy rather than foreign investors. By blunting any significant industrial development in Mozambique and by maintaining high tariffs on many non-Portuguese goods, it created a protected market. In 1945 Portuguese commodities represented 50 percent of all Mozambican imports, almost a threefold increase over the preceding decade. Mozambique's other critical economic role was to supply cheap raw materials and foodstuffs for the Portuguese economy. In 1938 the government imposed a cotton regime which, at its highpoint in the 1940s, forced almost 750,000 peasants, primarily women, to cultivate cotton rather than foodstuffs and other cash crops and to sell the fiber to Portuguese concessionary companies at prices well below the world market. Many growers earned less than five dollars for a year's labor. Under this highly regimented labor regime, cotton exports increased from under three thousand tons in the mid 1930s to more than twenty-five thousand tons in 1950, fueling the Portuguese textile industry. The imposition of a compulsory peasant rice cultivation scheme in 1942 also generated handsome profits for Portuguese rice companies.

Finally, the Salazar regime claimed a moral responsibility to bring Christianity and Portuguese culture to the "primitive" Africans. Since Africans simply represented a source of cheap labor, however, it made little sense to waste government resources to develop a colonywide public school system. Instead, Lisbon signed an agreement in 1941 with the Catholic Church entrusting to it the training of Africans. The church's mission was to provide a rudimentary education and to instill a sense of discipline and a work ethic. By the mid-1950s, less than 350,000 children, out of a total school-age population of approximately 3 million, attended classes, and virtually all were enrolled in the first three grades. After almost sixty years of formal colonial rule, more than 95 percent of the African population was illiterate.

The colonial policies of the Salazar regime had devastating social and economic consequences for most Africans living in the countryside. Through contract labor, chibalo, penal labor, and the migrant labor agreements, rural Mozambican communities lost hundreds of thousands of their most productive members. Forced cotton and rice production left little time for peasants to grow food crops. It also caused disruptions in the cycle of household production, with an attendant decline in food production, increased debt, famines, disease, and soil erosion. A 1955 nutritional study found that the diets of rural Mozambicans were neither adequate nor well balanced. Fragmentary data suggest that nutritional disease, particularly kwashiorkor, rickets, scurvy, beriberi and pellagra, were quite common. The minuscule allocation of state funds for rural health services and the shortage of doctors compounded health problems in the countryside.

For the relatively few Africans living in urban centers, life was equally harsh. Cities were basically segregated. Africans could not enter European restaurants, theaters, or social clubs. Most Europeans resided in modern apartment buildings or spacious private homes in the "city of cement." The vast majority of Africans lived in barrios or in Africanós (planned African neighborhoods) or in makeshift shantytowns ringing Lourenço Marques and Beira. Since cities were defined essentially as enclaves for the civilized, until the 1950s few serious efforts were made to provide basic social services in the shantytowns. Many assimilados and some more fortunate Africans, who were able to formally register

their holdings, lived in more comfortable townships, such as Xipaminine. Laws prohibiting urban Africans from organizing unions, de facto job reservation, chibalo, and the system of casual labor trapped them in the most low-paying menial jobs. By the 1960s, white workers, regardless of their qualification, earned about twenty times more than African workers. Prostitution, beer brewing, trading in the informal economy, and backbreaking labor in the cashew factories were among the few sources of income for African women.

Coping Strategies and Resistance

Despite the severity of the impact of colonialism, Mozambicans were not simply victims of oppression. They devised coping strategies to minimize the adverse effects of Portuguese labor policies and to help them and their families survive. Peasants coped with cotton-induced food crises by shifting to higher-yielding or lower-risk crops, such as manioc, sweet potatoes, pigeon peas, and corn. Faced with the loss of male labor, many rural women organized labor exchanges to ease their workload. Others assumed tasks colonial officials and their own male relatives presumed they were incapable of doing, such as chopping down heavy trees. In the cattle-keeping zones of southern Mozambique, thousands of women disregarded long-held taboos prohibiting them from working with cattle and began to use ox-drawn plows to ease their labor burdens.

Resistance in the countryside was also widespread. Occasionally it took the form of large-scale insurrections, such as the 1897 Maguiguana uprising, the Zambesian rebellion of 1917–1921, and the 1939 tax revolt in Mossuril. But rural Mozambicans rarely reacted openly or fully against their domination because their vulnerability made direct confrontation untenable. More often, they engaged in hidden forms of resistance. To gain some measure of control over their lives, thousands of peasants fled to Tanganyika (Tanzania), Nyasaland (Malawi), Rhodesia (Zimbabwe), and South Africa despite the colonial regime's use of force to curtail such cross-border migrations. Other deserters, reluctant to break all links with their families and their historic homelands, fled to sparsely populated backwater areas beyond the reach of the state. Covertly withholding a portion of their labor was probably the most widespread expression of defiance by peasants trapped inside the forced cotton and rice schemes.

Rural and urban workers, like their peasant counterparts, similarly engaged primarily in individual and sporadic actions to escape from or to minimize the effects of the colonial economic order. They fled before the labor recruiters arrived at their villages, deserted sisal and tea plantations in large numbers, "loafed," and occasionally sabotaged machinery or raw materials. There were also periodic labor actions and strikes, particularly at the Lourenço Marques port, such as the Quinhenta strike of 1933 and the work stoppage of stevedores in 1949. The struggles of peasants and workers were reflected in the writings of José Craveirinha and Noémia de Sousa, among others, who offered a powerful critique of Portuguese colonialism. It was not until the early 1960s, however, that the insurgent spirit of intellectuals, peasants, and workers was joined under the nationalist banner of the Frente de Libertação de Moçambique (FRELIMO) to fight for Mozambican independence from Portugal.

BIBLIOGRAPHY

Alpers, Edward A. *Ivory and Slaves in East Central Africa: Changing Patterns of International Trade to the Later Nineteenth Century.* London, 1975.

Beach, D. N. *The Shona and Zimbabwe, 900–1850: An Outline of Shona History.* London, 1980.

Bhila, H. H. K. *Trade and Politics in a Shona Kingdom: The Manyika and Their African and Portuguese Neighbours, 1575–1902.* London, 1982.

Capela, José. *O escravismo colonial em Moçambique.* Pôrto, Portugal, 1993.

Department of History, University of Eduardo Mondlane. *História de Moçambique.* Vol. 3. 1993.

First, Ruth. *Black Gold: The Mozambican Miner, Proletarian and Peasant.* Brighton, Sussex, and New York, 1983.

Harries, Patrick. *Work, Culture and Identity: Migrant Laborers in Mozambique and South Africa, 1860–1910.* Portsmouth, N.H., 1994.

Henricksen, Thomas H. *Mozambique: A History.* London, 1978.

Isaacman, Allen F. *Mozambique: The Africanization of a European Institution; The Zambezi Prazos, 1750–1902.* Madison, Wis., 1972.

———. *The Tradition of Resistance in Mozambique: The Zambesi Valley, 1850–1921.* Berkeley, Calif., 1976.

———. *Cotton Is the Mother of Poverty: Peasants Work and Rural Struggle in Colonial Mozambique, 1938–1961.* Portsmouth, N.H., and London, 1996.

Mudenge, S. I. G. *A Political History of Munhumutapa c. 1400–1902.* London, 1988.

Newitt, Malyn. *Portuguese Settlement on the Zambesi: Exploration, Land Tenure and Colonial Rule in East Africa.* London, 1973.

———. *A History of Mozambique.* Bloomington, Ind., 1995.

Pélissier, René. *História de Moçambique: Formação e Oposição, 1854–1918.* Lisbon, 1994.

Penvenne, Jeanne Marie. *African Workers and Colonial Racism: Mozambican Strategies and Struggles in Lourenço Marques, 1877–1962.* Portsmouth, N.H., and London, 1995.

Pitcher, M. Anne. *Politics in the Portuguese Empire: The State, Industry, and Cotton, 1926–1974.* Oxford and New York, 1994.

Vail, Leroy, and Landeg White. *Capitalism and Colonialism in Mozambique: A Study of Quelimane District.* Minneapolis, Minn., 1980.

ALLEN ISAACMAN

See also **Colonial Policies and Practice: Portuguese Policies; Nguni.**

MSWATI II (b. 1826?; d. 1865), Swazi king under whom Swaziland was unified as a nation. Mswati II was the first son, and hence the heir, of King Sobhuza I, the founder of Lobamba City (known today as Old Lobamba). Assuming the kingship in 1839, he gained fame throughout southern Africa as a great soldier, second only to King Shaka of the Zulu. He modeled his own armies after the efficient Zulu forces, recruiting non-Swazi fighters, including Sothos and Ngunis, to fight for him. In part due to the coeval decline of the Zulu empire, Mswati was successful in his raids of nearby Zulu territories as well as his domination of other surrounding terrain. His kingdom came to be known as Swaziland, after a European corruption of his name, "Swazi."

Also exerting his influence through diplomacy, Mswati avoided conflict with bordering states and sent his soldiers to settle disputes among neighboring chiefs. He signed a nonbelligerence treaty with the Afrikaner boertrekkers who then occupied the Transvaal and openly defended his own kingdom against European influences. Mswati died in Hhohho in 1868. His son, Mbandzeni, succeeded him and, through a series of grazing and mineral concessions to Europeans, began to lose control of Swaziland; the kingdom became a British High Commission Territory in 1906.

BIBLIOGRAPHY

Bonner, Philip. "Mswati II, c. 1826–65." In *Black Leaders in Southern African History,* edited by Christopher Saunders. London, 1979.

SARAH VALDEZ

See also **Mfecane; Shaka Zulu; Swaziland; Zulu.**

MUGABE, ROBERT (b. 21 February 1924), first president of Zimbabwe. A member of the Shona ethnic cluster, which comprises roughly 80 percent of the population of Zimbabwe, he was born at the Kutanma Catholic Mission at Zvimba, Rhodesia, and attended a Jesuit school there. He became a teacher and worked in Ghana when it became the first state in sub-Saharan Africa to free itself from colonial rule. There he married his Ghanaian wife, Sally Hayfron. After their marriage the couple returned to what was then Southern Rhodesia and entered politics.

When his party, the Zimbabwe African Peoples Union (ZAPU), split along ethnic lines, he stayed with the Shona-dominated Zimbabwe African National Union (ZANU). Mugabe was charged with "subversive speech" in 1963 and fled into exile in Tanzania. He returned and was jailed in 1964. He spent approximately ten years in detention while Ian Smith and his white administration ruled Southern Rhodesia; their rule brought an international boycott and sanctions, which eventually drove Smith from power.

As leader of ZANU-PF (ZANU–Patriotic Front) Mugabe won Zimbabwe's first free elections, which were held in 1980. The only effective opposition came from the minority Ndebele party, Joshua Nkomo's ZAPU. Their political rivalry deteriorated into civil war which ended with Nkomo's surrender. Throughout his career, Mugabe has incorporated rivals into his government; Nkomo became a vice-president of Zimbabwe.

Mugabe retained part of Smith's constitution that allowed him to appoint part of the legislature, which continues to ensure that his party dominates the parliament. Although a skilled fighter when necessary, Mugabe's true brilliance has perhaps lain in his ability to bring any opposition into the government, whether it has come from the Ndebele or from white landowners. For example, white Zimbabweans continue to rely on their influence within ZANU-PF rather than risk political marginalization by working outside it. Their economic power and international contacts continue to give them influence greater than their numbers. However, they are restrained by increasing calls for "indigenization" of the economy and by Mugabe's warning that former colonizers might return through "the economic door."

Mugabe faces no real opposition from within his party because it is riven by factionalism, which runs along both ethnic and regional lines. One focus for this factionalism is rivalry to be named as Mugabe's successor, whom Mugabe had not chosen by late 1997. That there were no public calls

Robert Mugabe. AP/WIDE WORLD

for him to nominate one was an indication of his great personal power within the party—he has made it clear that he does not wish to nominate a successor or to retire soon. It is also possible that he has allowed the party to remain weak, with ambitions focused on two vice presidents, one Shona and one Ndebele, so that his own influence within the party would be all the greater. Mugabe will be seventy-eight years old at the time of the next election, which is in the year 2002. His health and well-being were affected by the loss of his wife, who died in 1992. His continuing health may be a precondition for peace and stability in Zimbabwe.

BIBLIOGRAPHY

Smith, David, and Colin Simpson with Ian Davies. *Mugabe*. London, 1981.

ALEXANDER GOLDMAN

208

MUHAMMAD ʿABDALLAH HASAN. *See* **Hasan, Muhammad ʿAbdallah.**

MUHAMMAD AL-AMIN AL-KANEMI. *See* **Kanemi, Muhammad al-Amin al-.**

MUKHTAR, SIDI AL- (Sidi al-Mukhtar al-Kunti; (b. 1729; d. 1811), Sufi scholar and leader. Descendant of a prominent scholarly and saintly lineage, al-Mukhtar is considered by many Muslims to be the most important *mujaddid,* or rejuvenator of Islam, to appear in the central Sahara during the eighteenth century. He was a prolific scholar, authoring over eighty works, and was recognized as a *wali* ("friend of God") whose *baraka,* or spiritual grace, was said to protect all those who placed themselves under his spiritual authority. He was acclaimed as the shaikh of the Qadiriyya Sufi order in the central Sahara and was the founder of his own branch of that order, known as the Qadiriyya-Mukhtariyya. Through the expansion of this Sufi order, made possible by the renown of his scholarship and his spiritual stature, he built a network of clientage links with Muslim scholars which extended his religious authority throughout the region and into Sudanic western Africa. Al-Mukhtar was the first Muslim leader in the region to encourage a sense of exclusive identity in a Sufi order; he claimed that the Qadiriyya-Mukhtariyya was the only "pure" Muslim community that existed at the time and that the spiritual benefits it offered were superior to all others. The same mystical Islamic ideology also enabled him to extend both his political and commercial hegemony throughout the region and thus establish a voluntarist basis of social and political authority that contrasted with the Islamic statist models which were also emerging at the time, such as in the Sokoto Caliphate.

BIBLIOGRAPHY

Batran, A. A. "The Qadiriyya-Mukhtariyya Brotherhood in West Africa: The Concept of *Tassawwuf* in the Writings of Sidi al-Mukhtar al-Kunti (1729–1811)." *Transafrican Journal of History* 4, nos. 1–2 (1974): 41–70.

———. "The Kunta, Sīdī al-Mukhtār al-Kuntī, and the Office of *Shaykh al-Tarīqaʾl-Qādiriyya.*" In *Studies in West African Islamic History,* edited by John Ralph Willis. London, 1979.

LOUIS BRENNER

See also **Islam; Sufism.**

MULTIPARTY SYSTEMS. *See* **Political Systems.**

MUSEVENI, YOWERI (b. 1944), Ugandan political activist, guerrilla leader, and president of Uganda after Idi Amin. Museveni's political activism began in 1966, while he was a student in secondary school. At that time he organized Rwanda pastoralists in the Mbarara District of western Uganda against eviction from their lands. He attended the Tanzanian University of Dar es Salaam from 1967 to 1970, which he helped to form, and led the University Students' African Revolutionary Front. He spent September 1968 in areas of northern Mozambique that had been liberated from Portuguese control. There he gained his first experiences of guerrilla organization.

After graduation, he worked at the office of the then Ugandan president, Milton Obote, until Idi Amin's coup d'état in 1971. He fled to Tanzania, and soon after he formed the Front for National Salvation (FRONASA), training guerrillas to disrupt

Yoweri Museveni. REUTERS/POOL/ARCHIVE PHOTOS

Amin's rule. As leader of FRONASA, he returned to Uganda with the Tanzanian People's Defense Forces to help overthrow Amin in 1979. He served as minister of defense, minister of regional co-operation, and vice chairman of the military commission in the transitional Ugandan National Liberation Front government that replaced Amin.

Claiming that the election of the Uganda Peoples Congress Party, which returned Obote to the presidency in December 1980, was fraudulent, he left the capital in February of 1981 to again organize a guerrilla army, the National Resistance Army. This force was one of only two in Africa to successfully overthrow an independent government with only minimal external assistance.

Museveni became president of Uganda in January 1986, when his National Resistance Army seized control of Kampala, the capital of Uganda. His most important achievement has been the creation of a new and disciplined army that respected civilians and civilian rule. Under the leadership of his National Resistance Movement, Museveni reconciled several opposing factions by welcoming them into the broad-based interim government he formed upon taking power. His manifesto, the "Ten Point Program," united supporters during the guerrilla war and guided the government in its early years. In 1987 he committed the government to a program to liberalize and privatize the economy, policies he consistently supported and expanded over the years that followed. In 1988 he launched the process of writing a new constitution to restore democratic civilian rule. He promulgated the constitution in 1995. He served as chairman of the Organization of African Unity during 1990–1991.

BIBLIOGRAPHY

Museveni, Yoweri K. *Selected Articles on the Uganda Resistance War.* Kampala, Uganda, 1985.
———. *What Is Africa's Problem?* Kampala, Uganda, 1992.
Mutibwa, Phares. *Uganda Since Independence.* London, 1992.
Shamuyarira, N. M., ed. *Essays on the Liberation of Southern Africa.* Dar es Salaam, Tanzania, 1971.

NELSON KASFIR

See also **Amin Dada, Idi; Obote, Milton.**

MUSIC AND SONG

*[Coverage of music and song begins with an **Overview** and discussion of **Structure**. Four articles deal with Modern and*

*Popular Music: **Overview; Modern and Popular Music in Western Africa; Modern and Popular Music in Eastern Africa;** and **Modern and Popular Music in Southern Africa.** The entry concludes with articles on **Islamic Music** and music in **West African Savanna** and **Ethiopia.**]*

OVERVIEW

Language, Music, and Their Stylistic Affinities

Neither geographical boundaries nor physical characteristics of populations can be taken as determinants of culture. However, music in Africa is intimately linked with language, to the extent that much of its content and structure is difficult for linguistic outsiders to understand, and any appearance of comprehension occurs by reinterpretation. This holds true regarding both extra-African contacts and cross-cultural exchanges within Africa. In view of the close link between language and music in Africa, language can be identified as the most relevant parameter within which music operates. Speaking at a UNESCO gathering in 1972, J. H. Kwabena Nketia even postulated an analogy, speaking of the "musical languages of sub-Saharan Africa." Accordingly, the geographical notion of a sub-Saharan Africa is correlated here as much as possible with the broad linguistic picture of the continent.

Using his "cantometrics" scheme, Alan Lomax divided Africa, including Madagascar, into thirteen broad style areas, of which the ten following would cover sub-Saharan Africa: Western Sudan, Muslim Sudan, Guinea Coast, Equatorial Bantu, Eastern Sudan, Upper Nile, Northeast Bantu, Central Bantu, South Africa Bantu, and African Hunters. Lomax did not, however, postulate rigid boundaries. In fact, the world of African song and dance styles appears in fluctuating and often overlapping configurations.

Although Lomax's cantometrics project was criticized by some on methodological grounds, it has merit as the only attempt at a broad, comparative, stylistic sampling of vocal music across Africa. Certainly, it has produced some interesting, albeit controversial, results. His stylistic examination of single traits of a vast sample suggests the Guinea Coast and Equatorial Bantu as a sort of nucleus, if not dispersal center, of a formative African style world.

A remarkable characteristic in the present-day African cultural picture is the extremely interruptive, dissected contours of cultural-trait distribution areas. Very often, areas extremely distant from each other, and separated by divergent cultures, show stylistic affinities. In music, notable examples are the affinities between log xylophone music in northern Mozambique and in Liberia and Côte d'Ivoire. Strange affinities in harmonic part-singing style—with a tendency to equiheptatonic intonation—link the Chokwe, Luchazi, Mbwela, and others of eastern Angola to the Baule of Côte d'Ivoire. In Namibia the musical culture of the pastoral Herero is worlds apart from that of surrounding peoples. But in eastern Africa, especially in Nkore (western Uganda), western Tanzania, Rwanda, and Burundi, one finds compelling similarities to the Herero approach to song and movement.

This demonstrates the complex criss-crossing of the migratory paths of peoples and cultural influences in Africa's history. Some of the affinities may result from eighteenth- and nineteenth-century contacts; for example, northern Mozambique log xylophone styles could have been transplanted to coastal western Africa after 1815, with the dumping of liberated slaves from many parts of Africa in Sierra Leone and Liberia. But other analogies cannot be explained by recent contacts, such as the Baule-Chokwe affinities in homophonic multipart singing, particularly when associated with initiation.

The History of African Music

It is legitimate to reconstruct certain aspects of African music history by inference from a twentieth-century sample of sound recordings, as with Kubik's analysis of Nsenga-Shona harmonic patterns and their possible roots in San musical cultures of Zimbabwe and parts of Zambia during the first millennium C.E. Hypotheses, however, must be distinguished from verified historical facts.

Iconological Sources

The oldest iconological sources relating to African music history are rock paintings such as those in the Tassili N' Ajjer of the Sahara (in present-day Algeria), with many motifs depicting music and dance practice. A famous Tassili rock painting shows a six-string harp played in "vertical" position by a musician for a person in authority. It has been tentatively dated to around 700 B.C.E., in the so-called Period of the Horse. The picture suggests the presence of the harp in the central Sahara at that time and also, through componential analysis, the presence of a stratified society, with musicians who played for nobles, chiefs, or perhaps kings. The culture history of Sahara populations, as displayed in the rock art galleries of the Tassili, is of direct relevance to that of peoples south of the

Sahara at a later period. Linguistic reconstructions suggest that around 2500 B.C.E., Nilo-Saharan languages were spoken in areas much farther north than they are today. From about 8000 to 3000 B.C.E., much of the present Sahara passed through a wet period that gave rise to the development of what has been called an aquatic lifestyle. There are several indications that some of the Green Sahara population, speaking early forms of the Nilo-Saharan languages, gradually migrated southward as the Sahara became drier, continuing an aquatic lifestyle with modifications (such as the introduction of elements of a pastoral economy), as at Lake Chad, along the Upper Niger, and in the swamps of the *sudd* region of the Upper Nile in present-day Sudan. A number of the visual aspects of music and dance depicted in some of the oldest Saharan frescoes, such as a dance scene from the period of the Neolithic hunters (approximately 6000–4000 B.C.E.) showing elaborated body decoration, seem to be perpetuated today in certain areas of sub-Saharan Africa. In the case cited, perpetuation is as remote as in the *ndlamu* stamping dance of the Zulu of South Africa. The Sahara frescoes also include what could be representations of masks and initiation dances. The extensive resources of rock art in southern Africa also contain, to a lesser extent, motifs that could be interpreted as relevant to music and dance history in the areas concerned.

While the iconographic testimonies cited fall under the category of internal African sources because their authors were indigenous, many external pictographic documents are available from the fifteenth century to the present. One of the most interesting early illustrations in color is by traveler and explorer Jan Huyghen van Linschoten (1563–1611) and depicts a player of a braced musical bow, with the bowstick (not the string) passed by the lips. The performer was seen by van Linschoten somewhere on the Mozambique coast, where he landed during his passage to India, either at Sofala or close to Mozambique Island. It is the first record of a mouth-bow tradition that survives today in several areas of central and southern Mozambique; it persists in the *chipendani*, an instrument among the Chopi in the south; the *xipendani* among the Tsonga; the *chibendane* in Manica Province; the *chipindano* in Tete Province; and elsewhere.

Van Linschoten's illustrations and others, in particular those of Giovanni Antonio Cavazzi in 1687 and his original watercolors from his stay in the kingdoms of Kongo, Ndongo, and Matamba, can be analyzed for information about the organology of sixteenth- and seventeenth-century African musical instruments. Knowledge about their social setting, playing methods, and sometimes even the tuning layout can also be derived.

Iconological sources also include more recent materials, such as nineteenth- and twentieth-century illustrations: drawings, paintings, photographs, and so on. An example is the early-twentieth-century photographic collection from southern Angola kept at the Royal Anthropological Institute in London.

Archaeological Artifacts

There is a wide spectrum of artifacts related to African music history from Iron Age cultures. They include single and double bells, such as those excavated at Great Zimbabwe, Inyanga, and elsewhere, and even lamellae of lamellophones. Some of our earliest sources on music history in western, central, and southern Africa are archaeological. In western Nigeria, Frank Willett excavated several terra-cotta pots at a site in Ife, dated to between the eleventh or twelfth and fourteenth centuries, with reliefs depicting musical instruments. The Yoruba instruments depicted include drums of the *gbedù* type, demonstrating the early presence of a characteristic Guinea Coast method of creating drum-skin tension, the so-called cord-and-peg tension (prevalent today in drums of southern Ghana such as the *atumpan* and in *vodu* drums among the Fō of Togo and Dahomey). The artifacts also include horns (*edon*) and a double bell of the Guinea type, that is, with a smaller bell attached to the back of a larger bell, like a mother carrying her child. Willett's finds also reveal that between the tenth and fourteenth centuries, another ritual Yoruba drum, the *igbin,* was present in Ife. Even today this type of drum is used in religious contexts, for example at the shrine for *orisañla* or Obatala, the creator God. These artifacts demonstrate the relative antiquity of certain Yoruba musical instruments. Equally conclusive is negative evidence, such as the absence of the hourglass-shaped drums of the *dùndún* type, so prominent in Yoruba culture today and associated with the performance of praise poetry (*oriki*). There is no indication that they were used in Yorubaland during the so-called Classical period of Ife, corroborating the opinion that they were introduced (from the Hausa-speaking north of Nigeria) during a much later period.

The most famous artifacts relevant to the study of musical instruments and musical practice are Benin bronze plaques. They show the presence of a great variety of musical instruments, such as drums, including slit drums; bells; and even the pluriarc (or bow lute), still used in Benin culture. Archaeology has also contributed to the history of music in central and southeastern Africa, notably in southern Zaire, Zambia, Zimbabwe, and Mozambique. In excavations near Kisale, Zaire, artifacts dating from the tenth to the fourteenth centuries were recovered. Among these were several types of metal bells, an aerophone made of copper, and what might be the tongues of lamellophones.

Iron Age technology produced notable innovations in the repertoire of musical instruments in Africa, particularly during the period from the eighth to the fourteenth centuries. The history of the single and double iron bell in western, west-central, and southeast Africa has already been reconstructed in some detail, with new data added that close some area gaps in the sequence of diffusion, such as the Upper Sangha area in the present-day Central African Republic and the Congo. Iron bells are often associated with chiefship or kinship, and in music their present distribution across sub-Saharan Africa largely corresponds with the distribution of time-line patterns, another significant correlation. The proliferation of innovative types of lamellophones with iron lamellae from a dispersal center in southeast Africa (in Zimbabwe and the Lower Zambezi Valley) is another development to be ascribed to the rise of a new technology during the later Iron Age. Its inception in southern Africa is postulated by David W. Phillipson to have occurred in 1000–1100 C.E. In the ruins of Great Zimbabwe, several specimens of single and double bells have been excavated since Carl Mauch's first visit to the ruins in 1871. Also found were what could be lamellae of lamellophones, demonstrating the effects of the later stages of the Iron Age industrial complex on musical practice.

Written Sources

There is an abundance of external, and more recently also internal, written sources relevant to African music and its history. These include some New World sources, such as Alexandre Rodrigues Ferreira's account of the presence of a certain Angolan lamellophone type in northeastern Brazil toward the end of the eighteenth century. Yet contemporary written sources, especially from the era of the European discoveries and the subsequent colonial period, require critical evaluation by ethnomusicologists trained in historical methodology.

It is important to distinguish between primary source material, including the so-called prototestimonies, and secondary sources. Also, in each case the place, date, and circumstances of the writings and the author's sociopsychological background, opinions, value judgments, and so on, have to be scrutinized in order to separate factual information from personal opinions.

Written sources also include musical notations. Examples are the nineteenth-century attempts at notations of Asante and Fante music in Ghana by Thomas Edward Bowdich in *Mission from Cape Coast Castle to Ashantee* (1819) and notational outlines of Cape Hottentot music by Peter Kolb in *Caput Bonae Spei Hodiernum* (1719).

Sound Recordings

Recordings of sound are limited to the last decade of the nineteenth century and the twentieth century. They include wax cylinder recordings such as those made in Uganda by Sir Harry Johnston at the end of the nineteenth century, now stored in the British Library in London; the famous recordings of multipart singing from Missahöhe, Togo, made in 1905 by the German lieutenant J. von Smend and stored in the Museum für Völkerkunde in Berlin; acetate disc recordings; and analog tape recordings up to the more recent videotape and digital audiotape recordings. Sound-synchronized films and videos fall into the category of iconological as well as sound sources.

Students of African music history, proceeding from factual sources, cannot subscribe to the early-twentieth-century views of musicologists and cultural historians who projected evolutionary models upon African musical practice and relegated it to a stage of a universal cultural history. On the same methodological grounds, the historical study of African music cannot proceed from binary models such as the traditional versus modern dichotomy. The axiom of all historical research is the notion of history as a continuous process of datable change. Consequently, all African music documented on sound carriers in the twentieth century is, first of all, twentieth-century African music. Since there are no age-old, absolutely stable traditions, conclusions about earlier forms of African music drawn from a twentieth-century sample are possible only by inference and only to a limited extent. The historian's perception of African music history is that musical cultures in Africa have interacted, innovated, adapted, fused, and split from their beginnings—not just since the impact of colonialism or the introduction of industrially manufactured Western instruments.

African Music in Its Present Sociocultural Context

Any musical practice exists within a sociocultural context, and Africa is no exception. Some authors have stressed the contextual nature of African music and elaborated on the functions and roles of music in African social life. Some have postulated that African music is invariably a collective phenomenon, rigidly bound to social events such as rituals, religious ceremonies, and salient events in the life cycle. While applying to certain musical genres, this does not hold true as a generalization. African musical practice is no more and no less determined by sociocultural contexts than is the musical practice in any other region of the world. The researcher's objective, therefore, can only be to discover the specific contexts of specific genres of African music.

Of course, those contexts vary with the cultural profile of a society. For example, in societies where male or female puberty initiation is practiced, one is likely to encounter specific types of music linked to initiation ceremonies. These include the *myaso yakumukanda*, songs of the *mukanda* boys' initiation school as found in the large eastern Angolan culture area, and *nyimbo za chinamwali* girls' initiation songs in Chewa- and Nyanja-speaking communities of Malawi and Zambia. Without the social context of initiation, these types of music would not exist. In urban societies with a tradition of ballroom dancing, as at the *rebita* clubs in Luanda, Angola, or of gatherings around a radio or record player for dancing, as in many urban and semiurban areas of southern Africa, further divisions by age and sex may come into play. Class structures had a selective effect upon the composition of dancers and audiences in beer gardens or taverns in western Africa during the highlife era in the 1950s. Such spots attracted a certain social stratum of the population of cities like Accra, Ghana.

Religious beliefs, along with general ideas about the shape of musical instruments and their components that are derived from religious concepts, constitute another important cultural context of musical practice in sub-Saharan Africa. Frequently, anthropomorphic or zoomorphic ideas are projected into instrumental shapes. Thus, instruments usually have a head, a body, a back, and so on. For example, the harp (*ngombi*) in cult music among the Fon of Gabon is considered by priests to be the "house" of a female divinity.

Music and oral literature are so closely connected in many African societies that they are impossible to separate. This includes not only song texts or special traditions such as the "talking drum"—the drumming of poetry based on the tonality of languages—but any genres that combine these forms of expression. The fact that music also evokes strong nonmusical associations—various feelings, for example—confirms that it is difficult in many cases to delineate borders. Storytelling with integrated songs, for example, seems to display remarkably unified behavioral patterns across sub-Saharan Africa, from western Africa to speakers of Bantu languages in eastern and southern Africa. It is not by chance, therefore, that some word roots for "story" in the Bantu languages recur in comparable form in areas often distant from each other. For example, the root -simo appears as simo in the Kigogo language of Tanzania and visimo in the Ngangela languages of Angola; and ntano (or its variant -ngano) appears in several languages of eastern and southern Africa, even as far west as the Bantu language zone in R. Malcolm Guthrie's classification scheme, in northern Namibia and Angola.

Storytelling with songs is a community-oriented event involving relatively few people. It is somewhere halfway between large community gatherings and self-delectative music, such as the solo performance of a forager on his hunting bow transformed into a musical bow. Hugh Tracey was one of the first researchers to pay attention to the kinds of African music that are strictly individual in concept and performance. It was he who coined the term "self-delectative songs." Some music requires audience response, while other music does not. The lonely honey collector in a central African forest, the worker in the field, the likembe (lamellophone) player walking by himself to a mining center in the province of Shaba (formerly Katanga) in Zaire, all used to play for their own delight and for stress relief. Playing in solitude is often a dialogue with the instrument, from which strange oscillating voice lines seem to emerge from inherent instrumental patterns not actually played by the musician, like the voices of spirits.

The orality of African musical traditions requires from the field researcher an approach that is adapted to the circumstances. Orality implies that a certain range of variation can often be expected from performance to performance of the same song. However, this does not mean that the songs are not composed. In the past, African music was often called folk music, as if anonymous persons were its originators and everyone was a singer. Pointing to the contrary is the evidence emerging from some of the largest collections of field documentation now available, like that of the International Library of African Music in Grahamstown, South Africa, or the one at the Museum für Völkerkunde in Berlin. At one time every single item of African music recorded was composed by some individual (occasionally with the help of group members). In most cases the original composer of a song is soon forgotten by the community because of a lack of historical consciousness in rural communities (political hierarchies excluded); the work, however, is transmitted independently of the composer, to be picked up, adapted, and reinterpreted by other musician-composers.

As much as African musical practice is connected inseparably with the verbal realm of expression, equally there are cross-parallels to other forms of expression, notably in the visual arts. Costume patterning and decoration, as well as body paint in initiation ceremonies and masked dancing, often contain coded instructions for transforming musical patterns into movement. Recent research has revealed that some abstract geometrical designs of sub-Saharan Africa contain structures identical to those prevailing in music. For example, duple-, triple-, and quadruple-division interlocking are found in the mat plaiting of various areas of sub-Saharan Africa. In eastern Angola and northwestern Zambia survives a tradition of writing ideographs in the sand. Many of them, called sona in Chokwe and tusona in Luchazi, are constructed by interlocking two grids of dots laid out equidistantly. First, the mukwakusona (the writer of a kasona ideograph) impresses a series of equidistant parallel dots into the sand by using the first and third fingers of his right hand. Next, he inscribes into this basic grid a second series of dots interlocking in duple division. Finally, he inscribes and circumscribes the structure with diagonal lines. Inherent patterns emerge from the final product as in a picture puzzle, analogous to a similar phenomenon in some forms of African music. The inventors of these ideographs projected various ideas into their drawings, interpreting them, perceiving dream images, responding with metaphors, proverbial text lines, stories, and the like. Many of these interpretive texts have become a standard tradition associated with each ideograph, like the text lines of a song.

BIBLIOGRAPHY

Berliner, Paul. *The Soul of* Mbira: *Music and Traditions of the Shona People of Zimbabwe.* Berkeley, 1978.

Guthrie, R. Malcolm. *The Classification of the Bantu Languages.* London, 1948.

Kubik, Gerhard. *Zum verstehen afrikanischer Musik.* Leipzig, Germany, 1988.

Lomax, Alan. *Cantometrics: A Method in Musical Anthropology.* Berkeley, 1976.

Nahumck, Nadia Chilkovsky. *Introduction to Dance Literacy.* Grahamstown, South Africa, 1978.

Phillipson, David W. *The Later Prehistory of Eastern and Southern Africa.* London, 1977.

Tracey, Hugh. *Chopi Musicians.* London, 1948.

Willett, Frank. "A Contribution to the History of Musical Instruments Among the Yoruba." In *Essays for a Humanist: An Offering to Klaus Wachsmann.* New York, 1977.

GERHARD KUBIK

See also **Dance; Language Use; Oral Culture and Oral Tradition.**

STRUCTURE

Cognition and the Structure of Music

Although there is no such thing as "African music" as a singular, unified, pan-African expression, there are structural principles and patterns of behavior common to many musical cultures across the continent. These connecting threads are the result, first, of partly common histories of large agglomerations of people, especially within the Niger-Kordofanian superfamily of languages and even more pronounced within so-called Bantu languages, and, second, of cross-cultural exchanges between peoples, with varying intensity, for hundreds and even thousands of years.

African and European Concepts of Music

Some of these basic structural principles, encountered in various configurations and with varying degrees of intensity in different cultures, can be described. However, the conventional vocabulary of Western music theory is an insufficient tool for doing so and therefore has been largely replaced by a new terminology that comes as close as possible to the underlying African concepts and perceptual facts. In some African languages these concepts are expressed by a vernacular term (of analogous meaning, although different etymol-

ogy), while in others they are not expressed verbally but are silently implied.

In African musicology, most of whose results are published in European languages, the term "music" is still universally used as a blanket descriptive label. It is important, however, to keep in mind that the Latin word *musica* has no equivalent in African languages that would be congruent in its semantic field. Instead, most African languages have a term that can be translated as "song" (*oluyimbo* in Luganda, *mwaso* in the Nganguela languages, for example) but with a somewhat wider semantic field, because it includes instrumental representations of a "song." This reflects an idea found in most African cultures: that instrumental melodies "speak," that they can be verbalized, meaning that performances and listeners project verbal patterns, and quite often mere syllables with no verbal content, into sound structures. From the verbal interpretation of birds' "speech," as in eastern Angola, where *mwekuhandeka tuzila* means "what the birds speak," to the projection of text lines into inherent patterns emanating from an *ennanga* (bow harp) performance in Buganda's court music, there is a broad spectrum of verbalization permeating musical practice in sub-Saharan Africa.

Verbalization of musical patterns is also a tool in the educational transmission of African musical practices. It was only a matter of time until someone (Arthur M. Jones and J. H. Kwabena Nketia were among the pioneers) discovered the use of what we now call mnemonic syllables and verbal mnemonics (formerly called "nonsense syllables") in teaching. There is a never-ending opportunity for students of African music, by analyzing mnemonics, to discover how musical patterns are conceptualized by the carriers of those traditions themselves. In many teaching situations, musical patterns are taught by saying to the learner syllables or verbal phrases that in their kinetic structure and timbre sequences closely follow the pattern he or she is supposed to play. Among the patterns that have been published are some of those used for teaching melodic rhythmic phrases on an *akadinda* seventeen-key log xylophone in southern Uganda, and those of the *kora* bridge harp in the Gambia and Senegal as well as other Mandinka instruments. Other examples include the patterns for teaching a time line. Mnemonic syllables convey accent values and also express something about dance-beat relationships. For example, *cha* is a syllable used in many African musical cultures to transmit the notion of a rattle beat, always marking on-beat units. Nasals convey the idea of mute or empty pulses, and plosive sounds (such as *k, p,* and *t*) may convey strong timbre accents.

Principles of Timing

Attractive as the word "timing" sounds, it can be misleading. In very few African languages, if any, is music described in terms of time. To do so seems to be a characteristic Western mode of thought. Nketia coined the term in connection with Ghanaian music, but while it is applicable to European music, there is doubt that any comparable concept existed in the languages of Ghana before he introduced it. In two languages intensively researched—Cinyanja-Chichewa of Malawi and Zambia and Luchazi of Angola and Zambia—no trace of any temporal concept connected to music was found, except to performance speed. For example, when a rattle player in a musical group in southern Malawi is slow with his strokes, band members may say "*mukuchedwa!*" (You are getting late! You are delaying!). "Timing," therefore, is merely a crutch to express some observational facts relating to depth structures in African music.

Elementary Pulsation

Some forms of African music can be placed between song and speech, because they are in free rhythm. Examples are some forms of praise poetry, such as *izibongo* Zulu praise poetry in South Africa and *omuhiva* praise poetry of the Herero in Namibia. But most African music that is accompanied by some body movement (hand clapping, work movement, dance, and so on) is based on an orientation screen that can be described in English as the elementary pulsation. A. M. Jones, speaking of "smallest units," and Richard A. Waterman, speaking of a "metronome sense," were the first musicologists to express this concept, the former in terms of structure and the latter in terms of an inner experience.

The elementary pulsation is a fast, infinite series of pulses, made up of the smallest units of orientation in regular pieces. They form an unconscious orientation screen in the mind of performers (including singers, dancers, and instrumentalists) and audiences. In some kinds of instrumental playing, as with xylophone music from southern Uganda (*amadinda, akadinda,* and *embaire* music), it runs at the enormous speed of 600 (Maeltzel's metronome) and even more. Enculturation into African music begins with the gradual development of such an inner orientation screen, making the candidate ca-

pable of instantly recognizing the elementary pulsation in a piece of music, even when it is not objectified by any action units such as strokes, but barely forms a silent reference line in the back of the mind.

The elementary pulsation is not necessarily identical to the "smallest rhythmic units" in a piece of African music, although in most cases it is. There are traditions and musical styles—in Yoruba religious music, for example—where the line of elementary pulses is at some points further divided by certain (in-between) drum strokes. However, such subdivisions have no orientation function for the performers and often are merely ornamental; moreover, they are transient. The rule of thumb is that the elementary pulsation is made up only of those action units that suggest an uninterrupted flow; conceptually, the elementary pulsation is the line of reference that serves as a grid in the mind of the musicians to tell them where they are in relation to each other. Its function as an orientation screen promotes the development of what has been called the metronome sense in individuals.

The Beat

While the elementary pulsation is the primary reference level of timing in most forms of African music, of no less importance is the second reference level. In English it has come to be called the beat, derived from jazz terminology.

An infinite series of pulses such as the elementary pulsation has no pattern quality. However, the human perceptual apparatus superimposes patterns by grouping the infinite series into distinctive entities. These groups have a starting or inception point, a kind of "1," although it is not necessarily expressed that way in the languages concerned. In African music two, three, four, or more rarely five pulses are usually grouped together to constitute what can be called the beat.

The beat has several main structural characteristics. Although the beat in African (as in Western) music is an equidistant series of reference points, it is not in itself accented; that is, there is no notion of "strong" and "weak" parts of the meter. Melodic accents of a song can fall anywhere on elementary pulses to form autonomous phrase structures, on-beat or off-beat, a phenomenon for which Richard A. Waterman introduced the term "off-beat phrasing of melodic accents." In many forms of African music, melodic accents tend to fall on beat units 2 and 4 of a four-beat meter, which may give the impression of metrical accents on the "weak parts" of the meter. An example is South African *mbaqanga* music. Accentuation of such an intensity creates a strongly disorienting effect in listeners not used to those particular styles.

In principle, the beat in African music is a non-sonic concept as much as is the elementary pulsation; it is merely an inner reference scheme. But like the latter it can be objectified by action; sometimes it is, sometimes it is not. As much as performers, dancers, and the audience in African music must have internalized the perception of an elementary pulsation in order to operate, so is it necessary for dancers to internalize the beat for finding their steps. The steps can coincide with the beat; they can come in an even way, such as 1-2-3-4, and can take a binary form, such as left-right, left-right (or the reverse). But there are also traditions in which the beat is lifted; for example, in certain dance styles a dancer may lift a leg on beat units 1 and 3, and put it down on 2 and 4. In some central African dance traditions, particularly in certain forms of masked dancing of eastern Angola, the feet sometimes do not move during certain episodes, while the pelvis and shoulders are moved in isolation. In such cases, one of the kinemes (the smallest intraculturally conceptualized motional units) in the movement style coincides with the beat. Beat unit 1 (the point of inception) is often deliberately veiled through sound attenuation. For this reason, listeners to African music from other cultures often reverse African metrical schemes, perceiving, for example, beat units 2 and 4 as 3 and 1.

The Interlocking or Relative Beat

Many kinds of African music have a common beat to which all the performers, including dancers, refer. But there are also many kinds of African music with an interlocking or relative beat, where individual performers in one and the same ensemble operate from inner reference schemes that do not coincide with those of the other performers. There can be two or three different beat relationships among performers in one ensemble.

Jones discovered the existence of the interlocking or relative beat in some kinds of African music, and in the 1930s he vividly demonstrated an example in the *ngwayi* dance drumming of the Bemba musical culture in Zambia. At that time he called this phenomenon cross rhythm. However, it is not just rhythms that are crossed: what really cross are the internal reference schemes of the musicians playing together. In the *amadinda* xylophone music

of Uganda, for example, or in *mangwilo* xylophone music of northern Mozambique, performers who sit opposite each other at log xylophones placed over a banana-stem base would interlock with each other were they to stomp their feet, which they do not. This first type of interlocking is referred to as "duple-division interlocking."

The Cycles

The third reference level engraved in the mind of performers of African music is the cycle. Most African music is cyclic in form. The cycle is simply an entity created by the combination of elementary pulsation, beat, and the basic theme of a musical piece. For example, in the extract of a Yoruba story song the cycle is formed by the leader's phrase plus the chorus's response, against the orientation screen of the elementary pulsation, with the beat objectified by hand claps. The cycle number expresses repeating units, such as themes, by the number of elementary pulses that they cover. In notations of African music, cycle numbers replaced the conventional time signatures (as in Western music) beginning in 1960.

Another important structural element in African music is the tonal or tonal-harmonic segmentation of a cycle. In most African music the cycles are subdivided into two, four, or eight segments. Thus, a sixteen-pulse cycle will typically cover four or eight hand claps, dance steps, and/or tonal-harmonic progressions. For a twelve-pulse or twenty-four-pulse cycle, the segmentation will equally be 4 × 3 or 4 × 6 elementary pulses to form the segments. There are, however, notable exceptions—particularly, it seems, in some *mbira* and other music of the Shona of Zimbabwe, as studied by Andrew Tracey and Paul Berliner, and in the music of the Ganda, Soga, and related peoples in southern Uganda. For example, a cycle of thirty-six pulses in a song can be divided into three tonality segments, each covering twelve pulses. This is the so-called 3 × 12 segmentation. Recent urban musical styles display the common four-segment division of cycles almost exclusively. However, in Namibia, among the Nama and Damara, speakers of a Khoisan language, there is an urban dance style known as the Nama step; here the music is often constructed to form cycles that are divided into three or six segments.

Time-line Patterns

Time-line patterns are structured, short cycles of strokes, mostly at one pitch level. These patterns are used in some forms of music along the western African coast, in west-central Africa, and in parts of southeast Africa as a complex steering device. In contrast to the simple repeating beat of a bass drum, time-line patterns have an asymmetric structure. They are struck on instruments of penetrating sound, so that all members of the musical group, including the dancers, can hear them. Iron bells, the rim of a drum, or a glass bottle can be used for that purpose, but time-line patterns can also be produced by hand clapping.

Time-line patterns were first written down correctly by Jones (with the help of a transcription machine) from an informant who tapped them out on a copper plate. But although their structure is clear, there is still some controversy about how performers think of these patterns. Some scholars have formed the impression that west African musicians think of time-line patterns merely in relationship to the mnemonic syllables (and perhaps the elementary pulsation), but never in relation to a beat. However, recent comparative studies across western, west-central, and southeastern Africa suggest that intraculturally, time-line patterns are conceptualized in relation to multiple reference levels: the mnemonic syllables, the elementary pulsation, their own complementary images, and the performer's or dancer's inner beat. In those cases where the concept of a relative or interlocking beat steers a performance, different instrumentalists conceive of the permeating time-line pattern from their own relative viewpoints, that is, the time-line pattern is "hooked" on the inner beat of each ensemble member differently.

Tonal Systems

The European tonal system of twelve equidistant notes within an octave was imported into most parts of Africa with factory-manufactured instruments, and earlier with religious and school choir teaching. Although it has been widely accepted in Africa, there are still pockets of African cultures with tonal systems different from the tempered European twelve-note scale, and also large areas in Africa where the latter has been reinterpreted.

It is important, however, to distinguish between tonal systems and pitch intervals. Pitch intervals of nearly identical Cents values—such as perfect fourths of 498 and fifths of 720 Cents (Cents is a measuring unit to express intervals in any music)—can be found across the most diverse musical cultures of the world, let alone the octave, which seems to be universal. But the relationships of pitch

intervals to each other—their layout (in the form of a scale or other arrangement), their number, and so on—can form different tonal systems in the various cultures under study.

A preliminary inventory of tonal systems across sub-Saharan Africa by Gerhard Kubik (based on field research data from 1959 to 1994) suggests that broadly three families can be distinguished: (1) tonal systems derived from the experience of the natural harmonic series; (2) tonal systems derived from the experience of tone languages (and, in some cases, the experience of lower partials); and (3) tonal systems following the idea of "temperature," meaning that they tend toward an equidistant layout of the tonal material (that is, equipentatonic and equiheptatonic tunings).

Family 1

An important characteristic of family 1 is the presence (besides unisons and octaves) of simultaneous sounds suggesting interval sizes that are known from the natural harmonic series, such as bichords involving fourths or fifths, a somewhat flat major third (of 386 Cents), and a very flat minor seventh (of 969 Cents). In sub-Saharan Africa, there are several types of tonal systems that are derived from the experience of the harmonic series, depending on whether their basis is one or two (more rarely three) fundamentals, and on which section of the natural harmonic series is used to form the tonal system and, in particular, how high up.

For example, the tonal system of the !Kung (a Khoisan-speaking group found in southeast Angola and northeast Namibia) is derived from the experience of the mouth bow and the selective reinforcement of partials not higher than the fourth harmonic over two fundamentals. A !Kung performer can transform his hunting bow into either a vessel-resonated musical bow or a mouth bow by dividing the string by a tuning noose so that the two fundamentals give any interval that suits him—for example, an approximate major third.

Family 2

The relationship between language and music, particularly with regard to intonation of so-called speech cones in tone languages of western Africa's Kwa-speaking linguistic area, is still being investigated, despite considerable work already done on "tone and tune." Yoruba language and music are a case in point. With the exception of the Ilesha and Ekiti, most Yoruba-speaking people in Nigeria and neighboring countries have used (since their music was put on record) an anhemitonic pentatonic scale apparently with perfect fourths and fifths, and seconds and minor thirds as the constituent intervals. In this style, which is sometimes referred to as the Oyo style because it was concentrated in the Yoruba kingdom of Oyo, no multipart techniques are found that would accommodate simultaneous sounds other than octaves, unisons, and the occasional heterophony rising from overlapping call-and-response patterns in leader-chorus singing. This style is well preserved in children's songs of, for example, the *aló* type.

The question is how the ancestors of the Yoruba, the Fon, and other western Africans who share this tonal system arrived at it. In view of the absence of any particular partials-reinforcing techniques, at least in the Oyo Yoruba style and among the Fon, we can assume that the genesis of their common anhemitonic pentatonic system must have been different from that, for example, in southern Africa among various San groups. Our present data on language-music relationships suggest a vague relationship between the three acknowledged Yoruba tones in language (plus slides and perhaps intermediate tones) and musical pitch, but not in such a strict manner that a tonal step in language would neatly correspond to a musical interval. There is evidence demonstrating that intervals which in one performance of a Yoruba song appear as seconds can be intoned as minor thirds in the next. More important than the intervals is the direction of pitch movement for making the text understood. This would suggest that besides the factor of the tonal language there should be another, language-independent formative factor as the evolutionary basis of the specific anhemitonic pentatonic system shared by the Yoruba and some others in western Africa.

Family 3

In several areas of sub-Saharan Africa, field researchers have documented tempered instrumental tunings. These temperaments proceed from either a pentatonic or a heptatonic base. Therefore, they have been described as equipentatonic and equiheptatonic tunings in which the octave (a universal interval) is divided by ear into five or seven approximately equal steps. The concept of equidistance with regard to African instrumental tunings has been criticized in the general ethnomusicological literature. Recent experimental field research in Uganda and participatory research in southeast Africa, however, suggests that "pen-equidistance" (an expression coined by Klaus Wachsmann) is still a valid descriptive term.

Equidistant tunings proceed from audible pitch, not from the sound spectrum of a note. Therefore, the study of sonagrams is inconclusive with regard to equidistant tunings. Since instruments of different type, such as flutes and xylophones, or notes of the same instrument without uniform timbre, are tuned together by musicians, the auditory principle is always pitch abstraction, not timbre comparison.

In equipentatonic systems the octave (1,200 Cents) is divided by 5, resulting in a standard interval of 240 Cents (plus or minus 20 Cents margin of tolerance); in equiheptatonic systems, 1,200 divided by 7 equals 171.4 Cents (again with plus or minus 20 Cents, on the average, as a margin of tolerance). Musicians who tune their xylophones, lamellophones, zithers, and so on by ear cannot, of course, achieve accuracy down to decimal values. For structural reasons as well—such as the deliberate attempt at friction octaves (that is, octaves arbitrarily sharp or flat), as in tunings of southern Uganda—they would not aim at arithmetical accuracy. Therefore, equidistance in African instrumental tunings is always approximate.

How African instrumentalists eventually arrived at tempered instrumental tunings is an interesting historical issue. Some authors, including Erich M. von Hornbostel, Jaap Kunst, and Jones, have postulated that the idea was imported from southeast Asia with instruments such as xylophones. Such claims are difficult to verify, however, in the absence of factual sources. There can also be intraculturally valid motivations, such as the need for shifting patterns across the keyboard of a xylophone without risking their loss of identity. In the music of southern Uganda, musicians transpose the tone rows that constitute the instrumental themes through any of the five steps of a pentatonically tuned xylophone, without any modal concept. In *amadinda* music these shifts are referred to as the *emiko* of a theme. The unwritten compositional rules also only deal with standard intervals; they are valid irrespective of the *omuko* (pitch-level transposition) at which a theme is played on the xylophone. Obviously, a need must have been felt by musician-composers of the ancient court music tradition of the Buganda Kingdom (established in the fifteenth century) to create compromise tunings that would allow them to play the same songs in any transposition without their identity being lost.

There are some large areas in Africa with tempered instrumental tunings: southern Uganda (among the Ganda and Soga) and the southwestern Central African Republic for equipentatonic tunings; for equiheptatonic tunings, the Lower Zambezi Valley (among the Sena), southern Mozambique (among the Chopi), parts of eastern Angola, some parts of Mandinka-speaking western Africa (in Guinea, Mali, the Gambia, and elsewhere), and some cultures of Côte d'Ivoire. These are some of the prominent areas we know. But even in the vocal music of some of these regions, a kind of compromise intonation is often sought. The most famous example of this is the Chokwe in Angola: in their three-to-four-part singing style, long-held sounds in thirds are corrected constantly in their intonation by the singers, in the sense that minor thirds, where they would appear, are intoned toward neutral thirds. A similar phenomenon is found among the Baule of Côte d'Ivoire.

Multipart Singing

Closely related to the study of tonal systems in African music is the study of multipart patterns in vocal and instrumental performances. As suggested by Jones's harmony map, different styles and techniques of multipart singing exist in sub-Saharan Africa, with a somewhat patchy distribution. It has also been demonstrated that the tonal systems and multipart singing found in many African cultures are functionally linked. For example, parallelism in thirds is often associated with heptatonic systems, whereas in pentatonic traditions, fourth parallelism (sometimes interrupted by a single, structurally determined major third) often plays an important role.

There are two entirely different approaches to multipart singing in Africa. One is homophonic. In this case a group of people sing the same text together at different pitch levels. The emerging pitch lines then display an identical structure. The different voices usually move in intervals perceived as consonant (i.e., sounding well together). In some cases all the voices move together in parallel, but there are also many instances (particularly in eastern Angola) where parallel, oblique, and contrary motion are applied alternately within a song. The extent to which contrary motion is acceptable in a tradition depends on the degree to which a language is tonal. Languages with extreme tonality, such as those within the Kwa family of languages in western Africa, would not favor these kinds of motion, whereas other languages, such as Chokwe, Luchazi, and other Bantu languages in

Angola, accommodate contrary motion by singers. Regarding form, homophonic multipart singing by vocal groups is often combined with a leader-chorus responsorial scheme.

The other approach is polyphonic. In this case a group of people sing different text phrases (sometimes only syllables) without any common starting and ending points. Singing together, they interlock in various ways. Where the voices meet and produce simultaneous sounds, they are consonant. Polyphonic singing occurs among various San groups—particularly women—and among the central African pygmies. Contrary to earlier claims in the literature, these polyphonic styles are historically unrelated. More impressive polyphonic singing styles are found in Zimbabwe and central Mozambique, as in the threshing songs collected by Hugh Tracey among the Shona during the 1920s. In some cultures, polyphonic singing styles are practiced in particular by children, as among the Nyakyusa of Tanzania and other ethnic groups.

Sound and Body Movement

A common stereotype of African music is that it is rich in rhythm. However, in all the better-known African languages, there is no term that would be congruent in its semantic field with the Greek notion of "rhythm." Rhythm as a concept in isolation is probably not an African concept at all. If one analyzes instrumental performance in sub-Saharan Africa, such as "drumming" (to use a popular label), considering detectable kinemes (intraculturally significant motional-timbric units), one will discover that "drumming" in Africa is not merely "rhythm," but that the basic aim of a drummer playing with his hands (as opposed to a single-pitched bell) is to create language-related motional-timbric patterns. And he conceptualizes, in terms of timbre, units of discernible pitch rather than "rhythms." These units, according to which part of the drum skin or drum's body is struck, constitute a repertoire of sounds and phrases (patterns) often identified with mnemonic or teaching syllables. Therefore, to describe, let alone transcribe, drumming in Africa merely in terms of "rhythm" almost always misses essentials, an idea that is supported by the theoretical vocabulary in African languages referring to drumming.

A kinemic analysis of music and dance proceeds from the idea that motional patterns can be dissected into intraculturally conceptualized smallest units, called kinemes. Once these have been isolated, they can be explained in drawings and given notational symbols. Kinemic analysis embraces and connects the two areas of expression that are intimately linked in sub-Saharan Africa: sound production and body movement. In kinemic analysis one first isolates and lists the action units according to the musicians' own taxonomies. In many African musical traditions, each kineme has a specific syllable or mnemonic phrase attached to identify it. As an example we can cite an accompanying drum pattern used in *vipwali* drumming among the Nkhangala, Mbwela, Luchazi, Nyemba, and related peoples in southeastern Angola: *ma-cha-ki-li ma-cha-ki-li*, and so on. In order to discover these kinemes, one often can simply count the number of syllables in a mnemonic phrase; in the case cited, there are four. Therefore, the drummer must have conceptualized at least four different motional-timbric units. Next, one can attempt to check that result by watching the drummer's hands and discovering how those units are produced. For example, they can by produced by striking different areas of the drum skin, or by employing different parts of the hand for a stroke, or both. Finally, each kineme, thus isolated, is given a notational symbol—in the above case, the mnemonic syllables themselves. Then transcription can start, using these symbols, accompanied by an explanatory key.

Kinemic analysis can be employed as well for the structural analysis of dance movement. It follows the same principle. In contrast to conventional notation systems for dance, such as Laban or Benesh notation, it proceeds from an emic standpoint, using symbols adapted to the dance culture being analyzed, as different languages use different orthographic systems and not a single set of universal symbols.

In structural dance analysis, one first isolates the body areas that are acting, and then represents each area (like each drum) with a horizontal line. (Vertical lines represent the elementary pulsation.) Next, one identifies the number of kinemes used within each body area. For example, in a certain movement pattern used in various dance cultures of central Africa over a twelve-pulse cycle, two body areas (motional centers) are acting: first, the legs, and second, the pelvis (affecting the arms and upper torso).

While there is an extensive descriptive literature on dance in Africa, including several attempts at dance notation, sometimes under the ideological blanket of "dance literacy," very few emically relevant dance studies have been published. One of them is Azuka Tuburu's work on Igbo (Ibo) music and dance. Comparative works on dance in Africa include attempts at delineating broad geographical dance-style areas. Detailed stylistic analysis on a comparative basis is found in Alan Lomax's choreometrics scheme. A third area of attention was the cognitional dimension as reflected in verbalized concepts such as Robert Farris Thompson's "esthetics of the cool" and the study of behavioral patterns embracing body language.

BIBLIOGRAPHY

Berliner, Paul. *The Soul of* Mbira: *Music and Traditions of the Shona People of Zimbabwe.* Berkeley, 1978.

Ekman, Paul. "Movements with Precise Meanings." *Journal of Communication* 26, no. 3 (1976): 14–26.

Ekman, Paul, and Wallace V. Friesen. "The Repertoire of Nonverbal Behavior: Categories, Origins, Usage, and Coding." *Semiotica* 1, no. 1 (1969): 49–98.

Gunther, Helmut. *Grundphänomene und Grundbegriffe des afrikanischen und afro-amerikanischen Tanzes.* Studies in Jazz Research, no. 1. Graz, Austria, 1969.

Hornbostel, Erich Moritz von. "The Ethnology of African Sound-Instruments." *Africa* 6 (1933): 129–157, 277–311.

Jones, Arthur M. *Studies in African Music.* 2 vols. London, 1959.

Kubik, Gerhard. *Zum verstehen afrikanischer Musik.* Leipzig, Germany, 1988.

Lomax, Alan, et al. "Choremetrics: A Method for the Study of Cross-Cultural Pattern in Film." *Research Film* 6, no. 6 (1969).

Nahumck, Nadia Chilkovsky. *Introduction to Dance Literacy.* Grahamstown, South Africa, 1978.

Nketia, J. H. Kwabena. *The Music of Africa.* New York, 1974.

Thompson, Robert Farris. *African Art in Motion.* Los Angeles, 1974.

Tracey, Andrew. "The Original African *Mbira*." *African Music* 5, no. 2 (1972): 85–104.

Tracey, Hugh. *Chopi Musicians.* London, 1948.

Tuburu, Azuka. "Kinetik und sociale Funktion des Tanzes bei den Igbo." Ph.D. diss., University of Salzburg, 1987.

Waterman, Richard A. "African Influences on the Music of the Americas." In *Acculturation in the Americas,* edited by Sol Tax. Chicago, 1952.

Willet, Frank. "A Contribution to the History of Musical Instruments Among the Yoruba." In *Essays for a Humanist: An Offering to Klaus Wachsmann.* New York, 1977.

GERHARD KUBIK

See also **Dance; Language Use.**

221

MODERN AND POPULAR MUSIC

Overview

Modern African music has a history stretching back more than a century. Although early visitors and travelers brought hitherto unknown musical conventions to Africa, colonization was the main means for the introduction of Western musical instruments and concepts in Africa.

From the first half of the nineteenth century on, European musical traditions spread throughout the continent. In addition, Afro-American music (mainly in western and central Africa) and Arabic (which had arrived even earlier) and Indian music (both in eastern Africa) inspired new musics. Brass bands—forerunners were the fifteenth-century drum and fife bands on the west African coast—accompanied the arrival of the colonial armies and administration. After military music came the church music of the various Western denominations: the Protestants with hymns, the Catholics with liturgical chants. Next came the introduction of dance music, as well as the theatrical forms arising from the vaudeville and minstrelsy of North America.

With schools providing increasingly educated musicians, Africans performed in all spheres of musical activity. Soon they realized that imported musical forms could be adapted to local musical traditions, whether by providing fitting lyrics or by adding local percussive rhythmic structure or background, and they joined with the indigenist movements and what later became the nationalist or independence movements. Church hymns were sung in many of the African languages, and new compositions by African composers were drawing on local traditions. In the popular music context the amalgamation of different musical traditions resulted in many kinds of syntheses. They range from local folk music including Western instruments to Western instruments playing local folk music—or local instruments being used to play modern compositions. Western instruments were imitated—for example in Beni *ngoma*, for which gourds are grown to function as horns.

Musical Regions

The Sahel

The Sahel is dominated by what is called griot-style or Mandingo rock. (The Sahel covers more or less the area of the ancient Mandinka empire, from Senegal to Mali.) In the 1960s the popular dance orchestras, playing mainly Latin music, increasingly created a sound reminiscent of local string instruments (*kora*), xylophones (*balafon*), or drums. Local instruments were gradually reintegrated in the 1980s, such as the *tama*, a Senegalese drum. The vocal style took on the characteristics of the griots or griottes. Since the 1960s female singers have become stars, especially in Mali.

Since the 1960s national musical cultures have developed from similar roots. In Senegal, Youssou N'Dour created the *mbalax*. In Mali the Rail Band de Bamako produced some of the most famous African musicians: Salif Keita, singer; Mory Kante, singer and *kora* player; and Kante Manfila, guitarist. Both of them originally came from Guinea.

Coastal Francophone West Africa

In Guinea's national competitions Bembeya Jazz was crowned the best band in 1964; it subsequently became one of the favorite bands in west Africa. In Côte d'Ivoire Ernesto Djedje formulated *ziglibithy* in the late 1970s—a mix of Zairian rumba, Afrobeat, and francophone west African music. In the early 1980s Alpha Blondy presented Afro reggae. In the 1990s a new acoustic music, the Zouglou, sparked off a new movement of "neo-African" bands, especially at the university.

Anglophone West Africa

The anglophone west African states—mainly Sierra Leone, Ghana, and Nigeria—historically are strongly linked by their common British colonial past. They produced guitar bands and dance bands that played "highlife" after World War II. In Ghana, E. T. Mensah is considered the "King of Highlife." The guitar bands have Nana Ampadou as their greatest representative. In Nigeria, Bobby Benson was the leading artist of Nigerian highlife. Fela Anikulapo Kuti created the Afrobeat in the 1970s. Juju music, a Yoruba guitar band style, has been the prevailing sound since independence. After I. K. Dairo, Ebenezer Obey and Sunny Ade are the leading artists. Many other popular styles can be attributed to individual artists. Since the 1970s these have increasingly been female singers, mainly from a middle-class background.

Central Africa

After an initial period of copying Cuban rumba music, the Congo rumba began to evolve; Le Grand Kalle, Franco Luambo Makiadi, and Tabu Ley Rochereau produced hundreds of records. The big dance orchestras were musically questioned by the Zaiko Langa Langa guitar band in the 1970s. Zaiko developed into a "dynasty" and today competes with various classic formations.

Horn of Africa

Ethiopia's popular dance music in the 1960s was influenced by both jazz and soul. The sound was strongly Amharic. In the late 1980s and early 1990s, Aster Aweke and Mahmud Ahmed became the first Ethiopian artists to achieve international fame.

East Africa

East African music had its own guitar traditions connected with the Katanga/Shaba guitar-picking styles of the 1950s, such as those of Jean Bosco Mwenda, John Mwale, and George Mukabi in Kenya. In the 1980s the Luo-derived Benga beat began to evolve, thereby diminishing the influence of Zairian *soukous* bands. Singing was primarily in local languages—in Tanzania, in Swahili. *Taarab* is Swahili music (along the coast and on the islands, especially Zanzibar), played at all types of social events. Although seemingly Arabic, it draws its main roots from the mainland east African musics.

Central Southern Africa

In Zambia local neotraditional acoustic *kalindula* music was adopted in the 1980s by the electric bands, and Zamrock disappeared. Angolan and Mozambican styles developed, as did the music of the other African Portuguese colonies, under the influence of Portuguese folk music, including fado. In Mozambique, *marrabenta* became the name for modern dance music.

South Africa

In the townships, beginning in the 1950s, the music of the young boys was *kwela*. Electrified, it became *simanje-manje* and today is generally called jive or *mbaqanga*.

Recorded African Music

The first commercial recordings were made, in various parts of the continent, early in the 1920s. EMI chose west and south Africa; Odeon, east Africa. The musicians at that time were brought to Britain. In the 1940s and 1950s, mobile recording units or local studios within Africa supplied the musical products for the record companies in Europe. The projected market was Africa itself. The gramophone proved to be a practical implement, not requiring any electricity. As it became popular, a cross section of Euro-American popular and classical, as well as religious, music received the widest possible circulation. African record shop owners began to record local artists, and a small local

record production started, though the technical side was still done in Europe.

The 45rpm single and the 33rpm LP were introduced at the beginning of the 1960s. Local entrepreneurs started their own recording businesses—including pressing—and their labels competed with those of international companies. In the 1970s large modern studios were constructed in a number of countries, but in the 1980s the economic crisis hit most of them, and recording and producing returned to Europe. Paris has become the main center for the production of African music, even for formerly London-based anglophone artists. In South Africa the situation has been somewhat different. The large record companies operating there since the 1930s have survived. Nigeria, Senegal, Côte d'Ivoire, and Kenya still have their own recording industries. The main medium is the audiocassette. The vinyl record has largely disappeared. In Europe and America, African music is mainly distributed on CDs. Video has become another important carrier of African music; commercially produced videocassettes are available everywhere.

Organization of Modern African Music

Modern African orchestras generally have a leader who is at the same time the owner of the instruments, the manager, the copyright owner of all the material produced, the director, the main instrumentalist, the main vocalist, and the main composer and lyricist. The bandsmen—women are absent as instrumentalists except in a few all-female orchestras (e.g., Les Amazones de Guinée)—usually own nothing, are paid an hourly or weekly rate, and may be fired at any time. In some cases the hotel or bar owns the instruments and hires a bandleader to handle the rest.

Copyright, Piracy, and the Adaptation to New Poverty

Copyright is one of the biggest problems facing modern African musicians. Even though many states are signatories of international copyright conventions, governments do not support the execution of the rights. In Ghana, for instance, special legislation has been introduced to protect copyrights. Only on this basis can royalties be collected and musicians benefit from their work. Piracy is a common practice, much to the detriment of some musical cultures. In Sierra Leone it has led to the total disappearance of the orchestras. The increasing poverty following the economic decline in many countries since 1977 has had the same effect. Electric bands relying on expensive equipment and instruments could hardly survive. New acoustic groups started to operate in increasing numbers. Adapting to new economic conditions, they played local instruments that needed no amplification though some might be required for the vocalist. Their repertoire is a condensation of local popular tunes from various sources. The main aim is to provide a dense rythmic pattern for dancing. Examples are Milo Jazz (in Sierra Leone), Zouglou (Côte d'Ivoire), and Suede Suede (Zaire).

Song Lyrics

In African music there is rarely a piece that is solely instrumental. The lyrics are of utmost importance. It is the message of a song that the listeners are interested in. Most lyrics are in African languages, including creole and pidgin. English, French, or Portuguese songs are mostly signs of music in exile (for a foreign audience). In the case of tonal languages, such as Yoruba, the tonal pattern follows the melody. Lyrics are composed mainly by the vocalists themselves. The content varies greatly, from historical epos to love song, but seldom is overtly political, though hints may be hidden in cryptic expressions or familiar proverbs. Many songs are filled with religious references, even though they are not classified as religious.

BIBLIOGRAPHY

Andersson, Muff. *Music in the Mix: The Story of South African Popular Music*. Johannesburg, 1981.

Bemba, Sylvain. *Cinquante ans de musique du Congo-Zaïre (1920–1970): De Paul Kamba à Tabu-Ley*. Paris, 1984.

Bender, Wolfgang. *Sweet Mother: Modern African Music*. Translated by Wolfgang Fries. Chicago, 1991.

———, ed. *Perspectives in African Music*. Bayreuth African Studies Series no. 9. Bayreuth, 1989.

Berna, Marianne. *Paris wie die Wilden: Afrika, seine Musik, ihre Metropole*. Zurich, 1991.

Cathcart, Jenny. *Hey you! A Portrait of Youssou N'Dour*. Oxford, 1989.

Chernoff, John Miller. *African Rhythm and Sensibility: Aesthetics and Social Action in African Musical Idioms*. Chicago, 1979.

Clark, Ebun. *Hubert Ogunde: The Making of Nigerian Theatre*. London, 1979.

Collins, John. *Musicmakers of West Africa*. Washington, D.C., 1985.

———. *E. T. Mensah: The King of Highlife*. London, 1986.

———. *West African Pop Roots*. Philadelphia, 1992.

Conrath, Philippe. *Johnny Clegg: La Passion zoulou*. Paris, 1988.

Coplan, David B. *In Township Tonight! South Africa's Black City Music and Theatre*. Johannesburg, 1985.

Dibango, Manu, and Danielle Rouard. *Three Kilos of Coffee: An Autobiography*. Chicago, 1989.

Erlmann, Veit. *African Stars: Studies in Black South African Performance*. Chicago, 1991.

———, ed. *Populäre Musik in Afrika*. Berlin, 1991.

Euba, Akin. *Essays on Music in Africa*. 2 vols. Bayreuth, 1988–1989.

Ewens, Graeme. *Luamba Franco and 30 Years of O.K.Jazz: A History and Discography*. London, 1986.

———. *Africa O'Ye: A Celebration of African Music*. London, 1991.

Graham, Ronnie. *Stern's Guide to Contemporary African Music*. 2 vols. New York, 1988; London, 1992.

Konaté, Yacouba. *Alpha Blondy: Reggae et société en Afrique noire*. Paris, 1987.

Kubik, Gerhard. *The Kachamba Brothers' Band: A Study of Neotraditional Music in Malawi*. Zambian Papers no. 9. Lusaka, Zambia, 1974.

———. *Ostafrika. Musikgeschichte in Bildern*. Vol 1, pt. 10. Leipzig, 1982.

———. *Malawian Music: A Framework for Analysis*. Zomba, Malawi, 1987.

———. *Zum verstehen afrikanischer Musik*. Leipzig, 1988.

———. *Westafrika. Musikgeschichte in Bildern*. Vol. 7, pt. 11. Leipzig, 1989.

Lee, Helene. *Rockers d'Afrique: Stars et légendes du rock mandingue*. Paris, 1988.

Lonoh, Michel. *Essai de commentaire de la musique congolaise moderne*. Kinshasa, Zaire, 1969.

Low, John. *Shaba Diary*. Vienna, 1982.

Makeba, Miriam. *Makeba: My Story*. New York, 1987.

Moore, Carlos. *Fela, Fela, This Bitch of a Life*. London, 1982.

Nettl, Bruno, ed. *Eight Urban Musical Cultures: Tradition and Change*. Urbana, Ill., 1978.

Pongweni, Alec J. C. *Songs That Won the Liberation War*. Harare, Zimbabwe, 1982.

Ranger, Terence O. *Dance and Society in Eastern Africa, 1890–1970: The Beni Ngoma*. Berkeley, Calif., 1975.

Roberts, John Storm. *Black Music of Two Worlds*. London, 1973.

Stapleton, Chris, and Chris May. *African All Stars: The Pop Music of a Continent*. London, 1989.

Stewart, Gary. *Breakout: Profiles in African Rhythm*. Chicago, 1992.

Tenaille, Frank. *Touré Kunda*. Paris, 1987.

Wallis, Roger, and Krister Malm. *Big Sounds from Small Peoples*. New York, 1984.

Waterman, Chris. *Juju: A Social History and Ethnography of an African Popular Music*. Chicago, 1990.

Zindi, Fred. *Roots Rocking in Zimbabwe*. Gweru, Zimbabwe, 1985.

WOLFGANG BENDER

See also **Popular Culture.**

MODERN AND POPULAR MUSIC IN WESTERN AFRICA

In sub-Saharan Africa a large variety of acculturated popular music styles blend local elements with those from Europe and the Americas, including black diasporic influences ranging from ragtime to rap and from rumba to reggae. These syncretic forms evolved initially on the coast, the site of first contact with Europeans, and they have generally been associated with modern urban areas, the young, and the class of Africans who fall between the Westernized elite and the peasant class.

The Beginnings

The earliest documented case of such a syncretic genre is *goombay* (*gumbe/gumbeh/gombe*), which is played on frame drums. This neo-African drum dance of the Maroons of Jamaica was introduced in 1800 at Freetown, Sierra Leone, by freed Maroon rebels who were settled there by the British. It subsequently spread to what are now Ghana, Nigeria, Burkina Faso, Mali, Côte d'Ivoire, and Cameroon, where regional forms emerged. It was brought to Ghana, for instance, in 1900 by Ga artisans who had been working with Sierra Leoneans as contract laborers in the Congo Free State (later Zaire). A later wave, called *gome* in Ghana, was introduced into the country by Ga fishermen who had returned from Fernando Po. Related to *goombay* is the Sierra Leone *asiko* music, which employs frame drums and the musical saw.

Brass and fife marching band music was brought to western Africa in the nineteenth century by colonial armies and later by Protestant missionaries. A West Indian regimental band was established at Freetown as early as 1819, and in Ghana there was a native military band at Cape Coast Castle by 1840. From the outbreak of the Asante Wars in the 1870s, West Indian troops were stationed at Cape Coast, and they had regimental bands that played not only European dances and martial music but also syncopated Caribbean songs. By the 1880s they had inspired local Fante youths to form similar bands (e.g., the Lions Hearts) that developed an indigenous syncopated brass band music known as *adaha*, a forerunner of highlife that was prevalent in southern Ghana until the 1930s. *Konkomba*, a version of this marching/dance music using local instruments, appeared in the 1930s and subsequently spread as far as Nigeria.

"Palm-wine music" is a generic term for the syncretic music of the coast that evolved after the turn of the century into the Sierra Leonean *maringa*; the Ghanaian *osibisaba*, Asante blues, and guitar band highlife; Nigerian juju music and "native" blues; and the Cameroonian *makossa*. All of these originated from a fusion of indigenous coastal music with that of sailors: thus the use of local percussion instruments with the guitars, banjos, concertinas, and harmonicas of sailors. Besides foreign sailors, the maritime Kru people of Liberia were particularly important; they created the Africanized cross-rhythmic two-finger technique of guitar playing and disseminated their mainline, fireman, and *dagomba* styles throughout west Africa.

Guitar band music has been dominant since World War II. Some of its most important exponents in *maringa* are Ebenezer Calender and S. E. Rogie; in juju, I. K. Dairo, Ebenezer Obey, and Sunny Ade; in *makossa*, Manu Dibango, Sam Fan Thomas, and Mone Bile; in Ghanaian highlife, E. K. Nyame, Kwaa Mensah, the African Brothers, and the Kumapim Royals; in Nigerian highlife, the Three Night Wizards, Victor Uwaifo, Stephen Osadabe, the Warriors, the Peacocks, the Orientals, and Rokafil Jazz.

Through sheet music, recordings, and silent movies, American minstrel and ragtime music became the rage in anglophone west Africa early in the twentieth century. Among the local groups that were established was the African Comedy Company of Freetown (1915). In Ghana local minstrel and vaudeville shows originated from the Empire Day "concert parties" of Teacher Valley at Sekondi in 1918. In 1924–1926 there was a visit by the African-American comedy team of Glass and Grant; touring with them were Williams and Marbel from Accra and Williams and Nicol from Freetown. In the 1930s this previously coastal elite genre was taken over by Bob Jackson and the Axim Trio, who toured the interior and Africanized the concert party by performing in Akan and combining the blackface minstrel show with the mischievous Akan Ananse-the-Spider folk hero to form the "Bob" stage character. A further Africanization of the concert party occurred in the early 1950s when E. K. Nyame replaced the ragtime pieces and foxtrots of early concert parties with highlife music. There was a subsequent proliferation of concert party troupes (thirty in 1960, sixty in 1970), all modeled on Nyame's Akan Trio, and the genre spread to Togo.

World War II to Independence

World War II had a major impact on west African popular music, due to foreign servicemen being stationed there and to west Africans (e.g., Nigerian "Boma Boys") fighting in Burma and other countries. Nightclubs flourished in the cities where British and American troops were based—they enjoyed jazz, swing, calypso, Latin, and Afro-Cuban music. Local bands sprang up to play this music: the Mayfair Jazz Band of Freetown, the Eastern Progressive Swing Band of Lagos, and the Black and White Spots and Tempos of Accra.

When the foreign servicemen returned home, Ghana's E. T. Mensah reorganized the Tempos and and incorporated jazz, calypso, and Afro-Cuban elements into highlife. The new Tempos' sound spread throughout west Africa, helped by the band's proindependence sentiments. Mensah became known as the King of Highlife, and his small swing combo type of ensemble eclipsed the large dance orchestras (e.g., Excelsior, Sugar Babies) that had been favored in prewar times. The Nigerian Bobby Benson, who founded his jazz and swing group in 1948, influenced by the Tempos, became one of Nigeria's foremost highlife dance band musicians. Others were Victor Olaiya, Rex Lawson, E. C. Arinze, and Eddie Okonta.

Also in the immediate postwar era, Nigeria's equivalent of Ghana's concert party, Yoruba traveling theater, emerged. Through the various groups' performances a syncretic theatrical tradition that had been nurtured in the "native operas" and the cantatas of nativist churches entered the commercial, secular sphere. The first traveling theater was Hubert Ogunde's (1946); by 1971 the genre had its own trade union with almost 100 affiliated theatrical companies.

After the war, Latin and Afro-Cuban dance music became particularly admired in francophone west Africa, where numerous bands playing dance music were formed: Alfa Jazz of Dahomey (now Bénin), the National Bedama of Mali, the Star Band and Baobab Band of Senegal, Volta Jazz of Burkina Faso, and Habenera Jazz of Guinea. In what is now Zaire, that country's version of the rumba, known as Congo jazz (later *soukous*) helped increase the domination of Afro-Cuban music in francophone west Africa and Portuguese Guinea-Bissau until the 1970s.

Postindependence

Beginning in the 1970s, a fusion of Latin, Afro-Cuban, and indigenous dance music occurred in francophone west Africa, where there is a long tradition of professional griot, or *jali*, performers. Modern bands and artists that absorbed *jali* influences include Bembeya Jazz National and Mory Kante of Guinea; the Rail Band (with Salif Keita), Les Ambassadeurs (with Kante Manfila), and the musicians Ali Farka Touré of Mali; Ifang Bondi and Foday Musa Suso of Gambia; Super Mama Djombo of Guinea-Bissau; and Groupe Carnaval of Niger. In Senegal, Afro-Cuban and local music were blended by bands like Xalam, Touré Kunda, and Super Étoile. The best-known artist is the leader of Super Étoile, Youssou N'Dour, who in the 1980s created his electro-Wolof *mbalax* dance style and went on to work with many of the world's top pop stars.

Acculturated popular music really began to take off in the francophone areas only after independence. However, independence acted as a general catalyst throughout western Africa, not only through the establishment of indigenous mass communications and entertainment industries but also through women's appearing on the popular stage in some numbers and the stimulation of artistic indigenization.

Besides the effect of international pop stars (including South Africa's Miriam Makeba), women were encouraged to become popular entertainers from the late 1950s through the cultural and educational policies of the newly independent west African nations. Ghana's President Kwame Nkrumah set up Workers Brigade bands that employed women singers and actresses. The Nigerian government formed Maggie Aghumo's all-female Armed Forces Band, and Guinea's President Sékou Touré established a female gendarmerie band, Les Amazones de Guinée, that included the famous singer Sonia Diabate. Liberia's Fatu Gayflor rose to fame through her country's National Ballet Troupe, and Mali's cultural policy abetted a wave of female *jalis* or *djely mousso* (e.g., Fanta Damba, Fanta Sacko, and Tata Bambo Kouyate). Other top west African popular female performers of the postindependence period include Liberia's Miatta Fahnbulleh, Bénin's Angelique Kidjo, Côte d'Ivoire's Aicha Koné, Cameroon's Tity Edima, Cape Verde's Cesaria Evora, Bella Bellow of Togo, Asabea Cropper and Grace Omaboe of Ghana, and the Lijadu Sisters, Patti Boulaye, and Onyeka Onwenu of Nigeria.

Decolonization also brought more indigenous forms of popular entertainment to the fore. A striking example is the Portuguese *morna* music of Cape

Verde, which was eclipsed after independence in 1975 by the *batuco* and *furaca* polyrhythmic dance music styles. They had been denounced by the Portuguese authorities.

Independence institutionalized the "African personality," negritude, and Pan-Africanism. These, together with the contemporaneous African-American and Caribbean "black consciousness" and "back to roots" ideals, led to a self-conscious Africanization by many entertainers. Ghana's Koo Nimo and Cameroon's Francis Beby have become renowned for combining the acoustic guitar with traditional instruments. Nigeria's Duro Lapido helped pioneer the use of Yoruba myth and legend in popular traveling theater. "Doctor" Olah's *mailo* jazz-folk form of electric guitar band *maringa* music became the rage in Sierra Leone. The Ga group Wulomei created an acoustic form of guitar band highlife in Ghana. Ernesto Djedje of Côte d'Ivoire became successful with his electric *ziglibithy* rendition of local *bebe* music. Afro-rock, Afro-soul, and Afro-beat were blended by Ghana's Osibisa and Nigeria's Segun Bucknor and Fela Anikulapo-Kuti; the lyrics of the latter were particularly antiestablishment. The latest acculturated pop style is the Afro-reggae of Ghana's African Brothers, City Boys, K. K. Kabobo, and Kojo Entwi; and Nigeria's Sunny Okosun, Majek Fashek, Ras Kimono, and reggae queen Evi Edna-Ogholi. Alpha Blondy of Côte d'Ivoire had an international hit in the late 1980s with his "Apartheid Is Nazism."

BIBLIOGRAPHY

Bebey, Francis. *African Music: A People's Art.* Translated by Josephine Bennett. New York, 1975.

Bender, Wolfgang. "Ebenezer Calender—An Appraisal." In *Perspectives in African Music,* edited by Wolfgang Bender. Bayreuth, 1989.

———. *Sweet Mother: Modern African Music.* Translated by Wolfgang Freis. Chicago, 1991.

Bergman, Billy. *Goodtime Kings: Emerging African Pop.* New York, 1985.

Cathcart, Jenny. *Hey You!: A Portrait of Youssou N'Dour.* London, 1989.

Chernoff, John M. *African Rhythm and African Sensibility.* Chicago, 1979.

Collins, E. John. "Comic Opera in Ghana." *African Arts* 9, no. 2 (1976): 50–57.

———. "Ghanaian Highlife." *African Arts* 10, no. 1 (1976): 62–68, 100.

———. "Post-War Popular Band Music in West Africa." *African Arts* 10, no. 3 (1977): 53–60.

———. *Musicmakers of West Africa.* Washington, D.C., 1985.

———. *E. T. Mensah, King of Highlife.* London, 1986.

———. "Jazz Feedback to Africa." *American Music* 15, no. 2 (1987): 176–193.

———. *West African Pop Roots.* Philadelphia, 1992.

Coplan, David. "Go to My Town, Cape Coast! The Social History of Ghanaian Highlife." In *Eight Urban Musical Cultures: Tradition and Change,* edited by Bruno Nettl. Urbana, Ill., 1978.

Fosu-Mensah, Kwabena, Lucy Duran, and Chris Stapleton. "On Music in Contemporary West Africa." *African Affairs* (London) 86, no. 343 (1987): 227–240.

Graham, Ronnie. *Stern's Guide to Contemporary African Music.* 2 vols. London, 1992.

Haydon, Geoffrey, and Dennis Marks. *Repercussions: A Celebration of African-American Music.* London, 1985.

Hooker, Naomi Ware. "Popular Musicians in Freetown." *African Urban Notes* 5, no. 4 (1970): 11–18.

Horton, Christian Dowa. "Popular Bands in Sierra Leone: 1920 to the Present." *Black Perspective in Music* 12, no. 2 (1984): 183–192.

Ita, Chief Bassey. *Jazz in Nigeria: An Outline Cultural History.* Lagos, 1984.

Jegede, Dele. "Popular Culture and Popular Music: The Nigerian Experience." *Présence africain* n.s. no. 144 (1987): 59–72.

Kala-Lobe, Henri. "Music in Cameroon." *West Africa* (London) no. 3405 (November 1982): 2281–2283.

King, Bruce. "Introducing the High-Life." *Jazz Monthly* 12 (July 1966): 3–8.

Manuel, Peter. *Popular Musics of the Non-Western World.* Oxford, 1988.

Marre, Jeremy, and Hannah Charlton. *Beats of the Heart: Popular Music of the World.* London, 1985.

Mensah, Atta Annan. "The Impact of Western Music on the Musical Traditions of Ghana." *Composer* 19 (1966): 18–22.

———. "Jazz: The Round Trip." *Jazz Forschung/Jazz Research* 3/4 (1971/1972).

Oliver, Paul. *Savannah Syncopators: African Retentions in the Blues.* London, 1970.

Ricard, Alain. "The Concert Party as a Genre: The Happy Stars of Lomé." *Research in African Literatures* 5, no. 2 (1974): 165–179.

Roberts, John Storm. *Black Music of Two Worlds.* New York, 1972.

Sackey, Chrys Kwesi. *Konkoma: A Musical Form of the Fanti Young Fishermen in the 40's and 50's in Ghana, West Africa.* Berlin, 1989.

Smith, Edna M. "Popular Music in West Africa." *African Music* 3, no. 1 (1962): 11–17.

Stapleton, Chris, and Chris May. *African All Stars.* London, 1987.

Sutherland, Efua Theodora. *The Original Bob: The Story of Bob Johnson, Ghana's Ace Comedian.* Accra, 1970.

Van der Geest, Sjaak, and Nimrod K. Asante-Darko. "The Political Meaning of Highlife Songs in Ghana." *African Studies Review* 25, no. 1 (1982): 27–35.

Van Oven, Cootje. *An Introduction to the Music of Sierra Leone.* Freetown, 1981. *Supplement.* Freetown, 1982.

Ware, Naomi. "Popular Music and African Identity in Freetown, Sierra Leone." In *Eight Urban Cultures: Tradition and Change,* edited by Bruno Nettl. Urbana, Ill., 1978.

Waterman, Christopher Alan. *Jùjú: A Social History and Ethnography of an African Popular Music.* Chicago, 1990.

E. JOHN COLLINS

See also **Popular Culture.**

MODERN AND POPULAR MUSIC IN EASTERN AFRICA

Various modern or popular music styles have developed in eastern Africa since the 1930s. In local parlance, there is no commonly used term encompassing these various styles. However, the Swahili neologism *muziki wa dansi* (dance music), used for the Tanzanian national style, describes the common denominator and main purpose of most of these musical forms: to entertain audiences in (basically urban) dance halls, smaller clubs, or bars. All of these forms are widely distributed on records and cassettes, and are played on the radio. In Kenya, since about 1975, recording and media distribution has largely supplanted the live performance context. Until the 1960s and 1970s, most groups were organized as social clubs; since then, other organizational forms increasingly have come to dominate, the musicians being hired by state organizations or private businesses that own the instruments. Only in rare cases do the musicians own musical instruments or other means of producing their art.

A stylistic unity exists between the different forms in that almost all are based on the guitar as the main instrument. In Tanzanian dance music, trumpets and saxophones are added to a group generally consisting of up to three guitars, a bass, drums, and other percussion instruments. Despite this decidedly "modern" instrumentation, all styles are deeply rooted in the respective local musical traditions—in their use of melodies, rhythms, and general musical ideas. The most popular and widespread musical forms make use of the lingua franca Swahili. While a quasi-national outlook has always been a feature of Tanzanian music, in Kenya since about 1975, there has been a proliferation of regional styles sung in Gikuyu, Kamba, Luhya, and Luo. These have taken precedence over Swahili-language music, which had dominated since the 1950s. A similar situation exists in Uganda, where the bulk of popular music is written and sung in regional languages.

For musicians and audiences alike, the lyrics are a highly valued part of these musical forms. Dance-music songs usually comment on the conditions of everyday life, current affairs, or politics. Love and gender issues are the topics of many songs. Despite the severe underrepresentation of female artists, the lyrics often discuss female concerns, and many portray a questioning of male hegemony. Differences in "plot development" exist between the various genres. In some—for example, in the Luo and Luhya languages—songs are constructed as praise songs. The educative function of song is highly valued by the audiences, including the ruling elite, who sometimes make use of songs "to educate the masses." Yet the status of the musician is rather low, and the singer's or the songwriter's position is rather precarious and ambiguous. Musicians are often portrayed as loafers, drunkards, or drug takers. While the role of the singer as a social critic seems to be established, and a kind of poetic license is apparent, censorship and banning of songs regularly occur.

Not all new forms of music are linked to the urban dance hall. Various styles are connected to social occasions, particularly life-cycle celebrations. The most widely known and most popular among the latter is *taarab,* the wedding music of the Islamic Swahili-speaking people of the east African coast and adjacent islands. *Taarab* groups are found wherever Swahili-speaking populations live: in upcountry Kenya and Tanzania, Burundi, eastern Zaire, the Comoros. *Taarab* also has become a widespread form of popular music, distributed on cassettes and featured on the radio. Many *taarab* groups are still organized on a (social) club format, but organizational forms similar to the ones described for dance music are coming to the fore. In musical terms, *taarab* combines various elements from the musical cultures around the Indian Ocean: Arabic-Islamic, Indian, and African. The instruments include 'ud (a short-necked, plucked lute) and *qanun* (a plucked box zither or psaltery), violin, accordian, organ, guitar, and various percussion instruments.

Essentially, *taarab* is sung poetry conforming to the rules of classical Swahili poetics. Many songs are topically related to the wedding context, with love and relations between men and women dominating. Other topics are also current: society in general, philosophical matters, politics. Two types of *taarab,* so-called male and female forms, are distinguished. Male *taarab* has stronger leanings toward Arabic music, and the lyrics conform more strictly to received rules of etiquette. In recent years, female *taarab* has come to dominate; thus many of the songs voice concerns of women and show links to other forms of specifically female culture (e.g., on the Kenya coast and in mainland Tanzania, there are strong musical and textual links to *chakacha,* a female song and dance form). In contrast with other forms of popular music in eastern Africa, many women singers are active in *taarab.*

BIBLIOGRAPHY

Graebner, Werner. "Whose Music? The Songs of Remmy Ongala and Orchestra Super Matimila." *Popular Music* 8, no. 3 (1989): 243–256.

———. "Sources for the Study of Popular Culture in East Africa: A Select Bibliography and Discography." In *Sokomoko: Popular Culture in East Africa,* edited by Werner Graebner. Amsterdam and Atlanta, 1991.

———. "Tarabu—populäre Musik am indischen Ozean." In *Populäre Musik in Afrika,* edited by Veit Erlmann. Berlin, 1991.

Mekacha, Rugatiri. "Are Women Devils? The Portrayal of Women in Tanzanian Popular Music." In *Sokomoko: Popular Culture in East Africa,* edited by Werner Graebner. Amsterdam and Atlanta, 1991.

WERNER GRAEBNER

See also **Popular Culture.**

MODERN AND POPULAR MUSIC IN SOUTHERN AFRICA

The popular music of southern Africa reflects the region's integration into the modern world-system during the twentieth century. The evolution of performance genres, the changing social roles of performers, and the place of music making and dance in the cultural practices of rapidly changing societies and communities of southern Africa are all closely linked with the transition from predominantly agrarian, precapitalist social formations to commodity-producing, industrialized, or semi-industrialized modern nation-states. The impact of Western folk, sacred, and popular musical styles has been profound throughout the region, possibly even more so than in other parts of sub-Saharan Africa. Because of South Africa's economic and political dominance in the region, some of this music has in addition been influenced by styles originating from that country's major urban centers. In countries such as Malawi, Zambia, and Mozambique, as well as in parts of Angola, various styles

of Zairian *soukous* have also been a major influence. However, despite these homogenizing factors, the continuity of resilient local indigenous performance practices remains an important distinguishing element of the popular music on the subcontinent.

History

Among the earliest and most consequential agents of modernization and cultural innovation in southern Africa were the Christian missions. Seconded in part by the colonial military, they introduced European instruments and basic Western compositional techniques embodied in the Wesleyan church hymn. In addition to assimilating hymns, around World War I early popular performers such as the South African Reuben T. Caluza (1895–1969) eagerly absorbed what was available to them of the most advanced Western popular music: syncopated rhythms, ragtime, and vaudeville tunes. Labor migrants were responsible for blending these urban idioms with the rural traditions of their respective home areas, thus producing a wealth of local popular genres such as the *famo* dances of Basotho women, *mbube* choral songs of Zulu-speaking men, the *kiba* songs of Pedi migrants, and a rich variety of guitar and concertina styles.

From the 1930s, South Africa also developed its own variant of jazz. Absorbing, often under extremely restricted conditions, the best of American jazz, bands such as the Merry Blackbirds and the vocal quartet Manhattan Brothers blended swing with a local hymn-based style known as *marabi.* The influence of *marabi* is largely responsible for the strong local flavor in South African jazz, most clearly represented today in the music of pianist Abdullah Ibrahim (b. 1934). During the 1960s, fleeing ever more restrictive legislation and racial oppression, the most talented of these performers went into exile in Europe and the United States, where some—trumpeter Hugh Masekela (b. 1939) and singer Miriam Makeba (b. 1932), for example—embarked on major international careers. An offshoot of the swing era, albeit in combination with elements of rock and roll, is the *kwela* music of the 1960s. Performed on tin whistles, *kwela* and its derivatives such as sax-jive influenced musical forms in Zimbabwe (*tsaba-tsaba*), Zambia (*kalindula*), and Malawi (*simanje-manje*).

The predominant style of the 1950s through 1980s was *mbaqanga.* Created from the guitar music of Zulu-speaking migrants, the evolution of this style owes much to the work of pioneers such as

John "Phuzushukela" Bhengu (1930–1985), the all-female group Mahotella Queens, and the Soul Brothers. *Mbaqanga* is also at the root of a number of related styles elsewhere. In Zimbabwe, Oliver Mutukudzi has become popular for his *jit* music, a blend of *mbaqanga* and local Shona traditions, while in Zambia guitarist Alick Nkhata (d. 1978) pioneered *kalindula,* containing strong admixtures of Bemba music.

The 1970s saw the increasing influence of rock, pop, and a number of black styles such as soul. Fusing especially the former with *mbaqanga* and elements of Zulu migrant music, Juluka (later renamed Savuka), led by Johnny Clegg and Sipho Mchunu, emerged as one of the major recording groups of the 1980s. Clegg, who was also a prominent antiapartheid activist and a moving force in the formation of a South African musician's union, provided powerful images through his mixed-race band of a nonracial South Africa that had great appeal both within the country and internationally, particularly in France.

Another major historical turning point was the release in 1986 of *Graceland.* The Grammy Award–winning album by U.S. pop star Paul Simon showcased a wide range of musicians from west Africa and southern Africa, most notably the *mbube* choir Ladysmith Black Mambazo, which in 1987 with the album *Shaka Zulu* became the first southern African group to win a Grammy. Equally influential in focusing international attention on the struggle against apartheid and thereby making South African popular music known to wider audiences were musicals like *Sarafina!* by Mbongeni Ngema (b. 1955).

The renewed international interest in southern African popular music coincided with the demand for "world music," a term describing the growing commercialization beginning in the mid-1980s of traditional native music and its production for Western consumption. Many of the performers, besides those already mentioned, who have contributed to (and benefited from) this new expression of global culture are from southern Africa, especially Zimbabwe and South Africa.

Beginning with the visit by Bob Marley to Zimbabwe's independence celebrations in 1980, reggae became a major factor in the southern African popular music scene. Some of the world's most celebrated reggae performers, such as the South African Lucky Dube, probably the biggest-selling artist in his country, now come from this part of Africa. In the 1990s, other major genres of African American

popular performance such as rap have also caught on in South Africa.

Impact of the State and Mass Media

As elsewhere in Africa, the development of the popular performing arts was for a long time dependent on colonial policies. Certain dance forms considered bellicose or vaguely oppositional by the authorities, such as the *ingoma* dances of migrant workers in South Africa and certain forms of *mbira* music during the early colonial phase in Rhodesia, were banned. Other performance activities regarded as being conducive to the control of the labor force and the maintenance of public order, such as the *kalela* dances in the Zambian Copperbelt, were actively encouraged by the colonial state and mining companies.

The practice continued, in more subtle form, in the more autocratic postcolonial regimes such as that in Mozambique, where the ruling party, Frente de Libertação de Moçambique (FRELIMO), for a long time sought to gain control over the large Chopi *timbila* xylophone orchestras that had formerly been linked with the structures of colonial chieftaincy. In South Africa, apartheid legislation hampered the careers of an entire generation of exceedingly talented performers and effectively crippled the development of a solid institutional framework (music schools, etc.) and a healthy informal network of performance venues (clubs, etc.) open to performers of all races.

Equally obstructive with regard to the development of African popular performance were colonial broadcasting policies. With the exception of South Africa, where rudimentary forms of broadcasting for African audiences in both colonial and native languages started as early as the 1920s, most countries to the north only introduced broadcasting after the Second World War. While in large areas of Angola transistor radios were virtually unknown even until well into the 1960s, African-language programs in most of the British colonies featured a highly selective range of music, usually of rural origin. In South Africa by the 1960s, more than 90 percent of the population had access to a transistor radio, but with the institution of "Radio Bantu" (African-language services of the South African Broadcasting Corporation), until the mid-1970s and in line with the ideology of separate development, airplay was almost exclusively restricted to traditional music of an allegedly pure "ethnic" character.

The deregulation and democratization (and simultaneously the commercialization) of the media in the 1990s is moving apace in countries like South Africa and Zambia, thus opening the local markets up to an even greater influence of the international (i.e., U.S. and European) music industries.

Commercial recording on the subcontinent began in 1908 in South Africa and expanded with the opening of the first vinyl-record pressing plant in Johannesburg in 1932. It is during these years that Gallo (now a subsidiary of the media giant CNA) established itself as the leading record company in the region. Gallo, together with a number of labels owned by the major international companies (such as EMI and BMG) now controls virtually the entire southern African market. Besides the Gallo affiliate Teal, smaller companies operate in Zimbabwe (Gramma Records) and Zambia. A few isolated attempts at creating independent labels in South Africa (Shifty Records) during the 1980s were unsuccessful. In South Africa numerous state-of-the-art recording studios exist, but outside South Africa comparable facilities are few and far between: Zimbabwe is home to Shed Studios, while Zambia boasts a studio owned by the Teal company, DB Studios, and the independently owned Zambian Music Parlour, which characteristically operates in conjunction with a hairdressing salon. In countries with a once flourishing music industry of their own, such as Mozambique, national radio stations also provide studio space, but shortages of vinyl and locally manufactured affordable audio equipment have brought record production to a standstill.

Despite the considerable international acclaim southern African performers have gained, the situation of the vast majority currently remains precarious in their respective home countries. A combination of factors, among them the lack of a functioning infrastructure controlled by the musicians (studios, marketing networks, etc.), the ongoing dependence on South Africa for studio space and recording technology, massive bootlegging, and a general disregard by the state for popular musicians, has severely impeded the growth of truly democratic and viable local music industries. Thus in Zimbabwe, high import duties on musical instruments and unsupportive authorities have made it difficult for musicians, despite their role as cultural innovators, to survive as professional performers. The civil war in Mozambique from the mid-1970s to the early 1990s and a declining economy in Zambia in the 1980s have had an even more disastrous impact on the popular music scene.

Social Context of Popular Music

As a result of southern Africa's rapid economic growth, urbanization, and industrialization, the social occasions for popular performance reflect growing class and group differentiations and the constant readjustments of social identity, meaning, and values within the evolving modern societies. At the same time, some of these social contexts remain rooted—in modified form—in older forms of social interaction, many of them connected with the exercise of chiefly power and indigenous religious traditions. Thus in Zimbabwe, the *chimurenga* music of Thomas Mapfumo (b. 1945) has been influential in expressing the nationalist aspirations of the liberation movement, and because of its anchorage in the *mbira* music of the Shona ancestral spirit-possession cult it has been a significant factor in the selective reworking of precolonial traditions and in the revival of traditional performance practices.

Likewise in South Africa, popular performers played a crucial role in the antiapartheid struggle, either by directly confronting the minority regime in outspoken lyrics or, much more frequently, by providing images of black power and identity. Numerous performers openly declared their allegiance to the African National Congress and other antiapartheid organizations. Others, such as Ladysmith Black Mambazo, while never directly attacking the system, furthered African mass resistance by providing social commentary and by highlighting the resilience and indefatigability of black popular expression. At the same time, such broadly antihegemonic functions of popular music do not exclude a concern with gender issues and more narrow topics such as the assertion of local and ethnic identities.

BIBLIOGRAPHY

Ballantine, Christopher. *Marabi Nights: Early South African Jazz and Vaudeville.* Johannesburg, 1993.

Coplan, David. *In Township Tonight! South Africa's Black City Music and Theatre.* London and New York, 1985.

Erlmann, Veit. *African Stars: Studies in Black South African Performance.* Chicago, 1991.

———. *Nightsong: Performance, Power, and Practice in South Africa.* Chicago, 1996.

Graham, Ronnie. *The Da Capo Guide to Contemporary African Music.* New York, 1988.

Hamm, Charles. "'The Constant Companion of Man': Separate Development, Radio Bantu, and Music." *Popular Music* 10 (1991): 147–174.

Kubik, Gerhard. "Donald Kachamba's Montage Recordings: Aspects of Urban Music History in Malawi." *African Urban Studies* 6 (1979–1980): 89–122.

———. "The Southern African Periphery: Banjo Traditions in Zambia and Malawi." *World of Music* 31 (1989): 3–30.

———. "Muxima Ngola—Veränderungen und Strömungen in den Musikkulturen Angolas in 20 Jahrhundert." In *Populäre Musik in Afrika,* edited by Veit Erlmann. Berlin, 1991.

Vail, Leroy, and Landeg White. *Power and the Praise Poem: Southern African Voices in History.* Charlottesville, Va., 1991.

VEIT ERLMANN

See also **Popular Culture.**

ISLAMIC MUSIC

Islam presumably brought its musical practices to sub-Saharan Africa, along with other aspects of Muslim culture, in the early Middle Ages, but there is little evidence for this process other than references to musical instruments in medieval chronicles. Today, however, there is evidence for both specifically Islam musical forms and music influenced by them in a broad belt stretching from Senegambia to Malawi. The spheres of Islamic influence are usually divided into the west African, deriving from the trans-Saharan trade, and the east African, which evolved from contacts with the Indian Ocean. Northern Ethiopia has Muslim populations whose distinctive musical culture has evolved from contact with the Islamic peoples along the shores of the Red Sea.

West Africa

In west-central Africa there are Arabic-speaking peoples—for example, in Mali and Chad—who maintain a culture of purely vocal music. The unaccompanied chanting of genealogies and Islamic verses is not categorized as music. By contrast, in Mauritania, the Hassaniya people, described by Michel Guignard, have developed a highly elaborated musical culture based on the vertical harp, the lute, and a modal system resembling those found in North Africa. However, the richness of North African Islam finds its most complete expression in the courts of the west African savanna. Natural trumpet ensembles, the *algaita* shawm, some types of vertical flute, the *goge* (a one-stringed horsehair viol), and horse- or camel-mounted drums have been absorbed into the state music of the Hausa, Kanuri, and Kanembu peoples of Nigeria, Niger, and Chad. Islamic influences are also evident at other levels of society, most notably in the ecstatic trance music, *bori,* accompanied by the *goge,* that is widespread in the savanna region. Other traditions, such as the performance of folk epics by blind beggars narrating non-Qur'anic Islamic traditions, survive among the Hausa and Kanuri. Specific North African Islamic musical types and styles of vocal production have been largely replaced by locally evolved musical forms. In addition, some sub-Saharan Islamic musical forms were carried back to North Africa—for example, the performances of the *gnawa* musicians in Morocco. In Sudan, the rather more austere vocal styles of the *madih* and *qasida* solo songs and the *dikr* collective trance music reflect the influence of Sufism and the foundation of Islamic brotherhoods. The instruments used, especially the frame drums (*tar*) and the tambourine (*riqq*), have not spread to other regions of sub-Saharan Africa.

East Africa

Islamic culture is spread along the coast from Egypt to northern Mozambique, and inland as far as Zaire, encompassing enclaves in northern Madagascar. The Beja, Rashaida, and other camel nomads of the Horn of Africa accompany their lyrical songs with the lyre. Somali music is largely vocal, although the '*ud* (lute) and other instruments are played in towns. The Swahili culture represents a merging of local traditions and the Arabian and possibly Persian cultures brought by the maritime trade. Swahili music is the best-known and draws mostly from classical Persian and Arabian traditions. Instruments adapted from Islam include the shawm, the Swahili *nzomari,* the *mugole* fiddle of Mozambique, the '*ud,* and the *qanun* psaltery. Some of these, notably the shawm and fiddle, have spread inland to non-Islamic peoples as a result of the caravan trade. The popular Swahili music, *tarabu,* is accompanied by a large ensemble incorporating both classical and European instruments. Although it is intended to use Arab vocal styles and modes, recent observers have noted the tendency for these to be displaced by elements from Indian film music. Among the Swahili in northeast Kenya, more popular Islamic traditions, such as the sword dance (*hanzua*), also survive.

BIBLIOGRAPHY

Blench, Roger M. "The Morphology and Distribution of Sub-Saharan Musical Instruments of North-African, Middle Eastern and Asian Origin." *Musica Asiatica* 4 (1984): 155–191.

Guignard, Michel. *Musique, honneur et plaisir au Sahara.* Paris, 1975.

Kubik, Gerhard. *Ostafrika.* Musikgeschichte in Bildern. Leipzig, 1982.

Simon, Artur. *Dikr und Madih.* Museum für Völkerkunde Collection. Berlin, 1980.

R. M. BLENCH

See also **Islam.**

WEST AFRICAN SAVANNA

None of the languages spoken in the west African savanna employs a word which is equivalent to the European term "music." Instead, the terminology of music adopts words such as "playing," "performance," "dance," "song," "speech," or "beating an instrument." The perception of music is related to this semantic framework and combines language, physical motion, and musical activity with situations of high social significance. It is the effect of the music on the musician and audience, and eventually on the spirits and ancestors, which is of utmost importance. The creation of effects is not just a matter of the musical texture but also of the cultural context in which the music is performed: both are experienced as a unit and one would lose its meaning without the other.

Historical and Social Dimensions

In many societies of the savanna theoretical concepts about musical activities are expressed through historical accounts depicting the origin of music or an instrument. Apart from historical information, these stories help to decipher the cultural significance of music in the respective societies. Most Muslim musicians of the savanna, for example, will state that their musical ancestor was a follower of the prophet Muhammad, for whom the ancestor played. Due to the ambivalent relationship between musicians and the surrounding Islamic environment, this type of story is a way to legitimize and give standing to their profession. Music in non-Islamic societies is very often given religious meaning by linking the natural and the supernatural worlds. In their historical accounts the creation of music was either brought about directly by spirits or by people who were taught in dreams through spirits.

Since early times the savanna has been one of the largest migration areas in the world. Mainly due to the contraction and expansion of the Sahara Desert, people either moved over great distances looking for better ecological and economic conditions, or they confined themselves to certain areas which they had to defend against others. There is no doubt that the musical characteristic of the area is very much a product of these processes. As a result of these almost continual changes one observes nowadays a great diversity of languages and ethnic groups in the savanna. However, despite the heterogenity, some social, political, and religious factors seem to be related to certain musical behaviors. Three of these factors can be highlighted by the following statements:

- The music is dependent on the political situation; a kingdom, for example, requires different kinds of music than a nonhierarchical society.
- Music and its concepts are strongly related to the religious environment.
- Music is a mirror of the history of the area. The dynamic of musical change must be understood with the past in mind.

The kingdoms of the central Sudan were of great importance during precolonial and colonial history and are still in present times. In modern postcolonial nations titleholders are limited to fulfilling mainly representative roles. Nevertheless, they are the ones who keep the society together by creating identity in a rapidly changing world. The Ottoman Empire, as one of the superpowers over the last centuries, had great cultural influence on the whole area. This is seen clearly in the court-music instruments and ensembles; for instance in the combination of oboes, long trumpets, and barrel-shaped drums which is the standard ensemble in almost every court. Besides this example, one will often find other court ensembles which refer to various historical periods or local traditions. The court of the Shehu (king) of Bornu consists of at least four different musical ensembles: the standard ensemble, called *ganga kura,* with oboe (*al-gaita*), long trumpet (*gashi*) and barrel-shaped drum (*ganga kura*); a kettledrum ensemble, called *mara,* which can be seen as a remnant of the former dynasty; an ensemble of three large conical drums, called *tembal,* which reflects the influence of the Shuwa Arabs; and an ensemble which consists of an African version of a European snare drum (*terembel*) and a British-manufactured signal trumpet (*buruji*).

Most of the Islamic societies in the savanna show a clear ambivalence with regard to any kind of musical activity. Although the interpretations of the Qur'an concerning music are manifold, musicians live on the fringe of the society. Often they are seen and spoken of as beggars. This goes along

with strict marriage limitations allowing only endogamous marriages within the families of musicians. In their self-image, musicians see themselves
and each other as craftspeople following their trade
in accordance with certain codes and occasions. In
Northern Nigeria one of these regulations demands that all performances start first with praise
of Salala, an ancestor who played for the prophet
Muhammad, followed by praise of the musician's
teacher. Despite the musicians' castelike outsider
status, customers employ them for entertainment
during important Islamic festivities like 'Id al-Fitr
or 'Id al-Kabir, or for family occasions such as circumcisions and marriages. Next to the enjoyment
of dancing, the main entertainment stems from the
song texts and the praises that good musicians
are able to coin in the most appropriate ways. In
exchange for the social enhancement of the person
praised, the musicians expect payment. The dis-
crepancy between the expected and the received
sum often causes stress between the participants.
Many musicians adopt the strategy of continuing
the praise until the right amount of money is obtained. It might be this persistence which gives
them the reputation of beggars.

In some savanna societies musicians are under
the patronage of other professions, such as butch-
ers, blacksmiths, or hunters. In these cases one will
find an extensive repertoire of songs praising and
commenting on the profession. The following example, sung by Kanuri hunter-musician Makinta
Kolo, shows how he is able to depict the giraffe
while praising the other hunters and describing
the animal's relevance for the villagers.

1. *Oh, the trekking trader*
2. *The wandering trader of salt and potash* (the giraffe
   moves very long distances)
3. *Like Aisa from Mafiwo Fiyomi* (in the Fada area,
   Aisa is a praise name for the giraffe).
4. *If she is your mother you are lucky.*
5. *If she is your wife you are in a worry* (the giraffe
   is fearful and troublesome; lines 4 and 5 depict
   both sides of giraffe).
6. *So it is said that in the thick forest there cannot be
   a market.*
7. *Aisa my mother has made a road in the thick forest*
   (the killed giraffe has as much meat as a market,
   and the many people who go back and forth
   to carry the meat home trample a new road
   through the forest).
8. *When Aisa kills twelve* (hunters)
9. *She makes twelve* (other hunters) *climb trees.*

10. *The dog of Suluwe Bundimi* (a dead hunter)
11. *The dog of Audu Dogo Mbanji* (a certain dead
    Fulani)
12. *The man Malem Karumi*
13. *Of Mai Ciroma Cimba* (dead)
14. *Of Babburu.*
15. *My foolish mother is presented with the Gambara
    cloth* (a costly and nicely spotted dress).
16. *When I went to* (Lake) *Sambisa*
17. *When I went to* (Lake) *Abba Kuddum, there wasn't
    Aisa, Aisa was not there.*
18. *I went to* (Lake) *Gagaran*
19. *I went to* (Lake) *Dawu Kalimo.*
20. *The foolish trekking trader*
21. *The trader in salt and potash*
22. *The dog of the man Geschiri Fulata.*
(Recorded by the author, November 18, 1994)

Generally speaking, musical activity in the savanna follows either the annual cycle of planting
and harvesting, dry season and rainy season, or the
life cycle of birth, initiation, marriage, and death. It
can be said that non-Islamic societies especially
tend to focus strongly on the annual cycle. Often
life cycle and annual cycle are combined or fitted
into each other like cogwheels and structure the
yearly round. The type of music performed during
these occasions varies immensely among different
groups. Among those instruments which are used
frequently are drums, xylophones, and flute ensembles. In the course of the ritual activities the
differentiation between musicians and audience
becomes more and more inadequate, since every-
body is participating either in singing, clapping,
dancing, or generally supporting the whole occasion.

The same musical activity may take on a completely different meaning if the performance situation changes. For instance, the *tsinza* (xylophone)
music of the Bura in northeast Nigeria was traditionally, and for a small part of the society still is,
the key instrument during the extended funeral
rituals. The instrument and its player were highly
respected, as they helped the deceased to pass
safely over into the world of the ancestors. In the
seventeenth century, however, one section of the
Bura society came under the influence of the Islamic Bornu empire; for them the xylophone lost
its dominant position and became an instrument
which accompanies praise singers, who themselves
hold a rather ambivalent position in the society.
At the beginning of the twentieth century, due to
the presence of American Christian missionaries,

a large section of the Bura society became Christian and began to use the *tsinza* to accompany church songs. In all three examples the instrument as such has not changed in construction or tuning, and even the musical structure of the different compositions is not substantially different; nevertheless the meaning and status of the instrument could not be more diverse.

Musical Fundamentals

Most characteristic of the music of the savannah is the pattern structure within all compositions. These are relatively stable and well defined by the use of basic musical formulas or patterns which can be either a melodic, rhythmic, or speech phrase in frequent repetition. The duration of such patterns is measured by the shortest time unit or pulse. Usually, the rhythmic patterns last twelve or sixteen pulses, although longer phrases may be used where there is a strong influence from the Ottoman culture. An example of this is a phrase with 133 units played by the *ganga kura* drum during the opening composition (*mustre*) performed at the Shehu of Bornu's court.

Depending on the type of ensemble, compositions are usually built so that patterns with different lengths and metrical structures can be combined with each other. For example, a pattern with a duration of twelve units can be structured by the different instruments of a drum ensemble: one instrument plays a pattern with three units four times, another a pattern with four units three times, and a third a pattern with six units two times. As a result most of the compositions appear as a time web which repeats the pattern combination over and over again. The repetition is understood by the musicians and the audience as an increase in musical intensity due to the complex structure of the composition.

Most ensembles in the savanna consist of a couple of rhythm instruments, such as drums or rattles, which form the foundation on which solo instruments or singers create their own musical part. Depending on the situation, compositions might be either completely determined, as is often the case in rituals, or performed in a way that gives the soloist space for improvisation. Improvisation should be understood as a creative selection and successive combination of different patterns taken out of a larger standard repertoire. It is important for the musician that the meaning of the performance be understood by the audience; therefore, improvisations are usually far from being "free."

The better the musician the better his or her sensitivity is for the right phrase at the right moment. Differences between sung and spoken tones cannot be avoided. In the traditional praise-singing context, these differences rarely affect the understanding of the texts since the singers use mostly proverbial phrases that are understood despite tone variations.

The success of a performance partly depends on the soloist's ability to "speak" with his or her instrument. The foundation for the music is very much based on its semantic qualities. This is due to the tonal structure of the languages spoken in the area (with the exception of Arabic) having speech tones that determine the meaning of a word, so that speech itself is melodic. With the use of a musical instrument to copy the melodic qualities of a spoken phrase, the musician is able to convey messages to the audience. This is not to be taken as a static code system; it is rather a creative process which draws musicians and audiences together. Other factors, such as copying speech rhythms and the frequent use of proverbs or well-known praise phrases already established in the language, help to support the interaction.

The repertoire of played and spoken sentences needs to be shared by the musicians and the audience equally or an important part of the musical meaning is missed by one or the other. Every musical instrument that produces distinct tones can be used to speak: flutes, xylophones, many drums, harps, lutes. In the case of sung phrases the singer must combine two principles: he or she has to follow the tonal structure of the word, and he or she has to shape the melody in a pleasant and generally descendant manner. Differences between sung and spoken tones cannot be avoided, yet they do not disturb due to the general character of the song text. The musical repertoire of the artists is structured in well-defined compositions fulfilling the expectations of the audience and the occasion. Nevertheless, the musician tries to create a personal style which makes him or her special for the audience. In this respect the concept of composition as understood in European classical music needs adjusting to account for convention, improvisation, and interpretation.

During a musical performance the aspect of motion is fundamental. The rhythmic or melodic patterns are actually based on movement patterns which are related to dance as well. Besides its time dimension, savannah music gains a spatial quality through motion. Seen in this way, rhythms and melodies are not just structured time but also structured space. Often the movement determines the musical performance rather than the musical idea the movement. This perspective helps to explain the patterns not so much as repetitions in time but as circles in space. Musical elements with regard to the time dimension, like the beginning and end of a pattern or a composition, may be determined as much by the audience as by the musicians.

The tuning of musical instruments in the savanna is very much defined by the conventions of musicians and instrument makers. In many societies the tolerated margins for frequently variations are rather large. Pentatonic scales are dominant. It is futile to relate them to any occidental tonal system, as the musicians would not refer to the tuning in terms of seconds and thirds. The scale tones are often described as relationships to family members, as, for instance, among the Bura of northeast Nigeria, where the octave relationship between two xylophone tones is expressed as a relationship between father and son. In the savanna areas of Ghana and Côte d'Ivoire two or three remarkably different tonal systems exist within the same society, each of them related to certain occasions or rituals. In the more southern areas musicians sometimes adopt heptatonic scales which clearly point toward a coastal influence. Polyphony is a fairly rare phenomenon in the savanna. It may occur in antiphonal songs when a solo singer and choir overlap their phrases. In instrumental music heterophonic elements can be observed when two instrumentalists simultaneously play variations of the same melodic pattern.

Musical Instruments

The diversity of musical instruments in the savanna can be overwhelming. Furthermore, any attempt to structure them into an overall classification system meaningful to the individual instrument maker and player is bound to fail. Even slight alterations in terms of decoration or usage can completely change the instrument's importance and significance. Morphologically identical instruments might be for one event regarded as a toy and for another as a priestly device. A sort of grouping can be derived from the terminology used to describe the player's action. Many languages in the savanna differentiate between instruments that are struck, such as drums, lutes, harps, zithers, and plucked idiophones; instruments that are blown, such as flutes, trumpets, pipes, and

oboes; and instruments that are shaken or indirectly struck, such as gourd rattles and stick rattles.

Five main drum types can be distinguished in the savanna. The barrel-shaped double membrane drum can frequently be found in various sizes to accompany a solo instrument or a singer. In the Kanuri court orchestras a large version of this drum, the *ganga kura,* is identical with the Turkish *davul,* having an attached snare string and played in the same fashion with one thick drumstick and a thin flexible rod. The tall and narrow single membrane drum is widespread in many societies that belong to the Chadic language group and where Islam has very little footing. In shape, size, and playing position the instrument resembles the human body, and this is often expressed as well in the terminology depicting the different parts of the instrument. The double membrane hourglass drum with tension chords is usually played with a curved stick and held under the armpit; by pressing the chords with the arm, the musicians are able to produce within a fairly large tonal range every possible pitch. Furthermore, the drum has very effective sound qualities, making it suitable for all kinds of praising. One can assume, due to the importance of the instrument in the south, that the hourglass drum migrated north from southern areas. The double membrane conical drum is suspended from forked stakes and struck with two sticks. Mounted on camels, these instruments are often part of the court orchestras in the central Sudan and are dominant in areas with a large Shuwa-Arab population. A final type of drums cannot be described purely through morphological criteria. The instruments need to be classified in musical terms as accompanying, timekeeping drums. They are usually high-pitched and small, repeating short rhythmical patterns. The instruments can be shaped like an hourglass drum, kettledrum, or cylindrical drum.

Rattles are also frequently used for rhythmic accompaniment. They are constructed out of various materials, including calabashes, tins, and fruit shells and are designed either as containers or as stick rattles.

The large number of various lute instruments played in the savanna can be divided into two basic groups: spike lutes with a bowl-shaped resonator and inner-spike lutes. The first type points toward a strong Islamic influence. These instruments are related to a *rabab* type which is similar in its construction throughout the Islamic world. The second type is related to a North African tradition which goes back to an Egyptian inner-spike lute which is found on the wall paintings of pharaonic graves. Both lute types are played by praise singers who may or may not be accompanied by a supporting rhythm ensemble. The number of strings may vary, as may the length of the neck or the size of the calabash resonator.

In areas with little Islamic influence musical instruments such as xylophones or harps are of greater importance, although they tend to be distributed in small dispersed pockets which are not necessarily linked. Most xylophones are constructed as frame xylophones where the keys are positioned over resonators which amplify and alter the sound. To produce these sounds small vibrating membranes are attached to the resonators; a buzzing sound is created which hardly relates to the struck wooden keys. The size of the resonators, normally calabashes or cow horns, are always related to the key frequency; low frequencies demand a larger resonating volume than high ones. Usually, the keys are mounted in ascending order. Yet among the Bura of Northern Nigeria the keys are organized in a cycle: the two highest keys are not put to either side of the frame but in the middle next to their respective lower octave key. The circular form characteristic of the Bura's compositions is reflected in the construction of the instrument.

The westernmost examples of harp instruments, which are very much an east African tradition, can be found in the savanna of Northern Nigeria. The instruments are constructed with a bowed string carrier attached to the wooden resonator and covered with an animal hide. Unlike lutes, which are not designed to take a high string tension, the harps are nowadays fitted out with metal strings, making them sound over great distances.

Other instruments of a more personal character are in use as well. The most frequent one is the mouth bow, an instrument consisting of one string which is attached to a bowed piece of wood. The string is plucked or beaten, and through movements of the oral cavity a number of different partial tones can be evoked and used as compositional material. The songs accompanied by the mouth bow are very often self-reflective, usually describing the problems of life.

One of the few instruments traditionally played by female musicians is the calabash tube *jantu*, which is slapped against the player's calf and clapped with the fingers. The instrument is used to accompany marriage songs. The rhythms produced support the song structure and fill the end

of the phrase to avoid pauses, giving the singer time to mentally prepare new text phrases.

Two different flute traditions exist in the area side by side. The tradition of end-blown flutes with four finger holes, made out of corn stalks or tubes, is the more widespread, and seems to be of a more recent origin. In remote areas end-blown flutes with one or two finger holes, mostly made out of animal horns, are still in use. The main difference between the two instruments is the way they are played as ensemble instruments. The more recent type is either played by a soloist for personal enjoyment or by up to three flutists accompanied by a drum ensemble to provide dance music. The older type is played by all the men in a community simultaneously. They create a complex multivoiced composition through the interlocking of various two- or three-note patterns produced by each of the participants.

Throughout the whole area side-blown animal horns are played as speaking instruments, transmitting messages with text-related codes or signals. Usually, these instruments have a ceremonial function during rituals. There is also a wide range of sound-producing devices which may be of equal musical importance for a society. These are objects used for daily purposes—such as flails, grinding stones, pestels, and hoes—that are handled in a rhythmically structured manner to control, synchronize, and facilitate work such as threshing, pounding, or grinding.

BIBLIOGRAPHY

Ames, David W., and Anthony V. King. *Glossary of Hausa Music and Its Social Contexts*. Evanston, Ill., 1971.
Besmer, Fremont. *Hausa Court Music in Kano, Nigeria.* New York, 1971.
———. *Horses, Musicians and Gods: The Hausa Cult of Possession-Trance.* South Hadley, Mass., 1983.
Chernoff, John Miller. *African Rhythm and African Sensibility: Aesthetic and Social Action in African Musical Idioms.* Chicago, 1979.
DjeDje, Jacqueline Cogdell. *The One-String Fiddle in West Africa: A Comparison of Hausa and Dagomba Traditions.* 2 vols. Los Angeles, 1978.
———. "The Concept of Patronage: An Examination of Hausa and Dagomba One-String Fiddle Traditions." *Journal of African Studies* 9, no. 3 (1982): 116–118.
Erlmann, Veit. *Die Macht des Wortes-Preisgesang und Berufsmusiker bei den Fulbe des Diamarè.* 2 vols. Hohenschäftlarn, Germany, 1982.
———. "Trance and Music in the Hausa "bori" Spirit Possession Cult in Niger." *Ethnomusicology* (January 1982): 49–58.

Gottlieb, Robert. "Musical Scales of the Sudan as Found among the Gumuz, Berta, and Ingessana Peoples." *The World of Music* 28, no. 2 (1986): 56–76.

Gourlay, Ken A. "Long Trumpets in Northern Nigeria: In History and Today." *African Music* 6, no. 2 (1982): 48–72.

Kubik, Gerhard. "Pattern Perception and Recognition in African Music." In *The Performing Arts: Music and Dance,* edited by John Blacking and Joann W. Kealiinohomoku. The Hague, 1979.

———. "Einige Grundbegriffe und Konzepte der afrikanischen Musikforschung." *Jahrbuch für musikalische Volks- und Völkerkunde* 11 (1984): 57–102.

Kubik, Gerhhard, et al. *Westafrika.* Leipzig, 1989.

Mensah, Atta Annan. "Gyil: The Dagara-Lobi Xylophone." *Journal of African Studies* 9, no. 3 (1982): 155–163.

Simon, Artur, ed. *Musik in Afrika: 20 Beiträgen zur Kenntnis traditioneller afrikanischer Musikkulturen.* Berlin, 1983.

RAIMUND VOGELS

ETHIOPIA

Within the boundaries of present-day Ethiopia, the linguistic, cultural, and ethnic mix is extremely diverse. The same is true regarding music. Special attention has always been given to Ethiopian church music and the main ethnic groups, such as the Amhara, Tigre, Oromo, and Somali, whereas little or nothing has been published about the musical practice of the numerous smaller groups.

Music and Musical Instruments of the Ethiopian Orthodox Church

The Ethiopian church belongs to the Monophysite branch of Christianity. Roughly five decades after the Council of Chalcedon (451), which marked the break in Christian unity, the so-called Nine Saints, monks from Syria, introduced Monophysite beliefs into the kingdom of Aksum. The Ethiopian church retained its very elaborate liturgical practices through the centuries. In 1959 an autonomous Ethiopian patriarchate, independent from the Coptic church in Egypt, was established. The liturgy uses the ancient Sabean language Ge'ez. With exception of the Scriptures, which are read, the entire liturgy is chanted. According to the national tradition, Saint Yared, who lived during the reign of Gabre-Askal (550–570), claimed that he invented the chants, although it seems likely that they are rooted in a much older Judaic tradition. Religious studies are codified under *zema* (religious chant), *qene* (religious poetry), and *tergum* (interpretation). During the eighteenth century the city of Gonder became an important center for the teaching of religious dancing (*aquaquam*). The chants are written in six books: *qeddase,* comparable to the Latin missal; *zemmare,* a collection of eucharistic canticles; *deggwa* (hymns for the whole church year except those for Lent); *somma deggwa,* the Lenten hymns up to Palm Sunday; *mawase'et,* a special collection of hymns; and *me'eraf,* the common of the office.

The *dabtara,* church musicians and assistants to the priest, perform the chants in three musical genres—*ge'ez, 'ezl,* and *araray*—which should not be mistaken for modes, although they differ in their tonal structure as well as in their range. These genres are related to *serayu,* a large number of orally transmitted melodic formulas that constitute the basis of the compositions. Since the sixteenth century a notation system with marginal (*bet*) and interlinear (*meleket*) signs, which are a combination of interpretation marks and mnemonics, has been in use. The choir of the *dabtara* is usually divided in two parts that sing either simultaneously (*zahebrat*) or alternatively (*meltan*). The singers accompany themselves on three instruments: *magwamiya,* a prayer stick waved in the air and stamped on the ground; *kabaro,* a cylindrical or conical kettledrum, usually played by hand; and *sanasel,* a sistrum that consists of a wooden handle surmounted by a U-shaped silver frame pierced by two or three wires running from side to side, each wire with three small metal disks threaded on it.

Secular Music and Musical Instruments

The general occasions of singing and music making in Ethiopian society differ little from anywhere else in Africa. Music is rooted in daily life and is never seen as an isolated art. Due to the diversity of Ethiopia's ethnic makeup, an overall description of the musical features must remain unsatisfactory. Yet it can be stated that vocal music somehow prevails over instrumental music. The classical verses *qene* are composed and performed in Ge'ez for the praise of holy and secular leaders. Amharic is used for modern praise singing, which is performed by the itinerant *azmari.* The *azmari* accompany their songs on the *masenqo,* a bowed single-stringed spike lute with a tuning peg, and a parchment-covered, diamond-shaped box resonator related to the Arabian *rabab.* Two lyres are especially important for the Ethiopian tradition: a large box lyre, *beganna,* with eight to ten strings, and the smaller bowl lyre, *krar,* with six strings. The instruments resemble the ancient Greek *kithara* and *lyra.* The *beganna* is regarded as the instrument of the Ethiopian aristocracy, who use it to accompany religious songs and hymns in nonliturgical situations. Striking features of the *beganna* are the deep tuning of the strings, normally an octave below the voice, and the vibrating of the strings against the soundboard, which gives the instrument a characteristic buzzing sound. The *krar* is used for secular purposes, such as the accompaniment of ballads and love songs. Unlike the *beganna*, the *krar* may be played by women.

BIBLIOGRAPHY

Hannick, Christian. "Ethiopian Rite, Music of the." In *The New Grove Dictionary of Music and Musicians,* edited by Stanley Sadie. Vol. 6. London, 1980.

Lah, Ronald. "Ethiopia." In *The New Grove Dictionary of Music and Musicians,* edited by Stanley Sadie. Vol. 6. London, 1980.

Mondon-Vidailhet, C. "La musique éthiopienne." In *Encyclopédie de la musique et dictionnaire du Conservatoire.* Vol. 1, pt. 3. Paris, 1922.

Powne, Michael. *Ethiopian Music, an Introduction: A Survey of Ecclesiastical and Secular Ethiopian Music and Instruments.* London, 1966.

RAIMUND VOGELS

See also **Aksum; Ethiopian Orthodox Church; Literature; Musical Instruments.**

MUSICAL INSTRUMENTS. African traditional instruments are designed and built to express African ideas and musical values. Although many of these instruments belong to the same families as other world instruments, and in some cases share common origins, their construction and use are linked with specific African conditions—the musical principles of the continent and its ecology, history, and social organization.

Some of the values reflected in African music are the importance of human relationships, cooperation, independence, and rhythmic contrast between parts. African instruments have developed to express these values, and as a result have diverged significantly from the instruments of other parts of the world.

Tone Quality

In most African instrumental ensembles, it is important that every instrument be distinctly audible, keeping is own independent part. The concept of "blend" is largely subservient to that of "contrast." Given the structural principles of African music, where meaning depends to a great extent on the conflict of rhythms and meters, and on the interplay between musicians and between instruments, African musicians are strongly aware of tone quality and subtle differences in tone. Instruments are thus both carefully chosen and tuned so that each has its own recognizable "voice." This applies in mixed ensembles such as those including drums, rattles, and bells, and in groups of similar instruments like xylophones, mbiras, panpipes, horns, or steel drums; musicians try to fill up the whole sound spectrum. For example, drums are tuned to different pitches with heat, water, wax, or their own tensioning systems; idiophones of different types are chosen for their contrast; individual musicians blow or sound different pitches. The principle is also evident in vocal music in many parts of Africa, where each singer's voice is distinct from his or her neighbor's, and voice tone is open and "characterful" rather than sweet and blending.

In music which depends on rhythmic relationships, it is the exact moment of entry that is important, so most African instruments give a sharp, distinct onset of sound. Likewise, duration is largely of little importance, so even if capable of it, few instruments hold on long notes.

A widespread method of adding contrast and "bite" to instruments in Africa is to add buzzing devices. These vibrate sympathetically with the instrument, or with its individual notes. They can also act to amplify, prolong, or help carry the sound of an instrument, for instance in the open air or in noisy surroundings. Another effect is to selectively emphasize, either methodically or arbitrarily, certain notes or sounds, which can encourage the perception of inherent patterns. Buzz tone is an integral part of the tone quality of many African instruments, although generally considered irritating by Western musicians. It is found not only in Africa but also in some Indian and Chinese instruments, in the Guatemalan marimba, a xylophone of African ancestry, and in certain Western instruments of the Middle Ages, such as the flute and the tromba marina.

Buzzers are made of diverse materials, including loosely attached metal rings, bells, snail shells and other seashells, beads, seeds, lizard skin, string, grass, and bottle tops. Perhaps the most typical African buzz-tone is achieved with membranes known as mirlitons, found on most resonated xylophones, on some instruments of the mbira family, and on some drums. Wherever air moves as a result of the vibration of the body of an instrument, a mirliton can be used. On a resonated xylophone such as the *valimba* of the Sena of Malawi, a hole

239

on the side of each resonator gourd is fitted with a fine membrane affixed with wax. The membrane is tensioned to respond to the pitch of the wooden key and its equally tuned resonator. A mbira soundboard such as that of the *kankobela* of the Tonga of Zambia has a central hole, with the membrane on the underside. When the mbira is played over its resonating gourd, the air movement in the gourd, induced by the vibrating soundboard, operates the membrane. On a drum, which must have an enclosed airspace, such as the *ditumba da ndanya* of the Luba of Zaire, a membrane is pushed, using a piece of cylindrical calabash neck, into a hole below the pegs, until it is held in place by the calabash neck's tight fit into the hole and then tensioned with a finger. Typical substances for the membrane have included animal tissues such as from cow intestine, jerboa, bat, spider egg sac, cigarette paper, office carbon paper, and plastic bags.

Ecology and History

The distribution of African instruments gives a marbled map, the result of the interplay of the physical environment with social organization and the currents of history. Traditional instruments are largely made by the player, using materials growing or living at hand. Makers have an intimate knowledge of the properties of the local flora and fauna, not only for food, medicine, and other purposes but also for music. The ecology therefore determines to a large extent what instruments can be made. Wood determines the sound quality of many instruments; kiaat (*Pterocarpus angolensis*) and sneezewood (*Ptaeroxylon obliquum*) are commonly chosen in central and southern Africa for their resonance. African music is well suited to the varied sounds of many natural or found objects, from calabashes to pods to bottle tops and tins. The Chopi *timbila* xylophone of southern Mozambique is an ecological masterpiece, being constructed of at least fifteen natural materials, including gourds, beeswax, palm leaf, and rubber.

Two poles of African social organization can be distinguished which have a bearing on musical styles and instruments: the pastoral, centralized, hierarchical, living in grassy plains, where instruments are few and singing predominates, and the agricultural, small-scale egalitarian, where more instruments can be expected. The scale of the society likewise affects the scale of music making. Organized kingdoms, such as those of the Ganda, Yoruba, Zulu, and Asante, could have large and varied instrumental or vocal groups.

The chance contacts of a people's history affect their instrumentarium. Arabic music has made a deep impression on the west African savanna and on the Swahili east coast. The centuries-long association of the Nguni and Sotho peoples of southern Africa with the Khoisan led to their adopting the latter's bows and song and dance styles. The many invaders of Africa all brought their own musical instruments; Western instruments dominated urban music in Africa in the twentieth century.

Classification

Africa has several unique instruments, including those of the mbira family. All African instruments can be classed in the same families as other world instruments, however, revealing their wider connections. While African peoples have their own classification systems, based in most cases on the social uses of the instrument, the universal Sachs-Hornbostel classification considers the part of the instrument that vibrates to create the sound.

Aerophones, or Wind Instruments

Typical African examples of wind instruments are the widespread one-note reed-pipe or horn bands, where each player puts his one note into the total pattern at the right moments; panpipes, where more notes are available to the player; and end-, side-blown, and gourd flutes. Flutes, often associated, as in Hellenic times, with herdsmen, are now rare. Aerophones with vibrating reeds and finger holes, such as the oboe and clarinet, are rare, except in regions subjected to North African or Arabic influence.

Groups consisting of a number of instruments each of which gives only one note demonstrate a particularly African approach toward music making, one which demands a high degree of cooperation. Such groups, which may be formed of reed, bamboo, or metal tubes blown flute-style across the open end, or of animal, calabash, or wooden horns blown trumpet-style through a side mouthpiece near the tip, are widespread in Africa. The musicians often dance intricate step patterns while playing. As they involve the coordination of a large number of performers, they are often associated with important social occasions. The sound itself is not necessarily the only point of the performance; the entire attention of the dancer-musicians is given to the complexity of coordinating their correct note entries, which are different for each player, with the normally irregular dance steps that are shared by all as they move around in a circle. Such a musical group invariably accompanies a circle dance progressing to the right.

The *tshikona* bamboo-pipe dance of the Venda of northern South Africa is a formal men's dance, performed at the behest of royalty at both ritual and secular occasions, such as the installation of a chief or the opening of a store. It is also popular in Johannesburg, where Venda men play *tshikona* as a sign of their ethnic identity. The instruments are tuned heptatonically, and women play three drums in the center of the ring. Only one tune exists for *tshikona*, but there are many dance steps. The *dinaka* dance of the Pedi, neighbors of the Venda in South Africa, is similar in many ways to *tshikona*, but this dance employs reed-pipes tuned pentatonically, and a number of tunes exist for the ensemble.

The *nyanga* bamboo-panpipe dance of the Nyungwe in central Mozambique uses instruments of up to four notes each, and the technique involves both playing and singing. The principle is otherwise the same. This dance is performed on both ritual and secular occasions, especially when called to do so by the government of the day. Numerous named dance steps accompany only one *nyanga* tune. The women's part consists of singing selected inherent patterns arising out of the total sound of the men's pipe and voice parts, of which there may be over thirty, covering a range of three and a half heptatonic octaves.

The *amakondere* horn bands of the former and current kings of the Great Lakes region of east Africa use composite instruments of horn and calabash, which together with drums accompany formal duties of the ruler. Hutu horn bands in Rwanda used to accompany the dancing of the Tutsi. Some of the higher horns give two adjacent notes of the pentatonic scale, by means of a finger hole at the sharp end.

Chordophones, or Stringed Instruments

Africa shares with Europe the tradition of a singer accompanied by a chordophone. The instrument holds an ostinato pattern, often of great virtuosity, while a player sings against it in a musical dialogue. All four basic chordophone types, harp, lyre, zither, and lute, are present in Africa.

The harp has a body with a skin stretched over it for a soundboard, and one neck (or more than one in the "pluriarc" harp of the west-central coast); the strings are attached to the neck and come down into the soundboard, entering it perpendicularly without any intervening bridge. Harps are played in a long arc from the Great Lakes in the east to the savanna of west Africa. Some of them, such as the Ganda *ennanga*, show a remarkable resemblance to ancient Egyptian harps.

The lyre has a body normally covered in skin, two necks, and a yoke connecting the ends of the necks. The strings are attached to the yoke, pass parallel to the body over a bridge, and are fastened to the base of the body. Lyres are played in Ethiopia and neighboring countries of east Africa. The Ganda *endongo* lyre lacks a bridge; the strings buzz against the skin of the body. Both African harps and lyres are plucked, while some lyres, such as the *kibugandet* of the Kipsigis in Kenya, may also be strummed.

The zither has a body with the strings stretched parallel to it from end to end. A large family of zithers, known by names such as *bangwe*, *pango*, *ligombo*, and *nanga*, is found in Tanzania, Malawi, and northern and central Mozambique. They may be plucked or strummed. The strumming technique, as with the strummed lyres, is the same as that surmised for the ancient Egyptian lyre: the stretched fingers of the left hand are held between the strings, damping those strings that are not required at any given moment, while the right hand strums all the strings.

The lute has a skin-covered body with a neck extending from it. The strings are attached to the neck and pass parallel to the body over a bridge, being fastened to the base of the body. They may be plucked or bowed. The strings are stopped with the fingers of the left hand, not in most cases by pressing onto the neck, but simply by touching with the front or back of the fingertip. The plucked west African lutes from the savanna regions are fingered onto the neck; a connection with the American banjo has been proposed. The bowed lutes, such as the *molo* of the west African savanna and the many east African examples, including the Ugandan *endingidi*, are associated with North African or Arab influence.

The *kora* of Guinea and neighboring countries is perhaps the most magnificent of all African chordophones. Strictly a lute, it is usually called a "harp-lute" because of its visual resemblance to a harp, the twenty-one or so strings being stretched in two banks over a double-sided bridge. The body is a large spherical calabash, covered in skin. This is the prime instrument of the *jali* or griot, hereditary professional musicians formerly attached to rulers' courts.

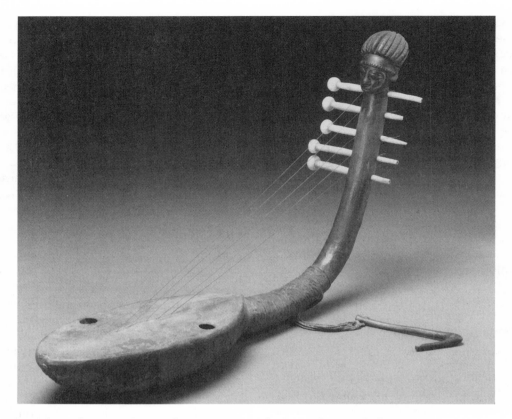

Bow harp by Azande peoples, Zaire. Wood, ivory, skin, and plant material. Height 54.5 cm. MUSEUM OF FINE ARTS, SPRINGFIELD, MASSACHUSETTS

The *zeze* lute of the Swahili coast and inland, now rare, may have had Indonesian connections. Played by itinerant entertainers, it consists of a narrow wooden body with three large built-in frets for the melody string, and one or two strings on the side which serve as drones, fitted with a chicken quill buzzer, and resonated by an attached half gourd.

Bows could technically be subsumed under the above types but are better considered separately. They may be curved or straight, with one string, or occasionally more, stretched from end to end, and may either have a gourd or other resonator attached or be mouth-resonated. They may be struck, plucked, bowed, rubbed—in the case of the southern African *chizambi* friction bow, where the notched bowstick is rubbed with another stick—or even blown, in the case of the *gora* mouthbow of the former Khoi of southern Africa. Unlike the musical bows of the Orient or North America, African bows give at least two fundamentals, either by bracing the string into two segments or by fingering. The harmonic series of each fundamental is

selectively resonated in the gourd or mouth to produce melody.

Membranophones, or Drums

Drums are considered to be the quintessential African instrument and are found almost everywhere, highly developed in west Africa, less so toward the south. There are significant areas, however, where drums were used little if at all, for instance in much of the southern African and other grasslands.

There is an enormous variety of shapes and sizes of drums, falling into two general acoustic types, the closed drum, with one or two membranes, which has a clearer musical pitch but little variety of sound, and the open drum, with one membrane, which is capable of more variety. The shape and materials of every drum body affect its timbre.

A drum plays patterns which are melodic as well as rhythmic; different hand, or stick, strokes give a variety of sounds, which are allotted "drum syllables" in some areas. An average drum group would consist of about three drums of different pitch. The leader, who is allowed more freedom, normally plays the lowest drum. The higher drums play more fixed patterns, and the highest of all often plays repeating "time-line" patterns, coordinating time-keeping devices for the group. These patterns may also be played on other high-pitched idiophones such as a bell, rattle, scraper, clapper, or a stick on the side of a drum.

Most villages have one set of drums for all purposes, but west African villages may possess several distinct drum families, each for a different social or ritual purpose. Drums often become symbols of political or ritual power. In the east African kingdoms, royal drums, some many centuries old, were considered the "crown jewels."

Some well-known examples of drums include the *djembe,* an open, goblet-shaped drum of Guinea and neighboring countries, which has spread worldwide with new-age youth; the hourglass-shaped, double-skinned pressure or "talking" drum, widely used in west Africa; the large, closed, laced, royal four-drum group of the Tutsi *omwami,* or ruler, of Rwanda; the *entenga* royal fifteen-drum chime, tuned to a pentatonic scale, of the Ganda of Uganda; the closed, goblet-shaped buzzing drums of the Luba of southern Zaire; the wax-weighted drums with cutout sides used for the *nyau* masked dance in Malawi; and the large, closed, bowl-shaped *ngoma* drum of Venda chiefs in South Africa.

Idiophones or "Self-Sounding" Instruments

Idiophones are instruments whose body itself, or parts of it, vibrates to produce sound. They include two of Africa's most important families of tuned instruments, those of the mbira or lamellophone (from *lamella,* thin plate) and of the xylophone. Otherwise, this family comprises most other instruments which are not included under the previous classes, such as the huge variety of rattles, bells, scapers, slit drums, and other small instruments which African musicians have a distinct talent for inventing and making.

The Mbira. The mbira family, of which more than two hundred types have been recorded, is widespread from northern South Africa through to Uganda and across to Sierra Leone, although not played everywhere. The name "lamellophone" has been coined to refer to the family, as no adequate Western word exists for it. However, proponents of an African name have suggested "mbira," "sansa," "likembe," and other names. In this article the name "mbira" is used, that of the Shona peoples of Zimbabwe and their neighbors, in whose hands the instrument reaches probably its greatest complexity, backed by five centuries of tradition.

A mbira consists of a wooden soundboard with several narrow metal tongues or keys fixed to it by means of a "backrest" and a "bridge"—which hold the tongue away from the soundboard—and a "bar" between the two, which presses the tongue toward the soundboard. The tongues are free to be plucked at one end by thumbs or fingers, each giving a different note of the local scale. The soundboard may be a single board, a hollow box, a bell shape (hollowed out from the bottom end), sometimes made of a tin can or other metal, in numerous inventive designs according to the region. In parts of the Zambezi area the tongues may be arranged in up to three "manuals"—that is, bent up so the tips form separate rows. The playing ends of the tongues are commonly arranged in a V-shape layout (lowest notes at the center) but may also be made "low-on-left" or in many local variants.

The mbira is mostly an informal solo instrument accompanying the voice, played while walking, at parties, to pass the time, as a paid entertainment, or as a solace for the player. Zimbabwe and the Zambezi valley seem to be the only region where it has a structured religious function, supporting the hypothesis of its great age and possibly even its origin here. It is played at all-night ceremonies during which ancestral spirits possess the bodies of mediums. Some songs for the *mbira dza vadzimu* are associated with Mutota, a historical ruler of the Zimbabwe kingdom in about the fifteenth century.

Examples of mbira types include the *dipela* of the Pedi of northern South Africa, the southernmost of all mbiras, tuned pentatonically in a V-shaped layout. This is one of the two known exceptions in the mbira family which are played not with the thumbs but with the fingers only, for instance with the instrument hanging from the neck and resting against the stomach of the player. The *mbira dza vadzimu* (mbira of the ancestors), of the Shona/ Zezuru of Zimbabwe, is a large instrument of twenty-two keys, V-shaped layout, and heptatonic scale. It is played inside a large calabash for resonance, in order to put mediums in touch with ancestral spirits. This ancient mbira type, with a three-octave range, is not only highly popular within Zimbabwe because of its prominence during the fight for independence but also has a considerable New Age following on the United States and Canadian west coast. Its music is based on complex harmonic sequences. It is normally played in pairs, with each player playing a complementary rhythm.

The *kalimba,* a small mbira with a fan-shaped body equipped with a buzzer mirliton and a minimum of eight keys, V-shaped layout, and hexatonic or heptatonic scale, is played over a small gourd for informal entertainment and walking songs in countries along the Zambezi valley. This instrument, it has been suggested, may be the most ancient form of the mbira in Africa. The *malimba* is a box-bodied mbira with V-shaped layout and pentatonic scale with several central sympathetic keys (keys that are not played but sound on their own when similar pitches are sounded), used in Tanzania by itinerant musician/entertainers.

The *likembe* is a box-bodied mbira with a vibrato hole or holes for the fingers on the reverse side. The keys are often tuned so that to play the descending heptatonic scale one would pluck alternately from left to right down toward the tip of the V-shaped layout. It has the widest distribution of all mbira types. Originating in the area of the Zaire River mouth, it has spread, originally by means of colonial porters who played as they walked, to most parts of central Africa as far as Uganda and Tanzania. The *kadongo,* a box-bodied mbira of the Soga of Uganda, is a variant of the *likembe* that is pentatonic, with a V-shaped layout, played in ensembles of four or more instruments of different sizes and pitch ranges. Smaller instruments are sometimes made of metal.

The *timbrh* is a large box-bodied mbira from southern Cameroon with bamboo keys tuned tetratonically, and a unique buzzing system consisting of a piece of stiff grass resting on top of the key, held in place at one end with wax. Like many other west coast mbiras from here down to Namibia, the keys are tuned with varying weights of black bee propolis attached under their tips. The *agidigbo* of the Yoruba of Nigeria, and other similar types of mbira played along the west African coast, are large box instruments often with no more than three or four keys, used less melodically than rhythmically. It is likely that the mbira reached west Africa relatively late. The *kondi* is one of several pentatonic and hexatonic V-shaped-layout mbiras played informally by individuals in Sierra Leone, the northwest limit of the mbira's distribution. This type has the distinction of being the only one played upside-down as other African players would see it—that is, with the thumbs, the tongues pointing away from the player. Lastly among the mbiras is the *marímbula* of Cuba and other Caribbean countries,

Mbira by Chokwe peoples, Angola. Date and artist unknown. Wood, metal, beeswax. Height 24 cm.
FROM THE CHARLES AND BLANCHE DERBY COLLECTION, NORTHAMPTON, MASSACHUSETTS

whither it was taken from west Africa during the slave trade. The *marímbula* is a large bass instrument with few keys.

The Xylophone. The xylophone is also widely played in Africa, with slightly less distribution than the mbira. It is a more social instrument than the mbira, strongly linked in many places with public events, rulers, dancing, and often with drums.

Some confusion exists between the words "xylophone" and "marimba." The latter is an African word used colloquially, under the influence of the Central and North American usage. They are in fact synonyms. "Marimba," however, is also used in some parts of Africa to refer to instruments of the mbira family.

Xylophones are idiophones consisting of a row of tuned wooden slats mounted on a frame so that they are supported at the correct nodal points. There are two basic types of xylophones in Africa: those with and those without resonators. The two types are not normally found in proximity.

Xylophones with resonators, which are usually gourds or calabashes but may also be horns, a wooden box, or a pit, are played with rubber-tipped beaters at the center of the key. The resonators usually have buzzing membranes on the sides. They may be played alone but more commonly are found in groups. Most resonated xylophones require a single player, but several styles involve the use of up to four players per instrument.

Some well-known resonated xylophones are the *mbila* of the Chopi of southern Mozambique, played in large orchestras of up to twenty or more players, with as many dancer/singers and several rattle players. The *timbila* are made in up to five different pitch ranges and have a compass of over four heptatonic octaves. Each instrument may have up to twenty keys. The *timbila* dance is one of the artistic peaks of African music/dance performance. Its continuity is currently in severe danger due to postwar conditions in Mozambique and the abolition of chiefs, its former patrons.

A west African xylophone, variously called the *balo, bala,* or *balafon,* is most often associated with the Malinke peoples of the Gambia, Guinea, Côte d'Ivoire, and Mali. This is a heptatonic frame xylophone of about eighteen keys, played by griots, either solo or in duo. The players have bells attached to their wrists as they play. Other instruments are pentatonic, such as the *gyil* of northern Ghana. The *valimba* of the Sena of central Mozambique and southern Malawi is a large instrument of about twenty-two keys, played by three or four boys on one side of the same instrument, accompanied by a drum and rattles, during night-time dances.

Xylophones without resonators are referred to as "log" xylophones because of their large, simple keys, often little more than tuned logs resting on two banana trunks or on a simple wooden frame. The large keys are loud enough not to need resonators. They are struck on the ends with plain sticks by two or more players sitting opposite each other, playing interlocking rhythmic parts. Most log xylophones are pentatonic.

The twelve-key *amadinda* and the seventeen-key *akadinda* xylophones of the Ganda in Uganda have been well studied by several ethonomusicologists and can now be heard as a result in many parts of North America, Europe, and Africa. These former royal court instruments are played at high speed, like most log xylophones, using a duple (*amadinda*) or triple (*akadinda*) interlocking technique between the two primary players. They are accompanied by several drums. The *mangwilo* xylophone of the Ashirima of northern Mozambique is a seven-key instrument played by boys for amusement and to keep birds and animals out of the crops. The *kponingbo* of the Azande of northern Zaire, the Central African Republic, and southwest Sudan is a large party instrument usually played together with a large slit drum and other drums.

Instrumental Tuning

Broadly, there are four scale types in use in sub-Saharan African music: tetratonic with four notes per octave, pentatonic with five, hexatonic with six, and heptatonic with seven. In this respect African scales form a single family with those of Europe. Approximately 40 percent of scales are pentatonic, 40 percent heptatonic, and the remaining 20 percent largely hexatonic with some tetratonic, the latter notably among the ancient populations of the Khoisan and Pygmies. The boundaries of scale areas are clearly defined and are closely related to language relationships between the peoples concerned.

The tuning of the notes themselves varies enormously, but two underlying tuning principles can be distinguished, although these by no means cover all African tunings. Firstly, where musical bows and/or the use of harmonics are found, tunings tend to be based on the notes of the natural harmonic series. This is the case for instance among the Gogo of Tanzania, many peoples in Congo, Gabon, and the Central African Republic, and the Nguni peoples of South Africa. Secondly, in several scattered regions such as the heptatonic lower Zambezi valley (mbira, xylophone, zither), Guinea (xylophone, *kora*), eastern Angola (mbira), and the pentatonic Great Lakes kingdoms of Buganda and Busoga (xylophone, harp, lyre, etc.), scales tend to be tuned in close to equal-spaced intervals. In a heptatonic scale this gives a uniform interval size of around 171 cents or six-sevenths of a Western tempered whole tone; in a pentatonic scale around 240 cents or one and one-fifth whole tones.

BIBLIOGRAPHY

Hornbostel, E. M. von, and C. Sachs. "Classification of Musical Instruments." *Galpin Society Journal* 14 (1961).

Kirby, Percival R. *The Musical Instruments of the Native Races of South Africa.* 2d ed. Johannesburg, 1965.

Tracey, Andrew. "The Original African Mbira?" *African Music* 5, no. 2 (1972).

———. "Kambazithe Makolekole and the Sena Valimba Xylophone." *African Music* 7, no. 1 (1991).

———. "The Nyanga Panpipe Dance." *African Music* 5, no. 1 (1971) and 7, no. 2 (1992).

Tracey, Hugh. "Towards an Assessment of African Scales." *African Music* 2, no. 1 (1958).

———. "The Mbira Class of Instruments in Zimbabwe." *African Music* 4, no. 3 (1969).

———. *Chopi Musicians: Their Music, Poetry, and Instruments.* Repr. London, 1970.

ANDREW TRACEY

MUSLIM POLITICAL ORGANIZATIONS.

Mass organization in Muslim Africa emerges with the Sufi brotherhood in the late eighteenth and early nineteenth centuries. The reasons for the organizational consolidation of the Sufi mystical tradition in Islam have still to be fully elucidated, but it appears to mark a response to decline in the Muslim world, political as well as religious, in the face of European expansion. While some Middle Eastern Muslim intellectuals sought to reform Islam by borrowing from the West, working in the direction of modernization or of nationalism, the founders of Sufi brotherhoods were intellectuals looking to the internal resources of Muslim societies, to the politics of the prodigious.

The centralized Sufi brotherhood (*tariqa,* or path) was firstly the creation of an outstanding Muslim personality, a *wali* (saint, or friend of God), credited by his disciples with miraculous achievements. Charismatic leadership here can also be seen as having been created by the needs and hopes of the disciples. A leadership cadre was constituted in each brotherhood by the family and close associates of the founder, a hierarchy with authority over a more or less extensive lay membership—the *tariqa* as mass party.

Organized Sufism in this brotherhood form is to be contrasted with the prior situation of either unaffiliated mysticism or decentralized *tariqa* affiliations, notably to the Qadiriyya "way," an association of the mystically learned rather than a structured organization. Affiliates to the Qadiriyya shared a particular form of supplementary prayer and also shared a reverence toward the memory of the association's founder, Abd al-Qadir al-Jilani of Baghdad (d. 1166). Although the affiliations of Qadiriyya could extend throughout the Muslim world, its social structure tended to be locally defined and lineage based. Pioneers of the new form of organized Sufi brotherhood, such as Sidi al-Mukhtar al-Kunti of Timbuktu (1729–1811), were then able to build a new brotherhood community (in this case the Qadiriyya-Mukhtariyya). Sidi al-Mukhtar used the brotherhood networks to consolidate his kinship relations, while his sainthood served to reinforce his authority as a neutral arbiter in disputes. This case may be compared for example with that of Muhammad 'Uthman al-Mirghani (1793/1794–1852), founder of the Khatmiyya brotherhood in the Sudan; or with that of the former slave Shaikh Ramiyya (1956–1931), builder of another independent branch of Qadiriyya in colonial Tanganyika.

Centralized Sufi brotherhoods such as these, actively seeking a mass membership, worked to unify society on a new principle: shared devotion to their saintly leader. Such organizations included an important kinship element, notably in the special place provided for the saint's family, but they also characteristically operated beyond the ties of blood relationship. The brotherhood could also provide for the social promotion of previously disadvantaged elements in society, as in the case of the up-country Africans of Tanganyika, who found in Shaikh Ramiyya's Sufi brotherhood an Islam free from Arab domination, or in the case of the slaves and casted people, who found in Amadu Bamba's Mouride brotherhood a welcome emphasis on the equality of disciples. Muslim brotherhoods such as these are bound together by a shared veneration for the saintly founder and for his successors, who are seen to have inherited his spiritual power, his blessing, or *baraka.* Regular tributary payments, offerings in cash or in kind, go to the brotherhood's aristocracy; such payments are perhaps the only enthusiastically paid taxes in Africa.

Differences between Sufi brotherhoods lie especially in matters of ritual, in the particular prayer formulas used by members in the sites chosen for local pilgrimage, and of course in the saint at the center of their veneration. Ritual rather than theological doctrine demarcates the different Sufi brotherhoods in sub-Saharan Africa, which remain on the whole firmly committed to Sunni orthodoxy. In sub-Saharan Africa the brotherhoods are seen as having provided an important missionary function, operating often on the geographic boundaries of Islam, winning new recruits to the faith from previously non-Muslim populations.

Sufi Muslim brotherhoods have often been characterized by their economic activism, working in trading diasporas where shared brotherhood membership is the basis of commercial trust in long-distance trading networks. Thus, the brotherhoods were equipped to take advantage of the improved market conditions provided by European colonial rule in Africa, with the Tijani followers of Ibrahima Niass cornering the market in beef supply from Kano to Ibadan in Nigeria, and the Mourides of Senegal moving from extensive groundnut production to an international street trading network which now reaches to New York and to the cities of the European Union.

While Muslim brotherhoods have on the whole adjusted well to the market, their relations with the state have been more ambiguous. The European rulers of the past were often apprehensive of the conspiratorial possibilities of the brotherhoods, especially of Tijaniyya, given its association with jihad movements in the nineteenth century. The brotherhoods developed political tactics of guarded cooperation with government. Such tactics have continued since independence through a businesslike exchange of services in which cooperation with government depends on the allocation of an adequate proportion of state resources, as well as suitable symbolic recognition of the brotherhood on state occasions. Brotherhoods can then contribute to the constitution of a civil society within the African state, an associational network between the state and the family, as notably in Northern Nigeria, Senegal, and Tanzania. The Islamists of the National Islamic Front in Sudan since 1985 have worked to co-opt that country's historically powerful brotherhoods, first infiltrating and then reforming them from the inside.

Sufi brotherhoods in general are threatened by reform movements in Muslim Africa, by mass diffusion of literacy in Arabic, and by the popularization of north African and Middle Eastern ideas in the politics of religion. Urban-based reform movements such as the Muslim Students' Society in Nigeria or Ibadou Rahmane in Senegal have taken a vanguard role, tending to learn from the example of the Iranian revolution of 1979. The Iranian example has been particularly noted among Muslim militants south of the Sahara, an example of non-Arab leadership in the world of Islam. Other forms of Muslim organization, again stressing a political militancy, are to be noted in states where Muslims are a minority. The Islamic Party of Kenya (IPK) for example, or Qibla in the Republic of South Africa, have drawn support from a younger generation: but the IPK has yet to be legally recognized, and Qibla speaks only for a minority within a minority. A majority of Muslim votes in Kenya still go to the governing Kenya African National Union (KANU), while most Muslims in South Africa seem to have voted for the National Party in that country's first nonracial elections in 1994.

Muslim vanguard associations have often attacked the leaders of Sufi brotherhoods for presenting themselves as intermediaries between the believer and the deity, for neglecting the educational function of the spiritual guide, for encouraging saint worship and pseudo-Islamic magical charlatanism. The brotherhoods in various ways have worked to reform themselves, notably with a greater emphasis on Arabic-language instruction, and they occupy a significant space within Africa's "triple heritage": Islam, Christianity, and traditional African belief.

BIBLIOGRAPHY

Cruise O'Brien, Donal B., and Christian Coulon, eds. *Charisma and Brotherhood in African Islam.* Oxford, 1988.

Karrar, Ali Salih. *The Sufi Brotherhoods in the Sudan.* London, 1992.

Nimtz, August H. *Islam and Politics in East Africa: The Sufi Order in Tanzania.* Minneapolis, 1980.

DONAL B. CRUISE O'BRIEN

See also **Education; Islam; Sufism.**

MUTAPA (Mwene Mutapa; Munhumutapa; Monomotapa; Mwanamutapa). The hereditary title of a dynasty of rulers of a state that existed in northern Zimbabwe and central Mozambique from before 1490 to the 1880s, the name Mutapa is also used by historians, following Portuguese practice, for the state itself, which comprised the territories of Mukaranga (on the northern Zimbabwean plateau), Chidima, and Dande (in the Zambezi Valley lowlands). The rulers, of the *nzou* or elephant clan, and most of their subjects were Shona speakers. It was once thought that the Mutapa state was established in the 1400s as a direct continuation of the southern Shona state of Great Zimbabwe. It is now known that Great Zimbabwe lasted until after 1500, whereas its main successor, the southwestern state of Torwa at Kame, had already been established by then.

The Mutapa state probably arose out of several outlying branches of the Great Zimbabwe culture on the northern plateau, and it was probably still expanding at the time of the civil war of around 1490, the first event in its history known to us. Construction and use of the fine stone enclosures of the Great Zimbabwe type ended between around 1512 and the 1530s, but the stockaded capitals of the rulers continued to be called *zimbabwe*. The northern frontier of Mutapa, on the Zambezi, was the most well-defined; the state's other borders remain unclear. A triangle from Zumbo to Harare to Tete includes the main state before around 1750. Mutapa rulers made repeated efforts to extend their rule to the coast before around 1550, but with indifferent success, as most of their forces sent to do this set up independent dynasties instead. The territory of Mukaranga, the heart of the state up to around 1723, included the best possible combination of arable land, grazing, and goldfields in the region. Here, most of the people spent their time in food production, but gold mining and elephant hunting were profitable sidelines for some. The state took about half of the gold and ivory, which made the Mutapa the greatest trader in the land, but individuals were then free to trade their share for imported cloth and beads. Trade involved either expeditions to the Zambezi and ocean ports or dealing with immigrant traders living under Mutapa rule. These were Muslims and, increasingly from the 1530s, Portuguese.

Despite an abortive Portuguese invasion in the 1570s, it was not until 1629–1693 that the Portuguese were able to conquer the state, exhaust its gold, and depopulate it. Oral tradition and documents tell us little of Mutapa internal history before 1600, but from then on civil wars became frequent and continued even after the Portuguese had been driven from Mukaranga in 1693. Itself moving to the dry Chidima region by 1723 and coexisting with the Portuguese in Tete, the Mutapa dynasty's power slowly decreased. Its final decline in the 1860s left little for the Portuguese to conquer in the 1880s. The Mutapa was never the most important Shona state, but its nearness to the Portuguese made it the best known.

BIBLIOGRAPHY

Beach, David. *The Shona and Their Neighbours.* Oxford, 1994.

Mudenge, S. I. G. *A Political History of Munhumutapa.* London, 1988.

DAVID BEACH

See also **Zimbabwe: Ancient Zimbabwe.**

MUTESA I (b. late 1830s; d. 1884), ruler (*kabaka*) of the kingdom of Buganda in eastern Africa (1856–1884). Mukabya Mutesa is regarded by the Ganda people as perhaps the greatest of their precolonial kings. At the death of his father, Kabaka Suna II, Mutesa was chosen from among sixty-one eligible "princes of the drum" by the prime minister, Katikkiro Kayira, who formed an alliance with Mutesa's mother, Muganzirwazza, and her Elephant clan. During his reign, powerful influences arrived from the outside world, most of which he welcomed. Coastal Swahili traders brought imported cloth, guns, and Islam. Mutesa became fluent in Swahili and literate in Arabic. He promoted Islam among his people and observed Ramadan from 1867 to 1876. He did not replace the indigenous Lubaale religion (whose deities included the spirits of former kings), but attempted to add Islam to it. The contradictions inherent in this policy led to a crisis of loyalty when young Muslim converts at court rejected Mutesa's leadership because he was uncir-

Mutesa I. COURTESY OF JOHN A. ROWE

cumcised and recognized other gods besides Allah. More than seventy of the Muslims were executed, becoming martyrs for their faith and signaling ominous new challenges to Ganda unity.

Simultaneously, Egyptian imperialism from the north threatened Buganda. The explorer Henry Morton Stanley visited Buganda in 1875, during the time of the Egyptian menace and suggested that British Christian missionaries be brought in to counter the Egyptian threat. At Mutesa's invitation the Church Missionary Society sent several missionaries in 1877. French Catholic "White Fathers" appeared, uninvited, in 1879 but were welcomed by Mutesa to offset the British Protestants. Mutesa then tried to play off the external forces against each other, creating new political-religious groupings that led to civil wars during the reign of his successor, Mwanga II. However, until his death of a venereal infection, on 9 October 1884, he presided over an era of Ganda power, influence, prosperity, and independence. He is remembered with awe and affection by his people.

BIBLIOGRAPHY

Kiwanuka, M. S. M. *Semakula: The Kings of Buganda*. Nairobi, 1971.

———. *A History of Buganda from the Foundation of the Kingdom to 1900*. New York, 1972.

Rowe, John A. "Revolution in Buganda 1856–1900. Part 1: The Reign of Kabaka Mukabya Mutesa, 1856–1884." Ph.D diss. University of Wisconsin, Madison, 1966.

———. "Historical Setting." In *Uganda: A Country Study*, edited by R. M. Byrnes. Washington, D.C., 1992

JOHN A. ROWE

MVEMBA NZINGA (Afonso I; b. 1465?; d. 1543), ruler of the Kingdom of Kongo. Baptized as Afonso in 1491 by Portuguese priests, he seized the kingdom following the death of his father in 1506. Though he has been portrayed by some historians as a naive collaborator with the Portuguese, other scholars have argued that he successfully used the Atlantic trade to strengthen his own position and to expand his kingdom. He controlled the supply of ivory, copper, raffia cloth, and subsequently slaves. By 1520 most slaves were supplied from the markets around Malebo Pool on the Congo River, and exotic imports were used to reward his officials and allies. The Portuguese settlers on São Tomé, however, frustrated his attempts to open up direct commerce with Lisbon.

Mvemba Nzinga practiced polygamy and adapted Christianity to provide ritual legitimation

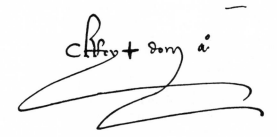

Mvemba Nzinga's signature. From Basil Davidson, *A History of West Africa* (London, 1977). BY PERMISSION OF BASIL DAVIDSON

for himself and his successors. He claimed miraculous intervention during his victory in 1506 and developed this legend to strengthen his dynasty. He was reported to be a keen student of Christian doctrine, and his correspondence with Portugal is full of biblical references. He sent numerous young relatives and noblemen to study in Lisbon, and his son Henrique was ordained and returned to Kongo as a bishop. During his reign, schools were established in Mbanza Kongo, the capital of the kingdom. He also built a central church on the site of the royal cemetery and had churches erected in the kingdom's provincial capitals.

BIBLIOGRAPHY

Brasio, António Duarte. *Monumenta Missionaria Africana*. Vol. 1. Lisbon, 1952.

Hilton, Anne. *The Kingdom of Kongo*. Oxford, 1985.

Thornton, John. *Africa and Africans in the Making of the Atlantic World, 1400–1680*. Cambridge, 1992.

RICHARD GRAY

MWINYI, ALI HASSAN (b. 1925), president of Tanzania (1985–1995). Born in Kisarawe District, Mwinyi earned a teaching certificate in 1944 and a degree from the University of Durham, in England, in 1956. He became principal secretary to the Zanzibar Ministry of Education in 1964. He was appointed to the union cabinet in 1970 and to the office of minister for health in 1972. In 1975 he was transferred to the Ministry of Home Affairs, from which he resigned, as a matter of honor, in

1977 after his subordinates were charged with misconduct. In 1982, he was appointed minister for natural resources and tourism and was later transferred to the vice president's office as a minister of state. He became president of Zanzibar in 1984 after president Aboud Jumbe's forced resignation due to secessionist accusations. When Tanzania's president, Julius Nyerere, stepped down in 1985, Mwinyi succeeded him, becoming the second president of Tanzania. He accepted the International Monetary Fund (IMF) and World Bank reform policies and made the ruling party, Chama cha Mapinduzi (CCM), endorse them in 1986. Under his leadership, in 1991 the party reversed one of the pillars of the Ujamaa—the leadership code. Under his presidency, Tanzania became a multiparty state in July 1992. He sanctioned Zanzibar's affiliation with the Islamic Conference in 1993. The constitutionality of that act was seriously questioned and was bitterly opposed by the Union parliament. Nyerere intervened, and Zanzibar was forced to withdraw from the Islamic Conference in August 1993.

LAUREAN NDUMBARO

See also **Nyerere, Julius Kambarage.**

MYTH AND COSMOLOGY

Concepts, Definitions, General Background

Myth and mythologies are conventionally defined in folklore and anthropology as sacred folktales whose content concerns the origins or creation of the world, deities, and a particular people or society. Part of oral traditions, these often express cosmological beliefs about the universe and are acted out in rituals. Mythologies have been of interest to scholars as a coded indication of the central values of a society; as a heavily symbolic metaphorical expression of perennial psychic and social tensions—for example, the Oedipus myth; as a charter validating social practices and institutions—for example, in Bronislaw Malinowski's theories; and as revealing, via the logics of myths, the universal structures of the human mind—for example, in the structuralist method of Claude Lévi-Strauss. The main poststructural objection to Lévi-Strauss's analysis of mythologies is that it is not clear how one can move beyond possible interpretations of the universal logics of myths when many of these interpretations seem arbitrary, abstracted as they are from social context and agency and leaving open alternate interpretations.

Despite African cultural diversity and the need for caution against overgeneralizing about continental Africa, there are some widespread motifs or common themes in many African myths and cosmologies: they concern deities; the creation of the universe, the origin of humans, human institutions, and values; the coming of death; animals; heroes and leaders; and powerful mediating figures associated with reproduction, sacred power, and conversion of natural into cultural substances. African myths and cosmological beliefs may be oral; carved on wood, clay, ivory, or stone; or enacted in dance.

Scholars have devoted considerable attention to the comparison of myth with history and written with oral expression. In V. Y. Mudimbe's view, two apparently distinct modes of thought and practice can coexist: one is critical and rational, aimed at mastering nature and its laws; the other is nonrational and ascientific, taking its meaning from objects' "irrational" investment in mythical propositions. Mudimbe opposes making a rigid dichotomy between oral and written in power, efficiency, and truth. He also attacks the hypothesis of a linear development from myth to history and science because such linear development negates an obvious fact: scientific discourse and practice can well coexist with myths.

Situating Mythology and Cosmology in History and Politics

Most scholars today recognize the fabricated nature of the geographical divisions into which the African continent is conventionally regionalized and have abandoned ethnocentric and racist classifications and ranking schemes. Many scholars also recognize that ethnographic perspectives on Africa are largely, though not exclusively, outgrowths of colonial connections.

Many anthropological approaches to African systems of thought developed in different directions during the colonial era. The British school of ethnography, until recently, concentrated on sociological aspects of African culture (kinship, politics) and tended to devote less attention to the cosmological and symbolic. When the British did turn to the latter, they were primarily interested in their function within the social system. A. R. Radcliffe-Brown and E. E. Evans-Pritchard developed a new approach: a shift from function to meaning. For example, Evans-Pritchard's account for Nuer religion and cosmology concentrates less upon sociological functions and more on linguistic categories.

The French school adopted an approach roughly opposite to early British functionalism: they focused upon symbolic-philosophical order, regarding this as the determinant of the social structure. Thus they made early advances in elucidating African cosmological systems and implicit philosophies, particularly in west Africa. This school tended to see social structure as a reflection of cosmology.

Besides various ethnographic approaches there is debate as to how much of the systematic character of cosmology may derive from the cognitive coherence of specific informants. For example, Marcel Griaule's study of the Dogon of Mali relied totally on a single atypical informant: Ogotemmeli, a hunter who had lost his sight as the result of an accident and was endowed with exceptional intelligence and wisdom. In thirty-three days, he introduced Griaule to a profound knowledge of Dogon belief. Griaule's *Conversations with Ogotemmeli* is organized around this one man's interwoven monologues on the creation and origin of social organization, a mythical decoding of the universe, and a symbolic interpretation of the foundation of history, culture, and society.

French structuralism has influenced more recent works on African mythology and cosmology. In his *African Religions,* Benjamin Ray reanalyzes Dogon myth structurally, according to its binary oppositions, and correlates it with its content. He shows how the structure expresses the central doctrine of the story: the world oscillates between order and disorder. The narrative proceeds through three temporal or diachronic phases: Creation, Revolt, and Restoration. In the first phase, Amma brings forth Thought, Signs, Seeds, Words, and Twins: the principles of order. Before this phase can be completed, it is interrupted by an oppositional phase, the revolt of Ogo, which introduces emotion, irrationality, sterility, and singularity: the principles of disorder. This is followed by a third and final phase which partially mediates the opposition between order and disorder and thus serves to restore the original order. Humans are direct descendants of Nommo, the son of Amma, the creator. Their task is to continually push back the boundaries of disorder, the tides of time and becoming, by spreading out the canopy of civilization over the Earth and by performing periodic rituals to restore its life. This role was predestined for humans from the beginning, and the myth provides the archetypal symbols that Dogon duplicate on Earth in social organization.

In 1965, Meyer Fortes and Germaine Dieterlen's *African Systems of Thought* initiated a collaborative attempt to integrate the British and French emphases and to show interconnections between two aspects heretofore separated by them: knowledge/beliefs and social organization. Most French and British anthropologists now agree that their perspectives are not contradictory but complementary. The objective today is to integrate social-functionalist and phenomenological approaches within a unified perspective.

Problems of Translation and Representation

In approaching African mythology and cosmology today, many scholars recognize the distortions arising from the historical and political situation of the academic disciplines in Africa. Recent work in anthropology and history acknowledges these difficulties and demonstrates an acute consciousness of the conditions under which the disciplines charged with representing the experience of others go about their tasks. The focus is on how the act of representing systems of thought in other cultures has political consequences, and sometimes political motives.

Another problem in previous studies of African mythology and cosmology was that Western scholars often began by looking at African supreme beings through the prism of Christian soteriology. For example, in creation myths about the early contiguity of earth and sky, some Western researchers interpreted these themes as equivalent to the idea of the Fall in Christianity.

Another issue pertains to the classification of logical systems of thought. The notion of "African philosophy" is a recent paradigm. At the beginning of the twentieth century, terms such as "primitive philosophy" and "philosophy of the savages" were used to refer to what today is called cosmology, modes of thought, or philosophy. African thought was considered to be merely a preliminary step toward a more progressive human capacity. Missionaries, anthropologists, and colonizers expounded means and techniques of changing Africa according to Western and Christian standards. In 1959, a Belgian missionary in Central Africa, Placied F. Tempels, published *Bantu Philosophy,* which expressed doubt concerning the supposed backwardness of Africans and proposed a new political policy. Yet many of Tempels' African critics as well as his followers remained concerned about making African philosophy agree with Western philosophical traditions and promoting a cultural integration of African thought with Christianity. In the late 1960s there was a movement in favor of restoring traditional African philosophies, called "ethnophilosophy," with a more secular outlook. Paulin Hountoundji has objected that ethnophilosophers present a mythologized African philosophy not located in real time, amid real problems, and that it is addressed primarily to a European audience. Thus philosophy and theology, mythology and cosmology, are political practices.

African Myth, Cosmology, and Society

Time and Space

While anthropologists and historians have begun to realize that describing African beliefs may tell us more about the assumptions brought to interpretations of non-Western formations than it does about the formations themselves, a number of studies of time and space in African myth and cosmology have attempted to avoid these errors of translation. John Middleton, for example, showed the complexities of the worldview of the Lugbara of northwestern Uganda. He sought to discover an order that lies not solely in the content of belief but also in contexts within which beliefs are invoked and uses to which the Lugbara put their beliefs. In Middleton's portrayal, the Lugbara are overwhelmingly pragmatic. The central theme that emerges is control of the evil they see around them. The local idiom of evil is inversion (reversal) in myths and cosmological explanations of past and present transformations. Through this idiom, the Lugbara display a combination of skepticism and faith. They express conflicting goals and attempt to influence forces perceived as affecting their lives.

By examining the Lugbara social and cosmological experience of time and space, one can move toward understanding mythologies of lost paradise, a widespread motif in Africa. These serve to categorize complex social and moral relationships. The Lugbara myth states that human society evolved through three social phases: first, a primordial, mythic, paradisal phase in which the world was the inverse of what is now (incest was possible; there was no marriage or bridewealth); second, a transitional, mythic-historical phase consisting of both inverse and normal characteristics; and third, the present sociocultural system. This tripartite scheme is fundamental to the Lugbara cosmology and serves as a conceptual model by which the Lugbara define both their present social circumstances and those of the recent past.

The myth also applies to recent historical experience. The Lugbara say that the first Europeans they met were cannibals, like the first ancestors who lived outside Lugbara territory: inverted people who could disappear underground and walk on their heads. Europeans who arrived later were associated with characteristics belonging to the second or "mythic-historic" phase. Like Lugbara heroes, Belgians and the first European district commissioner were regarded as magical people who performed miracles. Today, Europeans are regarded as normal people. This same scheme applies to contemporary experience. The local group to which the individual Lugbara belongs exists, as it were, at the center of a series of concentric circles, each representing a sphere at a greater social and spatial distance. The center is where normal, upright people live, one's kinship community. Outside this central area lies a larger social sphere containing other Lugbara and peoples of other societies who are not regarded as entirely normal. They possess magical powers and are suspected of sorcery. Further beyond lies the rest of the world, completely inverted and entirely outside the bounds of humanity. People there allegedly walk on their heads, eat rotten meat, and practice cannibalism and sorcery.

Contrasting conceptions of time and space are offered by Evans-Pritchard's studies of the Nuer, cattle herders who live in small villages widely dispersed over the flat riverine country of the upper Nile basin in southern Sudan. The Nuer are transhumant, moving about during the dry season and returning to their villages during the wet season to cultivate their fields. Nuer political organization is noncentralized and segmentary. Alliances are based on genealogical distance, built on kinship relations among dominant or aristocratic lineages on the village, clan, and subtribal levels. Hence the Nuer capacity, despite this decentralized system, for lengthy resistance against British colonial expansion and, more recently, the northern Sudan government in civil war. At the basis of this system are villages and family homesteads. The village is subject to the authority of elders of the dominant lineage. The homestead is subject to the authority of the father, who controls and protects the interests of his children.

Nuer cosmology is organized in much the same segmentary fashion, except that it is ultimately unified around the supreme god, Kwoth. Spirits of the sky are Kwoth's "sons." They are dominant or aristocratic powers, superior in rank to clan spirits, which are said to be "children of Kwoth's daughters." Each of these powers operates at a different level of social experience: family, lineage, village, clan, subtribe. The Nuer conceive of their relation to Kwoth in the idiom of kinship: they are his children and he their father and ancestor. Kwoth is the spirit of the homestead shrine and spirit of the village; he is the ultimate ground of family and village unity beyond clan spirits. He is also the spirit of all Nuer, and hence the basis of the widest ethnic unity, surpassing the limited scope of sky spirits. Thus the Nuer conceive of Kwoth in intimate, personal terms, as involved in all ritual occasions, and as inspirer of prophets. At the same time, however, they also refer to Kwoth in more transcendent terms as creator of the universe and as spirit of the sky. They say Kwoth sometimes seems far away and does not always heed their prayers; humans are mere "ants" in his eyes. Thus, although the Nuer see themselves as clearly separated from their creator, they do not experience this separation in radical form. The cause of separation is both accidental and natural; it did not stem from a moral breach. Kwoth remains their father and ancestor, transcendent in his authority and power, yet very close in moral and ritual terms.

Thus, in many African systems of thought, there is close coordination of cosmological time with the underlying dynamics of social context. Likewise, in concepts of space, there is often a close correspondence between humans and the world.

Dominique Zahan shows how African peoples organize space in order to situate themselves in the world and express concern with renewal. Everything concerning the house, for example, is determined by cosmic references. Among the Fali of northern Cameroon, the residence is conceived of and realized on the basis of symbolism which is at once cosmic, anthropomorphic, zoomorphic, and dendromorphic. The right side of the house, associated with the east, corresponds to earth and man, to the known world and the tortoise (the animal symbolic of one subgroup of Fali). The left side of the house, associated with sunset, corresponds to water and woman, to the unknown world and the toad (symbolic of the other subgroup of the Fali). Arrangement of the Fali home reproduces the successive phases of their myth of origin in terms of establishment, preparation, and possession by a human being of a "universe" cut to human scale. The single room of the primordial first cosmic house represents the primordial egg from whence issued man's earth, whose square form is reflected in the rectangular courtyard. The round shape of the Fali room suggests equilibrium of a nascent but already organized world, which contains its own future and whose completion will be marked by a large oval family enclosure divided into four sections connected two by two. This is the image of a "finished" world. The cycle will be completed by a circular shelter away from the family residence where the patriarch settles, detached from human activities and marking a return to the starting point.

References to the primordial myth involve the intervention of a dynamic principle correlative to the right-left symbolic dualism to which the construction of the house is related: the right side is associated with earth and man, the left side, with water and woman. The Fali house is likened to a living being, who is born, develops, and dies. The buildings are constructed in an order such that the right side of the house goes up at the same time as the left, and the construction of an edifice on the right is necessarily followed by that of another on the left. This back and forth movement is carried out in relation to the central post. Once completed and inhabited, the house, like humanity, is suited to procreation; it is also similar to the finished world.

Person and Agency

African cosmologies are not concerned solely with reproduction and temporal/spatial/ritual controls that may be exercised over it. There is a range of ideologies and experiences, both within a single culture and between different cultures. As Benjamin Ray points out, until recently, many Western scholars failed to appreciate the extent to which African mythologies and cosmologies are founded upon a systematic, indigenous anthropology and ethics, at the center of which lies a moral conception of person. The concept of person expressed by many African myths and cosmologies involves notions of personal identity, freedom, destiny, ancestors, and social ethics. Views of humanness strike a balance between collective identity as a member of society and personal identity as a unique individual. There is widespread definition of person in terms of the social groups to which he or she belongs.

Many studies now attempt to elucidate the dynamics of personhood in traditional African societies and signal a cognitive shift away from somewhat static structuralist approaches to the study of personhood characteristic of 1970s research. For example, accounts of cognitive experience have been amplified to include lived experience: the world of senses and emotions, of body, and of intuition and movement. Of central concern is the aspect of personhood that Marcel Mauss referred to as *moi*, awareness of self, as opposed to *la personne morale*, the ideological definition of personhood in terms of rules, roles, and representations. The focus is on idiosyncratic, inner, elusive experiences of self and not just upon the outer persona or mask that a person presents to the world. There are attempts to give equal value to culturally objectified and subjectively apprehended aspects of social and cosmological experience.

Anita Jacobson-Widding's work on the shadow in Congolese conceptions of personhood illustrates the dialectical relation between cultural thought models and lived experience. She argues that the ideologically privileged conception of personhood entails a shadowy, unofficial, countervailing set of ideas and experiences, often invoked in liminal moments of myth or intimate conversation. There is oscillation between formal and informal notions of person in several contexts: although orderly, rational, "white" worlds of matriclan and matrilineal ancestors are contrasted with the shadowy world of witches, sorcerers, and charismatic individuals, the latter domain is not unequivocally dark and negative. In private, many people cultivate strong, if ambiguous, emotional ties with marginal *nkuyu* spirits, sometimes identifying their deceased fathers with them. Formal, public interviews produced an official, sociocentric view of person as comprising an interior person, associated with matriliny, order, and collective identity, and an exterior person symbolized by bodily exuviae, a personal name, and the shadow, which was judged to be dark and negative. Informal, intimate conversations, however, tended to bring out a different view of person, one emphasizing emotions and specific events, and more concerned with an individual's power of agency than with static normative generalizations. In this latter discourse, the metaphor of shadow recurs, a metaphor for individual selfhood and agency.

This sense of choice and control is only occasionally achieved by the Talensi of northern Ghana; fate usually intervenes. Meyer Fortes, in his classic study of the concept of person among the Tallensi, describes how they recognize a basic polarity between a person's individual destiny and acquired social identity. Like some other African peoples—for example, the Yoruba and the Dogon—the Talensi see that a person's inner life is intimately related to the external social facts of his or her existence, but they also know that every person's life history is unique and individual. Like the Yoruba, they attribute this uniqueness to a person's prenatal or "spoken" destiny, which is chosen in heaven. This determines whether children will develop into human beings or whether they will fail and become social dropouts.

For the Talensi the exact nature of a person's destiny does not become known until he or she reaches maturity and begins to enter into responsible social roles. In the beginning, a child's prenatal destiny and social identity are closely merged with those of its parents; it is their destiny, especially the mother's, which controls the child's early life. But when the child reaches adolescence and begins to assume a certain social identity, his or her prenatal destiny becomes stronger and exerts more influence.

At this juncture in a boy's life, when his social identity begins to emerge, society steps in, under the guise of the ancestors, to mediate his maturing prenatal destiny. Each youth finds himself chosen by a specific group of guardian ancestors who will preserve and guide his life beyond the stage governed by his infantile and dangerous prenatal destiny. Under their guidance, the youth's destiny changes. It becomes what Fortes calls "a good destiny," shedding its evil propensities and assuming a more positive role.

A boy's destiny ancestors reveal themselves in critical adolescent experiences—for example, during a serious illness or when the youth first kills big game. When their presence is disclosed by divination, a destiny shrine is erected. Henceforth, the youth and his father make regular offerings of food and drink to the guardians, for they will determine the success or failure of the young man's life. This shift toward the ancestors also marks a crucial shift toward maturing and moral responsibility. In this way the youth moves out from under the arbitrary grip of his prenatal fate, over which he has no personal control, and acquires the freedom to assert his own personality. Hereafter, his moral behavior (subject to ancestral guidance), not his prenatal fate, will determine a large measure of his personal success or failure.

When first constructed, a youth's ancestor shrine is placed in his mother's quarters. When the young man marries, it is moved to his wife's quarters, though it still remains within the sphere of his father's compound. Until his father dies, a son lives within his father's household and remains subject to his father's destiny. The destiny of father and son are said to be opposed, especially when the son marries and has a child. This belief has a direct relation to inheritance and succession: the eldest son cannot inherit his father's legal and social position as compound head until his father's death.

Power

Related to concepts of person and human agency are concepts of power. William Arens and Ivan Karp critique accounts of exercise of power and political relationships that treat the latter as secularly based, even when religious activities are being described. As a consequence, many studies exhibit a tendency toward a universalizing stance, which many African philosophers have decried as ethnocentric. These accounts view power as almost always secular, unvarying in time and space. An alternative is to examine power as an aspect of a locally defined cosmos in the form of an immanent force derived from some "extrahuman" agency. This view of power illuminates African ideas about the nature of society, of nature, and of human actions.

Susan Rasmussen reports that smiths among the Tuareg, a seminomadic, stratified, Islamic people of northern Niger, act as oral historians, artisans, political intermediaries, and ritual specialists; nobles attribute mythical powers to them. Smiths are believed to be closer to the *jinn* spirits. Their powers cut across sacred and secular domains. Since smiths are outsiders of uncertain origins, who marry endogamously within their inherited social stratum, they derive freedom to mediate and transform. For example, in their work with metals and wood, smiths change natural substances into cultural substances. In their praise songs performed at noble weddings, smiths express critical social commentary. In contact between Tuareg society and the outside world of government functionaries and European tourists, smiths often serve as buffers and gatekeepers for nobles.

In her work on Wolof griots (included in Arens and Karp, *The Creativity of Power*), Bonnie L. Wright shows that occupational differentiation is based on a cultural ideology that distinguishes among powers held by categories of persons, which make these categories interdependent. Such interdependence affects the exercise of power. Domination by nobles is countered by their dependence on the griot (entertainers who function as oral historians), because of powers of speech that only griots have but that nobles require. In many African social sys-

tems, therefore, the exercise of political influence—both as the source of power to control others and the legitimization for actions—derives from access to and work upon natural and supernatural powers.

Mythology, Cosmology, and Social Change

Cosmological power, therefore, provides a useful lens through which to identify transformations that African social formations have undergone. A focus upon myth and cosmology need not create the impression that African cultures are static or unchanging. In *Womunafu's Bunafu*, David Cohen examines how a Soga community is captured by a state and transformed into a small-scale version of the state's court. All cosmological resources of the origin myth are put to the ideological purpose of legitimizing the establishment of authority in the community by the king's illegitimate offspring. The result is a radical transformation in community structure that entails systemic changes in meanings attributed to social forms and spatial arrangements. Hence reproduction at one level is change at another.

David Lan's *Guns and Rain* portrays religious innovation under conditions of rapid change and attacks colonialism's ancien régime. Lan builds on Lévi-Strauss's analysis of myth and shows that by expanding the reference of the political symbolism of local spirit mediumship, cult mediums (and perhaps most important among them, a medium associated with the power of war) were able to absorb guerrilla warfare within their mythology and cosmology. In one part of Zimbabwe, at least, the cult incorporated guerrillas, requiring them to conform to its logic, rather than the other way around. Lan relates that many *chimurenga* songs of the war of liberation sung by guerrillas and peasants celebrate the role of the ancestors and recognize the important part played by royal ancestor spirits in myths as protectors of the land and bringers of rains. Thus, despite political and economic changes, myth can actively influence new systems, even those defined as "secular."

Symbolism in African Myth and Cosmology

Many studies of African mythological and cosmological symbols have tended to take it for granted that symbols are intelligible as parts of semiological systems which are coherently related to social structure. Dan Sperber has questioned the premises of all semiologies of symbolism. He feels that the concepts "symbol" and "meaning," notoriously difficult to define, are categories of European culture, lacking universal or scientific value. He argues that what he calls semiological illusion results from a synthesis of academic and native theories.

Poststructural approaches to symbols in myth and cosmology attempt to avoid these problems and yield further insights into the problem of meaning. Alma Gottlieb, in her study of the Beng people of Côte d'Ivoire, sees in the local kapok tree, beneath which dances, sacrifices, folktales, and trials are held, symbolism of basic contradictions in Beng society. A kapok tree is ritually planted in each village. This symbol expresses inconsistencies, oppositions, and contradictions. Beng society is organized around a dominant pair of principles: "identity" and "difference." But the semantic field these terms cover and their contexts are varied. Although they appear opposed, the Beng do not see them as wholly incompatible. Each serves as a principle around which aspects of society are organized; together, they offer two quite distinct visions of how the world can be structured. Furthermore, despite the dualist division of Beng space into village and forest or Earth, Gottlieb cautions against associating such spheres with culture and nature as rigid oppositions. The Beng do not perceive or experience forest/Earth areas as anything akin to nature as Western culture understands that term. They do not experience the forest as formidable, chaotic, and dangerous. Rather, it is quite orderly and classified into zones: zones for spirits, for planting, for hunting and gathering.

Anomaly and Symbolic Mediation

The Beng principles of identity and difference shed additional light on the meanings of key mediating figures in Beng myths: Dog and Hyena. Dog acts now as ally, now as traitor to the human cause, wavering between maintaining identity with humans and asserting critical difference from them. Hyena plays the role of buffoon who is laughed at by audiences because of his immoral deeds but in life is the object of intense rites aimed at curtailing or counteracting the animal's anomalous behavior. Hence his dual connotations: he is laughable in one context, fatal in another. In myths Dog is responsible for both destruction and protection, and perhaps even creation, of humans. Dog is the alter ego for humans, embodying both hidden hopes and hidden frustrations. He represents positive and negative aspects of being human, alternately identifying with and protecting, yet differentiating from and creating disaster for, humans.

Accordingly, the Beng treat dogs inconsistently. They bestow nonhuman names on dogs, in non-Beng language or nonsense words, or in proverbs expressing negative views about fatalistic themes connected to dogs. The Beng do not eat, pet, or give human food scraps to dogs. Dogs baby-sit and survey fields. They are viewed as witches, or as good *and* bad, like human twins and political officeholders.

Hyenas are amusing and dangerous in different realms: in Beng oral literature, they prowl at night, scavenge on other animals' prey, howl, and are immoral. Hyena is associated with avarice, malice, and stupidity, the inversion of all admirable traits. His greed and stupidity prevent him from indulging to his full satisfaction; since he is foolish, he cannot achieve fully his greedy goals.

Audiences laugh at myths. In contrast, the Beng deal with hyenas in life quite seriously; ritual treatments highlight the hyenas' perceived defects. Thus myths and rituals concerning hyenas do not reflect but, rather, distort each other. Tales contain moral lessons: "That's how hyena is stupid." But perhaps people condemn while secretly admiring hyena's motives. Attitudes toward real hyenas condemn them for monstrous and anomalous features that set them apart. Like the pangolin of the Lele of Zaire analyzed by Mary Douglas, Hyena threatens categories which should remain discrete. Therein he derives anomalous status. By contrast, Dog, to the Beng, is more of a mediator, a bridging figure between domains. Dog and Hyena represent fine distinctions among symbolic anomalies. The Beng enact special rituals when they confront both animals, as the Lele do regarding pangolins, because these animals' similarly anomalous status alternately threatens and bridges categories in the local universe. These animals serve as creative means for making sense of the world and humanity.

Pollution

The Beng observe a number of forest/Earth-related taboos, many of which circumscribe human sexuality: couples may not have sexual intercourse in the forest or fields; men may not engage in sex the night before they eat meat from animals sacrificed to Earth; pregnant women may not eat food while walking on paths into or out of the forest; women in labor may not deliver in the forest or fields. Married women may not enter the forest or fields during menstruation. Yet, in contrast to some other assertions that menstrual taboos indicate "dirt" and/or "oppression" of women, Gottlieb explores the implications of taboos and revises previously androcentric interpretations of sexual pollution and restrictions in African cosmology. First, among the Beng, sexual taboos and pollution beliefs point to joint and mutual responsibility for pollution on the part of both men and women. Second, to the Beng, despite menstrual restrictions, menstrual blood is not "dirty"; rather, it is conceived as the symbol of human fertility. Separating it from the forest constitutes a ritual statement that human fertility must be separated from the kind of fertility that Earth-forest creates: crops. If these restrictions are violated, the Beng fear that offspring and crops may die. The Beng also prohibit women from eating Earth meat. According to myth, in the past, women ate Earth meat along with men; but once, a woman had falsely claimed that she had not had sex the night before eating the meat. Because she lied, she soon died. Henceforth, women are no longer trusted to tell the truth about their sexual activities and are no longer permitted to eat Earth meat.

This myth reveals a suspicion that women's speech is not to be trusted. Nevertheless, this androcentric view is counterbalanced: women participate in religion in other ways: they may offer sacrifices to Earth, may be diviners and healers, may apply paint and jewelry to their infants that attract or propitiate spirits, and may even be masters of Earth. Also, their allegedly unreliable speech can work in women's favor.

Voice and Authority

Gender Issues in African Mythology and Cosmology

The study of symbolism in African myth and cosmology therefore raises the issue of voice and authority, which Edwin Ardener has termed the problem of the ethnography of "the mute," social groups whose expression of their models of the world is impeded by megalophony of dominant groups in the system. He suggested that the models of society that women can provide are not the kind acceptable to men or to ethnographers, but they might, nonetheless, find indirect expression. This recognition that women's and other "muted" groups' models might constitute an alternative cultural ethnography has produced important insights. Marie-Claude Dupré describes frustrations of research into a twin cult when the researcher herself is the mother of twins. Batéké women appealed to Dupré to help them understand their

own experiences. Access to spiritual knowledge, which is the most fundamental aspect of ritual, appears to be continually weakened, forbidden, and perverted by masculine intervention. Women "discover" insignia of the rite, which men take over from them; moreover, during research, men continually insisted on making their own interpretations of what women's ritual meant. To the Batéké, the parrot is the bird of knowledge, knowledge that is possible but not yet acquired. Thus every mother of twins, who has carried in her body proof of having participated in the unusual, the disordered, wears a few red parrot feathers in her hair on feast days to show that she has been in contact with knowledge but that it has flown away, leaving only a sign of its existence. There is thus a sense that subordinate people are active producers of culture and not merely vehicles of it or victims of a dominant class.

African Responses to Western Scholarship

During the 1950s in African studies, the impact of anticolonialist movements and African critiques of anthropology resulted in a new discourse which was critical not only of colonialism but of all dominant colonial hegemonic culture. But despite liberation movements, some pre- and postindependence African policies seem predicated on the research of Western anthropology. Although local scholars have contributed significantly to the study of African myth and cosmology, Mudimbe feels that the paradox and problem is that most "modern" African thought is basically a product of the West. Most thinkers and leaders have received a Western education; thus their conceptual framework has been both a mirror and a consequence of their experience of European hegemony and cultural supremacy. This is exemplified by key works in cosmology. John Mbiti has argued that African concepts of the supreme deity spring from an independent reflection on the supreme God recognized in Judeo-Christian tradition. E. Bolaji Idowu has argued for a monotheistic interpretation of the Yoruba religion. The purpose of these theorists is theological and, because of their Western education, they choose metaphysics developed by Western theological thought.

African intellectuals acknowledge their estrangement from their own popular culture and the difficulty of escape from repeating some philosophical dichotomies embedded in European social thought: universalism/relativism; individualism/

collectivism; ideal/material. For the sake of ideological independence, certain writers have gone so far as to advocate an intra-African philosophic dialogue conducted in African languages. They argue that any practice of European sciences by African scholars tends to reproduce Western ideology, and the total rejection of the entire Western cosmology is the only way to liberation. Yet in such critiques and debates, Africans are already rewriting their own intellectual history from a non-Western stance and are thereby suggesting new directions for dialogues between African and Western scholars.

BIBLIOGRAPHY

Ardener, Edwin. "Belief and the Problem of Women." In *Perceiving Women,* edited by Shirley Ardener. New York, 1975.

Arens, William, and Ivan Karp, eds. *The Creativity of Power: Cosmology and Action in African Societies.* Washington, D.C., 1989.

Cohen, David William. *Womunafu's Bunafu.* Princeton, 1977.

Dupré, Marie-Claude. "Comment être femme: Un aspect du ritual mukisi chez les Téké de la République populaire du Congo." *Archives de sciences sociales des religions* 46, no. 1 (1978): 57–84.

Evans-Pritchard, E. E. *Nuer Religion.* London, 1956.

Fortes, Meyer. "The Concept of the Person." In *La notion de la personne en Afrique noire,* edited by G. Dieterlen. Paris, 1973. Reprinted in *Religion, Morality, and the Person,* edited by J. Goody. Cambridge, 1987.

Gottlieb, Alma. "Menstrual Cosmology Among the Beng of Ivory Coast." In *Blood Magic: The Anthropology of Menstruation,* edited by Thomas Buckley and Alma Gottlieb. Berkeley, Calif., 1988.

———. *Under the Kapok Tree: Identity and Difference in Beng Thought.* Bloomington, Ind., 1992.

Griaule, Marcel. *Conversations with Ogotemmeli.* London, 1965.

Hountoundji, Paulin. *On African Philosophy.* Bloomington, Ind., 1983.

Idowu, E. Bolaji. *African Traditional Religion: A Definition.* London, 1973.

Jackson, Michael, and Ivan Karp, eds. *Personhood and Agency: The Experience of Self and Other in African Cultures.* Uppsala, 1990.

Jacobson-Widding, Anita. "The Shadow as an Expression of Individuality in Congolese Conceptions of Personhood." In *Personhood and Agency: The Experience of Self and Other in African Cultures,* edited by Michael Jackson and Ivan Karp. Uppsala, 1990.

Lan, David. *Guns and Rain: Guerrillas and Spirit Mediums in Zimbabwe.* London, 1985.

Mbiti, John. *Introduction to African Religion.* Oxford, 1988.

Middleton, John. *Lugbara Religion.* Oxford, 1960.

Mudimbe, V. Y. *The Invention of Africa.* Bloomington, Ind., 1988.

Rasmussen, Susan. "Ritual Specialists, Ambiguity, and Power in Tuareg Society." *Man: The Journal of the Royal Anthropological Institute* 27, no. 1 (1992): 105–128.

Ray, Benjamin. *African Religions: Symbol, Ritual, and Community.* Englewood Cliffs, N.J., 1976.

Sperber, Dan. *Rethinking Symbolism.* Cambridge, 1975.

Tempels, Placide F. *Bantu Philosophy.* Paris, 1959.

Zahan, Dominique. *The Religion, Spirituality, and Thought of Traditional Africa.* Translated by Kate Ezra Martin and Lawrence M. Martin, Chicago, 1979.

SUSAN RASMUSSEN

See also **Anthropology and the Study of Africa; Dogon; Dreams and Dream Interpretation; Modes of Thought in African Philosophy; Nuer and Dinka; Oral Culture and Oral Tradition; Person, Notions of; Philosophy and the Study of Africa; Religion and Ritual; Symbolism; Tuareg.**

MZILIKAZI (b. c. 1790; d. 1868), military leader and founder of the Ndebele kingdom. As the most feared African leader after Shaka, Mzilikazi was the moving force behind the *mfecane* north of the Vaal River. In the early 1820s Mzilikazi served briefly as a lieutenant in Shaka Zulu's army. After winning a battle, Mzilikazi decided to herd the captured cattle back to his own kraal rather than send it as tribute to Shaka. The Zulu king sent men to investigate, and Mzilikazi cut the feathers from their headdresses, a grave insult.

To avoid the wrath that was sure to follow, Mzilikazi led a few hundred of his followers northwest from Zululand to the Transvaal. From there he built up his kingdom, incorporating Zulu refugees and conquering local Sotho clans. Mzilikazi's military methods were devastating: his army surrounded villages at night and attacked at dawn, rhythmically beating their shields, killing all but young men and women, and burning the village to the ground. The captured men were forced to join the age-set regiments (*amabutho*) that made up the army, and the women were taken as wives by the Ndebele.

Mzilikazi built a strong, centralized kingdom governed by an extensive law code that covered everything: farming, war, marriage, and taxation. Refugees joining the Ndebele for protection did forced labor, and young men were not allowed to marry until they had served in an *amabutho*.

"Lion Killers Presented to Matselikatsi [Mzilikazi]." Watercolor, 1835. CHARLES D. BELL/MUSEUMAFRICA

Mzilikazi moved the Ndebele often (1827, 1832, and 1837) in order to escape pursuing forces and to expand his base. By 1830 the Ndebele numbered some six thousand to eight thousand people and were a strong fighting force. When Shaka's successor, Dingane, sent the entire Zulu army in pursuit of Mzilikazi in 1832, the Zulu returned with some cows but lost three regiments in the fighting. In 1836 the Ndebele attacked the Afrikaners at Vegkop, losing 430 of their force of 6,000, and taking or killing thousands of Afrikaner sheep, cattle, and trek oxen. Mzilikazi moved his people from the area after attacks by an Afrikan-Griqua-Rolong alliance and other attacks by the Zulu.

Around 1840 Mzilikazi and the Ndebele (now fifteen thousand to twenty thousand strong) founded Bulawayo, a permanent capital in what is now southwestern Zimbabwe. From there Mzilikazi enlarged and protected his kingdom by conquering local Shona groups and fending off attacks from "trek-Boers" heading north (1847–1851). He forced the Afrikaners to sign a peace treaty in 1852, bringing stability to the area until gold prospecting in the 1860s ushered in a flood of European immigrants. Subsequent fights over land rights brought an end to the Ndebele kingdom under Mzilikazi's son, Lobengula.

BIBLIOGRAPHY

Rasmussen, R. Kent. *Migrant Kingdom: Mzilikazi's Ndebele in South Africa.* London, 1978.

THOMAS F. MCDOW

See also **Afrikaner Republics; Mfecane; Ndebele; Shaka Zulu; Zulu.**

N

NAIROBI. Nairobi, the capital of Kenya, is the largest city in Africa between Cairo and Johannesburg. It is also the financial, commercial, and tourist center of east Africa, famous as the high-rise backdrop to viewing rhinos and lions at the national park fifteen minutes from the city center.

Nairobi was founded at mile peg 317 in 1899 as a convenient stop for the 32,000 Indian laborers and British engineers building the railroad from Mombasa to Lake Victoria. They erected a tent camp, and the settlement took its name from a nearby Maasai watering hole. A railway works yard and depot were set up, and the camp grew into a small town. In 1905 Nairobi became the capital of the British East Africa Protectorate.

During the first decades of the twentieth century, Nairobi grew as a frontier town and commercial center. Indian merchants (some of whom had been laborers) set up bazaars, and Gikuyu people from the surrounding highlands brought agricultural goods to sell. White settlers, many of them from the English country set, also came, attracted by the fertile farmlands, temperate weather, and social freedoms. Big game hunting brought the first tourists to the area, including U.S. President Theodore Roosevelt, who came in 1909. Roosevelt, white settlers, and adventurers stayed in the Norfolk Hotel, an enduring landmark that still lends itself to the romanticizations of Karen Blixen (Isak Dinesen) and Denys Finch-Hatten.

As the Gikuyus became a greater urban force, they began to organize politically, especially because their families' lands were being taken by white settlers. During the state of emergency declared in 1952 in response to the Mau Mau uprising, thousands of Africans were arrested in a sweep of Nairobi and sent to de facto refugee camps in the countryside or detained in the town.

Kenya became independent in 1963, and under the conservative government of Jomo Kenyatta, commerce flourished and the capital grew. In the 1970s the population of Nairobi increased by 4 percent a year, outpacing available housing. Shantytowns sprang up around the city, and though some efforts were made by Kenyatta and his successor, Daniel arap Moi, to encourage the building of permanent housing, the official response (especially under Moi's rule) was often to bulldoze the squatters' camps.

In the 1990s the shantytowns were not apparent to the thousands and thousands of tourists who passed through Nairobi each year. Instead, many were struck by the cosmopolitan nature of the city. Cafés, bars, bookstores, discos, museums, and a university are sprinkled throughout the glass skyscrapers of downtown, and expatriates and well-to-do Kenyans live on lavish estates in the suburbs.

Tourism is by far the largest part of the ever-expanding service sector in Nairobi. The city is the east African safari gateway: Jomo Kenyatta Airport, served by more than thirty international carriers, is one of Africa's largest, and the most popular game parks (Amboseli, Tsavo, and Maasai Mara) are less than a day's drive from the capital. Nairobi's economy also benefits from industries that process food, make cigarettes and beverages, and

Nairobi, Kenya. View of part of the capital with the Jamia mosque.
HUBERTUS KANUS/PHOTO RESEARCHERS, INC.

manufacture plastics and other goods. Though the government is a major employer and the private sector is flourishing, there are not enough jobs in the city and throughout Kenya for the thousands of students who finish secondary school each year.

Unemployment and housing will be problems that continue to face the municipality in the next century. Nairobi's population was about 1.35 million in 1989 and is expected to be more than 3 million by the year 2000.

BIBLIOGRAPHY

Morgan, W. T. W., ed. *Nairobi: City and Region.* New York, 1967.

THOMAS F. McDOW

NAMIBIA

GEOGRAPHY AND ECONOMY

The Republic of Namibia is an immense (823,998 sq. km [318,146 sq. mi.]), arid (average rainfall less than 200 mm [7.8 in.]), and sparsely populated country (just below 1.6 million people) situated on the west coast of southern Africa. Roughly rectan-

gular in shape, Namibia is bordered in the north by Angola, in the northeast by Zambia, in the east by Botswana, in the south by South Africa, and in

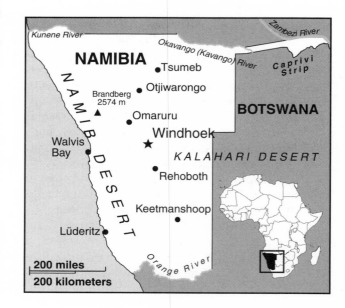

The Republic of Namibia

Population: 1,595,567 (1994 est.)

Area: 824,295 sq. km (317,260 sq. mi.)

Official language: English

Languages: Afrikaans, Damara, English, German, Herero, Kavango, Ovambo

National currency: Namibian dollar

Principal religions: Christian 90% (predominantly Lutheran, also Roman Catholic, Dutch Reformed, Anglican, and Methodist), traditional 10%

Capital: Windhoek (est. pop. 144,558 in 1996)

Other urban centers: Walvis Bay, Swakopmund, Keetmanshoop, Rehoboth, Lüderitz, Mariental, Oshakati, Karasburg

Annual rainfall: varies from less than 51 mm (2 in.) in western Namib and lower Orange River valley to less than 102 mm (4 in.) on southern border to over 508 mm (19.8 in.) in the northeast

Principal geographical features:

> *Mountains:*   Kaokoveld Mountains, Baynes Mountains, Auas Mountains, Huib, Tsaris, Naukluft-Hakos, Joutbertsberge, Khomas Highlands
>
> *Rivers:*   Orange, Kunene, Okavango, numerous seasonal rivers
>
> *Deserts:*   Namib, Kalahari

Economy:

> *GNP per capita:*   US$2,030 (1994)

Principal products and exports:

> *Agricultural:*   cattle, fish, Karakul sheep, maize, millet, sorghum, fruit
>
> *Manufacturing:*   fish and meat processing, cement, construction materials, mining equipment, beer, chemicals, timber milling
>
> *Mining:*   diamonds, uranium, lead, copper, zinc, gold, silver, tin, germanium, pyrites, tantalite, vanadium, arsenic, cadmium, tungsten

Government: German colony until World War I. Then administered by South Africa under League of Nations mandate until 1966. From 1966 until independence Namibia was under direct authority of the U.N., but South Africa maintained illegal occupation. Independence in 1990. Constitution approved 1990. Multiparty democracy. President elected for a maximum of two 5-year terms by universal suffrage. Bicameral national legislature: 72-member National Assembly elected for 5-year terms by universal suffrage and 26-member National Council nominated for 5-year terms by 13 regional councils. President appoints cabinet from members of National Assembly. For purposes of local government, there are 13 administrative divisions.

Heads of state since independence:

1990–: President Sam Shafiishuna Nujoma

1990–: Prime Minister Hage Geingob

Armed forces: President is commander in chief. Military instructors are from Kenya, Great Britain, and Canada.

> *Army:*   8,100
>
> *Marines:*   100

Transportation:

> *Rail:*   2,383 km (1,477 mi.)
>
> *Ports:*   Walvis Bay, Lüderitz
>
> *Roads:*   55,088 km (34,154 mi.), 7.5% paved
>
> *National airline:*   Air Namibia
>
> *Airports:*   Windhoek International Airport; airports at Tsumeb, Grootfontein, Walvis Bay. Numerous airstrips throughout the country.

Media: 4 daily newspapers, 4 weeklies. Radio and television service provided by Namibian Broadcasting Corporation.

Literacy and education:

> *Total literacy rate:*   38% (severely disproportional, by race). Since 1990 education has been free, universal, and compulsory to age 16. Higher education is available through University of Namibia, 4 teacher training colleges, and an agricultural college.

the west by the Atlantic Ocean. Namibia's border with Zambia runs along a strip of land—previously known as the Caprivi Strip and now the province of Liambezi—that extends to the Zambezi River. This geographical oddity is the result of the ill-informed colonial belief that the Zambezi was navigable and would thus ensure access to the Indian Ocean.

Namibia is dominated by a central plateau (elevation 900 to 1900 m [2,950 to 6,235 ft.]) on which most of its people live, and which is bounded by the Kalahari Desert in the east, the arid reaches of Namaqualand in the south, the Namib Desert in the west, and Kuvelai floodplain in the north. No permanent rivers flow from this central plateau; the only perennial rivers of the country are in the extreme north—the Kunene, Okavango, Mashi, and Zambezi—and in the extreme south—the Orange River. The cold Benguela Current, which flows northward along Namibia's coast, ensures that a low-pressure cell prevents extensive rains from falling on the interior. Most of Namibia is dependent on the remnants of the Indian Ocean monsoon rains that have been carried up and over the escarpment from the east. As a result, rainfall increases from the southwest, where no agricultural activity beyond extensive ranching is possible, to the northwest, where sufficient rainfall allows for the extensive cultivation of cereals. However, in a single season rainfall can be highly irregular and can vary extensively between years; droughts of longer than one year are not exceptional.

The Tropic of Capricorn runs through central Namibia 50 kilometers (31 mi.) south of the capital, Windhoek; thus, the country has distinct seasons. In Windhoek the average temperature in December is 75°F (24°C), with an average maximum of 88°F (31°C). In July the average temperature is 55°F (13°C), and the average maximum is 68°F (20°C). Most of the country's rains fall in the months of January, February, and March.

Namibia is characterized by extreme inequalities between rich and poor. In terms of the UNDP index for human development, which not only takes into account economic development but also considers economic inequality, education, health care, and the position of women, Namibia is ranked 116th in the world; if the index were to take solely Namibia's average annual income (in 1994, U.S.$1,820) into account, the country would be ranked thirty-seven places higher. In the past Namibia's economy was driven by the export of raw primary products, diamonds, base metals, uranium, fish, and livestock to South Africa. Since independence, Namibia has sought to lessen its economic dependence on South Africa. In the late twentieth century, its economy is boosted by fishing and tourism, which have ensured a real gross domestic product growth of 5.5 percent per year (1994). Strict controls have been imposed on the exploitation of fish stocks, which were seriously depleted in the 1980s, and it is expected that with the development of an indigenous fishing fleet, fishing will continue to be one of the growth factors in Namibia's economy. The other growth industry is the tourist trade, which since independence has been characterized by double-digit growth. In 1994 Namibia's external debt, primarily to South Africa, stood at a modest U.S.$444 million. Exports valued at U.S.$1.3 billion exceeded imports—primarily food, spirits, and vehicles—which were valued at U.S.$1.17 billion (1992 figures). Namibia's modest annual population growth of 3 percent will do little to restrict its economy. However, unemployment, which is estimated to run to as high 30 percent, unequal land distribution, extreme income disparity, the high illiteracy rate of 60 percent, lack of adequate schooling, food insecurity, and the specter of unresolved ethnic conflict will continue to hobble the Namibian economy in the years to come.

BIBLIOGRAPHY

Bley, Helmut. *South-West Africa Under German Rule, 1894–1914.* Evanston, Ill., 1971.

Gewald, Jan-Bart. *Towards Redemption: A Socio-Political History of the Herero of Namibia, 1890–1920.* Leiden, Netherlands, 1996.

Katjavivi, Peter H. *A History of Resistance in Namibia.* London, 1989.

Van der Merwe, J. H. *National Atlas of South West Africa.* Cape Town, 1983.

Wood, Brian, ed. *Namibia, 1884–1984: Readings on Namibia's History and Society.* London, 1988.

JAN-BART GEWALD

See also **Windhoek.**

HISTORY AND GOVERNMENT

By the early 1840s Oorlam raiders, who had originated on the cape colonial frontier, had established a string of small but highly centralized multiethnic polities in southern and central Namibia. In northern Namibia, Ovambo kingdoms had largely succeeded in deflecting slave traders operating out of Mossamedes region toward the headwaters of the

Zambezi. The central Namibian highlands, between the Ovambo kingdoms in the north and the Oorlam/Nama polities in southern Namibia, were occupied by Otjiherero-speaking pastoralists and Khoisan-speaking hunter-gatherers and pastro-foragers. During the 1850s central Namibia became increasingly drawn into the world system through the activities of traders operating out of Walvis Bay. In cooperation with these traders and Rhenish missionaries, a number of Herero were able to acquire firearms, with which they could defend themselves against Oorlam raiders, and with which they could in turn subdue and bind other Herero to themselves. Following extensive warfare a number of highly centralized Herero polities had been established in central Namibia by the early 1870s.

In the late 1860s, as Oorlam hegemony in central and southern Namibia crumbled, disenfranchised Basters from the Cape Colony trekked into central Namibia and established an independent Trekker republic centered on Rehoboth on the southern fringes of Hereroland. Alarmed by the establishment of this republic, Herero chieftains appealed for the establishment of a British protectorate over central Namibia. In 1876, anxious not to incur any excessive costs, Britain declared a protectorate over the immediate environs of Walvis Bay.

German Settlement

The late 1870s and early 1880s saw the reemergence of Nama polities in southern and eastern central Namibia. In southern Namibia, Hendrik Witbooi, the son of the chieftain of Gibeon, received a vision from God that instructed him to trek north with his followers to a promised land. As Hendrik Witbooi trekked north he and his followers were ambushed and driven off by Herero. As a result of this attack, Hendrik Witbooi unleashed an unrelenting guerrilla war on the Herero. At the same time a German entrepreneur, Adolf Lüderitz, sought to acquire land rights along the Namibian coast. In early 1884 the Imperial German government granted protectorate status to lands acquired by Lüderitz by means which it knew to be fraudulent. Shortly thereafter Germany annexed the Namibian coast, with the exception of Walvis Bay, from the Orange River in the south to the Kunene in the north. To fulfill the conditions agreed to at the Berlin Conference in 1884, German officials were sent to central Namibia in 1885 to sign protection treaties with Namibian leaders. In the immediate aftermath of an attack by Witbooi forces, Maharero Tjamuaha,

the most powerful of the Herero chiefs, agreed to sign a protection treaty with the Germans. Though the treaty proved to be ineffective in terms of protection, and the Herero annulled it and expelled the German officials from their territory in 1888, it did prove to be the basis for further German involvement in Namibia.

In 1889 German troops landed at Walvis Bay and seized control of the trade routes leading from the coast into the interior. Thus cut off from arms, and under continual attack from the forces of Hendrik Witbooi, the majority of Herero withdrew from central Namibia. In 1890 Maherero Tjamuaha died. In the ensuing succession dispute his son, Samuel Maherero, was able to mobilize the support of the Germans against his Herero succession rivals, as well as the forces of Hendrik Witbooi. In 1894 the future German governor, Theodor Leutwein, arrived in the territory. Through a mixed policy of divide and rule, and cooperation with a number of local chiefs at the expense of others, Leutwein was able to expand German control over the territory to the south of the Etosha plains. The rinderpest epidemic and ensuing drought and famine of 1897–1898 shattered the pastoral and pastro-forager economies of the indigenous communities of Namibia. Chiefs, who in the past had already sold large tracts of land to European settlers, were anxious to retain their power and influence; consequently they were forced to sell more and more of their land, and supply more and more of their subjects as laborers to the new colonial economy.

In early 1904, following a series of misunderstandings and the self-fulfilling fears of German colonists, war broke out. Under the command of General Lothar von Trotha, the German army waged a genocidal war against the Herero. An estimated 80 percent of the Herero died as they were summarily hung or shot, driven to die of thirst in the Kalahari Desert or incarcerated in concentration camps. At the time that a *Vernichtungsbefehl* ("extermination order") against the Herero was issued in October 1904, the Nama chieftains in southern Namibia, under the command of Hendrik Witbooi, took to war against the Germans. Nama survivors were driven into concentration camps, deported to Togo and Cameroon, or put to work as forced laborers. In any event, an estimated 75 percent of the Nama were killed, and though some Nama leaders continued a guerrilla war until 1908, the Nama, too, were defeated. After the war all Nama and Herero above the age of eight had to wear numbered metal tags, were prohibited from owning cattle or land, and were caught and confined within a web of labor laws.

As the Herero and Nama wars wound down, ranch land was allocated to German settlers, often former servicemen. In 1908 diamonds were discovered in southern Namibia, and along with the already established copper and zinc mines in northern Namibia, this led to a blossoming of the Namibian colonial economy. On account of the wars, there was an extreme shortage of labor in the colony, and consequently large amounts of labor were conscripted from north of the territory, in Ovamboland. Here rising population, declining hunting and export opportunities, as well as increasingly frequent battles with the Portuguese colonial armies in southern Angola, had led to ever greater economic hardship and impoverishment.

South African Domination

In 1915, during World War I, troops from the Union of South Africa invaded Namibia, and in a short campaign defeated the German troops. With the ending of German administration in the territory, thousands of Herero and Nama left their places of employment and migrated back to their ancestral areas. Their labor was replaced by Ovambo who fled south in the face of extreme drought in Ovamboland. Anxious to extend their control over Ovamboland, something that Germany had not done, Union forces defeated and killed Mandume, the Kwanyama king, in 1917. By 1918 Nama and particularly Herero had reacquired substantial herds of cattle and were able to pressure the new South African administration into assigning reserves to them. Following the treaty of Versailles, Namibia was granted to South Africa as a class C mandate: to all intents and purposes Namibia became a fifth province of the Union of South Africa.

Throughout the 1920s South Africa sought to strengthen its hold over Namibia, in part through the resettlement of hundreds of Afrikaner families from southern Angola on newly created farms in central Namibia. African resistance to the continued dominance of German missionaries in the churches led to the majority of the Herero and Nama leaving the church and beginning the establishment of independent "Ethiopian" churches. Dissatisfaction with the new South African administration meant that organizations such as the Universal Negro Improvement Association, as well as the Industrial and Commercial Workers Union of South Africa, were able to mobilize extensively in

the territory. However, the crushing by aerial bombing and the brute force of the Bondelswarts revolt in southern Namibia in 1922, the Rehoboth rebellion in central Namibia in 1924, and the Ukuambi revolt under Ipumbu in northern Namibia in 1935 ensured that all African opposition prior to World War II was thwarted.

Although Namibian soldiers had died fighting fascism in World War II, this did not prevent the election of the Nationalist party in the 1948 South African elections. As the new government enshrined racism in legislation, apartheid laws and policies were also applied in Namibia. The appointment of a Rhenish missionary, Dr. H. Vedder, to the South African senate, ostensibly as the representative of the African population of Namibia, finalized the breakaway of African communities from the mission church in Namibia. The majority of the Nama population found their spiritual home in the African Methodist Episcopal church (AME), while the Herero established their own independent church.

Intent on acquiring Namibia as a fifth province, the South African government sought to convince the outside world that Namibia's population had agreed to their formal incorporation into the Union of South Africa. Hosea Komombumbi Kutako was able to successfully mobilize opposition to the intended annexation of Namibia, and the U.N. rejected South Africia's claim. The South Africans prohibited a United Nations commission from visiting the territory, and Herero delegates were prevented from traveling to New York to put the Namibian case before the General Assembly. Through the interlocution of Chief Tshekedi Khama of the Bamangwato, and Chief Friedrich Maharero, the son of Samuel Maharero who was living in exile in Botswana, the Anglican priest Michael Scott went to Namibia in 1946 to collect information for submission to the U.N. General Assembly; this information was later backed up by Namibians who had been able to get scholarships to study abroad.

Resistance to South Africa

In the 1940s the African Improvement Society, a direct descendent of the UNIA, was founded primarily among Herero intellectuals. It was partly from these ranks that in 1959 the South West African National Union (SWANU) was founded. In Cape Town, Ovambo migrant laborers, inspired by the Congress movement in South Africa, formed the Ovambo People's Congress. In 1958 OPC leader Amdimba Toivo Ja Toivo was deported to

Namibia, where in 1959 the Ovamboland Peoples Organisation, which later became the South West African Peoples Organisation (SWAPO) was founded.

In keeping with apartheid legislation, the South African administration set about clearing "black spots." Africans were cleared off lands and deported to new "homelands" and "locations." In December 1959 things came to a head when more than ten people protesting against their forced removal from the "old location" in Windhoek were shot. In the ensuing crackdown many SWANU and SWAPO members fled the country. Undaunted, the South African administration continued its apartheid policies and established the Odendaal Commission, which recommended the "further extension of the system of apartheid throughout the Territory; and to make it the basic principle of political, economic, and social organization, as in South Africa."

During the course of 1966 SWAPO guerrillas entered northern Namibia and the armed struggle against South African rule began. In 1971 and 1972 wildcat strikes in the mining industry marked a turning point in the territory itself. With the independence of Angola in 1975, SWAPO forces became even more effective. This, coupled with the continued petitioning activities of SWAPO at the U.N., had by 1977 forced the colonial administration to attempt to reach an internal settlement advantageous to South Africa.

Starting in 1975 the South African administration organized the Turnhalle Conference. Namibians appointed by the South African administration as the representatives of ethnic communities which had been defined by that self-same administration, were expected to form an administration within what were effectively the confines of apartheid. Petty apartheid laws, such as the "mixed marriages act" were abolished, but legislation continued to be applied on the basis of race, and control and ultimate power remained in the hands of the newly appointed South African Administrator General. In 1977 all Namibian men above the age of seventeen became eligible for conscription in the South West African Territorial Force, which was formed as a South African proxy force in the territory. By 1980 there were an estimated eighty thousand men under arms in the service of the South African government in a territory populated by little more than a million people; added to this an estimated one hundred thousand Namibians had fled to neighboring states. Operating out of northern Namibia,

South Africa sought to eliminate SWAPO bases in southern Angola and became directly involved in the Angolan civil war. Northern Namibia was transformed into a war zone in which all local forms of civil government and administration were ended and made subservient to the South African military. Between 1977 and 1989 the Namibian economy went into decline, and the country's gross domestic product barely covered the annual military expenditure. At the same time the South African economy continued to decline. Social expenditure was equally high. In 1986 an estimated twenty-five hundred white South African soldiers lost their lives. This, coupled with continued urban unrest in South Africa, served to bring about less and less support for government policies from among the white electorate. In 1988 Angolan government forces, supported by Cuban forces, and SWAPO guerrillas, were able to turn the tide and inflict a heavy defeat on South African forces at Cuito Cuanavale in southern Angola.

Independence

In April 1989, on the basis of U.N. Security Council Resolution 435, the United Nations Transition Assistance Group (UNTAG) operating in conjunction with the South African Administrator General took over the administration of Namibia. A U.N.-supervised cease-fire got off to a shaky start as UNTAG forces were unable to confine South African forces to base and prevent them from attacking SWAPO guerrillas seeking to report to UNTAG forces. Elections under United Nations supervision took place in which SWAPO won 57 percent of the votes. On the basis of these elections, representatives were chosen for a constitutional assembly which drew up a charter guaranteeing minority, property, civil, human, and religious rights. South African troops were withdrawn and on 21 March 1990, Namibia gained its independence as the South African flag was lowered and the new Namibian flag raised in the National Stadium.

Independent Namibia has been fortunate in that it has been spared South African destabilization and has been able to establish good relations with its neighbours. Walvis Bay, Namibia's sole deep-water harbor, was handed over to Namibia shortly after independence and is being developed as a free-trade zone. Following independence, tourism has expanded with an average annual growth of 30 percent. Relative industrial stability and continued investor confidence have ensured that the Namibian economy has been able to show an average

2 percent growth in the first five years of independence. Major tasks facing independent Namibia are the extension of adequate schooling and health care, as well as the maintenance and development of infrastructure geared for the development of Namibia. Particularly daunting is the large number of unemployed, the majority of whom lack adequate formal schooling. Be that as it may, Namibian voters continued to express their support for a SWAPO majority government in the first post-independence elections, held in 1995.

BIBLIOGRAPHY

Diescho, Joseph. *The Namibian Constitution in Perspective.* Windhoek, Namibia, 1994.

Gewald, Jan Bart. *Towards Redemption: A Socio-Political History of the Herero of Namibia Between 1890 and 1923.* Leiden, 1996.

Grotpeter, John J. *Historical Dictionary of Namibia.* Metuchen, N.J., 1994.

Leys, Colin, and John S. Saul. *Namibia's Liberation Struggle: The Two-Edged Sword.* London, 1994.

JAN BART GEWALD

See also **Herero; Maherero, Samuel; Southern Africa; Witbooi, Hendrik.**

PEOPLES AND CULTURES

Namibia is one of the worlds's most sparsely populated countries. Its 1.56 million inhabitants are unevenly distributed, with some 55 percent living within 150 kilometers of the northern borders. Most of the rest are found in the central plateau, concentrated in the only metropolitan area, Windhoek. It is also a very young population, with 50 percent estimated to be less than eighteen years of age.

Such demographics and Namibia's long history of colonialism have significantly determined the cultural profile. With over 90 percent of its population professing Christianity, it has the highest ratio of Christians on the continent, yet until recently relatively few have belonged to Independent churches (those without direct origins to missionary efforts), a situation ascribable among other things to population distribution, church policy, and indigenous practices. A second striking cultural feature is the exceptionally high illegitimate birth rate and the large number of female-headed households found in both urban and rural areas, prominent since World War II and attributed by academic convention to poverty. They are supported largely by jobs in the cash sector, remittances from relatives, and earnings from *shebeens*. *Shebeens* are typically female-run bars selling traditional and European alcoholic beverages. Despite the colonial apartheid policy of trying to promote ethnic homelands, the necessity of migrant work has resulted in most Namibians being multilingual. English is the official language, although there are several national languages, such as Afrikaans and Oshiwambo. Most of the rural population is found concentrated in the central northern areas of Ovamboland and the eastern areas along the Okavango River.

The Huambo peoples occupy the grassy floodplains north of the Etosha National Park and extending into Angola. They are part of the so-called matrilineal belt of central Africa. Divided into eight tribes, their political arrangements have been characterized as feudal. The colonial policy of extensive indirect rule in this region, which served primarily as a labor reserve for the settler economy of the south, further entrenched this arrangement. Finger millet (*mahango*) is the principal crop of this region and some sanga cattle are bred, but the major source of cash is migrant remittances, which are redistributed through a vast network of *cuca* shops, a variant of *shebeens*. Population pressure has led, in addition to out-migration to central and southern Namibia, to gradual contiguous expansion into the west and south. Major Huambo groups include the Kwanyama, Ndonga, Kwambi, Mbalantu, Ngandjera, Kwaluudi, and Nkolonkathi-Eunda, some of whom still have kings.

Along the Okavango River and in the Caprivi Strip are also found numerically smaller matrilineal groups engaged in sedentary riverine living. The Kwangari, Mbunza, Shambyu, Geiriku, and Mbukushu are the most prominent among the over fifty ethnic groups recorded in the area, while the Mafwe and Masubia dominate in the Caprivi Strip. Scattered among these peoples are several mobile groups of foragers.

Beyond the towns, the mines, and the Ovambo-Okavango area, as befits the arid nature of the environment, the dominant mode of subsistence is foraging and pastoralism. Archaeological evidence points to a two-thousand-year pastoral sequence. The relationship between pastoralists and foragers is complex; given the unpredictable environment and lack of surface water, many people cyclically engage in both modes. Both make extensive use of local veld foods. Foraging is a variable process ranging in the past from scavenging and harvesting *nara* plants on the coast by the Topnaars to the well-documented foraging patterns of the contemporary !Kung. Several varieties of pastoralism are found, ranging from the agro-pastoralism of the Ovambo speakers to the capital-intensive ranching of the European settlers to nomadic pastoralism.

Khoikhoi-speaking nomadic pastoralists dominated the western and southern portions of the country by the fifteenth century. Linguistic evidence suggests that the various groups of Khoi pastoralists and foragers are closely related and that their economic differentiation was comparatively recent. Conventionally Khoi speakers are divided into the Damara (/Nu Khoe), the Nama, and the Hai//om. The Damara used to be forager-pastoralists. An important segment of the Nama is the Orlam, a Khoi people who migrated from the Cape Colony at the turn of the nineteenth century. These groups are characterized by extremely complex kinship systems. The Hai//om, along with smaller groups of Naron (in the central Kalahari) and Mbarakwengo (on the Okavango), are classified as San.

The other major category of pastoralists are Herero speakers who, most believe, migrated into the country around the seventeenth century and occupy a swath extending from western Angola through Kaokoland and central Namibia to Botswana. They include groups such as the Herero, Mbandero, Kaokoland Herero, Tjimba-Herero, Himba, Zemba, Hakaona, Tjimba, and Thwa. The largest group, the Herero, have a double-descent kinship system featuring seven matrilineal clans (*eanda*) through which individuals inherit cattle and productive property, and twenty exogenous patrilineal clans (*oruzo*) through which religious items like sacred cattle are passed. Historically the pastoralist peoples have had an uncentralized political system, but a number of previously nomadic groups among the Herero and Damara are currently in the process of establishing kingships.

Several of the Herero-speaking groups are forager-hunters, and some are renowned for their ironworking and divination skills. Most anthropological attention to date has been focused on the San, formerly called Bushmen. Major groups, apart from the Khoikhoi and Herero speakers, would include !Kung (also known as !Khu and Ju), //Khau//esi (also known as Makaukau and Nogau), /Nu//en, and /Auni. These people have no common name and should be called by their own names. Their status has been subject to considerable debate.

BIBLIOGRAPHY

Barnard, Alan. *The Bushman Myth: The Making of a Namibian Underclass.* Boulder, Colo., 1992.

————. *Hunters and Herders of Southern Africa.* New York, 1992.

Pendleton, Wade C. *Katutura, a Place Where We Stay: Life in a Post-Apartheid Township in Namibia.* Athens, Ohio, 1996.

ROBERT J. GORDON

See also **Animals; Herero; Khoisan; Kings and Kingship; Kinship and Descent; Ovambo.**

NATAL COLONY, HISTORY. The British colony of Natal was established in 1843–1845 in the territory between the Zulu kingdom in the north and that of the Mpondo to the south; in 1910 it became one of the provinces of the newly formed Union of South Africa. It had received responsible government in 1893 and incorporated Zululand in 1897.

The first white settler-traders established themselves at Port Natal (now Durban) in 1824, a time of great turmoil. Although the underlying causes of that turmoil remain controversial, its most proximate cause was the rise of the Zulu kingdom under Shaka. Victory over the Zulu enabled the establishment of a short-lived Republic of Natalia by boertrekkers (Afrikaners who departed the Cape Colony between 1835 and 1838). Concern over the trekkers' control of the southeast coastline, their negotiations with foreign powers, and their land and labor policies, which threatened to disrupt the Cape's eastern frontier, prompted British annexation, as a district of the Cape Colony in 1845. The Natal Colony was given crown colony status in 1856.

Throughout the nineteenth century, Natal's settler numbers remained extremely small. After British annexation, most Afrikaners moved to South Africa's interior, and were replaced by predominantly British colonists. Heavily outnumbered by the indigenous Nguni-speaking people, they had to come to terms with the strength of the surrounding chiefs as the new colonial state replaced Shaka's tributary state. Imperial decisions about Natal were dominated by absentee landowners who bought up land claimed by the boertrekkers and who were linked with Cape merchants. Rent was extracted from African producers while the landowners waited for an increase in white immigration to raise land prices. Their interests thus coincided with the imperatives of administrators anxious to avoid the open conflict with Africans that would have

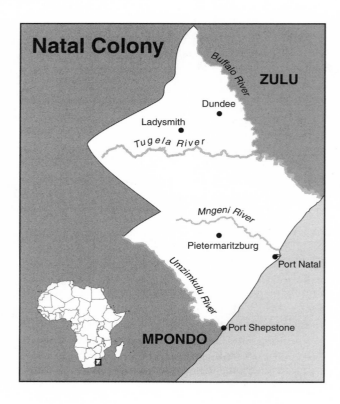

Natal Colony

BIBLIOGRAPHY

Duminy, Andrew, and Bill Guest, eds. *Natal and Zululand: From Earliest Times to 1910. A New History.* Pietermaritzburg, South Africa, 1989.

SHULA MARKS

See also **Afrikaner Republics; Cape Colony.**

NATIONALISM. In Africa, nationalism became a dominant ideology during and after the Second World War. In origins and motivations it may be usefully compared with the anti-imperialist nationalism of subject peoples in other multiethnic empires of the world, notably with those of Austria-Hungary and Ottoman Turkey in somewhat earlier times. Its primary aim was to devise and apply an effective politics of escape from the colonial systems installed by European imperialism, chiefly that of Britain and France. This promise of liberating renewal had obviously to mean different things to different sectors or classes of African society but was to be realized, given the constraints of imperialist policies, by transforming half a hundred subject territories, defined in or shortly before 1901 by frontiers of imperialist partition, into as many sovereign states. In achieving this, it was held, African peoples would be able to reverse the dispossession imposed by European invasion and its consequences.

With many difficulties and much counterviolence against the coercions of the colonial systems, this process of "decolonization," as it later became known, took some forty years to complete. It began in 1951 with the declaration of a "decolonized" kingdom of Libya. It continued across the continent, colony by colony, until 1990, with the formation of a southwest African republic of Namibia out of its quasicolonial status under white South African rule, and finally in 1993, with the self-liberation of Eritrea from that country's colonial condition within the now-defunct Ethiopian empire. Anticolonial nationalism, in short, was the political force wherewith Africans undertook the task of overcoming the disabilities imposed by imperialist dispossession. Its successes opened an entirely new period in the continent's history. In a real and continuing sense, these gave Africans a means of restoring their own identities. But these achievements inevitably brought a number of wounding disabilities.

resulted from direct expropriation. When, in 1860, sugar was successfully exploited, labor was provided by Mozambican migrants and indentured Indians in the face of widespread African refusal to undertake the work while homestead production was still intact. By the end of the century, however—as taxation was increased, Africans' cattle were decimated in the rinderpest pandemic, and land was increasingly in short supply—growing numbers were forced to seek work at white-owned mines and farms in South Africa.

The smallest of the South African colonies, and heavily dependent on the Transvaal, Natal's policies nevertheless provided many precedents for South Africa's later segregationist policies: the recognition of "traditional" authorities; the allocation between 1846 and 1864 of reserved lands for African communal occupation; the codification of "customary" law (from which Christian Africans were exempt); and the attempt to control urbanization through labor registration and pass laws. In contrast with the Cape Colony, Africans were effectively excluded from the vote: at the century's end there were barely half a dozen black voters on the rolls.

As in the internal European empires of the nineteenth century, nationalism had to be the program of newly literate social groupings; this was true even in lands of an ancient Islamic literacy, where the building of a dominant ruling class, or bourgeoisie, was envisaged as the means and guarantee of a liberating modernism. In the minds of the early African advocates of this nationalism—including the Sierra Leonean thinker James Africanus Horton (1835–1883)—Western education, modernizing still more than Christianizing, would enable Africans to stand clear of the "backwardness," as they saw it, to which history had condemned them. Then they could assume their rightful status of self-respect among the peoples of the globe. As another west African visionary, the Gold Coaster S. R. B. Attoh Ahuma (1863–1921), wrote in his then-influential book of 1911, *The Gold Coast Nation and National Consciousness*, "We must emerge from the savage backwoods and come into the open where nations are made." It was as if the whole long history of African community-formation, before European colonial enclosure, had never existed. This was a nationalism, in short, which thrust precolonial political and constitutional experience into a limbo of the lost. Adjusted to the imperialist and essentially racist ethos of the late nineteenth and early twentieth centuries, nationalism supposed a more or less complete break with the ways in which a majority of Africans were accustomed to think about themselves and their communities. For better or worse, nationalism in practice had to marry liberation with alienation. This produced a coupling that was to prove hard to sustain.

As matters stood, however, this project of a Western-educated few leading the uneducated many became the motor of a political rebirth, of a program of anticolonial change, that seemed the only option to those who advocated it. What other liberating project could induce the imperial powers to give way and eventually withdraw? Edward Wilmot Blyden (1832–1912), the Caribbean nationalist assimilated to west Africa, had answered long before: "An African nationality is the great desire of my soul. I believe nationality to be an ordinance of nature; and no people can rise to an influential position among the nations without a distinct and efficient nationality" (*Liberia's Offering*, 1862, p. v). To that end the enlightened few must lead the ignorant many. It was a powerful line of thought to which surviving kings and chiefs of a historical Africa were able to give only a muffled reply. Some

eighty-five years later the rising Nigerian nationalist Obafemi Awolowo (1909–1987) would still find this program a self-evident truth: "Only an insignificant minority have any political awareness" and "this articulate minority are destined to rule the country" (*The Path to Nigerian Freedom*, 1947, p. 63). As was said of Indian nationalists, who in some degree set the pace for those of Africa, the spokespersons of this deliberately moderate African nationalism, seeking advance against a still powerful imperialism, "saw in British officials their opponents but in British institutions their hope" (Percival Spear, ed., *Oxford History of India*, 3d ed., 1958, p. 782).

Along this route, in substance soon followed by nationalists in all the subject African territories at a time when European imperialism had lost the willingness and now the capacity to prolong its supremacy, even while withdrawal might still be much delayed, nationalism in Africa lost the opportunity to build on the state-forming trends or achievements of the African past. It acquired instead a program of nation-state formation on a pattern set by the English and French revolutions of the eighteenth and nineteenth centuries. The project of nationalism became that of a nation-statism the forms and objectives of which, greatly desirable as they seemed at the time, had to be those of models evolved in Western Europe.

That this nation building on an otherwise alien model might repress indigenous political cultures was well enough perceived at the time, and not only by kings or others with a privileged heritage. Yet no other route to effective postcolonial progress appeared to exist or, on the record, seemed likely to emerge. Nation building on the European model became Africa's destiny. For a while, even miniature white-settler minorities like those of Northern Rhodesia (Zambia in 1964) saw themselves as the founders of a nationhood. Even clan-structured peoples whose sense of inherent unity was weak or fractured—the Luo of East Africa would become a significant case, their near-neighbors the Gikuyu another—now began to press forward into the nation-forming arena. Whatever its hybrid origins, the program of nation-statism on the precedents of Western Europe carried all before it.

Origins and Equivocations

But the ambiguities remained. Memorable successes in hastening an end to colonialist overrule were achieved with the promises of a nationalism which had little or no awareness of the needs and constraints of modern nationhood. Such needs and duties might be written into elegant explanations aimed chiefly at non-African audiences, more willing after the lessons of World War II to listen to African voices. But in this immediate postwar era, the ideas of nationalism were powered not by fine rhetoric but by elemental emotions able to inspire the hope of immediate progress.

Very much as among the "submerged nationalities" of nineteenth-century Europe, this power was found in the word "freedom" and its African equivalents, such as *uhuru* in Swahili. Whatever else this freedom might then or later be thought to imply, the slogans of nationalism were accepted as passports to a new and nonracist equality of status and potentials in a world wherein Africans for generations had come to feel themselves woundingly disregarded or despised. So it was that nationalism in its evolved form was above all reactive, drawing its mobilizing strength from currents of self-defense against the racist discrimination which had characterized the rule of all the imperialist powers, if in varying degrees of coerciveness. Yet this mobilizing strength also promised to be creative, not only within the narrow limits of political action but also in cultural struggle, where it might eventually be able to signal the distant onset of a postimperialist culture.

In this creative sense, Africa's nationalism could be understood as a search for identity by peoples long subjected to the suffocating imposition of anonymity. Whatever else nationalism might be thought to imply could have little value; escape from subjection was what mattered. And this was a truth which helps to explain why no one much bothered to investigate the theoretical credentials of the nationalist project. "One thing's certain," exclaimed the Malagasy nationalist Jacques Rabemananjara in 1957 when lecturing a Paris audience: "As we use the word now, nationalism means the unanimous movement of coloured peoples against Western domination. What can it matter if the word should tell or fail to tell the precise nature of the phenomenon we apply it to!" (*Nationalisme et problèmes malgaches*, 1958, p. 122). Others down the years would enlarge on the same thought. In 1992 the notable writer Chinua Achebe, recalling that his own people, the Igbo (Ibo) of eastern Nigeria, had generally preferred to organize themselves in small-scale political communities, explained that self-identification by nationhood was only one of

the many "suits of clothes" that a people could prefer to wear, and that "Nigerian nationality was for me and my generation an acquired taste"— which, he might perhaps have added, had since gone sour in the mouth (*Guardian*, London, 7 May 1992).

For many others, also reared in a powerful awareness of their own histories, this taste for new nationality had to prove difficult to enjoy. To the west African Soninke in the modern republic of Senegal, whose remote history had made them the founders of ancient Ghana more than a thousand years earlier, or to Swahili townspeople in east Africa, whose ancestors not much later had founded cities of coral and commercial wealth, the notion that only a wider sense of nationality could provide a passport to self-respect and civilization had to seem strange and even perverse. The Soninke and Swahili were in no sense unique in remembering a prestigious heritage. Yet nationalism, however reductive of historical realities, had come to seem far more useful in its anticolonial and therefore liberating capacities than any celebration of a past which had so thoroughly and recently met with defeat by European invaders. The Soninke in their villages along the lower Senegal River have given little sign of nostalgia for a vanished past; they have accepted their membership in Senegal. The Swahili in their ancient cities recall the tales of their foundation. But their former "civilisation and urbanity are not merely matters of nostalgia for their golden past"; they "give strength in the present and for the future," since "Swahili civilization is not merely backward-looking or a vehicle of silent protest, but a statement of pride in their ability to survive in an oppressive world" (John Middleton, *The World of the Swahili*, 1992, p. 200).

This ambiguity, latent in the claims of modern nationalism, would emerge a little later when these or other peoples pressed gently or less gently into the nation-forming arena in the 1950s. They would then be denounced as the backward-looking agents of what was often, and often ahistorically, perceived as an anachronistic "tribalism." But meanwhile they were awkwardly out of place within an Africa now striving to shake itself free from colonial rule and the prejudices of racist domination. In Nigeria, for example, Igbo "tribalism" would afterward nourish dissent and civil war within the Nigerian nation-state.

But matters seemed different to those Igbo who took a moral and intellectual lead in promoting the concept of a Nigerian nationality during the years when colonial rule seemed so difficult to remove. For them, as for their west African forebears of the 1860s, escape by way of a pan-Nigerian nationalism uniting all "tribes" could be the only useful way ahead. In 1951, with independence from colonial rule looming close ahead, the prominent modern nationalist of Igbo origin Eyo Ita was clear in his belief that any reversion to the multiplicity of Nigeria's many ancient nations would be "out of date," for the future should be one of devotion to a "Nigerian nationality" (*West African Pilot*, Lagos, Nigeria, 23 January 1951). Six years earlier, when Eyo Ita was the foremost person in the nationalist Nigerian Youth Movement, he told the *West African Pilot* (2 June 1945) that "the greatest need of Nigerians today is to become a community" and to "evolve a national selfhood," which should be achieved by building "a strong national consciousness" from the "tribal unions" which had begun to be formed during the late 1920s.

Ideas and Personalities

These unions or associations, as they were often called, had been seedbeds of nationalism in its emergent anticolonial sense, as had similar entities within the internal European empires of the nineteenth century. They drew their recruits from ethnic- or language-defined groups of country people who had moved to the peripheries of colonial towns, seeking work or relief from hunger. Whether as "urbanized" peasants or migrant laborers, newly mingled peoples came together in these associations, which were initially devoted to the comforts of congeniality and neighborly self-help. Their directly political purpose took shape later with the emergence of anticolonial activists, both women and men. Their impulse stemmed from the anti-imperialist influences of World War I and, far more confidently, from those of World War II.

Taking encouragement from the growing independence movement in British India, and in a more subtle yet persuasive way from the early World War II European defeats at the hands of a non-European nation, Japan, these anti-imperialist influences counteracted the disunifying impact of a "tribal" past. They spoke for a new nationality principle that would carry all before it. The tribal associations proved to be this principle's handy and effective instruments, as evidenced by their rapid integration into parties of nationalism in British and French territories. Their natural ambiguity, as parties loyal both to a national vocation and to a sense of ethnic separatism, would become apparent somewhat later; for the time being, they did much to enable the nation-building few to achieve a wide audience among the masses. Much the same process occurred under culturally different conditions in northern Africa, including Egypt and Sudan. There, Islam had to face and attempt to resolve an increasingly abrasive contradiction between loyalties to the *umma*, the historical "family of Islam" divisible neither by nation nor ethnicity, and nation-state–forming nationalism, which was inherently separatist.

Along with the steady weakening of European imperialist self-assurance after World War II, the nationalist movements gathered strength. The various miseries that would accompany them in later years would obscure what seemed at the time to be—and what history may eventually confirm as—an irreversible assertion of African self-respect. Behind the rhetoric of national liberation were impressive realities of social, cultural, and even economic advance. In the former British and French colonies, though not elsewhere, substantial gains benefiting most of society were made until economic stringencies worsened after the middle 1970s. As the new nation-states took shape quite rapidly south of the Sahara, beginning with the independence of Ghana in 1957, these gains began to include a widening access to primary schooling and improved quality of education for populations hitherto largely or entirely deprived of any means of understanding the world beyond their frontiers. Fairly large numbers of primary-school age children were in school after the 1970s, when the colonial systems were reduced to Portuguese possessions and South Africa's indirect holdings in the far south.

Effectiveness varied, but here and there educational advances were dramatic. In Somalia, independent since 1960, nationalist initiative produced the invention and dissemination after 1972 of an effective means of writing Somali in a Latin script, Somali as a Cushitic language having proved resistant to an Arabic script. Consequently, a people governed for decades in Italian or English could look forward to governing themselves in their own language, even while the colonial legacy in Somalia degraded into chaos after 1978 in connection with Somali attempts to recover the Ogaden territory from Ethiopia.

Modernizing nationalism likewise strove to expand other public services, notably in health and communications. Many colonies had to begin almost from zero, but rapid if uneven progress was

273

made. Hospitals and medical schools were able to draw upon the graduates of expanding systems of public education. Towns and cities grew vastly, swollen by the arrival of impoverished rural peoples, and there too the nationalist promise of a better life could be initially upheld. If some assets were wasted on ceremonial or merely flamboyant presidential and other displays, efforts were also made to satisfy better the basic social needs of the expanding urban centers. Later on they would become vast cities whose chaotic traffic produced the congestion and pollution problems of Europe and America, but this was scarcely the fault of the nationalists. They had promised modernization, and if modernization created problems, that was only to be expected. Rural peoples might complain of neglect, but they were "backward peoples" low on nationalism's agenda.

The nationalists' programs of modernization in the habits and opportunities of everyday life, at least in the cities, provided new sources of self-respect after the humiliations of the colonial decades. Africans, now traveling the world as citizens rather than servants, found a welcome they had seldom received before. Platforms of worldwide debate, notably the United Nations, heard African men and women who spoke as confident equals. Great academies elected Africans to honored membership. At athletic festivals, Africans won famous prizes. Distant crowds received the same message of equality from touring African soccer teams. As never before, African identities became national identities. Famous runners did not cross the tape as Kalenjin or Gikuyu, Oromo or Amhara; they won their medals as Kenyans or Ethiopians. If Yoruba cities produced soccer players of grand renown, these played as Nigerians. If Fante dance music became popular worldwide, this appeared as Ghanaian music. By the 1970s, if not before, the new nation-states had imprinted their identities deeply into world consciousness.

With this assertion of specific identity, the nationalists secured an African dignity and value very capable of banishing debased racist caricatures and fantasies. With what to the old imperialist world might seem a disconcerting suddenness, there appeared a vivid range of African men and women, politicians or statespersons, scientists or poets, whose innovating self-assertion could not be questioned. In perhaps their greatest achievement, they brought to the world a new sense of African presence, an enlargement that was liberating as much as liberated.

As established leaders of their peoples or insurgent rebels in colonies not yet independent, the best of these men and women achieved fame across the globe. Among the early names on the list were those of Kwame Nkrumah in the Gold Coast colony that became Ghana in 1957, Jomo Kenyatta in Kenya, Benjamin Nnamdi Azikiwe in Nigeria, Félix Houphouët-Boigny in Côte d'Ivoire, Julius Nyerere in Tanganyika (which became Tanzania after formal union with the island of Zanzibar in 1964). They took the world to school in the matter of recognizing Africa, and this education continued as the decolonizing process advanced. After 1970 the hitherto unknown peoples of the Portuguese and Spanish colonies entered the world's consciousness with talented leaders such as Amílcar Cabral (Guinea-Bissau and Cape Verde Islands), Agostinho Neto (Angola), and Eduardo Mondlane (Mozambique). Far in the south, the voice of African self-assertion made itself known and respected through the agency of Nelson Mandela and his colleagues of the African National Congress, bringing with them fresh evidence of renewal in a world increasingly prepared to see colonialism as belonging to the sorrows of a rejected past.

The Limits of Nationalism

The dominant imperial powers, Britain and France, had withdrawn from Africa but with reluctance, demanding in effect that the peoples of the continent transform their colonial states into nation-states, this even as, notably in French West and Equatorial Africa and in British East Africa, strong anticolonial voices began to speak favorably of federal or regional solutions once the British and French had begun seriously to envisage their political withdrawal. Defined by the colonial partition, the new nation-states were obliged to accept from that partition a great deal more than frontiers. Given the social deprivation of most of the former colonies, these emergent states were in practice bound to take over the forms of government designed to meet colonial needs. Although pledged to parliamentary democracy, they found themselves chained to the habits and structures of administrative dictatorship. Neither the imperialist powers nor the nationalists offered long-term programs for development. Therefore, the new governments and their parties were left to accept bureaucratic habits and attitudes already in place even while the clearest minds foresaw that the resultant constrictions on democratic representation must promote the rise of dictatorial ambitions and perversions.

Two arenas of acute difficulty soon became apparent. The first was administrative. Rejecting precolonial precedents, the nationalist bureaucracies proved to be acutely centralizing structures. Colonial government had been resolutely "top-down," all effective power being concentrated at the apex of the administrative pyramid. This necessarily militated against any form of democratic development, whether derived from precolonial African experience or imported from Western Europe. In the few countries, most notably Mozambique, where the extremely centralized Soviet model was taken seriously, its impact was disastrous. The new governments found it hard to overcome this centralization of power. Many soon found it impossible. The second difficulty was economic. At least from the middle 1970s all progress in democratic development came into sharp conflict with the economic legacies of the colonial period. Decolonized into a world governed by the needs and interests of the industrialized powers, including the former imperialist powers, African nationalists had to meet the economic terms contingent on their sovereignty, which turned increasingly adverse.

All this combined gradually to ruin the hopes of the nationalists and reduce their nationalism to a caricature of what had been intended. They kept the peace among their nations in all but a few cases, and even in the exceptions the conflicts over frontiers were small. To that end their Organization of African Unity, launched in 1963, had performed as a useful, if limited, forum of intergovernmental diplomacy. Internally, however, many of the new states, for example Zaire and Somalia with many others to follow, found their nationalism swallowed by conflict, or even chaos, as economic stringencies transformed ethnic rivalries, or group rivalries dressed up as "tribalism," to a level of divisive violence against which the state bureaucracies proved increasingly helpless. Just as within the internal empires of nineteenth-century Europe, a liberating nationalism now appeared as a self-defeating scourge. With this decay, nationalists lost the vision and confidence displayed by the pioneers of the 1950s and 1960s. There were exceptions, but generally, it seemed, the nation-statist project had lost its creative power and potential.

A history of these many years of political and ideological decay after the early 1970s would reveal a deepening confusion and defeat. Linked to economic distress, rigidly centralized forms of government had the effect of increasingly confining social power to groups and family structures that could deploy force to use it. While the continent's international terms of trade grew ever more adverse, governments claiming a national vocation collapsed into one or other type of dictatorship by "strong men" or soldiers self-appointed to "save the nation." At best, they struggled against a sea of troubles; at worst, they degraded into banditry. Poverty widened while Africa, as was now realized, could no longer feed itself. Genuine food shortages caused by ecological strain or mistaken policies of development were overtaken or enlarged by internecine piracy and externally promoted subversion, as most tragically during the 1980s in Angola and Mozambique. In the 1990s, the disarray of nationalism appeared complete.

At the same time, as the twentieth century came to its end, the possibility of a different if still-distant prospect could be imagined. As a project of anticolonial restitution, nationalist ideology had delivered notable benefits, and the resultant nation-states would survive. But to survive in more than name or habit, they needed to be seriously reformed. There must somehow be an end to the suffocating centralism of these nation-states, derived from their colonial predecessors. Only this, it was now argued in countless debates at many levels, could rescue communities from the costs and losses of sectional strife and open the door to democratic renewal. Only this could enable African peoples to defend themselves in a world whose structures of investment and exchange strongly advantaged those with maturely industrialized economies. New thinking must be required. With all their merits, the nationalists belonged to the period of great-power imperialism. A postimperialist culture must call for other aims and solutions, perhaps regionalist, perhaps federalist, perhaps taking heart from Africa's centuries of precolonial autonomy. Meanwhile, as the millennium dawned, the public scene in most African countries displayed deepening frustration or despair.

Nationalism had encouraged but largely failed to promote political and social unities such as could induce the democratic development of postcolonial nation-states. In case after case observable as the old millennium ended, supposedly national governments were reduced to bureaucratic tyrannies or, in the worst examples, to militarized banditries. Wherever new "national movements" claimed attention, they appeared in practice to represent little more than the clamors of an extremist fanaticism, most obviously among the ancient Islamic communities of the Mediterranean fringe. These "fundamentalists" might promise a new and regenerative social morality, but whatever they achieved in practice was much more often a reversion to aggressive superstition and its destructive consquences. The high ambitions of national liberation, as these had been lived after the 1950s, had now to be set against the often grim realities of everyday life as most Africans found themselves obliged to live it. In the telling case of Angola, for example, the national movement of the 1950s had undoubtedly produced a sense and presence of national purpose, however much ravaged by externally promoted subversions and internal conflicts. But this had now proved too weak to stand against what had become a generalized process of disintegration.

Speaking on a nationwide broadcast of June 1996 to any of his fellow countrymen who would listen to him, the veteran Angolan president, José Eduardo dos Santos, spoke of a record of national failure to overcome a "crisis that everyone recognizes." Apart from offshore oil extraction, there was now "an extreme degradation of social facilities and equipment," superinflation touching an annual rate of 3,000 percent, an uncontrolled eruption of credit in an economy now virtually abandoned to itself. Health and education systems were "in near collapse." Respect for government and its institutions was barely to be found anywhere. He could have added that most people in Angola now lived within a "parallel economy" that was officially illegal, or they scarcely lived at all. "The poverty of the people is extreme," warned dos Santos, "and despair is entering many hearts."

Elsewhere the crisis of structure had sunk to levels sometimes even more chaotic. The relatively old states of Liberia and Sierra Leone were far gone in militarist confusion and self-frustration. In Liberia the republican order established in the nineteenth century by U.S.-backed "Americo-Liberians" had broken down without signs of possible repair: petty warlords relying on easily available automatic weapons repeatedly set their "armies" at each other without the least concern for any national cause. The little central African countries of Rwanda and Burundi were likewise deep in miseries of self-destruction. But elsewhere the picture was happily different: already there were exceptions to the record of failure. The much-abused country of Uganda, whose formal independence from British colonial rule in 1962 had been

followed by years of strife, at last entered a period of calm and reconciliation under a regime installed late in the 1980s. As peace gradually returned, this regime brought in constitutional initiatives which were drawn, to an important degree, from precolonial attitudes and arrangements, notably in regard to the devolution of authority whether on the national or local level. Something of the same line of postcolonial innovation, resting on the rural consciousness of past moralities, again proved valuable in an Eritrea released from successive phases of colonial usurpation. At the same time, in the far larger and highly populous republic of South Africa, an end to racist government by the white minorities, achieved early in the 1990s, promised to install a process of democratic social change in the wake of many decades of strife and dictatorship. Once again the necessary solutions were promulgated in terms of administrative decentralization from one or other form of colonial or paracolonial dispossession. Africa, it was argued by the reformists, could save itself if it would now draw upon its own experience and wisdom.

This was a lesson that met with resentment or dismissal by all those for whom Africa's indigenous history remained a closed book. Yet the reformists could and did argue, increasingly during the 1990s, that what they were advocating was no more than a modernized reflection or restatement of the thinking of the anticolonialist pioneers of a century earlier. Africa's own history, they maintained, could produce its own solutions, however perverse this advice might seem to commentators for whom precolonial history retained no more than a decorative or sentimental value. What the pioneering anticolonialist thinker J. E. Casely-Hayford (1866–1930) had proposed, a century earlier, notably in his *Gold Coast Institutions* (1903), could now be seen to possess a startling relevance to Africa's condition.

Hayford had argued in his writings, famous at the time though long forgotten, that colonial or paracolonial forms of rule must in any case fail, in that they would turn their back on the moral and political foundations of indigenous civility. And it was seen in due course that the British and their fellow dispossessors had made no effort, when withdrawing their power, to revitalize and reshape existing native institutions: they had left their colonial institutions in place, being sure that these must remain superior to anything that Africans might be able to devise. Leading African thinkers of the 1990s now argued that solutions of the postcolonial crisis must follow a reversal of this Eurocentric habit of thought: the problems of Africa must demand African solutions. For "the tragedy has been," wrote the leading Nigerian thinker Adebayo Adedeji in an acclaimed judgment of 1992, "that when the opportunity came (in the 1960s) to cast aside the yoke of imperialism, no effort was made to reassert Africa's self-determination by replacing the inherited foreign institutions and systems of government, and the flawed European models of nation-states, with rejuvenated and modernised African systems that the people would easily relate to and would therefore be credible" (ACDESS Bulletin 2, Ijebu-Ode, November 1992). How this crucial failure of postcolonial nationalism might now be made good, and by what possible diversities of local initiative and invention, had in fact become the central issues of the whole project of nationalism.

BIBLIOGRAPHY

Ayandele, Emmanuel A. *The Educated Elite in the Nigerian Society.* Ibadan, Nigeria, 1974.

Cabral, Amílcar. *Unity and Struggle: Speeches and Writings.* New York, 1979.

Coleman, James. "Nationalism in Tropical Africa." *American Political Science Review* 48, no. 2 (June 1954): 404–426.

————. *Nigeria: Background to Nationalism.* Berkeley, 1963.

Davidson, Basil. *The Black Man's Burden: Africa and the Curse of the Nation-State.* New York, 1992.

Hodgkin, Thomas. *Nationalism in Colonial Africa.* London, 1956.

————. *African Political Parties.* Harmondsworth, U.K., 1961.

Iliffe, John. *A Modern History of Tanganyika.* New York, 1979.

Isaacman, Allen F., and Barbara Isaacman. *Mozambique: From Colonialism to Revolution.* Boulder, Colo., 1983.

Joseph, Richard A. *Radical Nationalism in Cameroun: Social Origins of the U.P.C. Rebellion.* Oxford, 1977.

July, Robert W. *The Origins of Modern African Thought.* London, 1968.

Langley, J. Ayodele. *Pan-Africanism and Nationalism in West Africa, 1900–1945.* Oxford, 1973.

Markakis, John. *National and Class Conflict in the Horn of Africa.* New York, 1987.

Rothchild, Donald, and Naomi Chazan. *The Precarious Balance: State and Society in Africa:* Boulder, Colo., 1988.

Rotberg, Robert. *The Rise of Nationalism in Central Africa: The Making of Malawi and Zambia, 1873–1964.* Cambridge, Mass., 1965.

Simons, H. J., and R. E. Simons. *Class and Colour in South Africa, 1850–1950.* London, 1969.

BASIL DAVIDSON

See also **Boundaries, Colonial and Postcolonial; Colonialism and Imperialism; Colonial Policies and Practice; Decolonization; Development; Ethnicity and Identity; Independence Movements; Neocolonialism; Political Systems; Postcolonial State.**

NDEBELE. An ethnolinguistic group of peoples who also call themselves Amandebele, Ndzundza, and Manala, the Ndebele are an offshoot of the Nguni, who are Bantu speakers.

There are two branches. One, in Zimbabwe, primarily centered around Bulawayo, is descended from the military leader Mzilikazi (a former lieutenant of Shaka Zulu) and his son and successor, Lobengula. The other branch resides in South Africa, in the areas that were the "homelands" KwaNdebele and Lebowa. This second branch is descended from the leader Musi.

Both branches at one time fled the armies of Shaka Zulu and absorbed people from other groups who were also fleeing him. Both came into conflict with colonists; those in South Africa were rapidly subjugated, whereas those in Zimbabwe resisted long enough for their resistance to be remembered by the colonists as a war.

Like all Nguni peoples, the Ndebele cultivate corn (maize), reside in hamlets, and keep livestock. Urbanization has changed traditional lifestyles; its effect has been especially severe in South Africa, where work is often far from home and mining work has been particularly harsh.

In January 1997, the *New York Times* reported the election of the first female tribal chief, Singobile Mabhena. World feminism and the emergence of other female leaders in southern Africa may have influenced the elders. The other currents of change traversing the world will also leave their mark on the Ndebele.

BIBLIOGRAPHY

Bourdillon, M. F. C. *Where Are the Ancestors?* Harare, 1993.

McCaul, Colleen. *Satellite in Revolt: KwaNdebele—An Economic and Political Profile.* Johannesburg, 1987.

McNeil, Donald, Jr. "Zimbabwean Tribal Elders Air a Chief Complaint." *New York Times,* 12 January 1997, p. 3.

ALEXANDER GOLDMAN

N'DJAMENA. N'Djamena is the capital city of the Republic of Chad. Originally a French garrison (Fort-Lamy), N'Djamena became a permanent

N'Djamena. Formerly known as Fort-Lamy, N'Djamena is Chad's capital and most important trading center. VICTOR ENGLEBERT

settlement in 1900. The original civil population—Hausa, Kanuri, and Shuwa Arab—were forcibly brought in by the French.

The town expanded considerably during the colonial period following the free immigration of new elements producing a melting pot of several cultures. Arabic is now a principal language in urban N'Djamena.

Strategically and geographically located in the center of Africa, N'Djamena was the third busiest airport of the French union during World War II, and it is still an important transit center as well as a major stop on the west-east pilgrim route to Mecca.

BIBLIOGRAPHY

Decalo, Samuel. *Historical Dictionary of Chad.* Metuchen, N.J., 1977.

OLATUNJI OJO

NEGRITUDE. The word "negritude" first appeared in print in Aimé Césaire's long poem, *Cahier d'un retour au pays natal* (*Notebook of a Return to My Native Land,* 1995), published in an early version in the Parisian journal *Volontés* in 1939, and later expanded and revised for the definitive edition published in 1956. At least three related but distinctive meanings can be attributed to the word, coined by Césaire and employed by him in different contexts in the poem. The first meaning emerges from the poet's portrait of a poor black man encountered by chance in a streetcar, of whom he notes that "his negritude was fading under the action of a tireless tawing [curing of skin into white leather]" (p. 107). The visual image that lends substance to this meaning of the term as a physical attribute also functions as focus for a complex of associations symbolic of the degraded condition of the race to which both the poet and the character in question belong.

The second use of the word is at once more comprehensive and more pointed in its reference, and occurs in an allusion to the slave revolt in Saint Domingue (later Haiti) led by Toussaint L'Ouverture, which culminated in the establishment of the first independent black republic in modern history: "Haiti where negritude stood up for the first time and said it believed in its humanity" (p. 91). Here, the word serves as a collective designation for the black race, imagined as a historical and organic entity, the reference serving further to ground the theme of racial affirmation of which the poem itself is a development. This leads naturally, as it were, to the third occurrence in which the word "Negritude" acquires its full charge of meaning, denoting a unique racial endowment, celebrated by the poet in the well-known passage that constitutes one of the climactic moments of the poem:

> my negritude is not an opaque spot of dead water
>   on the dead eye of the earth
> my negritude is neither a tower nor a cathedral
>
> it reaches deep into the red flesh of the soil
> it reaches deep into the blazing flesh of the sky
> it pierces opaque prostration with its upright
>   patience.

(p. 115)

The three meanings may be said to have a common center in their bearing upon the acute racial consciousness, born of a problematic historical experience, that provides the driving force of Césaire's poem. It is of interest in this respect to note another occurrence of the word toward the end of the poem, where Césaire employs it in a context that leaves no doubt about this circumstantial aspect of his expression: "and negritude, not a cephalic index any more or a plasma or a soma but measured with the compass of suffering" (p. 125). This passage sums up the import of Césaire's poem as an exploration of the association between biological fact and existential condition, an association signified in this passage by the term "negritude."

Although fairly circumscribed in each of its various meanings in his poem, Césaire's coinage serves in the late twentieth century to designate in a comprehensive way the literary and ideological movement among French-speaking African and Caribbean intellectuals in their effort to formulate a new sense of black identity, founded upon a revaluation of African traditions. As a movement, "Negritude" represents a variant, conditioned by the circumstances of French colonialism, of the various forms of response by Africans and people of African descent to the historical experience of slavery, colonialism, and racism. As a concept it extends and brings to a culmination, in an impassioned imaginative register as well as in a highly articulated system of ideas, the process of self-reflection on the part of the black intelligentsia in Africa and the Americas provoked by the sentiment of historical predicament stemming from the collective experience of the race.

The Origins of Negritude

The origins of Negritude can be traced to the folk imagination in the diaspora, and in particular to Spirituals, which represent the earliest manifestation and aesthetic expression of black self-representation as a function of a modern experience determined by the African encounter with Europe. The Spirituals testify to an intense imaginative engagement with the condition of exile in America, and its reinterpretation in lyrical terms in relation both to the Western Judeo-Christian framework of the black slaves' existence in America and the sense of a common African origin that transplantation had generated among them. The African sentiment, as given voice in Spirituals, constitutes the thematic ground of diaspora expression, amplified in the work of French-speaking black writers and intellectuals. From this point of view, the Spirituals mark the distant ancestry of Negritude literature.

More immediate in terms of explicit content and medium was the early literature produced during the eighteenth century by educated blacks, whose acquisition of literacy in the European languages enabled them to bear witness to the experience of slavery, and thus to advance the cause of abolition. The master text of this early literature is Olaudah Equiano's autobiography, *Interesting Narrative of the Life of Olaudah Equiano* (1789), the prototype of what has come to be termed the slave narrative genre. Along with the writings of other figures preoccupied with the black condition, such as Ottobah Cugoano, James Gronniosaw, Ignatius Sancho, Phillis Wheatley, and Francis Williams, Equiano's work serves as literary antecedent to Negritude.

The relentless development of racist ideology in Western intellectual circles during the nineteenth century, with the negative image it projected of Africa as a land of unremitting savagery, and its postulate of the inferiority of the black race, exerted such pressure upon the minds of the emerging black elite that its members were compelled to take up the challenge presented to their sense of humanity by this ideology. Edward Wilmot Blyden undertook this task of racial retrieval from about the middle years of the century through a revaluation of the African continent and of its peoples, societies, and cultures. In the series of essays collected in the volume *Christianity, Islam, and the Negro Race* (1887), as well as other writings, Blyden endeavored to construct a new vision of Africa centered on the concept of "African personality," thus anticipating the theory of Negritude in many of its fundamental tenets.

The black elite in the French-speaking Caribbean also contributed to this early effort of racial affirmation. From the late eighteenth to the early twentieth century, such figures as Cyrille Auguste Bissette, Ismaël Urbain, Alexandre Issac, and Gratien Candace questioned the racial and cultural presuppositions of French colonial rule and promoted an awakening of racial solidarity and cultural nationalism that represented a significant precedent for Negritude. A similar thrust in the English-speaking Caribbean can be discerned in the work of J. J. Thomas, whose *Froudacity: West Indian Fables* (1889) constitutes an impassioned refutation of the racist arguments employed to justify slavery and colonialism. The influence of this book was a factor in motivating Henry Sylvester Williams to convoke the meeting, held in London in 1900, of black intellectuals and nationalists that has come to be regarded as the first Pan-African Congress. W. E. B. Du Bois, who played a minor role at that meeting, was later to expand the Pan-African movement through a series of historic meetings, notably those held in 1919 in Paris and in 1945 in Manchester, with significant consequences for developments in Africa. The influence of Du Bois was to extend beyond the English-speaking world to the black subjects of the French colonial empire.

Another African American, Marcus Garvey, also exerted a direct influence on the group of African colonials living in France during the interwar years, inspiring various anticolonial movements based on racial solidarity among black people. As the name implies, Kojo Tovalou-Houénou's Ligue Universelle pour la Défense de la Race Noire was modeled on Garvey's Universal Negro Improvement Association. The sentiment of racial grievance was central to the foundation of this and other organizations and publications, such as the Comité de Défense de la Race Nègre, founded by Lamine Senghor in 1926, with the journal *La voix des Nègres* as its mouthpiece, and Tiémoko Garan Kouyaté's journal, *Le cri des Nègres.* These were affiliated with the French Communist Party and advocated not only redress for the black race but also the rehabilitation of African culture.

These various movements provide the political and social context in which literary and cultural expression began to evolve among black students and intellectuals resident in Paris during the interwar years. Many had made the acquaintance of Du Bois's works, especially *The Souls of Black Folk* (1903). The impetus Du Bois's writings lent to the emergence of the Harlem Renaissance gave his pan-Negro ideas even wider resonance. The direct impact of the Harlem writers on the francophone black elite was also considerable. They identified with the works of Langston Hughes, Claude McKay, and Countee Cullen, which reflected their own preoccupations. Alain Locke's anthology, *The New Negro* (1925), with his introduction stressing the moral necessity for blacks to assert themselves, may have pointed the way to the affirmative tone that Léopold Sédar Senghor and Césaire were later, in their different ways, to adopt in the context of the Negritude movement.

Alain Locke's message was given new resonance in French by Jean Price-Mars, whose work *Ainsi parla l'oncle* (1928) was a statement of the dominant presence of Africa in the folkways and consciousness of the Haitian population. The book inspired a renewal of Haitian letters, marked by an original idiom newly attuned to the realities of Haitian life and experience. The literature of the so-called Indigenist movement in Haiti during the 1920s and 1930s, associated with Carl Brouard, René Bélance, Jacques Roumain, and Jacques Stephen Alexis, provides the first systematic development in the French language of the racial theme in black literature. The Haitian Renaissance may be considered the immediate predecessor of Negritude. Indeed, there is considerable overlap between the work of the writers involved in both movements. The parallel development in Cuba of the movement known as *negrismo,* with the ethnographic studies of Fernando Ortiz playing a similar role to that of Price-Mars, should also be noted. The Cuban movement was dominated in its significant phase by the work of Nicolas Guillén, who explored the theme of black identity and integrated folk beliefs into his poetry.

The sustained contact of the educated black elite with the Western literary and intellectual tradition meant that this tradition was bound to affect the structure of their ideas and their habits of thought. Marxism gave form and direction to black social consciousness, as a result of Lenin's association of capitalism with colonialism in his *Imperialism* (1917). Antedating the influence of Marx and Lenin was that of Johann Gottfried von Herder (1744–1803), whose organic conception of national identity underlies the racial nationalism of Blyden and Du Bois, for both of whom Africa represented the national home of the black race. Indeed, the cultural implications of Herder's idea of the Volksgeist, echoed in Du Bois's title, *The Souls of Black Folk,* compelled the affirmation of a universal black culture, with vital and profound links to Africa.

This affirmation was greatly facilitated in the case of the francophone black elite by the recognition that African art forms and black musical expression began to receive in the early years of the twentieth century in the Western world, especially in Paris. The revolution provoked by the encounter of leading European artists with African sculpture opened the way to modernism in art, and to an alternative aesthetics in the plastic arts that Georges Hardy sought to explore in his *L'art nègre* (1927). At the same time, the success of Blaise Cendrars's *Anthologie nègre* (1921) attested to a growing French interest in other areas of African creative endeavor. Of equal significance was the development in anthropology of relativism as a methodological principle. The new spirit of cultural tolerance which this promoted was reflected in the work of French scholars, notably Maurice Delafosse, Robert Delavignette, and later, Marcel Griaule, who fostered a new appreciation of African forms of social organization and thought systems. But it was above all the romantic vindication of Africa in the work of the German, Leo Frobenius, in particular *Histoire de la civilisation africaine* (1933), that had the greatest impact on French-speaking African and Caribbean intellectuals. Mention must also be made of Oswald Spengler's *The Decline of the West* (1918), a work that not only anticipated the dispirited mood of the West in the aftermath of World War I, but also contained a spiritualized conception of culture that both Césaire and Senghor took to heart. Finally, for the budding writers among the black francophone elite, surrealism offered an appealing theory of imaginative expression derived from Freudian principles, a theory that held out the promise of total moral and metaphysical liberation.

Precursors of Negritude

The literary and cultural affirmation of French-speaking black intellectuals began to take distinctive form with the publication of René Maran's novel *Batouala* (1920), which won the Prix Goncourt in 1921. Senghor has designated Maran as "the precursor of Negritude." The claims of his novel to attention reside less in its anticolonial stance than in its marked departure from the tradition of the French exotic novel with which the African theme had been bound up, as illustrated by Pierre Loti's *Roman d'un spahi* (1889). Maran's work was not only the first novel in French to portray Africans as fully developed characters; it also depicted a certain intensity of experience as essential to an African way of life.

The movement of feeling and ideas among francophone black intellectuals began to be developed in the years after the appearance of Maran's novel in a series of journals, beginning with the short-lived *La revue du monde noir*, published by the Nardal sisters, Paulette and Andrée, between November 1931 and April 1932. In 1932 Étienne Léro and René Ménil brought out the first and only number of *Légitime défense*; proclaiming their affiliation to Marxism and surrealism, they announced a principled repudiation of all previous Caribbean literature, along with a determined opposition to French political and cultural domination. The journal was immediately suppressed by the French

authorities, but was followed by *L'étudiant noir*, founded in 1935 by Senghor and Césaire. More moderate in tone, this journal served as a common platform of expression for Africans and Caribbeans.

These journals mark the first phase of a creative and intellectual collaboration between francophone black intellectuals that was interrupted by the outbreak of World War II. Already a new literary movement was under way: Léon Damas had published *Pigments*, his collection of poems, in 1937, and Césaire the first version of *Cahier d'un retour au pays natal* in 1939; Senghor's earliest poems had also begun to appear in the French review *Charpentes* in 1939. Returning to Martinique just before the outbreak of World War II, Césaire kept alive the momentum generated by the interwar activities among black students by founding the cultural review *Tropiques* (1941–1945). Césaire and his collaborators, including his wife Suzanne, brought to bear a formidable intellectual armory upon their examination of the social and psychological problems of their native island. They sought to circumscribe the nature of the Caribbean self by reference to the cultural ideas of Spengler and Frobenius, both of whom stressed the necessity to root oneself in a given environment for any meaningful self-awareness. The objective of the team grouped around *Tropiques* was to promote, through a process of self-knowledge, the emergence of an authentic Caribbean identity that would represent a full integration of the African component into the Martinican's cultural personality. *Tropiques* in effect began to formulate a vision of black experience that was to be central to the idea of Negritude.

Negritude as a Distinctive Movement

The ideological project of *Tropiques* was taken up and extended in the journal *Présence africaine*, founded in 1947 by Alioune Diop, with the collaboration of some of the most eminent French writers and intellectuals of the day. These included Jean-Paul Sartre, the leading French philosopher of his generation, who was to play a fundamental role in the development of Negritude. In 1948 Senghor published the historic *Anthologie de la nouvelle poésie nègre et malgache de langue française* (1948), conceived as a French equivalent of Locke's *The New Negro*. It was Sartre's essay, "Orphée noir," written as a preface to Senghor's anthology, that provided the first extended discussion and formulation of Negritude as a concept. But it was *Présence africaine* and the Société Africaine de Culture (SAC), a support organization for the journal, that crystallized Negritude as a distinctive literary and cultural movement. The two congresses organized by SAC, the first in Paris in 1956, and the second in Rome in 1959, have assumed historic significance, enshrined in the Congresses' published proceedings. The society was also reponsible for conceiving and planning the First World Festival of Negro Arts held in Dakar in 1966, under the patronage of Senghor, who had by then become president of the independent Republic of Senegal. It was also in this capacity that he organized the Colloquium on Négritude in Dakar in 1971 as a summing up, in the postcolonial period, of the ideas and achievement of the movement. By this time a substantial literary output and body of thought had become associated with Negritude, and the term itself had become established in the vocabulary of contemporary political and cultural discourse.

The primary character of the literature of Negritude is its unrelenting focus on the collective experience of the black race. It testifies to the lived actualities of black historicity marked by a problematic relationship to the West. This had to do especially with the moral discomforts of cultural dualism, given poignant expression in the poem "Trahison" by the Haitian Léon Laleau. Léon Damas uses irony to evoke the pain of self-denial, depicted in more straightforward accents in the poems of Guy Tirollien and Paul Niger. The dilemmas of culture contact are also explored in a realistic mode by the Senegalese writer, Ousmane Socé, in his novel *Karim* (1935). These works reflect the malaise of assimilation as a factor of lived experience, which became translated in the literature into the theme of alienation, summed up by Senghor:

> And this other exile, much harder on my heart
> The tearing apart of one self from the other.
> From my mother's tongue, from the ancestral skull
> From the tomtom of my soul.
>
> (*Éthiopiques,* in *The Collected Poetry,* p. 105)

Much Negritude literature revolves around this theme. Its classic statement came in Cheikh Hamidou Kane's introspective novel, *L'aventure ambigüe* (1961) (*Ambiguous Adventure,* 1963).

The deep anxieties generated by the cultural constraints of French assimilation policy in the francophone black elite account for the emotional energy of its literary revolt. The elite's recourse to literature as a mode of combat was predicated on a faith in the efficacy of imaginative discourse as a force in the world. In this they took their cue from the Harlem writers, who combined social protest with racial affirmation. This revolutionary stance of francophone expression is best exemplified in *Bois-d'ébène* (1945) by Jacques Roumain, and in *Minerai noir: Poèmes* (1956), by René Depestre, both Haitians. On a broader front, the literature of Negritude presents itself as a polemical contestation of colonialism, as in David Diop's *Coups de pilon: Poèmes* (1956) (*Hammer Blows,* 1975), and as an indictment of the West, as in Senghor's *Hosties noires* (1948) (*Black Hosts,* in *The Collected Poetry,* 1991). The bitter mood of the poetry also pervades the tone of many of the prose works which train a critical light on colonialism. In *Climbié* (1956), Bernard Dadié documents in an autobiographic mode the impact of the colonial experience on a young consciousness, also registered by the adolescent heroes of the two Cameroonian novelists, Mongo Beti and Ferdinand Oyono. It is, however, the poetry of Aimé Césaire, with its elaboration in surrealist imagery of an aesthetics of revolt, that marks Negritude as a literature of dissidence:

> A robust bolt of thunder flashes danger
> On the most untouchable brow in the world . . . .
>
> And beware the crow that does not fly it is my head which has broken loose of the centerpole of my shoulders uttering an ancient screech rending guts scattering watering holes.
>
> ("Soleil cou coupé," 1948;
> translated by F. Abiola Irele)

Césaire's poetry represents the ultimate expression of black revolt, revealing in its turbulent development the deep mechanisms that Frantz Fanon was later to analyze in clinical terms. But although the sentiment of revolt was given emphatic expression in the literature, the theme most closely associated with Negritude is that of rediscovery. The disaffection with the West dictated a movement of reconnection with a past that was felt to represent the true repository of the black self. The interest in the African past was reflected in the documentary manner of Paul Hazoumé's reconstruction of precolonial Dahomey (present-day Bénin) in his historical novel, *Doguicimi* (1938) (*Doguicimi: The First Dahomean Novel,* 1989). It also took the form of a lyrical statement of origins, as in Camara Laye's nostalgic recall of his childhood in *L'enfant noir* (1953) (*The Dark Child,* 1954), extended into a mystical vision of the African universe in *Le regard du roi* (1954) (*The Radiance of the King*, 1956). Birago Diop's celebrated poem, "Spirits," illustrates vividly the spiritualist temper of this aspect of Negritude literature:

> Listen to Things
> More often than Beings,
> Hear the voice of fire,
> Hear the voice of water.
> Listen in the wind,
> To the sighs of the bush;
> This is the ancestors breathing.
> (in Kennedy, ed., p. 152)

The poetry of Senghor provides the most sustained expression of Negritude's imaginative revaluation of Africa. The return to the source is identified with the recall of an antecedent state of grace, "le royaume d'enfance" (the kingdom of childhood). Senghor's comprehensive evocation of an African historical and mythical consciousness proceeds from a constant recourse to imagery drawn from the physical and human environment of his indigenous Serer background, which assumes meaning as the true realm of his being:

> I know that only this rich black-skinned plain
> Is worthy of my plowshare and the deep flow of
>   my virility"
> ("Shadow Songs," in *The Collected Poetry*, p. 29)

In Senghor's poetry the project of Negritude literature emerges ultimately as the effort to invest Africa with poetic significance. In a more general perspective, the literature of Negritude assumes innovative significance as the elaboration and actualization of a new aesthetics.

The thought processes reflected in the imaginative literature are clarified in the ideological writings. Indeed, these writings take up in discursive terms the themes expressed in images in the literary works. Thus, Damas details the inequities of French colonial rule in his *Retour de Guyane* (1938), while Fanon's *Peau noire, masques blancs* (1952) (*Black Skin, White Masks*, 1967) presents itself as a narrative, in the language of clinical psychology, of the pathos of black existence in a world regulated by the values of the white world. The combative orientation of Albert Tevoedjré's *L'Afrique révoltée* (1958) is evident from its title. The most trenchant indictment remains Césaire's tract, *Discours sur le colonialisme* (1950) (*Discourse on Colonialism*, 1972), marked by its aggrieved tone and insistence on the grave moral implications for the colonizer of the violations involved in the colonial adventure.

Theories of Black Identity

The effort to construct a theory of black identity represents a movement from the polemical to the constructive stage of Negritude. Ironically, it was a Frenchman, Jean-Paul Sartre, who provided the movement with its initial terms of discourse. Remarking in his essay, "Orphée noir," upon the intense fixation on the racial self in Negritude (what he calls "an anti-racist racism"), Sartre went on to dwell upon the sense of racial self-affirmation conveyed by Césaire's term. He thus described Negritude as an "an affective attitude to the world," and offered a definition of the concept in terms of the existentialist philosophy of which he was the foremost exponent in France, as "l'être-dans-le-monde du Noir" (the being-in-the-world of the Negro). He concludes by stressing the overdetermined nature and contingent status of the concept, which was bound in his view to fuse with the class consciousness of a universal proletariat.

While granting limited assent to Sartre's definition, Senghor has placed greater emphasis on Negritude as a cultural concept, with an objective expression in precolonial forms of life and modes of expression in Africa. Furthermore, Negritude constitutes for him an organic whole, what he calls "l'ensemble des valeurs de civilisation africaines" (the sum total of African values of civilization). As employed by him, the term serves to designate the common denominator of a global identity of the black race. The extension of the concept to include people of African descent in the Americas is justified not only by a common experience of historical adversity but on the grounds of the distinctive nature of African-derived subcultures in America, which Senghor considers as channels of a fundamental connection to the ancestral heritage. As such, they serve as institutional bearers of the racial memory.

The core of Senghor's theory of Negritude is constituted by his elucidation, in the series of essays written over a period of some twenty-five years and collected in *Liberté 1* (1964), of what he takes to be the essential nature of the African, as this is grounded in a racial disposition, and his exposition of an African mode of apprehension and the distinctive Weltanschauung it determines. For Senghor the preeminent trait of Africans is their gift of emotion, a highly developed faculty that underlies their intuitive grasp of phenomena and conditions an immediate participation in the profound reality of the world. This faculty enables a concrete experience that captures the inward scope of things and is therefore more complete than the limited understanding furnished by the discursive mode and analytical method of Western rationality. For Senghor the emotive experience constitutes accession to a higher mode of consciousness and is therefore expressive of a more vivid sense of life, one that informs African forms of social organization and cultural expression.

Senghor's Negritude represents a counter discourse to Western representations of Africa. His formulation proceeds by reversing the negative connotations of traits attributed to the black race in the colonial ideology, and endowing them with a new and positive meaning. This is especially the case with Count Arthur Gobineau's ascription of an emotive disposition to the black race as a sign of the genetic incapacity of its members for intellectual production, and Lucien Lévy-Bruhl's notion of a "primitive mentality" characterized by a prelogical mental structure, with mystic participation as its mode of experience, a notion he presents as the defining trait of non-Western races. Senghor reinterprets these European thinkers in the perspective opened up by the epistemology of Henri Bergson, with its reaction against the dominant tradition of positivism and its valuation of intuition as a valid mode of knowledge. Apart from Bergson's influence, Senghor's thinking is generally tributary of the antirationalist current of modern thought; thus, along with the "paieduma" of Leo Frobenius, Negritude incorporates the vitalist aestheticism of Nietzsche and owes much to the vatic conception of philosophy associated with Martin Heidegger, with its privileging of the "preconceptual" as the ultimate basis for our discovery of the world.

Senghor's Negritude defines itself as an alternative vision of the world to that proposed by the West. The presiding idea of his theoretical effort is a pluralism that not only grants recognition to all cultures within their respective frames of reference, but also enables productive encounters between the cultures of the world, as the dynamic of a multiple dialogue leading to their convergence in a universal civilization, what he calls "la civilisation de l'universel." For Senghor, then, Negritude is a new humanism derived from authentic African values. This aspect of Negritude prompted the investigation of African thought systems by francophone

African scholars in an effort to construct a coherent African philosophy, of which Placied Tempels's *La philosophie bantoue* (1949) (*Bantu Philosophy*, 1952) offered a precedent and model. The outstanding work of Alexis Kagame, in *La philosophie bantu-rwandaise de l'être* (1956) and *La philosophie bantu comparée* (1976), represents a development on Tempels and the centerpiece of a school, composed mainly of central Africans, whose work has come to be grouped under the rubric of "ethnophilosophy." Alassane Ndaw's *La pensée africaine* (1983) contains an expansive reformulation and synthesis of various ideas developed by this school. Beyond philosophical speculation, the postindependence situation also inspired a quest for the intellectual foundations of a new and focused sense of African endeavor. As with other African ideological leaders such as Julius Nyerere and Kwame Nkrumah, Senghor began to develop the concept of African socialism as an extension of Negritude, which thus came to serve as the conceptual framework for a social theory concerned with nation building and modernization in Africa.

Negritude has functioned as a central reference for what Molefi Asante has termed "a universal African consciousness" (*Afrocentricity*, p. 25). Its historical and thematic connection to black movements in the new world, and its integration of earlier black responses to a difficult history into a comprehensive vision of the race, account for its appeal and influence. As a form of cultural resistance to apartheid, Steve Biko's "black consciousness" is clearly related to the Negritude concept; the analogy is reinforced by the militant literature that accompanied Biko's movement, exemplified by the poetry of Oswald Mtshali, Sipho Sepamla, and Mongane Serote. In the Caribbean the ancestralism of Kamau Brathwaite draws its force from the example of Césaire. Negritude has also lent new impetus to African American movements since the 1960s. As a cultural expression of black power and the struggle for civil rights, the Black Aesthetics movement represents not only an extension of the Harlem Renaissance but also a reconnection to African antecedents. The avowed affiliation to Negritude of Asante's *The Afrocentric Idea* (1987) illustrates the cycle of reciprocities and commonality of themes between currents of thought and feeling in the black diaspora and on the African continent. Moreover, Afrocentrism acquires a special dimension by its attachment to the historiography by Cheikh Anta Diop and Theophile Obenga, given publicity by the controversy generated within the American academy by Martin Bernal's expansion of their work in his *Black Athena* (1987).

The Negritude Controversy

The intersection of Negritude with these various movements and trends reflects its focus on what Ralph Ellison has termed an "identity of passions" among black people (*Shadow and Act*, 1964). The concept has nonetheless been at the center of a controversy concerning its meaning and practical significance. Negritude met from the beginning with reservations in English-speaking Africa. Ezekiel Mphahlele called Negritude an "intellectual cult" in his *The African Image* (1962), while Wole Soyinka, who referred to it as "this magnitude of unfelt abstractions," mounted a full-scale attack on the concept in his *Myth, Literature, and the African World* (1976). Negritude also met with strong dissent from the radical wing of the French-African intelligentsia, who reject the biological determinism and idealism implied in the concept. Frantz Fanon, who took his early theoretical bearings from Negritude, came to dissociate himself from its hyperromanticism and to consider its culturalist emphasis as a form of accommodation with colonialism. He advocated instead, in *Les damnés de la terre* (1961) (*The Wretched of the Earth*, 1965), a revolutionary nationalism for Africa, conceived in terms of a Sartrian project of self-realization. The political uses of Negritude as state ideology in Senegal in the postindependence period and its association with "francophonie" has led to its being linked with internal conservative interests and neocolonial pressures. The mutation of Negritude into *authenticité* by the authoritarian regime of Mobutu Sese Seko in Zaire, imitated by Étienne Eyadema in Togo, has also fostered disquiet as to the less desirable implications of ideologies of African revival.

In the French-speaking Caribbean, the debate has developed as a reaction among the younger generation of writers and intellectuals against a universal Negritude undergirded by an African sentiment, with its postulate of an invariant essence of black people. Breaking with Césaire's romantic devotion to Africa, Édouard Glissant has advanced in his *Discours antillais* (1981) the notion of *antillanité* (Caribbeanness) as a more appropriate formulation of the differentiated and localized experience of Caribbean populations. Roland Souvélor has gone further to consider Negritude as another master discourse, exhibiting the same will to power as the Western discourse which it combats.

The general reaction against Negritude in the French Caribbean finds its most vigorous expression in *Éloge de la créolité* (1989), written jointly by Jean Bernabé, Patrick Chamoiseau, and Raphaël Confiant, a manifesto promoting an unfettered Caribbean consciousness and sensibility, and whose spirit corresponds to the heterogenous and unbounded imagination claimed for postmodernism.

Finally, Negritude has been involved in the current debate on the question of African philosophy. Kwasi Wiredu's scrutiny of its philosophical claims in his *Philosophy and an African Culture* (1980) connects directly with the comprehensive critique in francophone Africa of "ethnophilosophy" as an outgrowth of Negritude. This critique was undertaken by Marcien Towa in his *Essai sur la problématique philosophique dans l'Afrique actuelle* (1971), and especially by Paulin Hountondji in *Sur la "philosophie africaine"* (1977) (*African Philosophy: Myth or Reality*, 1983). The debate these works have generated centered upon an examination of the philosophical status of traditional systems of thought in Africa and their capacity not only of providing a satisfactory explanation of the world comparable to Western systems of knowledge, but also of ensuring the survival of Africa in a world regulated by the precepts of modern technological civilization. Against this background, V. Y. Mudimbe's *The Invention of Africa* (1988) presents itself as an effort of reconstruction in African philosophy, bent toward the promotion of a new mode of African rationality that departs radically from the Western, which he calls "gnosis."

The Negritude debate represents a significant phase in the intellectual adventure of contemporary Africa. The heightened consciousness denoted by the concept must be seen as inherent in the project of self-recovery necessitated by the historical experience to which it testifies. This is an inevitable component of cultural nationalism everywhere, all forms of which are parallels to Negritude. It is indeed no accident that, in its genesis, the Negritude movement owed much of its inspiration to the tradition of German nationalism that goes back to Herder and Johann Gottlieb Fichte, with its romantic exaltation of the German national spirit. The cultural revival of central and eastern Europe, manifested so powerfully in music, and the remarkable flowering of Irish literature in this century, inaugurated by the Celtic movement, offer examples of a creative impulse driven in each case by an intense national or ethnic consciousness. The motivating factor in these movements, as in

Negritude, is clearly the aspiration to establish what, in the American context, Ralph Waldo Emerson called "an original relation to the universe."

BIBLIOGRAPHY

Adotevi, Stanislas. *Négritude et négrologues.* Paris, 1972.

Bâ, Sylvia Washington. *The Concept of Negritude in the Poetry of Léopold Sédar Senghor.* Princeton, N.J., 1973.

Césaire, Aimé. *Cahier d'un retour au pays natal.* Paris, 1939. Rev. ed. Paris, 1956.

———. *Notebook of a Return to My Native Land.* Translation of *Cahier d'un retour au pays natal* by Mireille Rosello with Annie Pritchard. Newcastle upon Tyne, 1995.

Diop, Cheikh Anta. *Nations nègres et culture.* Paris, 1956.

———. *L'unité culture de l'Afrique noire.* Paris, 1959.

Fanon, Frantz. *Black Skin, White Masks.* Translation of *Peau noire, masques blancs* by Charles Lam Markmann. New York, 1967.

Hausser, Michel. *Pour une poétique de la négritude.* 2 vols. Paris, 1988, 1991.

Hountondji, Paulin. *African Philosophy: Myth or Reality.* Translation of *Sur "la philosophie africaine"* by Henri Evans with the collaboration of Jonathan Rée. Bloomington, Ind., 1983; 2d ed., 1996.

———. *Sur "la philosophie africaine."* Paris, 1977.

Kagame, Alexis. *La philosophie bantu-rwandaise de l'être.* Brussels, 1956.

———. *La philosophie bantu comparée.* Paris, 1976.

Kennedy, Ellen Conroy, ed. *The Negritude Poets: An Anthology of Translations from the French.* New York, 1975.

Kesteloot, Lilyan. *Les écrivains noirs de langue française.* Brussels, 1965.

Masolo, D. A. *African Philosophy in Search of Identity.* Bloomington, Ind., 1994.

Michael, Colette V. *Negritude: An Annotated Bibliography.* West Cornwall, Conn., 1988.

Mphahlele, Ezekiel. *The African Image.* London, 1962.

Mudimbe, V. Y. *The Invention of Africa.* Bloomington, Ind., 1988.

———. *Parables and Fables: Exegesis, Textuality, and Politics in Central Africa.* Madison, Wisc., 1991.

Ndaw, Alassane. *La pensée africaine: Recherche sur les fondements de la pensée négro-africaine.* Dakar, 1983.

Obenga, Théophile. *L'Afrique dans l'antiquité.* Paris, 1970.

Sartre, Jean-Paul. "Orphée noir." In *Situations III.* Paris, 1949.

Senghor, Léopold Sédar. *Nation et voies africaines du socialisme.* Paris, 1961.

———. "De la négritude: Psychologie du négro-africain." *Diogène* no. 37 (1962).

———. *Liberté 1: Négritude et humanisme.* Paris, 1964.

———. *Liberté 2: Nation et voie africaine du socialisme.* Paris, 1971.

———. *Liberté 3: Négritude et civilisation de l'universel.* Paris, 1977.

———. *Anthologie de la nouvelle poésie nègre et malgache de langue française.* Paris, 1948. 4th ed. Paris, 1977.

———. *The Collected Poetry.* Translated by Melvin Dixon. Charlottesville, N.C., 1991.

———. *Liberté 5: Le Dialogue des cultures.* Paris, 1993.

———. "Négritude: A Humanism of the Twentieth Century." In *The African Reader: Independent Africa,* edited by Wilfred G. Cartey and Martin Kilson. New York, 1970.

Soyinka, Wole. *Myth, Literature, and the African World.* New York, 1976.

Towa, Marcien. *Essai sur la problématique philosophique dans l'Afrique actuelle.* Yaoundé, Cameroon, 1971.

F. ABIOLA IRELE

See also **Invention and Images of Africa** (at the beginning of Volume 1); **Camara Laye; Césaire, Aimé; Diaspora; Diop, Alioune; Diop, Cheikh Anta; Du Bois, W. E. B.; Equiano, Olaudah; Fanon, Frantz; Garvey, Marcus Mosiah; Kagame, Alexis; Nationalism; Senghor, Léopold Sédar; Tempels, Placied.**

NEOCOLONIALISM. When most of the sub-Saharan African states achieved political independence in the early 1960s, a rift appeared between two groups. One proclaimed a political allegiance to the old colonial powers and the Atlantic powers in general and intended to rely on their support in the states' efforts toward development. The other group emphasized the significance of their liberation from the colonial yoke, choosing nonalignment in international relations, moving closer to the Soviet Union and the radical Arab states—particularly the Egypt of Gamal Abd-al Nasser—and declaring themselves socialist. The second group described the first as "neocolonial," coining a word that would become politically popular in the 1960s and 1970s and then fade gradually during the 1980s.

Colonial Policy After World War II

This rift was the inevitable result of the varying natures of the national liberation movements that led to the independence of these states. In certain countries, these movements mobilized large masses that often entered into violent conflict with the colonial administration. For these liberation movements, independence had not been granted by the colonial power but had been won in struggle against it. These countries became nonaligned and socialist. A granted independence, on the other hand, had occurred where the leaders of the national liberation movement not only had not antagonized the colonial administration but, won over to its strategies, had not even asked for the independence that was suddenly offered to them. These countries were dubbed "neocolonial."

The neocolonialism debate, therefore, must assess the strategies of the dominant imperialisms. At the end of World War II, the colonial powers—Great Britain, France, the Netherlands, Portugal, and Belgium—intended to maintain and reestablish, by force if necessary, the colonial regimes in Asia and Africa. To this end, they engaged in wars of colonial reconquest in Indochina, Indonesia, Malaysia, and the Philippines, or in the brutal repression of popular protests in the dependent colonies and countries, as with Algeria in 1945; Egypt in 1946; Madagascar in 1947; Kenya in the suppression of the Mau Mau during the 1950s; and the Cameroons in the suppression of the Union des Populations des Camerouns (UPC), also in the 1950s. Yet the colonial powers had to take into account important changes in the development of national liberation movements, whether they dated back to the end of the nineteenth century, as was the case in Asia and Egypt, or had crystallized immediately after World War II, as was the case in most African countries. Confronted with India's size, Great Britain had to rule out military intervention and so was forced to negotiate seriously for the first time, devoting its energies to dividing India up. Elsewhere, though, the strong-arm solution was always considered a possible alternative.

It is often said that the new hegemonic imperialism, that of the United States, advocated decolonization and therefore backed the liberation movements. Yet this claim is certainly wrong. The United States carefully distinguished between two kinds of movements. One kind was the "dangerous" movement, which opted for a policy of radical rupture, linking the recovery of independence to the running of an anti-imperialist, antifeudal social revolution, as in Vietnam and Southeast Asia generally. The other kind consisted of "moderate" movements, which did not challenge the integration of their economy into the worldwide capitalist system. The United States supported its allies against the radical movements, even taking over from the former if necessary, as was the case in Vietnam. Regarding the moderate movements, the United States pressured the two parties to promote negotiation.

The Soviet Union, which on principle supported the demands of every liberation movement, bourgeois or socialist, was isolated by the cold war that

the United States decided to impose upon the Soviets after it gained a monopoly on atomic weapons in 1945. Thus, Soviet support remained purely moral until the historic conference held in Bandung in 1955, which offered the USSR the possibility of allying itself with a new bloc of the non-aligned nations in Asia and the Middle East. The formation of this bloc and the financial support that the Soviet Union and China gave it led the colonial powers in Africa to rethink their relation with the continent.

In Africa, the national liberation movements were in no way insignificant, despite the intrinsic weaknesses of the region, with its small and scattered population, low level of urbanization and, especially, of education, almost total lack of local bourgeoisies and so on. Still, the variety of social and historical conditions across the continent gave the movements of each country their own character. On the matter of variation, there has been an emphasis upon the differing attitudes of the colonizers; contrasts have been made, for example, between the assimilationist politics of France (through the French Union) and Portugal and the so-called indirect rule of Britain. These differences, though, are more rhetorical than real in the case of Africa, where in actual practice direct colonial administration was the dominant approach.

Internal African Conditions

The distinctive characteristics of internal conditions in Africa are salient. In Africa a number of colonies, protectorates, and a formally independent dominion had significant white populations: Algeria and, to a lesser degree, Morocco, and Tunisia in North Africa; Kenya, Southern Rhodesia (later Zimbabwe), and, especially, the Union of South Africa, in sub-Saharan Africa. Here the national liberation movements were confronted with the issue of the future of the white colonizers. In the extreme cases of South Africa (1948) and independent Rhodesia (1965, formerly British Southern Rhodesia), where the white minority had seized exclusive political power, the movements had to deal with the issue of apartheid (South Africa) and quasi-apartheid (Rhodesia). Yet, as a whole, the continent had been integrated into the capitalist world as an exporter of tropical agricultural products supplied by a peasantry of small market producers, with mining enclaves here and there, especially in the Belgian Congo and in southern Africa. Through these various forms of capitalist exploitation, the local bourgeoisie was reduced to subordinate mercantile roles, which, moreover, were often carried out by foreign communities of Lebanese or Indians. Furthermore, the statuses of the land, inherited from earlier periods and roughly maintained by colonization, did not permit the formation of latifundiary commercial properties as occurred in Latin America, the Middle East, and northern India. The great landowner class in those areas benefited from integration into the world market and, through the same process, from the support of imperialist domination. This class, which was quickly labeled feudal even though its members were in fact great commercial landowners, failed to take hold in Africa. In its place the colonial administration entered into an alliance with chiefdoms that were supposedly traditional. Some of these really were traditional, and being linked to the political and administrative management of the colony, as in northern Nigeria, for example, they gave the appearance of a feudal system and indirect rule. Yet several others were not traditional, having been created out of whole cloth by the colonizing power, which needed a negotiator who at least seemed to represent the scattered peasantry. The so-called district chiefs in these entities quickly fell into bad repute among the peasants. They were correctly seen as servants without genuine power, in the pay of the administration.

Despite these general shared characteristics, which prevailed throughout sub-Saharan Africa, the degrees to which colonial market capitalism and its forms penetrated local societies were fairly varied and created conditions for national liberation movements that were themselves diverse. One effect of the commercialization of production was the differentiation of the peasantry in the regions where the penetration of capitalism was most advanced. This resulted in the emergence of a relatively well-to-do class of peasants, confronting a semiproletariat of landless workers, many of whom had immigrated from other ethnic regions. This was the case in the colonial Gold Coast (present-day Ghana), western Nigeria, Togo, and Uganda, for instance. The political position of the more well-to-do class was ambiguous: it participated very much in the national liberation movements but adopted moderate, even conservative, positions.

In other regions the creation of a bourgeoisie from elements in the peasantry was hindered for various reasons. In some cases, the social control exercised by the chiefdoms prevented the peasantry from acquiring any historical legitimacy. This

was frequently the case in the regions long Islamized, where a class of often religious leaders (the brotherhoods, such as the Mourides in Senegal and the Ansar in the Sudan) monopolized the best lands and assumed the role of partners in the mercantile system. It was equally true in the regions where the precolonial apparatus of state or parastatal control was maintained, as in Uganda, Rwanda, Burundi, and Swaziland. In other cases the original society, based on equality among lineages, offered strong resistance to the differentiation of access to the soil. This often occurred in central Africa. There, as a result, the administration was forced to establish venues of pseudo-solidarity among the peasants—that is, village farming communities oriented to commercial production. The results, however, remained poor; commercial production was low and extremely dispersed. Also, the penetration of the market economy remained superficial where distance from the coast considerably reduced an area's profitability, as in the Sahelian region, or where communities were in isolated regions. In some areas a combination of these reasons were at work. In every case the peasantry—inclined to radicalism but without the ability to organize itself—constituted an important reserve labor force that could be mobilized by the national liberation movements.

In these general circumstances, the urban petty bourgeoisie was the catalyst of the national liberation movements. Of course, this class was not isolated from the rest of society. Thus, according to circumstances, it tilted to the left, seeking to establish its principal alliance with the rural masses victimized by the exploitative colonial mercantile system, or to the right, crystallizing the ambitions of the nascent rural bourgeoisie or of the traditional notables and their mercantile partners. In these cases, the weight of ideologically driven decisions was important, sometimes even decisive, in choosing allies. In the French and Portuguese colonies, the metropolitan Communist parties played an important role in this regard, providing training for the African political elite. In the British and Belgian colonies, the influence of the churches—Catholic in the Belgian case, Protestant in the British—was more striking, often moderating or even polarizing the political struggles around the churches' own conflicts, as occurred in Uganda.

If the working-class proletariat was embryonic, it nonetheless existed, playing a role disproportionate to its size. Nearly everywhere, colonization had led to the creation of railway and port infrastructures. Railroad workers were reckoned among the most radical supporters of the postwar trade union movement, especially in the Sudan. In southern Africa the large mining proletariat formed a trade union; in South Africa, the most disciplined members of the African National Congress (ANC) and the Communist Party (PC) come from the mine-workers' union. In this area, therefore, the national bourgeois leadership shared its responsibilities with worker officers. Nonetheless, as a result of various forces, throughout sub-Saharan Africa generally trade unionism was dominated by teachers, nurses, and other government and business employees.

The New Nations

These objective facts explain what took place around 1960, when Great Britain and France decided to "decolonize" while trying to transmit power to their political clients. In this period, the anti-imperialist front of Bandung, which supported African struggles for independence, was still in its expansion phase. Followers of Nasser and of Ghana's Kwame Nkrumah chose socialism. The war in Algeria was at its height, forcing the moderates in Morocco and Tunisia to confront France. In 1951, the Rassemblement Démocratique Africain (RDA) in the French colonies had extricated itself from alliance with the Communists in order to move closer to the power center in Paris. Now, it separated itself from France, adjusting to the anticipated "no" vote of Ahmed Sékou Touré's Guinea in the referendum proposing the establishment of a so-called French community; the vote accelerated the evolution of the RDA elsewhere. The Congolese crisis, sparked by Belgium's refusal to grant its colony independence, crystallized the choices to be made by the various countries in the 1960s between neocolonialism and radical nationalism. Based on whether they supported Congolese radical Patrice Lumumba or moderate Joseph Kasavubu in Léopoldville and the secessionists of Katanga and Kasai, the African states were constituted on two adversarial lines. The radicals, called the Casablanca bloc, formed behind Nasser, Nkrumah, Touré, and Modibo Keita of Mali. The moderate grouping, known as the Monrovia bloc, consisted of the clients of Paris, London, and Brussels. It was during this rift that the neologism "neocolonial" appeared, intended to indicate the choices made by the Monrovia group.

This rift lasted three years, until the Congolese imbroglio was overcome by the call for national unity and the elimination of secessionism in 1963. Haile Selassie then took the initiative of inviting the two African blocs to merge in order to create the Organization of African Unity.

Yet the two groups remained in opposition until the beginning of the 1980s. It is important, however, to relativize the differences in their strategies: although at the time these differences were experienced as opposites, there was common ground. All national liberation movements that became governments shared what might be called an ideology of development, which left a mark on the entire postwar period from 1945 to the 1980s. This ideology, which animated every national liberation movement, held that political independence created the conditions necessary for the modernization of the state, society, and economy in order to reproduce the Western model at an accelerated pace. But while Asia and Latin America involved themselves in the industrialization process during the postwar years, the same cannot be said for Africa, which after three decades of independence still found itself confined to specializations in agriculture and mining. Colonialism and then neocolonialism are largely responsible for this.

The Neocolonial States

The neocolonial option proposed to do more rapidly what colonization was supposed to have initiated already. Political independence was separated from economic and social reform because in these latter two areas, the transformations implemented by colonization were judged to be positive and modernizing, even though insufficient. Therefore, neither social reform—such as agrarian reform—nor a shake-up of economic structures were addressed. Foreign property was allowed to retain its central role in the modern sectors of activity, and the openness of local markets to the world economy was reaffirmed, indeed even reinforced. The integration of sub-Saharan African institutions into the worldwide capitalist system was maintained. Examples include such regional integrations as the western and central African monetary unions, submitting member countries to the management of their money by France, and the community of eastern Africa. For its part the European Economic Community (EEC), the formation of which had begun just prior to the era of African independence with the Treaty of Rome in 1957, supported traditional African agricultural and mining exports (as opposed to African industrialization) by means of the conventions of Yaoundé and then Lomé.

The fact that the neocolonial option was founded upon economic liberalism by no means ruled out strong state intervention on its behalf. Moreover, such intervention was not devised by the socialists within Africa, but by the colonial powers themselves when they first began instituting a state-run system to supervise the peasantry and to collect and commercialize their market products (through marketing boards, for example). Under the conditions then facing the continent, there was hardly any other way to extract a surplus out of the peasantry. But under neocolonialism such a surplus was intended to finance the administration and the activities of the infrastructure and to feed the profits of foreign capital. The neocolonial state thus maintained, in fact reinforced, the structures of exploitation. Here yet again, there was no means for the new African political bourgeoisie to assert itself and accumulate profits other than through its control of the state. This choice of historical continuity with colonization ruled out democracy for the same reason as in the colonial period: the peasant majority had to be kept under control. Neocolonialism thus favored the single party and the supervision of mass organizations (unions and cooperatives), reproducing the Soviet model in a caricatured way. Few saw the contradiction of neocolonial countries copying the Soviet Union, and the postponement of democracy to a later time was legitimized by the priority given to this type of development.

The neocolonialists assumed axiomatically that development occurred in stages. The "takeoff," to be based on the profits of agriculture and mining, was bound to create by itself, gradually and spontaneously, a market for industry (at first, to take the place of imports, then capable of generating exports), which would attract foreign and local capital, both public and private. The EEC and the World Bank asserted this axiom without hesitation. In fact, however, the automatic transition from one phase to the next has obviously not taken place, the reason being that it presupposed that the state would actively adopt objectives (toward democracy and free enterprise) that were excluded by the neocolonialist option. Certain countries managed to create the illusion of economic success, as with the "miracles" of Côte d'Ivoire, Kenya, and Malawi but they rapidly discovered their limits, which were those of the agro-mining exporter model. The growth and enrichment of the new bourgeoisie offered the prospect of a small industry of import substitution. This new bourgeoisie, which arose from the accentuation of income inequality, and which was grafted on this narrow economic base, could only guarantee the inflated profits of the foreign capital that controlled it, thanks to state protection.

The model did not prepare the way for its own supercession, either economically or politically. On the contrary, it nurtured regressions, including the disenfranchisement of the peoples subjected to the clientelist dictatorships; the intensification of the parasitic character of an urbanization unaccompanied by industrialization; the slower growth, or even decline, of food production; and the increasing corruption of the political bourgeoisie. The clash of these contradictions, slowed by recourse to foreign debt in 1975–1980, was manifested from the beginning of the 1980s. Starting then, the neocolonial states submitted to plans for structural readjustment stemming from exclusive focus on debt service to the detriment of development. Henceforth development was handicapped by, among other things, the collapse of the systems of education, health, and infrastructures; disinvestment; the delegitimization of the state; and the splitting apart of society.

The Radical Nationalist Alternative

Neocolonialism ended in a dramatic (though foreseeable and foreseen) failure, but hopes were also invested in the apparently opposite choice, radical nationalism. The Bandung model, which was popular in Asia and in the Arab world as of the 1950s, inspired a wave of successive movements for Pan-African unity erected on a base of radical liberation movements. Guinea, Ghana, and Mali chose this option in 1960. Later, Tanzania and Congo-Brazzaville (now People's Republic of the Congo) followed suit. Then Somalia, Bénin, Burkina Faso, Zambia, Uganda, Madagascar, and Ethiopia joined, as did the former Portuguese colonies after they gained their independence in 1975; Zimbabwe entered their ranks in 1980 with the establishment of black majority rule.

Theoretical discourse on the significance of radical nationalism takes as its starting point the concept of rupture with colonization as opposed to historical continuity. Rupture sometimes implied moderate social reforms, but above all it involved an attempt at the national level to control the processes for the accumulation of wealth through the mastery of the internal market; the ownership of capital through nationalization; the prioritizing of the public sector and currency management; the reproduction of the work force through the administration of wages and prices; and, at least rhetorically, the acquisition of a technology. The will to speed up industrialization was also declared. The limits of this approach resulted from the fact that it did not envision disconnecting itself from the worldwide capitalist system but instead envisioned forcing that system to adapt to the demands of the internal development of the countries affected. Africa, even more than other regions in the developing world, lacked the means for forcing such coherence. For example, the radical African states also accepted the logic of the Lomé agreements. In these conditions, developmental strategies have not been so different from those enacted in neocolonial countries, despite socialist proclamations and exterior anti-imperialist alliances. The same regressions as in the neocolonial states, again brought about by the refusal to become democratic (based on the same arguments—the need for state intervention and foreign capital and in consequence of social and economic reform—reinforced here by Soviet ideology), have led to similar crises since the start of the 1980s.

Conclusion

Neocolonialism has passed through the general crisis of the worldwide capitalist system, neocolonialism's own collapse, and that of its alternative, radical anti-imperialism (in intentions, at least), yet is unable to overcome its own internal limits. The subjugation of Africa to external powers over the entire continent has reduced to nothingness the differences between paths of development asserted during the preceding decades; the Africa of the ruling classes no longer has a plan for development, whether neocolonial or parasocialist. This regression, which has often been described as "fourth-worldization" as opposed to the semi-industrialization of the "third world," creates new openings in the world market and summons a kind of "recolonization" of the continent, cynically carried out by the dominant powers. The neocompradore form that the local state as much as the dominant classes takes in these circumstances—replacing the illusions of radical bourgeois nationalism and neocolonialism—is incapable of convincing society of their legitimacy. Thus, this form entails a political chaos that will be overcome only when new systems of popular social power succeed in crystallizing around a project that offers an alternative to the utopia of capitalist internationalization.

BIBLIOGRAPHY

Adotevi, Stanislas. *De Gaulle et les Africains.* Volume 10, *Afrique contemporaine.* Paris, 1990.

Amin, Samir. "Le développement du capitalisme en Afrique noire." In *En partant du "Capital,"* edited by Victor Fay. Paris, 1968.

———. *The Class Struggle in Africa.* Cambridge, Mass., 1969.

———. "Underdevelopment and Dependency in Black Africa: Origins and Contemporary Forms." *Journal of Modern African Studies* 10, no. 4 (1972): 503–524.

———. *Neo-colonialism in West Africa.* Harmondsworth, U.K., 1973.

Amselle, Jean Loup, and Elikia M'Bokolo, eds. *Au coeur de l'ethnie: Ethnies, tribalisme, et état en Afrique.* Paris, 1985.

Arrighi, Giovanni, and John S. Saul. *Essays on the Political Economy of Africa.* New York, 1973.

Benot, Yves. *Les indépendances africaines: Idéologies et réalités.* 2 vols. Paris, 1975.

Chrétien, Jean-Pierre, and Gérard Prunier. *Les ethnies ont une histoire.* Paris, 1989.

Davies, Ioan. *African Trade Unions.* Baltimore, 1966.

Gibson, Richard. *African Liberation Movements: Contemporary Struggles Against White Minority Rule.* New York, 1972.

Gutkind, Peter, and Immanuel Wallerstein, eds. *The Political Economy of Contemporary Africa.* Volume 1 in Sage Series on African Modernization and Development. Beverly Hills, Calif., 1976.

Hodgkin, Thomas. *African Political Parties: An Introductory Guide.* Gloucester, Mass., 1961.

Lovejoy, Paul E., ed. *The Ideology of Slavery in Africa.* Volume 6 in Sage Series on African Modernization and Development. Beverly Hills, Calif., 1981.

Piault, Marc, ed. *La colonisation: Rupture ou parenthèse.* Paris, 1987.

Suret-Canale, Jean. *Afrique noire occidentale et centrale.* 3d. ed. Volume 2, *L'ère coloniale.* Volume 3, *De la colonisation aux indépendances.* Paris, 1968.

SAMIR AMIN

See also **Colonial Policies and Practice; Colonialism and Imperialism; Decolonization; Independence Movements; Nationalism; Postcolonial State.**

NETO, AGOSTINHO (b. 1922; d. 1979), anticolonialist revolutionary and first president of independent Angola. Born at Bengo in the Catete district of western Angola, Antônio Agostinho Neto was the son of a Protestant pastor of Mbundu linguistic origin. In 1947 he left the all-pervasive racism of ruling Portuguese culture in Angola and went to Lisbon to study medicine. With like-minded African students in Portugal at the end of World War II, he began to campaign for Angola's independence. This was necessarily subversive in the eyes of the ruling dictatorship, and Neto was drawn into socialist and communist agitation. In 1958 he returned to Angola and established a medical practice. In 1960 he was arrested by the Portuguese political police, the Polícia International de Defesa de Estado (PIDE) and exiled first to Santo Antão in the Cape Verde archipelago, at that time a Portuguese colonial possession, and then to Portugal.

In 1962 Neto escaped from Portugal and at once assumed leadership of the widespread anticolonial insurrection which had erupted in Angola during 1961. His leadership of the Angolan independence movement, the Movimento Popular de Libertação de Angola (MPLA), was repeatedly confirmed through the years of struggle which brought independence to Angola in 1975, with Neto as president. The nascent Angolan state was at once threatened with disaster by full-scale military invasion from an apartheid-ruled South Africa. Narrowly failing to destroy Angolan independence, the incursion was frustrated and finally defeated by Cuban military intervention.

South African withdrawal still left the Angolans, at the end of 1976, not only riven by their own problems but subject to the destructive miseries of the East-West cold war and the hostility of the United States. It would not be until the termination of the cold war in the late 1980s that prospects for eventual reconstruction in Angola could be envisioned. This was too late for the man who had captained Angola's history of self-emancipation. Although disabused of his youthful faith in the Soviet state, Neto remained an unwilling captive of the politics of his time. He died in a Moscow hospital in 1979, leaving the republic he had founded to a difficult survival. A notable poet in Portuguese, Neto produced a volume of verse published initially in Tanzania in 1974 and entitled, in its English translation that year, *Sacred Hope*.

BIBLIOGRAPHY

Khazanov, A. M. *Agostinho Neto*. Translated by Cynthia Carlile. Moscow, 1986.

BASIL DAVIDSON

Agostinho Neto. DANIEL TOPOLSKI/CAMERA PRESS LONDON/ARCHIVE PHOTOS

NGUGI WA THIONG'O (James Ngugi; b. 1938), Kenyan author. Born into a polygamous Gikuyu peasant family at Kamiriithu, near Nairobi, Ngugi was educated at Alliance High School, the premier colonial secondary school in Kenya. He later attended Makerere University College in Kampala, Uganda, where he began to write (B.A., 1964), and Leeds University in England, where his political views turned left.

Joining the University of Nairobi's Department of English in 1967, Ngugi was its first African staff member. In this role he exercised a twofold influence on Kenyan cultural life: as the first Kenyan to publish anglophone creative literature, and as the proponent of an Afrocentric curriculum that was influential in other African universities. His protests against repressive government policies led to his imprisonment for a year (1978); while in prison, he resolved to write only in Gikuyu.

Denied reinstatement at the University of Nairobi upon his release, Ngugi resumed his work in theater, only to encounter renewed governmental suppression during rehearsals. In 1982, threatened with arrest, he went into exile, first in London and later in the United States, where he has taught at Yale and New York University. Ngugi is known

Ngugi wa Thiong'o. HEINEMANN AFRICAN WRITERS SERIES

for his steadfast criticism of neocolonialism and his espousal of writing in African rather than colonial languages.

BIBLIOGRAPHY

Sicherman, Carol. *Ngugi wa Thiong'o: A Bibliography of Primary and Secondary Sources 1957–1987.* Bibliographical Research in African Written Literatures, 1. London, 1989.

———. *Ngugi wa Thiong'o: The Making of a Rebel. A Source Book in Kenyan Literature and Resistance.* Documentary Research in African Written Literatures, 1. London, 1990.

CAROL SICHERMAN

NGUNI. The cluster of Bantu-speaking peoples of southeastern Africa usually held to have been the vanguard of the southward movement of Bantu peoples across Africa are called the Nguni. Many Nguni use "clicks" as gutturals, which is usually taken as sign of their having absorbed the aboriginal Khoisan who at one time occupied southern Africa. The Nguni do not form a single society but a congeries of culturally similar but politically independent groups. Nguni have traditionally been mixed farmers growing grains and keeping cattle. During the first half of the nineteenth century, they became organized into several powerful kingdoms that engaged in long wars with the European colonial intruders of the time. Today they live in both their own homelands (such as KwaZulu and the Transkei) and the towns of the region. The best-known Nguni societies include, in South Africa, the Zulu, the "Cape Nguni" (Xhosa, Pondo, Tembu, Pedi, Bomvana, Bhaca, and others), and the Ndebele of the Transvaal. Other Nguni include the Swazi of Swaziland, the Ndebele of Zimbabwe, and the Ngoni of Malawi.

BIBLIOGRAPHY

Hammond-Tooke, W. D., ed. *The Bantu-Speaking Peoples of Southern Africa.* 2d ed. London, 1974.

JOHN MIDDLETON

NGUNI REGION. The word "Nguni" is today commonly used to refer to the black peoples who historically have inhabited the region of southern Africa which extends from the eastern Cape northward through KwaZulu-Natal as far as Swaziland. The languages spoken by these peoples have since colonial times been known as Xhosa, Zulu, and Swazi. This broad meaning of "Nguni" was first given currency by white academics in the 1920s and 1930s. Before that, it had been used by the black inhabitants of southeastern Africa in a number of more restricted senses. Strictly speaking it should be used only as a linguistic term—Nguni languages, Nguni-speaking peoples—and not as an ethnic or cultural label. From a historical perspective, the idea of the "Nguni region" is an artificial one, for the region does not form a coherent unit of study.

The Precolonial Period

Archeological research since the early 1970s suggests that the remote ancestors of the Nguni-speaking peoples were Iron Age farmers whose ultimate origins lay in east Africa. From around 100 C.E., communities of these farmers were colonizing the eastern coastlands of southern Africa. By about 500 C.E. they had reached as far as the southern limits of the summer rainfall region in the eastern Cape, and by about 1500 they had extended inland to the foothills of the Drakensberg Mountains in the north and the edge of the arid Karroo in the south. Among them lived groups of San speakers, who are thought to have subsisted mainly by hunting and gathering. The nature of their relations with the farmers is an ongoing subject of study by archaeologists. In the far south, the territories occupied by the farmers overlapped with those of Khoi pastoralists.

A dozen surviving accounts of journeys in, or visits to, the Eastern Cape–KwaZulu–Natal region made by European castaways and traders from 1550 to 1750 touch on the way of life of local farming societies. From a handful of oral traditions recorded in the nineteenth and early twentieth centuries, we get glimpses of community histories that in some cases extend back to around 1700. These sources indicate that, as late as the middle of the eighteenth century, farmers throughout the region lived in small chiefdoms under hereditary chiefs whose authority over their adherents was relatively limited.

By the later eighteenth century, officials, traders, and travelers from the Dutch colony at the Cape and the Portuguese outposts on the coast of Mozambique were beginning to come into more frequent contact with the African communities of the eastern Cape and of the Delagoa Bay area, respectively. From this time onward, written records form an increasingly important source of evidence on the history of these communities. In the same period, the impact of the expansion of European commerce and colonization was beginning to be widely felt across the subcontinent. European influences impinged in different ways on the Xhosa-speaking chiefdoms on the borders of Cape Colony and on the ethnically diverse chiefdoms in the hinterland of Delagoa Bay, and these influences stimulated different kinds of reaction from them.

The Xhosa-Cape Frontier

By the late eighteenth century the dominant Xhosa chiefdoms were that of the Gcaleka north of the Kei River and that of the Rharhabe to the south of it. To the north and west were a cluster of Thembu chiefdoms, and to the northeast were the chiefdoms of the Mpondo.

At that time, conflicts over grazing land, agricultural land, and trade were pushing the southernmost Xhosa chiefdoms westward across the Fish River. More and more they came up against groups of Dutch pastoralists from the Cape who were expanding in the opposite direction. Competition for

land and cattle led to a series of violent clashes between different groups of Xhosa, Khoi, and Dutch. In intervals of peace, numbers of Xhosa took up work on colonial farms, and Dutch frontiersmen hunted and traded deep into Xhosa territory.

For forty years neither the Xhosa nor the Dutch were able to establish domination over the frontier zone that developed west of the Fish. The balance was finally tipped against the Xhosa by the intervention of the British, who had taken control of the Cape in 1806. To try to stabilize the frontier, in 1811–1812 the British launched regular troops in a fierce assault on the Xhosa communities west of the Fish, drove them into the already occupied territories east of the river, and seized large numbers of their cattle.

This was the first in a long and destructive series of wars in which the British, assisted by Xhosa, "Mfengu," and Khoi clients, raided cattle from resistant Xhosa chiefs and their followers, and seized land for occupation by Dutch and, from 1820, British colonists. Ongoing rivalries among the Xhosa chiefdoms made the process easier. In 1847 the British authorities extended their rule as far as the Kei River, and began working actively to destroy the power of the western Xhosa chiefs and to force their people to go out to work among the colonists. A major rebellion in 1850–1853 was followed by the confiscation of more land and the further tightening of the often arbitrary and brutal rule of colonial officials.

By the 1850s, increasing numbers of Xhosa, made desperate by deepening poverty, the crumbling of the world they understood, and the feeling that their chiefs were failing them, looked more and more to prophets and visionaries for guidance. The devastation of the herds of many Xhosa communities by an epidemic of lung sickness in 1855–1856 gave major impetus to this movement. By far the most influential of the prophets was a young woman named Nongqawuse. Her messages, which were passed on to the public by intermediaries, were believed to have come from the ancestors. Their content seems to have been influenced in part by the teachings of Christian missionaries, who had been active among the western Xhosa since the 1820s. Following her instructions, in 1856–1857 thousands of Xhosa, including many of the still-independent Gcaleka north of the Kei River, held back from planting crops, slaughtered their cattle, and awaited a day of resurrection and purification when all evildoers would be swept away, and the dead would rise and bring new crops and cattle.

The so-called Xhosa cattle killing (some historians have argued that the destruction of crops was even more significant than the destruction of cattle) has been widely seen as a national rising of chiefs and commoners against oppressive colonial rule. More recently, some scholars have argued that it was in part an attempted revolution of commoners against the chiefs and aristocracies who, through their control of cattle, held sway in Xhosa society. Others see as a significant element in the movement the resistance of women to the domination exercised by male homestead heads.

In any event, at least forty thousand people died of starvation, and community life over wide areas completely collapsed. The colonial authorities under the governor of the Cape, Sir George Grey, were quick to seize the opportunity to strike further blows at Xhosa political and cultural autonomy. Numbers of chiefs were jailed, often on trumped-up charges, for violence against their followers or for resisting the orders of magistrates. Thousands of starving men, women, and children were channeled into the labor force of Cape Colony. More lands were confiscated and cleared for settlement by white farmers. The cattle killing brought to an end eighty years of Xhosa resistance to colonial rule, and finally destroyed the independence of Xhosa society.

The Southern Hinterland of Delagoa Bay

The paucity of source material makes it difficult to discern patterns of change among the northern Nguni-speaking chiefdoms until the later eighteenth century. After about 1760 the impact of European expansion was increasingly felt through the growth of international trade at Delagoa Bay. British and Indian merchants from India were active in buying ivory from local chiefdoms in return for cloth, beads, and metal goods. Though the outbreak of the French revolutionary wars in the 1790s sent the ivory trade into decline, it was in part replaced by a trade in cattle to U.S. whaling ships.

The rise of this commerce seems to have played an important role in stimulating a struggle among the chiefdoms around Delagoa Bay and in its hinterland for control of trade routes and sources of ivory and cattle. By the end of the eighteenth century a number of chiefs were simultaneously expanding the territories they controlled and tightening the authority they exercised over their followers. In the region south of the bay the most important chiefdoms were those of the Maputo, Ndwandwe, and Mthethwa. The effects of their political rivalries were felt throughout Natal and as far south as northern Transkei.

By the late 1810s the struggle for supremacy between the Ndwandwe and the Mthethwa was coming to a head. Some historians argue that the conflict between them was intensified by the contemporary rise of a trade in slaves at Delagoa Bay to Brazilian merchants. The defeat of the Mthethwa by the Ndwandwe left the way open for the rising Zulu chiefdom under Shaka to establish its domination in the south of what is now called Zululand. The breakup soon afterward, for reasons that still need to be adequately explained, of the Ndwandwe chiefdom provided the opportunity for the Zulu to extend their domination farther north. By the early 1820s the Zulu leaders were busy consolidating an authoritarian form of rule over a partially militarized state which dominated much of what is now the KwaZulu-Natal region.

In the hilly country north of the Phongola River, a cluster of chiefdoms, dominated by the Dlamini under Sobhuza (Somhlolo), managed to hold out against Zulu raids. By the late 1830s, these chiefdoms were consolidating into the nucleus of what became the Swazi kingdom.

A commonly held view is that the expansion of the Zulu kingdom was an explosive and bloody affair which touched off a widespread chain reaction of wars and migrations known as the *mfecane*. A number of historians have recently challenged this notion. They argue that the size and strength of the Zulu kingdom have been heavily exaggerated by successive generations of white and black historians and that there is little evidence to support the notion of a "Zulu explosion." These historians do not deny that the 1820s were a period of upheaval in much of southeastern Africa, but they argue that the prime cause lies in the destabilizing impact the expansion of European trade and colonization was having on the indigenous societies of southern Africa from the middle of the eighteenth century onward.

BIBLIOGRAPHY

Hamilton, Carolyn, ed. *The Mfecane Aftermath: Reconstructive Debates in Southern African History.* Johannesburg, 1995.

Mostert, Noel. *Frontiers: The Epic of South Africa's Creation and the Tragedy of the Xhosa People.* London, 1992.

Peires, Jeffrey B. *The Dead Will Arise: Nongqawuse and the Great Xhosa Cattle-Killing Movement of 1856–1857.* Johannesburg, 1989.

Wright, John, and Carolyn Hamilton. "Traditions and Transformations: The Phongolo-Mzimkhulu Region in the Late Eighteenth and Early Nineteenth Centuries." In *Natal and Zululand from Earliest Times to 1910*, edited by Andrew Duminy and Bill Guest. Pietermaritzburg, South Africa, 1989.

JOHN WRIGHT

See also **Cape Colony; Cape Dutch Settlements; Mfecane; Nongqawuse; Shaka Zulu; Sobhuza I and II.**

NIAMEY. The capital of the Republic of Niger, Niamey was originally a small Songhai fishing settlement on the left bank of the Niger River. Because of Niamey's strategic location, the French established a military post there at the beginning of the twentieth century. In 1926 it became the capital of the colony of Niger, supplanting the town of Zinder in that role. Niamey's location on two major regional roadways (the Nigeria-Mali and the Burkina Faso–Chad roads) encouraged its growth and development: by the mid-1970s the population of the city numbered over 220,000, and by the late 1980s the city's population had more than doubled in size. Niamey is the commercial center of Niger as well as a center for national culture.

BIBLIOGRAPHY

Decalo, Samuel. *Historical Dictionary of Niger.* Metuchen, N.J., 1979.

OLATUNJI OJO

NIGER

GEOGRAPHY AND ECONOMY

The Republic of Niger is a landlocked country 700 kilometers (435 mi.) north of the Gulf of Guinea, 1,200 kilometers (745 mi.) south of the Mediterranean, and 1,900 kilometers (1,180 mi.) east of the Atlantic. Four-fifths of the territory is in the desert and subdesert zones. Agricultural and pastoral activities requiring rain are possible only on its southern fringe, where the annual rainfall exceeds 350 millimeters (13.7 in.). This area has long been called the useful Niger.

Niger is a country of plateaus and plains partly covered by dunes held in place by vegetation, with shifting dunes in the Ténéré Desert, east of the Aïr. The Aïr, a massif with a maximum elevation of 2,020 meters (6,628 ft.), extends over 400 kilometers (248 mi.) south of the Algerian border. The Niger River, crossing the southwest region of the country, flows all year. Its tributaries on the right bank flow seasonally, whereas those on the left bank make up a vast fossilized network. To the south, the Majia and the Goulbi of the Maradi flow seasonally, as does the Komadougou Yobé, which empties into Lake Chad, on the border between Chad and Nigeria.

From the north to the south, as rainfall increases, the level of vegetation increases from absolute desert through a steppe region covered in thorny shrubs and, at the very south, the low-bush savanna. Some vegetation is specific to the terrain—for instance, in the plateaus, thickets and small shrubs predominate, whereas in the valleys, *Acacia albida* and *Hyphaene thebaïca* flourish.

The northern zone, that is, the southern Saharan and northern Sahelian, is devoted to pastoral nomadism involving camels, cattle, sheep, and goats. Moving from north to south, the number of cattle increases and that of camels decreases. The southern Sahelian zone is devoted to agropastoralism, which at the fringe of the Sudanian zone becomes essentially agriculture.

Niger has a population of 8,702,800 (1994) and an area of 1,267,000 square kilometers (489,189 sq. mi.), for a population density of 6.9 people per square kilometer (17.8 per sq. mi.). This population is distributed unevenly, increasing gradually from a density of less than 1 per square kilometer in the north (0.3 per km^2 in Agadez Province) to 33 per square kilometer in Maradi Province (from 14.6 in the district of Dakoro to 81.2 in the district of Madarounfa, on the Nigerian border). The population, essentially rural, is moving to the cities; Niamey, the capital, has 391,876 people (1992). Two other cities have a population greater than 100,000: Zinder has 120,160; Maradi, 110,739, Niger's urbanization rate is 15.2 percent. By province, Agadez has the highest rate (43.7 percent), and Tillabéry has 25.7 percent, because the populations of industrial and mining centers (Arlit, Akokan) have a greater effect on the urbanization rate in a region that is otherwise sparsely populated, as is this desert region. Between 1977 and 1988, the proportion of the population under fifteen years of age increased from 44 percent to 49 percent, and the cities almost doubled in size, with an annual growth rate of 5 percent.

In Niger, there are five main ethnolinguistic groups, corresponding to the five national languages, in addition to French, which is the official

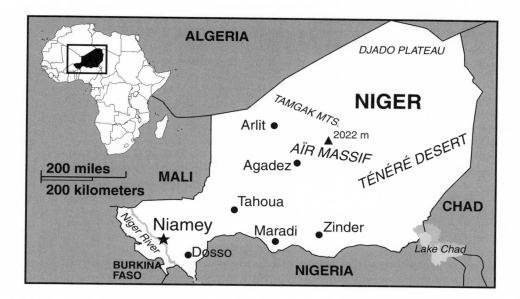

language. In descending order of number of speakers, they are Hausa, Zerma-Songhai, Fulani (Fulbe), Tuareg, and Kanuri. Each of these groups extends across national borders, and the Hausa, who make up the majority of Nigeriens, are few compared to the Hausa in Nigeria. Sunni Islam is the national religion, although traces of ancient religions are widespread.

Millet and sorghum are the staple food crops: the satisfaction of the country's food requirements depends on the success of their harvest, which in turn depends on the summer rains. Among cash crops, the peanut was long the most important export. Peanut production almost doubled between 1960 and 1970. Animal husbandry and fishing also play important roles in the country's economy, whether for domestic sale or for export. Since 1970, uranium has been the principal export: production of uranium ore, after quadrupling between 1974 and 1979, represented 80 percent of exports and 50 percent of the gross national product of the country. After 1980, the uranium market collapsed and Niger's income tumbled.

BIBLIOGRAPHY

Bernus, Edmond. *Touaregs nigériens: Unité culturelle et diversité régionale d'un peuple pasteur.* Paris, 1981.

Grégoire, Emmanuel. *Les Alhazai de Maradi, Niger: Histoire d'un groupe de riches marchands sahéliens.* Paris, 1986.

Raynaut, Claude. *Structures normatives et relations électives: Études d'une communauté villageois Haoussa.* Paris, 1972.

Olivier de Sardan, Jean-Pierre. *Les sociétés songhai-zarma, Niger-Mali: Chefs, guerriers, esclaves, paysans.* Paris, 1984.

EDMOND BERNUS

See also **Niger River; Sahara Desert.**

HISTORY AND GOVERNMENT

Several great precolonial empires have successively left their imprints on Niger's provinces. In the fifteenth century, they were under the influence of the Songhai to the west and the Bornu Empire to the east. In the nineteenth century, the Fulani Empire of Sokoto was established through a holy war (jihad) from the Niger River to the Hausa states, which had been at their apogee in the eighteenth century. To the north, the sultanate of the Aïr had played an important role since 1400.

The French moved from west to east and gained the allegiance of many prestigious chiefdoms: the kingdom of Say, the sultanates of Kebbi and Zinder, and others. To the north, the conquest met fierce resistance from the Tuareg, who, led by their chief, Kaocen, organized a general uprising in the Massif Aïr in 1916–1917, which was severely repressed. The pacification of the territory was assured when it became the French Colony of Niger (1922).

After the Second World War, French colonial policy softened: the constitution of 1946 permitted Niger to elect a representative to the French National Assembly. Local political life was dominated by the Parti Populaire Nigérien (PPN; Nigerien People's Party) of Diori Hamani and the African Socialist Movement (MSA Sawaba) of Djibo Bakary.

République du Niger

Population: 8,702,800 (1994 est.)

Area: 1,267,000 sq. km (489,189 sq. mi.)

Official language: French

Languages: French, Fulani, Hausa, Songhai, Tuareg

National currency: CFA franc

Principal religions: Muslim 90% (mostly Sunni), Christian 5%, traditional 5%

Capital: Niamey (pop. 391,876 in 1992)

Other urban centers: Zinder, Maradi, Tahoua, Dosso, Agadez, Arlit

Annual rainfall: varies from 500 mm (20 in.) in the south to 100 mm (4 in.) at Agadez to almost 0 mm in the far north

Principal geographical features:

Mountains: Tamgak Mountains, Aïr Massif

Lakes: Lake Chad

Rivers: Niger River, other seasonal rivers

Desert: Ténéré Desert

Economy:

GNP per capita: US$220 (1995)

Principal products and exports:

Agricultural: millet, sorghum, cowpeas, groundnuts, cassava, rice, livestock

Manufacturing: agricultural product processing, textiles

Mining: uranium, iron, tin, tungsten, coal, calcium phosphates, gold, some oil

Government: Independence from France, 1960. Multiple constitutions: 1960, suspended in 1974; revised 1989, suspended in 1991; 1992, suspended in 1996; 1996. Military dictatorship moving toward multiparty democracy. President elected for 5-year term by universal suffrage. 83-member Assemblée Nationale, inaugurated in 1993, was suspended in 1996. Next elections scheduled for 2000 (legislative) and 2001 (presidential). National government headed by appointed prime minister and Council of Ministers. Local governmental organization based on 7 departments headed by prefects, 32 arondissements, and 150 communes.

Heads of state since independence:

1960–1974: President Hamani Diori

1974–1987: Lieutenant Colonel Seyni Kountché, chairman of the Supreme Military Council

1987–1989: Colonel (later General) Ali Saïbou, chairman of the Supreme Military Council

1989–1993: President Ali Saïbou

1993–1996: President Mahamane Ousmane

1996–: Colonel (later Brigadier General) Ibrahim Baré Mainassara, chairman of the National Salvation Council

1996–: President Ibrahim Baré Mainassara

Armed forces: President is commander in chief. Two-year conscription.

Army: 5,200

Air force: 100

Paramilitary: 5,400

Transportation: Principal transport is by the Niger River to Nigeria, controlled by the Société Nigerienne de Transports Fluviaux et Maritimes.

Roads: 39,970 km (24,836 mi.), 8% paved

Airline: Trans Niger

Airports: 30 usable airports. International services at Niamey.

Media: One daily newspaper: *Le Sahel.* One weekly: *Le Sahel Dimanche.* 15 periodicals. One book publisher: L'Imprimerie Nationale du Niger. Radio is a state monopoly: Office de Radiodiffusion-Télévision du Niger (also called La Voix du Sahel). Télé-Sahel broadcasts only French-originated television programming.

Literacy and education:

Total literacy rate: 13.9%. Education is free, universal, and compulsory for ages 7–15. A great proportion of schoolchildren attend traditional Qur'anic schools. 1996: Postsecondary education provided through Université de Niamey, Université Islamique du Niger, École Nationale d'Administration du Niger, Centre Régional de Recherches et de Documentation pour la Tradition Orale.

The law of 23 June 1956 gave Niger's politicians even more voice in the management of their country by establishing a government council presided over by the governor; its vice president (Djibo Bakary) was elected by the Territorial Assembly. Two years later, the new constitution adopted by referendum permitted creation of a republic (18 December 1958) with Diori Hamani at its head. Independence was proclaimed on 3 August 1960.

President Hamani Diori (1960–1974) suppressed all political opposition so well that the PPN controlled the entire country. At the end of the 1960s, a rising generation of bureaucrats criticized the inaction of the government, which seemed unable to improve the lot of the rural population. To respond to this dissension, Diori Hamani wanted to call an extraordinary session of the PPN to plan the means of assuring durable development. The military coup d'état of 15 April 1974 prevented him from doing so.

The new chief of state, Lieutenant Colonel Seyni Kountché, suspended the constitution and restored order so as to alleviate the famine ravaging the country. He built his authority upon an image of integrity sorely lacking in the preceding government. Apart from attempted coups d'état (1976 and 1983), President Kountché was, from 1974 until his death in November 1987, the uncontested master of Niger, which he governed with rigor. In October 1983, he reoriented his regime by designating a civilian prime minister of Tuareg origin, and he frequently changed the responsibilities of his ministers and senior public servants and carried out new nominations for these positions in order to avoid a feeling of exclusion among members of the political elite. General Ali Saïbou, army chief of staff, succeeded him.

More liberal, General Saïbou adopted a new constitution (1989) and created a unique party, the National Movement for a Development Society (MNSD): a first step was taken toward the return to a state of law. This liberalization of government favored the protest movements of students and unions that led the general to accept the principle of multiple parties (November 1990) and later to hold a national conference.

The National Conference, which held its first session on 29 July 1991, proclaimed itself sovereign. It suspended the constitution, dissolved the National Assembly and the government, but retained the president of the republic. It designated Amadou Cheiffou as prime minister of the transition government and made him responsible for organizing democratic legislative and presidential elections and managing the country until the installation of the new government.

The Alliance of the Forces of Change (AFC), which consisted of all the parties opposed to the MNSD, won the legislative elections, and soon afterward, Mahamane Ousmane was elected president of the republic for five years (27 March 1993). The supporters of the Kountché regime entered the opposition, and the army withdrew from the political scene. Mahamadou Issoufou was named prime minister. Disagreeing with the president's policies, he resigned eighteen months later and his party (the PNDS, one of the largest member parties of the AFC coalition) left the AFC, upsetting the existing alliances.

With the secession of the PNDS, the AFC no longer held a majority of the seats in the General Assembly and President Ousmane had to dissolve the Assembly. The new legislative elections, held in January 1994, democratically restored the MNSD to power, in a new alliance with the PNDS. The new prime minister was Hama Amadou. His relations with the president became ever more aggravated with the approach of the date by which the constitution authorized the president to dissolve the General Assembly, if he saw fit. On 27 January 1996 President Ousmane was preparing to dissolve the Assembly, designate a new prime minister unconstitutionally, and fire the army chief of staff. The prime minister, for his part, was preparing to outlaw the president's party, the Convention Démocratique et Sociale (CDS). To national economic bankruptcy and the general insecurity created by the Tuareg rebellion was added this unprecedented political and constitutional crisis that led the army to stage a coup d'état and take power again.

The new strong man, Colonel Ibrahim Baré Mainassara, justified the coup d'état by the fact that law and order and the unity of the country were threatened. However, he promised a rapid return to democracy; a new presidential-type constitution was put to a successful referendum, followed by presidential and legislative elections. In a contested election, on 7 July 1996 Colonel Mainassara became president of the Fourth Republic of Niger. The election of a new General Assembly, held on 23 November 1996, was boycotted by the largest parties, including the MNSD, the PNDS, and the CDS. Dissident members of these parties and a number of smaller parties had, however, organized the Comité du Soutien d'Ibrahim Baré (COSIMBA), and the election gave their candidates a majority. In forming his government, President Mainassara, who was then promoted to the rank of general, appointed civilians from the top ranks of all the political parties to ministerial positions, including that of prime minister. Nevertheless, the parties that boycotted the elections then regrouped into a new coalition opposed to the government, called the Front pour la Restauration et la Défense de la Démocratie (FRDD). COSIMBA was then structured into a political party under a new name, Rassemblement pour la Démocratie et le Progrès (RDP).

BIBLIOGRAPHY

Baier, Stephen. *An Economic History of Central Niger.* Oxford, 1980.

Fuglestad, Finn. *A History of Niger, 1850–1960.* Cambridge, 1983.

Grégoire, Emmanuel. *The Alhazai of Maradi: Traditional Hausa Merchants in a Changing Sahelian City.* Translated and edited by Benjamin J. Hardy. Boulder, Colo., 1992.

Séré de Rivières, Edmond. *Histoire du Niger.* Paris, 1965.

EMMANUEL GRÉGOIRE

PEOPLES AND CULTURES

Niger comprises many ethnic and linguistic groups. Populations with a sedentary agricultural or fishing base include the Hausa (56 percent of the population), the Zerma-Songhai and Dendi (22 percent), and the Kanuri and Manga (4.3 percent). Populations with a history and ideology favoring nomadic pastoralism include the Tuareg (8 percent) and Fulani (8.5 percent). Niger also has small populations of Zarab, Tougou, and Gourmantche (1.2 percent). Each of these groups has cultural, historical, and political affinities across national boundaries. Tuareg populations, for example, are drawn into the political orbit of Libya and Algeria, while Hausa speakers often look to northern Nigeria for patronage and support.

Despite Niger's arbitrary colonial boundaries, populations within the national borders share significant cultural and historical commonalities. Although Niger has a small minority of non-Muslims, the region has been influenced by Islam for centuries, and all of Niger's major ethnic groups share many Muslim beliefs and practices, including a respect for Islamic scholarship in Arabic. Most have nevertheless retained elements of pre-Islamic cultural and political life, such as spirit possession and bilateral (as opposed to strict patrilineal) kinship patterns. The occupation of shared territories across ecological zones has contributed to both symbiosis and conflict. Historically, Tuareg nomads could not survive without the agricultural production of their Buzu slaves; Fulani pastoralists relied upon Hausa farmers for access to pasture; Kanuri traders had close ties with Hausa crafts-workers.

All share the legacy of French colonial rule, although they have been quite differently positioned within the colonial and postcolonial regimes as a result of that history. Despite strong initial resistance to French rule, Zerma speakers benefited more from the employment, education, and infrastructure of the colonial era than other groups and have therefore come to dominate political life and the civil service. Hausa speakers bore the economic brunt of peanut cropping under colonialism, strengthening their sense of affinity with Hausa speakers across the border in British Nigeria and contributing to the emergence of a powerful Hausa merchant class. Tuareg and Fulani pastoralists have been at a disadvantage in the colonial and postcolonial periods. Sustained Tuareg resistance to colonial rule contributed to French hostility toward the nomads. With the colonial conquest, Tuareg migration and military domination of agricultural populations were disrupted, while the growing commercial economy, based upon sedentary practices, French education, and cash cropping increasingly passed them by.

Subdivisions within each of these ethnolinguistic groups exist which can occasionally be more salient than differences between ethnic groups. Precolonial societies often distinguished nobles and Islamic scholars from commoners and slaves; merchants from farmers, herders, and fishers; and warriors from producers. Individuals with similar precolonial socioeconomic roles were often channeled into the same colonial and postcolonial structures, such as the military, the civil service, and the industrial workforce. Members of traditional aristocracies, scholarly clans, merchant classes, and laboring classes can therefore have much in common with one another across ethnic lines because of their positions within the modern political economy, even when their identities are grounded in local ethnic idioms. Distinctions within ethnic groups often have tremendous importance in local politics, while at the national level rivalries between ethnic groups can be significant despite these crosscutting forms of social differentiation. These competing strands of ethnicity and interest structure Niger's identity and politics.

BIBLIOGRAPHY

Bernus, Edmond. *Touaregs nigériens: Unité culturelle et diversité régionale d'un peuple pasteur.* Paris, 1981.

Dupire, Marguerite. *Peuls nomades: Étude descriptive des Wodaabe du Sahel nigérien.* Paris, 1962.

Nicolas, Guy. *Dynamique sociale et appréhension du monde au sein d'une société hausa.* Paris, 1975.

Stoller, Paul. *Fusion of the Worlds: An Ethnography of Possession Among the Songhay of Niger.* Chicago, 1989.

BARBARA M. COOPER

NIGER-BENUE REGION, HISTORY. The headwaters of the Niger are relatively close to those of the Senegal. The Niger flows from the northeast in a great sweep through Sahelian and desert latitudes, and its waters helped sustain a series of great civilizations. It then flows south to the sea, through what is now Nigeria, dividing into the myriad branches of the Niger Delta. The Benue is a great tributary, flowing from the east and joining the Niger at much the geographic center of Nigeria. Most of the peoples who live near the lower Niger speak languages which belong to the Kwa branch of the great Niger-Congo language family or phylum—Nupe, Yoruba, Idoma, Igala, Ebirra, Igbo (Ibo), and Ijo, this last the language of the delta. Linguistic evidence shows that these peoples have lived in much their present homes for a very long period. The Tiv, who crossed the Benue in the nineteenth century, in the course of a migration from the southeast, speak a Bantoid language, part of a vast language family which includes Zulu, spoken in South Africa, and Swahili, the lingua franca of the east African coast. Bantu is a subdivision of Benue-Congo, another branch of the Niger-Congo phylum; significantly, the languages of the other subdivisions are all spoken in the Benue or Cross River area. They include Jukun.

We rely on archaeology for our knowledge of the early history of the Niger-Benue region. The Nok culture refers to a series of sites located over an expanse three hundred miles long, extending both north and south of the Benue. It flourished from around 500 B.C.E. to around 300 C.E. and had a striking and distinctive tradition of terra-cotta sculpture. It had also entered the Iron Age, one of a number of sites in sub-Saharan Africa where iron was smelted as early as the sixth century B.C.E.

The people now known as the Igbo number perhaps twenty million. Most of them live east of the Niger; in the past, they lived in over two thousand small independent village democracies. (The novels of Chinua Achebe give a vivid picture of their life in the past, and of the changes brought by the twentieth century.) A minority lived west of the Niger. Although they now regard themselves—and are regarded by others—as a single ethnic group, their dialects are so different that they are best seen as separate languages, and there was no sense of pan-Igbo identity in precolonial times.

Several Igbo centers had considerable impact on a wider environment. Arochukwu, on the Igbo-Ibibio borderland, was famous for its oracle. Most Igbo relied primarily on yam farming, but the Aro were famous as long-distance traders. The blacksmiths of Awka were another group who, like the Aro, systematically traveled along well-defined routes to practice their craft. Nri was a famous ritual center which sent out ritual specialists east and west of the Niger to purify the Earth from abominations. They carried no weapons and abhorred bloodshed.

Igbo-Ukwu is a village about twenty miles east of the lower Niger, close to Nri; here, a treasure hoard and the burial grounds of a great dignitary were excavated. The finds, which include intricate works of art in bronze, have been dated to the ninth century C.E. The dignitary is thought to be an *eze* (sacred king) Nri. The peoples of the delta and of the Igbo hinterland developed reciprocal trade relations, described by an early European visitor at the beginning of the sixteenth century. The Igbo were efficient farmers but lacked salt and protein. Delta people exported salt and dried fish but in many areas lacked the acreage for agriculture. The resultant trade took place in large canoes, through the delta creeks and along the lower Niger.

The Atlantic slave trade, which in this area reached its height in the eighteenth century, modified the relationship with the interior, which now purchased various commodities from Europe in exchange for slaves. Some were obtained from peoples further north, but the vast majority were Igbo, often obtained by kidnapping, a process facilitated by the region's political fragmentation. The autobiography of Olaudah Equiano tells the story of an Igbo who was enslaved, but who finally won his freedom and settled in England.

The peoples of the Benue Valley also had a reciprocal trade relationship with those who lived to the north, on the Jos plateau. The Benue Valley was well endowed with brine springs, and salt was exported in return for the iron processed by the expert metallurgists of the plateau.

In modern times, the people who are generally known as the Jukun (a Hausa name) but who call themselves Wapan, live in a number of settlements in the Benue Valley; the largest is at Wukari. Their ritual knowledge is widely respected, and the sacred king, the *aku* of Wukari, enjoyed a spiritual preeminence similar to that of Eze Nri further south. Hausa records refer to a southern state called Kwararafa, which is thought to have invaded both Hausaland and Bornu in the sixteenth and seventeenth centuries. This region has sometimes been identified with the Jukun, but they have no tradition of war making. The identity of Kwararafa is a mystery, but it seems likely that the name referred to a coalition of non-Muslim peoples—perhaps created in response to a particular situation, and perhaps made up of different peoples on different occasions. In the nineteenth century, the life of the region was disrupted by the incursion of the Tiv from the south and the Chamba from the east, and by the creation of new emirates on the southern boundary of the Sokoto Caliphate.

Several major states had their origins on the Niger, above the confluence. The Oyo capital was not far from the Niger, to the south. (The present Oyo, far to the south, was a nineteenth-century foundation.) Early Oyo was a small state; in about 1500, its kings were driven into exile by Nupe forces and did not reoccupy their capital until the early seventeenth century. Later, Oyo expanded far to the south, attaining its greatest extent shortly before its collapse as a result of a succession of crises in the late eighteenth and early nineteenth centuries.

Nupe was another state which grew up on or near the Niger. Tradition ascribes its foundation to a prince called Tsoede, the son of an Igala king; there are many such founding heroes in Nigerian traditional history, and it is not easy to know if they represent real personages or are a kind of symbolic shorthand for an epoch of historical experience. Nupe was strategically located for long-distance river trade; a long-distance trade route which carried kola from the Asante forests to Hausaland also ran through Nupe.

The Niger, like the Benue, experienced the impact of the jihads which created the Sokoto Caliphate. In 1817 a new state was created—the emirate of Ilorin—and a Fulani teacher and his son replaced the ancient royals of Nupe, founding a new royal line.

BIBLIOGRAPHY

Isichei, Elizabeth. *A History of the Igbo People.* New York, 1976.

———. *A History of Nigeria.* London, 1983.

Isichei, Elizabeth, ed. *Studies in the History of Plateau State, Nigeria.* London, 1982.

Last, Murray. "The Early Kingdoms of the Nigerian Savanna." In volume 1 of *History of West Africa*, edited by J. F. A. Ajayi and Michael Crowder. New York, 1985.

Obayemi, Ade M. "The Yoruba and Edo-Speaking Peoples and Their Neighbours Before 1600 A.D." In volume 1 of *History of West Africa*, edited by J. F. A. Ajayi and Michael Crowder. New York, 1985.

ELIZABETH ISICHEI

NIGER DELTA REGION. The Niger Delta has been formed by deposits brought down by the rivers Niger and Benue over ten thousand to seventy-five thousand years. The number of tributary rivers discharging Niger waters into the Atlantic has shrunk to the area between the Forcados River in the west and the Brass River in the east. The network of creeks and lagoons extends westward beyond Lagos and eastward beyond the estuary of the Imo River. The region, which represents an extension of the Nigerian mainland into the Atlantic, has been a reservoir of diverse fauna, flora, and human resources, ranging from marine products to palm oil, and crude oil in recent times. A diversity of landforms has contributed to the richness of life-forms and history. The coast is ringed by a thin, sandy beach ridge, succeeded by a wide saltwater mangrove swamp forest and a freshwater swamp rain forest.

The region is bordered by four large Nigerian groups: the Yoruba to the west, the Edo of Benin to the northwest, the Igbo (Ibo) to the northeast, and the Ibibio to the east. The core inhabitants of the region, based on location, population, and longevity of settlement, are the Ijo (Ijaw), who are spread over its length and breadth. On the peripheries are located numerous other groups culturally affiliated to the Ijo or the larger mainland groups. These groups include the Itsekiri, Urhobo, Isoko, Epie-Atissa, Engenni, Ogba, Echie, Ekpeye, Ogbia, Abua, Ogoni, and Andoni.

Linguistic studies have greatly improved our understanding of the traditions of origin of the peoples of the Niger Delta. Ijo has been classified as a language cluster with at least four groups of dialects that may be considered languages, and separated from Yoruba, Edo, and Igbo up to eight thousand years ago. Ijo has, therefore, had a long time to develop in the Niger Delta, and the only language with close affinities to it is Defaka (Afakani), spoken in the eastern Delta periphery. The history of the four dialect clusters is quite complex. The members of the Eastern Ijo dialect cluster (Kalabari, Bile, Okrika, Ibani, and Nkoro) have traditions of migration from original homes in the central Niger Delta, in the freshwater swamp zone. The Nembe-Akassa dialect cluster (Nembe, Akassa) also has traditions of migration from the central Niger Delta, as well as accounts of relations with or of migrants from the Benin (Edo) kingdom. The Izon dialect cluster (Bumo, Eastern Tarakiri, Oporoma, Olodiama, Bassan, Apoi, Ikibiri, Ogboin, Ekpetiama, Kolokuma, Gbarain, Mein, Seimbiri, Tuomo, Western Tarakiri, Kabowei, Kumbowei, Operemo, Oyakiri, Ogulagha, and Iduwini) forms the central group of Ijoid, along with Nembe-Akassa. The Inland Ijo dialect cluster (Biseni, Okodia, and Oruma) has been located in an area of diversification that could provide evidence for an early point of dispersal of proto-Ijo speakers.

A history of dynamic interactions between groups in the Niger Delta is suggested by the language position (relationships with other languages) in some Ijo groups in the western delta. The Apoi, Arogbo, Furupagha, Olodiama, Egbema, Gbaramatu, Ogbe, and Obotebe of this region show varying degrees of acculturation to Yoruba, Edo, and Itsekiri.

In the western Niger Delta, Itsekiri is classified as a Yoruba dialect, although its speakers' political institutions and history are more closely related to those of the Benin kingdom. Urhobo and Isoko are related to Edo. The traditions of origin of many sub-groups cite Benin as a place of origin; others cite locations in the Igbo country. The Epie-Atissa, Engenni, and Degema of the northern central delta also belong to the Edo family and recount traditions of origin from the west. Groups in the northeastern areas of the delta have the following historical relationships indicated by linguistic affinities:

1. The Ekpeye, Ikwerre, Ogba, Egbema, Ndoni, and Echie are classified as Igboid and exhibit close historical ties to the Igbo, although some groups also relate traditions of contact with the Benin kingdom.
2. The Ogoni group, comprising Kana/Khana, Gokana/Gokhana, Eleme, and Ogoi, is related to the Cross River languages and evidently entered the Niger Delta from Ibibio country to the east.
3. The central delta group of languages (Abua, Odual, and Ogbia) belong to the Benue-Congo language family to the east of the Niger Delta.

The movements within the region indicated by the traditions and the linguistic relationships are

datable only to the last millennium. Radiocarbon dates for excavations in the eastern and central delta date to periods no earlier than about 800 C.E. However, palynological data indicate the presence of the oil palm about three thousand years ago and suggest conditions conducive to human settlement in the Nembe area. Excavations at Onyoma, Ke, Ogoloma, Okochiri, and Saikiripogu, in the eastern saltwater mangrove swamp and sandy beach ridge zones, have yielded shellfish, pottery, terra-cotta figurines, local and imported smoking pipes, manillas (copper bangles used as currency), and evidence of limited metalworking. These artifacts suggest internal long-distance trade prior to the Atlantic overseas trade. Sites at Agadagbabou, Koroama, and Isomabou in the freshwater swamp delta have produced fewer artifacts because of less favorable conditions for the preservation of artifacts than the shell midden mounds of the saltwater delta. There is, however, similar evidence of internal and external contacts. Sites in the Ogba area of the northeastern delta fringe have produced dates earlier than the last millennium, confirming the relationship with the long-established populations of the hinterland.

Most of the communities of the region apparently had village-level political organizations, often with age as the basis for authority. The migrations from the freshwater delta to the saltwater delta to the southeastern delta zone led to the creation of state structures based on population centers at Bonny, Elem Kalabari, Okrika, and Nembe. These communities developed institutions called houses, which were headed by chiefs whose trading canoes were also war canoes; their power bases were under the control of the *amanyanabo* ("owner of the town"). These states of the eastern Niger Delta traded with the western delta in pottery, locally manufactured salt, dried fish, and cloth from the Yoruba country and the Itsekiri. They also exchanged bronze art objects or technology and political and cultural ideas with the Benin kingdom. These states traded north into the Igbo hinterland for agricultural produce and established relations with the religious and cultural centres of Nri, Awka, and Arochuku. Preliminary studies of pottery and clay figurines suggest contacts up the Niger River with centers of the Nok culture.

The state centers of the eastern Niger Delta and the Itsekiri metropolis of Warri in the western delta were the focus of European trade from the late fifteenth century. These city-states or trading states supplied the slaves from their established trading areas in the hinterland and, from the mid-nineteenth century, the palm oil and palm kernel, that their Atlantic trading partners required. The expanded opportunities of the Atlantic trade triggered other internal structural changes, and intensified contacts between the delta communities and those of the Nigerian hinterland.

By the last decade of the nineteenth century, the British had become well enough entrenched in the region to assume political control. Christian missions had preceded the formal establishment of colonial rule, and their converts were internal agents of change in religion and society. The formal education that the mission schools brought unified the new Niger Delta elite with those of the rest of Nigeria to fight for the creation of the nation-state of independent Nigeria. The pattern of the creation of and demands for autonomous political units within the Nigerian federation in recent times suggests an increasing desire to reestablish the identity of earlier communities and political entities.

BIBLIOGRAPHY

Alagoa, Ebiegber, Joe. *A History of the Niger Delta: An Historical Interpretation of Ijo Oral Tradition.* Ibadan, 1972.

Alagoa, Ebiegberi Joe, F. N. Anozie, and Nwanna Nzewunwa, eds. *The Early History of the Niger Delta.* Hamburg, 1988.

Alagoa, Ebiegberi Joe, and Tekena Tamuno, eds. *Land and People of Nigeria: Rivers State.* Port Harcourt, Nigeria, 1989.

Dike, Kenneth Onwuka. *Trade and Politics in the Niger Delta, 1830–1885.* Oxford, 1956.

Jones, Gwilym Iwan. *The Trading States of the Oil Rivers: A Study of Political Development in Eastern Nigeria.* London, 1963.

E. J. ALAGOA

NIGER RIVER. At 2,585 miles in length, the river Niger is the third-longest in Africa, after the White Nile and the Zaire, and the fourteenth-longest in the world. It rises in the Kouranko Mountains on the Sierra Leone–Guinea border at latitude 9°5′ north, less than 200 miles from the Atlantic Ocean. From its headwaters, it flows north and east into the southern Sahara at latitude 17° north and then south and east until it enters the Atlantic Ocean through a broad delta in Nigeria. Among the Mandinka people of Mali it is known as the Joliba, among the Songhai of the great bend in the river it is called the Issa Ber, while among the Nupe and Yoruba of Nigeria it is called the Kwara. The name "Niger" is of uncertain origin but first appears in European literature in the *Description of Africa* of Leo Africanus in the mid-sixteenth century. It is possible that he took the name from an Arabic translation of the *Geography* of the Greco-Egyptian scholar Claudius Ptolemy (fl. c. 150 C.E.), and it may be related to the Berber word *n'gher* (river).

The river has a number of notable natural features. After descending from the highlands of Guinea, it becomes a broad, slow-moving mass of water, about 1,000 yards wide at Bamako, the capital of Mali, and is joined by other smaller rivers, notably the Sankarani upstream from Bamako, and the Bani, which flows into it in the southern reaches of the next notable feature, the Inland Delta. When the Niger enters this flat plain just beyond Segu, it branches into a number of subsidiary channels, creating a network of waterways that overflow their banks when the runoff of the heavy annual rains (over 80 inches a year) that fall in the highlands of Sierra Leone and Guinea brings down floodwaters in late August. Over the ensuing months, this flood creates a massive, shallow "lake" up to 150 miles wide and 300 miles in length, while at the northern end of this flood zone are a number of lakes of more-or-less permanent character that are replenished by the annual flood. Like the Nile in Egypt, this annual flood lays down a rich layer of silt that makes the region an ideal agricultural zone where grains can be grown for human consumption and various grasses, clover, and similar plants can be raised for horses and cattle to graze on.

The flood zone reaches as far north as Kabara, the port of Timbuktu, and in good years a channel reaches Timbuktu, some 7 miles away from the riverbed. In former times this rendered the city an ideal meeting place for caravan traffic and riverine transportation, while its proximity to the larger flood zone assured its supply of grain. Prior to about 7500 B.C.E., the Niger flowed northward to Timbuktu and terminated in an inland delta in Azawad. During this wet period, another independent river rose in the Adrar-n-Ifoghas Mountain range (Adrar des Iforas), some 250 miles east. This was fed by other rivers that rose in the Aïr massif (present-day Dallol Bosso and Dallol Maouri) and emptied into the Atlantic. At some stage this more easterly river "captured" the western river to form the present course of the Niger. Eventually, as the Sahara began to dessicate after 5000 B.C.E., the

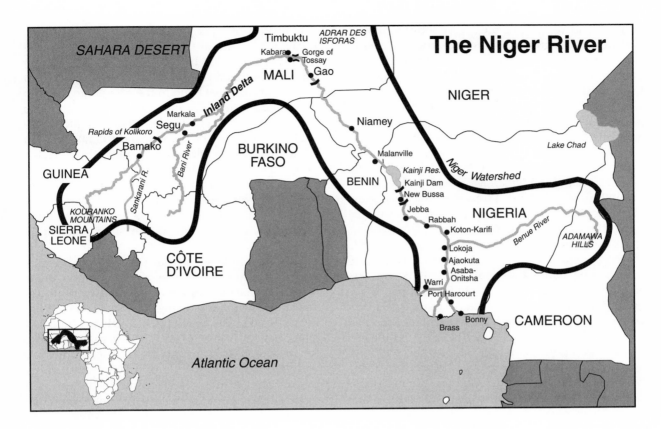

The Niger River

SAHARA DESERT

Timbuktu ADRAR DES ISFORAS
Kabara Gorge of Tossay
Gao
MALI
NIGER

Markala
Inland Delta
Niamey
Segu
Rapids of Kolikoro
Bamako
Malanville
Lake Chad
Niger Watershed
BURKINO FASO
Bani River
Kainji Res.
Kainji Dam
BENIN
New Bussa
GUINEA
Sankarani R.
Jebba
Rabbah
NIGERIA
KOURANKO MOUNTAINS
Koton-Karifi
SIERRA LEONE
Benue River
ADAMAWA HILLS
Lokoja
Ajaokuta
CÔTE D'IVOIRE
Asaba-Onitsha
Warri
Port Harcourt
Bonny
CAMEROON
Brass
Atlantic Ocean

eastern river dried up, though flood torrents still course down stretches of the fossil valleys leading to the Niger during brief and erratic annual rains in July and August. Downstream from Kabara as it passes through the zone of capture, the Niger becomes narrower again, moving through the gorge of Tossay before turning south on its journey to the sea. Some 250 miles from the Atlantic the river Niger is joined by another major watercourse, the river Benue, which brings down water from the hills of Adamawa straddling Nigeria and Cameroon. Together they flow due south to the sea, their silt building up a broad, fan-shaped delta dissected by numerous channels that create swampland in which mangroves flourish.

The full course of the Niger was not drawn on European maps until after 1830. Hitherto, European dependence on medieval Arab maps had led mapmakers to posit a connection between the Niger and the Nile or to show the Niger originating in a lake (in the general region of Lake Chad) and flowing westward to Senegal. The theory favored by Arabic geographers, such as al-Idrīsī (who wrote his *Nuzhat al-mushtaq* for the Norman king Roger II of Sicily in 1150), was that of a single river source

in central Africa which flowed via two lakes and various branches into a vast swamp. Out of this swamp flowed the two "Niles," one going north to Egypt and the other—the *Nīl as-sudan* (Nile of the blacks)—flowing west and emptying into the the Atlantic Ocean in Senegal. Al-Idrīsī's work was published in Rome in 1592, and an Italian translation followed in 1600. Leo Africanus's *Description*, published in Italian in 1550, also appeared to confirm an east-to-west flow. The west-to-east flow of the river was finally established by the Scottish traveler Mungo Park when he saw the river near Segu in 1796 and traced its course during his second journey as far as Boussa. Still searching for the river's outlet to the sea, Captain Hugh Clapperton was told by Sultan Muhammad Bello of Sokoto (Nigeria) in 1824 that the "Nile/Niger" flowed on toward Egypt. Other authorities proposed that it drained into a swamp in the Lake Chad region or flowed on to join the Congo (Zaire) River. In 1830 Clapperton's servant Richard Lander with his brother John undertook an expedition that finally established the course of the river below Boussa and showed that it flowed into the Atlantic Ocean through its delta in the Bight of Benin.

The lower reaches of the Niger soon became a highway for European—more particularly British—explorers, missionaries, and merchants. The Lander brothers were recruited by Macgregor Laird for an exploratory trading mission in 1832 in which thirty-nine out of forty-eight Europeans fell prey to disease. In 1841 three naval captains, William Allen, Bird Allen, and D. H. Trotter, set off on a new expedition to suppress slavery, open up legitimate trade, and establish a small settlement on the banks of the Niger. Missionaries, including Samuel Ajayi Crowther, a freed Yoruba slave from Sierra Leone (later a bishop), accompanied them. Again the toll from malaria and other tropical diseases was heavy, and nothing permanent resulted. More successful was the Scottish doctor William Baikie, who commanded an expedition up the Niger in 1852 and, on a second expedition in 1857, pushed up into Nupe country, signing a treaty with its emir and creating a more permanent settlement at Lokoja on the Niger-Benue confluence. These expeditions paved the way for the activities of the Royal Niger Company, founded in 1886, which under its chief officer, George Taubman Goldie, not only gained a commercial monopoly in the lower Niger region but also political and military influence along the Niger. It thus became the precursor of more formal British colonial control. In 1898 Brigadier General Frederick Lugard was dispatched to the area to halt French attempts to push into the Niger Valley through their colony of Dahomey (now Bénin), and his efforts ended with the conquest of most of what became Northern Nigeria by 1903.

Elsewhere on the Niger, far upstream in what is now Mali, the French began to move in from their colony of Senegal in the 1880s, dismantling piece by piece the Islamic empire established by al-Hajj 'Umar al-Futī based at Segu and, after his death in 1864, divided among his sons. In 1890 Colonel Louis Archinard took Segu and seized the royal library, which was sent back to France where it is still kept at the Bibliothèque Nationale in Paris. By 1894 French forces had conquered as far inland as Timbuktu, and by the end of the nineteenth century they had completed the conquest of the territories bordering the Niger up to the area the British were busily bringing under their control in what became Nigeria. By the end of 1960, however, both the British and the French had withdrawn from their colonial territories along the Niger, and four sovereign independent nations had emerged: Guinea, Mali, Niger, and Nigeria.

Many diverse peoples live along the banks of the Niger. The largest groups are the Bambara (Bamana) in the region between Bamako and Segu in Mali, the Songhai around the northern and eastern reaches of the great bend in the river, merging into the related Jerma (Zarma or Zerma) in Niger, the Nupe in central Nigeria, the Igbo (Ibo) along the southern reaches of the river, and the Ijo (Ijaw) in the delta. We should also mention the Sorko—Songhai-speaking fisherfolk, hippopotamus hunters, and boatbuilders—who move up and down the Niger from the Gulbin Khebbi tributary in Nigeria to the Inland Delta in Mali where the Bozo and Somonou, who engage in similar activities, live.

The Niger has been a vital artery of communication historically. It is navigable for much of its length by shallow draft boats, the only serious impediments to passage being the rapids of Kolikoro near Bamako, the rapids just north to the Mali-Niger border, and the rapids of Boussa in Nigeria, where Mungo Park lost his life in 1806. During the period of the Songhai Empire (1464–1591) large canoes carried grain to Gao and Timbuktu, and ferried dignitaries and military personnel from one end of the empire to the other. At the present time there is still much private river traffic, and a Malian government ferry operates during the high-water season between Kolikoro and Gao.

Several bridges cross the Niger: two in the Malian capital, Bamako; one at Segu; one at Niamey, the capital of Niger; and one at Malanville on the Bénin-Niger border. There are several bridges in Nigeria: one just south of the Kainji Dam; two at Jebba (road and rail); one at Koton-Karifi (just upstream from the Niger-Benue confluence); one at Ajaokuta (where an iron and steel complex is sited); and one at Asaba-Onitsha linking the southeastern and southwestern halves of Nigeria. A ferry links Gao in northeastern Mali to a road that runs back to Bamako.

In the 1990s the Niger is still only partially exploited. In Mali a natural arm of the river between Markala and Sokolo was cleared by the French in the 1930s to form a canal, and hundreds of miles of irrigation channels were dug. Cotton was grown there, and since the 1970s, rice and sugar have been cultivated. A supervisory body, called the Office du Niger, was created as early as 1932 and continues to function. At Kainji in Nigeria there is a major high dam which was completed in the late 1960s, creating a lake that flooded old Boussa. Its hydroelectric turbines are a major source of electricity for Nigeria and Bénin. In the Niger Delta region in Nigeria, oil and natural gas have been exploited since the 1950s. In 1993 the two largest concessions were owned by the Nigerian National Petroleum Corporation and Shell, followed by Elf and Gulf Oil. There are refineries at Port Harcourt and Warri, and oil terminals at Brass and Bonny. Oil accounts for 98 percent of Nigeria's export earnings and 75 percent of government revenue.

BIBLIOGRAPHY

Africanus, Leo. *Description de l'Afrique.* Translated by A. Epaulard et al. 2 vols. Paris, 1956.

Dike, Kenneth O. *Trade and Politics in the Niger Delta, 1830–1885.* Oxford, 1956.

Dubois, Felix. *Timbuctoo the Mysterious.* Translated by Diana White. New York, 1896.

Flint, John E. *Sir George Goldie and the Making of Nigeria.* London, 1960.

Gallais, Jean. *Le Delta intérieur du Niger et ses bordures.* Paris, 1967.

Gramont, Sanche de. *The Strong Brown God: The Story of the Niger River.* London, 1975.

Hallett, Robin. *The Penetration of Africa.* Volume 1, *To 1815.* New York, 1965.

Hollett, Dave. *The Conquest of the Niger by Land and Sea: From the Early Explorers and Pioneer Steamships to Elder Dempster and Company.* Abergavenny, U.K., 1995.

Lloyd, Christopher. *The Search for the Niger.* London, 1973.

Requin, Édouard. *Archinard et le Soudan.* 1921.

Roberts, Richard. *Warriors, Merchants, and Slaves: The State and the Economy in the Middle Niger, 1700–1914.* Stanford, 1987.

JOHN HUNWICK

See also **Niger-Benue Region; Niger Delta Region.**

NIGERIA

GEOGRAPHY AND ECONOMY

The Federal Republic of Nigeria was formed from the British colony and protectorates of Northern and Southern Nigeria, which came into existence on 1 January 1900. It gained its political independence from Britain on 1 October 1960 and became a republic on 1 October 1963. The country lies between 3° and 15° east longitude and 4° and 14° north latitude. It is bounded on the south by the Gulf of Guinea, on the east by Cameroon, on the north by Chad and Niger, and on the west by Bénin. It has a total land area of some 923,768 square kilometers (356,669 sq. mi.) and a population of 88.5 million (according to the 1991 census). Fairly reliable estimates, however, exceed 100 mil-

lion. The Federation has grown from three regions (1960) to four states (1963), twelve states (1967), nineteen states (1976), twenty-one states (1987), and thirty states (1991), and has a new federal capital city at Abuja. Until December 1991, Lagos was the capital.

Geography

Large areas of the country, especially in the northern, central, and western parts, are underlain by very old igneous and metamorphic rocks of the basement complex. They comprise granitic as well as basaltic rocks, the latter in areas of volcanic activity such as the Jos, Biu, and Mambilla plateaus. By contrast, the northwestern and northeastern areas, the valleys of the Niger and Benue Rivers, most of the eastern areas, and the coastal belt are underlain by young sedimentary rocks including sandstones and limestones.

In terms of relief, Nigeria is part of the great western lowland zone of tropical Africa. Much of the country lies below 1,000 meters (3,300 ft.). The main highlands are the Jos Plateau, almost in the center of the country, the Biu and Mambilla Plateaus, and the Adamawa and Mandara Mountains in the eastern borderlands. All are highly dissected. They slope down to upland areas such as the central Hausa high plains in the north and the Yoruba uplands in the south. These upland areas are dotted everywhere with striking rocky outcrops and inselbergs. To the northeast and northwest are the lowlands of the Lake Chad depression and the Rima Basin, respectively. In southeastern Nigeria, the sedimentary rocks give rise to a distinctive topography of scarp lands marked by spectacular gully erosion and small, beautiful lakes. The coastal areas are notable for their mix of sand beaches, creeks, and lagoons that merge imperceptibly into the delta of the Niger River.

The Niger River and its principal tributary, the Benue, are the two most important rivers. Both rise outside the country, the former in the Futa Jalon highlands of the Republic of Guinea, the latter in the Adamawa highlands of western Cameroon. After their impressive confluence at Lokoja, they continue south to enter the Gulf of Guinea through a large network of creeks and distributaries forming the Niger Delta. Virtually all Nigerian rivers north of the Niger-Benue Valley rise from the Jos Plateau. They include the Sokoto, Kaduna, and Gongola as well as the Komadugu-Yobé, which drains into Lake Chad. Rivers draining south of the Niger-Benue Valley are usually short and flow

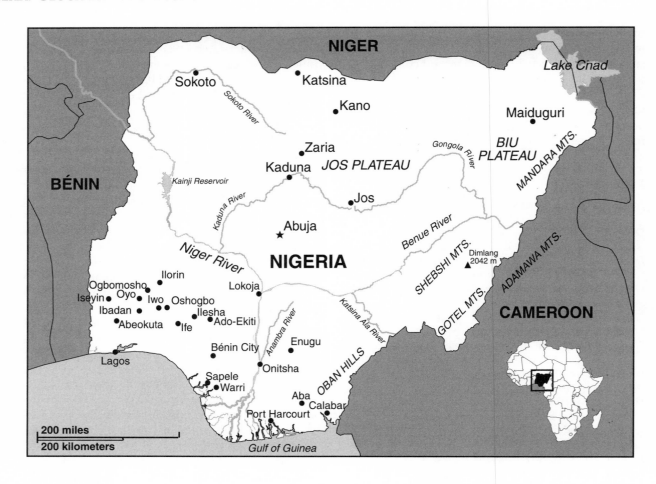

either into the Niger-Benue system or directly to the ocean. As in other parts of Africa, rapids and falls are common on Nigerian rivers. These make them unnavigable over any great distance but indicate some significant potential for hydroelectric development.

Temperatures are high throughout the year. Except on the plateaus, maximum temperatures range from 27° to 40°C (81°–104°F), the minimum from 18° to 25°C (64°–77°F). Rainfall is the critical climatic element. It decreases progressively northward from 3,800 millimeters (148 in.) per annum in Port Harcourt on the coast to about 625 millimeters (25 in.) in Maiduguri in the extreme northeast. Seasonal variation in rainfall becomes very pronounced as one moves northward, with the dry season varying from less than one month on the coast to as much as seven months in the northeast.

Total rainfall and its seasonality determine soil characteristics and vegetation patterns. Most parts of the country are covered by ferruginous tropical soils derived from both the basement complex and old sedimentary rocks. On the north-central Hausa high plains, more fertile soils have developed on the drift deposits covering the basement complex. To the south, clayey and sandy ferralitic soils occur. Low in humus content, they are not the best soils for agriculture. These become hydromorphic and still less fertile as one moves into the Niger Valley, the Niger Delta, and the coastal creeks and lagoons.

The vegetational pattern changes in consonance with the rainfall and soil conditions. It varies from the mangrove forest of the delta, creeks, and lagoons of the coast, to the rain forest of the southern lowlands, to the succession of the derived, Guinea, Sudan, and Sahel grassland belts and the inliers of mountain vegetation on the Jos and other plateaus. Forests still cover about 10 percent of the land area, and in the south they yield abundant timber that has been exported since colonial times.

Economy

Much of the vegetation has been transformed by human activities, especially through farming and

The Niger River in southern Nigeria. BRUCE PATON/PANOS PICTURES

mining, the former now utilizing some 40 percent of the land. In terms of agricultural production, the country can be divided into three broad zones: the southern root crop zone; the northern grain zone; and the middle (mixed crop) belt. The major staples from the southern zone are yams, cassava, and cocoyams. Until the introduction of rice in the twentieth century, corn was the only grain produced in the zone. Agricultural exports are cocoa, palm oil, palm kernels, rubber, and timber. The northern zone produces millet, sorghum, rice, beans, tomatoes, and onions as well as peanuts and cotton for industrial processing and export. Because of its relative freedom from the scourge of the tsetse fly, this zone, along with the plateau areas, contains most of the major livestock population, particularly cattle, goats, and sheep. The middle belt, which can produce both root crops and grains, is emerging as the major food basket of the country.

Mining locations and products are determined largely by geology. Metamorphic rocks of the basement complex offer such metallic minerals as tin and columbite mined on the Jos Plateau; gold, an important export commodity since colonial times; and iron ore, mica, feldspar, marble, and a host of other minerals of unproven economic significance. The sedimentary rocks, especially of the coastal areas and the southeast, yield fossil fuels of various types. Initially, sub-bituminous coal was mined in the Enugu region. Since the late 1960s, petroleum has been produced (and exported) both offshore and onshore within the Niger Delta. In 1991 production stood at 705 million barrels, of which 599 million barrels were exported. The same area offers large quantities of natural gas, with reserves estimated at over four trillion cubic meters. Major development, production, and export of natural gas, begun in the late 1990s, promise to bring a renewed upturn in the economy of the country. There is also abundant lignite. All these are in addition to such industrial minerals as lead, zinc, limestone, kaolin, talc, sand, and clay.

Until the railway network of some 3,505 kilometers (2,178 mi.) was established by the colonial administration between 1896 and 1927, there was only limited internal exchange or overseas export of any significance. Transportation development, particularly the improvement of the ports of Lagos-Apapa and Port Harcourt in the first two decades of the twentieth century, transformed economic conditions in Nigeria. Road development followed after World War I but was closely controlled because of its competition with the railway. Restrictions were relaxed after World War II because the railway proved inadequate for transporting the vastly increased agricultural production from interior locations. Since then the road network has expanded tremendously, amounting in the mid-1990s to some 124,000 kilometers (77,000 mi.), nearly half of which are paved. More ports have been developed at Tin Can Island in Lagos; at Warri, Koko, Burutu, and Sapele in the delta; at

309

The Federal Republic of Nigeria

Population: 108,500,000 (1994 est.)

Area: 923,774 sq. km (356,669 sq. mi.)

Official language: English

Languages: Edo, Efik, English, Fulani, Ibibio, Hausa, Igbo, Ijaw, Nupe, Tiv, Urhobo, Yoruba

National currency: Naira

Principal religions: Muslim 50%, Christian (Roman Catholic and Protestant) 40%, traditional 10%

Capital: Abuja (Federal Capital Territory)

Other urban centers: Ibadan, Lagos, Ogbomosho, Kano, Ilorin, Oshogbo, Abeokuta, Port Harcourt, Ilesha, Onitsha, Zaria, Iwo, Ado-Ekiti, Kaduna, Maiduguri, Calabar, Enugu, Ife, Oyo, Bauchi, Mushin, Benin City, Aba, Sokoto, Jos, Offa, Katsina, Jimeta, Akure, Minna, Warri, Makurdi, Owerri, Ikeja, Yola

Annual rainfall: Highly variable, 1,700–4,310 mm (70–170 in.) from west to east along the coast; 500 mm (20 in.) in the extreme north

Principal geographical features:

Mountains: Mandara Mountains, Shebshi Mountains, Alantika Mountains, Mambilla Mountains, Gotel Mountains, Jos Plateau, Biu Plateau

Lakes: Lake Chad, Kainji Reservoir, Tiga Reservoir

Rivers: Niger, Benue, Katsina-Ala, Gongola, Sokoto, Kaduna, Anambra, Yobe, Benin, Ogun, Escravos, Forcados, Sombreiro, Cross, Kwa, Imo, Calabar

Economy:

GNP per capita: US$260 (1995)

Principal products and exports:

Agricultural: palm kernels, palm oil, cocoa, rubber, cotton, coffee, groundnuts, sesame, yams, cassava, plantains, maize, sorghum, millet, rice, cowpeas, potatoes, fruit, livestock, fish, timber

Manufacturing: oil refining, iron and steel production, agricultural product processing, textiles, sugar refining, pulp and paper mills, cement, vehicle assembly, soap and detergent, brewing, cigarettes, footwear, pharmaceuticals, chemical fertilizer

Mining: petroleum, natural gas, tin, coal, columbite, iron, gold

Government: Independence from Great Britain, 1960. Constitution, 1960, sections suspended in 1966. New constitution approved in 1970, suspended in 1983. New constitution approved in 1989, suspended in 1996. Military rule. Since the suspension of the constitution, government is by decree of the 26-member military Provisional Ruling Council (previously named the Armed Forces Ruling Council and the Supreme Military Council). There is an essentially powerless cabinet, the Federal Executive Council. Federal law and decrees prevail over those promulgated by individual states. Since 1994, a constitutional conference exists but has not produced a constitution.

Heads of state since independence:

1960–1963: Governor General Benjamin Nnamdi Azikiwe

1960–1966: Prime Minister Abubakar Tafawa Balewa

1963–1966: President Benjamin Nnamdi Azikiwe

1966: Major General Johnson Aguiyi-Ironsi

1966–1975: Lieutenant Colonel (later General) Yakubu Gowon

1975–1976: Brigadier (later General) Murtala Ramat Muhammed

1976–1979: Lieutenant General (later General) Olusegun Obasanjo

1979–1983: President Shehu Shagari

1984–1985: Major General Muhammadu Buhari

1985–1993: Major General Ibrahim Badamasi Babangida

1993: Interim President Ernest Shonekan

1993–: General Sani Abacha

The Federal Republic of Nigeria *(continued)*

Armed forces: Head of state is commander in chief. Voluntary enlistment.

Army: 62,000

Navy: 5,000

Air force: 9,450

Paramilitary: 2,000

Forces abroad: 5,000 (ECOMOG)

Transportation:

Rail: 3,505 km (2,173 mi.), operated by the Nigerian Railway Corporation

Waterways: 8,575 km (5,316 mi.), principally the Niger and Benue Rivers

Ports: Lagos-Apapa, Tin Can Island, Delta Port Complex (Warri, Koko, Burutu, Sapele), Port Harcourt, Calabar, Bonny, and Burutu for petroleum shipping

Roads: 108,000 km (66,960 mi.), 28% paved. Trans-Africa Highway links Lagos with Mombasa.

National airline: Nigerian Airways (government owned). Air Nigeria is a joint government-private venture. Kabo Air and Okada Air are private.

Airports: Murtala Muhammed International Airport in Lagos. There are 17 other airports throughout the country.

Media: More than 26 dailies, including *Daily Times, Nigerian Observer, Punch, Nigerian Herald, Nigerian Tribune, New Nigerian.* 88 periodicals as of 1988. Major Nigerian publishers include Fourth Dimension, Skevium, Nalthouse, and Gaskiya. There are also several multinational publishing companies: Oxford University Press, Longman, Evans, Macmillan, Heinemann, Thomas Nelson. There are also several university presses and publishers specializing in local vernacular publications. The government owns Federal Radio Corporation of Nigeria and the Nigerian Television Authority. External radio service provided by Voice of Nigeria. Other outlets include Radio-Television Kaduna and Western Nigeria Radiovision Service. Film production began in 1970.

Literacy and education:

Total literacy rate: 51% (1990). Education is free, universal, and compulsory for ages 6–12. 31 universities, including Ahmadu Bello University, University of Benin, University of Calabar, University of Ibadan, Obafemi Awolowo University, University of Ilorin, University of Jos, University of Lagos, University of Maiduguri, University of Nigeria, University of Port Harcourt, and Usman Dan Fodio University. Numerous technical schools.

Calabar; and at Bonny and Burutu for petroleum shipping.

Waterways were important for transporting goods during the colonial era. For some months of the year, some 8,600 kilometers (5,300 mi.) of waterways were navigable on the Niger River from the coast up to Jebba, and on the Benue up to Garuoa (in Cameroon). Internal air transportation has become very important since the 1980s, with the removal of the monopoly previously enjoyed by Nigeria Airways. Many of the state capitals are now linked to Lagos and Abuja by a number of private carriers with many flights each day.

The period after World War II saw the beginning of serious industrialization. However, instead of promoting the industrial use of local raw materials, it encouraged the importation not just of machinery and equipment but also of semiprocessed raw materials for producing goods and articles the country had formerly imported. It thus placed a high premium on port location, and so a high percentage of industrial capacity came to be concentrated in Lagos and to a lesser extent in Port Harcourt. Industries established include food processing, textiles, vehicle tires and other rubber products, printing and packaging, vehicle assembly, and metalworking. Important industrial concentrations developed inland in Kaduna, Kano, Jos, Enugu, and Aba.

In spite of consuming a large proportion of the foreign earnings of the country, manufacturing in 1992 accounted for less than 9 percent of the gross domestic product (GDP). In that year, the GDP (at 1984 constant factor cost) was 98.42 billion naira (N) (U.S.$5.3 billion). Agriculture contributed

Farmland in northern Nigeria. ANNA TULLY/PANOS PICTURES

38.5 percent, and mining (including crude petroleum), 13.2 percent. They also employed over 70 percent of the total labor force. Wholesale and retail trade, which employs a substantial proportion of the female labor force, contributed some 12.5 percent of the GDP.

By 1992, while nonoil exports stood at only N4.2 billion (U.S.$227,000) (oil exports were N201.4 billion), nonoil imports rose to 43.2 billion (U.S.$2.3 billion) (oil imports were N19.6 billion). Capital goods and raw materials for industries accounted for some 60 percent of imports. By the late 1970s, this heightened import dependence, deriving from the strategy of industrialization, had placed Nigeria in the league of internationally indebted countries. By 1993 the external debt of the country stood at U.S.$32.53 billion. In 1986 the inability to repay much of this debt had forced the country to adopt a structural adjustment program. This program aims to curb the high propensity to consume imports while increasing the volume and value of exports. It also seeks to reduce the excessive level of government spending, which often has given rise to high budget deficits. An important element of the program has been the deregulation of the economy and the privatization of most of the enterprises previously owned totally or in part by government.

The naira was allowed to float and find its exchange value in a free market. The resulting sharp fall in value wrought untold havoc on the standard of living and quality of life of most Nigerians. In terms of structurally adjusting the economy, the effect to date has been very mixed. Consequently, some revision of the program has occurred, involving the reimposition of some degree of regulation. This has left the prospects for a stable and growing economy far from certain. Nigeria is, however, a well-endowed country. Its fairly large population of enterprising individuals offers the prospects that with time, the country's economy will again become vibrant, strong, and stable.

BIBLIOGRAPHY

Aina, Tade Akin, and Ademola T. Salau, eds. *The Challenge of Sustainable Development in Nigeria.* Ibadan, Nigeria, 1992.

Arya, Pyare L. *Structure, Policies, and Growth Prospects of Nigeria.* Lewiston, N.Y., 1993.

Buchanan, Keith M., and J. C. Pugh. *Land and People in Nigeria.* London, 1958.

Ihoya, F. E., et al., eds. *Self-Reliance, Politics, and Administration in Nigeria.* 2d ed. Ekpoma, Nigeria, 1995.

Nnoli, Okwudiba. *Ethnicity and Development in Nigeria.* Brookfield, Vt., 1995.

Oguntoyinbo, J. S., O. O. Areola, and M. O. Filani, eds. *The Geography of Nigerian Development.* Ibadan, Nigeria, 1983.

Onokerhoraye, Andrew G. *The Impact of the Structural Adjustment Programme on Grassroots Development in Nigeria.* Benin City, Nigeria, 1995.

Watts, Michael, ed. *State, Oil, and Agriculture in Nigeria.* Berkeley, Calif., 1987.

AKIN L. MABOGUNJE

See also **Niger River.**

HISTORY AND GOVERNMENT

Nigerian Republic Since Independence

History

Nigeria obtained its independence from Britain in 1960. Ever since, its history has been one of hope and frustration: hope because it is expected that it should be able to use its abundant resources to achieve rapid economic development; and frustration because this expectation is unfulfilled and political stability is not in sight.

Nigeria's political history is dominated by military rule, with few interruptions by democratic governments. The First Republic, presided over by Prime Minister Abubakar Tafawa Balewa and with a nominal president (Nnamdi Azikiwe), lasted from 1960 to January 1966. Plagued by intense regionalism, declining revenues, and bitter power rivalry, the First Republic moved from one crisis to another until it was overthrown by the military. The first coup, led by Patrick Nzeogwu, was badly planned, and an officer who was not involved in it, Johnson Aguiyi-Ironsi, became the country's head. Nzeogwu and Ironsi were Igbo (Ibo), and both the coups and the policies that followed were interpreted as an attempt to achieve Igbo domination. A countercoup occurred in July 1966, leading to the emergence of Yakubu Gowon as the new head and generating a bitterness that led to the massacre of Igbo in the north, and a secession by the east, led by Odumegwu Ojukwu. The Igbo established the short-lived Republic of Biafra, and a civil war followed to reunite the country.

The 1970s were marked by dramatic changes. The civil war ended in 1970, for a short while abating the danger of ethnicity but introducing the problem of postwar reconstruction and rehabilitation. An oil boom gave the country tremendous opportunities to expand and develop into a regional power. There were coups and countercoups, leading to the overthrow of Gowon in 1975, and the emergence of the well-liked Murtala Muhammed, who was killed seven months later. Olusegun Obasanjo assumed leadership and became the first to voluntarily relinquish power to a civilian, Shehu Shagari, president of the Second Republic from 1979 to 1983. The later 1980s were dominated by the military, first by Muhammadu Buhari and later by Ibrahim Babangida, who ruled for eight years, during a time of massive corruption and indifference to public opinion. Babangida's failure to manage a successful transition led to the inauguration of an interim government, headed by Ernest Shonekan, which was unable to generate trust and offer strong leadership. He was overthrown in November 1993 by General Sani Abacha, whose excessive political style has generated domestic protest and international condemnation.

All governments have considered foreign relations an important component of policy. The First Republic pursued a conservative policy of promoting friendship with the West, distancing itself from the Soviet Union, and playing soft on major international issues. Under Gowon, the support of the Soviet Union to win the civil war encouraged the broadening of relations with the East, and oil wealth was spent to build a positive international image. The late 1970s was characterized by radicalism, with Nigeria championing the liberation of Angola and condemnation of apartheid South Africa. Since the 1980s, economic downturn has weakened the country's ability to assert itself.

Government

Nigeria is supposed to be a federal secular state. The First Republic was administered by a parliamentary system, whereas the Second Republic tried an American-style presidential system. The post-1979 constitution is based on federalism, a strong executive president, and political parties that cut across ethnic and religious groups. Whenever it is inaugurated, the Third Republic is expected to operate on the basis of a presidential constitution, federalism, and a multiparty system. In the meantime, five political parties have been established and approved by the government, and elections were held in 1997 to appoint leaders for the local government. The military has promised to hand over power in 1998, but the Nigerian political situation is always volatile and unpredictable.

The military has ruled Nigeria for most of the time and has succeeded in building a strong center that controls power and resources. While this has helped to minimize tensions among the states, it has increased the competition for control of the center. The military is part of the country's problem: its officers are power hungry, while the rank and file is divided by ethnic and religious differences.

The military rules by decrees that supersede the constitution. There is a vibrant judiciary, but it is powerless to deal with bad laws and unable to use the legal system as a basis of social justice. There are a dynamic, mature newspaper industry and government-controlled electronic media. The civil service has grown more in size than in experience and has become a major avenue to wealth and power.

The emergence of democracy is made difficult by the excessive interest of the military in government, the failure of civilian political actors to rise above self-interest, and the weakness of the civil society to constitute a respectable public opinion and opposition to dictatorship.

No government has been able to sustain lasting popularity or confidence among the populace because officials use power to promote selfish ends and to defend parochial, religious, and ethnic interests. When the public complains, the government resorts to intimidation and press clampdown. Nevertheless, individuals and organized groups continue to criticize the government, protest authoritarianism, and demand reforms. The failure to meet the demands and expectations of a large population, ensure human rights and freedom, manage the economy well, and govern in a democratic manner means that Nigeria will be prone to more conflicts and civil rebellion. Without a committed government and an active civil society, the country is unlikely to move forward, in spite of its enormous natural resources, talented intelligentsia, and large size.

BIBLIOGRAPHY

Falola, Toyin, et al. *The Military Factor in Nigeria: 1966–1985.* Lewiston, N.Y., 1994.

Forrest, Tom G. *Politics and Economic Development in Nigeria.* Boulder, Colo., 1993. Rev. ed. 1995.

Kirk-Greene, Anthony H. M., and Douglas Rimmer. *Nigeria Since 1970: A Political and Economic Outline.* New York, 1981.

TOYIN FALOLA

Northern Nigeria, from c. 1900 until Independence

The Protectorate of Northern Nigeria was created, largely as a takeover from the chartered Royal Niger Company, on 1 January 1900, with the capital momentarily at Lokoja before moving upriver to Jebba. To the first high commissioner (1900–1906), Sir Frederick Lugard, much of the subsequent colonial administrative structure and ethos can be attributed. After occupying the Sokoto Caliphate in a campaign culminating in the fall of Kano and the defeat of Sokoto in 1903, Lugard set about devising, as an economic expedient rather than from any prior blueprint, a system of close cooperation with and ruling through the traditional leaders (emirs and chiefs), relying on such existing institutions as local administration and courts. He directed his officials to act as advisers rather than as rulers. This system, eventually exported (with varying measures of success) to most of British Africa other than Kenya, became known as indirect rule, or native administration. Northern Nigeria became its showpiece. It was a policy adopted by Lugard's successors in Zungeru, where the capital next moved; the policy was also misguidedly urged by Lugard for extension to the Southern Provinces, which lacked the hierarchical structure of authority on which its success in the northern provinces depended.

That the essence of Lugard's policy lay in the principle of effective collaboration should not conceal the fact that resentment and protest were equally an element of the relationship between the ruled and their alien rulers. The grassroots revolt at Satiru and the resistance at Hadejia in 1906 were but two of the most violent manifestations. Of the three options which had been open to the emirs of Northern Nigeria and their subjects when confronted by the threat of foreign overlordship at the turn of the century, two were frequently resorted to and the third from time to time turned to: armed resistance, at first on the battlefield and later in sporadic unrest; collaboration, at least superficially, in the perceived best interests of their people; and flight, whether relocation over the border to Niger or Cameroon, or across the western Sudan toward the ultimate haven of Mecca.

In 1914 Northern Nigeria came under the control of the governor-general in Lagos, following the amalgamation of the Northern and Southern Protectorates. The Northern Provinces, as the protectorate was restyled after 1914, received additional territory at the end of World War I by the award of the League of Nations mandate for part of the German Kamerun. During the so-called Cameroon campaign of 1914–1916, Yola in the northeast became an important part of the war theater. In 1917 the capital was moved again. Neither Sokoto, the caliphate, nor Kano, the prominent commercial center, was selected; rather, it was shifted from Zungeru to the colonial town of Kaduna. In 1926 a total reorganization of the provinces took place. The 1939 division of the Southern Province into the Eastern and Western Provinces had a psychological rather than a physical effect on the North.

If the North achieved some economic progress with the building of the railway to Kano in 1911 and the development of major export trades in groundnuts, tin, hides and skins, and later cotton, and if it continued to be characterized by a system of administration which worked and was orderly without being recognizably developmental, its constitutional and educational position was markedly behind that of the South up to 1950. This was partly due to the Muslim emirs' suspicion of the evangelizing efforts of the mission schools and partly due to the decision to keep the North outside the jurisdiction of the central legislature. As governor of Nigeria in the 1930s, Sir Donald Cameron's aim to liberalize the straitjacket of indirect rule through a redirected interventionist policy of indirect administration had a limited impact. Similarly, his successor, Sir Bernard Bourdillon, found it hard to modernize the attitude of the emirs toward political reform.

It was not until after World War II that some sort of conciliar local government was introduced into the native administration, albeit still hesitantly. At the national level, the restructuring of Nigeria in 1914 had, significantly, been no more than an administrative amalgamation. Furthermore, the North was excluded from the jurisdiction of the Legislative Council, set up in Lagos in 1914 and expanded in 1922; the governor legislated for the North at his own discretion. It was to be nearly twenty-five years before any Northern Nigerian voice was heard in the central legislature.

From 1945, however, the North began to assume its proper place in the government of Nigeria. The 1946 Constitution created a regional House of Assembly, with a majority of unofficial members (though not yet all elected), in each part of the country, along with a House of Chiefs for the North. For the first time there was, however minimal, a representative Northern presence in Lagos. The 1951 Constitution introduced elected members both at the center and in the regions, and in 1954, under the Lyttleton Constitution, the North became a self-contained region within the Federation of Nigeria, with its own premier, government, and judiciary. These constitutions, approved by the Colonial Office in London, were stages in the policy of planned advance toward self-government.

Political party activity, which had been low-key and uncoordinated in the emirate-dominated Northern society, burgeoned in the 1950s. The dominant parties were the traditionalist Northern People's Congress (NPC), a cultural organization turned political party, forcefully led by Alhaji Ahmadu Bello, Sardauna of Sokoto, who in 1954 became the regional premier, and the radical Northern Elements Progressive Union (NEPU), led by Aminu Kano. While the power base of both parties lay in the Muslim Hausa homelands, their support was largely divided by class. In the lower part of the North, riverine and predominantly Christian or animist, the United Middle Belt Congress (UMBC) emerged as the major opposition, calling for a separate region to be carved out of the Muslim North. The question of allaying the fears of minorities, ethnic and religious, lay at the heart of the inquiry of the Willink Commission in 1957, on the eve of independence, which did not recommend the creation of more states within these regions. For all its expanding prominence in central government, the NPC never seriously campaigned for votes outside the North before 1960.

During the heyday of party politics in Nigeria—that is to say, between the first general election of 1951 and the first military coup in 1966—the NPC symbolized the North both internally and outside, even though that North was never so monolithic as it superficially appeared. Its motto was "One People, One North," and its guiding principle, with a generous resonance of status quo and attachment to tradition and legitimate authority, is best defined as that of continuity within change. Its three main internal challenges came from the traditional Fulani (Fulbe) rulers, the radical urban youth, and the non-Muslim Northern peoples outside the emirates but within the Northern Provinces.

The traditional rulers were wooed and won over thanks to the charismatic personality of the premier, Ahmadu Bello, himself a member of the royal house of Sokoto and hence indisputably, in the eyes of the emirs, "one of us." While, as traditionally fathers of their people, chiefs were supposed to remain aloof from the new sport of politics, the evolving symbiosis between them and the Northern political leadership soon reached the stage where the NPC could not have succeeded without the approval of the emirs, and the emirs could not have survived without the endorsement of the NPC.

The urban youth sought their solace in the welcoming arms of the radical NEPU. As for non-Muslim peoples, after some anxious moments in the early 1950s when the irredentist Northern Yoruba flirted with the idea of joining with their kinsmen south of the Niger, and again in the mid-1950s when the movement for an excised Middle

Belt state threatened to crystallize among the non-Muslims, the NPC leadership was astute enough generally to accommodate and incorporate such opposition rather than to drive it underground. In this, the tactic of "we" in the North against "them" in the South proved a successful move to ensure regional unity. So dominant was the NPC in shaping the new political North that its legacy and its image were still alive and recognizable thirty-five years, several governments, and numerous coups beyond independence.

With independence palpably in sight by 1954, the North's biggest challenge was to catch up with the educationally advanced (in Western terms) and politically sophisticated (in Westminster terms) South so as to be able to play its proper role in the Federation according to its rights as the region with the largest population. This criterion meant that the decennial census became a matter of intense political excitement and significance instead of being a routine administrative exercise. The period from 1954 to 1959 was characterized by a vigorous campaign of "Northernization": accelerated education and training at all levels so as to create a reservoir of Northern talent, not only to localize the regional bureaucracy but also to ensure that the North at least filled its quota of posts in the new federal institutions like the civil service, the military, and eventually the diplomatic corps. At its own request, the North postponed internal self-government until 1959, two years after it had been granted to the West and East.

Although the federal election of 1959 resulted in a marriage of convenience at the center between the NPC, which in Alhaji Abubakar Tafawa Balewa had provided the prime minister since the inception of the office in 1957, and its arch rival in the Northern election, the eastern-based National Council of Nigeria and the Cameroons (NCNC), there was little doubt when Nigeria became independent on 1 October 1960 which political party and which region would dominate the country's immediate political future. And so it proved. Northern Nigeria, which in terms of party competition and educational record had entered Nigeria's final decade of colonial status as the least advanced of the country's component parts, had by 1960 staked its claim as the unquestioned leading force in the Federation.

BIBLIOGRAPHY

Ayandele, Emmanuel A. *The Missionary Impact on Modern Nigeria, 1842–1914: A Political and Social Analysis.* London, 1966.

Crowder, Michael. *The Story of Nigeria.* Rev. ed. London, 1978.

Dudley, Billy J. *Parties and Politics in Northern Nigeria.* London, 1968.

Ikime, Obaro. *The Fall of Nigeria: The British Conquest.* London, 1977.

Kirk-Greene, Anthony H. M. *The Principles of Native Administration in Nigeria: Selected Documents, 1900–1947.* London, 1965.

Nwabueze, B. O. *A Constitutional History of Nigeria.* London, 1982.

Whitaker, C. Sylvester. *The Politics of Tradition: Continuity and Change in Northern Nigeria, 1946–1966.* Princeton, 1970.

ANTHONY KIRK-GREENE

See also **Bello, Ahmadu; Hausa States; Kano, Alhaji Aminu; Lugard, Frederick Dealtry; Sokoto Caliphate; Tafawa Balewa, Abubakar.**

Southern Nigeria from c. 1850 until Independence

Developments of 1849–1899

For Africans in the communities that later made up Southern Nigeria, the nineteenth century was critical in several ways. All of them came to realize the significance of the familiar saying that weak states invite attack. Group after group, they also came to understand that sovereignty is indivisible. By treaties, agreements, coercion, conquest, or annexation, these communities first lost to foreigners authority over their external affairs, then surrendered internal control. Unable or unwilling to confront common foes decisively, they succumbed, under progressive attacks, to forces superior to them in firepower if not in will and guile. As these communities declined and fell, one after another, they paved the way for dramatic changes which affected the course of events well beyond the nineteenth century. For them and for their early-twentieth-century successors, the interplay of the key factors of time, circumstance, and leadership left indelible marks.

Ill-equipped in men and resources to defend themselves against a European incursion, Africans in these groups failed to respond effectively to new changes and challenges in their environment from the beginning of and throughout the nineteenth century. In the end, their largely uncoordinated response failed to deter an enemy seeking to exercise more and more jurisdiction, power, and authority in their lands.

British abolition of the slave trade in 1807 and of slavery in 1833 led to regular patrols in west

African waters by a preventive or "humanitarian" squadron. Simultaneously, European traders either persisted in the trans-Atlantic slave trade or sought alternatives in legitimate commerce such as palm produce (palm oil and kernels). About the same time, Christian missionaries began to be active in the region, first along the coast and later in the hinterland. The pursuit of these interests gradually encouraged officials of the British government (in particular of the War, Foreign, and Colonial Offices) to adopt measures in favor of informal empire (through colonies and protectorates) where opportunities encouraged these efforts. As the nineteenth century wore on, British spokesmen such as Joseph Chamberlain (of the Colonial Office) did not hesitate to preach the doctrine of breaking African eggs to make imperial omelets.

How ready, then, were Africans to resist these efforts? In the southwest, the decline and collapse of the Old Oyo Empire and protracted warfare among successor states, in addition to incessant attacks from Dahomey (present-day Bénin), weakened much of Yorubaland. War weariness inclined communities, such as those of New Oyo and Ibadan, and the Ekiti, Egba, Ijebu, Egbado, and Ijesa, among others, to sue for peace through British pressures in the 1880s and 1890s. By 1893, these efforts had brought a measure of peace to parts of Yorubaland.

Events at Lagos and its vicinity resulted in a different solution. In the 1840s, the British feared competition from the French close to Badagri. Moreover, dynastic disputes between claimants to the throne of Lagos created intense rivalries between Kosoko, Akitoye, and Dosunmu and their supporters. Thus, the weak monarchy in Lagos failed to stop creeping British consular jurisdiction from 1851. The annexation (or cession) of Lagos in August 1861 surprised no one.

In the southeast, a similar combination of weakness among the city-states and communities of the Niger Delta and the Cross River plus dynastic rivalries resulted in the establishment of consular jurisdiction in 1849 and its expansion and consolidation thereafter. The declaration, in 1885, of the Oil Rivers Protectorate, renamed Niger Coast Protectorate in 1893, came in the wake of the Berlin Conference, 1884–1885, and Brussels Conference, 1889–1890. Step by step, the era of the "paper protectorate" of the 1880s gave way to one in need of "effective occupation" from the 1890s.

Correspondingly, African rulers, chiefs, and common people, unwilling to cooperate with British consular officials of the 1880s and 1890s, paid dearly for their opposition—mainly through deportation. Notable deportees included Ja Ja of Opobo (1887), Nana of the Itsekiri (1894), Ibanichuka of Okrika (1896), Koko of Nemba-Brass (1896), and Overami, or Ovonramwen, of Benin (1897). As Ralph Moor, commissioner and consulgeneral, proclaimed at the end of the 1897 expedition against Benin, the British crown would brook no rival "king" in any part of the Niger Coast Protectorate.

The new era in the Niger Coast Protectorate tolerated only collaborators, with or without "warrants," who were given minor judicial and administrative roles as members of native courts and councils, the successors, in the 1880s and 1890s, of the informal "courts of equity" begun in the 1850s. About the same time, another fundamental change occurred: from men and measures to principles. In particular, the meaning of a British "protectorate" became more fluid. Its interpretation varied, since the law officers of the British crown said one thing in faraway Whitehall, while the local officials said another.

Along the lower Niger (Idah, Akassa, Onitsha, Asaba, Aboh) a different dispensation occurred during the 1880s and 1890s. The Royal Niger Company, in 1886, received a British charter to combine its trading activities with those of administration (including the dispensation of justice). Its arbitrary exercise of power led to severe confrontations such as the Akassa Raid (1895) and conflict with an Igbo war cult, the Ekumeku (also called the League of the Silent Ones), in Asaba hinterland (1898). The company lost its charter in 1899 as part of new arrangements for the "Niger territories" or "districts," effective from 1900.

Developments of 1900–1960

The prevailing environment in Southern Nigeria did not favor a meaningful partnership in support of the "indirect rule" of the Lugardian school. In the Southern Nigeria of the 1890s and the 1900s, the true "rulers" in central and local institutions were the British officials who dictated policies. The administrators these officials tolerated were collaborators assigned minor executive functions.

In parts of Southern Nigeria, advocates of the old order, however, found some refuge in secret societies and cults which met the needs of the informal sector, though prohibited under the Unlawful Societies Proclamation (1905). Members of secret societies were not immune from detection and punishment by vigilant officials, however. The Ekumeku disturbance in Asaba hinterland in 1898, which recurred in 1903–1904 and 1910, illustrated how entrenched were these conflicts and confrontations between advocates of the old and new orders in Southern Nigeria.

Through a variety of means, Britain expanded and consolidated its rule over territories to the west and east of the Niger from 1900. The new era in the government of these territories witnessed various strategies and tactics, which included both diplomatic and coercive measures. The personalities of the British administrators east and west of the Niger were more decisive than those of distant controlling agencies such as the Colonial Office and the British Parliament.

Also, British public opinion failed to change significantly the direction of events in Southern Nigeria. Even so, some humanitarian organizations based in the United Kingdom endeavored to make their voices heard. Among these were the Third Party (led by Mary Kingsley, John Holt, and E. D. Morel), the Anti-Slavery and Aborigines Protection Society, and the Native Races and Liquor Traffic United Committee.

In southwest Nigeria, a few unofficial and nominated members of the Lagos legislative council and a vocal press, based in the colony, sought to give vent to criticisms by the chiefs and people of the Colony and Protectorate of Lagos. Less effective outlets for public opinion and criticism were available to those of the Protectorate of Southern Nigeria before the 1914 amalgamation.

Thus, agreements, pledges, understandings, and treaties of peace, friendship, and commerce between the Lagos government and the chiefs and people of Yorubaland, between 1886 and 1893, in addition to judicial agreements which supplemented these during 1904–1908, gave more diplomatic cover than was available in the Protectorate of Southern Nigeria. Indeed, after the Ijebu's unsuccessful military campaign against the British in 1892, and the bombardment of the *alafin's* palace at Oyo in 1895, few episodes of that kind occurred in the Protectorate of Lagos.

In the Protectorate of Southern Nigeria, British punitive expeditions or patrols were more the rule than the exception. Wherever the British went, Maxim guns, rifles, and seven-pounders went with them. Military campaigns occurred yearly, during the dry season, until 1912. Of these, the most famous was the Aro Field Force, 1901–1902, which covered Arochukwu, Ikot-Ekpene, Itu, Uyo, Abak,

Owerri and Bende. One of its major objectives was the destruction of the Aro Long Juju, Chuku Ibinokpabi. The "pacification" of Igboland, however, took much longer, as the Women's Riots of 1929–1930 and Enugu Colliery Incident of 1949 testified.

The various programs of "pacification," expansion, and consolidation of British rule paved the way for a major political event: amalgamation. By 1898, representatives of the British government had agreed on the consolidation of the Niger territories as a conscious policy goal to be implemented gradually, in installments. The deciding factor was economic or financial: to reduce the burden of the public debt on the British Treasury. Northern Nigeria, British officials acknowledged, was then not as economically viable as its southern counterpart, whose resources were needed to support the government of a combined territory. Thus, amalgamation proceeded in stages: the Colony and Protectorate of Southern Nigeria was created in 1906 and that of Nigeria in 1914. Whatever the merits of amalgamation, from the British point of view it was not a creation based on broad Nigerian opinion. The 1914 amalgamation achieved the beginning of "one country," but not of "one people" or "one system" of government. Nigeria's subsequent development, as a multicultural federal state, prevented any precipitate embrace of unitarism among people with different histories and modes of governance.

The southern component of these developments can now be briefly examined. At amalgamation, Nigeria comprised two provinces: southern and northern. In 1939, the southern provinces were subdivided into eastern and western. A Nigerian Council, 1914–1922, a mere advisory and deliberative body for Northern and Southern Nigeria, performed a cosmetic role along with a Legislative Council for the colony. Under a new constitution named after Sir Hugh Clifford in 1922, the principle of elective representation was introduced only for electorates in Lagos colony and Calabar municipality. The Richards Constitution, 1946, merely expanded the basis of representation in the Central Council to the annoyance of critical Southern politicians. Concessions for responsible government were made under the Macpherson Constitution, 1951, and Lyttelton Constitution, 1954, largely because of more agitations by the leaders of southern political parties. Thus, the transition from representative to responsible government through "dyarchy" (of ministerial partnership between British and Nigerian representatives) also witnessed the growth and development of two southern-based parties (known, after 1961, as the National Council of Nigerian Citizens and the Action Group) as well as the Northern People's Congress and the United Middle Belt Congress. From 1954, federalism became a marked feature of Nigeria's constitutional growth and development.

Through several constitutional review exercises, such as the General Conference at Ibadan, 1950, and others in Lagos and London between 1953 and 1958, Nigerian politicians and British officials sought to resolve conflicts (including the pace of self-government, the status of Lagos, ethnic minorities, among others) and agreed to independence on 1 October 1960. Independence, however, failed to bury the legacy of Southern Nigeria's colonial past: controversial sociopolitical events and vexatious arguments concerning the 1914 amalgamation which led to secessionist attempts and a bloody civil war in 1967–1970.

BIBLIOGRAPHY

Ajayi, J. F. Ade. *Christian Missions in Nigeria, 1841–1891.* London, 1965.

Coleman, J. S. *Nigeria: Background to Nationalism.* Berkeley, Calif., 1958.

Dike, K. O. *Trade and Politics in the Niger Delta, 1830–1885.* Oxford, 1956.

Nicolson, I. F. *The Administration of Nigeria, 1900–1960.* Oxford, 1969.

Tamuno, Tekena N. *The Evolution of the Nigerian State: The Southern Phase, 1898–1914.* London, 1978.

TEKENA N. TAMUNO

See also **Colonial Policies and Practice; Lugard, Frederick Dealtry; Niger Delta Region, History; Oyo; Slave Trade: Western Africa.**

PEOPLES AND CULTURES

Northwestern Nigeria

Northwestern Nigeria comprises the present states of Sokoto, Kebbi, and parts of Niger. There are many ethnic groups in this region, but they have similar religious and sociopolitical values. Prior to the development of the Sokoto Caliphate, the Hausa, who constituted the largest indigenous group, had raided many of their neighbors to the south and west for slaves. Gradually, many of these peoples were absorbed into Hausa culture and became indistinguishable from their overlords. Many groups, however, in spite of the jihad in the early nineteenth century and the emirate system, continued to maintain their own identities.

A number of states in this region, including Borgu, Kebbi, Dendi, Zaberma, Arewa, and Gobir, were hostile to the caliphate. Although they were initially subjugated, they could not be permanently held. Some groups who are actually Hausa speaking do not identify with the Hausa/Fulani. These include Dendi, Busa, and Tienga. The Dendi are a branch of the Songhai of the middle Niger and speak a language of the independent Songhai family. The Busa and Tienga languages belong to the Mande branch of the Niger-Congo language family.

The Kabbawa, Dakarkari, Kambari, Arawa, Dandawa, Zabarmarwa, Fakkawa, and Dukawa ethnic groups are distinct, although they still retain their linguistic affinity to the Hausa/Fulani. The Kabbawa of Argungu in Sokoto, apart from resisting Fulani conquest, are further distinguished by their maintenance of conspicuous pre-Islamic religious practices, including the Argungu fishing festival and the Uhola festival. The Dakarkari, who are predominant in what is now Kebbi state, also celebrate the Uhola festival in the towns and villages of the Zuru emirate. It conveys the people's gratitude and commitment to their ancestral god, Asilo, for the rains and good harvests. It is also a puberty rite for young boys and girls.

The people of the region are generally farmers and pastoralists. They also engage in local crafts such as weaving and leather working. The existence of mineral resources such as limestone, kaolin, salt, gypsum, and phosphates has also made the area a focus of industralization. The region boasts a university, schools, an airport, hotels, and a network of roads and railway lines. Places of interest include the Sokoto Museum and the tomb of Shaikh 'Uthman dan Fodio.

BIBLIOGRAPHY

Adeleye, R. A. "The Sokoto Caliphate in the Nineteenth Century." In *History of West Africa*, edited by J. F. Ade. Ajayi and Michael Crowder. 3d ed. London, 1985.

Nelson, H. D., et al. *Area Handbook for Nigeria*. 4th ed. Washington, D.C., 1982.

OLUTAYO ADESINA

See also **Sokoto Caliphate; 'Uthman dan Fodio.**

Northeastern Nigeria

The peoples of northeastern Nigeria inhabit that part of the country which borders on the Republic of Niger and Lake Chad to the north and northeast, on the Mandara Mountains and Cameroon to the east, on the Benue River region to the south, and on the area around Gombe and Potiskum to the west. The region covers most of the present Bornu, Yobe, Adamawa, and Taraba States and has a population of about eight million people. The major cities are Maiduguri, Damaturu, Yola, and Jalingo.

Throughout its history the area has been inhabited by a large number of ethnic and linguistic groups, producing the complex cultural situation that exists in the area today. In the northern part, in and around Bornu, Islam has been present since the eleventh century, and as a result of jihad movements in the nineteenth century, centralized Islamic states emerged in what became the emirates of Dikwa, Fika, Bedde, Adamawa, Muri, Gombe, and Biu. The remaining parts of the region were inhabited by a large number of smaller ethnic groups, many of which claimed to have migrated into the area from the east by the eighteenth or early nineteenth century. Some of them—such as the Jukun, the Chamba, and the Bata—tried to establish larger centralized states, but the majority were organized in small-scale chiefdoms or in decentralized political systems based on subsistence farming. Most of these groups actively resisted attempts by the Muslim Fulani at conquering the region during the nineteenth-century jihads.

This dual cultural tradition is clear today. The region is still populated by a large number of ethnic groups, probably more than fifty, most of them speaking separate languages of the Niger-Congo, Chad, and Saharan families, yet united by the widespread use of the Hausa, Fulfulde (or Fufulde), and English languages. The politically dominant peoples are the Kanuri in Bornu and the Fulani in the western and southern parts of the region. Together, they probably constitute about half the population of the area; both are predominantly Muslim.

Kanuri society is highly stratified, headed by a royal lineage that centers on the political and religious head, the *shehu;* the majority of the people are commoners. Kanuri village households consist of nuclear or polygynous families living in walled compounds. Kanuri farmers grow millet, Guinea corn, corn, and peanuts; many Kanuri engage in local trade, some of it with Fulani and Muslim Shuwa Arab nomads.

The Fulani are either pastoralists, settled in towns, or farmers. Both pastoralist and town Fulani own cattle; the pastoralists travel widely with their herds, building temporary houses where grazing conditions are good. The Fulani emirates are based on hierarchical systems of bureaucracy and taxa-

tion derived from the Islamic tradition, and the emirs are paramount political leaders with great influence on Fulani as well as non-Fulani communities. Compared with the town Fulani, the pastoralists have a more egalitarian social structure.

The other ethnic groups in the region include, in the northern part, the Bolewa, Bura, Gamargu, Glavda, Kotoko, Lamang, Manga, Margi, Ngweshe, Pabir, Shuwa Arabs, and Sukur, and, in the southern part, the Bille, Bura, Bwatiye (Bachama and Bata), Chamba, Gaanda, Gudu, Higi, Kanakuru, Kilba, Koma, Longuda, Mumuye, Waja, and Yungur.

These peoples vary in number from less than 50,000—such as the Glavda, the Sukur, and the Gudu—to 300,000 to 500,000—such as the Shuwa Arabs and Margi in the northern part of the region and the Bwatiye, the Chamba, and the Mumuye in the southern part. Besides the Kanuri and the Shuwa Arabs, many of the peoples in the north are influenced by Islam but also practice their traditional religions, as do many of the peoples in the south. The number of people who practice the traditional religions exclusively is generally falling. In Adamawa and Taraba states, Christianity (whether Protestant, Roman Catholic, or local Nigerian churches) is now as strongly established as Islam is in the northern part of the region. These world religions provide their adherents with regional and national organizations; affiliation with the Islamic brotherhoods or with Christian church fellowships such as the Tarayyar Ekklesiyoyin Kristi a Nijeria (the Fellowship of the Churches of Christ in Nigeria) transcends local loyalties.

Some of the smaller ethnic groups—such as the Bwatiye and the Kilba—are organized in hierarchically structured chiefdoms in which the chiefs both exert traditional political authority and act as salaried government officials with specified legal powers, as well as being the religious heads of the people. Other groups—such as the Mbula—were originally organized in decentralized and nonhierarchical political systems, but developed chieftaincy systems during the colonial period in the first half of the twentieth century. In all the groups, descent remains the primary principle of social organization and identity and provides the social framework of traditional beliefs and rituals, which are centered on local spirits and ancestors. It is also an important organizing principle in the primary economic activities of the region: farming (the main crops being yams, millet, Guinea corn, rice, peanuts, cassava, and corn), fishing, and local trade.

The nineteenth-century jihads between Muslims and non-Muslims have had a great impact on contemporary relations between the ethnic groups. Considerable tension and competition exist between the Kanuri and Fulani, on the one hand, and many non-Muslim groups, on the other. Since social identity and religious affiliation are closely linked, ethnic and religious tensions are often indistinguishable, and political conflicts are frequently the product of Muslim-Christian antagonism. Direct religious confrontations have been widespread: large-scale violent clashes between different Muslim groups and between Muslims and Christians broke out in Maiduguri in 1982, in Yola in 1984, and in Gombe in 1985. Religious tensions continued throughout the 1990s, strengthened by active Muslim and Christian missionary work. In addition, ethnicity and religion are often the decisive criteria for access to government resources, business contracts, and personal careers, emphasizing the great importance of local traditions in the modern state.

BIBLIOGRAPHY

Abubakar, Sa'ad. *The Lamibe of Fombina: A Political History of Adamawa, 1809–1901.* Zaria, Nigeria, 1977.

Cohen, Ronald. *The Kanuri of Bornu.* New York, 1967.

Kirk-Greene, Anthony H. M. *Adamawa, Past and Present: An Historical Approach to the Development of a Northern Cameroons Province.* 2d ed. London, 1969.

Lukas, Renate. *Nicht-islamische Ethnien im Südlichen Tschadraum.* Wiesbaden, Germany, 1973.

Wente-Lukas, Renate. *Die materielle Kultur der nicht-islamischen Ethnien von Nordkamerun und Nordostnigeria.* Wiesbaden, Germany, 1977.

NIELS KASTFELT

See also **Bornu Region; Hausa States; Sokoto Caliphate.**

Southwestern Nigeria

Southwestern Nigeria consists of territory lying to the west of the Niger River and south of the Benue River. It occupies six states (Edo, Lagos, Ogun, Ondo, Osun, and Oyo) and parts of three others (Delta, Kogi, and Kwara) of the Federal Republic of Nigeria's thirty states (excluding the Federal Capital Territory). In 1991 the population of these areas exceeded 20 million. The terrain ranges from tropical rain forest to open savanna countryside. The economy is based on agricultural production including cocoa, kola, rubber, maize, yams, oil

Fishing village near the mouth of the Escravos River in southwestern Nigeria. AP/WIDE WORLD

palm, and cassava; extensive trade and some industrial production; and, historically, fishing, hunting, and crafts. Two-thirds of the men were farmers in 1950. Women seldom farm, but are involved in extensive trade and marketing networks. Educational attainments are the highest in the country.

This area is dominated by Yoruba-speaking peoples who spill into neighboring states of Bénin, Togo, and Ghana. Other major groups are Edo (Bini), Egun, Urhobo, Ijo, Ishan, Isoko, and Itsekiri. The term "Yoruba" is applied to a large language-sharing family of peoples: Anago, Awori, Egba, Egbado, Ekiti, Ibadan, Ife, Ifonyin, Igbonima, Ijebu, Ijesha, Ketu, Kwara, Ondo, Owo, Oyo, and Shabe. There has been extensive contact among these groups, and consequently much cultural blending.

Archaeological evidence indicates Stone Age inhabitants were in the area between the tenth and second centuries B.C.E. By the time Ife emerged in the ninth century C.E., iron making and agriculture had long been developed. Ife reached an artistic and political zenith between the twelfth and fourteenth centuries and is mythologized as the cradle of all Yoruba. Internal trade was important from earliest times, and external trade grew rapidly from the seventeenth century after the increase in the New World demand for slaves.

At contact Yoruba peoples were organized in hundreds of minor polities ranging from villages to city-states and to large centralized kingdoms of which there were about twenty. Communities varied in size from hunting and farming camps to large cities inhabited by twenty thousand to sixty thousand people by the 1850s. Indigenous capitals were circular, densely settled, and protected by earthen walls. At the center were royal compounds of several acres and a market; clustered around them were residences of chiefly and commoner families. Agricultural lands lay outside the walls and farmers commuted from town to farm.

Precolonial political systems consisted of a ruler and advisory council of chiefs who represented important sectors of the society; descent, military, and religious groups, age grades, markets, and secret societies. The ruler performed rituals, conducted external affairs, kept the peace, and wielded the powers of life and death over subjects. Chiefs advised, adjudicated, and administered. Palace officials were intermediaries between a ruler and heads of outlying towns and tributaries. Today the ancient political systems survive with new functions as arms of local government, modeled initially on British governmental structures.

Kinship relationships continue to be significant in marking status, providing security, and regulating inheritance. Status is also differentiated according to sex, age, and wealth. In the past, elder males held most positions of civic authority; senior women occasionally rose to prominence. Today's class distinctions are calculated according to wealth, education, and occupation.

Introduced religions of Christianity and Islam are embraced in roughly equal proportions. Ancient religious practices are performed simultaneously or blended with introduced faiths. The Yoruba system has a pantheon of deities who underpin an extensive system of cults. Rituals are focused on the life cycle, ecological and civic calendars, and appeasing or gaining favor.

Yoruba are known for their arts. Life-size bronze heads and terra-cottas, sculpted in a classical style between 1000 and 1400 C.E., have been widely exhibited. Other art forms are poetry, myth, dance, music, bodily decoration, weaving, dyeing, embroidery, pottery, calabash carving, leather and beadworking, and jewelry and metalworking.

BIBLIOGRAPHY

Forde, Cyril Daryll. *The Yoruba-Speaking Peoples of Southwestern Nigeria*. London, 1962.

Keyes, Carolyn. "Ade: Cloth, Gender, and Social Change in Southwestern Nigeria, 1841–1991." Ph.D. diss., University of Wisconsin–Madison, 1993.

SANDRA T. BARNES

See also **Yoruba States.**

Southeastern Nigeria

Southeastern Nigeria is about 78,612 square kilometers (31,445 sq. mi.; 8.51 percent of Nigeria's total area). It is bounded by Cameroon on the east, the Bight of Bonny on the south, and the Niger River on the west. Its northernmost towns are Nsukka, Ogoja, and Obudu. It comprises Abia, Anambra, Akwa Ibom, Cross River, Enugu, Imo, and Rivers States.

Southeastern Nigeria includes both coastal and forest regions. The coastal region is intersected by an intricate network of rivers and creeks that are tributaries of the Niger River. These abundant waterways plus frequent rainfall explain why this part is made up of mangrove swamps. Immediately north of the coastal region is dense mangrove forest.

There are more than thirty ethnic and linguistic groupings. They include the Igbo (Ibo), Anang, Efut, Ibibio, Ijo (Ijaw), Ogba, and Ogoni. A remarkable feature in precolonial times was the absence of centralized political authority. Only the Nri, a subgroup of the Igbo, some western Igbo communities, the Efik, and much later the Ijo were exceptions to this general phenomenon. Secret societies like the Ibibio Ekpo featured prominently in law enforcement among some groups.

Occupations in the zone include farming, fishing, saltmaking, pottery, weaving, blacksmithing, and wood carving. With the advent of the slave trade in the fifteenth century, the area became a major source of supply and the center of evacuation of slaves to the Americas. With abolition of the slave trade by the mid-nineteenth century, the area became the major palm produce belt of Nigeria. It is now the center of crude oil production. Traditional religion has considerable following in the zone, but Christianity has become the most widely practiced religion.

Following political upheavals soon after independence, southeastern Nigeria made a secession bid under the banner of Biafra from 1967 to 1970. Today the peoples are fully reintegrated. Some of Nigeria's largest commercial centers, such as Onitsha, Aba, and Port Harcourt, are located there. The zone has about ten universities, with secondary and primary schools running into thousands. Furthermore, there are four airports, one of which is international. In addition, there are two seaports, Calabar and Port Harcourt. According to the 1991 census, the population is 18,921,872 which is 21.4 percent of Nigeria's total.

BIBLIOGRAPHY

Talbot, Percy Amaury. *The Peoples of Southern Nigeria.* London, 1926. Repr. 1969.

Udo, Reuben Kenrick. "Environments and Peoples of Nigeria." In *Groundwork of Nigerian History,* edited by Obaro Ikime. Ibadan, 1980.

C. OGBOGBO

Central Nigeria

The central Nigerian region, usually referred to as the Middle Belt, is one of the most ethnically heterogeneous areas of the country. The peoples are agriculturists and heirs to the famous Iron Age Nok culture (perhaps the earliest in sub-Saharan Africa), which flourished between 900 B.C.E. and 200 C.E. The village of Nok and other sites in the region have yielded scores of terra-cotta artifacts. Central Nigeria has two major subdivisions.

Niger-Benue Confluence Area

The most numerous peoples in this area are the Nupe, Igala, Tiv, Bassa Kano, Idoma, Alago, Afo (Eloyi), Koro, Gade, Gbari (Gwari), Igbirra (Ebira), and O-kun Yoruba. The Nupe and the Igala alone in this area of segmentary political institutions have centralized political systems going back several centuries. Linguistically, the Yoruba, Igala, Bassa Nge, Nupe, and Idoma belong to the Kwa language subgroup; the Koro, Afo, and Tiv, among others, fall under the Benue-Congo subclassification. Several linguistic groups in the area coexist without clear-cut territorial boundaries. Some settlements, such as Koton Karifi in Kogi State, are occupied by several groups. Consequently, there is considerable cultural admixture in spite of linguistic and other differences.

Indigenous religions, both before and after the coming of Islam, display many similarities. So also do rites in respect of ancestors.

In the precolonial period, trade occurred along north-south and east-west routes. Commodities on the former included salt, copper, and horses in exchange for slaves. The east-west route, based on the Niger-Benue River system, was used by the Igala and Nupe, who traded salt and brass products, which have been important in the confluence area since prehistoric times.

The Bauchi Plateau and the Upper and Middle Benue Region

The eastern section of the central Nigerian region is also a region of diverse ethnic groups, some of them recent immigrants. For example, the Jukun, formerly found along the Gongola and in the Upper Benue Valley, at present live in the middle Benue region. The Gamba and the Bata predominate along the Upper Benue and the adjoining areas. North of the Upper Benue Valley are the Higi, Gude, Fali, Kilba, Gabun, Hona, Lala, Gudu, and Margi, among others.

Throughout the precolonial period, the Jukun, under the *aku* (ruler), were the only group with centralized political institutions. The *aku* was the center of Jukun social and political life and of the fortunes of his people.

Guinea corn and millet are the chief staple crops in the Bauchi Plateau region and Benue basins. Tin and columbite are mined around the plateau. Associated with the tin are deposits of kaolin (a clay used in making ceramics) that are worked commercially. The mineral wealth and the favorable climate have attracted to the Plateau region, especially Jos and its environs, large numbers of other Nigerian peoples, including Hausa, Igbo (Ibo), and Yoruba, as well as expatriates.

BIBLIOGRAPHY

Forde, Daryll, Paula Brown, and Robert G. Armstrong. *Peoples of the Niger-Benue Confluence.* London, 1955.

Isichei, Elizabeth, ed. *Studies in the History of Plateau State, Nigeria.* London, 1982.

S. ADEMOLA AJAYI

See also **Hausa; Igbo; Niger-Benue Region; Tiv; Yoruba.**

NILE RIVER

GEOGRAPHY

The Nile is the longest river in the world, flowing south to north 6,737 kilometers (4,187 mi.) over thirty-five degrees of latitude through civilizations of great antiquity. The Nile Basin embraces some 3 million square kilometers (1.2 million sq. mi.) of equatorial and northeast Africa. The river flows through every natural formation, from mountainous highlands to barren deserts, and through nine independent states—Rwanda, Burundi, Zaire, Tanzania, Kenya, Uganda, Ethiopia, Egypt, and Sudan. The Nile is unique among the great rivers of the world. The civilizations of dynastic Egypt (3000 B.C.E.–332 B.C.E.) and the Kingdom of Kush, which flourished in Nubia from 805 B.C.E. to 350 C.E. and six hundred years after the occupation of Egypt by the Greeks and Romans, were as

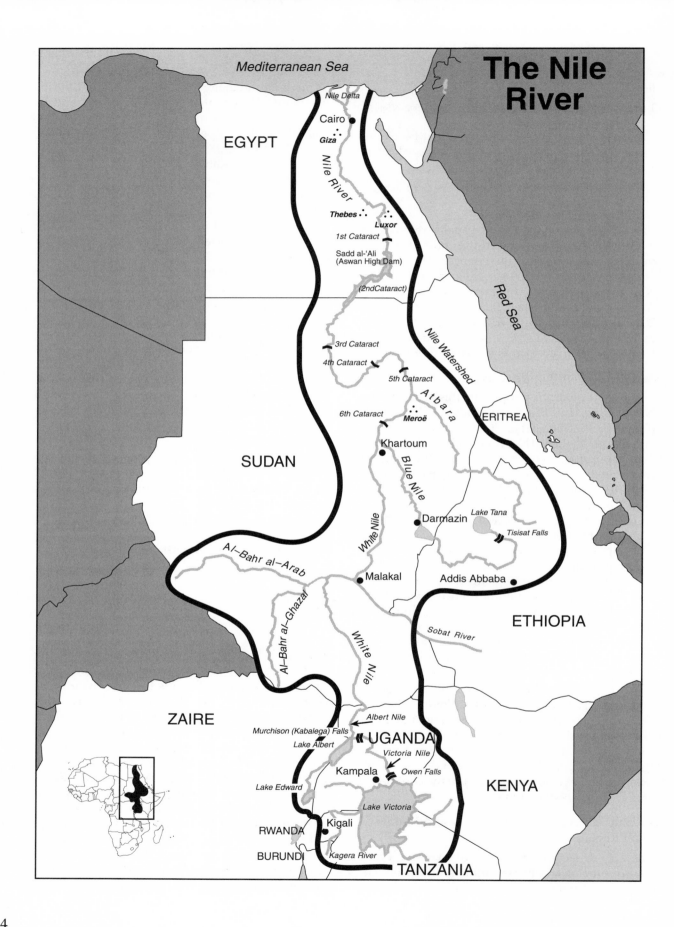

The Nile River

Mediterranean Sea

Nile Delta

EGYPT

Cairo

Giza

Nile River

Thebes

Luxor

1st Cataract

Sadd al-'Ali
(Aswan High Dam)

(2nd Cataract)

3rd Cataract

4th Cataract

5th Cataract

6th Cataract

Meroë

SUDAN

Khartoum

Nile Watershed

Red Sea

Atbara

ERITREA

Blue Nile

White Nile

Darmazin

Lake Tana

Tisisat Falls

Al–Bahr al–Arab

Al–Bahr al–Ghazal

Malakal

Addis Abbaba

Sobat River

ETHIOPIA

White Nile

ZAIRE

Albert Nile

Murchison (Kabalega) Falls

Lake Albert

《UGANDA

Victoria Nile

Owen Falls

KENYA

Lake Edward

Kampala

RWANDA

Kigali

Lake Victoria

BURUNDI

Kagera River

TANZANIA

324

dependent upon the waters of the Nile as the Christian and Muslim states that have succeeded them in the last two thousand years. Humanity cannot survive without water, and so when the inhabitants of the Sahara began to drift out of the desert five thousand years ago to escape its desiccation, they came completely under the control of the annual Nile flood, which could create destruction if too great and famine if not great enough.

The most southern source of the Nile, the "Caput Nili Meridianissimum," is a spring in the Kangosi Hills in the Republic of Burundi. Its eastern and hydrologically most important source is the holy spring of Sakala at the foot of Mount Gish in the heartland of the Ethiopian highlands.

From its southern source in Burundi, not discovered until 1937, the waters of the spring are soon joined by a myriad of streams which coalesce into the Luvironzia and Ruvuvu to form the Kagera River, which flows into Lake Victoria, the second largest body of fresh water in the world (67,000 sq. km; 35,800 sq. mi.). It is situated on the plateau between the two great rift valleys of Africa, with only one outlet, at Jinja, 5,600 kilometers (3,400 mi.) from the Mediterranean Sea. Jinga was first brought to the attention of Europe in 1862 by John Hanning Speke. West of Lake Victoria rise the Mfumbiro (Virunga) volcanoes and the Ruwenzori Range (the Mountains of the Moon). These slopes collect the torrential, tropical rains blown out of the South Atlantic and across the rain forests of Zaire to flow into a series of equatorial lakes—George, Edward, Albert (Mobutu Sese Seko)—lying at the bottom of the Western Rift Valley and connected by the Semliki River. Here the waters of the Victoria Nile pass out of the lake to flow north through the marshes of Lake Kyoga. They then head west, plunging over the escarpment of the Western Rift Valley, 43 meters (142 ft.) through rock walls only 6 meters (20 ft.) wide at Murchison (Kabalega) Falls, to meet the waters of Lake Albert. Now known as the Bahr al-Jabal (the Mountain River), the Nile proceeds northward out of the Western Rift Valley and into the sudd (in Arabic, *sadd*, meaning obstacle), the great swamps of the Nile the size of Belgium. There the river meanders 370 variable kilometers (230 mi.) absorbing its western tributaries—the Bahr al-Arab, the Bahr al-Ghazal, and the numerous rivers flowing northeastward from the Congo-Nile watershed, whose waters are mostly evaporated, however, by 30,000 square kilometers (12,000 sq. mi.) of aquatic vegetation. Emerging from the sudd at Lake No, the

White Nile (Bahr al-Abyad) now contains only 14 percent of the total Nile waters (from the agreed standard of measurements at Aswan for all Nile flows) until joined by the significant contribution (14 percent) of the Sobat River and its tributaries, the Baro and Pibor Rivers. These surge out of the Ethiopian plateau to double the size of the White Nile at Malakal, "Where Africa Begins." From here the river flows another 1,000 kilometers (600 mi.) through flat, arid plains into the reservoir behind the Jebel Aulia Dam, 47 kilometers (30 mi.) south of Khartoum. Here the basin of the equatorial Nile has brought downriver an average of only 28 percent of the total water available to Egypt at Aswan.

From its eastern source at the spring of Sakala, first seen by a European, Father Pedro Páez, in 1613, the Nile descends down the Little Abbai into Lake Tana. This lake is dotted by islands, upon which are monasteries, churches, and the tombs of Ethiopian emperors. Its only outlet is near Bahar Dar on the southern shore. From the lake, the Blue Nile, known in Ethiopia as the Abbai, soon disappears over the lip of Tisisat Falls (Amharic for "the smoke of fire") and then careers through a zigzag gorge, gouging out of the Ethiopian plateau a grand canyon nearly a mile deep and absorbing thousands of streams and steep-flowing rivers—the Giamma, Muger, Guder, Finchaa, Diddessa, and Balas—to swell the Blue Nile with water and the nutrients from the sediments of the highlands. The Blue Nile descends onto the plains of Sudan at the Bumbode River and into the reservoir of the Roseires Dam at Damazin, 1,000 kilometers (600 mi.) from Lake Tana. Beyond the dam are flat, arid lands between the Blue and the White Niles, upon which lie the irrigated cotton scheme known as the Gezira (Arabic for "island"), while east of the Blue Nile the Sudanic plains are broken by two seasonal rivers, the Dinder and the Rahad. Some 3,000 kilometers (1,800 mi.) from the Mediterranean Sea, the Blue Nile reaches its confluence with the White Nile at the Mugran (Arabic for "meeting") of Khartoum, carrying 59 percent of the total Nile waters as measured at Aswan.

From the capital of the Sudan, the Nile flows northward through deserts; the inhabitants of Sudan and Egypt congregate along its banks. The river receives no additional water except from the Atbara, 320 kilometers (200 mi.) north of Khartoum. Rising in Ethiopia, the Atbara River is a seasonal, spate river, dry from January to June. During its flood it contributes a significant 13 percent to the total annual flow of the Nile. Beyond the Atbara the Nile makes its great S-bend, with its point at Abu Hamed and depression at Ed Debba. It rolls over three cataracts and along the Dongola Reach to flow placidly into the reservoir impounded by the Aswan High Dam, the Sadd al-'Aali, the waters of which are known in the Sudan as Lake Nubia and in Egypt as Lake Nasser. At Aswan, the Nile is only 87 meters (287 ft.) above sea level, yet the waters are made to flow another 1,180 kilometers (700 mi.) through barrages designed to raise the level of the river for passage into a myriad of irrigation works downstream; beyond Cairo, a labyrinth of canals weaves through the Nile Delta. Forming an inverted pyramid with its pinnacle at Cairo, the river bifurcates into two branches, the Damietta flowing northeast and the Rosetta passing northwest, to form a delta 160 kilometers (100 mi.) deep and 310 kilometers (180 mi.) along the Mediterranean coast. Here live 60 percent of the population of Egypt, who absorb the last of the waters of the Nile.

BIBLIOGRAPHY

Butzer, Karl W. *Early Hydraulic Civilization in Egypt: A Study in Cultural Ecology.* Chicago, 1976.

Collins, Robert O. *The Waters of the Nile: Hydropolitics and the Jonglei Canal, 1900–1988.* Oxford, 1990. Repr. Princeton, 1996.

Howell, P. P., and J. A. Allan, eds. *The Nile: Sharing a Scarce Resource: A Historical and Technical Review of Water Management and of Economic and Legal Issues.* Cambridge, 1994.

Howell, Paul, Michael Lock, and Stephen Cobb, eds. *The Jonglei Canal: Impact and Opportunity.* Cambridge, 1988.

Hurst, H. E. *The Nile: A General Account of the River and the Utilization of Its Waters.* Rev. ed. London, 1957.

Waterbury, John. *Hydropolitics of the Nile Valley.* Syracuse, N.Y., 1979.

ROBERT O. COLLINS

See also **Ecosystems; Irrigation and Flood Control.**

HISTORY AND CULTURE

The Nile dominates northeast Africa geographically and historically. Geographically, it is the world's longest river, at 4,187 miles. The main Nile has three major sources. Its longest is the White Nile, which flows from Lake Victoria in east Africa. The greatest volume of water is carried by the Blue Nile, flowing from Lake Tana in Ethiopia to meet the White Nile at Khartoum, the capital of modern-day Sudan. Just north of that junction, the Atbara, also from Ethiopia, flows in. The Nile basin is thus huge in area and links the lush areas of highlands and mountains at its sources with the arid Sahara Desert, which it crosses in northern Sudan and upper Egypt before reaching the Mediterranean via the river's delta.

Historically that connection was central to the flowering of one of the world's oldest civilizations, in Egypt some five thousand years ago. The annual floodwaters brought by the Blue Nile from Ethiopia left the area downstream of Aswan in particular covered in rich alluvial deposits. Egypt's farmers grew abundant crops, the surplus from which made possible the development of the three-thousand-year rule of the pharaohs. Egyptian influence in turn ascended above Aswan into Nubia; and later, after the decline of Egypt, Meroitic civilization emerged from the third century B.C.E.

Religion too was carried up the Nile. Egypt was the home of Coptic Christianity, which spread along the Nile to the independent kingdoms of Nubia. Nubia succeeded Meroë from the sixth century C.E. and went on to dominate the Ethiopian highlands, from where the Coptic church maintained its connections with Egypt through the centuries.

From the seventh century, the Arab invasion of North Africa brought the spread of Arabs and Islam up the Nile (as well as from Arabia), but this influx took several centuries to overcome the Christian kingdoms of Nubia, while the Ethiopian highlands remained predominantly Coptic Christian. Meanwhile the swamps of the upper Nile and the powerful Nilotic peoples of southern Sudan prevented the southward march of Islam and the Arabs into east Africa.

Beginning in the nineteenth century, a keen rivalry developed for dominance of the Nile basin. Mohammed Ali, as ruler of Egypt in the early nineteenth century, conquered Sudan; his successors had dreams of an empire stretching to the east African coast. But Egypt overreached itself, and it was left to the major European powers, Britain and France, to take up the rivalry for the Nile. This included the much proclaimed search for the source of the White Nile, eventually discovered by John Hanning Speke in 1862. Rivalry for control of the river's headwaters was delayed by the Mahdist state in Sudan from 1885 until 1898, when Britain's Lord Kitchener, fresh from victory over the Mahdists at the battle of Omdurman, confronted the young French captain Jean-Baptiste Marchand at Fashoda in southern Sudan. There was talk of war between the two powers before the French retreated, leaving Britain the dominant power on the Nile from the delta to Lake Victoria.

During the British domination of the Nile basin, control of the river developed rapidly. Measures of control in lower Egypt had been undertaken in the earliest times, but now there were developments to control the whole of its length in order to expand the areas of irrigation along it. Demand was rising from the growing population in the arid lands of northern Sudan and Egypt. In addition, though the Nile is long, it does not carry a particularly large volume of water, and apart from the annual flood it is generally sluggish across the flat plains of Sudan and Egypt, making conservation and management vital. A dam was completed at Aswan in 1902 to improve irrigation in Egypt; in 1925 another was built in Sudan at Sennar on the Blue Nile to enable operation of the Gezira Scheme, a major cotton-growing enterprise. A Nile waters agreement was signed between Egypt and Sudan in 1929, which disproportionately favored Egypt. Britain encouraged independent Ethiopia to build another dam at Lake Tana; the British built new dams at Jebel Aulia on the White Nile near Khartoum, in 1937, and later at Owen Falls in Uganda in 1959.

With the retreat of British imperialism and the spread of independent statehood in the Nile basin, problems of the river's management occurred as a result of both international and domestic developments. The two countries most in need of the Nile waters were Egypt and Sudan, but agreement between them on a more equitable distribution than that of 1929 proved difficult to reach. They eventually came to an understanding in 1959, with Sudan's share being raised to 20 percent, and both countries then completed new developments. The best known was Egypt's construction of the High Dam at Aswan, designed to generate hydroelectricity as well as for irrigation. Meanwhile Sudan extended the Gezira Scheme into the adjacent Managil area, and the country built new dams at Roseires on the Blue Nile and Khashm al-Girba on the Atbara (the latter for the use of Sudanese Nubians displaced by the rise of Lake Nasser above the High Dam at Aswan). There were even plans in the 1970s for the two countries to cooperate on the long-proposed Jonglei Canal in southern Sudan to improve the flow of water around the *sudd*. However, the start of Sudan's second civil war in the south in 1983 prevented completion of the project, and by the mid-1990s work on the canal had not resumed.

Cooperation over the development of the Nile has given way to growing rivalries as international differences have been compounded by rising domestic water needs all along the river. With no new agreement on the share-out of water, Egypt, with its fast-growing population, has gone ahead with its own plans. Projects include a new canal from Lake Nasser above the Aswan High Dam to relieve population pressure in lower Egypt, and plans to dig the so-called Peace Canal to irrigate parts of Sinai. Although Sudan does not use all of its quota under the 1959 treaty, there has been talk of plans for new dams and irrigation schemes. Ethiopia has also come into the picture. The erratic rainfall in northern Ethiopia contributed to famine in the 1970s and 1980s, and with peace now restored to that country the government has proposed two new dams utilizing the Blue Nile waters.

The international disagreements and domestic conflicts which have afflicted the Nile in the years since independence have checked collaborative efforts in the region. The Nile is the most developed river basin in Africa, and cooperation is necessary if further development is to be achieved without recriminations over unilateral actions which could undermine the development of the basin as a whole. This has been recognized, and the possibility of creating an authority for the river has been discussed. But thus far the very real differences that exist between the independent riparian states have promoted as much fear of rivalry as hope for cooperation over the Nile.

BIBLIOGRAPHY

Adams, William Y. *Nubia: Corridor to Africa.* Princeton, N.J., 1977.

Collins, Robert O., and Robert L. Tignor. *Egypt and the Sudan.* Englewood Cliffs, N.J., 1967.

Hurst, H. E. *The Nile: A General Account of the River and the Utilization of Its Waters.* Rev. ed. London, 1957.

Waterbury, John. *Hydropolitics of the Nile Valley.* Syracuse, N.Y., 1979.

PETER WOODWARD

See also **Egypt.**

NILOTES. The Nilotes are a cluster of peoples of eastern Africa, related linguistically rather than politically, and in all numbering more than four million people. Almost all Nilotes are transhumant pastoralists, although a few groups practice sedentary agriculture. They are usually divided into the western and the eastern Nilotes. The main groups of the former include the Nuer, Dinka, Shilluk, and others of the Upper Nile region of the Sudan; the Acholi and Lango of Uganda; and the Luo of Kenya. The eastern Nilotes, culturally distinct from the former, include the Maasai, Samburu, Turkana, and Kalenjin of the Rift Valley area of Kenya; the Karamojong and Teso of Uganda; and the Bari of the Sudan. Most western Nilotic groups are organized into patrilineal clans, with much authority given to ritual leaders and prophets, and only the Shilluk having any form of kingship. The eastern Nilotic groups also recognize the power of prophets and diviners; in addition, all are organized into elaborate systems of age sets based on the initiation of young men and in the past forming military groups for cattle raiding and warfare.

The eastern Nilotes have often been known as Nilo-Hamites, a clumsy term that refers to an outmoded view, the Hamitic hypothesis, which claims that they originated in ancient Egypt and moved southwards with other "Hamites." These so-called Hamites were by this theory the originators in Africa of forms of pastoralism, divine kingship, and other elements of "civilization" that many Europeans at the time thought could not have been invented by black Africans. There is no historical evidence for this theory and it is now generally discarded.

BIBLIOGRAPHY

Vossen, Rainer von. *The Eastern Nilotes: Linguistic and Historical Reconstructions.* Berlin, 1982.

JOHN MIDDLETON

See also **Nuer and Dinka.**

NJINGA MBANDI ANA DE SOUSA (b. 1582?; d. 1663), Mbundu ruler of the kingdoms of Ndongo (1624–1629) and Matamba (1630–1663), in what is modern Angola. In 1624, Njinga seized power in Ndongo. Opposing interests, shaped mostly by the Atlantic slave trade, led to a break with the Portuguese, who expelled her from Ndongo with the help of a puppet rival in 1626–1629. Njinga ensured her survival through alliances with the feared Mbangala (Jaga), assuming their ideology of war and their laws and rites, which were generally perceived as brutal and repulsive.

After the successful conquest of Matamba around 1630, Njinga had free rein and created a new basis of power without giving up her claim to power over Ndongo. Matamba, an impregnable

barrier between areas lying to the east and west, became one of the most important states acting as brokers in the slave trade.

During the Dutch occupation of Angola (1641–1648), Njinga again became a dangerous opponent of the Portuguese. But after the Portuguese drove the Dutch out of Angola in 1648, always thinking pragmatically, she sought a balance of power. In 1656, Njinga, who had been baptized Ana de Sousa in Luanda in 1622, returned to the Catholic faith. A year later she signed a peace treaty with the Portuguese, ending clashes that had raged for thirty years.

Njinga, the most important female political figure in Angola's history, was a remarkable personality. Unscrupulous and unbending in the pursuit of her interests, power-conscious and possessing great diplomatic talent, she was at once shrewd and magnanimous. In recent times, she has become a national symbolic figure of African resistance against colonial rule.

BIBLIOGRAPHY

Heintze, Beatrix. "Das Ende des unabhängigen Staates Ndongo (Angola): Neue Chronologie und Reinterpretation (1617–1630)." *Paideuma* (Stuttgart) 27 (1981): 197–273.

———. *Studien zur Geschichte Angolas im 16. und 17. Jahrhundert.* Cologne, Germany, 1996.

Thornton, John K. "Legitimacy and Political Power: Queen Njinga, 1624–1663." *Journal of African History* 32 (1991): 25–40.

BEATRIX HEINTZE

NJOYA (b. 1873?; d. 1933), Bamum ruler. Njoya Ibrahim ascended to the throne about 1886, after his father, King Nsangu, was killed in a war with the Nso kingdom. His mother, Queen Njapundunke (d. 1913), acted as regent until he had reached adulthood. About 1894, a group of palace servants tried to usurp power. Njoya resisted the uprising with the help of Lamido Umaru, the ruler of the Islamic Banyo kingdom. In gratitude for the support, Njoya and his court converted to Islam.

In 1902, Bamum came under German domination as part of the colony of Kamerun. Njoya, a pragmatic politician, tolerated the colonial power in order to maintain the autonomy of his kingdom. This strategy allowed him to pursue numerous innovative projects, such as the introduction of a Bamum script, the fostering of art production at the palace, and the adoption of new styles of

Njoya. BASEL MISSION ARCHIVE

NKRUMAH, FRANCIS NWIA KOFI (Kwame Nkrumah; b. 1909; d. 1972), Pan-Africanist leader and first prime minister and president of Ghana. Born in the British colony of the Gold Coast (present-day Ghana), Nkrumah was educated in Roman Catholic missionary schools and attended Achimota College in the colony. He continued his studies abroad, earning degrees from Lincoln University and the University of Pennsylvania, in the United States, and the London School of Economics in England. While in the United States, Nkrumah read Marx, Lenin, and Marcus Garvey. He served as president of the African Students Association and met W. E. B. Du Bois and George Padmore, ardent Pan-Africanists. In London, Nkrumah wrote and published *Towards Colonial Freedom: Africa in the Struggle Against World Imperialism* (1947), a book that set forth his ideas on fighting colonialism and liberating colonized peoples.

architecture. As a result of World War I, the Germans withdrew from Bamum in 1915, and the kingdom came under French rule. The French perceived Njoya as a German ally and a threat. In 1924, they stripped him of his powers. Seven years later, they exiled him in Yaoundé, the capital of the colony, where he died. Njoya is remembered as a reformer and innovator, a patron of the arts, and the author and editor of one of the most unusual works of African historiography, a detailed chronicle of the Bamum kingdom.

BIBLIOGRAPHY

Geary, Christraud M. *Images from Bamum: German Colonial Photography at the Court of King Njoya, Bamum, Cameroon, West Africa, 1902–1915.* Washington, D.C., 1988.

Njoya, Sultan of Bamum. *Histoire et coutumes des Bamum.* Mémoires de l'Institut Français d'Afrique Noire, Centre du Cameroun. Série: Populations, no. 5. Edited under the direction of Njoya. Translated by Henri Martin. Dakar, Senegal, 1952.

Tardits, Claude. *Le royaume Bamoum.* Paris, 1980.

CHRISTRAUD M. GEARY

Francis Nwia Kofi Nkrumah, first prime minister and president of Ghana. ARCHIVE PHOTOS

Invited to serve as the secretary-general of the United Gold Coast Convention (UGCC), Nkrumah returned to the colony in 1947 to put his ideas into practice. In 1949 he split with the UGCC and founded the Convention People's Party (CPP), an organization dedicated to strikes, civil disobedience, and noncooperation to bring about independence. The CPP attracted followers and won local elections. In 1950 Nkrumah was sent to jail for his role in a CPP strike; he was released early in order to take a seat in the Legislative Asssembly. Named prime minister in 1952, he guided the Gold Coast to independence in 1957 as the nation of Ghana.

Nkrumah considered this triumph over the colonial system as a blueprint for others and used his position as postindependence prime minister to herald Pan-Africanism. Ghana's strong economy, based on the high price of cocoa on the world market, was strong enough to support Pan-Africanists abroad and an aggressive development program at home.

Nkrumah saw himself as a leader and spokesman for Africa and Pan-Africanist ideals, and he envisaged a united Africa. In 1959 Ghana and Guinea agreed to form a union, with Mali to join later. The Ghanaian constitution of 1960 created a republic and had provisions to surrender the country's sovereignty to a Union of African States. On 1 July 1960 Nkrumah became first president of the republic following a plebiscite.

While Nkrumah's international reputation grew with the publication of his book *Africa Must Unite* and the founding of the Organization of African Unity (1963), he became less popular and more autocratic in Ghana as the country's economy shrunk with falling cocoa prices in the early 1960s. As president of the republic Nkrumah survived several assassination attempts: after each one he increased his personal control, eliminated rivals through arrest and detention, and in 1964 created a one-party state with himself as president for life.

On 24 February 1966, while Nkrumah was on a trip to Beijing and Hanoi in an effort to end the war in Vietnam, his government was toppled by a military coup. Nkrumah settled in Guinea, where President Sékou Touré appointed him copresident. Though his fall weakened the Pan-African movement, Nkrumah continued to write for the cause. In exile he published *Handbook of Revolutionary Warfare: A Guide to the Armed Phase of the African Revolution* (1968) and *Class Struggle in Africa* (1970), before dying of cancer in 1972.

BIBLIOGRAPHY

Budu-Acquah. *K. Kwame Nkrumah.* Accra, Ghana, 1992.

THOMAS F. MCDOW

NONGOVERNMENTAL ORGANIZATIONS, or NGOs, have become firmly entrenched in the political, social, and economic fabric of sub-Saharan Africa since the late 1970s. Ranging from Oxfam to the Undugu Society in Kenya, NGOs are, as their name implies, organizations that operate outside the sphere of national government and are vital actors within civil society. Geographically, they are indigenous as well as based in countries outside Africa. Almost all NGOs have some local presence. They range in size from small, grassroots organizations at the community level to large-scale global operations with a network of local field offices throughout Africa. Their membership is equally diverse, ranging from community volunteers (for example, Home Area Associations in Burkino Faso) to professionally staffed organizations such as the World Wildlife Fund. The approach NGOs take in conducting operations is equally diverse. Some take a participatory approach, while others follow a more top-down strategy. Lastly, NGOs have varying orientations, including humanitarian assistance, research, technical support, managerial support, development, conservation, and famine relief.

Proliferation of NGOs

The number and role of NGOs in Africa are an outgrowth of the political and economic vacuum that stemmed from the structural adjustment and austerity programs of the 1980s. As African governments tightened their belts, they cut social programs and services. Given these conditions, states found it difficult to provide adequate services, including health care, agricultural extension, famine relief, education, and family planning. In many cases the rise of NGOs had its roots in religious organizations, such as missions and churches, that switched their focus from charitable work to community development, health services, and welfare. NGOs also have entered the African civil landscape as a result of the decline in foreign aid transfers. In the wake of the cold war, Africa has increasingly taken a backseat to efforts to develop other parts of the globe, notably central and eastern Europe. While funding has dried up for many government programs, European, Asian, and American donors have increased their funding of African NGOs, thus helping to fill this economic vacuum.

Another reason for the proliferation of NGOs is that they perform functions for which national governments are either underfunded or ill-equipped to handle. This is especially true in the case of disaster-relief services, such as famine relief in Somalia, Ethiopia, and the Sahel, and assistance to refugees from civil strife in Rwanda, Burundi, and Zaire. The effects of these events are international, and difficult for a single state government to handle. In addition, given the scarcity of funds, aid organizations and donors seek to make the best use of the limited amounts available by maximizing the return on their investment. Thus, aid organizations have increased funding to NGOs, which claim to be closer to people targeted for funds and assistance, and assert that, consequently, they spend less money on overhead. The Canadian International Development Agency and the World Bank have both increased their lending to NGOs. The Kenyan government states that NGOs provide more than one-third of all development funds, as well as almost one-half of family planning services. Therefore, NGOs have become a powerful force in African democratization and development.

NGOs originally stemmed from the two world wars. Oxfam was formed in 1948 and has been involved in Africa since 1954, when it began feeding refugees from the Mau Mau in Kenya. Since the late 1970s, the number of NGOs has increased dramatically. In 1975 there were 124 NGOs in Kenya; twenty years later there were some 500. It is estimated that of the 6,000 to 8,000 NGOs working in developing countries, 4,500 work in Africa. They are, however, unevenly distributed in sub-Saharan Africa for various reasons: the local political and economic climate, acceptance of NGOs by local governments, and the willingness of international NGOs to invest in a particular area. While there are many NGOs in Kenya, Nigeria, Rwanda, Burkina Faso, Senegal, and Zimbabwe, there are few in Ethiopia, Cameroon, Chad, and the Central African Republic.

Focus of NGOs

As NGOs have proliferated, they have changed their focus. The earliest NGOs were largely oriented toward charitable giving, humanitarian services, and agricultural extension, whereas the new crop of NGOs is oriented toward more productive, developmental activities. They include financial management (the Partnership for Productivity in Togo); primary and community-based health care (Tokombere Health Promotion Centre in Camer-

oon); technical support for agriculture, livestock, crafts, and small-scale businesses (the Centre for Cooperative Research and Training in Rwanda); development-oriented relief services (the Catholic Relief Services of Madagascar); and increased attention to proactive solutions to natural and human-made disasters, such as drought preparedness (the Churches Drought Action in Africa).

The proliferation of NGOs has led to some problems vis-à-vis the state. States fear that NGOs threaten their power by providing services and funding once provided by the state. As NGOs grow in number as well as power, they play a stronger role in policy decisions that can affect how governments interact with communities. For instance, international wildlife NGOs play an increasingly strong role in the conservation of wildlife and natural areas in Africa. Conservation policies, often initiated through NGOs, are carried out by wildlife services of African countries, and sometimes lead to conflicts over land and resources that states must confront. The increasing power of NGOs also makes some national governments wary. Thus, NGO autonomy and the political ramifications of the proliferation of NGOs are being challenged by states whose hands are tied by austerity programs, debt, and funding problems. However, the reverse is also true. Many African states welcome NGOs in an effort to secure funding and resources for programs they can no longer support.

Perhaps the best-known NGO in Africa is Oxfam. Founded as the Oxford Committee for Famine Relief, to help rebuild Europe after World War II, it has played a pivotal role in Africa. Oxfam had its beginnings in providing food to war-weary people during the Mau Mau uprising, and subsequently provided funds, assistance, and medical support during the Congo famine of 1961, the Sahelian and Ethiopian famines of 1973, and the famine in Ethiopia in 1984–1985. Oxfam's mission has always been to side with the poor, providing humanitarian assistance regardless of politics. Oxfam has broadened its scope, and funds projects, including rural development and family planning, designed to reduce the vulnerability of the poor to natural and human-caused disasters.

While some of the best-known NGOs are international—such as Oxfam, the World Wildlife Fund, and Médecins sans Frontières (Doctors Without Borders)—others are indigenous, locally based organizations that play an important role in African civil society. One such organization is the Undugu Society of Kenya. It works with Kenya's urban poor and street children. Begun in 1973 by a Dutch Catholic priest, Father Arnold Grol, Undugu has more than twenty programs in communities throughout Kenya. It operates youth centers, conducts cleanup campaigns, and provides apprenticeships and employment opportunities to Kenya's urban poor. It also offers a glimpse of how NGOs interact with states. Undugu has grown over the years and is now a large, registered NGO in Kenya. As such, it must carefully navigate between the goals of the state and its own mission. This relationship highlights the careful balancing act NGOs must perform in order to achieve their goals and objectives.

Future of NGOs

The future of NGOs in Africa is uncertain. While the number of NGOs has proliferated since the late 1970s, their quality and effectiveness depend upon a number of political and economic considerations outside their control. International funding is crucial to many NGOs. For example, Kenyan and Zimbabwean NGOs depend on foreign sources for more than 90 percent of their funding. In addition, the rapid proliferation of NGOs means that they now compete with each other for funding. This may mean that funding will increasingly be based on political rather than social considerations. In addition, instability of international funding means that if political winds change, funding for NGOs also may change, which could endanger long-term relations and programs.

The local political climate is of paramount importance for the growth of NGOs. Given the dependence of NGOs on foreign sources of funding, African governments are often wary about the agendas, directions, and goals of NGOs. NGOs also threaten sources of government funding. Prior to the 1970s, governments were the main beneficiaries of development funds flowing into Africa. This has changed as donors have shown their preference to fund NGOs rather than national governments. Thus, while the enabling environment for NGOs is strong in countries such as Bénin, Ethiopia, and Ghana, in countries such as Zambia and Namibia the political environment is not as friendly. Finally, NGOs face the question of how effective they can be in empowering local communities. In many cases they are successful, as is the Undugu Society, but in other cases, community involvement, though a stated goal of NGOs, is weak. For example, international conservation NGOs call for "people's participation" in wildlife conservation, yet this is hampered by a lack of understanding of local communities, the need to work with national governments, and the top-down approaches still used by many NGOs. Nevertheless, NGOs are powerful actors in African civil society. They empower local communities and are valuable resources for development, humanitarian assistance, welfare, health services, and family planning.

BIBLIOGRAPHY

Clark, J., M. Brown, B. Ricci, and K. O'Connor. *Non-Governmental Organizations and Natural Resources Management: An Assessment of Eighteen African Countries.* Washington, D.C., 1993.

Farrington, John, and Anthony Bebbington. *Reluctant Partners?: Non-Governmental Organizations, the State, and Sustainable Agricultural Development.* London, 1993.

Langley, P. *Non-Governmental Organisations in Africa and Rural Development.* Pan African Institute for Development Report no. 15E. Limbe, Cameroon, 1995.

Ndegwa, Stephen N. *The Two Faces of Civil Society: NGOs and Politics in Africa.* West Hartford, Conn., 1996.

Wellard, Kate, and James G. Copestake, eds. *Non-Governmental Organizations and the State in Africa.* London, 1993.

DAVID SMETHURST

See also **Christianity; Development; Health Care: Hospitals and Clinics; Human Rights; Hunger and Famine; Postcolonial State; Refugees; Wildlife.**

NONGQAWUSE (b. 1840?; d. 1900?), Xhosa prophet. Nongqawuse was an orphan raised by her uncle, Mhlakaza, near the Gxarha River in the Transkei region of South Africa. She began to prophesy in April 1856, telling the people that they must kill all their cattle, destroy all their corn, and throw away all their magical devices, because the dead were going to rise, bringing with them a new and perfect world. The blind would see, the deaf would hear, the old would become young; new cattle and corn would appear in abundance; and nobody would ever again lead a troubled life.

After fifteen months of cattle killing (April 1856–June 1857), about 40,000 Xhosa had starved to death, and another 150,000 had abandoned their homes in search of food. The power of the Xhosa kingdom, which had blocked the expansion of the Cape Colony for more than eighty years, was broken, and most of Xhosaland was divided among the white settlers.

Nongqawuse. COURTESY OF THE SOUTH AFRICAN LIBRARY, CAPE TOWN

The callous manner whereby Governor Sir George Grey manipulated the crisis led many Xhosa to conclude that he somehow bribed or deceived Nongqawuse into uttering the fatal prophecies. There is no direct proof of this, but in any case, other factors need to be taken into account: the military stalemate between the Xhosa and the colonists; the devastating bovine pleuropneumonia (lung sickness) epidemic of 1854–1857, which led the Xhosa to believe that their cattle were bewitched; and the influence of Christianity through Mhlakaza, a lapsed and frustrated Christian convert. Thus, the cattle-killing millennium was not conceived entirely within an indigenous cultural framework, but was a tragic synthesis of Xhosa creation myths and ancestor beliefs with Christian ideas concerning the Resurrection and the Apocalypse.

We know almost nothing about Nongqawuse as a person. The only firsthand Xhosa description we have states that she was "a girl of about sixteen years of age, has a silly look, and appears to me as if she was not right in her mind" (Peires, p. 87). She was the only person who saw the spirits of the dead and conversed with them. But her communications were incoherent, and were explained to the Xhosa by Mhlakaza.

As pressure upon her grew, Nongqawuse became "sick" and stopped talking altogether. Many of her immediate circle, including Mhlakaza, starved to death. Nongqawuse was captured by the colonial police and taken to Cape Town. The authorities tried to get her to implicate the Xhosa chiefs in punishable crimes, but she would not do so. There are no official records concerning her release from custody, but apparently she ended her days quietly, among relatives on a white farm near Alexandria in the Eastern Cape.

BIBLIOGRAPHY

Gqoba, William W. "The Tale of Nongqawuse." In *Towards an African Literature*, edited by A. C. Jordan. Berkeley, 1973.

Peires, Jeffrey B. *The Dead Will Arise: Nongqawuse and the Great Xhosa Cattle-Killing Movement of 1856–7.* Johannesburg, 1989.

JEFF PEIRES

See also **Nguni Region; Prophetic Movements; Xhosa.**

NORTHERN AFRICA

IN RELATION WITH
SUB-SAHARAN AFRICA

Before the Rise of Islam

The area we now call the Sahara (from an Arabic word meaning desert) has appeared and disappeared several times during the history of humankind. Most recently it began to emerge during a period of continuing dessication from about 2500 B.C.E. By around 300 B.C.E., the process was almost complete, and the herding populations that had once inhabited the grasslands of the Sahara had dispersed north and south. Isolated groups of agriculturalists remained behind in better-watered areas, and their descendants form the basal element of the *haratin*—darker-skinned, low-status agriculturalists—who are to be found in oases from southern Morocco to the Niger. The oases of the Fezzan in southern Libya probably also originally contained similar populations; an early Islamic legal text describes the Fezzanis as "one of the peoples of the blacks." As the Sahara dried up, contact

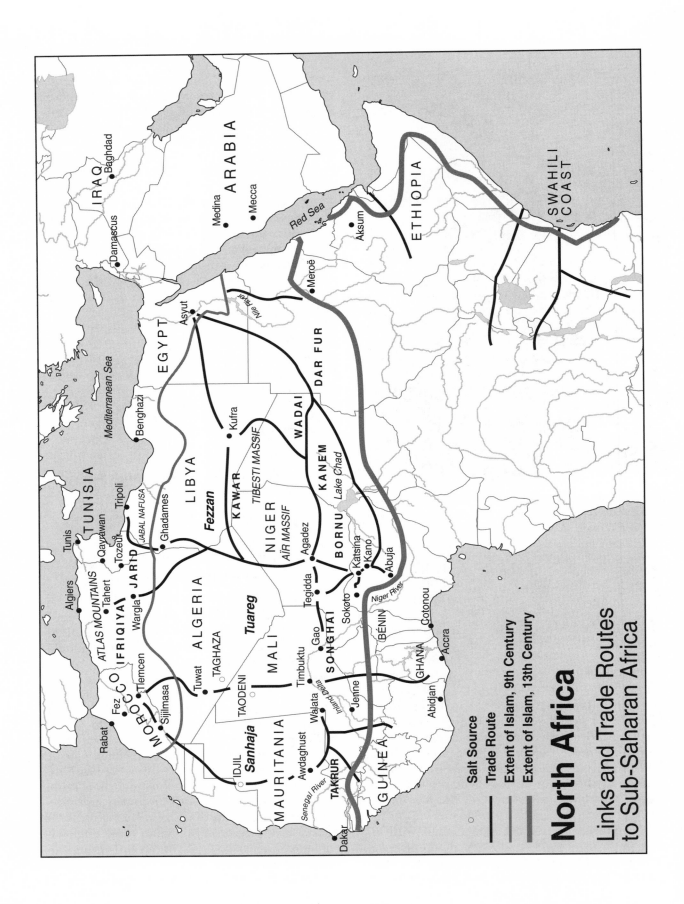

North Africa
Links and Trade Routes to Sub-Saharan Africa

Salt Source
Trade Route
Extent of Islam, 9th Century
Extent of Islam, 13th Century

IRAQ
Baghdad
Damascus
ARABIA
Medina
Mecca
Red Sea
ETHIOPIA
SWAHILI COAST
Aksum
Meroë
Nile River

Mediterranean Sea
EGYPT
Asyut
DAR FUR
WADAI
Kufra
TIBESTI MASSIF
KANEM
Lake Chad
BORNU
KAWAR
NIGER
AÏR MASSIF
Agadez
Katsina
Kano
Abuja

TUNISIA
Benghazi
Tunis
Qayrawan
Tozeur
Tripoli
JABAL NAFUSA
Ghadames
LIBYA
Fezzan
Tegidda
Sokoto
Niger River
BÉNIN
Cotonou
Accra
GHANA
Abidjan

Algiers
Tahert
ATLAS MOUNTAINS
IFRIQIYA
Wargla
JARID
ALGERIA
Tuareg
TAGHAZA
MALI
Gao
SONGHAI
Timbuktu
Jenne

Rabat
Fez
MOROCCO
Tlemcen
Sijilmasa
Tuwat
TAODENI
Inland Delta
Walata
Awdaghust
MAURITANIA
Sanhaja
IDJIL
Senegal River
TAKRUR
Dakar
GUINEA

between the populations of the Mediterranean African lands and those of west Africa gradually diminished, but not before knowledge of copper and iron working had passed into west Africa around the middle of the first millennium B.C.E. Early in the Christian era, the introduction from the Middle East and the spread in North Africa of the one-humped camel (*Camelus dromedarius*) made a nomadic existence in the Sahara possible, and Berber-speaking groups began to move deeper into the desert. Those who have come to be known as the Tuareg appear to have originated in Libya, perhaps obtaining camels from Roman legions stationed there, and then moved south and west, eventually occupying large areas of modern Niger, southern Algeria, and northern Mali. To the west, the Sanhaja—like the Tuareg, wearers of the face-veil (*litham*)—moved into the deserts lying between the southern Atlas Mountains and the Senegal and Niger Rivers.

Both of these nomadic groups played an important role in sustaining contact between Mediterranean and sub-Saharan Africa, especially during the Islamic period when their intimate knowledge of the Sahara and their camel resources made possible the organization and safe passage of trading caravans. Prior to the Islamic era, there was very little direct commerce between the two sides of the Sahara. Rock drawings of horse-drawn chariots (probably belonging to the first millennium B.C.E.) point to possible routes from Fazzan to the Niger around Gao, and from western Algeria through western Mauritania and then eastward to the Niger at the northern end of the Inland Delta. However, their significance is difficult to gauge, and it is unlikely that such fragile vehicles and sensitive animals could have served the needs of either regular commerce or periodic warfare. Arguments have been made for a trans-Saharan trade in gold during late Roman times, but the evidence is tenuous. Romans had other, more accessible sources of gold, and on the west African side there is little evidence of the emergence of significant polities until after the middle of the first millennium C.E. Certainly, North Africans had contacts with Saharan oases, and there were various Roman exploratory probes into the Sahara and warfare with the Garamantes of the Fezzan; but fuller, more direct and substantial contacts between North Africa and sub-Saharan Africa only become apparent after the establishment in the seventh and eighth centuries C.E. of a huge Islamic empire that stretched from the Atlantic Ocean in the west to the Indus River in the east.

The Islamic Period (c. 670–1900)

The Arab conquest of North Africa began in earnest with the founding of the garrison city of Qayrawan (in modern Tunisia) in 670 C.E. By the early years of the eighth century a strip of territory 100–200 miles deep had been brought under Arab control all the way from the borders of Egypt to the Atlantic coast, with significant southerly extensions into the Fezzan and into the Sus region of southern Morocco. From both of these regions probes were undertaken into lands to the south, but no conquests took place. Early trading contacts probably began in the latter part of the eighth century following the arrival of schismatic Kharijites of the Ibadi and Sufri sects, who sought refuge in North Africa from determined attempts by the Abbasid caliphs (from 750 C.E.) to stamp them out in the central lands of Islam. These sectarians established themselves in areas relatively remote from the Arab garrisons: in Jabal Nafusa (a mountainous region south of Tripoli); in Tozeur, in the marshy Jarid region of southern Ifriqiya (Tunisia); in Tahart, in the central Atlas Mountains (Algeria); and at Sijilmasa, an oasis in Tafilalt beyond the Moroccan Atlas. From these locations they established trading contacts with existing or emerging polities on the Saharan fringes of west Africa.

The principal trade routes of the early centuries of Islam appear to have been a westerly route from Sijilmasa down to Awdaghust (Tegdaoust in southern Mauritania), and from there to the kingdom of ancient Ghana astride the region between the Senegal and the Niger Rivers; an easterly route from Jabal Nafusa through the Fezzan and down through the Kawar oasis toward the Lake Chad region where the kingdom of Kanem emerged in the late tenth century; and a central route from Tahert via Wargla (where it was joined by a route from Tozeur) down to the Niger at Kaw Kaw (also Gawgaw or Gao). These routes were apparently established by the early ninth century, since the names Ghana, Kaw Kaw, and Zaghawa (a nomadic group associated with the founding of the Kanem kingdom) appear in the *Surat al-ard* of al-Khuwarizmi, an early work of geography otherwise mainly based on the *Geography* of Claudius Ptolemy (c. 150 C.E.) and written between 813 and 842 C.E.

These three axes remained the principal avenues of trade between Mediterranean and Sudanic Africa down to the early twentieth century, though precise routes varied from period to period. From early on there was also a transverse route which connected ancient Ghana with Egypt via the Middle Niger, the Aïr massif, and Fazzan, and various sectors of it remained active over the centuries, especially as a route for pilgrims traveling to Mecca. By about the mid-fifteenth century, the northern Hausa cities of Kano and Katsina (in modern Nigeria) were linked more directly to trans-Saharan trade by routes that led north through Agadez or the Tegidda region to the west of it to Ghadames and Tripoli, or northwest to Tuwat and thence to Tlemcen and Fez. In the seventeenth century, after the conversion of the ruler of Wadai (in contemporary eastern Chad) to Islam, a route was opened up from the Lake Chad region to Dar Fur and the Nile Valley, leading to Mecca via the Red Sea, and to Egypt down the Nile Valley. A route also led up from Wadai through the Kufra oasis to Benghazi. This latter route was especially active after Sanusi *zawiya*s were established (in contemporary southern Chad) in the late nineteenth century and was probably the last route used for bringing slaves across the Sahara.

The items traded across the Sahara in both directions were many and varied. Southward went horses, rock salt, cloths—both of European (from the fifteenth century at any rate) and North African weave (especially the thick blanket material called *hanbal*, corrupted to *lambens* by the Portuguese)—swords, chain mail and horse trappings, copper and brass vessels (brass bowls from Mamluk Egypt have turned up as shrine objects in modern Ghana), mirrors, scissors, needles, perfumes, paper, and cowrie shells (*Cypraea moneta*, brought from the Indian Ocean), which were used as currency in several states bordering the Sahara. Northward went slaves, ivory (and perhaps hippopotamus tusks), grain (to Saharan oases), goat hides, senna, and cola nuts (*Cola nitida*), among other items of tropical produce. There is little doubt, however, that the lure of gold was the primary incentive for North African merchants to undertake the perils of a Saharan crossing. Al-Fazari, an astronomer contemporary with al-Khuwarizmi, characterized Ghana as "the land of gold," and gold is the leitmotiv of all subsequent Arab writing about the region. Gold dust was obtained from pits in Bambuhu, a region lying between the Faleme and Bafing Rivers, southern tributaries of the Senegal River, and somewhat later from Bure on tributaries of the Upper Niger. From the late fourteenth century, Muslim traders also obtained gold mined in the Akan forests (in modern Ghana) bringing it up to Jenne and thence to Walata or Timbuktu. The most important item bartered for the gold was rock salt, obtained from pans in the central Sahara (Idjil, Taghaza, Taodeni, and others less easily identified), carried down to the Niger or Senegal on the backs of camels and loaded onto large river canoes. As late as the 1970s this trade was still in existence, though no gold was then being exchanged for the salt.

Far to the east in Kanem there was no gold in which to trade, and the chief commodity was most probably slaves. Earlier, the Romans had obtained slaves via intermediaries from the Tibesti massif to the north of Kanem, so a southerly extension of this trade should not surprise us. Black slaves appear in the North African record as early as 826, when laborers revolted in the Jarid area, and later in that century the Aghlabids of Ifriqiya used some as soldiers. In fact, slaves became the second major item of commerce in the trans-Saharan trade along all routes, right down to early years of the twentieth century. Prior to the nineteenth century, slaves were most often bartered for Barbary horses, in ratios of up to fifteen slaves for one horse, depending on the time and place and the age and sex of the slaves. Although horses were to be found in west Africa before the Islamic era, they were small compared to the Barbary horse, which could carry a rider wearing chain or quilted mail and thus furnished a war machine or a long-distance raider—both usages serving to provide yet more slaves for exchange. The slaves thus transported to North Africa were primarily used in domestic service, including concubinage. (Two-thirds of the slaves taken over the Sahara in the nineteenth century were females.) The next most common usage was as soldiers. Many regimes thus employed them, while in Morocco under Mulay Ismail (1672–1727) a vast slave army was raised by impounding all black slaves in the empire. The army's strength was later maintained by marrying the male slaves to black female slaves and training up the resultant offspring—boys for the army, and girls for palace service. Relatively few slaves were used for agricultural or industrial tasks, the opportunity in North Africa for intensive labor in such occupations being limited. Some were reexported. Prior to 1492 some black slaves were sold into Andalusia. From the seventeenth century the trans-Saharan slave trade provided the Ottoman sultans with eunuchs to guard the harem of the Topkapi palace, while others were sent to serve in the Prophet's mosque in Medina or the Mosque of the Kaaba in Mecca.

In the absence of an Arab-Muslim conquest of west Africa, the way was open for political relations between Sudanic and Mediterranean African states based on mutual interest. The way was also open for the conversion of west Africans to Islam at their own pleasure, devoid of the pressures brought by conquest and colonization. In the eleventh century—some two and one-half centuries after initial contacts—a number of rulers of states on the southern Saharan fringes formally accepted Islam: the ruler of Takrur, a small state on the Senegal River; the ruler of the state based on Kaw Kaw (perhaps as early as the late tenth century); and the ruler of the state of Kanem. Also in the eleventh century, a militant religious movement arose in the western Sahara among the nomads of the Sanhaja. These Almoravids, as they became known (from the Arabic al-murabitun, "warriors for the faith"), attacked Sijilmasa around 1055, swept on into central Morocco, and before the end of the century into Andalusia, briefly uniting a vast region from central Spain to the southern Sahara under their banner. Their role in the demise of ancient Ghana is disputed, as is the possible role of a segment of the movement in the affairs of the state based on Gao. Tombstones recording the deaths of "kings" and "queens" buried there in the period 1088–1120 have been shown to originate in Almeria, then under Almoravid control, but the precise identity of these royal figures is unclear.

Sudanic states established diplomatic relations with North African and Middle Eastern states at various times. Kanem exchanged gifts with the Hafsids of Tunis in the thirteenth century; Mali had close ties with the Marinids of Fez in the mid-fourteenth century; Bornu's rulers turned to the Mamluk sultan of Egypt for help against marauding Arab nomads later in the same century, and in the late sixteenth century sent missions to the Ottoman sultan Murad III and to the Sadian sultan of Morocco, Ahmad al-Mansur, in a bid to obtain firearms. Subsequent rulers of Bornu maintained close relations with the Ottoman governors of Tripoli during the seventeenth century. Relations between Songhai under the *askiyas* (1493–1591) and the Sadians were less friendly. The Sadians used both diplomacy and force to wrest the salt pans of Taghaza from Songhai's control, and in 1591 a Sadian force dominated by Spanish renegades crossed the Sahara and overthrew the reigning *askiya* of Songhai, Ishaq II. From then until the early nineteenth century, the Middle Niger was governed by descendants of these and other Moroccan soldiery sent to Timbuktu, who ruled with the title *basha*. Even in the late nineteenth century, the citizens of Timbuktu appealed to the Alawid sultan of Morocco to protect them against the invading French—needless to say, to no avail.

Religious and Cultural Relations

Whatever the military impact of the Almoravid movement on the region may have been, one thing seems sure: it was in the wake of this movement that the Maliki school (*madh'hab*) of Islamic law—the school vigorously promoted by the Almoravids—became dominant in west Africa. Its sway remains undisputed, even though in the twentieth century its scope is limited mainly to family law. The principal law books of the school, still studied with their manifold commentaries, originated in North Africa, where the school also predominates, and in Egypt. West African scholars themselves have written many a commentary or gloss on the *Risala* of Ibn Abi Zayd of Qayrawan (d. 997) and the *Mukhtasar* of Khalil b. Ishaq of Alexandria (d. 1374) and have also studied, taught, and commented upon the writings of many other Muslim scholars of North Africa, Andalusia, and Egypt.

Historically, relatively few west African scholars went to North Africa to study, though many visited Egypt on their way to or from the pilgrimage to Mecca. North African scholars, however, did visit west Africa, sometimes spending years teaching or holding judicial positions. Among the most influential was Muhammad ibn 'Abd al-Karim al-Maghili (d. 1504) from Tlemcen, who spent some years in both Kano and Gao and advised their rulers in the 1490s. He is said to have left behind some male children in Kano, and their putative descendants still play a role in Kano court and religious life in the late twentieth century. In the nineteenth and twentieth centuries, a religious movement originating in Morocco has had a profound influence in west Africa. The Tijani "congregation," a Sufi "way" (Arabic *tariqa*, "path"), owes its origins to the teachings of Sidi Ahmad al-Tijani (d. 1815), a mystic from Ain Madi in the Algerian Sahara. Disciples spread his teachings in Mauritania, and from there the Tijani Way was carried into what became Senegal and Guinea. Al-Hajj 'Umar ibn Sa'id Tal (d. 1864), a scholar from Futa Toro (Senegal), was made a secondary leader of the Way by a deputy of al-Tijani's during his pilgrimage to Mecca. On his return to west Africa, he recruited disciples and eventually led a militant movement (jihad) which carved out a considerable state in what is now Mali. On his way home he had initiated a number of people into the Way in Bornu and Sokoto (both in modern Nigeria). From the 1930s through the 1960s, the Tijani Way garnered large numbers of adherents in Senegal, Ghana, and northern Nigeria through the exertions of Shaikh Ibrahim Niasse (d. 1975) of Kaolak (Senegal), who gained international repute within the order and within such pan-Islamic organizations as the Islamic World League.

North African culture has influenced west Africa in many domains other than the purely religious. Domestic and royal architecture along the Saharan fringes show signs of such influence, especially in the flat-roofed, cube-shaped houses and the multiple courtyards of palaces with distinct "harem" quarters. Styles of men's robes also show North African influence, and the narrow men's loom was probably introduced from there, though having more distant origins. Some food crops came to west Africa from the Mediterranean lands, especially through returning pilgrims. Onions and tomatoes are two of the more important, while names for maize often reveal its path of introduction: *masar hayni* in Songhai and *dawar masara* in Hausa both mean "Egyptian millet," while *makka*, the Tamajeq word for maize, clearly hints at the pilgrimage route. Above all, Arabic language and script has been a strong influence in the cultural life of sub-Saharan African Muslims. Arabic was the principal language of literacy for a thousand years down to the colonial period, and the forms of Arabic script used in west Africa all derive from North Africa or Andalusian hands. Many African languages have been written using slightly modified forms of Arabic script (e.g., Fufulde, Hausa, Kanembu, Wolof), though they have now been largely abandoned in favor of the Roman script. West African languages spoken by Muslim peoples have absorbed a considerable number of Arabic loanwords, some of them through North African dialectal usage.

There have also been influences the other way. Some of the Arabic writings of west African Muslim scholars such as Ahmad Baba of Timbuktu (d. 1627), Muhammad b. Muhammad of Katsina (d. 1742), Salih al-Fullani of Futa Jallon (d. 1804), and Muhammad Bello of Sokoto (d. 1837) found their way into North Africa and the Middle East; Salih al-Fullani, who had a noted teaching career in Medina (in modern Saudi Arabia), became better known in India than in west Africa. Bornu was famous for its Qur'anic calligraphy, and copies of the sacred text penned there were sold for high prices in Tripoli. At another level, the *bori* possession cult practiced among the Hausa (more particularly by non-Muslims) was carried into Tunis and Tripoli by slaves. The so-called *diwan*s of Sidi Bilal, quasi-Islamized possession and exorcism cults that have flourished in Algeria (as well as other sacrificial cults), have west African origins; as does the *gnawa* cult (cf. Berber *igginaw*, "black") long practiced in Morocco, but now reduced to the status of folklore and performed for tourists.

Finally, we may recall that the writings of medieval Arab authors from North Africa, Andalusia, and Egypt constitute the sole written sources for the history of west Africa before the arrival of Europeans on the coast in the fifteenth century and the beginnings of local historiographical traditions in Arabic in the sixteenth. Such sources have many weaknesses, of course, most notably the lack of firsthand knowledge of west Africa on the part of most of their authors; continued dependence on ancient Greek writers (notably Claudius Ptolemy of Alexandria, fl. 150 C.E.); and certain prejudiced notions about black people, partly derived from Greek sources and partly from the close relationship of blackness to slavery in the Arab world. Three authors, however, benefited extensively from information gathered from visitors to the region or from west Africans who visited the Arab world: al-Bakri (d. 1087), an Andalusian who has left us a precious description of ancient Ghana; al-Umari (d. 1349), a Syrian who wrote an encyclopedia for bureaucrats which included a description of ancient Mali; and Ibn Khaldun (d. 1406), who gave a brief dynastic history of Mali in his general history of Islamic civilization. To these we should add the account of the great fourteenth-century world traveler Ibn Battuta, who visited Mali and the Middle Niger region in 1352–1353 and described these areas from the point of view of a tourist.

The Contemporary Period

Physical links between North and west Africa have become tenuous with the cessation of caravan traffic. The French dreamed of building a trans-Saharan railway to link their territory in Algeria with their west African possessions via Timbuktu, but this was never more than a dream. Although there is now a paved road from Algiers to the central Algerian Sahara at Adrar in Tuwat, and a similar one from Cotonou in Bénin to the

Niger-Mali border, this still leaves a gap of some 900 miles. As of 1994 traffic on land routes through Mali and Niger was virtually at a halt, since militant action by Tuareg seeking greater autonomy had rendered the area insecure. Air services between the two regions of Africa are few and far between, and travel between west and North Africa is swiftest via Paris or Rome. North African states retain diplomatic representation in the more important west African capitals such as Abuja (Nigeria), Accra (Ghana), Abidjan (Côte d'Ivoire), and Dakar (Senegal), and this is reciprocated by those countries in Rabat, Algiers, Tunis, and Tripoli. All the countries of both regions however, belong to the Organization of African Unity, and many also belong to the Organization of the Islamic Conference, the cultural division of which is based in Rabat and is active in west African countries.

BIBLIOGRAPHY

Barkindo, Bawuro. "Early States of the Central Sudan: Kanem, Borno, and Some of Their Neighbors to c. 1500 A.D." In volume 1 of *History of West Africa*, edited by J. F. A. Ajayi and Michael Crowder. 3d ed. London and New York, 1985.

Bovill, E. W. *The Golden Trade of the Moors.* 2d ed. London, 1968.

Camps, G. "Beginnings of Pastoralism and Cultivation in North-West Africa and the Sahara: Origins of the Berbers." In *Cambridge History of Africa.* Volume 1, *From Earliest Times to c. 500 B.C.*, edited by J. Desmond Clarke. Cambridge, 1982.

Devisse, Jean. "Routes de commerce et échanges en Afrique occidentale en relation avec la Mediterranée: Un Essai de commerce médiéval du XIᵉ au XVIᵉ siècle." *Revue d'histoire économique et sociale* 50 (1972): 42–73, 357–397.

Hopkins, J. F. P., and Nehemia Levtzion. *Corpus of Early Arabic Sources for West African History.* Cambridge, 1981.

Hunwick, John. "Songhay, Borno, and the Hausa States, 1450–1600." In volume 1 of *History of West Africa*, edited by J. F. A. Ajayi and Michael Crowder. 3d ed. London and New York, 1985.

———. *Les Rapports intellectuels entre le Maroc et l'Afrique sub-saharienne à travers les âges.* Publications de l'Institut des Études Africaines, Université Mohammed V. Rabat, Morocco, 1990.

Konare, Adam Ba. *Les Relations politiques et culturelles entre le Maroc et le Mali à travers les âges.* Publications de l'Institut des Études Africaines, Université Mohammed V. Rabat, Morocco, 1991.

Levtzion, Nehemia. "The Sahara and the Sudan from the Arab Conquest to the Rise of the Almoravids." In *Cambridge History of Africa.* Volume 2, *From c. 500 B.C. to A.D. 1050*, edited by J. D. Fage. Cambridge, 1978.

Mauny, Raymond. "Trans-Saharan Contacts and the Iron Age in West Africa." In *Cambridge History of Africa.* Volume 2, *From c. 500 B.C. to A.D. 1050*, edited by J. D. Fage. Cambridge, 1978.

Savage, Elizabeth, ed. *The Human Commodity: Perspectives on the Trans-Saharan Slave Trade.* London, 1992.

JOHN HUNWICK

See also **Arab World, African Relations with; Arabs; Berbers; Ibn Battuta; Islam; Maghili, Muhammad ibn ʿAbd al-Karim al-; Sahara Desert; Sudanic Empires of Western Africa; Sufism; Tijani, Ahmad; Travel and Exploration; Tuareg; ʿUmar ibn Saʿid Tal (al-Hajj).**

PEOPLES AND POPULATION MOVEMENTS IN RELATION WITH SUB-SAHARAN AFRICA

North Africa as discussed here comprises Morocco, Algeria, Tunisia, and Libya. The most prominent geographical features of the area are the Sahara in the south and in the north the Atlas Mountains, with a high point of 4,165 meters at Mount Toubkal in Morocco. A broad coastal plain borders the Atlantic in Morocco, and in Tunisia a small one faces eastward, while in Algeria there are pockets of cultivable land along the coast. In the interior are narrow valleys and some high plains. Mountain chains often extend to the Mediterranean coast. There are few rivers, and many inland areas do not drain to the ocean. In Libya the Sahara reaches nearly to the Mediterranean.

Environment

Rainfall follows the characteristic Mediterranean pattern of a wet winter and a dry summer. There is considerable variation from one year to the next, and a good agricultural year depends as much on the timing of the rain as the total amount. Winter wheat and barley are the main crops. Herding sheep and goats has historically been the best method to utilize these marginal lands with their unreliable climate. But pastoral nomadism has now largely disappeared, and livestock raising is combined with farming. Irrigation has long been present in pockets throughout the area and has spread considerably with modernization since the 1950s. Irrigated areas are largely devoted to fruits and vegetables, though occasionally cereals are cultivated. Sedentary agriculture has spread with the growth of irrigation, the growth of the population, and the presence of a market for the crops.

Language

North Africa is part of the Arab world and is known in Arabic as the Maghreb, the "occident" or Arab

West. Arabic is the predominant language of the people and of government. There are, however, substantial numbers of Berber speakers. The various Berber languages are older in the area, and Arabic is intrusive, beginning with the Muslim conquest in the seventh century. The Berber languages and the Semitic languages, such as Arabic, are both part of the Afro-Asiatic language family. Arabic is written, while Berber languages generally are not. Arabic is characterized by diglossia, a distinction between the formal written language and the common colloquial spoken language, which itself varies by locality.

Various Berber languages are spoken in mountain areas in Morocco and Algeria, and also in isolated desert and oasis settings throughout the four countries. The bulk of the Berber speakers are in the Atlas and Rif Mountains of Morocco and in the Kabylia and Aures Mountains of Algeria. There are Berber-speaking enclaves in southern Tunisia, on the island of Djerba, in the Dra and Ziz Valleys of Morocco, in the oases of the Algerian Sahara, as well as in the Nafusa escarpment, Augila oasis, and elsewhere in Libya. The southernmost Berber language is Tamashek, spoken by the Tuareg, who are found as far south as Mali, Niger, Burkina Faso, and Nigeria. There are small groups of Berber speakers in Mauritania. The easternmost contemporary outlier is the oasis of Siwa in the Western Desert of Egypt.

Elsewhere in the area Arabic speakers are found, in the villages, plains, and cities, and among the pastoral tribes. Overall, Berber speakers represent perhaps a third of Morocco's population and a quarter of Algeria's, while they are less than 1 percent in Tunisia and about 5–10 percent in Libya. But the figures are approximate, given the high rate of bilingualism between the Berber languages and Arabic. Many Arabic speakers of today doubtless descend from the Berber speakers of yesterday. French is a common second language in Morocco, Algeria, and Tunisia, though English is much more common than it was.

Peoples

The population of the four countries in the mid-1990s was over 65 million, slightly more than Egypt's 60 million. Morocco and Algeria each had over 26 million people, Tunisia nearly 9 million, and Libya 5 million. Growth rates are high, ranging from 2 percent to 4 percent annually.

The North African population is roughly half urban. The largest cities are Casablanca, Algiers, Tunis, and Tripoli. The urban centers house the educated elite and the national ruling classes but also include numerous slums and other poor areas which have grown as a result of rural to urban migration and overall population growth. In the rural areas the plains are dominated by large capitalist estates while villages are concentrated in the mountains.

There are pockets of phenotypically black populations, particularly in the Saharan oases and in the cities. The groups in the Sahara sometimes represent remnant populations of a more substantial original black population that was submerged by Berber expansions and Arab invasions. Other Saharan groups and the urban people reflect the residue of the slave trade. Some communities, such as those in the Dra and Ziz Valleys of Morocco or in southern Tunisia, are Berber-speaking. Some nineteenth-century accounts refer to Hausa-speaking blacks in North Africa.

North Africa historically had a Jewish population. In 1952 percentages ranged from 1.5 percent in Algeria to 3.5 percent in Libya, with Morocco (2.7 percent) and Tunisia (2.9 percent) in between. The majority of the Jews were urban and small-town craftsworkers and traders who linked the urban and rural sectors. The Jews were of diverse origins: some nineteenth-century immigrants, others ancient parts of North African society. With the creation of Israel in 1948 and the independence of the North African countries between 1951 and 1962, almost all the Jews have emigrated. The most significant community is now in Morocco, and it is a shadow of its past.

Life

North Africans are virtually all Muslim, and in the vast majority they are Sunni Muslims of the Maliki rite. There are a few Berber-speaking Ibadhites (or Kharijites, early Muslim schismatics) in the Mzab oases of the Algerian Sahara, on the Tunisian island of Djerba, and in the Libyan Nafusa escarpment. Sunnis of the Hanafi rite are found in the coastal towns, where they reflect Turkish influence during the period of Ottoman domination. There is no indigenous Christian population, nor are there Shia. Throughout North Africa one finds "popular" religious practices, often centered around saints' shrines, some of which are transformations of nature cults focused on springs, mountains, exceptional trees, or rock outcroppings. These cults are often closely connected with local politics and social organization, since they also incorporate ancestors and descent. Thus cemeteries often serve as symbols of the integrity of local communities. Other popular religious practices (such as those of the Hamadsha or *gnawa* in urban Morocco or the Stambouli in Tunis) are locally believed to have come into North Africa from south of the Sahara. Despite these influences, popular Islam is more Middle Eastern than African. Many Islamic institutions were supported through religiously endowed property (*awqaf* or *hubus*) which provided an income to religious specialists. Modern Islam is more universalistic and engages the identity of the entire population rather than its segments.

Despite the diverse historical origins of the population, there is remarkable homogeneity throughout North Africa. The dominant social process has been one of absorbing diversity into a common pattern. Only in Algeria has ethnic diversity become a political issue, through Kabyle Berber specificity. The Berber-speakers of the Kabyle area often refer to themselves as Imazighen (glossed as "free men") and to their language as Tamazight, and they seek an official recognition of their language and culture. The intellectual centers of this Amazigh movement are in the Algerian town of Tizi Ouzou and in France. This ethnic dispute is confused with differences of opinion over the role of Islam, the task of the state, and other more specifically political issues. Class differences, however, based on education, wealth, and lifestyle, do provide an axis of distinction.

Family relations are patrilineal and patriarchal. A strict division of labor along gender lines is common outside sophisticated urban circles. Polygyny is prohibited in Tunisia and elsewhere is permitted but rare. Female genital mutilation is unknown, but male circumcision is universal. The restriction of women's ability to maintain an independent life outside home and family is justified by appeals to family honor and by notions that female sexuality would threaten family integrity if not socially circumscribed.

Local social units in some parts of North Africa are villages, in other parts tribes. "Tribe" here refers to a social group marked by common descent rather than by cultural characteristics. Property rights are vested in both groups and individuals; over the last century, individual rights have dominated. The historical existence of individual rights in land, based on Islamic law, distinguishes North Africa from much of sub-Saharan Africa.

In the 1996 United Nations Development Programme's Human Development Report, Libya ranked 59th, Algeria 69th, Tunisia 78th, and Morocco 123d, of a total 174 countries. Libyans had a life expectancy at birth of 63 years, and a literacy rate of 74 percent. The figures for Algeria were respectively 67 years and 59 percent, for Tunisia 68 years and 64 percent, and for Morocco 64 years and 42 percent. Men are more likely to be literate than women. Thanks to oil wealth, the adjusted real gross domestic product per capita was slightly higher in Libya and Algeria than in Tunisia, with Morocco ranking lower.

Politics

Morocco, Algeria, and Tunisia were under French colonial rule, and Libya under Italian. Tunisia became independent in 1956 as a monarchy and established a republic in 1957. Algeria became independent in 1962 as a republic, while Morocco remained a kingdom after independence in 1956. Beginning in 1975 with the Green March, King Hassan II extended Morocco's boundaries southward to incorporate former Spanish colonial territories, some of whose people claimed independence as the Saharawi Arab Democratic Republic. Libya, under United Nations' trusteeship after the defeat of Italy in World War II, became independent as a kingdom in 1951. The king was overthrown, and the country became a republic in 1969. Multiparty elections in all countries have been respected occasionally in name but rarely in practice. The legitimacy of the government and the ruling elite is an enduring political issue, though the regimes in all four countries have been relatively stable. Currently the major challenge to the regimes comes from parties advocating a more Islamic government.

Algeria and Tunisia went through considerable social change in the post-independence period as the result of strong government policies. A major feature of this socialist period was land reform and the formation of cooperatives. Libya underwent radical change as a result first of the discovery of oil in the 1950s, and then as a result of Colonel Muammar Qaddafi's idiosyncratic theory of anti-bureaucratic administration.

Links to the South

North Africa has been politically linked to the rest of the African continent through the Organization of African Unity (OAU) and through mutual support during and since the struggle for independence. There are various forms of cultural exchange, of which sports is the most prominent.

North African national and club teams compete in continent-wide championships in football, basketball, volleyball, handball, and other sports, sometimes for both men's and women's teams. North Africa also participates in the Pan-African Games and in occasional Pan-African cultural celebrations.

Islam forms a common framework for North and west African countries, reflecting their common history. Some North African countries maintain cultural centers in west African countries that give a large role to religion. However, Egypt and Saudi Arabia are probably more important in this respect than the Maghreb.

Commercial links are present but not strong, as both North and sub-Saharan Africa are more closely tied to the developed world than to each other. There is not much movement of people across the Sahara; the major exceptions are African students in North African universities, clandestine migrants transiting from west Africa to Europe, and occasional merchants from the northern Sahara drifting south. There is a modest amount of traffic across the Sahara, especially between Libya and Chad and across the Algerian Sahara, and there are air links between each of the four North African countries and the neighboring west African countries.

BIBLIOGRAPHY

Bourdieu, Pierre. *The Algerians.* Translated by Alan C. M. Ross. Boston, 1962.

Crapanzano, Vincent. *The Hamadsha: A Study in Moroccan Ethnopsychiatry.* Berkeley, 1973.

Davis, John. *Libyan Politics: Tribe and Revolution.* London, 1987.

Geertz, Clifford, Hildred Geertz, and Lawrence Rosen. *Meaning and Order in Moroccan Society: Three Essays in Cultural Analysis.* Cambridge, 1979.

Gellner, Ernest, and Charles Micaud, eds. *Arabs and Berbers: From Tribe to Nation in North Africa.* London, 1973.

Hammoudi, Abdellah. *The Victim and Its Masks: An Essay on Sacrifice and Masquerade in the Maghreb.* Translated by Paula Wissing. Chicago, 1993.

Paques, Viviana. *L'arbre cosmique dans la pensée populaire et dans la vie quotidienne du nord-ouest Africain.* Paris, 1964.

Zghal, Abdelkader. "The Reactivation of Tradition in a Post-Traditional Society." *Daedalus* 102, no. 1 (1973): 225–237.

NICHOLAS S. HOPKINS

See also **Arab World, African Relations with; Berbers; Tuareg.**

NUBIA. Since the early Middle Ages, the toponym "Nubia" has been applied to that portion of the Nile Valley which lies immediately upriver from Egypt. It is not a political term, for there never was any single nation specifically called Nubia, and today the region is divided between the republics of Egypt and of the Sudan. Nubia takes its name rather from a distinctive ethnic group who call themselves Nubians and who speak languages of the Nubian family.

The Nubian-speaking peoples seem to have migrated from the Kordofan and Dar Fur regions of the western Sudan to the Nile Valley in a series of waves, beginning perhaps two thousand years ago. Initially they settled within the territories of the Sudanese empire of Kush, became its subjects, and absorbed much of the culture of the riverine farmers along the Nile. Gradually, as their numbers became predominant, their languages supplanted the older, Meroitic language of Kush. By the time the empire of Kush broke up, in the fourth century C.E., it appears that all of the peoples of southern Egypt and the northern Sudan spoke Nubian languages and were called Nubians. The northern boundary of Nubia was, and still is, just to the south of Aswan, in Egypt; the southern boundary was somewhere well to the south of modern Khartoum, perhaps around Sennar.

For about two centuries after the fall of Kush, there is almost no historical record relating to the Nubians and their country. We know from extensive archaeological excavations that in the most northerly part of Nubia (commonly called lower Nubia) a fairly powerful kingdom persisted and still carried on some of the traditions of Kush. It derived its prosperity from trading with Byzantine Egypt. However, in the sixth century C.E., when Christian missionaries from Byzantium entered the country, they found three well-established Nubian kingdoms. In the north, on the borders of Egypt, was Nobadia; farther upstream, and centered in the Dongola region, was Makuria; and in the region around the confluence of the Blue and White Niles was Alodia, known in later medieval texts as Alwa.

All three of the Nubian kingdoms accepted the Christian faith with extraordinary rapidity, and it appears certain that conversion was complete by the end of the sixth century. The Nubian church became, and for nearly a thousand years remained, an integral part of the Coptic Orthodox Church of Egypt, and all its bishops were appointed by the Coptic Patriarch of Alexandria. The conversion set the stage for a flourishing of religious architecture, art, and literature, which were the hallmarks of medieval Nubian civilization.

Less than a century after the Christianization of Nubia came the Arab conquest of Egypt. The conquerors also twice invaded Nubia, in 642 and in 652, but on each occasion the invasion was repulsed. The Arab commander, Abdallah ibn Sa'd, then concluded a treaty with the kingdoms of Nobadia and Makuria which guaranteed the Nubians against any further Arab incursions or any forcible imposition of Islam for the next six hundred years. In exchange for the guarantee of peace the Arabs received an annual tribute of slaves. This document, called the *baqt,* laid the foundations for medieval Nubian peace and prosperity.

Sometime in the eighth century the two kingdoms of Nobadia and Makuria were merged under a single king, whose capital was at Dongola. There was not however a complete merger of administrations; the two regions were always separately named in documents, and each had its own administrative hierarchy. Nobadia, the northern region, was a free trade zone in which Arab traders were allowed to travel and even to settle, and where Egyptian coinage was in circulation. Administration was in the hands of a representative, or viceroy, called the eparch of Nobadia. Makuria was much more directly ruled by its king: here all foreign commerce was a royal monopoly, and no money was in circulation. The peoples of Nobadia and Makuria spoke different though closely related Nubian languages, as do the present-day inhabitants of those regions.

The united kingdom of Nobadia and Makuria prospered for several centuries through its trade with Islamic Egypt, sending gold, ivory, slaves, ebony, and ostrich feathers, and receiving in exchange fine textiles, glassware, glazed pottery, and wine. At the same time, however, the Nubians made very elaborate decorated pottery of their own, adorned with designs derived from medieval manuscript illumination. These vessels, together with the brightly colored paintings on church and cathedral walls, were the outstanding artistic achievements of medieval Nubian civilization.

The weakening and eventual destruction of the Christian kingdoms began when the Mamluk sultans seized power in Egypt in 1250 C.E. They repudiated the *baqt* treaty and launched a series of incursions into Nubia, none of which, however, resulted in any lasting conquest. Much more destructive in the long run were the mass migrations of nomad Arab tribes, some from Egypt and some directly from the Arabian peninsula. In the fourteenth and fifteenth centuries they overran the territories of Alwa and most of Makuria, and the formerly unified kingdoms were divided into a series of petty, warring principalities under Arab warlords. Throughout these regions the Nubian languages were gradually replaced by Arabic.

The far north, including Nobadia and the northern part of Makuria, was spared the Arab invasions because of the extreme desert conditions of the Nile hinterland. Here, a splinter Christian kingdom called Dotawo persisted until the end of the fifteenth century, after which the historical record becomes entirely silent for several centuries. Archaeology has demonstrated, however, that when lower Nubia was annexed to the Ottoman Empire, in the latter half of the seventeenth century, there was no surviving trace either of the medieval Christian kingdoms or of the Nubian church. Gradually, in the seventeenth and eighteenth centuries, the Nubians converted to Islam, as Islamic teachers from northern and western Africa came to settle among them. They continued however to speak Nubian rather than Arabic, as they do down to the present day.

The Nubians today are thus a linguistic enclave surrounded on all sides by Arabic-speakers, some of whom were speakers of Nubian languages until a few centuries ago. The name Nubia, which was once applied to the whole of southern Egypt and the northern Sudan, is now applied only to that area actually occupied by Nubian-speakers, a region extending from Aswan in Egypt to Ed Debba in Sudan. However, a very large part of Nubia was flooded in the 1960s by the building of the Aswan High Dam, and the inhabitants have been resettled in distant regions in Egypt and Sudan. There are today about 1.2 million Nubian-speakers, about equally divided between Egypt and Sudan.

BIBLIOGRAPHY

Adams, William Y. *Nubia, Corridor to Africa.* Rev. ed. 1984.

Dafalla, Hassan. *The Nubian Exodus.* 1975.

Fernea, Robert A., and George Gerster. *Nubians in Egypt.* 1973.

Monneret de Villard, Ugo. "Storia della Nubia Cristiana." *Pontificium Institutum Orientalium Studiorum, Orientalia Christiana Analecta* 118 (1938).

WILLIAM Y. ADAMS

See also **Egypt; Exploration and Travel; Nile River.**

NUBIANS, NUBA, NUBI. There is often confusion between Nubians, Nuba, and Nubi, due to the similarity of their names and of their histories. Nubians are the occupants of the riverine region known as Nubia, in the Nile Valley between Wadi Halfa and Khartoum, much of which was submerged as part of the Aswan Dam project in the 1960s. The present-day Nubians, speaking languages of the Nubian branch of the Nilo-Saharan family, comprise some half-dozen small groups living on the Nile itself, with outliers in the region of Kordofan in the western Sudan. They number in all some 300,000 people and are dependent mainly upon agriculture; most have accepted Sunni Islam and much Arab culture from the north.

The Nuba are the occupants of the Nuba Hills in Kordofan and are divided into six main groups, mostly farmers. They are unrelated to the Nubians and have not voluntarily accepted Islam. Since the mid-1980s, they have been deprived of their lands and have suffered much brutality, enslavement, and forcible conversion to Islam by Arab invaders, with the approval of the Sudanese government.

Nubi is the name given in the southern Sudan and Uganda to the mostly urbanized descendants of the nineteenth-century Egyptian troops who were cut off from the north by the disturbances associated with the rise of the Mahdi, and who linked themselves to Emin Pasha (Edward Schnitzer). They have intermarried with local populations but distinguish themselves by speaking a form of Arabic and by being Muslims. Like the Nubians, their women practice the genital mutilation known as infibulation. The best-known Nubi in recent history has been former dictator of Uganda, Idi Amin Dada.

BIBLIOGRAPHY

The best sources include HAMED AMMAR, *Growing Up in an Egyptian Village: Silwa, the Province of Aswan,* New York, 1973; H. M. FAHIM, *Dams, People, and Development: The Aswan High Dam Case,* New York, 1981; and PETER GEISER, *The Egyptian Nubians: Resettlement and Year of Coping,* Cairo, 1986. The best account of the Nuba is S. F. NADEL, *The Nuba: An Anthropological Study of the Hill Tribes in Kordofan,* London, 1947. There is no single comprehensive account of the Nubi.

JOHN MIDDLETON

See also **Nubia; Sudan: Peoples and Cultures; Uganda: Peoples and Cultures.**

NUER AND DINKA. The origin of the Nilotes, a group of which the Dinka and Nuer are members, is contested. Historians have suggested that Nilotes were a group of agriculturalists who settled in the Bahr al-Ghazal region of the southern Sudan, where they acquired the techniques for domesticating cattle. With a predominantly cattle economy, the Nilotes began to migrate from the Bahr al-Ghazal during the fifteenth century. The Dinka and Nuer did not move far. They occupied the swamplands around Lake No and the Bahr al-Jebel. The Nuer live in the Upper Nile and the Dinka in both the Upper Nile and Bahr al-Ghazal, where they eke out their existence by cattle herding; their system and area are known as the "cattle complex."

Nuer and Dinka identity must be examined from the perspective of the transformative impact of the ongoing civil war, which resumed in 1983, between the north and various southern groups, predominantly the Sudan People's Liberation Army (SPLA). Because the immediate realities of Dinka and Nuer identity and tribal boundaries are swiftly changing, the consequences of the war must be seen in a broader historical perspective. It is necessary when documenting people's notions of identity and survival, especially when those people are threatened by endemic war, to use oral testimonies to voice the thoughts and experiences of marginal groups. These can serve as both a research tool and an ideology for action to alleviate suffering.

Shared economic resources, similarities in language and cultural norms, and myths of genealogical connection all create a sense of collective identity. This identity is built on the sentiment of a shared historical experience: the self-identified "blacks" and "Africans" who are marginalized by "Arabs" and "Muslims." Their collective identity also depends on the cultural similarity that distinguishes them from other Nilotic neighbors. Yet, "Dinka" and "Nuer" are not definite identities because they are made up of many sections with remarkable regional variations, especially between western and eastern Nuer, and between western and eastern Dinka. They are not as bounded, homogeneous, and static as they are ethnologically portrayed.

Two issues have enforced their distinct "tribal" identities in recent decades. First, there is hostility between and within the two groups. Many cultural practices, such as initiation (removal of lower incisors and head scarification), and artifacts (e.g., spears and shields) are maintained as identification marks in cattle raiding, and more recently in well-armed fights instigated by rival factions of the SPLA. Second, the Dinka and Nuer form the largest part of southern resistance against the north, yet they frequently turn weapons against each other. These internal hostilities have been traced to their shared economic features, cattle and pasturage. In addition, the modern hostilities have resulted from elites' struggle for leadership, causing many Dinka and Nuer to question each other's patriotism and concern for the national cause, and others to wonder if there is anything, apart from the northern enemy, that binds the two groups. For the majority of the rural population, Dinka and Nuer identities precede the national identity of southern Sudan. The consequences of the present war can attest to this claim.

The causes of the war, which began in 1955 and had a ten-year hiatus (1972–1983), are rooted in deep-seated struggles over natural resources and in religious and ethnic identity. The Dinka and Nuer believe they are victims of their limited resources. The result has been economic transformation, famine, and the displacement of 1.5 million Dinka and Nuer to the north and another 800,000 to Ethiopia, Kenya, and Uganda. Yet the Dinka and Nuer have actively intervened in these historical forces that are shaping their identity. Despite their plight, rural populations have shown extraordinary survival techniques.

The present dilemmas, the results of both civil war and the government's effort to incorporate the Nuer and Dinka into the nation-state, combine mixed feelings about state regulations, widespread distribution of guns, and violence; changing notions of leadership, kin and gender relations, and marriage and divorce; and commodification of their value systems. To face these dilemmas, the Dinka and Nuer have produced a formula for survival, resorting to old ways in response to new challenges, and adopting new strategies to deal with failures of the antiquated. The Dinka and Nuer, so gradually thrust onto the global stage, have had trouble coming to terms with values that may have been theirs all along, but had never come to the fore as challenges. To both groups, the concepts "Dinka" and "Nuer" as nations are vital. Their ideology, which holds that livelihoods must be guided by religion, is based on the vitality of cattle in connecting human worldly matters with what lies beyond human control. With the cattle culture threatened, the whole ideology is endangered. In sustaining the sense of self, Dinka and Nuer are caught up in a struggle between Christianity and indigenous religions, tradition and modernization, ethnic identities as nations and the identity of southern Sudan, and individual and kin.

The Dinka and Nuer have not been stagnant, and the signs of change are heartening. Despite decades of destructive war, they have taken up trade to supplement the cattle economy, shifted to social networks, and altered concepts of disease, albeit with nostalgia for the old days. Such evidence suggests a culture that is seeking to reshape itself for assault on the global system—assault for both immediate survival and future prosperity. Their involvement in the war is based on questions about what it means to be Dinka and Nuer, and that is to remain so, even in the context of a modern nation-state.

While the artificial integration into the nation-state is the legacy of government, many southern Sudanese cling to their ethnic nationalities. The Dinka and Nuer have continued to perceive the nation-state as a temporary, migrant world—a locale for modern amenities. Yet the Sudan government struggles to coerce the allegiance of these groups to the nation-state, and the educated southerners promote the identity of a unified southern Sudan. Doubtless only a culture so deracinated could pose the question of identity with such insistence as it has been posed historically for the Dinka and Nuer. In understanding their plight, it is important not to erase the traces of multiple locations that they occupy, multiple identities that they maintain—or the evidence of a unified location, of shared historical experience, of one identity.

BIBLIOGRAPHY

Hutchinson, Sharon E. *Nuer Dilemmas: Coping with Money, War, and the State.* Berkeley, 1996.

Jok, Jok Madut. "Women, Sexuality, and Social Behavior in Western Dinka: The Impact of War on Reproductive Health in South Sudan." Ph.D. diss., UCLA, 1996.

Keen, David. *The Benefits of Famine: A Political Economy of Famine and Relief in Southwestern Sudan, 1983–1989.* Princeton, 1994.

JOK MADUT JOK

See also **Ethnicity and Identity; Nilotes.**

NUJOMA, SAMUEL SHAFIISHUNA (b. 12 May 1929), Namibia's first elected president since the country's independence, from South Africa, on 21 March 1990. Nujoma was born in Ongandjera in the far north of Namibia. He attended a Finnish mission school before relocating to Walvis Bay (1946) and later to Windhoek (1948). He was fired from the South African Railways (1957) for union organizing and then worked as a city clerk while attending night school.

In 1958 Nujoma helped to found, and was elected president of, the Ovamboland Peoples Organization. In 1959 he helped mobilize resistance to the forced removal of blacks from Windhoek. In March 1960 he fled into exile; the newly founded South West African Peoples Organization (SWAPO) elected him president. In June 1960, he appeared before the U.N. Committee on South West Africa. He was arrested on his return to Windhoek and was deported. He subsequently established SWAPO provisional headquarters in Dar es Salaam, Tanzania, and embarked on armed struggle. The following three decades he spent galvanizing international support for Namibian independence and directing SWAPO's military activities.

Nujoma returned from exile in September 1989 and was chosen president-elect in balloting by the Constituent Assembly on 16 February 1990. However, he did not assume office until the date of

Samuel Shafiishuna Nujoma, 1993. AP/WIDE WORLD

independence, 21 March 1990. As president of Namibia, Nujoma has received widespread praise for his steady-handed stewardship of democracy. He chairs weekly cabinet meetings and is personally involved in agricultural and drought relief projects. He delegates the tasks of daily governance to his prime minister.

BIBLIOGRAPHY

Katjavivi, Peter H. *A History of Resistance in Namibia.* London, 1988.

JOSHUA BERNARD FORREST

See also **Independence Movements; Postcolonial State.**

NUMBER SYSTEMS. Through the ages the peoples of sub-Saharan Africa have invented hundreds of numeration systems, both spoken and symbolic, that use body parts or objects to count or to represent numbers.

Verbal Numeration

The most common way to count bigger quantities—without inventing completely new number words—is to combine existing number words and rely on the arithmetic relationships between the involved numbers.

In the Makhwa language of Mozambique, "*thanu*" (five) and "*nloko*" (ten) are the bases of the system of numeration. One says "*thanu na moza*," or "five plus one," to express "six." "Seven" becomes "*thanu na pili*," or "five plus two." To express "twenty," one says "*miloko mili*," that is, "tens two" or "10 × 2." "Thirty" is "*miloko miraru*," or "tens three."

The most common numerical bases in Africa are ten, five, and twenty. Some languages, like Nyungwe (of Mozambique), use only base ten. Others like Balanta of Guinea Bissau use five and twenty as bases. The Bété language of Côte d'Ivoire uses three bases: five, ten, and twenty. For instance, fifty-six is expressed as "*golosso-ya-kogbo-gbeplo*," that is, "twenty [*golo-*] times two [*so*] plus [*ya*] ten [*kogbo*] (and) five [*gbe-*] (and) one [*blo*]." The Bambara of Mali and Guinea have a ten-twenty system. The word for twenty (*mugan*) means "one person," the word for forty (*debe*) means "mat," refering to a mat on which husband and wife sleep together: jointly they have forty digits.

As languages are never static, variants for number expressions may be found over time, or different combinations may be used in different regions. For instance, among the Huku of Uganda, the number words for thirteen, fourteen, and fifteen may be formed by addition of one, two, or three to twelve. Thirteen is expressed as *"bakumba igimo,"* meaning "twelve plus one." The decimal alternatives $10 + 3$, $10 + 4$, and $10 + 5$ were also known.

A particular case of the use of addition to compose number words is the duplicative principle whereby both parts are (almost) equal. For instance, among the Sango of Zaire, 7 is expressed as *"na na-thatu"* ($4 + 3$), 8 as *"mnana"* ($4 + 4$), and 9 as *"sano na-na"* ($5 + 4$).

In several African languages, along with additive and multiplicative principles, subtraction has also been used in forming number words. For example, in the Yoruba language of Nigeria, sixteen may be expressed as *"eerin din logun,"* meaning "four until one arrives at twenty."

In those contexts where it was necessary to have number words for relatively large numbers, there often appear completely new number words or ones that express a relationship with the base of the numeration system. For instance, among the Bangongo of Zaire, one says *"kama"* (100), *"lobombo"* (1,000), *"njuku"* (10,000), *"lukuli"* (100,000), and *"losenene"* (1,000,000).

Gesture Numeration

Gesture counting was common among many African peoples. Many variants have been invented. For instance, the Yao of Malawi and Mozambique represent one, two, three, and four by pointing with the thumb of their right hand at one, two, three, or four extended fingers of their left hand. Five is indicated by making a fist with the left hand. Six, seven, eight, and nine are indicated by joining one, two, three, or four extended fingers of the right hand to the left fist. Ten is represented by raising the fingers of both hands and joining the hands. The Shambaa of Tanzania and Kenya use the duplicative principle. They indicate six by extending the three outer fingers of each hand, spread out; seven by showing four on the right hand and three on the left; and eight by showing four on each hand.

To express numbers greater than ten, the Sotho of Lesotho employed different men to indicate the hundreds, tens, and units. For example, to represent 368, the first person raises three fingers of the left hand to represent three hundreds, the second one raises the thumb of the right hand to express six tens, and the third one raises three fingers of

the right hand to express eight units. In fact, here we deal with a positional system, as the position of each man determines whether he indicates units, tens, hundreds, thousands, and so on.

Tally Devices

Many types of tally devices were used in sub-Saharan Africa. An example of using knotted strings can be found among the Makonde of Mozambique and Tanzania; pregnant women tied a knot in a string at each full moon, to keep track of when they were about to give birth. In order to register the age of a person, two strings were used. A knot was tied in the first string at each full moon; once twelve knots had been tied, one knot was tied in a second string to mark the first year and so on.

Other Visual Numeration Systems

A variety of numeration systems in Africa are written in one way or another. The Fulani of Niger and Nigeria place sticks in front of their houses to indicate the number of cows or goats they possess. One hundred animals are represented by two short sticks placed on the ground in the form of a V. Two crossing sticks, X, symbolize fifty animals. Four sticks in a vertical position, | | | |, represent four; two sticks in a horizontal and three in a vertical position, — — | | |, indicate twenty-three animals. For example, the following was found in front of the house of a rich cattle owner:

VVVVVVXII,

showing that he had 652 cows.

The Akan peoples of Côte d'Ivoire, Ghana, and Togo used money weights, that is to say, they used stone or metal figurines or vegetable seeds as coins. Many figurines display graphic signs representing numbers. Although in the languages spoken by the Akan peoples, like Anyi, Baule, Aboure, Attie, and Ebrie, only base ten is used, base five is also found on their money weights:

$$5 = \mathsf{G}$$
$$6 = 5+1 = \mathsf{G}$$
$$7 = 5+2 = \mathsf{G}_c$$
$$8 = 5+3 = \mathsf{G}_\epsilon$$
$$9 = 5+4 = \mathsf{G}_-$$

Duplication may be observed in the transition from one of the expressions for six:

$$6 = \wedge\wedge\wedge$$

347

to an expression of twelve:

$$12 = 6+6 = \text{〰〰〰〰〰}$$

BIBLIOGRAPHY

Gerdes, Paulus. "On Mathematics in the History of Sub-Saharan Africa." *Historia Mathematica* 21 (1994): 345–376.

———, ed. *Numeração em Moçambique.* Maputo, 1993.

Kane, E. A. *Les systèmes de numération parlée des groupes ouest-atlantiques et Mandé: Contribution à la recherche sur les fondements et l'histoire de la pensée logique et mathématique en Afrique de l'ouest.* Lille, 1987.

Zaslavsky, Claudia. *Africa Counts: Number and Pattern in African Culture.* Boston, 1973.

PAULUS GERDES

See also **Geometries.**

NUTRITION

African Food Culture

The main component of a meal in sub-Saharan Africa is a starchy porridge made of tubers or cereals with a stew as accompaniment. The usually thick porridge can be prepared from tubers such as yam, cocoyam, and cassava and cereals such as maize, sorghum, and millet. The stew contains cooked vegetables and, depending on the economic situation of the household, pieces of meat or fish. In practical terms the porridge provides the energy and the stew the quality of the daily diet. In Ethiopia *enjera,* a pancake made from teff (*Eragrostis abyssinica*), is a favorite dish. African cuisine is basically a rural cuisine, derived from a rural way of life. This does not mean that dishes are simple. West Africa in particular is known for its great variety of elaborated fermented maize dishes.

Not all foods are consumed by the various ethnic groups, and food avoidances or food taboos exist. It is useful to make a distinction between permanent and temporary food avoidances. Muslim Africans avoid pork. Other foods may be avoided when they are closely associated with the history of someone's clan, for instance certain kinds of antelope or dogs. The nomadic pastoralists have an aversion for fish, based on a contempt for the way of life of fishing communities. Besides these permanent food avoidances, there are also foods which cannot be consumed during certain critical periods of the life cycle, including infancy and childhood, during pregnancy and lactation, or when suffering from various diseases. Pregnant women may for instance avoid green leafy vegetables out of fear that they may harm the unborn child.

Women play a crucial role in the supply and distribution of food at a household level. Household members will not always eat together from the same dish. Sometimes three eating groups can be observed: men, women and very young children, and the older children under the guidance of an elder sister. Foods are not always equally divided, and men may get the best part of the food, in particular a good piece of meat or fish. This is not necessarily detrimental to the children's nutrition. Women may get a lower intake of proteins, which can lead to a diminishing nutritional status.

In rural areas children are breast-fed up to more than a year. The crucial period for infants is the introduction of weaning foods. At six months or even later the infant will receive a soft carbohydrate pap, while breast-feeding continues. Poor hygienic conditions and the low protein content of the traditional weaning foods cause problems of malnutrition. The expensive, imported, industrially processed infant foods are out of reach for most mothers. In several countries small-scale enterprises have been set up to produce low-cost weaning foods, based on available local materials.

Beverages

Sub-Saharan Africa has an age-old beer tradition. This explains the presence of flourishing modern breweries in many African countries. Beer brewing from sorghum, millet, or maize is traditionally a female activity. Apart from being a pleasant beverage, beer plays an important role in ceremonies. In savanna Africa, when assistance is requested from neighbors in harvesting food crops, beer has to be provided as a compensation. In the forest zones the sugary sap of certain palm trees is drained and left to ferment into palm wine. Ethiopia is well known for its mead, a liquor of fermented honey and water. Coffee is indigenous to the highlands of the Horn of Africa. The preparation of coffee is an important ceremony in Ethiopia.

Ecological Dimensions

The choice and use of available foods has an ecological component. In the humid forest zones the diet is based on roots and tubers, while in the drier zones cereals form the staple of the diet. In the humid tropics milk and dairy products are absent in the traditional diet, because the climate is unfavorable for keeping cattle, while milk and dairy products are part of the diet of the cattle-keeping nomads and cattle-keeping agriculturists of the

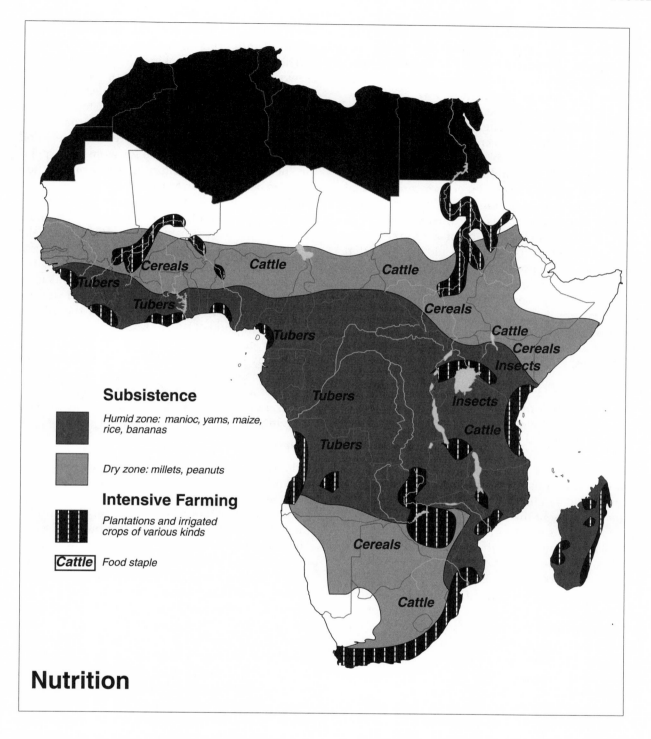

Subsistence

Humid zone: *manioc, yams, maize, rice, bananas*

Dry zone: *millets, peanuts*

Intensive Farming

Plantations and irrigated crops of various kinds

Cattle *Food staple*

Nutrition

sahel and east African highlands. The importance of insects as a food source is often underestimated. Edible insects include caterpillars, flying ants, and grasshoppers or locusts, well known in rural equatorial and eastern Africa. Taxonomically, these insects are not so far removed from shrimps, which are considered a delicacy in Europe and North America.

Seasonality and Food Habits

In regions with a distinct wet and dry season, only one harvest is possible, and rural households have to build up food stocks. Important social events such as marriages will take place after the harvest. A frequent phenomenon is the so-called hungry season, when at the beginning of the wet season food stocks are getting low before the new harvest is available. Households have an already-developed coping strategy for seasonal shortages, involving a decrease in food consumption by reducing the number of meals a day, reducing the portions, and diluting the meals with water. When the shortage lasts longer, nonconventional foods will be consumed, known as "hungry foods." In the savanna zones it is not unusual for groups of women to search for seeds of wild grasses, tubers, and wild fruits, which would not be eaten otherwise. Sometimes the seasonal food shortage may last longer than could have been foreseen. Households may then turn to an extremely hazardous measure: the consumption of seeds reserved for sowing and planting. Rules of hospitality such as offering food and local beer will disappear at such times.

Changing Food Habits

The food habits of a society are never static. A major aspect of the dynamics of food consumption is the diffusion and acceptance of new foods in the past and at present. For Africa it has been estimated that 50 percent of the major food crops originated from the Americas, for instance cassava, maize, tomatoes, and condiments such as red peppers (*Capsicum*). At present the main forces in changing African food habits are the monetization of rural areas, population growth, and the process of rapid urbanization.

With modern economic development, agriculture is often directed toward cash crops and marketing. This process may have harmful side effects on the local diet. Nutritious food crops are likely to be replaced by cash crops such as cotton, cocoa, or coffee. Another danger is a weakening of the old farmers' wisdom: build up a food stock after the harvest.

Population growth has two main effects on food habits: more mouths have to be fed and less fuelwood is available for cooking. In many African countries population growth has caused a shift from indigenous food crops such as sorghum, millet, and yam to cassava and maize. Cassava and maize give a higher yield in food energy per acre but are less nutritious than yam, sorghum, and millet. And with more people to feed, the stew,

once richly provided with meat or fish, can become a thin watery gruel with a few vegetables only.

The main fuel for cooking in most households is wood, supplemented with crop residues and sometimes animal dung. Wood collecting is predominantly a task for women, assisted by their children. Present population growth surpasses the natural increase in wood. Decreasing fuelwood availability means more time for women to spend on the heavy task of collecting. Food preparation will also be affected. In Malawi, for example, economizing on fuel caused a substitution of vegetables for pulses in the diet, which need much less cooking energy. Such a substitution implies a gradually diminishing protein intake, which in the long run may lead to a weakening nutritional status. Other reactions to the lack of fuelwood are the consumption of cold or warmed-up leftovers and the use of already prepared foods for sale in the village. The consumption of cold or insufficiently warmed-up leftovers, stored under poor hygienic conditions, may cause diarrheal diseases. Diarrhea may lead to malabsorption of nutrients, dehydration, and mortality. The use of already prepared foods in rural areas will add to an increase in the cost of living.

The Effects of Urbanization

Urbanization affects food patterns in two ways: urban influences modify food habits in the rural areas and new food patterns develop in the cities. Urban food habits include a greater demand for imported foods such as wheat (for bread, biscuits, and other products based on wheat), canned meat and fish, powdered milk and milk products, hard liquor, bottled beer, and soft drinks. (The success of the various kinds of soft drinks is striking.) The urbanite is receptive to new foods that are quick and easy to prepare, requiring less fuel. It is a challenge for the local food industry to develop African food products suited to an urban way of life.

Urban food habits comprise three components. First, rural culinary traditions are still strong at the household level; outside the household the social pressure of the urban environment prevails. Second, food habits are influenced by working conditions and by people with different ethnic backgrounds. A third component is the possibility for more individual food choices. In the city one can select food outside the household, without the constraint of having to share expensive foods with others.

The increasing demand for food by a growing urban population has stimulated the development of street foods: ready-to-eat foods and beverages prepared and sold by vendors and hawkers in streets and public places. Women play a major role in the urban food supply, and street foods are largely the domain of women. Prepared meat and meat snacks, however, are mainly sold by men. Street foods are well suited to the needs of poorer consumers. They are ready to eat, which means saving time and fuel, and they are often less expensive than the same foods prepared at home. For poor urban households it can be more economical to purchase street foods than to prepare food on a daily basis. A point of concern remains the hygiene and quality of the street foods.

Despite insufficient employment, overcrowding, inadequate cooking facilities, and expensive housing, comparisons with country folk show that urbanites have a more varied diet, with a greater assortment of fruits and vegetables, more meat, and less seasonal variation. The situation may differ from country to country, and between those living in the shantytowns and in the planned urban districts.

An interesting development in the francophone cities is the emergence of a new type of restaurant, the *maquis*, offering African dishes to local middle-class customers, sometimes with a touch of French culinary art. In African cities new food habits and new kinds of foods are continually being incorporated into the local food culture. Despite this, the modern urban diet remains in essence an African diet.

BIBLIOGRAPHY

Bricas, Nicolas, et al. *Nourrir les villes en Afrique subsaharienne.* Paris, 1985.

Garine, Igor de, and George Koppert. "Coping with Seasonal Fluctuations in Food Supply Among Savanna Populations: The Massa and Mussey of Chad and Cameroon." In *Coping with Uncertainty in Food Supply,* edited by Igor de Garine and Geoffrey A. Harrison. Oxford, 1988.

Goody, Jack. "The Impact of the World System." In *Cooking, Cuisine, and Class: A Study in Comparative Sociology,* by Jack Goody. Cambridge, 1982.

Hladik, Claude M., Serge Bahuchet, and Igor de Garine, eds. *Food and Nutrition in the African Rain Forest.* Paris, 1990.

Van Liere, Marti J., Inge D. Brouwer, and A. P. den Hartog. "A Food Ethnography of the Otammari in North-Western Benin: A Systematic Approach." *Ecology of Food and Nutrition* 34, no. 4 (1996): 293–310.

Webster, David J. "The Political Economy of Food Production and Nutrition in Southern Africa in Historical Perspective." *Journal of Modern African Studies* 24, no. 3 (1986): 447–463.

ADEL P. DEN HARTOG

See also **Agriculture; Animals, Domestic; Food; Fuel; Hunger and Famine.**

NWAPA, FLORA (b. c. 1931; d. 1993), Nigerian writer. Flora Nwapa was born at Oguta in eastern Nigeria. She received her primary and secondary education at Archdeacon Crowther's Memorial Girls School and CMS Girls School in Lagos, took an arts degree at University College, Lagos, in 1957, and in 1958 was awarded a diploma in education at Edinburgh University. Upon returning to Nigeria she took a post as a women's education officer and subsequently accepted positions as a teacher of English and geography at Queen's School, Enugu, and as assistant registrar at the University of Lagos. Following the Biafran War, Nwapa served for five years on the East Central State Executive Council. She published her first novel, *Efuru*, in 1966. Published in London by Heinemann, *Efuru* is a portrait of a fiercely independent Igbo (Ibo) woman who secures a respected place in her rural society, not as a wife and mother but as an autonomous trader and a devotee, eventually a priestess, of Uhamiri, the divine lady of the lake. It was the first English novel to be published by a black African woman and thus marks Nwapa's dual significance as one of Nigeria's most important novelists and as a foundational figure in African women's writing. In addition to *Efuru*, Nwapa has published four novels: *Idu* (London, 1970), *One Is Enough* (Enugu, 1981), *Women Are Different* (Enugu, 1986), and *The Lake Goddess* (Trenton, N.J., 1995). She has also authored *Never Again*, a memoir of the Biafran War (Enugu, 1975); two collections of short stories, *This Is Lagos, and Other Stories* (Enugu, 1971) and *Wives at War, and Other Stories* (Enugu, 1980); and numerous books for children. Nwapa was also a publisher. In 1977, discontented with the Euro-American monopoly on the publication of African literature, Nwapa established her own publishing house, Tana Press, which was dedicated to publishing works by African women and books for children. The entrepreneurial spirit that animated Nwapa's decision to establish the Tana Press, a spirit that emerged from her conviction that African women could liberate themselves only by securing their economic independence, weds one of the central achievements of Nwapa's life to the social ethic and aspiration of many of her characters. The recipient of numerous awards during her lifetime (including the Officer of the Order of the Niger in 1982 and the Ife Merit Award for Authorship and Publishing in 1985), Nwapa died of pneumonia on 16 October 1993.

IAN BAUCOM

See also **Literature.**

NYAKYUSA. The Nyakyusa (Niakiusa) settled in what is now Tanzania between 1550 and 1650, in an area bordered by Mount Rungwe in the north, the Songwe River in the south, and Lake Malawi (Lake Nyasa) in the east. They called the region Unyakyusa; it is now called Mbeya. They speak a Bantu dialect called Inyakyusa and are related to the Ngonde and the Kinga (most of the Nyakyusa chiefs were originally from the Kinga).

Unlike the other ethnic groups around Lake Malawi, the Nyakyusa developed an elaborate sociopolitical system that encompassed three separate and distinct village formations: one group shared land rights in common; a second was based on allegiance to a particular chief; and the third is known as the "age village."

In the age-village system, boys leave their homes at puberty and move away to start their own villages. Until they are married, they return to their villages daily to work with their fathers and to eat with their mothers. Under British colonial rule, the system of age villages was greatly weakened.

Each Nyakyusa village has a headman appointed by the district chief. There is no single central authority, but rather a council of chiefs. Belief in an afterlife, a fear of death, a fear of the "breath of men" (the action of witchcraft), and belief in the supernatural powers of divine monarchs constitute the traditional religion of the Nyakyusa. They have many ceremonies to purify the land and to ensure posterity. Within the family the brother, then the elder son, inherits the land and wife or wives. Because of the high bridewealth and polygyny, there develops an imbalance between single men and single women in which most women are married but most men are not. Village economy rests on agriculture, both for subsistence and cash cropping, as well as trade in iron, cloth, pottery, and salt.

BIBLIOGRAPHY

Wilson, Monica Hunter. *Good Company: A Study of Nyakyusa Age-Villages.* London, 1951.

———. *Rituals of Kinship Among the Nyakyusa.* London, 1970.

GARY THOULOUIS

NYERERE, JULIUS KAMBARAGE (b. 1922), nationalist leader and president of Tanzania (1962–1985). *Mwalimu* (teacher), as Nyerere is popularly known in Tanzania because of his original profession, led the nationalist struggle for the independence of Tanganyika from British rule. Independent in thought and innovative in his actions, he has based his political career on the pursuit of liberation and social advancement in Africa.

Julius Kambarage Nyerere, 1963. AP/WIDE WORLD

In the early days of independence, Nyerere, like many of his contemporaries, believed in the variously defined African socialism. In the late 1960s and early 1970s, he relentlessly and single-mindedly pursued a policy of *ujaamaa* (socialism and self-reliance) in Tanzania. Despite its proclaimed intentions, this policy resulted in the disruption and dislocation of agricultural production, neglect of industry, and intensification of external dependence. Nyerere refused to acknowledge these failures.

Nyerere also had some notable successes. Propelled by his unwavering commitment to social justice, he supported liberation struggles in southern Africa and beyond and turned Dar es Salaam into the haven of liberation movements in Africa. In the 1970s Nyerere was one of the most articulate and committed believers in global interdependence and a defender of the developing world's failed quest for a New International Economic Order. He later became the first chairman of the South Commission, established in 1987. The commission's primary task was to study the many problems and common experiences of the southern countries and draw lessons for regional cooperation with the hope of attaining a collective self-reliance.

Although Nyerere established authoritarian rule in Tanzania, many who perceive him as a benevolent dictator believe that he was driven by good but misguided intentions. Others believe that he was essentially Machiavellian. In any case, his personal integrity is generally acknowledged. He became converted to democracy and multiparty rule after he relinquished the presidency. He is skeptical about party proliferation, however, and is equally suspicious of Western motives in making democracy a condition for economic aid. In retirement, as "Father of the Nation," Nyerere has agitated for prudent and honest government as well as fair play in politics.

Nyerere has written extensively on political and social issues and has remained an ardent defender of developing world interests. He has consistently opposed the International Monetary Fund and World Bank structural adjustment policies. Nyerere has been a tireless fighter for African freedom, dignity, and global social justice. Ironically, his passion for these goals has frequently clouded his judgment on how to attain them. He became a lone crusader mainly because he had little tolerance for criticism and dissent.

BIBLIOGRAPHY

Duggan, William Redman, and John R. Civille. *Tanzania and Nyerere.* Maryknoll, N.Y., 1976.

Hatch, John Charles. *Two African Statesmen: Kaunda of Zambia and Nyerere of Tanzania.* Chicago, 1976.

Nyerere, Julius. *Freedom and Unity.* London, 1967.

———. *Freedom and Socialism.* Dar es Salaam, Tanzania, 1968.

———. *Freedom and Development.* London, 1974.

———. *Crusade for Liberation.* Dar es Salaam, Tanzania, 1978.

Smith, William Edgett. *We Must Run While They Walk: A Portrait of Africa's Julius Nyerere.* New York, 1971.

MWESIGA BAREGU

See also **Independence Movements; Nationalism; Postcolonial State.**

O

OBASANJO, OLUSEGUN (b. 1937), Nigerian statesman. Born in Abeokuta, Ogun State, Obasanjo was educated at Baptist Boys' High School, Abeokuta. He enlisted in the Nigerian army in 1958 and received his military training at the Mons Officers' Cadet School, Aldershot, England, and at other military institutions in Britain and India. He was commissioned second lieutenant in the Nigerian Army in 1959 and achieved the rank of general by 1979. Obasanjo served in the Congo (later called Zaire) in 1960 and in the Nigerian civil war (1967–1970). As commander of the Third Marine Commando Division, he took the surrender of the Biafran forces in January 1970. In 1973 Obasanjo was appointed federal minister of works and housing, and in 1975 as chief of staff (Supreme Headquarters). He was head of state of the Federal Republic of Nigeria (1976–1979) and has the distinction of being the only Nigerian leader, to date, who has willingly relinquished power at the end of his tenure. Obasanjo is a member of the Inter Action Council of Former Heads of States and Governments, member and cochairman of the Commonwealth Eminent Persons Group on South Africa, and founder and chairman of the Africa Leadership Forum and Foundation. Obasanjo's numerous published books include *My Command* (1980), an account of his experiences in the Nigerian civil war. He was arrested in Lagos in March 1995 on the charge of concealment of treason and, after a secret trial, was sentenced to life imprisonment (later commuted to fifteen years).

Olusegun Obasanjo, 1986. UPI/CORBIS-BETTMANN

BIBLIOGRAPHY

Eke, Kenoye Kelvin. *Nigeria's Foreign Policy Under Two Military Governments, 1966–1979: An Analysis of the Gowan and Muhammed/Obasanjo Regimes.* Lewiston, N.Y., 1990.

A. L. MABOGUNJE

See also **Military Governments and Armies; Post-colonial State.**

OBOTE, MILTON (b. 1924), two-time president of Uganda. Apollo Milton Obote, born near Akoroko, studied at Makere University in Kampala for one year before he was expelled by colonial officials for political activity. He worked in Kenya as a laborer and salesman, joining Kenya's nationalist political organizations in the early 1950s, at the time of the Mau Mau uprising. Upon his return to Uganda, Obote became active in the Uganda National Congress Party (UNCP) and set up local branches in his home area.

Elected to the newly formed Legislative Council in 1958, Obote was critical of British colonial policy. When the UNCP split the next year, Obote established the Uganda People's Congress (UPC) to oppose the traditionalist-royalist Kabaka Yekka (KY) party, which sought to reestablish the Buganda Kingdom, the largest and most influential of Uganda's kingdoms. After the UPC's defeat in 1961, however, the party formed a loose alliance with KY, and Obote was elected prime minister under the colonial government in early 1962. Independence was granted later that year, and a quasi-federal system was established with the Bugandan king, Mutesa II, as president and Obote as prime minister. In this post Obote was important in organizing the East African Community.

Accused of gold smuggling with army officer Idi Amin in 1966, Obote moved to consolidate power, suspending the constitution and declaring himself executive president. He managed to rule Uganda without Bugandan support by using the army to dismantle the kingdom and force Mutesa into exile. Though the army was his means of centralizing power, it twice proved his undoing. He alienated the military with his political shift to the left, announcing the Common Man's Charter in 1969 and the nationalization of 60 percent of the foreign interests in 1970.

While Obote was out of the country in 1972, Idi Amin escaped house arrest, led an army coup, and took over the government. Obote, exiled in Tanzania, returned to Uganda after the Tanzania People's Defense Force pushed Amin's army out of the Kagera Salient and Amin's regime fell in 1979. Obote was elected president of Uganda in 1980. He faced the difficult task of reviving a ruined economy and restoring order to a lawless country

Milton Obote declares victory of his Uganda People's Congress party in the 1980 parliamentary elections. AP/WIDE WORLD

in the wake of Amin's mass killings and deportations. Unable to control an increasingly ruthless army and faced with a rebellion led by 1980 electoral contender Yoweri Museveni, Obote lost favor with Ugandans. He was deposed in 1985 by the army (which was in turn overthrown in 1986 by Museveni's National Resistance Army). Obote escaped to exile in Zambia.

BIBLIOGRAPHY

Ingham, Kenneth. *Obote: A Political Biography.* London, 1994.

THOMAS F. McDOW

See also **Amin Dada, Idi; Museveni, Yoweri.**

ODINGA, OGINGA (Jaramogi; b. 1911; d. 1994), Kenyan nationalist and politician. Odinga, born at Nyamira Kango, Kenya, graduated from Makerere University College in 1939 and became a teacher. He is the author of *Not Yet Uhuru,* published in 1967.

Odinga was a nationalist who spearheaded Kenya's struggle for independence from the British. He remained a central figure in the country's political development and was a statesman committed to democratic governance, as attested to by his struggle for multiparty politics.

A founding member of the Nationalist Party that formed the first postcolonial government, Odinga served as the country's first vice president. In 1966 he resigned from government and formed an opposition party, the Kenya People's Union. In 1969 the party was banned and Odinga was detained. In 1988 he formed the National Democratic Party, which was denied registration by the state. Odinga did not give up his quest for political pluralism, however. In 1990 he founded the Forum for the Restoration of Democracy (FORD), and transformed it into a political party in 1992. Odinga was a presidential candidate in the 1992 elections, and was the official leader of the opposition in Parliament and chairman of the Public Accounts Committee until his death at Kisumu, Kenya.

BIBLIOGRAPHY

African Perspectives, no. 1 (September–October 1977).
Gertzel, Cherry J. *The Politics of Independent Kenya 1963–68.* Evanston, Ill., 1970.
Gertzel, Cherry, Maure Goldschmidt, and Don Rothchild, eds. *Government and Politics in Kenya: A Nation-Building Text.* Nairobi, 1969.

Oginga Odinga. COURTESY PETER WANYANDE

Goldsworthy, David. *Tom Mboya, the Man Kenya Wanted to Forget.* Nairobi, 1982.

PETER WANYANDE

OGBOMOSO. The second-largest town in Yorubaland, Ogbomoso was founded sometime between 1680 and 1720. It attracted a number of refugees after the early-nineteenth-century collapse of Oyo, and by 1850 it had become a cosmopolitan town and the most important commercial center between Ilorin and Oyo, thirty miles north of Ibadan. The arrival in 1854 of Thomas Jefferson Bowen, of the Southern American Baptist Convention, later transformed Ogbomoso into a major center of Christian evangelism and educational development.

Located in the semisavanna region, its increasing population prospered on the cultivation and marketing of food rather than cash crops. As the colonial railways bypassed Ogbomoso, Oshogbo soon replaced it as the commercial center. Ogbomoso tried cotton unsuccessfully, then tobacco, but could not stem the tide of large-scale emigration of its people, who became well-known traders in other Nigerian cities such as Oshogbo, Lagos, Jos, and Kano, as well as abroad in Ghana and Côte d'Ivoire.

The Christian presence in what would otherwise have been a major Islamic center is remarkable. Ogbomoso and its environs are today home to more than four hundred churches, a theological seminary, and a famous Baptist hospital, not to mention a number of small- and medium-scale industries, a farm settlement, and a university founded in 1992.

BIBLIOGRAPHY

Ayegboyin, D. I. "Baptist Mission Enterprise at Ogbomoso, 1855–1915: Analysis of the Social Significance of Mission." M. A. diss., University of Ibadan, 1983.

Whirley, Carlton F. *The Baptists of Nigeria: A Story to Tell.* Nashville, Tenn., 1988.

S. ADEMOLA AJAYI

OGUNDE, HUBERT ADEDEJI (b. 1916; d. 1990), Nigerian actor, playwright, and acclaimed doyen of modern popular Yoruba theater. Ogunde was born in Ososa in Ogun State of Nigeria, where he was educated. He was a pupil teacher in Ijebu-Ode from 1932 to 1940. He served in the Nigerian police force from 1941 to 1945, after which he established the Ogunde Theatre and the Ogunde Record Companies in 1946. He later expanded his scope with the establishment in 1966 of the Ogunde Dance Company and the Ogunde Film Company. He wrote and presented over fifty plays in addition to several films. His folk opera and musical morality plays performed in Yoruba are frequently seen on stage, television, and cinema houses in all parts of Nigeria.

Ogunde founded and became president of the Nigerian Dramatists and Playwrights Association. He was also a founding member of the Association of Nigerian Theatre Artists. Until his death, he led the Nigerian National Troupe. He was honored in 1982 with membership in the Order of the Niger (MON), and the Universities of Ife and Lagos awarded him honorary degrees in 1985 and 1986 respectively.

Hubert Adedeji Ogunde, 1965. UPI/CORBIS-BETTMANN

BIBLIOGRAPHY

Clark, Ebun. *Hubert Ogunde: The Making of Nigerian Theatre.* London, 1979.

C. OGBOGBO

See also **Popular Culture; Theater.**

OLYMPIO, SYLVANUS EPIPHANIO (b. 1902; d. 1963), first president of Togo. Sylvanus Olympio is a significant figure in African history because he was the first president of an independent country to be overthrown by the wave of military coups of the late 1960s. His career flourished at the height of African optimism, and his violent end marked the beginning of African disillusionment.

Born to a wealthy family, he was educated in the German system prevalent in Togo and studied at the University of Vienna and the London School of Economics and Political Science. He had a successful career with the United Africa Company, rising to district manager for Togo, a post he held from 1928 to 1938. At that time, it was the highest post held by an African working for a colonial multinational company.

He entered politics, was banished from Togo, but returned after World War II when President Charles de Gaulle of France allowed elections in French African colonies. Olympio was president of the Territorial Assembly from 1946 to 1952, when his party lost power to the Parti Togolais du Progrès (PTP), which was supported by the colonial authorities.

Olympio came to power again in 1958 and campaigned for Togolese independence, which was achieved in 1960. In 1961 he was elected first president of the new republic. His authoritarian rule, coupled with austerity measures taken to balance the budget, made him unpopular in some quarters. Because his government was largely composed of Ewe people from southern Togo, northerners felt they were excluded. Juvento, a radical branch of his party, wanted Togo to cut itself off from France completely, while Olympio was attempting to bring in foreign investment (there was significant investment in the phosphate industry in 1962), and he suppressed Juvento's leaders ruthlessly. Finally, he refused the army's demands for more pay and more personnel, and it was the army's enmity that destroyed him. He was killed on 13 January 1963 as he was running to the American Embassy in Lomé.

Sylvanus Epiphanio Olympio, first president of Togo; shown here in 1963. AP/WIDE WORLD

BIBLIOGRAPHY

Kokouvi Agbobli, Atsutse. *Sylvanus Olympio: Un destin tragique.* Abidjan, Côte d'Ivoire, 1992.

ALEXANDER GOLDMAN

See also **Togo.**

ORACLES. *See* **Divination and Oracles.**

ORAL CULTURE AND ORAL TRADITION. The concept of African "oral culture" is closely related to "oral literature" and "oral tradition." Whereas oral literature designates the various forms of literature delivered by word of mouth, the broader notion of "oral culture" shifts the focus away from the product, that is, the text, and includes the historical circumstances and the social setting in which the delivery of the oral text takes place. In addition, oral culture refers to all practices and habits related to the use of the spoken word and draws attention to the consistency of the practices of oral communication. In what follows, the various products of oral culture will be referred to as oral literature, whereas the term "performance" designates the actual delivery of the oral text.

Oral tradition is an essential component of a society's oral culture. All societies need to pass down their cultural heritage and human experience to succeeding generations. In many African cultures, this body of inherited human experiences, insights, and customs is passed down through the spoken word. Both the process of oral transmission and its results, the oral texts, are called "oral tradition." The crucial defining characteristic of an oral tradition text is that it has been passed on by word of mouth over at least one generation. Oral tradition text does not deal exclusively with past events and practices. In some contemporary African societies, the relevance of oral tradition to major parts of the population is even higher than written historical evidence is to the societies of contemporary Europe and the United States.

From the late nineteenth century on, European colonial officials and travelers collected African oral texts, such as songs, tales, riddles, and proverbs. In the view of these Europeans, only written texts constituted literature and were acknowledged as works of art; as they saw it, written texts required a higher level of sophistication from both their creators and their consumers. In contrast, the collected texts of oral performances were seen not as products of an African artistic imagination but as "mere folklore." One reason for this initial condescending view was that Europeans were used to distinguishing between a "high" culture of the educated European elites, which they associated with the written word, and a "low" culture of the popular masses, a population that did not read and write. Ruth Finnegan's 1970 book, *Oral Literature in Africa,* marked an important departure from this view because it acknowledged oral art as a form of literature. Today, there is a widely shared agreement that oral performances are a form of literature. To distinguish written language from spoken texts, some authors refer to the latter as "orature."

However, scholarly discussions of the late 1990s were still reminiscent of the earlier condescending view. One example is the controversy over the differences between "literate" cultures that rely strongly on written texts and "oral cultures" whose practices are mostly shaped by oral communication. Some authors argue that the use of written texts invests a society with higher skills of technological innovation and of the rationalization of everyday life. The problem with this view is that it tends to emphasize differences between orality and literacy and to see them as opposites, thereby neglecting the fact that the "use" and the mental implications of either written or oral texts can be understood only in consideration of their actual relevance and use in a specific society.

Classification of Oral Literature

No general agreement exists on the classification of the diverse kinds of oral literature. This is partly because for many oral literature forms, no clear-cut demarcation can be drawn. Scholars classify oral literature according to various criteria, such as the form and the structural composition of oral art forms, their themes, the situation in which they are delivered, and their social use. To follow the classifications that the people themselves establish is not always useful, because these classifications rarely respond to the Western search for neat differentiation and clearly bounded classificatory concepts. Also, similar to nonscholarly definitions of literature in the West, within one African community various criteria (such as content, setting, purpose of the performance, and musical accompaniment) may not always be used in a consistent way to distinguish between different oral art forms.

Thus, it is important to keep in mind that the following categories are not intended as clearly delineated categories, but that they should facilitate our approach to the diverse oral art forms. Important types of oral art are songs; recitations (chants); poetry (art forms in which language is subject to certain rules of tonal and rhythmic patterning); epics and other narratives that deal with a real or imaginary past; dramatic and musical forms in which actors enact and represent ideas and symbolic figures (these productions often accompanied by rhythmic or melodic instruments); and, finally, concise verbal expressions reflecting the speaker's rhetorical and intellectual competence, such as puns, proverbs, and riddles. (This classification comes close to Isidore Okpewho's characterization.) Many of these forms of oral artistry belong to the body of a society's oral tradition.

In societies such as the Akan of Ghana and the Yoruba in Nigeria, some dramatic forms and proverbs are played on the "talking drums" that imitate the tonal patterns of human speech.

Functions of Oral Art

Depending on the cultural community in which they are created and performed, oral art forms serve a wide array of functions. Some are performed in ceremonies of sacrifice and worship. Another frequent function is the enhancement of the public renown of an individual or a group on whose behalf a song or recitation is performed. Other oral art forms, or slightly revised versions of the same art form, may serve to distract, amuse, and even to educate the audience on formal occasions (such as official celebrations of communal interest) or informal gatherings of friends or family members. The performance of a particular art form is sometimes restricted to female or male artists.

During a performance, many senses are activated simultaneously and complementarily. Visual and aural aspects are essential elements of the performance. Also, the contents of the perfomer's speech are often less important than the ways in which it is presented. Thus, members of the audience might declare that a performance was particularly well done, not because of what the oral artist said but because of how he or she said it. Oral art forms include, in varying degrees, musical accompaniment and rhetorical improvisation. The oral artist also draws on paralinguistic resources, means of expression that do not rely on the spoken word, to highlight aspects of the performance. The most frequent paralinguistic resources are body movements, gestures, and the use of implements. Dancing is another effective way to underscore the importance of key narrated events and to enhance the visual and dramatic impression of the performance. In performances of some oral art forms, such as the recitation of heroic legends and epics, the musical accompaniment increases the aesthetic complexity of the performance. The accompanying instruments may offer another rhythmic pattern and thus provide a kind of counterpoint to the rhythm of the spoken word. Also, musical accompaniment may stress certain verbal expressions or add to the meaning of the spoken text. For instance, the recitation of the heroic epic of Sundjata Keïta, the legendary warrior king of the medieval Mali empire of the western Sudan, gives ample opportunities to the oral artist to enrich his speech through the rhythm. The performer accompanying his recitation on a stringed instrument may suddenly change the rhythm and play the pattern associated with the hero Sundjata or with one of his followers. These rhythmic allusions are not only a tribute to past heroes but also a gesture of praise and flattery directed to their descendants, who may well be in the audience.

Stylistic Techniques

Like written literature, oral literature displays a wide range of stylistic techniques to embellish or highlight certain aspects of the recounted story or the performed song. Important stylistic features are the use of parallel or chiastic sentence construction; the repetition of key words or sentences, such as the attributes of a main protagonist; the manipulation of vocal sounds to establish a tonal counterpoint; and the successive arrangement of lines that transfers key expressions from one line to the following line. Especially the use of metaphors, allusions, symbols, and onomatopoeic words adds to the performance's sensual and dramatic effects on the listeners' imaginations. In texts of oral tradition, specific techniques are often employed to help the artist remember the text and rhythmic patterning. Among these are cueing, scanning, and the use of mnemonic devices, such as a metaphor representing a particular idea, personality, or event.

Performers of Oral Art

In all societies, there are women and men with extraordinary memories and rhetorical talents. They are particularly well placed to retain and pass down many details of local history and thus to be repositories of oral tradition and history. For these skills they will be highly respected, especially if they combine their erudition with musical talents. Some of them may acquire a widespread reputation as an eminent artist, whereas others will be known only in their home community. In some societies, oral artists do not make a living from their performances, and their artistic activity is not considered a profession. In other societies, however, oral artists belong to a professional group whose members specialize in social communication and the management of social relations. For example, the griots of the western Sudan belong to a separate social group whose members combine various tasks of social mediation with their mastery of the word.

Whether they are members of a specialized group or not, men and women have to be genuinely talented to fulfill the requirements of oral artistry. The mastery of the spoken word requires a high competence in performance skills, and the future artist will therefore go through a long period of training. During that time the apprentice is often affiliated with an artist considered to be a master of the spoken or chanted word. The apprenticeship and training vary in the degree of organization. Apprentices often learn their skills—such as the memorization of large bodies of text, the learning of rhetorical techniques and idioms, or the accompaniment of their chants on an instrument—by imitating or accompanying their master. Their training is not restricted to formally declared instruction sessions. Therefore, Western researchers, who are accustomed to the formalized instructional setting of the Western school system, may not immediately recognize a training event.

Early research on African oral art portrayed it as the unsophisticated outgrowth of African peoples' cultural inventory. This view tended to underestimate the imprint that individual performers leave on a work of art. It is therefore important to note that oral art is not the product of an anonymous populace but reflects the individual techniques and performance skills of particular artists. Even where oral art forms demand the artist's "faithful" delivery of historical events or of a group's cultural heritage, the performer enjoys a certain freedom of artistic improvisation, rearrangement, and innovation. This does not exclude the possibility that a particular work of oral art—for instance, a song—may lose over time, through its repetition and reinterpretation by other artists, the personal imprint of its original composer. Therefore, the concept of an "original" and "authentic" version makes no sense in relation to many works of oral art.

Differences Between Oral and Written Literature

Among the most important differences between written and oral literature is that any work of oral art is created in the presence of and in interaction with an audience. Spectators and listeners usually interject comments and statements of approval or disapproval, and thus force the performer to readjust the course and the contents of the performance in consideration of their responses. Performers do not consider audience interventions as an impediment to the delivery of the "authentic" version of the piece, song, or text. On the contrary, they recognize the audience's contribution to the performance as one of its constitutive elements and a sign of the audience's sustained attention. Many performers acknowledge the audience's importance in their speech or chant. An artist is often assisted by other performers who may structure and enrich the performance through melodic or rhythmic accompaniment or, as speakers, regularly insert remarks of approval and encouragement. The fact that the performing artists constantly readjust the textual, musical, and paralinguistic features of the performance to the expectations of the audience implies that the artists do not merely deliver a work of art, but instantaneously create it during the performance. Repetitions of the performance will often result in different versions of the same piece. The fluid nature of oral art forms and the participation of the audience in the creation of the work of art are clear differences from written literature.

There are also substantial differences between written and oral literature in the degree to which the social situation of the author has an effect on the qualities and contents of the work of art. Performers of oral literature are dependent to a greater degree on the social setting in which they live and perform. The artist creates the work of art in interaction with the audience, and the particular position of the performer in society will be more evidently reflected in the work of art than in a written form. Therefore, any interpretation of the oral art has to take into consideration the circumstances in which the performer lives and works. Appreciation of the sociopolitical situation of the performer will enhance the understanding of the social and political relevance of the performance.

In contrast to the widespread assumption that African oral literature reflects the communal spirit of a traditional African society, oral performances usually display the views of particular groups or of individuals. Because oral texts are fluid and open to improvisation, they may be used for purposes of political domination and legitimation, but also to express criticism and mockery. The political relevance of oral performance is particularly evident in texts that deal with an imaginary or real past and are part of a society's body of oral tradition. For example, during the performance of historical narratives, the performing artists may not explicitly say so, but often they voice the interests of particular members of the audience. Therefore, to grasp the subtleties of the text and historical accounts, one must determine the historical situation in which they were delivered and that gave rise to the reinterpretation of previous versions.

Another limitation of oral tradition as historical evidence is that not all historical details survive the process of transmission: some details may be repeatedly left out by the performer and thus will be lost over time. There are usually several people in a society who pass on accounts of past events to the next generation. As a result, some current oral traditions are the product of several earlier versions that have been fused into a single narrative. Because many historical accounts lack a consistent chronology, they render the absolute dating of events and personalities difficult. Also, the independent confirmation of events through other oral sources is often hard, if not impossible. Finally, some historical accounts have a symbolic, rather than a "factual," significance—they may express certain norms and attitudes rather than report the observation of real events. For all these reasons, oral history has to be interpreted carefully when used as a historical record.

Oral Arts and Patronage

In the past, many oral historians and artists lived as clients of wealthy patron families whose interests they were expected to express and defend in exchange for the patron's provision of certain goods and services. Many royal families provided food, housing, and protection for oral artists and their families. One task of eminent political significance was management of the reputation of royal patrons. For example, the *umusizi* at the royal courts of Rwanda would, on occasions of public importance, laud the legendary past and the achievements of current members of the patron family. These public displays of the royal family's power and prestige contributed importantly to the maintenance and the legitimation of the family's leadership position. Among the Xhosa and the Zulu in southern Africa, the *imbongi* specialized in enhancing the prestige of the ruler. At public events, he reported the history of the royal family, yet presented it as if this account reflected the past of the entire community. In some societies, the tasks of remembering and of passing down traditions were divided between different individuals or families of specialists.

Today, there are still many oral artists who perform on behalf of patron families or individuals. Since the imposition of colonial rule, processes of economic, political, social, and technological change have undermined the basis of these patronage relations and thus have altered the working conditions for oral artists. The artists can no longer count on material support from patrons because the latter have lost much of their wealth and political influence. These changes have seriously altered the social position, tasks, and recognition of many artists, as well as their influence as managers of public opinion. However, the revolution in communications technology has not always been to the disadvantage of these representatives of African oral culture. For instance, in the cities of Guinea, Senegal, Gambia, and Mali, some griots who in the past performed on behalf of patron families have resourcefully adapted to the new working conditions and especially to the availability of broadcasting technology. Their songs and historical narratives are broadcast on television and on national and international radio stations. They reach even remote rural areas because their performances are widely circulated on cassette tapes. As a consequence, some of these artists have become highly successful pop stars, sometimes achieving international renown.

BIBLIOGRAPHY

Finnegan, Ruth H. *Oral Literature in Africa.* London, 1970.
Goody, Jack. *The Domestication of the Savage Mind.* Cambridge and New York, 1977.
Miller, Joseph C. Introduction to *The African Past Speaks: Essays on Oral Tradition and History.* Folkestone, Eng., and Hamden, Conn., 1980.
Okpewho, Isidore. *African Oral Literature: Backgrounds, Character, and Community.* Bloomington, Ind., 1992.
Street, Brian V. *Literacy in Theory and Practice.* Cambridge and New York, 1984.
Tonkin, Elizabeth. *Narrating Our Pasts: The Social Construction of Oral History.* Cambridge and New York, 1992.
Vansina, Jan. *Oral Tradition: A Study in Historical Methodology,* translated by H. M. Wright. Chicago, 1965.
———. *Oral Tradition as History.* Madison, Wis., 1985.

DOROTHEA E. SCHULZ

See also **Dance; Epics and Epic Poetry; Historiography; Music and Song; Myth and Cosmology.**

ORGANIZATION OF AFRICAN UNITY. The Organization of African Unity (OAU) is the symbol, embodiment, and culmination of the various Pan-African movements that originated in the black diaspora between 1900 and 1945. The leading

OAU Secretariat, Addis Ababa, Ethiopia. COURTESY OF ORGANIZATION
OF AFRICAN UNITY

figures of these movements were African Americans, West Indians, and Africans: W. E. B. Du Bois, the father of Pan-Africanism and the driving spirit of the Pan-African Congresses (1900, 1919, 1921, 1923, 1927, 1945); Henry Sylvester Williams; Marcus Garvey (Universal Negro Improvement Association); George Padmore; and Kwame Nkrumah (the first president of Ghana). It was after the 1945 Pan-African Congress in Manchester, England, that Pan-Africanism took on an African dimension aimed at self-government and independence. However, between the 1900 Pan-African Congress and the historic Conference of Independent African States in Addis Ababa, Ethiopia, in 1963, which led to the founding of the OAU, many attempts were made to achieve freedom, independence, and unity in Africa.

The major landmarks in this struggle for African solidarity and unity are:

- The National Congress of British West Africa (1920–1930)
- The Ghana-Guinea Union of November 1958, which Mali joined in April 1961
- The Pan-African Movement for East and Central Africa (PAFMECA)
- The Casablanca Group (January 1961), composed of Ghana, Guinea, Mali, Morocco, Egypt, and Algeria

- The Monrovia Group (May 1961), composed of Liberia, Nigeria, Cameroon, Chad, Côte d'Ivoire, Congo (Brazzaville), Dahomey (now Bénin), Upper Volta (now Burkina Faso), Gabon, Central African Republic, Ethiopia, Libya, Malagasy Republic (Madagascar), Mauritania, Sierra Leone, Somalia, Tunisia, Niger, Senegal, and Togo
- The Brazzaville Group (October 1960), composed of Dahomey (now Bénin), Upper Volta (now Burkina Faso), Cameroon, Central African Republic, Chad, Congo (Brazzaville), Côte d'Ivoire, Gabon, Malagasy Republic (Madagascar), Mauritania, Niger, Sierra Leone, Somalia, Tunisia, and Senegal. The Brazzaville group joined the majority of English-speaking African countries outside the Casablanca group in May 1961 to form the Monrovia group.

These attempts at regional cooperation culminated in the creation of the OAU on 25 May 1963 at Addis Ababa. The charter of the OAU was signed on that date by the thirty-two leaders of the independent African states.

Principles and Objectives

The principles and objectives of the OAU are stated in articles II and III of the charter: (1) to promote the unity and solidarity of the African states; (2) to coordinate and intensify their cooperation and efforts to achieve a better life for the peoples of Africa; (3) to defend their sovereignty, territorial integrity, and independence; (4) to eradicate all forms of colonialism from Africa; and (5) to promote international cooperation, with due regard for the charter of the United Nations and the Universal Declaration of Human Rights.

To achieve these aims, member states agreed to harmonize their policies by cooperation in the areas of politics and diplomacy, economics, education and culture, science and technology, and defense and security. Member states also agreed to the following principles: the sovereign equality of all member states; noninterference in the internal affairs of states; peaceful settlement of disputes; condemnation of subversion; emancipation of the African territories still under colonial rule; and affirmation of a policy of nonalignment. The founding member states envisaged a unity "transcending ethnic and national differences." Membership was open to all of "the Continental African States, Madagascar and other Islands surrounding Africa."

Institutions

Article XX of the charter created six specialized commissions. They were subsequently reduced to three by a 1965 amendment: the Economic, Social, Transport, and Communications Commission; the Educational, Cultural, Health, and Scientific Commission; and the Defense Commission.

When necessary, ad hoc commissions have been established by the OAU to aid in its peacemaking efforts. They include the Ad Hoc Committee on the Algero-Moroccan Dispute, created in 1963; the Ad Hoc Committee on Inter-African Disputes (the 1979 Uganda-Tanzania conflict); and the commission established by the OAU Council of Ministers resolution on the Tanganyika military mutiny of 1964, which made possible the replacement of British troops (which had been invited by the government) with Nigerian troops.

The headquarters of the OAU General Secretariat is located at Africa Unity House in Addis Ababa, Ethiopia. The General Secretariat is the permanent organ responsible for servicing OAU meetings and implementing decisions and resolutions adopted by the OAU heads of state and government. It houses the OAU archives and coordinates the activities of member states in the fields stated in the charter. Since the signature in 1992 of the Abuja Treaty establishing the African Economic Community (AEC), the General Secretariat is also

serving as the secretariat for that body. The General Secretariat is headed by the secretary-general, assisted by five assistant secretaries-general appointed under articles XVI and XVII of the charter. The main policy organs are the Assembly of Heads of State and Government and the Council of Ministers.

Achievements and Failures

There is general consensus that the OAU has been moderately successful, particularly in the promotion of solidarity, and sometimes a certain degree of unity, among the African states, especially in times of crisis, and when there is a perception of a common external threat or the common experience of a negative external economic environment (e.g., declining terms of trade, unsustainable external debt burden, protectionism, and the negative impact of macroeconomic policies of industrialized countries). The OAU has responded to these developments by creating consensus among member states and taking initiatives in cooperation with the United Nations Economic Commission for Africa and the African Development Bank. It has developed a common African position on external debt, the environment, democracy, human rights and popular participation in development, and population and development. The OAU has had its successes and failures but, on the whole, has stayed true to its mission and embodies the collective will and aspirations of Africa. When its founding-member states became independent, they had no experience of modern government and international organizations, but they were able to use the OAU to project an African identity and articulate common positions on international affairs, especially within the United Nations, on issues of peace, decolonization, and economic development.

The OAU has been criticized for being ineffective in preventing or solving inter-African conflicts and for its inability or unwillingness to condemn despotism and promote democracy and socioeconomic development. While some of the criticism is fair, most observers agree that the blame cannot be laid at the door of the OAU, because the organization is only as effective as its fifty-two member states, with their conflicting interests, want it to be. Poor governance and economic management, and political instability arising therefrom, cannot be attributed to the OAU. The OAU can act effectively only when there is consensus or common purpose among its membership and, in the case of peacekeeping, when resources permit and member states fulfill their obligations, as evidenced in the OAU peacekeeping operation in Chad (1977–1982), which was difficult and frustrating.

Since its establishment, the OAU has seldom condemned unconstitutional rule, military take-overs, and serious interethnic conflicts, on the grounds that these are matters internal to the governments concerned, in accordance with Article III.2 of the charter. However, it must be acknowledged that since the late 1980s, particularly following the dissolution of the former Soviet Union and the end of the cold war, the OAU has taken commendable steps in articulating and actively promoting ideas on good governance, human rights and the rule of law, and democracy and popular participation. It was involved in mediation in Rwanda before the massacres of 1994 and in helping to resolve the interethnic conflict in Burundi, taking the unprecedented step in 1996 of calling for economic sanctions against that country aimed at the restoration of constitutional rule and other conditions conducive to social and political stability. In response to the devastating economic crisis of the 1980s, it adopted the African Priority Programme of Economic Recovery (APPER). In 1987 it initiated and guided the establishment of the OAU African Commission on Human and Peoples' Rights, which publishes annual reports on the performance of African governments in the field of human rights. National human-rights commissions have been established in some African countries.

The 1990 Addis Ababa summit clearly articulated Africa's understanding of the economic and political dimensions of the post–cold war era and its implications for democracy, development, and economic cooperation and integration. This was reflected in the resolution of the Assembly of Heads of State and Government titled "The Political and Socio-Economic Situation in Africa and Fundamental Changes Taking Place in the World," and in the African Peoples' Charter of Popular Participation in Development (1990).

A noteworthy achievement of the OAU has been its longtime concern for refugees. The Bureau for the Placement and Education of African Refugees (now the OAU Commission of Fifteen on Refugees) was established in 1968, and the OAU Convention on the Status of Refugees was signed in 1969. However, internal conflicts have increased, the most recent being in Somalia, Rwanda, and Burundi, and the OAU has not been successful in effectively

mediating these conflicts beyond facilitating the preliminary negotiations, except in Burundi, where, following renewed interethnic violence and the overthrow of a democratically elected government, it has taken the initiative in calling for economic sanctions aimed at restoring constitutional rule. The main reasons for this failure are the lack of financial and logistical resources to mount and sustain peacemaking and peacekeeping operations, and the inadequacy of existing mechanisms within the OAU to manage conflicts. Recognizing the root causes of conflicts—poor governance, the politics of intolerance and exclusion, and economic mismanagement—the OAU articulated the importance of peace and security based on democracy, the rule of law, and popular participation as indispensable conditions for stability and sustainable development.

After the Dakar (1992) and Cairo (1993) summits, the OAU began to address the complex problems of interstate and intrastate conflicts and established a mechanism for conflict prevention, management, and resolution, acting through the Bureau of the Assembly of Heads of State and Government rather than the Commission of Mediation, Conciliation, and Arbitration or the Defense Commission, which were provided for in the charter but had not been effective in managing conflicts. The OAU Peace Fund was established to support the conflict management activities of the new mechanism. The 1993 Cairo summit declared, "No single internal factor has contributed more to the socio-economic problems on the continent that the scourge of conflicts within and between countries," thus recognizing that whatever the internal problem, it is essentially an African problem. A committee of experts was appointed to review the charter in the light of the OAU's conflict management mandate and its new development orientation, especially the implementation of the Abuja Treaty, which created the African Economic Community.

In the cultural area, the OAU organized the first All-African Cultural Festival in Algiers (1969), which adopted the Pan-African Cultural Manifesto. The Cultural Charter of Africa was adopted in 1976.

With decolonization and the end of apartheid, the three major challenges to the OAU in the 1990s and into the twenty-first century are managing conflicts, promoting democracy and human rights, and implementing the Abuja Treaty while maintaining its political character.

BIBLIOGRAPHY

Amate, C. O. C. *Inside the OAU: Pan-Africanism in Practice.* Basingstoke, U.K., 1986.

Cervenka, Zdenek. *The Unfinished Quest for Unity: Africa and the OAU.* New York, 1977.

Gassama, M. I. S. "The OAU Does Care." *New African* no. 317 (April 1994): 20.

Geiss, Imanuel. *The Pan-African Movement.* New York, 1974.

Langley, J. Ayo. *Pan-Africanism and Nationalism in West Africa, 1900–1945.* Oxford, 1973.

Wolfers, Michael. *Politics in the Organization of African Unity.* London, 1976.

J. AYODELE LANGLEY

See also **Development; Geopolitics; Human Rights; Independence Movements; Nationalism; Postcolonial State; Refugees; Warfare.**

OROMO. Since the sixteenth century the Oromo have been a formidable force in Ethiopian political history. Speaking a language that belongs to the Eastern Cushitic family of Ethiopic languages, akin to Saho and Somali, Oromo may constitute 40 percent of the Ethiopian population. The six major territorial groups spread across the flanks of the central highlands, from Wallaga on the west to Harer on the east, and south of the Webe Shebelle River. Sixteenth-century migrations onto the central Ethiopian plateau brought Oromo into contact with Amhara-Tigrinya cultural and economic patterns of life, including village settlements and Christianity and Islam. Pastoralism, once practiced by all Oromo, survives in slightly attenuated form as the dominant economic way of life among the Boran and Arusi. The *gada* system of age-sets and grades remains a significant feature of political organization. In the nineteenth century, the spread of Islam strengthened petty Oromo states in the Gibe Basin, enabling them to expand their trading networks into Christian Ethiopia. The Jimma kingdom, last to survive, was conquered by Menilek II in the unification of Ethiopia.

BIBLIOGRAPHY

Loo, Joseph van de. *Guji Oromo Culture in Southern Ethiopia.* Berlin, 1991.

Mohammed Hassen. *The Oromo of Ethiopia: A History, 1570–1860.* Cambridge, 1990.

WILLIAM A. SHACK

See also **Islam; Menilek II.**

ORTHOGRAPHIES. *See* **Writing Systems.**

OSEI BONSU (b. 1779?; d. 1823), *Asantehene* (ruler of Asante). Osei Tutu Kwame Asibe Bonsu (r. 1804–1823) became king following a period of domestic conflict in the region, which is part of present-day Ghana. The *Asantehene* Osei Kwame (1777–1803) had been forced to abdicate, and his successor, Opoku Fofie, died a few weeks after coming to the throne. Domestic stability was restored under Osei Bonsu. Concerning himself with regulating trade with the European establishments on the coast, Osei Bonsu engaged in successful campaigns against the Fante in 1806–1807, 1811, and 1816. Once Asante had gained effective control of trade routes from the northern hinterlands to the coast, several European emissaries came to negotiate trade and friendship. Numerous Muslim traders and clerics also came to the capital at Kumasi.

Osei Bonsu continued and improved bureaucratic reforms begun in the mid-eighteenth century. Though the king remained primus inter pares in relation to state rulers of the Asante confederation, Osei Bonsu appointed civil officers in Kumasi and provincial administrators who were directly responsible to him. Their close regulation of external trade ensured economic prosperity for the nation. Notwithstanding such achievements, Osei Bonsu was disappointed by the British failure to sign a treaty of trade and friendship negotiated in 1820. In fact, at the time of his death and before his successor, Osei Yaw Akoto, came to the throne, Asante was at war with the British. Charles McCarthy, the British governor of Sierra Leone and the Cape Coast Castle, was killed in this conflict.

BIBLIOGRAPHY

Bowdich, Thomas. *Mission from Cape Coast Castle to Ashantee.* London, 1966.

Dupuis, Joseph. *Journal of a Residence in Ashantee.* 2d ed. London, 1966.

Owusu-Ansah, David. *Islamic Talismanic Tradition in Nineteenth-Century Asante.* Lewiston, N.Y., 1991.

Wilks, Ivor G. "Aspects of Bureaucratization in Ashanti in the Nineteenth Century." *Journal of African History* 7, no. 2 (1966): 215–232.

———. *Asante in the Nineteenth Century: The Structure and Evolution of a Political Order.* London, 1975.

DAVID OWUSU-ANSAH

See also **Akan Region, History; Colonial Policies and Practice.**

OSEI TUTU (b. 1636?; d. 1717), first Asante king (*asantehene*). Succeeding his uncle Obiri Yeboah of the Oyoko clan as *kumasihene* (ruler of Kumasi) about 1685, Osei Tutu continued his predecessor's wars of expansion, and succeeded in consolidating the territorial base of the Oyoko dynasty. He united the nuclear Asante states for the conquest of Denkyera (1699–1701). The military union provided the framework of Asante unity and the machinery for Asante political expansion. In the course of the eighteenth century, it resulted in the creation of greater Asante, embracing most of present-day Ghana and eastern Côte d'Ivoire.

Osei Tutu built Kumasi as the capital of the Asante kingdom and introduced enduring incorporative institutions for its further expansion. First was the Golden Stool, the seat used in the ritual installation of the *asantehene*. Mystically incorporating all existing stools, it became the supreme shrine of the Asante people, embodying their collective soul. Identified with the nation, it defined an Asante as its subject. Second, *odwira* (first fruits), an annual national festival, was given precedence over other festivals; it brought together all Asante for both secular and ritual purposes. Third was a set of laws that the Asante regard as the framework of their nationhood.

The Asante union established by Osei Tutu remains intact, known to the constitutions of Ghana since 1959 as the Ashanti Regional House of Chiefs. Relations between the *asantehene* and the heads of the constituent state remain modeled on the rules promulgated by Osei Tutu. The rites of communion with the ancestral spirits culminating in the annual *odwira* festival are still observed, and the Golden Stool is known as the stool of Osei and Poku, his immediate successor.

BIBLIOGRAPHY

Freestone, Basil. *Osei Tutu: The Leopard Owns the Land.* London, 1968.

Reindorf, Carl Christian. *A History of the Gold Coast and Asante.* Basel, 1895.

Wilks, Ivor G. *Asante in the Nineteenth Century: The Structure and Evolution of a Political Order.* London, 1975.

NANA ARHIN BREMPONG

See also **Asante.**

OUAGADOUGOU. Founded about 1050, Ouagadougou is the capital of Burkina Faso, a major regional capital, and home of the traditional ruler (*mogho naaba*) of the Mossi people. The tenth *mogho naaba*, Nyadfo, who lived in the mid-seventeenth century, was the first *mogho naaba* to live in Ouagadougou. The city, however, did not become the permanent capital until the reign of the twenty-first *mogho naaba*, Zombere, in the 1750s. The twenty-fourth *mogho naaba*, Doulougou, built the first mosque in Ouagadougou in the early nineteenth century.

The first European known to have visited Ouagadougou was Gottlob Adolf Krause, in 1886. The French captured the city ten years later. Between 1934 and 1954 Bobo-Dioulasso, the other major city in Burkina Faso, outstripped Ouagadougou in terms of industry and population; it remains the "industrial capital" of the country.

Ouagadougou is located close to the center of Burkina Faso and is equidistant from the Red Volta and the White Volta. It is 302 meters (991 feet) above sea level. March and April are the warmest months, and August is the coolest. From November to April there is little rain; monsoons occur in July and August. The 1986 census, the most recent, counted 448,000 inhabitants.

BIBLIOGRAPHY

Skinner, Elliott P. *African Urban Life: The Transformation of Ouagadougou.* Princeton, 1974.

JESSE A. DIZARD

See also **Mossi; Mossi Region, History.**

OUSMANE, SEMBÈNE. *See* **Sembène Ousmane.**

OVAMBO. At approximately 700,000 people, the Ovambo make up the largest population group of present-day Namibia, about 50 percent of the total population. They inhabit the Cuvelai floodplain, which straddles the national boundary between Angola and Namibia. Linguistically the Ovambo belong to the Southwestern Bantu family. They began settling between the Kunene and Okavango Rivers between 700 and 100 B.C.E. Their language, which is spoken in a variety of dialects, is called Osivambo. Political secession and fission led to the different groups and polities that today constitute the Namibian and Angolan Ovambo: the Kwanyama, Kwambi, Ndonga, Ngandjera, Kwaluudi, Kolonkadi, Ombalantu, Eunda, Mbandja, Evale, Ehanda, Ndombodhola, Eshinga, and Onkwankwa. The political structures of these groups range from highly centralized kingdoms to rather loosely structured polities in which elders and the clan constitute the important offices.

The Ovambo were, originally, a sedentary, agro-pastoralist-hunting population; their economic and social structures were largely determined by ecological factors such as rainfall, good soils, and an abundance of game. The onset of colonialism from the north, through Portugal, and the south, through the British at the Cape of Good Hope, as well as the ensuing trade networks, resulted in important changes in the social fabric. Droughts and cattle epidemics, such as the rinderpest epidemic of 1897, reinforced these processes. Missionary activity was started in 1872 by the Finnish Mission Society. Social stratification became more pronounced, resulting in considerable poverty. Poverty in turn led to conflict over leadership and succession in some of the communities, such as the Kwanyama and Ndonga; it also made young men leave the area for economic reasons and satisfied the somewhat later need for migrant labor in the colonial economies of southern Africa.

Despite considerable efforts of the Portuguese, colonial pacification of the Ovambo only happened as late as the 1910s, and Portugal suffered repeated crushing defeats. The latter fact, together with the Herero-German War of 1904 and the remoteness of Ovamboland, convinced the Germans not to subjugate the region militarily. A series of protection treaties between the rulers of the more numerous groups and the German colonial government was concluded by 1910 to secure a steady flow of migrant contract labor for the now fully operating colony.

When South Africa took over as the succeeding colonial power in 1915, Ovamboland was conquered by military means, and the most important king, Mandume of the Kwanyama, was fatally wounded. A council of headman was appointed by the colonial government to rule the group. King Iipumbu of the Kwambi was banished from his throne in 1932, again by military means. The economy of colonial Namibia—its mining, fishing, and agriculture—depended on the contract labor supplied from Ovamboland. Ovamboland was the main site for the liberation struggle against the South African colonial administration, waged by the South West Africa Peoples Organization (SWAPO) of Namibia from 1966 on. As such it has suffered disproportionately. Today it is one of the poorer regions of Namibia.

BIBLIOGRAPHY

Hayes, Patricia M. *A History of the Ovambo of Namibia, c. 1880–1935.* Ph.D. diss., University of Cambridge, 1992.

WOLFRAM HARTMAN

See also **Namibia.**

OYO. Oyo, a Yoruba town in southwestern Nigeria, was founded in about the fourteenth century A.D. by Oranmiyan, a prince of Ife. The new kingdom was forced by pressures from neighbors and internal problems to move its capital to Igboho for about two centuries. After the return from Igboho, the kingdom was expanded and consolidated. It prospered from the Atlantic slave trade and built a strong army. The emergent empire was plagued by internal problems from the eighteenth century. Revolts by vassals and slaves were followed by the incursion of Muslim elements connected to the Sokoto jihad. In the late 1820s Oyo was sacked and forced to move 190 kilometers (120 mi.) southward, where it remains today.

Oyo was conquered by the British in 1895, but the king, or *alaafin,* continues in office under British overrule. Oyo is today a predominantly Muslim town, although the American Baptist mission is active in the town.

BIBLIOGRAPHY

Johnson, Samuel. *The History of the Yorubas.* 2d ed. Lagos, 1976.
Smith, Robert S. *Kingdoms of the Yoruba.* London, 1969.

OLATUNJI OJO

See also **Yoruba States, History.**

P–Q

PAN-AFRICAN AND REGIONAL ORGANI-ZATIONS. *See* **Organization of African Unity; Western African Regional Organizations.**

PASHA, EMIN. *See* **Schnitzer, Eduard.**

PATRIARCHY AND PATRILINY. *See* **Kinship and Descent; Kinship and Marriage; Marriage Systems.**

PATRONAGE. Also referred to as "clientelism" or "patron-client relations," "patronage" denotes a relationship between individuals of unequal power, wealth, or status. The superior, or patron, provides benefits in the form of wealth or security to the inferior, or client, who is in return expected to offer loyalty and obedience to the patron. The relationship is thus in essence a transactional one, from which each party benefits. It is, however, often reinforced by a vocabulary of moral obligation, which in the southern European societies from which much of the social science analysis of the concept derives, classically took the form of god-parenthood.

Although in essence a two-person relationship, patronage may readily be expanded into a much wider set of relationships, often described as a patronage or clientelist system. This is constituted first by a set of societal values which place high emphasis on interpersonal but hierarchical relationships, and second by the networks of linkages built up between individual patrons and clients.

Since each patron may have many clients, since rival patrons compete for clients against one another, and since an individual who is a client in one capacity may also be a patron with a set of subordinate clients, such networks are often widespread and complex. An individual who is simultaneously client and patron is often referred to as a middleman, whose independent relationship with his own clients is classically expressed in the Ethiopian proverb "A dog knows his master, but not his master's master." Patronage systems are normally male-dominated, though female patrons are by no means unknown.

Patronage occurs to some degree in all political systems, but its importance varies significantly between systems. It particularly characterizes those in which the value placed on personal relationships is high, and in which commitment to universalist values is low. As a relationship between unequals, it is also salient in societies with high levels of inequality; in such societies, subordinate individuals may be better able to achieve their goals by attaching themselves to a patron than by collaboration with other individuals in the same position as themselves. Patronage thus undermines class-based political action and helps to account for the relative insignificance of class politics in many societies with evident class inequalities. Since patronage runs counter to such universalist values as efficient administration, impartial allocation, and national interest, it is readily regarded as corrupt.

African societies possess to a high degree the features that characteristically induce patronage, which is consequently an important feature of

African political and social life. Precolonial African social relationships, as in almost all agrarian and pastoral societies, tended to emphasize personal obligations. The imposition of colonial rule created pronounced inequalities, not only between colonizers and colonized but among Africans themselves. Although nationalist leaders generally attempted to create a sense of common political identity, this was difficult to achieve within the territories artificially created by colonialism. In those parts of the continent where social mobilization was relatively weak and local notables exercised considerable authority, patronage provided the only way to create effective political parties. Parties such as the Northern Peoples' Congress in Nigeria and the Sierra Leone People's Party in Sierra Leone could be characterized as "patron parties," while elements of patronage were present even in such radical nationalist movements as Kwame Nkrumah's Convention People's Party in Ghana.

Most of all, however, patronage politics was enhanced by the structure of the African state, which in the years after independence exercised a monopoly of power, wealth, and authority which no rival institution could challenge. African leaders, inheriting political office within artificial states with fragile economies, understandably turned to patronage as a means of maintaining both their own power and the structure of the state itself. Compared with the alternative of dependence on force, patronage could be regarded as relatively benevolent. Its classic expression was the single-party state, in which loyalty to the leader was rewarded with political office and opportunities for self-enrichment. Local party bosses in turn served as middleman, maintaining their own clients at the local level.

At the same time, national leaders could also be regarded as middlemen within an international patronage system, responsible for delivering the loyalty of their own state to a superpower or ex-colonial patron which in turn provided economic benefits (in the form of aid) and security (in the form of military protection or arms supplies). Such relationships, as for example between President Valéry Giscard d'Estaing of France and President Mobutu Sese Seko of Zaire or President/Emperor Jean-Bédel Bokassa of the Central African Republic, readily became highly personalized. While by no means all African leaders succumbed to them, they provided a tempting option to leaders whose domestic hold on power was uncertain, and in turn

reduced the accountability of those leaders to their own societies. The effects were perhaps most intense in the Horn of Africa during the cold war era, when leaders such as Haile Mariam Mengistu in Ethiopia and Siad Barre in Somalia could call on superpower patrons to supply armaments which greatly exacerbated the problems of security and governance in the region.

Patronage was thus readily identified as one of the major pathogens in the failure of the African state, which became evident from the 1970s onward. By concentrating power in the hands of a dominant national leader, it encouraged autocracy and, in some cases, the grossest forms of abuse. Internationally, it signaled increased dependence and reduced accountability. In economic terms, it led not only to individual corruption but to the maldistribution of scarce resources, and especially to a bias against politically less significant rural producer interests and toward urban consumer ones. Eventually, it helped promote widespread public alienation from the political process and encouraged the formation of opposition movements.

The attack on patronage therefore became a guiding theme in the challenge to the African state which emerged in the 1980s and 1990s, from both indigenous opponents and international actors. The structural readjustment programs imposed by lending agencies such as the International Monetary Fund cut at the basis of patronage through state allocation of resources. Demands for democratization and good governance were likewise intended to replace patronage by accountable and efficient administration. The end of the cold war greatly reduced the ability of African governments to call on the patronage of major world powers. The main problem for African states in the face of these changes was whether they were capable of reforming themselves in the way that their critics required, given the continued importance of many of the factors which had promoted patronage politics in the first place.

BIBLIOGRAPHY

Clapham, Christopher, ed. *Private Patronage and Public Power: Political Clientelism in the Modern State.* New York, 1982.

Eisenstadt, S. N., and René Lemarchand, eds. *Political Clientelism, Patronage, and Development.* Beverly Hills, Calif., 1981.

Rothchild, Donald, and Naomi Chazan, eds. *The Precarious Balance: State and Society in Africa.* Boulder, Colo., 1988.

Schmidt, Steffen W., et al., eds. *Friends, Followers, and Factions: A Reader in Political Clientelism.* Berkeley, 1977.

CHRISTOPHER CLAPHAM

See also **Bokassa, Jean-Bédel; Ethnicity and Identity; Kinship and Descent; Mengistu Haile Mariam; Mobutu Sese Seko; Nkrumah, Francis Nwia Kofi; Postcolonial State.**

PEASANTS, PEASANTRIES, AND LAND SETTLEMENT

[Peasants' livelihoods are inextricably tied to the land. This composite entry covering the various regions of sub-Saharan Africa surveys the experiences of peasants and major land-settlement efforts that, in many cases, complicated rather than helped their lives. The preliminary **Overview** *explains the controversy surrounding the meaning of the word peasant.]*

OVERVIEW

The reference to African farming populations as "peasantries" seems more apposite to some places than to others. The term only reached a tentatively general acceptance among scholars in the 1970s. And it is still a matter of controversy how useful it is to draw more attention to the similarities between African farmers and, for example, Chinese or medieval European peasantries, than to the differences. The similarities are clear: these are usually family-based enterprises, using nonmechanized technologies for cultivation and processing, producing for both home consumption and regional markets. The differences hinge on two characteristics generally taken as definitional of peasantries: they are generally assumed to be "part" economies and societies that "produce mainly for their own consumption and [also] for the fulfilment of obligations to the holders of political and economic power" (Saul and Woods, p. 240). Political subordination has usually been associated with a style of production at the intensive end of the extensive-intensive continuum of land use. Only in a few African societies did farmers of the past submit to state control of resources, and in even fewer places did they practice intensive agriculture. Ethiopia is the single fairly unambiguous case. Hence the sense of unease among scholars about grouping the past and present rural economies of Africa, for comparative purposes, with the classic peasantries of the world.

To add to the confusion, the French term *paysan* has a different enough connotation from the English term "peasant" to have been generally ac-cepted in the literature on French West and Equatorial Africa long before controversy arose in anglophone circles. A *paysan* was someone who made a living from the *pays*, the countryside. One of the early classic studies of African farmers, by Paul Pélissier, was entitled *Les paysans du Sénégal: Les civilisations agraires du Cayor à la Casamance* (1966). The famous Belgian schemes for modernizing agricultural techniques in the Congo during the colonial period were called *paysannats*. Ironically, the cultivators of the Zaire River basin are perhaps among the least likely, in all of Africa, to fit neatly into a "peasant" mold. Where they developed intensive techniques (as they did in fishing) it was in nonstate political structures, and the centralized polities were more based on the profits of trade than of production. But in relationship to a French-speaking colonial government, all rural producers could conveniently be assimilated to the concept of *paysans*.

Indeed, it was really the changes at the end of the colonial era that made English-speaking scholarship warm to the analytical prospect of "peasants." Whatever the situation in the past, African cultivators were by then definitively integrated into state structures and world markets, and as a result many were practicing more intensive and specialized agriculture than their forebears. In 1955 M. G. Smith wrote of the Hausa economy of Northern Nigeria that it was based on "two differing interest groups, the peasants and their rulers" (p. 4). In 1961 Lloyd Fallers—working from his study of one of Africa's stronger state structures and more intensive agriculture systems, the Baganda—posed the question bluntly: "Are African cultivators to be called 'peasants'?" Rural-based political movements in the 1960s made it clear that, whatever they were called, African farmers were ready to make some claims against the state and to react to markets, taxes, duties, and other institutions of the world economic system in a fashion that seemed closer to peasant politics than to anything else.

By that time, however, a great deal of new research had been published on the history of employment of rural-based populations outside of agriculture altogether, or on European-owned farms. Oscillating migration in South Africa was simply the most formalized version of a general pattern of male and youth employment for long periods of time outside of their home areas. This finding put a dent into another of the diacritics of a peasantry: family-based cultivation. In fact, it was suggested by Ester Boserup in 1970 that African farming was better depicted as feminized farming than as household production. In brief, scholarship had no sooner become more or less comfortable with the idea of a peasantry "than they were confronted with the fact that in vast parts of Africa peasants had already been made into proletarians" (Cooper, p. 284).

The debates may seem sterile, but in fact they have been productive, because each effort at definition has drawn African cases into a different comparative context with respect to the rest of the world. Robert Netting, for example, abandoned the criterion of state subjection altogether, to pursue the criterion of intensive household production. As a result, some African local economies figure alongside Chinese and Swiss farming while others do not. Sara Berry, by contrast, emphasized the particular nature of African state intervention, regardless of the intensity of agricultural technique. She argued that the relationship between African farmers and postcolonial states is a partial one, where the state intervenes in production but only enough to produce uncertainty rather than decisive change. Other work, particularly in west Africa, with its tradition of production for commercial markets, suggests that cultivators of food for rapidly growing urban populations are indeed intensifying and also accommodating to government, but in ways that come forward from their own history rather than primarily through either political subjection or adoption of well-known world techniques of intensification such as irrigation or manuring.

Specialists are still debating these issues, less to fix on an acceptable terminology than to expand on an understanding of the social, political, and technical dynamics of rural livelihood. The idea of a peasantry can be very useful, but in African studies it is usually combined with other concepts that set the comparative frame in other ways. West Africa, with its long tradition of commerce and urban life, is a particularly difficult case to categorize. For the past, it may make sense to consider the Hausa producers as peasants, as long as we encompass the fact that farm slavery was also very widespread in the nineteenth century. For the present, it is altogether less clear that we capture the dynamics of change adequately for these long-specialized populations without teasing out the separate influences of factors that the term "peasant" groups together: techniques and social organization of production, relationship to the state, and engagement with the market.

BIBLIOGRAPHY

Berry, Sara. *No Condition Is Permanent: The Social Dynamics of Agrarian Change in Sub-Saharan Africa.* Madison, Wisc., 1993.

Boserup, Ester. *Woman's Role in Economic Development.* London, 1970.

Cooper, Frederick. "Peasants, Capitalists, and Historians: A Review Article." *Journal of Southern African Studies* 7, no. 2 (1981): 284–314.

Fallers, Lloyd. "Are African Cultivators to Be Called 'Peasants'?" *Current Anthropology* 2 (1961): 108–110.

Guyer, Jane I. *An African Niche Economy: Farming to Feed Ibadan, 1968–1988.* Edinburgh, 1997.

McCann, James C. *People of the Plow: An Agricultural History of Ethiopia, 1800–1990.* Madison, Wisc., 1995.

Netting, Robert McC. *Smallholders, Householders: Farm Families and the Ecology of Intensive, Sustainable Agriculture.* Stanford, Calif., 1993.

Pélissier, Paul. *Les paysans du Sénégal: Les civilisations agraires du Cayor à la Casamance.* Saint-Yrieix, France, 1966.

Saul, John S., and Roger Woods. "African Peasantries." In *Peasants and Peasant Societies,* edited by Teodor Shanin. Harmondsworth, Eng., 1971.

Smith, M. G. *The Economy of Hausa Communities of Zaria.* London, 1955.

JANE I. GUYER

See also **Agriculture; Production Systems.**

WESTERN AFRICA

The savannas include extensive grassland areas, interspersed with woodlands of varying densities, that cover an immense area of western Africa: the southern parts of the sahelian countries of Senegal, Mali, Burkina Faso, and Niger; and the northern, or sudanian, areas of the coastal countries of Côte d'Ivoire, Ghana, Togo, Benin, Nigeria, and Cameroon. Agriculture is the most important feature of savanna peasant livelihoods, accounting for the work done by more than 80 percent of the labor force in the sahelian countries and about two-thirds of the labor force in the coastal countries, where industry and commercial and service activities are more developed. Other common activities include agropastoralism, fishing, hunting, craft production, commercial activities (especially petty trade), and on-farm and off-farm wage work. Savanna agriculture depends on rainfall, which varies from 150 millimeters (6 inches) to 900 millimeters (35 inches) per year in the sahelian zone and may reach 1,800 millimeters (70 inches) per year in the more southerly sudanian zone. Rainfall distribution has a markedly seasonal character, often occurring during a single rainy season that lasts three to four months (May/June to July/August). During the rainy-season months, peasant households are intensely involved in the production of a variety of crops. Cereals, principally millet and sorghum, are the most important food crops in the sahelian zones of the western African savannas. Peasant farmers often use production systems that are based on infields, outfields, and rotating bush fallow. Infields surround village communities and often benefit from the fertilizing effects of household rubbish and manure from household livestock; infields are cultivated yearly. The more distant outfields rarely benefit from animal manure. They are cultivated for a period, followed by several years in fallow when crops are not planted. Fallow fields gradually revert to bush, permitting the soil to regain a measure of fertility. New outfields are obtained by clearing fallowed fields and rotating them back into production or by clearing previously uncultivated areas when available. A major contrast to this approach occurs in the immense interior delta areas of the Niger River as it courses through central Mali. Here, annual flooding of the river gives peasants a critical opportunity to cultivate rice for domestic consumption. Important rain-fed food crops in the savannas include cassava, groundnuts, cowpeas, okra, and a variety of condiments. Rural dwellers use the fruits and by-products from naturally occurring trees, such as the shea (*Butyrospermum parkii*), the baobab (*Adansonia digitata*), the tamarind (*Tamarindus indica*), and palm tree species (*Hyphaene* and *Borassus*). They also plant fruit tree varieties including mango, guava, and citrus. In the southern or woodland savanna areas, maize replaces millet and sorghum as the dominant crop. Peasant farmers in these southern areas also more frequently plant root crops such as yams, cocoa yams, and sweet potatoes. Despite the predominance of a particular crop type in a given area, considerable crop diversity occurs throughout the savannas due to the common practice of intercropping, in which peasants cultivate several crop varieties within their fields. Frequent intercropping combinations include types of millet or sorghum as principal crops, with groundnuts, okra, sorrel, and cowpeas as secondary crops. Intercropping provides households with dietary variety and takes advantage of local variations in soil quality, land slope, and water availability. Peasants in western Africa frequently raise livestock, particularly sheep, goats, and poultry (chicken, ducks, guinea fowl). They also raise cattle, horses, and donkeys. They may raise pigs in areas where Islam is not widely developed.

Men play a central role in producing major cereal and root crops such as millet, sorghum, and yams. Women are also key players in the agriculture of western Africa and are often involved in planting and harvesting cereal crops. But women are much more active in producing vegetables and condiments on smaller garden plots that they manage on their own. Women may virtually monopolize the production of more specialized crops such as shallots and sesame, and they collect much of the wild fruit from indigenous trees for sale or processing (shea butter, tamarind). Likewise, women play an important commercial role in community and market-based sales of local fruits, condiments, and smaller quantities of cereals and other staple crops. Women are the chief producers of goats and poultry in many areas, while men are more likely to take charge of raising cattle and sheep. Peasant households cultivate crops primarily to satisfy their own consumption needs, but they may also sell or trade some portion of their harvest every year. Crops that are important as a source of cash income include groundnuts, cotton, cassava, tobacco, cowpeas, sugarcane, rice, and garden vegetables. Savanna peasants do not often use mechanized technology for their farming. Well under 20 percent of all households use oxen- or donkey-drawn plows for farming; the use of tractors is rare. The vast majority of peasant households rely on manual labor and simple, well-adapted cultivating tools such as hoes and other implements, including axes and machetes. Finally, more specialized pastoral peasant groups move cyclically with their livestock from north to south and back across the savannas every year.

Peasant Livelihoods

We observe a diversity of specific livelihood strategies among peasants in western Africa, but two major patterns of activity are particularly noteworthy: agricultural production and pastoralism. Each approach reflects important differences in how peasants endeavor to use the natural resource base for their well-being. While distinctive, these approaches are also interlinked in important ways.

Agriculturalists
Social life in peasant communities in western Africa is focused on a shared sense of values and norms

and a strong sense of membership in a community of origin, often having deep historical roots in a particular geographical location. Households often claim privileged access to arable land in areas around their communities. These areas include many of the natural resources (land, wooded areas, grazing resources, game and fish, water, and so on) that peasants identify as essential for their livelihoods. Their claims to land and other natural resources are based on their kinship relation, by blood or by marriage, to ancestors who settled in the area generations earlier and who claimed the surrounding land and its resources themselves. Typically, peasants in western Africa assert their right to use land, not to own it. Nonetheless, land is loaned, rented, occasionally pawned, and, increasingly, sold. Land sales are relatively infrequent in rural areas where land quality is poor, where the population density is low, or where there is no ready access to markets. By contrast, a series of factors have contributed to an increased but uneven pace of land sales in the savanna areas. These factors include increasing population pressure on available land combined with the widespread use of extensive, rather than intensive, agricultural practices. They also include competing demands for land, particularly in growing peri-urban areas and other areas having better soil for agriculture, proximity to water for irrigation, and greater access to markets. Agricultural production in these areas is often commercial in nature. Despite their primary concern with self-provisioning through agriculture, peasant households in western Africa often do not satisfy all of their consumption needs. Household members also need a variety of items for everyday life that they do not produce, ranging from cloth and shoes to cooking pots to salt. Peasant households rely on the market to obtain these goods and to cover shortfalls in their own food production. As a result, peasants in western Africa are involved in a wide range of market relationships that link them to other communities and with economies in distant regions, different African countries, and other parts of the world. Peasants in western Africa widely use, for example, inexpensive rubber sandals, kerosene lamps, and flashlights manufactured in southeast Asian countries; they also use French sugar, Italian tomato paste, Moroccan sardines, and Dutch cloth.

Pastoralists

The land-use patterns of western African pastoralists, who rely primarily on the dairy products de-

rived from their herds rather than on crops, differs from the patterns we have seen among the agriculturalists. Pastoralists have developed highly mobile livelihood strategies (transhumance) with which they move with their livestock between areas that offer the grazing and water resources that their herds need. During the rainy-season months, pastoralists graze their livestock on the annual grasses that grow in the northern savannas. As the quality of northern pastures declines, the pastoralists gradually move toward the southern savanna and woodland areas inhabited by peasant agriculturalists, looking for better-quality grazing and forage for their livestock. At these times of the year, sedentary agriculturalists' fields may benefit from the fertilizing effects of livestock manure as the pastoralists' herds browse among the dry crop residues remaining from the year's harvest of grain crops.

Historically, this seemingly complementary relationship between the nomadic pastoralists and the more sedentary agriculturalists has been strained by tension and conflict. Pastoralists may arrive with their livestock in agricultural areas before the harvests are complete. Then, agriculturalists seek to protect their end-of-harvest crops and woodlands from incursions by pastoralists and their herds, and there often are conflicts over access to natural resources. With the onset of the next rainy season, the pastoralists move northward again, and for a while, the tensions between the agriculturalists and pastoralists subside.

Challenges to Complementarity and Livelihood Strategies

In the western African savanna, the longer-term viability of both the relationship between peasants having different livelihood strategies and also the distinctive cultures of both agriculturalists and pastoralists face major challenges. Many peasants are too poor to invest in technological improvements in agricultural production or are unwilling to do so because of the risks that are associated with rain-fed agriculture in the savanna. Unable or unwilling to improve agricultural productivity, peasant agriculturalists frequently practice extensive agriculture in an effort to increase total production. One important result of this practice has been that the agricultural frontier has "drifted" northward into more marginal, low-rainfall areas. This northward expansion of rain-fed agriculture has important long-term implications for many peasants in western Africa.

First, the increased cultivation of marginal areas having lower annual rainfall places the well-being of agriculturalists at risk. The largely unimproved agricultural practices of many peasant households, whose increasing numbers are fueled by continuing high fertility rates, have contributed to increased pressure on arable land areas and, because many peasants cannot afford to invest in land improvements, to the gradual degradation of the natural resources on which peasant livelihoods depend. In addition, reports of shortened fallow cycles and of the cessation of fallowing altogether are common in western Africa. As the practice of rotating bush fallow declines, so does a very effective practice for restoring soil fertility. While there is plenty of land in western Africa, there is much less good-quality agricultural land, and the low level of investment in maintaining soil quality bodes ill for the agricultural future of the region. Finally, the expansion of cultivated areas into pastoral zones places added pressure on the well-being of pastoralists who discover that their access to traditional grazing areas is declining.

Diversification and Mobility

Peasant societies in the western African savanna face a number of challenges: varying and unreliable rainfall; declining or very limited increases in agricultural production on account of a lack of access by peasant households to capital and improved agricultural technology; continuing population growth relative to finite access to good land; and the long-standing effects of uneven economic development in western Africa, which has favored the coastal areas at the expense of the hinterland savanna areas. Western African peasants' efforts to deal with these challenges have resulted in strategies to diversify their access to the resources they need for their livelihoods and to manage risks in their operating environments. Their attempts to diversify their income sources by including both on-farm and off-farm activities have contributed to the hallmark characteristic of these peasants: massive mobility. Typically this mobility takes the form of seasonal migrations by men both within their own countries and over large areas of western Africa, but increasingly women also participate in these migrations. Many western African peasants travel long distances each year in search of economic opportunities. The willingness and ability to migrate to resources have given western African peasants a noteworthy resilience and have enabled them to moderate, to a degree, the effects of a harsh physical environment, which have been periodically made more difficult by several major droughts, particularly since the late 1960s. Likewise, these diversification strategies have enabled peasants to moderate the frequently negative impacts of government policies and, on a larger scale, the effects of several decades of economic stagnation that have affected all of sub-Saharan Africa. The resilience of peasant societies in the western African savannas does not mean that they are impervious to social change. While the pace of change has differed from one group and area to another, all peasant societies in western Africa have been affected at the individual, household, community, and regional levels by the uneven yet inescapable impact of environmental and demographic change, by socioeconomic development, by political change, and by integration in a larger and interdependent world economy.

BIBLIOGRAPHY

Barker, Jonathan. *Rural Communities Under Stress: Peasant Farmers and the State in Africa.* Cambridge, 1989.

Bernstein, Henry, Ben Crow, and Hazel Johnson, eds. *Rural Livelihoods: Crises and Responses.* Oxford, 1992.

Berry, Sara. *No Condition Is Permanent: The Social Dynamics of Agrarian Change in Sub-Saharan Africa.* Madison, Wisc. 1993.

Hopkins, A. G. *An Economic History of West Africa.* New York, 1973.

Painter, Thomas M., James Sumberg, and Thomas Price. "Your 'Terroir' and My 'Action Space': Implications of Differentiation, Mobility, and Diversification for the *Approche Terroir* in Sahelian West Africa." *Africa* 64, no. 4 (1994): 447–464.

Richards, Paul. *Indigenous Agricultural Revolution: Ecology and Food Production in West Africa.* London, 1985.

Sautter, Gilles. *Parcours d'un géographe: Des paysages aux ethnies, de la brousse à la ville, de l'Afrique au monde.* Paris, 1993.

Thomas, M. F., and G. W. Whittington. *Environment and Land Use in Africa.* London, 1969.

Watts, Michael J. "The Agrarian Question in Africa: Debating the Crisis." *Progress in Human Geography* 13, no. 1 (1989): 1–41.

THOMAS M. PAINTER

See also **Ecosystems; Exchange and Market Systems; Gender; Production Systems**

EASTERN AFRICAN PEASANT SOCIETIES

The term "peasantry" gained currency in eastern Africa during the 1960s, coincident with the rejection of the colonial denotation of African agricultural producers as "natives." Borrowed from European history, "peasantry" was given theoretical rigor in academic debates of the 1970s on the nature of the relationship between African agricultural producers and the state. In the policy arena of the 1980s and 1990s, the term "peasantry" has been increasingly supplanted by "smallholders."

Peasants in eastern Africa, as elsewhere, are identifiable by three main characteristics: sedentary agricultural practices, an internal social organization based on family labor, and external subordination to state authorities as well as the regional or international markets through which peasant surpluses are siphoned. The geographical incidence of peasant societies has been variegated due to the presence or absence of a suitable combination of conditioning factors arising from differences in ecology, population density, the emergence of state power, and external influences such as market demand and the spread of world religions.

Many parts of eastern Africa, specifically areas of low rainfall, poor drainage, or tsetse infestation, have been sparsely populated and poor in natural resources, making the development of surplus production and the emergence of surplus-extracting elites and peasantries unlikely. Even where the natural resource base and population densities have been favorable, peasantries have not arisen without a degree of investment in infrastructure and agricultural innovations making surplus extraction physically feasible. The stimulus of the market and the organizational role of the state in developing roads and communications is critical.

Geography has had a strong influence on state and market expansion and on the emergence of peasantries. The East African Rift that runs from north to south through eastern Africa creates striking differences in altitude and climate. Rainfall and agricultural potential tend to be correlated with altitude. Innovation, trade, and investment have been influenced by eastern Africa's two main routes to the outside world, namely the Nile River and the coastline of the Indian Ocean. Both routes, however, have been restrictive in terms of intercontinental contact. Given the long journeys required around the Cape by sea to eastern Africa prior to the opening of the Suez Canal, the Indian Ocean linked eastern Africa with Asia rather than Europe. The Nile, flowing into the Mediterranean, has not served as eastern Africa's gateway to Europe on account of its numerous cataracts, which are obstacles to navigation. The vast swamplands of the sudd have posed a barrier to frequent traversing.

Nonetheless, the main conduit of migratory people and agricultural innovation has been in a southerly direction along this axis.

Ancient and Modern Peasantries

There is evidence of the existence of an ancient Nile Valley agrarian kingdom, the Kerma culture, as early as 1600 B.C.E. in what is now the Sudan. It is believed that this kingdom was absorbed by the imperial expansion of Egypt in 1500–1000 B.C.E. More recent Christian kingdoms of the Nile Valley were established from the seventh century C.E. onward. Despite the drought-prone nature of northern Sudan, the use of waterwheels and plows created localities of relatively high agricultural productivity and the possibility of tribute-paying peasants. Peasants performed labor services and paid taxes in kind. The system of taxation was structured to gather goods of potential export value, such as cotton. In the fourteenth century, the elites of most of these agrarian kingdoms adopted Islam. Market influences emanating from the Mediterranean began to undermine the foundations of the kingdoms in the eighteenth century. Merchants grew in power, amassing land by foreclosing on indebted peasants and switching to reliance on the labor of imported slaves from the south for large-scale plantation production. Some of the dispossessed peasants were destined to become slave raiders, seizing neighboring tribal people by force to supply labor to the northern merchant class as well as to the imperial ambitions of the Egyptian government under Muhammad 'Ali Pasha (1769–1849).

Ethiopia has been strongly identified with peasant agriculture throughout its long-recorded history. The combined power of the Ethiopian church and a succession of highland kingdoms has constituted an enduring apparatus of surplus extraction. The adoption of ox plows sometime before 1000 B.C.E. resulted in higher-yielding agriculture and more densely populated settlements than in the surrounding, drier lowlands. The Aksum kingdom flourished from 100 to 700 C.E. The Aksumite king Ezana converted to Christianity around 330 C.E. It is apparent that although slave labor was used in Ethiopia during the last millennium, the constraints placed on active engagement in slave trading by the Christian scriptures restricted the spread of slavery. Thus, the family labor system of the Ethiopian peasantry predominated. With the waning of the Aksum kingdom, a succession of kingdoms followed until the mid-eighteenth century, when the nobility triumphed over the monarchy. Peasants had claims on land through *rist* ancestral descent, but the nobility demanded tribute in the form of agricultural products and labor under the *gult* system of surplus appropriation.

Environmental and climatic extremes of the regions to the south—namely, the arid lowlands of Ethiopia, Somalia, northern Kenya, and northern Uganda, as well as the dry-wetland complex of southern Sudan—proved to be a barrier to the establishment of high-yielding sedentary agricultural systems. At relatively low levels of population density, pastoralist forms of livelihood and tribal social organizations were most common. The pastoralist belt, spanning the width of eastern Africa and running through southern Sudan and Ethiopia, Somalia, and the drier parts of Kenya, Uganda, and Tanzania, marked a clear boundary line between the different agrarian traditions of the northern and southern zones of eastern Africa. The latter is an older agrarian tradition that is identified with many crops unique to Ethiopia, for example enset, or "false banana" (*Ensete ventricosum*), and teff (*Eragrostis tef*). While there were early Cushitic food producers in Kenya and Tanzania by 1000 B.C.E., evidence suggests that agricultural specialization based on Iron Age hoe technology and the cultivation of grain crops such as sorghum and millet, which would come to characterize the southern zone, spread with the migration of Bantu-speaking peoples from the north sometime after 500 B.C.E.

Hoe agriculture was associated with the kingdoms and tribute-paying peasants of various high rainfall areas in Kenya, Uganda, and Tanzania that European explorers encountered in the mid and late nineteenth century. In the intralacustrine region where Uganda, Tanzania, and Rwanda meet, Tutsi pastoralists ruled over peasant cultivators. In other areas—for example, Uhaya, Uchagga, and Usambara, in Tanzania; and Buganda, in Uganda—the ruling class was not occupationally distinct from those it ruled. The wealth of these agrarian kingdoms rested on extremely high-yielding banana production. In the dryer savanna areas, there was a complex mosaic of tribal communities practicing a mixture of shifting cultivation, pastoralism, and hunting and gathering. During the nineteenth century, these communities were increasingly subject to slave raiding and to the economic stimuli of traders associated with the Omani commercial empire that eventually headquartered itself on Zanzibar Island.

Madagascar, physically removed from continental Africa and subject to Indonesian migration in the first half of the first millennium C.E., experienced a succession of militarized kingdoms beginning in the seventeenth century, that of the Sakalava in the western part of the island, the Betsimisaraka in the east, and finally the powerful Merina kingdom which had gained possession of firearms and was the last kingdom before the imposition of French colonial rule. Whereas the former kingdoms had strong seafaring influences and were based on trade, which included slaves, the Merina kingdom had a primarily agrarian foundation. Peasant producers achieved high yields practicing intensive forms of terraced rice cultivation in the kingdom's highland areas. The Merina king Andrianampoinimerina was reported to have declared that "the seas are the limits of my rice-fields." Large-scale public works were initiated to construct irrigation canals which, for the first time, made possible two crops of rice per year.

When Mauritius—hitherto unpopulated—was settled by the Dutch in 1638 (just one of many colonial ventures in the western Indian Ocean during the seventeenth century), the island became a center for sugar production that was based on slave and indentured labor, rather than peasant labor. One is left to speculate if the lack of an indigenous population precluded the development of a Mauritian peasantry.

Peasantries During the Colonial Period

European colonialism and the influence of the world market asserted itself in the rest of eastern Africa at the close of the nineteenth century. The opening of the Suez Canal in 1869 made continental eastern Africa economically accessible to Europe for the first time. The European "scramble" for Africa began soon after. Colonial annexation encompassed all eastern African territories with the exception of Ethiopia, where military resistance was successful largely because of the ability of the state to call on a continual supply of peasant conscripts.

The imposition of European rule incorporated the existing peasantries and created peasant societies in ecological zones which had hitherto posed obstacles to generating and collecting surpluses. The result was the peasantization of vast expanses of eastern Africa. Peasantization was accomplished through colonial taxation, increasingly collected in cash rather than in kind, and through the attendant introduction of new crops and promotion of peasant commodity production.

It is significant that a similar process of monetization and widening surplus appropriation took place in Ethiopia under Menilek and later Haile Sellassie as the country developed into an imperial state in which tax collection became more standardized. Hitherto, the state had tended to depend on local intermediaries as tax collectors—that is, quasi-state officials, church functionaries, and soldiers—which had led to a great deal of local variation in the amount and form of peasant taxation. With deemphasis on the role of local intermediaries as tax collectors, rising levels of corruption and extortion from peasants on the part of the displaced intermediaries occurred in addition to official taxation.

Hut and poll taxes and tariffs on external trade were the main forms of colonial taxation. To pay taxes, peasants were obliged to be in possession of cash earned by selling either their labor or commodities. In either case, certain technical innovations and captial investments had to be undertaken by the state. In many areas, colonial government officials or missionaries introduced cash crops such as coffee, cocoa, cotton, tea, and sisal. Irrigation schemes were devised to facilitate the spread of cotton cultivation in the Sudan and sugar and banana production in southern Somalia along the Juba and Shabelle Rivers. Furthermore, investment in transport infrastructure was vital. Railroads from coastal entrepôts were built at the turn of the century to tap the main commodity-producing regions of the hinterland. Road building was a continual colonial preoccupation in up-country districts. Given the vulnerability of peasants to harvest fluctuation, particularly in agricultural systems where food surpluses were neither large nor reliable, colonial famine prevention was a necessary counterbalance to government taxation policy.

While slavery was outlawed and peasant societies expanded dramatically during the colonial period, it should be stressed that peasant production was not ubiquitous throughout eastern Africa. Various agricultural patterns evolved. For the first half of the twentieth century, Uganda and Ethiopia represent the clearest examples of states whose policies fostered the conditions for maintaining and taxing peasant production. In Sudan, it was originally the intention of the British to create an extensive peasantry associated with the new irrigation works, but the emergence of an indigenous rural landowning class was not checked, and labor tenancy followed. In Kenya, European settlers succeeded in getting colonial government support for the appropriation of land and the creation of an African tenant class in the service of European planters. In Tanganyika (part of present-day Tanzania), while peasant production was encouraged in various areas, other areas of European land appropriation gave rise to a plantation sector which siphoned African labor from the more remote parts of the country where peasant commodity production was not considered viable because of the lack of transport infrastructure.

Independence and After

After roughly eighty years of colonial domination, one by one most eastern African countries gained their political independence during the 1960s. In many countries, the new ruling elites successfully mobilized peasant support for their struggle against the colonial powers. The national governments, not surprisingly, were heavily laden with agrarian values regarding the necessity for ensuring the basic subsistence needs of their populations, particularly with respect to the priority placed on ensuring national food security.

Independence resolved political tensions while creating new economic contradictions. Colonial governments had tended to operate with tightly restricted budgets and skeletal staffing, and they had few welfare goals. Postcolonial governments, however, won support on the basis of promises of far-ranging improvements to the living standards of the national population. In addition, they had modernizing ambitions which took the form of industrialization and rapid urbanization. Their taxation strategies had to accommodate heavy state expenditure. Yet peasants associated taxation, particularly poll taxes, with colonialism, and the new national governments risked deep unpopularity by imposing such taxes.

Governments increasingly relied on indirect taxation, which they realized by controlling the terms on which peasants marketed commodities. Peasant producer prices were depressed relative to world market prices, boosting government revenues, as illustrated by export crop pricing in Tanzania during the 1970s. International financial institutions (IFIs), such as the World Bank and the International Monetary Fund (IMF), argued that lower prices had disincentive effects on peasant commodity production.

In the 1960s and 1970s, many countries had considerable success in achieving their welfare goals.

Investment in health care and education led to measurable improvements in infant mortality rates and peasant life expectancies in rural areas. One outcome was a steady increase in population and, consequently, demographic pressure on land. In some countries, the problem of decreasing rural land availability was alleviated when peasants migrated to urban jobs. But in other countries, the strain was very severe and expressed itself in an increasing incidence of food shortages culminating in devastating famines, such as the ones experienced in Ethiopia and Sudan in the mid-1970s and then repeated less than a decade later in the 1980s.

In the countries where environmental stress was not so extreme, the mid- to late 1970s was a period of economic crisis arising from the oil price boom. Given the vast distances over which African agricultural goods travel to get to shipment points, the oil price rise dealt a severe blow to the international competitiveness of commodities produced by peasants on the continent. Peasants in many eastern African countries lost significant amounts of their share in international markets for important exports like coffee, cotton, and tea. The peasants' losses translated into diminished tax revenues and thus into cutbacks in social services and a rapid decline in the social and economic welfare of many segments of the rural population. Heavy reliance on external donor funding and increasing foreign indebtedness ensued.

Given the context of economic uncertainty, the political legitimacy of many eastern African states was being questioned in the 1980s and early 1990s by both internal and external forces. Sudan went through several upheavals, Uganda was highly unstable until the late 1980s, Ethiopia's military regime was toppled in 1991, and Somalia erupted in the early 1990s. More generally, an increasing reliance on foreign aid made the eastern African states subject to the insistence of the World Bank and IMF that these states reform their domestic economic policies, notably government control over peasant smallholder crop marketing.

Under pressure, eastern African governments implemented structural adjustment programs throughout the region beginning in the 1980s. Market liberalization was a central component of the programs, justified in terms of the need for the comparative advantage of smallholders' commodity production in the world market to emerge. However, these policies were implemented at a time when the terms of trade for eastern Africa's most important peasant commodity exports were extremely low. In partial recognition of this fact, IFIs promoted the establishment of "nontraditional" export crops, notably horticultural products, which were transported by air to Western consumer markets. Producing these crops required substantial capital investment.

It is uncertain who will be the long-term beneficiaries of structural adjustment policies. In the short term, the agricultural producers who can respond to the market are those in climatically favorable areas with good road access. There has been a strong bias in much economic policy and practice toward large-scale commercial producers rather than peasant smallholders. Evidence from several countries suggests that a land aggregation process is unfolding. Government officials, retrenched by structural adjustment policies, are often leading actors in the acquisition of peasant land. Unwittingly, peasant producers may have been quietly jettisoned by structural adjustment policies originally intended as the means of providing the right financial incentives for eastern African smallholders.

BIBLIOGRAPHY

A general reference on eastern African peasantries is not available. Information can be gleaned from relevant chapters in the *Cambridge History of Africa* (Cambridge, 1982–1984) as well as books and articles covering the histories of individual countries and groups of rural people. The following list attempts to provide at least one reference for each country in the eastern African region and should be considered a starting point from which further references can be traced.

Bahru Zewde. *A History of Modern Ethiopia, 1855–1974.* London, 1991.

Brett, Edwin Allen. *Colonialism and Underdevelopment in East Africa: The Politics of Change, 1919–1939.* London, 1973.

Bryceson, Deborah Fahy. *Food Insecurity and the Social Division of Labour in Tanzania, 1919–1985.* New York, 1990.

Iliffe, John. *A Modern History of Tanganyika.* Cambridge, 1979.

Kapteijns, Lidwien, and Jay Spaulding. "History, Ethnicity, and Agriculture in the Sudan." In *The Agriculture of the Sudan,* edited by G. M. Craig. Oxford, 1991.

Kitching, Gavin. *Class and Economic Change in Kenya: The Making of an African Petite Bourgeoisie, 1905–1970.* New Haven, Conn., 1980.

Kongstad, Per, and Mette Mönsted. *Family, Labour, and Trade in Western Kenya.* Uppsala, Sweden, 1980.

Lewis, Ioan M. *A Pastoral Democracy: A Study of Pastoralism and Politics Among the Northern Somali of the Horn of Africa.* London, 1961.

Leys, Colin. *Underdevelopment in Kenya: The Political Economy of Neo-Colonialism, 1964–1971.* Berkeley, 1975.

McCann, James. *From Poverty to Famine in Northeast Ethiopia: A Rural History, 1900–1935.* Philadelphia, 1987.

North-Coombes, Alfred. *A History of Sugar Production in Mauritius.* Mauritius, 1993.

Ogot, Bethwell A., and John A. Kieran, eds. *Zamani: A Survey of East African History.* Nairobi, Kenya, 1968.

Pankhurst, Richard. *Economic History of Ethiopia, 1800–1935.* Addis Ababa, Ethiopia, 1968.

Raison, Jean-Pierre. *Les hautes terres de Madagascar et leur confins occidentaux: Enracinement et mobilité des sociétés rurales.* Bondy, France, 1984.

Spaulding, Jay. *The Heroic Age in Sinn-ar.* East Lansing, Mich., 1982.

DEBORAH FAHY BRYCESON

See also **Agriculture; Archaeology and Prehistory; Colonial Policies and Practice; Development; Ecosystems; Postcolonial State; Production Systems.**

EASTERN AFRICAN LAND REFORM AND RESETTLEMENT

Eastern Africa has seen several of the continent's boldest official attempts to change human attachments to land, and among these, some of its most spectacular failures. Some have been "land reforms" to redistribute people and their activities over land, as by resettlement or the consolidation of fragmented holdings. Others are "land *tenure* reforms" to change rules about rights and duties in land or about modes of access to it. The most important attempts of both kinds have been designed and implemented by colonial or national governments—some, since the mid-twentieth century, with the initiative and financial and managerial backing of foreign nations and the World Bank and other international agencies. In most cases the designs of central planners and implementers have been profoundly affected by local actors with their own understandings, assumptions, and intentions, and by ecological conditions not always well understood or fully appreciated by policymakers. Directed reforms often have undirected outcomes.

Overlapping claims of individuals and groups have long been the essence of African landholding and use. In most rural areas the precise mix of competing claims varies seasonally. Landholding is tightly woven together with social identity, particularly among agrarian peoples. At all times in written and oral histories, eastern African kings, chiefs, clan and lineage heads, and senior age-set members have, in their various settings, claimed different powers to reallocate land in occupancy and usage, human and animal. In many areas, however, these powers have seldom been exercised in practice. They do not add up to "insecurity of customary tenure," as some Euro-American reformists have supposed. What can be described as insecure is tenure under remote national regimes that is subject to shifting policies and market forces controlled in cities or overseas, or subject to competing modes of law. Two main kinds of reforms removing tenure from local control have been individuation and socialization.

Individual Titling

Strengthening the land claims of some persons means weakening those of others, who may include dependents or neighbors. An early colonial attempt to reform property rights in eastern Africa was the Uganda Agreement of 1900, which designated about eight thousand square miles of land in the Ganda kingdom for titling as individual estates, which acquired the name *mailo.* Originally planned for one thousand holders, the program actually gave out about seventeen thousand titles by its closure in 1936, and the numbers on the registers have continued to multiply. Allocated mostly to chiefs and wealthy men at the outset, *mailo* holdings were soon subdivided into shares of quite unequal sizes and qualities. Several other smaller-scale titling initiatives have also been attempted in Uganda. The Rujumbura Pilot Land Registration Scheme, launched in 1958 in Kigezi District, showed by the late 1980s a possible statistical increase in farm input investments, apparently as a result of titling, but little increase in use of credit, for better or worse.

Kenya has become Africa's preeminent test case of individual titling since the 1950s, when its British colonial government extended titling from "scheduled" (European settler) areas to what were classed as "native reserves"—that is, it attempted tenure reform nearly nationwide. The tenure reform proposed in the 1954 Swynnerton Plan was passed into law as the Native Land Tenure Rules of 1956, superseded by the Native Lands Registration Ordinance of 1959 and the comprehensive Registered Land Act of 1963. The titling program has continued with little modification since independence in 1963. From the outset the program's immediate aims have been twofold: to consolidate fragmented holdings into larger units and to register rural land as marketable (freehold) individual property. Its deeper motives have been several, including visions of making land usable as collateral for loans (as in a mortgage system); increasing individual incentives to develop and conserve land, allowing able or energetic farmers to obtain more land; and through consolidation, making mechanization more feasible and rewarding. A hidden ulterior motive, in a time of Mau Mau insurrection, was to form a yeoman middle class with vested interests in political stability. Making rural land taxable has been another motive for continuing the "reform," but one not widely broadcast in the countryside.

Kenyans had by the 1990s titled most of the country's arable lands, but debates, misunderstandings, and litigation continue to hinder the reform process. Farmers broadly refuse to continue reporting to government bureaus their land transactions, often for sound reasons. Doing so can require high fees, bribes, or both; it can involve time-consuming travel and red tape; it exposes the transactants to legal scrutiny they may not welcome; and for sellers or lenders, it closes possibilities of later retaking the land by fair means or otherwise. This has made the land register tend to obsolesce in practice. Consolidation of holdings has succeeded in some areas and been stiffly resisted (again for sound ecological and economic reasons, it turns out) in others. As some 95 percent of registered titleholders by the late 1980s were male, women had been, in a formal sense, legally dispossessed. But many unofficial rights and duties persist, sometimes conflicting with official ones.

The economic and financial ambitions of this program have remained largely unfulfilled. Institutional lenders have refused to accept land titles as a sufficient condition for loans. Where farmers lived among kin and near ancestral graves, as they do in most of Kenya's farming areas, it turned out politically difficult or impossible for lenders to foreclose on mortgages and sell off rural land once borrowers had fallen into arrears or defaulted. Doing so risked violence. The promise of credit—which also means debt—has thus in no way justified the sweeping land tenure reform.

Other justifications are elusive too. There are no sound indications that individual titling increases farm yields. Nor is there clear evidence that land buyers and their heirs or assignees are any more productive farmers and herders than are sellers—many are urban-based speculators. But these remain open questions. In some areas resettled by members of different ethnic groups with different traditions of landholding and inheritance, a state-imposed titling system, if free of political abuse,

would appear to help establish common understanding and agreement about claims. The future of landholding in Kenya's large but thinly settled pastoral grazing areas—places where private titling seems least suited of all—remains uncertain.

The most important potential effect of Kenya's tenure reform, speeding a concentration of holdings into fewer hands, was in fact part of its original design. Such a trend is hard to measure, partly because of smaller countertrends to proliferate claims. With titles, individuals can more easily pledge or sell land out from under their unknowing or unwilling families to speculators and others. In all, the results of the grand titling experiment are hardly encouraging for Africans elsewhere.

Also fraught with problems have been the results of Somalia's attempts at land tenure reform since British and Italian colonial times. Through capitalist and socialist regimes since independence in 1960, the nation's assault on clan control over landholding has been fairly constant, remitting only with the collapse of the Somali government in civil war in the late 1980s. By then, under the national Agricultural Land Law (1975), some 10 percent of rural land was titled as leasehold. Further registration was slow and easily manipulated by elites. Attempts to settle pastoral nomads have been resisted and resented.

In individuation programs, rural landholders' reasons for acquiescing to titling do not always correspond to the official rationales of the programs. Some seek titles so that they can migrate or cease farming without giving up land claims. Others accept titling by one branch of government for protection against other branches (for instance, the park service, military, or parastatal crop authorities) or persons acting under their names.

Socialist Reforms and "Villagization"

Eastern Africa's socialist land and tenure reforms have worked out no better than its capitalist ones, and arguably worse. Tanzania's and Ethiopia's governments have both attempted bold nationwide villagization programs (grouping scattered rural populations into larger or more tightly nucleated settlements) in conjunction with broader, doctrinally inspired socialist economic programs. The two nations' experiments have had different starting points but roughly parallel outcomes.

Tanzania's socialist reform officially began in 1967, with the Arusha Declaration. Basing its political rhetoric on the ideal of national familyhood (in Swahili, *ujamaa*), the government of Julius Nyerere officially abolished private landowning over most of the country. Over the next few years the government established some eight thousand registered, nucleated, cooperative villages for about five million people it compulsorily or voluntarily resettled. An announced goal was to bring people closer to basic services like water, health, and schooling.

Ethiopia's socialist reform, begun under the newly established Derg in 1975, nationalized land, dispossessed a rather feudalistic nobility, set up farmer associations, prohibited alienation except by inheritance, and ostensibly guaranteed a minimum holding under usufruct to any needy family. Populistic measures evolved into statist ones in Ethiopia as in Tanzania as villagization, rural producer cooperatives, and state farms promised to provide conveniently located services but proved as much to be, in both cases, ways of extending state political control over the countryside. Ethiopian farmers found tenure of state-allotted lands insecure, and migration hard. Production rose somewhat, then declined, and despite economic policies favoring collective farms, smallholder peasant farms kept outproducing them.

A basic problem of compulsory villagization is that the resettled people tend soon to exhaust the land resources immediately surrounding the new villages. To farm, to collect firewood, or even to find water, villagers must then travel farther and farther on a daily basis or else split up their families to establish outstations. Villagization is thus usually least appropriate where soils are thin and other resources scarce to begin with.

The major socialist reforms have also been beset with problems of work incentive. Where farmers have both individual and collective plots, they tend to spend far more time on the former to the neglect of the latter, the personal rewards of which are less sure or direct.

The effects of socialization and villagization are analytically distinguishable; though these programs coincided in the cases of Tanzania and Ethiopia, they need not do so in others. In these two countries, both villagization and the broader socialist reforms were followed within a few years by rural countermovements and backmigrations—and eventual official policy reversals. Tanzania's government embarked in the 1990s on a new policy of registering village titles to land and allowing villages some autonomy over internal land administration.

Land Nationalization

Among the state tenure reforms discussed above, some have included proclamations that all land is public or state property. Three examples, all in 1975, were Ethiopia's land reform, Uganda's Land Reform Decree, and Somalia's Agricultural Land Law. National governments always claim ultimate sovereignty or eminent domain, and such proclamations when explicit are sometimes used as cover for dispossession of disfavored ethnic minorities and for land grabs by civil servants or other well-connected persons. Officials who can classify land as idle and unoccupied often deny the needs of long-term fallowers; other intermittent users such as water, firewood, or thatch collectors; or herders who graze animals on others' crop stubble after harvest. "Rights" includes the right to exclude.

Local Resettlements

Eastern Africans have experienced local voluntary and involuntary land resettlement of various kinds. Early-twentieth-century displacements of Africans by European farmers have been partially redressed by state resettlement programs to repurchase and subdivide such farms for a new generation of African settlers. East Africa's largest such program, a voluntary and relatively successful one, has been Kenya's Million Acre Scheme, inaugurated in mid-1962. By the time of completion in 1971, it had transferred about four hundred seventy thousand hectares (1.16 million acres) in the fertile central and western highlands from 970 European to about thirty-five thousand African titled holders, many with state loans; other schemes in Kenya raised the numbers higher. Not all these people, however, came from the land poor or landless strata as had been widely hoped. Many appear to have been chosen instead because officials deemed them likely to be able to repay.

Rural people in numerous eastern African settings have been resettled from areas taken over for cash-crop plantations (as in western Kenya's tea and sugar estates), airports, and so on, or from river-basin areas flooded by new dams. The experiences of these people, in eastern Africa as worldwide, seem generally to have been unhappy ones.

Monetary compensation for land expropriated, as for setting up plantations, almost never satisfies its recipients lastingly, and the money seldom arrives as promised anyway. Resettlement tends to shake public confidence in local leaders, partly for the self-evident reason that they have failed to prevent it, and the loss of symbolic landmarks can be profoundly disorienting, psychologically and culturally. Harmful psychological effects can merge into physiological ones as grief over perceived loss of lands and culture contribute to problems like depression, alcoholism, homicide, and suicide.

Irrigated settlements for cash cropping, which once seemed like a possible panacea for dealing with African droughts and poverty, have raised yields in some settings but given rise to many unanticipated political, economic, and ecological problems as well as more easily identifiable technical and logistical ones. Irrigation programs have been mainly administered through statal or parastatal bodies such as irrigation boards. Sudan's schemes, begun in the 1920s, are the largest, covering over 1.6 million hectares (4 million acres) and including some three hundred thousand tenant families; they incorporate, among others, the giant Gezira (al Jazirah) scheme and its Managil extension; the Zande, Kinanah, and New Halfa schemes (mostly planned for cotton growing); and movements associated with the Jonglei Canal's drainage of the sudd. Other smaller irrigation projects elsewhere include the Tana River (Mwea, Bura) and Lake Victoria (Nyanza) Basin schemes (Ahero, Bunyala) in Kenya.

Generally, irrigation-scheme inhabitants have suffered from hasty program planning and rigid, top-down bureaucratic control of their lives. Dependence on cash cropping has meant vulnerability to volatile world prices. Factors like these have driven many irrigation-scheme inhabitants into intermittent labor migration, dividing their families. Women's interests have tended to be overlooked in the allocation of land, labor, and cash rewards. Flooding has entailed intractable water-related public health problems like malaria and schistosomiasis. These are things hard to weigh precisely against the benefits of raised agricultural production or, in the case of dams, hydroelectric power.

Some east African cities, including Nairobi, have experienced coercive local clearances of spontaneously settled peri-urban shanties. Often unpredictable, and carried out in the name of economic development or law, these forceful removals sometimes involve government-implemented attacks on particular ethnic enclaves or voter concentrations, and their effects remain poorly understood.

International Migration and Resettlement

Wars have always caused migration and resettlement in eastern Africa as elsewhere, and disparities in economic opportunity and political liberties have always caused slower demographic flows. In the late twentieth century, substantial movements across borders have accompanied civil disturbances and famines in Uganda, Sudan, Ethiopia, and Somalia. Within Ethiopia in the 1970s and 1980s, the government forcibly resettled northeasterners, notably from Wollo, Tigre, and Eritrea, to the southwest, partly for political reasons disguised as economic ones.

Movements of Hutu and Tutsi speakers from war-torn Rwanda and Burundi into Tanzania, Zaire, and other surrounding countries, and (for some) back, in the 1990s have been among Africa's most dramatic recorded mass migrations, with numbers into several millions. Settlement camps have been organized by migrants themselves, by host governments, and by numerous international relief agencies, at the risk of permanent dependency, but some migrants have spread themselves among local populations. Governments distrust and disrespect migrants. Refugees frequently lack public services and protection by their old or new states, and while their welcome by host populations can vary between warm accommodation and suspicious persecution, they are seldom accorded high status.

Research on the social effects of resettlement, in eastern Africa and elsewhere, shows that migrants experience recognizably phased periods of adjustment, involving a period of social shock and cultural conservatism followed by a period of looser experimentation and innovation and sometimes one of broader assimilation. But if such sequences are fairly predictable, the duration of the phases is not. Helping keep communities intact through resettlement, when their members have chosen, has sometimes helped their adjustments.

Conclusion

Land and land tenure reforms have proved both difficult and dangerous, in eastern Africa as elsewhere, even though experiences have varied widely by ecozone and by ethnic group. Broadly, African people have thwarted and transmuted ideologically rooted property reforms meant to turn them into capitalists or socialists. Policymakers' attempts to force what they see as social evolution—however defined—usually fail. No kind of "development" initiative proves more damaging to lands and livelihoods than compulsory resettlement. Forced settling of nomads, in particular, leads almost inexorably to impoverishment and misery.

Human feelings about belonging are deep, complex, and generally inadequately understood in their cultural, psychological, and political ramifications. They cannot easily be reengineered from national or international capitals, for this usually means reworking the roots of human societies themselves. Knowing what tenure reform and resettlement initiatives might merit official support means heeding which ones people have begun on their own, and such intervention proves least disruptive if it involves a feeling of participation or representation by the people directly concerned.

BIBLIOGRAPHY

Bassett, Thomas J., and Donald E. Crummey, eds. *Land in African Agrarian Systems.* Madison, Wisc., 1993.

Colson, Elizabeth. *The Social Consequences of Resettlement: The Impact of the Kariba Resettlement upon the Gwembe Tonga.* Manchester, U.K., 1971.

Davison, Jean, ed. *Agriculture, Women, and Land: The African Experience.* Boulder, Colo., 1988.

Dessalegn Rahmato. *Agrarian Reform in Ethiopia.* Uppsala, Sweden, 1984.

Downs, R. E., and S. P. Reyna, eds. *Land and Society in Contemporary Africa.* Hanover, N.H., 1988.

Glazier, Jack. *Land and the Uses of Tradition Among the Mbeere of Kenya.* Lanham, Md., 1985.

Goheen, Miriam, and Parker Shipton, eds. "Rights over Land: Categories and Controversies." *Africa* 62, no. 3 (1992). Special issue.

Hansen, Art, and Anthony Oliver-Smith, eds. *Involuntary Migration and Resettlement: The Problems and Responses of Dislocated People.* Boulder, Colo., 1982.

Hyden, Goran. *Beyond Ujamaa in Tanzania: Underdevelopment and an Uncaptured Peasantry.* Berkeley, 1980.

Malkki, Liisa H. *Purity and Exile: Violence, Memory, and National Cosmology Among Hutu Refugees in Tanzania.* Chicago, 1995.

Okoth-Ogendo, H. W. O. *Tenants of the Crown: Evolution of Agrarian Law and Institutions in Kenya.* Nairobi, Kenya, 1991.

Salem-Murdock, Muneera. *Arabs and Nubians in New Halfa: A Study of Settlement and Irrigation.* Salt Lake City, 1989.

Shipton, Parker. "Land and Culture in Tropical Africa: Soils, Symbols, and the Metaphysics of the Mundane." *Annual Review of Anthropology* 23 (1994): 347–377.

West, Henry W. *Land Policy in Buganda.* Cambridge, 1972.

PARKER SHIPTON

See also **Agriculture; Colonial Policies and Practice; Development; Economic History; Labor; Land Tenure Systems; Law; Mau Mau; Nyerere, Julius Kambarage; Postcolonial State; Refugees.**

CENTRAL AND SOUTHERN AFRICA

Peasants are small-scale tillers of the land and keepers of livestock whose ultimate economic and social security lies in their land rights and family labor teams. They may hire extra labor or themselves work for wages, but the focus of their lives is the family farm and the satisfaction of family needs. Their self-sufficiency and autonomy are highly valued ideals that are never attained; peasants are always part of a larger social system in which they occupy a subordinate political position. Peasants must regularly provide food or labor for public works projects and perform military service. They are obliged to pay tribute, rent, or tax in one form or another to their ruling classes.

Although there were tribute-paying peasantries in precolonial central and southern Africa, many writers on peasant societies in these regions are interested mainly in the period of an expanding colonial capitalist economy. They have studied the impact upon peasant societies of the colonial capitalist economy in which peasants participate as migrant workers or small-scale, cash-crop farmers or both. Radical scholars postulated the proletarianization of the peasantry as a logical outcome of the process of peasant differentiation under capitalism, and thus saw peasants as a transitory category of rural Africans. Poor peasants were expected to abandon their increasingly small and infertile plots of land and become dependent on wages, while rich peasants would expand production and become capitalist farmers. However, there has been no uniform process of peasant differentiation, and the uneven pace of development has produced different outcomes in different countries.

From Wage Labor to Peasant Farming in Zambia

Peasant societies in central Africa resemble those in southern Africa in many ways, but capitalist economic development has a longer history and has had a greater social impact in southern Africa. There are more European settler farmers in South Africa and Zimbabwe than in Botswana, Zambia, or Malawi; wherever European farmers have settled in large numbers, large-scale farming enterprises have developed, rendering many peasants landless in the process. In such countries, wars of liberation have been fought over land as well as over democratic rights.

Central African peasant societies still farm on a small scale, using hand tools and, occasionally, ox-drawn implements. Malawi, Zambia, and Mozambique have a combination of large estate, plantation, and peasant agriculture. In these countries, peasants are not separate from the capitalist economy; in fact, the viability and growth of peasant farming depends on peasants' participation in the capitalist economy. Remittances and savings of migrant workers, as well as the sale of produce in the towns and cities, play a crucial role in peasant societies. Equally important in the past was the role played by the colonial and national governments in promoting sections of the population and helping them to make the transition to market-oriented farming. In Zambia, the involvement of state agencies in farmers' training and credit programs, and even the marketing of produce, was crucial in pushing peasants further into the capitalist economy.

The Zambian economy long relied upon the copper mines as the major employer and earner of foreign exchange. The contribution of peasant farmers to the national economy was so low that they were generally dismissed as subsistence producers. The steady decline in the mining industry and the national economy generally since the 1970s has made peasant farming more important for the survival of the low-income sections of the population and has made the movement from wage employment to peasant farming feasible. Zambian government statisticians estimate the urban population to be about half of the total; but though the country may appear to be urbanized, it is common for people to straddle the urban and peasant economies as a matter of necessity.

Peasants Under Socialism in Mozambique

Peasants in Mozambique have experienced the problems of both capitalist- and socialist-oriented development, as well as the stress caused by prolonged war, drought, and famine. Beginning in the colonial period, peasant society was influenced by the migration of male laborers to the gold mines in South Africa, to farms in South Africa and Southern Rhodesia (now Zimbabwe), and to Portuguese-owned plantations within Mozambique. In some areas the forced production of cotton also disrupted village life. As a result, self-provisioning was greatly undermined, thereby making wage labor and the purchase of food common in many Mozambican peasant societies.

After Mozambique's independence in 1975 the Marxist FRELIMO (Mozambique Liberation Front) government, in a campaign against exploitative capitalist relations, tried to stop its citizens from working in the South African mines. Agricultural production soon fell due to the lack of resources for farm implements, fertilizers, and other inputs. The campaign against exploitation put peasant societies under economic stress. For Mozambicans,

as for Malawians and Zambians, security lies in creative straddling of the urban and rural economies by both peasants and the urban poor, thereby blurring the distinction between peasant and proletarian.

Peasants' attempts to protect their autonomy against the socialist state continued to use the tactics developed during the colonial period. Thus, if government-controlled corn prices were lower than those for beans, peasants planted beans. When the cassava price was deregulated, they switched to cassava. When money became worthless, as a result of prolonged economic crisis, barter became the norm. Corn was exchanged for fruits and vegetables even by government agencies. Under such circumstances, peasants could prosper until the civil war reached their village.

During the civil war of the 1980s, many of Mozambique's peasant societies were destroyed. People fled to neighboring countries or were displaced internally, separated from their families. In the chaos of the civil war, especially attacks by the Mozambique Resistance Movement (RENAMO) on rural communities, the parallel economy became more important, as did the Mozambican peasants' dependence on international relief and labor migration to South Africa. Thousands of Mozambicans risked the electrified fence and the wild animals in Kruger National Park to find security, though not a normal life, in South African refugee camps.

Southern Africa's Proletarianized Peasant Societies

In recent years, researchers in rural southern Africa have found that wages, remittances from migrant workers, and pensions, rather than self-provisioning agriculture, provide most rural people with their livelihood. This would seem to suggest that the process of proletarianization has been completed and that there are few peasant societies left in southern Africa. Swaziland and Botswana, more than Lesotho and South Africa, can claim to be predominantly peasant societies. In all countries, however, the shortage of land has made peasant farming unviable. At the same time, rural farmworkers and tenants still hope for, and are campaigning to regain, their land rights.

If the democratically elected government of national unity were to transfer large tracts of land to the rural population, a viable peasant agriculture could be reestablished. In general, the experience of Lesotho, which turned from a grain-exporting peasant economy into a food-importing labor reserve of South Africa, exemplifies the sort of underdevelopment that other parts of rural southern Africa have experienced. Transkei and the Orange Free State also recorded periods of growth in peasant economies that made a major contribution to capital accumulation in South Africa. The boom ended when the ecological optimum was reached, and both the human and the livestock populations exceeded the carrying capacity of the available land. The land laws of 1913 and 1936 decreased the ability of African peasants to sustain their growth even more because they were not allowed to obtain land outside their reserves. Although the Nationalist party government's Tomlinson Commission of 1955 noted that Africans in the rural reserves needed more land, there was never a major redistribution of land to the landless. Some of the problems experienced by the rural population were a consequence of government policy, and the demands of many black former landowners that the new government correct the wrong policies of the past are very strong in former peasant communities.

Peasant societies in both central and southern Africa need much more than land reforms for their well-being and development. As a part of the global economy, they participate in a market where anything from secondhand American clothes to electronic goods from Taiwan may be exchanged for their crops, and where changes in international currency exchange rates may render them poorer overnight. In the final analysis, the fate of peasant societies depends on the success of their national and regional economies.

BIBLIOGRAPHY

Bundy, Colin. *The Rise and Fall of the South African Peasantry.* Berkeley, Calif., 1979.

Chipungu, Sam N. *The State, Technology, and Peasant Differentiation in Zambia: A Case Study of the Southern Province, 1930–1986.* Lusaka, Zambia, 1987.

MacIntosh, Maureen. "Mozambique Case Study." In *Agricultural Pricing Policy in Africa.* Edited by Charles Harvey. London, 1988.

Murray, Colin. "Lesotho: From Granary to Labour Reserve." In *Transformations on the Highveld: The Tswana and the Southern Sotho.* Edited by William F. Lyle and Colin Murray. London, 1980.

Sandbrook, Richard. *The Politics of Africa's Economic Recovery.* Cambridge, 1993.

Saul, John, and Roger Woods. "African Peasantries." In *Peasants and Peasant Societies.* Edited by Teodor Shanin. 2d ed. Oxford, 1987.

OWEN SICHONE

See also **Agriculture; Development; Economic History; Gender; Production Systems.**

SOUTHERN AFRICA

In both the colonial and postindependence periods, many African countries have experienced substantial population resettlement. Resettlement is distinguished from other kinds of population movement in that relocation is compulsory. People are either forced by the authorities to move from their homes or, as in the case of refugees, they feel constrained to flee in order to escape violence or famine. Where they are to go and the conditions of their resettlement may or may not be planned for by the authorities. In Africa, the major causes of resettlement have related to dam construction and agricultural schemes, the establishment of socialist villages, and the refugee crisis—with some fifty million people uprooted since World War II.

Over the years, and particularly since the beginning of the apartheid policy in 1948, South African society has been organized along the lines of the administrative and territorial separation of race groups. South Africans have been legally divided into four separate race groups: Black, Coloured, Indian, and White, with the Whites having been accorded ownership of or control over approximately 87 percent of the land surface. Resettlement has occurred principally in terms of this policy of racial separation, reaching its height during the apartheid years.

The Surplus People Project, a nongovernmental organization based in Cape Town, provides the most comprehensive overview of resettlement in South Africa and argues that, up to 1982, the apartheid policy was responsible for the resettlement of more than 3.5 million people. Several important causes led to this resettlement:

- Black farm laborers were turned off or left White-owned farms as, inter alia, mechanization led to a reduced demand for labor and to less favorable conditions of employment (1,129,000 people);
- Removals occurred under the Group Areas Act, which set aside separate residential areas for the different official race groups, and which was related to the concomitant separate administration and use of facilities such as schools (834,000 people);
- Urban relocation was government policy. Black people staying in towns or cities in South Africa were required to live in officially proclaimed Black

townships, usually on the outskirts of the city. A number of these townships were deproclaimed, with people being resettled in newly established centers within the homelands (also known as reserves or bantustans), which had been set aside for Black occupation under the 1913 Natives' Land Act and 1936 Native Trust and Land Bill and subsequent apartheid legislation (730,000 people);

• Homeland consolidation and "Black spot" removals were undertaken. The government sought to make the homelands into units that were as geographically consolidated as possible. Small, separate sections that hindered this process were deproclaimed, and some adjacent White areas were incorporated into homelands. "Black spots"— Black settlements anomalously situated in non-homeland South Africa—were likewise redefined. In both cases people had to move to enable the political jigsaw to fit together (614,000 people).

Other causes of resettlement include "betterment planning" and agricultural settlement schemes. Betterment planning was a government initiative that sought to combat erosion and improve agriculture in the homelands through what planners saw as a more rational land-use plan. Settlements were divided internally into separate arable, grazing, and residential areas, with people having to move into newly established residential areas, particularly from the 1950s through the 1970s. Betterment planning has been by far the largest single cause of resettlement in South Africa, accounting for the displacement of at least three million people. Agricultural settlement schemes were established with the intention of creating jobs and promoting commercial agriculture for both White (e.g., the Vaalharts Irrigation Scheme) and Black farmers (e.g., the Mooifontein maize project in the homeland of Bophuthatswana). These schemes, however, did not involve the compulsion to move integral to the definition of resettlement.

Both betterment and agricultural schemes have been directed primarily toward agricultural rather than explicitly political concerns. Nevertheless they do relate to the overall policy of racial separation when one takes into account the disparities in land allocation, as well as the fact that Black and White agriculture have been administered and financed separately since the Union of South Africa was established in 1910. While White agriculture fell under the Department of Agriculture, Black agriculture fell under the then Department of Native Affairs (subsequently renamed several times and abolished in the early 1990s).

Finally, not to be discounted as a cause of resettlement is the flight from violence. The civil war in Mozambique has led to a considerable number of people seeking safety in neighboring countries, including South Africa, where a number of Mozambican refugees have settled—particularly in the homeland of Gazankulu. The violence in some Black townships and rural areas in South Africa has similarly led to sporadic flight from these areas, whether on a temporary or more permanent basis.

At least 7 million people (equivalent to one-fifth of the South African population in the 1980s) have thus felt the impact of resettlement—largely for political reasons. They have overwhelmingly been people other than those legally defined as White. Some scholars argue that resettlement should be understood not only in the narrow political sense of effecting physical separation of the various race groups, but also in terms of the apartheid policy serving the interests of capital, by allowing for more effective control of the rural proletariat. While this may have been true at certain periods, priorities and alliances have altered over time, both within and between the political and the economic sectors. The gap between possible "real" motives and the frequently ad hoc nature of resettlement on the ground suggests a bureaucracy which, while clearly operating within the paradigm of racial separation, was often involved in crisis-management rather than efficient and coherent long-term collusion.

Involuntary resettlement is an almost universally disruptive and stress-inducing process which involves both geographical and social displacement. Relationships predicated on kinship or territorial ties are disrupted as associates are separated from one another in new residential patterns; people's access to and distance from basic resources such as arable and grazing land, water, and wood, are changed—often for the worse. People may either lose their jobs as a result of the move, or have to travel much farther to work, and find themselves further from basic social services. Involuntary resettlement thus places people at risk of impoverishment.

The greater the degree of spatial change, the greater the disruption and the necessary adjustment. While people undergoing resettlement in South Africa have almost always found themselves in denser and more socially diverse settlements than before, the scale of socio-spatial change has varied according to the type of settlement situation. Betterment-planning areas have usually

389

experienced the least such change, for in such cases people were moved within their own settlement areas (usually a move of not more than a mile or two). They therefore remained within walking distance of friends, relatives, and fields, although patterns of association and conflict have increasingly become predicated on membership of the new residential areas. In many cases people have found themselves with less arable land—in some cases, even no land—as planners sought to implement what they saw as a more rational land-use plan, re-zoning land they regarded as unsuitable for cultivation.

A related kind of resettlement has been the removal of Black communities from their home areas to "trust" land, acquired by the state from White farmers for Black occupation under the 1936 Native Trust and Land Bill. These trust areas (over which the state retained ownership) were often considerable distances from the home areas and involved a much greater degree of change and disruption. A number of these areas have subsequently become unofficial receiving areas for people moved out of non-homeland areas for various reasons, and are therefore overcrowded. Group Areas removals and urban relocation have involved greater distances than betterment resettlement, while yet allowing some—but by no means all—people to be close enough to their former homes to keep contact with their former associates and to keep their jobs. While state housing has been provided for many of these relocatees, people find themselves having to spend more on accommodation, on travel to work, and on goods at local shops, because they live farther from urban shopping areas. Urban relocation to homeland towns has usually involved greater distances and socioeconomic disruption than Group Areas removals, as well as placing people under often unpopular homeland administrative systems.

The greatest spatial change and suffering has been experienced by those people moved to closer settlements in the homelands. They have either been moved to these areas or have had to move there to find a place to stay as they have been turned off of or have left White-owned farms, Black spots, or urban areas. Closer settlements have usually arisen in a fairly ad hoc fashion with minimal planning and service provision, and incomers have generally had to construct their own accommodation. The homeland of Qwaqwa provides the most extreme case of a closer settlement. Between 1969 and the mid-1980s, the population of this homeland of 480 square kilometers increased from roughly twenty-four thousand inhabitants to

Residents of Vryburg, South Africa, facing eviction. PAUL VELASCO/ ANTHONY BANNISTER PHOTO LIBRARY

nearly half a million, as people streamed in from the rest of South Africa, whether officially designated as citizens of this southern Sotho apartheid homeland or not. In the vast majority of cases, obtaining any arable land has been simply out of the question under such severe population density. Many people moved as separate families or even individuals, as circumstances permitted or dictated. Kin and colleagues accordingly were scattered widely. With minimal if any socioeconomic continuity, people have had to start forging new relationships in conditions of severe overcrowding and impoverishment—often leading to conflict within, and restructuring of, primary social units.

Resettlement in South Africa has thus taken place in terms of the overriding ideology of racial separation, and must be understood in light of the socio-spatial change that has resulted from it. Given the transition to a post-apartheid society (a process that will take many years), it is perhaps ironic that yet more resettlement will have to take place as historical imbalances are addressed.

BIBLIOGRAPHY

Cernea, Michael. *Poverty Risks from Population Displacement in Water Resources Development.* Development Discussion Paper No. 355, Harvard Institute for International Development, Harvard University, 1990.

de Wet, Chris. *Moving Together, Drifting Apart: Villagisation in a South African Homeland.* Johannesburg, 1995.

James, Deborah. *The Road from Doornkop.* Johannesburg, 1984.

Niehaus, Isak. "Relocation into Phuthaditjhaba and Tseki: A Comparative Study of Planned and Unplanned Removals." *African Studies* 48, no. 2 (1989): 157–181.

Platzky, Laurine, and Cherryl Walker. *The Surplus People: Forced Removals in South Africa.* Johannesburg, 1985.

Sharp, John. "Relocation and the Problem of Survival in Qwa Qwa." *Social Dynamics* 8, no. 2 (1982): 11–29.

Western, John. *Outcast Cape Town.* Minneapolis, Minn., 1981.

CHRIS DE WET

See also **Apartheid; Development; Refugees.**

PEREIRA, ARISTIDES MARIA (b. 1924), president of Cape Verde. Born in Boa Vista, in the Cape Verde archipelago, of Roman Catholic parents, Pereira completed his secondary education in Santiago, Cape Verde, before joining a Portuguese trading company. In 1956 he became one of the six founding members of the Partido Africano de Independência da Guiné e Cabo Verde (PAIGC), the

Aristides Maria Pereira, 1978. UPI/CORBIS-BETTMANN

anticolonial movement launched clandestinely by Amílcar Cabral. When armed resistance finally proved necessary to the movement's survival as well as to its eventual success, Pereira played a leading role in the guerrilla war that led to independence for Guinea-Bissau in 1974, and for Cape Verde a year later. He then returned to Cape Verde and was elected president of the new republic. An architect of his country's modernization and democratization, he also acted as a skilled diplomat on the continental scene. In 1990 Pereira presided over the introduction of a multiparty system in Cape Verde. When he and his party were voted out of office in legislative elections in 1991, Pereira and his colleagues accepted this verdict without complaint, seeing their defeat as a logical development of the democratic principles for which they had fought, and for which many of them had risked or lost their lives.

391

BIBLIOGRAPHY

Davidson, Basil. *The Fortunate Isles: A Study in African Transformation.* Trenton, N.J., 1989.

BASIL DAVIDSON

See also **Cabral, Amílcar Lopes.**

PERSON, NOTIONS OF

[*There are vast differences between African cultures, both over time and at any point in time. In this entry "African" refers to features that many, if not most, African cultures have in common, whether on the African continent or throughout the African diaspora. Similarly, "European" refers to societies sharing a European language and culture, whether in Europe or not. Many of the peoples on the North American continent are "European" by this definition. Comparisons such as those attempted in this essay are about cultural forms and social actions. People can live in more than one culture at one and the same time and may experience no difficulty "being African" and "European," just as many people can speak two or more different languages.*]

The ideas and actions that make up the "category of the person" are substantive universals, part and parcel of the culture of all societies at all times and in all places. In different cultures ideas about the person are similar in function but exhibit differences that can be attributed to the ways in which ideology, history, and social organization affect the interpretations people make of their experience of self and other. In the disciplines of philosophy and anthropology the term "personhood" is used as a shorthand for describing and interpreting different solutions to a universal existential dilemma: the problem of reconciling the lived experience of our changing physical bodies and sets of discordant experiences with the sense that there are unifying themes mediated through a single entity, which we call a person. Philosophers tend to seek justifications for choosing among different concepts of personhood, while anthropologists have pioneered the investigation of different vernacular concepts of the person, located across time and space. Both disciplines attempt to understand the underlying assumption or grounds that enable people to say the movement of a body through time and space and the accumulation of a set of experiences denote a single person, or exhibit a definable personhood, the characteristic or quality of being a person.

Commonsense answers to the dilemma of personhood often refer to attributes of the person such as character traits or social status, so that it may be said that someone is a person because of his or her standing or office or because he or she exhibits characteristic patterns of behavior. Nor is this simply a matter of classifying others. The interpretation and knowledge of self is as much a problem of personhood as understanding others.

However, no society relies on common sense alone. All peoples have evolved theories of the person that provide guides to classifying different people and categorizing the experience of self and other. These theories explain why people act the way they do, interpret their experiences, and predict their actions and fates. The terms these theories use are derived from religious and moral concepts or from cosmology. They encode ideas about physical and social growth and development, motivation and personality, and the consequences of action.

Ideas about the person also entail descriptions of the capacities and powers that persons have to carry out their actions and locate these powers and capacities in the image of the body. In the traditions of European societies, for example, dualistic models using categories such as body and soul (in religion) or the body and mind (in psychology and philosophy) define the basic terms of a theory about the person that makes a radical distinction between physical capacities and powers on the one hand and mental and moral capacities and powers on the other hand.

In many African cultures mental and moral capacities and powers are located in the body rather than opposed to the body. Among the Iteso people of Kenya and Uganda, for example, the heart, *etau*, is the seat of emotions, while the head, *akou*, is the seat of experience. The head guides the heart, which provides vitality and energy to the body. At first sight the Iteso model appears very similar to European commonsense discourse about the person, in which the heart is often made equivalent to the soul or is the seat of emotions, and the mind is located in the activities of the brain, operating through the senses found primarily in the head.

Contrasts Between African and European Concepts of Personhood

In most, if not all cultures, vernacular concepts of the person use the body as a model for constructing the person. Hence it is not surprising to find similarities between the African and European concepts of personhood. For comparative purposes, however, the differences count far more than the shared ideas and attitudes. There are at least four significant differences between the African models of the person, such as the Iteso have, and European models of personhood. First, the European model tends to be more metaphorical; it uses bodily experience as a metaphor for certain experiences, such as emotions, which are not thought of as being actually embodied, rather than define specific powers as an activity of the embodied person, as the Iteso model does. This is an instance that shows how the dualistic emphasis of European culture and cosmology shapes the use of the body as a model for experiencing the world, in contrast to more monistic African models.

Second, in the European view each person is customarily defined as separate from other persons. Hence, the powers and functions of the person are restricted to the single individual. Relationships between persons tend to be defined more in terms of the effect one person has on another rather than in terms of relationships among persons. In contrast, among the Iteso people and many other peoples throughout Africa and the world, the body is not simply a container of powers and attributes set in a world with other bodies containing their own attributes and powers. For the Iteso the body is at most separated from other persons as the end points of relationships. The Iteso model of personhood recognizes both the effects of one person on another and the relationships that bind one to, or divide one from, another. This model operates in a large portion of Iteso ritual and ceremony, which is devoted to defining, creating, or maintaining relationships, "making paths," among persons. The model of the person among the Iteso and in other African societies is not dualistic, nor are people seen as isolated from other persons. No people, African or otherwise, has been known to think about the person only in terms of effects or relationships. The contrast drawn here is one of emphasis and degree rather than an absolute one. Yet we may say that the Iteso and most other African concepts of personhood are relational rather than material, and that the boundaries of the body are defined as more permeable and less discrete in Africa than in many European settings.

A third difference between European and African concepts of the person such as those held by the Iteso has less to do with body image and personal experience than with ideas about action and agency, the ways in which actions are conceived and the judgments made about the person who undertakes or is affected by an action. One feature that people in both settings share is that they show

a lively awareness of differences in character and disposition. The Iteso have a well-developed vocabulary that distinguishes various emotional states and dispositions, although shame plays a greater role than guilt in their attribution of emotions to themselves and others. Yet the reactions to and judgments people make about seemingly similar emotional states and motives can be very different. Early on, American children may learn the moralizing rhyme, "Sticks and stones can break my bones but names will never hurt me." Later they learn that words can indeed hurt, but also that hurtful words can be rescinded and relationships often repaired. Many utterances among the Iteso operate in much the same way, but certain words are taken as clear and unambiguous indications of dispositions that cannot be altered. No Iteso person would hear the words "I could kill you for that" as an idle threat. Even the more innocuous sounding "We will see what happens" is taken as a serious and probably unrepairable breach of a relationship. As the Iteso people explain it, these words express homicidal intent. A person who would say such things has a heart so angry ("hot") that nothing can alter that state. For the Iteso the disposition is permanent and not a transient state of affairs. A statement of homicidal intent is taken as an expressed desire that will be acted upon as soon as circumstances permit. Hence, even though Iteso recognize differences in character and disposition, they do not define emotional states and their relationship to actions as Europeans do. A similar contrast could be drawn between Iteso and European ideas about love and passion. The romantic concept that "being in love" overwhelms other cognitive and emotional capacities is not so prevalent in Iteso thinking about and judgments made of persons.

The fourth and final contrast to be drawn between the African example of the Iteso and European concepts of the person has to do with ideas about fate and destiny. In capitalist society the historical tendency has been increasingly for the fate of the person to be seen as a growth from within rather than an imposition from without. Fate is increasingly seen as a matter of personal responsibility and not the product of external, often extrahuman, even supernatural, forces. This development, termed "disenchantment" by Max Weber, is manifested in the individualism characteristic of social relations under capitalism and is connected to a world view that is often mechanistic and materialist in a reductionist sense.

By contrast, African concepts of the person are far more often articulated in a worldview that defines individual fate as not only imposed from without, but the responsibility and concern of coalitions activated during circumstances of crisis and focused on resolving the breaches in social relations that are perceived as an underlying cause of the misfortune that it has been the fate of the afflicted person to suffer. Once again this contrast is more a matter of degree than absolute contrast. The development of therapeutic models in European healing systems, such as family therapy, tend to recognize that influences on a person's fate can be the result of another person's actions and that solutions are dependent on working within the social network of the afflicted person.

Few European forms of group therapy are as elaborate as the therapy groups that emerge in contexts of illness and affliction in many parts of Africa. There is no doubt that stress and mental illness are effectively dealt with in the context of African healing, and European psychotherapies have been shown to be no more successful in remedying psychological illnesses or reconciling social antagonisms.

The Study of Personhood in Africa

The literature on personhood in Africa owes its inception to Marcel Mauss's seminal eassay on the concept of the person, "Une catégorie de l'esprit humaine: La notion de la personne, celle de moi." In this essay Mauss reminded his audience that etymologically "person" derives from the ancient Latin *persona*, which referred to the mask and role performed by an actor in a play. Mauss argued that the Roman concept of the person evolved into what he termed "la personne morale," which refers to the social definition of the person in terms of its status and roles and rules governing actions and social relationships. Relying on evolutionary assumptions, Mauss postulated distinct stages in the development of concepts of the person, culminating in the evolution of the "moi," the individual self, which he believed to be characteristic of capitalist societies. There is some justification for applying to whole societies the traits that Mauss attributed to each of his theoretical stages. The contrast between the extreme individualism attributed to capitalist society and the more socialized concept of personhood and social relations in Africa and elsewhere seems valid and is reflected in the contrasts between African and European concepts of personhood drawn above. What is untenable in

Mauss, however, is the assumption that non-European or noncapitalist societies had no concept of individual selfhood.

For any society, the distinction between what the anthropologist Meyer Fortes termed "person" and "individual" is critical for understanding the significance of concepts of personhood in everyday life. Looking at it from the objective side, the distinctive qualities, capacities, and roles with which society endows a person enable the person to be known to be, and also to show himself to be the person he is supposed to be. Looked at from the subjective side, it is a question of how the individual, as actor, knows himself to be—or not to be—the person he is expected to be in a given situation and status. The individual is not a passive bearer of personhood; he must appropriate to him or herself the qualities and capacities of personhood, and the norms governing its expression.

The distinction between person and individual transforms Mauss's evolutionary framework into a form of analysis that seeks to understand behavior not as it has evolved from one society to another but in terms of context and social situation, in relationship to everyday life. One of the most significant aspects of the concept of the person addressed by Fortes's distinction between person and individual is the complex and changing relationship between the socially prescribed and the individually experienced, in which locally based, vernacular interpretations about personhood are developed.

There are no better examples of how Africans distinguish between person and individual than those described in Fortes's essays on personhood among the Tallensi people of Ghana. In "On the Concept of the Person Among the Tallensi," Fortes shows us that African solutions to the dilemma of identity as manifested in concepts of the person have epistemological and social dimensions; norms defining the person are generally experienced only by deviations from them or failures to conform to them—just as individuality is experienced only through conformity to or deviation from norms. This is not just a matter of conformity but rather is part of an elaborate cosmology and set of social ideas that Tallensi use to make sense of social and individual experiences. This Fortes illustrates in *Oedipus and Job in West African Religions* (1959), his study of Tallensi interpretations of fate and destiny.

The inability or failure to live up to the most fundamental aspects of Tallensi concepts of the person, such as exhibiting the capacity to bear children, are interpreted as the product of an impersonal agency called *nuor-yin,* which Fortes translates as "evil prenatal destiny." Illnesses are more usually attributed to conflict between living persons or the result of failure to propitiate the ancestors. Other Tallensi spirits are related to healthy growth and development and to the quality of life in community and kinship group. With these elements taken together, Fortes describes a very elaborate cultural complex through which people interpret their life in society and their experience of one another, and through which they debate about the ultimate ends of existence and the means through which to achieve them.

The Tallensi view represents only the best-described example of a widespread and complex concept of the person that has not only been evoked by anthropologists and historians of religion but is the cultural framework for some of the most important African novels and stories, such as Wole Soyinka's *The Interpreters,* Ben Okri's *The Famished Road,* and Buchi Emecheta's *Joys of Motherhood.* In the first of these examples, a novel of social change, all the main characters represent a different Yoruba power or *orisha,* and through this device Yoruba concepts of the person are connected to contemporary events. The protagonist of Ben Okri's book is a child born of an evil prenatal destiny, and the novel tells the story of his adventures in a world in which he did not choose to live. Buchi Emecheta's novel ends with the core of an Igbo (Ibo) person, her *chi,* afflicting her ungrateful children. Each of these novels is a major work of African fiction. They show in different west African social and cultural settings how west African ideas about personhood, agency, and fate are used to organize everyday experiences and provide an armature for products of the imagination ranging from popular culture and forms of religiosity to imaginative literature itself.

This discussion of concepts of the person has brought together bodies of Africanist literature that are normally kept separate. These include African philosophy, the anthropology and history of religion, studies of symbolism and ritual process, vernacular ideas about society and agency, and oral and written literature. In addition the vast literature on topics such as witchcraft and sorcery and spirit possession are relevant to discussions of African concepts of personhood. Witchcraft and sorcery beliefs are forms of moral discourse, exhibiting African ideas about the nature and use of power and about good and evil. It has often been

noted that inversion characterizes the image of the witch, that witches seem to have attributes and practices that invert the most fundamental moral norms of society. This is the domain of culture that Thomas O. Beidelman calls the "moral imagination," in which people think through their most profound aspirations and fears. Ideas about the person or their negation are fundamental components of the shared imaginative life of peoples. In other spheres of social life, such as cults of spirit possession, aspects of personhood are suspended, negotiated, and even contested.

Iteso culture can provide another example. Women assume male attributes and powers in the cult of possession among the Iteso, and they set up spheres of social life that are exempt from male domination, at least when cult groups meet. Many of the problems that women say are caused by possession, such as the death and illness of children, are precisely those fundamental aspects of Tallensi personhood that Fortes described as the product of an evil prenatal destiny. In cults of possession, male interpretations of these problems are marginalized, as women assume male prerogatives and acquire the symbols of male power. We may say that the shifting definitions of gender and the person displayed in cults of possession are used to constitute epicenters of power, in terms of which women define the causes of their affliction and acquire means to deal with their difficulties in asserting all the attributes of the adult person. Cults of possession are a privileged arena in which the discrepancies between person and individual are articulated.

This example, like much of the literature on the concept of the person in Africa, shows the importance of relating work done within different disciplines and on seemingly different aspects of African life. Academic disciplines tend to fragment deleteriously the ways in which Africans conduct their lives, unless they use integrative points of view embodied in concepts like that of personhood.

BIBLIOGRAPHY

Beidelman, Thomas O. *The Moral Imagination in Kaguru Modes of Thought.* Bloomington, Ind., 1986.

Dieterlen, Germaine, ed. *La notion de personne en Afrique noire, Paris 11–17 octobre 1971.* Paris, 1973.

Fortes, Meyer. "On the Concept of the Person Among the Tallensi." In *La notion de personne en Afrique noire, Paris 11–17 octobre 1971,* edited by Germaine Dieterlen. Paris, 1973.

———. *Religion, Morality, and the Person: Essays on Tallensi Religion.* Cambridge, 1987.

Jackson, Michael, and Ivan Karp, eds. *Personhood and Agency: The Experience of Self and Other in African Cultures.* Washington, D.C., 1990.

Karp, Ivan. "Power and Capacity in Rituals of Possession." In *Personhood and Agency,* edited by Michael Jackson and Ivan Karp. Washington, D.C., 1990.

Lienhardt, G. "Self: Public and Private, Some African Representations." In *The Category of the Person: Anthropology, Philosophy, History,* edited by Michael Carrithers, Steven Collins, and Steven Lukes. Cambridge, 1985.

Mauss, Marcel. "Une catégorie de l'esprit humaine: La notion de la personne, celle de moi." *Journal of the Royal Anthropological Institute* 68 (1939): 263–282.

Riesman, P. "The Person and the Life Cycle in African Social Life and Thought." *African Studies Review* 29, no. 2 (1986): 71–198.

Turner, Victor Witter. *The Drums of Affliction: A Study of Religious Processes Among the Ndembu of Zambia.* Oxford and London, 1968.

IVAN KARP

See also **Gender; Literature; Modes of Thought in African Philosophy; Philosophy and the Study of Africa; Religion and Ritual; Soyinka, Wole; Yoruba.**

PESTS AND PEST CONTROL. Most African agriculture takes place in tropical climates, on small landholdings with little access to machinery and agricultural chemicals. These conditions influence the type and severity of crop pest problems, constrain management options, and make pest control in sub-Saharan Africa distinct from pest control in industrialized, temperate regions. Farmers in tropical agroecosystems are challenged with a comparatively rich variety of major and minor pests; and the combination of warm temperatures and abundant rains during the growing seasons support many pest generations per year. However, subsistence farmers and small-scale growers with little access to costly farm inputs such as pesticides, herbicides, and synthetic fertilizers must place strategic importance on cultural practices, such as the selection of crop varieties resistant to pests and the use of crop mixtures, to reduce the impact of pests on particular crops.

Average yield losses due to insects attacking crops in the field have been estimated at 9 to 15 percent, with additional losses varying from 10 to 50 percent during storage, processing, and marketing. Targeted research on pests and pest management in Africa increased in the late twentieth century. It has become obvious that knowledge derived from studies in the temperate zone—usually on commerical varieties of industrial crops grown in mechanized, chemical-intensive, large, single-crop fields—has limited application to the majority of African growers, 80 to 90 percent of whom are involved in subsistence-crop production. Until the 1980s, research on African pests and pest control focused mainly on the 15 percent of agricultural enterprises devoted to industrial crops, such as coffee, tea, cotton, groundnuts, and tobacco. Technical knowledge is beginning to advance on pests attacking the major staples (cassava, maize, sorghum, millet, teff, and legumes) and minor food crops (such as sweet potato, plantains, and wheat), which comprise over 80 percent of the agriculture in African countries. Very little has been documented on the pests of the more than two thousand native grains, roots, fruits, and other food plants that are grown traditionally in different regions of Africa.

Common pests of African crops range widely in size, feeding habits, and mobility. Insect pests number in the thousands and include native and introduced species. Common pests native to the African continent range from the large migratory locusts to the minute, solitary bean flies. Migratory locusts are four to five centimeters long, have a single generation per year, periodically fly in swarms covering 100 to 1,000 square kilometers, with up to 50 million insects per square kilometer, and descend to devour almost all green parts of crops, shrubs, and trees. In contrast, bean flies measure two millimeters long, complete each generation in twenty to thirty days, and feed internally as stem-boring maggots only on plants in the bean family. Introduced species such as the greenbug aphid on cereals, the cassava mealybug, and the sorghum panicle bug were transported accidentally from other parts of the world. These introduced pests often multiply rapidly and cause devastating losses. Arriving in the early 1970s from South America, the newly established cassava mealybug threatened the major staple of over 200 million people across the African continent.

Insect pests attack every crop in every field in Africa, but vertebrate pests and weeds also cause substantial crop losses. Relatively few species of birds, notably those that form large feeding groups such as weaverbirds, cause crop destruction in the field. Weeds reduce crop yields through competition for light, nutrients, and moisture, with especially devastating effects from parasitic plants such as witchweed, which attaches to the roots of grain legumes and cereal crops. Along with insects, rodents destroy a large proportion of stored food products. Stored-food pests are particularly critical in regions with long dry seasons during which subsistence-based families must rely on these stores until the next harvest. Termites, which live in large, social colonies, can devour not only crops in the field but, with the help of gut bacteria that digest cellulose, they can feed on the structures that house stored food products.

Pest-control methods selected for most African crops can be relatively labor intensive and may take advantage of local knowledge, resources, and flexibilities in the design of cropping systems. Physical, cultural, and biological control methods are the cornerstones of pest management for resource-poor farmers. Examples of physical methods include the use of brushes and tarred paper dragged over crops to crush or remove insects, the use of barriers such as metal sheaths around storage bins to deter termites, and the use of traps with baits or synthetic chemical attractants to capture and destroy pests in large numbers. Storage pests can be killed through the use of dusts which abrade their protective waxy cuticle and allow dessication, or through airtight containers or high temperatures.

Cultural control methods based on manipulations of crops and land have rich traditional histories. Shifting agriculture, crop rotation, and intercropping are examples of widely practiced cultural controls against the proliferation of insect pests, diseases, and weeds. Additional measures include the destruction of crop residues and alternative hosts of pests as well as the selection of planting and harvest dates to avoid peak pest populations or prevent pest development. The selection of pest-resistant varieties from locally grown seed stock is an effective and common practice in crops grown on small landholdings, and the use of hybrids resistant to pests and disease is practiced for many industrial crops in Africa. Malawian subsistence farmers, for example, routinely incorporate varieties that tolerate attack by bean flies to reduce the risk of crop loss. Farmers who were not familiar with the tiny insects themselves selected the bean varieties that showed fewer symptoms of dried stems (caused by the maggots as they feed on the passageways for water movement up the stem). Resistant cultivars can also be toxic to pests, such as certain young sorghum plants that are protected from attack by the release of hydrogen cyanide

gas when chewed by insects or rodents. Because resistance traits are genetically inherited, farmers develop cultivars that thrive despite attack from local pests.

Biological control by naturally occurring beneficial organisms is encouraged through cultural methods when farmers increase the suitability of the crop habitat for herbivores that feed specifically on weeds and predators or parasitic insects that kill crop pests. Pest regulation is also enhanced by introducing beneficial organisms through mass releases into the field or through importation from other geographic areas. The cassava mealybug which caused losses of 80 percent of the root crop in west Africa was reduced dramatically after the importation and establishment of a small parasitic wasp from the Americas which kills cassava mealybugs. The wasp deposits its eggs only in the body of this type of mealybug, and the young feed and develop on the internal tissues and vital organs. Biological control through carefully planned introductions of specific natural enemies of appropriate pests is a relatively inexpensive and potentially permanent management tactic for reducing pest outbreaks but remains an underexploited area of research in many parts of the world, including Africa.

Appropriate cultural and biological pest-control methods often require knowledge of the biological and ecological characteristics of the species. Identifications of insect pests can be relatively accurate and simple, as with the six common species of migratory locusts, or extremely difficult. Several species of bean flies are identical as adults and can be distinguished morphologically only by examining the internal reproductive organs of male flies. Despite their similarity in appearance, bean flies respond differently to management tactics. One species is attacked relatively heavily by parasitic wasps which regulate its density, and this species is not sensitive to changes in soil quality. Another species tends to proliferate in beans growing in fertilized soil and is rarely killed by parasitic wasps.

Of all the pest-control methods available to growers in tropical Africa, chemical controls may be least sensitive to specific biological differences among pest species. Most commercial pesticides and herbicides are formulated to have broad-spectrum toxicity effective against a wide range of insects, pathogens, or weeds. Although common synthetic pesticides such as organophosphates and pyrethroids used in response to imminent pest outbreaks are often cost effective in commercial

Helicopter spraying larvicide into a river in the north of Côte d'Ivoire, 1995.
AP PHOTO/JEAN-MARC BOUJU

crops, recommendations originating outside tropical Africa are subject generally to climatic and socioeconomic constraints. Problems with relying on imported pesticides for crop protection in Africa include the reduction of persistence and efficacy of pesticides under frequent, heavy rains and elevated temperatures, the scarcity of capital for farmers to purchase and apply pesticides, and the human and environmental health hazards magnified by the costs of protective measures and the labeling of imported materials in foreign languages.

Experts in African pest-management research, policy, and practice promote a range of innovative strategies for reducing yield losses in African agriculture. Some favor the importation and adoption of technological advances such as precision sprayers, hybrid seed–fungicide-fertilizer packages, and genetically engineered crop varieties, while others promote the exploration of indigenous farmers' knowledge and development of strategic farming practices using locally available materials as the major tools of pest management.

BIBLIOGRAPHY

Abate, T., and J. K. O. Ampofo. "Insect Pest of Beans in Africa: Their Ecology and Management." *Annual Review of Entomology* 41 (1996): 45–73.

Gahukar, R. T. "Role of Extension in Protecting Food Crops of Sub-Saharan Africa." *Outlook on Agriculture* 19 (1990): 119–123.

Greathead, D. J. "Opportunities for Biological Control of Insect Pests in Tropical Africa." *Revue de zoologie africaine* 110 (1986): 85–96.

Herren, H. R., and P. Neuenschwander. "Biological Control of Cassava Pests in Africa." *Annual Review of Entomology* 36 (1991): 257–283.

Hill, Dennis S. *Agricultural Insect Pests of the Tropics and Their Control.* 2d ed. Cambridge, 1983.

Kumar, R. *Insect Pest Control: With Special Reference to African Agriculture.* London, 1984.

National Research Council. *Lost Crops of Africa.* Vol. 1, *Grains.* Washington, D.C., 1996.

Odhiambo, Thomas R. "International Aspects of Crop Protection: The Needs of Tropical Developing Countries." *Insect Science and Its Application* 5 (1984): 59–67.

Sridhar, M. K. C. "African Researchers on Pesticide Use and Poisoning." *African Environment* 6 (1989): 69–102.

DEBORAH K. LETOURNEAU

See also **Agriculture; Ecology; Plants.**

PEUL; PEULH. *See* **Fulani.**

PHILOSOPHY. *See* **Modes of Thought in African Philosophy.**

PHILOSOPHY AND THE STUDY OF AFRICA

European Philosophy and the Study of Africa

Plato and Aristotle say relatively little about Africa. Aristotle refers in his works on natural history to biological and meteorological curiosities from Egypt and Ethiopia, as when, for example, in book 4, chapter 4 of *De Generatione Animalium,* he remarks that "monstrosities occur more often in regions where the women give birth to more than one child at a time, as in Egypt"; or, in book 2, chapter 14 of *De Caelo,* he reports that different stars are visible in Egypt than can be seen farther north; or in book 1, chapter 5 of the *Historia Animalium,* where he reports that there are flying snakes, without feet, in Ethiopia. He also observes, in book 1, chapter 1 of *Metaphysics,* that the mathematical arts originated in Egypt, because the priests had the time to develop them (this is part of a general argument for the view that theoretical knowledge is the fruit of leisure). In the *Politics,* he discusses various features of the Egyptian constitution and social structure as well as observing that in Ethiopia social position is said to be determined by height. Egypt is important to Aristotle because, as he says in book 7, chapter 10 of the *Politics,* the Egyptians appear to be the most ancient of all peoples and to have laws and a constitution that have existed from time immemorial.

Plato says rather less, but in the *Phaedo* he does refer to the Egyptian practice of embalming, and in the *Laws* the Athenian Stranger remarks on the superiority of Egyptian laws limiting innovation in music and painting. In the *Statesman,* the Eleatic Stranger refers to the priestly powers of the Egyptian monarchs; in the *Timaeus,* there are a few remarks about the warrior caste in Egypt. Egypt is most frequently invoked in Plato, however, when characters in his dialogues swear "by the dog of Egypt."

There is, in fact, fairly little discussion of Africa or African ideas, beliefs, and practices in the works of the major writers of the European philosophical canon, even in Saint Augustine, who was, of course, born in Roman North Africa in Tagaste (though, it should be said, some of the heresies he combatted originated, as he did, on the African continent).

This fact should be relatively unsurprising. While the European philosophical canon reflects in many obvious ways the particular traditions of the cultures of those who wrote it, much of that work proceeded on the assumption that it was addressing the most general questions about the nature of reality, questions whose answers did not depend on where you asked them or on accumulating particular facts knowable only in particular places. When Aristotle in the *Metaphysics* asks the most general question about Being, he is not asking a question whose answer requires evidence from Africa: he would have been interested, we can be sure, in any answers to his questions that came to him from Africa (as he was in the natural historical works), but on the central questions of metaphysics he relied largely on his own arguments and Greek texts.

The first philosophers in the European tradition to take cultures and nations as topics of serious philosophical reflection were in the European Enlightenment, and probably the most important of these were Johann Gottfried von Herder (1744–1803) and George Wilhelm Friedrich Hegel (1770–1831). Both of these philosophers made contributions to the philosophy of history that reflected a sense of the profound *philosophical* significance of national or cultural traditions. Nevertheless, for two major reasons, much of the very little the Enlightenment philosophers had to say about Africa and Africans was negative.

First, by the mid-eighteenth century it had become conventional to distinguish between the "Negro" population, which is mostly found in what we now call sub-Saharan Africa, and the mostly lighter-skinned Arabic-speaking North African populations of the Maghreb, and the well-known negative observations of many philosophers of the European Enlightenment about Africa were associated with a negative view of the Negro race. Few contemporary readers are likely to be undisturbed when they discover the moments when Africa is banished from Hegel's supposedly universal history and when David Hume declares, in the essay on "National Characters," that blacks are incapable of eminence in action or speculation (likening in the same place Francis Williams, the Jamaican poet, to a "parrot who speaks few words plainly").

Second, very little was known in Europe about the intellectual life of non-Muslim Africa until late in the nineteenth century; and it is, of course, the intellectual life of this part of the continent that European philosophy would need to address, if it were to take up the possibility that African peoples had something to contribute to the evolution of human understanding.

As a result, the philosophical engagement of the European tradition with Africa had essentially to wait until the period after World War II: then two forces combined to give salience to the question of how philosophy should take its place in Africa. First, the critique of scientific racism that had begun in the first part of the century was continued and extended in the face of the Nazi Holocaust and the recognition that racism had led to moral catastrophe on an unprecedented scale in the heart of the "civilized world." Second, an increasing number of African scholars trained in European philosophy began to teach in the new African universities in the 1950s and 1960s.

Non-European Literate Traditions

In North Africa, where Muslim philosophers are able to draw on a long literate philosophical tradition that itself goes back to Plato and Aristotle, we are dealing with work that belongs within the world of philosophy in Arabic; while these works are plainly African in location, this article will not address them further, since to do so would require substantial contextualization within the world of Arab cultures and of Islam.

For similar reasons, the literate philosophical traditions of Ethiopia, which go back to the translation into an Ethiopian language (probably in the fifth century C.E.) of a Greek text, *The Physiologue,* constitute a substantially distinct tradition—one that has been excavated recently by Claude Sumner working in Addis Ababa. *The Physiologue* is largely a work of Christian natural theology. The later *Book of the Philosophers* is a sixteenth-century translation of a (probably ninth-century) Arabic collection of philosophical sayings, heavily influenced by Greek (and, more particularly, Platonic and neo-Platonic) sources. *The Life and Maxims of Skendes* has a similar history—a Greek original, translated into Ethiopic from an Arabic version. It is only when we come to the seventeenth-century treatises of Zara Ya'iqob and his student Walda Heywat that we begin to get a distinctive and original Ethiopian tradition, which Sumner has characterized as rationalist.

Colonial Legacies

The role of academic philosophy in sub-Saharan Africa cannot be understood without acknowledging the radical differences between the colonial and postcolonial educational histories of anglophone and francophone states—differences that themselves reflect differing national approaches to philosophy and to colonial education in Britain and France.

When, in the early part of this century, Gottlob Frege replaced Hegel as the tutelary spirit of En-glish philosophy, Continental historicist modes of thought were largely expelled from the philosophy faculties of English (though, curiously, not from Scottish) universities. In England, the most influential body of philosophical practice through the mid-century derived from the transfer, through such figures as Ludwig Wittgenstein and Alfred Ayer, of the logical positivism of the Vienna Circle to Oxford and Cambridge into the context provided by the critique of idealism which had been begun by Bertrand Russell. The tradition that resulted came to be known as "analytical philosophy." Analytical philosophy was centered in the philosophy of language and in epistemology, and its method was conceptual analysis.

In France, on the other hand, historicism survived and was supplemented by the introduction of Husserlian phenomenology, under the influence of Jean-Paul Sartre. Metaphysics and ontology remained central topics, and a good deal of intellectual effort was also devoted to normative questions and, in particular, to political philosophy in a broadly Marxist tradition.

This difference in approach to philosophy was exacerbated by the differing approaches to education in general and colonial education in particular. In France and in the francophone states, philosopy was a central part of secondary education for those with a serious vocation to intellectual life. Philosophy was also central to university education. Because French colonial policy aimed to create a class of "evolved" Africans, fully educated to the highest standards of French civilization, it was natural that philosophy should gain the attention of some of the most successful African students in the francophone educational systems, and given the centripetal pull of Paris, it is unsurprising that significant numbers of them were educated in philosophy there.

The difference with the anglophone world could not be more striking. Philosophy was almost exclusively a university subject, and it was the province, almost everywhere except Oxford, of a relatively small number of students. (At Oxford, many students studied some philosophy, but there, too, relatively few specialized in that subject exclusively.) And the aim of colonial education was not, on the whole, to create "black Englishmen." Even if it had been, philosophy would not have played a central role in the process, since philosophy was not regarded as central to an English education at home.

As a result it is important to distinguish the trajectories of philosophy in anglophone and francophone spheres. (The Portuguese devoted no resources to tertiary education in their colonies and few to the tertiary education of their colonial subjects; contemporary philosophical traditions in Angola, Guinea-Bissau, and Mozambique owe much to the influence of Marxism in the anticolonial movements in Lisbon, where figures such as Agostinho Neto and Amílcar Cabral were educated.)

Francophone Philosophy

Negritude

The essential background to modern African philosophy in French is in the theories of Negritude. While the Negritude movement is rightly seen as the product of the extraordinary convergence of Léopold Sédar Senghor, of Senegal, and Aimé Césaire, from the Antilles, who coined the term that gave the movement its name, the first philosophical statement of Negritude was made by Jean-Paul Sartre, in the essay "Black Orpheus." Sartre framed Negritude in the existentialist terms he had developed in *Being and Nothingness*: Negritude was the "being-in-the-world-of-the-Negro." And, Sartre argued within the historicizing narrative of Marx, the movement was the anti-thesis to European racism and a stage in a dialectical process that would produce in the end a synthesis in which both race and class would be transcended.

Senghor went on to articulate the movement as the basis for an understanding of African cultural and intellectual life that was to endure through decolonization, and for him, at least, the key to Negritude was a fundamental difference between European and African modes of experiencing the world. For Senghor (following the French anthropologist Lucien Lévy-Bruhl) Africans engage the world cognitively not, like Europeans, with reason but with their emotions, knowing objects in the world by "participating" in them.

Bantu Philosophy

The second major source of modern francophone philosophy is in the work of Placied Tempels, a missionary priest in what was the Belgian Congo, now Zaire. The first French edition of *La philosophie bantoue*, which was written originally in Dutch, was published in the Belgian Congo in 1945. (An English-language version was published by Présence Africaine in 1959.) Tempels argued that the thought of the Bantu-speaking Luba had at its center a notion of Force, a notion which occupied the position of privilege of the notion of Being in Western (by which, as a Catholic, he meant Thomist) thought; and his articulation of that notion

owed a good deal to the French philosopher Henri-Louis Bergson.

There has been much controversy both about Tempels's methods and his claims about the thought of Bantu-speakers. But his work provided an influential model of how philosophy in Africa might be conceived. He constructed what was later to be called an "ethnophilosophy": exploring and systematizing the conceptual world of a culture, as expressed in the central concepts embedded in its language. As a result, a significant amount of academic philosophical work in Africa in the postwar period has been in the form of ethnophilosophy, which amounts, in effect, to adopting the approach of a folklorist: studying the "natural history" of traditional folk-thought about the central issues of human life. Among the most influential of Tempels's followers was the Rwandan intellectual Alexis Kagame, whose *La philosophie bàntu-rwandaise de l'être* (1957) sought to extend Tempels's work in his own Kinyarwanda language. But there has also been a significant body of work in what Valentin Y. Mudimbe has called the "school of Tempels," much of it by Catholic clerics concerned with missiology.

Where Senghor's Negritude had insisted on a distinctive African epistemology, ethnophilosophy has tended to insist that what is distinctive is African ontology and ethics, focusing, in particular, on the role of belief in spirits and ancestors in understanding reality and in shaping normative life.

Critique

Criticism of Negritude and of ethnophilosophy developed in parallel with each of them. Frantz Fanon argued implicitly against Negritude in *Les damnés de la terre* (1961) when he insisted that African culture should be seen as shaped by political struggle, not by an essence reflected in folklore. (Though Fanon was born in the French Antilles, he died an Algerian citizen, and his political writings were grounded in his experience of colonialism and decolonization in his adopted country.) But perhaps the most philosophically substantial critique begins in the *Essai sur la problématique philosophique dans l'Afrique actuelle* (1971) of the philosopher Marcien Towa and reaches its apotheosis in the work of the Béninois philosopher Paulin J. Hountondji.

Sur la philosophie africaine: Critique de l'ethnophilosophie (1977)—which has also been influential in its English translation, *African Philosophy: Myth and*

Reality (1983)—collects some earlier essays in which Hountondji had mounted an assault on ethnophilosophy, an attack that is fundamental within the francophone tradition in that it opposes assumptions common to Negritude and to ethnophilosophy. Hountondji makes his major objections to ethnophilosophy in the first three essays, which appear in their original order of publication. Beginning with a recapitulation of Césaire's political critique of Tempels as a "diversion," he moves on to discuss the work of Kagame, whose *La philosophie bàntu-rwandaise de l'être* "expressly and from the outset, establishes its point of view in relation to Tempels' work as an attempt by an autochthonous Bantu African to 'verify the validity of the theory advanced by this excellent missionary' " (p. 39). While endorsing some of Kagame's specific criticism of Tempels, Hountondji objects to what he calls their shared "unanimism," their conviction that there is a collective system of thought at the heart either of black African cultures generally (Negritude) or of particular cultures in Africa (Tempels, Kagame), and to their conviction that the articulation of this body of thought would constitute an African (or Bantu, or Rwandan) philosophy. (He refers at one point to "the description of an implicit, unexpressed world-view, which never existed anywhere but in the anthropologist's imagination" [p. 63].)

Along with his attack on ethnophilosophy's unanimism, Hountondji has an unflattering analysis of its motivations. Ethnophilosophy, he alleges, exists *"for a European public"* (p. 45). It is an attempt to cope with feelings of cultural inferiority by redefining folklore as "philosophy," so as to be able to lay claim to an autochthonous philosophical tradition.

The most original of Hountondji's objections to the ethnophilosophers derives from an essentially Althusserian view of the place of philosophy. Hountondji cites a passage from *Lénine et la philosophie* where Louis Althusser says that philosophy "has been observed only in places where there is also what is called a science or sciences—in the strict sense of theoretical discipline, i.e., ideating and demonstrative, not an aggregate of empirical results" (p. 97), and then Hountondji himself goes on to argue that if "the development of philosophy is in some way a function of the development of the sciences, then . . . we shall never have, in Africa, a philosophy in the strict sense, until we have produced a history of science" (p. 98; meaning by "science" here, of course, systematic knowledge in

the French sense). Hountondji then develops in Althusserian language an insistence on the development of a critical tradition. The project of philosophy is not one of describing concepts but one of engaging with them in order to seek out the truth. Hountondji essentially argues that African philosophers cannot commit themselves to a singular heritage, because there isn't one—this is part of the critique of unanimism—and then argues that there is, in any case, no reason to hold to ideas because they come from "our" (African) traditions, unless they can stand up to critical ("scientific") scrutiny.

In later work, Hountondji has moved away from some of the universalism of the essays in *Sur la philosophie africaine*, examining in a more pragmatic spirit the possible roles of philosophy in Africa and exploring the ways that philosophy in Africa can address the project of intellectual modernization, a task that requires the development of a critical sociology of knowledge in countries that are, like all African countries, in "the periphery" of the world-system. For these purposes, Hountondji has now come to concede that the materials of ethnophilosophy can provide a useful starting point.

A final crucial figure in the development of the francophone tradition is the Zairian philosopher, philologist, and novelist Valentin Y. Mudimbe, whose work has had a significant impact in the English-speaking world, both through anglophone translations and commentary and through those of his own works that have been published in English since he has come to be based in the American academy. Mudimbe's work can be seen as a vast and systematic interrogation of the various Western discourses about Africa. In *L'autre face du royaume* (1973), for example, he conducted a scathing attack on ethnology, which he called a "langage en folie"; and in *The Invention of Africa* (1988), probably his best known theoretical work, he pursued a rigorous examination of anthropology and of African studies, arguing that Africa, as a subject of inquiry, is an invention of a Western episteme. Mudimbe's explicit methodological debt to Michel Foucault is substantial; he is pursuing an archeology, in the Foucauldean sense, of Africanist knowledge.

Anglophone Philosophy

Because of the very different roles that philosophy occupies in British and French cultures, the history of philosophy, in the strict sense, in anglophone Africa cannot be said to have been as central to late colonial and postcolonial intellectual life as it has been in the francophone areas of the continent. Nevertheless, two important streams of anglophone thought can be identified that are distinctive.

Conceptual Analysis

First, there is a tradition of conceptual analysis of African concepts and conceptual systems that is somewhat different from the tradition of francophone ethnophilosophy because its engagement with those concepts and systems is critically argumentative, in rather the sort of way that Hountondji can be taken to have been proposing. This tradition's earliest text is probably *The Akan Doctrine of God: A Fragment of Gold Coast Ethics and Religion* (1944), by the Ghanaian political leader Joseph Boakye Danquah, who took a doctoral degree in philosophy at London University. This text explores Akan conceptions against an Aristotelian background, and while it celebrates Akan traditions, it does so, in contrast to Tempels, by finding them close to European (Aristotelian) notions rather than remote from European (Thomist) conceptions. Since Danquah's work was by a distinguished anglophone African public figure—it was he who invited Kwame Nkrumah to take up the leadership of the independence movement—it is somewhat puzzling that his work has had so much less influence than the English translation of Tempels's *La philosophie bantoue*, which appeared in 1959. It is tempting to speculate that in the period of African independence it suited American, European, and African intellectuals to focus on a text that made an exciting claim for the distinctiveness of African thought rather than a more careful exploration of connections between ideas in one African cultural zone and early European philosophy. This may also account for the rather substantial success of *The Mind of Africa* (1962) by the Oxford-trained Ghanaian philosopher Willie E. Abraham. This book sought to characterize African modes of thought in the manner that Hountondji was later to criticize as unanimist, focusing, as it did, on features of the intellectual life of African cultures such as ethical communitarianism and the belief in ancestral spirits. (Abraham's work has the advantage over Tempels's, however, that many of the generalizations he makes are both quite intelligible and roughly ethnographically correct.)

Since these works a number of Ghanaian philosophers, among them Kwame Gyekye in his *An Essay on African Philosophical Thought: The Akan Conceptual Scheme* (1987) and Kwasi Wiredu in his *Phi-

losophy and an African Culture* (1980) and the more recent *Cultural Universals and Particulars: The African Perspective* (1996) have explored questions in epistemology, ontology, metaphysics, ethics, and the philosophy of religion with careful attention to a particular (Akan) conceptual world; and Barry Hallen and J. O. Sodipo in their *Knowledge, Belief, and Witchcraft: Analytic Experiments in African Philosophy* (1986) have carried out an extended exploration of Yoruba epistemology. Other work of this sort has been carried out in other traditions.

If this work is not the sort of descriptive (and often exoticizing) ethnophilosophy that Hountondji was criticizing, it is also not what the Kenyan philosopher Odera Oruka identified as "sage philosophy," something that he and his students pioneered, which entails the detailed exposition of the views of "wise elders" untrained in the methods and the themes of European philosophy. This work is unlike ethnophilosophy in identifying the philosophical systems it explores as the product of (culturally situated) individual thinkers, but it is also unlike the works of Gyekye, Wiredu, and Hallen and Sodipo (all of whom draw to varying degrees on respectful conversation with philosophically untrained interlocutors in the languages they discuss) in that it does not seek to engage in conceptual analysis of its own. (Oruka went on, later, to characterize the work of Gyekye, Wiredu, and Hallen and Sodipo as "hermeneutical," engaged with the philosophical exploration of an African language "to help clarify meaning and logical implications.")

Nationalist-Ideological Philosophy

Oruka also identified a significant body of philosophical writing as "nationalist-ideological": and it is here that we find the second body of distinctive anglophone writing. For many of the African political leaders of the independence generation wrote works of political theory. Nkrumah published one work that was somewhat technical in its philosophical style while he was president of Ghana, a book entitled *Conscientism: Philosophy and Ideology for De-Colonization* (1964). While the most interesting of the philosophical claims in this work are hard to defend—they include an attempt to defend the compatibility of materialism and belief in spirits by way of a doctrine of categorical conversion that is far from clear—Nkrumah insisted, like Senghor, on the African roots of his ideas, and especially of his socialism. After his fall from power, Nkrumah published a substantial body of further work on decolonization and on non-colonialism, including *Neo-colonialism: The Last Stage of Imperialism* (1965) and *Class Struggle in Africa* (1970).

Less philosophically opaque work in political theory can be found in the writings of Kenneth Kaunda of Zambia (for example, *A Humanist in Africa*, 1966, and *Kaunda on Violence*, 1980) and Julius Nyerere of Tanzania (*Nyerere on Socialism*, 1969). These compare favorably in originality and clarity with analogous francophone work, such as the extensive Marxist works of President Sékou Touré of Guinea, though none of them has had the influence of the work of Frantz Fanon.

It is, finally, worth insisting that in the discussion of recent philosophy in Africa, this article has focused on arguments and trends *distinctive* of philosophy in Africa; there have, of course, been philosophers in Africa trained in Europe and North America who have pursued the standard fare of the traditions in which they were trained. African philosophy journals, such as the anglophone *Second Order*, have published articles on Aristotle and Locke on substance, for example; and francophone philosophers, like Valentin Mudimbe, have taught and written about Michel Foucault. This work constitutes the bulk of what Odera Oruka dubbed "professional philosophy."

Given the peculiar circumstances of the intellectual trained in a Western philosophy with very little historical engagement with Africa (almost none of it positive), it is not surprising that since decolonization began there has been a very substantial discussion alongside all the work this article has described on the question "What is African philosophy?" This can often usefully be glossed as asking what African philosophers with Western trainings should be doing. Tsenay Serequeberhan excerpts most of the crucial essays in this debate in his *African Philosophy: The Essential Readings* (1991). This article provides a sketch of the wide variety of answers that Africa's philosophers have implicitly endorsed in their practice over the last few decades.

BIBLIOGRAPHY

Abraham, Willie E. *The Mind of Africa*. Chicago, 1962.

Danquah, Joseph Boakye. *The Akan Doctrine of God: A Fragment of Gold Coast Ethics and Religion*. London, 1944. Repr. London, 1988.

Fløistad, Guttorm, ed. *Contemporary Philosophy*. Vol. 5, *African Philosophy*. Boston, 1987.

Gyekye, Kwame. *An Essay on African Philosophical Thought: The Akan Conceptual Scheme*. New York, 1987. Rev. ed. Philadelphia, 1995.

Hallen, Barry, and Sodipo, J. O. *Knowledge, Belief, and Witchcraft: Analytic Experiments in African Philosophy*. London, 1986.

Hountondji, Paulin J. *African Philosophy: Myth and Reality*. Translated by Henri Evans. Bloomington, Ind., 1976. Repr. London, 1983.

———. "Pour une sociologie des réprésentations collectives." In *La pensée métisse: Croyances africaines et rationalité occidentale en question*. Paris, 1990.

———. "Démarginaliser." Introduction to *Les savoirs endogènes*. Dakar, Senegal, 1994.

Kagame, Alexis. *La philosophie bàntu-rwandaise de l'être*. Brussels, 1956.

Kaunda, Kenneth D. *Kaunda on Violence*. Edited by Colin M. Morris. London, 1980.

Mudimbe, Valentin Y. *The Invention of Africa: Gnosis, Philosophy, and the Order of Knowedge*. Bloomington, Ind., 1988.

Nkrumah, Kwame. *Consciencism: Philosophy and Ideology for De-Colonization*. London, 1964, 1970.

Nyerere, Julius K. *Nyerere on Socialism*. Dar es Salaam, Tanzania, 1969.

Oruka, Odera H. *Trends in Contemporary African Philosophy*. Nairobi, Kenya, 1990.

———. *Sage Philosophy: Indigenous Thinkers and the Modern Debate on African Philosophy*. Nairobi, Kenya, 1991.

Serequeberhan, Tsenay, ed. *African Philosophy: The Essential Readings*. New York, 1991.

Sumner, Claude. *Classical Ethiopian Philosophy*. Addis Ababa, Ethiopia, 1985.

Wiredu, Kwasi. *Philosophy and an African Culture*. Cambridge, 1980.

KWAME ANTHONY APPIAH

See also **Fanon, Frantz; Kagame, Alexis; Kaunda, Kenneth; Negritude; Nkrumah, Francis Nwia Kofi; Nyerere, Julius Kambarage; Religion and Ritual; Touré, Sékou.**

PHOTOGRAPHY

*[Photography has a long history in Africa and today is an important activity in modern African culture. This double entry deals with both the **Development** of photography in Africa and its modern **Social and Cultural Aspects**.]*

DEVELOPMENT

Although the precise history of photography in Africa has yet to be written, one can delineate major developments, discuss the work of important photographers, and examine the European views of Africa that affected the images of this continent. Attention must be paid to the long-neglected work of indigenous African photographers and photographers of Indian origin in eastern and southern Africa.

The Early Years

In the mid-nineteenth century, several historical and technical developments coincided. The first photographic process, the daguerreotype, was introduced in 1839. Over the next decades, photographic technology developed from the cumbersome early processes, such as the calotype and the wet-collodion process, to the dry-plate process of 1871, which facilitated the taking of pictures. Another breakthrough occurred with the invention of handheld cameras in the late 1870s and finally with the arrival of box cameras and celluloid film.

The second half of the nineteenth century was a period of systematic exploration and the subjugation of the African continent and the growth of physical anthropology and ethnography as disciplines that began to use photography. By the turn of the twentieth century, both professionals and amateurs were practicing photography around the globe. Images had a wide distribution, first through photographic albums and in the forms of lithographs and engravings, and finally through halftone reproductions in contemporary books and on postcards.

Travelers, artists, scientists, and later professional photographers from all over Europe began taking images in Africa immediately after the introduction of the first photographic processes in 1839. The nineteenth-century fascination with Egypt drew artists and photographers to the Nile. Adventurous travelers along the African coast also used photography, among them a helmsman by the name of Vernet traveling with Charles Guillain to Madagascar and the east African coast in the years 1845–1848. His daguerreotypes are now in the archives of the Musée de l'Homme in Paris.

Studios and Explorers

This phase of "incidental" photography gave way to the establishment of photographic studios. Europeans opened commercial photographic studios in Egypt and in South Africa in the Cape as early as the 1840s. Establishments in other cities, such as Luanda in Angola and Freetown in Sierra Leone, followed in the 1850s and 1860s. Studio photographers catered mainly to expatriate patrons who wanted their portraits taken; they also sold collectible photographs such as city views and sets of "native types."

In east Africa, many photographers were originally from India, where indigenous photography had begun early on. Goans settled on the Kenyan and Tanzanian coasts and in Zanzibar and established large commercial studios. Among the best known were A. C. Gomes (active from about 1868) and his son P. F. Gomes, who died in 1932. Their studio on one of the main streets of Zanzibar exists to this day. They worked closely with the Goan Coutinho Brothers in Mombasa, both excellent photographers who had adopted the conventions of Western photography and sold albums with large prints and later postcards as well.

While studio photography flourished, several famous explorers and travelers began to employ photography during their expeditions to the interior of Africa. John Kirk, a botanist on David Livingstone's Zambezi expedition of 1858–1862, took some of the earliest images of buildings, boats, and vegetation in the interior of Africa. Later on, the Nile brought photographers into eastern and central Africa, among them the Austrian artist Richard Buchta (1845–1894), whose pictures of the upper Nile and northern Uganda, taken with a dry-plate apparatus during 1878–1879, became famous and were distributed in both albums and print.

Anthropologists, Missionaries, and Adventurers

From the 1880s, photography proliferated and the pace of the exploration of Africa increased in conjunction with imperial claims, scientific projects, and the effort to convert peoples under colonial rule. As photography was no longer the domain of a few specialists, anybody could take photographic equipment to Africa. Military people, colonialists, scientists, and missionaries now produced images that served multiple functions, from personal mementos to research and propaganda to entertainment for popular audiences. According to their backgrounds and interests, photographers often emphasized particular aspects of their experience and followed certain preoccupations and photographic conventions.

Anthropologists early on developed a standardized code of representation of Africans as racial specimens, producing some of the most dehumanizing images of Africans. Their collections, among them the oeuvre of the German anthropologist Gustav Theodor Fritsch (1838–1927), who conducted research in southern Africa from 1863 to 1866 and in Egypt from 1898 to 1899, remain in many archives and ethnographic museums. The tradition of the traveler and anthropologist as photographer has continued into the present. Among the most famous are Bernhard Ankermann (1859–1943, German) in Cameroon, Franz Stuhlmann (1863–1928, German) in east Africa, Leo Frobenius

(1873–1938, German) during several research expeditions, Robert Sutherland Rattray (1881–1938, British) in Ghana, Charles Gabriel Seligman (1873–1940, British) in Sudan, and Pierre Verger (1902–1996, French) in Bénin.

Photographers of different backgrounds were also eager to contribute to science and followed anthropological conventions in their photography, relying on photographic instructions written for amateurs. Melville William Hilton-Simpson (1881–1936, British) accompanied the Hungarian explorer Emil Torday (1875–1931) to central Africa in 1907–1908 and, after 1912, also photographed in Algeria. The Austrian merchant Rudolf Oldenburg (1879–1932) purposefully produced photographic records in Guinea and Cameroon to serve anthropology. He sold series of prints to many ethnographic museums in the German-speaking part of Europe. The German-American taxidermist, collector, and mammalogist Herbert Lang (1879–1957) in 1909–1915 created a fabulous set of images of the Mangbetu, which are now in the American Museum of Natural History in New York.

The work of missionary photographers reflected the missions' "civilizing" influence. Since missionaries were often the first Westerners to reach an area, their images are of great importance to historical and cultural studies. The African-American missionary William Henry Sheppard (1865–1927) was among those who entered unknown territory and was the first visitor to the Kuba kingdom. His photographs are now at Hampton University in Virginia. A few of the missionary photographers were women. Anna Rein-Wuhrmann (1881–1971, Swiss), for example, created evocative portraits of nobility in the Bamum kingdom of Cameroon, where she worked for the Basel Mission from 1911 to 1915. Her images, now in the Basel Mission Archive in Switzerland, are beautifully composed, rising beyond mere documentation.

After World War I, anthropological interest in the study of race declined. Nevertheless, the conventions and requirements of anthropological and ethnographic photography still influenced the type of imagery produced. Austrian travel writer and photographer Hugo Bernatzik (1897–1953) created magnificent images of peoples in Guinea and Sudan. He was one of several traveling photographers who sought recognition as both an artist and an anthropologist. While photography was still widely practiced, film became the medium of choice for travelers and hunters, who depicted their African adventures and contributed to the

A young Wolof man from Senegal depicted in a "carte de visite," c. 1880. NATIONAL MUSEUM OF AFRICAN ART, SMITHSONIAN INSTITUTION

creation of knowledge about the continent. In films and illustrated books, Martin and Osa Johnson (1884–1937 and 1894–1952, American) fascinated and delighted the American public with their safaris while the Italian hunter, filmmaker, and photographer Attilio Gatti (b. 1896) appealed to European audiences.

News and Propaganda Photography

One of the major uses of photography for the colonial governments in Africa was as a tool for propaganda. Even in the years before 1914, the German Reichskolialamt mandated that all photographs by colonials in government service be presented to

Portrait by Anna Rein-Wuhrmann, 1914. © BASEL MISSION. REFERENCE NO. QE-30.006.0143

the office, which retained the right to keep images that might serve its purposes. In the 1920s, new genres of photography, such as photo reportage and news photography, came into their own, increasing the already major pictorial output on Africa to a flood of images from the continent. In the 1930s and 1940s colonial picture services, such as the Belgian Centre d'Information and Documentation (later Congopresse), and research institutions, such as the Institut Français de l'Afrique Noire, headquartered in Dakar, hired documentary photographers. Photographers worked for magazines, for example George Rodger (b. 1908, British) and Eliot Elisofon (1911–1973, American) for *Life* magazine, and Volkmar Kurt Wentzel (b. 1915, American) for *National Geographic*. It should be noted here that one of the most unusual journals was *Drum,* first published as *African Drum* in 1951 in Cape Town, South Africa, but later covering the entire African continent. The *Drum* also employed African photojournalists, among them Peter Magubane (b. 1932,

South African), whose fame drew attention to the contributions of African photographers.

African Photography

Compared with the number of European photographers at the turn of the twentieth century, Africans who established photographic studios or carried out their business as itinerant photographers were a small minority. In many instances, we know only the names of African photographers working at the turn of the century and into the 1930s and 1940s. Among the better-known was Alex Agbaglo Acolatse, who was active roughly from 1900 to 1950. Born around 1880 to the ruling family of Keta in the then Gold Coast, he moved to Lomé, the capital of German Togoland, around 1900. He was among the first professional African photographers during the German colonial period. Some of his images can be found in the Bremen Staatsarchiv in Germany.

Among the most prolific practitioners were Creole photographers of Sierra Leone. The brothers Alphonso and Arthur Lisk-Carew had a studio and business establishment in Freetown. The older brother, Alphonso (1888–1969), opened the studio in 1905. In 1918, Arthur joined him in the business, which eventually included the sale of photographic materials, stationery, postcards, so-called fancy goods, and toys. The Lisk-Carews' clients included affluent Creoles, who cherished photography as a means to present a sense of self, and British colonials. The brothers also worked on commission for the British and recorded many official government events. Many of their images can be found in British repositories, such as the archives of the Royal Commonwealth Institute, now in Cambridge. They also produced postcards, which were widely distributed and used well into the 1950s.

N. Walwin Holm and J. A. C. Holm were a father-and-son team from Ghana who established several successful studios. The father, N. Walwin Holm, was born in 1865 and started his photographic business in Accra, Ghana, around 1883. In 1896, he moved to Lagos and opened a studio there. In 1897, the year the British destroyed the Benin kingdom in Nigeria, N. Walwin Holm became a member of the British Royal Photographic Society. His son, J. A. C. Holm (b. 1888) joined the Lagos family business around 1906, and later reestablished the Accra branch. Many of the Holms' commissions came from the British colonial administration and their images are preserved in photographic albums

407

and archives to this day, although not always identifiable, because they were not signed. These early African photographers were extraordinary individuals and entrepreneurs who often learned their craft from Europeans and followed classic Western photographic conventions when taking their subjects. At the same time, photography slowly spread to the interior and to smaller towns in Africa.

After World War I, African photographers opened numerous small studios to serve the growing needs of their African clientele, who patronized such studios in greater numbers after colonial authorities demanded that indigenous Africans carry identification. Photographs became a necessary and desirable part of life for Africans, especially as a means to project a modern image. In the 1940s and 1950s, studios sprang up everywhere, ranging from sheds to elaborate commercial buildings. Their owners were often well-traveled entrepreneurs who had been in the colonial service and thus were well acquainted with technology. Itinerant photographers catered to a less affluent clientele in the streets. All of them shared the ability to adapt photographic techniques to the conditions under which they had to work, and develop original modifications of the process.

Only in the late twentieth century had researchers and collectors begun to document the often extraordinary work of these photographers. Among them are Meissa Gaye (1892–1993) and Mama Casset (1908–1992) and his brother Salla Casset (1910–1974) in Senegal, who ran successful studios in Saint-Louis and Dakar. In the 1940s, Seydou Keïta (b. 1923, Malian) took up photography in Bamako, Mali. Their portraits follow similar conventions. The client stands or sits in front of either a pictorial or plain backdrop and assumes poses that demonstrate his or her sophistication and worldliness. Studio photographers often had props at hand, such as wristwatches, Western-style suits, telephones, and radios—in short, visual symbols of modernity.

The days of the African studios have come to an end. With the introduction of color photography in the 1960s, the proliferation of minilabs for the processing of images, and the increased availability of cameras and film, the business of the studio photographers declined, while the business of ambulatory "street corner" photographers, who make use of autofocus cameras and have their pictures printed in minilabs, seems on the upswing, a development that should be closely followed. Only future research will further reveal the creativity and ingenuity of African photographers, be they studio photographers, photojournalists, or artists.

"Types of the Lagos Fire Brigade." Postcard by Ghanaian N. Walwin Holm, c. 1900. NATIONAL MUSEUM OF AFRICAN ART, SMITHSONIAN INSTITUTION

BIBLIOGRAPHY

Center for African Art. *Art/Artifact: African Art in Anthropology Collections.* New York, 1988.

Edwards, Elizabeth, ed. *Anthropology and Photography, 1860–1920.* New Haven, Conn., 1992.

Geary, Christraud. *Images from Bamum: German Colonial Photography at the Court of King Njoya, Cameroon, West Africa, 1902–1915.* Washington, D.C., 1988.

Guggenheim Museum. *In/Sight: African Photographers, 1940 to the Present.* New York, 1996.

———. "Historical Photographs of Africa." *African Arts* 24, no. 4, special issue (1991).

Killingray, David, and Andrew Roberts. "An Outline of Photography in Africa to ca. 1940." *History in Africa* 16 (1989): 197–208.

Untitled portrait by Seydou Keïta. SEYDOU KEÏTA

Royal Commonwealth Society. *Commonwealth in Focus: 130 Years of Photographic History*. Sydney, Australia, 1982.

Theye, Thomas, ed. *Der geraubte Schatten: Die Photographie als ethnographisches Dokument*. Munich, 1989.

Viditz-Ward, Vera. "Photography in Sierra Leone, 1850–1918." *Africa* 57, no. 4 (1987): 510–517.

CHRISTRAUD GEARY

See also **Cinema.**

SOCIAL AND CULTURAL ASPECTS

Photographs—in addition to mirrors—provide the most important means by which we are able to see ourselves and to create self-images as well as self-representations. Research in visual arts and culture has taken considerable interest in the photographic practices of non-Western cultures, focusing on two related questions: What can we find out about other cultures by studying their photographic images? And inversely, what do we learn about the nature of photography itself by studying the way other cultures adapt it as their visual practice?

History and Technology

Photography was invented in 1839, at the dawn of European imperialism, when the scientific exploration and colonization of Africa were already well under way. The new technology was used extensively in the encyclopedic effort to invent, define, categorize, and dominate "the Other." Photographic anthropometrics tried to establish racial and ethnic types. Between 1844 and 1864, inspired by the orientalism then in vogue, various traveling photographers (George Bridges, Félix Teynard, John Beasley Green, Maxime Du Camp, and others) published albums illustrating Egyptian antiquities and scenes. The ubiquity of such imagery, printed in mass numbers, obscures, however, the existence of works by African and Indian photographers, who were starting to appropriate and transform the new technology for their own purposes. Commercial studios were first set up in Egypt, Algeria, and South Africa, then later in Sierra Leone, the Gold Coast (present-day Ghana), Angola, and Zanzibar. Unfortunately many of the names of those pioneers are lost to history.

Indian photographers from Goa had been doing business in Zanzibar since the 1860s. A. C. Gomes opened his studio in 1868 and went on to establish a branch in Dar es Salaam; others—such as E. C. Dias and J. B. Coutinho—followed suit. Along Africa's west coast, the earliest photographers were probably itinerant merchants who traveled on European steamers between the major ports. In 1857, a Freetown newspaper announced the arrival of a daguerreotyper named A. Washington, probably an African American. Local photo studios were to be found in Freetown as early as the 1880s. In the Gold Coast, the first native photographers were Gerhardt L. Lutterodt and N. Walwin Holm, both mulattos whose grandfathers originally came from Germany (Lutterodt) and Britain (Holm). Holm, who opened his studio in Accra in 1883, was the first African photographer to become a member of the Royal Photographic Society fourteen years later. Lutterodt started out as a traveling photographer in the various coastal towns between Freetown and Douala in the early 1870s. He eventually settled in Fernando Po, where he trained his nephew Freddy R. C. Lutterodt (1871–1937) and his son Eric P. Lutterodt (1884–1959). In the late 1890s they began to operate the two principal photo studios in the Gold Coast capital, Accra (the Duala Studio and the Accra Studio).

A first change in this pioneer period of African photography (1840–1880) occurred after the invention of the silver-bromide-gelatin dry plate in 1871, which replaced the cumbersome wet-collodion technique and made the photographic procedure much easier. Soon thereafter, the mass-produced postcard was introduced. Both factors caused a significant increase in the number of studios. At the turn of the twentieth century photo studios were to be found in nearly all African capitals and the major peripheral cities as well. Photography was developing into a distinct profession with its own formal apprenticeship and work ethic. Customers included Europeans and Indians as well as members of the local elite, teachers, priests, and clerks. Imagery from this period of early urban African photography (1880–1940) is still to be found on historical postcards, in family albums, and in glass-covered wooden frames in the halls of bourgeois houses. Most of these photographs are quite stern and rigid Victorian-style portraits or group pictures which often evoke a sense of bereftness, of figures uprooted from their social context. Because of the low sensitivity of the available emulsions, exposure times running up to several minutes had to be given. The photographers operated bulky "box cameras" without shutters, exposing large-size glass negatives (four by five and five by seven inches), which were carefully retouched and printed as contact prints in daylight.

By the 1920s, the first locally manufactured cameras appeared in the Gold Coast and in Nigeria. The main modification to the European models was the integration of a darkroom into the camera body. This permitted production of a negative on printing paper and immediate processing; this negative was then snapped again in front of the lens—producing, after processing, the positive. This extremely practical and ingenious technique, popularly known as "wait and get" photography, led to a new type of ambulant actor who offered comparatively cheap portraits and passport pictures to the growing number of urban poor and farmers from remote areas visiting the towns. The result was a democratization of access to individual photographic representations, which had been an exclusive privilege of the urban economic and educated elites. However, the majority of Africans first encountered photography while taking identity photos, thus being symbolically subjected to the public eye of the colonial administration, which sought to impose individual identities and responsibilities where corporate ones had prevailed.

This early urban African photography led during the 1940s to a period which many photographers refer to today as the golden age of black-and-white studio photography. Electrification reached more and more towns, permitting installation of artifical studio lights. European, American, and Asian companies introduced medium-size cameras (for roll film) and low-cost enlargers. The customers diversified, as did their reasons for requesting pictures for "future remembrances." Photographers were increasingly invited to cover their clients' rites of passage (baptisms, "outdoorings," weddings, and funerals), as well as local political events, such as the enstoolment of a new chief or the dedication of new buildings. Some work of this generation—mainly from francophone west African countries—was exhibited and published in catalogs and booklets in the 1990s (Alex Acolatse, Seydou Keita, Malick Sidibe, Samuel Fosso, Salla Casset, Augustt Azaglo). In South Africa—and to a lesser extent in Nigeria—magazines such as *Drum* stimulated the development of African photojournalism.

Another structural change within the photographic sector occurred in the 1980s, when manual black-and-white photography was gradually replaced by quasi-industrial color photography. The new laboratories, mostly run by foreigners of Asian or European origin and supported by significant capital, took over the market in developing and printing. Studio photographers lost their former monopoly, and more and more studios were forced to close down. A similar situation existed in postwar Europe; instead of leading to large-scale amateur photography, as happened in Europe, however, a new actor was brought onto the scene: the young "roving" photographer, who often served as an agent for one of the color labs. Compared with the highly stylized and often enlarged black-and-white photographic images of earlier decades, later production was more heterogeneous and colorful, smaller, and impressive in volume.

Social and Cultural Embeddedness

In the early days, local beliefs about stealing souls and shadows made for considerable resistance to photographers. Picture taking was feared because it was thought to make people weak or their blood thin. In many African languages, the word for "negative" is the same as for ghost or dead spirit, and cameras were often literally referred to as "shadow-catching machines." However, the initial fear seems to have abated quickly. Photography has become widely accepted and integrated into the canon of pictorial traditions.

Early photographers in Africa found themselves in direct competition with other image makers. In order to compete, they blended their European and Indian aesthetic legacies with existing local conventions. But they also offered services to peoples who until then had been deprived of having their likenesses preserved. Since in Ghana, for example, potters had imagined and rendered the dead long before the coming of photography, it was not surprising that photographers would attempt to emulate that custom, too. In the long run, they drove the potters out of business. Photographers started to depict their customers in the locally idealized manners and produced images that were considered appropriate to be displayed on walls. Photography became a practice of splitting off the ideal from the social self, thus transforming images of individuals into virtually eternal image allegories and potential objects of religious veneration. All over the continent, photographs increasingly became integrated into ancestor worship. This tendency to assimilate photography into the realm of "tradition" was paralleled by the new practice of keeping photo albums, and not only by young people. The presentation of photo albums became part of the protocol of visiting and hospitality. The visitor is symbolically introduced to the life and family of the host or hostess by flipping through his or her collection of photographic stand-ins. Finally, photography became important in what one might be tempted to call a custom of "generalized image circulation and exchange." People appreciate giving and receiving pictures as reminders of events, as signs of friendship or love, and as indicators of modernity and social achievement. This exchange is, however, subtly regulated by distance and proximity. People are eager to give out their pictures to a person who lives far away—and ever less willing as the proximity increases. In hierarchical as well as conflictual relations, pictures are not exchanged at all. The growing significance of photographs within this system of image circulation and exchange is connected to people's increased migration and mobility. Here, pictures clearly serve as substitutes for absent persons as well as for events in which one was not able to participate, thus symbolically counteracting the loss of social cohesion. Sometimes photographs are used for healing and harming. Along the Kenyan coast, for example, so-called waganga use photographs to diagnose as well as to identify persons who are attacking and harming their clients. In love magic, photographs are widely "worked on" to bring back a beloved who has run away or fallen in love with another person. In the 1950s, when photography spread through the villages of western Kenya, many people feared that their likenesses would be used by witches or sorcerers to kill them. As a means to counter this threat, the practice of holding or posing with a Bible while being photographed evolved as a protective device.

As elsewhere in the world, African photography serves the purpose of preserving memories of happy times—even creating them. Photography (and videography) are deeply embedded into a culture of performance and social consumption where social positions are negotiated. During feasts like weddings marking the life cycle, as well as Christmas and Islamic celebrations, photographs are used not only to document a particular ritual passage, but the act of photography itself becomes part of a more comprehensive ritual of self-representation. Photography "crowns the celebration," as a photographer in Mombasa put it. During weddings, for example, the quantity and quality of photographs produced and distributed among the guests and relatives serves as an index of a host's social standing. As in a potlatch, his status can be raised or be destroyed. And, in addition, photographs will be used to remember this event. However, as Islamic fundamentalism spreads, men are making greater attempts to control and limit the circulation of women's photographs. The Islamic interdiction of representing a person is heavily debated among scholars and believers. In Lamu, a center of Islamic scholarship, for example, photographs are no longer to be seen in studio display cases. However, paradoxically, the segregation of men and women has allowed a few female photographers to become professionals and to specialize in taking pictures of women during feasts.

One of photography's main functions is to provide a means to remember. Picture taking—and to a lesser extent writing—has in many significant ways replaced other bodily forms of memory and has become one of the primary means by which twentieth-century Africans remember. A current practice consists of remembering events by clothes and clothes by photographs. That African photography is linked with clothing can also be seen in the fact that—at least in some west African countries—many photographers started out as tailors. The boundaries of these two professions often overlap; both are highly experienced in creating appearances. In some areas, a kind of repertory of photographic gestures has developed. Many of these gestures are meant to visualize proverbs or adages; others are expressions of suffering as well as of wishes and desires. Here, however, the viewer must be familiar with the local canon of body gestures in order to understand the motive or to guess the event that is to be remembered by a particular photograph.

Aesthetics

A comparison between late-nineteenth-century black-and-white pictures and later color ones reveals a continued focus on the human figure. Landscapes and other motifs are almost completely lacking. The composition is mostly formal, characterized by the desire for centrality, frontality, stability, and completeness. The main subject is nearly always in the center of the picture and in full figure,

Two Ghanaian studio portrait, c. 1970s. FRANCIS K. HONNY

whether sitting or standing, singly posed or in a group. Writing about Nigeria, Stephen Sprague emphasized that the model for such body posing and image framing might have derived from conventions of sculpture. Nigerian photographers are less interested in depicting individual idiosyncrasies than social types. The Yoruba ideal of *jijora* postulates a mimetic balance between abstraction and individual likeness. Ghanaian photo criticism stresses the preservation of body integrity—no body parts are to be cut off in the framing or cropping of a photograph, or else the photographer will have "killed his image." Other aesthetic criteria used by Ghanaians as well as by Kenyans to evaluate photographic appearances of persons include the ideals of coolness, roundness, and smoothness.

For many decades, retouching has been standard practice in beautifying black-and-white photographs. An investigation of retouched negatives is particularly illuminating as it reveals the African ideals of beauty. Retouching with graphite pencils as is done in Ghana lightens the complexion and is mostly done to facial wrinkles. An old Ghanaian photographer put it: "Retouching can make you young and moreover change your face entirely." As regards scarifications, opinions differ. Some photographers retouch them, too, because they consider them to be "savage tribal marks" of olden days; others, however, refuse to do so, since they feel that the photographed persons might no longer be recognizable. Retouching is also done to protruding veins and bones, especially collarbones, since their visibility is thought to signify malnutrition and poverty. Faces are usually made fuller and rounder. The eyes, especially the corneas, are lightened—as "white eyes" suggest coolness, calm, and kindness, whereas "red eyes" are associated with heat, disorder, and witchcraft. Retouching is supposed to "cool" one's face by transforming it into a mask of the cool. As on statues, neck rings, denoting prosperity, sometimes are drawn on the negatives. They serve as indices of body prosperity.

With the introduction of color film, which does not lend itself to retouching, the practice is gradually disappearing; so are photomontage and double and multiple exposures, which were extraordinarily popular in the "golden age" of black-and-white photography. Human figures were excised from an already existing picture, placed on a new image and photographed again. Photographers were image magicians, and even today, studio names such as Magic Photo Studio or Mr. Magic

refer to this uncanny aspect of photomontage. The most common practice was probably the rematching of body and head, which was usually done when a person had died without leaving behind a full-figure picture. The image of the head was then taken from an identity shot and mounted on the body of someone else. In addition, villagers and migrant workers who had no good clothes for a photo session were able to order their likenesses on the bodies of elegantly dressed men.

Such montage techniques were sometimes integrated into ritual contexts, such as the Yoruba twin cult. When one of the twins had died, before they had been photographed together, the surviving one was photographed alone, and the photographer printed this negative twice, so that the two twins appeared to be sitting together. This was supposed to maintain their spiritual integrity. If they were of opposite sexes, the surviving twin was photographed once in male clothing and once in female clothing. Sprague also notes that such photographs were increasingly replacing earlier wooden *ibedji* sculptures and kept on altars. Some of these photomontages are quite obvious, some are more subtle, and the others are so sophisticated that it is nearly impossible to determine how the pictures came into being. One encounters montages such as a newlywed couple on a TV screen or a woman inside a beer bottle. Sometimes double exposures consist of one subject in two poses: a man reading a book to himself or helping to light a cigarette for himself. This multiplying device could perhaps be seen as an image allegory or as an African response to the puzzling experience of an age termed by Walter Benjamin as the "age of technical reproducibility."

African photo studios provide their customers with many hand props and clothes. In Ghana, coats and ties are supplied; they are often complemented by prestigious *kente* cloths, royal sandals, hats, umbrellas, watches, imitations of gold ornaments, and ceremonial swords. One Asante photographer declared himself to be a "kingmaker." He had on hand all the items necessary to dress men as chiefs and women as queen mothers. In the monarchistic Asanteman, following the death of a queen mother, women of all social classes hurry to photographers' studios to dress and be shot as queen mothers themselves. Elsewhere backdrops are used with painted Durbar scenes including a royal umbrella, in front of which a customer may be photographed seated on a chief's stool.

413

The studio lighting is usually strictly frontal. Side and head lights to create the impression of depth—typical for Western photographic portraiture—are not used. In African practice, less shadow makes better lighting. Dramatic lighting effects are categorically refused, as they would subvert the ideals of "smoothness" and of blending figures into their backgrounds—which is clearly opposed to the Western option of differentiating figure and ground. African photographs thus appear to the Westerner as flat and shallow, sometimes creating the impression of persons who have been corroded into their backdrops.

The environment of African photo studios and their hand props and backdrops reflect, above all, a male gaze. Nearly all studio owners and roaming photographers are men, and only a few have allowed female apprentices to acquire photographic skills and to work for them. These women are in subordinate positions that do not permit them to influence the setting.

Painted backdrops with landscapes, clouds, and bourgeois living room interiors were originally introduced by Europeans. They were first copied by local artists and then continuously adapted to the taste of the African studio visitors. Each decade developed its own favorite motifs, such as urban scenes with multistory buildings, city streets lined with street lights, skyscrapers, airports and airplanes, parks and benches, waterfalls and national tourist sites, and "room dividers" laden with the icons of modernity and social promotion (refrigerator, TV, sound system, and VCR). Whereas in some parts of Africa very crude perspectives that make no attempt at realism prevail, a strong tendency to trompe l'oeil compositions in which people interact with their painted environment has developed in Nigeria and Ghana. Here, the photographic practice has shifted from providing simple symbolic presences to that of true illusions.

African photography forms part of what Susan Vogel has called "new functional art"; it has had a significant impact on other pictorial arts (such as painting and sculpture) as well as on shaping modernity. Photography in Africa does not attempt to document social reality. Instead, it is considered to be a modern way of seeing the world and improving one's standing in the world. People enjoy

Studio portrait, taken in Côte d'Ivoire, 1996. AKANI LUKUMAN

being seen in the act of being photographed and thus showing that they can afford it. In addition, the photo as an object stays there to be seen and remembered by others. Not only the practice but also the result of this practice proves the subject-owner's modernity.

In its nearly 150 years of existence, African photography has left an immense legacy of visual documents and chronicles revealing shifts in identity formations (individual as well as collective ones), social memories, human desires, ambivalences, memento mori, and much more. Unfortunately, photography archives are not yet part of the African cultural scenario. African photography has only recently been officially recognized as an art through the increasing number of exhibits, done mostly in France and in the United States. However, many of these exhibitions have focused on individual artists and motifs sure to appeal to Western narcissism. African photography still needs to be seen holistically as the widespread modern-day cultural phenomenon that it is.

BIBLIOGRAPHY

David, Philippe. *Alex A. Acolatse, 1880–1975: Hommage à l'un des premiers photographes togolais.* Lomé, 1993.

Deberre, Jean-Christophe, ed. *Cornelius Yao Augustt Azaglo: Photographies, Côte d'Ivoire, 1950–1975.* Paris, 1996.

Fondation Cartier pour l'Art Contemporain. *Malick Sidibé.* Exhibit catalog. Paris, 1994.

Guggenheim Museum. *In/Sight: African Photographers, 1940 to the Present.* New York, 1996.

Hambourg, Maria M. "Extending the Grand Tour." In *The Waking Dream: Photography's First Century,* by Maria M. Hambourg et al. New York, 1993.

Jewsiewicki, Bogumil. "Representations of Congolese Memories: Mermaid, Belgian Colony, and Lumumba." Paper given at the Conference Images and Empires, Yale University, February 1997.

Killingray, D., and A. Roberts. "An Outline History of Photography in Africa." In *Photographs as Sources for African History.* Collection of papers presented at a workshop at SOAS. London, 1988.

Macmillan, Allister, ed. *The Red Book of West Africa.* London, 1920.

Monti, Nicolas. *Africa Then: Photographs, 1840–1918.* New York, 1987.

Ouedraogo, Jean-Bernard. "La figuration photographique des identités sociales: Valeurs et apparences au Burkina Faso." *Cahiers d'études africaines* 141–142 (1996): 25–50.

Pivin, Jean-Loup, ed. *Mama Casset: Les précurseurs de la photographie au Sénégal, 1950.* Paris, 1994.

Sprague, Stephen. "Yoruba Photography: How the Yoruba See Themselves." *African Arts* 12, no. 1 (1978): 52–59, 107.

Theye, Thomas, ed. *Der geraubte Schatten: Eine Weltreise im Spiegel der ethnographischen Photographie.* Munich, 1989.

Viditz-Ward, Vera. "Alphonso Lisk-Carew: Creole Photographer." *African Arts* 19, no. 1 (1985): 46–51.

———. "Photography in Sierra Leone, 1850–1918." *Africa* 57 (1987): 510–518.

Vogel, Susan. *Africa Explores: Twentieth-Century African Art.* New York and Munich, 1991.

Werner, Jean-François. "Produire des images en Afrique: Le cas des photographes de studio." *Cahiers d'études africaines* 141–142 (1996): 81–112.

HEIKE BEHREND
TOBIAS WENDL

See also **Cinema.**

PIDGINS. *See* **Language Families.**

PLAATJE, SOL (b. 1876; d. 1932), writer, founding member of the African National Congress, and activist for the preservation of the Setswana (Tswana) language. Born in Boshof in the Orange Free State of South Africa, he received his elementary education at the Lutheran Church Missionary School in Barkly West. He worked as a pupil-teacher and as a mailman before he was sent to Mafeking in 1898 to serve as an interpreter for Lord Edward Cecil at the Court of Summary Jurisdiction and then in the Native Affairs Department.

Plaatje was in Mafeking when the Anglo-Boer war broke out in 1899. During that year, he kept a journal of the Boers' siege as they attempted to gain independence from the British. Having discovered himself as a writer, Plaatje left government service in 1901 to begin a newspaper, *Koranta ea Becoana* (The Tswana Gazette). The paper was printed in both Tswana and English and was the first Setswana newspaper. In 1908, Plaatje returned to Kimberly to found a second newspaper, *Tsala ea Batho* (The Friend of the Bechuana).

Plaatje's interest in politics grew through his journalism, and in 1912 he helped to organize the South African Native National Congress (SANNC), which eventually became the African National Congress (ANC). Elected the group's first general secretary, he was key in their first action in opposition to the Native Land Act of 1913. The colonial government had begun segregating the land and had passed the act to prevent Africans from owning or living in territories that the British had declared their own. As a member of the SANNC, Plaatje went as part of a delegation to London to protest. Though unsuccessful with the British government, Plaatje stayed in England to lecture on racial problems in South Africa while he worked as a language assistant at the University of London. Fiercely believing in the preservation of his culture, Plaatje also wrote three books during his three years in London: *Native Life in South Africa Before and Since the European War and the Boer Rebellion*, *The Sechuana Phonetic Reader*, and *Sechuana Proverbs, with Literal Translations and Their European Equivalents*, all of which were published in 1916. A scathing observer of the happenings in his country, Plaatje wrote in *Native Life*:

> What have our people done to these colonists, we asked, that is so utterly unforgivable, that this law should be passed as an unavoidable reprisal? Have we not delved in their mines, are not a quarter of a million of us still laboring from them in the depths of the earth in such circumstances for the most niggardly pittance? . . . Have we not obsequiously and regularly paid taxation every year, and have we not provided the Treasury with money to provide free education for Dutch children in the "Free" State and Transvaal, while we had to find additional money to pay the school fees for our own children?

Plaatje continued to travel in order to make known the worsening racial tensions in South Africa. In 1919, he joined another SANNC delegation to the Versailles Peace Conference, despite the conference's refusal to acknowledge their presence. That year in Paris, he also attended the Pan-African Congress before he returned to London, where he met Prime Minister David Lloyd-George and made an appeal for Blacks in South Africa. In 1921, Plaatje traveled to the United States to meet with publishers of the American edition of *Native Life in South Africa*. That year he also published his *The Mote and the Beam: An Epic on Sex-Relationship 'Twixt White and Black in British South Africa*.

In 1923, Plaatje returned to South Africa and earned a living as a journalist while he continued to work for the preservation of his native language. He translated Shakespeare's *Comedy of Errors* into the Setswana *Diphoshophosho*, and *Julius Caesar* into *Dintshontsho tsa Bo-Julius Kesara*. His final novel, *Mhudi: An Epic of South African Native Life a Hundred Years Ago*, was published in 1930. Plaatje died of pneumonia during a trip from Kimberly to Johannesburg.

BIBLIOGRAPHY

Willan, Brian. *Sol Plaatje, South African Nationalist, 1876–1932*. Berkeley, Calif., 1984.

SARAH VALDEZ

See also **Literature; Publishing.**

PLANTATION ECONOMIES AND SOCIETIES. Many of sub-Saharan Africa's most important agricultural export crops—coffee, cocoa, sugar, tea, palm oil, tobacco, sisal, and bananas—are typically associated with plantation agriculture (table 1). However, in most African countries, plantations have not become a dominant feature of the agricultural economy and rural society as is the case in tropical America and Southeast Asia. Where they have become the dominant institution in the agricultural economies, the centralized, hierarchical, and regimented production systems that typify plantations have resulted in social, economic, and ecological problems that are difficult to resolve. Sub-Saharan Africa's ecology, high land-to-labor ratio, social institutions, and technologies combine to make the production of export commodities under plantations uneconomic. As a result, most of Africa's agricultural commodities are produced by small farmers with holdings considerably smaller than 50 hectares (125 acres). Nonetheless, plantations have been important in the development of agricultural exports and the introduction of new crops and technologies into Africa. Their role remains significant for some key exports for several African states.

Plantations are a special type of large farm, normally over one hundred hectares, which is distinguished by the way that production is organized and channeled. Modern plantations are social and economic institutions run by merchant or industrial capital for the production of tropical export crops. Among their key features are specialization in one or two tropical crops for export, with some processing of the export crop done on the plantation; there is some preference for perennials or tree crops. Typically, plantations maintain a large, disciplined, unskilled labor force with sharp differences between managerial-technical staff and field labor. Plantations often depend upon imported labor, which must be housed and fed. Thus, labor costs are the highest factor in total cost of production. The failure of plantations to dominate the continent's production of agricultural exports highlights the indigenous social institutions, ecology, and history of infrastructure development in Africa, which made plantations profitable only in cases where they received considerable direct and indirect concessions and subsidies from the colonial or postcolonial state. These were in the form of cheap or free land, coerced labor, export monopoly, and price guarantees or subsidies.

Origins and Evolution of Plantations in Sub-Saharan Africa

The African islands of Cape Verde, São Tomé e Príncipe, Bioko (Fernando Póo, Equatorial Guinea), Zanzibar, Mauritius, and Réunion have the longest history of plantations. Early sugar plantations on Cape Verde and São Tomé e Príncipe were crucibles for the development of the classic plantation systems of the tropical Americas. Early attempts by the Portuguese in the late fifteenth and the sixteenth centuries to establish sugar plantations based on slave labor did not last due to slave insurrections, poor processing technologies, and the more favorable land conditions and greater control over labor that was possible in the Americas. The sugar plantations established by French and Dutch planters in southern Africa and the Indian Ocean proved more successful. This was due in part to better technology, improved cane varieties, and the ability to import indentured labor from South Asia and Indonesia following the collapse and abolition of slavery in the early and mid-eighteenth century. Sugar plantations are still important in South Africa, Swaziland, Madagascar, and Mauritius.

Europeans and creole African traders established plantations in the eighteenth and nineteenth cen-

TABLE 1. Total Values of Plantation Export Crops from Sub-Saharan Africa, 1994 (in U.S. dollars)[1]

Coffee	1,516,540,000
Cocoa	1,235,567,000
Sugarcane	862,982,000
Tobacco	730,805,000
Tea	418,995,000
Rubber	199,360,000
Banana	115,650,000
Sisal	19,462,000

[1] From FAO statistics

SOURCE: Taken from David B. Grigg, *The Agricultural Systems of the World: An Evolutionary Approach.* London, 1974.

turies along the upper Guinea coast from the Casamance River in Senegal in Guinea and Sierra Leone. Sugar, groundnuts, and palm oil were the main exports upon which these were based. As economic institutions they were short-lived since production reverted back to indigenous small farmers with Europeans and creoles acting as buyers and middleman. The growing demand by Europe for plant oils used in soap manufacture and as lubricants in the early pre-petroleum industrial age led to the establishment of large oil palm plantations in west Africa in the early nineteenth century. These plantations were established and managed by African and creolized African elites. In Dahomey the kings and court officials established palm plantations worked by slaves. The same was true in the neighboring Yoruba chiefdoms of Egba and Ijehu. Slave revolts in the latter half of the nineteenth century and eventual conquest by France and Britain in the last decade of the nineteenth century put an end to this west African plantation system. Around the same time, another indigenous plantation system arose on the Swahili coast on the island of Zanzibar. Here the sultan of Zanzibar and the Omani-Swahili elite established clove and coconut plantations also worked by slaves. While the labor regime had changed, these plantations remained at the end of the twentieth century.

The heyday of plantations in Africa was the early part of the twentieth century, particularly before World War I. Portuguese planters and bankers established large cocoa and coffee plantations in São Tomé and Príncipe; coffee plantations in Angola; and cotton, sugar, and coconut plantations in Mozambique. German companies established cocoa, banana, and coffee plantations in their west African colonies of Kamerun (present-day Cameroon) and Togo. In German-ruled Tanganyika (present-day Tanzania) sisal and coffee plantations were established. In southern Africa and the Indian Ocean, sugar has been the main plantation crop, dominating the agricultural-export economies of Swaziland, Réunion, and Mauritius. The Belgian colony of the Congo produced many of the same plantation crops—rubber, coffee, oil palm—but state-supported companies preferred to coerce African farmers to produce them rather than invest in the capital and management structure of large settler-run plantations. The large Kenyan coffee and tea estates were under settler control. Low-cost land grants, protected markets, and laws forbidding Africans from growing coffee made white-owned plantations viable ventures despite the inherent diseconomies of this system in a free market.

Plantations continued in some cases even under socialist state ownership, as was the case in Angola, São Tomé and Príncipe, Mozambique, and Tanzania. The collective and industrial character of plantation production of cocoa, coffee, coconut, tea, and sisal appealed to the Marxist notion of a rural proletariat which could participate in the management of the plantation under state ownership. These nationalized plantations failed to match the earlier and already low production levels of the colonial planters. The added costs of state patronage and bureaucratic management did little to improve incomes for the workers or profits for the state. The experience of state-owned plantations illustrates how the plantations' social and political characteristics, useful in the control of a populace and natural resources, may override any economic rationale for profitable production of export crops. The contemporary agro-industrial plantation in Africa exemplifies this.

In contemporary sub-Saharan Africa, plantations are an important exception to the smallholder production which predominates. For example, coffee and cocoa, the most valuable agricultural exports in sub-Saharan Africa, are now predominantly pro-duced by African smallholders. The modern agro-industrial plantation is best represented by the efficiently managed and technologically advanced sugar estates of Mauritius, Swaziland, and South Africa. Other agro-industrial plantations were established by multinational corporations such as Unilever for oil-palm production in west Africa, and Firestone Rubber for plantations in Liberia. A Japanese company in Liberia operates the largest single rubber (*Hevea brasiliensis*) plantation in the world. Civil strife in that small country over ten years has reduced rubber production to the occasional and uncontrolled tapping of existing trees with little maintenance and no investment. Tobacco plantations in Malawi, Zimbabwe, and South Africa still employ large labor forces and are linked to multinational tobacco corporations. While southern African and Indian Ocean sugar and tobacco estates are still competitive and benefit from significant research and development, labor remains a problem. Plantation work is a low-status and onerous job that is avoided when other options are available. As economies develop and the rights of laborers are affirmed, obtaining and managing a highly regimented labor force on the estates becomes a problem. Migrant laborers are one option, but increasingly the agro-industrial plantation is being

Laborers at a tea plantation in Tanzania. © BERNARD PIERRE WOLFF/
PHOTO RESEARCHERS, INC.

supplanted by the system of contract growers dependent upon a centralized processing unit or sugar mill.

In Equatorial Guinea and São Tomé e Príncipe, the plantation has survived even under state ownership. The expatriate planters are now being invited back, and new investors, including international development banks, are being wooed. In Somalia, banana plantations were a major element in the national export economy until the total breakdown of security in the early 1990s. Even in times of terrible drought, Somalia's banana plantations were always assured a supply of water.

African agricultural entrepreneurs supported by multinational fruit export companies have revived plantation systems in Côte d'Ivoire for the production of pineapple and bananas. A state-owned company for the promotion of rubber production in Côte d'Ivoire also established large industrial rubber plantations, but even here the emphasis is increasingly being placed on organizing and providing technical support to smallholders while providing central processing and purchasing services. Foreign companies in Côte d'Ivoire continue to play an important role in the export of plantation crops, but they are increasingly moving out of plantation production and concentrating on the processing and evacuation of the product for export. There is also a trend toward greater control over plantations by national investors or parastatal companies. Plantations owned by large multinationals are more likely to have labor unions which can press for higher wages and improved housing and health conditions. The multinational companies in turn are working hard to reduce labor costs and overcome labor scarcity by investing in laborsaving technologies, as has already happened in tropical America.

Future Trends for Plantation Systems in Sub-Saharan Africa

Recent studies of plantation economies in Africa, Asia, and tropical America conclude that plantations will continue their downward trend. Prices for the traditional tropical export crops grown on plantations have been declining or stagnant for the last twenty years. Africa's productivity in these crops is declining relative to competitors in Asia and America. Africa's products even face competition from temperate crops grown in industrialized countries. For example, production of sugar beet and maize sweetener all contribute to the de-

pressed prices for sugar. Guaranteed export quotas and prices such as those the European Union extends to the former colonies is one reason that Mauritius, Swaziland, and Réunion can continue to depend on export income from sugar plantations. Palm oil and coconut oil face similar competition from soybean, corn, and rapeseed oils. Tobacco prices for African planters have remained stable, thanks to the growing markets of China, eastern Europe, and the former Soviet Union, but they, too, face stiff competition from new producers. Plantation production of fresh fruits such as pineapples and bananas requires efficient post-harvest handling, packaging, and transport infrastructures, conditions which are still lacking in many African states. With more efficient marketing and handling facilities, smallholders could meet the demand for tropical exports without the heavy investment and management infrastructure of a plantation. This trend is already apparent as established plantations are evolving into centralized processing units for small farmers referred to as "outgrowers."

For nearly all tropical export crops grown in Africa, there seem to be few, if any, economies of scale derived from large-scale plantation production. Economies of scale are, however, clearly present in the processing and evacuation of the product for export. Nonetheless, a well-organized system for grading, transporting, and pricing the output of small producers has shown itself to be more efficient than plantation systems, as the comparison of west African cocoa production from plantations and small producers has shown.

As a source of employment it is unlikely that large plantations can extend their contribution. A curious feature of plantation economies is that plantations often experience labor shortages in areas of high rural unemployment. This has much to do with the nature of the labor regime that essentially defines plantations. Africa's peoples have traditionally lived in societies where land is abundant and where, with the exception of cases such as feudal Ethiopia and the Zanzibari sultanates, central authorities were seldom able to regiment or deny farmers access to the land and control of their own labor. As a result, only rarely and through some form of coercion were African farmers obliged to become plantation laborers. Where plantations did predominate, such as in the case of insular Africa, plantation labor was composed primarily of migrants brought to work as slaves or indentured laborers. Countries such as São Tomé e Príncipe and Equatorial Guinea, where the plantation system came to dominate society, are still coping with the polarized institutions and inherent social and economic problems produced by the plantation.

Mauritius was a classic sugar plantation society facing social instability and high unemployment at the time of independence. The planters were mainly based in the country and were able to use the export and industrial infrastructure as well as the capital and management experience generated by its sugar industry to diversify into industry. Herein lies perhaps the most important contribution that plantations can make to sub-Saharan Africa's economic development. In the early stages of development, plantations can provide a basis upon which to build an export infrastructure and managerial experience which can eventually be used to diversify the economy around the major plantation crops. However, there are serious social and political inequities entailed in the labor regimes of many plantation systems. Plantations tend to monopolize an inordinate share of natural resources, land, water, and vegetation in those sectors where they predominate. Growing concern for environmentally sound production is also promoting to greater importance African smallholder production with its traditional use of crop diversity and low levels of external inputs. While a combination of social, economic, and ecological factors argue against any expansion of plantation production in Africa, a particular appeal of the plantation sector has been its centralized production, which can provide a more reliable source of tax revenue in countries where plantations are not themselves recipients of government subsidies. It is the strong linkage between centralized political power and plantation systems that continues to promote this system in many African countries. As a counterbalance, technological advances in crop production and new modes of management and communication are increasingly able to provide the means to coordinate production of tropical export crops without the economic and social cost of hierarchical and centralized systems of production that are embodied in the plantation.

BIBLIOGRAPHY

Beckford, George L. *Persistent Poverty: Underdevelopment in Plantation Economies of the Third World.* Oxford, 1972.

Chembezi, D. "Modelling Acreage Response with Risk Consideration: The Case of Malawi." *Agricultural Systems* 36, no. 4 (1991): 427–438.

Davies, S. "Plantations and Rural Economy: Poverty, Employment, and Food Security in Kenya." *IDS Bulletin* 18, no 2 (1987): 15–20.

Epale, S. J. *Plantations and Development in Western Cameroon, 1885–1975: A Study in Agrarian Capitalism.* New York, 1985.

Evans, Julian. *Plantation Forestry in the Tropics.* 2d ed. Oxford, 1992.

Fall, B. "Économie de plantations et main-d'oeuvre forcée en Guinée-Française: 1920–1946." *Travail, capital, et société* 20, no. 1 (1987): 8–33.

Giusti, J. *The Kenya Plantation and Agricultural Workers' Union.* Geneva, 1987.

Kimaro, D. N., B. M. Msanya, and Y. Takamura. "Review of Sisal Production and Research in Tanzania." *African Study Monographs* 15, no. 4 (1994): 227–242.

Kirk, C. *People in Plantations: A Review of the Literature and Annotated Bibliography.* Brighton, U.K., 1987.

Lele, Uma J. *Smallholder and Large-Scale Agriculture in Africa: Are There Tradeoffs Between Growth and Equity?* Washington, D.C., 1989.

Loewenson, Rene. *Modern Plantation Agriculture: Corporate Wealth and Labour Squalor.* London, 1992.

Maddox, G. H. "Famine, Impoverishment, and the Creation of a Labour Reserve in Central Tanzania." *Disasters* 15, no. 1 (1991): 35–42.

Mendis, P. "A Survey of Estate Size and Tea Productivity Debate in India, Sri Lanka, and Kenya." *Marga* 11, no. 4 (1991): 72–79.

Ndegwe, N. A. "An Appraisal of 'Turnkey' Oil Palm Production in Rivers State, Nigeria." *Agricultural Administration and Extension* 29, no. 3 (1988): 185–196.

Ogbu, O. M., and M. Gbetiouo. "Agricultural Supply Response in Sub-Saharan Africa: A Critical Review of the Literature." *African Development Review* 2 (1990): 83–99.

Pryor, F. L., and C. Chipeta. "Economic Development Through Estate Agriculture: The Case of Malawi." *Canadian Journal of African Studies* (1990): 2450–2474.

Sajhau, Jean-Paul. "Employment, Wages, and Living Conditions in a Changing Industry: Plantations." *International Labour Review* 125, no. 1 (1986): 71–85.

Sajhau, Jean-Paul, and Jürgen von Muralt, eds. *Plantations and Plantation Workers.* Geneva, 1987.

Tiffen, M., and M. Mortimore. *Theory and Practice in Plantation Agriculture: An Economic Review.* Overseas Development Institute. London, 1990.

Vaughan, M., and G. H. R. Chipandae. *Women in the Estate Sector of Malawi: The Tea and Tobacco Industries.* Geneva, 1986.

PABLO B. EYZAGUIRRE

See also **Agriculture; Development; Economic History; Labor Systems; Land Tenure Systems;**

Production Systems; Slavery and Servile Institutions; Trades Unions and Associations.

PLANTS

[*This double entry explores the major plants grown in the many climates of sub-Saharan Africa. The first part examines* **Origins and Domestication,** *the second* **Varieties and Uses.**]

ORIGINS AND DOMESTICATION

With its diverse array of climates and environments, sub-Saharan Africa is home to a wide range of indigenous domesticated plants and methods of crop production. The domesticated plants of sub-Saharan Africa can be divided into three major agro-environmental complexes: the savanna, Ethiopian, and forest margin (table 1).

The savanna complex is the most widespread and characteristic of the three groups and is composed of a wide range of oils, fruits, pulses, and cereals adapted to the grasslands and woodlands encompassing much of sub-Saharan Africa. The most economically significant crops are the cereals including sorghum, pearl millet, fonio, and rice. Sorghum is undoubtedly the most important crop, grown over more hectares than any other African food plant. Botanists have identified four wild and five domesticated races of sorghum, each of which has a specific geographical area of distribution. However, all belong to the same biological species, *Sorghum bicolor.*

The Ethiopian complex is composed of a small group of crops native to Ethiopia. These include teff, the principal cereal of Ethiopia; coffee (*Coffea arabica*); noog, an edible oil plant; enset, a banana-like plant rich in carbohydrates; a number of root and legume crops; and possibly finger millet.

Crops of the forest margin complex include oil palm, yam, guinea millet, kola nut, coffee, cowpea, and other plant foods first domesticated in the savanna/tropical forest ecotone or within the tropical forests of western Africa.

Unfortunately, the origins of these domesticates remain poorly studied. This is due in part to a past focus by archaeologists on early hominid and Iron Age studies rather than the Neolithic (stone-tool-based food production), as well as problems in the archaeological recovery of African domesticates, many of which preserve poorly. Nevertheless, this has not prevented scholars from formulating numerous theories to explain the origins of sub-Saharan African plant domestication.

TABLE 1 Major Cultivated Plants of Sub-Saharan Africa

Latin Name	Common Name
Plants of the Savanna Complex	
Colocynthis citrullus	Watermelon
Digitaria exilis	Fonio
D. iburua	Black fonio
Oryza glaberrima	African rice
Pennisetum glaucum	Pearl millet
Polygala butyracea	Black beniseed
Solanum aethiopicum	African tomato
Sorghum bicolor	Sorghum
Voandzeia subterranea	Earthpea
Plants of the Ethiopian Complex	
Avena abyssinica	Tetraploid oats
Catha edulis	Chat
Coffea arabica	Arabica coffee
Eleusine coracana	Finger millet
Ensete ventricosum	Enset
Eragrostis tef	Teff
Guizotia abyssinica	Noog
Plants of the Forest Margin Complex	
Brachiaria deflexa	Guinea millet
Coffea canephora	Robusta coffee
Cola acuminata	Kola nut
Dioscorea bulbifera	Air potato
D. rotundata	White guinea yam
Elaeis guineensis	Oil palm
Lablab niger	Hyacinth bean
Plectranthus exculentus	Hausa potato
Solenostemon rotundfolius	Piasa
Sphenostylis stenocarpa	Yampea
Vigna unguiculata	Cowpea

SOURCE: Adapted from Harlan (1992).

In general these theories can be placed within two major groups. The first group argues for the independent domestication of plants in distinct biogeographical regions. During the first half of the twentieth century, the Russian agronomist Nicolai I. Vavilov proposed Ethiopia to be one of eight world centers of origin for cultivated plants. He was soon followed by other agronomists, geographers, botanists, cultural anthropologists, and archaeologists who also considered Ethiopia as well as the western and eastern Sahel to be independent centers of plant domestication where local hunter-gatherer populations devised methods of domesticating, producing, and processing wild plant foods.

The second and more prevalent group of theories views the physical migrations of agriculturalists and the spread of crops through cultural diffusion as the main stimuli for the establishment of agriculture. One of the most common themes has been to argue for the migration of farming peoples from the Near East who introduced domesticated plants and agricultural methods (not to mention their genes) to the indigenous foragers of northern and eastern Africa. Alternatively, scholars have suggested that the "idea" of Near Eastern farming was introduced through stimulus diffusion to those northern African populations who were "preadapted" to cereal agriculture in that they were already intensive grain collectors. Once African groups established farming, they subsequently introduced agriculture to neighboring populations.

Perhaps the most common and influential example of the use of migration theory to account for the spread of agriculture in African populations relates to the purported movements of Bantu-speaking populations out of western Africa. These iron-using farming communities are often argued to have been responsible exclusively for introducing agriculture to much of central, eastern, and southern Africa over a two-thousand-year period.

Why foraging populations would shift to food production was a question initially rarely asked by researchers, probably because it was commonly assumed that once foragers were introduced to farming they would readily accept it as an inherently better way of life. However, environmental change at the end of the Pleistocene or mid-Holocene epochs was to become one of the most common explanations, as it was argued that regional shifts from humid to more arid environments forced hunter-gatherer populations to turn to alternative modes of food procurement, including plant domestication. Some archaeologists have considered demographic and social stress as causal explanations for independent plant domestication, while others have concentrated upon uncovering the processes involved in the change from foraging to farming rather than on any specific cause.

Historical linguistic evidence suggests that as early as eight thousand years ago, proto-Nilo-Saharan-speaking peoples in southern Egypt and Sudan were engaged in the cultivation of cereals of unspecified type, with sorghum or pearl millet being grown by 5000 B.P. (years before present).

Unfortunately, direct archaeological evidence for the origins of savanna complex crops is meager. At the site of Nabta in southern Egypt, excavations have uncovered numerous charred remains of wild plants, including seeds of sorghum. Securely dated at around 8000 B.P., the seeds are, however, morphologically wild, although biochemical data suggest they may be cultivated. At the Neolithic site of Kadero in central Sudan, grain impressions of sorghum and finger millet were found on pottery shards dating to the seventh millennium B.P.

Since it is impossible at these early Neolithic sites to be certain if the cereals represent wild or cultivated species, the earliest secure evidence for any African food crop comes from India—not Africa—where dates of around 4000 B.P. for sorghum are interpreted by some scholars to represent a minimum age for African cultivation. However, the earliest unequivocal evidence for domesticated sorghum (*S. bicolor*) in Africa dates to around 2200 B.P. from such Sudanese sites as Jebel Moya and Meroë. Similarly, in the savanna regions of western Africa, the earliest dates for sorghum, pearl millet, and rice come from the site of Jenne-jenno, situated along the Niger River in Mali and dating to around 2000 B.P.

On historical linguistic grounds, the spread of savanna complex domesticates south into eastern Africa is argued to have taken place soon after 5000 B.P. However, direct archaeological evidence for any cultigens is conspicuously absent until the arrival of Bantu-speaking, iron-using farming communities around two thousand years ago. The same can be said for central and southern Africa, where the earliest direct evidence of sorghum and millet dates to no earlier than the first millennium C.E.

Except for finger millet, which may have been initially domesticated outside Ethiopia, the unique crops of the Ethiopian complex evidently were not introduced during prehistoric times to other regions of Africa, as were cultigens of the savanna complex. Historical linguistic data propose that by 7000 B.P. "proto-Cushites" in the northern and central Ethiopian highlands were cultivating such cereals as teff and finger millet, while in the southern highlands early Omotic-speaking peoples were engaged in the domestication of enset.

Because of the lack of archaeological research on the Ethiopian Neolithic, there is remarkably little direct archaeological evidence for early cultivation. In the 1970s, excavations at Gobedra rock shelter in northern Ethiopia produced surprisingly

Workers winnowing teff, a major Ethiopian food grain. MARTIN ADLER/PANOS PICTURES

fresh-looking uncharred seeds of cultivated finger millet from strata bracketed by radiocarbon dates of 9000 and 5000 B.P. However, later radiocarbon accelerator dating of the actual seeds indicated they are intrusive and are only about one thousand years old.

Excavations at the site of Ona Nagast on Bieta Giyorgis hill overlooking the ancient capital of Aksum have produced the first direct evidence for domesticated teff. Here teff as well as lentil and grape seeds were recovered from strata dating to around 400–700 C.E. Another team of researchers excavating in the domestic area of ancient Aksum have discovered the first remains of noog, as well as a range of unspecified pulses and crops of Near Eastern origin, dating to around the sixth century C.E. These finds, however, only provide minimal age estimates for the cultivation of Ethiopian complex crops, which surely are of much greater antiquity.

Turning to crops of the forest margin complex, historical linguistic evidence suggests a great antiq-

uity for many of these plants, especially the yam and oil palm. However, as with the other two complexes, direct archaeological evidence for these crops is very limited. Charred oil palm nuts and cowpeas dating to about twenty-five hundred years ago have been recovered from Kintampo period and other sites in Ghana, Liberia, and Nigeria and are assumed to be cultivated varieties (although this still remains uncertain). Virtually nothing is known about the origins of yams and other tubers, as preservation problems have so far prevented archaeologists from recovering the remains of these important domesticates.

Research into the origins of sub-Saharan Africa's domesticated plants was still in its infancy at the close of the twentieth century, as only a handful of archaeological sites had provided direct evidence for the age and distribution of early domesticates. Many more problem-oriented, long-term archaeological projects will be needed before there is a significant improvement in the database necessary to test the various hypotheses generated to explain the evolution of African plant domestication.

BIBLIOGRAPHY

Bard, Kathryn A., and Rodolfo Fattovich. "The I.U.O./B.U. Excavation at Bieta Giyorgis (Aksum): An Interim Report." *Nyame Akuma* 44 (1995): 25–27.

Bower, J. "Early Food Production in Africa." *Evolutionary Anthropology* 4 (1995): 130–139.

Clark, J. Desmond, and Steven A. Brandt, eds. *From Hunters to Farmers: The Causes and Consequences of Food Production in Africa.* Berkeley, 1984.

Harlan, Jack R. "Indigenous African Agriculture." In *The Origins of Agriculture: An International Perspective,* edited by C. Wesley Cowan and Patty Jo Watson. Washington, D.C., 1992.

Harlan, Jack R., Jan M. J. de Wet, and Ann B. L. Stemler, eds. *Origins of African Plant Domestication.* The Hague and Chicago, 1976.

Phillipson, David W. *African Archaeology.* 2d ed. Cambridge and New York, 1993.

———. "The B.I.E.A. Aksum Excavations, 1995." *Nyame Akuma* 46 (1996): 24–33.

Shaw, Thurstan, et al., eds. *The Archaeology of Africa: Food, Metals, and Towns.* London and New York, 1993.

Sutton, John E. G., ed. "The Growth of Farming Communities in Africa from the Equator Southwards." *Azania* 29–30 (1994–1995). Special double volume.

STEVEN BRANDT

See also **Agriculture; Archaeology and Prehistory; Ecosystems.**

VARIETIES AND USES

Throughout sub-Saharan Africa, the savannas, woodlands, and forests supply many products and services essential to the well-being of rural communities. Even urban dwellers receive a host of inputs from plant-based resources. By and large, plant products are from natural systems, or their modified derivatives, not from planted exotic species, except in the obvious case of agricultural crops, such as maize and cassava. Natural or seminatural systems are the primary source of energy, in the form of firewood and charcoal, and a crucial source of essential subsistence goods. Important products include poles and construction materials, timber, tool handles, household utensils, wild foods, medicines, leaf litter, grazing, and browse. In addition, natural systems have a service role in controlling soil erosion, providing shade, modifying hydrological cycles, and maintaining soil fertility. Religious and cultural customs that relate to designated areas and certain tree species are vital to the spiritual well-being and effective functioning of rural communities.

A number of studies have been carried out on species use and the species preferences of users. These studies show that species use is highly selective, providing preferred species are available. In a study in Malawi, nearly ninety tree and shrub species were identified by villagers, and a number of uses or attributes were ascribed to each of them, though the number of preferred species for a variety of uses were relatively few.

Wood Products

Firewood

Women are the principal collectors and consumers of firewood for domestic uses and are highly selective in the species used. The characteristics of favored firewood include burning with a hot flame, producing little smoke, and having long-lasting embers. Different sizes and species of wood are selected for different purposes: smaller pieces that catch fire easily are used for kindling, and large logs are used for preparing food that has to cook for a long time; hot- or cool-burning wood may be selected, depending on the type of cooking required. Dry wood of small dimensions is preferred, because it is easier to collect and transport than wood of living trees.

Men are generally responsible for the collection of firewood in larger quantities and diameters, such as for brick burning or fish smoking. They often use a sledge or cart to transport the wood and are not so particular about the species collected.

Traditional beliefs forbid the use of certain species. For example, in Malawi it is taboo to use the wood of *Psorospermum febrifugum* for fires, because it is believed that its smoke causes family conflicts (its local name means "trouble stirrer").

The forests and woodlands are a vital source of firewood and charcoal for urban populations. While fuelwood markets are relatively uncommon in rural areas, urban households are generally dependent on the market to meet their energy needs. In Mozambique, annual fuelwood consumption is estimated at 16 million cubic meters. In Tanzania, around 91 percent of all energy consumed in the country is from fuelwood. Wood is also important as a fuel for some industries. The cheapest source of fuel for the Malawian tobacco industry is wood. Wood for tobacco curing, accounting for an estimated 17 percent of the country's total energy consumption in the late 1970s, comes from the unlicensed clearance of woodlands.

Timber

There are many fine timber species in sub-Saharan Africa. One of the most important in eastern and southern Africa is *Pterocarpus angolensis,* the timber of which is very durable, works well, and shrinks very little in drying. It is one of the most valuable timbers in Africa. Another notable species is *Dalbergia melanoxylon,* considered one of the best turnery woods in the world and used for making musical instruments. Most of the accessible stock of *P. angolensis* has been felled in southern Malawi, and the furniture industry relies on supplies from across the border in Mozambique. In Zimbabwe, where *P. angolensis* has been heavily exploited in the past, warning has been given that the exploitable stock will be exhausted by the beginning of the twenty-first century if current extraction rates are continued. Mozambique still has large stocks of valuable indigenous hardwoods, and commercial logging operations have increased since the cessation of the war. The timber is being exported as logs to South Africa, Portugal, and Germany.

Employment in enterprises based on inputs from forests and woodlands is an important part of total employment in some countries. In Malawi these enterprises are estimated to employ over 150,000 people, perhaps 15 percent of the total number employed in the small- and medium-scale enterprise sector.

Poles and Construction Materials

The supply of construction materials is still a vital role of woodlands and forests, though in places where the resource has become degraded, the large-diameter posts of durable timber traditionally used have become scarce or unavailable. House and barn construction requires many poles of many different dimensions, weights, and durability, as well as rope fiber for tying them together and grass for thatching, which has to be replaced at frequent intervals. Rope fiber, made by peeling strips from beneath the bark, needs to be strong, long, and easily separated from the tree stem and the bark.

Household Implements and Curios

Wood is the principal material for making domestic implements: hoe and axe handles, pestles and mortars, cooking sticks, plates, bowls, bows and arrows, drums, knobkerries, walking sticks, ox harnesses, and oxcarts. It is also important for carved curios, an important income earner and sometime source of foreign exchange. As with firewood, specific attributes are required of the wood for each express purpose: hunting tools, such as knobkerries and arrows, are made from dense heartwoods such as that of *Swartzia madagascariensis,* and bows are made from light, durable, and flexible woods such as *Diplorhynchus condylocarpon* and *Cordia abyssinica.* For axe and hoe handles, species with woods having interlocked grain at the root collar, and that are strong, resist splitting, and sand to a smooth finish, such as *Julbernardia paniculata,* are preferred. *Terminalia sericea* is the preferred species for yokes, because of its flexibility. In Zimbabwe, *Artabotrys brachypetalus* and *Sterculia quinquiloba* are commonly selected to make musical instruments. For carving utility items, a durable wood with good form and density is desired, such as *Pericopsis angolensis* and *Sclerocarya birrea* for pestles and mortars.

Wild Foods

The woodland of the Lumbumbashi region in Zaire reportedly produces more than fifty edible plants, including fruits of *Strychnos* and *Chrysophyllum bangweolense;* drupes of *Vitex, Parinari,* and *Uapaca;* flowers and seeds of *Stenostylis;* tubers of *Dioscorea;* bulbs of *Cyanastrum johnstonii;* and young shoots of *Adenia gummifera.* While the consumption of fresh fruit is still very important, some publications indicate that the use of other edible woodland products has declined. In southern Zimbabwe, there has been a shift from foodstuffs gathered in woodlands toward "weeds" and "pests" collected from arable and disturbed land. Indigenous foods are of great importance in the diet of rural people; their role in the cash economy appears to be much more variable.

Fruit

Wild fruits are abundant in tropical forests and woodlands. In Tanzania eighty-three species of indigenous fruit trees have been recorded. Wild fruits are mostly consumed by children but also are eaten by adults while they are walking through the bush, herding animals, or collecting other products. Wild fruit is not normally a major constituent in the diet but is an important supplementary source of food, supplying vitamins and nutrients. Many fruits are a major source of iron, and some have a high crude protein and calcium content. Wild fruit is consumed mainly in the hot, dry season and the early rainy season, before the cultivated crops are ripe. Wild fruits are more important in remote areas and during times of famine. *Grewia flavescens* fruits, ground and made into a porridge, comprised nearly 25 percent of the food items during the dry season in a remote communal area in northern

A woman uses thatch to cover the roof of a hut under construction in Maun, Botswana. ORDE ELIASON/LINK PICTURE LIBRARY

Zimbabwe after the 1981–1982 drought. Few examples are reported of fruit processing.

Mushrooms

Many woodland types have abundant and diverse mushroom populations. In Malawi sixty species of edible fungi have been documented. In the savanna climates, the mushroom season coincides with the rainy season. Mushrooms are eaten both fresh and dried. Fresh mushrooms are eaten in both well-off and poor rural households; dried mushrooms are eaten only by poorer households. In a village in the Kasungu district of Malawi, 16 percent of journeys to the woodlands in a six-month period were for mushroom collection—second only to firewood collection trips. During the rains, mushrooms are widely sold along roadsides, particularly by women and children.

Insects

Insects are widely consumed in Africa and constitute a valuable source of protein, vitamins, and energy. They are often eaten as a "relish" to supplement a generally starchy staple diet. Although woodlands are well known as a source of honey,

their value as the major source of edible caterpillars in Africa is less widely recognized among planners and policymakers. To rural people, however, this is a resource of great importance that influences public attitudes to management and conservation. A recent survey of public attitudes to Kasungu National Park in Malawi found that the resources the majority of people wanted to harvest from the park were honey and caterpillars, with fuelwood, building materials, and mushrooms all of lesser importance.

Fourteen species of edible caterpillars were recorded in Kasungu district, Malawi, of which four species were preferred, partly because of taste, partly because of availability. Caterpillars are consumed fresh and also are dried and stored for up to six months; they are an important source of protein. In Zimbabwe the availability of caterpillars is reported to have diminished markedly; of fourteen species commonly said to have been consumed in the past, most have decreased in abundance and some are very rare. Caterpillars are harvested by shaking the tree or a branch, though there are cases reported of people cutting trees to obtain them. Some trees are defoliated by edible caterpillars but recover after the rains have started. Termites are another important source of relish. In Zimbabwe, soldier termites are considered a food for the poor and elderly.

Traditional management practices by local chiefs to control the collection season for caterpillars are recorded from Zambia and from Zaire, where a magical fetish is used to prevent collection until the caterpillars have reached near maximum size. Customary regulations among the Yansi people in Zaire prohibit the cutting of live branches from certain tree species during caterpillar collection. Yansi women are recorded burning savanna woodland to promote the leaf regrowth and increase caterpillar abundance.

As commercial harvesting for local markets or export has escalated, these controls have weakened under massive demand for the seasonally available resource. The quantities harvested are immense. In southwestern Zaire, commercial harvest of dried caterpillars averaged 185 tons (170 tonnes) per year. Mopane worm sales of 1,600 tons (1,500 tonnes) per year) are recorded in South Africa, while in Botswana, a single businessman is recorded buying 5,000 bags of mopane worms. Harvesters are mainly women, who collect an average of 18 kilograms (40 lbs.) (wet weight) of caterpillars per hour; the caterpillars are then eviscerated, dried, and sometimes smoked for a longer shelf life. Recent records from mopane woodland in South Africa show that harvesters can earn U.S.$715 in seven weeks, almost 95 percent of the average farm worker's income in this area. Since each bag contains about 80,000 caterpillars, and up to six hundred women are recorded harvesting from one area of *Colophospermum mopane* woodland, there is concern that edible caterpillars "are too profitable for their own good."

Leaves and Roots

Wild plant leaves and roots are another important source of food derived from woodlands and forests. Rural households in Lushoto, Tanzania, were found to consume at least fifteen species of wild leaves. In central Zambia, ten species of edible wild leaves and four species of edible roots were recorded.

Honey and Beeswax

Apiculture is a traditional occupation throughout the woodlands and savannas, but rapidly disappearing forests have led to a decline in honey and beeswax production in some areas. Productivity estimates from Tanzania indicate that 1 square mile (2.6 km²) can support forty-four bee colonies producing 0.1 ton beeswax and 1.3 tons of honey per year. Honey and beeswax are important foreign currency earners in Tanzania: approximately U.S.$0.5 million and U.S.$2.6 million through exports in 1989 and 1991, respectively. Tanzania's exports are destined for the Middle East, Japan, Germany, and the United Kingdom.

Medicines

Woodlands and forests, to diviners and herbalists, are much more than the sum of species with various uses. They are also, through certain plants, a link with the supernatural world. Use of traditional medicines for strengthening, protection, or purification rituals is particularly important during periods of conflict, social upheaval, or uncertainty, when it is important to draw on supernatural power. In rural areas, for example, plants are used to protect homes and crops, in hunting or warfare, or to pomote success (or failure of opponents). An example from Zimbabwe is the key role played by *mhondoro* spirit mediums during the liberation war in that country. Traditional medicines are also used and traded in urban areas for medical as well as symbolic and traditional religious purposes, and it is important to understand the background of the "magical" use of traditional medicines. High unemployment, a psychologically stressful environment, and crowded living conditions are features of many urban areas in Africa. Labor migration also creates the need for men to maintain relationships with wives, or find girlfriends in the urban environment. For these reasons, much of the traditional medicinal plant and animal material sold in urban markets is for symbolic or psychosomatic value. The protective and cleansing functions of medicinal plants offer one way of dealing with this conflict-ridden and competitive environment, where individuals become "polluted" through proximity to undesirable people, discarded medicinal charms, or the activity of sorcerers. It is not surprising, therefore, that employment opportunities for traditional healers are increasing. In Zimbabwe, the urban demand for traditional remedies is reflected in a higher ratio of traditional healers to total population (1 : 234) than in rural areas (1 : 956).

The roots, leaves, and bark of many different species are used in health care, both as medicine and for magic. Plant material combinations are used in self-treatment of common ailments, such as coughs, headaches, sores, and diarrhea. People generally are very knowledgeable about which plants can be used and how to prepare them. In a number of African languages the words for "tree" and "medicine" are the same or similar.

In Malawi, traditional birth attendants offer plant medicines to women for contraceptives, for barrenness, and for childbirth. Traditional healers are consulted for more serious complaints, and they travel long distances to find materials they need. The general lack of formal health-care facilities in the rural areas means that people are very dependent on plant medicines, which are normally regarded as more effective than "European" methods. The disappearance of woodlands makes it harder to find the traditional materials and is identified by rural people as a factor in reducing their well-being.

In addition to the importance of medicinal plant compounds for local use, some are internationally marketed, such as quinine, which earns foreign currency for Tanzania. Medicinal plants appear to be widely traded in the region, although in-depth information is lacking, mostly because herbalists do not wish to divulge information on their trade. Plant medicines are often sold dried and occasionally are kept in water. Urban traditional herbalists frequently purchase their supplies from wholesale collectors who move far afield in search of prized species. There is an informal export trade in medicinal plants—for example, from Mozambique to neighboring countries, mostly South Africa and Zimbabwe.

Leaf Litter

Small-scale farmers often use leaf litter from forests and woodlands to increase soil fertility in arable lands. Leaf litter is of particular value to farmers who lack access to other soil fertilizing inputs and is critical to those who have no land other than their home yards.

Browse

The dry season flush of leaves that occurs in many woodlands is a vital forage resource at a time when grasses are dry, a month or two before the rains. At this time cattle can spend up to 60 percent of their feeding time on trees. The new leaves are high in crude protein and mineral content. Cattle, goats, and wild animals browse leaves from regeneration, short trees, and shrubs.

Tannins, Dyes, Oils, Resins, Gums

A wide range of other useful products comes from trees, including tannins, dyes, oils, resins, and gums. Many of these products are unknown outside the area in which they are used, and there exists a high potential for added value and commercialization.

Service Functions of Woodlands and Forests

Other benefits of woodlands and forests include soil retention, stream-flow regulation, shade, and shelter from strong winds. Woodland often provides watershed protection to soils prone to erosion by heavy seasonal rains, and rapid regrowth from well-developed root stocks provides bush fallow for shifting cultivation. Water conservation is a frequent justification for protection, and trees play a role in protecting the source of streams.

Spiritual and Cultural Values

Throughout sub-Saharan Africa, trees and woodlands are important in the spiritual and cultural life of local residents. Territorial cult religions, in which natural resources are believed to be guarded by the spirits of ancestors, are common to most of the indigenous people of the region. There are various rules and taboos that govern the use of resources; these must be obeyed, or misfortune and disaster will, it is said, result. Sacred groves, often burial sites for ancestors, are used for a variety of important cultural and religious ceremonies.

BIBLIOGRAPHY

Banda, A. S. M., and H. De Boerr. "Honey for Sale." In *Indigenous Peoples and Protected Areas: The Law of Mother Earth,* edited by E. Kempf. London, 1993.

Campbell, B. M. "The Use of Wild Fruits in Zimbabwe." *Economic Botany* 41, no. 3 (1987): 375–385.

Campbell, B. M., ed. *The Miombo in Transition: Woodlands and Welfare in Africa.* Bogor, Indonesia, 1996. Includes the following articles: T. Brigham, A. Chihongo, and E. Chidumayo, "Trade in Woodland Products from the Miombo Region"; J. Clarke, W. Cavendish, and C. Coote, "Rural Households and Miombo Woodland: Use, Value, and Management"; and A. B. Cunningham, "Saturniid Subsidy: Cash and Protein from Edible Caterpillers of Zambesian Woodlands" and "Medicinal Plants and Miombo Woodland: Species, Symbolism, and Trade."

Cunningham, A. B. *African Medicinal Plants: Setting Priorities at the Interface Between Conservation and Primary Health Care.* Paris, 1993.

DeFoliart, G. R. "Edible Insects and Minilivestock." *Biodiversity and Conservation* 4 (1995): 306–321.

Fleuret, Anne. "The Role of Wild Foliage Plants in the Diet: A Case Study from Lushoto, Tanzania." *Ecology of Food and Nutrition* 8, no. 2 (1979): 87–93.

Gauslaa, Y. "Management and Regeneration of Tropical Woodlands with Special References to Tanzanian Conditions: A Literature Review." *Lidia* 2 (1989): 37–112.

Gelfand, M., S. Mavi, R. B. Drummond, and B. Ndemera. *The Traditional Medical Practitioner in Zimbabwe.* Gweru, Zimbabwe, 1985.

Grundy, I. M., B. M. Campbell, S. Balebereho, R. Cunliffe, C. Tafangenyasha, R. Fergusson, and D. Parry. "Availability and Use of Trees in Mutanda Resettlement Area, Zimbabwe." *Forest Ecology and Management* 56 (1993): 243–266.

Holden, S. "Edible Caterpillars: A Potential Agroforestry Resource?" *Food Insects Newsletter* 4 (1991): 3–4.

Lan, David. *Guns and Rain: Guerrillas and Spirit Mediums in Zimbabwe.* London, 1985.

Lowore, J., and P. G. Abbott. *Initial Regeneration of Miombo Woodland Under Three Silviculture Systems.* Zomba, Malawi, 1995.

Lowore, J. D., H. C. Coote, P. G. Abbott, G. B. Chapola, and L. N. Malembo. *Community Use and Management of Indigenous Trees and Forest Products in Malawi.* Zomba, Malawi, 1995.

Malaisse, F. P. "The Miombo Ecosystem." *Natural Resources Research* 14 (1978): 589–606.

McGregor, Joann. "Gathered Produce in Zimbabwe's Communal Areas: Changing Resource Availability and Use." *Ecology of Food and Nutrition* 33, no. 3 (1995): 163–193.

Mkanda, F. X., and S. M. Munthali. "Public Attitudes and Needs Around Kasungu National Park, Malawi." *Biodiversity and Conservation* 3 (1994): 29–44.

Morris, Brian. "Woodland and Village: Reflections on the 'Animal Estate' in Rural Malawi." *Journal of the Royal Anthropological Institute* n.s. 1, no. 2 (1995): 301–315.

Muyay, T. "Insects as Human Food." Translated by D. Turk. *Food Insects Newsletter* 4 (1991): 5–6.

Pegler, D. N., and G. D. Piearce. "The Edible Mushrooms of Zambia." *Kew Bulletin* 35, no. 3 (1980): 475–491.

Quin, P. J. *Foods and Feeding Habits of the Pedi.* Johannesburg, 1959.

Schoffeleers, J. M. *Guardians of the Land.* Limbe, 1978.

Williamson, J. *Useful Plants of Malawi.* Rev. ed. Limbe, Malawi, 1974.

Wilson, K. B. "Trees in Fields in Southern Zimbabwe." *Journal of Southern African Studies* 15, no. 2 (1989): 369–383.

B. M. CAMPBELL

See also **Agriculture; Ecosystems; Food; Healing; Production Systems.**

POLITICAL MOVEMENTS. *See* **Independence Movements; Muslim Political Organizations; Prophetic Movements.**

POLITICAL SCIENCE AND THE STUDY OF AFRICA. Political science is relatively new to the African scene. While anthropologists and historians were actively involved in the study of Africa during the colonial period (although historians tended to study only European history in Africa), political scientists began their first explorations on the eve of independence, in the 1950s.

A major reason for this difference is that the colonial powers did not encourage the study of politics. The subject was taboo to colonial administrators, who wanted to keep their colonies free from politics because it was associated with African nationalism and opposition to colonial rule. Having it recognized and confirmed by academics was not only against policy but also an admission that things were not the way they were supposed to be in the colonies. Academics from the colonizing countries, notably Britain and France, therefore, did not take an active interest in political phenomena in Africa. To the extent that politics was studied at all in the colonial period, it features subtly in the publications of anthropologists and historians.

This situation changed in the 1950s when American scholars were prompted by the emerging cold war to study other continents including Africa, a continent that fascinated many political scientists because they could detect the strength of nationalism there. Working primarily under the auspices of the Committee on Comparative Politics of the Social Science Research Council and the newly established Fulbright program, American political scientists set off to study African nationalism and the transition from colonialism to independence. They included David Apter, Margaret (Peggy) Bates, Gwendolen Carter, James S. Coleman, Gus Liebenow, and Carl Rosberg, all of whom made their mark on the study of African politics in subsequent years.

The early focus on decolonization and nationalism gave way in the 1960s to other themes in the study of African politics. During the 1960s and 1970s, political scientists were particularly interested in three areas that reflected the political events and trends in Africa south of the Sahara. The first was ethnicity. African states had been created by the colonial powers with little regard for precolonial boundaries. Most colonial states consisted of many ethnic groups. It was natural, therefore, that political scientists concerned themselves with the role of the ethnic factor in politics in the newly independent states. For instance, in his study of politics in the Congo (later Zaire),

Crawford Young, one of the pioneers of this genre, concluded that ethnicity is not a primordial factor in African politics but is quite malleable and adjustable to social circumstances. This was confirmed several years later by Nelson Kasfir in a study of ethnicity in Ugandan politics.

The second theme was the role of the military in African politics. Many governments had been overthrown by the military in the late 1960s and early 1970s, and these events attracted scholarly interest. Much of the literature in this area centered on the question of whether the military was a stabilizing or destabilizing force and whether its officers were better placed than civilians to provide the necessary competence for governing Africa's modernizing societies. Scholars who have contributed to our understanding of the military in African politics include Samuel Decalo and Robin Luckham.

The third theme that emerged in the 1960s as significant among political scientists related to Africa's role in the global economy. African states had gained political independence in the 1960s, but their economies remained bound to the former colonial powers. Studies of international political economy tended to emphasize the neocolonial character of African states, that is, their extensive dependence on external economic forces that limited their sovereignty. This area was dominated by students who drew their theoretical and ideological inspiration from Marxism. Although not political scientists per se, Samir Amin, an Egyptian, and Walter Rodney, a citizen of Guyana, were particularly influential. Also notable were Colin Leys, a Briton, and such African scholars as Issa Shivji, Mahmood Mamdani, and Okwudiba Nnoli.

In the 1980s scholarly interest among political scientists crystallized in a focus on the African state. Much of this interest stemmed from what was perceived as the inability of states in Africa to perform the roles conventionally associated with such institutions. States were not successful in maintaining law and order. Nor did they do a good job of collecting public revenue. In promoting development they tended to do particularly poorly. What were the reasons for such poor performance, and what were the consequences for society? In answering this and related questions, scholars began to see that there was an informal side to African politics that could not be ignored. What mattered were not the formal rules but informal relations among key political actors. The concept of neopatrimonialism was generally adopted to refer to this

most prominent aspect of African politics, the personalized nature of rule and the inclination to use patronage to secure support. Scholars whose names are associated with this orientation include Thomas Callaghy, Naomi Chazan, René Lemarchand, and Donald Rothchild.

Some of this emphasis continued into the 1990s, but it has taken second place to the study of efforts by African countries to democratize their political systems. Africa south of the Sahara, like other regions of the world that were not democratic prior to 1990, has been under pressure to create more open polities, in which party competition is permitted and the rule of law is adhered to. This transition has not been easy, and political scientists not only have taken an academic interest in this set of issues but have also served as consultants and advisers to international organizations concerned with funding and supporting these efforts in African countries. Political scientists who have written on this subject include Joel Barkan, Larry Diamond, John Harbeson, and Richard Joseph.

It is important to include some specific references here to the evolution of the discipline of political science in Africa. Although most young African academics were ideologically opposed to the role that the United States played in Africa during the cold war days, many received their academic training in U.S. universities, often under the guidance of the first generation of American Africanists. A professional association—the African Association of Political Science—was started in 1973 with headquarters in Dar es Salaam, Tanzania. Now headquartered in Harare, Zimbabwe, it is affiliated with the International Political Science Association and has two representatives on the latter's governing council. Its membership is drawn from all over the continent, including northern Africa. It works through local chapters, which exist in some, but not all, countries. African scholars who have made a contribution to the discipline at large include Claude Ake and Peter Ekeh from Nigeria, Michael Chege and Ali Mazrui from Kenya, George Nzongola-Ntalaja from Zaire, Issa Shivji from Tanzania, Mahmood Mamdani from Uganda, and Sam Nolutshungu from South Africa.

BIBLIOGRAPHY

Bates, Robert H, Valentin Y. Mudimbe, and Jean O'Barr, eds. *Africa and the Disciplines.* Chicago, 1993.

Coleman, James S., and C. D. R. Halisi. "American Political Science and Tropical Africa: Universalism vs. Relativism." *African Studies Review* 26, no. 3/4 (1983): 25–62.

Sklar, Richard L., and C. S. Whitaker. *African Politics and Problems of Development*. Boulder, Colo., 1991.

GORAN HYDEN

See also **Neocolonialism; Patronage.**

POLITICAL SYSTEMS

[Sub-Saharan Africa has had many political systems. **State Formation** *examines the different types of political organizations, from age-sets to large states, from the earliest times until the sixteenth century;* **Since Independence** *outlines the major postcolonial arrangements.]*

STATE FORMATION

Sub-Saharan Africa was home to a great many different political forms, from independent villages in which no one leader held supreme authority to grand empires whose rulers held the power of life and death; from small bands of hunters and foragers who cooperated with one another and shared food to states dominated by wealthy aristocrats.

The history of changing political organization is not a straight-line movement from small to large or from simple to complex. When people on the African continent created new political institutions, they did not abandon the old ones; they added on the new ones alongside them. Tiny communities of people who lived by foraging for wild foods and by hunting continued to maintain their own political forms even after farmers created new kinds of political organizations based on the independent village. The two kinds of communities came to live alongside each other and to influence each other. People in independent villages, for their part, often maintained their independence just beyond the borders of large kingdoms. It was the diversity of forms, all existing side by side, that defined the character of early political processes on the continent.

"Stateless" Societies

The history of political organization needs to be understood, first of all, within the context of the changing economy. In earliest times, people lived entirely by foraging for wild foods and by hunting or fishing. At different historical periods in the different parts of the continent, people began to domesticate animals or to farm. Sometime after 3500 B.C.E. people in northern Nigeria and Ethiopia began to raise crops and to herd cattle, although the earlier economic practices never disappeared completely.

Among those people who lived by foraging and hunting there were practical limits on the emergence of stratification and of political centralization. Judging from studies of foragers in the twentieth century, most communities had between 25 and 50 people and were unlikely to grow beyond 150. One such community would occupy a fairly large territory, since wild foods are spread more thinly across the landscape than are cultivated ones. Larger groups could emerge where people lived by year-round fishing. Communities of foragers (sometimes called bands) were relatively egalitarian. They needed to share their food if they wished to ensure the survival of children whose mothers were pregnant or whose parents had died. It is likely that leaders in these small societies held a relatively informal and noncoercive kind of authority. Some helped to organize community rituals. Others coordinated the decision on whether a stranger would be permitted to enter the group and share the resources of its territory.

When farming communities emerged, the foraging communities lived beyond their fringes and interacted with them. In a number of places throughout central and southern Africa, in later centuries, the foragers and hunters served chiefs and powerful farmers in order to win their protection. Sometimes individual foragers entered into regular relationships of gift exchange and mutual help with partners in farming communities.

People practiced farming and herding in all the regions of the continent, with varied political, cultural, and linguistic traditions. Eastern, central, and southern Africa were regions where Bantu languages spread, at first within a very narrow core, and then more widely after 1000 B.C.E. Most Bantu speakers lived clustered together in villages, achieving higher population densities than forager-hunters. The earliest Bantu languages included words that tied leadership and honor to wealth and also to the act of giving, showing that wealthy village leaders attracted clients and built up followings. At an early stage, leadership involved some kind of relationship to the ancestors. In the earliest period, leadership was also tied linguistically to healing, by establishing correct relations with the ancestors and in other ways. Another important leader was the diviner, who had special skills at finding the moral causes of practical events.

A different kind of leadership, beginning in the first millennium B.C.E., was exercised by the smelter of iron. The master smelter coordinated the work of a number of people, because iron production required charcoal preparation, furnace building, and the collection and preparation of ore and other raw materials. Smelters were prominent economic leaders; the iron they produced was one of the most valuable commodities of the time.

Societies with only small-scale leadership—that of the wealthy villager, the local healer, the diviner, or the smelter—are sometimes defined in works of history or anthropology as "stateless." They are labeled in this way because they did not have great class differences or centralized institutions capable of forcing many people to obey a single set of leaders. The word "stateless," however, tells us only about the absence of the state; it does not tell us, in a positive way, about the particular forms of leadership. In preconquest Africa these forms were many and varied, and a number of them had ancient roots. In some parts of eastern Africa, for example, especially those where Nilotic languages were spoken, people organized themselves in age-sets, which began to emerge by the first millennium C.E. As the institution was practiced in more recent times, a group of adolescent boys formed an age-set when they were initiated together. A single set moved through several grades together, beginning as young initiates, then becoming warriors, and still later elders. The age-sets made it possible for people to cooperate and to organize fighting forces over areas taking in a number of villages.

In some places the prominent men of a village or district would gather together in councils to decide public affairs through open discussion. Some kinds of affairs were also decided in women's councils. Another form of nonstate authority emerged in places where deep segmentary kinship groups took on some of the work of creating public order. These emerged in the Sahara by the first centuries C.E. but likely are much older. They also played an important role in eastern Africa. People within each kinship group saw themselves as descended from a common ancestor or ancestors. Each kinship group was then subdivided into many units. A large group, for example, might remember the story of the founder's two sons or daughters, each of whom founded a smaller subgroup. The leaders of each subgroup, then, would settle their own internal disputes and defend their own territory, but they would join together with the other subgroup to respond to larger threats.

Some African societies managed highly complex affairs without relying on state institutions. People in the Igbo-speaking areas of southeastern Nigeria, for example, created a wide range of political insti-tutions, most of them lacking forms of hierarchy. Within this region people had a dense network of markets, which moved periodically in four- or eight-day cycles to make it easy for merchants to travel from one to another, and also a network of long-distance trade fairs. By late in the first millennium C.E. the region was importing substantial quantities of trade goods overland from the Mediterranean. Egalitarian councils maintained peace in the markets, and the agents of religious oracles communicated over long distances. Artisans practiced numerous crafts. The region's history shows that societies without states could manage dynamic economies.

Shrines and oracles were important in creating forms of dominance and order in Igboland. In this, Igboland resembled many other regions of the continent. In southern Uganda, by the first half of the second millennium C.E. (and probably earlier), local shrines had a central position. Mediums at important shrines—leaders who were a channel of communication with major spirits—advised people on how to deal with misfortune, whether individual illness or widespread epidemic, war, or hunger. Lesser mediums were able to travel widely and likely helped to organize trade in basic commodities.

Intermediate Forms

The sharpness of the imagined division between states on the one hand and stateless societies on the other proves misleading when we examine the records of the African past. There were many intermediate political forms, more centralized than societies called stateless, yet with only modest degrees of inequality between rulers and ruled. They were unstable in their centralized rule, which often fragmented. Some chiefdoms fell apart when a chief died, leaving his heirs to fight over succession. Others split up when subordinates grew in strength and declared themselves independent.

Small-scale leadership originally grew out of the institutions of nonstate leadership. Some leaders built up their power by taking in refugees as clients. These might be people whose relatives had died or who had been cut off from family during a period of warfare or other disaster. The growth of centralization out of clientage advanced in the inner Zaire basin, for example, in the early centuries of the second millennium C.E. At that time people began to believe that a whole village took its identity from its founder's kinship group, and the original identities of the clients became less important.

In another region nearby, where the Kongo kingdom later arose, some matrilineal kinship groups grew in power by taking in more clients, by engaging in trade, and by requiring that weaker groups send tribute. In many cases, local leaders acquired more authority and became chiefs by performing rituals to ensure that the land would be fertile or that the rains would come at the appropriate time. In most cases a chief gained greater authority by showing skill in settling disputes among subordinates and in defending the common territory.

In every region of sub-Saharan Africa, large numbers of these small chiefdoms grew up. In some cases they formed clusters of a kind anthropologists came to know from studies of the Alur, a people living on the border between Uganda and Zaire. In the case of the Alur a chief who was rising in power sent a son to a place where there were no chiefs. The local people might welcome the son as the carrier of his father's rain medicines, as someone who could settle disputes, and because the original chief would not attack an area where his son was ruling. By sending out many sons, a chief expanded the area under his control. But over time the sons and their dependents often would declare their independence, especially after the father's death. The Alur state came to be called a segmentary state because each secondary chief, in each place, had all the same powers as the chief at the center—the power to hear cases, to collect tribute, to organize warfare—and also because the state, as it grew, tended to segment into many small states.

The many chiefdoms, all across Africa, formed a kind of substratum of social organization, from which larger states might arise. Where this happened, the chiefdoms served as subordinate units, districts of the larger kingdom. Nonstate institutions—shrines, age-sets, kinship groups, and others—also continued to exist even in places where large states emerged. The chiefdoms and nonstate institutions played roles of central significance within states because they became institutions through which local leaders could oppose the wishes of a great king.

Large States

Historians do not have precise knowledge of when large states began to emerge in each of the regions of sub-Saharan Africa because we have only an incomplete record of what happened in early African history. For every early state about which scholars have knowledge, there were many others at the same time about which they are ignorant.

It is likely that kingdoms were emerging in Nubia by the second millennium B.C.E. In northern Ethiopia the kingdom of Aksum, which took part in the Red Sea trade in gold and ivory, had emerged by the first century C.E. By that time states were probably also beginning to form in the far west of Africa, just south of the Sahara. Ghana and Takrar, for example, were known to Muslim travelers by the eleventh century but had earlier roots. The great empire of Mali, in this same region, took shape by the thirteenth century. The forest states of west Africa were also emerging by that time, including Benin, in what is now southern Nigeria. Archaeologists who have studied the earthworks around Benin's capital say they would have taken 150 million hours of work to construct.

In central Africa, states were beginning to emerge by the tenth century. Archaeologists have found symbolic royal objects dating to that period near what was later the Luba kingdom's heartland, in Zaire. Farther south, the capital of Great Zimbabwe (in what is now the modern nation of Zimbabwe) was occupied in the first millennium C.E. The most important parts of the stone-built settlement at the heart of this state were constructed in the thirteenth and fourteenth centuries; at its height, eighteen thousand people lived there. The examples could be multiplied, but the general point is that sub-Saharan Africa had a long and rich history of state formation over many centuries.

As we have seen, the places where kingdoms emerged usually already had vigorous and effective political institutions. The central job of a state builder was, therefore, to link the earlier smaller units and lead them to direct their attention toward a single center. This could be achieved in a number of ways, and it was common to combine several of them.

Some techniques were widely used all around the continent. State builders often began as heads of chiefdoms who were successful in making alliances with neighboring chiefs. The state builder would then try to find the resources with which to dominate his or her partners, perhaps by using the combined fighting force to raid more distant neighbors for booty or to exact tribute. Another technique involved taking control of important trade goods or of key transit points on long-distance trade routes.

The chief who emerged as the king of Kongo in the early fifteenth century, for example, controlled a river crossing that was important for the copper trade. The kings of Ghana and Mali expanded their borders so as to achieve maximum control over the trade in salt from the north and gold from the south. Aksum controlled trade routes along which gold and ivory were transported from the interior of Ethiopia on the way to the Red Sea trade. Zimbabwe participated in the gold trade to the east African coast, which then linked up with Asia's trade.

As a kingdom expanded, the fringe area from which the ruler exacted tribute in one generation could become a core area in a later generation. This happened in many kingdoms. In the Christian Solomonid kingdom of Ethiopia in the fourteenth and fifteenth centuries, the king absorbed new territories by establishing monasteries and colonies of Christian soldiers in them. These Christian settlers often succeeded, over time, in undermining the semi-independent chief or king and bringing the territory more firmly into the empire.

There were many different techniques for reducing the independence of a kingdom's provinces so that it could no longer split apart in the manner of a segmentary state. The king of Mali was one of many who built standing armies so as not to be at the mercy of the separate district armies. The Solomonid kings of Ethiopia required the heads of tribute-paying states to send children to the royal court as hostages and there indoctrinated them in the culture of royal rule. In Benin, a large town at the center of the kingdom held so many influential social groups that civil war would have been possible only if the town itself were torn apart. Because of this, challengers to the throne did not secede with their chiefdoms (as they would have done in some segmentary states); they fled, instead, to the capitals of neighboring states. In the kingdom of Kongo, the king moved provincial governors from one province to another every three years, so as to prevent them from building up groups of followers within a single locality.

Nonstate institutions continued to play a major role, both beyond the borders of the large kingdoms and within them. Successful state builders usually left most of the preexisting nonstate institutions in place. These then took part in political contests and shaped the political process. In the great kingdom of Benin, for example, the heads of the preexisting chiefdoms continued to have some influence over affairs, as did village heads, tributary chiefs, and members of the *uzama n'Ihnron*—a council of the guardians of custom into whose villages the king could not enter. In the kingdom of Kongo, the heads of predynastic matrilineal territo-

ries continued to have influence, as did territorial priests.

Within every African kingdom there were institutions that survived, and continued to evolve, from the times before royal power was centralized. This complexity of structure, in which institutions from old periods survived and new ones were added, meant that there was some possibility for checks and balances within African kingdoms. It meant, also, that in virtually every kingdom one could see, in the very structure of the kingdom's institutions, the remnants of many historical eras.

BIBLIOGRAPHY

Ajayi, J. F. A., and Michael Crowder. *History of West Africa.* 3d ed. Harlow, Essex, Eng., 1985.
Vansina, Jan. *Paths in the Rainforests: Toward a History of Political Tradition in Equatorial Africa.* Madison, Wis., 1990.

STEVEN FEIERMAN

See also **Aksum; Dahomey; Ethiopia; Hausa States; Postcolonial State; Production Systems; Sudanic Empires of Western Africa; Urbanism and Urbanization.**

SINCE INDEPENDENCE

Once it became clear that independence was inevitable, the colonial authorities belatedly attempted to create democratic constitutional political systems in their colonies. Thus, in many states a rich array of political parties emerged to compete for office. In the decade following independence, however, military coups and civilian executive abuses of power conspired to end democratic rule in all but a handful of African states. Instead, authoritarian political systems emerged in which political parties were either eliminated or limited to a single party under the control of the government. By the mid-1980s, it was possible to distinguish several types of regimes based on their party system.

First, a handful of states retained multiparty systems: Botswana, the Gambia, Mauritius, Senegal, and Zimbabwe all allowed a number of political parties to participate in competitive elections, albeit often in the context of press censorship, human-rights abuses, and some government intimidation. After its independence, in 1990, Namibia joined this select group. Only in Mauritius, however, did elections lead to a peaceful transfer of executive power: in 1982, Prime Minister Seewoosagur

Ramgoolan and his Mauritius Labor Party were swept from office. In the other five countries, the incumbent executive or dominant party won every election held. In all five of these states, however, at least one opposition party, and often many more, were allowed to compete actively for national political office.

All other African states had authoritarian political systems with a single legal political party, but it is possible to make distinctions between them, based in part on the strength and role of the single party. These categories are fluid, and during the three decades after independence states may have belonged to more than one of the regime types discussed. Thus, a second category includes the military-led states in which all parties are banned. Upon taking power in states such as Bénin under Mathieu Kérékou, Mali under Mouassa Traoré, and, at different times, Ghana and Nigeria, the military hierarchy quickly outlawed all parties in order to weaken civilian politicians, to limit political participation, and to strengthen their own power. As military regimes consolidate, however, they find it difficult to mobilize the population on behalf of regime objectives without some kind of party structure; thus, they have often created one. This has been particularly true of radical and populist military regimes such as Ethiopia under Mengistu Haile Mariam, Ghana under Jerry Rawlings, and Burkina Faso under Thomas Sankara and Blaise Campaoré. Thus, these "no-party" regimes have often been transitional. Nonetheless, as long as the military remains in power, it is clear that the single party is never endowed with much political power, which remains circumscribed to a small coterie of officers and senior administrators.

In a third category of states, authoritarian rulers used a single party largely as a vehicle to mobilize support for the regime and to provide patronage opportunities for the president. No significant competition was allowed within the single party, which was put at the center of various participatory rituals meant to demonstrate plebiscitary support for the regime. Thus, for example, these regimes frequently organized elections that provided no other choice to the electors than to vote for the hand-picked candidates of the single party. Countries such as Zaire, Cameroon under Ahmadou Ahidjo, Gabon under El Haj Omar Bongo, and Madagascar under Didier Ratsiraka would fit this category. The single party in such states rarely enjoyed much popular legitimacy.

Finally, in a fourth category of states, significant political competition continued after the termination of multiparty politics. In Kenya, Côte d'Ivoire, Zambia, and Tanzania, for example, regular parliamentary elections provided voters with choices among several candidates from the single party, in what amounted to competitive party primaries. In these competitive one-party regimes, the single party typically retained some popular legitimacy, in part because its officials and candidates were at least somewhat responsive to their constituents' needs.

In the late 1980s, this typology of states was upset by a wave of democratization unique in Africa's postcolonial history. Between 1989 and the beginning of 1994, significant political liberalization occurred in more than half of all African states, and multiparty elections were held in roughly twenty-five states. In some states, political liberalization was ephemeral. In Sudan, this period actually witnessed an increase in the level of repression. But the clear pattern, throughout the continent, was one of opening up. In eight states (São Tomé, Cape Verde, Bénin, Zambia, Congo, Mali, Madagascar, and Niger) elections marked a smooth transition in which the incumbent was defeated, accepted the results, and allowed a new leader to enter office. At this time, the Republic of South Africa also engaged in a successful, peaceful transition to majority rule, instituted a multiparty democracy, and held a general election in 1994. One direct consequence of political liberalization and democratization was the reintroduction of multiparty politics to many African states. The sustainability of these political reforms is difficult to predict, but several characteristics of the new political parties are emerging. First, many are not so new and can be directly linked to parties that existed during the nationalist period and then disappeared or were repressed. In some cases long-exiled party leaders returned to the country once they believed it safe and useful to do so.

Second, apart from the old single parties, most parties exhibit little organizational or financial strength. They lack dues-paying members and are too poor to maintain even skeleton professional staffs, relying for the most part on temporary volunteers during campaigns. As a result, parties are overrepresented in the capital and large cities, and weak or completely absent from much of the countryside. Where the old single party has managed to win a reasonably free and fair election, as in Côte d'Ivoire in 1990 and in Ghana in 1992, it was largely because it retained a stronger organizational presence in the provinces than did the newer parties.

Third, party competition is typically more motivated by ethnic and personal rivalries than by ideological or policy concerns. Many new parties are little more than the personal vehicles of political entrepreneurs with a following that may not extend outside the immediate clan or district. Loyalty is sought on the basis of patronage and clientelism rather than policy objectives, which are rarely enunciated clearly or precisely. One result has been a proliferation of small and weak parties. By 1991, some seventy-six parties had been officially recognized in Cameroon, forty-two in Guinea, twenty-seven in Gabon, and as many as two hundred in Zaire (present-day Democratic Republic of the Congo).

BIBLIOGRAPHY

Bratton, Michael, and Nicolas van de Walle. *Democratic Experiments in Africa: Regime Transitions in Comparative Perspectives.* New York, 1997.

Collier, Ruth. *Regimes in Tropical Africa.* Berkeley, Calif., 1982.

Hyden, Goran, and Colin Leys. "Elections and Politics in Single-Party Systems: The Case of Kenya and Tanzania." *British Journal of Political Science,* 2 (1972): 389–420.

Zolberg, Aristide. *Creating Political Order: The Party States of West Africa.* Chicago, 1966.

NICOLAS VAN DE WALLE

See also **Ahidjo, El Hajj Ahmadou; Mengistu Haile Mariam; Military Governments and Armies; Rawlings, Jerry.**

POLYGAMY. *See* **Family; Kinship and Marriage; Marriage Systems.**

POPULAR CULTURE

[The many aspects of popular culture—from the musical genre of highlife to the Onitsha market literature—are explored thematically in **Popular Culture and Political Ideology** *and* **Popular Literature,** *and regionally in* **Western Africa, Eastern and Central Africa,** *and* **South Africa.***]*

POPULAR CULTURE AND POLITICAL IDEOLOGY

It is difficult to analyze popular culture in relation to politics. The simplest way to roughly define the scope of such a field of creativity and social activities would be to imagine two partially overlapping circles that represent, respectively, culture and politics. Yet this undertaking is difficult, and we have not yet even included the notion of the popular. Symbolic productions—speeches as well as objects—are connected to the exercise of political power: craftwork and works of art, including such mass products as postage stamps, banknotes, printed portraits of politicians, televised images; and such group individual behavior as the distribution of a press photo or a televised image, the "sidewalk radio" (street gossip, the rumor mill), and so on, are linked to the practice of political power. Is it necessary to place within this analytic field the notions of culture and political representation, which are so important for political analysis? What does one make of such vague but fundamental notions as the nonpolitical, that is, the radical exclusion of the political field?

To anticipate the line of reasoning in this article, let us consider one example. In Zaire in 1990, at the beginning of the process of democratization, the fifty-zaire bill was put into circulation. New notes are routinely introduced in order to adjust the nominal value of the currency for inflation. The image on this note—the mountain gorilla, a protected species—dragged the country into the realm of international ideology. The "sidewalk radio," soon followed by a press recently freed from censorship, seized upon an alleged admission by the state that this new currency would only be "monkey money" (worthless money). There followed a long and spirited public discussion, with the participation of various "experts" and witnesses, including several former government ministers, regarding the alleged presence of Satanic symbols on the banknotes. Their presence would prove the existence of a pact binding the forces of evil to the president and to two or three other personalities whose positions illuminate the partnership between culture and politics. The spiritual head of the Kimbanguist church, the most famous musician in the country, and eventually the president's personal Senegalese marabout all came to be involved. Except for President Mobutu Sese Seko, all died within a few years, which lent support to the rumor.

Some people refused not only to accept the fifty-zaire note, but even to touch it, for fear of being thereby delivered to Satan through the agency of the market. The unrest lasted for several months because, sharing a fundamentally Christian imagination, the people acknowledged Satan as the generic figure of all evil, including sorcery. Some particularly wide-ranging views included Islam because of the role of the Senegalese marabout. The arts were involved because of Franco, a famous singer whose work supported the government as often as criticizing it. All three—Mobutu, the marabout, and Franco—became rich because they sacrificed not only their family members but also the entire Zairean people.

The popular indignation over the image of the gorilla on a banknote bears witness to a long cultural memory in Zaire, since most Zaireans were born after 1960. The word *macaque* (a genus of monkeys) was the common racist insult in the colonial era. It stuck so strongly in people's minds that a banknote with a monkey image on it was taken as synonymous with calling ordinary people *macaque*, just as whites had done before independence. People felt they were being called uncivilized, savages, persons without political existence, mere fodder for the state.

In Africa, political history offers a long list of the excluded: the natives during the colonial period (who had previously been slaves), women, the young, foreigners. The notion of foreigner has been manipulated in postcolonial Africa in many ways. He can be at the same time a relative, that is, a member of the same kin group, and a noncitizen. Even if he becomes a high-ranking civil servant, is a native of the country, and comes from an old family line of several generations, he still will not be recognized as a citizen if his male ancestors were born in a location that a colonial border had placed in another country. The presidents of Côte d'Ivoire and Zaire have often had the reputation for surrounding themselves with noncitizens (Senegalese and Rwandans, respectively). The constitution of Zaire, prepared by the National Sovereign Conference in 1993, is devoted to removing all noncitizens from power. These would include the sitting president, Mobutu Sese Seko, who is rumored to be from what became the Central African Republic, as well as Prime Minister Kengo Wa Dondo, born in Zaire of a Rwandan mother and a Polish father. The plundering of the country thus is seen as the result of a conspiracy of foreigners, especially mulattos.

In political culture, obsession with the foreigner must be seen in light of the difficulty of defining "we, the people." This is a colonial legacy as well as the cultural explanation of why ethnicity is central to every contemporary political process. Since the colonial period, the notion of "foreigner" has

been increasingly confused and manipulated politically, possibly because a detour through culture made it possible to avoid speaking of "the citizen." For the most part, colonial states were states without citizens, since neither the natives nor the whites living there were their citizens. The persisting political rumor in the Belgian Congo, Rhodesia, and Kenya, which was taken seriously by various colonial administrations, spoke of the state devouring people. The whites of the state, aided by black assistants, were feeding on blacks or were trading in their flesh and blood. This image helps us grasp the gist of the "popular" perception of the modern political field: "Le pouvoir se mange entier" (Power is eaten whole), "Ebi Te Yie" (Some sit well), "Un siège n'a qu'une place" (Only one at a time can sit on the seat), and so on, as lyrics or images in theater, song, and popular art constantly restate this theme. The state is a mechanism of exclusion for the benefit of certain "whites," whether white by skin color or by social status. In any case, in sub-Saharan Africa the term "white" now connotes power rather than race.

The popular has now worked its way into our discussion. A rather broad descriptive definition is suitable: "Popular culture is culture that is popular; culture that is widely accessible and widely assessed; widely disseminated, and widely viewed or heard or read" (Davis, 1992, p. 1413). To this I would add, with Anthony Appiah, that "in Africa, the distinction between high culture and mass culture . . . corresponds by and large to the distinction between those with and those without Western-style formal education." It is imperative to situate popular culture in Africa within the historical context of industrialized and urbanized societies, and to link it directly to the economy, market societies, and commodification. Yet this last characteristic, which appears in the better works on popular culture in sub-Saharan Africa, seems to be put forward more timidly and with some hesitation with regard to the popular arts.

In the context of Africa's contemporary societies, delimiting the field of popular culture is particularly difficult. Where Islam and Christianity have advanced noticeably, secularization is weak. These religions favor the broad participation of diverse social strata, without alleviating or suppressing social inequality. Within the African Christian churches, some prayer meetings are held at the Intercontinental Hotel, while others take place on a dusty piece of land. In Nigeria, everyone dances to the music of a modern orchestra (Ebenzer Obey) at a great traditional feast (the enthronement of the *oba* of Ondo). Nevertheless, some dance in the festival hall while others dance the same steps in the streets.

Contemporary African societies are consumer societies. Even if the majority of the population does not have the means to live the internalized values, many cultural goods originate in local or global mass culture. Literate culture, whether Western or Muslim, is accepted as the model of high culture, which seems to separate it from the "nationalist" objectives of the state. In that culture originated the intentional confusion of democracy and acculturation, of social "distinction" and cultural and political "betrayal." One "forgets" that even the most "traditional" rituals today incorporate manufactured objects acquired in the market, and the most modern politics never fails to resort to the most "traditional" symbols. Examples are the plastic dolls in the Ibeji ritual and the battle between the African National Congress and the Inkatha Freedom Party over the question of the "modern" legitimacy of "traditional" Zulu men's appearance including arms-carrying in the industrial centers of South Africa.

Social actors do not consciously consult a set of norms of behavior that regulates what they do or defines who they are. Nevertheless, they are as a rule aware that such norms exist. Because of this awareness, Jomo Kenyatta, for example, could use published ethnographies to construct a cultural "bible" of traditional practices and values. In everyday life, social actors do not behave as Yoruba, Swahili speakers, or Kinois (inhabitants of Kinshasa) even if, in certain circumstances, particularly in the context of mass tourism or in the face of political enemies, they behave especially like Yoruba, Zulu, or Kinois. Festive behaviors are ways to parade distinctions of cultural, social, or political status. Examples include the highlife in Lagos and Ghana, dance clubs in the cities of the Belgian Congo in the 1920s and 1930s, and the Zulu immigrant workers' Inkatha gatherings.

It is impossible to provide an exhaustive description of the ways in which cultural deeds relate to all other facts. I organize the following account in five sections that discuss the dominant activities.

Religious Thought

In Africa today, the religious is the central site of the development of social thought. It is a place of identification, where one interprets a particular statement according to a norm, a totality. Fabian has drawn our attention to the relation between popular culture and the place of the secular in the religious thought of the African Christian churches. Identity, legitimacy, and authority are actively debated within various churches and religious groups as well as by African philosophers. In Zaire the testimony, a life narrative presented publicly in order to attest to divine intervention, is laden with these matters. Numerous testimonies circulate in photocopies and on cassettes along with "model examples" taken from the Western charismatic movements. They offer a new ethic and a new aesthetic of daily life. The proselytism of Muslim and Christian fundamentalists emphasizes the presence of a global framework. They offer structures of circulation and funds in order to convey audiocassettes and videocassettes, books, and other materials to even the most remote corners of Africa. The social sciences, influenced by the historical evolution of Western universities toward secularization, have had difficulty acknowledging that in Africa the religious can accommodate a more open discussion than is possible under national states calling themselves secular.

The paradigm constructed around the relations between sin and healing, grace and forgiveness, emerges as the dominant structure for bringing meaning to popular culture, especially in relation to politics. The new dynamic of transformation operates largely on society's base, but there is also increasing participation of both "traditional" and "modern" intellectuals as well as politicians. It has been correctly claimed that industrialization and new technologies do not lead to the obliteration, but rather to the expansion, of popular cultures; in contact with mass culture, they integrate the culture of the elites and the elites themselves. The measure of contemporary popular culture is the international market, the global culture.

Communication

Forming part of popular culture, communication, which is still essentially verbal, is inherently post-scriptural because it refers to writing even though it is distinct from it. The visual has grown rapidly in popular culture because television and videocassettes have been added to the printed, photographic, and painted images that have been part of daily life for two generations. The distinction among communication, appearance, and the arts is arbitrary but nonetheless useful, because the media are increasingly penetrated by the organization appropriate to mass production and are increasingly dominated by capital and by international cultural products. South Africa has long led in this regard, whether one considers the press, television, or music. Elsewhere, this is above all the case with music. Up to the 1970s this industry was essentially local, even if the capital was foreign. Music, video to a lesser degree, the press, and publishing are torn between integration into a global market, which was interrupted by an economic crisis, and the informal distribution of foreign mass cultural products acquired with no regard to copyright ownership.

One cannot speak of communication without also speaking about the vernacular, which escapes the standardization imposed by writing and, especially, printing. Creolization allows language to be closer to the real world and to better express representations while participating in globalization. Creole and pidgin are as much the materials as the grammars of popular culture. It is impossible to understand the cultural dynamic without understanding their function. As a young Senegalese from Dakar said to Leigh Swigart: "'People speaks French but they speaks it with a Wolof accent.' . . . He said this in order to show [the Frenchman] that 'You have given us French, but we are not obligated to use it in the way you wish.'"

The "sidewalk radio" (gossip) is a literary genre and a medium of communication particularly important for the functioning of every political regime. The popular comic strip and, since the liberalization in 1990, the popular press, and especially the satirical cartoon that depends heavily on it, are genres virtually ignored by researchers. Possibly they should be considered a single medium. In Zaire, where there has almost never been a free press for Africans, the free Kinois press of 1990 was assimilated into the "sidewalk radio." The overwhelming majority of readers learn what is in the newspaper by perusing copies spread out on the ground by the seller, who is constantly surrounded by a tight circle of readers. As a result, the circulation of information is the responsibility of the "sidewalk radio," the orality of which is postscriptural.

Radio and television, as well as videocassettes, where foreign television programs are found, require special attention because of their growing presence in popular culture. Foreign programs such as *Dallas*, the action films of Bruce Lee, and videocassettes of sports competitions, such as soccer and wrestling, are the material of popular culture in the same way that secondhand clothing is the material of appearance. The soundtrack is usually unintelligible; the spectators who watch the image have to reconstruct the meaning, taking into account their own aesthetic of reception. Paul Richards and Stephen Ellis suggest that the violent action films watched by young people at the mobile video shows in Liberia and Sierra Leone constitute a point of initiation into violence. In Lubumbashi, Zaire, the young people who prefer these films appreciate them only for their violent scenes. Videos offer a virtual reality where, by proxy, one has useful experiences. The men who attend the showings of erotic films offer a similar reason for it: they get "technical training" there. People from cultures that value dream experience are more receptive to virtual reality.

Popular Arts and Letters

Popular arts and letters constitute another specific sphere. The internal logic of the field of popular culture does not justify this division, but the international market, where a work of popular art can be appropriated as a curio, something to be collected or displayed, makes the arts a separate field because they have a distinct market. The biggest problem has little to do with the pertinence of the Western bourgeois distinction between art and craft. Rather, it has to do with the impossibility of separating, using internal criteria, the aesthetic of the beautiful and the epistemology of the true; of what is socially pertinent and what is merely pleasant to look at. To forbid ourselves an aesthetic appreciation of the popular arts of Africa would be discrimination. Nonetheless, one must be explicit regarding the appropriation of objects detached from their context.

At the heart of what is considered Western art is its separation from what is "commercial" and thus might be considered less profound, less intimate. This separation, which resembles the deeply held conviction of many Catholic missionaries for whom every belief system, even the "heathen," can be religious, contains a grain of monotheism. Popular arts in contemporary Africa operate in a context of commodification. Neither the material used nor the amount of time an artist works escapes it; objects circulate through market exchange, and the subsistence of the artists is worked out through the market. The artists forced to leave the market because of lack of buyers—as has happened to many Zairean popular painters—suddenly find themselves unable to work in their chosen field. Without a canvas, without paints,

Popular painting of a pro-democracy demonstration in Zaire.
COURTESY BOGUMIL JEWSIEWICKI

they become farmers, unskilled laborers, or traveling vendors—a fact that does not authorize us to question their inner need to paint. Should favorable circumstances arise, with some start-up capital or an advance on a commissioned work, they will become painters again.

In the long run, new technologies, new materials, and new possibilities of commercialization favor the expansion of popular arts in spite of economic poverty. Popular arts do not deteriorate when artists incorporate new contributions and challenges. Studio photography, the practice of which in Africa is little studied, has stimulated rather than supplanted the practice of portrait painting. There is no indication that radio and video have marginalized popular theater. The phonograph, the radio, and the cassette recorder have made the expansion of popular music possible. New instruments, new techniques for recording and pressing disks and then cassettes, and local and international capital have transformed the artisanal activities of musicians into an industry. Music and popular painting have changed, thanks to commodification and new markets offering possibilities for expansion. The number of artists has exploded, thus making possible the affirmation of new talents. Popular paintings and the words of contemporary songs offer a reflection of society: they discuss social values and propose social norms.

Often of populist inspiration, research on popular culture emphasizes the political critique, the subversive character of the text. Yet it must be admitted that at least as often, songs praise the incumbent regime, conveying its values and transmitting its structure. Franco, one of the most popular contemporary Zairean musicians, sang as much to glorify the Mobutu regime as to criticize it. Decorated with the country's highest distinction for his praise, he was stripped of that honor and imprisoned for his criticism.

Song, as genre, takes a more systematic interest in social questions and great existential problems than in political struggles. Its political impact is most acute when a metaphor focusing on social justice or social harmony meets with a political situation. This was the case with "Ebi Te Yie" (Some sit well) by the African Brothers in Ghana, and "Voisin" (Neighbor), the chorus of which yells "Fuck off" in French when Mobutu announces the end of his regime. The proverbial use of a song title, passage, or tune shows that it enjoys lasting success. Sometimes the "subversive" reading of a song or of a series of songs, where the words and music often fit together, is due to the zeal of the censor, who, catching a whiff of subversion, thereby creates a political reading of the message. Such seems to me to have been the case in Nairobi with the campaign against a group of songs broadcast in the *watatu* (public taxis) in July 1990. The popularity of the songs thus politicized did not outlive the event, unless their aesthetic value assures them independent life. "Etike Revo Wetin," a song with Wole Soyinka's lyrics that was issued in reaction to the Nigerian elections of 1983, is an example of a song popular long after the political event to which it referred.

In an excellent and exhaustive presentation of the literature on the subject, Karin Barber writes: "Popular arts penetrate and are penetrated by political, economic, and religious institutions in ways that may not always be predictable from our own experiences." Several genres have benefited from excellent analyses, some of which have become classics. The "Africa Explores" exhibit at the Museum for African Art in New York and its catalog sensitized people to the political impact of works of art.

Popular writing—trade literature, autobiographies, testimonies, religious writings, and the popular press—is the least studied of popular arts and letters. Yet in this domain the political element is important. Faced with a vast international literature by African novelists writing in English or French, the literature of everyday life seems, by formal standards, awkward. Written in pidgin or creole, it provides a platform for debates about ethics, the problems of social justice, political legitimacy, and so on. John Lonsdale has analyzed Mau Mau texts as social and political writings. The African authors of missionary periodicals and religious writings also have been studied.

Appearance

Appearance is fully registered in popular culture, often serving as an instrument of political confrontation and propaganda. Produced in great quantities, the printed fabric that drapes the female body (the loincloth) is an important vehicle of the political image in western and central Africa. A man often asserts his social status through what his wife wears, as people are quite aware of whether the loincloth is of local or foreign origin and how much it conforms to the latest fashion. Monarchs, heads of state, and even Pope John Paul II have had their likenesses exhibited on the ample derrieres of women whose dress indicates the social standing of the men who support them.

In authoritarian political regimes, citizens deprived of any real exercise of voting power often have to express their support for the rulers through dress made of fabric distributed free of charge by businesses anxious to show their support of the regime in a public place. By the late twentieth century, such a display of support had become limited to specific political manifestations; to wear such clothing every day had become an admission of poverty.

The name of a fabric, of a specific pattern, or of an article of clothing can carry a political message. In Zambia in the 1990s, *chiluba* is a jacket typically made from secondhand clothing. Frederick Chiluba, the first democratically elected president, symbolized Zambia's transition to a market economy. The object and its name together take on political significance. To be sure, *chiluba* commemorates the new liberty by reference to the dress and the new managerial style of the president. People remember well the austerity of life under the previous regime and the austere dress of Kenneth Kaunda. Nevertheless, the fact that *chiluba* comes from *salaula* (to select from a pile, in KiBemba)—that is to say, used clothing imported from the West—recalls the profound economic crisis that the country experienced. It is possible that the collective memory still recalled the mercantilist liberation preceding the colonial period, during which time only the leaders were affluent enough to wear used clothing from Europe. If such was the case, the derision directed toward these same leaders in the colonial literature would still be alive in the people's memory, and *chiluba* would signify a reproach for what people experienced as recolonization.

Whether in Nigeria, South Africa, or the Congo, the grammar of various modes of appearance lies at the heart of political representations. An example is the South African debate of the early 1990s over what constituted legitimate attire for a Zulu worker at political gathering. In Zaire, the 1972 ban on suits and ties for men and on slacks and short skirts for women was part of Mobutu's politics of authenticity, which included the banning of Christian first names. At the same time, by virtue of bourgeois and Christian missionary norms, decency as decreed by civil servants dictated that women had to wear bras, even during the most "traditional" village ceremonies.

The importance of one's physical bearing and manner of dress is an urban fact. In the cultural milieu of Congo-Zaire, the *sape* ("elegant appearance") indicates one's lifestyle, as does the origin of the clothing (upscale ready-to-wear clothes) one wears. The phenomenon is comparable with the highlife in Nigeria and Ghana. There are several specific manifestations of it in South

Africa. It combines appearance with a lifestyle, music, the places of leisure one frequents, and so on. The musicians in vogue are often its leaders—for example, Papa Wemba in Zaire, as seen in the film based on his life story, *La vie est belle*. They launch a fashion, a musical style, a dance step. The popular culture of appearance follows the same tendency as elsewhere in the industrial world: at the level of everyday social life, aesthetics takes over from ethics.

Along with appearance, we should mention that whether and how people drink and smoke can be a sign of identity, the political calling card of a Muslim or a member of an African Christian church. Alcohol, tobacco, and hemp, as well as the places where they are consumed, whether they are established bars or clandestine spots, are political places par excellence. For several governments, keeping people supplied with beer and cigarettes and keeping these commodities affordable in relation to the buying power of low salaries have been properly political issues. Controlling and infiltrating the places where they are consumed has had a definite influence on political stability. Group and individual identities are asserted, confronted, and negotiated there.

Sports Spectacles

I propose to consider the spectacle that sports competitions offer, as well as the gatherings, the demonstrations, and the public appearances of political personalities, as a singular domain of popular culture. There is a fundamental difference between the urban spectacle considered here and the performance in the preindustrial rural context. The invention of leisure activities and their specific organization in a time and place set aside for this purpose have in two ways altered the meaning and the form of the spectacle, the product instead of the performance. On the one hand, there is a sharp separation between the audience and the performers; on the other hand, the management of leisure activities is directly associated with the management of a society that is expected to be rational. The spectacle of sports draws close to the political spectacle because the two are essentially occasions to publicly construct and confront collective identities, in principle nonviolently.

The fact that the sports arena constitutes a preferred location for political gatherings is not just a matter of its being able to accommodate large crowds. Since the colonial period, the use of sports, especially soccer matches, as spectacle has been considered a way to channel social energies toward

political objectives. This practice of depoliticization inevitably reveals its political character. Numerous major political events have begun at a sports competition. At first, it had to take the place of the urban performance of "tribal" dances. However, it was quickly seized upon by the logic of the construction of identity that prevailed in both black and white colonial popular culture. In the Belgian Congo, a model colony at that time, the first anticolonial urban riot took place in 1957, at the close of a soccer match between a Congolese and a Belgian team. It had already been indicated that, on certain occasions, "in the mind of the crowd, the game quite rapidly took on the look of an interracial clash." In its 25 June 1957 edition, the Belgian newspaper *La Libre Belgique* indicated that the white colonials, not having appreciated the victory won by the Congolese team a little earlier, had publicly "uttered some unsportsmanlike remarks regarding the Congolese . . . players." Thus, as happened all over the world, soccer stadiums became specific locations for confrontations over identity and points of political uprisings. *La Libre Belgique* therefore reconsidered its correspondent's assertion. In its 21 June edition, the newspaper had painted a picture of the culture, or rather the absence of culture, of the black spectators responsible for the incidents. It stated that only a few hundred highly advanced people were able to truly appreciate the match; 80 percent of the other Congolese did not know anything about the sportsmanlike ideal of fair play. Four days later, the newspaper acknowledged the responsibility of the European spectators but made no reference to European culture.

New technologies today make it possible to replace the actual spectacle with the quasi-virtual and portable one of the video recording. Itinerant small businessmen equipped with a television monitor, video recorder, and electric generator have put video recordings within the reach of millions of viewers, who are increasingly isolated by civil wars, the destruction of communications networks, and poverty. Consider the Zairean example of the wrestling matches in Lubumbashi. The local popular culture, in particular that of the young, has invested these competitions with the ideal of individual self-affirmation, achieved through one's own strength. Yet this strength must be protected and increased by recourse to magical powers that come from the villages or from "foreign" places. In contrast with what happens in a video spectacle of a wrestling match, in this case the opponents show off and praise not only their physical power but also, in fact especially, their so-called magical power. The spectators are under the illusion of having privileged access to the grammar of individual success. Thus, in the popular culture structured by the market and by commodification, sports competitions, in whatever form the spectacles are produced, retain their role as the places where identity is constructed and confronted.

BIBLIOGRAPHY

Appiah, Anthony. *In My Father's House: Africa in the Philosophy of Culture.* London, 1992.

Barber, Karin. *West African Popular Theater.* Bloomington, Ind., 1997.

Jewsiewicki, Bogumil. *African Historiographies: What History for Which Africa?* Beverly Hills, Calif., 1986.

MacGaffey, Wyatt. *Art and Healing of the Bakongo, Commented by Themselves.* Bloomington, Ind., 1991.

Masolo, D. A. *African Philosophy in Search of Identity.* Bloomington, Ind., 1994.

BOGUMIL JEWSIEWICKI

See also **Art; Cinema; Literature; Music and Song; Photography; Sports; Theater.**

POPULAR LITERATURE

''Popular literature'' can be a misleading term when applied to a body of writings from a part of the world with a high rate of illiteracy. In Africa the situation is complicated further by a remarkable multiplicity of languages—more than a thousand in all, most of which have never been written down. In such circumstances it is impossible to conceive of any published literature becoming known and appreciated by millions of readers. In Africa, popular literature is not mass literature because the masses either cannot all read the same language or cannot read at all.

Those Africans who are literate tend to live and work in urban areas, where they earn incomes considerably higher than the national average. Their education has prepared them for a style of life quite different from that of the unschooled peasant or common laborer. Except in the Muslim north, where Arabic remains the dominant medium of instruction, they have been exposed in school to a Western-style curriculum and have absorbed Western culture and Western habits while learning a Western language. They are an urbanized, acculturated elite, and their reading tastes tend to reflect their new interests and enthusiasms as well as their adjustment to conflicting sets of values and to modern city life. It is only among such people—a rela-

tively small fraction of the total population—that it is possible to speak of the emergence of African popular literatures.

The growth of such literatures has been both stymied and stimulated by available publishing opportunities. Until relatively recently there were few well-established independent publishers in Africa. Publishing in African languages was done mainly by missionary presses and government publishing houses as a way of promoting literacy. Writing in a European language offered authors a greater range of publishing options, enabling them to reach audiences beyond their own ethnic group; but to have access to the widest possible readership, they still had to find a publisher able to distribute books nationally or, better yet, internationally. Since local firms did not have such extensive distribution networks, many authors turned to educational or commercial publishers based in Europe. The books that have sold most widely in Africa are those produced by multinational publishing firms in London and Paris. So if we define African popular literature as a type of indigenous written discourse accessible to a large indigenous reading public, we have to begin with African writings published in Europe in European languages and sold throughout the African continent.

Multinational Publishers

The most successful multinational publisher in Africa has been Heinemann Educational Books, which launched its influential African Writers Series in 1962. Although intended initially as a source of books suitable for school and university use, the series grew rapidly, eventually expanding its compass to include literary works that were experimental in form and political in orientation. The all-time bestseller for Heinemann Educational Books was the very first title in its African Writers Series: Chinua Achebe's *Things Fall Apart,* a novel describing the impact of European colonialism on an African village community. This classic of contemporary African literature, which became prescribed reading in African schools and universities, has sold over eight million copies worldwide, a greater number than all the rest of the more than 250 titles in the series combined. The extraordinary success of Achebe's novel, and of the series that launched it, was due in part to the increasing Africanization of the English-literature syllabus at secondary and tertiary levels throughout Africa in the decades following independence from colonial rule, but it is likely that such a well-written narrative ultimately

443

would have made its way in the wider world on the strength of its literary merits alone. Heinemann's African Writers Series merely increased its availability within Africa, thereby accelerating its rise to prominence and popularity.

Other European multinational publishing firms have sought to emulate Heinemann's success by establishing their own series aimed at African readers. Macmillan's Pacesetters series and Longman's Drumbeat series, launched in the late 1970s, tried to provide an alternative to the African Writers Series by publishing formulaic adventure stories and romances for teenagers. These books, according to a Macmillan catalog, were "developed to fill the gap between school readers and adult fiction," and to "deal with contemporary issues and problems in a way that is particularly designed to interest young adults, although the stories are such that they will appeal to all ages." Tales of crime, passion, intrigue, and suspense were common, but they tended to be wholesome, moralistic narratives free of any earthiness or vulgarity. Such books were aimed at literate Africans looking for something to read for pleasure, not for passing exams. The Macmillan and Longman series have been viable publishing enterprises but have not approached the impressive sales figures of the Heinemann African Writers Series.

Local Publishing

Although their markets have been relatively small, usually not extending beyond their own national boundaries, local publishers have produced some of the liveliest popular literature on the African continent. Examples from anglophone areas of western, eastern, central, and southern Africa reveal varying patterns of production and dissemination, but the underlying purpose of all such ventures remains basically the same: to supply reading matter that the literate public will find engaging or amusing, and therefore will desire to buy. Commerce and creativity are thus indissolubly conjoined, with the publisher eager to make a substantial profit on the wares offered for sale. This is a literature conditioned and compromised by the marketplace. Anything goes, so long as it will sell. School boards, examination syndicates, and foreign editors have no influence here.

Nigeria

The earliest and most vigorous indigenous publishing industry in anglophone Africa started after World War II in Onitsha, a busy Nigerian market town on the Niger River. The availability of print-

ing presses, the expansion of primary and secondary schooling, the robustness of small-scale trade, and the democratic spirit of the Igbo (Ibo) people in Onitsha have been cited as factors promoting the development of a literature of, by, and for working-class people. This was an inexpensive, unpretentious pamphlet literature catering to the newly literate townspeople who sought both instruction and entertainment in what they read.

Some of the booklets published and sold in Onitsha were didactic handbooks offering helpful advice to those interested in self-improvement: *How to Succeed in Life; How to Write Good English Letters and Compositions; How to Speak in Public and Make Good Introductions; How to Avoid Enemies and Bad Company; The Way to Avoid Poverty.* There were also "courtesy" books covering a range of topics closer to the heart: *How to Speak to Girls and Win Their Love; How to Write Love Letters; How to Get a Lady in Love and Romance with Her; How to Marry a Good Girl and Live in Peace with Her.* But from a literary standpoint, the most interesting of these booklets were the narratives or dramas focusing on problematic love relationships which usually ended in disaster. Titles such as *Veronica My Daughter, Agnes the Faithful Lover, Miss Cordelia in the Romance of Destiny, "Innocent Grace" and Her 23 Husbands, Mabel the Sweet Honey That Poured Away,* and *True Confessions of a Convent Miss* were formulaic romances with characters and incidents of a decidedly melodramatic stamp. Unfaithful boyfriends, fallen women, star-crossed lovers, interfering parents, and unscrupulous rogues populated their pages, playing their customary roles. Heartache, desertion, or dishonor were apt to lead to attempts at suicide or self-reformation. Each story served as an exemplum illustrating a moral. As in the handbooks and "courtesy" books, the purpose of such writing was to improve or caution, not merely to amuse. The lightweight medium often carried a heavy message.

Some Onitsha "chapbooks" sold hundreds of thousands of copies and were reissued as soon as stocks fell low; others made a brief appearance, then disappeared from sight forever. The "how to" books were addressed mainly to a male readership; the romances appear to have been read with equal avidity by males and females. Nearly all the authors were men, but when they told love stories, they preferred to concentrate on the problems of women, sometimes writing from the perspective of a disappointed or betrayed heroine. The most successful authors—J. Abiakam, Thomas

Iguh, Nathan Njoku, Ogali A. Ogali, Okenwa Oli-sah—were quite prolific, producing more than twenty booklets each.

Chapbook publishing in Onitsha reached its peak in the mid-1960s, then lost momentum during the Nigerian civil war (1967–1970) when the Onitsha market was destroyed. After the war the market was rebuilt and a few new titles appeared, but the pattern of local publishing in Nigeria gradually began to change as advances in computer technology made desktop publishing a viable commercial alternative to the earlier print culture. In the 1990s popular literature was produced in many Nigerian cities and towns, some of it crime, spy, or space fiction. Onitsha chapbooks have been displaced by slick paperbacks put out in more sophisticated formats. Nonetheless, Onitsha writing, with its crude vibrancy and ebullience, played an important inspirational role in the development of a popular publishing industry in Nigeria.

Ghana

Nigeria was not the only western African nation to produce a substantial homegrown popular literature in English. There was a similar phenomenon in Ghana, where writers published and sold their literary wares in the bookshops and market stalls of Accra, the nation's capital. Though not as extensive or varied as the pamphlet literature available in Onitsha, Ghanaian chapbooks, with titles like *Woman Is Poison, Parted Lovers, The Tears of a Jealous Wife,* and *The Troubles of a Bachelor,* exploited some of the sentimental themes favored by young, urban Nigerian readers. The main focus was on affairs of the heart, and even the most tawdry of tales emphasized the virtue of living a moral life. In a typical story a young woman or man learned through bitter personal experience the importance of adhering to socially accepted codes of conduct. Anyone who behaved foolishly or irresponsibly toward family, friends, or lovers was roundly condemned. As one author succinctly put it, "Love either makes or mars a life." Romantic potboilers thus served conventional, social didactic purposes.

The most commercially successful popular writer in Ghana was Samuel Asare Konadu, who established his own publishing house, Anowuo Educational Publications, to market his books. With print runs ranging from eight thousand to thirty thousand copies, and with reprints boosting sales of at least one title beyond one hundred thousand copies, Konadu rapidly became the most widely read of locally published authors. But since several of his books were adopted for school use in Ghana, he may have owed some of his success to a large student readership—a captive audience rather than a captivated one. Even so, he must be recognized as a resourceful entrepreneur who made storytelling pay rewarding dividends.

Kenya

Popular writers elsewhere in anglophone Africa have tried to follow the same path to success. David Maillu of Kenya and Aubrey Kalitera of Malawi have established their own publishing houses, seeking to capitalize on a public hunger for entertaining, instructive reading matter. Maillu's Comb Books, launched in 1973 as a vehicle for publishing some of his manuscripts that had been rejected by established multinational and indigenous publishers, recorded impressive sales in the mid-1970s by issuing a series of novellas and long narrative poems on urban themes.

His prose works typically dealt with wastrels who ruined their lives by overindulging in sex and alcohol. The central characters were Nairobi civil servants or white-collar workers with a voracious appetite for women, especially office secretaries willing to do anything to retain a job or earn a promotion. Usually these jaded bureaucrats suffered for their sins, ultimately losing their overpaid sinecures in the civil service and thereby forfeiting riches, reputation, and respectability. They were high-class rogues brought low by loose living, picaros of the paperwork empire.

Maillu's books were extremely popular among office workers in Nairobi and among young people in rural areas who aspired to live and work in the city. None was adopted for school use, yet each new title sold between ten thousand and fifty thousand copies in a year or two. Profits on sales grew so substantial that within three years Maillu was able to expand Comb Books from a one-man vanity press to a thriving publishing house employing seven or eight workers who did all the editing, typesetting, layout, and design work, using the most modern publishing equipment. Since Maillu wrote most of the volumes published by Comb Books, no one else can claim credit for the extraordinary success of his press. Comb Books was an indigenous eastern African publishing phenomenon, and Maillu was the driving force behind it from the start.

Unfortunately, Maillu eventually overextended himself financially, and unpaid creditors closed Comb Books down. But Maillu didn't stop writing;

he simply sought other outlets for his work, publishing some of his love and adventure fiction in the Macmillan Pacesetters series until he could set up another company of his own, David Maillu Publishers, which began operating in 1979. He no longer brought out new books at the swift earlier pace, but he remained an important figure on the Kenyan literary scene, supplying books that readers turned to for pleasure.

Malawi

Aubrey Kalitera, like Maillu and Konadu, was a self-made literary entrepreneur. After establishing a successful short-story magazine that he filled with his own fiction, Kalitera decided to bring together some of these stories in book form. He typed his manuscripts on stencils, ran them off, bound them, and sold them in shops and offices in Blantyre. He called his firm Power Pen Books, and to keep it going, he began producing full-length novels, choosing romantic themes he calculated to be of great interest to lower-middle-class readers.

Nearly all of Kalitera's narratives dealt in one way or another with the making and breaking of contracts of the heart. He wrote about men who abandoned their girlfriends after getting them pregnant, about women who abandoned or killed their children in order to live a life of luxury unencumbered by parental responsibilities, about sons and daughters who deserted or neglected their parents, about fathers and mothers who interfered in the marriages and romances of their grown-up children. But most of all he wrote about marital infidelity, focusing on complications in the love affairs of men and women who cheated on their spouses and fiancés.

This was the stuff of romantic fiction the world over, but Kalitera grounded his tales in a milieu that was unmistakably Malawian, so that his readers could easily identify with the men and women caught in these highly emotional entanglements. The landscape, the names, the material culture, the predicaments were all recognizably local, not foreign or exotic. There was also a fairly explicit message appended to some of the stories, giving even the most titillating of them a trace of traditional moral earnestness and the aura of a didactic parable or folktale. Kalitera, though operating in a popular medium of widespread international currency, kept his feet planted in his native soil.

After bringing out eight of his own novels in three years, Kalitera sought to expand his enterprise by employing others to do the production work and by hiring agents to sell Power Pen Books up-country. Some of these agents never returned, and he experienced his first losses. By the mid-1980s he was out of business, and though he tried to make a comeback by turning one of his novels, *To Ndirande Mountain with Love,* into Malawi's first locally made feature film, he failed as a filmmaker, too. Power Pen Books is now little more than an interesting footnote in Malawi's literary history.

South Africa

In South Africa, where during the apartheid era (1948–1994) local publishing was closely monitored by the state, popular literature aimed at a Black audience took a variety of forms. Initially it surfaced as short fiction, a form generated by the appearance of the first pulp magazines in English for Africans, the most important of which was *Drum,* established in 1951. *Drum's* annual short-story competition attracted hundreds of entries, some of them flavored with strong social and political protest. The top prizes usually were awarded to stories combining a memorable mixture of crime, violence, and sex. A more politically committed literature filled the pages of a handful of liberal, radical, and Communist magazines, but by 1963 all such publications were banned under the provisions of the all-encompassing Publications and Entertainments Act, which facilitated government censorship of the media. Some writers fled into exile and continued their literary activities by publishing antiapartheid fiction, poetry, drama, and autobiographical narratives abroad; Alex La Guma, Dennis Brutus, Lewis Nkosi, and Bloke Modisane were among the best-known of these émigrés. The writers who remained at home tended to fall silent, having few indigenous outlets for their work.

In 1971 that silence was shattered by the publication of Oswald Joseph Mtshali's *Sounds of a Cowhide Drum,* a book of poems that blended poignant personal reflections with sharp political observations. There was a strong element of protest latent in such verse, but government censors were willing to let it pass, possibly because it would have been difficult for them to justify banning such ambiguous lyrics.

Mtshali's success in finding a way to express politically charged ideas without incurring censorship encouraged other poets to come forward, and soon there was a small boom in poetry publishing. Mongane Wally Serote, James Matthews, Sipho Sepamla, and Pascal Gwala led the way with increasingly militant volumes of verse that articulated an ideology of Black Consciousness. As this confrontational "Soweto poetry" grew louder and shriller, the government began trying to suppress it through censorship and intimidation. New collections of Black verse were banned, Matthews was arrested and imprisoned, Serote went into exile, and the strong flow of antiapartheid lyricism was momentarily interrupted.

To fill the void and continue protesting, Black creative artists turned to other modes of self-expression, particularly to oral poetry and drama, modes that did not require a literate audience. By building upon age-old traditions of improvisional performance, poets could communicate effectively with masses of working-class people who could not be reached through printed texts. The principal performance poets who emerged in the 1980s—Alfred Qabula, Mi Hlatswayo, Nise Malange, Mzwakhe Mbuli—were workers associated with trade-union movements. They created a populist liberation poetry praising the stubborn struggles of the proletariat in a brutally oppressive capitalist economy. Their recitations, composed in a mixture of African languages and English, were recorded and subsequently published.

Another tradition of performance that assumed prominence in the 1980s was township drama. Although melodramas and comedies by Sam Mhangwane, Gibson Kente, and others had been performed in South African Black townships in the preceding decades, they did not have much impact on the national scene. Black musicals such as *King Kong*, *Umabatha*, and *Ipi Tombi* were far more successful, playing to large audiences at home and abroad. Conforming to strict censorship regulations, most of these entertainments had little to say about current political realities in South Africa.

After the Soweto uprising of 1976, an angrier group of dramatists began to assert themselves. Zakes Mda, Julius Maqina, Matsemela Manaka, and Maishe Maponya wrote and directed plays informed by Black Consciousness, plays that challenged the prevailing apartheid order. Mbongeni Ngema and Percy Mtwa teamed up with Barney Simon to produce *Woza Albert*, a hilarious satire in which Jesus Christ visits South Africa and gets arrested as a terrorist. Ngema and Mtwa went on to stage a series of musicals—*Asinamali!*, *Bopha!*, *Sarafina!*—that combined song and dance with current political commentary. These plays and musicals addressed serious South African problems without losing their appeal as popular entertainment. They have been oppositional works that captured the public imagination.

In South Africa, then, popular literature has been part and parcel of the antiapartheid struggle. Writers, performance poets, and dramatists have adopted innovative strategies to circumvent censorship and express rebellious ideas. Irony, parody, burlesque, and other forms of ridicule have been among their most effective weapons of political protest. Now that multiracial democracy has been achieved in South Africa, it is possible that these writers and artists will begin to move in the direction of their tropical African counterparts, producing entertainments that focus on love rather than hatred, on family ties rather than racial or class differences.

BIBLIOGRAPHY

Barber, Karin. "Popular Arts in Africa." *African Studies Review* 30, no. 3 (1987): 1–78.

Chapman, Michael, ed. *Soweto Poetry*. Johannesburg, 1982.

———. "More Than Telling a Story: *Drum* and Its Significance in Black South African Writing." In *The "Drum" Decade: Stories from the 1950s*, edited by Michael Chapman. Pietermaritzburg, South Africa, 1989.

Lindfors, Bernth. *Popular Literatures in Africa*. Trenton, N.J., 1991.

Obiechina, Emmanuel. *An African Popular Literature: A Study of Onitsha Market Pamphlets*. Cambridge, 1973.

Orkin, Martin. *Drama and the South African State*. Manchester, U.K., 1991.

Priebe, Richard. "Popular Writing in Ghana: A Sociology and Rhetoric." *Research in African Literature* 9 (1978): 395–432.

BERNTH LINDFORS

See also **Achebe, Chinua; Apartheid; Education; Language Use; Literature; Independence Movements; Publishing; Theater.**

WESTERN AFRICA

"Popular culture" describes a complex and variable range of social phenomena. Throughout west Africa these are found both in forms generally recognized as part of the arts—such as music, song, theater, sculpture, painting, portrait photography, and writing—but also in a wide range of activities such as coffin making, joking and storytelling, hairstyles, hand-dyed and factory-printed cloths, house decoration, commercial billboards, and television soap opera. Indeed, popular culture can exploit any medium. Furthermore, this diversity is often fluid, seemingly ephemeral, as it changes in response to changing social conditions and possibilities.

But such an obvious yet ambiguous term proves resistant to easy definitions. "Popular" is a description open to social contestation, though in recent years there has been much debate about the overloaded assumptions entailed by the use of the term "culture"—especially in its intersections with the processes of globalization. But it is a debate that is particularly applicable to localized forms of popular culture, which often appropriate and reconstitute products, ideas, and social practices from across local, regional, and international boundaries.

"Popular culture" as a term has gained its currency by emphasizing the contrast between the actions of the mass of people compared with the elites who control the infrastructures and institutions at local, regional, and national levels. It identifies social practice situated or generated at the level of ordinary, often economically impoverished, people who lack the resources of elite social networks. However, these masses are not homogeneous; rather, they are differentiated into social layers. Often the producers of this popular culture are within the skilled classes, usually literate or semiliterate, sometimes migrants. At the outset of the twentieth century they were often converts to Christianity or Islam. Moreover, the contrast between the masses and the elites is often highly ambiguous and ambivalent. A prominent example is the recent role of soccer in west Africa; sponsored and encouraged by the state, it has a mass appeal, especially with the successes of the Cameroon, Ghanaian, and Nigerian national teams, that situates it under the umbrella of popular culture. Other examples are the state-sponsored cultural exhibitions of the First World Festival of Negro Arts held at Dakar in 1966 and the Second World Black and African Festival of Arts and Cultures (FESTAC) held in Nigeria in 1977, which presented a range of popular and elite cultural forms.

At times popular culture seems critical of elite social ideologies; for instance, in 1984 Fela Anikulapo-Kuti's constant criticism of the Nigerian government in his Afro-beat music resulted in his incarceration for twenty months. At other times it seems indifferent to the existing political order or even to aspire to elite status, as the popularity of wearing cloth embellished with Rolls-Royce logos or Mercedes Benz cars attests. The elites and masses often share many aspects of the same popular culture, as the pidgin poems of Major General Mamman Vatsa, a former member of the Supreme Military Council of Nigeria, demonstrate. But however popular culture is constituted at any given time, as social practice it provides a means for people to participate in and relate to events within society. Hence the term is here considered open-ended and used descriptively. But such is its scope in west Africa, regionally and historically, that the emphasis will be on a few salient examples.

Popular culture has always been a dynamic feature of west African societies and preceded the colonial enclosures. One such expression, masquerade, is found all over west Africa. It takes many forms and is situated in many different and often overlapping contexts. Some of its contexts can be understood in terms of the construction of social categories and the legitimation of political authority, whether it is initiation of the young into adulthood or the exercise of authority by the elders, as exemplified by the men's *poro* and women's *sande* societies that range across Sierra Leone and Liberia. But masquerade can provide entertainment as well as present the views of the ordinary people. In this context it is used to castigate and satirize the activities of the elite groups, whether elders, eminent chiefs, or, nowadays as likely, local politicians. Such examples are the *okumpka* masquerades of the Afikpo of southeastern Nigeria and the *efe* song night of the Gelede masquerade tradition among the Yoruba-speaking peoples who range from southwestern Nigeria to Bénin.

The advent of the colonial powers at the end of the nineteenth century in west Africa engendered new social formations. This was particularly evident in the urban areas, where the bureaucracies required for administering the colonial enterprise produced new social groupings that acquired new skills, often with an added emphasis on literacy. The conurbations developed or expanded to accommodate the exigencies of colonial rule and provided a fertile ground for the development of popular culture across west Africa. Populations in the urban areas were diverse and heterogeneous in comparison with the rural areas, although the rural populations also were affected by the new transport infrastructures, commodity crop production, and the expansion of various media of mass communication. Change and innovation in religious expression also played a part in the shaping of new forms of popular culture. Mass conversion to Islam and Christianity at the beginning of the century led to new and dynamic forms of religious organization, such as the Islamic brotherhoods and the independent African churches. The development of new roles and contexts of identity cut across prior social boundaries to create innovative forms and traditions. These combined with the media of mass communication to create new and potent forms of local popular culture.

Music

The development of highlife music across anglophone west Africa exemplified these developments from its inception in the 1920s in Ghana. Drawing on a constellation of elements, migrant and local musicians catered to the heterogeneous city audiences, offering a wide range of musical styles and instruments. They included marching bands that emulated the colonial regimental and police bands but played traditional melodies and rhythms; the "palm wine" music of the acoustic guitar bands that combined guitars, drums, and claves and thumb pianos (the guitar took the place of many indigenous stringed instruments, such as the Akan lute in Ghana); the large dance orchestras that played European music as well as concert parties and vaudeville shows. At first the spread of Christianity had encouraged the replacement of indigenous musical instruments, which had too close an association with pagan practices, with Latin American percussion (although subsequently the churches have returned to the use and development of indigenous musics). In addition, the burgeoning independent African churches, with their emphasis on indigenous contexts of performance, introduced Christian hymnal singing elements to this musical form.

Highlife was quickly taken up throughout anglophone west Africa, developing local variants and strands wherever it was established. With the introduction of electric amplification in the 1940s, it became the dominant idiom of popular music in anglophone west Africa, with such notable musicians as the Ghanaian E. T. Mensah. Highlife lyrics commented from the male viewpoint on the changing social mores, particularly changes in gender roles with the rise of economically independent urban women. In Nigeria it was constantly reworked and changed by the various ethnic groupings, who blended in local musical forms and language—resulting, for example, in the development of juju music among the Yoruba-speaking peoples. In the 1970s, juju replaced highlife as the dominant idiom in southwestern Nigeria.

In colonial francophone west Africa the state intervened far more directly, leading to the develop-

ment of a state-sponsored cosmopolitan culture that maintained close links to the European metropoles. The hereditary griot traditions derived from the Mandinka and Wolof kingdoms persisted as a popular form of music, with the added patronage of business entrepreneurs and, in Senegal, of the Islamic brotherhoods. These separate state-managed and popular musical trajectories contrasted with the development of musical traditions in anglophone west Africa, where elite elements had contributed to popular styles to create innovative forms such as highlife.

In Mali, with the gaining of independence in 1960, music was organized in terms of national and regional orchestras, but with a new emphasis on developing popular regional idioms in the construction of a national identity (a similar situation prevailed in Guinea and Guinea-Bissau on gaining independence). Much of these popular musical traditions lay in the hands of the hereditary griots, men who played instruments and sang. They were accompanied by women singers, and women in the audience participated through clapping, singing, and beating out rhythms on iron percussion. Often women were favored as singers of the praise songs that recounted the achievements and origins of the noble families. Such women, known as *djely mousso*, gained great economic and social independence through the often lavish sponsorship of their patrons. Women singers such as Fanta Damba were incorporated into regional orchestras and recorded through state sponsorship, with mass dissemination by Radio Mali. With the eclipse of national and regional orchestras in the 1980s, male singers such as Kassemady Diabate and Salif Keita (exceptionally a nongriot singer) sought international recognition. There has been an exodus of francophone musicians to the European capitals, particularly Paris.

Griot forms were further extended by women singers such as Fanta Sacko (and later by Ami Koita), who introduced a more cosmopolitan style incorporating elements of music heard on Radio Conakry of neighboring Guinea and its visiting musicians. In recent years the great status and independence achieved by these women have encouraged other nongriot women, such as Coumba Sidibe and Oumou Sangare, to develop musical styles based on the traditions of music from the Wassoulou area.

In Senegal and Côte d'Ivoire, the colonial separation of popular and elite culture was maintained after independence, although for very different

449

purposes. President Léopold Senghor of Senegal, in his development of the concept of Negritude, directed state resources into supporting an elite culture, establishing government-funded art, dance, and music schools. During the early years after independence, the musicians of Dakar and Saint-Louis reproduced Latin American music, such as Cuban rumba music. However, toward the end of the 1960s groups such as Star Band of Dakar and Baobab Orchestre, controlled by the nightclub owners who owned the equipment and venues, began to introduce elements from neighboring countries such as Guinea, Mali, and Nigeria—with the influential presence of the saxophonist Dexter Johnson. In the mid-1970s young singers such as Youssou N'Dour, Thionne Seck, and Elhadji Faye became well known through singing in the griot tradition at circumcision ceremonies, wrestling matches, and other ceremonial social events. Youssou N'Dour joined the Star Band of Dakar and Thionne Seck the Baobab Orchestra when these musical groups started to introduce occasional songs sung by guest griot singers. But with increasing success, Youssou N'Dour split away to form the seminal Etoile de Dakar with Elhadjji Faye and began to introduce new forms underpinned by the lyrics and *mblax* rhythms of griot traditions.

The development of a cassette industry in the 1970s, with its capacity for small-scale entrepreneur mass reproduction of music, established the musicians' autonomy from the nightclub owners. This cheap mass dissemination, with cassettes being copied and recopied until the music dissolved into white noise, gained them national and ultimately international recognition. However, these bootleg profits eluded the musicians, who still had to earn their living through performance. By the 1980s a younger generation added a more political commentary and introduced elements from jazz, reggae, and fusion music while replacing the conga drums with the sabar, the original griot drum. Musicians such as Baaba Maal produced music in their own languages (his was Tukulor), rather than using Wolof, which had become the lingua franca of Senegal. Since the early 1990s there has been a resurgence of griot artists such as Kine Lam and Dial Mbaye being recorded and, as in Mali, there is an emerging identification of this griot-influenced music with a national identity.

Pictorial Art

The dynamic development of the Islamic brotherhoods has been paramount in Senegal, and every cassette has at least one song dedicated to the marabout (holy men) founders of these brotherhoods, such as Cheik Ahmadou Bamba of the prominent Mouride brotherhood. The popular art of painting on glass, derived from Islamic North Africa at the beginning of the century, produced many devotional pictures of these Islamic brotherhood leaders. It was an art form inspired by the then costly photographic reproductions that it copied, as well as by chromoliths and postcards. Its close relation to photography as a direct record of the world and its devotional intent combined with its provenance from northern Africa may have made it acceptable despite Islamic prohibitions on figurative representation. However, its subject matter soon encompassed all aspects of social life, often from a humorous and lively viewpoint. Its sources of imagery also drew upon popular Islamic prints from Cairo and French comic books such as *Tintin,* named for the French cartoon hero.

The composition of glass painting retains the formal-portrait representations of photography with their frontal axis, symmetry, and shallow ground. The forms are outlined in black ink, and then the areas mapped out are filled with evenly rendered, bright enamel colors. Spaces and forms are intentionally flattened and perspectives tilted to accommodate the fields of uniform color. The picture is painted on the underside of a thin sheet of glass, so that it is protected. However, the color gives the appearance of floating on the surface to achieve a luminous and saturated quality. It was learned by apprentices from masters of the craft and was cheap to reproduce. However by the 1950s its original consumers had replaced it through easy access to studio photography and the small printing works that could offer cheap mechanical reproduction. Now demand is maintained by tourists and its gradual incorporation as a commodity into international art markets.

By way of comparison, in recent times in Senegal, as support from the state has been withdrawn, some artists, such as the cooperative group Laboratoire AGIT-Art, are seeking to bridge the gap to popular culture by producing an avant-garde art that incorporates masks and similar artifacts. They situate these works in unexpected public contexts, such as busy markets and, on one level, compete with the signboards and barbers' signs that are vigorous manifestations of popular art.

Theater

The independent African churches, with their reshaping of Christianity to west African contexts, also have precipitated new forms of popular culture. In Lagos, Nigeria, the Yoruba Church of the Lord (one of a cluster of independent African churches known as the Cherubim and Seraphim) commissioned Hubert Ogunde to compose "native air operas" in 1944. The enormous success of these religious productions encouraged Ogunde to form his own traveling company two years later. He presented productions written and produced by himself (including musical arrangements) and became actor-manager of his ensemble. He promoted his first play by advertising for paid actresses, who made up the bulk of his ensemble. It was the first time that professional actresses appeared in their own right in Yoruba theater.

Ogunde's plays proved to have enormous popular appeal. He drew on concert-party traditions, using indigenous musical instruments and referring to the *egungun* masquerade tradition of *apidan* or *alarinjo* theater—especially in the glees with which his performances started. His productions centered on topical themes of the day, whether a craze for an exorbitantly expensive and fashionable cloth or a strike in Jos. For the latter production, he was briefly arrested by the colonial authorities. His arrest made him a national hero in the struggle for an independent Nigeria.

By the 1950s Ogunde's outstanding success in both urban and rural areas led to the formation of many rival traveling theaters, such as those of E. K. Ogunmola and Duro Ladipo, which introduced new elements: spoken (instead of sung) Yoruba and English dialogue to broaden their appeal, the use of popular folklore as a new theme, and the introduction of Western instruments to draw on highlife and juju influences. In the 1970s and 1980s many of the troupes appeared regularly on local radio and television in performances and series. A number of films were made, such as *Ajani Ogun* (1976), produced by Ola Balogun and featuring Duro Ladipo, and *Aiye* (1980), with Hubert Ogunde. Their filmic explorations of contemporary concerns and their relations to the past gained large audiences.

New forms of popular theater are not confined to the urban areas. In Benue State, Nigeria, among the Tiv people, *kwag hir* (which translates as "marvelous thing") puppet theater developed in the late 1950s from a long tradition of resistance to colonial authority. *Kwag hir* combines a long-established form of storytelling about the magical world of *adzov* (which also legitimized the popular resistance) with innovative jointed puppet figures in theatrical performances. It articulates a Tiv sense of identity by placing the contemporary world in this mythical world of *adzov*—whether the story enacted is about the construction of a new road or about a lake from a popular folktale. It is a popular theater that through performance provides a counterpoint in the construction of ethnicity within Nigeria, what is described as Tiv "traditional" theater in state-sponsored tours.

Religion

Apart from the Christianity and Islam, local religions and cults provide dynamic and popular forms of culture in both urban and rural areas. New deities have developed in this century, such as Mami Wata, a river goddess with long, flowing hair, who is found throughout west Africa in varying forms. She is associated with a contemporary lifestyle that includes fast living, popular music, sweet drinks, and smoking. Some devotees perform with a harmonica or guitar in their rituals. Mami Wata's appearance and her associations with a fast-living contemporary lifestyle have provided a basis for describing the dangers and seductions of urban living. Mami Wata imagery appears in music and in paintings in bars and elsewhere.

Other innovative forms have emerged, such as the Ode-lay societies in Freetown, Sierra Leone, which also are concerned with the lifestyle of the young. In this multiethnic urban setting, gangs of young men have formed Ode-lay secret societies in marginal areas of the city. These groups espouse a freethinking lifestyle, much influenced by the precepts of the Jamaican religion of Rastafarianism, which includes the smoking of marijuana. Group identity and prestige centers on the masquerade processions through the city that form the core of their activities. These processions are ritual events in which Ode-lay societies engage in physical and aesthetic contest with each other. The masquerades either emphasize their fighting capabilities as creatures of the bush, loaded with potent and dangerous medicines, or elaborate a fanciful and ornate appearance, using rich materials and decorations.

Other masquerades and processions in Freetown include the lantern festivals. These developed during the nineteenth century in Senegal and Gambia and had spread to Freetown by the 1930s. The lanterns, lit by candles within wire structures, range from handheld to elaborate mobile floats representing ships, human figures and animals, cars, mosques, and other objects. In Freetown, lantern festivals usually take place at the end of

Ramadan and are sponsored by the Young Men's Muslim Association, whereas in the Gambia they are Christian affairs.

Clothing

Clothing and fashion have played an important part in popular culture. One example is *adire* cloth, which is an indigo resist-dyed cloth produced in the Yoruba-speaking area of southern Nigeria. The starch resist is applied freehand or through metal stencils. The process was further developed with the access to factory-woven cotton shirting, which provided an even ground. In the 1930s and 1940s *adire* flourished with a dazzling array of images, often set in squares side by side on the same cloth: geometric shapes, frogs, watches, umbrellas, koran boards, sugar lumps, even the pillars of the Ibadan municipal town hall on a cloth called *ibadandun* ("Ibadan is sweet," meaning that life is good there). A popular design was *olokun,* named after the Yoruba river goddess. One of the most striking was *oloba* ("It has King," meaning that the cloth portrays a king), which contained a central oval over which were the words "King George and Queen Mary." It was a form of popular visual culture that took account of and participated in the diversity of the colonial world.

By the 1960s *adire*'s appeal had diminished. It was replaced by Kampala, a form of wax resist-dyed cloth that has molten wax poured on it before the dying process. This process probably stems from dyeing techniques used in Senegal and Sierra Leone by the Mandinka diaspora. It was introduced into Nigeria during the civil war at the time of the Kampala peace conference—an example of the way popular culture links and encapsulates historical events.

With the gaining of independence by west African countries, there was a renewed emphasis on local dress and fabrics. In Nigeria the *agbada,* a long sleeved gown worn by men, became necessary for important occasions, irrespective of status. Hausa and Nupe embroidery on the top pocket and neck opening crossed ethnic boundaries and religious divides to become essential to any *agbada.* The Hausa embroidery consists of a range of patterns based on Islamic calligraphy, such as the simpler long, triangular shapes of "Three Knives" and the squares known as "Houses," to more elaborate combinations. In Mali in the 1980s there was a revival of *bogolan,* a mud-dyed cloth, which derived from Bambara traditions of fabric dyeing. It was used in state-sponsored cultural drama and dance

productions in the 1960s and gradually became an emblem of Mali nationality, transcending its original ethnic boundaries.

Literature

Printed images and words have played their part in shaping popular culture, such as the Indian prints that inspired Mami Wata imagery; prints of Al-Buraq, the horse that took Muhammad to Jerusalem and up to heaven in a night; and the posters and picture calendars that present collective images of associative life. The printed word has effloresced throughout the conurbations of west Africa. Onitsha market literature of the 1950s and 1960s is one example (printed initially in the market town of Onitsha, Nigeria) in which a vigorous and direct reworking of English-language stories and pamphlets describes the protagonists overcoming the difficulties of adversity or the trials of love to gain success in the urban environment.

Its audience was a new literate class composed of the semiskilled, low-level white-collar clerks, primary school teachers, small-scale entrepreneurs and traders, mechanics, and taxi drivers. Its stories drew on people of popular foreign films (Indian, American, Hong Kong) that appealed to the cosmopolitan aspirations of this social stratum. Although Onitsha market literature died out during the Nigerian civil war at the end of the 1960s, it contributed in Nigeria to a confidence in the local uses of English, resulting in a dynamic literature being produced, such as *The Palm-Wine Drinkard* by Amos Tutuola and, more recently, plays such as *Katakata for Sofahead* by Segun Oyekunle.

Films

In contrast to printed matter that can be produced comparatively easily by small entrepreneurs, film requires a large capital outlay. This has greatly shaped its trajectories in west Africa. Before the 1960s, filmmaking remained in the hands of Europeans, although some west Africans gained technical experience working for the British Colonial Film Unit or, in francophone west Africa, working for the French filmmaker Jean Rouch. It is only since independence that filmmaking in west Africa has flourished.

With independence, France initiated a new policy of economic and cultural cooperation with its former colonies that encouraged west African filmmakers in their productions. These filmmakers from the former French colonies adapted the medium to represent African realities and concerns, thereby attracting mass audiences of their compatriots. One of the first filmmakers to emerge was Sembène Ousmane from Senegal, who embraced the aim of critically exploring key issues in Senegalese society. He has consistently related contemporary concerns to key historical issues, particularly in films such as *L'Empire songhay* (1963), *Ceddo* (1976), and *Camp de Thiaroye* (1988), the last codirected with Thierno Faty Sow. Several of his films were censored, and *Ceddo* was banned for its critique of precolonial politics in Senegal. Souleymane Cissé from Mali produced short government-sponsored documentary films and a body of fiction that explores urban and rural concerns before producing his high-budget film *Yeelen* (1987), which explores a mythic world of the Bambara. Other notable francophone filmmakers are Idrissa Ouedraogo and Gaston Kaboré from Burkina Faso and the woman filmmaker Safi Faye from Senegal.

Anglophone west Africa has developed an independent film industry that has mainly produced feature films blending comedy and melodrama. In Ghana notable filmmakers are King Ampaw, with films such as *They Call It Love* (1972) and *Juju* (1986), and Kwaw Ansah, who had great success with *Love Brewed in the African Pot* (1980), a film about a love affair between a girl from an elite family and a fisherman's son. Both filmmakers explore the clash between the contemporary world and the past to strike a deep chord with their audiences. Indeed, *Love Brewed in the African Pot* was a sellout success in Sierra Leone, Liberia, and Kenya. In the 1990s filmmaking in west Africa is characterized by a diversity of themes and styles.

Television

Television has played an important part in training many filmmakers, but it has also been an important medium of popular culture in its own right since the 1960s, despite usually being controlled by the state. Not only does television portray aspects of popular culture through its programming of cultural events, but it also creates new forms of popular culture, such as the genre of soap operas. It reconstitutes elite artistic productions in terms of popular culture reaching a mass audience that otherwise would be excluded. For example, in Nigeria, Wole Soyinka's *My Father's Burden* was televised in 1960 to a mass audience, and Chinua Achebe's novel *Things Fall Apart* was televised in Igbo as a series to such popular acclaim that it was reshown with English dubbing (and packaged as a video in 1988). Mass access of video recorders is creating a

shift to low-cost video productions, where the mass market now resides.

BIBLIOGRAPHY

Barber, Karin. "Popular Arts in Africa." *African Studies Review* 30, no. 3 (1987): 1–78.

Bender, Wolfgang. *Sweet Mother: Modern African Music.* Translated by Wolfgang Fries. Chicago, 1991.

Bettelheim, Judith. "The Lantern Festival in Senegambia." *African Arts* 18, no. 2 (1985): 50–53, 95–97.

Brincard, Marie Therese, and Maurice Dedieu, eds. *Treasures of a Popular Art: Painting on Glass from Senegal.* New York, 1986.

Deliss, Clementine, ed. *Lotte, or the Transformation of the Object.* Graz, Austria, 1990.

Diawara, Manthia. *African Cinema: Politics and Culture.* Bloomington, Ind., 1992.

Drewal, Henry John, and Margaret Thompson Drewal. *Gelede: Art and Female Power Among the Yoruba.* Bloomington, Ind., 1983.

Jeyifo, Biodun. *The Yoruba Popular Travelling Theatre of Nigeria.* Lagos, 1984.

Nunley, John W. "The Lantern Festival in Sierra Leone." *African Arts* 18, no. 2 (1985): 45–49, 97.

———. *Moving with the Face of the Devil: Art and Politics in Urban West Africa.* Urbana, Ill., 1987.

Picton, John. *The Art of African Textiles: Technology, Tradition, and Lurex.* London, 1995.

Secretan, Thierry. *Going into the Darkness: Fantastic Coffins from Africa.* New York, 1995.

Vogel, Susan Mullin, ed. *Africa Explores: Twentieth-Century African Art.* New York, 1991.

Waterman, Christopher Alan. *Juju: A Social History and Ethnography of an African Popular Music.* Chicago, 1990.

CHARLES GORE

See also **Achebe, Chinua; Art; Cinema; Dance; Literature; Mami Wata; Music and Song; Negritude; Soyinka, Wole; Theater.**

EASTERN AND CENTRAL AFRICA

"Popular culture" generally refers to communicative expressions that grow from, are possessed by, and are significantly associated with the people. Following Karin Barber, popular culture is neither elitist nor traditional but "unofficial" in the Bakhtinian sense: novel, syncretic, and urban-oriented (though drawing from rural-based arts). It transcends ethnic, geographical, and national boundaries because it can be disseminated by electronic and print media or by roving performers beyond the boundaries of its place of creation. Popular culture raises the consciousness of the people insofar as it opens avenues for self-reflection and comprehension. Indeed, it is recognition of this consciousness-raising role that has set in motion major popular cultural movements linking culture with social change in Kenya, Uganda, Botswana, Zambia, Zimbabwe, Malawi, and Tanzania.

Music

Popular culture in eastern and central Africa did not come with Western colonialism. On the eastern African coast there is evidence of the tremendous influence of the Arab and Indian culture in decorations and *taarab* music going back to 900 C.E. Whereas colonial and postcolonial popular culture is clearly distinctive in its innovativeness, within the traditional setup limited innovation was allowed. *Gicandi* dialogue poetry among the Gikuyu, *gungu* in the islands of Lamu and Pate, and *kibati* oral poetry on Pemba operated within a poetically consistent canonicity convention. They were public performances of spontaneous poetic dueling.

Popular culture grows out of a convergence of thought and practice between the alien and the local or between cultural intellectuals and the ordinary people. During the struggle for independence the precolonial culture was collaboratively reactivated and redefined to reflect the current struggle. The Mau Mau songs of Kenya, the Pungwe and Chimurenga songs of Zimbabwe, music and dance on dictatorship in Uganda, and the liberation poetry of Mozambique, though created for political mobilization through the efforts of an elite, were appropriated by the people and made an integral part of their culture.

Most east African secular musicians focus on relationships as the principal domain of concern, be it in the popular *taarab* music of the coast, the rumba derived from west African rhythms, the reggae rhythms derived from the Caribbean, or the *benga* beat from upcountry Kenya. Political and social commentaries are also made to a significant degree through popular songs, which are available in all languages, but more so in the region's major languages—notably Swahili, English, Dholuo, Gikuyu, Shona, Bemba, Ganda, Lingala, and Luhya. Religious music by artists like Festus Munishi, Mary Wambui, and Mary Atieno has taken root over the years. Secular songwriters focus in their compositions on love, marriage, betrayal, money, power, life, and death. They include Fred Sebatta, Wamucii Benson, Ochieng Kabasseleh, Anne Mwale, Thomas Mafumo, Oliver Mutukudzi, Simon Chimbetu, Stella Chiweze, Mechanic Manyeruke, Samba Mapangala, Jane Kakai, Fundi Konde,

George Ramogi, Daudi Kabaka, Them Mushrooms, and Wangonya Success.

Popular Arts

Popular culture stems from the need for self-expression and may serve a variety of intrinsic and extrinsic functions. For example, popular arts in the form of concerts, theater, stickers, music, fiction, art in bars, and *matatu* and *daladala* taxis (in Kenya and Tanzania, respectively) are being used for financial advantage. Moreover, every major town has an array of commercial popular entertainment in the form of American, Indian, British, and Chinese movies, records, cassettes, novels, and television dramas. The region is replete with evidence of Western mass-culture, especially in the world of film, and there is an overwhelming urge to develop an indigenous film industry. Images from Western popular culture are manifest almost everywhere. In addition, tourist art—such as carvings, baskets, paintings, and performance of music, dance, masquerade, and acrobatics, provided either through the ministries of tourism and culture or the informal sector—is financially motivated. Political leaders and government bureaucrats, like the tourists, see troupes perform forms of "traditional" dances modified to fit the occasion. The troupes may be rewarded individually or collectively after the performance.

There are also non–financially motivated popular art forms, such as those found in home decorations, paintings, and recreational music and dance. Moreover, the elite, in pursuance of developmental policies and consciousness raising, promote the growth of "developmentalist theater" as a way of reaching the people, as is happening in Tanzania, Uganda, Kenya, and Zimbabwe. Indigenous theater styles and *ngonjera* (poetic drama) were used to propagate the Ujamaa philosophy in Tanzania, and nongovernmental organizations are using popular culture to an impressive degree in the transmission of political and health-related messages in Uganda.

Popular theater that is people-based may also be seen as subversive, as happened in the 1977 Kamiriithu Theatre Project in Kenya, which led to the detention of Ngugi wa Thiong'o and the exile of most of his associates. Ngugi and his team had set out to revive the Kamiriithu Community Educational and Cultural Centre by working with workers and peasants to make adult education a liberating process. The collaboration was seen as a threat to the political establishment.

Popular culture is essentially dynamic, free, ever-changing, and playful (by bridging the performer-audience gap) and resists containment. It challenges and collapses the dichotomies between traditional and modern, foreign and indigenous, official and unofficial. In all cases, alien popular culture is localized, appropriated, and redefined through being assigned new meanings and modes of representation. That is precisely what the popular Beni dance did, after growing out of the European brass tradition. The Beni, a militaristic mime, combined indigenous dance forms and the colonial military parade.

The Novel

In a (1982) article on the Tanzanian popular novel, Rajmund Ohly asserted that the popular novel is generally simple; targets the emotions rather than the intellect; is easy to read; and sets out to entertain rather than to educate. A more sympathetic view of the popular novel in eastern and central Africa would view it as emanating from the Western elite novel, on the one hand, and from the oral narrative, on the other, but rebelling against them by not conforming strictly to their conventions. The urban novel in Tanzania is almost exclusively rendered in Swahili, the national language, and there is a visible influence of the Western detective novel in, for instance, those of Mohammed Said Abdulla and Faraji Katalambula. Some popular fiction in Tanzania appears in newspaper serials. Likewise, Kenyan Swahili dailies, especially *Taifa Leo*, *Kenya Leo*, and *Taifa Jumapili*, carry serialized fiction.

The Ugandan urban novel is mainly available in English and Ganda. Okello Oculi, Eneriko Seruma, Michel Kayoya, and Davis Sebukima have written on love, wealth, alienation, prostitution, and unemployment in postcolonial Ugandan cities. Okot p'Bitek uses gentle, genial satire in his popular narrative poetry, which carries the rhythm of indigenous oral poetry, to reflect the cultural and political alienation of the African people in the region, especially in the urban areas. His popular poetry includes *Song of Lawino* (1966), *Song of Ocol* (1970), *Song of Prisoner* (1971), and *Song of Malaya* (1971). Okot p'Bitek was the founder of the Gulu Festival and director of Uganda's National Theatre and Cultural Centre. He went into exile when Idi Amin took over leadership in Uganda. Alumidi Asinya has written *Abdulla Salim Fisi* (1977), a beast fable on the career of Idi Amin.

In Kenya the urban novel is predominantly in English and Swahili. Struggles in the money economy are central to these novels. In *Voices in the Dark* (1970), for example, Leonard Kibera depicts the struggles of the present-day urbanite through the eyes of Gerald Timundu, a radical playwright in love with the daughter of a wealthy businessman. As the novel develops, we witness the contrasts between the emerging political and economic elite, on the one hand, and the beggars who are the main characters in Timundu's plays, on the other. The negative attitudes, values, and practices of the people on Etisarap (Parasite) Road are subjected to satirical treatment.

The foremost Kenyan urban novelist is Meja Mwangi. His novels *Kill Me Quick* (1973), *Going Down River Road* (1976), *The Cockroach Dance* (1979), *The Bread of Sorrow* (1987), *The Bushtrackers* (1979), and *Weapon of Hunger* (1989) explore urbanicity, especially as it relates to unemployment, economic and social stagnation and regression, and crime and punishment in the lives of the majority of the people. There are ethnic and racial tensions, dislocations and uncertainties, illicit drink, drugs, prostitution, and intraclass and interclass criminality in settings replete with individualism. These issues also are treated in the works of Charles Mangua, especially in *Son of Woman* (1971), *A Tail in the Mouth* (1972), and *Kanina and I* (1994), and those of Mwangi Ruheni, in *What a Life!* (1972), *What a Husband* (1979), *The Future Leaders* (1973), and *The Minister's Daughter* (1975).

In recognition of the place of the crime novel in the region, Heinemann Publishers launched the Spear series in 1975 and published such titles as *The Ivory Merchant* (1976), *Lover in the Sky* (1975), and *Mystery Smugglers* (1975) by Mwangi Gicheru; and *A Prisoner's Letter* (1979) by Aubrey Kalitera. These titles now appear under the East African Educational Publishers Spear series. There are other popular novels in the Spear series, including *Life and Times of a Bank Robber* (1988) by John Kiggia Kimani, *Agony in Her Voice* (1982) by Peter Katuliiba, *Unmarried Wife* (1994) by Sitwala Imenda, *The Girl Was Mine* (1996) by David Karanja, and *My Life in Crime* (1984) and *Son of Fate* (1994) by John Kiriamiti. East African Educational Publishers also started the Peak series in 1995 and published *From Home Guard to Mau Mau* by Elisha Babu, *Hearthstones* (1995) by Kekelwa Nyaiywa, and *Links of Chain* (1996) by Monica Genya. These works are fast-paced and critical of the region's social and political direction.

Macmillan publishers started the Pacesetters series in 1977 and Trendsetters in 1995. Personal, social, and political betrayal, urban crime, corruption, poverty, wealth, misuse of power, and human relationships are some of the themes covered in this series. Some of the popular novels in the Pacesetters series include *Child of War* (1985) by Ben Chirasha of Zimbabwe, *Thorns of Life* (1988) by David Maillu, *Poisoned Bait* (1992) by James Ngumy, *The Shadow of a Dream* (1991) and *Desert Storm* (1992) by Hope Dube, *Double Dating* by Walije Gondwe (Malawi's first female novelist), and *Love on the Rocks* (1981) and *Rassie* (1989) by Andrew Sisenyi of Botswana.

Longman (Kenya) launched the Crime Series in which it published *The Men from Pretoria* (1976) by Hilary Ng'weno, and *Master and Servant* (1979) by David Mulwa. These titles now appear in the Longhorn Masterpiece series. Other Masterpiece popular novels include *Shrine of Tears* (1993) by Francis Imbuga and *The Mixers* (1991) and *Two in One* (1984) by Mwangi Gicheru.

The slowly changing patterns of life among the Maasai people is depicted in popular form in the writings of Henry Ole Kulet. In *To Become a Man* (1990), for example, he depicts the cultural and social expectations of Maasai youth. In *Moran No More* (1990), through the experiences of Roiman, he portrays the challenges posed to Maasai youth, caught up in the cultural, social, political, and economic dynamics of postcolonial Kenya. Ole Kulet also depicts the tensions between cultural expectations and postcolonial reality in his other novels, such as *Is it Possible?* (1971), *Daughter of Maa* (1987), and *The Hunter* (1985).

In addition, Longhorn has published the fiction of Yusuf Dawood, the writer of the *Sunday Nation* column "Surgeon's Diary," which first appeared on 25 May 1980. Some of the stories in the "Surgeon's Diary" have been published in *Yesterday, Today, and Tomorrow* (1985), *Behind the Mask* (1995), and *Off My Chest* (1988). Dawood has also written *The Price of Living* (1983) and *Water Under the Bridge* (1991). In his novels and short stories, Dawood examines the relationship between surgeons and their patients, their different problems and how they cope with them, ethical behavior, wealth, and power. *In the Price of Living,* for instance, he explores the relationship between morality, money, and power. In a world that is shaped through competition and immorality, Maina Karanja judges success through the eyes of money and power. As he comes to find out, there are things that money cannot buy.

Money and power is also the subject of Sam Kahiga's *Paradise Farm* (1993). This popular fiction is a portrayal of the intense, though at times turbulent, love between Joe and Janet in the Kenya Highlands, Nairobi, Mombasa, and the dark alleys of New York's Harlem, where the novel reaches its climax. *Paradise Farm* is also about the difficult search for the meaning of life, race relations, and supernatural forces that influence the activities and experiences of human beings.

Another interesting novel in the Longhorn Masterpiece series is *Sunrise at Midnight* (1996) by Ongoro wa'Munga. In this novel, a business magnate, Carlysto Baronner Sakwa, conspires with the prime minister of an island kingdom to persuade the old and sick founder of the nation to declare himself king so that they can start a dynasty between them. In the process, Carlysto grabs 14,000 acres of land from his clansmen, plans the death of many citizens who are opposed to his activities, and attempts to force his daughter to marry the prime minister's son. The daughter, however, commits suicide rather than succumb to a forced marriage. Moreover, before the king becomes fully manipulated, the nation is saved by one of his close confidants, Mrs. Patricia Odiero. On learning the truth about his prime minister, the king restores power to the people.

The Oxford University Press New Fiction from Africa series included *Murder in Majengo* (1976), a crime thriller by Marjorie Oludhe Macgoye. Also in the 1970s, Foundation Books started its African Leisure Library series, and John Nottingham launched the Afroromance series.

It has been claimed by, among others, Bernth Lindfors, that while Onitsha market literature (printed initially in the market town of Onitsha, Nigeria) is fresh, vigorous, and imaginative, Kenyan popular fiction is pornographic and cynical. Stephen Arnold has said that Kenyan popular fiction is escapist, compensatory, and titillatingly fantasizing and charges that it evades social issues, uncritically approves of capitalist values of competition, individualism, and money worship, or indulges sex and sadism. David Maillu has been accused by the Tanzanian authorities of being pornographic, and his novels have been withdrawn from circulation. His Comb Books, such as *Unfit for Human Consumption* (1971), *Troubles* (1974), *After 4:30* (1974), *My Dear Bottle* (1973), and the 850-page narrative poem *The Kommon Man* (1975), are so sexually explicit as to be devoid of aesthetic appeal. He is, however, more aesthetically conscious and optimistic in perception when writing for children. Under the Pyramid series, he has written, among other titles, *The Last Hunter* (1992), *Journey into Fairyland* (1992), and *The Government's Daughter* (1996).

The claim that popular fiction in the region is cynical is only partly true and cannot, in any case, be made with regard to the popular novel in Swahili or other African languages, an area that is here best represented by Gakaara Wanjau, who has been writing in Gikuyu since the 1940s and is widely known for his Wanduta series. There are many other popular works available in Swahili and other languages of the region, including the writings of Said Ahmed Mohamed, Euphrase Kezilahabi, J. M. Simbamwene, Katama Mkangi, Mohamed Said Mohamed, Ben Mtobwa, and Zainab Burhani, the foremost female Swahili novelist in Kenya.

BIBLIOGRAPHY

Arnold, Stephen H. "Popular Literature in Tanzania: Its Background and Relation to 'East African' Literature." *Kiswahili: Journal of the Institute of Kiswahili Research.* 51, nos. 1–2 (1984): 60–86.

Barber, Karin. "Popular Arts in Africa." *African Studies Review* 30, no. 3 (1987): 1–78.

Lindfors, Bernth. "A Basic Anatomy of East African Literature." In *Design and Intent in African Literature,* edited by David F. Dorsey et al. Washington, D.C., 1982.

Liyong, Taban Lo, ed. *Popular Culture of East Africa.* Nairobi, 1972.

Mlama, Penina Muhando. *Culture and Development: The Popular Theatre Approach in Africa.* Uppsala, 1991.

Ngugi wa Thiong'o. *Decolonising the Mind: The Politics of Language in African Literatures.* London, 1986.

Ohly, Rajmund. *Aggressive Prose.* Dar-es-Salaam, 1981.

———. "Swahili Pop Literature: The Case of Munda Msokile." *African Marbugensia* 15, no. 1 (1982): 43–55.

Searle, Chris. "The Mobilisation of Words: Poetry and Resistance in Mozambique." *Race and Class* 23, no. 4 (1982): 305–320.

KIMANI NJOGU

See also **Art; Cinema; Dance; Literature; Music and Song; Radio and Television; Theater.**

SOUTH AFRICA

Any consideration of popular culture in Africa must differentiate this (admittedly imposed) category from "traditional" or "recreational" culture associated with rural peasants. The determining dimension is summarized sociologically as "modernization," "industrialization," "urbanization," "social (class) differentiation," and even "capitalist penetration." The difference being drawn is that between what have been viewed (wrongly) as organic, autonomous, self-sufficient (culturally at least) communities possessing access to the means of production, and the urban, class-structured society that results from migration and wage labor. Social anthropology has, however, demonstrated over the last half of the twentieth century that this dichotomy does not accord with the situation on the African ground. Rural people are thoroughly integrated into the wage economy even if they are not migrant laborers, and in South Africa forced population movements created as well the phenomenon of "rural urbanization." In the towns, conversely, rural styles of performance are maintained and elaborated by people for whom home (as opposed to residence) will always be somewhere in the countryside.

Nor is Western city life a product of the twentieth century, or even the nineteenth in South Africa. Cape Town, settled by the Dutch in 1652, was by the eighteenth century both a great port of call and a seat of empires with many layers, both polished and rough-hewn, of cosmopolitan, hybridized culture. In seaside taverns, at creole "rainbow balls," and even on rural Dutch plantations, slave musicians from the East Indies, India, Madagascar, and the interior of southern Africa (Khoisan and Bantu) learned to perform on violins, woodwinds, horns, snare and bass drums, and guitar. The music and the dancing rapidly localized as distinctive syncretic Cape (*kaapse*) styles, expressing the experience of race and place, emerged in South Africa's "mother city." Even distinctive institutions such as the illegal house-tavern, where black and brown people were sold and even served their grog in the back kitchens of private houses, originated in Cape Town under Dutch East India Company rule in the seventeenth century. In the late nineteenth century, immigrant Irish vice police in Cape Town gave these taverns the Gaelic sobriquet that has stuck ever since: *shebeens* (little shops).

The forms of indigenous popular culture associated with nineteenth- and twentieth-century South Africa virtually all have their origins in the cultural fusion of European and African forms that accompanied the colonial penetration of the interior and the resulting growth of towns, mining camps, and their associated black ghettos. Often first on the scene from the outside were Christian missionaries, who brought European hymnody and forms of display (school concerts and plays) into an African environment in which a capella choral music and group dance were the dominant form in both religious and recreational contexts. Starting more than a century ago and continuing to the present, formidable African choirs have made world tours and enlivened religious, ceremonial, and competitive local events.

The emergence of a distinctively South African Afro-European performance culture was further enhanced by the influences of the English music hall and the American minstrel and light operatic traditions that touring companies brought from abroad starting in the latter half of the nineteenth century. The urban workplace as well as the small-town churches spread this choral music-and-movement form to non-Christian rural labor migrants, who soon developed it into a range of thoroughly local styles. Among these, the *isicatam-iya* of Zulu-speaking Natal, researched by Veit Erlmann and David B. Coplan, has been brought to the world by the Durban-based Ladysmith Black Mambazo.

South African popular culture in general entered its second and most significant phase of development with the rise of the "Diamond City" of Kimberley in the 1870s and Johannesburg, "City of Gold," in the late 1880s. The pattern of segregated urban life and culture established in these centers remained the template for popular cultural development even at the end of the twentieth century. Among the white population, those of English and the "better" class of Dutch descent continued to import their cultural forms and interests from Europe. The strictly Calvinist Afrikaners, for example, used a High Dutch Bible; the local Dutch-based creole, Afrikaans, was not thought a worthy vehicle of the Lord's word until a Bible appeared in the language in 1933. The rural and urban working-class Afrikaners (including the "Coloured people" of mixed racial descent), however, developed games, cuisine, and styles of folk speech, performance, and sociability that were strongly influenced by the indigenous people among whom they lived and upon whose labor they depended. But it is only after the formal dismantling of apartheid that Afrikaans culture is being liberated from its fitfully hegemonic, racially exclusive governmentality and is jostling with renewed creative energy for a place among the other indigenous language cultures of the land.

Black popular culture was likewise produced and organized around markers of transforming social identity, and the display of cultural capital necessary for the establishment of claims to urbanized status and social class. In the domain of performance culture this led to the emergence, by the 1920s, of a range of petit bourgeois and working-class styles, venues, and occasions of concertizing, popular dance, and local jazz music. For the small professional and salaried class, it was ballroom dance, choir music, mission church sodalities, football clubs, and boxing. For laborers, it was raucous *marabi* African jazz, urbanized rural-style dance competitions, and independent African folk gospel churches. Of course there was social movement. Domestic servants, eager to acquire Western cultural capital, were the most ardent enthusiasts of ballroom dance. Middle-class Africans, attuned to Count Basie and Duke Ellington, began to enjoy the localized compositions of an emerging, distinctively African dance band and entertainment world. From this world developed the "classic" South African jazz called *mbaqanga*, or simply "African jive," of the postwar period, made famous abroad by performers such as Miriam Makeba and Hugh Masekela.

This world was nearly destroyed by the enforced removal of black people from the inner-city and near-suburban residential "locations" to distant, anomic, and anonymous government "townships" such as Soweto in Johannesburg and Mamelodi in Pretoria during the 1960s. But with characteristic reconstitutive social creativity, black people made homes and communities bloom amid the barren, squalid rows of four-room brick "matchbox" houses that made it so difficult to find one's way around or to tell one township from another. American, specifically African American, popular culture was once again mobilized to produce resilient, rough, and energetic new cultural styles and forms that not merely reflected but challenged social experience. The way was opened for the emergence of a popular dance-balladry and theater that examined dislocations within black community life and stubbornly protested the political dispensation that so severely exacerbated them. So in the 1970s and 1980s, the meaning of "popular" in South African black culture shifts political gear from the expression of social reality to its active rejection. The youth culture of the time, fueled by the "black consciousness" of its African American materials and models, made modernist rebellion into a nationalist cultural style. The expressions of this style

South African performers Miriam Makeba and Ray Phiri join Paul Simon on his Graceland tour. ZIMBABWE MINISTRY OF INFORMATION

not only in performance, but also in dress, funerals, leisure, education, and political activity, played a large role in creating the modes of solidarity that kept the antiapartheid Mass Democratic Movement moving through the dark and tortuous tunnel of the 1970s and 1980s to the light of the 1990s.

As liberation approached, television, previously neither much directed at nor much watched by township residents, began to play a leading role in the conscious development of new popular cultural models for a self-creating society. The transformation of SATV into a genuinely public broadcaster has not only democratized language programming to better serve all of the country's eleven language groups (with the exception of the dramatic decrease in programming in Afrikaans); it has also sponsored the scripting and production of local dramatic and comedy series that focus unblinkingly, if somewhat naively, on salient issues of a tumultuous, dynamic, democratizing society. On SABC radio, democratization has enabled a host of new regional, metropolitan, and community stations serving previously neglected audiences to find airspace. Further, new regulations which require that 30 percent of all music played over the radio feature South African performers have begun to spur a renaissance in South African music that is reworking and developing stylistic blends and influences from virtually everywhere into the familiar framework of popular local genres.

As the struggle for liberation began to achieve its political (if not yet social) aims, the energies of militant township youth that had been absorbed in this struggle found in part a new focus in the creation of a performance- and media-oriented youth popular culture. "Culture clubs" and youth clubs sprang up in black communities throughout the country's urban areas, and by the early 1990s almost half of township youth were involved in associations of this kind. Their hope is that the educational, vocational, and cultural programs of these clubs can make up in some measure for the failings of their schools, and offer at least the possibility of a way out of the cycle of violence, poverty, and stagnation that rules life in the townships and shantytowns in the midst of South Africa's remarkable political renaissance.

BIBLIOGRAPHY

Coplan, David B. *In Township Tonight! South Africa's Black City Music and Theater.* London, 1985.
Erlmann, Veit. *African Stars: Studies in Black South African Performance.* Chicago, 1991.

———. *Nightsong: Performance, Power, and Practice in South Africa.* Chicago, 1996.

DAVID B. COPLAN

See also **Apartheid; Dance; Music and Song; Radio and Television; Theater; Urbanization.**

POPULATION DATA AND SURVEYS. There is less certainty about sub-Saharan Africa's population data than there is for any other major world region. This is true in spite of the region's unusually interesting population phenomena, namely the world's highest birth, death, and growth rates. Nevertheless, it is clear that by 1994 the population of the region had exceeded 550 million, constituting slightly less than one-tenth of the world's population and almost four-fifths of that of the whole African continent. So rapid is population growth that projections suggest that, when the world achieves near-stationary population growth, perhaps by the end of the twenty-first century, the people of sub-Saharan Africa will constitute almost one-fifth of humankind.

Before the twentieth century there was no reliable information on the region's population. The United Nations employed a figure for the whole continent, from the seventeenth through nineteenth centuries, of 100 million, based on estimates from three prominent authorities. These estimates, however, were influenced by each other and rested ultimately on the interest in the mysticism of numbers of a priest in Bologna, Giambattista Riccioli, who in 1651 published a book about the population of the world. When attempts to modify these estimates were first made, they were based on the backward projection of securer figures from post–World War II censuses. The true continental population figure for the seventeenth century may have been nearer 50 million, because there was undoubtedly subsequent population growth made possible, after the arrival of Europeans on the sub-Saharan African coast, by new food plants such as corn, manioc, and Asian yams.

Regional population estimates began to be reported by explorers in the eighteenth and nineteenth centuries. These figures commonly appear to have been overestimates resulting partly from their authors' enthusiasm for their new discoveries. Also, the explorers usually traversed the most densely populated country along coasts, rivers, and trade routes. When later counts found fewer people, the thesis of continuing depopulation was born. The usual way of estimating population until well into the twentieth century was to accept the numbers paying poll tax as a reasonably accurate estimate of the adult male population and then to use a multiplying factor (3.1 in Kenya and 4.5 in Tanzania) to take account of the women and children. Much of this information for British Africa was gathered together by Robert R. Kuczynski in the first two volumes of his *Demographic Survey of the British Colonial Empire,* published in 1948 and 1949. As the author recognized, the compilation showed primarily that very little of this information could be trusted.

Nevertheless, the census was to prove a necessity for African administration. It was the sole source of comprehensive data on a range of matters which, in more statistically developed regions, were gathered by other routine administrative methods. The poor censuses during most of the colonial period are explained by a lack of both financial and human resources. The amount spent per capita on censuses in anglophone western Africa multiplied in the thirty years after 1931 by a factor of up to 100, far in excess of inflation. Later censuses have depended for their success on great numbers of educated enumerators, particularly schoolteachers, a resource not available in the earlier period. There was often resistance to the census, most often because of the fear that it would identify people for the poll tax.

The Early Censuses

Although the British Colonial Office decided that censuses should be carried out in British territories beginning in 1871, nineteenth-century censuses were largely confined to such areas as Lagos Colony, the Gambia, the colony in Sierra Leone, and the large "native reserves" in southern Africa which became Lesotho and Swaziland. The situation changed after the turn of the century, and starting in either 1901 or 1911, most British colonies held decennial censuses in the first year of each decade, as did Britain. They were joined by Portuguese colonies with the taking of a census in Mozambique in 1940 and in Angola, São Tomé, and Príncipe in 1950. In that same year the Spanish colonial administration carried out a census in Spanish Guinea (now Equatorial Guinea).

These were not censuses in the modern sense. R. R. Kuczynski calculated that five-sixths of the population supposedly counted in the nineteenth century was only estimated. Usually, at the best, the censuses were little more than head counts, and as late as the 1921 census of the Northern

Territories of the Gold Coast (now Ghana), much of the counting was done by villages sending in calabashes of beans representing men, groundnuts women, and stones children. The only well enumerated populations were resident Europeans and, to a lesser extent, Asians. The French colonies carried out no censuses until well after the Second World War. In all colonies there were local administrative counts, often based on village population registers; these were used for estimates, and appear to have formed a significant part of the British colonial censuses. They reached their high point in the card-index system of the Belgian Congo (now Zaire) in the 1950s.

The Emergence of the Modern Census

After the Second World War, the census began increasingly to be seen as a necessary instrument for development planning and as an essential part of the preparation of colonies for independence, particularly when the enumeration was also used to prepare lists of voters. In British West Africa the 1950 census of Lagos was used as a trial for the 1952–1953 census of the whole of Nigeria, which was staggered over time to allow skilled personnel and other resources to be moved from one region to another. The 1948 censuses of Uganda, Kenya, Tanganyika (now part of Tanzania), and the Gold Coast (now Ghana) were landmarks. In each of them a simple census was complemented by a longer questionnaire administered to a subsample. Although administrative lists were undoubtedly consulted during the censuses, the latter proved their worth by enumerating considerably more people than were on the lists.

A new emphasis on censuses around the developing world led to an increasing United Nations role in setting standards and providing experts. A key event was its publication in 1954 of *A Handbook of Population Census Methods,* which provided procedural guidelines and lists of essential and important questions to be included. The first African census to meet these requirements was held in Ghana in 1960, with a post-enumeration survey or supplementary sample survey held three months after the main census. This showed that independent African countries could carry through a modern census. However, limited resources meant that although the census volumes appeared within a few years, the post-enumeration results were not available until 1971.

Similar censuses were held later in the 1960s in Nigeria, Kenya, Tanzania, and Uganda, while francophone countries continued to rely on administrative censuses compiled from local records, increasingly supplemented by demographic sample surveys. However, in 1971 the United Nations Population Commission established the African Census Program, funded by the newly established United Nations Fund for Population Activities (UNFPA). During the rest of the decade censuses were held as part of this program in twenty-two sub-Saharan African countries, including eleven francophone ones. Similar programs were undertaken in the 1980s and 1990s, so that by 1990 at least one census had been held in every sub-Saharan country, with Chad being the last country to complete a census. South Africa held its first census in 1904 (although component parts of the country had held much earlier ones) and continues to conduct regular censuses, although undercounts apparently occurred in 1993, probably because of the volatile political situation.

There were still problems, as shown by the Nigerian censuses of 1962, 1963, and 1973. Over-enumeration could occur because of ethnic and political rivalries or because promised resources would be based on population counts. Some countries, like Liberia in 1962 and the Central African Republic in 1965, suppressed censuses, apparently on the grounds that smaller populations were revealed than their national prestige demanded. This was expected by many to be the fate of the 1993 Nigerian census after the coup late that year, but by mid-1996 this had not occurred.

Problems in the Interpretation of African Census Data

Much demographic analysis depends on accurate age statement. In one sense, age is important in many African cultures because of the formation of age cohorts as males reach maturity and because of strongly held concepts of seniority in relationships. Nevertheless, age cohorts may be broad and overlapping, as traditional societies did not observe birthdays or identify people by exact age. As a result, age statement is worse than in any other world region. This in turn accounts for the imprecision in fertility, mortality, and growth estimates. Even the 1960 census of Ghana, the most educated country of sub-Saharan Africa, showed three- or fourfold differences in the numbers of people enumerated at successive single-year ages, although five-year age groups were much more regular. Pre–World War II censuses tended to use four or five major age groupings, or even just divide the population into men, women, and children. Since 1960 there has been an almost universal attempt to collect single-year age data, but success in this effort depends very much on the achievement of near-universal schooling. Observation of enumeration in 1969 in southwest Nigeria showed that only 43 percent of males and 34 percent of females even attempted to report their own age, and the majority of estimates came from the enumerators or other people. Experiments with the use of historical calendars to assist the memory have done little to improve the situation.

Problems with defining marital status have made the analysis of marriage very difficult. Minor variations in the wording of a survey or census question can result in striking differences in the proportion reporting that they have ever been married. In Botswana, for instance, the contrast is between 96 and 30 percent for twenty- to twenty-four-year-old women in two successive surveys. Part of the problem is that in many societies getting married has traditionally been a continuing process rather than an instantaneous one; part is that practices are changing. The first anglophone census to attempt to obtain marriage data was taken in 1957 in Tanganyika, where men were asked how many wives they had. Current marital status was first asked for in the 1960 Ghana postcensus enumeration survey. The data are still inadequate for establishing trends satisfactorily. If marriage questions are asked, then a question on polygyny should be included, but answers can be misleading where polygyny is illegal, as in Zaire or South Africa.

In the absence of adequate vital registration data, and with a growing interest after World War II in fertility rates, attempts were made in the 1948 censuses of British East Africa and Ghana to obtain information on births. Questions were asked in East Africa on the total number of live births to each woman and on her births within the previous 12 months. The information was clearly inaccurate because, from what is known of the timing of family-building, the responses to the two questions were incompatible for the whole society. Efforts were also made to obtain mortality data by seeking information on deaths over the previous year and on the numbers of children women had lost. These data too usually appeared to be implausible.

African censuses have frequently sought information on ethnicity, mother tongue, religion, literacy, education, and physical condition. Ethnicity and religion are invaluable social measures, but they have been increasingly charged with causing internal competition and conflict and both were omitted from the 1993 Nigerian census. Literacy is very sensitive to the measure used, as is shown by the fact that in Nyasaland (now Malawi) the 1945 census recorded a literacy level only one-eighth of that reported by the 1931 census. Data on physical condition were thought to be related to the needs of colonial plantation and mining economies and disappeared from the postindependence censuses, although they are now reappearing in some surveys because of an increased interest in health.

Vital Registration

Efforts have been made for almost two centuries to enforce the registration of births and deaths, but, as most of the population does not need passports or seek employment where birth certificates are needed, usable systems exist nowhere. Sierra Leone declared registration compulsory in 1801, the Gambia in 1845, Lagos in 1892, selected towns of the Gold Coast in 1912, and other Nigerian towns in 1926.

Only in some island colonies did registration ever exceed 90 percent. Lagos has been quoted as a success story because birth registrations yielded plausibly high fertility levels, but the evidence seems to be that, while many Lagos births were not registered, other babies from outside Lagos were registered as born in the city so that the children would later be eligible to attend the city's schools. Research in Ghana showed that registration officials accepted birth registration from all applicants and had no clear idea of the boundaries of the registration district, thus making it impossible to calculate birth rates by comparing registration and census population data. In South Africa vital registration for Whites has been complete for all of the twentieth century and for Indians and Coloureds since the 1940s, but it is still far from complete for the Black population.

An alternative approach to state registration was to make it a responsibility of Native Administrations. This was done with considerable success from 1904 in the kingdom of Buganda and by 1930 in most of Uganda. A similar approach was adopted in Northern Nigeria early in the twentieth century and in some cities, notably Katsina, a high level of coverage was achieved. The nearest approach to complete national registration appears to have developed in the Belgian Congo in the 1950s. Nowhere have such systems been successfully used for demographic analysis.

In the early 1970s several projects were organized with external help to establish dual record schemes whereby data could be obtained from at least two different sources (e.g., a registration system and periodic surveys), so that births and deaths could be estimated from the degree of overlap between the two systems. Experience in Morocco, Liberia, and Malawi yielded estimates of fair quality, but the schemes were too expensive to continue and did not meet the legal and other needs for which national registration systems are usually employed.

New Demographic Methods and Data Collection Systems

The problems of obtaining plausible fertility and mortality estimates from African census and other population data were so challenging that they gave rise to new methodologies. The resultant demographic analytical approaches have been widely applied to contemporary data from developing nations and historic data from developed countries. Faced with the incomplete data of the 1948 East African censuses, beginning in 1953 William Brass published papers on how to obtain acceptable fertility estimates from biased retrospective birth reporting. Beginning in 1956 he made available his methodology on estimating child mortality from retrospective reporting of child deaths. Later, methods were devised for estimating adult mortality from information on whether the respondents' parents (or, in some cases, other relatives) were still alive. An alternative approach to fertility estimation, requiring only information on the age structure of populations, was developed by Ansley Coale using stable population models which he and Paul Demeny published in 1966. At the Princeton University Office of Population Research, these three and others applied their methods to African census and survey data in the first attempt to obtain demographic estimates for the whole region, *The Demography of Tropical Africa*, published in 1968.

Sample Censuses and Post-Census Surveys

Southern Rhodesia (now Zimbabwe) conducted a sample census in 1948, and sampling was also used in the 1955–1956 Sudan census. Post-census sample surveys were undertaken in Uganda, Kenya, Tanganyika, and the Gold Coast in 1948. The sample censuses were more expensive than anticipated and subsequent evidence suggested that they underestimated population numbers compared with full censuses. The post-census surveys allowed information on fertility, mortality, and migration to be collected through multiple questions.

Francophone Demographic Surveys, 1954–1961

In the absence of censuses, French colonial administrators, supported by French statistical and demographic agencies, carried out ten demographic surveys in French sub-Saharan African colonies between 1954 and 1961. A demographic survey was also carried out by the Belgian administration in the Belgian Congo in 1955–1957. Some of these surveys attempted to be representative of whole countries but others chose restricted and unrepresentative areas. The relatively small scale of the enquiries allowed a density of demographic questions and an intensity of fieldwork that permitted the new demographic analytical techniques to be fully used.

The most detailed analyses of Princeton University Office of Population Research's African Project of the early 1960s, published as *The Demography of Tropical Africa*, concentrated on these surveys, although less detailed analyses were also carried out on the censuses from anglophone countries and Portuguese colonies. For the first time, it was possible to map estimated fertility levels for much of sub-Saharan Africa. The pattern was one of high fertility, six or more live births per woman, with the level rising to over eight in a significant number of populations. But areas of Africa were revealed where a considerable proportion of women—almost half in some districts—had never borne a child, with resultant total fertility rates under four. The largest area of pathological sterility of this type was in the central portion of Africa, embracing Gabon, Río Muni, and considerable parts of northern Zaire, the Central African Republic, southwest Sudan, and Cameroon. The analyses also showed that much of sub-Saharan Africa had infant mortality rates over two hundred per thousand live births (i.e., 20 percent of babies died in the first year of life). Consequently, life expectancy at the time of birth was below thirty-five years and often below thirty years.

World Fertility Survey, 1980–1984

The World Fertility Survey (WFS) was an international program of demographic surveys (collecting mortality as well as fertility data), supported by the United Nations Fund for Population Activities as well as many national governments and other organizations. It originated in 1972, but all the sub-Saharan surveys were carried out in the early 1980s so as not to interfere with the 1970 African census round. The program provided standardized questionnaires and analysis, as well as a great deal of technical assistance. Surveys were held in Kenya, Lesotho, Senegal, Cameroon, Ghana, Bénin, Côte d'Ivoire, and Nigeria, and also in Mauritania and northern Sudan. The surveys had a good coverage of the west African coast but a very limited coverage elsewhere.

The program published its own reports and analyses, which were supplemented in professional journals. Only one book concentrated on the region: *Reproduction and Social Organization in Sub-Saharan Africa,* edited by Ron J. Lesthaeghe (1989). This book used the World Fertility Surveys and a range of other sources to map marriage patterns, showing significant regional differences in age at first marriage (women marry earliest in the savanna regions of western and central Africa; men marry latest in western and southern Africa) and in age differences between spouses at first marriage (greatest in western Africa, especially in the far west, where the gap is typically over nine years). Patterns of polygyny were also shown, with the proportion of wives in polygynous marriages exceeding 40 percent from Senegal to western Zaire, except for the small minority of matrilineal areas; the rates were 30 percent in eastern Africa and below 20 percent in most of southern Africa.

Demographic and Health Surveys from 1986

A new international demographic survey program, the Demographic and Health Survey (DHS), funded by the United States Agency for International Development (USAID), published its first African survey report in 1985 and by the end of 1993 had issued reports on twenty-one sub-Saharan African countries. The new program focused on fertility levels more than on the determinants of these levels, and on contraception and various health measures. A major publication in 1994 was *The Population Dynamics of Sub-Saharan Africa,* arising from a National Research Council of the National Academies of Sciences and Engineering research project with the same title, directed by Samuel Preston. The project was able to confirm that fertility had begun to fall in three African countries, Botswana, Zimbabwe, and Kenya, as had the fertility of Black South Africans a decade earlier. It also drew together childhood mortality data showing levels and trends for most sub-Saharan African countries. It appears that child mortality fell steeply from at least 1945 until 1980 and that adult mortality had

also improved. Between 1945 and 1980 life expectancy at birth for the whole region had probably increased from little over thirty years to more than forty-five years, although it was still the lowest in any world region. There was some evidence of a slower mortality decline in certain countries during the economically troubled 1980s.

Fertility Control

The first surveys of fertility and family planning had been carried out in the early 1960s as part of the KAP (Knowledge, Attitudes, and Practice of Family Planning) survey program. Fertility control was also a component of all WFS and DHS surveys as well as more specialized programs such as the Contraceptive Prevalence Surveys (CPS). In the 1950s few couples of reproductive age used contraception, but by 1994 the level was 50 percent in South Africa, 43 percent in Zimbabwe, and 33 percent in both Botswana and Kenya. Levels were highest in anglophone countries but were still below 5 percent in some francophone countries.

Conclusion

Sub-Saharan African population data are still less secure than those of any other major region of the world. Nevertheless, nearly every country in the region has had at least one census, and for most there is additional demographic information from surveys. We probably know the regional population within 5 percent of the true figure and currently estimate it to be around 550 million, up from 100 million in the 1920s and 130 million in 1950. Regional mortality has probably been falling all this century while the regional fertility level has not fallen and may even have risen. As a result, the regional rate of population growth is now the world's highest at 3 percent per annum and the population may well double in little more than 30 years. There has been much debate about why this region has been the last in the world to attain any effective level of fertility control, but in the late 1980s the first sub-Saharan African fertility declines were recorded.

The census data are available in published volumes in national capitals and colonial archives, but few are as yet stored electronically. The WFS and DHS data disks are available from these organizations. The most important regional studies based on these sources are listed below.

BIBLIOGRAPHY

Brass, William, et al. *The Demography of Tropical Africa.* Princeton, N.J., 1968.

Caldwell, John C. "The Social Repercussions of Colonial Rule: Demographic Aspects." In *General History of Africa*, volume 7, *Africa Under Colonial Domination, 1880–1935*, edited by A. Adu Boahen. Berkeley, 1985.

Caldwell, John C., and Chukuka Okonjo, eds. *The Population of Tropical Africa*. New York, 1968.

Caldwell, John C., et al., eds. *Population Growth and Socioeconomic Change in West Africa*. New York, 1975.

Evalds, Victoria K. *Union List of African Censuses, Development Plans, and Statistical Abstracts*. Oxford, 1985.

Foote, Karen A., Kenneth H. Hill, and Linda G. Martin, eds. *Demographic Change in Sub-Saharan Africa*. Washington, D.C., 1993.

Ominde, Simon H., and Charles N. Ejiogu, eds. *Population Growth and Economic Development in Africa*. London, 1972.

Page, Hilary J., and Ron Lesthaeghe, eds. *Child-Spacing in Tropical Africa: Traditions and Change*. London, 1981.

Pinfold, John R., ed. *African Population Census Reports: A Bibliography and Checklist*. Oxford, 1985.

Van de Walle, Étienne, Patrick O. Ohadike, and Mpembele D. Sala-Diakanda, eds. *The State of African Demography*. Liège, Belgium, 1988.

Van de Walle, Étienne, Gilles Pison, and Mpembele D. Sala-Diakanda, eds. *Mortality and Society in Sub-Saharan Africa*. Oxford, 1992.

JOHN C. CALDWELL

See also **Fertility and Infertility; Mortality.**

PORT-LOUIS. The capital and principal port of Mauritius since 1730, Port-Louis is situated on the northwestern part of the island. It is the seat of government, the most populous town (142,000 in 1994, which is 14 percent of the populace), and the main trading center of the island. Protected from storms by a range of mountains, and therefore a safe harbor, Port-Louis was preferred as the capital, rather than Grand Port, by the French governor Maupin. It was probably named after King Louis XV (r. 1715–1774), although it has been suggested that it may have taken its name from a Breton port near Lorient. Under French rule, Port-Louis rapidly developed into a major Indian Ocean port. It also became an important naval base and a center for regional trade.

BIBLIOGRAPHY

Simmons, Adele S. *Modern Mauritius: The Politics of Decolonization*. Bloomington, Ind., 1982.

Wright, Carol. *Mauritius*. Newton Abbot, U.K., 1974.

JESSE A. DIZARD

PORTO NOVO. The official capital of the People's Republic of Bénin (formerly Dahomey), Porto Novo was formerly Ajase, capital of the Yoruba state of Popo. It was called Hogbonou by its Gun (Goun or Egun) inhabitants and Aklon by the Ahori (Awori).

In the eighteenth century, Ajase (as it was then known) became an important seaport for the Oyo slave trade with the Europeans. In about 1752, the name was changed to Porto Novo by Portuguese merchants. Following the decline of the Oyo empire, Porto Novo faced attacks from Dahomey, Egba Badagry, and Lagos. In the nineteenth century, dynastic rivalries in Porto Novo and competition among European powers led to its being ceded by Portugal to France. In 1863, the king of Porto Novo sought French protection against Abomey.

Porto Novo became a French protectorate in 1882. The late nineteenth and early twentieth centuries witnessed the immigration of a sizable number of Brazilian returnees. The institution of kingship was abolished by the French, following the death of King Toffa in 1908. In 1970, Sourou-Migan Apithy called for the cession of Porto Novo to Nigeria.

Since the 1970s, Porto Novo has been surpassed in economic importance by the deep seaport town of Cotonou. Nevertheless, it remains the official capital, with its administrative buildings such as the library, the National Archives, and the sciences division of the Institut d'Enseignement Supérieure du Bénin.

BIBLIOGRAPHY

Akinjogbin, I. A. *Dahomey and Its Neighbours, 1708–1818*. Cambridge, 1967.

Decalo Samuel. *Historical Dictionary of Dahomey (People's Republic of Bénin)*. Metuchen, N.J., and London, 1970.

OLATUNJI OJO

See also **Yoruba States.**

PORTUGUESE COLONIES. *See* **Colonial Policies and Practice.**

POSTCOLONIAL STATE

WESTERN AFRICA

In sixteen of the seventeen present states of western Africa colonial rule came to an end between 1957 and 1974. (The seventeenth, Liberia, had never become a formal colony of a western state.) The timing of the colonial era's end, in most instances, depended more upon the politics and economics of the metropolitan power than on those of the former colony itself. The British colony of the Gold Coast (now Ghana) led the process of decolonization; the Portuguese colonies of Cape Verde and Guinea-Bissau, after a protracted interval, and in the latter case a lengthy armed struggle, brought it to its formal conclusion.

But none of the contemporary states of western Africa (not even Liberia or Guinea-Bissau) became a separate sovereign state within its current boundaries through the exercise of military force and political authority generated within those boundaries—that is, through its own coercive and organizational efforts. None as yet has drastically altered its territorial boundaries since the formal end of colonial rule (though these were rearranged importantly in some cases in the closing years of colonial authority). As yet, none has formally subjugated another (or even explicitly claimed sovereignty over it as a whole). None, furthermore, has yet openly abandoned the attempt to sustain sovereign governmental authority over its own national territory. There is no guarantee that any of these characteristics will continue to hold good indefinitely. But for the present, and taken together, they define the range of postcolonial variation within the state forms of western Africa.

For all their striking contrasts in scale, population size, resource endowments, economic development, and political experience, all of these states today are states in the same sense and of essentially the same kind. They take their political form from the cosmopolitan legal and organizational model pioneered in western Europe several centuries ago, and extended to almost the entire world as a prescribed format through the United Nations Charter in the aftermath of the Second World War. The essence of this format, internally, is the claim to monopolize the legitimate use of force within its own territories; to define for itself what is legitimate within those confines; and to define externally, through agreement with its sovereign peers, just where those territories terminate.

The state so conceived is a composite of spatial and demographic elements, subject to a single supposedly coherent system of rule; a territory; a people recognized by other states and peoples as fully entitled to rule itself; and a legally specified system through which that rule is carried out. In none of the postcolonial states of western Africa do the peoples now deemed to be sovereign or the territories over which they hold authority, coincide with

peoples and territories which existed as distinct units prior to colonial rule. (In the case of Liberia, again, the political and territorial construction of the present state was closely constrained by the extension of colonial rule around it and by the intervention of ecclesiastical and economic interests from the United States.)

Inaugurating Constitutional Legitimacy

At the end of colonial rule, the legitimate constitutional authority of the new governments was in each instance developed, with varying reluctance and grace, from the departing colonial ruler. In the earlier phases of decolonization, first by Britain and then by France, sovereign authority was transferred not merely to an apparatus of government with its own supposedly loyal army and police force. It was also transferred to a formal structure of constitutional authority which prescribed how those who controlled the government should and should not make laws, how judicial power should and should not be exerted, and how future holders of governmental power should and should not acquire it. Only in the former Portuguese colonies, where the colonial rulers came close to being expelled by protracted and relatively successful guerrilla struggle, was the newly sovereign political authority able to prescribe from the outset the constitutional terms on which it proposed to rule.

The constitutional systems established at independence varied in form; more, for example, were unitary rather than federal states. But Nigeria, by far the most populous and powerful state, had a complicated federal constitution from the start. Its accompanying administrative structure, which drew extensively from the colonial arrangements, has persisted through all the subsequent disruptions of Nigerian politics and the elaborate reorganizations which these have prompted. In all of the colonies of France and Britain, the successor governments won power in the approved manner, through the organization of a political party and its successful struggle for the popular vote.

There remains sharp disagreement about the real sources and intensity of popular commitment to these parties, both up to the point of independence and since. What cannot be disputed is that this process of accumulation and transfer has produced a form of authority which has proved markedly flimsy in subsequent use, and one which has by now been abandoned or supplanted for substantial periods of time in almost every country in question.

This is in no way surprising. The claim to legal authority is itself essentially formal. The constitutional framework which initially defined the terms on which western Africans could compete to secure it was in no sense an initiative of western Africa's own populations and could therefore call on few local loyalties. The appropriateness of that framework had always been inherently disputable and had often been keenly contested in practice. The power to rule had often enjoyed a high degree of prestige in African societies (not least in the wealthier and politically better consolidated). The spoils of office in the wake of colonial rule were more than handsome. The struggle to redefine the framework through which they might be won in the future was intense, turbulent, and predictably disruptive. It brought out, and at least for a time rewarded, some of the most brilliant entrepreneurial talents and most active social imaginations in every country concerned: qualities, above all, of improvisation, daring, guile, ruthlessness, and steadiness of purpose.

The contrast between the constitutional and ideological pretensions and the organizational realities of western Africa's independent governments has been in many respects as acute and as distressing as anywhere in the world over the same span of time: less genocidal at its worst, but also far less successful at economic, political, and social development than in virtually any other area of comparable size in any other continent. Judged by the stern cosmopolitan standards of comparative economic efficiency, all of western Africa's postcolonial states have in some measure failed, though some plainly, at different times, have failed far more grimly or odiously than others. This verdict is naturally unwelcome to those who sit in the seats of government and has therefore been vigorously disputed throughout the postcolonial epoch. But by now it would be hard to find evidence that it is still genuinely doubted by a majority of the population in any western African state.

Constitutional Legitimacy and Organizational Reality

The burden of failure has emerged as clearly in the discontinuities in constitutional authority as it has in the falling living standards of most of the population. It has come out, too, in the persisting difficulty in securing public order in many of the countries, and in the prevalence of illegal exactions in the exercise of governmental authority from summit to base of their apparatus of rule. In several

of the countries, above all recently in Liberia and Sierra Leone, the state itself has virtually collapsed over large areas of its territory in face of competing groups of armed bandits, leaving a condition closer to anarchy than to well-defined civil war. Only in Nigeria, the leading western African power, has the state as a whole been riven for a time (within a few years of independence) by full-scale civil war between opposing units of its own professional armed forces, a war terminated only by the emphatic victory of the federal army.

By now the cumulative impact of these political and military mishaps has inflicted massive additional damage on the fabric of economic and social life, as it could scarcely have failed to do. But the scale of disruption and consequent damage is itself a measure of the fragility of the economies of these countries at the point of independence. The key question for understanding the postcolonial history of western Africa is why these economies were already so fragile, and why the states which supposedly existed to protect their populations against the hazards of this fragility have proved so ill-equipped to do so.

The Failure of the Armies

To grasp this failure, it is necessary to focus on what the states themselves really were. Set over against their subject populations, they consisted not simply of a formal body of law supposedly sovereign within their territorial limits, and of a set of persons formally entitled to rule through this body of law, but also of a range of organizational realities. At independence the formal locus of sovereign authority shifted crisply from metropolitan power to holders of political office drawn from the nation itself. But the organizational realities of government shifted less rapidly and far less clearly. This was most important at the center of the state. There, rule at first could only be through a civil administration and a fiscal structure constructed by the colonial powers for their own purposes, enforced by an army and police force devised by the same agents for the same purposes. The legitimacy of the new rulers came from the publicly expressed support of the people in whose name they ruled. But their capacity to rule still came predominantly from the apparatus of control constructed by their colonial predecessors. This created an inherently unstable situation.

For the most part, the former French territories were the least unstable, particularly Senegal, but also to a lesser degree Côte d'Ivoire. Both had extended experience of competitive representative politics and powerful nationalist political parties. They also had a considerable measure of continuing military support from the former colonial power for rulers of great political skill who had acquired their claim to legitimacy through institutions installed by the French state to dignify its own departure. (For some time, the tiny riverine Republic of the Gambia sustained a comparable level of domestic stability without the ambiguous benefit of foreign military guarantors.) But the larger states were uneven in development across their regions and had shorter and correspondingly uneven experience of democratic representation. There, the relations between sovereign pretension, in the hands of elected politicians, and organizational realities, at first largely in the hands of career officers, civil servants, and "traditional" rulers who had benefited greatly from the systems of indirect rule, could be kept stable only by conspicuous political skill and appreciable good luck.

The hardest organizational reality to keep subordinate was the army itself. (Armies were by far the largest of the postcolonial armed forces, and unlike navies or air forces, they could and often did take decisive political action for themselves.) Military coups, in one case (Ghana) with key police assistance, removed from office Ghana's first president, Kwame Nkrumah, in February 1966, during the ninth year after independence, and Nigeria's federal premier, a month earlier, in the sixth such year. In both countries (as in most other western African states) there have been numerous unconstitutional changes of regime since. In almost all of these changes of power, the armed forces, under one leadership or another, have in the end acted as a single unit and effectively imposed their own will on the remainder of the population. In each country, accordingly, many senior officers in the armed forces (including some initially not so senior), along with their friends and relations, have amassed large fortunes.

As the decades since independence have gone by, both army and state have lost markedly in popular appeal. In Ghana and Nigeria, it is now barely disputable that decades of military misrule have wrecked their economies and done much to ruin the life chances of most of their inhabitants. This outcome was not the initial intention of anyone who inaugurated this grim pattern; and many, outside and inside the armed services, have struggled valiantly to try to reestablish a sounder balance and a less destructive mode of government. In

Ghana, for example, in very different styles, the first military regime, that of the National Liberation Council in the late 1960s, and the electorally refurbished regime of Jerry Rawlings in the early 1990s, each for a time achieved some success in the endeavor to improve the government.

The Failure of the Parties

Virtually no one at the point of independence anticipated such a ruinous pattern of change (least of all the officers of the army). What was widely anticipated (and purposefully attempted) by those with a keen interest in politics was the construction, extension, and consolidation of political parties as prospective agents of government—in part supplementary to, and in part in lieu of, the colonial apparatus of administration and coercion. The point of this venture was open to a variety of understandings. From the viewpoint of those at the summit of parties in government, no doubt, it was largely to consolidate their own political control. But this, naturally, was not how they described the parties' merits to their followers or opponents (perhaps not even to themselves). Its overt point, rather, was as obvious as it was initially compelling: to turn structures of authority, which remained conspicuously alien in pretension and imaginative content even after their alien builders had largely departed, into more convincing expressions of local will, taste and purpose, and thus into distinctly more trustworthy and effective instruments for defending local interests.

The existence of at least two strong parties in each state was a prerequisite for the pluralist model of effective electoral competition. But the mechanics of electoral competition in weakly institutionalized states with strong local divisions of language, culture, and political allegiance posed from the start a clear threat to political stability. The will to replace a plurality of parties with single ruling parties—whether on a loose and ideologically vague footing, or on a tauter and more didactic cosmopolitan model drawn from Soviet experience that claimed explicitly to privilege some local interests over others—was expressed with varying frankness in every western African state. This drive made greatest headway where it was least interrupted by the intervention of the armed forces.

In the long run, this pattern of political aspiration revealed more about the centrifugal forces with which all African states have to contend than it did about potentially effective means for countering those forces. The distinctively African eligibility of the one-party state came widely to be seen, domestically as well as internationally, as a threadbare fiction, certain in application to protect and reproduce extensive corruption and maladministration, but offering no firm assurance of either stability or ethnic harmony. Furthermore, the cosmopolitan model of single-party rule on behalf of legitimate local interests was discredited in its own territory of origin. Even the will to escape definitively from alien tutelage, so vividly expressed in the struggle for independence, has been sapped by the experience of protracted economic failure, and largely defeated by the imposition of World Bank and International Monetary Fund structural adjustment programs.

These programs are explicitly designed to shrink the organizational reality of the state; to favor private economic interests, local and international, against state-owned enterprises; to reduce the numbers and emoluments of state officials; and to render rulers and administrators more accountable to those over whom they rule. The intended gains in economic efficiency of the programs have been slow in coming. The immediate costs, economic and political, have in every case been heavy. The promise to render rulers more accountable to their subjects, always presumptuous in international agencies confronting a sovereign state, has been tantalizing rather than effective.

Almost four decades after independence, the states of western Africa have made little headway in securing the interests of most of their own citizens. And it would be hard today to argue that any existing body of political doctrine, or site of political or social scientific judgment, shows clearly how they can hope to do fundamentally better over the next four decades.

BIBLIOGRAPHY

Austin, Dennis. *Politics in Ghana, 1946–1960.* New York, 1964.

Bayart, Jean-François. *The State in Africa: The Politics of the Belly.* Translated by Mary Harper, Christopher Harrison, and Elizabeth-Harrison. New York, 1993.

Coleman, James S., and Carl G. Rosberg, eds. *Political Parties and National Integration in Tropical Africa.* Berkeley, 1966.

Cruise O'Brien, Donal, John Dunn, and Richard Rathbone, eds. *Contemporary West African States.* New York, 1989.

Dunn, John, and A. F. Robertson. *Dependence and Opportunity: Political Change in Ahafo.* London, 1973.

Dunn, John, ed. *West African States: Failure and Promise.* New York, 1978.

————. *Modern Revolutions.* 2d ed. New York, 1989.

————. ed. *Democracy: The Unfinished Journey, 508 B.C. to A.D. 1993.* Oxford, 1993.

————. "Introduction: Crisis of the Nation State?" In *Contemporary Crisis of the Nation State?* edited by John Dunn. Cambridge, Mass., 1995.

Luckham, Robin. *The Nigerian Military: A Sociological Analysis of Authority and Revolt, 1960–1967.* Cambridge, 1971.

Morgenthau, Ruth Schachter. *Political Parties in French-Speaking West Africa.* Oxford, 1964.

Sklar, Richard, L. *Nigerian Political Parties.* New York, 1963.

Stremlau, John J. *The International Politics of the Nigerian Civil War, 1967–1970.* Princeton, N.J., 1977.

Whitaker, C. S., Jr. *The Politics of Tradition: Continuity and Change in Northern Nigeria, 1946–1966.* Princeton, N.J., 1970.

Zolberg, Aristide R. *Creating Political Order: The Party-States of West Africa.* 1966.

JOHN DUNN

See also **Development; Geopolitics; Government; Law; Military Governments and Armies; Neocolonialism; Political Systems.**

EASTERN AFRICA

The concept of the "postcolonial state" became prevalent in social science discourse after the majority of African and Asian countries became independent from colonial rule in the 1960s. Much earlier, it had been argued that political independence made very little difference to the social, political, and economic life of the former colonized peoples; the new states were regarded as neocolonial, having only changed guards in terms of political rulership.

While recognizing continuity of processes, institutions, and structures from colonial to postcolonial times, the concept of the postcolonial state went a little further. It sought to conceptualize the nature of political power in postcolonial societies in terms of class structure and its bearing on politics within the domestic and international settings. Theories of the postcolonial state ranged from those which fully embraced dependency to those which analyzed the state as a factor of cohesion in class-divided society not necessarily permanently ensconced in a relationship of external domination.

In eastern Africa, the Dar es Salaam school of the 1960s and 1970s did extensive work on the postcolonial state in Tanzania in particular and in eastern Africa in general. Most influential in this debate was Issa Shivji's *Class Struggles in Tanzania*

469

(New York, 1973). It characterized the state not just as an extension of its colonial predecessor but also as an arena of class struggles in which the comprador bourgeoisie was hegemonic. This is the bourgeoisie of African nationalists who, having gained access to state power, was bent on using it to consolidate its class interests in terms of property ownership (through the ideology and economic program of Africanization) and monopoly of political power (through the ideology of African socialism and the authoritarianism of the one-party system). In this context, ethnic and racial relations were largely subordinated to the political game plan of the single-party regime.

In Tanzania, Julius Nyerere, so adept at articulating the dominant socialist ideology, made it difficult for other competing interest groups, including ethnic ones, to penetrate the political arena. Since the Tanzania African National Union/Chama Cha Mapinduzi (TANU/CCM) came to power in the 1960s, Tanzania has remained a stable one-party state where the ruling class has not faced any major challenge from the masses or any sector of the competing elites. Parliamentary and local government elections have been held regularly, albeit on a semicompetitive basis, thus providing legitimacy for the regime through a well-orchestrated circulation of elites. Because of deteriorating socioeconomic conditions over the years, and with the onset of structural adjustment programs in the mid-1980s, Tanzania—like its neighbors in eastern Africa—has had to face the growing threat of internal conflicts. The most threatening tension is that of the rise of Islamic fundamentalism and Zanzibari nationalism.

But nowhere have internal conflicts been more debilitating to political stability and socioeconomic progress than in Sudan, Somalia, Ethiopia, Eritrea, and Uganda. In Sudan, Somalia, and Ethiopia there have been long-standing disputes regarding the legitimacy of the central power to govern certain sections of the subject peoples. Those rebelling against central authority have regarded themselves as autonomous ethnic communities forcibly put under the political domination of minority central authorities who monopolize political power by armed might. Southern Sudan, for example, has challenged the legitimacy of the government of Khartoum, regarding the latter as Arab-dominated and therefore committed to the Islamization of the whole country. In terms of resources and opportunities for development, the south—predominantly

Kenneth Kaunda, premier of Northern Rhodesia (now Zambia); Julius Nyerere, president of the United Republic of Tanganyika and Zanzibar (Tanzania); Jomo Kenyatta, premier of Kenya; and Milton Obote, premier of Uganda, 16 October 1964. UPI/CORBIS-BETTMANN

black and of Christian and traditional religious affiliation—has felt discriminated against by the north: it has remained relatively backward while the north prospers on resources including agricultural produce and oil perceived to be obtained in large part from the south.

The Sudanese civil war, going back to the early 1960s, has led to a major refugee problem in Africa, not to mention a tremendous loss in human life and a general retardation of socioeconomic development. The Khartoum regime, legitimizing its authority by Shari'a law, is largely regarded as autocratic and sectarian, hence not amenable to a democratic and peaceful solution of the Sudanese crisis. In the mid-1980s, the Sudan People's Liberation Movement (SPLM) proposed, during discussions with the central authorities, a national reconciliation program based on "a democratic and a new Sudan," but the proposal was rebuffed. Since then, it has become increasingly unlikely that Sudan can hold together as one state. The solution to the internal conflict perhaps lies only in the birth of two Sudans fashioned along the lines of the ethnic divide between the north and south.

Siad Barre's regime in Somalia was in a similar predicament of conflict with the people before it was overthrown in 1991. The difference, however, is that Somalia presents a case of general political disintegration growing out of untenable policies of repression by an increasingly impoverished state. The challenge to central authority, mounted by antagonistic clans rivalling each other for political power, finally degenerated into separatist and secessionist movements almost impossible to contain in one political community. Attempts to reconstitute the state through military action and a negotiated settlement have so far been elusive, leaving the future of the Somalia nation-state in doubt. With each armed group demanding self-determination of some kind, the Somalia scenario presents a bleak picture of the viability of nationhood in multiclan societies in Africa. Fortunately, the Somalia tragedy is not typical of the general crisis of state legitimacy in eastern Africa.

Since Eritrea achieved its independence in 1993 following the overthrow of the Stalinist government of Mengistu Haile Mariam in Addis Ababa, it has moved to establish a liberal and market-oriented republic; meanwhile, Ethiopia struggles to find an acceptable governing coalition for its different ethnic elites. Regarded as one of the poorest countries in Africa, Ethiopia enjoys the unique status of being the oldest empire on the continent;

hence, it is also weighed down by the political and economic backwardness of its feudal past. Whether the new regime will succeed in creating a culture of democratic governance will largely depend on how much progress is made in socioeconomic reforms and development. The latter, as elsewhere in Africa, is now jeopardized by major cuts in international development assistance programs at a time when all economic indicators show the need for an increase in the flow of resources toward Africa to stimulate economic growth. With growing poverty and very little to expect from Addis Ababa, ethnic nationalism is unlikely to subside in Ethiopia. While its internal conflicts may not necessarily reach the tragic level of Somalia, the internal instability will for some time delay the emergence of a republican nation-state—a project first conceived by Mengistu Haile Mariam.

Uganda's program of socioeconomic recovery, initiated by the National Resistance Movement (NRM) government of Yoweri Museveni in 1986, has been impressive. Not only have economic activities resumed with inflation reduced to single-digit proportions, but positive steps toward institutionalizing democracy have also been taken. Inter-ethnic suspicions, after decades of inter-ethnic conflicts, still abound. But these can only be assuaged by letting pluralist politics take place within legitimate institutions. The north, regarded as the center of power in the pre-NRM days, was devastated by civil war under both Idi Dada Amin and Museveni and still remains the area least integrated into the new political system of government through Resistance Councils. The restoration of democracy in Uganda will depend largely on the success of the NRM government in building a national coalition that will support a republican constitution embracing traditional values—like ethnic kingdoms—and modern, competitive party politics. But since capitalist development has stratified society largely along ethnic lines in the past, competition for resources—among the elite as well as the masses—remains ethnicized. A highly centralized political system may still be identified as that of the ethnic group from which the president comes and hence regarded as illegitimate by other ethnic groups. This crisis of illegitimacy is not confined to Uganda.

Kenya's authoritarian presidential regime, established under Jomo Kenyatta in 1964, remained stable and economically prosperous until the early 1980s when Danial Arap Moi was beginning to consolidate his power. The loss of revenue from export agriculture on account of deteriorating terms of trade beginning in the mid-1970s reduced the foreign-exchange earnings of the state, limiting its ability to reward or pay off the propertied elites from various ethnic groups on which it relied for support. The result was an escalation in bureaucratic corruption, leading to a series of intra-elite conflicts that heralded the rise of multiparty politics in the early 1990s. Without substantially transforming the institutions of the single-party state, the establishment of multiparty politics has remained as tenuous in Kenya as it is in Madagascar and the Seychelles. The ruling Kenya African National Union (KANU) stays in power through "carrot and stick" politics; that is, repression mixed with the buying of support from influential elites.

In eastern Africa, Mauritius remains the only prosperous, liberal democratic nation. Democracy in Mauritius has grown on the fertile ground of economic prosperity. In terms of promoting citizens' economic interests, Mauritius has done much better than its other Indian Ocean neighbors: the Comoros, Madagascar, and the Seychelles. The latter three, still very much dependent on France, have remained classical cases of underdevelopment in the service of external interests. In the Comoros, an authoritarian regime has held sway since the islands attained independence.

BIBLIOGRAPHY

Allen, Philip M. *Madagascar: Conflicts of Authority in the Great Island.* Boulder, Colo., 1995.

Holcomb, Bonnie K., and Sisai Ibssa. *The Invention of Ethiopia.* Trenton, N.J., 1990.

Issa-Salwe, Abdisalam M., and Cabdisalam M. Ciisa-Salwe. *The Collapse of the Somali State: The Impact of the Colonial Legacy.* London, 1994.

Mutibwa, Phares Mukasa. *Uganda since Independence: A Story of Unfulfilled Hopes.* Trenton, N.J., 1992.

Okwema, Michael. *Political Culture in Tanzania.* Lewiston, N.Y., 1996.

Sidahmed, Abdel Salam. *Politics and Islam in Contemporary Sudan.* New York, 1996.

Solomon, Joel A. *The Democratic Challenge: Freedom of Expression in Multi-Party Kenya, 1993.* Washington, D.C., 1994.

PETER ANYANG NYONGO

See also **Amin Dada, Idi; Ethnicity and Identity; Kenyatta, Jomo; Mengistu Haile Mariam; Moi, Daniel arap; Museveni, Yoweri; Neocolonialism; Nyerere, Julius Kambarage; Political Systems; Refugees.**

CENTRAL AFRICA

An enormous and diverse area, central Africa stretches from the Central African Republic and Gabon in the north and west to Zimbabwe and Mozambique in the southeast. This region's political heritage is equally disparate, having emerged as it did from hundreds of indigenous societies and cultures, as well as from four distinct colonial empires: British, Portuguese, Belgian, and French. Given these different backgrounds, it should not be surprising that since independence the thirteen states in this region have ranged from the relatively tranquil to those which have suffered from violent ethnic conflict, near-continuous civil war, and an almost complete dissolution of the state itself. Although the politics of the region's states thus defy facile generalization, it is nonetheless possible to discern broad patterns of political institutions and political behaviors which have occurred with some regularity throughout this area. But the timing and sequencing of these patterns have often varied markedly from state to state.

The Reign of Repression

With the exception of the Portuguese, whose own democratic regime was not fully in place at the time their empire—consisting of central Africa of Angola, Mozambique, and São Tomé and Príncipe—ended in the mid-1970s, the other colonial powers sought to bequeath to their former colonies some semblance of democratic governance. In general, the institutional forms of a particular colony were patterned after those of its controlling colonial power, or "metropole." The French left Congo, Gabon, Chad, and the Central African Republic with a state closely modeled on that of the strongly centralized presidential regime of the Gaullist Fifth French Republic. The British, of course, preferred to leave their former territories of the Central African Federation (Zambia, Rhodesia/Zimbabwe, Malawi) with states created in the image of the Westminster model of parliamentary democracy. The Belgians, beating a hasty retreat from empire in the early 1960s, sought to leave their former colonies (Congo/Zaire, Rwanda, Burundi) with governments resembling Belgium's constitutional monarchy. But however democratic these forms of governance might have been in Europe, their transplanted institutional roots did not long survive in African soil.

In the former British territories, ostensibly democratic regimes soon gave way to the realities of single-party rule under a politically dominant president in the person of Zambia's Kenneth Kaunda and Malawi's Kamuzu Banda. In 1970 the latter declared himself president-for-life, and the former might as well have done the same thing, for he thoroughly dominated Zambia's single-party government from 1964 until 1991. In Rhodesia the same pattern of strong presidential rule emerged after Ian Smith's Unilateral Declaration of Independence from Great Britain in 1965—but this time with the twist of an authoritarian state devoted to the interests of a white racial minority. Although Smith's regime gave way in 1980 to an independent, majority-ruled Zimbabwe after more than a decade of revolutionary guerrilla warfare, the new government of Robert Mugabe remained, in many ways, a less than democratic single-party–dominant regime under strong presidential leadership.

On the French-speaking side of the region a similar pattern also appeared, this time encouraged by occasional assistance from France. Whether civilian or military, strong, dictatorial, presidential figures soon dominated the political landscape. Both soldiers and civilians often felt the advisability of cloaking their rule in the garb of the then legitimate single-party system. This was certainly the case in Congo under a succession of military leaders culminating with Denis Sassou-Nguesso, as well as in the Central African Republic under the brutal tyranny of Jean-Bédel Bokassa. In Chad international interventions, civil war, and serious ethnic strife resulted in a drastic erosion of the state itself. In Gabon, French interventions ensured the continuity of single-party rule first under Léon Mba, and then under his chosen successor, Omar Bongo.

Zaire, Rwanda, and Burundi—former Belgian colonies—have suffered tragic fates. Ill-prepared for decolonization, the democratic fig leaves left in place by the departing colonial power did not last terribly long. All three of these states eventually followed the Mobutiste model of governance: centralized, tyrannical, and presidential rule by a "big man" through a patrimonial state and a single party. Mobutu Sese Seko seized power in a military coup in 1965 after years of civil strife, ethnic violence, and external interventions motored by the cold war.

Most Zairians initially welcomed his coup, and Mobutu enjoyed widespread legitimacy for a time. But by the mid-1970s falling copper prices, poor economic policy decisions, military adventures in Angola, excessive centralization, and an increasingly oppressive single-party regime all increased popular dissatisfaction. His regime became increasingly dependent on the dual props of internal repression (the political police and the armed forces) and external support (from France, Belgium, and the United States) to remain in power. High on Mobutu's agenda was using the state to accumulate personal wealth, and social class formation was an important subscript of political life among the rapacious Zairian bourgeoisie. In Rwanda and Burundi, however, the "big men" and those behind them had an agenda that seemed to place priority on ethnic factors. Tragically, both Rwanda and Burundi have been the scenes of postcolonial genocide.

Angola and Mozambique, the largest of the region's three lusophone states, have also been principal players in a political tragedy. Both states achieved independence in the mid-1970s after years of armed struggle against the Portuguese. Angola became a major theater of the cold war, with powerful external actors intervening militarily on the side of their preferred Angolan movements. Nationalist struggle, civil war, and cold war overlapped with devastating consequences. While a Marxist-Leninist regime under Agostinho Neto and then José Eduardo Dos Santos emerged in 1975, it was never able to control significant portions of the countryside. Mozambique also suffered, largely because a successful Mozambique was not in the interests of neighboring South Africa and because the latter state did all it could to subvert Samora Machel's Marxist-Leninist government.

The end of the cold war has ended the dominance of single-party, presidentially dominated regimes in central Africa. In the late 1980s and early 1990s, long-serving tyrants began to encounter populations who were no longer willing to suffer and erstwhile international allies who had lost interest in supporting them against their own people. Demand for multiparty regimes increased everywhere, as long-ruling autocrats left the political scene either peacefully through elections or national conferences (Kaunda in Zambia, Sassou-Nguesso in Congo, Banda in Malawi) or through more violent means (Juvénal Habyarimana in Rwanda). Other leaders, such as Zaire's Mobutu, were increasingly besieged but were able, at least for a while, to hijack democratic movements and still cling to power.

The Reasons for Repression

Central Africa has been an area characterized by repressive authoritarian rule for several reasons.

First, the colonial experience was not democratic. Colonialism was a system of political control, not political freedom. When independence arrived, therefore, this authoritarian model was the most proximate and influential historical referent for most of the peoples of the region.

Second, the colonial powers did not create an independent bourgeoisie. Their main economic goal was the exploitation of primary materials, not the creation of a class of African entrepreneurs and industrialists capable of competing with metropolitan economic interests. African opportunities for capital accumulation were restricted. And because these were so limited, when independence came politicians usually used the state as a resource-in-itself. The state thus became the major source of wealth because there was only a minimal private sector and virtually no industrialization. Since the state was the only resource available, political struggles for its control often became zero-sum games. Losing political power also meant losing economic wealth and security.

Third, the easiest way to mobilize political support in these struggles has been through appeals to ethnic identity. Even if their aim is not ultimately an ethnic one, politicians have cynically manipulated their own identities as well as those of others to achieve power. In this regard, perhaps because they have been afraid to lose power and wealth, many politicians in the region have failed to educate the population. They have been content, in other words, to resort to the same thinly veiled ethnic appeals about what will happen to "our" slice of the "national cake" if one of "them" is elected, selected, or chosen instead of one of "us."

Fourth, politicians in the region have served themselves rather than serving their compatriots. Many of them have displayed, and profited from, an extraordinary cupidity. Furthermore, considering points three and four together, it is difficult to escape the conclusion that there has been a failure of political leadership.

Lastly, international forces (apartheid, the cold war) have contributed to political dynamics that have been detrimental to democratic rule. A stable, authoritarian regimen was often better suited to Western interests than a more unpredictable democratic one. Similarly, the Soviets usually encouraged variants of their own Marxist-Leninist dictatorship.

Unfortunately, the results of these factors have been a series of human tragedies: political repression, ethnic violence, civil wars, external interventions, declining economies, and the dissolution of the state coupled with a serious tear in the fabric of civil society. But the region is complex and diverse; Zaire has fallen farther than Zimbabwe, Gabon is not Rwanda. Whether any of these political, social, or economic catastrophes can change under the sway of the new, more liberal political currents sweeping the region remains to be seen.

BIBLIOGRAPHY

Finnegan, William. *A Complicated War: The Harrowing of Mozambique.* Berkeley, Calif., 1992.
Gaulme, François. *Le Gabon et son ombre.* Paris, 1988.
Kriger, Norma. *Zimbabwe's Guerrilla War: Peasant Voices.* New York, 1992.
Lemarchand, René. *Burundi: Ethnocide as Discourse and Practice.* Washington, D.C., 1994.
Marcum, John A. *The Angolan Revolution.* 2 vols. Cambridge, Mass., 1969, 1978.
Newbury, Catharine. *The Cohesion of Oppression: Citizenship and Ethnicity in Rwanda, 1860–1960.* New York, 1988.
Schatzberg, Michael G. *The Dialectics of Oppression in Zaire.* Bloomington, Ind., 1988.
Young, Crawford, and Thomas Turner. *The Rise and Decline of the Zairian State.* Madison, Wis., 1985.

MICHAEL G. SCHATZBERG

See also **Banda, Kamuzu; Bokassa, Jean-Bédel; Colonial Policies and Practice; Genocide, Violence, and Civil Society; Geopolitics; Kaunda, Kenneth; Mobutu Sese Seko; Mugabe, Robert; Neto, Agostinho.**

SOUTHERN AFRICA

Postcolonial southern African states are distinctive for their relative administrative capacity and their fairly effective governance. Analysis of African states has identified a prevalent set of weaknesses: uncertain territorial jurisdiction, underperformance, overconsumption of limited resources, external dependency, corruption, and the privatization of public resources by unproductive ruling groups. No southern African state is entirely free of these shortcomings, but they affect the functioning of government less in this region than elsewhere in Africa. Southern African states differ from most African postcolonial states in having stronger or at least longer established traditions of legitimation and political continuity. In several countries the formation of the modern state has been facilitated by the congruence of frontiers with precolonial political boundaries: Lesotho, Botswana,

Swaziland, Zimbabwe, and in certain respects South Africa have benefited from this. In the cases of South Africa and Zimbabwe especially, complete sovereignty, or at least considerable political autonomy for most of the century, has enabled their administrations to develop a degree of social impermeability. State autonomy is also facilitated by what are in African terms quite well-developed capitalist class structures in relatively diversified economies; especially in South Africa, Zimbabwe, Botswana, and Swaziland, the state is less significant than elsewhere on the continent as a nexus of class formation and hence can function more independently of specific social forces. These qualities reflect the comparatively sophisticated bureaucratic development required to administer a labor-repressive mining economy that evolved at the turn of the century; fairly extensive secondary industrialization in South Africa and Zimbabwe, and sharply differentiated social structures that include large and well-organized working classes and correspondingly vigorous industrial, commercial, and agricultural bourgeoisies.

Four criteria are helpful in assessing state capacity in developing countries: institutional autonomy, social penetration, legitimate authority, and bureaucratic rationality. Autonomy refers to the extent to which the state is distanced from society and can determine and implement its policies unrestrained by particular social interests. Social penetration is evident in the degree of control the state can exercise over society, its extractive capability, and the extent to which it meets social needs. Authority can rest upon ideological and legitimating devices as well as the effectiveness of repressive agencies. Bureaucratic rationality is expressed in the relative absence of corruption, the existence of an institutional corporate culture within state agencies, and the levels of professionalism and competence of civil servants.

Institutional Autonomy

Until recently, racial exclusiveness helped to reinforce the state's autonomy in South Africa, as did a degree of social and cultural distance between political and economic elites. Independence from these elites is partly attributable to the relative strength of what David Yudelman has termed a "legitimation imperative" arising from the institution of democratic politics (for whites) before the creation of an industrial society (*The Emergence of Modern South Africa*, pp. 38–39). This helped to explain the state's attentiveness to the needs of farm-

ers despite the competing labor claims of business. In relatively economically diversified Zimbabwe the state has been able to maintain a balance between the interests of different sectors of capital, notwithstanding the powerful influence exercised by settler agriculture; in certain respects the ascendency of an African nationalist governing class in 1980 has strengthened state autonomy. The government has been able to resist urban pressures for cheap food and maintain pricing policies that are generally favorable to rural producers and to smallholder peasants especially. Crop marketing boards remain exceptionally efficient and, in contrast to the experience north of the Zambezi, continue to invest their surpluses in the countryside. Sophisticated financial regulatory institutions developed during the Unilateral Declaration of Independence period had been by 1990 rather successful in directing foreign investment to promote a more competitive domestic industry; these gains have since been largely dissipated by overhasty tariff reductions.

Representative politics established relatively early for Namibian settlers also helped to advance the fortunes of a commercial farming class, but until independence, state policies remained subordinate to South African economic priorities and this ruled out any local manufacturing or processing. Democratic politics under a government of former guerrillas has accelerated a growing Africanization of the ranching class. This, together with the purchase of equity shareholding in the diamond industry (which supplies about half of public revenues) helps to keep government policies business-friendly and social reform gradual. With respect to Botswana, the social connections of a landowning rancher class and the political elite are very intimate; here the state's measure of social insulation is a reflection of the idiosyncratic preferences of an aristocratic ruling group whose economic base was well established before decolonization. Retaining the services of a large group of expatriate technocrats helped to protect the bureaucracy from social pressure.

Several of the structural predeterminants of Botswana state autonomy were present in early postcolonial Malawi and Swaziland, most notably the existence of a landowning class; the possibility of capital accumulation outside the state already existed. In the case of colonial Malawi, estate agriculture was foreign-owned and the creation of an indigenous group of commercial farmers depended upon public finance. Much of the sector was to be owned by President Kamuzu Banda's personal parastatal, Press Holdings. In Swaziland plantation revenues from multinational corporations supplied the capital of a royal holding company, the Tibiyo Taka Ngwane. In these two countries, in contrast to Botswana, state power was employed to create huge patrimonial estates in which the distinction between the private and public domain became very blurred indeed. In Lesotho an extreme degree of external fiscal dependence places severe contraints on state autonomy; for over two decades after independence a government representing junior chiefs consolidated the fortunes of this group through adroit exploitation of donor agencies' susceptibilities to accord Lesotho a special position in their priorities. Of all the southern African countries, though, Zambia resembles the most stereotypical "economy of affection." There, the state served as the main motor of indigenous class formation and a swiftly expanding public sector supplied a generous field of political patronage. Notwithstanding the presence of an expanding entrepreneurial class within the bureaucracy, state activity was mainly geared to consumption rather than accumulation, much of it in the form of generous subsidies to strategically placed political constituencies.

Social Penetration

In Angola and Mozambique violent decolonization allowed insurgent elites to capture political power. In Angola three separate liberation struggles left state power in the hands of an *evolué* grouping already well represented in the colonial civil service and largely drawn from a creole elite in Luanda. In Mozambique the victorious guerrilla leadership embraced a wider social range, but FRELIMO's urban leadership's antipathy to the chiefly colonial collaborators ensured hostility to its policies in many parts of the countryside. In both cases the ruling groups were ideologically and culturally distinctive, and their initial policies suggested a freedom from the communal and moral restraints that bound other African states to prevalent social conventions. Even without the force of external military aggression, though, the frail and permeable foundations of state power in these two territories would have made the "revolutions from above" contemplated by their governments impossibly ambitious. In each of the four territories in which the state's internal freedom of maneuver was quite limited—Lesotho, Zambia, Mozambique, and Angola—the government developed extreme external fiscal dependency and foreign indebtedness that today detract significantly from their sovereignty.

With the exception of the former Portuguese territories, state reach in southern African countries is extensive either because it reflects substantial bureaucratic systems of repression and control developed during the colonial period in quite diversified modern economies (as in Rhodesia [later, Zimbabwe], Namibia, and South Africa) or because of the very small size of the territories (Swaziland and Lesotho) or the relative density or concentration of population and social networks (Malawi and Zambia). Until the mid-1980s South Africa maintained an extensive apparatus to control the geographical movement of black workers, in this process arresting three hundred thousand "pass offenders" every year. The degree of administrative social penetration deepened in the 1960s with the institution of almost universal primary education and the provision of (very meager and racially inequitable) pensions to all adults. To maintain these services an enormous bureaucracy developed, employing 1,081,000 people in 1994. In Lesotho and Malawi state penetration was chiefly manifest in the power of repressive agencies that were built on earlier networks of pervasive nationalist mobilization, which themselves reflected the depth of proletarianization through migrant labor. State access to mineral wealth permitted the expansion of subsidies, welfare services, and social security on a considerable scale in Zambia during the 1960s and early 1970s and, more recently, in Botswana. Relatively efficient state distributive networks in Botswana date from an unusually effective colonial famine-relief system, an institutional response to an especially harsh climatic environment.

In Zambia, Lesotho, and Malawi shrinking resources and foreign indebtedness have led to a geographical contraction of the state and its effective disappearance from remoter rural areas. Counterinsurgency campaigns in Rhodesia and Namibia during the 1970s and 1980s encouraged colonial states to reorganize settlement and expand welfare services to an extent well beyond the normal reach of colonial states elsewhere in Africa. Counterinsurgency in Mozambique and Angola also strengthened state capacity and supplied some of the impetus for postcolonial social engineering efforts in former "protected villages." Civil wars and South African "destabilization" put an end to any efforts to expand the scope of state institutions in Mozambique and Angola, and in contemporary peacetime Mozambique the state's fiscal dependency has led to a direct usurpation of its functions by foreign nongovernmental organizations.

Authority

Obviously, state authority is closely tied to the effectiveness of its repressive and welfare components. To be sure, that authority can be considered legitimate simply if the majority of a repressive state's subjects perceive no conceivable alternative to its rule; outside of South Africa before 1976, and Rhodesia before the inception of peasant-based guerrilla warfare, no southern African state possessed coercive power on a sufficient scale to rule without ideological forms of legitimation. Even in South Africa, racially limited representative democracy and accompanying liberal institutions formed a significant component of state rule and probably affected values and expectations among a large section of the disenfranchised. Liberal democracy has shaped the postcolonial histories of Botswana, Namibia, and Zimbabwe. In Zambia the existence of a strategically placed and very well-organized labor movement quite independent from the control of the ruling party compelled the state to invest heavily in ideological activity and to allow measures of freedom and choice within the constraints of one-party politics. In Swaziland traditional patrimonialism, and in Lesotho and Malawi neotraditionalist discourses, help to sustain the state's authority, but in these cases ideology probably has had less to do with the long survival of autocratic government than the relative ease of governing geographically small countries, and in the case of Swaziland, the state's relative wealth. In Angola the state's ideological legitimacy was contested from its inception and it has yet to obtain territorial hegemony; this reflects an especially fragmented expansion of colonial society in three distinctive regions within the country. In Mozambique the postcolonial state might have fared better had it not adopted ideologies and programs so much at odds with the beliefs and aspirations of most rural people.

Bureaucratic Rationality

To what extent has postcolonial southern Africa been administered by effective and rule-regulated bureaucracies geared to developmental ethics? South Africa, Namibia, settler Rhodesia, and modern Botswana evolved professionalized and technically competent bureaucracies, and direct political interference remains quite limited. Arguably, in the case of South Africa, socially exclusive recruitment detracted from efficiency, but the Public Service Commission generally succeeded in curbing personalized forms of patronage by politicians. In Malawi, as in Botswana, the long period during which expatriate experts were retained helped to socially insulate the civil service. Compared with many African countries, relatively slow rates of bureaucratic expansion have helped to maintain bureaucratic quality. In Zambia and Lesotho bureaucratic growth was from very modest starting points, for in both these countries colonial governments delegated administrative and welfare functions to private agencies to an unusual extent. Zimbabwe's administration expanded swiftly after 1980, matching the proliferation of services, but this growth merely maintained the momentum of the counter-insurgency period and included a significant demilitarization. After South Africa, the largest public service is Zambia's but its 180,000 workforce of 1995 remains smaller than the Ghanaian bureaucracy in 1960.

Civil services have been least effective where their functions have been replicated by party or parastatal structures and where political leaders have prevailed in recruitment and promotion; Zambia, Lesotho, Mozambique, and Angola are all cases in point. In South Africa, Zimbabwe, Botswana, Swaziland, and more arguably, Malawi and Namibia, the state has been rather successful in promoting local accumulation of capital both within and outside the public sector; in Lesotho, Mozambique, Zambia, and Angola the state's deployment of resources has tended to be more wasteful, geared toward either consumption or warfare. In all these territories the factors that are generally held to cause political corruption—the persistence of precolonial tributary obligations, the status insecurity of emergent (as opposed to established) elites, institutional expansion and proliferation, and comparatively undifferentiated social formations—have been less of a feature of the political system than elsewhere in Africa, and hence bureaucratic venality has generally been less pervasive.

Conclusion

As noted above, the historical roots of modern states are deeper in this region than elsewhere in Africa; in addition, the existence in the region of diversified and complex capitalist economies as well as the bureaucratic requirements of large-scale labor mobilization help to explain the evolution of

477

comparatively resilient and effective state structures in southern Africa. To this might be added, notwithstanding its damaging effect on the former Portuguese territories, the impact on state formation of militarization and warfare, as well as the integrative role played by fairly vigorous working-class mobilization, and relatively early development of state programs of legitimation arising from the presence of enfranchised settler minorities. Finally, the existence of developmentally effective states in the region seems more or less to coincide with those societies in which early modern state formation was closely linked to the consolidation of a local agricultural bourgeoisie. Southern African state hardness is derived from structural features of the region's political economy and historical characteristics that distinguish it quite sharply from the rest of postcolonial Africa.

BIBLIOGRAPHY

Birmingham, David. "Angola Revisited." *Journal of Southern African Studies* 15, no. 1 (1988): 1–14.

Bratton, Michael. "The Public Service in Zimbabwe." *Political Science Quarterly* 95, no. 3 (1980): 441–464.

Finnegan, William. *A Complicated War: The Harrowing of Mozambique.* Berkeley, Calif., 1992.

Good, Kenneth. "Interpreting the Exceptionality of Botswana." *Journal of Modern African Studies* 30, no. 1 (1992): 69–95.

Herbst, Jeffrey. *State Politics in Zimbabwe.* Berkeley, Calif., 1990.

Lehman, Howard P. "The Paradox of State Power in Africa: Debt Management Policies in Kenya and Zimbabwe." *African Studies Review* 35, no. 2 (1992): 1–34.

Leys, Colin, and John Saul, eds. *Namibia's Liberation Struggle.* London, 1995

Mhone, Guy C., ed. *Malawi at the Crossroads: The Post Colonial Political Economy.* Harare, Zimbabwe, 1992.

Picard, Louis A. *The Politics of Development in Botswana.* Boulder, Colo., 1987.

Seegers, Annette. "Towards an Understanding of the Afrikanerisation of the South African State." *Africa* 63, no. 4 (1993): 477–497.

Strom, Gabrielle. *Migration and Development: A Study of Lesotho.* Uppsala, Sweden, 1986.

Trapido, Stanley. "Political Institutions and Afrikaner Social Structures in the Republic of South Africa." *American Political Science Review* 57, no. 1 (1963): 75–87.

Turok, Ben. "Zambia's System of State Capitalism." *Development and Change* 11, no. 3 (1980): 455–478.

Yudelman, David. *The Emergence of Modern South Africa.* Westport, Conn., 1983.

TOM LODGE

See also **Apartheid; Class, Rank, and Caste; Colonialism and Imperialism; Development; Education; Gender: Social Contexts; Government; Law; Minerals and Metals; Professionalization.**

POTTERY. Pottery is among the oldest arts of Africa. In Kenya it is documented from the Upper Paleolithic era and in Saharan sites from as far back as the eighth millennium B.C.E. Its prevalence is in part accounted for by the wide availability of clay across Africa, where it is a very versatile material. Apart from its use in the manufacture of vessels for cooking, storing, and measuring bulk items, clay in various forms is also used to make jewelry, wigs, furniture, paint, coffins, beehives, toys, essential elements of architecture, sieves, grindstones, musical instruments—even rattraps. At the other end of its career, pottery has value in its broken form as gaming chips, floor tiles, spindle weights, roundels, and grog (powdered terra-cotta to temper clay) for making new pots.

Although molds may nowadays be used in industrial production, sub-Saharan pottery has traditionally been handmade without the use of the wheel. The technical simplicity of African pottery has made possible the existence of itinerant potters. Modern analyses have tended to stress the distinctiveness of traditional pottery styles rather than the ways in which they overlap and interrelate. Common traditional techniques include coiling, pulling, and beating (where a depression in the ground or an old pot may be used as a form for new pots.) Such techniques, while extremely simple, require great manual skill and produce pottery more quickly, inexpensively, and of greater strength than is possible on a wheel. Baking may be done over an open bonfire or in fires using retaining walls or pits, or in simple kilns. Decorative finishes come from burnishing, incised patterning, roulettes, colored slips, and vegetable infusions. African pottery combines total utility and great beauty.

Those west African cultures studied by art historians—Jenne, Sao, Igbo-Ukwu, Nok, and Ife—are known among other things for their terra-cotta works, which show great continuity with contemporary pots. Igbo-Ukwu pottery of the ninth and tenth centuries, for example, shows strong stylistic similarities with modern Igbo forms.

The West normally divides clay objects into the figurative (art) and the functional (craft). The distinction coincides approximately with one often made in Africa between figurative forms, which

Three linked human figures. COURTESY OF THE
TRUSTEES OF THE BRITISH MUSEUM, LONDON

are largely made by men, and functional vessels made by women. It is a widely held belief in Africa that making images of animals or men in clay endangers female procreative powers. Domestic pots are overwhelmingly made by women and the physical skills involved—kneading, grinding, plastering—are often those gained elsewhere in female life. Potting in Africa has few of the genteel associations it has in the West. It is demanding physical labor, and pots must often be transported for long distances before sale. Yet the male/female distinction is far from hard and fast and in terms of local gender definitions, postmenopausal or politically and ritually powerful women may well be classed as male. Since such women are allowed to make images, much early ethnography becomes difficult to interpret; to understand the rules of pottery production, age as well as sex must be known. In eastern Africa, women may model images but only in unbaked clay, as among the Cewa. It is clear

that in contemporary Africa, traditional divisions between male and female modeling have had to be stretched to cope with the successful introduction of cement sculpture. To determine which gender makes it, a decision must be made about whether it is pottery or sculpture, and different cultures come to different conclusions. Moreover, there are areas, such as Grasslands Cameroon, where both genders pot but use different techniques. Women may form clay while men carve it. Since earliest contacts, however, Europeans have found that the most publicly important pots tend to be made exclusively by a few old women and have wrongly taken this as firm evidence that pottery in Africa is an art form about to disappear.

As in the West, vessels classify contents, users, and events. Palm wine is not drunk out of the bowl that sauce is cooked in. A widow might well have to use a vessel formally distinct from that of a married man or a child, so different classes of pots lend themselves to the marking off of different classes of people. Thus, the Sirak use a vegetable pot to bury the placenta of a baby girl but a meat pot for that of a boy, while a fertile mother may have her tomb marked by a flour storage bowl. While he is in an urban beer hall a Zulu man might drink out of a jam jar or plastic cup, but on formal occasions he would use a burnished clay bowl with an ornate cover (*imbenge*) and demonstrate great care for the etiquette of precedence. Nowadays that cover might well be woven from multicolored telephone wire, but the patterns would be traditional. In the everyday grammar of use, African pottery competes with wooden, basketry, and calabash vessels as well as china, aluminum, and enamelware. While in some parts of the continent pottery is being displaced by expensive imports and increasingly restricted to a ritual role, in others it is staging something of a comeback in elegant urban settings and even moving into the "art" category. The status of pottery differs across contemporary sub-Saharan Africa.

Pots are not only commodities in the African marketplace but instruments of patron-client relations. There is a widespread convention that the price of a pot is the grain that it can contain. Since their price is not subject to negotiation, pots have a special place in exchange relationships, being outside the commerical sphere.

A factor tending to complicate neat Western distinctions is that, at the village level, African pottery often moves quite easily between "ritual" and "everyday" uses. Potted vessels may act as containers of all sorts of spiritual forces, transforming domestic utensils into articles of spiritual significance. A pot that has served for years for the hauling of water may overnight become the dwelling place of a dead woman's spirit (*dowayo*), and the rough handling of a Shona woman's quite ordinary kitchen pots by her husband may be seen as the most explicit of formal insults in a complex language of female sexuality.

It is often said glibly that the West uses the models of natural science to talk about society whereas Africa uses social models to talk about nature. Yet the technology of pottery is widely used in African social thought to inform ideas of the body, life, disease, death, and female powers. It is a common basis for myths of creation but acts much more widely as what George Lakoff has termed a "scenario"—that is, a basic experience used to structure other experiences. A frequent model in west Africa is a woman who is both potter and midwife while her husband is smith and undertaker. The marginal, caste-like position of such artisanal groups—which are often endogamous, live apart, and have strongly regulated contact with outsiders—has long been something of an obsession with Western researchers. Many different arrangements for the production of pots have been documented, from individual women working alone or in groups to rigid guild-like arrangements.

The ritual importance of pottery has been almost totally obscured by a Western preoccupation with metalworking as an epoch-making male activity, the potter being seen as a mere domestic adjunct of her husband. Pottery, however, is just as likely to enter into rituals of transformation and the "thermodynamic philosophies" of cool and hot as are male metalworking skills. To generalize enormously, very broad themes can be traced across sub-Saharan cultures whereby the childbearing powers of women are seen as analogous to the potting process. Parts of bodies (especially women's) are regularly equated with pottery forms, so that death involves the breaking of old pots while marriage involves the making of new ones. Pottery, however, is a versatile idiom. Grinding down a shard from an old vessel and recasting it as part of a new one is a powerful way of creating identity through time, while the molding of new pots over old among the Senufo offers a culturally acceptable vision of the relations between successive generations.

Inevitably, this involves questions of power. Among the northern Sudanese villagers studied by Janice Boddy, gestation is equated with the preparation of dough in a special leakproof vessel, different from the porous jar used for storing water. Miscarried fetuses are buried in such a watertight pot inside the house. In this culture of pharaonic circumcision, marriage of close kin, and inward-focused architecture, pottery reflects social boundaries and the control of female apertures.

The decoration of sub-Saharan African pottery raises fundamental questions of interpretation. Given the frequent linkage made between pots and the human form in Africa, it is hardly surprising that many of the patterns on pots are the same as those on bodies. Cicatrization is among body arts of sub-Saharan Africa most neglected by scholars, being simultaneously under attack from Islam and secular modernism. Sub-Saharan pottery similarly stresses incised or embossed differences of texture rather than color and warns us that in both pottery and the arts of the body, we may be dealing with an African aesthetic very unlike that dominant in the West, one of touch rather than vision, of the hand rather than the eye.

BIBLIOGRAPHY

Aschwanden, Hans. *Symbols of Life.* Zimbabwe, 1982.

Barley, Nigel. *Smashing Pots: Feats of Clay from Africa.* London, 1994.

Boddy, Janice. "Womb as Oasis: The Symbolic Context of Pharaonic Circumcision in Rural Northern Sudan." *American Ethnologist* 9, no. 4 (1982): 682–698.

Cline, Walter. *Mining and Metallurgy in Negro Africa.* Menasha, Wis., 1937.

Heusch, Luc de. "Heat, Physiology, and Cosmogeny: *Rites de Passage* among the Thonga." In *Explorations in African Systems of Thought,* edited by Ivan Karp and Charles S. Bird. Bloomington, Ind., 1980.

Lakoff, George. *Women, Fire, and Dangerous Things: What Categories Reveal about the Mind.* Chicago, 1987.

Leith-Ross, Sylvia. *Nigerian Pottery: A Catalogue.* Ibadan, Nigeria, 1970.

Röeschenthaler, Ute. *Die Kunst der Frauen: Zur Komplimentarität von Nacktheit und Maskierung bei den Ejagham im Südwesten Kameruns.* Berlin, 1993.

Rubin, Arnold, ed. *Marks of Civilization: Artistic Transformations of the Human Body.* Los Angeles, 1988.

Sterner, Judy. "Who is Signalling Whom? Ceramic Style, Ethnicity, and Taphonomy among the Sirak Bulahay." *Antiquity* 63 (Sept. 1989): 451–459.

Stössel, Arnulf. *Afrikanische Keramik: Südlich der Sahara.* Munich, 1984.

Yoshida, Kenji. "Masks and Transformation among the Chewa of Eastern Zambia." *Senri Ethnological Studies,* no. 31 (1992): 203–274.

NIGEL BARLEY

See also **Art; Geometries; Symbolism.**

PREHISTORY. *See* **Archaeology and Prehistory.**

PREHISTORY AND THE STUDY OF AFRICA

Archaeology and the "Roots of Backwardness"

> If in any sense there is a single "Africa problem" it is nothing less than to bring civilisation to Africa—life more abundant for all its inhabitants. . . . It is no flattery to the intelligence of Africans to suppose them lacking in ambition to acquire not only our mechanical and material efficiency, but that spiritual freedom, unknown to tribal society. . . . Against the fear and insecurity of primitive life unaided, Africans have shown themselves powerless. For the first time science and the arts give them real hope. (W. M. Macmillan, *Africa Emergent*, 1938, pp. 13, 16–17)

> By comparison with the role it played during the earlier stages of prehistory Africa had . . . already relapsed into provincialism during the late Pleistocene. From this time much of the continent remained a kind of cultural museum in which archaic cultural traditions . . . continued to adapt to ecological change and even on occasion to display idiosyncratic variations without contributing to the main course of human progress. (Grahame Clark, *World Prehistory*, 1969, p. 181)

These quotations illustrate how the scientific conclusions of archaeology came to reinforce the colonial enterprise. The first quotation was written by one of the British Empire's leading academics and propagandists in a book that became the obligatory reading for aspiring postwar colonial administrators. The spirit of the age was captured in chapter headings such as "The Mission of Civilisation in Africa" and "The Roots of Backwardness." Here, in the supposed primitiveness of African society, lay the justification for the colonial enterprise, and with it the wholesale introduction of Western civilization.

The second quotation comes from an influential textbook written by the late Sir Grahame Clark, a leading prehistorian of his generation, setting out what remained a widespread view until as late as the 1970s. In an earlier edition (published in 1961), Clark claimed that in Africa, primitive Lower Paleolithic cultural traditions continued down to recent times, and that by 30,000 B.C.E., Europe was already superior to some modern African societies.

For much of its past, African society was indeed prehistoric, in the sense that written sources do not survive, or were written by outside, partial observers. Archaeologists, for whom the absence of written documents is of no great concern, should have been uniquely placed to challenge the colonial orthodoxy that Africa was a primitive backwater, ripe for Western improvement, with their own evidence.

But it is only now, a full generation after the "winds of change," that a new and radical view of African prehistory is emerging. According to this view, Africa is not a museum piece, a meaningless gyration of "tribes" but a dynamic and innovative continent that made major contributions to the development of the ancient and medieval worlds. While details of many of these new views can be found in the archaeological entries in this encyclopedia, I have chosen examples that I believe highlight this new thinking in African prehistory.

The Origins of Humankind

One of the main achievements of African archaeology in recent years has been its contribution to the debate about the origins of humankind. From the first suggestions of Charles Darwin—"It is somewhat more probable that our early progenitors lived on the African continent than elsewhere. But it is useless to speculate upon the subject" (1874, p. 240)—to the discoveries of Australopithecines in southern Africa and the pioneering work of the Leakeys in eastern Africa, culminating in claims for the genus *Homo* at 1.8 million years, with its clear links to a stone-tool industry known as the Oldowan, few now doubt that Africa was the main center of early human evolution.

However, it has been on the subsequent stages of the evolutionary story that recent opinion has been sharply divided. Two schools of thought have developed. One, the "multiregionalist," accepts only one radiation, around 1 million B.P., of early hominids from Africa—probably *Homo erectus*—with its associated Acheulean industry, and then postulates that evolution continued across the Eurasian landmass, through a common gene pool, to archaic *Homo sapiens*, *H. sapiens neanderthalis*, and *H. sapiens sapiens*.

The "out of Africa" school suggests that sub-Saharan Africa was the center of several stages in human evolution. There were successive *Homo* radiations out of Africa; each successive radiation, because of improved intellectual ability and developed culture, displaced the more primitive *Homo* populations. The evolution of modern humans can be recognized in eastern and southern Africa, during the period 200,000–150,000 B.P., from both skeletal and cultural remains associated with a very advanced Middle Stone Age. The populations of modern humans moved into western Asia and Europe around 100,000 B.P., displacing Neanderthals by around 50,000 B.P. This model not only has impressive archaeological support but is also predicated on global population studies of mitochondrial DNA.

This debate has wider implications. One concerns the nature of human racial differences. According to the multiregional model, the racial differences of modern populations extend back to the very early spread of *Homo* a million years ago, whereas the "out of Africa" model stresses how very recent these differences are, and that they are heavily dependent upon environmental factors. The prehistory of Africa, if the "out of Africa" model proves to be correct—and it is supported by the overwhelming proportion of academic evidence—shows how modern human populations are closely related, and that perhaps up to around half the time that modern humans have existed, it was in sub-Saharan Africa.

Environmental Solutions

One of the accusations of colonial writers has been that African society was slow to climb the "ladder of civilization"—there was no Neolithic revolution able to generate surpluses enabling the development of towns, writing, states, and thus civilization. At the base of this ladder lie the human food revolution and the observation that in Africa, crop production developed many millennia later than in western Asia.

A basic question that the prehistory of Africa poses is why bother to domesticate at all. From the modern studies of hunter-gatherer communities, from the !Kung and Hadza, it is now widely recognized that these groups are well adapted to their environment, and are able to survive with relatively little time devoted to food collection. They were, in Marshall Sahlins's classic phrase, the "original affluent society." Domestication is an option for societies that mismanage or are unable to cope with their environment. In the African environment, with the longest tradition of human occupation, modern humans had worked out how to live successfully without the need to domesticate crops.

Attempts to find evidence of a Neolithic revolution in sub-Saharan Africa, comparable with that in Asia, have largely failed, and there still is very little evidence for the early domestication of crops

in sub-Saharan Africa. This is partly due to problems of preservation in the archaeological record; the desiccated soils of the Near East preserve cereals, whereas the tropical soils of Africa are less likely to do so. Certain African domesticates, such as yams, have only recently been recovered archaeologically and survive only under certain conditions. Ironically, the earliest evidence for domesticated African crops—sorghum, finger and pearl millet—comes not from Africa but from Oman and India. This could imply an early trade in African crops or the exchange of wild cereals that were later domesticated in Asia. Where Near Eastern domesticates spread into sub-Saharan Africa, they are found generally after 4000 B.P. in Ethiopia and do not extend significantly further south until the colonial period.

One reason may be that the domestication of basic food crops was not sufficiently advantageous to African society. This was partly due to the nature of the tropical African plants themselves, with their relatively low yields and a much less spectacular increase through domestication than was achieved by Near Eastern barley and wheat. Large areas of available wild cereals, and few geographical restraints on movement across the savannas of eastern Africa and the Sahel, exerted little pressure to intensify production. An unstable climate pattern during the early Holocene may have been a further disincentive.

Linked to this debate is the evidence that Africa was the earliest global center of cattle domestication; perhaps as early as 10,000 B.P. is suggested by recent finds in the eastern Sahara. These finds are up to 2,000 years older than evidence found in the Near East, and while this evidence remains controversial, it is certain that cattle keepers were present in the Sahara at the same time as cattle were in the supposed center of domestication in western Asia. The Sahara was, even in the early Holocene, a very difficult place to live, and is a likely place for environmental pressures to encourage the domestication process.

The African pastoralist groups spread south and west with the changing climate and eventual desiccation of the Sahara, and by 5000 B.P. they occupied much of the Sahel and savannas. There is no evidence that they cultivated crops; rather, they relied upon the skilled collection of wild cereals and plants, which were processed using stone bowls. The pastoralist societies of this area today are successful managers of a fragile environment, having developed social and economic means to live in an area that Western agriculture is unable to exploit.

The development of crop-based economies across much of sub-Saharan Africa dates to 2500 B.P., and was based on a mixture of locally domesticated crops and the introduction of non-African plants, such as bananas and plantains from Southeast Asia. There is no doubt that this led to an increased population, the exploitation of tropical forested areas, and the spread of farmers to areas previously occupied by hunter-gatherer groups.

When colonial administrators and settlers first came in contact with African communities, they were quick to condemn their farming practice, which was often based upon swidden or slash-and-burn systems; they argued this was wasteful of land and uneconomic. The archaeological record shows that African farmers were quite able to adopt intensification practices where conditions were suitable—examples include Nyanga terraces in eastern Zimbabwe, Engaruka in central Tanzania, and the Sirikwa complex in Kenya. But for much of the continent, these systems were quite unsuited, and Western-inspired attempts to intensify indigenous agriculture have almost always failed.

Technology and Art

African society is often seen as technologically conservative and backward. Throughout Eurasia, archaeologists can follow a broad progression from Stone Age to Bronze Age to Iron Age—the three-age system that underpins much of chronological and cultural classification. The system had its origin in eighteenth-century Scandinavia, where it was used to classify ancient artifacts, and was then applied to northern European and later to Mediterranean and Asian prehistory.

In Africa the three-age system does not work. There is no Bronze Age, and the so-called Stone Age continued in some areas into the modern era as hunter-gatherer communities. The Iron Age spread rapidly across Africa, from center and west to the east and south, in the hands of migrating farmers who, it is widely believed, displaced the hunter-gatherers and pastoralist groups with their new technology. Since this new technology—ironworking—was comparatively complex, compared with the working of copper and bronze, many prehistorians and archaeologists looked for an outside agency for its introduction. Meroë was seen as the main candidate; its large slag heaps provided evidence for iron production on an industrial scale, and it was located at the southern end of a trade route that followed the Nile to Europe and the Mediterranean.

In recent years, evidence has built up against this interpretation. In the first place, the technology of African iron smelting is quite different from that observed at Meroë, and second, radiocarbon dates of iron from central and eastern Africa considerably predate any of the Meroitic ironworking. While other routes across the Sahara are possible, it is now broadly accepted that African ironworking developed independently, with distinctive furnace designs, bellows, the use of preheated air, and the production of various types of steel.

A similar case can be made for other metalworking technologies. The extraordinary copper, bronze, and brass objects of central and western Africa were based upon a mastery of highly complex operations. Despite many attempts to see outside agencies as the prime movers in these magnificent works of art, the consensus remains that much is of indigenous origin, with a clear, logical development from the use of terra-cotta to the use of metal. The use of lost-wax casting and the mining and refining of copper are certainly local achievements and do not need to be the result of trans-Saharan contact.

A fundamental problem in assessing art and technology is that so little survives. This is partly because perishable materials were often used and, with an architectural tradition that preferred timber and mud to stone, there were few places to store artifacts over long periods of time. For materials before the sixteenth century, archaeological finds have to be relied upon. Many sites that are known to contain artistic artifacts are increasingly under threat of looting and illicit excavation, and such objects, when they reach the art markets of the West, are effectively stripped of their cultural or chronological context.

African Urbanism

It is often maintained that early African society was largely rural and nonurban. Where are the great urban centers of ancient Africa comparable with Athens and Rome, the Near Eastern cities, or even the urban centers of Mesoamerica? The new archaeological evidence suggests that Africa contained urban communities as complex as these other regions, but that they have been neglected.

One such community was Kerma, located on the Middle Nile, which flourished between 2500 and 1500 B.C.E., a period contemporary with the Old and Middle Kingdoms of ancient Egypt. Here

483

excavations in the early twentieth century uncovered "royal" burials in massive mounds containing numerous human sacrifices. The excavations are now providing the urban context for Kerman society: temples, public spaces, a royal palace, and town walls. They are also showing that Kerma was not a pale derivative of ancient Egypt but a dynamic and long-lived African state, which, after its destruction by the Egyptians of the New Kingdom, reemerged as the Kingdom of Kush around 850 B.C.E. While the urban complex at Napata is little known, its successor at densely populated Meroë, with public buildings, temples, and palaces, survived until around 350 C.E. Meroitic society was literate (substantial quantities of written material have survived), but modern scholarship is still unable to translate much of this material.

Modern archaeological research is uncovering other examples of complex urban societies across much of tropical Africa. These projects range from urban studies in the inner Niger Delta, especially at Jenne-jeno, to Ethiopia and the research at Aksum, to the Swahili coastal towns of eastern Africa, and survey work at Great Zimbabwe which demonstrates that it was a major center of population, not just a ceremonial or royal complex serving a rural community.

The difficulty in recognizing urbanism in Africa is due not just to the lack of fieldwork but to a broader problem of classification. Studies of urbanism, from V. Gordon Childe's "urban revolution" in the Near East to those of modern urban geographers, have relied upon trait lists to define urbanism. American midwestern towns required three banks and a Woolworth's store; ancient cities needed craft specialization, appropriation of economic surplus, public architecture, social stratification, art, trade, and writing. In practice, African towns satisfy only a few of these widely accepted criteria, which suggests that they were not true "towns" in a universal sense.

My view is that African urbanism should not be compared unfavorably within these classification schemes, which have their origins in Western society and, ultimately, in Greek philosophical ideas. The economic basis of African society is distinctive, with a heavy reliance upon cattle pastoralism across much of the continent. In the West and Near East, as well as Mesoamerica, crop surpluses were used to support large urban populations, and such redistribution was at the heart of their economic organization. Within sub-Saharan Africa, as a result of environmental and botanical constraints, crop surpluses were not so readily available. Accumulated surpluses were stored as livestock, especially cattle, which formed the basis of exchange systems within the economy. Because cattle rather than crops were the underpinnings of urban development in Africa, the resulting towns differ from the standard preindustrial city of Western society.

Ancient Africa and World Economic Systems

The Victorian image of "darkest Africa" implied not only the darkness of the skins of the inhabitants but also a continent, cut off from the rest of humanity, that could be rescued from obscurity by intrepid explorers and brought triumphantly onto the world stage. Even today, the notion of precolonial Africa as isolated from the world still underlies much historical thought.

In fact, the evidence shows that continental Africa was no more shrouded in obscurity than other parts of the Old World. Links between the Mediterranean, Egypt, and sub-Saharan Africa can be shown to go back into the Predynastic period (before c. 3000 B.C.E.), and trade with Punt—a broad term for areas of northeastern Africa reached via the Red Sea—was maintained over some 2,000 years, until about 1000 B.C.E. The Puntites may even have sailed to Egypt on their own trading missions. The supply of Nubian products was a major factor behind the prosperity of ancient Egypt. Medieval links between Egypt and sub-Saharan Africa continued, via trans-Saharan trade, through the Christian kingdoms of Nubia and Ethiopia, and through Islamic trade along the Red Sea to the Indian Ocean and eastern Africa.

The east African coast, forming part of the rim of the Indian Ocean, has a long history of contact with a wider world through a monsoonal-based trading system. Firm archaeological evidence for this begins in the sixth century C.E., and since then specialized traders, the Swahili, have supplied African products in exchange for manufactured goods such as ceramics, textiles, and glass. It was once maintained that the Swahili network extended along a narrow coastal strip and hinterland, and that long-distance trade with the interior was a nineteenth-century innovation. Trade with the far interior had, if fact, begun very much earlier, and the Indian Ocean was one of the main destinations of gold, copper, and iron mined in southern Africa. There appears to have been a particularly close link in the fourteenth century between the Swahili coast and Great Zimbabwe.

Long-distance trade into the Sahara may have originated with the so-called chariot routes, which date to the first millennium B.C.E.; with the camel, long-distance trade was viable. Dates for domesticated camels, at Qasr Ibrim (about 900 B.C.E.) raise the possibility of very early trans-Saharan travel, and Kerma may have been trading directly with the Nile Delta via the desert oases before 1500 B.C.E. The heyday of trans-Saharan trade with western Africa was during the Islamic period, and the main export commodity was gold. Indeed, so reliant was medieval Europe upon these supplies of African gold that when the flow was interrupted in the late fourteenth century, Europe plunged into a bullion crisis and economic depression. Some have argued that the search for new sources of gold was the true motive behind European voyages of discovery in the late fifteenth century.

It has been fashionable to place the origins of the world economic system in the sixteenth century, with European expansion into the wider world. African products played a fundamental part in this process, not least in the supply of slaves to work the plantations of the New World, which in turn generated wealth for colonial expansion, industrialization, and the progress of the West. However, from the perspective of the archaeologist, it is clear that the role of African society, as a supplier of valuable commodities—not just slaves, but also gold, ivory, and, in the ancient world, valuable wood, incense, and animal skins—goes back a very long way. The sixteenth century saw an intensification of a deeply embedded, unequal relationship whose origins lay in the first Egyptian expeditions to Punt.

The nature of this unequal relationship lies at the root of the Western misunderstanding of Africa. This has polluted much of the historical record, and it is to be hoped that archaeological methods—albeit rooted in the Western scientific tradition—provide a means of giving the proper perspective on the African past and an understanding of African cultural achievements.

BIBLIOGRAPHY

Clark, J. Desmond. *The Prehistory of Africa*. New York, 1970.

Leakey, L. S. B. *Stone Age Africa: An Outline of Prehistory in Africa*. London, 1936.

Phillipson, D. W. *African Archaeology*. Cambridge, 1993.

Robertson, Peter, ed. *A History of African Archaeology*. London, 1990.

Shaw, Thurston, et al., eds. *The Archaeology of Africa: Foods, Metals, and Towns*. London, 1993.

MARK HORTON

See also **Agriculture; Aksum; Archaeology and Prehistory; Climate; Human Evolution; Jenne and the Saharan Borderlands; Leakey, Louis and Mary; Meroë; Production Systems; Sahara Desert; Zimbabwe; Ancient.**

PREMPEH, AGYEMAN (b. 1871? d. 1931), thirteenth *asantehene* (king of Asante). Agyeman Prempeh became *asantehene* after winning a war of succession (1884–1888). From 1888 to 1896, Prempeh engaged in restoring peace among the central Asante and asserting his authority over the rebellious northern Asante, with some success. Concurrently, the British were consolidating their rule on the Gold Coast, and their hesitation about further imperial expansion kept the Asante disunited. Prempeh's refusal of their offer of protection led the British to invade Kumasi in 1896 and exile Prempeh to Sierra Leone and, in 1900, to the Seychelles Islands. In exile (1896–1924), Prempeh learned English and was baptized in the Anglican Church, taking the name Edward. Owing to his exemplary life, the pressure of Asante nationalism, and the requirements of indirect rule, Prempeh was allowed by the British to return to Kumasi as a private citizen in 1924. Since the Asante still regarded him as their king, and the British needed his help to advance indirect rule, he was installed as

Prempeh. FROM BASIL DAVIDSON, *HISTORY OF WEST AFRICA*

kumasihene (ruler of Kumasi) in 1926. Between 1926 and his death in 1931, he accomplished the political and legal reorganization of the Kumasi state and created the conditions for the restoration of the Asante confederacy on 31 January 1935.

BIBLIOGRAPHY

Ghana National Archives. *The Life of Nana Prempeh I, 1872–1931, Incorporating History of Nana Prempeh's Adventure During His Thirty Years of Captivity, Namely Elmina, Sierra Leone, and Seychelles.* Accra, Ghana, n.d.

Lewin, Thomas J. *Asante Before the British: The Prempean Years, 1875–1900.* Lawrence, Kans., 1978.

Tordoff, William. *Ashanti Under the Prempehs.* London, 1965.

NANA ARHIN BREMPONG

See also **Asante.**

PRETORIA. Modern Pretoria has been the administrative capital of South Africa since 1910, when the country was established as the Union of South Africa. Previously the city served as the capital of the Afrikaner state, the South African Republic (SAR), and as such was at the center of political and military battles between the Afrikaners and the British at the end of the nineteenth century. Pretoria was occupied by the British during the South African War; the peace treaty, the Peace of Vereeniging, was signed there on 31 May 1902. The origins of Pretoria go back to the 1840s, when *voortrekker* migrants from the Afrikaner Cape Colony settled in the Transvaal on the banks of the Apies River. There Pretoria—known originally as Pretoria Philadelphia—was founded in 1855 by Marthinus W. Pretorius, the first president of the SAR (1857–1877), as a meeting place for the Afrikaner parliament, the Volksraad.

Pretorius named the city for his famous father, Andries, who is remembered primarily for two reasons. In January 1852, he negotiated with the British the Sand River Convention, which established the Transvaal as an independent Afrikaner territory. In December 1838 he led some 500 *voortrekkers* into the Zulu kingdom (in Natal) and there, beside the Ngome River, directed his party in defeating an attacking Zulu force that has been estimated to be 10,000 strong. This battle is commemorated in Pretoria on the engraved stone walls that circle the Voortrekker Monument, a massive, elaborate structure erected in the 1940s to honor all who participated in the Great Trek. Pretoria abounds in other monuments to Afrikaner history, including statues of the two Pretoriuses, father and son; a statue of Paul Kruger (president of the SAR, 1883–1900); and a statue of Louis Botha (commander of the Boer forces during the South African War; later first prime minister of the Union of South Africa, 1910–1919).

Pretoria is the largest city in South Africa, though only the fourth most populous: a million people live in the greater metropolitan area, but only about 500,000 reside in the city proper. Cape Town, by contrast, has 850,000 inhabitants, while Durban and Johannesburg, the next two biggest cities, each have populations of about 700,000. The residential patterns of Pretoria still reflect a history of apartheid that dates back to the beginning of the century: whites, blacks, Cape Coloured people, and Indians each congregate in largely segregated neighborhoods that surround the center of the city, which is occupied primarily by the offices of the national government and those of the Guateng Provincial Administration, as well as commercial and industrial enterprises.

The latter include food processing, engineering, and—most important—diamond, iron, and steel mining companies: the general area where Pretoria is located is one of the most abundant in minerals in South Africa. Industry in the city is facilitated by the national rail system, as well as by the nearby international airport. So, too, is tourism: tourists come to see not only the monuments but also the famous jacaranda trees—there are 70,000—which produce their purple blooms in October and November. Other attractions include the National Zoological Gardens of South Africa, known especially for its work in wildlife conservation, and the important collections of South African art and old Dutch masters on exhibit at the Pretoria Art Museum. The University of South Africa, the University of Pretoria, and the world-renowned Onderstepoort Veterinary Research Institute are in Pretoria. Not surprisingly, this city—where Nelson Mandela was inaugurated in 1994—also serves as the headquarters for a number of Afrikaner political organizations, including the Conservative Party of South Africa, which has sought to establish an independent Afrikaner state.

BIBLIOGRAPHY

Elliott, Aubrey. *Pretoria.* Cape Town, 1975.

Hattingh, P. S., and A. C. Horn. "Pretoria." In *Homes Apart: South Africa's Segregated Cities,* edited by Anthony Lemon. London, 1991.

MARGARET ALISON SABIN

See also Apartheid; Afrikaner Republics; Cape Colony; Kruger, Paul.

PRODUCTION SYSTEMS

[This entry consists of six parts: Overview; Hunting and Gathering; Agriculture and Horticulture; Pastoralism; Peripatetic; and Fishing.]

OVERVIEW

For the most part, traditional African societies—whether hunters and gatherers, pastoralists, or farmers—have been rural peoples whose livelihood depended on the land.

Natural Constraints

The deserts were areas of limited resources, which placed constraints on the peoples who lived there. Their dependence upon elementary technology made these groups especially vulnerable to natural conditions. The regional variability of rainfall was one particularly decisive factor in their survival. Desert peoples like the Khoisan of the Kalahari were forced to forage for food and search daily for scarce water supplies. Sometimes they were enslaved by nomadic pastoralist groups, as in the Sahara.

In the Sahel, rainfall is limited to two or three summer months. This region, which lies directly to the south of the Sahara and extends from the Atlantic coast to the semi-desert of the Horn of Africa, was best suited to transhumant cattle pastoralists (Tuaregs in the west, Maasai and Somali in the east) who moved their livestock seasonally up and down according to the rains. A similar ecosystem exists along the northern border of the Kalahari, which is inhabited by Tswana cattle pastoralists. In the intertropical zone, a longer rainy season is followed by a brief humid season in the winter months. This climate permitted the development of savannas. The economic complementarity between agriculture and the raising of large and small livestock here ensured a relative degree of prosperity. The staple crops were cereals: sorghum and millet. In the equatorial zone proper, abundant rains give rise to the great forests, long inhospitable to agriculture except in the form of root crops (originally yams, then manioc introduced by the Portuguese). This was the territory of hunting, fishing, and foraging peoples such as the Pygmy groups, for whom the dense forests provide a refuge even today. It was not until the twentieth century that colonizers established plantations in this region for the cultivation of export crops (cocoa and coffee).

In east-central Africa the stark division of the continent into climatic zones is moderated by the effect of higher altitudes, which result in a better balance of temperatures and rainfall and which gradually gave rise to agropastoralist societies such as the Gikuyu in Kenya and the Tonga of Zambia. Their economies, too, were based on the complementarity between cattle-keeping and farming. From the sixteenth to the twentieth centuries, maize, imported from the Americas, progressively transformed these agrarian societies by shifting productive energies to a crop that could be grown not only for subsistence but also for export. Beginning in the early twentieth century, an analogous role was played by rice, which was imported in great quantities by the colonial powers.

The ecological vulnerability of much of Africa's regions is accentuated by other unfavorable conditions. The climate characteristically provides too much or too little rain. The soils are generally poor: in the arid regions, rapid evaporation causes mineral salts to rise to the surface and form hard lateritic crusts that have to be broken up with a pick before the land can be farmed. In the wet zones, on the other hand, the rains leach the nutrients from the soils, so that they form heavy lateritic clays. In addition, in many areas sleeping sickness, which affects both humans and livestock and has been known from earliest times, militates against keeping large livestock, whose dung could be used as fertilizer. The only fertilizer traditionally used here resulted from the practice of burning the ground cover off fields prior to planting—the ashes provide some soil nutrients. To avoid sterilizing the soils, cultivated land here therefore needs to be left fallow for long periods, on the order of fifteen to twenty-five years. This implies a semi-itinerant farming system. The traditional unit of production was made up of all the local members of two successive generations—the household or village collective. They would periodically move off as a group to clear new lands when the current farm became less productive. This practice explains how a relatively small number of people could clear vast expanses of land. For example, the Gabonese forest today is entirely second-growth, not primary; this is believed to be the result of human activity, although people have never been many.

Except in the Nile Valley, Africa has no vast alluvial plains comparable to the river deltas of Asia. There are no fertile volcanic soils except in very

A man cuts down trees for slash-and-burn farming near Evinayong, Equatorial Guinea. © SEAN SPRAGUE/IMPACT VISUALS 1994

limited areas, such as in northern Rwanda or the slopes of Mount Cameroon. Irrigation was known, but appears rarely to have been developed, despite archaeological evidence discovered in the Sahel. This is probably because settlement along the river banks was interdicted by ancient, recurrent endemic diseases: malaria (known since prehistoric times), bilharzia (caused by parasitic worms and resulting in blood loss and tissue damage), and oncocerchiasis, also called "river blindness."

Demographic Factors

The birthplace of humanity, Africa, was no doubt populated for millions of years by groups of hunters and gatherers whose modern descendants could be the Khoisan-speaking peoples now limited to the desert regions. Our knowledge of these peoples begins around 8000 B.C.E. with the beginning of the desertification of the Sahara. The peoples of the Sahara migrated southward, giving rise to the linguistic groups of the Nilo-Saharan family (for example, the Songhai). From this first migration, sometime around 1000 B.C.E., there arose a linguistic group on the interior Nigerian plateau, between the Niger and Benue Rivers, and in the Congo Basin. This great language family, called Niger-Congo, gave rise to the Bantu-speaking peoples who progressively spread out over central, western, and southern Africa. There is ample evidence of iron working having developed here rather earlier than among contemporaneous peoples who, apparently, still used stone tools. The iron-working people were farmers who spread the use of iron across the continent. They created the first great intercontinental trade routes, exchanging two commodities that were universally necessary but not universally available. Salt, produced only in the desert, around the great lakes of the eastern Rift, and on the coasts, was exchanged for the iron that was needed to manufacture that widely used farming tool, the hoe.

The Bantu expansion was stimulated by the arrival of the banana, brought by the Indian Ocean trade toward the end of the first millennium C.E., and then by the introduction of the new plants from the Americas (cassava, maize, beans). These

488

new crops completely transformed rural agriculture in the Congo Basin, stimulated a marked population increase, and made possible the formation of the great empires of the African interior. Unfortunately, the slave trade—particularly the Atlantic slave trade—dealt a harsh blow to this demographic growth throughout the eighteenth century. The massive European penetration of the continent in the nineteenth century and the first phase of the colonial era, in turn, caused a further demographic recession, largely because of the uncontrollable spread of major endemic diseases (rinderpest, a cattle disease introduced on the continent in the 1880s; sleeping sickness; and venereal disease). Nevertheless, by the end of the nineteenth century, the total population of sub-Saharan Africa had regained the level achieved five centuries earlier (about one hundred million).

Social Factors

Naturally, given the diversity of the African environment, there has never been a single, uniquely African form of social organization. However, at a certain level of generalization, the modes of organization that exist show some undeniable similarities. The reason for this is twofold. First is the long history of cross-cultural contacts within sub-Saharan Africa, arising from long-distance regional trade (for example, salt for iron, salt for gold, and farm products for the products of pastoralists). Second, the continent as a whole has undergone successive shared experiences: the Bantu expansion during the first millennium B.C.E.; the spread of Islam beginning in the eighth to tenth centuries; contact with the West since the mid-1500s; direct European colonization during the nineteenth and twentieth centuries; and independence, gained largely through the efforts of a single generation (1956–1980).

Within this difficult context, African agrarian societies built up social institutions designed to protect their environment, conserving much in order to maintain a balance among the needs of production, demographic uncertainties, and political imperatives. Marxist scholars of the 1960s and 1970s viewed these institutions as "modes of production," but it seems less reductionist today to speak of them as total social systems: although production is a major concern for these societies, it is not their only preoccupation. In these preindustrial societies, everything was expressed in social and ideological terms: beliefs, institutions, and rules of life made up a complex whole in which it is impossible to isolate what is deterministic of economic imperatives and what is determined by them. Furthermore, today it is known that these social and ideological structures do not survive only as a part of a particular mode of production, but have remained in place long after that mode of production has disappeared.

It is clear, however, that rural preindustrial societies were initially organized for survival: to provide food, shelter, and clothing, and to guarantee the continuity of the household were the overriding imperatives. Subsistence concerns had an impact upon production for profit. Use values were separate from market values. An entire series of effects arise from this fact, which the analysis of modes of production has helped us to understand.

The mode of production defined by Marx makes a distinction between two levels: the productive forces (the means of production) and the social relations of production. In rural Africa, productive forces were limited to the generalized use of the hoe. Although the rock art of the Sahara demonstrates that the wheel was known, it was not adopted outside of Ethiopia. This had important technological consequences because the wheel was useful not only for transport but above all as an energy source, enabling the use of the plow or intensified irrigation techniques. The reasons why Africans did not adopt the wheel are many and controversial. They include a recognition of the fragility of the environment (as the unhappy experiments with industrial agriculture during the 1950s and 1960s confirm); weak demographic pressure, which failed to generate a need to intensify production; the absence of hierarchical societies that could support specialization of production beyond the subsistence level; the lack of a perception of the individual that would encourage the development of an entrepreneurial spirit—in brief, a whole constellation of ideological and social structures.

These structures were a part of the social relations of production in a system wherein, whether one was a farmer, a pastoralist, or a hunter-gatherer, the single most important means of production was the land. The land was therefore protected. Truly inalienable and sacred, the land was a gift from the gods and the ancestors and could be neither bought nor sold. Placed in the care of a ritual specialist, the "chief of the land," access to land was the condition upon which the survival of the community was based. Such access was often strongly inegalitarian: the most powerful lineages controlled it. But in principle, no one could be deprived of access to it: one needed only to put oneself under the protection of one of the dominant lineages, either as a dependent or as a slave, in order to participate in the subsistence of the group.

The mistaken Western view that this kinship-based organization of production was egalitarian arose largely from an outmoded belief that household- or village-based communities lived in an amiable "primitive communism." In agricultural societies, and even more so among pastoralist groups, there was a clear inequality between elders and juniors, dominant and dependent lineages, masters and slaves, men and women, aristocrats and commoners. This inequality was great even in groups that lacked a state hierarchy. In equatorial Africa, the Pygmy hunting groups served the Bantu farming communities. In exchange for their meat they received a very small portion of the Bantu agricultural harvest. Even within the dominant lineages, a sometimes fierce hierarchy existed between the elders—the keepers of knowledge and power—and the juniors, from whom respect and labor were expected. In order to maintain social and political equilibrium, it was the elders who negotiated marriage exchanges between lineages. They alone possessed the cattle needed for the bridewealth required for a junior to acquire a wife.

Lacking technology, the productive force was limited to what an individual could produce with his hands and a hoe. But the hoe was, without exception, a tool used exclusively by women. This was because a man's wealth was measured not in goods but in the people, particularly the women, that he possessed, or in the livestock that served as the means of exchange for women. In this system, women were simultaneously prized and despised. They were prized because, without exception, they did the bulk of the farm work (and, in pastoralist societies, were responsible for milking the cattle), and also because their fertility was the best indicator of the reproductive success of the group. But they were also despised because, even in matrilineal systems where they had a relative right to inherit power, they almost never exercised that power directly. Slaves or free, young women generally constituted the lowest social level of any group, subordinate to the mother-in-law and to the men, young and old, of the family unit.

The Role of Trade

Exchange has always played an important role in traditional society: exchanges of women, of goods, and of slaves, whether on the local, regional, or international level. Local exchanges were most often handled by women, who had direct responsibility for the household's subsistence. Indeed, in certain regions such as the Gikuyu states, it was only colonialism that displaced the women from their earlier role as merchants. But in broader markets, where goods from distant venues acquired a higher value due to their rarity, commerce was controlled by the chiefs. The chiefs conducted transactions among themselves, through intermediaries who were their direct dependents, or entrusted the trade to carefully controlled outsiders. The ancient empires of the savanna (Ghana, Mali, Songhai) built their wealth on the gold and salt trades. They did not directly control production: salt was brought in by the Arabs, while gold was locally mined by small producers. Similarly, between the twelfth and fifteenth centuries, the ruler of Great Zimbabwe controlled the trade of gold, from regions that were not necessarily under his rule, for the rare goods that came to him by caravan from Sofala on the Indian Ocean.

For some time scholars contended that the power of these states was derived from exclusively external elements, and two nearly impermeable systems were distinguished: "rural communists" on the one hand, and state aristocracies on the other. Today this analysis appears too simplistic. Certainly, in Africa there is less evidence of the state's direct exploitation of the peasantry than was the case in medieval Europe where the wealth of the sovereigns, based primarily on the trade in wheat, required the direct exploitation of the peasantry. But the power of the state was directly felt by the peasantries of the great medieval African empires, which participated in the slave trade as much as in the trade of gold. All the products to be traded had to be handled, transported, and transformed. At the time of the Atlantic slave trade, the ruler of the ancient kingdom of Dahomey (present-day Bénin) built up his authority by alternating his military and mercantile power. Every dry season, he led his army in raids on the neighboring people, from whom he took prisoners of war who then were sold as slaves. During the rainy season, he negotiated with Europeans for the arms and prestige goods that he needed to maintain his power. Nearby, during the same period, one of the fundamental bases of the Asante king's wealth was his control of the neighboring Dyula merchant communities and the kola nut trade that they monopolized. These nuts had to be gathered, processed, and transported by local peasants. The formation of the early African states cannot be conceived of as independent of the local societies upon which they were built, because what we call a "state" was essentially a capital city and an army. Most of the time, the soldiers were simply the subjects of the ruler and could be drafted at his command. The capital city was inhabited by people whose activities were only marginally agricultural: their existence, and the existence of a court, presupposes the existence of a rurally based provisioning complex where the peasantry—dependents or slaves—was directly involved.

Future Prospects

Nonetheless, it remains surprising that these often highly elaborate and powerful societies did not in the precolonial past make the transition from subsistence-based to production-based economies. Surely this was in part because their ensemble of social values was based on a different conceptual universe in which their ideas of poverty, time, wealth, and value were not the same as those of Western societies. Doubtless, too, the linkage between internal production processes and the external resources available to the states did not develop in Africa in the same way that it did in the West. The great merchant systems of Africa foundered with the disappearance of the foreign markets upon which they depended (the Muslims of the Mediterranean, the Atlantic slave trade). This underscores the importance of a third factor: these societies found themselves dependent on foreign markets, long before colonial conquest, a situation that time and again served to thwart the internal dynamism of African states.

One final point must be made. Certainly, institutions and ideologies inherited from the past often appear maladaptive to the new economic and political conditions that arose from the events of the past two centuries. Nonetheless we must reject the outmoded paradigm of tradition versus modernity. Traditional societies were never static. Concepts and circumstances were constantly evolving. It would require another article to detail the strategies by which customary political authorities have adapted in order to retain a portion of their economic power, and above all how these strategies involved not only adaptation but also the innovation of rural peoples seeking a place in this new context. The colonial era, characterized by the introduction and development of cash crops grown for export, gave rise to the internal social reorgani-

zation of powerful groups. A new class of entrepreneurs has arisen, for example, on the cocoa plantations of the Gold Coast (now Ghana), or among the Hausa pastoralists who sold livestock to the colonial settlements on the western coast of Africa. Since independence, these trends have continued wherever they have not been thwarted or interrupted by war. Finally, since the 1970s, corresponding to the great global recession, the impoverishment of the lands has inspired the invention of new modes of production. Thus the need to supply the towns tends more and more to reorganize production and exchange of subsistence goods: market gardens and farms within or surrounding urban areas are springing up. Meat markets are being developed for the pastoralists. All these modes of production, called "informal" by the Western economists who understand them poorly, still await serious study and analysis.

BIBLIOGRAPHY

Anderson, Benedict. *Imagined Communities.* New York, 1983.

Berry, Sara. "The Food Crisis and Agrarian Change in Africa." *African Studies Review* 27 (1984): 59–112.

Bohannan, Laura, and George Dalton, eds. *Markets in Africa.* Evanston, Ill., 1972.

Boserup, Esther. *Women's Role in Economic Development.* New York, 1970.

Coquery-Vidrovitch, Catherine. "On an African Mode of Production." In *Perspectives on the African Past,* edited by G. Wesley Johnson. Boston, 1972.

———. "The Political Economy of the Peasantry and Modes of Production." In *The Political Economy of Contemporary Africa,* edited by Immanuel Wallerstein and T. Hopkins. Beverly Hills, 1977.

Coquery-Vidrovitch, Catherine, and Paul Lovejoy, eds. *The Workers of African Trade.* Beverly Hills, 1985.

Crummey, Donald, and Charles C. Stewart, eds. *Modes of Production in Africa.* Beverly Hills, 1981.

Goody, Jack. *Technology, Tradition, and the State in Africa.* London, 1971.

Iliffe, John. *The African Poor: A History.* Cambridge, 1987.

Jewsiewicki, Bogumil, ed. "Modes of Production: The Challenge of Africa." *Canadian Journal of African Studies,* special issue 19 (1985).

Klein, Martin, ed. *Peasants in Africa: Historical and Contemporary Perspectives.* Beverly Hills, 1980.

Méillassoux, Claude, ed. *The Development of Indigenous Trade and Markets in Africa.* London, 1981.

———. "The Economic Bases of Demographic Reproduction: From the Domestic Mode of Production to Wage-Earning." *Journal of Peasant Studies* 11 (1983): 50–61.

———. *Maidens, Meals, and Money: Capitalism and the Domestic Community.* Cambridge, 1991.

Palmer, L., and N. Parsons, eds. *The Roots of Rural Poverty in Central and South Africa.* London, 1977.

Smith, A. K., and C. E. Weleh. "Peasants in Africa." *African Studies Review* 20, no. 3 (1977): 1–127.

CATHERINE COQUERY-VIDROVITCH

See also **Dahomey; East African Interior; Economic History; Exchange and Market Systems; Slave Trade; Sudanic Empires of Western Africa; Zimbabwe, Ancient.**

HUNTING AND GATHERING

Articulated relations of property, production, labor, and exchange have, until recently in a few studies, been erroneously treated as being absent from hunter-gatherer social formations. Equally inhibiting to an understanding of these relations has been a tendency, when such relations are addressed, to equate production in such societies with energetics rather than social processes. An adequate discussion of this subject thus requires that attention be given to two interrelated subtopics: first, the received model of hunting society and its critique; second, the new model with emphasis on institutions of land tenure upon which production is based and the social relations that govern exchange systems.

The means of production in hunting-gathering systems are varied and complex. Methods of hunting include the use of snares, spears, bow and arrows, net traps, pitfalls—sometimes in conjunction with animal drives and running an animal to ground. Snares and simple pitfalls are placed in paths habitually used by particular species (ranging in size from small mammals to hippopotamuses); unobtrusive barriers of brush are often erected to ensure that the prey does not sidestep the trap. These methods plus bow-and-arrow hunting are usually carried out by one man acting alone, although small hunting parties are not infrequent. By contrast, net traps and pitfall drives require the cooperation of a large number of people. In both methods, the trap—net or pit—is established at a suitable location and is attended by several persons (usually men); animals are driven to this location by many other persons (among them women and children) who, having fanned out at some distance away, force the prey to run into the traps where they are killed with clubs and spears. Spear hunting is most successfully carried on with dogs trained to bring prey to bay; during the twentieth century, horses have been used to chase animals and spear them from the mount. The gathering of plant foods, on the other hand, requires little other than carrying devices—bags, slings, pouches—and a sharpened stick to dig tubers.

Archaeological and historical evidence increasingly demonstrates that few peoples have relied solely on these methods for at least several centuries. Almost all societies in which hunting-gathering has been important during this time, certainly all in Africa, have engaged to some degree in animal husbandry based on some combination of cattle, sheep, and goats, either as owners of livestock or as herders for others. Sorghum, millet, sweet-reed (a kind of sugarcane), cowpeas, and melons have been widely grown for an equally long time; cassava and maize were added by Europeans from the sixteenth century. The degree to which these domesticated products play a role in hunter-gatherer economies and the length of time they have done so is hotly contested by adherents of the received and new models, and indeed in many cases the question cannot yet be satisfactorily answered.

The Received Model

Hunter-gatherer societies were initially characterized by nineteenth-century scholars who based their theories on the work of French sociologists and British and American evolutionary anthropologists. In both of these theoretical frameworks, a distinction was made between simple, "mechanical" societies and complex, "organic" ones—the former functioning entirely according to the static (mechanical) rules of nature, the latter evolving through the interposition of social (organic) rules between persons and nature. The economic form of mechanical society was said to be hunting and gathering: its attributes were listed as small, self-sufficient groups of individuals, all possessing identical abilities and skills; mobility of individuals among groups restricted only by ecological factors; reciprocal access to resources and land, all held collectively; undeveloped material culture limited in variety and amount by nomadic life; and division of labor based only upon age and sex. In this economic form, production—as the creation of artifactual products through acts of labor—could not exist; humans were themselves the instruments of production, in Marx's sense of being the direct means of harvest with few tools (other than rudimentary ones of stone, bone, and wood) intervening in the process. This model was posited to be the original form of human society and, thus, was seen as the initial, "Stone Age" stage of human social evolution.

This theoretical approach held that, while the intervention of social rules produced the whole range of organic agricultural and industrial societies known in the nineteenth century, the imperative, mechanical rules of nature did not allow hunting-gathering societies to evolve. Thus, peoples in Africa, Asia, the Americas, and Australia encountered by Europeans from the sixteenth century onward who appeared to subsist entirely or substantially by hunting and gathering were thought to be relics of the Stone Age. As such they were studied for the light they might throw on the origin of human society.

Although, in the early twentieth century, this model was temporarily abandoned, it was revived in the 1960s by, principally, American anthropologists working in the new paradigm of evolutionary ecology. In its new form it was called variously the hunting model, the band level of sociocultural organization, or the foraging mode of production. But the attributes of the original model were largely unchanged. Two significant contrasts, however, distinguish the revived model from the original. First, and most important, it acknowledged the existence of production among hunter-gatherers—although it was a restricted kind of production with division of labor still based solely on "natural ascriptions" of age and sex, and individuals were still viewed as instruments of production subservient to nature. Second, while in the nineteenth century the lives of hunter-gatherers were usually thought to be "nasty, brutish, and short," now anthropologists set out to demonstrate that theirs was "the original affluent society." These anthropologists, like their predecessors, turned to living peoples as a window through which to witness paleolithic affluence. While at first apparently successful, their results were soon shown to be flawed by the constrictions of the model.

These efforts stimulated a reexamination of supposedly simple hunter-gatherer relations of production. This led to the formulation of a new model which articulates these relations with the other domains of social life. This model proposes that production in hunter-gatherer societies (as in all other societies) is the emergent result of the interplay of social status, land entitlement, propinquity of other peoples, investment opportunity, and the historicity of the region in which it takes place. In the first instance, hunter-gatherer access to the forces and means of production resides in kinship practices which are, in turn, ineluctably enmeshed in relations to land.

The New Model

Land Tenure

In contrast to the ecological concept of territory, which focuses on productivity and the means of production, the constitution of land tenure locates people within the social matrix of relations to the land upon which productive activity must take place. A number of hunter-gatherer societies in Africa share structural elements of property relations and tenure in common. Property law in these societies defines not so much rights of persons over things, as obligations owed between persons with respect to things. Being in a property relationship involves being bound within a set of reciprocal obligations among persons and things; entitlement to land and rights to its use must be subject to a complex of claims arising from this social matrix. It is not, however, land itself that is inherited. What actually is inherited is a set of status positions binding individuals to a network of obligations owed among persons through which they are entitled to land.

Among southern African Khoisan, a person's primary entitlement is that person's birthplace; there is a very high probability that this birthplace will be in at least one parent's entitlement. An individual's tenure in land is acquired bilaterally through a regional kinship net defined initially by birth into a local descent group and later reinforced by

Khoisan woman gathering edible roots in Botswana. © JASON LAURÉ 1993

marriage. East African Okiek divide land into lineage-owned, patrilineally transmitted tenures; the local group is a significant association of identity which incorporates affines (relatives by marriage) into its residential units. The Lese-Dese and the Efe pygmies of central Africa respectively organize themselves as segmented patrilineages and exogamous patriclans each with its own traditionally transmitted tenure. It is thus apparent that hunter-gatherer kinship is a form of conjectural history the elements of which—both the positions potentially open to persons and the connections among these positions—are subject to manipulation in conjunction with wider social and economic concerns.

Social Relations of Exchange

Exchange networks play important integrative roles in this social-spatial structure. While land is owned communally, the means of production—weapons, tools, containers, transporting devices, as well as the products of individual labor—are private property. This private nature of production makes possible the specialization of productive activity and the consequent necessary interdependence of producers via exchange. Among the Khoisan-speaking Zhu, 62 percent of reciprocal exchange occurs between grand relatives and 82 percent between great-grand relatives; a high proportion of this exchange is associated with marriage negotiations. Comparable statistical data are not available for eastern and central Africa, but the outlines of reciprocal exchange appear similar. Historically, this dialectic between independent private production and dependent community sociality formed extensive exchange networks that tied together diverse, disparate goals and strategies—the political conditions of their labor—of families, homesteads, kin, and neighbors.

If political practice is that activity which produces and transforms social relations, it becomes evident that, among the people we have been examining, kinship is the arena in which political practice takes place. Exchange, then, is the product of strategies oriented toward the satisfaction of material and symbolic interests and organized by reference to a determinate set of economic and social conditions. It emerges as relationships that can be read in different ways by participants in them. In keeping with the necessary interdependence of private producers via exchange, no local descent group can independently reproduce itself within the parochial limits of a single land tenure. For this reason, a significant number of marriage ties are negotiated with strategically placed collateral affines in adjacent and nearby tenures. Adults with mature children choose to gain strength through intensified exchange and other forms of cooperation with people in specific tenures because they are concerned with finding spouses in those tenures for their children.

There is also "foreign" exchange. Exotic products are transferred over distances far greater than those to nearby tenures; a web of extensions of individual relationships stretches for hundreds of kilometers through many hands. Persons closer to each other in any direction along the network are closer relatives or affines; those farther away, both in geographical distance and along the links of transfer chains, are progressively more tenuously related. Marriage negotiations form part of the strategies employed to tie desirable trade partners more closely together and to give generational continuity to these arrangements. Partnerships are passed in inheritance from parent to child, and inheritors strive to solidify anew those partnerships that offer continuing advantageous access to material and social resources. That is, the role of exchange in the reproduction of the conditions of production is an incorporative one; it is through delicate, complex balancing of individual interests in a fluid field of options that the parochial bounds of local groups are opened to a necessary wider social sphere.

BIBLIOGRAPHY

Bailey, Robert. *The Behavioral Ecology of Efe Pygmy Men in the Ituri Forest, Zaire.* Ann Arbor, 1991.

Barnard, Alan. *Hunters and Herders of Southern Africa: A Comparative Ethnography of the Khoisan Peoples.* New York, 1992.

Berry, J. W., et al., eds. *On the Edge of the Forest: Cultural Adaptation and Cognitive Development in Central Africa.* Berwyn, Pa., 1986.

Kratz, Corinne A. *Affecting Performance: Meaning, Movement, and Experience in Okiek Women's Initiation.* Washington, D.C., 1994.

Wilmsen, Edwin N. *Land Filled with Flies: A Political Economy of the Kalahari.* Chicago, 1989.

EDWIN N. WILMSEN

See also **Anthropology and the Study of Africa; Kinship and Descent; Land Tenure Systems; Marriage Systems.**

AGRICULTURE AND HORTICULTURE

Two kinds of small-scale farming units grow food crops (grains, root crops, vegetables, small livestock) and commercial crops (cotton, coffee, tea, cocoa, and other products) in sub-Saharan Africa. Each of them has variants adapted to different ecological, social, and political conditions.

Kin-Group Farming

To grasp the range of differences in agricultural and horticultural systems, it helps to consider first the small-scale farming that predominated in most of sub-Saharan Africa before the early 1900s. It remains one of the types found in most parts of Africa. The system thrived where the labor supply was limited and land was abundant.

A group defined by kinship farms a few hectares of land each year, changing the particular plots cultivated every few years as crops deplete the soil. The old fields are left fallow for periods of up to twenty-five years, to maintain soil fertility. The farming group grows a basic food crop and several garnish crops, supplying most of their food needs and selling or exchanging a small amount of the food or special crops on local or wider markets. Both men and women do farm work, but they have different tasks and women generally work more hours over the year than men do. Farming operations are carried out with hand-held tools. During planting and harvest, when the demand for labor is intense, the group recruits additional labor through cooperative work groups, labor exchange, or hiring outside labor.

The basic food crops in drier regions are millet and sorghum, whereas in wetter forest zones they are plantains (cooking bananas) or root crops like yams or manioc. In some river valleys and coastal regions, rice is the staple grain. Surplus food crops are sold or exchanged, often on local markets. There is a long history of trade in cola nuts, sesame, and gum arabic. In addition to the main industrial export crops of the twentieth century—cotton, peanuts, cocoa, tea, and coffee—many other crops are locally important, from cashew nuts to pyrethrum to seasonal vegetables and flowers.

The system has eight key elements. Each of these elements follows a basic pattern upon which changes and variations combine to form a wide assortment of farming units.

- Land-use regime. Farm families invest their limited amount of labor over a large expanse of land, employing fallowing to keep soil fertility high. Because land is in short supply around cities, in especially fertile and accessible areas, and in regions of high population density, land use in many places is becoming more labor intensive.

- Technology. People using hand-held tools supply most of the energy and skill for farmwork. Animal power is used on some of the larger farms in those savanna areas that are free of tsetse flies. The use of ox- or horse-drawn plows has become commonplace in parts of Senegal, Uganda, Zimbabwe, and Zambia, for example. Tractors are found mainly on commercial farms, although rental services are available to small-scale mixed food and cash crop farms in some places. Farmers use selected seeds, fertilizer, and pesticides on cash crops when prices and earnings warrant and when the supply system is adequate.

- Food crops. Farming groups produce a large proportion of the food they consume. Cash crop production, need for money income, cheap grain imports, and changing tastes have decreased the degree of food self-sufficiency in many regions.

- Labor supply. A set of close or extended relatives supplies most labor for farming. The productivity of a farming unit is likely to expand as children reach the age of useful work and to decline as adults age and lose their physical capacities. At times of high labor requirements, more and more farms resort to hiring workers instead of calling on kinship groups or cooperative labor groups.

- Division of tasks. Men often do initial soil preparation and women often do most of the weeding and food preparation. In practice, however, there is variation in the distribution of tasks, and cultural differences are great. As men have moved into wage work, women have shouldered an increasing burden of farm labor.

- Management. The head of the farming unit, often the senior man, manages some of the farming tasks or plots of land while junior members of the farming group have independent control of other tasks or plots of land. The increasing numbers of women left independent by divorce or the death of a husband, or labor migration by men, has increased the proportion of farms managed by women.

- Market connections. The group or its members purchase some tools and agricultural inputs and sell some agricultural products. Market connections are an integral aspect of farming units in most regions, although, in regions afflicted by war (such as much of Mozambique in the 1980s) or by government neglect (such as much of Zaire in the 1980s and 1990s), groups have often moved away from market production to self-provisioning, frequently at an impoverished level.

• Political and economic subordination. Community or state authorities accord use rights to and collect taxes from people who farm. They may seek to influence choice of crops and farming practices through extension advice, credit conditions, administrative intervention, or pricing and marketing policies.

Farmers adapt this kin-group farming unit to changing conditions, altering each of the aspects just listed. The result is a large number of different types of farming unit. Some of the most common variants are:

• Labor-intensive farm. In the densely settled zones around cities in northern Nigeria, in eastern Nigeria, in the fertile hills of Rwanda and Burundi, and in several other places, rotational fallow has given way to permanent cultivation. Farmers return nutrients to the soil by penning livestock on fields after the crop is harvested, by spreading household waste on the land, and by interplanting and rotating crops. Some also use commercial fertilizers.
• Labor-exporting farm. Where markets and prices of potential cash crops are not favorable, the women members of a farming unit and the older men often maintain self-provisioning while the young men seek off-farm work and send remittances to help support those left on the farm.
• Cash-crop kin-based farm. Men and women work intensively on cash-crop farming while continuing to supply most food needs for members of the production unit. The unit hires labor for harvesting and may purchase pesticides and animal-powered technology. Farming practices are influenced by marketing and extension agencies. The large regions of Africa that produce peanuts, cotton, cocoa, coffee, and tea have evolved several variants of this farming unit.
• Small-scale market-gardening farm. Members of a small farm unit intensify work on land to produce food crops beyond their own needs for sale on urban markets. They may purchase fertilizer and hire labor to increase production, and sell the crop on a competitive market managed by traders and transporters.

Commercial Farming

Another set of farming units in sub-Saharan Africa has a different origin and distinctive characteristics. Commercial farms were started by settlers, notably in Kenya, Zimbabwe, Zambia, Mozambique, and Angola. These farms, some of them now owned and managed by Africans with no settler heritage, continue to produce significant output in the first three of these countries. In parts of most countries in sub-Saharan Africa, urban businesspeople, professionals, civil servants, and army officers have established commercial farms as a business investment or as a secondary activity for some family members. Although the dividing line between mixed food- and cash-crop farms and small commercial farms is not sharp, on the whole commercial farms are quite different from family-based farms.

Commercial farms hire most of their labor and sell most of their product. Managers, who may be employees rather than owners, have strong central control. Some commercial farms are very large and on average spread labor over much land, but they use labor and machinery intensively on some parcels of land. Historically governments have supported settler farms and elite-owned commercial farms, protecting them against competition and subsidizing their inputs and services. As with family farms, the elements of commercial farms combine to form different kinds of units.

• Project farms. One kind of farm is established in conjunction with a government program that makes new land available at low cost, supplies crucial inputs at subsidized prices, purchases crops at favorable prices, or otherwise assures the financial viability of the farms, if not of the project that supports them. Nigeria has had several such programs. Several countries, including Nigeria, Senegal, and Mali, have irrigated projects with associated farms. In Sudan there are extensive rain-fed farm projects that have only seasonal residents and use only hired labor and rented equipment.
• Contract farms. Contract farming often combines commercial farming management with household farmland and labor. The extent to which control over the farming operations passes to the contractor depends upon the terms of the contract. The farmer agrees to supply a certain crop at a certain time. He or she may also agree to follow a particular agronomic regimen and to purchase and use particular inputs. The contractor may undertake to supply inputs and technical assistance, and may agree to purchase a certain quantity at a certain price. It is a growing form of agriculture for nontraditional export crops like flowers and seed beans, and for crops that require immediate processing like sugarcane, tea, and

tobacco. In the early 1990s more than 15 percent of Kenya's smallholders were farming under contract.

BIBLIOGRAPHY

Anthony, Kenneth R. M., Bruce F. Johnston, William O. Jones, and Victor C. Uchendu. *Agricultural Change in Tropical Africa*. Ithaca, N.Y., 1979.

Barker, Jonathan. *Rural Communities Under Stress: Peasant Farmers and the State in Africa*. Cambridge, 1989.

Berry, Sara. *No Condition Is Permanent: The Social Dynamics of Agrarian Change in Sub-Saharan Africa*. Madison, Wis., 1993.

Heyer, Judith, Pepe Roberts, and Williams Gavin, eds. *Rural Development in Tropical Africa*. New York, 1981.

Hill, Polly. *The Migrant Cocoa-Farmers of Southern Ghana: A Study of Rural Capitalism*. Cambridge, 1963.

Little, Peter D., and Michael J. Watts, eds., *Living Under Contract: Contract Farming and Agrarian Transformation in Sub-Saharan Africa*. Madison, Wis., 1994.

Richards, Paul. *Indigenous Agricultural Revolution*. London, 1985.

Siddle, David, J., and Kenneth Swindell. *Rural Change in Tropical Africa: From Colonies to Nation-States*. Oxford, 1990.

JONATHAN S. BARKER

See also **Agriculture; Exchange and Market Systems; Gender; Labor Systems; Land Tenure; Urbanism and Urbanization.**

PASTORALISM

Pastoral production plays a greater role in the economies of African societies than in those of any other continent. At times, pastoralism represents the principal or even exclusive economic activity and is generally associated with a nomadic way of life. More often, these societies are based on various combinations of agriculture and animal husbandry, except in forested zones infested by the tsetse fly. Climatic and ecological conditions help explain the role of animal husbandry. The continent contains vast arid or semiarid zones. Those in which the annual rainfall is less than 500 millimeters (20 in.) are mainly used by specialized pastoralists. In zones with rainfall between 500 and 1,000 millimeters (20–40 in.), husbandry continues to play a major role.

In order to understand the role that pastoral production has assumed in African societies, one must refer first of all to history. The predominance of pastoralism developed quite early in the Neolithic period in northern Africa and the Sahara. These pastoralists were gradually driven south by the desiccation of the Sahara. Sedentary pastoralists appeared in Mauritania around the fourth millennium B.C.E. The cattle culture attested by the Saharan rock paintings of humpless, long-horned cattle date from this period. From the second millennium, there is evidence of humpless, short-horned cattle in the Sahel and the northern Sudan. Cattle, sheep, and goats were in eastern Africa between 3000 and 1000 B.C.E.; there is evidence from this later date of numerous Neolithic pastoral cultures in this region and even more in the south. The introduction of the zebu, better adapted to arid and semiarid zones, took place in eastern Africa 2,000 years ago. The introduction of the horse, by way of the north of Africa, occurred earlier (second millennium B.C.E.), and that of the camel still earlier (third millennium B.C.E.), although camels diffused across the arid zone toward northern Africa quite slowly.

These historical circumstances explain the two forms taken by specialized pastoralism and agropastoral systems in Africa. Cattle societies, the most numerous in sub-Saharan Africa, are the heirs, sometimes directly, of the "savanna pastoral Neolithic." Camel societies (Bedouin societies) were formed in a more recent context.

Cattle Societies

Even though cattle husbandry often takes place alongside sheep and goat husbandry and various forms of grain agriculture, the principal characteristic of African pastoral societies is the value they place on cattle husbandry, whatever its value in production.

The Fulani (Fulbe) of western and central Africa represent one of the archetypes of cattle societies. The Wodaabe, a part of the Fulani, lived exclusively on cattle raising. They gradually moved as a migratory group, organized on a lineage basis, occupying new grazing areas as a result of agreements negotiated with the agricultural or pastoral societies that welcomed them. In the course of these pastoral migrations, the Fulani formed exchange relations (milk and animal manure for grains) with farmers that integrated them into regional economic and political systems. In this context, the Islamization of these societies facilitated the formation of states by the Fulani aristrocracies from the end of the eighteenth century onward (Futa Toro, Massina, Sokoto).

Another model of the cattle societies exists in eastern Africa. Whether we consider the agropastoral Nuer or the Maasai, exclusive cattle raisers,

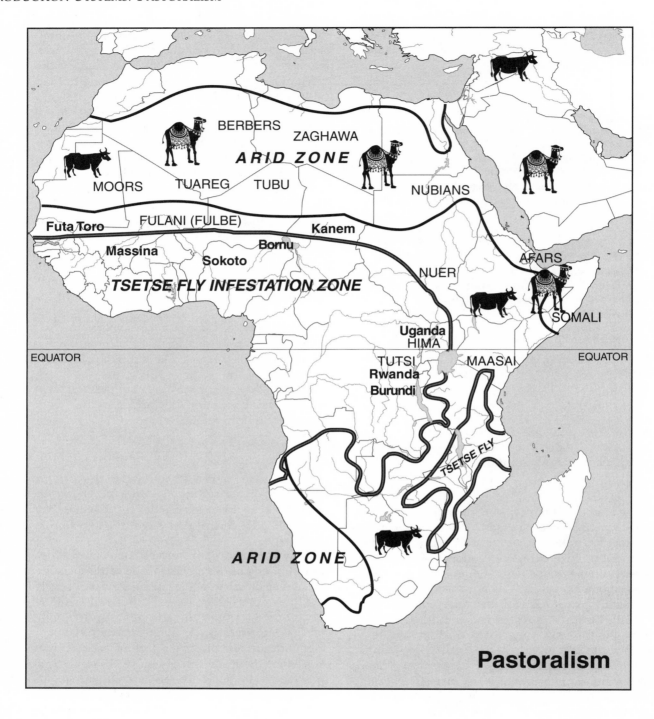

Pastoralism

cattle are at the center of social practice and ideology. The relations established through the circulation of cattle—whether as bridewealth or other social relations, age systems characteristic of certain of these societies, or even sacrificial relation with the supernatural—are regarded as the very framework of society. Yet the products of cattle husbandry, including those of small livestock husbandry, cannot satisfy all human needs; as a result, regional systems of exchange are organized. They not only take an economic form but also undergo several social mediations.

There are comparable forms of pastoral societies in other regions of Africa, particularly in the south

Samburu herdsmen near the Losioco escarpment, Kenya.
© GERALD CUBITT

(e.g., the Tswana). Another original form exists in the sacred kingships of central Africa (Rwanda, Burundi, Uganda). Here pastoral aristocracies (Hima, Tutsi) have established states in which social differentiation depends on access, or lack of access, to cattle. The cultural codes of sacred kingship are based on the pastoral values.

In these cattle societies, the central place of cattle in social values does not predetermine their actual economic value in production. This is true for both specialized pastoral and agropastoral societies. The central value given to cattle helps explain the social dynamic, including, as in the case of the Fulani or the interlacustrian kingships, the formation of states that developed for regional exchange systems and interethnic authority.

Camel Societies

The introduction of camels radically altered the nature of the African societies. Above all, camel societies are organized around the use of the animal for caravan transport, in particular across the arid zones separating sub-Saharan Africa from the rest of the world. International or regional caravan commerce (for example, Saharan salt) contributes to the organization of these societies. It provides them with the goods of exchange for agricultural products that make their pastoral specialization possible; it facilitates their settlement in sub-Saharan Africa, where they play a major economic, political, and military role.

The adoption of camel husbandry and the caravaneer functions of the Berbers of the western and central Sahara, the Tubu and the Zaghawa of the

central Sahara, and the Afars and the Somalis in the Horn of Africa, came at the very beginning of these civilizations, which were strongly influenced by Islam. Camel husbandry is not the only pastoral specialization in these societies, however; some subgroups simultaneously develop cattle or small livestock husbandry. These societies also practice rain-fed or irrigation agriculture—for example, raising date palms.

In certain areas, Islamization was accompanied by the Arabization of societies, this being as much a consequence of the process of internal transformation as of an Arab "conquest." This was the case with the Moors of the western Sahara and the Berbers and Nubians of the Sudan, who were Arabized between the fourteenth and sixteenth centuries. Arabization occurred a little later in Chad.

Social Constants in Pastoral Production

The diversity of social structures shown by pastoral and agropastoral societies is compatible with common characteristics found in both cattle and camel societies. Examples of such structures include the tribal and lineage organization and age-sets found in eastern Africa and the interlacustrine states.

These common characteristics are related both to the economic and social value given to livestock and to the role that livestock play in defining social relations. Insofar as ownership of the herd is individual or familial, and the family provides the labor necessary for development of the herd, the structure of the domestic herd and of the family are closely linked. Nevertheless, there are forms of slave and tributary labor, especially in camel

499

societies. Much like the polygynous family structure in eastern Africa, these forms allow for a diversification of production to include several types of husbandry or combinations of husbandry and agriculture.

Whatever the value given to livestock in these societies, husbandry alone can never satisfy all their needs. They must enter into exchange relations in order to obtain agricultural and craft products. Such exchanges include market activity (selling salt and dates in order to buy millet, in the Sahelian zone), bartering (milk for millet among the Fulani), or adopting other types of social relations (matrimonial, interethnic, and so on).

In the case of African pastoralists, the ownership of herds by individuals or families conflicts with the collective ownership of pastoral land that gives these societies their specific character. The use of natural pastures, the scarcity and dispersion of plant and water resources, and their seasonal variations often necessitate the more or less regular movement of humans and animals that is characteristic of nomadism or the various systems of transhumance. In the precolonial period, this control of space was sometimes translated to the geopolitical plane and favored the conquests of nomadic pastoralists and the establishment of states bringing together nomads and sedentary populations. In other circumstances, however, the pastoralists were integrated into the African states—as occurred, for instance, in Kanem and Bornu.

Modern Developments

Modern developments, colonization in particular, are manifested in the reorganization of pastoral space. The mobility of pastoralists has been constrained by the creation of national borders. The development of agriculture, whether indigenous or colonial, has led to the restriction on use of land once utilized for travel routes. The social and political structures of pastoral societies, and to a lesser degree of agropastoral societies, have been shaken to the core.

In other respects, pastoral production has become integrated into a regional economy that is increasingly mercantile as a result of demographic developments, urbanization, and, more generally, the development of monetary relations and income-producing agriculture. The development of a livestock market has witnessed the emergence of a new social category, tradespersons and brokers, and has altered the conditions of pastoral specialization.

The desiccation and general degradation of the arid and semiarid environments, which have resulted as much from human factors as from overgrazing, have contributed to the accelerated marginalization of several African pastoralist groups. The geopolitical importance of the zones these groups occupy, especially at the southern limits of the arid zone, from the Atlantic to the Horn of Africa, helps to explain the political unrest there (such as the Western Sahara war; the Tuareg uprising; the Chad, Sudan, Somalia, and Djibouti conflicts).

BIBLIOGRAPHY

Almagor, Uri. *Pastoral Partners: Affinity and Bond Partnership Among the Dassanetch of South-West Ethiopia.* Manchester, U.K., 1978.

Amadu, Mahdi, and A. H. M. Kirk-Greene, eds. *Pastoralists of the West African Savanna.* Manchester, U.K., 1986.

Dahl, Gudrun, and Anders Hjort. *Having Herds: Pastoral Herd Growth and Household Economy.* Stockholm, 1976.

Dupire, Marguerite. *Peuls nomades: Étude descriptive des Wodaabe du Sahel nigérien.* Paris, 1962.

Équipe Écologie et Anthropologie des Sociétés Pastorales, ed. *Pastoral Production and Society.* Cambridge, 1979.

Evans-Pritchard, Edward Evan. *The Nuer: A Description of the Modes of Livelihood and Political Institutions of a Nilotic People.* Oxford, 1940.

Galaty, John G., and Pierre Bonte. *Herders, Warriors, and Traders: Pastoralism in Africa.* Boulder, Colo., 1991.

Kelly, Raymond C. *The Nuer Conquest: The Structure and Development of an Expansionist System.* Ann Arbor, Mich., 1985.

Monod, Théodore, ed. *Pastoralism in Tropical Africa.* London, 1975.

Simpson, James R., and Phylo Evangelou, eds. *Livestock Development in Subsaharan Africa.* Boulder, Colo., 1984.

PIERRE BONTE

See also **Animals, Domestic.**

PERIPATETIC

Africanist anthropology has long been tied to a simple typology of productive strategies. Rural people were hunter-gatherers, agriculturists, or pastoralists. Numerous minority groups, which recently have been referred to in comparative analyses as peripatetics and service nomads, do not easily fit into this typology. Hunter-gatherer groups like the Waata and the Thwa of eastern and southern Africa, the "gypsy-like" Yibir, Dupi, and Fuga from the Horn of Africa; and casted craftsmen like the west African LawBe, the Saharan Inaden, and the Sudanese Halab make their living entirely or periodically by supplying services to a dominant population. Recently formed groups, like the Nigerian Yan Goge, wandering urban musicians, and the Karretjies, itinerant sheepshearers in the semiarid South African Karroo, show that minority groups are increasingly entering this niche.

All of these groups share common features and are described by Aparna Rao as "primarily non–food producing, preferentially endogamous, itinerant communities, subsisting mainly on the sale of goods and/or more or less specialized services to sedentary and/or nomadic customers." Peripatetics usually are generalists offering services to host populations that range from fortune-telling to ritual activities to handicrafts. This does not prevent some peripatetics from occasionally hunting or herding small stock, and others from migrating only occasionally. Typically, their activities are held in contempt by the dominant societies. Furthermore, all these groups are despised minorities within a larger setting and experience marked forms of symbolic and sometimes even violent rejection. However, their position is ambiguous; although deemed to be outcasts and thought to be antisocial, they frequently are courted as diviners and ritual specialists who are indispensable for the spiritual well-being of their clients.

After delineating productive strategies in seven exemplary groups, the major productive strategies will be summarized and contextualized.

Halab

Traditionally the Halab, or Nile Valley gypsies, were associated with manufacture of metal goods. In addition they acted as veterinarians and livestock traders. As entertainers they generated income as musicians, snake charmers, monkey trainers, and tightrope walkers. Halab women earned money as diviners and healers. Nowadays, Halab in Omdurman, Sudan, specialize in forging, thus extending their traditional skill in ironwork. Their small-scale enterprises are located within the informal sector and typically are small, family-based businesses that hire day laborers. They produce metal drums, pans, troughs, and water tanks, mainly from recycled metals, as well as simple machines (e.g., coffee grinders and sausage machines).

The endogamous Halab are despised in Sudan. Their access to rural resources has been legally restricted, and they are forced to be mobile. Urban Halab are more sedentary, although the dominant population sees them as rather unstable and mobile.

LawBe

The LawBe are one group of casted craftspeople in west Africa's Sahel. In the past they were nomadic, traveling from village to village, whereas today there is a marked tendency to sedentarization in towns. LawBe mobility is not confined to the territory of one host society, and they cross ethnic boundaries rather frequently. They offer their services to a number of patrons, who are obliged to show generosity to craftsmen who continuously supply them. Casted people are even entitled to small donations from their customers beyond payment for their goods. Occasionally they are given small plots of land to supply their households, but typically they do not have property rights in the land they till. LawBe men produce wooden utensils, mortars, pestles, milking equipment, and occasionally canoes. Frequently they travel to villages where they know they can buy trees to be used for carving. They obtain permission to cut trees at the fringe of the village and later work them into goods for sale. LawBe women are hairdressers and have a reputation of being prostitutes. Like other groups of casted craftspeople of the Sahel, the LawBe are endogamous. Recently their woodcarving economy has been boosted by tourists' demand for exotic, hand-carved items.

Yan Goge

The Yan Goge, the "children of the bowed lute," are itinerant entertainers in the Hausa towns of northern Nigeria and are culturally linked to the Sahelian griot tradition. With the griots they share the marginalized position of entertainers in a Muslim context. The Yan Goge are people who have been estranged from their traditional social context due to personal fate or to societal pressures against professional musicians and dancers. They are organized in several smaller groups: male dancers, female dancers, musicians, praise singers, and a manager. Their clients are wealthy urban dwellers and, in recent times, political parties that rely on the praise singers to popularize their programs and hope for the advertising effect of the dance companies. Additional income is earned from prostitution, shoe shining, and go-between jobs, such as taking odd bits of information as oral or written accounts from a customer to a specified person or group.

Yibir

The Yibir are part of the *sab*, a despised group of hunters, beggars, and craftsmen among the Somali.

They were estimated by I. M. Lewis to number about 1,300 individuals in the early 1960s. Some of them are attached to noble Somali pastoralists, and others offer services to various households. In the late nineteenth century a traveler described them as beggars, buffoons, fortune-tellers, tanners, saddlers, and producers of charms. Soothsaying, magic, surgery, hairdressing, and circumcision are other income-generating activities. They were entitled to customary gifts that allegedly had to be paid as a form of blood money because a major Yibir ancestor was killed by an early Somali hero. In return for these obligatory alms, they blessed their clients. The Somali attribute great supernatural powers to the Yibir and fear their curse. The Yibir are strictly endogamous. They trace their ancestry to pre-Islamic times and mention a pagan sorcerer as their ancestor, a fact that is not highly esteemed in an Islamic context. Apparently they use an argot to protect themselves or to cause curiosity among their clients. In recent times many Yibir have settled in towns of northern Somalia, where they earn their livings as craftsmen and merchants.

Fuga

The Gurage of Ethiopia call all despised craftsmen Fuga and then differentiate them into blacksmiths, tanners, and the Fuga proper, the woodworkers. In other southwestern Ethiopian groups, such as the Kambata and Janjero, tanners and potters are subsumed under the term "Fuga." The Fuga are not confined to tribal territories and move about to offer their services in various southern Ethiopian societies. From the perspective of the sedentary farmers, they are nomads who have no settled abode, yet in actuality they may oscillate between sedentary and mobile periods. Several authors have reported that they use an argot for communication among themselves. In most Ethiopian host societies they were prohibited from owning land and thereby were barred from investing labor and capital in agriculture; in a few societies they were permitted to hold small sections of rented land. Due to this legal discrimination they were forced to generalize their service activities: among the Gurage they specialized in woodworking, felling trees, cutting wood, and constructing parts of homesteads. Among the Kambata they served as potters and leatherworkers and earned additional income as musicians at weddings and funerals and as ritual experts. As was typical for southern Ethiopian minorities, they were despised and feared at

the same time. They were circumcisers and performers of funeral rites and were considered indispensable when a curse on a field had to be removed. At the same time they were described as irreligious by members of the dominant societies and were suspected of turning into hyenas at night.

Waata

The Waata of Ethiopia and Kenya were described by Philipp Viktor Paulitschke as "nomadic gypsies" who occasionally hunted and at other times acted as musicians. Enrico Cerulli translated "Waata" as "wandering magician" in Tigrinya. Waata groups who today live among the Boran, Sidamo, Gabbra, Orma, and coastal Bantu of Ethiopia and Kenya are generally described as foragers. Although all ethnographies report that they do some hunting and gathering, they engage in numerous other activities: they tan skins, make pottery, act as grave diggers, and offer ritual services. The endogamous Waata are held in contempt for breaking food taboos, being irreligious, and pursuing a life "outside culture," yet they are indispensable in many rituals of their host societies. The pastoral nomadic Gabbra of northern Kenya do hardly any ritual without significant contribution by the Waata. The latter follow a complex pattern of spatial mobility; as long as the economy of their hosts flourishes, they will attach themselves to patrons; when it declines, they will survive as foragers for some time.

Thwa

The Thwa of southwestern Angola are small-scale pastoralists who earn a major part of their living by offering services to diverse host populations. The men are ironsmiths who produce bracelets and various types of knives and spears; the women are expert potters. The Thwa conduct rituals for spirit-possessed clients and cure various diseases. In order to conduct these rituals, they move to the client's household for some weeks. According to their traditions, they have experienced a complex history of shifts between various modes of production. During the ivory boom of the late nineteenth century, they became expert elephant hunters and either acted as hands for commercial hunters or hunted on their own account and exchanged the ivory later on. Their oral traditions still convey an expert knowledge of elephant hunting. After the ivory boom was over, they found new income-generating activities in a growing demand for iron products, pottery, and ritual services among rich pastoral and agropastoral neighbors. The Thwa are despised and are frequently accused of thievery and sorcery. They are strictly endogamous; should a man from another group have a liaison with a Thwa woman, he has to undergo a costly purification. Most of the Thwas' services are paid for in livestock, and since healing spirit-possessed customers has become a good business, their livestock holdings have expanded considerably.

Major Strategies Within the Peripatetic Mode of Production

The peripatetic niche is determined by the dominant mode of production, the social environment, and the technological capacity of the minority group. Some occupational activities occur often and are frequently combined. In the field of handicrafts, smithing, leatherwork and tanning, pottery, and weaving are typical for peripatetics. They frequently offer ritual services like circumcision, grave digging, magical curing, fortune-telling, and divination. Begging and various kinds of entertainment also provide income. Not all these activities are highly regarded by the dominant population but are urgently needed to fulfill certain material or spiritual needs. Peripatetics in Africa frequently use subsidiary food-producing strategies. They occasionally hunt and gather, pursue small-scale horticulture on rented fields, or raise small stock. Frequently the dominant population restricts their access to resources, and they are not entitled to own resources in their own right. Because they are always dependent on a large number of clients, they are mobile. The degree of mobility is determined by the density of potential customers in an area. Some peripatetics live directly attached to their clients and migrate with them, whereas others follow independent migratory cycles. In the first case the host family is often regarded as the owner of the peripatetic group, who end up in a slavelike position of exploitation and social marginalization. In the latter case, peripatetics move between clusters of clients and act as go-betweens connecting them. The Yibir of the Somali and the Tuudi smiths of the Tubu have been reported to negotiate between warring tribes or factions. Typically, peripatetics are deemed to be neutral and nonaligned, indispensable qualities for brokers within a multiethnic setting. Neither the Fuga nor the Waata nor the Manna of Ethiopia took part in wars of the dominant societies, and the nyeenyBe craftsmen of the Wolof had a special status during times of violent conflict.

Peripatetic groups are generally assigned ritual powers by the host society, and this belief in their supernatural capacity defines other income-generating strategies for them. In many west African societies peripatetics are deemed to be experienced sorcerers and magical healers. The Aouloube, casted craftsmen among the Malian Tukulor, are reported to be specialists in curing venereal diseases, and the Enkyagu, smiths of the Marghi in northern Nigeria, act in addition as cicatrizers of females, diviners, doctors, and grave diggers. The Awka, traveling smiths among the Nigerian Igbo (Ibo), act as agents of a famous oracle and earn income as diviners, circumcisers, and healers. The Fuga of the Ethiopian Gurage, the Janjero, and the Kambata are indispensable specialists in rites of passage, organize burials, and conduct circumcisions. Their skills as healers and producers of magical potions are frequently used by members of the host society. The Thwa of southern Angola specialize in healing spirit possessions. They produce the most effective charms and amulets to repulse sorcery and evil spirits. The Sarwa of Botswana conduct trance dance sessions for their hosts, who on other occasions would be reluctant even to eat with them.

Many peripatetic minorities have clung to an original language in spite of their minority status or have developed an argot to shield internal communication against a hostile social environment. Yet many of them act within a multiethnic setting and consequently are bi- or even trilingual. This "language policy" ensures that they are conversant in the cultural codes of several host societies and at the same time maintain "secret knowledge" against outsiders. This ambiguity is reflected in the myths of origin of many African peripatetic societies. These myths integrate them into dominant tales of genesis and cultural development, and at the same time explain their marginal economic and social situation. An early ancestor of the Fuga was said to have offered a mythical king rotten meat, and therefore was cursed. The ancestor of the Yibir, a pagan witch doctor, fought with a Muslim Somali ancestor and tried to kill him with magic. An ancestor of the west African LawBe craftsmen had the impudence to wound Muhammad in a fight. Pollution and sin are dominant themes in these tales of origin and explain the low status of these groups.

An Evolutionary Perspective on Peripatetic Societies

The evolution of hunter-gatherer groups in a complex post-Neolithic setting does not necessarily lead to food production. The cases in which foragers move into a peripatetic niche, combining generalized productive strategies with spatial mobility, are rather frequent in Africa and Asia. The hallmark of their economy and social organization is flexibility, which allows them to adapt optimally to their clients' changing demands. Many hunter-gatherers, like the Waata, Dorobo, and San, pursue foraging strategies in times of stress and adopt non-food-producing strategies when the economy of the dominant society flourishes.

African peripatetic groups did not develop solely out of forager societies, which have been losing ground to food-producing societies. Other peripatetics originated in a peasant setting, driven from their land by war, famine, or expropriation. The itinerant sheepshearers of the South African Karroo, the Karretjies, are just one example. Urban unemployment and poverty, a flourishing informal sector, and a growing refugee population seem to open new fields for the emergence of peripatetic groups. The Halab of Khartoum, as specialized ironworkers, and the Yan Goge of northern Nigeria, as professional itinerant entertainers, show that peripatetic strategies are an option for the urban as well as the rural future.

Peripatetic economic strategies and social organization in Africa have not been important topics of anthropological research. Ethnographers frequently deal with them only in passing and mainly reproduce the opinions of host societies about them. There is very little knowledge from within. Due to their mobility patterns, which are not confined to tribal territories, and their despised status, research on peripatetics is difficult. However, more scientific interest in this specific mode of production may elucidate new perspectives on economic change and the transmission of knowledge, and could have an impact on the development of crafts in many African societies.

BIBLIOGRAPHY

Bollig, Michael. "Ethnic Relations and Spatial Mobility in Africa: A Review of the Peripatetic Niche." In *The Other Nomads: Peripatetic Minorities in Cross-Cultural Perspective*, edited by Aparna Rao. Cologne, 1987.

Casimir, Michael J. "In Search of Guilt: Legends on the Origin of the Peripatetic Niche." In *The Other Nomads: Peripatetic Minorities in Cross-Cultural Perspective*, edited by Aparna Rao. Cologne, 1987.

Cerulli, Enrico. *Folk-Literature of the Galla of Southern Abyssinia*. Cambridge, Mass., 1922.

Dahl, Gudrun. *Suffering Grass: Subsistence and Society of Waso Borana*. Stockholm, 1979.

Dupire, Marguerite. "A Nomadic Caste: The Fulani Woodcarvers. Historical Background and Evolution." *Anthropos* 80, no. 1–3 (1985): 85–100.

Hallpike, C. R. "The Status of Craftsmen Among the Konso of South West Ethiopia." *Africa* 38 (July 1968): 258–269.

———. *The Konso of Ethiopia: A Study of the Values of a Cushitic People*. Oxford, 1972.

Hayden, R. M. "The Cultural Ecology of Service Nomads." *The Eastern Anthropologist* 32, no. 4 (1979): 297–309.

Lewis, I. M. *A Pastoral Democracy: A Study of Pastoralism and Politics Among the Northern Somali of the Horn of Africa*. London, 1961.

Olofson, Harold. "Children of the Bowed Lute: Organization and Expressive Culture of the Hausa Urban Itinerant Entertainers." *Anthropos* 75, no. 5–6 (1980): 920–929.

Paulitschke, Philipp Viktor. *Ethnographie nordost-Afrikas*. Berlin, 1893–1896. Repr. New York, 1967.

Rao, Aparna. "The Concept of Peripatetics: An Introduction." In *The Other Nomads: Peripatetic Minorities in Cross-Cultural Perspective*, edited by Aparna Rao. Cologne, 1987.

Shack, William A. "Notes on Occupational Castes Among the Gurage of South West Ethiopia." *Man* 64 (March–April 1964): 50–52.

MICHAEL BOLLIG

See also **Class, Rank, and Caste; Capitalism and Entrepreneurship; Economies, Alternative.**

FISHING

Dried, smoked, and salted fish and shellfish were traded as early as the fifteenth century along the west African/Sahelian trade routes. There is some evidence that commercial fishing was significant by at least the sixteenth century. For instance, the Sorkawa and the Boza, who fished the middle Niger River, paid their taxes to the Songhai Kingdom exclusively in dried fish. As of the late 1990s, Africa's fishing industries are both a major source of animal protein for domestic consumption and an important source of foreign earnings. Of the forty-six states in sub-Saharan Africa, thirty-two are maritime, and fourteen are landlocked. It is estimated that eight million people in sub-Saharan Africa are directly or indirectly employed in the fisheries sector. On a global scale, marine fishing off the coast of Africa accounts for less than 5 percent of the world marine harvest, and inland fishing accounts for approximately 12 percent, of the world freshwater harvest. With rare exceptions, Africa's marine fisheries are fully exploited or overexploited. Its inland fisheries are generally underexploited, although inland fisheries in Kenya and Uganda are overexploited, and those of Ghana, Malawi, Tanzania, Zaire, and Zambia are fully exploited.

Data on African fisheries are extremely inconsistent, inaccurate, and often based on compilations, extrapolations, and interpolations from a variety of unreliable sources. This situation results from inadequate scientific funding, facilities, and equipment to collect reliable data on fisheries exploitation and management. Furthermore, fisheries science is often dependent on the political and economic considerations of fishing companies and states; most fisheries studies are conducted in conjunction with access and management negotiations between states under the United Nations Convention on the Law of the Sea (UNCLOS). Finally, unlike terrestrial agricultural systems in sub-Saharan Africa, fisheries have been relatively neglected in the social analysis of food provisioning.

The Hydrosphere of the Coast

The Atlantic Ocean

The major fishing areas on the west coast of Africa are the eastern central Atlantic and the southeast Atlantic, which cumulatively extend from the Strait of Gibraltar to Durban, South Africa. The richest fishery zones are defined by the extent of the continental shelf and the existence of cold upwellings and currents. Continental shelf ecosystems provide rich plankton growth, and thus an abundance of fish, in three main areas: from the Canary Islands to Sierra Leone; from Cape Palmas to Togo; and from Gabon to the Cape of Good Hope. The Canary Current and the warm Guinea Current, in addition to a permanent upwelling off the coast of Senegal, provide nutrient-rich flows of water along the coast of western Africa. A seasonal upwelling occurs between Côte d'Ivoire and Togo. The cold Benguela Current flows along the southwestern coast of Africa. Productive fishing zones also are associated with the outflow of the Congo River and an upwelling off the coast of Angola.

The principal pelagic fisheries adjacent to the western coasts of Africa are sardines (*Sardina*), tuna (*Thunnus*), and mackerel (*Scomber*). The principal demersal fisheries are hake (*Merluccius*), octopus (*Octopus*), grouper (*Epinephelus*), and snapper (*Lutjanus*). Shellfish, crustaceans, and turtles are also taken for local trade and subsistence consumption.

The Indian Ocean

The principal marine fisheries of eastern Africa are associated with coral reefs. The continental shelf along Africa's eastern coast is relatively thin and in many places is nonexistent. The principal fisheries are located along the coast of Mozambique; along the western coast of Madagascar; in the Mozambique Channel; and along the Mascarene Ridge, which extends southeast from the Seychelles to Mauritius. Pelagic fisheries include tuna and sardine. Principal demersal fisheries include various reef fishes, sharks (*Selachimorpha*), rays (Elasmobranchii), and shrimp.

Inland Fisheries

Inland fisheries in sub-Saharan Africa are often associated with the introduction of aquaculture systems since the 1970s, although trout (*Salmo*) farming was established in Kenya and Madagascar in the 1920s, and tilapia (*Oreochromis*) was first farmed in Kenya in 1924 and in Zaire in 1946. Early aquaculture enterprises were abandoned in the 1960s as a result of poor returns, lack of stocking material, drought, and political unrest. The resurgence of freshwater farming has often been in conjunction with irrigation and dam development projects.

Inland fisheries in sub-Saharan Africa are mostly in freshwater environments, but recently there has been an upward trend in use of coastal brackish waters, particularly in Nigeria and Kenya. The major inland fisheries are located in Nigeria, Côte d'Ivoire, Zambia, Kenya, Zaire, Ghana, Togo, Congo, Madagascar, and Sudan. Over thirty species of fish are cultured in inland sub-Saharan Africa, particularly tilapia and carp. Stocking material is supplied by public production centers.

The basic production units for inland fisheries are small, earthen ponds which range in size from 100 to 1,000 square meters (1,076–10,760 sq. ft.)—subsistence level to small-scale commercial level. Larger, privately owned, commercial farms exist in Kenya, Malawi, Nigeria, Zambia, and Zimbabwe and range in size from 2 to 30 hectares (5–75 acres). Some producers use tanks, raceways, and net pens. In Madagascar, irrigated rice fields are commonly planted with paddy and stocked with fish. The application of organic fertilizer is widespread in African aquaculture; mineral fertilizers are used when affordable.

Stocks and diversity of lacustrine fishes in sub-Saharan Africa have declined since the 1890s due to overfishing and the introduction of exotic species to create new fisheries. The introduction of the Nile perch (*Lates niloticus*) to Lake Victoria is thought to be responsible for the largest mass extinction of lake fauna in modern times. Fifty different exotic species have been introduced into six of sub-Saharan Africa's nineteen major lakes, prominently Nile perch and various freshwater sardines (*Stolothrissa tanganicae* and *Linnothrissa miodon*, for instance). Most of these lakes are located in the Rift Valley of eastern Africa.

Artisanal Fisheries

Africa's artisanal fishing industries are characterized by locally designed technologies, intensive communal and seasonal labor, and production mainly for domestic and subsistence consumption. Due to the scarcity and the expense of livestock, fish provides up to 70 percent of the animal protein in the African diet. In both inland and marine fishing communities, equipment typically consists of wood dugout canoes, various designs of fish and shellfish traps and nets, and hooks and lines. Since the late 1950s, African fishers have adopted the use of imported motors, hooks, and synthetic nets and lines; imported vessels have not been widely adopted.

Central to most of Africa's artisanal fishing industries is the highly seasonal nature of fish migrations and spawnings. In order to sustain year-round income from fishing in the absence of reliable refrigeration, various methods of processing, preservation, and marketing have been developed. Salting, drying, and smoking are the three main techniques of preservation. Smoking ovens and storage systems have been independently developed throughout Africa and allow marketers to efficiently control the distribution of their commodity. Fisher migrations are also essential to year-round harvests and profits. The Fante fishers of Ghana, for instance, make short- and long-term migrations from Senegal to Cameroon to exploit a succession of harvests which follow current and upwelling patterns along the coast of western Africa. As a result, Fante canoe, net, and oven designs have diffused to many fishing cultures along the west African coast.

Gender and kinship systems are integral to the division of labor in Africa's artisanal fishing industries. Both women and men participate in inland fishing and nearshore collection of shellfish, crustaceans, and urchins; only men fish on the open sea and on large lakes. Several African coastal ethnic groups place cultural and religious restrictions against women setting foot in fishing canoes, such as the Ewe of Ghana and Togo, and the Swahili of Kenya and Tanzania. Women are usually responsible for processing and marketing of fish and in this way have become dominant players in local

fishing economies and communities. Communal and familial labor is often employed in artisanal fishing. Particularly in marine and large lake fishing, groups of workers are necessary to drive fish into nets, to cast and haul large nets, and to paddle and crew large canoes. Groups of workers are also imperative in large-scale fish processing, which demands the completion of multiple tasks in a brief window of opportunity. Communal labor and relationships between fishers and marketers typically center on kinship and household arrangements. However, as a result of recent economic restructuring and fisheries environmental degradation throughout sub-Saharan Africa, these kinds of familial networks are giving way to wage, credit, and contract arrangements between individual fishers, marketers, equipment owners, and laborers.

Worldwide, inland fishing accounts for only 16 percent of the total production, but inland fishing plays a tremendous role in sub-Saharan Africa. Landings of inland fish in sub-Saharan Africa account for almost 60 percent of the over 3 million metric tons (3,306,000 tons) of fish that are landed annually on the continent. In eastern Africa, for example, over 95 percent of Kenyan fish landings are from inland fisheries, despite Kenya's abundant coastal reef fishery and 200-mile Exclusive Economic Zone (EEZ) in the Indian Ocean. While sub-Saharan Africa's inland fisheries have not been developed for the international market, development projects have focused on aquaculture techniques to meet local demands. Small-scale aquaculture is generally a secondary activity to terrestrial agriculture and is taken up by male farmers, although pond management and labor are usually performed by women. Medium-sized commercial fleets exist on Lake Volta in western Africa; Lake Chad in the Sahel; and Lakes Victoria, Tanganyika, and Nyasa in the Rift Valley. These fleets fish primarily for distribution to African countries, although there is a growing market for fresh Nile perch in Europe and the Middle East. Kenyan and Ugandan exporters ship frozen Nile perch products as far as Australia and North America. In 1991, for instance, Kenya and Uganda together exported approximately 11,000 metric tons (12,122 tons) of Nile perch fillets, with a total value of over U.S.$21 million.

In response to declining catches in both marine and lacustrine artisanal fisheries, fishers throughout Africa have resorted to desperate practices such as the use of dynamite and poisons. This kind of fishing not only overexploits the fisheries but also causes severe and irreversible damage to marine and inland aquatic ecosystems, further degrading the future of Africa's fishing industries.

Commercial Fisheries

Unlike Africa's inland fisheries, commercial fishing for international export is highly developed in Africa's marine fisheries. European and Russian fishing fleets have exploited the eastern central Atlantic fisheries off the coast of western Africa for over a century, whereas the coastal waters of southern and eastern Africa remained out of reach for most Western commercial fishers until recently. The first attempts to export marine fish and shellfish from sub-Saharan Africa were made by various colonial governments, but on a very small scale. During World War II, there occurred simultaneously a surge in the demand for canned fish and the beginning of catch declines from perennial overfishing in many of the world's fishing grounds. Improvements in fishing technology, particularly of nets and radar equipment, gave Western fishing companies a further incentive to expand their operations to distant (often Southern Hemisphere) waters, such as those around the African continent.

Today, Africa's marine fisheries are exploited mainly by European, Russian, North American, and Asian distant water fleets. There are many African-based commercial fleets in operation, but the nebulous politics of vessel flagging and joint ventures obscure the ownership and headquarters of many commerical fleets which appear to be African-owned and -managed. Spain and Russia report the highest catches of the most valuable species from the eastern central Atlantic. Japan, Russia, and South Africa outharvest the well-established commercial fleets of Namibia and Angola in the southeastern Atlantic. Pakistan and India are the dominant fishers in the western Indian Ocean adjacent to eastern Africa, although Japan and France take the highest catches of tuna. High-grade species are immediately exported, fresh and frozen, by air or by "over-the-side" deals with larger courier ships. Lower-grade species are boxed and frozen, or processed into meal and oil aboard factory ships. Of the few large-scale commercial processing operations which exist in African ports, most are owned by multinational corporations, such as the Starkist tuna-canning facility in Tema, Ghana.

Attendant to the structural adjustment loans that many African states took out in the 1980s, develop-

ment projects have promoted nontraditional exports to raise foreign currency. Among sub-Saharan Africa's coastal states, the nontraditional export of fish has been encouraged by international aid and loan projects which are used (a) to upgrade and establish commercial fleets, (b) to construct port and harbor infrastructure, (c) to expand port services and post-harvest operations, (d) to introduce aquaculture, and (e) to increase training and research. Ironically, as debt and malnutrition in sub-Saharan Africa have increased since the mid-1980s, so have the exports of nutritionally valuable fish products to the supermarkets, livestock feed-lots, and fertilizer factories of the developed world. Per capita consumption of fish in sub-Saharan Africa has declined from 9 kilograms (19.8 lbs.) in 1990 to less than 7 kilograms (15.4 lbs.) in 1994.

Since 1983, most coastal states have claimed a 200-mile exclusive economic zone (EEZ) over the seas which extend from their coastlines. The EEZ is one of the main principles of the UNCLOS and is thought to promote better management of marine resources through the national privatization of marine space. With the exception of Eritrea, every African state has signed UNCLOS, although rights to claim an EEZ are also supported by customary international law of the sea. Many coastal African countries signed UNCLOS with a view to negotiating access fees and other deals for foreign entry into their EEZs. However, given the frontierlike quality of the high seas, access to the EEZ is difficult to enforce for poor African states which cannot afford the necessary high-tech surveillance vessels or military power.

While the exploitation of marine fisheries off the African coasts has increased substantially since the 1970s, catches have either remained level or declined. The reported catch of crustaceans in Africa has remained at around 100,000 metric tons (110,200 tons) since 1987; the catch of demersal fish has averaged at 525,000 metric tons (578,550 tons) since 1985; and the catch of pelagic fish has dropped from a high of 2.5 million metric tons (2,755,000 tons) in 1987 to 2.2 million metric tons (2,424,400 tons) in 1993. Artisanal and commercial marine fishers alike complain not only of reduced numbers of fish but also smaller sizes of fish. Given the poor management practices in both sectors, the future of Africa's marine fisheries is doubtful.

BIBLIOGRAPHY

Carr, Claudia. "The Legacy and Challenge of International Aid in Marine Resource Development." In

Freedom for the Seas in the 21st Century, edited by Jon M. Van Dyke, Durwood Zaelke, and Grant Hewison. Washington, D.C., 1993.

Coche, André, et al. *Aquaculture Development and Research in Sub-Saharan Africa*. Food and Agriculture Organization of the United Nations. Rome, 1994.

Haakonsen, Jan, and M. Chimière Diaw, eds. *Fishermen's Migrations in West Africa*. Programme for Integrated Development of Artisanal Fisheries in West Africa. Cotonou, Bénin, 1991.

Kaczynski, Vlad. "Foreign Fishing Fleets in the subSaharan West African EEZ: The Coastal State Perspective." *Marine Policy* 13, no. 1 (1989): 2–15.

Marine Resources Service. *Review of the State of World Fishery Resources: Marine Fisheries*. FAO Fisheries Department Circular no. 884 FIRM/C884 (En). Rome, 1995.

Pitcher, Tony J., and Paul Hart, ed. *The Impacts of Species Changes in African Lakes*. London, 1995.

BARBARA LOUISE ENDEMAÑO WALKER

See also **Ecosystems: Coastal Environments.**

PROFESSIONALIZATION. The paradigmatic profession possesses (1) a set of *technical skills* that are acquired through an extended period of training, (2) a set of *norms* governing the behavior of its practitioners that is oriented toward service either to clients or the general community, and (3) some degree of *autonomy* and ability to regulate at least the technical quality of the work of its members. Particular occupations differ in the extent to which these three attributes are realized, but the more prominent the traits the more likely it is that the consequences usually associated with professionalization will be found. Economists tend to focus on only the skills part of the preceding definition, but sociologists have long insisted that all three attributes are important, and the rest of the social sciences have tended to follow their lead. Those who write on professionalism differ among themselves as to the relative importance of the three traits and about the causal sequence between them, but all agree that their presence has important consequences.

The prototypical professionals are lawyers, doctors, and university professors. The clergy, veterinarians, accountants, and pharmacists also usually approach the defining criteria. In Africa economics, journalism, teaching, and nursing might be called aspiring professions. They possess only some of the three attributes of a profession (or possess them only to a limited degree) but tend to aspire to all of

them. The legal profession has received the largest amount of scholarly attention in African studies.

Development of the Professions

The professions clearly were a colonial creation and played an important part in integrating Africa into a Western-dominated international market and value system. Initially, professional training had to be acquired in the West, and well after independence, standards and organizational forms were still derived from the metropolitan countries. Despite their imperial origin and function, however, the professions often became an important source of indigenous adaptation and resistance to colonialism. For example, law has played a dual role as an instrument of colonial domination and penetration by international capital, on the one hand, and as an instrument of indigenous groups attempting to mold those forces to their own advantage, on the other, a development documented particularly well for Ghana.

The professions are not as well developed in Africa as they are in most industrial democracies (with the partial exception of southern Africa, where the presence of substantial numbers of non-Africans heavily influences all the "commanding heights" of society). The technical qualifications of Africans approach those of their metropolitan counterparts in some fields, but the local professions of which they are a part usually have less autonomy and give less attention to ethics. Nonetheless, in societies in which the state dominates most organizations that cross ethnic boundaries and in which normative systems oriented toward the collective interests of all of society are weakly developed, even the limited degrees of autonomy and ethical development that the professions do possess in Africa can be quite important.

The degree to which a profession has autonomy from the state depends on the importance of the private sector in that economy and the proportion of that particular occupation employed outside the state. Private practice has been particularly important in the early and sustained ability of the law profession to challenge governments in Africa. The development of the professions was much more dominated by the state in France than it was in Britain, for the state essentially monopolizes education and regulation for most professions in the former, whereas autonomous institutions play a much larger role for both functions in the United Kingdom. As a result professions tend to be more autonomous in anglophone than in francophone Africa.

The breakdown of the state and the expansion of an independent private sector in many African countries has reinvigorated many professional associations that had been atrophying. As economies have liberalized, professionals have had to reorganize to protect their interests and to develop self-regulatory mechanisms to supplant the ineffective supervision of the state. So far, outside of southern Africa the self-protection functions of professional associations are reemerging more vigorously than the self-regulatory ones. However, the needs to give consumers confidence in their services and to justify their political claims for greater autonomy are forcing the professional associations gradually to give more attention to policing their own members.

Consequences of Professionalization

Scholars have stressed very different effects of professionalization in Africa and have made contradictory evaluations. In the historical literature, some have emphasized the role the professions played in the penetration of Western capital and culture, while others have highlighted their role in indigenous adaptation and resistance.

With regard to the present, scholars such as Ragia Abdin and his colleagues see professions as antisocial groups, raising qualifications and imposing monopoly for self-aggrandizement. For example, their case study of the Pharmaceutical Society of Ghana shows it struggling to require inappropriately high, metropolitan qualifications for practitioners in order to justify larger salaries for its members.

Other scholars, however, praise the professions for providing support to those who would stand above ethnicity and pursue the public interest in political, administrative, and regulatory settings that generally are narrow and selfish. In this regard, the international connections of the professions are seen as a lifeline in a hostile sea of patronage and corruption. Thus, David K. Leonard credits the professional identities of key civil servants for turning some narrow political pressures into programs with broad community benefit in Kenya.

A third theoretical perspective, best exemplified in the work of Robin Luckham, holds that the professions have had all the preceding consequences, with their apparent contradiction and mixture of good and bad.

Most recently, the professions have been recognized as central to "civil society" and have been credited with a key role in the democratization movements of the 1990s. Lawyers, both through their relatively autonomous professional organizations and as the guardians of judicial independence, and the clergy, as the one profession wholly outside state employment and dependent directly on society for its income, have been particularly prominent and important in resisting state autocracy. The Bar Association was an important and visible source of resistance to the Nkrumah, Busia, and Acheampong regimes in Ghana and even organized a strike of professional bodies in 1977. In Kenya the Law Society and the clergy have been key sources of criticism of the government of President Daniel arap Moi. And in South Africa the independence of the judiciary was responsible for curbing some of the excesses of the apartheid regime, although questions were raised as to the extent to which physicians respected their professional code of ethics in the treatment of political prisoners.

BIBLIOGRAPHY

Abdin, Ragia, Paul Bennell, Olufemi Fajana, Martin Godfrey, and Bachir Hamdouch. *A World of Differentials: African Pay Structures in a Transnational Context.* London, 1983.

Anibaba, Musliu O. *A Short History of the Accountancy Profession in Nigeria.* Lagos, Nigeria, 1990.

Dias, C. J., R. Luckham, D. O. Lynch, and J. C. N. Paul, eds. *Lawyers in the Third World: Comparative and Developmental Perspectives.* New York, 1981.

Hyden, Goran, and Michael Bratton, eds. *Governance and Politics in Africa.* Boulder, Colo., 1992.

International Commission of Jurists. *The Independence of the Judiciary and the Legal Profession in English-Speaking Africa: A Report of Seminars Held in Lusaka from 10 to 14 November 1986 and in Banjul from 6 to 10 April 1987.* Geneva, 1988.

Kalu, Onuka. *Modern Journalism in Africa: A Newspaperman Looks at His Profession.* Owerri, Nigeria, 1989.

Leonard, David K. *African Successes: Four Public Managers of Kenyan Rural Development.* Berkeley, 1991.

——. "Professionalism and African Administration." *IDS Bulletin* 24, no. 1 (1993): 74–79.

——. "Structural Reform of the Veterinary Profession in Africa and the New Institutional Economics." *Development and Change* 24, no. 2 (1993): 227–267.

Rayner, Mary. *Turning a Blind Eye? Medical Accountability and the Prevention of Torture in South Africa.* A Report of the Committee on Scientific Freedom and Responsibility of the American Association for the Advancement of Science. Washington, D.C., 1987.

DAVID K. LEONARD

See also **Education; Health Care; Law.**

PROPHETIC MOVEMENTS

[This entry consists of six parts: Overview; Western Africa; Eastern Africa; Central Africa; Kongo Region; and Southern Africa.]

OVERVIEW

Prophetic movements have been a pronounced feature of sub-Saharan Africa since the mid-nineteenth century. They have increasingly drawn on Christian and, in some areas, Muslim ideas and symbols but are grounded in indigenous models of religious inspiration and organization. The term "prophet," now widely used to denote inspired religious leaders whose revelation concerns matters of common or public import and tends to generate an organized following, is drawn from the Judeo-Christian tradition. Here its main meanings were one who announces or reveals divine judgment or moral law, and, in a more oracular sense, one who makes predictions about future contingencies. In much current usage by historians and social scientists, there is also the implication (deriving largely from Max Weber's view of prophets as a supreme type of charismatic leader) that a prophet is an extraordinary kind of religious leader who stands in sharp contrast to more routine practitioners such as diviners or spirit mediums. While this may be true of the major figures, it is unwise to overemphasize it, since it prevents appreciation of the local cultural roots of African prophecy, the traditions that shape both the prophets and those who respond to them.

Indigenous Roots of Prophecy

The range of indigenous revelatory and inspired practices from which African prophets have emerged is extremely varied. Revelation of the hidden sources of human and social well-being and malaise, and of the steps needed to attain or remove them, is universally a concern of African communities and gives rise to a variety of diviners and seers (though the simplest techniques are usually available to anyone). Sometimes their procedures involve no special inspiration but depend on the mastery of relevant bodies of knowledge and technique, as with Yoruba Ifa diviners (*babalawo*) or the practitioners of the Ebony Oracle among the Uduk (Sudan). The interpretation of dreams is widespread and merges into something more likely to be considered inspirational or indicative of unusual personal powers: visions or waking trances, from which guidance may be derived. Revelation and inspiration come fully together in the case of spirit mediums: people whose possession by a spirit enables them to transmit messages from spirits to humans. (Mere possession by a spirit, without mediumship, is much more widespread.) The identity of the possessing spirits varies widely: the "prophets" of the Sudanese Dinka (*ran nhialic*, which may be translated as "men of divinity") may be possessed by both clan and free divinities; among the Shona of eastern and central Zimbabwe, spirits of deceased chiefs (*mhondoro*) speak through mediums; and among western African peoples like the Akan and Yoruba, deities with local shrines—*abosom* and *orisha*, respectively—possess their priests or otherwise enable them to "see." Only rarely are the messages derived from a "high god" like the oracular sky deity Mwari of western Zimbabwe.

Usually, becoming a diviner or a medium is not determined by birth or descent but depends on personal choice and aptitude, or on being "called" by the spirit. But some priesthoods of Yoruba *orisha* may be "owned" by families, and among peoples like the Maasai and Nandi of Kenya, the functions of *loibon* and *orkoiyot* (both loosely rendered as "seer" or "prophet") are restricted to the members of particular lineages. Even in these cases, though, the special nature of the role is felt to imply an unusual inherent capacity or personal election by the spirit.

With the routine, local-level demand for guidance from the spirits in dealing with sickness, crop failure, and other misfortunes, the diagnostic (rather than predictive) functions that are the primary source of African prophecy tend to be closely allied with healing and "magic" (or thaumaturgy). Diviners are often healers too, and cures may be taken as evidence of the genuineness of the spirit medium as well as of the power of the spirit. Yet a differentiation of these functions also occurs, particularly as the spatial and temporal scale of society expands. Thus, in their "religious commissions" (as MacGaffey terms them), the Kongo distinguish between the *ngunza* (prophet) and the *nganga* (magician or healer). Although both deploy mystical power derived from the dead to enhance life, the key distinction between them is that the *ngunza* does so for public ends and the *nganga* for private or personal ones. In the case of the Nuer, their prophets (*guk*)—men possessed by a spirit whose mouthpiece they were—were expressly regarded as having nothing to do with magic.

Prophets, Crisis, and Change

Compared with the forms of inspired revelation that address themselves to fairly routine kinds of

Kongo prophets of the Church of the Holy Spirit in Africa performing "the healing," Manianga region, Zaire. COURTESY JOHN M. JANZEN

distress and uncertainty, there are some that occur in more exceptional circumstances and seem to qualify more decisively as prophetism. Throughout a large region of central Africa there is a well-established pattern of recurrent social renewal through prophet figures like the Kongo *ngunza*. Periodically—roughly every generation or so—there accumulates a sense that the incidence of sickness and social malaise has reached an intolerable level; this is interpreted as indicating that the charms or fetishes (*nkisi*) that protect the community against witchcraft have lost their power. There arises a charismatic visionary who proclaims the destruction of the old fetishes and the elimination of witches. He reveals new protective charms and establishes new shrines and rituals; his adherents set about institutionalizing the new religious order—which will last until it, too, is judged to have lost its efficacy.

Though these prophets innovated, they did so in relation to circumstances that recurred, and their innovations were closely limited by the prevailing culture. A greater degree of novelty was found where indigenous visionaries confront the unprecedented upheavals that attended the advance of European power. The prophet Rembe, active among the Lugbara of Uganda and Zaire in the 1890s, introduced a water cult that yielded a new protective war charm and also created wider social loyalties than existed before. The latter is also true of the Nuer prophets who, in the name of their encompassing deity Kwoth, articulated opposition to colonial pressure in the 1920s and 1930s. In the uprising of 1896–1897 against British rule in Rhodesia, however, it was not the priests of the wide-ranging sky deity Mwari, but some of the more localized *mhondoro* mediums of the Shona, who played a significant role in encouraging resistance. Likewise, over a wide area of Ruanda (now Rwanda) and adjacent parts of Uganda, Congo, and Tanganyika (now Tanzania), mediums of an established possession cult, Nyabingi, promoted resistance to colonialism into the 1920s. Among the Gikuyu, there emerged by the 1930s, from an indigenous tradition of prophets (*arathi*) now partially Christianized, the sect called Watu wa Mungu (People of God), who offered a radical and populist, but apolitical, critique of colonial society.

Thus, there are several overlapping criteria by which we may distinguish prophets in a fuller sense from the mediums, seers, and diviners whom they partly resemble, and from whom they have often arisen. Their revelations pertain to problems in the public sphere, not just the ills of individuals and households; they come to the fore during extraordinary, rather than routine, times; and they tend to propound new solutions, rather than old solutions more effectively. This last point might be put in terms that recall Weber's emphasis on the world-historical significance of what he called "ethical prophecy": thaumaturgy gives way, at least in part and for a while, to social re-formation. Two further traits (which are implied by the foregoing) have tended to feature in African prophecy in the twentieth century: a greater degree of orientation toward the future and a growing tendency for the Supreme Being to figure as the source of prophetic inspiration. These features may have been inherent in the combination of the African heritage and the colonial situation, but they were given a definite boost by the spread of Christianity and of Islam.

Influence of the World Religions

The world religions offer both exemplars of prophecy and new theological and eschatological ideas. In a strict sense, Islam allows no prophets (Muhammad is regarded as the last to receive direct inspiration from God); but a Muslim charismatic might follow Sufi mystical paths, or take the role of a *mujaddid* (renewer), or like the Sudanese Mahdi, be guided by visions and dreams of the Prophet and saints. The Muslim figures whom the French in West Africa called marabouts—Sufi leaders and specialists in amulets, Islamic lore, and dream interpretation—might play functions similar to those of pagan seers or Christian prophets, including the articulation of opposition to colonial rule. Amadu (Ahmad) Bamba, who after the French defeat of the Wolof of Senegal in 1886 was led by visions to found a new Sufi brotherhood, stood in this marabout tradition, calling himself not "prophet" but "servant of the Prophet."

Yet the Muslim term *nabi* (prophet; closely cognate with the Hebrew) entered African languages: the increasingly Christian Kuria (western Kenya) came to call their most notable seers of the past *abanaabi* (from Arabic through Swahili). The Yoruba Christian word for a prophet, *woli*, derives from a word widely current in Islamic West Africa for a Sufi mystic or "saint." The earliest we know of the Kongo term *ngunza* is as the word used for "prophet" in the Bible translation made by the Baptists.

Though Christianity undoubtedly gave more legitimation to African prophecy, both it and Islam shared the most vital new ideological component: millennialism, the notion that the world might be made anew and enjoy a thousand-year reign of peace and justice, a notion that might mesh with indigenous ideas of a community cleared of witches. In Islamic thought, the Mahdi is the savior who will be sent to expel the Antichrist and establish Islam. Mahdist ideas inspired the leaders of many of the western African jihads, including 'Uthman dan Fodio, founder of the Sokoto caliphate. Millennialist doctrines (which had a more definitely predictive character then most traditional prophecy) might be directly inferred from a reading of the Bible, but were especially liable to be taken up where they were expressly part of a missionary church's teaching, as was the case with Jehovah's Witnesses, very influential in central Africa, or the American Zionists, who had a large influence in South Africa after 1904. Being less exceptional, such missionary practices as mass baptisms and calls for the destruction of charms and idols—both of which were powerfully redolent, for Africans, of purification from evil and a new beginning—were readily incorporated into the repertory of African prophecy.

Millennial Ideas in Southern Africa

Christian ideas of the millennium had the most explosive effect where they were combined with the traumas of settler colonialism—military defeat, land loss, cattle disease, taxation, and forced labor migration—and might be present, combined with the desire to restore a lost traditional order, even among non-Christians. Thus, among the Xhosa of the eastern Cape, prophets or diviners on several occasions in the early nineteenth century preached purification from witchcraft and sacrifice to the ancestral shades and offered new charms to drive the whites from the land. In 1856–1857, the prophetess Nongqawuse added to these basic elements a much more millennial note: if the people would refrain from sowing and would kill their cattle, the dead heroes would return and the whites would be swept into the sea. The destruction of wealth was, in effect, a massive act of sacrifice in order that death might be annulled. The tragic irony of the "cattle-killing" was that it subordinated the Xhosa to white settler control even more rapidly.

In the early twentieth century, millennialism of a more "orthodox" kind became most deeply entrenched in central Africa. Doctrinally, its point source was Joseph Booth, a radical English Baptist who came to Africa in 1892. Booth combined a fervent desire to promote Africa's material development with a questing religious zeal that eventually led him through Adventism to the apocalyptic vision of the Brooklyn-based Watch Tower Bible and Tract Society (later known as Jehovah's Witnesses). It was a convert of Booth's, Elliott Kamwana, a Tonga from northern Nyasaland (now Malawi), who dramatically indigenized Watch Tower ideas, allegedly baptizing more than 10,000 people in 1909 alone and predicting the millennium for October 1914. This movement expressed both initial popular hopes of Christianity as a vehicle of purification and plenty and then dismay at the harsher realities of taxation and colonial rule. Despite the failure of 1914, Kitawala (as Watch Tower came to be known) diffused throughout the entire region from Zaire to Zimbabwe, graduating from apocalyptics to the earnest petit bourgeois congregations of Jehovah's Witnesses.

This trajectory from utopian endeavor to practical self-improvement was crossed in the opposite direction by Booth's closest African disciple, John Chilembwe. Having built up his Providence Industrial Mission in the Shire Highlands of southern Nyasaland, an area with large European estates, Chilembwe was gradually radicalized by worsening African conditions. The outbreak of war provided the final spark: in January–February 1915, he led an uprising to overthrow white rule that was rapidly and brutally put down. Though Chilembwe was not in the strict sense an inspired prophet, the eschatological strand in his project was very pronounced and implies that he should be placed within the range of religious leaders that includes witchfinders and diviners, prophets traditional and Christian, rather than set against them as a "secular" figure. The essential point is the unity or connectedness of the social values that animated African "prophecy" of any kind.

The spread of Christian ideas and idioms of prophecy did not mean that older notions of evil and its expulsion were made redundant—indeed, they were often incorporated into them. In the Mwana Lesa movement, founded in Northern Rhodesia (now Zambia) in 1925 by a former Kitawala adherent, Tomo Nyirenda, adventist and millennial preaching about the return of the dead and the expulsion of the whites tended to give way to witchcraft eradication. In central Africa there were numerous small-scale witch-finding movements (generically known as *mcape*) in later decades, often combined with healing and increasingly incorporating Christian elements.

Farther south, millennialism as such had less effect. Zionist prophets like Isaiah Shembe of the Nazarites and the Lekyanyane brothers of the Zion Christian church responded to the intense pressures of the South African system, not by envisaging the worldly reversal of Satan's order in the millennium, but by creating cult centers where an alternative order was continuously or periodically available to the members, and by doctrines of a heavenly state where the injustices of the color bar would be reversed. Nevertheless, the mundane focus of Zionist religion was still upon healing, guidance through dreams and visions, and negating the activity of witches and other evil forces.

Prophets in Western Africa

In the absence of both settler colonialism and any strong input of millenarian teaching from outside, prophecy in western Africa shows greater continuity with precolonial forms, despite its Christian content. As elsewhere, the 1910s provided strongly facilitating conditions: the entrenchment of colonialism through taxation and the courts, followed by the disruptive effects of the outbreak of war and the influenza pandemic of 1918. The two earliest movements affected coastal regions. William Wade Harris, a Grebo Episcopalian, received his prophetic call in 1910 while in prison for treason against the Liberian state. Wearing a white robe and carrying Bible, rod, and calabash of water, he traveled eastward along the lagoons of Côte

d'Ivoire as far as the western Gold Coast (now Ghana). He preached that people should renounce their old gods and fetishes and that witches should confess, and he offered baptism freely. Though expelled from Côte d'Ivoire by the French at the end of 1914, he left thousands of adherents, some of whom were later recruited by the Methodists, while others eventually founded the Église Harriste as well as a number of smaller healing and antisorcery cults. A comparable figure was the Kalabari prophet Garrick Braide, known to his followers as Elijah II, who in 1915 broke from the Anglicans in the Niger Delta to preach the destruction of charms, mass confession, and baptism (i.e., witchcraft purification). Braide died in 1918, but many of his followers were organized into the Christ Army Church, which emphasized healing and powerful prayer.

The largest movement of this general type was Aladura (from the Yoruba *adura*, prayer). It had its origins in several prayer groups—one set up at Ijebu-Ode, Nigeria, during the 1918 influenza pandemic, another (the Cherubim and Seraphim) established as a result of visions at Lagos in 1925—but it coalesced only in the early 1930s, years of depression in the Yoruba cocoa economy, when a number of prophets (*woli*) drew enormous crowds to their revivals. The greatest of these was Joseph Babalola, who preached the renunciation of idols and juju, and through prayer sanctified stream water in order to confer healing and fertility. Witchcraft confession was present, but not usually a dominant concern. For a while in 1930–1931 there was also a millenarian note—prophecies of the overthrow of the government and some preaching against taxes—but this was minor and transient. The enduring outcome of the Aladura revivals was a group of independent churches emphasizing healing, prayer, and visions that (through their overseas contacts) became the main vehicle for the spread of Pentecostalism in Nigeria.

The message of the great Congolese prophet Simon Kimbangu had much the same religious content as those of Harris, Braide, and the Aladura. A former Baptist catechist, Kimbangu received his first call during the epidemic of 1918, but his prophetic career lasted for only a few months in 1921. Despite his focus on healing and the evils of witchcraft and fetishism—great quantities of *nkisi* were handed in for destruction—the Belgian authorities imprisoned him for sedition. By the time of his death (still in prison) in 1951, his name and example had inspired a diverse sequence of movements, some mainly political in emphasis, some of a more nativist character. As with Harris, a church in his name, the Église de Jésus Christ sur la Terre par le Prophète Simon Kimbangu, was founded after his death; it has become a major element in the religious life of contemporary Zaire.

Kimbanguism raises the question of how these movements, which in some respects are so manifestly Christian, relate to traditional belief and practice. In phenomenological terms, just how different was the revival of Prophet Babalola at Ilesha in 1930 from, say, the activities at Abeokuta in 1855 of one Akere, whom the missionaries called a prophetess of the river goddess Yemoja? Like Babalola, she was inspired to sanctify the water of a stream with prayer and attracted vast crowds of people to take it for healing and fertility. Popular definitions of the ends of religious action, much of its symbolic language, and even much of the *woli's* role were given in the prevailing pre-Christian culture. It has not been argued that in western Africa, healing and witch-finding movements occur in a repeating, cyclical pattern like that proposed for western central Africa, where the Kongo are found. There Kimbangu stood in a line of *ngunza*, prophets who arose periodically to cleanse society of its evil and offered water as a medium of healing, empowerment, and renewal. A generation earlier, in 1888, British Baptist missionaries had been amazed at their sudden breakthrough, in what they called the "Pentecost of the Congo." They little understood that in the eyes of the Kongo, a people yearning for the renewal of their society, they conformed so well to the cultural template of the *ngunza*.

Christian prophets like Kimbangu and Babalola, who take the experiential realities of African lives in the same way the traditional religion does, are thus likely to act in ways that are culturally prescribed for healers or witch finders. But they may begin to innovate radically within these templates. Since the healing is ascribed to the power of a God who is jealous as well as high, the renunciation of fetishes is broadened into an attack on all other cults, and idolatry is assimilated to witchcraft, the perennial evil. Working with other forces of rationalization in the society (like literacy, wage labor, and bureaucratic administration), the prophets may thus be a significant force for cultural change.

Prophets and Politics

The relevance of prophecy to African politics has been explained in two main ways. First, it is argued that African cultures posit a particularly close con-

nection between "religion" (action oriented to spirits, gods, and other forces based in some unseen or other world but operative in this one) and "politics" (the working out of power relations in human society). This is true, but the spheres are not usually merged, at least where political authority is distinct from kin- and gender-based roles. Even though they usually have some sacred legitimation, the roles of chiefs, headmen, and kings are nearly always distinguished from those of priests, spirit mediums, diviners, and seers. *Okomfo* (priest) Anokye established the sacred charter of the Asante state, but he was not an *ohene* (chief), and among the Shona, the mediums of former chiefs (*mhondoro*) had a role sharply in contrast with, but complementary to, that of the chief.

The links between the religious and the political become relevant when political leaders or institutions are judged to have failed or where circumstances find them inadequate or lacking. The failure calls for a fresh attempt to determine the unseen—the spiritual—conditions of the social well-being that political leaders are expected to deliver and without which their legitimacy fades. Prophecy is thus like divination writ large: it diagnoses where things are wrong and proposes a new ordering of them. Since things can go wrong in various ways—sickness, witchcraft (i.e., general malaise), military defeat, and social dislocation being the commonest forms—we may ask whether all are equally political in import. Never was prophecy so saliently political—in the sense of directly addressing issues in the public sphere—as in the early colonial period, particularly in eastern and central Africa.

Though sickness and witchcraft can never be unconnected with this—the sick body being a powerful sign of the disordered society—where these concerns come to the fore, the direct political relevance of prophecy recedes. When healing and other forms of thaumaturgy for individuals become routine, the wider sociopolitical order is implicitly accepted: it is implausible to treat, say, Zionist churches in South Africa as expressing any kind of political resistance. Conversely, the political potential in Kimbangu's manifest concern with healing, witchcraft, and fetishism was realized only when the colonial regime suppressed him. Some of Kimbangu's successors, such as André Matswa, were quite overtly political, and the movement made its contribution to Congolese nationalism. But when the ban was finally lifted, the outcome was a bifurcation of religion and politics: a

Kimbanguist church with thaumaturgical concerns, and a Kongo-based political party (ABAKO) that held Kimbangu's memory in honor. By the 1970s no church supported Mobutu Sese Seko's state more strongly than the Kimbanguists.

Despite great growth in healing and Pentecostal churches, there have been fewer prophets of political import since the end of colonialism. Two rather unusual cases, both involving a visionary who found a particular local (and class) basis for a movement that offered a moral challenge to the political elite, were Alice Lenshina Mulenga's Lumpa Church in Zambia, which after coming into conflict with local branches of the ruling party was forcibly suppressed in 1964, and the Maitatsine movement in Northern Nigeria, led by an Islamic preacher highly critical of elite corruption, which provoked riots and was put down with force in 1980. Lesser prophets—offering healing, visionary guidance, protective rituals, and charms—have appeared in many of the episodes of civil war in Africa since the 1960s. Such were the Aladura prophets who predicted (and so helped to effect) the final collapse of the Biafran lines in the Nigerian civil war, and the prophetess Alice Lakwena, whose Holy Spirit Movement, syncretizing Christian and traditional mediumistic motifs, emerged in the chaos of Uganda in the late 1980s. Prophecy, in all its forms, continues as a potent force in African life.

BIBLIOGRAPHY

Anderson, David M., and Douglas H. Johnson, eds. "Diviners, Seers, and Prophets in Eastern Africa." *Africa* 61, no. 3 (special issue) (1991).

———. *Revealing Prophets: Prophecy and History in Eastern Africa.* London, 1995.

Beattie, John, and John Middleton, eds. *Spirit Mediumship and Society in Africa.* London, 1969.

Craemer, Willy de, Jan Vansina, and Renée C. Fox. "Religious Movements in Central Africa: A Theoretical Study." *Comparative Studies in Society and History* 18, no. 4 (1976): 458–475.

James, Wendy. *The Listening Ebony: Moral Knowledge, Religion, and Power Among the Uduk of Sudan.* Oxford, 1988.

Johnson, Douglas H. *Nuer Prophets: A History of Prophecy from the Upper Nile in the Nineteenth and Twentieth Centuries.* Oxford, 1994.

Haliburton, Gordon M. *The Prophet Harris.* London, 1971.

Lan, David. *Guns and Rain: Guerrillas and Spirit Mediums in Zimbabwe.* London, 1985.

Lienhardt, Godfrey. *Divinity and Experience: The Religion of the Dinka.* Oxford, 1961.

MacGaffey, Wyatt. *Modern Kongo Prophets: Religion in a Plural Society.* Bloomington, Ind., 1983.

Peel, J. D. Y. *Aladura: A Religious Movement among the Yoruba.* London, 1968.

Peires, Jeffrey B. *The Dead Will Arise: Nongqawuse and the Great Xhosa Cattle-Killing Movement of 1856–77.* Johannesburg, 1989.

Ranger, Terence O. "Religious Movements and Politics in Sub-Saharan Africa." *African Studies Review* 29, no. 2 (1986): 1–69.

Shank, David A. *Prophet Harris: The "Black Elijah" of West Africa.* Abridged by Jocelyn Murray. New York, 1994.

Shepperson, George, and Thomas Price. *Independent African: John Chilembwe and the Origins, Setting, and Significance of the Nyasaland Native Uprising of 1915.* Edinburgh, 1958.

Sundkler, Bengt. *Bantu Prophets in South Africa.* 2d ed. London, 1961.

Van Binsbergen, Wim. *Religious Change in Zambia.* London, 1981.

Weber, Max. *The Sociology of Religion.* Translated by Ephraim Fischoff. Boston, 1963.

J. D. Y. PEEL

See also **Braide Garrick; Christianity; Divination and Oracles; Harris, William Wadé; Healing; Islam; Kimbangu, Simon; Lenshina, Alice; Nongqawuse; Religion and Ritual; Shembe, Isaiah; Spirit Possession; Sufism; Witchcraft and Sorcery.**

WESTERN AFRICA

The history of west African Christianity since independence has been dominated and shaped by prophetic church movements and groups (often called Aladura churches) and by Evangelical Pentecostal-charismatic churches. These churches and movements fall within a long cultural and religious interdependence that began in the last decades of the nineteenth century when a group of church leaders seceded from the mission-established churches to form what are now called the Ethiopian or African churches. These churches, rooted in the nationalist fervor of the period and reacting to the Western colonial missionary enterprises, were founded mainly to protest the European domination and control of the mission churches. They seceded in order to form a new church that would be under African leadership and that would adopt African customs and traditions. Nevertheless, the African churches retained much of the structure and liturgy of mission churches.

Prophetic (Aladura) Churches

Genuine African initiative in the Christian tradition began with a second independent African church movement called the prophetic churches. In western Africa, especially in Nigeria, they are generally called Aladura (people of prayer) as an indication of their fervent prayers; in Ghana they are called spirit churches, emphasizing the importance of glossolalia (speaking in tongues) in the church. These were churches founded by African charismatic men and women who felt themselves called by God to be prophets, to begin a new mission of prayer, healing, and prophecy among their own people. The formative period of these churches was the first half of the twentieth century, after which some of them became well-established, large Christian denominations and highly routinized. The earliest and oldest of the Aladura churches established in Nigeria were the Church of the Lord (Aladura), Christ Apostlic church, the Garrick Braide movement, and the Cherubim and Seraphim church. The most popular and the fastest-growing independent churches today are the Celestial Church of Christ and the Brotherhood of the Cross and Star, also first established in Nigeria but today found in other parts of the world, especially in Europe and America.

Most of the prophetic Aladura churches originated in anglophone western Africa, where the Anglican, Methodist, and Baptist churches have taken deep root. Most of these churches first appeared in Nigeria, Ghana, and Liberia, though they spread very quickly to other countries in the region. Very few of the churches began in the French-speaking countries, the churches of Prophet William Wadé Harris being a notable example. The paucity of prophetic churches in the French-speaking areas may be related to two factors. First, the regions were predominantly Roman Catholic, a denomination that hardly witnessed the phenomenon of secession by its members. Second, the region has a large Muslim population, which at that time did not have compelling reasons to convert to prophetic churches.

The sizes of these churches vary from fewer than one hundred members to several thousand members. While most of them remain influential largely in their area of origin, a few have expanded far beyond their founders' "homeland."

The prophetic churches are loosely structured and are not based on any coherent doctrinal and liturgical practices, especially early in their development. Unlike mission churches, the organizational setups of the independent churches differ from one another very greatly. Also, neither their doctrines nor their liturgy is well laid out, in contrast to mission churches. The sole authority lies with the founder, regarded as divinely guarded; his utterances, instructions, and pronouncements, often backed by revelations and visions, are regarded as divinely inspired and therefore infallible. The prophetic churches allow for more ingenious creativity in worship and are very true to the African tradition of orality and the use of nontextual materials.

A distinguishing mark of the liturgical practices of these churches is their use of indigenous African instruments, such as drums, gongs, and flutes, and the emphasis they place on African dances and local lyrics and music. Even where they borrow from the liturgical text of the mainline churches, these are rendered into African words and music. As members of the Christian church, most of them observe Holy Communion, saints' days, and matrimony; in contrast to the practices of the mission churches, they have adopted personal and communal rituals of cleansing and healing. Taboos and prohibitions are put in place to ensure holiness and purity of individual members, especially in the places of worship. For example, menstruating women are prohibited from entering the church after sexual intercourse. Some of these churches designate and consecrate certain mountains, hills, rivers, and lands around them as holy places where members withdraw for special prayers, vigils, and ritual activities. As visions and prophecy recommend, special ritual births take place in these sacred rivers and streams, often located within the church precincts and consecrated by the church for such use. For example, in the Celestial Church of Christ, healing prayers occur at a place in the precinct of the church called "mercy land." This church also calls its founder's home place, Imeko, the Celestial City, and members go there on annual pilgrimages of prayer and worship.

Pentecostal-Charismatic Churches

The Pentecostal-charismatic churches' phenomenal rise in number and membership since the late 1970s has made them the largest single movement in western Africa. Pentecostal-charismatic churches are Evangelical groups that emphasize reconversion of members from their nominal Christian status to a more radical fundamentalist and evangelical stance, often called "born again" Christianity, through baptism of the Holy Spirit. It is assumed that members are holier and spiritually superior to nominal Christians. Like earlier African churches, these churches emphasize speaking in tongues and the performance of divine healing and miracles. They also emphasize material success or prosperity of their members.

The origin of the charismatic churches in Nigeria has been traced to college and university student ministries, which began in the postcolonial period as prayer and scriptural groups on college campuses (for example, the Scripture Union and Campus Christian Fellowship). Their leaders, upon graduation, began ministries in cities among educated groups. Some of the west African Pentecostal and charismatic churches originated in Europe and America but were adapted to African situations on arrival. Examples are the Assembly of God and the Full Gospel Business Men's Fellowship International. While some of these churches are interdenominational and have members who retain their membership in denominational churches, in recent years several of the charismatic churches, such as the Deeper Life Bible church and the Redeemed Christian church, have become distinct denominations with memberships larger than the mainline churches.

Since the 1980s the charismatic churches have begun to have significant appeal among Christian communities in western Africa. Some of the mainline churches have adapted their evangelical practices, including the use of electronic media, open-air services, and large revival meetings. The use of cassette tapes, videos, and electronic keyboards, have enhanced their appeal among the west African Christian communities. To maintain strong contact with a large array of adherents, the churches provide weekly and monthly literature like Gospel tracts, and prayer and Bible guides, in both English and local languages. The global orientation of the charismatic churches can be seen in the frequent visits of their leaders to international revival meetings in Europe, Asia, and America, and the frequent visits made by prominent Western charismatic church leaders to western Africa.

In contemporary western Africa, there is a second type of Pentecostal-charismatic churches, called the neocharismatic renewal groups. Originating within such Western denominational churches as the Roman Catholic and the Anglican, members of these groups often maintain their identity within the denomination to which they belong. The classic example is the Catholic charismatic renewal churches found all over western Africa.

Continuity of Prophetic and Pentecostal-Charismatic Churches

In spite of the attempt in the scholarly literature to project a sharp distinction between the pro-

phetic and charismatic groups, there is a clear continuity between them. Both are preoccupied with what could be said to be the primary concern of African religious communities: the quest for healing, well-being, material success, and long life. Although both of them have condemned indigenous practices and beliefs as "paganism," they recognize the persistence of such beliefs as witchcraft and sorcery, as defined in the indigenous cosmology and thought system. Both also have waged incessant wars against indigenous religious institutions, and ritual practices and ritual places, by burning shrines, destroying medicine and amulets, and casting out what they consider to be "demons" inhabiting people's bodies. However, the African worldview and practices manifested in visions, dreams, healing, the use of consecrated water, prophetic experiences, spirit possession, and prayer are in most cases distinct marks of the Pentecostal and charismatic traditions.

Rise of African Independent Churches

The phenomenal explosion of the African independent church movement (Pentecostal, charismatic, and Aladura types) in the last decade of the twentieth century can be explained in a variety of ways. First is the local cultural context of the movement: its primary success seems to lie in the new Christian response to Africans' perennial religious quests. At the base of Africans' traditional culture and society is a spirituality inseparable from the well-being of *Homo religiosus*. The social, economic, political, and spiritual aspects of life are interwoven; human welfare and the sacred are conceived as inseparable. Religion, therefore, is a way of life. The Western notion of religion as a belief system that can operate outside the scope of human welfare and human values is foreign to the African thought system. Whereas the mission churches, which had been constructed in the image of the Western worldview, denied this African reality, the African churches accepted it. In their theology, God is not worshiped only for his own sake or for the sake of gaining paradise, but also for guaranteeing human happiness and material success. We may call this the spirituality of matter.

Second is the social and historical context of the explosion of African indigenous churches in western Africa. The euphoria of nationalism and nation-state quickly disappeared in the mid-1960s after most African countries had obtained independence. This was followed by a series of military coups and at times one-party rule by African dictators. By the 1980s it was obvious that the African continent was entering its own dark age at a time when other regions of the world were making progress. In the midst of the contemporary chaos, religion became one of the most viable media of protest against the excesses of the state, especially in places where other arms of the civil society—such as the mass media, trade unions, and university associations—had been thoroughly repressed.

The African churches constitute the most formidable threat to the uncontrolled power of the state in sub-Saharan Africa. While some scholars tend to associate the movement with a form of political dormancy, that is not always the case. In countries like Nigeria, where the state has allied itself with Islam to impose hegemony over the political and religious life of a people of many religions, the African church leadership has responded forcefully against the repressive power of the state. The churches also have empowered their adherents to respond to the oppressive power of the state in very subtle ways. For example, if we examine their theology, the notion of evil includes both spiritual and human principalities and power. Thus, it encompasses the corrupt state.

The independent African churches have achieved a high degree of success in the processes of inculturation and indigenization. What liberation theology meant for Latin American countries, inculturation meant for African churches. The Pentecostal independent churches emphasize "oral" theology, whereby the Gospel is communicated through visual and verbal symbols (music, dance, and arts), oral traditions, stories, and proverbs. This unique contribution to global Christianity is noteworthy. These churches have also made possible the incarnation of the Christian message on African soil. For example, it is not uncommon to find references to Christ as an African healer, a king, or a prophet.

Beyond the use and adaptation of African indigenous symbols, rituals, and images, Pentecostal churches provide a meaningful, powerful synthesis of the African worldview and biblical revelation. For example, for the followers of Samuel Oschoffa, the founder of the Celestial Church of Christ, their prophet's personal life, prophetic journey, and death parallels biblical examples as well as the indigenous worldview. Oschoffa's prophetic call occurred on 23 May 1947. As he was in a canoe on his way to a nearby village to buy some planks, there was an eclipse, during which he heard a voice telling him to go out into the world to convert "pagans" to the true worship of God. The voice also gave him power to wake the dead and perform all types of miracles in the name of God. In response to this visionary experience, Oschoffa formed the nucleus of the Celestial Church of Christ. The first clue to our understanding of this religious experience lies in the founder's life history. Significant aspects of Oschoffa's birth and early life are embedded in both traditional and religious cosmology and biblical worldviews in a way that provides the most essential paradigm for the new movement. The founder's biographical epic contains striking parallels with the events surrounding the birth of the biblical Samuel. Members are able to identify with these biographical stories and events, and cognitively appropriate the founder's experiences into their own worldview, thereby providing paradigmatic truth for reordering their previous life patterns.

African and World Christianity

Also significant is the contribution of the African churches to the evolution of a national and global Christian culture and identity. I am tempted to call this the emergence of a Christian *umma*, in the manner of the Islamic *umma*, a community in the largest sense of the term. I shall describe the Christian *umma* as a transethnic, even transnational, community of Christians for whom Christianity is viewed as tradition, culture, and civilization, not just religion. For students of African Christianity this is quite important, given the fact that with mission churches, Christianity in Africa never attained the status of culture and tradition. Christians were always seen through the prism of Western culture and civilization. The nature of the Western missionary enterprise was partly responsible for this because of its hostility to indigenous cultures and religions. The mission churches were soon regarded as foreign. The often-quoted verse of the literary tradition (Ifa divination) of the Yoruba people of Nigeria provides a case in point: *Aye la ba Ifa, Aye la ba Imole, Osan gangan ni Igbagdo de.* (We met indigenous religion [Ifa] on earth, we met Islam on earth, Christianity arrived all of a sudden [in the afternoon].) The Yoruba and several other African groups embraced Islam centuries before Christianity, and the two traditions interacted amicably for a long period of time. But when mission Christianity arrived in the late nineteenth century, boasting about its moral and religious superiority, it was labeled "foreign tradition." The Ifa's description of the Christian situation seems to be echoed by Ali Mazrui's popular film *African Triple Heritage.*

Celestial Christian visionaries and healer during a healing ceremony in Cotonou (Bénin). © 1994 HENNING CHRISTOPH/FOTOARCHIV/BLACK STAR

When Mazrui made his film, he subsumed the Christian contribution to the African continent under Western civilization, whereas indigenous African religion and Islam were identified as providing authentic African contributions to African civilizations. Contrary to the apparent "foreignness" of Christianity, in the late twentieth century the African churches espousing a new Christian culture and tradition are setting the pace for the emergence of popular national indigenous culture. In highly heterogeneous, multiethnic, and multireligious countries like Nigeria and Ghana, there is undoubtedly a "hallelujah revolution" of charismatic churches going on and influencing the society's cultural landscape. One proof of this new Christian culture that African churches have contributed to national popular culture is that contemporary music, arts, and dance in several African states are heavily influenced not by secular or Islamic culture but by Christian metaphors and symbols.

Last, the contribution of women to the growth and identity of African churches is unique in Christianity. Although few west African churches were founded and controlled by women, women do play significant roles in the management of some, as in the Cherubim and Seraphim. The development of a Christian-inspired popular culture was made possible by them, and the most significant aspect of this is what is often called indigenous gospel music. Through their musical creativity women have produced a new liturgical tradition that reflects the changing role of religion in African society. Their music is used for entertainment and ceremonial purposes, and reflects the influence of indigenous music in several places. The music also has a liberative motif, creating a niche and a voice for women in patriarchal west African society.

BIBLIOGRAPHY

Babalola, E. O. *Christianity in West Africa.* Ado-Ekiti, Nigeria, 1976. Repr. 1981.

Bond, George, Walton Johnson, and Sheila Walker, eds. *African Christianity.* New York, 1979.

Clarke, Peter B. *West Africa and Christianity.* London, 1968.

Hayward, Victor E. W., ed. *African Independent Church Movements.* London, 1963.

Omoyajowo, J. A. *Cherubim and Seraphim: The History of an African Independent Church.* New York, 1982.

Peel, John D. Y. *Aladura: A Religious Movement Among the Yoruba.* London, 1968.

Sanneh, Lamin. *West African Christianity.* Maryknoll, N.Y., 1983.

Turner, Harold W. *History of an Independent African Church: Church of the Lord (Aladura).* 2 vols. London, 1967.

JACOB K. OLUPONA

See also **Braide, Garrick Sokari; Christianity; Dance; Harris, William Wadé; Music and Song; Musical Instruments; Oral Culture and Oral Tradition; Religion and Ritual.**

EASTERN AFRICA

Eastern Africa has a long history of prophetic movements and cults, some linked to indigenous or "traditional" deities and spirits, some to Christianity, and others to Islam. These movements were reported from the earliest periods of colonial administration and missionary endeavor. Some were recognized as being efforts to overcome drought, famine, and other natural disasters; others were considered to be anti-European, often as atavistic manifestations of "heathen superstition," and as destructive of the "order" brought about by colonial administrations and therefore to be put down by force. It has often been held that these movements were early examples of "resistance" to colonial overrule, but many were in existence long before the colonial interlude. Although some have indeed been part of resistance movements, all have been more than mere responses to colonial rule and have been concerned also with divisions and conflicts within and between local societies and their various elite and commoner groups.

Eastern Africa has had many kinds of prophets, priests, diviners, mediums, healers, oracle operators, witch-finders, religious reformers, and religious innovators, all claiming some form of divine knowledge and wisdom. Only prophets, diviners, and mediums are generally held to have the power to see beyond and behind the everyday world by means of trance or possession. A distinction should also be made between, on the one hand, healers and diviners who are consulted by individual clients and, on the other hand, prophets and reformers who attract and lead wide groups of followers and whose activities have political aims and consequences. Most of the recent prophetic movements have had as their immediate aim the religious purification of Christian and Muslim religious institutions, with the ultimate intended consequence of reforming and purifying the whole of society. In some movements a religious ideology has been paramount; in others the emphasis has been on political and military resistance. In this article only those who have tried to form a moral community wider than preexisting groupings—clan, ethnic group, multiethnic community—are mentioned.

The Earlier Prophets

There is no space here to discuss more than a few of these various movements. The earliest were those led by the prophets of the Nuer and Dinka peoples of the southern Sudan. Of these, the most famous was the Nuer prophet Ngundeng Bong, who in the 1870s built an immense earthen pyramidal mound where divine power became manifest to and in him. He claimed to predict the future and to purify his people, who saw in his person the immanence of Divinity. He and the many other prophets were the central ritual experts and peacemakers of the Nuer and Dinka peoples, and these prophets saw the advent of colonial rule as a continuation of Arab slave raiding earlier. They were concerned mostly with problems of finding land and pasturage in the ever-changing riverine environment of the southern Nile region and attempted to protect their peoples from the drought or famine. Nonetheless the colonial administration saw them as hostile, and tried for many decades to weaken the prophets and to destroy their pyramids.

A second prophetic movement was that which guided the Maji Maji rebellion against the Germans in Tanganyika in 1905–1907. The movement's ideology was spread by a prophet, Kinjikitile, who was believed to obtain prophetic powers from the deity Bokero at a pool of mystically powerful water, the drinking of which was held to make people immune to German bullets and inspired them to join together to fight the German administration.

A third early prophetic movement was the Yakan cult among the Lugbara of northwestern Uganda, in which the prophet, Rembe, was not Lugbara but Kakwa. Here much the same pattern emerged: a cult, centered on a prophet who was believed to possess divinely given knowledge and mystical power, was transformed into a movement with an anticolonial ideology that inspired an armed uprising. Rembe was first sought by Lugbara in the 1880s, to help them fight epidemics of human and cattle sickness as well as the plague of Europeans and Arabs that was destroying the "traditional" ways of local life and livelihood. When these epidemics reappeared Rembe was again called and entered Lugbaraland in 1915. There he established himself at a pool in which there lived a rainbow-colored serpent with a monitor lizard's head. While possessed, Rembe received messages from the serpent. Men and women from a wide area drank the pool's water, which was held to make them immune to bullets, to bring back the ancestors and dead cattle, and to cause Europeans and Arabs to vanish. The movement culminated in a small revolt in 1916 which was soon put down. Rembe was taken to the Sudan and hanged at Yei. The cult still existed in the

1950s, in a nonprophetic form of belief in a possession spirit called Yakan. (Yakan means "the force that makes people tremble.") The overt similarities with the Maji Maji cult are striking, but there appears to have been no historical connection between them.

A longer-lasting movement was that known as Nyabingi among the Kiga people of southwestern Uganda. This dates back to the seventeenth century with the appearance of a "goddess" called Nyabingi. During the nineteenth century the cult opposed the growing strength of the rulers of Rwanda and Ankole, and its leaders united local territorial and descent groups into wider defensive groupings. About 1910 a Nyabingi prophetess named Muhumusa led the general resentment against the use of Ganda agents by the new British administration. She was deported and imprisoned until her death in 1945. The cult continued, however, leading attacks upon Ganda agents and Christians. In the late 1920s these agents were finally withdrawn and replaced by Kiga, who were mostly Christians and unsupportive of the Nyabingi movement, which then died out.

There may also be mentioned early Islamic movements: that led by el-Mahdi in the Sudan; that of Sayyid Muhammad 'Abdallah Hasan (known by the British as the "Mad Mullah") of Somaliland; and the movement led by Muslim reformers among the Swahili of the east African coast in the later years of the nineteenth century. The first two were overtly political, the aim being mainly to oust the colonial (and Christian) conquerors from Muslim lands. The third was concerned more with purifying the Islam practiced by patrician merchants of the coastal towns and with bringing former slaves into the mainstream of coastal society. The most famous reformer was Sayyid Saleh ibn Alwy ibn Abdullah Jamal al-Layl (known more familiarly as Shaykh Habib Swaleh), who came to the town of Lamu from the Comoro Islands about 1880 and built the great Riyadh Mosque that has attracted pilgrims and scholars from throughout eastern Africa and beyond ever since.

Later Christian Movements

Other prophets have been reported from all parts of eastern Africa throughout the twentieth century. They have been in varying ways and to varying degrees linked to the advent of Christianity, in the sense that either the leaders have been considered emissaries of indigenous divinities sent to oppose Christianity, or have been African Christians attempting to purify and Africanize "mission" Christianity brought and controlled by European missionaries. Virtually all of them at one time or another became overtly political, with the aim of freeing their members and local societies from colonial rule, and so became part of "resistance" movements. To make a rigid distinction between "traditional," Christian, and Muslim prophetic leaders and their movements would be misleading, as all during the colonial period these prophets saw themselves, and were seen by their followers, as having similar aims. All took elements of whatever religious beliefs and rituals they found as part of what Wendy James has called their "cultural archive" and did not invent new beliefs, although their emphases and interpretations were new.

We may discern certain common or widespread processes in the histories of these movements. One was that prophets have usually been concerned with fighting witchcraft and sorcery, seen as signs of societal and cultural confusion and breakdown; as reformers they have tried to purify society by appeal to the believed traditional moralities of their societies. The basic criterion for defining these leaders as prophets has been their ability to transcend local social and religious groups and moralities and to construct new moralities that are acceptable to culturally diverse groups over wide areas. In most cases traditional divinities have come to be seen as outmoded and ineffective, as former "tribal" systems became obsolete in the modern world and inter-"tribal" relations became more important.

Many of these movements have been local and temporary, but others have been long lasting and have entered history and tradition as events of central importance in African history. The successive prophetic cults and movements among the Gikuyu of central Kenya merit mention. Here the first reported were overtly political associations such as Harry Thuku's Young Kikuyu Association in the early 1920s, concerned with offsetting the effects of land alienation and treatment of laborers. Soon there appeared in this and other associations a breach between older and younger people, the former adhering to traditional religious beliefs and the latter rather to Western education and Christianity. In 1929 the so-called "circumcision controversy" defined these conflicts more clearly. This was a conflict between Gikuyu and the European missions (especially the Church of Scotland and the Africa Inland Mission) which wanted to stop the practice of the clitoridectomy of girls. This led not only to conflict between Gikuyu and the Europeans but also between the more traditional and landowning elders (supported by the administration) and younger educated and generally landless men and women, considered untrustworthy citizens by the administration. Most Gikuyu Christians left the missions and established their own churches and schools, the two most important being the Kikuyu Independent Schools Association and the Kikuyu Karinga Educational Association, the latter the more radical and linked to the leading political group of the time, the Kikuyu Central Association. The former was linked to the African Independent Pentecostal Church and the latter to the more anti-mission African Orthodox Church.

While this overtly Christian controversy was being engaged, another strand appeared, from the 1920s' Watu wa Mungu ("People of God") led by traditional Gikuyu seers, who refused European clothing and objects, worshiped facing Mount Kenya (where dwelt the traditional Gikuyu High God), and became linked to the Kikuyu Central Association, whose secretary-general was Jomo Kenyatta (whose book, *Facing Mount Kenya,* had its dustcover showing Kenyatta wearing the attire of the Watu wa Mungu). Although details are unreliable, there seems to have been a historical link with the later Mau Mau movement. Today the Mau Mau conflict is seen as a striking example of anticolonialist resistance, but the internal struggle between landed and landless Gikuyu was at the time equally as important.

There have been many other and not dissimilar prophetic movements in Kenya. The first for which there is reliable information was that known as Mumbo among the Gusii of western Kenya. They believed in Mumbo, a god who had homes in the sky and in Lake Victoria and who appeared in a vision to a prophet called Onyango among the Luo to the immediate northwest. Mumbo took the form of an immense snake linking sky and lake and promising a future of ease and prosperity to those who accepted its message. Adherents were to sacrifice to it and follow certain rules: to wear skins instead of European-style clothes; not to wash or cut their hair; and to perform traditional dances. Also, they were allowed or perhaps encouraged to smoke bhang (hashish). The cult's message spread among the Gusii in the early 1920s. The Gusii had suffered military defeat by the administration in 1905–1908 and heavy losses of men recruited as carriers in World War I; also their indigenous political leaders had been ignored by the administration and young educated men had been appointed in their place. In the 1930s the cult spread fast after a period of drought and famine. There were several

Gusii prophets of Mumbo, the most powerful being a former prophet called Zakawa and a woman, Borairiri. The cult made sporadic appearances and attacks until the 1950s, when it died out. Its message was strongly against the European administration and mission Christianity; hostility was largely directed against local administrative chiefs and officials. Mumbo seems not to have been a totally new cult, and certainly there had been a long history of prophetic movements among the Gusii.

A later movement was the Dini ya Msambwa among the Luhya and Pokot of western Kenya, an area that had long suffered from external interference from the time of the Arab-Swahili slave raiders during the mid-nineteenth century. Mumia, chief of the Luhya subgroup called Wanga, had been a central figure in the trade with the coast in slaves and ivory, and welcomed the British colonial administration, carefully placing many of his close kin as subchiefs throughout Luhya. These appointees were resented by the younger Christian-educated men who found their political careers blocked. Missions had been active throughout the region since the early years of the century, and some of the missionaries established and led widely popular voluntary associations for local social betterment.

During the interwar years European settlement had increased throughout Kenya, with alienation of land and continual demands for labor by European farmers. The first third of the twentieth century brought little prosperity to the Luhya and little hope for their future as independent peasant farmers. In the late 1930s a prophetic leader, Elijah Masinde, appeared. A former Quaker mission convert, from the Bukusu or Vugusu subgroup of the Luhya, his aims were to expel the European administrative, settler, and mission presence and to return to the traditional religion of the Luhya, although retaining European material wealth. The movement spread rapidly within and beyond the Vukusu, with sporadic outbursts of destruction of European property and threats to mission supporters. In 1945, Masinde was committed to Mathari Mental Hospital, and although he was soon released he quickly lost his former influence. By the mid-1950s the movement was fading rapidly. The word *basambwa* means those ancestors to whom offerings are made, and Msambwa was the term also used to describe the creator divinity, Wele. Wele was associated with Mount Elgon and a lake near its peak, which the movement referred to as Zion. The water of the lake purified sinners, and gave strength to the movement's members, among other things making them immune to bullets. Masinde was assisted by other minor prophets and mediums, mostly men, with only a few women. Throughout their teaching continual reference was made to the Bible and its accounts of millenarian society in which foreign oppressors had no place. By the 1950s or so the movement was no longer a Vukusu movement only but had spread widely. It was proscribed after Kenyan independence, in 1968.

The Dini ya Msambwa led also in the 1950s to religious activity and prophecy among the Pokot, north of the Luhya; they followed a prophet of their own, Lukas Pkech. The aims were similar, and ended in 1950 with a military affray at Kolloa in which Pkech and many followers and several European administrative and police officers were killed. The administration exacted heavy penalties and the movement came to an end.

Both Mumbo and Dini ya Msambwa were clearly political movements with religious ideologies, the latter based on Christian themes but at heart a "nativistic" movement. Any purification of Christianity was a minor aspect of its aims and activities; reversion to or revival of the traditional faith remained central. Christians were counted as enemies, although their Book could be used as text to support the prophecies made by the leaders.

The colonial history of Kenya provided a central factor in the rise and nature of these two movements (and there were many other minor ones, all rather similar, throughout western Kenya). Uganda had a very different colonial history. There the best-known movement was that known as Abalokole ("the saved ones"), first among the Kiga and Hororo of southwestern Uganda and later among the Ganda and other groups. The movement began in the Ruanda Mission, an offshoot of the (Protestant) Church Missionary Society that had long worked among the Ganda. It established a mission at Kabale in 1921, many of its members being Canadian Pentecostalists. After the Nyabingi revolts of the late 1920s, in which traditional female diviners had been supplanted by men, the women moved to the Kabale mission. During the 1930s the movement developed into a full-scale revival movement, largely under the guidance of a medical doctor, Joe Church. Membership required public confession of sins (actual and intended sins being equally serious), repentance, and the renunciation of alcohol, personal adornment, and dancing; charismatic behavior in the form of trance and glossolalia (speaking in tongues) was common. Salvation was sent by Christ and was not considered as resulting from an individual's act of will. The movement estab-

lished itinerant teaching teams, some three-quarters of the members being women. It spread rapidly to Buganda and then to the rest of the country. (It reached the Lugbara of far northwestern Uganda in the late 1940s as a women's movement.) In Buganda during World War II some of its leaders were imprisoned for advocating civil disobedience and nonpayment of taxes. However, the (British) bishops refused to expel Balokole members and retained them in the main body of the Church of Uganda on the premise that they were sincere even if misguided Christian reformers. Balokole members and supporters have since played an important role in church affairs throughout Protestant Uganda. It has had few directly political aims but was intended to purify the church by the moral purification of church incumbents and by "Africanizing" the church hierarchy. Its political impact has nonetheless been considerable in areas such as the choice of political leaders throughout southern Uganda.

A final movement may be mentioned, that of the present-day Holy Spirit Movement among the Acholi of northern Uganda. This began in 1985, when it was believed that the Christian God sent a prophet called Lakwena to Uganda, where he spoke through a medium, an Acholi woman, Alice Auma. She built up the military arm of the movement, known as the Holy Spirit Mobile Force, to fight the Uganda government, whose army was devastating northern Uganda. This military arm was clearly modeled on the colonial army of World War II, in which many Acholi men had served. Its aim was to cleanse the world of evil and to build a new world in which humans, the spirits, and the forces of the environment would live together in peace. Alice guided the military engagements on Lakwena's instructions until late 1987, when the force was defeated by the Ugandan army. Alice fled from Uganda and is today a refugee in Kenya; her followers, under the name of the Lord's Resistance Army, are still fighting in Uganda.

Conclusion

Despite their differences in beliefs, symbols, and social consequences, these and other eastern African movements shared certain basic features.

Prophets were believed to be emissaries sent by Divinity (God), themselves often coming from outside the particular society. A problem was that of the identity of the Divinity concerned, whether traditional, Christian, or Islamic. The first was tied to a particular society, the others were universal. Yet most of these movements conceived of them as forming a single source of power: the differences were in their respective congregations. The conventional Christian distinction between God and Satan, stressed by the mission churches, was not of great significance. The second point is that of the person of the prophets. They were sacred persons, given knowledge and power by the Divinity and not by their followers (here prophets differ from priests). A prophet had the ability to contact Divinity by possession and glossolalia and was linked to the rainbow snakes that linked earth and sky. The often-reported prophetic behavior was the reversal of everyday behavior in matters of sexuality, attire, food, often of gender. Prophets were not limited by ordinary constraints of time and space; they did not die, and might travel through the air; they could prophesy only at night or in the wilderness; they were able to turn bullets into water; and so on.

Prophets came in response to crises, to signs of breakdown or threat to a society's sense of order, certainty, and accepted primordial traditioning. Their messages were those of purification and reform in order to restore those traditions and the form of society as the people stated or imagined them once to have been. The prophetic messages were typically restatements of these traditions, by reconstruction and recombination of traditional elements deemed the opposite of those of the present day. It may be assumed that there were always many potential or would-be prophets at any time, with their own ambitions and messages. Most of them failed and vanished from history. Only a very few were accepted and gained followers: the "prophetic movement," in Marcia Wright's words, had not yet arrived.

In the cases given earlier, there already existed certain basic conditions: the wretchedness and uncertainty in the lives of peasant farmers or urban laborers under the colonial and postcolonial regimes; long and dangerous epidemics striking humans and livestock, thought to be sent by Divinity, whether deserved or not; an increasing uncertainty about women's roles; worsening change and conflict in the relations between old and young, men and women, rich and poor, landed and landless, educated and noneducated, indigenous and stranger, free and slave or ex-slave.

These conditions, however, had persisted for long periods without the appearance of prophets or reformers. For this there was need of a flashpoint, a sudden impulse for people to act together to set perceived wrongs right, a "prophetic movement," as with the Kenya missions' deciding to stop Gikuyu clitoridectomy or the German administration's imposition of compulsory cotton planting. It was at such moments that a prophet was sought or appeared. A prophetic message purported to reveal the Divine truth and the ultimate meaning that lay behind the existing conditions and events. It transformed a human historical event into a moral and spiritual one; it removed the actors from everyday time and space and convinced them that they were endowed with the creative power of Divinity as manifest in the prophet's person. The sacred was typically defined in terms of the reversal of the everyday, and the prophet's adherents were told to reverse or invert their everyday behavior so as to remove themselves symbolically from everyday earthly authority and to share in Divinity. To reform society its members had themselves to be reformed through the process of a *rite de passage* or rite of transformation. As in all such rites the creative phase of liminality and "communitas" was demonstrated by inverted behavior, only after which could the transformed persons begin to reform society, to make it as it had been and should again become.

BIBLIOGRAPHY

Anderson David, and Douglas Johnson, eds. *Revealing Prophets.* London, 1995.

Behrend, Heike. *Alice und die Geister: Krieg im Norden Ugandas.* Munich, 1993.

Hansen, Holger Bernt, and Michael Twaddle, eds. *Religion and Politics in East Africa.* London, 1995.

Johnson, Douglas H. *Nuer Prophets: A History of Prophesy from the Upper Nile in the Nineteenth and Twentieth Centuries.* Oxford, 1994.

Middleton, John. "The Yakan or Allah Water Cult Among the Lugbara." *Journal of the Royal Anthropological Institute,* 1963.

Robins, Caroline. "Conversion, Life Crises, and Stability Among Women in the East African Revival." In Bennetta Jules-Rosette, ed., *The New Religions of Africa.* Norwood, N.J., 1979.

Wipper, Audrey. *Rural Rebels: A Study of Two Protest Movements in Kenya.* Nairobi, 1977.

JOHN MIDDLETON

See also **Ethnicity and Identity; Maji Maji; Myth and Cosmology; Religion and Ritual.**

CENTRAL AFRICA

The terms "independent" and "prophet" designate contrasting modes in Africa's Christian evangelization by Africans. With the caveat that those modes are not always separable, a convenient shorthand is to think of the independent mode as proclaiming new goals, and the prophet mode as proclaiming new gifts or new revelations. "Ethiopian," "Pan-Africanist," and "separatist," on the one hand, and "Zionist," "healing," and "spiritual," on the other, mark an approximately similar distinction. Hence, the constitution of Jordan Msumba's Last Church of God and His Christ proclaimed new goals when it declared, around 1925 in colonial Nyasaland (Malawi), that "Africa [was] in need of a church that would correspond with her God-given customs and manners" (Rotberg, p. 341). And when beautiful hymns and the gift of healing erupted from the visions of Alice Lenshina, in colonial Northern Rhodesia (Zambia) of the 1950s, a huge prophet movement was born—but, to recall the caveat, Lenshina's movement evolved into the independent Lumpa Church. That the Lumpa Church ended in 1964 amid millennarian prophesying, and through bloody confrontation with the newly independent government, shows that both modes have political resonance.

Even so, the essence of any religion is the content of its promise, and the promise of Christianity in all its forms is salvation. Therefore, the fundamental question about Africa's Christian evangelization of itself is "Salvation from what, and for what?" Every central African evangelizer's biography has intersected with the economic, political, and religious realities of a vast region subject to British rule from the 1890s until the 1960s. Therefore, picture first the peoples of Nyasaland, Northern Rhodesia, and Southern Rhodesia (now Malawi, Zambia and Zimbabwe, respectively) as suddenly dispossessed of land and sovereignty, and as thenceforth linked with one another, with South Africa, and with the world economy. Now add colonial taxation as an early tool of labor recruitment to mines, farms, and other enterprises, thus moving men out of their villages, often on foot, back and forth across the length and breadth of the region. Think of the Zambian Copperbelt, the Zimbabwean coal mines, and the South African gold mines not only as places of work and of new urban experiences, but also as places that both inspired and met new needs, individual and collective, secular and spiritual.

Insert South Africa again, therefore, this time as a luxuriant garden of churches, some representing "mainline" Christianity and others, a great variety of energetic nonconformisms. The term "Zionist," for one mode of African Christianity, is taken from an American Pentecostal mission to South Africa, with headquarters in Zion City, Illinois. The Watch Tower Bible and Tract Society (whose adherents

at first called themselves Bible Students and after 1931, Jehovah's Witnesses) made many converts there, black and white. Now add periodic crises as well: harsh mobilizations during two world wars; widespread joblessness in the 1920s and again in the 1930s; the (successfully contested) establishment in the 1950s of the Central African Federation and, with it, settler domination of all three territories. Finally, add not simply Christianity but diverse and sometimes competitive Christianities—against the background of the first to take root, the Church of Scotland and Free Church of Scotland missions to Nyasaland (separate Presbyterian entities after the "Disruption" of 1843), established at Blantyre and Livingstonia in 1875–1876.

Catholics, Anglicans, Baptists, Methodists, and various nondenominational Protestant evangelicals followed soon thereafter, along with scores of others, including imports from America such as Seventh Day Adventists and the African Methodist Episcopal Church, in addition to Pentecostal groups and the Watch Tower Bible and Tract Society. All missions built networks of churches and schools; all manned them largely by training African evangelists and catechists. Now, bisect the whole with a thoroughgoing color bar. Its significance in matters religious is well conveyed by the lifelong Zambian Free Churchman Paul Mushindo, who for fifteen years collaborated with Rev. R. D. McMinn on the creation of a Bemba Bible: "McMinn . . . loved me as a man loves his best tool. . . . He often said, 'Mushindo is my right hand' " (Fields, p. 13). Some chose not to rise above such contradictory bonds but to annul them.

The earliest missionaries had little success in the environment of religious choice that prevailed until full "pacification" in the 1890s (which, in Southern Rhodesia, included the defeat of the Chimurenga Rising, inspired by the Shona prophetess Nehanda and her colleagues). In the midst of the rapid growth that then ensued, the exit routes from mission Christianity became visible right away. By 1900, Nyasaland had its first independent church. John Chilembwe established the churches and schools of the Providence Industrial Mission, with the encouragement of the missionary radical Joseph Booth and with the support of African-American Baptists. Chilembwe's preaching against colonial exactions of all kinds and against the constant indignities of the color bar laid out the political and economic routes away from missions. He embraced the religious and cultural forms that the missionaries at Blantyre purveyed while disputing their sole authority to purvey them. In addition, he advanced a Protestant ethic for Africa that owed much to the teachings of Booker T. Washington, his American contemporary.

Between the mid 1900s and mid 1910s, other mission-educated Africans increasingly joined more specifically religious disputes. Missionary magazines such as *Livingstonia News* depict an emerging map of long-term dissensus: the meaning of baptism; long probation before baptism; slow ordination of Africans; increasing church dues and school fees; proper interpretation of the Bible; material inequality between black and white Christians; the missions' community of interest with colonial regimes; the missionaries' support of wartime mobilization; and finally—not least—the cultural content of European Christianity. Were indigenous customs and tastes in religious expression condemned as "pagan" by the Bible or merely by authoritarian missionaries? What of participation in traditional ceremonies, the use of African beer, and polygamy (men and women differing)? Was witchcraft not an evil from which to seek deliverance? And did full-scale African Christians not have a legitimate say?

To varying degrees like Livingstonia in this regard, Protestant missions generally deemed such issues fundamental enough to help define entrance into, discipline within, and dismissal from the Christian community. They preached salvation as the highest good and held that there was "no salvation outside the church." But, at the same time, their principles held that, of the many called, few would be chosen—slowly—even as missionaries continued a steady sifting-out. In sum, not surprisingly for groups that had begun institutional life as breakaway sects, the doors of the churches were narrow for coming in and wide for going out. Protestant missions grappled with salvation at those doors.

Catholic missions displayed a different institutional structure and heritage. Salvation was to be grappled with inside the church, sinners and saints together. Hence, they baptized far more freely and more easily took a pragmatic posture on cultural issues other than divorce. That many Catholic missionaries were of peasant origin, unlike their mainly city-reared Protestant brethren, surely affected the tone of Christian life. It mattered, too, that their money demands were small. Congregational self-reliance was not their missionary ideal; and in any case, costs could be kept relatively low. An unmarried priesthood could do without the expensive domestic establishments that elsewhere

evoked the color bar—and it did not at first attract African would-be emulators. Perhaps most consequentially of all, the early emphasis of Catholic missions was on the rapid development of churches rather than of schools—and, correspondingly, of catechetical teaching by rote rather than preparation for firsthand encounters with the Bible. Bible literacy invites diverse interpretation that in turn invites schism.

Such differences do not mean, however, that Catholic missions escaped all religious dissent and invention. For example, in the 1920s, when interest in schooling was becoming widespread and resolute, they became vulnerable to complaints. That catechists began losing respect, compared with their better-educated Protestant counterparts, made the weaknesses of the initial strategy obvious. Likewise, they were not always fully protected against new revelation. In the 1930s, Catholics were among those who welcomed the *bamucapi* medicine men to deal with economic and interpersonal stress, phrased in the idiom of witchcraft. And in the 1950s, Lenshina's movement drew large numbers of people earlier claimed as Catholic. Meanwhile, the Catholic magazine *Le Petit Écho* reported on a short-lived Catholic movement that arose in the same era and area. Emilio Mulolani, a third-generation Catholic, apparently rediscovered through ultra-asceticism the antinomian heresy that faith alone, not obedience to the moral law, was necessary for salvation. The private communal life and public parades of his mixed coterie of young men and women led to public turmoil and a quick response by the Catholic Church. Mulolani was sent to Rome for a psychiatrist and a new confessor. But such dramas were uncommon. The Protestants' early-developed, long-lived map of religious invention had no full-scale Catholic counterpart.

As suggested earlier, the idiom of witchcraft as a manifestation of evil is one strand in the story of indigenous thought patterns that produced various inspirations, variously related to all of the mission Christianities. Since none of the Christianities approached spirits, possession, exorcism, divination, and witchcraft with pragmatic ease, solutions fell to others. In a spectacular sweep during the intense public crisis of the Great Depression, *bamucapi* from Nyasaland and Northern Rhodesia (many of them returned labor migrants and some, former mission pupils) pressed whole villages at a time to confess witchcraft, renounce it by surrendering their amulets for public destruction, and partake of a communal meal treated with a special medicine. Then and later, missionaries and officials sometimes held on only by using similar tactics preemptively.

In Southern Rhodesia, the public crisis of those same years converged with the private crisis of a Shona artisan, Johane Masowe (born Shoniwa Mutedza Tandi Moyo). Masowe's crisis led to visions and millennarian expectation, and then, like John the Baptist's, to continuous preaching and baptizing despite many arrests. He baptized by total immersion in rites called "Jordans" that drew large followings in many localities and, inevitably, drew the attention of the police, who considered him subversive. Anglican by birth, Masowe addressed his new revelation not only to ceaseless demands by Europeans for church dues and taxes throughout the Great Depression but also to other practical problems. To cure spirit illnesses and witchcraft, he conducted services of healing, confession, and the surrender of amulets. To cure material unease, he proclaimed an ethic of self-sufficiency through skillful labor within a close community of the saved. With their schools and workshops, the Masowe Apostles (also called the Korsten Basketmakers) have prospered as well as suffered persecution. They are a large group today (estimated at some 500,000), with a history that spans nine countries.

Think of Masowe's revelation and career as spanning the continuum between the visible spirit of capitalism and the invisible spirits of Europe and Africa. At one extreme of that continuum are neotraditional inspirations that are bound to Christianity by their explicit rejection of it. In Malawi, the Church of the Black Ancestors provides an example. Founded in the late 1960s, it preaches the restoration of lapsed ancestor observances and the prestige of elders, once powers within communities of kin. But, whatever success it may achieve, the very notion of mobilizing a church, through the voluntary recruitment of individuals, presupposes the organizational mode of the imported religion it rejects.

No African Christian initiative so fully illustrates the whole continuum as does the African "Watchtower" or "Kitawala." Because it has a phenomenally broad geographic scope and was for decades controlled by Africans, it embodies the ungeneralizable diversity of independent and prophet churches as a phenomenon. Besides, Watchtower ideas and methods have influenced and inspired other religious initiatives. Its origin in the region

goes back to 1907, when Elliott Kenan Kamwana, a former prize pupil at Livingstonia, returned to Malawi from South Africa. There, with the religiously peripatetic Joseph Booth, he had studied the teachings of an American, Charles Taze Russell, founder of the Watch Tower Bible and Tract Society. In Kamwana's version of Russell's ideas, the end of the world would mean British defeat and the end of Africans' living as powerless strangers in their own lands. Preaching, furthermore, that missions had withheld Bible truth and baptism while demanding money from the people, he baptized many thousands by total immersion— "without preparation," said the missionaries, who besides detected new and unsettling connotations of the rite.

Thus did Kamwana plant the first charge of a millennarian explosive—both religious and political—that repeatedly shook all three territories. In 1917, police in Southern Rhodesia planted the next two, when they expelled seven mine laborers who continued their "subversive" activities as they returned on foot to their villages in Northern Rhodesia and Nyasaland. With stunning effectiveness in the war-ravaged north of Northern Rhodesia, Watchtower preaching and baptizing announced the coming Kingdom—and denounced the one ruled by collaborating chiefs and the British. Thereafter, the result of the colonial governments' continued exclusion of the society's missionaries was to lend Watchtower ideas a protean adaptability according to place, time, and the interests of preachers and their hearers. Only two features of those ideas can be generalized. First, all Watchtower congregations adhered, in one way or another, to the society's principle against political engagement and allegiance to governments of this world. Therefore, all were persecuted for noncompliance with the mobilizations of World War II. Second, virtually all adopted the society's practice of baptism by total immersion, a practice that converged with the practical need for deliverance from witchcraft. In that way, the rite was free to take its proper place alongside other interests that baptism into a Christian community connoted for many villagers. It typically did so. (On occasion, however, witchcraft eradication predominated—spectacularly, in the murders connived at during 1925 by Shaiwila, a chief in Northern Rhodesia, and Tomo Nyirenda, a migrant laborer from Nyasaland).

Like indigenous African Christianity as a whole, the Watchtower exhibits a body of imported ideas undergoing continual modification as they percolate through an immense region. Some had political themes on the surface, as in the role many Watchtower preachers played in the Copperbelt strike of 1935, whereas healing and interpersonal concerns predominated in others. The militant revival of 1917 had both. Hanoc Sindano, among the boldest veterans of 1917, formed a law-abiding community of the saved, called Jerusalem, that lasted into the 1950s. We find the Bible rejected or else made central (with the Old and New Testaments taken together, valued unequally, or read with different emphases). Organization followed overseas models, indigenous ones, or a synthesis of both. Thus, for example, while Livingstonia hesitantly adapted to the absence of men by instituting the office of deaconess, Watchtower deaconesses evangelized so prominently that colonial officials and chiefs collaborated in the enactment of rules designed to end their missionary travels. (By contrast, despite Lenshina's role as its prophetess, men were the powers in the Lumpa Church, as in the nearby missions and in most independent and prophetic churches.)

Some groups expressed open contempt for constituted authority, African or European; others took care to obey every law that conscience permitted; still others were jostled into antigovernment conflicts by passing circumstances or heavy-handed officials. Some aspired to, while others rejected, European cultural habits in matters as diverse as marriage, dress, housing, and education. Some groups ran quiet, and others ecstatic, worship services. The codes of conduct taught ranged from antinomian violation of established rules to teachings indistinguishable from those of the missions. Hence, the reports in areas remote from one another were that nighttime funeral drumming, fought for decades by European missionaries, ceased instantly as a result of Watchtower conversions in a locality. Elsewhere, however, some groups practiced ritual incest, a rite called the "baptism of fire." When, in the 1930s, the society's missionaries were at last allowed conditional freedom to evangelize, they struggled for many years to stamp out that notorious rite. Despite this and other deviations, they nevertheless found as well a broad base of experienced leaders and committed members on which, and with whom, to rebuild. Today, there are many Jehovah's Witnesses in all three countries, and the Luapula area of Zambia was said in the 1970s to have the highest concentration of Jehovah's Witnesses in the world. During the region's struggles for independence as well as in the postindependence era, they have attracted

suspicion and suffered persecution. Quite different political regimes have opposed the political disengagement they affirm as their Anabaptist heritage.

In summary, it can be said that independent and prophet churches are endlessly diverse in doctrine, practice, leadership, and organizational forms. That diversity has prevailed not only between different churches in different places but also within individual churches over time. What all share with one another is their common heritage in post-Reformation Christianity, whose keynote is boundless variety as a result of internal change, schism, and fresh evangelization. Today that heritage finds expression in such marked activity in both overseas and indigenous churches that one can speak of a "second Christianization" in the region.

In the 1890s, only a relative handful of people professed Christianity. Proportions in the mid 1990s are estimated at 75 percent in Malawi (out of a population of 9.3 million persons), at 50 to 70 percent in Zambia (out of a population of 8.53 million persons), and at 55 percent in Zimbabwe (out of a population of 10.64 million persons) (all population figures are 1993 esimates). Since published estimates of the larger denominations in Malawi account for only about 200,000 church members, the large remainder undoubtedly reflects the work not only of missions but also that of at least ninety churches created between 1900 and 1979 outside mission auspices. Likewise, Zambia and Zimbabwe are home to many overseas missionary groups too small to be reported, as well as to a comparably effervescent indigenous creativity. Therefore if, a century ago, Europeans could speak of "planting" Christianity in the region, it must be said today that African indigenous churches, as a group, represent the transplanting that has enabled Christianity to flourish.

BIBLIOGRAPHY

Dillon-Mallone, Clive Mary, S. J. *The Korsten Basketmakers: A Study of the Masowe Apostles, an Indigenous African Religious Movement.* Manchester, 1978.

Fields, Karen F. *Revival and Rebellion in Colonial Central Africa.* Princeton, 1985.

Linden, Ian, and Jane Linden. *Catholics, Peasants and Chewa Resistance in Nyasaland, 1889–1939.* Berkeley, Calif., 1974.

Marwick, Max G. "Another Modern Anti-Witchcraft Movement in East Central Africa." *Africa* 20, no. 2 (1950): 100–112.

Ranger, Terence O. *Revolt in Southern Rhodesia, 1896–97: A Study in African Resistance.* Evanston, Ill., 1967.

Richards, Audrey I. "A Modern Movement of Witch-Finders." *Africa* 8, no. 4 (1935): 448–461.

Rotberg, Robert I. *A Political History of Tropical Africa.* New York, 1965.

Schoffeleers, J. Matthew. "Economic Change and Religious Polarization in an African Rural District." In *Malawi: An Alternative Pattern of Development,* edited by William Beinert et al. Centre of African Studies, Seminar Proceedings no. 25. Edinburgh, 1984.

Shepperson, George, and Thomas Price. *Independent African: John Chilembwe and the Origins, Setting and Significance of the Nyasaland Native Rising of 1915.* Edinburgh, 1958.

KAREN E. FIELDS

See also **Chilembwe, John.**

KONGO REGION

Religious movements are an ancient phenomenon in Africa, but the part of the continent occupied by Kongo speakers, on the Atlantic coast between about 3° and 7° south of the equator, is unique in the amount of documentation and the antiquity of its tradition of independent churches. In 1491, the Kongo king and members of the aristocracy eagerly accepted baptism from Portuguese missionaries, but the Christianity to which they "converted" seemed to them to be like the religious programs with which they were familiar. Christianity in sixteenth- and seventeenth-century Kongo can be described as an independent church because European missionaries were few, the king insisted on controlling the role of missionaries, and parishes were mostly in the care of indigenous secular clergy.

The kingdom disintegrated in 1665, but some forty years later a young woman called Kimpa Vita (who had been baptized Beatrice) attempted to revive it, saying that she was guided (or possessed) by the spirit of Saint Anthony of Padua. The resulting Antonine movement lasted for several years, although Beatrice was burned as a heretic (and, perhaps more to the point, as a political nuisance) on the orders of the royal council of King Pedro.

Between 1886 and 1920, the Kongo converted to Catholic and Protestant Christianity in large numbers. The Christianity of this period is not usually labeled "independent" because it was firmly under the control of mission churches and colonial governments, but there was considerable evidence of the assimilation of the Gospel, once again, to indigenous categories. By this time, the territory of the Kongo had been distributed among the French (Moyen Congo), the Portuguese (Cabinda and Angola), and the Belgians (Belgian Congo). These powers were greatly disturbed in 1921 by the outbreak of a religious movement inspired by a Baptist convert, Simon Kimbangu, which they saw as a political threat, possibly provoked by foreign interests. Kimbangu himself died in prison in 1951, but Kimbanguism continued underground, eventually giving rise in 1957, three years before the independence of Belgian Congo, to the Church of Jesus Christ on the Earth by the Prophet Simon Kimbangu. This church, led by Kimbangu's sons, was admitted to the World Council of Churches in 1969.

The underground influence of Kimbanguism contributed to three movements with much more definite political aims: Matswanism in French Congo, Mpadism in Belgian and French Congo, and Tokoism in Angola. In France, in 1926, André Matswa founded a Congolese friendly society (l'Association Amicale des Originaires de l'Afrique Équatoriale Française), active in defense of the rights of labor. Confrontations with the government multiplied during the 1930s and 1940s. Although Matswa, who died in prison in 1942, was not religiously motivated, his followers awaited his coming again; in the 1950s they founded a Matswanist church. In the Belgian Congo, Simon Mpadi founded the militant Khaki Movement, some aspects of which merged in French Congo with Matswanism; Mpadi's militancy and his several reportedly miraculous escapes from prison gave him a notoriety exceeding his real influence. In 1959, greatly reduced in scale, this movement became the Black Church. Simão Toko, after contact with Kimbanguists, began a movement in the 1950s that the Angolan government effectively suppressed. Other movements originating in the 1930s include Lassyism in French Congo, and in Belgian Congo, various movements called "ngounzist" that consider themselves to be the true heirs of the legacy of Kimbangu.

In urban areas of Zaire, successor to Belgian Congo, small independent churches multiplied during the 1980s, among the Kongo and particularly among the Luba, in response to the ruling dictatorship. These churches come and go. All have grand aspirations but rarely amount to more than a few congregations. The most successful are most likely to splinter into factions, reflecting in this respect the segmentary nature of the indigenous political system. No current information on the number or size of such churches exists.

BIBLIOGRAPHY

MacGaffey, Wyatt. *Modern Kongo Prophets: Religion in a Plural Society.* Bloomington, Ind. 1986.

Sinda, Martial. *Le Messianisme congolais et ses incidences politiques*. Paris, 1972.

WYATT MACGAFFEY

See also **Christianity; Kimbangu, Simon; Kimpa Vita; Spirit Possession.**

SOUTHERN AFRICA

Although disputed on grounds of political correctness, the term "African Independent Church" (AIC) aptly describes a religious association, exclusively African in membership, that is free from white administrative supervision and spiritual tutelage. First appearing at the close of the nineteenth century, these churches have historical roots that can be traced to developments early in the century, when white expansion northward from Cape Colony began to overwhelm predominantly pastoral societies with superior technology, turning them into vassals dispossessed of their land. Foremost in African experience of this invasion were the inroads of foreign missionary societies into indigenous cultures and religious beliefs. It was in the gradual conversion of these societies into the Christian proletariat that the seeds of religious independence were planted.

The AICs in southern Africa took two divergent forms arising from different sets of circumstances in the experience of the colonized: missionary discrimination and repression of workers. The discriminatory practices of the missionaries produced churches called Ethiopian, the first of their kind appearing in 1892. Although they preached a Christian creed of egalitarianism, the missionaries were reluctant to promote black pastors to positions of responsibility and refused to interact with them as equals. The educated lower clergy eventually rebelled by establishing separate African churches in Johannesburg that were free from white control but in all other respects were replicas of their parent bodies. Ethiopia was chosen as a rallying point because it was the biblical prototype of Africa and because contemporary Ethiopia embodied the ideal of political independence. In 1904 the first charismatic Zionist church appeared among exploited farm workers in a remote rural area. As a response to conditions of near enslavement, the workers adopted a Pentecostal strain, imported from working-class America by a white missionary, which empowered them with the Holy Spirit to provide a novel form of healing that was neither scientific nor African.

Since the beginning of the twentieth century, the AICs have grown phenomenally and have spread geographically throughout southern Africa, following the migrant routes from the South African mines to present-day Zimbabwe, Zambia, Malawi, and Zaire. Within South Africa alone, according to the official enumeration in 1990, AIC members constitute 30 percent of the total African population. Since they are most numerous in northeastern South Africa and are heavily concentrated in the densely populated urban areas around Johannesburg and Durban, their proportional representation in these cities is in the region of 40 percent or beyond. There is an unmistakable correlation between AIC expansion and the transformation of rural migrants into a settled urban population. Although no exact figures are available, there is every indication that this development has favored the growth of Zionist rather than Ethiopian churches.

While retaining the doctrine and organization of their missionary forebears, the "Ethiopians" strive to project an image of Christian autonomy under black leadership. Typically, the ministry is moderately educated with some scriptural training, often by correspondence, ironically from Bible colleges established by the churches from which they originally seceded. Once strongly committed to African emancipation through alignment with nationalist movements, "Ethiopians" are now dormantly respectable Christians with middle-class aspirations. They have not attracted much in the way of recent scholarly attention, but the available evidence indicates that they are in decline, with nothing distinctive to offer and unable to recruit replacements for their largely aging membership. A few of their leaders have achieved some prominence by claiming to be spokesmen for AICs in general, but without the support of the Zionist majority.

There are several thousand Zionist churches in existence at any time, some expanding while others decline, and new ones arising at a rate faster than those dying out. Nobody can claim to speak for Zionists in general because, lacking a semblance of central organization or an agreed canon of orthodoxy, they are characterized by wide variation of belief and observance and by obsessive disunity. Many retain a sense of authenticity and orthodoxy by tracing historical links to the first Zionist foundation and by preserving the tenets of the early founders. These groups take pride in calling themselves "Christian" Zionists and distance themselves from "new" Zionists, whose pretensions they disparage. "New" Zionists, some old in years of existence, are undoubtedly in the majority, if only because anyone inspired by a spiritual vision and prophetic message can set up a church and woo followers by borrowing selected elements of Zionism, mixing them with features of African religion, and reconstructing these to fit the founder's own esoteric design. Still other charismatic churches are not Zionist in any sense. Also of spontaneous prophetic origin, these churches are attempts to adapt traditional religion to modern needs and are often led by several generations of a particular family. Some—for example, the Zion Christian Church near Pietersburg, under the leadership of Lekyanyane, and the Nazareth Baptist Church outside of Durban, identified with Shembe—are spectacularly large, although both churches exaggerate the size of their followings. Most Zionist churches are of very modest size because of an inherent tendency to segment and subdivide, to which even the large "traditionals" are not entirely immune.

While the range of differences expressed in Zionism defies generalization, some salient features may be singled out for comment, predominantly in connection with "Christian" Zionists. Most Zionist churches seek to alleviate the condition of the poor, with varying success. The two main strategies are economic uplift and healing. The first is an economic package blending a disciplined way of life, sobriety, abstemiousness, hard work, saving, and mutual support. The maintenance of discipline is entrusted to a preaching hierarchy of preacher, who preaches to a local congregation and may recruit converts; evangelist, who in addition to a preaching function has the right to baptize and process entry into full church membership; and bishop, who oversees several congregations normally controlled by a minister. These positions can be embellished at will with the addition of contingent offices. The preaching function draws on the Bible as a source of moral precept and exemplary precedent. At the Christian end of the Zionist spectrum, the preaching ranks are monopolized by married men; "newer" Zionists admit women to the ministry, and there are even female bishops. The ministry, however, is unspecialized; unwaged and without formal training, incumbents must work for a living, and since leaders are seldom more than barely literate, education is not a qualification for office. Apart from founding a church of one's own, entitlement to office rests upon experience, endurance, and an ability to recruit followers.

Healing draws on a different kind of expertise, that of the prophet; and here the difference between "Christian" and "new" becomes more manifest. Later strains of Zionism restored ancestors to their healing role, commonly in some form of partnership with the Holy Spirit, and prophets in their healing work derived their insights into the nature of illness and remedy from these twin sources. With this goes a marked tendency for prophetic healing to become the dominant or sole concern of these "newer" churches, to the virtual exclusion of Bible-centered preaching; prophet leadership then becomes the norm, with corresponding female ascendancy. Mainstream "Christian" Zionists recognize both male and female prophets, but male prophets are given a better hearing and all prophets are subordinate to the male preaching hierarchy. Healing power and prophetic inspiration are derived from the Holy Spirit alone, and healing is not divorced from preaching. Preachers are charged with drawing on the Bible to stir up the enthusiasm of the congregation and to arouse the Holy Spirit among them, in such a way as to build up a wave of spiritual power than can be used by the prophet in healing the sick. A major concern is alleviating the damage done to individuals by sorcery and equipping them with symbolic protective devices suffused with the power of communal prayer.

The Zionist AICs are churches of the poor and uneducated, seeking to meet the needs of the hard-pressed, for whom the primary appeal is the healing service. The attraction is greater for women, who outnumber men among members by at least two to one; they gain not only from healing attentions and communal support but also from marriage to a disciplined, frugal breadwinner or, failing that, the possibility of converting a spouse into a reliable Zionist provider. Zionism, therefore, values and promotes the stability of the family unit in an urban environment not conducive to it, and it rewards good family men with status and office. Economically and therapeutically, for men and women alike, Zionist churches provide havens of safety and order in the perceived chaos of urban society. Set apart by their chosen lifestyle, Zionists are separated from normal patterns of association and, accordingly, behave as isolates in the workplace and other public spaces. Part of their refusal to participate fully in relations with outsiders, with whom they have little in common, is their consistent avoidance of any political activity. This apolitical stance did not endear them to supporters of the liberation struggle, and it left them doubly exposed to the bitter street fighting between rival contenders for power in the preelection period. Paradoxically, it ultimately earned them a kind of political respectability, as party leaders went in search of votes among this very large constituency.

BIBLIOGRAPHY

Comaroff, Jean. *Body of Power, Spirit of Resistance: The Culture and History of a South African People.* Chicago, 1985.

Daneel, M. L. *Old and New in Shona Independent Churches.* Vol. 2. Gweru, Zimbabwe, 1974.

Fogelqvist, Anders. *The Red-Dressed Zionists: Symbols of Power in a Swazi Independent Church.* Uppsala, Sweden, 1986.

Johnson, Walton R. *Worship and Freedom: A Black American Church in Zambia.* New York, 1977.

Kiernan, James P. *The Production and Management of Therapeutic Power in Zionist Churches Within a Zulu City.* Lewiston, N.Y., 1990.

Sundkler, Bengt Gustaf Malcolm. *Bantu Prophets in South Africa.* London, 1976.

West, Martin Elgar. *Bishops and Prophets in a Black City: African Independent Churches in Soweto, Johannesburg.* Cape Town, 1975.

JAMES P. KIERNAN

PROSTITUTION. Few aspects of women's work are as mystified as prostitution in modern Africa. Even after an eighteenth- and nineteenth-century vision of African sexual license had vanished from polite society, social scientists and reformers looked at prostitution in Africa and saw it as "natural" and "cultural"—confusing Africans' public tolerance for what women had to do to survive with a cultural condoning of the sale of sex for money. Following from this, a range of observers from the 1950s on have looked at the sale of sexual relations in Africa and labeled and hierarchized them without regard for the strategies that informed the ways women practiced prostitution. An emphasis on which women were in bars, who formed short-term liaisons, who did not demand cash and who did was replaced, by the 1980s, by studies of HIV and risk behaviors that created new hierarchies based on researchers' imaginings of how much choice women had of their customers.

In all of these cases, prostitutes were located in generalized notions of culture, but never in their families, households (those headed by themselves and those headed by husbands and lovers), and homesteads. Indeed, a close reading of the literature on prostitution in twentieth-century Africa reveals the flaws in such hierarchies: women went from bars to short-term liaisons in an evening; they demanded cash when their need for it was urgent and did not demand cash when they were negotiating another kind of relationship with a man. What women sought from their customers had less to do with the woman's personality and culture than it did with the labor market of the place where she worked: demanding cash from a man with low wages may have been far more advantageous than trying to establish a long-term relationship with him; forming a short-term liaison with a man whose job included housing might have been extremely advantageous to women who worked in cities where rents were high.

For most prostitutes in Africa, past and present, sex work was a way to earn money; a successful Nairobi prostitute who worked in the 1940s explained that most prostitutes did not seek jobs "because it was unlikely a woman would find a job that paid as much as 30 boyfriends" (White, 202). The absence of pimps throughout the continent enabled women to keep most of their earnings; even where there were taxi or rickshaw drivers, touts or go-betweens to arrange sexual encounters, these were usually paid by the man, not the woman. The kind of prostitution a woman chose to practice, however—whether she was on the street, in a house, or sitting outside her house—had to do with whom she was earning money for.

Streetwalking is generally considered the most contemptible form of prostitution, the work chosen by down-and-out desperate women whose moral character is even lower than those who work as prostitutes indoors. Such a crass generalization has little to support it, however. Streetwalkers maintained to this researcher that while working on the streets was difficult, the rewards were worth the difficulties—the streets were a place to earn a lot of money in a reasonably short period of time. If a woman was sending money home to support family and kin in depressed rural Africa, streetwalking was often the best strategy. The greatest risk, streetwalkers maintained, was repeated police harassment; they claimed they had more control over the customers they chose—and refused—than did women who "stayed inside their rooms."

For these reasons, streetwalking was a form of prostitution that homeless women could practice until they earned a month's rent, and hence it was the way many immigrants to urban Africa entered city life, but it was not a form women abandoned once they could rent accommodation. Indeed, many women rented rooms in areas where it was nominally illegal for Africans to live in order to be close to the most lucrative markets: men returning from work or men in cars ("a man with a car cannot tell you he has no money") were well worth a monthly investment of rent several times greater than it would have been in African areas.

But the risks and high financial costs of streetwalking meant that most women did not stay in it very long. As a form of prostitution into which women were often driven by crises at home, many women returned home and abandoned prostitution when the crisis had passed. Maasai women in early colonial Kenya, for example, whose cattle-keeping families had been devastated by the rinderpest epidemics of the late 1890s, were numerous among Nairobi's prostitutes in the first decade of this century; when Maasai herds were restocked by about 1911, Maasai women left prostitution and returned to the homes they had subsidized for years. At other times—in port cities when fleets arrived or during wartime—many prostitutes engaged in streetwalking briefly because the financial rewards were so high.

Women who stayed inside their rooms—a form of prostitution that had various names throughout the continent—have been mystified again and again. These women helped construct the mystification, maintaining that "no one could tell I was a prostitute." But there was much to support this fiction: unlike streetwalkers, these women were invisible to authorities and thus free from police harassment and public condemnation. As important was that these women provided a range of services to their customers, of which sexual relations was only one. A man who spent the night with a prostitute in her room in Nairobi from the 1920s on could expect breakfast and bathwater heated for him; men on the Zambian Copperbelt from the 1920s to the 1950s referred to the women they visisted in their rooms as "good friends" who could cook for them and do their laundry. Such services were strategic; if women asked for payment when the encounter ended, she could charge for every cup of tea provided. Such a strategy produced a slower rate of accumulation than streetwalking did, but almost all women agreed that in the long run earnings in the aggregate were worth the wait, even including the times men refused to pay or delayed payment as long as they could.

More to the point, they were not selling sexual relations but domestic relations, those that men could only obtain through marriage. What men purchased when they visited and were served by a woman in her room was not only a fiction of marriage rights, but a vision of the proper relations of women to men. In Northern Nigeria, *karuwai*—who were generally divorced women who lived together and catered to men's needs—sang, cooked, and had sexual relations with men in exchange for money. In much of the region, where divorce was frequent, men frequently stated a wish to marry *karuwai*, not to save them from a life of degradation, but because only women who had been *karuwai* knew how to look after a man. Where these prostitutes did not live together, they tended to be well-regarded, if not respected, members of their communities. In 1930s and 1940s Johannesburg, before the intense segregation of apartheid was in place, prostitutes in urban yards blended into neighborhoods of shopkeepers, families, and migrant laborers. Many colonial and postcolonial officials observed the social service these women provided by allowing the migrant labor system to function smoothly, which did not require the higher wages a family presence would.

But the women who chose such a deferential form of prostitution seem to have done so because they were earning money for the most radical of lives: these women were not supporting families in rural Africa, and only occasionally were they supporting any kin but their children in town. Rather, they had established themselves as independent heads of households. The slow and steady saving by the women who stayed inside their rooms, measured in cups of tea and nights of conversation, was for women who had for the most part cut their ties with rural households and kin.

In very many cases, these women took their slowly acquired earnings from prostitution and invested in urban property, sometimes in legal townships and more often in squatters' settlements, where the risks of losing one's investment could be offset by the high rents charged there. It was this particular relationship of prostitutes to laboring men, and the states for whom they labored, that was most troubled: the same women officials saw as protecting the migrant labor system also provided the accommodation that gave a sense of place and belonging to the very laborers the states wanted to maintain as migrant. Thus when there have been attacks on prostitutes who practiced this form of prostitution, it has invariably been on the status and legality of these women's property ownership rather than anything to do with their prostitution.

Prostitution in Africa does not simply break down into neat dichotomies of women in their homes and on the streets. African prostitutes go to bars and nightclubs, of course. One well-known and frequently cited vision of that life comes from Cyprian Ekwensi's 1960s Nigerian novel *Jagua Nana*, in which the heroine is herself both a loyal lover to one man and a prostitute and which points to some of the ambiguities of successful nightclubbing and successful prostitution. Indeed, most working streetwalkers maintain that going to bars or nightclubs is only a good strategy when used occasionally. Being well known in one bar could lower a woman's nightly earnings considerably, as men could argue that they should be charged what their friend paid last month. Besides, the overhead costs of a night on the town are not always easily recouped.

In many parts of Africa (as in many parts of the world, in fact) a form of prostitution developed that responded to several economic factors, including the density and high rents of the urban areas and the increasing poverty of the rural areas. The form of prostitution in which women sat outside their rooms has often scandalized observers, who were at worst horrified to hear women calling low prices out to men passing by, and at best called it "commercialized prostitution," a telling comment on what some social scientists thought about women who stayed in their rooms. But in fact most women sat outside their rooms because their rooms were too small for anything but a bed; often the rooms were illegal structures added to urban housing and measuring under forty square feet.

The women who sat outside, known as *wazi-wazi* in Nairobi (from the Swahili word for open, as in exposed) or *tu tu* in west African towns (for the number two, as in two shillings), did so to make themselves and their prices well known. Other established local prostitutes were horrified by women shouting out low prices: these prices fixed pay rates for women. There was no negotiating and no need to prepare tea or food. "If a man knew in advance that he could go with me for 1 shilling, he would. . . . I wouldn't have to spend money on tea in the hopes that he would give me a few pennies in the morning" (White, 197). This was a form of prostitution favored by women who were supporting families at home—often they were the daughters of cash-crop producers impov-

erished by the decline in commodity prices during the depression. Often they came to Africa's cities in groups, living close together. They did not care for the niceties of looking after men, or of blending into the neighborhood: in Nairobi, *wazi-wazi* women were remembered for being the first prostitutes to fight fiercely with men if they refused to pay; they would call in their neighbors for physical support. The small rooms were tolerable for these women because they did not intend to stay for long. *Tu tu* prostitutes in Abidjan, Accra, and other west African towns had a fixed price and no protracted urban relations and could take their earnings back to northern Ghana and Burkina Faso whenever they liked. As an old woman said of the women from northwest Tanzania who dominated the *wazi-wazi* form in Nairobi in the late 1930s, "They didn't want to be rich here, they wanted to be rich in Tanganyika" (White, 114).

This form of prostitution combined its most aggressive aspects and was practiced by women who were earning as the most dutiful of daughters; it was generally engaged in by individual women for only a short time. It provided high earnings at tremendous social costs to the women, and for it to be financially successful required high male employment. But as rural households faced decline after decline, this form of prostitution became the choice of many rural women seeking to better the conditions of their families.

Prostitution in Africa—like prostitution anywhere else—is not a form of social pathology or cultural predisposition. It is one of the ways that women's work supports their families, and the specifics of the ways women in Africa have prostituted themselves have to do with the specific kinds of families they are supporting and creating, and the specific kinds of support their families require at the time.

BIBLIOGRAPHY

Bujra, Janet M. "Women 'Entrepreneurs' of Early Nairobi." *Canadian Journal of African Studies* 9, no. 2 (1975): 213–234.

Chauncey, George W., Jr. "The Locus of Reproduction: Women's Labour in the Zambian Copperbelt, 1927–1953." *Journal of Southern African Studies* 7, no. 2 (1981): 135–164.

Cohen, Abner. *Custom and Politics in Urban Africa: A Study of Hausa Migrants in Yoruba Towns*. Berkeley, 1969.

Hoelmann, Ellen. *Rooiyard*. Rhodes-Livingston Papers. Lusaka, 1948.

Southall, Aiden W., and Peter C. W. Gutkind. *Townsmen in the Making: Kampala and Its Suburbs*. Kampala, 1956.

White, Luise. *The Comforts of Home: Prostitution in Colonial Nairobi.* Chicago, 1990.

LUISE WHITE

See also **Disease; Labor Migration; Sexuality; Urbanism and Urbanization.**

PROVERBS AND RIDDLES. Proverbs and riddles are among the poetic verbal art forms of most African societies. Compared to other poetic forms, and indeed to all other forms of verbal art, they are extremely short—in the case of riddles sometimes as brief as a word or a sound. Of the two, proverbs, by far the more important, have attracted the attention of more collectors and scholars. They are ubiquitous in African societies, with the possible exception of the Khoisan of southern Africa, and the Nilotic and Hamitic groups residing in a stretch from the area of the Horn north and west along the Mediterranean coast.

Their appeal to collectors and scholars reflects their popularity in traditional discourse. The Igbo (Ibo) of eastern Nigeria describe them as the palm oil with which words are eaten, while the Yoruba, their compatriots to the west, say proverbially that proverbs are the vehicles of speech; when communication goes awry, proverbs come to the rescue.

Proverbs are incisive in their propositions and terse in their formulation. They are deduced from close observations of life, the characteristics and habits of life forms, and the environment and natural phenomena, and from sober reflections on these. Because they are held to express unexceptionable truths, resort to them in a discussion or argument is tantamount to appeal to incontrovertible authority. This is one reason they are virtually indispensable in formal and informal verbal interactions; their absence in speech reduces its impact, while their apt use significantly enhances it. They even pervade all other (major) forms of verbal art, in which their use confers greater effectiveness. Archer Taylor must have had the general acceptance of their sagacity and veracity in mind when he described proverbs as "the wisdom of many and the wit of one": the artistry involved in their formulation is one person's (usually anonymous), but their truth is accepted by all ("The Wisdom of Many and the Wit of One," *Swarthmore College Bulletin* 54 [1962]: 4). Yet no society's proverbs speak with one voice, a society's repertoire being a record of the plurality of views, opinions, and attitudes that society has known. For every proverb that makes a judgmental assertion, one would most probably find others expressing a contradictory view. This eclectic quality makes them invaluable archives of the intellectual and ideational history of the community.

Proverbs not only lend rhetorical effectiveness to speech but also perform important social functions. They may indicate the sort of behavior society considers appropriate, as does, for example, the Jabo (Liberia) proverb, "a grown-up who emulates children is a fool," or they may comment on an occurrence, as with the Zulu saying, "the beast has fallen on its horns," referring to a person's prostration by misfortune. The Fulani of Nigeria say "before the old woman made soapsuds the tick bird was clean," a rebuke to a person who erroneously believes that he or she is indispensable to another's well-being. Perhaps most importantly, proverbs' cryptic and indirect manner of expression make them most useful in African societies which, being close-knit in general, place great stock in relational delicacy and tact.

Riddles are closely related to proverbs in that they are also brief and based on close observation of nature. Some riddles are a mere word or sound long, for example the Kamba (Kenya) riddle "seh!" whose answer is "A needle stabbed the sand," "seh" being the sound the needle supposedly made on entry. Essentially they are metaphorical; they pose questions (implicit or explicit) to be solved by identifying a thing whose characteristics match those indicated in the question. The analogy might be of sound, rhythm, tone, or appearance, and it might be simply metaphorical, as in the Sotho riddle from South Africa, "a tree on which all birds sit"—a chief.

Proverbs are usually not associated with special occasions but occur virtually any time people speak; riddles, by contrast, are confined to a few special instances of verbal gaming and are for that reason less popular. Some scholars have dismissed them as being of minor and childish interest, meant for mere entertainment rather than education. That judgment is only partially correct, though. Among the Yoruba, for example, riddling is typically a preliminary to evening storytelling. The riddles exercise the intellect and bring it to a state of heightened alertness before the telling of the tales from which the listeners must extract important morals. Riddles are thus kin to dilemma tales, which also demand the application of intelligence to solving difficult problems.

The closeness between proverbs and riddles is evident in the following Yoruba proverb-riddle:

"The elephant died and Mangudu ate it; the buffalo died and Mangudu ate it; Mangudu died but found no creature to eat it." As a proverb it could refer to a person who always came to the aid of those in need, but found no succor in his or her own time of need. As a riddle its answer is the grave.

BIBLIOGRAPHY

Finnegan, Ruth. *Oral Literature in Africa.* Oxford, 1970.
Harries, Lyndon. "The Riddle in Africa." *Journal of American Folklore* 84 (1971): 377–393.
Okpewho, Isidore. *African Oral Literature: Backgrounds, Character, and Continuity.* Bloomington, Ind., 1992.
Seitel, Peter. "Proverbs: The Social Use of Metaphor." In *Folklore Genres,* edited by Dan Ben-Amos. Austin, Tex., 1976.

OYEKAN OWOMOYELA

See also **Language Use; Oral Culture and Oral Tradition.**

PUBLISHING

[This double entry deals with the publishing of books and journals within Africa itself rather than publications about Africa produced in Europe and elsewhere.]

BOOKS

Although Africa's association with printing and literature goes back many centuries, publishing in Africa began with the advent of Islam, and by the seventeenth century various Arabic scripts were in circulation in the main urban and trading centers of the western Sudan. Literacy was restricted to a select few, mostly professional scholars and scribes. Distribution was limited, there was no real book trade in any sense, and the only libraries that existed were private collections.

It was not until the spread of Christianity in the nineteenth century that publishing began to establish itself, and it was largely through the influence and activities of the Christian missions that the book made its first real impact in Africa. In Nigeria, for example, the first mission printing press was established as early as the mid-eighteenth century, to be followed by several more in the nineteenth century. Similar developments took place around that time in Kenya, and in southern Africa local printing presses were established by missionaries at Lovedale in the Eastern Cape in 1861 and at Morija in Basutoland (now Lesotho) in 1874. These presses are still in existence today.

From the nineteenth century to World War II there were mission presses in most of the colonial territories that published primarily translations from the Bible, along with hymnbooks, devotional literature, and evangelical tracts in African langugages. This was followed in the 1930s by the establishment, in various parts of the continent, of Vernacular Literature Bureaus, which published simple readers and other material in African languages. These literature bureaus were run not as commercial enterprises but as government departments.

In the immediate postwar period, publishing for schools and other educational institutions was the domain of British and French publishing houses. Independence in many African countries subsequently created an education explosion, and educational publishing for Africa became big business. With independence also came the establishment of the West African and the East African Examinations Councils. Invariably these boards, largely staffed by expatriates, encouraged and recommended the use of schoolbooks published by the British, and several British firms opened branches in Africa in the early 1950s. Although local manufacture was established on a substantial scale in Nigeria and Kenya, many of the books produced by the United Kingdom multinationals continued to be written by expatriate authors and colonial officers. In the early days much of the content of these books reflected colonialist attitudes. Sometimes the market was flooded with special "African editions," which frequently amounted to no more than putting an African face on the cover of a book or making other minor cosmetic changes. The result was a broadside of books which were sometimes insensitive to African needs, frequently not suitable for the environment of an African child, or which portrayed stereotyped images of Africa. It was not until the late 1960s that the metropolitan firms started to reduce this one-way traffic and began to develop books that originated in Africa, written by African authors.

Multinational Publishers

The role and dominance of foreign and multinational publishers in Africa has been the subject of a great deal of debate. They have been accused of commercial opportunism and of being excessively profit minded, of determining which African manuscripts become books and dictating what gets published, of neglecting literacy and young people's materials and the indigenous languages. Some of these accusations have not been without foundation, and the multinationals' sometimes exploitative role has been rightly exposed and criticized. However, there is plenty of evidence that the multinationals are now engaged in publishing African-oriented books and literature, conceived and published in Africa.

The much-maligned multinationals, which so dominated the publishing scene in the 1960s and 1970s, are now largely out of favor with African governments, or certainly no longer play such a dominant role. In some countries, they now coexist relatively peacefully alongside indigenous publishers, and in other cases former branches of the multinationals have paved the way for new indigenous companies.

Indigenous Publishers

Even though the multinationals—with their ready access to capital and expertise—have much working to their advantage, this has not prevented the establishment of a lively indigenous book industry, beginning in the early 1960s. During the following three decades indigenous publishing in Africa, despite enormous problems, came of age. The International Conference on Publishing and Book Development in Africa, held at the University of Ife in Nigeria in 1973, can be regarded as a milestone in the development of an autonomous publishing capacity in Africa. By that time indigenous publishing had become an established reality in many African countries and was poised to challenge the previous monopoly of foreign publishers. An awareness was growing in all African nations of the need for homegrown publishing, geared to the requirements and experiences of the local people.

If the 1970s were a decade of expansion for the African book industries, the 1980s can only be described as a decade of crisis, a crisis that was becoming even more acute in the 1990s. The constantly deepening economic recession and chronic balance of payments problems in most African countries took a severe toll on publishing and book development. Moreover, few African governments had taken decisive action to support their book industries, certainly not in the private sector, and in many countries the book industry and library development have had to take a backseat in the pursuit of national development. Although there have been a few instances of positive government support, government participation in book publishing in Africa has been generally ill conceived. State-aided companies were either hampered by bureaucracy or inefficiency or have led to publishing monopolies which have stifled the growth of independent publishers—a situation whereby books are written, approved, published, and distributed by the same state monopoly, leaving the private publishing sector out in the cold.

Key Issues

The development of the book industries in Africa has been affected, and will continue to be heavily affected, by infrastructure problems and by the progressively worsening economic conditions in most parts of the continent. There are also many social and cultural dimensions which compound the problem: a multiplicity of languages, high illiteracy (over 50 percent Africa-wide), poor transportation and communications, and lack of training and expertise. All have played their part to hinder the development of the reading habit and the growth of a healthy book industry. Effective distribution is still the main headache, although some publishers have tried to come to grips with the problem and have explored novel and innovative ways of getting books to the marketplace. Moreover, one of the most fundamental issues for publishers and writers alike is the question of language. Whether to write in an African or in a European language has been vigorously argued, and debates about new norms, new ways for writers to reach the people, are recurring themes. The language issue greatly affects publishing developments: on the one hand the vast number of languages creates special problems for African publishers; on the other, African governments' decisions on language policy will significantly influence future publishing developments in general and the success and viability of publishing in the African languages in particular.

Despite the difficult economic conditions, the lack of government encouragement, and the many obstacles facing the indigenous book industries, innovative new publishing ventures are still being started in many places. A wide range of books of the highest quality has emerged from some African countries, there is evidence of great intellectual vigor, and a number of privately owned firms in particular have demonstrated imaginative entrepreneurial skill in the midst of adversity. Although mortality has been high, by the mid-1990s there were around three hundred active indigenous firms with fairly sizable publishing programs, plus several hundred small imprints, though most of these live a somewhat precarious existence. Whereas many of the indigenous publishers still find it difficult to compete with the multinationals in real terms, there are especially dynamic autonomous publishing companies in Zimbabwe, Kenya, Nigeria, Ghana, and South Africa, as well as in a few francophone countries, notably Senegal and Côte d'Ivoire.

Another aspect of indigenous publishing is the much-written-about phenomenon of Onitsha market literature. Consisting of chapbooks or pamphlets containing pulp fiction written by the common man for the common man, it was hawked by traders in the main market of Onitsha in eastern Nigeria, which flourished in the 1960s. Over two thousand titles were published during that period, until the market was destroyed in the civil war that began in 1967.

Mass-market publishing has since emerged elsewhere in Africa, notably in Kenya, many publishers having apparently suddenly awakened to the fact that money was to be made in such literature. The books are similar to the Onitsha titles, but are rather more sophisticated, more elitist, and better produced. Some of this literature subsequently came under fire for its sometimes cheap morality, and fears were expressed that some of Africa's best serious creative writing was about to be drowned in a swamp of pulp. Nevertheless, African-produced mass paperbacks of popular fiction have created a new readership and have also created an appetite for reading among people who did not in the past want to read books other than those required for passing examinations. The spread of popular literature in Kenya, Nigeria, and elsewhere has probably also caused many ordinary readers to progress to more serious works of creative writing.

New Approaches

In the 1990s there has been a great deal of new thinking on how to develop indigenous publishing, and recognition of the need for new approaches to tackle, with renewed determination, the many problems faced by the African book industries. In February 1991 a major international seminar on publishing in developing countries was convened at the Rockefeller Conference Centre in Bellagio, Italy, bringing together a group of prominent publishers from Africa and Asia, as well as representatives of donor organizations. The goal was to review and assess various approaches to foster book publishing in the developing world and examine strategies for improvement. The book that came out of the conference, *Publishing and Development in the Third World* (London, 1992), pres-

ents what is probably the first full-scale discussion of publishing in developing countries. The conference also led to the establishment of the Bellagio Group of donor organizations, which aims to strengthen indigenous African publishing through the promotion and funding of activities in various areas.

There is also a growing trend toward collective approaches to address the issues and challenges of book publishing in Africa. A major initiative, launched in 1992, is the African Publishers' Network (APNET), based in Harare, Zimbabwe, which aims to give a clear and unified voice to publishers in Africa, and which, among other activities, is developing a program to train publishing personnel throughout the continent. Outside Africa, the Oxford-based African Books Collective, a self-help initiative set up by a group of African publishers in 1989, is trading with increasing success, bringing the wealth of African publishing to the shelves of libraries and bookshops in Europe, North America, and other places outside of Africa and providing more visibility for African books, while promoting

Insignia of the members of the African Books Collective. COURTESY OF THE AFRICAN BOOKS COLLECTIVE LTD.

African scholarship, African writing, and African cultural identity.

An earlier initiative, the Noma Award for Publishing in Africa, has significantly contributed to both substantive progress and international recognition of African books. It owes its establishment and endowment to the philanthropic spirit of the late Shoichi Noma, former president of the Japanese publishing house Kodansha Ltd., who saw the need to encourage African authors and publishers to achieve their proper place in world scholarship and literature. Established in 1979, it is offered annually for an outstanding new book published in Africa by an African writer or scholar, in three categories: academic and scholarly books; books for children; and literature and creative writing. The Noma Award has now become the major book prize for Africa. It enjoys a high reputation both for the quality of the works it has crowned and for the success it has achieved in its main mission, to promote publishing in Africa and thus contribute to increased publishing activities all over the continent.

BIBLIOGRAPHY

Information on book publishing in sub-Saharan Africa can be found in a number of sources. Two books on the subject are PHILIP G. ALTBACH, ed., *Publishing and Development in the Third World,* London, 1992; and EDWINA OLU-WASANMI, EVA MCLEAN, and HANS M. ZELL, eds., *Publishing in Africa in the Seventies: Proceedings of an International Conference on Publishing and Book Development Held at the University of Ife, Ile-Ife, Nigeria, 16–20 December 1973,* Ile-Ife, Nigeria, 1975. HANS M. ZELL has edited two references resource: *African Books in Print/Livres africains disponibles,* 4th ed., 2 vols., London, 1993; and *The African Book World and Press: A Directory/Répertoire du livre de la presse en Afrique,* 4th ed., London, 1989. The most comprehensive bibliographic reference work to date is *Publishing and Book Development in Sub-Saharan Africa: An Annotated Bibliography,* by HANS ZELL and CÉCILE LOMER, London, 1996, which cites over 2,200 references on all aspects of publishing and the book trade in Africa. Journal sources include *The African Book Publishing Record,* published quarterly in London since 1975 by Hans Zell Publishers; *African Publishing Review,* issued six times a year in Harare, Zimbabwe, since 1992 by African Publishers' Network; and *Bellagio Publishing Network Newsletter,* published quarterly in Buffalo, N.Y., since 1991 by Bellagio Publishing Network.

HANS M. ZELL

See also **Education; Language Use; Literacy; Literature.**

NEWSPAPERS AND PERIODICALS

Mass communication is a potent force in human society and is crucial in politics, industry, business, culture, and lifestyles. The media are vital not only as sources of information, but also as points of reference for the shaping of ideas, decisions, and actions. They select and call to public attention ideas, trends, and events. For instance, newspapers and magazines have been known to set political and economic agendas, in addition to informing their readership about national and international events.

Overview

The problems faced by the media in Africa include distribution, low levels of literacy, poor surface transport, costly airmail, and production difficulties caused by lack of generating power and chemical and newsprint mills, among other things. In spite of these hardships, the publishing of newspapers and journals in African states continues to thrive, albeit not as impressively as in other developing nations in Asia and Latin America.

Because the existence of newspapers and journals is correlated to levels of literacy, such literature is a fairly recent phenomenon in sub-Saharan Africa, although there was an active press in South Africa in the early nineteenth century. Prior to the introduction of the press in Africa, there were oramedia (oral media) which were collectively owned and grounded in indigenous cultures. Oramedia, as systems of social interaction and transmission of information, have existed in a variety of forms in Africa to reinforce group values, maintain social relationships, and redirect the thinking of people. Moreover, with the emergence of formal Western education, and changes in patterns of economic production, social relations, and political structures, print, electronic, and oramedia began interacting to reshape African societies. During the colonial era, oral and print media were crucial in the mobilization of the masses for nationalistic and developmental sentiments and goals. Currently, oramedia are being reactivated in many African countries to represent contemporary problems related to health, environment, agriculture, the status of women, moral decay, and democratization.

Modern newspaper and journal publishing, predicated on literacy, was introduced in Africa through the colonial experience and contact with major industrialized economies. Initially, production of print media was spearheaded by the colonial government through, for example, the publication of gazettes, and through mission societies, which mainly published in indigenous languages for evangelical purposes. With improved literacy and political consciousness, private individuals and nationalist organizations set up their own presses.

In Africa, basic figures on the number and circulation of daily newspapers indicate the levels of literacy, press freedom, and economic development. With greater political democratization and increases in levels of literacy, these figures are likely to change. For a long time, governments in Africa, driven by the urge to protect their own political positions and the economic interests of those in power, have mainly been concerned with intervention in media programming rather than with the role the media can play in national development. As a result, there have been numerous cases of press harassment and intimidation, including detention, imprisonment, and deportation of journalists, and the withdrawal of vital government advertising. Generally, the media serve the interests of particular social classes, help maintain and legitimize power structures, and encourage or hinder the entry of ideas that may disrupt the political and economic status quo. There is little doubt, however, that communication is important for development, and a number of African countries are using the print media, however minimally, for communication in the improvement of health, nutrition, agriculture, family planning, and environmental management. This utility of the media can be expanded with greater press freedom, literacy, and the economic empowerment of the people.

A Survey of the Press in African States

During the colonial era in Africa, the European-owned press was mainly, although not totally, concerned with maintaining colonial relationships and structures. In Kenya, many newspapers acted as the voice of the settler community and occasionally opposed government inclinations to relinquish colonial power, whenever that became imperative. There also existed an oppositional press, such as *Muiguithania*, which attempted to mobilize the Kenyan people in the struggle for independence. An underground press was vibrant. In the 1990s the Kenyan dailies were the *East African Standard*, originally owned by Lonrho but currently owned by, among others, Mark Too, the deputy director of Lonrho East Africa; *Daily Nation*, owned by the Aga Khan, but with local shareholding; and the *Kenya Times*, owned by the ruling party, the Kenya African National Union (KANU). Foreign-owned newspapers and magazines condition their policies with regard to the role of foreign investment, and editors, sensitive to the idea of a free press, are under pressure from different forms of censorship by the state to toe the political line of the ruling party. They attempt not to be abrasive. The *Nation* is Kenya's most popular daily, with a circulation of 190,000 (2,500 in Uganda and 2,000 in Tanzania), while the *East African Standard*'s average sales is 50,000. The *Sunday Nation* has a circulation of 202,000 and is clearly ahead of the other papers.

Before the emergence of the *Kenya Times* in 1983, print media in Kenya had been dominated by the *Nation* and the *Standard*. The acquisition of the paper by the ruling party, and its subsequent role as an organ of the party, quickly denied it the role of a credible and objective competitor. The *Kenya Times*, which has the bulk of government advertising, carries stories that are uncritical of the government and the ruling party. Its daily circulation is only 5,900 copies. In contrast, *The People*, a weekly tabloid owned by Kenneth Matiba, chairman of the opposition party Forum for the Restoration of Democracy-Asili (FORD-Asili), has a knack for investigating powerful political exclusives which cut across the ruling party and the opposition divide. *The People* has been at the center of exposing some of the most bizarre cases of corruption involving top government officials and their associates. In the mid-1990s it was selling 47,000 copies a week against a print order of 54,000.

In the political magazine field, Hilary Ng'weno's pioneering *Weekly Review*, founded in 1975 and with a circulation of 20,000, and the *Economic Review*, founded in 1992 and edited by Peter Warutere, are the main weeklies. Peter Kareithi's *Financial Review*, banned by the government in the late 1980s because of its exposure of high-level corruption, would have been a welcome addition. *Parents*, founded in 1986 by Eunice Mathu and with a circulation of 42,000, and Evelyn Mungai-Eldon's *Presence*, founded in 1984 and with a circulation of 8,000, dominate social and gender issues. The human interest magazine *Echo* folded after the departure of its editor Joseph Odindo, now editor of the Nation Group's weekly, the *East African*, which is quickly carving a special place for itself as a reliable tabloid on east African political and economic issues.

The 1980s marked the emergence of new media in Africa promoting pluralism, government accountability, and freedom of expression. These media have contributed significantly toward greater democratization and economic liberalization in Africa. In December 1991, the Kenya government gave in to national and international pressure to repeal a law enacted in 1982 which turned the country into a de jure one-party state. With the reentry of multiparty political participation, a number of oppositional magazines emerged and articulated positions different from those of the ruling party. These magazines included the *Nairobi Law Monthly, Beyond, The Option, Society,* and *Finance.* They have contributed to the exposing of high-level corruption, and various editors have been subjected to harassment and imprisonment for publishing allegedly seditious articles. The *Nairobi Law Monthly,* edited by Gitobu Imanyara, is targeted at legal practitioners and the human rights community, and it has been removed from the streets on numerous occasions by security forces. Njehu Gatabaki, the editor of *Finance,* has been threatened, detained, and jailed on a number of occasions for articles in his publication. *Beyond* was banned by the government.

Government censorship has not been restricted to the magazines. The *Daily Nation* has been accused by President Daniel arap Moi of undermining security, fanning tribalism, and promoting political violence. Other newspapers and magazines in Kenya include *African Medical News,* published by African Sciences; *Coast Week,* a tabloid edited by Adrian Grimwood; *The Crusader,* published by Leafray Ltd.; *The Business Chronicle,* published by Media House Ltd. and edited by Wanjiru Ciira; *The Executive,* a monthly magazine for the business and financial community; the *Jua Kali News,* a bi-monthly that covers news from the informal sector; and *Ngao,* a newsletter published by the Network for the Defense of Independent Media in Africa. There are also other journals including *PC World East Africa, Enterprise News, Farming News, Character, NG, Media Focus,* and *Media Insider.* Newspapers and journals in Kenya's indigenous languages are expanding quickly. They include *Mwihoko, Mumenyereri, Kihooto,* and *Mutiiri,* written in Gikuyu, and *Nam Dar* and *Otit Mach,* written in Dholuo.

Since 1986, when the National Resistance Army, under the leadership of Yoweri Kaguta Museveni, took over political power in Uganda, the independent press has had a significant measure of freedom, including the freedom to criticize the government. The *Uganda Confidential,* a periodical launched in 1989, is fairly abrasive in its stories and

there are moments the president has responded in the pages of the paper. Most of the papers in Uganda are written in English and Luganda. They include the *Citizen; The Economy; The Exposure; Ekitangala; Focus; The Market Place,* a weekly with a circulation of 20,000; *The Monitor,* with a circulation of 28,000; *The People; The Tribune,* with a circulation of 30,000; and *The Shariat,* targeted at the Islamic community and with English and Luganda versions.

In Malawi, before President Kamuzu Banda's acceptance of pluralism in June 1993, there were only two newspapers, the *Daily Times* and the *Malawi News,* both of which were under the control of the ruling Malawi Congress Party. In the late 1990s, there were over fifteen publications commenting on political, economic, and social issues. These included *The Daily Times, The Democrat, The Enquirer, The Independent, The Focus,* and *The Monitor.*

The publishing of newspapers and journals in Angola has been hampered by the political conflicts involving the ruling Movimento Popular de Libertação de Angola (MPLA) and União Nacional para a Independência Total de Angola (UNITA) since independence from Portuguese colonial rule in 1975. As a result, most publications are short-lived. Newspapers and journals in Angola are available in Portuguese and include *Batuque Amana,* published by the Partido Social Democrata de Angola; *Comércio Actualidade,* a weekly with a circulation of 10,000 published by Artimagen; and *Journalismo Hoje,* a monthly publication by Sindicato dos Jornalistas Angolanos.

South Africa has a long history of publishing newspapers and journals. On 16 August 1800 the first bilingual newspaper in South Africa, *The Cape Town Gazette and African Advertiser/Kaapsche Stads Courant en Afrikaansche Berigter,* was published. It articulated government policy. The publishers, Alexander Walker and John Robertson, were not supposed to offer any personal comments on political subjects. Thomas Pringle (1798–1834) and John Fairbairn (1794–1864) published a magazine, the *South African Journal,* in January 1824 but discontinued it immediately due to government interference. Their names are closely associated with the struggle for press freedom in South Africa. Sir Larry Cole signed Cape Ordinance 60 of 30 April 1829, which ensured relative freedom of the press, although with the adoption of apartheid as a political ideology, the press was significantly stifled. The government of President Nelson Mandela, leader of the African National Congress, is restoring press freedom in an impressive way.

The first Afrikaans newspaper, *Di Patriot,* published between 1876 and 1904, was a mouthpiece for the Afrikaners. It encouraged readers to write in their own languages and was an important vehicle for the consolidation of Afrikaans as a language. When the Afrikaan Language Movement was set up in 1875, it established its press. Its magazine *Om Klyntji* (1896–1906) was crucial in the propagation of Afrikaans as the language of the future, a reality that emerged when Dutch was replaced by Afrikaans as one of the official languages of the Union of South Africa in 1925. The first black newspaper, *Imvo Zabantsundu,* was published in Kingwilliamstown in 1884 and was edited by the first black South African journalist, John Tengo Jabavu. It is still in circulation, especially in black townships.

There are certain newspapers and race-specific magazines targeted at blacks. These include *Drum,* first published in 1951 by Jim Bailey, with east African editions; *True Love; Family; Thandi;* and *Tribune.* The articles in *Drum* are in various African languages and English, but the advertisements are mainly in English. The business magazine sector includes publications such as *Black Enterprise, The Business Magazine, Black Manufacturer, Black Farmer, African Business,* and *Chamber of Commerce Review.*

In 1889 Francis Dormer founded one of the largest newspaper and publishing groups. Since its inception, Argus Printing and Publishing Company Ltd. has continued close links with mining entrepreneurs like Cecil John Rhodes and major mining companies. Argus newspapers include *The Star* (Johannesburg), the *Argus* (Cape Town), *Pretoria News* (Pretoria), *Daily News* (Durban), *Post Natal* (Natal), *Sunday Star* (Johannesburg), *Sunday Tribune* (Durban), *Sowetan* (Johannesburg), and *Diamond Fields Advertiser* (Kimberley). Newspapers in South Africa are widely read. The *Sunday Times,* published by Times Media, has a circulation of over 538,000 and the *Sowetan* of over 210,000.

In addition, there are specialized magazines, which include those for the motorist (*Car, Wiel, The Motorist/Die Motoris*); the sportsman and traveler (*Caravan and Outdoor Life, Gateway, Hengel/Angling, SA Garden and Home, SA Sports Illustrated, SA Yachting, SA Athlete*); the businessman (*Finance Week, Financial Mail,* and *Finansies & Tegniek*); and youth (*Blush, Youngtime, Early Times,* and *T-Mag*). In South Africa, the general-interest consumer magazines are *Huisgenoot,* the nation's largest magazine; *You* and *Personally;* the black magazines *Pace, Bona,* and *Drum;* and downscaled magazines *Keur*

and *People.* There is also the international magazine *Reader's Digest,* established in 1948. Other magazines include *Style,* published since 1980, and *De Kat.*

Other than the international editions of *Time, Newsweek,* and *U.S. News and World Report,* which are available in many African countries, there are also news magazines which are targeted at the sophisticated reader. In South Africa these include *To the Point,* which folded in 1978 during the information scandal when government funding for the magazine was revealed; *Frontline,* published by Dennis Backett and, since 1991, incorporated into the *Sunday Star; Insig,* established in 1987; and *Vrye Weekblad.* Due to strict censorship laws in the country, sexually explicit magazines have been few. International magazines of this kind such as *Playboy, Hustler,* and *Penthouse* are banned in many countries in the continent because they are seen to be morally inappropriate.

There are also trade journals, which include *Marketing Mix, Medicine Today, Wynboer, Servanus, Black Enterprise, Plastics Southern Africa, Hotelier and Caterer,* and *Vector.* Moreover, most professional associations publish magazines or professional journals for their members. These cover domains such as journalism, medicine, engineering, education, and commerce. There are also farming and agricultural magazines, which span such areas as computerization, irrigation, geology, wildlife management, meteorological research, and the environment. These include *African Wildlife, Farmer's Weekly,* and *Wood Southern Africa.* Most magazines in South Africa are owned by Nasionale Tydskrifte, based in Cape Town, and Republican Press, based in Durban.

Despite the quick succession of military regimes in Nigeria, the press has maintained its vibrancy. The country has over twenty daily newspapers, twenty-two weekly newspapers, and nineteen weekly newsmagazines, the majority of which are independent. Furthermore, each of the thirty states has its own newspaper. There are approximately a hundred publications nationwide. This may be explained by the country's large population, which stands at over a hundred million, and a relatively high literacy rate of about 50 percent.

The press in Nigeria has been far from free. On 11 June 1994 armed antiriot policemen and agents of the notorious State Security Service stormed the premises of Punch Nigeria Limited, publishers of *The Punch* (daily), *Sunday Punch,* and *Toplife* (weeklies), and sealed off the offices. On the same day, another team of security officers sealed off the premises of Concord Press Nigeria Limited, publishers of *National Concord* (daily), *Sunday Concord, Business Concord, Idoka, Isokan, Weekend Concord,* and *African Concord* (weeklies). Both groups were later proscribed for six months. Also proscribed were the titles of the Guardian Newspapers Limited—*The Guardian* (daily), *Guardian Express* (afternoon daily), *Financial Guardian, Lagos Life,* and *African Guardian.* The three groups have been vociferous agitators for a democratic Nigeria. General Sani Abacha, the current head of state who took power by overthrowing General Ibrahim Babangida, has done everything in his power to muzzle the press in that country.

After President Mathieu Kerekou of Bénin relinquished power to Nicéphore Songlo in April 1991, there was initial euphoria and hope in the country that freedom of the press might be upheld. But this was short-lived as the government started instigating libel cases against journalists who were critical of the new regime. For instance, Edgar Kaho, editor of *Le Soleil,* was imprisoned in May 1993 for two articles published the previous year accusing the president's wife of corruption following a trip to Paris in which she was alleged to have spent FCFA 10 million (U.S.$20,000) inappropriately. Tabloid papers in Bénin include *L'Avenir,* published by Claude Firmin Grangbe since June 1995; the *Forum de la Semaine,* published in France by Bruno Sodehou since 1989, with a circulation of 17,500; and the weekly *La Gazette du Golfe,* published by Maurice Chabi since 1987. Other newspapers include *Nouvelle Vision, Le Matin Concorde,* and *Bénin-Info.*

Until 1982, the only newspaper in Botswana was the government-owned *Daily News,* launched in 1964 as a free two-page newsletter. The growth of newspapers and magazines in Botswana is slow. This may be due to the country's small population, and low literacy rate, the inaccessibility of certain parts of the country, and competition from the press in South Africa, notably the *Weekly Mail, Johannesburg Star,* and *New Nation.*

Cameroon continues to practice prepublication censorship of the press. Under Article 14 of the Freedom of Mass Communication bill enacted into law in December 1990, newspapers are required to submit their copies to the senior divisional officer for censorship before they are printed. Moreover, Article 17 empowers the senior divisional officer to seize publications viewed as having overstepped political bounds. A number of publications have experienced the wrath of government either through arbitrary seizure of the papers or the im-

prisonment of the editors. Some of the controversial papers in Cameroon include *Le Messager, Dikalo, La Nouvelle Expression,* and *Galaxie.*

The ruling party in Zimbabwe, the Zimbabwe African National Union–Patriot Front (ZANU–PF), continues to control the print media through the government's majority shareholding in Zimbabwe Newspapers Limited (Zimpapers), set up in 1980 to buy out the Argus Group of South Africa. Although Zimpapers is an independent company, the majority shareholder is Mass Media Trust, which always acts on behalf of government. The country has a thriving independent press, but journalists tread carefully due to occasional government paranoia. Newspapers and magazines in Zimbabwe include the *Financial Gazette, The Financial Telescope, Horizon, Living On, Mahogany, Moto, The Northern News, New People, Southern African Economist, Parade, The People, Sunday Gazette, Sunday Times,* and the *Village Voice.* The *Parade* is a monthly magazine published by Thomson Publications and has a circulation of over 90,0000. The *Sunday Times* has a circulation of over 50,000.

Julius Nyerere, the first president of Tanzania, was ideologically committed to the centrality of the Party in national development. His political philosophy of Ujamaa was extensively legitimized, promoted, and propagated by the media. After the country accepted the principles of participatory democracy in 1992 and enacted the 1993 Broadcasting Services Act, independent radio and television stations quickly emerged. A number of newspapers and journals were also licensed. Although the Information Services Department attempts to control the media, it is only partially successful. Problems of poverty and inaccessibility of certain regions restrict newspaper and magazine readership to the rural areas. The papers in Tanzania include the *Daily News, The Guardian, Majira,* and *Nipashe* (dailies); *Business Times, Cheche, Motomoto, Wasaa, Rai, Tazama,* and *Dimba* (weeklies); *The Express, Heko,* and *Mfanyakazi* (biweeklies); and the bimonthly *Family Mirror.* Other papers include *Raha Leo, Watu, Mwananchi, Mtanzania,* and *Alasiri,* an afternoon daily. Most of the media utilize KiSwahili, Tanzania's official and national language.

Future Prospects

The development of print media in Africa is closely related to the status of the various languages in the continent. Most of the media are available in English, French, and the specific country's national language(s), which are mainly acquired through formal education. Countries with low literacy rates and undemocratic governments are more likely to have inferior media. Nonliteracy, political intolerance, and financial difficulties are some of the reasons limiting the growth of the media in Africa; increased alleviation of poverty, higher literacy rates, and the consolidation of participatory democracy are likely to bring about a more vibrant media throughout the continent. When this happens, some of the problems that confront Africa, such as ethnic factionalism, corruption, and disease, can be exposed and deliberated. If fully utilized within a democratic environment, newspapers and journals can contribute to much-needed development in Africa.

BIBLIOGRAPHY

De Beer, A. S, ed. *Mass Media for the Nineties: The South African Handbook of Mass Communication.* Pretoria, 1993.
Maje-Pearce, Adewale, ed. *Directory of African Media.* Brussels, 1995.
Okigbo, Charles, ed. *Media and Sustainable Development.* Nairobi, 1995.
Reeves, Geoffrey. *Communications and the "Third World."* London, 1993.

KIMANI NJOGU

PYGMIES, a number of peoples in central Africa, classified as distinct by Europeans since Herodotus, and by many other Africans, on account of their short stature and their typical occupancy of forest habitats. There is long-standing controversy as to whether they form a distinct racial group (known as Negrillo) or whether their stature results from long-enforced dwelling in forest habitats. They do not use languages of their own but those of their non-Pygmy neighbors. There is no single "Pygmy" society or culture, their social organization being that of many small and autonomous bands, without chiefs or any holders of distinct political authority. Most bands are isolated from other "Pygmy" groups and linked to neighboring non-Pygmy farming peoples, with whom they form symbiotic relationships based on exchange of forest products for commodities such as iron, salt, and grain. Some "Pygmy" groups also fish, and others traditionally provide hunters and soldiers for neighboring chiefs.

There are generally accepted to be four main "Pygmy" groups: the Aka or BaBinga of the Congo, Gabon, and the Central African Republic; the Mbuti of the Ituri forest in Zaire; the Twa of Rwanda and Burundi and neighboring areas; and the Gesere near Lake Kivu. "Pygmies" have been greatly romanticized and little is really known of their cultures and forms of social organization.

BIBLIOGRAPHY

Two works dealing with the Mbuti are Colin M. Turnbull, *Wayward Servants: The Two Worlds of the African Pygmies,* Garden City, N.Y., 1965, and Paul Schebesta, *Among Congo Pygmies,* London, 1933.

JOHN MIDDLETON

QUAQUE, PHILIP (Philip Kweku; b. 1741; d. 1816), cleric and educator at the Gold Coast (present-day Ghana), first African to be ordained a priest in the Church of England. Born at Cape Coast, Ghana, he was a protégé (some sources implausibly say the son) of the local chief, Caboceer Cudjoe, who maintained good relations with the British and helped preserve Cape Coast within the British sphere of influence. At the age of thirteen Philip was sent to England for education, sponsored by the Society for the Propagation of the Gospel in Foreign Parts, known after its initials as SPG. During his study in England he was ordained first as deacon of the Anglican church by the bishop of Exeter at the Chapel Royal in St. James on 25 March 1765, then as priest on 1 May 1765, by the bishop of London. He was the first African to be ordained an Anglican priest. He married an English woman, Catherine Blunt, in London in 1765, and returned to Cape Coast in 1766 as the Reverend Philip Quaque, with the official title of "Missionary, School Master, and Catechist to the Negroes on the Gold Coast." He went there in the joint service of the SPG and the Company of Merchants Trading to Africa, an association of British merchants engaged in the slave trade. Quaque was also designated chaplain at Cape Coast Castle. He died at Cape Coast on 17 October 1816, aged seventy-five.

Quaque's career can be divided into two parts. The first part centered on his religious duties as missionary and chaplain, and it was the less distinguished of the two. As chaplain at Cape Coast Castle, with responsibility sometimes extending to Dixcove, Sekondi, and Komenda, Quaque propagated "fortress Christianity," with the inevitable consequence of sealing the religion from any genuine indigenous response. Second, fortress Christianity had its fate tied to the vestiges of medieval Christendom by targeting chiefs and rulers, the fittest of the fit, as worthy of Christian baptism.

Since these chiefs and rulers acted from rules of political expedience, they resisted baptism for fear of compromising their authority by unwittingly conceding sovereignty to some foreign Christian monarch. After some forty-five years of dogged attempts, Quaque finally wrote to London in October 1811 admitting failure as a missionary. He was beaten by what he called African indifference.

The second part of his career concerns his educational work, and here also he had mixed success. As an organized institution, Quaque's school was for the most part an ad hoc affair. He tried but failed to construct a new building for the school, and enrollment fluctuated wildly, between sixteen at its highest to one or none at all. The shadow of fortress Christianity had fallen over it, too. In 1789 Quaque was reporting that the school was being reestablished in the fort as a charity boarding school for needy mulatto children. However, the reports of progress the school was making by 1791 proved premature, for decline soon set in. Support for the work from the European Castle community and its African clients was lost, and Quaque felt the local population was too hostile to the school to fill the gap. However, one tangible result of the school was the few individuals who were trained there and who in turn became teachers, thus perpetuating the tradition of primary school education at Cape Coast and in similar Fante areas.

Quaque himself paid a personal price for having become a protégé of fortress Christianity. He lived under the constraints of castle politics, cultivated the English style, manners, and customs, and abandoned the Fante tongue for English. He relied on translators in his dealings with Africans. In less challenging times, all of that might have turned him into nothing more curious than an eccentric, but in those early pioneer years eccentricity was tantamount to cultural rejection. Garrisoned in his trading enclave, Quaque failed to become an effective mediator between Africa and Europe. On the African side, he complained often of unreasonable demands and expectations. His second and third wives after the death of Catherine Blunt in November 1766 were African, and that entailed extended family duties and obligations. Yet Quaque resented those duties and obligations as unwarranted, so Westernized had he become.

It is the unalterable nature of the duties and obligations that African family life brought with it that offers us a rare glimpse into how Africa's encounter with Europe as represented in Quaque as a Westernized African would falter in cultural

misunderstanding. As such, it demonstrates the importance of mutual understanding where relations existed between Europeans and Africans. It was a role Quaque as a transitional figure could have filled to great consequence, but he did not.

However, Quaque's proximity to chiefs and rulers allowed him to observe at close hand the nature and functioning of indigenous institutions, and their responses to Western influences. He was positioned at the strategic intersection of Cape Coast, the center of Fante politics, and Kumasi, the hub of Asante power, and that makes him extremely valuable as a source in understanding late-eighteenth- and early-nineteenth-century political relations in that part of western Africa. Similarly, his comments on the ambivalent attitude of chiefs and other members of the political aristocracy to the European presence at Cape Coast reveals the limited value of chiefs, whom Quaque said created obstacles rather than bridges, in efforts to establish Christianity in Africa. In Quaque's judgment, chiefly authority thus filled an ambivalent role in facilitating Western contact with Africa, while, on the other hand, it deflected it, too. Such a mixed verdict is appropriate to Quaque himself.

BIBLIOGRAPHY

Bartels, F. L. "Philip Quaque, 1741–1816." *Transactions of the Gold Coast and Togoland Historical Society* 1 (1995): 153–177.

Priestley, Margaret. "Philip Quaque of Cape Coast." In *Africa Remembered: Narratives by West Africans from the Era of the Slave Trade*, edited by Philip D. Curtin. Madison, Wis., 1967.

LAMIN SANNEH

See also **Christianity; Colonial Policies and Practice; Education.**

QUEENS AND QUEEN MOTHERS. Men dominate in African monarchies: the model of the king's authority is based on the kind of patriarchal authority exemplified by heads of kin groups and households. However, in most monarchies one or two high-ranking women participate in the exercise of royal power and occupy a position complementary to that of the king. It should be noted that in the published literature the translations into English of indigenous terms for these positions is often both confused and confusing.

Few instances are known in Africa of women ruling in their own right as queens: the Lovedu of the Transvaal are the best-known example; others include the Merina and Sakalava of Madagascar. In each of these cases their gender is ambiguous: the Merina use a non-gender-specific term: "the person who rules"; the Sakalava "queen" was spoken of familiarly as if a whore yet addressed in male terms and given the prerogatives of a man—she was prohibited from bearing children. It is probably significant that in these three cases, women took over from previous reigns of men in the nineteenth century, when the kingdoms were coming under colonial rule. These changes appear related to efforts to evade direct colonial administration by removing the seat of indigenous kingship to a less obviously political (i.e., nonmale) context.

The classic case of a woman ruling in her own right in Africa is that of Mujaji, the Rain-Queen of the Lovedu, a small kingdom in the Transvaal, South Africa. Mujaji I came to the throne about 1800, following previous reigns of male kings; her successors have all been women. These "queens" have exercised little political authority. With only the powers of persuasion, not of coercion, they rely on strategy, diplomacy, and power derived from their control of rain medicine throughout the region. They have a reputation for being able to turn the clouds into rain. Their mystical powers are said to have originated as a consequence of royal incest: Mujaji is said to have been conceived through incest between her mother and her mother's own father, the previous king.

The Rain-Queen occupies the center of a complex network of political links and obligations expressed in the idiom of kinship. Symbolically she is both masculine and feminine. She has no husband and should bear no children, but she has many wives, given to her by chiefs and nobles in return for rain, and she allocates these wives to nobles, their children recognizing her as their father. She dies by her own hand, taking poison, and is buried secretly at the royal mausoleum far from ordinary eyes. (She was the subject of H. Rider Haggard's 1887 novel *She: A History of Adventure,* which concerns a mythical queen of fair complexion, rumored to have powers over the "intrepid explorers" who penetrated to her secret realm.)

Although most African monarchies do not have regnant queens, in most of them certain senior women serve important roles as royal wives, queen mothers, queen sisters, or as regents for immature kings-to-be, who are too young to be given the powers of rulership. Such women are deemed to be "essential ingredients" (Ronald Cohen, Luc de

Heusch) of royal power and authority. Symbolically and politically these female officeholders' positions largely resemble gender relations in the wider society, in which men dominate in the political sphere yet are dependent on women for nurturing and regeneration. Regnant women, further, are often given symbolic attributes of sacredness and of maleness. These women's positions complement that of the male king, but their role may also allow them to supplement, modify, soften, or even publicly correct a king's behavior or political decision.

There are many variations on how this basic principle is realized in actual organization and behavior. The male and female elements of a single kingship may be separated in space, time, political and ritual status, legal roles, and a great number of symbolic attributes and forms of behavior. The Lozi of Zambia divide their kingdom into north and south and have two identical capitals 40 kilometers (25 mi.) apart: the southern one is ruled by a sister of the king (who has her own chiefs, councillors, and army) and is a sanctuary from the king's anger. Among the Akan of Ghana and Nyoro of Uganda, "queen mothers" or "official sisters" have exercised secular authority similar to that of senior chiefs; among the Luba of Zaire, such women are more similar to spirit mediums or tomb-guardians. The queen mother of the Shi of eastern Zaire (who holds as her private domain approximately half the land in the kingdom) may rule as regent for years until her son comes of age and is powerful enough to end her rule; she is a symbolically complementary aspect of the kingship, and both she and her son share a single essence which embodies both masculine and feminine traits. In a parallel fashion, the Alund (Lunda) king of southwestern Zaire is both a father and the nurturing female who possesses regenerative power for his people. He is secluded and symbolically sexless, without bodily orifices, and outside everyday ordinary human and social exchange; his body is guarded by his senior wife, and it is held to assure the unity and well-being of the people, animals, and crops.

Kings in Africa almost always have (or had) many wives, following the model of the polygynous family. Many wives were a symbol of high status, and their children could enhance the influence of their father, or (in a patrilineal kingship) build up his lineage. The wives, as representatives of their various clans, could exercise influence on behalf of their own clan heads, but at the same time they jointly bound the kingdom together. Royal spouses were given different titles and attached to the king in various ways. Among the Swazi, representative headmen from throughout the country provided the bridewealth for the kings' main wife (who was rarely, if ever, his first wife). A king's wives seldom "reigned" alongside the king as did his sister or mother, and it should be noted that the indigenous term designating a king's wife is frequently used metaphorically for the numerous attendants who serve the king, regardless of their sex.

Among the Luba of Zaire, important female officeholders include certain of the king's wives and the Mwadi, a female spirit medium who incarnates the spirit of a deceased king and inherits his emblems, titles, and residence. Forbidden to have sexual relations and provided with wives of her own, the Mwadi was treated as though she were a king herself. At the beginning of the colonial period, there were said to be at least four reigning Mwadi wielding greater authority than the then-ruling king.

The role of the queen mother among the Asante and other matrilineal Akan peoples of Ghana has attracted both scholarly attention and flights of imagination. To begin with, she is not a queen mother in the English sense of the term—that is, she is not the actual mother of the ruling king (she might, indeed, be his sister); neither is she a woman who rules, nor is she the king's wife. Further, she is not a high priestess of a cult associated with women and the moon (as has been fancifully asserted by some writers). Her authority is respected, but she has little formal power. And while the term "queen mother" is a gender-specific one for chief (*ohene* plus the female suffix *mea*), the *ohemmea* is not simply a female chief. Her royal status is that of a man: she adjudicates issues as the only woman among men; she dresses as a man; and (in Asante) when she is married, unlike other women, she is not bound exclusively to her husband.

The Akan kingship structure is replicated at different levels of Akan society: the word *ohemmea* was adopted originally for the elder woman of the king's lineage, but the title in the last three or four decades of the twentieth century has been used far more loosely to refer to honorary queen mothers, market queen mothers, and the like. The Akan queen mother is symbolically and politically important, but she is not the symbol of the kingship as is the king. Rather, whether or not she actually

has children, she personifies nurturing "motherhood" and is the affective link to the matrilineal ancestors. (She is the first publicly to weep for the previous year's dead in the annual royal purification rite.) She is invoked in arbitrations as the symbolic creator and destroyer, the ultimate arbiter in decision making, but she is also appealed to as an advocate. In Asante her judicial court is less costly than that of the king and the members of her court are men. In the past in some Akan kingdoms, the queen mother took part in rites pertaining to women: puberty, naming rites for infants, and ridding the town of pollution. Politically most important is that she symbolizes the lineage that produced the king, and her "wisdom" (i.e., her "knowledge" of genealogy that is held to derive from her biological role in reproduction) enables her to legitimate the selection of the king and to advise and rebuke him as well. She continues to reign whether or not the ruling king's position falls vacant, and she must take part in the selection of his successor.

The complex field of roles played by royal women is exemplified by the Ganda of Uganda. The kingship is divided between, on the one hand, the living ruler and the wife or wives, one of whom will bear the future heir to the kingship in a palace at Mengo, the kingdom's capital in Kampala, and, on the other hand, the deceased king with a palace in the form of a complex of royal shrines several miles away. The gender-neutral title of *kabaka* is used for the regnant king and the effigy of the deceased king as well as for several women, including the queen mother (his actual mother), the queen sister (the senior of his sisters or half-sisters), and, it seems, the chief wife who is in charge of the king's "charms." Also important is the royal midwife, who is the queen mother's sister. There is no royal clan: the king belongs to his mother's clan by matrifiliation. After the king's accession his mother is traditionally forbidden to see him, and she may bear no further children. She becomes queen mother with her own lands, subjects, palace, and court officials. Ganda princesses, including the queen sister, who undergoes her brother's accession rite jointly with him, must have no children and are called by male names. At her brother's death, the queen sister retires to guard his relic (jawbone) in his shrine and acts as a medium when he is consulted by his successors. These women, although highly powerful in a temporal sense, owe the king neither tribute nor political obedience; yet together they form an integral part of the total kingship.

A widespread but not ubiquitous concept associated with kings and these female royal kin is that of an original act of royal incest from which the line of kings descended. The brother-sister or father-daughter incest which figures in the royal myths of origin removes the actors from an ordered moral world, and their offspring are thereby set apart, given the dangerous status of the sacred, and placed above the everyday conflicts of interest within the kingdom itself. De Heusch suggests that this incest sacralizes sexual relations and fertility throughout the kingdom and has to do with the perceived opposition and complementarity of the sexes. Monarchy, he says, is founded on the sacred triad of king, sister, and mother.

Other well-known examples of queen mothers are found in the kingdoms of Mundang in Chad, those of the Cameroon Grasslands, the Benin of Nigeria, and Zululand. They differ primarily only in detail from those described above.

In sum, divine kingship in Africa has a long history. The kings were (and are) surrounded by a proliferation of courtiers and titled officials as well as by their queen mothers, sisters, and consorts. These women held (and hold) uniquely prestigious and powerful positions in the political hierarchy of the kingdom. Their status was equivalent to that of high-ranking male chiefs, they generally possessed their own court with chiefs and retainers, and their power was often expressed visually in art and ritual regalia.

BIBLIOGRAPHY

Boeck, Filip de. "Of Trees and Kings: Politics and Metaphor among the Aluund of Southwestern Zaire." *American Ethnologist* 21, no. 3 (1994): 451–473.

Cohen, Ronald. "Oedipus Rex and Regina: The Queen Mother in Africa," *Africa* 47, no. 1 (1977): 14–30.

Feeley-Harnik, Gillian. "Issues in Divine Kingship." *Annual Review of Anthropology* 14 (1985): 273–313.

Gilbert, Michelle. "The Cimmerian Darkness of Intrigue: Queen Mothers, Christianity, and Truth in Akwapem History." *Journal of Religion in Africa* 23, no. 1 (1993): 2–43.

Heusch, Luc de. *The Drunken King or The Origin of the State.* Translated by Roy Willis. Bloomington, Ind., 1972.

Krige, E. Jensen, and J. D. Krige. *The Realm of a Rain-Queen: A Study of the Pattern of Lovedu Society.* London, 1943.

Ray, Benjamin C. *Myth, Ritual, and Kingship in Buganda.* New York, 1991.

Roberts, Mary Nooter, and Allen F. Roberts, eds. *Memory: Luba Art and the Making of History.* New York, 1996.

MICHELLE GILBERT

See also **Akan Region, History; Gender; Kings and Kingship; Kinship and Descent; Kinship and Marriage.**

R

RABIH BIN FADLALLAH (b. 1845; d. 1900), slave trader and freebooter. He is also called Rabih Zubayr, and in French accounts he is referred to as Rabah, Rabbi, or Rabat.

Rabih was born in Salamat al-Basha, on the southeast side of Khartoum. He belonged to the Hamaj group of the southern Blue Nile. As a young man, Rabih joined a Sudanese battalion of the Turco-Egyptian army. He went to the province of Bahr al-Ghazal in the late 1850s and was assistant head of a slave-trading company. When his company was taken over by the government, Rabih was employed by Zubayr Rahma Mansur, the biggest slave trader in the region. After Zubayr's departure to Egypt in 1875, Rabih was employed by Sulayman ibn Zubayr. Following Sulayman's defeat by the government forces in 1879, Rabih reassembled the remainder of his slave army and fled to Azande territory. In the early 1880s, he raided non-Muslim groups such as the Banda, Kreish, and Sara in the Oubangui-Chari region. After defeating a French expedition in 1891, Rabih occupied Bagirmi. In 1894 he invaded Bornu, where he was joined by Haiyatu, ruler of Adamawa, who married his daughter. In 1899, Haiyatu was killed by Rabih's son Fadlallah. During the same year, Rabih defeated a French force at Togbao. In response, the French sent an expedition under the leadership of

The palace of Rabih bin Fadlallah as it stands today in Maiduguri.
FROM W. K. R. HALLAM, *THE LIFE AND TIMES OF RABIH FADL ALLAH* (ILFRACOMBE, DEVON: ARTHUR H. STOCKWELL, LTD.). REPRODUCED WITH PERMISSION OF THE PUBLISHERS

Émile Gentil, the governor of Chari, near Lake Chad. After a series of skirmishes, Rabih was killed at Lakhta on 22 April 1900.

BIBLIOGRAPHY

Adeleye, R. A. "Rabih b. Fadlallah, 1879–1893: Exploits and Impact on the Political Relations in Central Sudan." *Journal of the Historical Society of Nigeria* 5, no. 2 (1970): 223–242.

Babikir, Arbab Djama. *L'empire de Rabeh*. Paris, 1950.

Cordell, Dennis. *Dar al-Kuti and the Last Years of the Trans-Saharan Slave Trade*. Madison, Wis., 1985.

Hallam, W. K. R. *The Life and Times of Rabih Fadl Allah*. Ilfracombe, U.K., 1977.

Hill, Richard. *A Biographical Dictionary of the Sudan*. 2d ed. London, 1967.

AHMAD ALAWAD SIKAINGA

RACE. *See* **Human Evolution.**

RADAMA I (b. 1793?; d. 1828), second king (r. 1810–1828) of the Merina kingdom in central Madagascar founded by Andrianampoinimerina, his father. Radama I was responsible for two developments critical to the kindgom's history: the expansion of the kingdom from Antananarivo, the capital, into an island-spanning empire, and an alliance with the British government. The two developments were intimately connected. Actively negotiated by Radama I in 1816, the British alliance provided the king's peasant army with military training and equipment and his administration with a literate elite trained in schools run by the London Missionary Society. In exchange Radama agreed to ban the export trade in slaves from his kingdom, cleverly pleasing the British while at the same time undercutting the efficacy of his political opponents who benefited from the trade. The social price of Radama's military campaigns was paid by the peasantry through prodigious death rates in his army and the loss of male labor to increasingly feminized Merina households. He was opposed most vocally by women, who staged a revolt in 1822 when Radama I cropped his plaited hair in the European fashion. Sometimes called Madagascar's Napoleon, Radama was in his middle thirties when he died of an unknown disease.

BIBLIOGRAPHY

Valette, Jean. *Études sur le regne de Radama I$_{er}$*. Antananarivo, Madagascar, 1962.

PIER M. LARSON

Radama I.

See also **Andrianampoinimerina; Antananarivo; Ethnicity and Identity; Slave Trade.**

RADIO AND TELEVISION. Cultural forms of television, radio, video, and the print media are pivotal in the development of thoughts, sentiments, and behavior. They arouse strong feelings and reactions in individuals and governments. Consequently, in colonial and postcolonial Africa, national broadcast stations have been publicly owned and state controlled. During the colonial era, governments used the electronic media for entertainment and for the articulation of colonial political and cultural policies. In the postcolonial era, governments have used the media to propagate their positions on national issues. In the late 1980s, due to pressure from inside and outside the continent, private stations began emerging, despite the reluctance of governments to liberalize the airwaves because of the political implications of a vibrant electronic media. Mass media play crucial roles in constructing, internalizing, and contesting national ideologies. Whereas liberalized airwaves would provide for alternative voices, especially oppositional ones, government-controlled stations lack a sense of balance, owing in part to the fact that senior management is appointed by government. Heavy central control, lack of effective competition between channels, and limited funding have led to stodgy and biased programming. In certain cases, governments stipulate that the media are free but in practice keep them under tight control.

The control of the electronic media is mainly felt in rural areas, where most Africans live, and there have been calls by opposition leaders and donor agencies for the free flow of information as a prerequisite to democracy. Governments have devised various strategies to deal with this pressure, such as restricting what may be broadcast and forming partnerships with private media entrepreneurs. For instance, the Kenyan government has a financial interest in the country's five television stations, Kenya Television Network (KTN), Stella Television (STV), Kenya Broadcasting Corporation (KBC), KBC Channel 2, and Cable Television Network (CTN). Generally, news in Kenya's electronic media is censored and imbalanced in favor of government. KBC is received nationally and carries stories in support of government and the ruling party. KTN occasionally carries stories that are critical of government. This may be allowed due to the network's restricted reach; its audience does not extend beyond Nairobi and its suburbs. In the late 1990s, radio licenses were still confined to FM frequencies which, like the television stations, are not received far beyond the city.

In sub-Saharan Africa, radio is the most widespread electronic medium because its receivers are relatively cheap and widely distributed. Moreover, it is easy to maintain continuous programming at a relatively low cost. Education, information, and entertainment have continued to be the main functions of radio and television broadcasting in Africa. There have been efforts to utilize broadcasting to espouse values and ideas on equality, rights, democracy, economy, development, and cultural integration, but success has not been significant be-

cause of government restrictions on what is transmitted. Adult literacy programs are also carried by many national radio stations. There have been advances in television broadcasting with the formation of the Regional African Satellite Communications System (RASCOM), the Pan African Telecommunications Network (PANAFTEL), and the Union of National Radio and Television Organizations of Africa (URTNA).

URTNA, an association of African broadcasting institutions, was established in 1962 to promote inter-African cooperation for the development of broadcasting activities and services in Africa. The major activities of URTNA include the exchange of radio and television programs, training of broadcasting personnel, research on technical aspects of broadcasting, organization of seminars to enhance the application of media in national and regional development, coverage of international sporting and cultural events, and international promotion and marketing of African television programs. The association is financed by its member organizations, international organizations, the United Nations, and bilateral agencies.

Institutional structures have been put in place so that URTNA can realize its objectives. The General Secretariat was established in Dakar, Senegal, in 1964 and it is responsible for the coordination and supervision of all URTNA activities. Moreover, the secretariat is responsible for mass media research and the dissemination of information. It also publishes a bilingual journal, *URTNA Review*. The association has a technical center, launched in Bamako, Mali, in 1966, which handles technical matters including the monitoring of radio transmissions, provision of advice on frequency interference, evaluation of rural telecommunications, and publication of technical research reports and monographs. The Programme Exchange Centre, established in 1977 in Nairobi, promotes and coordinates the exchange of radio and television information, as well as broadcast information among URTNA members; promotes and markets international African television programs internationally; produces commissioned radio and television programs; and organizes the annual African Television Program Screening Session. The Inter-African Centre for Rural Radio Studies was set up in 1978 in Ouagadougou, Burkina Faso, to offer professional training courses on techniques of rural radio production to broadcasters from francophone Africa. There is also the Television News Coordinating Centre in

Algiers, which was started in 1991. The center coordinates television news transmitted via satellite.

Broadcasts in the region are also available in indigenous, national, and official languages. For example, in South Africa approximately eight million television viewers receive broadcasts in Zulu, Xhosa, Venda, Tswana, Sotho, English, and Afrikaans, and about twenty languages are used in broadcasting to the fourteen million people who listen to twenty-five radio services.

Broadcasting Stations in Sub-Saharan Africa

Most stations are either owned, controlled, or directly censored by government. In Algeria the national broadcasting company is the state-controlled Enterprise Nationale de Television, and Radio Botswana is government controlled and concentrates on programs that promote government policy. Botswana does not have a television station, but entrepreneurs receive and relay BOP-TV, TVI, and TV3 from South Africa to viewers in their immediate environment. Some countries in francophone Africa are served by Canal Plus Horizon.

Radio Gambia was established in 1962 and operates as a government department, whereas the Ghana Television Service (GTS) was started in 1965, and in 1967 commercial broadcasting was begun in radio and television. Three radio stations, of which Radio Ghana is the most powerful, broadcast in the most widely spoken languages. The first community FM radio station was introduced in 1987, and over the last few years other FM stations have been launched in Accra and Kumasi. The external service broadcasts in English and French. The television network has four channels transmitting in English and five indigenous languages.

In Kenya the national broadcasting station, Kenya Broadcasting Corporation (formerly Voice of Kenya), was fully controlled by the government until 1989 when it became a state corporation. In spite of the change, the corporation continues to articulate the position of the ruling party. The service mainly broadcasts in English and KiSwahili, although there are short programs in Kenyan indigenous languages. In 1970 an additional television station was opened in Mombasa, with a microwave link to Nairobi. The national station has been central in the pursuit of national development through educational programs and documentaries. However, most critics view its coverage as imbalanced in favor of government institutions.

The Lesotho Television Service has been in existence since 1988 and broadcasts for thirty minutes daily. There are about twenty-five hundred television sets in Lesotho which also receive spillover signals from the South African Broadcasting Corporation and M-Net. There is also a national radio service which competes with transmissions from South Africa. The Malawi Broadcasting Corporation was established in 1964. Radio programs are broadcast in Chichewa, the national language, and English, the official language. Mozambique has a state-owned experimental television station called Television Experimental (TVE). There is also a national Portuguese radio service, Radiodifusão Portuguesa (RTP). Namibia Broadcasting Corporation is controlled by the government and it offers radio services in indigenous languages such as Oshivambo and Oshiherero. The television service, which broadcasts in English, Afrikaans, and indigenous languages, is received in Windhoek and its suburbs, Swakopmund, and Oshakati.

Broadcasting in Tanzania was started in 1951 by the British government. The first station was Sauti ya Dar es Salaam (the Voice of Dar es Salaam). Like many stations in the colonial days, it was used to entertain expatriates and discourage political involvement by the African people. In the 1960s and 1970s, the Tanzanian government used the radio extensively to argue for the ruling party's Ujamaa philosophy. In the 1990s the government liberalized the airwaves and a number of private radio and television stations emerged. Radio Tanzania Dar es Salaam (RTD) is the national station; it has two main services, Swahili and English. Some of the private radio stations include United Radio (Arusha), Radio Five (Arusha), Radio Free Africa (Mwanza), Radio Tumaini (Dar es Salaam), and Radio One (Dar es Salaam). Television is strictly an urban phenomenon; some of the stations include Independent Television (ITV), Dar-es-Salaam Television (DTV), Coastal Television (CTN), and Entertainment Cable Television (ECT).

Nigeria in 1959 was the first country in sub-Saharan Africa to introduce its own television service and, until 1976, the federal and regional states were permitted to set up their own television stations. Thereafter, control became centralized under the Nigerian Television Authority (NTA). Currently, NTA controls twenty-three television stations. Nigeria has approximately 4.5 million television sets. All federal states operate radio stations which are regulated by the Federal Radio Corporation of Nigeria. They broadcast in English and a variety of Nigerian languages, including Yoruba, Igbo, and Hausa, and are funded by the federal government and commercial services.

Uganda has six television stations broadcasting in English, Luganda, and other indigenous languages. Uganda Broadcasting Corporation is state run. Other stations include the Central Broadcasting Corporation, Capitol Radio, Sanyu Radio, and Radio One. In February 1997 the British Broadcasting Corporation launched a twenty-four-hour FM radio station in Kampala as part of the expansion of the British World Service in Africa. The station covers a radius of five miles and captures an estimated five million listeners. Zambia National Broadcasting Corporation is run by the state. There are also private FM radio stations. Zimbabwe has two national television channels, one commercial and the other educational. Both are operated by the Zimbabwe Broadcasting Corporation, which is controlled and owned by the state.

The first radio program in South Africa was broadcast from Johannesburg on 18 December 1923, but regular broadcasting started on 1 July 1924. The South African Broadcasting Corporation (SABC) was launched on 1 August 1936 and carried programs in English and Afrikaans. The external service of the SABC went on air on 21 December 1950, and on 1 May 1966 it was replaced by Radio South Africa (RSA). Radio South Africa is funded by the Department of Foreign Affairs.

A bilingual commercial service, Springbok Radio, went on the air on 1 May 1950. On 1 January 1962, Sotho and Zulu programs were broadcast on FM for the first time, and on 1 July they were presented in Northern Sotho and Tswana. Regional stations included Radio Highveld, Radio Good Hope, and Radio Port Natal. Approximately forty-seven radio stations operate in South Africa, and SABC is the most dominant. SABC operates a number of national radio stations including Radio 5, Radio South Africa, Radio Suid Afrika, Radio Lotus, Radio Orion, Radio 2000, and Radio Metro. SABC also operates regional radio stations.

The history of television in South Africa up to the early 1990s is closely linked to the SABC and the discourse of separate development encapsulated in the apartheid ideology. By the 1980s, SABC was using eleven languages on radio and television to reach an audience of approximately fifty million people. Its television services include TV1, CCV, and TSS. TV1 broadcasts in English and Afrikaans. CCV (Contemporary Community Values Television) broadcasts mainly in English. It was introduced in 1990 to replace TV2 and TV4. TSS broadcasts sports, educational, and public-service programs. The total viewership for SABC is approximately eight million. SABC is financially independent of the state.

Bophuthatswana started the first television service in competition with SABC on 31 December 1983, and in 1986 a religious television broadcasting service, Trinity Broadcasting Network, was launched in Ciskei. M-Net is a subscription service and began operating on 1 October 1986. It carries films, entertainment, documentaries, drama series, and, since July 1991, news documentaries.

The South African Broadcasting Corporation operates under the Broadcasting Act (Act 73 of 1976), which has provisions on broadcasting in general. Private broadcasters are not subject to statutory broadcasting control, although they are licensed and allocated frequencies by the Postmaster General's office within the provisions of the Radio Act of 1952.

Programming

Radio and television programming in Africa includes dramas, features, talk shows, and documentaries on health, environment, agriculture, culture, and religion. Dramas have been used to entertain and educate on socially relevant issues such as the status of women, health, the environment, and economic empowerment in Kenya, Tanzania, Uganda, Zimbabwe, and Nigeria. These dramas, though fictional, are extremely realistic. There are also children's programs and sports.

In addition to local stations, African nations receive international radio and television broadcasting. These include Voice of America, CNN, British Broadcasting Corporation, Radio Netherlands, Radio Moscow, and Deutche Welle. Newscasts constitute only part of the material that international broadcasting stations transmit to Africa. There are, for instance, features specifically produced for the region, and these are transmitted in the targeted language services. "African Panorama," a daily thirty-minute program in the Voice of America's Africa Service, focuses on events in Africa and those around the world that affect Africa.

Critics of international media have over time asserted that when Western media pay attention to events in Africa it is usually during occasions when events, such as political instability, seem to threaten economic exchanges beneficial to the West. More criticism revolves around certain television programs, especially movies and dramas, imported from the West. They are seen to be violent, aggressive, linguistically inappropriate, and too sexually explicit. Soap operas from the United States, Mexico, and Australia such as *Days of Our Lives* (U.S.), *The Young and the Restless* (U.S.), *Wild Rose* (Mexico), *The Lady of the Rose* (Mexico), *The Rich Also Cry* (Mexico), *No One But You* (Mexico), *Dallas* (U.S.), *The Bold and the Beautiful* (U.S.), *Neighbors* (Australia), *Falcon Crest* (U.S.), and *Santa Barbara* (U.S.) are transmitted in many African countries. Unlike the indigenous soap operas such as *Egoli: The Place of Gold* (South Africa), *Tausi* (Kenya), *Tushauriane* (Kenya), *Ushikwapo Shikamana* (Kenya), *Twende na Wakati* (Tanzania), and *Zinduka* (Tanzania), which focus on social and cultural themes, the entertainment value of the Western dramas is significantly higher than their educational value. Western television soap operas mainly target the emotions of their audience in their representation of the glamour and excesses of the Western lifestyle. However, they have a loyal audience in the urban areas.

In view of technological advances, the videocassette recorder (VCR) has become a popular information and entertainment medium, especially in major urban centers. Popular movies from the United States, Britain, China, and India are rented or bought and screened either at home or in public parlors. These videos are either pirated or legally acquired. Owing to the availability of VCRs, video cameras are used by certain members of society to cover important ceremonies such as weddings, parties, and funerals.

Media critics, in addition to calling for the total liberalization of the airwaves, have argued for an end to "media imperialism." This phrase refers to the transplanting of media from colonial powers, and their present-day counterparts, to areas they either influence or possess, directly or indirectly. It is also used to described the unidirectional flow of material from a small number of industrialized countries to less developed countries in Africa and elsewhere. This unidirectionality, it is argued, leads to the development of a market-oriented consumerism detrimental to Africa.

Prospects

Radio and television will continue to play an important role in development, at the individual and national levels. The radio is destined to be the main source of information, education, and entertainment in Africa's rural areas, and television will expand its reach in the urban centers. While uniting different people of the world and broadening viewers' domains of knowledge, the electronic media also has the potential of offering convivial and at times controversial topics for conversation in homes and public places. Moreover, radio and television have the capacity to contribute toward national development and the reshaping of national attitudes and ideologies. However, for them to do so more effectively, they need to operate within more democratic and tolerant environments.

BIBLIOGRAPHY

Barwise, Patrick, and Andrew Ehrenberg. *Television and Its Audience.* London, 1988.

De Beer, A. S., ed. *Mass Media for the Nineties: The South African Handbook of Mass Communication.* Pretoria, 1993.

Head, S. W., ed. *Broadcasting in Africa.* Philadelphia, 1974.

Jeter, James P., et al. *International Afro Mass Media: A Reference Guide.* Westport, Conn., 1992.

Onuora, E. Nwuneli. *Mass Media in Nigeria: A Book of Reading.* Enugu, Nigeria, 1986.

Tomaselli, K., et al., eds. *Currents of Power: State Broadcasting in South Africa.* Bellville, South Africa, 1989.

Ziegler, Dhyana, and Molefi Asante. *Thunder and Silence: The Mass Media in Africa.* Trenton, N.J., 1992.

Kimani Njogu

See also **Political Systems.**

RAINFORESTS. *See* **Ecosystems.**

RANAVALONA, MADA (b. c. 1788; d. 1861), queen of Madagascar. The daughter-in-law of Andrianampoinimerina, who reunited the Merina kingdom on the plateau of Madagascar around 1797, Ranavalona called herself Rabodonandrianampoinimerina, "the beloved daughter of Adrianampoinimerina." She was a blood relative and the wife of Radama I (r. 1810–1828), who extended the Merina kingdom through much of the island. Radama had not chosen a successor, and when he died Ranavalona became queen, consolidating her power with the Merina military leaders and nobles. Putting to death any rivals, she became an absolute monarch determined to uphold Malagasy tradition and avoid interference by European powers (while adopting European dress and manufactured goods such as firearms, sugar, and alcohol).

She terminated British protection. When negotiations about trade with the British resumed in 1836, the queen's position was to allow trade only at ports controlled by Malagasy governors. There the traders were subjected to interference and put under the jurisdiction of Malagasy law, including

Ranavalona and her niece Marie Louise, in a portrait dated 6 July 1901. CULVER PICTURES

forced labor and *ganguin,* ordeal by poison; the British withdrew. Britain and France bombarded the port city Tamatave (later Toamasina); when the queen impaled the heads of the corpses on the beach, the European powers turned back. Ports were opened again in 1853.

While the king had welcomed Christianization by the London Missionary Society, Ranavalona persecuted Christians at various times by suppressing their religion, murdering them, and exiling missionaries. She did this because Christian teachings undermined devotion to ancestral idols and to an oligarchy ruling a society stratified by castes and based on slavery. In 1835 all the Malagasy were forbidden to convert to Christianity, and in 1836 and 1840 the queen brutally martyred Protestant Christians.

The borders of the Merina kingdom established by Radama I remained essentially in place during Queen Ranavalona's reign, but control was con-

solidated. Some ethnic groups (Sakalava and Ambongo in the west, Tanala in the south, and Antanosy to the southwest) retained their independence. In the south the Antesaka rebelled in 1852 and were massacred by Merina warriors. By this time the Merina army had degenerated from the organization established by Radama I into a group of unscrupulous plunderers.

For manufacturing goods the queen relied on a shipwrecked Frenchman, Jean Laborde, who set up a small manufacturing city, employing over a thousand laborers. The items they manufactured included guns, tiles, cement, and ribbons; he also built a zoo and a wooden palace for the queen. His future, however, was tied to the ill-fated "Lambert Charter." Jean Lambert, a French businessman-adventurer, made a secret agreement in 1857 with the queen's son, Prince Rakoto, to allow for development of the island and creation of a French protectorate. Upon discovery of the plot, the suspicious and superstitious queen banished all Europeans, tortured Christians, and asked for confessions by criminals and sorcerers, murdering and imprisoning over a thousand people. Upon her death, Prince Rakoto became Radama II, having been designated by the aged and ill queen as her heir.

BIBLIOGRAPHY

Gow, Bonar A. *Madagascar and the Protestant Impact.* New York, 1980.

Kottak, Conrad Phillip. *The Past in the Present: History, Ecology, and Cultural Variation in Highland Madagascar.* Ann Arbor, 1980.

Raison-Jourde, François. *Les souverains de Madagascar: L'histoire royale et ses résurgences contemporaines.* Paris, 1983.

NANCY G. WRIGHT

See also **Andrianampoinimerina; Christianity; Radama I.**

RAS TAFARI. *See* **Haile Sellassie.**

RAWLINGS, JERRY (b. 1947), Ghanaian head of state. Born in Accra, the illegitimate son of a Ghanaian (Ewe) mother and a Scottish pharmacist father, Jerry Rawlings John (as he was named at birth) attended the prestigious Achimota Secondary School before joining Ghana's air force as a flight cadet in 1967.

Angry at the corruption and economic incompetence of the I. K. Acheampong–F. W. K. Akuffo military regime (1972–1979), Rawlings led an unsuccessful mutiny on the night of 14 May 1979, for which he was imprisoned. He was freed from jail on 4 June to head the Armed Forces Revolutionary Council (AFRC). The AFRC carried out a radical and sometimes violent populist program of "house-cleaning," which included the execution of eight senior officers and former officers, before handing over power to a freely elected civilian government, headed by President Hilla Limann, on 24 September 1979.

Disillusioned with the Limann administration, Rawlings returned to power by coup d'état on 31 December 1981. His initially radical, neo-Marxist Provisional National Defence Council evolved into a pragmatic, authoritarian administrative regime and implemented an International Monetary Fund/World Bank–approved structural adjustment program commonly regarded as the most successful in Africa. Accused of extensive human-rights abuses by his political opponents, Rawlings nonetheless retained sufficient popularity to win a reasonably free and fair presidential election in November 1992.

BIBLIOGRAPHY

Gyimah-Boadi, E., ed. *Ghana Under PNDC Rule.* London, 1993.

Jeffries, Richard. "Ghana: The Political Economy of Personal Rule." In *Contemporary West African States,* edited by Donal B. Cruise O'Brien, John Dunn, and Richard Rathbone. Cambridge, 1989.

Jeffries, Richard, and Clare Thomas. "The Ghanaian Elections of 1992." *African Affairs* 92 (July 1993): 331–366.

Okele, Barbara E. *Four June: A Revolution Betrayed.* Enugu, Nigeria, 1982.

Rothchild, Donald, ed. *Ghana: The Political Economy of Recovery.* Boulder, Colo., 1991.

Shillington, Kevin. *Ghana and the Rawlings Factor.* London, 1992.

RICHARD JEFFRIES

See also **Postcolonial State.**

REFUGEES. The forced displacement of populations and the social processes of incorporation, integration, and exclusion in sub-Saharan Africa have been continuous phenomena since ancient times. Had there been state boundaries in Africa then, such forced migrants would have been regarded as refugees according to definitions in use now, especially those set out in the 1969 Organization of African Unity (OAU) Convention Governing Specific Aspects of Refugee Problems in Africa. This convention incorporates and expands on the definition of the term "refugee" as laid down in the 1951 United Nations Convention and Protocol Relating to the Status of Refugees. As will be discussed below, the integration of the African continent into the global state system, and of its refugees into the international legal and humanitarian regime, has adversely affected the traditional processes of incorporation and integration of the "stranger."

Migration and Refugees in the Precolonial Period

Throughout the known history of the African continent, environmental factors, famine, disease, and competition for resources have led to wars, flight, and resettlement. For example, the presence of Ewe in western Africa, Ndebele in Zimbabwe, and Nguni in Mozambique is the result of migrations caused by war. The Ndebele, from farther south, fled into present-day western Zimbabwe. En route they plundered other groups and displaced the Shona, giving rise to continued tensions between themselves and other communities which regard themselves as the original owners of the land—a problem which is quite general throughout sub-Saharan Africa.

In western Africa, Islam, in particular the religious duty to make the *hajj*, became a force for the movement and permanent displacement of people across the continent along routes leading to the Red Sea ports; many people were unable to complete the journey to Mecca, or to return home. Today, one of the major challenges in Sudan is the position of its minority population of west Africans—Nigerians, Chadians, even some Sierra Leoneans—who either failed to reach Mecca or were unable to return home. Still perceived as "foreigners," they are called *fellata*.

From at least the ninth century C.E., trade in human beings became another major cause of involuntary population movements. The Arab slave trade affected large sections of the continent and was the cause of displacement within and beyond it. Although quite different from plantation slavery, domestic slavery, as practiced by many African societies, continued into the twentieth century; Mauritania legally abolished this institution only in 1972. Slaves became members of families through marriage, but they continued to occupy lower socioeconomic positions within the societies in which they lived. For example, the classical Arab word *ab'ed*, meaning "slave," is still used by Arabic speakers to designate all peoples of African descent.

From the fourteenth century, the introduction of arms and the capture and sale of slaves by Europeans, and by Africans to Europeans, caused further large-scale movements of people, including the loss of millions of the most able-bodied from throughout western Africa. The British abolished the slave trade in their colonies in 1807. In its attempts to enforce the abolition, the British navy patrolled the seas of western Africa, capturing slave ships en route to the Americas. Rather than being returned to their homelands, the human cargoes were deposited in Freetown, a colony established for liberated slaves in 1787.

Colonialism and Forced Migration

Throughout the eighteenth and nineteenth centuries, competition among the European powers for trade and influence on the African continent, culminating in the Treaty of Berlin (1885), which defined the boundaries of colonial governments, further disrupted African communities. World War I (1914–1918), which included local battles for control, drew Africans into conflicts. This process was continued during World War II (1939–1945), particularly affecting the people in former Italian colonies.

Although slavery had been officially abolished, the need for labor in some of the colonies continued. This problem was addressed in Sierra Leone, for example, by paying local leaders to recruit workers to what, in practice, constituted forced labor migration. Throughout the colonial period, Africans were forcibly dispossessed of their land; in Rhodesia, for example, the Land Apportionment Acts (1930, 1931) were mechanisms of displacement.

The extraction of resources, both mineral and agricultural, required substantial labor forces, and throughout sub-Saharan Africa, people were "motivated" to earn cash through the imposition of various systems of taxation. In many cases, the search for paid employment forced workers to travel great distances. For example, Mozambicans and Malawians went to work in the mines of South Africa, and thousands of Nigerians went to work on the Gezira cotton scheme in Sudan.

Forced Migration, Decolonization, and the Cold War

Decolonization following the Second World War was rarely a peaceful process. Major independence wars–beginning with Algeria and including all the major Portuguese colonies, Kenya, and the still un-resolved colonial situation of the Western (Spanish) Sahara (which has been claimed and occupied by Morocco with the support of France, the United States, Britain, and other nations that support the war for this territory)—all produced refugees.

At the conclusion of the Second World War, the world was partitioned into new zones of influence. Supporting the movement toward the independence of African colonies for both strategic and material advantages, the superpowers competed for ideological control. For example, both the Soviet Union and the United States were eager to have access to the uranium and cobalt resources in the Congo (now Zaire). This newly independent country became the first subject of superpower competition in Africa; in one way or another, almost all European nations were involved in the war against the government of Patrice Lumumba. This war, which broke out soon after the Congo declared independence on 30 June 1960, and which involved territorial disputes and ideological differences, led to the death and displacement of unknown numbers of people.

Much of the fighting in the Horn of Africa from the mid-1960s to the mid-1990s was exacerbated by the cold war, during which the superpowers financed and armed various governments, as they have done throughout Africa. Haile Sellassie, emperor of Ethiopia, for example, received more than half of the U.S. military allocation to sub-Saharan Africa, a good deal of which he spent in the war against Eritrean independence. U.S. support of the emperor was small, however, compared with the funds the Soviet Union bestowed on the military regime which overthrew him in 1974. The region has been awash with weaponry and displaced persons ever since.

The catastrophes in Somalia were precipitated by changes in alliances in 1976, when the Soviet Union and the United States switched sides in the Somalia-Ethiopia conflict. The real problem, however, originated with the postindependence division of Somalis among four countries: Kenya, Ethiopia, Djibouti, and Somalia itself. In 1978 Siad Barre invaded the Ogaden, launching the first of many waves of refugees in and out of Ethiopia.

In the decades since independence, the issue of self-determination has been the principal source of conflict on the continent and has created refugees and enormous numbers of internally displaced persons. Examples include the secessionist wars in Sudan, Ethiopia, and Nigeria. Other disputes over the arbitrary boundaries created by the

Refugee tent town at Khayalitsha Township (near Cape Town). PHOTOGRAPH BY GUY TILLIM. © AFRAPIX/IMPACT VISUALS

colonialists and defended by the Organization of African Unity include the wars fought in pursuit of "greater Somalia" and the war between Upper Volta (now Burkina Faso) and Mali in 1974.

The southern African states have produced the second-largest number of refugees in the post-1945 period. The protracted wars for independence in Mozambique and Zimbabwe produced thousands of refugees. The apartheid system in South Africa forcibly uprooted millions within the state itself and forced thousands of others to seek safety in neighboring countries and abroad.

The Republic of South Africa's role in destabilizing its neighbors has been a major cause of forced migration, especially in Mozambique. In Namibia, South Africa's refusal to hand over power resulted in a long war and led to large numbers of refugees. In Angola, its support for rebel UNITA (National Union for the Total Independence of Angola) forces, led by Jonas Savimbi, has created refugees since the mid-1970s. Even after being defeated in an election, UNITA has continued its war against the Angolan government.

Expulsions

Mass expulsions of minority groups, orchestrated by many newly independent states, have been a cause of forced migration and have dealt a shattering blow to the ideas of pan-Africanism, naturalization, and the integration of immigrants. The expulsion of 40,000 Asians from Uganda in 1972 was perhaps the most widely publicized in Africa. However, in post-Amin Uganda, Milton Obote's government adopted a scorched earth policy in northern Uganda during the 1980s, sending more than 350,000 of its citizens into exile in Kenya, Sudan, Zaire, and elsewhere. In addition, Uganda expelled some 300,000 Banyarwanda to Rwanda in 1982, among them Rwandese (Tutsi) refugees who had lived in the country since 1959. Nigeria, in 1983 and 1985, expelled some three million migrant workers.

Guineans were expelled from the border area of Senegal in 1965; Ghanaian fisherman who had lived in Sierra Leone for generations were ousted in 1967; in 1969, Ghana expelled 200,000 migrant workers from Nigeria, Niger, and Upper Volta, following the introduction of the Aliens Compliance Order; and in 1971, Zambia expelled 150,000 migrants, mostly Rhodesians, Botswanans, Zairians, Tanzanians, and Somalis. Perhaps the most violent ouster, which led to a cascade of displacements, began in 1989 with Mauritania's expulsion of its "black" populations, including large numbers of migrants from sub-Saharan Africa. This triggered revenge killings of Mauritanian traders scattered throughout Senegal.

Independent Africa's Response to Forced Migration

In 1969 the OAU promulgated the Convention Governing Specific Aspects of Refugee Problems in Africa. Incorporating all the provisions of the 1951 UN convention (as amended by the 1967 protocol), the OAU definition of "refugee" was broadened from applying only to "individual persecution" to include "every person who owing to external aggression, foreign domination or events seriously disturbing public order in either part or whole of his country of origin or nationality is compelled to leave his place of habitual residence in order to seek refuge in another place outside his country of origin or nationality" (Article I [2]).

By 1993, forty-three states had ratified the 1969 OAU convention. South Africa was in the process of doing so, and Zimbabwe, Swaziland, and Sudan had introduced domestic legislation incorporating, to varying degrees, the provisions of the convention. However, at least three major factors have rendered the protection and incorporation of refugees problematic.

Refugees and the Interests of States

The OAU convention was written in the context of the formation of states which sought to establish their legitimacy and to consolidate internal control of their populations. The cornerstone upon which the OAU was built was the sanctity of existing borders and the principles of territorial integrity and noninterference in the internal affairs of member states. The convention puts the interests of states above the protection of refugees. States have the right to determine when the circumstances which gave rise to flight have ceased to exist, and the convention denies refugee status to any persons "guilty of acts contrary to the purposes and principles of the OAU or the UN." It forbids any "subversive action" against any member of the OAU (Article III [1] and [2]). Seeking to ensure the depoliticization of refugees, it advises that they be settled away from borders, denies them freedom

of speech and association, and declares the granting of asylum to be a humanitarian, and not "an unfriendly" act, in relation to the state of origin (Article II [2]).

Refugee Status as Temporary

The founders of the OAU apparently believed that once the colonial wars had ended, there would be no more situations on the continent which could give rise to forced migration. Whereas the 1951 UN convention does not mention repatriation except in negative terms forbidding the *refoulement* (forced repatriation) of a refugee, the OAU convention specifically includes provision for voluntary repatriation and rehabilitation once conditions in the country of origin permit (Article V).

While the 1951 UN convention provides for "most favored" treatment of refugees, including the right to education, employment, and ownership of property, and Article 34 recommends that states facilitate their assimilation and naturalization, the emphasis upon repatriation in the OAU convention has allowed its signatories to ignore these provisions (even though it includes all of the rights of the UN convention) and has led African states to regard refugee status as temporary. This assumption has had enormously negative consequences on traditional practices concerning the incorporation of the stranger and has, with few exceptions, both directed the development of state policy toward refugees and legitimized the approach to refugee assistance orchestrated by the international humanitarian establishment.

Assisting African Refugees

Whenever there is movement across borders, the first to assist the refugees are the local people. Most refugees in Africa have never received international assistance but have settled among their hosts, on whose goodwill their security and economic survival depend. All African societies have some method of incorporating the stranger into their membership, but the subject has been inadequately researched. In southern Africa, for example, the chiefdoms made provision for strangers, whose status depended on their class and on whether they were coming in as individuals or as members of a large group with a leader of their own. For example, during the wars of 1820–1837, which spread from Zululand to the highveld, and north and south along the coast from the Save River to the Mthatha, thousands of African people were displaced and scattered. Some were absorbed as individual refugees into other communities, others were accepted as groups under their own leaders to whom land was allocated, and still others established conquest states, such as those of the Nguni under Soshangane, the Ndebele under Mzilikazi, and the Kololo on the Zambezi River. The aftereffects of slavery and colonialism undermined the capacity of African societies to incorporate and integrate involuntary migrants into their communities.

At least one society, the Luo of Kenya, made special provision for refugees. They recognized three categories of strangers: prisoners of war (*wasumbini*); migrants, who were provided land and could marry within the community (*jodak*); and refugees (*jomotur*). Refugees were either attached to individual families, especially when the numbers were small, or, after consultation with the elders, settled separately in parts of clan land which were not under cultivation. Islamic law makes the granting of asylum a religious duty on the part of both the individual and the polity.

International Policies and African Response

Given the poverty of most host states in Africa, it is generally assumed that international aid is required, and the OAU convention calls for "burden sharing." However, rather than channeling this assistance through governments, the Office of the UN High Commissioner for Refugees (UNHCR) and its "implementing" partners, the foreign nongovernmental organizations, have become the main conduits for international funds.

Although the major solution to the refugee problem in Africa promoted by UNHCR up to the 1980s was local integration, its policy of settling refugees in camps has had the opposite effect, creating islands of either privilege or destitution. This approach, rather than allowing refugees to be incorporated into and to contribute to their host's economy, involves labeling and the perpetuation of refugees as a "problem," resulting in their "capture" by international assistance agencies and their being frozen in a state of permanent marginality in their host societies. Thus, in order to receive international assistance, states have been forced to stop the spontaneous settlement of refugees among their own populations and to comply with the international policy of encampment in order to make the refugees countable and visible. This has created great insecurity among self-settled refugees and has led to serious violations of the fundamental rights of refugees, including the regular use

of the military to force them into camps—as is done, for example, in Zambia.

This action has been justified on the grounds of "security," but in fact the refugees who represent the greatest security risks for host states are seldom forcibly encamped. For example, refugees from South Africa enjoyed freedom of movement in the countries that hosted them, even though South Africa mounted military operations on the host countries' soil. Even today, and in spite of the consequences for its relationship with the Khartoum government, many Sudan People's Liberation Army supporters from southern Sudan have relative freedom within Kenya and even have the power to decide who goes to the camps. At least two nations—Sierra Leone and Guinea—have declined offers of international assistance. Guinea received large numbers of refugees from the liberation war in Guinea-Bissau, but withstood pressure to establish a UNHCR office there. Tens of thousands of Fula-speaking people fled Sékou Turé's Guinea and were peacefully received by Sierra Leone. They were not labeled as refugees, no international assistance programs were mounted, and no camps were set up for them. The government permitted their integration into the national economy, and their leadership was absorbed into the local Islamic religious community.

Growing Restrictionism in Africa

There is a growing tendency for African states to adopt the industrialized countries' anti-integration and restrictionist policies toward refugees. The OAU convention provides for the recognition of refugee status en masse by nationality. Only recently have some African states introduced procedures for the determination of individual status, the application of which is governed by political considerations. For example, the close association of Zimbabwe with Mozambique during the former's freedom struggle was a factor in the acceptance of Mozambican refugees en masse while its domestic legislation (introduced in 1985) provides for claims to be reviewed on an individual basis. Although there is no domestic refugee legislation in Kenya, over the years asylum seekers who lacked access to networks of social support or, more important, were without political influence were likely to find themselves confined for long periods of time in the Thika reception center while their asylum claims were decided. And Swaziland is being encouraged to introduce "first country asylum" rules, which would allow it to return refugees (the case of immediate concern being the Bosnians who sought asylum from the war in the former Yugoslavia) who have entered through another "safe country."

Since the early 1980s, as a consequence of donors' frustration with the failure of the camp policy to make refugees self-sufficient, UNHCR has been promoting repatriation. With the threat of international aid being withdrawn, few states have resisted agreeing to, or implementing, repatriation agreements. The policy to promote repatriation has also provided a convenient vehicle for realizing the political objectives of certain state authorities.

Refugees have always been a pawn in intra- and interstate politics. For example, throughout Muhammad Nimeiri's rule of the Sudan, depending on his relations with the Ethiopian government, the offices of the Eritrean political fronts were allowed to be open or were forcibly closed. And in Kenya, with the introduction of multiparty politics and the ensuing internal security problems, refugees became a convenient scapegoat for explaining

unrest in the historically volatile northeastern region. Consequently, the government supported the policy to return Somalis, on the grounds that they were the source of arms and the resulting insecurity.

Conclusion

Although 1994 marked the twenty-fifth anniversary of the promulgation of the OAU convention on refugees, sub-Saharan Africa continued to be the major theater of population displacement, with an estimated seven million refugees and twenty million internally displaced persons. The collapse of Somalia and the collapse of Rwanda provide a glimpse of the future as African states fail to grapple with the more general political, economic, ecological, and social crises that grip the continent. The violation of human rights, conflicts between states, ethnic strife, the struggle for religious hegemony, natural disasters, lack of democratic practice, the failure of development, global economic inequalities, and ideological rivalries have all

Katale refugee camp, near Goma in Zaire, home to over 250,000 refugees who fled Rwanda in July 1994. Lacking many basic facilities, the camp was situated partly on a two-year-old lava flow from the nearby volcano. HOWARD DAVIES/PANOS PICTURES

561

contributed to the degeneration of Africa into an arena of conflict and turmoil. It is evident that conventional attempts to resolve the refugee phenomenon through encampment have been iatrogenic.

The challenge for the future is to address the fundamental political issues which have beset the continent and have led to forced displacement on an unparalleled scale. From the international perspective, donors must review the impact of current aid policies on the region. The recognition of the right to self-determination, exemplified by the newly independent Eritrea, and the willingness to discuss the recognition of an independent Somaliland suggest that, at last, the OAU is beginning to address the issue of colonial boundaries, one of the major causes of forced migration in sub-Saharan Africa.

BIBLIOGRAPHY

Adelman, Howard, and John Sorenson, eds. *African Refugees: Development Aid and Repatriation.* Boulder, Colo., 1994.

Allen, Tim, and Hubert Morsink, eds. *When Refugees Go Home: African Experiences.* London, 1993.

Anand, Renu M. *African Refugees: An Overview.* New Delhi, 1993.

Brooks, Hugh C., and Yassin El-Ayouty, eds. *Refugees South of the Sahara: An African Dilemma.* Westport, Conn., 1994.

Bulcha, Mekuria. *Flight and Integration: Causes of Mass Exodus from Ethiopia and Problems of Integration in the Sudan.* Uppsala, Sweden, 1988.

Comité-intermouvements auprès des évacués, INODEP, and Mouvement International d'N'Krumah. *Africa's Refugee Crisis: What Is to Be Done?* Translated by Michael John. London, 1986.

Deng, Frederick M. *Protecting the Dispossessed: A Challenge for the International Community.* Washington, D.C., 1993.

Forsyth, Frederick. *The Biafra Story.* London, 1969.

Goodwin-Gill, Guy S. *The Refugee in International Law.* Oxford, 1983.

Greenfield, Richard. *The OAU and Africa's Refugees.* Oxford, 1983.

Hamrell, Sven. *Refugee Problems in Africa.* Uppsala, Sweden, 1967.

Harrell-Bond, Barbara. *Imposing Aid: Emergency Assistance to Refugees.* Oxford, 1986.

———. "Pitch the Tents: An Alternative to Refugee Camps." *The New Republic,* 19–26 September 1994, 15+.

Melander, Goren, and Peter Nobel, eds. *African Refugees and the Law.* Uppsala, Sweden, 1978.

Platsky, Laurine, and Cherryl Walker. *The Surplus People: Forced Removals in South Africa.* Johannesburg, 1985.

Shack, William A., and Elliott P. Skinner, eds. *Strangers in African Societies.* Berkeley, 1979.

Waldron, Sydney R. *Resettlement in Ethiopia: Where Angels Fear to Tread.* London, 1986.

BARBARA HARRELL-BOND
MARK CHINGONO
ENOCH OPONDO

See also **Colonial Policies and Practice; Decolonization; Genocide, Violence, and Civil Society; Human Rights; Labor Migration; Pan-African and Regional Organizations; Slave Trade; Strangers; United Nations Agencies in Africa.**

RELIGION AND RITUAL

Issues and Arguments

The religions of Africa have been the subject of much interest, argument, and misunderstanding. Most accounts of them have been written by non-Africans, often on the basis of European classifications and definitions. There has been a failure to understand these religions as systems of thought and action of particular societies in particular social and historical contexts. In addition, most accounts have separated "indigenous" or "local" religions from the "world" religions of Christianity and Islam.

A question commonly asked about African religions is that of their "truth." This question reflects early Eurocentric views that African religions were "juju" or "black magic," that they were made by the Devil, and so on—views with no foundation in reality. The question of "truth" also often reflects the view that "world" religions, being literate and usually possessing sacred books, are "higher" and thus more "true" than those of Africa, which are "lower" and thus less "true." It makes more sense to perceive African religions within their social and historical contexts, as functioning systems that may (or at times may not) give coherence and meaning to both social organization and individual sense of place and order, as being part of the exercise of power, of social competition, and even of dispute and intrigue.

There is no word in most African languages that may properly be translated by the English word "religion." Most African words so translated might better be translated as "custom," "proper behavior," or some similar notion: most African societies do not construct rigid boundaries between the "religious" and other forms of social behavior.

It is often asked whether there is one "religion" or many "religions" in Africa. Many non-African travelers and modern Afrocentric scholars claim there is only one; others, including most Africans, claim that there are as many as there are particular societies, each with its own culture. There is also the question of whether African religions are in some way unique or are essentially similar to those of the remainder of the world. It is clear that religions found in Africa are comparable with those found elsewhere even though they vary in cultural detail both from others and among themselves.

We know virtually nothing of indigenous African religions before the earliest colonial contacts. Apart from the records of early travelers and of archaeological excavation, we have little knowledge, and both those sources present grave difficulties of interpretation. But it should not therefore be assumed that they have ever been, or are today, unchanging. If we take it that any particular African society has or has had its own religion, we may assume that when societies change, as they have done throughout history, so have their religions. Religions, as social constructs, do not remain unchanging, and have never done so.

Myth

Every known African religion has a corpus of myths, of which there have been many interpretations. "Myth" is another Eurocentric notion, but provided we rid ourselves of the popular fallacy that it means merely an untrue story, it is useful even if, again, there may be no precise term for it in any particular African language. Myths are typically considered by those who tell and hear them to be "true" narratives of ancestral origins, historical events, and divinely given experience. In many cases they may be historically accurate records, but in most cases, even where they refer to actual historical personages and events, they are used to resolve what the people consider as the moral and social paradoxes and contradictions of the present. The past is used to explain the present, and as present paradoxes change over time, so are the relevant myths likely to do so in order to accommodate the changes. Myths are thus "true" in a moral sense, as explaining the present and providing a cosmology, a cognitive representation or "map" of the particular society and its place in the world and in history. No myths of any particular people have fixed versions or interpretations: tellers accommodate them to the vagaries of the present, and listeners (or participants) give them meanings that they find relevant to their own problems: men, women, and children, rich and poor

find different significances in a single mythical recitation.

A universal problem throughout Africa resolved by myth is the cosmogony or creation of the world by the Divinity (a less ethnocentric term than the more usual "God") and the subsequent formation of the particular society, usually by heroic ancestors. Creation and social formation may be related in a single myth or in separate ones, but all African peoples have such myths, some simple and others elaborate. All have similar elements: the divine creation ex nihilo, the appearance of sacred or semisacred heroic figures using "magic" to form society, and the later historical growth of that society now peopled by "ordinary" living people.

These myths place the Divinity and the living in their present relationship, which frequently arose from separation between the sky and earth, in which the moral fault for the separation was human disobedience of the Divinity, so that humans were separated (as in the Tower of Babel story), given their own nondivine languages, and made subject to the vagaries of death and sickness. In essence these myths define space and time, which came into human awareness after the separation, when "history" began.

The other universal problems of cosmology are those of the similarities and relations between human and nonhuman animals (which are recognized by all African peoples) and between the natures of women and men. These myths have many forms, those of tales of moral and immoral behavior and the rewards of each perhaps being the most widespread.

Myths are statements about the validation of the distribution and exercise of power and authority among the living. They explain the world and human society, and time and space in human experience: if it is explained, the world becomes controllable and then predictable. It is generally accepted as divinely made and inspired, its meanings unknowable by ordinary people but knowable at least in patches by those whose skills, learning, sanctity, and devotion make that possible. One of the most common errors made in so many accounts of African religions is to suppose that Africans lack sophisticated and devout thinkers. To the contrary, theological argument is one of the central areas in all African thinking.

The Structures of Religion

In all religions of sub-Saharan Africa the believed or accepted identities of mystical agents that can affect living people are essentially similar. They are headed by a Creator Divinity, in most cases considered male, often ruling in conjunction with some form of Mother or Earth Goddess, and dwelling in the sky. The Divinity is typically defined as otiose, having created the world and then retired from the living, although many African religions hold that the Divinity continues to determine both an individual's fate or destiny and the time and manner of death. The Divinity is given the typical attributes of the theological argument known as the *via negativa;* that is, the Divinity is defined by criteria that are the opposite of those defining the living: being everlasting, beyond life and death, omnipotent, beyond human comprehension or control—qualities defined in terms of responsibility for all life, death, disease, or whatever fates may befall the living.

Whether in a particular myth the identity of the Divinity is that of an indigenous African religion or that of Islam or Christianity, the attributes used by the living to describe the Divinity are everywhere similar. But there is one crucial difference. In the former religions the Divinity is that of the particular society and essentially cares only for his own creatures—helps and punishes them—and is unconcerned with others. On the other hand, in both Islam and Christianity the Divinity is considered universal, caring for all humankind.

"Below" the Divinity there is typically thought to be an immense array of lesser mystical or spiritual beings of various kinds and powers. They act as intermediaries between the Creator Divinity and the living, and it is among them that the principal differences among African religions are found. These intermediaries may be divided into those that are living and those that are not. The nonliving essentially comprise spirits and ancestors of many kinds. Spirits are refractions or aspects of the Divinity, under divine control, holding many powers over the living, not immediately known to or understood by them, and only occasionally partially under their control. They are usually considered to be without known number, without known shape, to be invisible, unhearable, unsmellable (although at times they may choose to become visible, hearable, and smellable, and then take on shapes that the living may see). They may be associated with particular places in that they either dwell there or use them as loci or shrines for contact with the living. They may be great or small in power, be male or female, be associated with particular alien groups, have their own languages, and so on.

Then there are the ancestors. A dead person is not automatically an ancestor: ancestors are made so by the performance of mortuary rites. Only a few of the dead may be selected: those remembered in genealogies; men who have begotten children or only sons; or women who have been firstborns and so are "like men." Which ones are selected and made individual ancestors, to whom sacrifice or prayer may be made, varies between societies. In the literature various terms are used to distinguish what we might call the effective dead from those who are forgotten as individual beings: ghosts, shades, and so on. The ancestors are typically considered as members of the clans, lineages, and families of their living descendants, may be able to see and hear them, and both protect them and punish them for disloyalty or harm to the group. In most African societies the kinship group remains the basic and long-lasting social unit, and relations within it—and thus between living and ancestors—must be those of amity and trust.

Contact and communication between living and nonliving are at the heart of almost all African religions. They are of two main kinds. One is initiated by the living, or more precisely by their ritual intermediaries or representatives, such as priests; the other is initiated by the mystical intermediaries or by the Divinity. There are many kinds of living mediators who can contact mystical agents: priests, diviners, prophets, rainmakers, seers, and elders who are given sacrificial authority. Few are specialists or professionals. Some act by virtue of genealogical position and age—for instance, the heads of families who may sacrifice to the ancestors; others are given power and skill by various rites of initiation. All, at least while acting as mediators, are given some degree of sacredness, not an innate quality but one acquired by training and initiation.

These various roles involve the possession and exercise of power and authority, which may be important politically as well as ritually. Religious belief and ritual involve forms of knowledge that may be learned from teachers, invented, acquired from spirits, inherited from ancestors, bought from other practitioners, shared, sold, lost, or forgotten. Religious knowledge, in Africa as elsewhere, is one element in many forms of social and mystical relationships, whether between living people or between the living and the dead and spirits. In particular, acts of ritual, possession, and divination, and the believed activities of witches, are associated with knowledge that may be sacred, secret, mystical, or evil, or may be more technical (such as knowledge of healing herbs). Undergoing a religious rite brings change in social status and in knowledge of oneself: new spiritual experiences can bring new knowledge. We may see these religious functionaries in this light: they possess a secret knowledge, they are attributed sacredness in varying degrees, they exercise power and authority beyond those of ordinary people, and, as everywhere, the boundary between religious and political position and authority is often slight.

Sacrifice and Possession

Sacrifice takes many forms, may be largely secret or confined to a narrow congregation, and is intimately linked to the exercise of familial and political authority.

Ritual communication initiated by the living is of many kinds: prayer sacrifice, vision, prophecy, silent devotion; that initiated by the mystical agents of the Divinity almost always takes the form of possession of the living. Both forms of communication involve a change, temporary or permanent, in the social and psychological personality of the living vis-à-vis both mystical agents and other living people, effected by sacrificial purification. There are in general two main kinds of sacrifice: that performed regularly at stated intervals or on regular occasions, and that performed to remove sickness or physical or psychological harm. Both bring about purification, the one from the pollution of an existing condition and the other from that of taboo, sin, misdemeanor, or the malevolence of others.

Regular sacrifices are those made as part of rites of transition or transformation, generally known as rites of passage: the most widespread are at initiation and at death; others occur at birth, marriage, the reaching of various age and generation classes and grades, and the gaining of political or religious positions such as king or priest. The central part of these rites is the period of seclusion, when the initiands are symbolically, and often physically, separated from the everyday world and then undergo transformation. This period typically begins and ends with rites of sacrifice, which "make sacred," and therefore pure, those passing into a new grade or status. The phase of seclusion may be long or short but is invariably marked by forms of symbolic reversal, such as eating normally taboo foods, wearing normally forbidden or different clothing, or other symbolically reversed observances, such as "wild" dancing, going into an ecstatic state, or psychological dissociation, usually

signs of the proximity of the initiand to the sources of divine and spiritual power.

At death there occur rites of disposing of the corpse (usually by burying or exposure), of transforming the deceased into an ancestor, and of purifying the mourners so as to re-form the local group that has been disrupted by the death. Rites may be elaborate and drawn out, or simple and short. Which they are is determined mainly by the status of the deceased, a king or chief having the former and infants the latter: the rites for women are usually less than those for men. Sacrificial offerings may also feature in the "rituals of rebellion" in certain kingdoms, by which kings and kingships are purified from the pollution of a preceding year or other period.

Sacrifices for physical and moral healing are universal in African societies. Purification is effected by oblation, usually that of a living animal, although some involve only the offering of nonanimal foods. The oblation is typically offered to the dead and to spirits, much less commonly to the Divinity. Animal sacrifice follows a common pattern: consecration of the animal for sacrifice; identification with the person for whom the rite is being performed, so that it will carry with it his or her pollution from sin or misdemeanor; killing and immolation; and consumption by the congregation, whose members thereby share food with the dead or other agents and with one another, thus redefining and strengthening the bonds that unite them. The sin that has led to sickness is carried away by the immolation, and the breach of kin or other relations and solidarity that has occurred is mended.

The other main form of ritual communication is possession, the seizing of a living person by a spirit or ancestor. The victim typically enters a state of trance or of violent physical seizure while the body and mind are taken over by the possessing agent. There are two main forms of possession: in one it is a sign of a mystical link between agent and victim that singles the latter out as being joined to the world of spiritual powers; in the other the possessed person is given the power of divination and mediumship. Later, as part of professional skill, possession may be self-induced by dancing, hyperventilation, drugs, or other means of dissociation. Although both women and men may be possessed, the majority in Africa are women. Well-known examples are the *bori* cult of northern Nigeria and the *zar* cult of northeastern Africa, in which women possessed by *bori* and *zar* spirits form cult groups around the particular possessing spirits. As with

A shrine of Shango at the court of the Temi of Ede, furnished with
figures of women devotees for the annual Shango festival.
Shango is the Yoruba god of thunder. COURTESY HIS HIGHNESS OBA
LAOYE 11. WERNER FORMAN ARCHIVE/ART RESOURCE

sacrifice, one effect of possession is the purification
of the victim and a change of social and moral
status, such as being removed from some of the
everyday uncertainties and obligations of familial
and other authority, and coming under the greater
authority of the possessing spirit. Possession is still
little understood as a physiological and psychological phenomenon. It takes place, voluntarily and
involuntarily, induced by the self or others; often
the possessed person, especially if also a medium,
has little or no recollection of being possessed.

A necessary part of sacrifice is divination to determine the mystical agents to whom the oblation
must be made. Divination takes many forms, which
may be divided into mediumship and oracular consultation, although the distinction is often hazy.
Mediumship typically involves possession or
trance, and with practice a diviner can enter a
trance easily. Diviners often wear clothing or eat
foods that represent the "wilderness" whence
comes their knowledge. They are often featured
by travelers and filmmakers as "witch doctors" in
order to show them as "primitive." Oracular con-

sultation involves devices such as the throwing of
pebbles or shells or the examining of animal en-
trails, which the diviner interprets as having hidden information about the causes of sickness or
harm.

To understand sacrifice in African religions (and
in any other), we must consider sin, taboo, atonement, and restitution, highly complex notions that
need long and careful analysis for their understanding. They concern purity, pollution, and danger and essentially involve the breaking or abandonment of culturally determined symbolic
boundaries that are established and validated by
myth and tradition. Breaching a taboo, associated
especially with the differences between the Divinity and human, between human and animal, and
between men and women, rarely appears to be
taken as a purposeful and heinous moral act. However, deliberately harming others, breaching ordered boundaries through disobedience or misdemeanor that destroys amity, trust, and identity of
kinship and neighborhood groups, may be considered sin. It may lead to sickness or other response

from the Divinity, ancestors, or spirits that must be cured by atonement, sacrifice, and often restitution by material compensation.

The Problem of Evil

Notions that might properly be translated as "evil" are part of all African religions. Evil comes in many forms: as sudden or cruel death, as undeserved sickness, as unfortunate event or coincidence, as unexpected poverty or failure, as bad dreams or visions. All are held to originate outside the individual and may affect the body and cause its internal dissolution. The occurrence of evil may be unexpected, may spring from a sense of guilt, or may be retribution for an antisocial action. To explain and to counter forms of evil, people use divination to identify its senders, who in small-scale interpersonal communities are thought likely to be other people rather than spirits or the Divinity. Harm sent as justifiable retribution, punishment, or "teaching" by the dead is typically diagnosed by diviners and removed by expiatory sacrifice. Harm that is malevolent and diagnosed as unmerited is typically attributed to other persons, those known in the literature as witches and sorcerers.

It used to be held by the travelers and missionaries that African peoples are characterized by witchcraft and its terrors. This is everywhere an exaggeration, although there have been instances of mass witch epidemics, at times of serious and sudden disasters, that have been countered by prophetic reformers. There is no reliable evidence of any actual existence of witches: what do exist are belief, fear, suspicion, and accusation of actual people thought to practice witchcraft, who may be sought out and punished by so-called witch doctors or witch-hunters.

The distinction between witches and sorcerers is not found in all African societies. It is rarely made in European societies, and observers have tended to confuse and conflate the terms. General anthropological usage is that a witch has an innate mystical power to harm others merely by volition (there may also be physical manifestations of the power, such as red eyes or a gray complexion), whereas a sorcerer can harm others only by the deliberate use of material substances, usually known as "medicines." Both may be men or women.

It appears universal in African societies that bewitching and ensorcellment are expressions of envy, jealousy, or hatred between rivals, whether kin or unrelated neighbors. Evildoer and victim must generally, therefore, know each other, and

divinatory procedures are based on this fact. Suspected or accused witches or sorcerers are typically made to withdraw the sickness or misfortune; they may at times also be punished, ostracized, or even killed, especially in cases where the same person is accused on many occasions, usually an indication of long-standing unpopularity within the local community. It follows that witchcraft and sorcery accusations will be found as much in modern urban settings as in the more "traditional" rural ones: it is not merely a matter of education or conversion.

European travelers and missionaries have tended to characterize African religions as being largely devoted to "magic," especially the "black magic" of sorcery. This term, with its implications of superstition and "primitive" thought, is used essentially to refer to beliefs and practices that the observer cannot accept as being "natural" or "religious," an ethnocentric view that is best discarded.

Prophets and Reformers

No African society or social group is unchanging, and African history is filled with the comings of prophets who have tried to reform or reshape a society and its religion in the face of wide disaster, whether natural or man-made. It is typical for the sources of the disaster to be thought to lie outside the community. Typical prophets also come from outside society, claiming their charismatic authority is given by the Divinity so that they can rebuild the identity and well-being of the "besieged" community. We know little of past prophets but may assume that most failed and left no record of their activity. During the twentieth century most prophets have been Christian with new messages from the Christian Divinity; indeed, most early missionaries were first taken to be prophets.

Christianity and Islam are both of great antiquity in sub-Saharan Africa, but their spread throughout the continent, especially that of Christianity, is very recent. Today, indeed, Africa is the scene of the most rapid and widespread Christian conversion in the world. If we look at the religious thought and behavior of any particular people in sub-Saharan Africa, and whether they claim adherence to an indigenous faith or to Islam or to Christianity, it is clear that except for a few geographically remote peoples, any religion includes elements of all these faiths, amalgamated, perhaps uneasily, into a single living religious system. It also becomes clear that every such religious system comprises the structure of mystical agents that has been described, despite cultural variation between the societies concerned.

Christianity came first to sub-Saharan Africa at Aksum in the fourth century and has persisted in Ethiopia ever since. Islam spread along the eastern coast of the continent and the southern edge of the Sahara beginning in the ninth century. Christian priests came to Africa during the colonial period, at first as chaplains to coastal European trading posts and then as priests to the kings of Kongo and Benin. Later, in the period of high colonialism in the eighteenth and nineteenth centuries, Christian missionaries entered the interior and spread across the continent. Today, most European missionaries have given way to African missionaries working in association with European-based missions and to the leaders of the ever-growing African independent, charismatic, and "separatist" churches.

The Christian missions of the colonial period were almost all in the hands of non-Africans of diverse churches and sects, with differing aims and methods, and with varying degrees of conversionary impact. African adherents in general held lower positions despite protestations (often sincere enough) of "brotherhood" and equality. Non-African missionaries held far greater authority yet paradoxically were dependent upon their inferiors, and both sides knew it. The consequence was that during the middle and later twentieth century, missions tended to divide, with African evangelists splitting off (often as new prophets) to establish their own separatist churches, and the structure and face of Christianity in Africa changed.

Most mission and church records have been concerned with rates of conversion, of "sincerity" or otherwise of converts, often in terms of an African theology as opposed to a non-African one. These data tend to be misleading, to imply that the break between "traditional" local religions and the "intrusive" religions was total, with an implicit conversionary movement from the former to the latter.

Much has been written on "religious syncretism," but its precise meaning remains unclear. Other than any presumed primordial "ur-religion," all religions of which anything is known are "syncretic," although devout believers of any religion rarely care to admit it. In Africa the term has come to have the rather explicit meaning of a mingling of local religions with either Christianity or Islam. But observation shows little such doctrinal mingling as far as behavior is concerned. The more devout converts to a world religion may be adamant in shunning "heathen" belief and ritual, but most ordinary people accommodate to one or the other according to the situation of the moment.

There is more to conversion than "a change of heart." It is also a matter of the widening scale of local and culturally discrete societies that today become parts of larger economic and political systems. One consequence is the realization that local divinities lose their power, and so new ones with wider power over many societies may be accepted. The obvious such Divinity is the Christian or Islamic Divinity, and people come to adhere to one of them. Yet they may at times appeal to their traditional divinities to help them in traditional situations and with traditional problems. If it appears more likely that, for example, a sickness may best be removed by traditional ritual, then that is followed; the opposite holds good as well. However, the situation with regard to independent Christian churches and sects may perhaps be called syncretic, in that the new leaders may take beliefs from both "indigenous" and "intrusive" faiths and form them into new sets of beliefs. This process occurs especially in those parts of Africa where traditional local forms of organization have given way almost completely to wider regional and national organizations, as in most of South Africa.

Conclusion: The Nature of Religion in Africa

There are three main conclusions to be drawn about religion in sub-Saharan Africa: (1) there are as many religions as there are distinct societies; (2) the conventional distinction between "indigenous" or "traditional" religions, on the one hand, and the "intrusive" or "world" religions of Islam and Christianity, on the other, is untenable as far as understanding actual social behavior is concerned; and (3) African religions are essentially similar to all religions throughout the world, even though they present certain local particularities. It is from the details of these local variations that the nature, functions, and histories of African religions may best be understood, both by Africans who wish to learn of the cultural and religious variety and richness of their continent, and by non-Africans who wish to learn from Africa to widen their knowledge of the world as a single whole.

BIBLIOGRAPHY

There are an immense number of writings on African religions, including reports of missionary endeavors, ethnographic monographs (the most useful, but typically limited to the study of single "local" religions), and collections of essays on African religions. The better of the last category are listed below.

Blakeley, Thomas D., Walter E. A. van Beek, and Dennis L. Thomson, eds. *Religion in Africa: Experience amd Expression.* London, 1994.

Horton, Robin. *Patterns of Thought in Africa and the West.* Cambridge, 1993.

King, Noel Q. *African Cosmos: An Introduction to Religion in Africa.* Belmont, Calif., 1986.

Parrinder, Geoffrey. *Religion in Africa.* New York, 1969.

Ray, Benjamin C. *African Religions: Symbol, Ritual, and Community.* Englewood Cliffs, N.J., 1976.

Taylor, John. *The Primal Vision.* London, 1963.

JOHN MIDDLETON

See also **Anthropology and the Study of Africa; Christianity; Healing; Initiation and Transition Rites; Islam; Judaism; Prophetic Movements; Sacrifice and Purification; Spirit Possession; Taboo and Sin.**

RÉPUBLIQUE CENTRAFRICAINE. *See* **Central African Republic.**

RESEARCH AND KNOWLEDGE

[This article consists of eight parts: **Biological Sciences; History; Humanities; Natural and Physical Sciences; Social Sciences; Responsibilities of Africanist Scholars; Scholarly Resources;** *and* **Western Research Aims and Achievements.***]*

BIOLOGICAL SCIENCES

The growth of biological knowledge in sub-Saharan Africa can be considered in two broad phases: the informal precolonial phase and the formal colonial/postcolonial phase. We shall consider these two broad phases in turn.

The Precolonial Phase

Biology is the conscious (formal or informal) accumulation of knowledge of living systems. Such knowledge became very important for survival of the human species. At what exact point in the evolution of man—from *Homo habilis* to *Homo sapiens*—such a conscious accumulation of biological knowledge took place, we will probably never know. The process is gradual and unobtrusive, in that a body of unconscious instinctive knowledge is transformed into a corpus of conscious communicable ideas. But conscious knowledge it definitely became when Lucy's descendants began using the communication skills known as language.

Of all forms of knowledge, biology is the most natural and the most immediate for the survival of man in a given environment. This is true for *Homo sapiens* and its probable evolutionary precursors. Man requires a knowledge of biology to understand, exploit, and protect himself from the environment. In short, man's survival is intimately related to his capacity to foresee environmental changes which are either useful or injurious to his survival and to take appropriate action in response to those changes. Early man, who by all accounts first evolved in Africa, had to constantly learn about environmental changes and how to adjust to them.

Searching for and acquiring food are the first prerequisites of survival for any organism. The coordination of a group of animals in the acquisition of food is manifested by a number of social animals. Watching a pride of lions conducting what seems to be a carefully planned attack (particularly upon the larger herbivores) makes it difficult to believe that such action is not a result of a carefully discussed plan. We know from the early works of Karl von Frisch that it is possible for a honeybee to "inform" other bees of the whereabouts of food several kilometers away. And yet in both these cases these maneuvers toward the acquisition of food cannot be attributed to either a rational analysis of a given situation or to an articulation of an information exchange between one member of a social group and others. Nor is there any debate. Debate is the ultimate test of interactive communication. It is probable that even after the evolution of a true modern hominid like *Homo sapiens*, speech, and thus the capacity for debate, was a later development.

Searching for and acquiring food—probably the starting point of humankind's domination of planet Earth—were pursuits which moved beyond the realm of instinctual to that of intellectual activity. Although the borderline between instinct and intelligence is indistinct, if we accept the thesis that higher primates are more intelligent than other animals, a selective advantage is thereby conferred on higher primates. This selective advantage would be reflected in the ability to learn which plants and animals are nutritious and which are poisonous. In the case of the latter, man has of course gone further in that he has found or devised ways of detoxicating otherwise poisonous foods. This might be a determinant factor between survival and death in a given environment.

Between Lucy and early man and between early man and the colonization of Africa by both Arab and European powers, African biology was in the hands of the indigenous African, although it would be wrong to think of this latter as a geographical fixture. Humans are a mixture of the migratory and the stationary natures. Humans tend to remain in a given environment so long as that environment can provide for all their survival needs. There were probably very few environments that yielded continuous year-round sustenance, providing a basis for a stable community which could then develop the complex social and other structures which we call civilization. Civilization is a product of biological stability, which in turn is a product of a reliable year-round food and water supply and freedom from physical and biological dangers.

By the time early man evolved to a modern African, he had acquired and transmitted a great deal of knowledge about the biology of the African environment. He could identify what plants and what animals constituted healthy food and which had to be avoided. He could read the signs written in the skies and integrate such information with regular and thus predictable climatic and environmental changes which in turn told him not only about the imminent availability of food but also its impending scarcity. He learned how to predict the rains and, with that, both which plants and animals to cultivate for food and how to cultivate them. He learned how to recognize different diseases that afflict him and his animals and perhaps even his plants, and he developed a variety of cures for these diseases.

It is easy to dismiss this learning as not being bona fide research, but clearly such a view would not stand serious examination. What all these generations of *Homo sapiens* did was to build a solid base of know-how which qualifies as scientific knowledge. This scientific knowledge served him well and enabled him to survive in a hostile environment for millennia before the advent of foreign powers.

The Pre–World War II Colonial Period

A major change occurred in the cultural ecology of Africa through the continent's colonization by European powers. The changes wrought by the European colonization of Africa were of bigger magnitude than anything that had hit Africa before or since. Its best legacy was probably to bring Africa into contemporary world civilization. Its worst legacy was to seek to recreate Africa in the image of Europe, and the African in the image of the European. From the viewpoint of research and knowledge, the arrogant and sweeping assump-

tion that nothing in African culture is worth knowing let alone worth preserving denied contemporary science a wealth of knowledge.

The first European biologists came into Africa in expeditions. They concentrated on compiling a taxonomic database, which included much information that was new to formal European science. With respect to the international nomenclature of plants and animals, the introduction of African flora and fauna did constitute new scientific information, though Europeans tended to subscribe to the view that the plants and animals had been "discovered," giving the impression that they were new to humanity.

The early colonial collections of biological specimens were destined for exhibition in European museums. Later, live specimens were sent to European zoos. The British Museum (Natural History) in South Kensington, like its French, Belgian, Spanish, and Portuguese counterparts, continue to house rich collections of African animals and plants.

By the end of World War I, there was a shift from a pure collecting zeal to that of seeking some understanding of the ecological relationships of the diverse components of the African biota. The historical scientific expeditions which came to Africa to collect specimens of animal and plant life were now increasingly replaced by those which tried to study the relationship of African plants and animals to each other and the balance between the various environmental components. In the late 1920s the Graham expedition to Lake Victoria resulted not only in the naming of a new tilapia species, *Tilapia esculenta* (now *Oreochromis esculentus*), but also in determining the effect of newly introduced gill nets, whose mesh sizes were deemed by the Graham expedition to be too small for the continued survival of the endemic Lake Victoria species. Perhaps the most important of the investigations of the inland waters of Africa were undertaken by Worthington in 1929 and 1932; reports of the latter included the results of a 1930–1931 expedition sponsored by Cambridge University. One member of the Cambridge Expedition was a young Cambridge graduate, Leonard C. Beadle, who in 1950 became the first professor of biology (and later, of zoology) at Makerere. The results of some of these expeditions continued to be published into the 1990s.

The Postwar Period

World War II brought about a major change in the political ecology of Africa. With the returning

African war veterans who had fought and died alongside their white colleagues, particularly in Burma and Malaysia, the distinction between the ruler and the ruled became less clear. Agitation for independence was in the air. As the victors of World War II, the major European colonial powers were Britain, France, and Belgium, with Portugal and Spain being reduced to relatively minor roles. The Axis Powers of Germany and Italy were required, as a consequence of their defeat, to cede their colonial territories to the Allies as Mandated Territories.

With the sweep of socialism in Europe, there was an anticipatory mood of political independence in the colonies. India and Pakistan became independent in 1947. These were followed ten years later with the first African colony to attain independence: Ghana, formerly the Gold Coast.

These events were not without due effect on the development of African biology. An urgent need was felt by colonial scholars and administrators to redefine the structures of research along more pragmatic lines. In the British Colonial Office, the buzzword of the time was "federation." French colonial philosophy was revolving along the same lines except that the French preferred to regard the francophone colonies as part of metropolitan France. Thus, before the granting of independence to Ghana and later Nigeria, the idea of a West African Federation was put forward. In Central Africa, Roy Welensky and his white-dominated Central African Federation was bitterly undermined by African political leadership, in particular by that of Kamuzu Banda of Malawi.

These various political moves did not occur without impact on the organization and running of research in Africa. Thus in the immediate postwar East Africa, there was formed in 1948 an East African High Commission, a kind of joint high command of the three British East African governors and their Zanzibar counterpart, the British Resident. Under this body, instruments of economic advancement and integration were formed, such as the East African Currency Board, the East African Posts and Telecommunications, the East African Railways and Harbours, and the East African Airways. At the same time, a number of research institutions were set up. These were the East African Medical Research Organization at Mwanza (Tanganyika), and the East African Agricultural and Forestry Research Organization and the East African Veterinary Research Organization at Muguga, a few kilometers northwest of Nairobi (Kenya). On the Kenyan side, the East African Leprosy Research

Organization was established, while in Uganda the East African Freshwater Fisheries Research Organization at Jinja and the East African Trypanosomiasis Research Organization at Tororo were set up. The East African Marine Fisheries Research Organization was based in Zanzibar. All these organizations were engaged in the fields of applied biological research.

One seed for the future expansion of biological research and knowledge was in the founding and expansion of institutions of higher learning. Ibadan in West Africa and Makerere in East Africa became the nuclei of a wide catchment base of higher education that transcended, in the case of Makerere, "national" boundaries. Thus in the early 1950s students attending Makerere came not only from the four East African states of Kenya, Uganda, Tanganyika, and Zanzibar, but also Malawi and Zambia. In Ghana, the foundations of the University of Ghana were also laid. In the Central African Federation before its breakup into the three later independent states of Malawi, Zambia, and Zimbabwe, a Federal University College at Salisbury was founded during this phase of the colonial era, although in reality this was a white-dominated institution.

The Early Postindependence Period

By the 1960s many African countries were either politically independent or on the way to becoming so. Most African countries that gained independence had a national university or the nucleus of a national university. In rare cases, a few countries banded together to support a federal university. The University of Botswana, Lesotho, and Swaziland (UBLS) is a case in point. While this institution was still in operation in 1997, the University of East Africa, which also started as a federal university to be shared between Kenya, Uganda, and Tanzania, did not survive for long. The component University Colleges of Dar es Salaam, Makerere, and Nairobi soon parted ways in 1970, each to become a separate university.

In the early postindependence period, an interest in more fundamental, theoretical aspects of biology were taking shape in the universities. Although applied aspects of these fundamental studies were not necessarily relegated to other institutions, the freedom—indeed, desire—to take a longer view of biological research was both healthy and necessary. New linkages with universities in Europe and to a lesser extent in America led to international partnerships between universities and research institutions. Granting bodies such as

Ford, Rockefeller, Nuffield, Wellcome, and Munitalp Foundations began to support university research in Africa in significant ways. The Rockefeller Foundation, in particular, developed a program to support the indigenization of East African universities with training scholarships and fellowships for African academic staff. In the wake of this, strong growth in contemporary biological research took place in a number of African countries.

Both the numbers and the quality of the publications in biological research began to rise steeply and significantly. There was worldwide recognition of African biological research. More and more conferences were held in Africa as a mark of respect for the research quality emanating from Africa. The holding of the first International Symposium in Comparative Endocrinology in Kenya in 1974 was both an acknowledgment of the quality of research being done in Africa in this very fundamental aspect of biology and a recognition of the potential of new biological insight through the understanding of tropical endocrine mechanisms. By the mid-1970s, therefore, African biological research reached its peak and institutions like the International Centre for Insect Physiology and Ecology (ICIPE) and the International Laboratory for Research in Animal Diseases (ILRAD) attained enthusiastic international support.

The Late Postindependence Period

The 1980s and 1990s saw a general decline in African university research. Many factors contributed to this situation. The improved health of African nations resulted in reduced infant and child mortality and a dramatic increase in the number of young people in the general population. This resulted in political pressure on African governments to increase the level of enrollment in public universities. At the same time, financial and equipment resources for scientific research diminished. Competition for international funds became greater worldwide, demanding the ever higher quality of research proposals and supporting references. University staff remuneration decreased. The indications are that with an increasing sense of financial realism in African countries hitherto buffered during the cold war period by aid from both sides of the ideological divide, the situation will improve. The post-Gorbachev era brought a sharp rejoinder to African countries that Western countries were demanding a number of political and financial targets in return for the injecting of funds into the African economy. This in turn is beginning to have

a deep impact on the management of university financial resources. From a previous hand-to-mouth annual subvention (which sometimes existed only on paper), African universities have begun to take a far more strict approach to management of their financial resources. More market-oriented approaches will probably lead to a more realistic fee structure and a consequent improvement in both staff remuneration and in research funding. In the mid-1990s, however, African biological research had yet to recover to its post-independence boom. Once the reorientation in the general economy has taken place, modern tools of communication will surely see a resurgence of African biological research and the growth of biological knowledge to a hitherto unprecedented level.

BIBLIOGRAPHY

Graham, M. *The Victoria Nyanza and Its Fisheries.* London, 1929.

Worthington, E. B. "Scientific Results of the Cambridge Expedition to the East African Lakes, 1930–1931." *J. Linn. Soc.* 381 (1932): 99–119.

MOHAMED HYDER

HISTORY

Modern research in the history of Africa by African scholars was greatly accelerated by the establishment of the universities of Ibadan in Nigeria, Legon in Ghana, Makerere in Uganda, and Khartoum in Sudan, beginning around 1948. The practice of the discipline was, however, advanced by Africans trained in European universities in Western traditions of historiography: Kenneth Onwuka Dike and Saburi Biobaku in Nigeria, Adu Boahen in Ghana, Bethwell A. Ogot in East Africa, Yusuf Fadl Hassan in Sudan, and others, starting in the 1950s. The first heads of the new departments of history were, however, non-Africans, except for Dike in Ibadan. The situation has now changed with the proliferation of universities throughout Africa. The shortage of resources for research, teaching, and publication, however, ensures that African scholars continue to rely on support from outside the continent, and the contribution of scholars from outside the continent continues to be significant.

At the first representative gathering of African historians at the University of Lagos, Nigeria, in 1977, sponsored by the Association of African Universities, it was discovered that most African universities had changed the colonial content of education in history from concentration on the colonial power, or imperial expansion, to African history or local history. Anglophone Africa appeared to have moved farthest in that direction, followed by francophone Africa and the universities of northern Africa, which tended to pay greater attention to Arabic or Islamic history. It was noted that contacts between historians from different parts of Africa were limited or nonexistent, and that the proposed Association of African Historians had not been realized. The association was started in 1975 by the francophone scholars of western Africa with the financial support of their governments. Its purpose was to establish a forum through which intellectuals could promote action through their ideas; however, it did not go beyond the publication of an issue of its journal, *Afrika Zamani*, at the University of Yaoundé, Cameroon. The workshop proposed courses on the philosophy of history to support training in the techniques of historical method.

The departments of history in African universities became the focus for research and publication. National historical societies were formed in Nigeria in the 1950s, Ghana in the 1960s, and eastern Africa in the 1970s. These societies became the media for carrying out changes in the curricula and teaching methods in secondary and primary education; they also served as pressure points to influence decisions of government and the thinking of ruling elites. The primary function of the historical societies and the goal of African scholars remained the advancement of research and publication. In this area, too, differences in orientation among the universities became observable. An Ibadan school devoted to empirical research and publication became distinguished from a more ideologically oriented school based at the University of Dar es Salaam, Tanzania.

The national historical societies provided outlets for publication, such as the *Journal of the Historical Society of Nigeria, Tarikh, Transactions of the Historical Society of Ghana,* and *Transafrican Journal of History,* which was published through a collaboration of the universities in Uganda, Kenya, Tanzania, Zambia, and Malawi. Historians trained in the Ibadan school initiated the Ibadan Series of historical monographs, published by Longman (edited by Dike through the 1960s and J. F. Ade. Ajayi from the 1970s). Historians in the various societies produced collaborative national or regional histories. The east Africans began with *Zamani: A Survey of East African History,* edited by Bethwell Ogot and J. A. Kiernan,

published by the East African Publishing House in 1968 and 1973. The Historical Society of Nigeria published *Groundwork of Nigerian History* in 1980, edited by Obaro Ikime and published by Heinemann. *History of West Africa* was edited by J. F. Ade. Ajayi and Michael Crowder for Longman in two volumes from 1971. The climax of these publication activities was the publication, beginning in 1981, of the eight-volume UNESCO *General History of Africa,* edited by African scholars; it is comparable to the established *Cambridge History of Africa: Methodology and African Prehistory,* edited by Joseph Ki-Zerbo; *Ancient Civilizations of Africa,* edited by G. Mokhtar; *Africa from the Seventh to Eleventh Century,* edited by M. El Fasi; *Africa from the Twelfth to Sixteenth Century,* edited by D. T. Niane; *Africa from the Sixteenth to Eighteenth Century,* edited by B. A. Ogot; *The Nineteenth Century until 1880,* edited by J. F. Ade. Ajayi; *Africa under Foreign Domination, 1880–1935,* edited by A. A. Boahen; and *Africa since 1935,* edited by A. A. Mazrui.

The rationale for collaborative publication is the interdisciplinary nature of African historiography—it requires the combined contributions of many scholars in many disciplines to do justice to a general history of the continent, a nation, or a region. The one notable general synthesis by an African scholar is Joseph Ki-Zerbo's *Histoire de l'Afrique noire* (1978).

Publication outlets have decreased in many countries of Africa with shrinking economies and unstable governments. Many local journals are unable to keep up their circulations and subscriptions. Local publishing houses, too, are unable to publish without subsidies from the scholars. The Paris-based *Présence africaine* and the Senegalese *Bulletin de l'Institut Fondamental d'Afrique Noire* (Dakar, Senegal) appear to be the exceptions.

The progress of historical research in Africa has been slowed by poor funding. National governments have not provided research money to their universities, and there are no foundations or nongovernmental organizations offering grants or fellowships. Archives, museums, and other institutions for the conservation of evidence and provision of research facilities are in desperately short supply. Thus even the centers for the study of oral tradition set up by the United Nations Educational, Scientific, and Cultural Organization (UNESCO) at Niamey, Niger, for western Africa, at Zanzibar for eastern Africa, and in central Africa have atrophied since being handed over to the Organization of African Unity (OAU). This severe failure of resources has delayed the full development of the potentials of African historians to move the center of the study of African history to the continent.

The special focus of African historians is the oral tradition as the principal document and methodology—even ideology and philosophy—of history. The oral tradition also provides the means of reaching urban as well as rural populations, as many younger urban historians search for relevance to present realities on the continent through a social historical approach to the present. Yet others insist on a greater effort by African historians to appropriate the legacy of ancient Egypt, an activity to which Cheik Anta Diop, from Senegal, devoted a lifetime of study.

At the end of the twentieth century, oral traditions no longer form a subject of concentrated discussion among African historians. The number of scholars pursuing studies in oral tradition in the mid-1990s was small, compared with the well-funded projects conducted by Dike on Benin (1953) and Biobaku on the Yoruba (1956). The situation is, in part, the result of a shortage of local funds for scholarly research in the field. In Nigerian universities, for example, most work in the collection and interpretation of primary data is carried out by candidates for the bachelor's degree in history, and by a smaller number of candidates for master's and doctoral degrees. However, lack of special attention by scholars is, in part, the result of a feeling that oral tradition is now established as a valid orthodox historical source and is available within communities to any scholar as a routine component of research; it is not seen as a subject for study in itself.

African historians have legitimate complaints against the political elite for their lack of historical consciousness and neglect of the lessons to be learned from history. But most urban dwellers and workers show interest in oral history of the recent past; and the rural populace, in the oral traditions of their communities, since many current inter- and intracommunal conflicts and disputes are grounded in historical claims or grievances. Accordingly, the data of oral tradition and oral history provide the scholar with access to historically conscious urban working and rural populations. Indeed, in Nigeria there have been cases of community development associations in the cities contributing money to assist scholars in preparing histories of their communities. However, African scholars have not yet come to grips with the problem of devising cheap and efficient ways of collect-

ing, transcribing, translating, and publishing oral traditions. The Jos Oral History and Literature Texts, published by the Department of History, University of Jos, Nigeria, and texts published by the University of Ibadan's Institute of African Studies are pilot projects in this field that have been forced to stop for lack of funding.

The euphoria of the 1960s that came with the independence of many nations is partly restored by the new government of South Africa, with its resources and promise of a historiography divorced from racism. It is hoped that South African historiography may revive the vigor of the 1960s as well as restore balance to the interpretation of the African historical record.

Can African historians develop an authentic voice for the interpretation of the critical problems of the continent to its people and the world? To do this, it is necessary to harness the resources of Africa's multiple traditions of historiography: the oral tradition, which forms the basis of all historical traditions; the Islamic tradition, which became part of a native African tradition over most of northern Africa and the Horn, down to the Sudan belt and coastal eastern Africa; and the Western tradition, which has become a part of the African heritage even since the departure of the colonial rulers. Such an integrative historiography would present a fundamentally African contribution to an increasingly international science of history.

BIBLIOGRAPHY

Alagoa, E. J. "Communicating African History." *Storia della storiografia*, no. 15 (1989): 75–89.

———, ed. *The Teaching of History in African Universities: Being Proceedings of a Workshop Sponsored by the Association of African Universities at the University of Lagos, September 21–24, 1977.* Accra, Ghana, 1978.

Falola, Toyin, ed. *African Historiography: Essays in Honour of Jacob Ade. Ajayi.* Harlow, U.K., 1993.

Jewsiewicki, Bogumil, and David Newbury, eds. *African Historiography: What History for Which Africa?* Beverly Hills, 1986.

Neale, Caroline. *Writing "Independent" History: African Historiography, 1960–1980.* Westport, Conn., 1985.

Ranger, Terence O., ed. *Emerging Themes of African History: Proceedings of the International Congress of African Historians Held at the University College, Dar es Salaam, October 1965.* Nairobi, 1968.

Vansina, Jan, Raymond Mauny, and L. V. Thomas, eds. *The Historian in Tropical Africa: Studies Presented and Discussed at the Fourth International African Seminar at the University of Dakar, Senegal, 1961.* London, 1964.

E. J. ALAGOA

See also **Education; Historiography; History and the Study of Africa; Oral Culture and Oral Tradition; Publishing.**

HUMANITIES

The conquest and colonization of Africa by the West was accompanied by the negation of the possibility of an indigenous world outlook and systems of knowledge on the part of Africans. Instead, the colonial order imposed a Euro-Christian episteme and a dominant ideological discourse that affirmed Western superiority and resonated with the rhetoric about a "primitive" Africa. Africans were denied histories and cultures, and a knowledge that was about but not of Africa was invented. This new knowledge of Africa, canonized as the legitimate colonial archive, appropriated the intellectual space hitherto occupied by Africa's organic intellectuals. It reigned unchallenged both in academia and in the everyday discourses of the colonizers, but also in the consciousness of the emergent African intelligentsia, which could not disengage itself from the totalizing hegemony of Western thought. In art, philosophy, religion, literature, anthropology, language, and history, Africa was sharply contrasted with Europe, creating a process of dichotomization and polarization in which Africa occupied the bottom and Europe the top positions on the civilizational scale. The Africa that the "world" came to know through its Western representation was a European social construct.

The decolonization of learning that followed in the wake of political independence in Africa was likewise an ideological project. This process included the reinvention of Africa in the academe, this time as a distinct but worthy subject of study, evidencing a continental cultural unity and dynamic culture histories, and with a contribution to make in the cross-fertilization of the universal. It also involved the assertion and insertion of African content into the Western academic disciplines. The pioneers in this enterprise had to persuade the West about the possibility of an African gnosis and of African rationality. Next they had to make explicit their method for the recovery of knowledge from orality; that is, from the spoken word, memory, and performances of primary oral societies—the "preliterate" peoples, in colonial parlance. The production of knowledge thus involved the crafting and refinement of research methodology, the timely publication of research results, and a specific pedagogy aimed at reintroducing the African into the world. The study of oral traditions was born within this milieu.

The Historian's Craft

The common starting ground for humanities research in Africa has been primary orality, with the lead being taken by the first generation of historians appointed to university positions from the late 1940s. Jan Vansina's pathbreaking *De la tradition orale: Essai de méthode historique* (1961), translated into English in 1965, has greatly influenced subsequent scholarship. Whereas Vansina started work among the kingdom peoples of central Africa, his methodology was appropriated and refined by Bethwell A. Ogot, who made it applicable to the study of a wide range of noncentralized Luo peoples including the Padhola of Uganda and the Kenya Luo. Embraced by J. B. Webster at Makerere University in Uganda and later at Chancellor College in Malawi, Ogot's usage of oral traditions gave history to hundreds of communities big and small in eastern Africa. E. J. Alagoa did the same for the many acephalous communities of the Niger delta. An important aspect of Vansina's scholarship was his continual refinement of methodology, keenly undertaken by his students as well, which gave this method an invaluable internal critical capacity. Much of this methodological criticism was published in David Henige's *History in Africa,* a journal that has subjected both the oral traditions and the written archives to the same high standards of scholarship. Indeed, methodological rigor has been one hallmark of this historical scholarship as it has sought to subject itself to the same canons as Western historical scholarship. African historiography has been changed by this practice, most evidently in the concentrated studies of precolonial Asante by Ivor Wilks and T. C. McCaskie; the Senegambia by Philip D. Curtin and Boubacar Barry; northern Angola before 1830 by John K. Thornton and Joseph C. Miller; the aftermath of the Zulu conqueror Shaka's *mfecane,* or forced migration, in southern Africa by J. D. Omer-Cooper and Carolyn Hamilton; and the extended researches on spirit mediums in central and southern Africa initiated by the early work of Terence Ranger and by J. M. Schoffeleers.

The European treatment of Africans as a people without history has provoked an abiding concern with the deep past of Africa—the Africa before the age of Europe. This has led to keen interest by historians in the contribution of archaeologists and historical linguists to the study of Africa. Their results have been incorporated into arguments for the African origins of classical Egyptian civilization. Archaeology has been a useful handmaid in providing a coherent chronology, since the beginning of radiocarbon dating in 1951, for the material cultures of early civilizations, and recent efforts by archaeologists themselves to interpret the nature of early complex societies, for example at Jenne-jeno, has further enhanced its utility. This influence is most marked in Roland Oliver's interpretations of the African iron age in his 1991 history of the continent. The work of the historical linguists has likewise had an impact on Vansina's interpretation of the migrations and settlements of the forest-savanna peoples of central Africa. On a wider scale, the debates about "Bantu genesis" served to caution scholars about the limits of these sources.

Africa's involvement with Europe and the Atlantic world from the fifteenth century onward has inevitably led to engagements in wider debates within Atlantic Africa regarding the origins, extent, and impact of the slave trade on African life. As well, it has led to engagements with the nature of domestic slavery in Africa, and into comparative studies of slavery globally. Philip Curtin's pioneering census on the Atlantic slave trade has endured decades of scrutiny and revision, and work continues on this terrain by Joseph E. Inikori and others. The trade has been magisterially explored in its tricontinental dimension by Miller, while the place of the trade in African life, studied by Patrick Manning, its prosperity in the Sokoto Caliphate, and its slow death in both east and west Africa have been extensively examined. *How Europe Underdeveloped Africa* by Walter Rodney (1972) was timely in its linkage of Africanist scholarship to developments in the wider Atlantic basin, and influenced approaches to the study of colonialism and underdevelopment in both east and west Africa for two decades; it was also the most popular history being read by nonhistorians. Its heuristic value lay in its partial explanation of the failure of the state and the increasingly evident manifestations of underdevelopment and dependence in Africa in the 1970s.

Oral historical narratives about the twentieth century have been subjected to the same critical analysis as the oral traditions of the precolonial era, and with the same rigor as the colonial archive, which has provided a reliable chronological frame while being the subject of skepticism in its representation of both the colonizer and the colonized.

The two sources have been used complementarily in writing the new social histories of Africa. This new strategy has propelled the historiography of "the African voice"; the role of African spirit mediums in the resistance to colonialism; biography; village history; the historical anthropology of peasant discourses; colonial medicine; negotiated identities; gender and history; urban labor history; leisure; the moral economy of the Mau Mau; and the political consciousness of Zimbabwe guerrillas. Historical explanation has been pushed in new and refreshing directions, situating twentieth-century Africans as participants in the terrain of creation, contestation, and occupation as they sought to exercise choice and control over their location, identity, and security, as Phyllis M. Martin has observed.

Likewise, sustained researches in African women's history began in the mid-1970s and have continued unabated, ranging from studies of women under slavery and under colonialism to women as liberation soldiers; a testimony to the success of the global agenda on women, as presented by Catherine Coquery-Vidrovitch in 1997. In the 1990s the construction and reconstruction of social relationships beyond the reach of the colonial order placed gender at the core of the study of social change in the twentieth century. Deconstructing the male-dominated kinship model of colonial historiography, these studies have revealed and deepened understandings about power and process, of the exchanges of signs and substance as parties seek to gain mastery over others through the colonization of consciousness, of the embeddedness of culture in power struggles, and of culture as process, by exploring the ways in which individuals, households, and communities have invested in other people for production and reproduction of material and ideological life, and in explicating how people have used power to get power. The historiography of South Africa since the 1970s in particular has been wholly transformed as a result of the researchers' concerns with social history. The cumulative impact of this historical endeavor has been summarized thus by Roland Oliver, the doyen of historians of Africa: "On the more enduring stage of historiography in the English language we shall have made our mark."

African Philosophy

The development of philosophy as a subject of intellection and research in Africa had the added urgency of being a political project, embraced by the scholar-statesman Léopold Sédar Senghor as an affirmation of a renaissance Africanity; by Tanzanian president Julius Nyerere as the basis of African socialism, Ujamaa; and by Ghana's first president, Kwame Nkrumah, as "consciencism," an ideology of decolonization and development. Within the academy, philosophy's initial grounding in the seminaries and in the religious studies departments in the new African universities made it a discipline engaged with the colonial archive right from the start. Its early and extended concern with the rationality debate (which argued about the existence of a "primitive" versus a "modern" mentality) from the mid-1960s was symptomatic of the inherited Western episteme. Later philosophical developments were informed by the existing imperative to practice philosophy the Western, scientific way in order that it qualify as philosophy at all. In this enlightenment discourse, the universality of the European Idea was an uncontested given. Thus contemporary African philosophy has been driven by the encounter between the African world and European "modernity" and with the need to define itself as of and yet outside that inscription.

The first steps involved a critique of Eurocentrism. Negritude, a formulation of Senghor and Aimé Césaire in the Paris of the interwar years, contested the identity imposed on Africa by Europe. Later critiques of Eurocentrism have involved an extensive rereading of the colonial archives, a revisitation of Hume, Kant, and Hegel, and the hermeneutical elucidation of their texts to expose the complicity of continental European philosophy in empire and colonialism. This project is seen as necessary for mental liberation and for the appropriation of the intellectual heritage of Europe on African terms. It is seen as an essential stage in the emancipation of the practice of philosophy in Africa from the hegemony of European ideas, and in the quest for a hermeneutic that grows from lived African experience.

The quest for the lived African experience has led back to the study of African traditions and facilitated research and production of knowledge on the subject of ethnophilosophy. Placied Tempels' book *La philosophie bantoue* (1945) provided a convenient launching pad in its claims for the wide Bantu world. The work and the debates surrounding it in missionary circles inspired Alexis Kagame, from a study of the Kinyaruanda language, to analyse the concept and categorical structure of Being as conceived by the interlacustrine Bantu speakers,

and to make general statements concerning Bantu metaphysics. Subsequent work has focused on the explication of the thought systems of specific speech communities. Detailed researches have sought to articulate the fundamental Akan conceptions and the discursive principles which underlie Akan conceptions of personhood and agency, morality, and the idea of God as a cultural universal. At the microlevel, Marcel Griaule's *Conversations with Ogotemmeli: An Introduction to Dogon Religious Ideas* (1965) encouraged the reliance on knowledgable informants. This possibility of the individual mind and voice led to the search for the authentic African voice, and to the foregrounding of their voices, their African subjectivity, as sagacity. In creating what has come to be called "sage philosophy," Odera Oruka defined the task of the African philosopher as the fostering of the authentic African identity. Critics of sage philosophy have pointed out that it is a method that has built-in assumptions about the place of Africans in the world and the nature of African rationality in the context of an imaginary worldview of collective wisdom. While accepting its assertion that African philosophy must be rooted in Africa and not simply philosophy that happens to be done in Africa, critics have objected to its assumption that the object of study must be African traditions. Alternatively, they have suggested that African philosophy should be concerned with the definition of the social processes that will enable local production of knowledge as a function of the articulation of the complexities of the world of experience. "In fact," argues Bruce Janz, "African traditions must inform African Philosophy, but the object of study must be human experience as it manifests itself and as it comes to self-understanding" (p. 235).

Religions

John S. Mbiti's *African Religions and Philosophy* (1970) straddled the two fields mentioned in the book's title, for Mbiti asserted that philosophical inferences could be derived from the everyday practices of indigenous African religions through the study of their languages. Mbiti's contributions to the study of African traditional religion (his own coinage and trope, with E. Bolaji Idowu) lay in his providing an anthropocentric ontology based on the hierarchical categories of God, the originator and sustainer of man; the spirits that explain the destiny of man; man, at the center of the ontological hierarchy; and the plants, animals, and natural phenomena that constitute the living environment.

Second, Mbiti provided an ontological concept of time that had two parts: a deep past, *zamani*, and a lived present five generations in depth, *sasa*; the future was nonexistent. Mbiti's critics accused him of scholasticism, of smuggling Hellenic religious thoughts about a unified and transcendental Socratic God, of explaining African ideas through Greek metaphysics, thus essentially Christianizing African religions and in the process obscuring the reality of African thought. The call has been for a study of these systems of thought on their own terms. Once again the plea has been entered for a theory of and for Africa, a task easier called for than accomplished, as the debates between Robin Horton and his critics, including Jean and John Comaroff, have testified.

The study of Christianity in Africa focusing on mainline churches has given extensive coverage to the church in Ethiopia, the missionary movement into Africa, the role of the churches in Western education and in the making of a Christian elite, the interface between African traditions and Christianity, and colonial evangelism. Later discourses centered on an African theology and on missiology, inculturation, and translation in the process of reinventing Christianity. They are about "religious statesmanship," in Lamin Sanneh's words, as African theologians seek to make Christians of Africans without the presumption of cultural rejection by the receiving societies. But inculturation is not intended to compromise the church's basic faith as defined by the papacy in Rome. In the 1970s Archbishop Milingo's error was to attribute causation to African agency by describing affliction and practicing healing on African terms. The culminating publication on mainline Christianity, by Elizabeth Isichei, is a "cognitive map" of the Christian epoch in Africa that is sensitive to the roles of lay people and to the "pools of autonomy" created by women within the mainline churches through the revivalist movements.

Autonomous African initiative and agency has been best exemplified in the studies of African appropriations of Judaism by the Falashas of Ethiopia and of Christianity, earlier referred to as independency. African prophecy drew early attention and categorization, and the scholarship on the messianic, apocalyptic, and eschatological understanding of the two most popular prophets, William Wadé Harris and Simon Kimbangu, has been advancing over the years. The clash between the state and the prophets is a running theme. The humanistic approach—the study of religion without making any assumptions about its metaphysical grounds or object, in Benjamin C. Ray's words—has been successfully deployed by Cynthia Hoehler-Fatton in a study of the role of women in one of the earliest Holy Spirit movements in East Africa, the Roho church of Alfayo Odongo Mango.

The late twentieth century has witnessed the proliferation of religious pluralism, a manifestation of popular religion with myriads of both indigenous and exogenous pentecostal, evangelical, and spiritual science organizations in both rural and urban areas. Africa is experiencing a boom in "the church industry," a multiplicity of religious organizations drawing into their ranks people who have become dissatisfied with conventional religious worldviews and who are searching for new sources of meaning and spiritual power, that is, according to Rosalind I. J. Hackett, in "world building." An exploration of these modes of popular religious consciousness has demonstrated the successful appropriation of endogenous Tswana and exogenous Zionist ritual by the marginalized populations.

African Islam

The extensive researches on Islam, based on both chirographic and oral sources, have yielded expansive knowledge about western African societies from the tenth century A.D. West African Islam has been constructed through the usage of Arabic sources that document the penetration of Islam in the medieval period, the nature of the Almoravid intervention, the influence of the Maliki law school, the rulings of Muhammed ibn abd al-Karim al-Maghili in the late fifteenth century, the influence of the *hadith* school of Medina, and the creation of Sufi congregations of the Tijaniyya, Qadiriyya, and Khatmiyya persuasions. The modern period has spawned researches on the revolution in Islamic thought and polity ushered in by the jihad and the teachings of 'Uthman dan Fodio; the expansion of Muslim communities in the savanna and the role of the 'ulama; and the emergence of the Mourides. Colonial conquest provoked numerous wars of Islamic resistance that have inspired both folklore and scholarly research. The works on the twentieth century portray the relationship between Islamic society and the secular state, the interaction between Islam and Christianity, traditional religions and resultant worldviews, and the return of Islam to the center of social thought regarding identity and political practice in both east and west Africa and the wider Islamic world.

Oral Performance Traditions

Researches in oral performance traditions have intensified since the work of Ruth Finnegan in the 1960s, inspiring explorations into songs and chants, narratives, riddles, puns and tongue twisters, proverbs, and folktales. It is acknowledged that African researchers as native speakers of the languages have enhanced the field by emphasizing African subjectivity and aesthetics. The performers in oral traditions have included those who have worked within restricted contexts, such as royal courts. These include the griots, performers in the western Sudan; the *kwadumfo,* court poets of the Asante state; the *imbongi,* Zulu praise singers; and the *umusizi,* Rwandan court poets. This heroic royal poetry has attracted much research and interpretation. In addition to being praise this literature is about power, how it is won and retained. In the *Sundiata* epic the griot Bala Faseke describes the Mali legendary king as "the husband of power" and provides instructions on the culture and traditions of the Mande that would enable him to rule wisely. A second variety of performance is for entertainment. This genre includes the Yoruba *oriki,* variously translated as praises or praise poems, which come in various categories, such as *oriki ilu* in praise of towns, *oriki orile* for lineages, and *oriki olanije* for the prominent living and dead. It also includes the vocal tonal *ijala* poetry of the Yoruba hunters. Among the nonkingdom peoples, the Dinka cattle songs take pride of place, as does the oral poetry of the Somali. A third tradition, literature as children's entertainment, has flourished in translations such as Pamela Kola's *East African Why Stories* (1971) and Cyprian Ekwensi's *An African Night's Entertainment* (1962). This genre has been little researched. The most significant studies on the oral-written interface have been on the epic, prose, myth, folktale, and songs and chants, oral narratives, and witticisms.

The recording, transcription, translation, study of, and commentary on African languages by Africans remains surprisingly scanty, in spite of the dedicated beginnings of pioneers such as Kagame on Kinyarwanda, A. C. Jordan on Xhosa, Wande Abimbola on the Yoruba Ifa, and the indefatigable J. P. Clark, whose work is considered a model. It is argued that this kind of research requires an inordinate investment in time in the field and in the study of philology, while at the same time the master bards are disappearing. Swahili literature has thrived in both oral and written forms. The traditional *utenzi* or *utendi,* a genre of epic and narrative poetry, flourished in the written form in the nineteenth century. Works in this genre include *Utendi wa Lyomo Fungo,* which tells of a hero protector of the city-state and its wells, *Al-Inkishafi,* a homily, *Diwani wa Muyaka,* a discourse on political factionalism in Mombasa, and *Utendi wa Mwana Kupona,* a poem that is ostensibly about wifely virtue, but is also a subversion of this theme.

African poetry written in European languages started as protest literature proclaiming African culture in the face of its negation by colonial Europe. It gave birth to the poetry of the negritude movement, whose most prolific exponent was Léopold Sédar Senghor. The most popular of such protest literature in English was *Song of Lawino: A Lament* (1968) by the east African Okot p'Bitek. Within east Africa this work inspired a flood of pastoral nostalgia: Jared Angira's *Juices* (1970) is fairly representative of narratives published in its wake. But it was Christopher Okigbo, whose Euro-modernist poetry in English, *Labyrinths* (1971), and poetic individualism in *Heavensgate* (1962), set the tone in the early 1960s. His work stands in sharp contrast to the traditionalist poetry of Mazisi Kunene, who draws heavily from the oral poetry of the Zulu people. The extensive corpus of poetry has in turn given birth to literary criticism, concerned not just with the elucidation of art but also with the development of a literary tradition for Africa.

Colonialism and the Postcolonial Novel

Milestones in African prose include Apolo Kagwa's early-twentieth-century publications based on extensive research into the history and culture of the Baganda, the vernacular *Basekabaka be Buganda* and *Ekitabo kye mpisa,* works that entered the canon of Ganda studies. Of equal long-term significance was Paulo Mboya's *Luo Kitgi gi Timbegi* (1938), a researched work on Luo history and culture that was strikingly original, being uninfluenced by the otherwise ubiquitous Christian missionary. D. O. Fagunwa's *Ogboju Ode* (1936), better known in its English translation as *The Forest of a Thousand Daemons: A Hunter's Saga* (1982), marked a high point in the orality/literacy dialectic, and its protagonist has remained, in Wole Soyinka's words, "a compound of spells" in the literary imagination, interrogating modernity "immanently." This work inspired, as did the equally famous *The Palm-Wine Drinkard and His Dead Palm-Wine Tapster in the*

Dead's Town (1952) by Amos Tutuola, generations of critics in west and east Africa. The most famous epic prose in an African language, Thomas Mofolo's *Chaka* (1925), sought to correct the image created by the Europeans of Shaka as the bloodthirsty Zulu tyrant. The African novel in English and French likewise initially took the form of "writing back," challenging the "conditioned imagination" and the inscriptions of colonial writers such as Joyce Cary and James Conrad, and counterfactualizing the colonialists' definitions of an Africa that was presumed to be dark and mute. Camara Laye's *L'enfant noir* (1953) and Chinua Achebe's *Things Fall Apart* (1958) both created an idealized picture of village Africa at the moment of its spoliation by the West, as did Ferdinand Oyono in *The Old Man and the Medal* (1969). In the hands of Ayi Kwei Armah, this idealization became transformed into a metaphysical vision of an Africa before the Europeans, a long history of harmony designated as "our way" in *Two Thousand Seasons* (1973) and in *Why Are We So Blest?* (1971).

The second stage of creative writing reflected the contradictory emotions provoked by the pull of Western education. Ngugi wa Thiong'o's early novels, *Weep Not, Child* (1964) and *The River Between* (1965), both wrestle with this contradiction, this desire for "civilization," as does Buchi Emecheta's *Head Above Water* (1984). The conflict between Western-influenced "civilizational values" and local mores are portrayed most clearly through the dialectical reasoning in Cheikh Hamidou Kane's *Ambiguous Adventure* (1969). The totality of the colonial project and the dialectical contradictions inherent in it is best captured in Sembène Ousmane's *Les bouts de bois de Dieu* (1960; published in English in 1962 as *God's Bits of Wood*), a novel staged in the 1940s which depicts a struggle for social change and a quest for a new social, political, and economic identity. But what has most engaged the postcolonial novelist has been state power, seen through the lenses of independence struggles that have been betrayed by the incumbent dictators and their supportive elites in a "season of anomie." Chinua Achebe's *Anthills of the Savannah* (1988) is a sensitive rendition of this postcoloniality among the many nationalist novels. Nuruddin Farah's novels—*From a Crooked Rib* (1970) and *Maps* (1986)—both design women as metaphors for male oppressive patriarchy and of the nation as it emerges from independence into living under dictatorship. The trope of double jeopardy is extended to include male and Islamic oppression in Mariama Ba's *Une si longue lettre* (1980; published in English in 1981 as *So Long a Letter*). The prostrate and latterly prostate nation awaiting its redemption is the paradigmatic analogy deployed by Ngugi wa Thiong'o in his postcolonial novels on Kenya—*A Grain of Wheat* (1967), *Petals of Blood* (1977), and *Matigari* (1989); Ngugi's overdetermined characters move in a Manichaean world of betrayal and capitalist evil on the one side, and selfless revolutionary correctness and socialist vision on the other. In contrast, the works of Nadine Gordimer complexify and enrich our understanding of the legacy of colonialism, in this case the perdition of apartheid, her gaze having been trained on a heady vision of what Gordimer herself saw as a South African society whirling and swaying through revolutionary change, a lived world of possibility in a promised land of error, explored through four decades of transition from innocence and guilt in *The Lying Days* (1953) to revolutionary commitment and "actions springing from emotion, knocking deliberation aside" in *My Son's Story* (1990).

A tradition of literary criticism has developed in the wake of this literary output, initially beholden to the Western canon although empathetic to the nationalist agenda, as seen in the writings of Emmanuel Obiechina, growing into the counter-Africanistic nativism of Chinweizu, later advocating Marxist perspectives, establishing the canons for criticism, and embracing the Black Atlantic. Analysis of the enormous range of black South African writing has yet to be carried beyond the prism, poison, and prison of apartheid lenses. Continentally, the frequent claims to an autonomous African literary theory remain unrealized.

Synthesis

Beyond protest, Wole Soyinka, Africa's leading humanist thinker, has urged intellectuals to regain the former conditions of mind through reeducation, a project whose aim is "self-apprehension" through a conscious reimmersion into the "deepest mythopoeic resources," that is, the endogenous cultural heritage, an act of self-retrieval into a newly articulated African identity. Isidore Okpewho has referred to the processualizing of this act as "conversing with" the culture. Soyinka makes explicit the philosophical grounds for this stance in his *Myth, Literature, and the African World*, a statement of the author's sense of history wherein, in the words of Abdulrazak Gurnah, he "sees history both as time past and as a dynamic myth contextualizing the present and the future." History becomes a social paradigm in Soyinka's works of tragic vision such as *The Interpreters* (1965), *Death and the King's Horseman* (1975), and *The Road* (1965), as well as in the embodiment of the political unconscious in his autobiographical narratives *Aké: The Years of Childhood* (1981), *Isara* (1990), and *Ibadan* (1994). Likewise, Soyinka has more than any other writer made the symbols of indigenous African mythology the basis of his poetry, as in the collection *Idanre and Other Poems* (1967) where the Yoruba god of iron, Ogun, becomes the revolutionary artist as protagonist.

The work of Ben Okri best signifies the movement of African literature beyond the cultural-national paradigm into the terrain of postcolonial theory. In both *The Famished Road* (1991) and *Songs of Enchantment* (1993), Okri comfortably enmeshes his education in the English of Europe, the writings of Amos Tutuola and D. O. Fagunwa, the consciousness of Yoruba oral-narrative forms, and the obvious enjoyment of Soyinka's virtuosity. He uses this multiple heritage in new ways when deploying an indigenous category of thought, *abiku*, the spirit child, to confront the contemporary Nigerian experience. In doing so he arrives at a literature that according to Margaret Cesair-Thompson, "presents the generative forces of *replacement* rather than the debilitating colonial legacy of *displacement* and therefore moves beyond the historical catalepsy which has marked so much of postcolonial writing" (p. 34). In conclusion, the crisis in the production of knowledge on and of Africa started with the encounter with European modernity. It must end with an exit from it. As the philosopher Paulin Hountondji wrote in 1995:

> First we have to appropriate, assimilate and make entirely ours, with lucidity and a critical mind, all the international heritage now available. . . . Secondly [we must] . . . reappropriate our own ancestral heritage and the creativity, adaptability and ability to innovate that made our ancestors what they were. This is not traditionalism but the exact opposite. (p. 9)

BIBLIOGRAPHY

Abdalaziz, Mohamed H. *Muyaka.* Kenya Literature Bureau. Nairobi, 1979.

Abimbola, Wande. *Ifa: An Exposition of Ifa Literary Corpus.* Ibadan, 1976.

Abun-Nasr, Jamil M. *The Tijaniyya: A Sufi Order in the Modern World.* London, 1965.

Ajayi, J. F. Ade. *Christian Missions in Nigeria, 1841–1891: The Making of a New Elite.* Evanston, Ill., 1965.

Alagoa, E. J. *A History of the Niger Delta: An Historical Interpretation of Ijo Oral Tradition.* Ibadan, 1972.

Allen, J. W. T. *Tendi: Six Examples of Swahili Classical Verse Form.* New York, 1971.

Andrzejewski, B. W., and I. M. Lewis. *Somali Poetry: An Introduction.* Oxford, 1964.

Appiah, Kwame A. *In My Father's House: Africa in the Philosophy of Culture.* New York, 1992.

Asante, Emmanuel. *Towards an African Theology of the Kingdom of God.* Lewiston, N.Y., 1995.

Babalola, S. A. *The Content and Form of Yoruba Ijala.* Oxford, 1966.

Barnes, Sandra T. *Patrons and Power: Creating a Political Community in Metropolitan Lagos.* Bloomington, Ind., 1986.

Barry, Boubacar. *Le royaume du Waalo: Le Sénégal avant la conquête.* Paris, 1972.

Bates, Robert H., V. Y. Mudimbe, and Jean O'Barr. *Africa and the Disciplines: The Contributions of Research in Africa to the Social Sciences and Humanities.* Chicago, 1993.

Beidelman, T. O. *Colonial Evangelism: A Socio-historical Study of an East African Mission at the Grassroots.* Bloomington, Ind., 1982.

Berry, Sara. *Fathers Work for Their Sons: Accumulation, Mobility, and Class Formation in an Extended Yoruba Community.* Berkeley, 1985.

Biebuyk, Daniel, and Kahombo C. Mateene, eds. and trans. *The Mwindo Epic from the Banyanga.* Berkeley, 1969.

Brenner, Louis. *West African Sufi: The Religious Heritage and Spiritual Search of Cerno Bokar Saalif Taal.* Berkeley, 1984.

Cesair-Thompson, Margaret. "Beyond the Postcolonial Novel: Ben Okri's *The Famished Road* and Its 'Abiku Traveller.'" *The Journal of Commonwealth and Comparative Literature* 31, no. 2 (1996): 33–45.

Chapman, Michael. *South African Literatures.* London, 1996.

Chinweizu, Onwuchekwa Jemie, and Ihechukwu Madubuike. *Toward the Decolonization of African Literature.* Washington, D.C., 1983.

Clark, J. P. *The Ozidi Saga.* Ibadan, 1977.

Cohen, David W., and E. S. Atieno Odhiambo. *Siaya: The Historical Anthropology of an African Landscape.* Athens, Ohio, 1989.

———. *Burying SM: The Politics of Knowledge and the Sociology of Power in Africa.* London, 1992.

Comaroff, Jean. *Body of Power, Spirit of Resistance: The Culture and History of a South African People.* Chicago, 1985.

Comaroff, Jean, and John Comaroff. *Of Revelation and Revolution: Christianity, Colonialism, and Consciousness in South Africa.* Chicago, 1991.

Comaroff, Jean, and John Comaroff, eds. *Modernity and Its Malcontents: Ritual and Power in Postcolonial Africa.* Chicago, 1993.

Cooper, Frederick. *Decolonization and African Society: The Labor Question in French and British Africa.* Cambridge, 1996.

Coquery-Vidrovitch, Catherine. *African Women: A Modern History*. Boulder, Colo., 1997.

Cruise O'Brien, Donal B. *The Mourides of Senegal: The Political and Economic Organization of an Islamic Brotherhood*. Oxford, 1971.

Curtin, Philip D. *The Atlantic Slave Trade: A Census*. Madison, Wisc., 1969.

———. *Economic Change in Precolonial Africa: Senegambia in the Era of the Slave Trade*. Madison, Wisc., 1975.

Deng, Francis M. *The Dinka and Their Songs*. Oxford, 1973.

———. *Dinka Folktales: African Stories from the Sudan*. New York, 1974.

Diop, Cheikh Anta. *The African Origin of Civilization: Myth or Reality*. Translated by Mercer Cook. Paris and New York, 1974.

Farsy, Abdallah S. *The Shafi'i Ulama of East Africa, ca. 1830–1970: A Hagiographical Account*. Madison, Wisc., 1989.

Feierman, Steven. *Peasant Intellectuals: Anthropology and History in Tanzania*. Madison, Wisc., 1990.

Fields, Karen E. *Revival and Rebellion in Colonial Central Africa*. Princeton, N.J., 1985.

Finnegan, Ruth. *Oral Literature in Africa*. London, 1970.

Gikandi, Simon. *Reading the African Novel*. London, 1987.

———. *Reading Chinua Achebe: Language and Ideology in Fiction*. London, 1991.

———. *Maps of Englishness: Writing Identity in the Culture of Colonialism*. New York, 1996.

Gurnah, Abdulrazak. *Essays on African Writing*. Volume 1, *A Re-evaluation*. Oxford, 1993.

Guyer, Jane I. *Money Matters: Instability, Values, and Social Payments in the Modern History of West African Communities*. London, 1995.

Gyekye, Kwame. *An Essay on African Philosophical Thought: The Akan Conceptual Scheme*. Cambridge, 1987.

Hackett, Rosalind I. J. *Religion in Calabar: The Religious Life and History of a Nigerian Town*. Berlin, 1989.

Hamilton, Caroline. *The Character and Objects of Chaka: A Reconsideration of the Making of Shaka as Mfecane "Motor."* Johannesburg, 1991.

Harries, Lyndon, ed. and trans. *Swahili Poetry*. Oxford, 1962.

Hiskett, Mervyn. *The Sword of Truth: The Life and Times of the Shehu Usuman dan Fodio*. New York, 1973.

———. *Some to Mecca Turn to Pray*. St. Albans, 1993.

———. *The Course of Islam in Africa*. Edinburgh, 1994.

Hoehler-Fatton, Cynthia. *Women of Fire and Spirit: History, Faith, and Gender in Roho Religion in Western Kenya*. New York, 1996.

Horton, Robin. *Patterns of Thought in Africa and the West: Essays on Magic, Religion, and Science*. Cambridge, 1993.

Hountondji, Paulin J. *African Philosophy: Myth and Reality*. Bloomington, Ind., 1983.

———. "Producing Knowledge in Africa Today." *African Studies Review* 38, no. 3 (1995): 1–10.

Hunwick, John O. *Sharia in Songhay: The Replies of al-Maghili to the Questions of Askia al-Hajj Muhammad*. London, 1985.

Iliffe, John. *Africans: The History of a Continent*. New York, 1995.

Inikori, Joseph E., and Stanley L. Engerman, eds. *The Atlantic Slave Trade: Effects on Economics, Societies, and Peoples in Africa, the Americas, and Europe*. Durham, N.C., 1992.

Irele, Abiola. *The African Experience in Literature and Ideology*. London, 1981.

Isichei, Elizabeth. *A History of Christianity in Africa: From Antiquity to the Present*. Grand Rapids, Mich., 1995.

Janz, Bruce. "Alterity, Dialogue, and African Philosophy." In *Postcolonial African Philosophy*, edited by Emmanuel C. Eze. Cambridge, Mass., 1997.

Johnson, John William, ed. and trans., and Fa-Digi Sisoko. *The Epic of Son-Jara: A West African Tradition*. Bloomington, Ind., 1986.

Jordan, A. C. *Towards an African Literature: The Emergence of Literary Forms in Xhosa*. Berkeley, 1973.

Kaba, Lansine. *The Wahhabiyya: Islamic Reform and Politics in French West Africa*. Evanston, Ill., 1974.

Kagame, Alexis. *La philosophie bantou comparée*. Paris, 1976.

Kaplan, Steven. *Fils d'Abraham: Les Falashas*. Turnhout, Belgium, 1990.

Karrar, Salih A. *The Sufi Brotherhoods in the Sudan*. Evanston, Ill., 1992.

Kriger, Norma J. *Zimbabwe's Guerrilla War: Peasant Voices*. Cambridge, 1992.

Kunene, Daniel P. *Heroic Poetry of the Basotho*. Oxford, 1971.

———. *Thomas Mofolo and the Emergence of Written Sesotho Prose*. Johannesburg, 1989.

Kunene, Mazisi. *Zulu Poems*. London, 1970.

———. *Emperor Shaka the Great: A Zulu Epic*. London, 1979.

Lan, David. *Guns and Rain: Guerrillas and Spirit Mediums in Zimbabwe*. London, 1985.

Last, Murray. *The Sokoto Caliphate*. New York, 1967.

Levtzion, Nehemia. *Muslims and Chiefs in West Africa: A Study of Islam in the Middle Volta Basin in the Pre-Colonial Period*. Oxford, 1968.

Levtzion, N., and J. F. P. Hopkins. *Corpus of Early Arabic Sources for West African History*. Cambridge, 1981.

Liyong, Taban Lo. *The Last Word: Cultural Synthesism*. Nairobi, 1969.

Lonsdale, J. M. *Unhappy Valley*. 2 vols. London, 1992.

MacGaffey, Wyatt. *Modern Kongo Prophets: Religion in a Plural Society*. Bloomington, Ind., 1983.

Manning, Patrick. *Slavery and African Life: Occidental, Oriental, and African Slave Trades*. Cambridge, 1990.

Marks, Shula, and Richard Rathbone, eds. *Industrialisation and Social Change in South Africa: African Class Formation, Culture, and Consciousness, 1870–1930*. New York, 1982.

Martin, B. G. *Muslim Brotherhoods in Nineteenth Century Africa*. Cambridge, 1976.

Martin, Phyllis M. *Leisure and Society in Colonial Brazzaville*. Cambridge, 1995.

Masolo, D. A. *African Philosophy in Search of Identity.* Bloomington, Ind., 1994.

McCaskie, T. C. *State and Society in Pre-Colonial Asante.* Cambridge, 1995.

Miller, Joseph C. *Way of Death: Merchant Capitalism and the Angolan Slave Trade, 1730–1830.* Madison, Wisc., 1988.

Molyneux, K. Gordon. *African Christian Theology: The Quest for Selfhood.* San Francisco, 1993.

Mudimbe, V. Y. *The Invention of Africa: Gnosis, Philosophy, and the Order of Knowledge.* Bloomington, Ind., 1988.

———. *Parables and Fables: Exegesis, Textuality, and Politics in Central Africa.* Madison, Wisc., 1991.

———. *The Idea of Africa.* Bloomington, Ind., 1994.

Mulago (Gwa Cikala), Vincent. *Une visage africain du christianisme.* Paris, 1956.

Nassir, Abdalla ibn Ali ibn. *Al-Inkishafi.* Nairobi, 1972.

Ngara, Emmanuel. *Stylistic Criticism and the African Novel: A Study of the Language, Art, and Content of African Fiction.* London, 1982.

———. *Art and Ideology in the African Novel: A Study of the Influence of Marxism on African Writing.* London, 1985.

———. *Ideology and Form in African Poetry: Implications for Communication.* London, 1990.

———. *New Writing from South Africa: Authors Who Have Become Prominent Since 1980.* Portsmouth, N.H., 1996.

Niane, Djibril Tamsir. *Soundjata; ou, L'épopée mandingue.* Paris, 1960.

Nkrumah, Kwame. *Consciencism: Philosophy and Ideology for Decolonization and Development with Particular Reference to the African Revolution.* London, 1970.

Obiechina, Emmanuel. *Culture, Tradition, and Society in the West African Novel.* Cambridge, 1975.

———. *Language and Theme: Essays on African Literature.* Washington, D.C., 1990.

Ogot, Bethwell A. *History of the Southern Luo.* Volume 1, *Migration and Settlement.* Nairobi, 1967.

Okot p'Bitek. *Song of Lawino: A Lament.* Nairobi, 1968.

———. *African Religions in Western Scholarship.* Nairobi, 1971.

———. *The Horn of My Love.* London, 1974.

———. *Hare and Hornbill.* London, 1978.

Okpewho, Isidore. *The Epic in Africa: Toward a Poetics of the Oral Performance.* New York, 1979.

———. *Myth in Africa: A Study of Its Aesthetic and Cultural Relevance.* Cambridge, 1983.

———. *African Oral Literature: Backgrounds, Character, and Continuity.* Bloomington, Ind., 1992.

Oliver, Roland. *Africa and Africans.* London, 1991.

Oloruntimehin, B. O. *The Segu Tukulor Empire.* London, 1972.

Omer-Cooper, J. D. *The Zulu Aftermath: A Nineteenth-Century Revolution in Bantu Africa.* Evanston, Ill., 1966.

Oruka, H. Odera. *Sage Philosophy: Indigenous Thinkers and Modern Debate on African Philosophy.* Leiden, 1990.

Osa, Osayimwense. *African Children's and Youth Literature.* New York, 1995.

Paden, John N. *Ahmadu Bello, Sardauna of Sokoto: Values and Leadership in Nigeria.* London, 1986.

Parrat, John. *Reinventing Christianity: African Theology Today.* Trenton, N.J., 1995.

Quayson, Ato. "Wole Soyinka and Autobiography as Political Unconscious." *Journal of Commonwealth Literature* 31, no. 2 (1996): 19–32.

Ranger, Terrence. *Are We Not Also Men?: The Samkange Family and African Politics in Zimbabwe, 1920–1964.* Harare, 1995.

Ricard, Alain. *Literatures d'Afrique noire: Des langues aux livres.* Paris, 1995.

Robinson, David. *The Holy War of Umar Tal: The Western Sudan in the Mid-Nineteenth Century.* New York, 1985.

Samatar, Said S. *Oral Poetry and Somali Nationalism: The Case of Sayyid Mahammad Abdille Hassan.* Cambridge, 1982.

Sanneh, Lamin O. *The Jakhanke: The History of an Islamic Clerical People of the Senegambia.* London, 1979.

———. *Translating the Message: The Missionary Impact on Culture.* Maryknoll, N.Y., 1989.

———. *Encountering the West: Christianity and the Global Cultural Process.* Maryknoll, N.Y., 1993.

———. *Piety and Power: Muslims and Christians in West Africa.* Maryknoll, N.Y., 1996.

Schoffeleers, J. M., ed. *Guardians of the Land: Essays on Central African Territorial Cults.* Salisbury, 1978.

Senghor, Léopold Sédar. *The Collected Poetry.* Translated by Melvin Dixon. Charlottesville, Va., 1991.

Serequeberhan, Tsenay. *The Hermeneutics of African Philosophy: Horizon and Discourse.* New York, 1994.

Shank, David A. *Prophet Harris, the "Black Elijah" of West Africa.* Abridged by Jocelyn Murray. Leiden, 1994.

Soyinka, Wole. *Myth, Literature, and the African World.* Cambridge, 1976.

Sundkler, Bengt. *Bantu Prophets in South Africa.* 2d ed. London, 1961.

Tamrat, Taddesse. *Church and State in Ethiopia, 1270–1527.* Oxford, 1972.

Ter Haar, Gerrie. *Spirit of Africa: The Healing Ministry of Archbishop Milingo of Zambia.* London, 1992.

Thornton, John K. *The Kingdom of Kongo: Civil War and Transition, 1641–1718.* Madison, Wisc., 1983.

Van Onselen, Charles. *The Seed Is Mine: The Life of Kas Maine, a South African Sharecropper, 1894–1985.* New York, 1996.

Vansina, Jan. *Oral Tradition as History.* Madison, Wisc., 1985.

———. *Paths in the Rainforests: Toward a History of Political Tradition in Equatorial Africa.* Madison, Wisc., 1990.

Vaughan, Megan. *Curing Their Ills.* Cambridge, 1991.

White, Landeg. *Magomero: Portrait of an African Village.* Cambridge, 1987.

White, Luise. *The Comforts of Home: Prostitution in Colonial Nairobi.* Chicago, 1990.

Wilks, Ivor. *Asante in the Nineteenth Century: The Structure and Evolution of a Political Order.* London, 1975.

Willis, Justin. *Mombasa, the Swahili, and the Making of the Mijikenda.* Oxford, 1993.

Wiredu, Kwasi. *Philosophy and an African Culture.* Cambridge, 1980.

E. S. ATIENO-ODHIAMBO

NATURAL AND PHYSICAL SCIENCES

In his only surviving book, *The Meadows of Gold and Mines of Gems,* Abu al-Hasan al-Masudi narrated his sea journey in about the year 925 C.E. down the east African coast on "the sea of the Zanj" (the sea of the black people), which was much later renamed the Indian Ocean. In vivid terms he described the Kingdom of the Zanj, ruled by the Waqlimi, who was the supreme lord, the king of kings. The kingdom of the Waqlimi had established an enabling environment for international trade in technology-oriented industrial goods more than a millennium before al-Masudi's time. Al-Masudi's narrative demonstrated that the kingdom extended as far south as the State of Sofala, on the coast of present-day Mozambique, as well as that gold, ivory, and iron were the key items of the then-flourishing export trade. More than two centuries later, in 1154 C.E., the Andalusian historian al-Idrisi, then living in Sicily, observed that Indonesians regularly visited the State of Sofala in order to purchase smelted iron, "which they carry to the continent of India and sell . . . there at a good price, for this iron is a material of big trade and consumption in India." In return, the merchants of Sofala were sold white cottons, red cottons, porcelain, and copper. The State of Sofala acted as the maritime point of commodity exchange for the inland kingdoms of stone-built Zimbabwe, which ruled western Mozambique and extended westward into what is the present-day Republic of Zimbabwe.

These cosmopolitan and vibrant economic relations were shattered half a millennium later, at the beginning of the seventeenth century, when able-bodied captives from Africa became the basis of a large and increasing commodity trade for the next three centuries. Other systems of trade, patterned on international commercial exchange of technological goods which had plied for centuries around the Sea of the Zanj and the well-worn trade routes across the Sahara Desert, were snuffed out amid recurring raids for captives and periodic punitive wars against resisting kings. This profoundly dark age was largely ended only in the 1950s and 1960s as a result of the post–World War II national and pan-African movements for political independence. Thus, for a period of approximately four hundred years, Africa south of the Sahara had seen

its political peace, social tranquility, and economic base violated, trampled under, and subjected completely to alien control.

The price paid by Africa has been horrendous: civilization, and its associated technological innovations and incremental economic growth, became immediately frozen, and it then progressively regressed to the extent that the world at large, and latterly Africa itself, has tended to believe that Africa never had a heritage in science, technology, and indigenous art. Conveniently forgotten, for example, is that the first known sculpture of exceptional character and quality was practiced on an almost industrial scale in Ife, Nigeria, in the fifth or fourth century B.C.E.; that the western Sudanic savanna of the Sahel region has seen the sequential rise of great empires and civilizations, having their own cosmopolitan centers of learning, such as the Kingdom of Awkar and the Empire of Ghana (from the sixth to thirteenth centuries C.E.); that the Kingdom of Mali had a center of advanced mathematics, science, and learning in Timbuktu (from the thirteenth to fifteenth centuries); that the Songhai Empire had a center of advanced learning in Gao (in the fifteenth and sixteenth centuries); and that the Yoruba, in present-day western Nigeria, had established an international reputation for robust trading enterprise, metalworks, and sculpturing in terra-cotta and bronze. The eastern and southern continental regions had analogously well-endowed civilizations, stretching for close to two millennia until the start of the great cataclysm of African civilization around 1600.

The four-hundred-year gap in the growth of African civilization and, by implication, in advanced study, research, scientific discoveries, and technological innovations—at exactly the period when northwestern Europe (and European emigrants) was aggressively making advances in science and technology which would incrementally change humanity's concept of its place in the scheme of nature—profoundly derailed the subcontinent from its own path of scientific and technological endeavors, its international trade in industrial goods, and the building and nurturing of its own international centers of discovery and knowledge. In the latter sphere, the subcontinent fell behind, particularly in the natural sciences.

The theme of this article is the state of research and knowledge of the natural and physical sciences in contemporary Africa south of the Sahara. For this vast subcontinent, with forty-four nation-states, a great range of economies, and approximately three thousand languages, it is not possible in a short narrative to provide more than a snapshot of the present-day status of each of the major branches of the natural and physical sciences, and of the subcontinent's degree of success in shifting from the former colonial powers' agendas to those of the newly independent nation-states.

The Colonial Science and Technology System

During the heyday of foreign imperial power in the first half of the twentieth century, the countries of the subcontinent—other than the nominally independent states of Ethiopia, Liberia, and the then Dominion of South Africa—cooperated scientifically with the science and technology institutions of the metropolitan powers. There was, in contrast, an insignificant degree of inter-African scientific cooperation, except among areas located within the same colonial jurisdiction, such as the Belgian zone (present-day Democratic Republic of the Congo, Burundi, and Rwanda), or the French central African zone (present-day Congo, Gabon, the Central African Republic, Cameroon, and Chad), and the British southern African zone (present-day South Africa, Namibia, Botswana, Lesotho, and Swaziland).

The nature of the scientific work consisted predominantly of adapting known technologies designed and developed in Europe for the production in Africa of large quantities of low-priced basic commodities for industrial processing in Europe, whether agricultural and forest products, marine fish products, raw minerals, or crude vegetable and mineral oils. For instance, an enterprise which had enormous support from the colonial powers was botanical exploration of the tropics. The eighteenth and nineteenth centuries became known as "an era of economic botany, when the usefulness of new plants to the nation's economy was prominent in the minds of all but the purest taxonomist. Every plant was being scrutinized for its use as food, fibre, timber, dye or medicine" (Vernon H. Heywood in *Systematic Botany*, 1988). In this respect the Royal Botanical Gardens at Kew (England), Leiden (the Netherlands), and Paris (France) played a central role as the anchor stations for the planning and coordination of the expeditions, subsequent research, follow-up agronomic and breeding work on the selected plant species, and overall economic evaluation of their value for plantation production in the tropics and subsequent processing in Europe. The intellectual by-products of such long-term missions—taxonomic monographs, plant guides and directories, plant atlases, and national and regional floras—are classical outcomes of these venturesome endeavors. In this genre several major works were published in the nineteenth and early twentieth centuries as repositories of economic intelligence data as well as floristic information for the discerning botanist, phytogeographer, and evolutionist: *The Flora of Tropical Africa; Flora Capensis; Flora of West Tropical Africa; Die Blütenpflanzen Afrikas; Flore du Congo Belge et du Ruanda-Urundi; Flora of Tropical East Africa;* and others.

A second focus area of science and technology in the colonial period was the earth sciences, as opposed to the purely physical sciences. This area can be forcefully illustrated with the scientific work of what later became known as the Geological Survey of Nigeria (GSN) which, as early as 1903, began a detailed exploration of the territory's mineral wealth. A major find in the early years, from 1903 to 1913, was the discovery of the Enugu coalfields in northern Nigeria. In 1928 the GSN began the exploration and exploitation of groundwater, down to a depth of 100 meters. Oil prospecting companies arrived in the territory in 1937 and greatly accelerated exploration, which had previously been undertaken by government geologists. These explorations continued at the end of the twentieth century, with many of the foremost university geophysicists participating directly, beginning with the University of Ibadan's establishment of its Department of Petroleum Engineering in 1972. Several universities of technology, founded in Nigeria beginning in the early 1980s, have made mining engineering and associated technologies a central feature of their curricula.

Inter-African cooperation in science and technology began in the early 1950s, by the then-metropolitan powers—Belgium, France, Portugal, and the United Kingdom—acting together with two of the then dominion-type administrations in Africa (the Federation of Rhodesia and Nyasaland, and the Union of South Africa). They initiated intergovernmental planning steps that eventually led to the establishment in 1950 of the Commission for Technical Co-operation in Africa South of the Sahara (CCTA), with its headquarters in London, for mutual assistance in science and technology among governmental entities. A parallel initiative among scientists from these same six countries led to the creation in the same year of the Scientific Council for Africa South of the Sahara (CSA), with its headquarters in Bukavu, Democratic Republic of the Congo, for cooperation in science and technology among practicing scientists. The two organizations worked closely together, with the CSA acting as the principal scientific advisory body to the CCTA, especially in regard to policy development and implementation, while the CCTA became the managerial executive and financial authority. Within this framework, and on the basis of the CCTA Establishment Agreement signed in London in January 1954, all the existing regional science and technology establishments were placed under the CSA umbrella: the Inter-African Bureau of Epizootic Diseases; the Tsetse Fly and Trypanosomiasis Permanent Inter-African Bureau; the Inter-African Bureau for Soils and Rural Economy; the Inter-African Labour Institute; and the Inter-African Pedological Service. Provision was made for other institutions to be added subsequently.

The philosophy undergirding the establishment of the CCTA was informed by the fragmentation of the subcontinent into small states whose autonomous development in the fields of science and technology needed strong cross-border cooperation and networking. This was highlighted by E. B. Worthington's seminal book for the CCTA, *Science in the Development of Africa* (1958):

> In the competitive world of the 20th century, it is difficult for any small country to be independent of its neighbours and at the same time provide the requirements of modern civilization for its people, unless it is unusually well endowed with natural and human resources. This principle has special force in Africa where local conditions have led to economic specialization, not merely in one major industry such as agriculture and mining, but in particular sections of it, such as cotton, cocoa or copper. Any measures of pooling the resources of neighbouring countries with different specialities lead to all-round advantages in reducing the economic risks. As in economics, so in science, considerable specialization has taken place in different territories, so that collaboration, or even a full exchange of information, could give great benefits. (p. 3)

To further implement the concept of cooperation and networking in science and technology, and in anticipation of geopolitical changes caused by the accelerating continental movement toward wholesale political independence, the CCTA at its seventeenth session held in Abidjan, Côte d'Ivoire, in February 1962, and the CSA the same year at its thirteenth meeting held in Mugaga, Kenya, decided, first, to drop the words "South of the Sahara" from the full title of the commission; second, to initiate negotiations for entry into the CCTA and CSA of the noncolonized states in the subcontinent (Ethiopia, Sudan, and Togo) and of the countries in north Africa which had been left out of the original CCTA constitution; and third, to cease all relations with Portugal (the last active colonial power) and the Union of South Africa. Thus, the whole continent of Africa, with the sole exception of apartheid South Africa, came under the umbrella of CCTA and CSA. In the words of the CCTA, expressed in its strategic paper on inter-African cooperation in 1992, "CCTA, an instrument of African solidarity, is likewise a bridge between Europe's science and Africa's needs. There are other, wider bridges which may carry more traffic, but the one built and maintained by the Commission will remain open whatever political fluctuations may occur."

Among the issues dealt with by the First Ordinary Session of the Council of Ministers of the newly established pan-African geopolitical organization, the Organization of African Unity (OAU), held in Dakar, Senegal, in August 1963, was the future of the CCTA. While affirming the continued need for "health, sanitation, and nutritional cooperation" and "scientific and technical cooperation" so as "to coordinate and intensify their cooperation and effort to achieve a better life for the peoples of Africa," the council decided immediately to transform the CCTA into the OAU Scientific, Technical and Research Commission (STRC), and the CSA into the OAU Scientific Council of Africa (SCA), with virtually the same mandates as previously, although their separate headquarters were moved in 1964 to Lagos, Nigeria, and Addis Ababa, Ethiopia, respectively.

The promise that STRC and SCA evinced at the beginning of their new Africa-centered transformation in 1964 has not been realized to any extent: the hope of these organizations becoming the bridge between Europe's science and Africa's needs has not been assiduously cultivated, nor have these institutions made a manifest mark on achieving a better life for African people. This is in spite of the fact that Africa remains the world's last frontier in science and technology and is overdue for indigenous initiative and external assistance for development. All the science and technology indicators for Africa during the three decades since the creation of the STRC and SCA demonstrate clearly that overall achievements and related budgetary support for science and technology are growing rapidly, but are still grossly inadequate for Africa's own needs and in comparison with other regions of the world, or even with other developing regions.

Baseline Science and Technology Indicators

Science and technology indicators have been characterized in UNESCO's *World Science Report 1996* as "quantitative units of measurement of the parameters defining the status and dynamics of research and technology systems." Such indicators are important yardsticks with which to review national science policymaking, as part of strategic analysis by decision makers of the scientific research and technological development institutions, and for those planning for their nations' industrial production and supporting resources, such as human capital, financial resources, and physical infrastructure. Although none of the science and technology indicators currently in use are perfect, they are widely employed as approximate measures for comparative purposes between nations and regions, and as planning instruments for science-led national development.

Three science and technology indicators are commonly employed the world over. The first is the measurement of research and development expenditure and professional scientific staff. The second indicator is the measurement of scientific production. It monitors the number of scientific publications (what has come to be known as "science bibliometry"), taking them as one of the basic products of scientific work. It is calculated from the databases of the Science Citation Index and Compumath, both founded by the Philadelphia-based Institute for Scientific Information, which indexes some 3,500 scientific journals in eight disciplines. But it is to be noted that this particular indicator is biased against developing countries, because the journals published by the industrialized countries, and those published in English, are overrepresented in these databases. The third indicator is the measurement of technological production. It monitors patents (hence "patent bibliometry"), which reflect the level of inventiveness and creativity in technology for competitive industrial production. This indicator is imperfect, however, as its raw data are derived only from patents registered in the two principal "open markets" of the United States and Europe (the combined European Union and the European Free Trade Area); further, it tells nothing of technological fields in which no patents are granted (such as those derived from indigenous knowledge systems). Even though the three science and technology indicators are imperfect when taken separately, they have meaning when considered together.

One generation after the onset of political independence in sub-Saharan Africa, the subcontinent was in a dismal situation in regard to all the science and technology indicators (as estimated in 1992–1993). The subcontinent scored very poorly relative to all other regions (other than north Africa), including west Asia and Latin America, in the gross volume of funds devoted to research and development (R & D), even when these are considered as a proportion of the gross domestic product (GDP), as shown in table 1. Similarly, the subcontinent suffers from a relatively low number of research and development scientists and engineers; indeed, there are only four of these specialists per ten thousand population—a position analogous to that in Latin America, Asia, and the Middle East except for the newly industrializing countries (NICs), where the proportion is nearly four times that number (table 2). On the other hand, brain drain is a major crisis for the subcontinent: about 6 percent of the students from the subcontinent study abroad, the highest number of any region except Israel (table 3). Many of these students never return. Yet the subcontinent receives very few students from other regions.

The subcontinent's share of the entire world's scientific production was a mere 0.8 percent in 1993, and it had hardly increased from a decade before (table 4). On the other hand, when one disaggregates this production into broad disciplines, the subcontinent shows manifest comparative strength in biology, clinical medicine, and earth and space sciences (table 5). The major technological capabilities, according to the patents registered in the United States and Europe, predominate in the United States, Europe, and Japan. The NICs are beginning to be significant players, but all other regions play a negligible role (table 6).

It is a truism that in sub-Saharan Africa, women traditionally are educators and transmitters of traditional values and customary norms. Therefore, if Africa's economic and social development is going to be truly science led, it is pivotal that science and technology become, once again, part and parcel of African culture all the way from the household level. Yet contemporary African women are severely disadvantaged in the science field: teachers' attitude toward girls enrolled in scientific disciplines, and the girls' own attitude toward the study of science, are negative; they regard science as a male domain. Consequently, it is not surprising that of the large number of students enrolled in the natural sciences in universities in Ethiopia, Kenya, and Zimbabwe, only 6 percent, 15 percent, and 19 percent, respectively, are female. Nor is it surprising that of the lecturers in the science faculties in ten selected universities (of Botswana, Ghana, Ibadan,

TABLE 1. Gross Domestic Expenditure on Research and Development (GERD), Gross Domestic Product (GDP), and GERD/GDP Ratio for Sub-Saharan Africa in Comparison with Other Areas of the World, 1992

	GERD* (calculated in purchasing power parity; GERD measures all sources of finance combined, including those from abroad)	GDP* (calculated in current purchasing power parity)	GERD/GDP Ratio (%)
Sub-Saharan Africa	1.09	245	0.4
North Africa	0.72	160	0.4
Middle East and Near East	3.11	598	0.5
United States	167.01	5,953	2.8
European Union	117.67	6,079	1.9
Latin America	3.93	1,063	0.4
Japan	68.31	2,437	2.8
Newly Industrializing Countries	10.73	824	1.3
China	22.24	3,155	0.7
India	7.10	940	0.8
WORLD TOTAL	428.58	24,295	1.8

* In U.S. $1.0 billion.

SOURCE: Modified from Pierre Papon and Rémi Barré, "Science and Technology Systems: A Global Overview," in *World Science Report, 1996,* Paris, 1996, p. 13.

TABLE 2. R & D Scientists and Engineers and Population Ratios for Sub-Saharan Africa and Other Areas of the World, 1992

	R & D Scientists and Engineers (thousands)	Population (millions)	R & D Scientists and Engineers per 1,000 Population
Sub-Saharan Africa	176.8	482.6	0.4
North Africa	81.6	219.7	0.4
Middle East and Near East	117.4	465.9	0.3
United States	949.3	257.5	3.7
European Union	740.9	369.0	2.0
Latin America	158.5	464.6	0.3
Japan	511.4	124.8	4.1
Newly Industrializing Countries	136.7	92.5	1.5
China	391.1	1,205.0	0.3
India	106.0	887.7	0.1
WORLD TOTAL	4,334.1	5,563.1	0.8

SOURCE: Modified from Pierre Papon and Rémi Barré, "Science and Technology Systems: A Global Overview," in *World Science Report, 1996,* Paris, 1996, p. 14.

TABLE 3. International Mobility of Students from Sub-Saharan Africa and Other Regions of the World, 1992

	Total Student Population (thousands)	Students Studying Abroad (thousands)	Proportion of Students Abroad (%)
Sub-Saharan Africa	1,393	84	6.0
North Africa	1,834	90	4.9
Middle East and Near East	3,407	153	4.5
Israel	149	23	15.4
United States	14,556	25	0.2
European Union	10,740	232	2.2
Latin America	7,715	73	1.0
Japan	2,918	55	1.9
Newly Industrializing Countries	2,581	132	5.1
China	2,302	129	5.6
India	4,936	43	0.9
WORLD TOTAL	68,408	1,354	2.0

SOURCE: Modified from Pierre Papon and Rémi Barré, "Science and Technology Systems: A Global Overview," in *World Science Report, 1996,* Paris, 1996, p. 22.

Lesotho, Malawi, Nairobi, Swaziland, Tanzania, Zambia, and Zimbabwe), only 12.3 percent are female, of the senior lecturers only 9.6 percent are female, while among the professors a mere 3.8 percent are women. A profound change needs to be brought about in the subcontinent by creating an institutional framework to build up and maintain a strong human capital base, including a rapidly increasing female component.

Human Capacity and Institution Building

It may be instructive to highlight three case studies to indicate both the deep structural problems as well as the enormous human-resource potential in the natural sciences in sub-Saharan Africa today. Two of the case studies pertain to two of Africa's oldest nation-states, Ethiopia and South Africa, with the focus on botanical research and university training in the sciences, respectively. The third case study will focus on research and human-capacity building at the doctoral level in tropical insect science at an Africa-initiated center of research and training excellence, the International Centre of Insect Physiology and Ecology (ICIPE), established in April 1970 and based in Nairobi, Kenya.

Botanical Research, Ethiopia

Taxonomic botany is the philosophy and practice of naming, classifying, and documenting plant data and retrieving it so that it is available for research, economic, pharmacological, natural products chemistry, or plant-breeding purposes. The study of taxonomic botany is basic to any advance in the production and utilization of plants and is especially important in the tropics, where the great majority of plants originate. It is no surprise, then, that there exists a vast corpus of indigenous knowl-

TABLE 4. Scientific Production in Sub-Saharan Africa and Other Areas of the World, Measured by Publications, 1993

	World Share 1993 (%)
Sub-Saharan Africa	0.8
North Africa	0.4
Middle East and Near East	0.6
United States	35.3
European Union	31.5
Latin America	1.5
Japan	8.1
Newly Industrializing Countries	1.4
China	1.2
India	2.1
WORLD TOTAL	100

SOURCE: Modified from Pierre Papon and Rémi Barré, "Science and Technology Systems: A Global Overview," in *World Science Report, 1996,* Paris, 1996, p. 15.

TABLE 5. Scientific Production per Discipline in Sub-Saharan Africa and Other Regions of the World, 1993

	Sub-Saharan Africa (%)	North America (%)	Latin America (%)	Europe (%)	Newly Industrializing Countries and Japan (%)
Biology	2.1	43.6	2.5	31.5	7.6
Clinical Medicine	1.2	41.4	1.3	41.0	8.1
Earth and Space Sciences	1.2	45.5	2.1	32.7	4.1
Mathematics	0.6	39.7	1.6	38.0	6.3
Biomedical Research	0.5	44.9	1.3	36.9	9.5
Chemistry	0.5	27.9	1.3	36.9	14.0
Engineering Sciences	0.4	44.0	0.9	29.6	12.6
Physics	0.3	32.8	1.9	34.4	11.7
ALL DISCIPLINES	0.8	39.8	1.5	36.5	9.5

SOURCE: Modified from Pierre Papon and Rémi Barré, "Science and Technology Systems: A Global Overview," in *World Science Report, 1996,* Paris, 1996, p. 16.

edge on tropical African plants, their roles in the ecosystem, and their uses in food, nutrition, medicine, and other utilitarian purposes. But their formal study in situ in the tropics is very recent. In Ethiopia the first formal phytotaxonomic work by an indigenous Ethiopian was undertaken in 1962 by Tekle H. Hagos on the leguminous genus *Parkia*. There immediately followed a very active period of Ethiopian taxonomic research and publication by Amare Getahum in 1974 on common medicinal and poisonous plants used in Ethiopian folk medicine; by Tadesse Ebba in 1975 on the Ethiopian indigenous cereal, teff (*Eragrostis tef*); and by Getachew Aweke in 1979 on the revision of the genus *Ficus* (family Moraceae). It soon became apparent that there was a paramount need for good taxonomic studies to underpin ecological research and conservation work within Ethiopia.

TABLE 6. Technological Production in Sub-Saharan Africa and Other Regions of the World, Measured by Patents Granted in Europe and USA, 1993

	1993 World Share, European Patents (%)	1993 World Share, U.S. Patents (%)
Sub-Saharan Africa	0.1	0.1
North Africa	0.0	0.0
Middle East and Near East	0.0	0.0
United States	27.3	48.7
European Union	45.4	18.6
Latin America	0.1	0.2
Japan	20.9	25.0
Newly Industrializing Countries	0.5	1.3
China	0.0	0.1
India	0.0	0.0
WORLD TOTAL	100	100

SOURCE: Modified from Pierre Papon and Rémi Barré, "Science and Technology Systems: A Global Overview," in *World Science Report, 1996,* Paris, 1996, p. 17.

As a consequence, the Ethiopian Flora Project (EFP), which had been brought up for discussion in 1970 at a congress in Munich, Germany, of systematic botanists of the Association pour l'Étude Taxonomique de la Flore d'Afrique Tropicale (AETFAT), was actually launched in April 1980.

The EFP, which is expected to embrace some six thousand to seven thousand flowering plant species and to publish eight volumes, has already established a National Herbarium based at the biology department of Addis Ababa University (AAU) and has close working relations with other older, specialized herbaria within Ethiopia (at the Alemaya University of Agriculture, the Institute of Agricultural Research, the Forestry and Wildlife Training Institute at Wondo Genet, and the International Livestock Research Institute in Addis Ababa). The project is a truly functional multinational partnership, with four working stations: Addis Ababa (at AAU's biology department, its lead institution, where the deputy project leader is based); Asmara, Eritrea (at the University of Asmara, where the project leader, an Eritrean, is located); the Royal Botanic Gardens, Kew, England (for comparative taxonomic studies); and Uppsala, Sweden (at the Department of Systematic Botany, Uppsala University, for major taxonomic research and postgraduate training, and where the European coordinator is based). The supporting funds for the EFP, which is regarded as long term, are jointly provided by the Ethiopian government and the Swedish Department of Research for Cooperation with Developing Countries (SAREC). The EFP has continued uninterruptedly, even during the long years of civil war in Ethiopia.

Postgraduate training, mostly at the doctoral level, has from the very beginning of the EFP been an integral and vital component of the entire partnership project. Trainees do their fieldwork in Ethiopia and Eritrea, while the postgraduate degree is completed in Swedish and Danish universities. Shortly, by the end of the project, both Ethiopia and Eritrea will possess a far better institutional and human capital base in systematic botany than any other African country and may well begin to be competitive with most developed countries in this field, whose attraction is dimming in the face of the escalating interest in molecular biology.

University Training in the Sciences, South Africa

The contrast of progress in Ethiopia and Eritrea with the capacity of South Africa's indigenous Africans in science and technology could not be more stark. On the eve of the historic emergence of a democratic South Africa in May 1994, a searching science and technology policy mission established in 1992–1993 to design a nationwide, people-sensitive scientific research and service organization for national development found that the republic's policy formulation for science and technology was a very selective process, serving what the senior science and technology officials termed "the first world" within South Africa to the exclusion of its "third world," that it served to buttress the apartheid regime, and therefore that it was captive to South Africa's strategic and military interests.

> Where else but in South Africa could one find a state that had created 15 parallel departments of education, 15 departments of health, and 14 departments of agriculture under the guise of giving different groups responsibility for their "own affairs," while systematically depriving all but one racial group of adequate resources to manage those affairs. (*Building a New South Africa*, vol. 3, *Science and Technology Policy*, 1995, p. 1)

The implicit assumptions held by many South African scientists and countered by the mission were that science and technology developments are apolitical, that science and technology policy is a technical subject, and that only the best research and development institutions should be awarded research grants. Such assumptions ignored the importance of science and technology for development, which requires that crucial social and economic problems of the nation as a whole be tackled and that unrealized talents of the majority of citizens be utilized.

In this context South Africa sees its tertiary educational system compartmentalized into two broad groups: "historically white universities" (HWUs), with almost entirely white faculties and a smattering of black students, and "historically black universities" (HBUs), with all-race faculties and largely black student bodies. While the HWUs have all the usual faculties expected of a modern university and attract the lion's share of research funding allocated on the basis of excellence, the HBUs tend to have only some of the faculties, mostly of the humanities and arts. Only one HBU has a faculty of engineering, and the HBUs have a low success rate in attracting competitive research funding. These disparaties in research funding are huge, as can be surmised from table 7.

TABLE 7. Research Support in South African Universities, 1993, in Rand (Millions), with Exchange Rate of U.S. $1.00 = 3.4 South African Rand

| | Sources of Research Funding (Million Rand) | | | | |
	Government	Tertiary Sector	Business Sector	Foundation and Foreign	Total
Natural Sciences					
HBUs	0.5	21.9	1.2	0	23.6
HWUs	50.5	212.6	42.5	1.0	306.6
Human Sciences					
HBUs	0.5	14.3	0.2	0	15.0
HWUs	4.7	110.7	7.8	1.6	124.8

SOURCE: Modified from International Development Research Centre, *Building a New South Africa*, vol. 3, *Science and Technology Policy*, Ottawa, 1995, p. 41.

Equally, there are utter distortions in the enrollment in tertiary education, especially among those opting for the sciences. For every ten thousand children entering first grade, only twenty-seven receive the matriculation exemption necessary to enter a university, and only one will gain entry into science, mathematics, or engineering programs. Transforming this reality to one which generally reflects the true science potential in South Africa is going to take time, tremendous interracial goodwill, and a prodigious amount of effort, just what the rest of the subcontinent has realized in comparison to the situation in the developed, industrialized nations.

Research in Tropical Insect Science

The third case study is related to a unique network created for three-year postgraduate studies at the doctoral level, designed and partnered by the ICIPE. This network links hands-on project work and postgraduate coursework, on the one hand, and on the other hand, a group of twenty-two participating universities in west, east, and southern Africa. The universities select the students, examine them, and award them doctoral degrees on successfully passing the thesis project and examinations.

The program stemmed from a recognition of the central role of insect science in the bioeconomy of the African tropical ecosystems, as well as the burgeoning need for such specialists in national and regional scientific institutions and university establishments. Insect science comprises all scientific disciplines that impinge directly on insects as the objects of study, including taxonomy, functional morphology, behavior, physiology, bio-chemistry, molecular biology, chemical ecology, genetics, ecology, evolution, population management, insect-host relations, parasitology, and population biostatistics. The ensuing dialogue, which included representatives of African universities, Africa-based research institutions, and international partners, resulted in the convening of the International Conference on Postgraduate Education in Insect Science, held at the Rockefeller Foundation Bellagio Study and Conference Centre at Lake Como, Italy, in 1981. The pivotal and immediate product of this Bellagio Conference was the establishment in 1983 of the African Regional Postgraduate Programme in Insect Science (ARPPIS), based at the ICIPE, but encompassing many African universities in an interactive network.

From 1983 to 1993, the ARPPIS graduated ninety-five Ph.D.s, all of them working in Africa, and all of them leaders in their own specialties. This novel collaborative mechanism for postgraduate education, which brings out the best of scientific talent in the graduates, and at the same time confirms them in their scientific commitment to Africa, is well worth emulating in other fields of the natural and physical sciences.

Summary of Key Factors for Success

In both the Ethiopian Flora Project and the ARPPIS doctoral program, a few key factors appear to have been at play to make these two novel approaches so innovative and so effective. First, each of the capacity-building projects has established a clear measurable goal for a major identified need, to be implemented within a workable time frame. Second, each project has created an enthusiastic, home-grown intellectual environment that can be sustained indefinitely by committed scientific leadership, functioning within an enabling geopolitical climate. Third, each project established a strong regional and international network of partnerships in the defined specific area of concern. Fourth, supporting funds have been mobilized to energize each of the projects over a medium-term perspective. Thoughtful leaders in the subcontinent should be capable of employing these and related factors to amplify these success stories in other scientific endeavors.

The beginnings of such noteworthy advances may be found in several new research and development institutions that have sprouted on the subcontinent since the 1960s. In a survey titled *Profiles of African Scientific Institutions* (1992), published by the African Academy of Sciences, 186 institutions in thirty-six countries have been profiled, 40 percent of which are located in francophone countries. In the 1950s these scientific institutions would have been preponderantly university related; in this directory, however, only 19 percent derive from the university sector, and another 17 percent are private-sector institutions. As would be expected, the majority of the institutions are in the agricultural sciences (32 percent), the biological sciences (27 percent), the physical sciences (21 percent), and in the medical sciences (16 percent).

In broad terms, the senior African scientists resident in the region reflect these quantitative relations: 25 percent of the senior scientists are engaged in the agricultural sciences; 23 percent in the physical sciences; 15 percent in the biological sciences; and 14 percent in the medical sciences, as indicated in *Profiles of African Scientists* (1996). The institutions and the human capital are present; what is seldom available is the set of the four incentive factors referred to above.

Regional Perspectives and Concerns in the Physical Sciences

Nigeria

Nigeria's formal history of engagement in research in the physical sciences other than geology (which, as we have seen, started early in the twentieth century through colonial government fiat) is of very recent character, starting in the late 1940s and early 1950s with the establishment of the University of Ibadan. Even so, the federal research system in science and technology possesses a complex range of major fields of research endeavor covering geophysics (the oldest of the physical sciences in Nigeria), experimental solid state physics, radiobi-

ology and health physics, solar energy, space physics, radio astronomy, electronics, mathematical physics, theoretical plasma physics, theoretical nuclear physics, elementary particle physics, theory of general relativity, chemistry, and the earth sciences. Perhaps Nigeria's most productive prospects seen in a wider continental framework are in the fields of geophysics and natural products chemistry.

Research in physics is based mainly in the universities, as the nation's first National Physical Laboratory was only just coming into functional being in the mid-1990s at the newly built Sheda Science and Technology Complex, some eighty kilometers from the federal capital, Abuja, which also houses the National Chemical Laboratory and the National Biotechnology Laboratory, all advanced centers of research. Physics research formally began in Nigeria at the University of Ibadan in 1950, with an all-British staff, by initiating research in geophysics, an opportune choice, since Ibadan is only four degrees north of the magnetic equator. The initial research was given impetus by the acquisition of a Union Ionosonde on loan from the U.K. Department of Industrial Research, at Slough. This was followed in 1952–1960 by the initiation of a very active program of studies on the physics of the equatorial ionosphere (based on a geomagnetic observatory that was newly established at Ibadan), on geomagnetism, and on the equatorial electrojet. It was during this period that Olu Ibukun, an engineer-turned-physicist, became the first Nigerian to join the Department of Physics at Ibadan. Ibukun, in concert with a second Nigerian lecturer, D. F. Ojo, then initiated research on atmospheric radio noise. In the early 1960s a new field was added to the geophysical research portfolio of the department: research on atmospheric electricity, including lightning and the phenomena associated with tropical thunderstorms, employing various charge configurations.

From Ibadan, research and postgraduate training in geophysics has spread to other university campuses across the nation. Research in meteorology is flourishing at Ife. At Ahmadu Bello in Zaria, intense studies are being carried out on the "harmattan haze," a cold, dusty weather condition that prevails over most of Nigeria and neighboring countries between November and January and is attributed to the Sahara Desert–originated southwesterly winds. And as of the mid-1990s at Jos, Professor Deborah Enilo Ajakaiye was leading a vigorous research group taking gravity profiles across the geologically interesting parts of the country and mapping them out in detail, while carrying out combined airborne magnetic, electromagnetic, and radiometric measurements. Such surveys have led directly to the evaluation of mineral potentials of large areas of the country, often inaccessible at ground level, and to consultative arrangements with Nigeria-based mineral and oil-prospecting corporations.

Research in chemistry has developed in a similar way, with formal research starting at the University of Ibadan in 1948 by an all-British staff. Since 1960, many more Nigerians by far have taken postgraduate training and research in chemistry than in any other natural science.

The majority of Nigerian chemists work in the area of natural products chemistry, especially on indigenous tropical plant species with bioactive medicinal properties, in connection with terpenoids, alkaloids, heterocyclics, and aromatics. For instance, through such research, the folkloric anti–snake venom plant, *Schumanniophytum magnificum* (family Rubiaceae), has yielded a series of novel chromone alkaloids. Similarly, the chemical prospecting of the medicinal plant of the *Erythrophleum* species (family Rutaceae) has yielded an anesthetic with an intense local action, a cardiac-stimulating agent, and the characterization of an alkaloid, *couminque*.

South Africa

The profile and development of the physical sciences, including the earth sciences, in South Africa has taken a very different path from that in Nigeria, not least because of the two countries' differing geopolitical and cultural history in the last nine decades, their dissimilar economic development paths, their varied natural resource endowments, and their differing human capital profiles. Two fields of research of special interest are astronomy and astrophysics, and experimental nuclear physics. These fields are explored in other countries on the subcontinent, but not as intensely and with as much investment as in South Africa.

Astronomy in South Africa was initiated in the late nineteenth century and is a branch of the physical sciences in which South Africa has excelled, for three reasons. The first is the geographical position and climate of the country, the southernmost point of which is adjacent to Antarctica. Second, there has been heavy investment in observatory facilities for optical and infrared wavelengths (concentrated at the Sutherland site of the National Observatory, the South African Astronomical Observatory [SAAO], with the main library, workshop, and computer facilities at the SAAO headquarters in Cape Town), radio wavelengths (based mainly at the Hartebeesthoek Radio Astronomical Observatory, HartRAO, located in the Transvaal), and gamma ray wavelengths (concentrated at the Physics Department of the University of Potchefstroom, using a telescope array which detects the Cerenkov radiation generated by extraterrestrial gamma rays as they travel through the atmosphere). Third, investments have been procured for a small but strong school of astronomy.

Because of these factors, South African astronomers play an important collaborative role in international research in the southern hemisphere. Several examples of international collaboration can be given: the twenty-four-hour-a-day coverage of rapidly varying objects viewed with the "Whole Earth Telescope" project, of which SAAO is a part; the ongoing large-sky survey; the so-called Edinburgh-Cape blue-star survey, which involves specialized facilities in Scotland, South Africa, and Australia; and the project to obtain high-resolution radio images of quasars and similar objects through worldwide Very Long Baseline Interferometry (VLBI) work, in cooperation with Australia, the United States, Germany, and Russia. In-country astronomical research, as well as that undertaken under international cooperative arrangements, has added significantly to our knowledge of the universe, and on the practical side, it has also led to the development of very sensitive infrared detectors.

An ancient science, astronomy is often used to generate an understanding of science among the general public, and to establish a broad scientific culture in the country. In this context, however, it should be a matter of public concern that in their submission, the science and technology policy formulation mission prior to the launching of a democratic South Africa stated: "There is no objective guideline to suggest how much a country should spend on fundamental science. In the end, it is largely a political decision based on how much the country can afford" (*Building a New South Africa*, vol. 3, *Science and Technology* [1995]).

The pure science case for experimental nuclear physics in South Africa is more tenuous even than that of astronomy. The investment is heavy on facilities and annual research funding, obtained directly from Parliament. This investment roughly equals the whole budget of South Africa's Foundation for Research Development in support of university research in the natural sciences and engineering. South Africa's experimental nuclear physics is largely based at the National Accelerator Centre (NAC), located at Faure, near Cape Town, but cooperating with a smaller group at the Schonland Research Centre for Nuclear Sciences located at the University of the Witwatersrand. The Faure facility encompasses a separated sector cyclotron, which produces 200 MeV protons, and a new injector cyclotron, which enhances the capacity of the former with the provision of a wide range of heavy ions and polarized protons. Other research facilities include a 5.5 MeV pulsed van de Graaff (single-ended) accelerator at Faure (used for nuclear analysis in solid state physics and chemistry); a 2.5 MeV single-ended van de Graaff accelerator at the University of Pretoria (used exclusively for material science research); a tandem van de Graaff accelerator, with the capability of protons-to-heavy-ions production, at the Schonland Research Centre for Nuclear Sciences. The accelerator is used for nuclear physics heavy-ion research, including the pioneering development in that country of the scanning proton microprobe, scanning heavy-ion microprobe capability, and scanning transmission-ion microprobe, while also extending the tandem accelerator's capability to accelerator mass spectrometry, thus opening up the field of "minerals physics." Although the NAC and other nuclear physics facilities are well engineered, the question is seriously being raised whether the investment in these facilities should continue to be made.

Prospects for the Future

There is no doubt at all that, in reviewing the transformation of the natural and physical sciences in sub-Saharan Africa over the second half of the twentieth century, four to five decades after the onset of the movement toward political independence from colonial and apartheid governance, there is exuberance and vigor in the development of the natural sciences, despite debilitating economic setbacks of the 1980s and 1990s stemming from unpayable external debts, declining terms of trade, uncompetitiveness in the international marketplace, ethnic civil wars, and escalating brain drain. The challenge for the geopolitical and geo-economic leaders, and the science and technology community in the subcontinent, is to link research

and development to their vision for national development in the twenty-first century. The natural and physical sciences are the mother lode of technology, and sub-Saharan Africa must nurse them along, together with their practitioners, within an enabling environment for the sake of the development future of this subcontinent.

BIBLIOGRAPHY

African Academy of Sciences. *Profiles of African Scientists.* 3d ed. Nairobi, 1996.

African Academy of Sciences and Network of African Scientific Organizations. *Profiles of African Scientific Institutions.* Nairobi, 1992.

African Regional Postgraduate Programme in Insect Science, ARPPIS. *Proceedings of the International Conference on Capacity Building in Insect Science in Africa: Field Experience and Evaluation of the Impact of ARPPIS.* Nairobi, 1991.

Davidson, Basil. *The Search for Africa: A History in the Making.* London, 1994.

Demissen, Sebsebe, and Mesfin Tadesse. "Contributions of Systematic Botany to Different Disciplines: The Ethiopian Experience." In *Systematic Botany: A Key Science for Tropical Research and Documentation,* edited by Inga Hedberg. Uppsala, Sweden, 1988.

Ellis, George F. R. *Science Research Policy in South Africa: A Discussion Document.* Cape Town, 1994.

Hedberg, Inga, and Sue Edwards, eds. *Flora of Ethiopia.* Vol. 3, *Pittosparaseae to Araliaceae.* Addis Ababa, 1989.

Heywood, Vernon H. "Tropical Taxonomy: Who Are the Users?" In *Systemic Botany: A Key Science for Tropical Research and Documentation,* edited by Inga Hedberg. Uppsala, Sweden, 1988.

International Centre of Insect Physiology and Ecology. *Insect Science Education in Africa: The ICIPE Graduate School Model.* Nairobi, 1991.

International Development Research Centre. *Building a New South Africa.* Vol. 3, *Science and Technology Policy.* Ottawa, 1995.

Maduemezia, Awale, S. M. C. Okonkwo, and Ephraim E. Okon, eds. *Science Today in Nigeria.* Lagos, 1995.

Makhubu, Lydia P. "Women in Science: The Case of Africa." In *World Science Report, 1996.* Paris, 1996.

Odhiambo, Thomas R., and T. T. Isoun, eds. *Science for Development in Africa.* Nairobi, 1989.

Odhiambo, Thomas R. "Africa." In *World Science Report, 1993.* Paris, 1993.

Oliver, Roland. *The African Experience.* London, 1991.

Papon, Pierre, and Rémi Barré. "Science and Technology Systems: A Global Overview." In *World Science Report, 1996.* Paris, 1996.

Piel, Gerald. *Only One World: Our Own to Make and Keep.* New York, 1992.

World Bank. *World Development Report 1991: The Challenge of Development.* Oxford, 1991.

Worthington, E. B. *Science in the Development of Africa.* London, 1958.

THOMAS R. ODHIAMBO

See also **Ecology; Ecosystems; Education; Plants.**

SOCIAL SCIENCES

The social sciences, as generally understood in the academic world, include the following disciplines: anthropology, economics, geography, political science, and sociology. This entry provides an overview of the evolution of the social sciences in Africa, beginning in the colonial period. In so doing, this article looks at the major research orientations in the social sciences, the training of social scientists, the organization of the social sciences for research in and on Africa, and the interaction between social scientists in Africa and the United States.

Major Research Orientations

Social science research in Africa began in earnest in the period between World War I and World War II, when the social structures of African societies became an object of scholarly investigation among academics, U.S. foundations, and colonial administrators alike. Building on an intellectual tradition that had been established in the late nineteenth century by scholars such as Émile Durkheim, these anthropologists were interested in identifying what was universal about all of humankind and tracing the evolution of human society through its successive stages.

Research on the indigenous peoples of Africa initially involved scholars from the main colonizing powers, Britain and France, but other Europeans joined in as well. While much of the work done by French anthropologists was ethnographic in character and conducted for museums, it also included research on African thought, particularly on the meaning of ritual, myth, and symbol. Marcel Griaule's work on the Dogon people of Mali had special significance for the development of anthropological work in French-speaking countries, but it was British social anthropologists who dominated theory building in these early days of social science research in Africa. The influential "systems" model of society was created out of the African experience. This work was concentrated at the International African Institute in London (funded by the Rockefeller Foundation) and two leading anthropology departments: those at Oxford (under the leadership of A. R. Radcliffe-Brown, E. E. Evans-Pritchard, and Meyer Fortes) and the London

School of Economics (under Bronislaw Malinowski, Audrey I. Richards, and Lucy Mair). It had an impact not only within anthropology but also in neighboring disciplines such as political science. In their *African Political Systems,* published in 1940, Fortes and Evans-Pritchard divided African systems into two types, those with centralized systems of rule and those without, using a model of analysis that highlighted the universality of functions in human society. This structural-functional approach to the study of social and political phenomena was subsequently developed by sociologists such as Talcott Parsons. It formed the core of the modernization theory that Parsons and political scientists such as Gabriel A. Almond and Karl W. Deutsch helped develop in the 1950s. Less academically influential but still significant was the work of anthropologists directly employed by the Colonial Office in London, such as R. S. Rattray in Ghana.

While some anthropologists in the colonial days focused on supposedly isolated African precolonial societies, others concentrated their research on modernity and its impact on contemporary phenomena that fitted into the dominant structural-functionalist paradigm. Studies were conducted on social change, migration, and cities. One research question that became quite contentious in those days was how much of the "tribal" system African migrants took with them into town. How much of their old values survived in the new setting? How much gave way? This gave rise to two contending schools, one emphasizing the breakdown of African cultures, the other stressing the ability of African urban immigrants to adjust without giving up old customs. Work conducted at the Rhodes-Livingstone Institute in Northern Rhodesia (now Zambia) by Godfrey and Monica Wilson was influential in shaping the first approach, while that of Clyde Mitchell, A. L. Epstein, and Max Gluckman shaped the second. This debate subsequently carried over into the discipline of political science; scholars such as Crawford Young in the early 1960s demonstrated with research from Kinshasa, Zaire (the former Belgian Congo), that African urban immigrants were quite flexible in determining their identity, and that ethnicity, far from being "primordial," was determined by context and social competition. A state of disruption or anomie was not likely to be the outcome of Africans incorporating new and modern values into their existing worldviews.

Not all social anthropologists had connections with British or French colonial authorities—even when "indirect rule" was practiced—but anthropology became the subject of much controversy as African countries achieved political independence in the 1960s. Anthropologists were assumed to have been quiescent students of African societies in colonial days, and their emphasis on the integrity of African "tribes" was incongruent with the new emphasis on nationalism at the expense of such "tribal" identity. In the 1960s, therefore, anthropologists faded into the background, and the leading modernization paradigm was carried forward largely by political scientists and sociologists. Drawing their inspiration both from anthropology and new models in development economics that identified stages of economic growth, notably that of W. W. Rostow, much social science research was devoted to examining the key variables that determine a society's development. For example, leading political scientists such as Almond and James S. Coleman were interested in identifying how a range of social and economic variables such as education, socioeconomic status, media exposure, and residential location (urban or rural) were affecting political attitudes. Although many social scientists in the 1960s operated with other theoretical constructs, there was a remarkably broad agreement in those days that development of African societies was essentially a matter of replicating the "functional" aspects of modern Western societies while displacing the "traditional" aspects of African societies, a view shared by African ruling elites and many African nationalists. Using the structural-functionalist paradigm to conduct this broadly comparative work, the ultimate objective was the "scientific" goal of discovering social laws that would guide both future research and development policy.

Toward the end of the 1960s, it had become increasingly evident that development was a much more multifaceted and complex enterprise than modernization theory had assumed. Not only had social scientists failed in identifying scientific laws, but they had basically fallen short in making operational their theory in ways that facilitated empirical research on issues of practical or academic interest to scholars. Economists continued much of their research on how to stimulate economic growth using a demand-driven model, in which additional public resources provided through foreign aid played a key role and were relatively undisturbed by the increasing controversies surrounding structural-functionalism. The most significant changes, therefore, affected political science and

sociology, the two disciplines that had been in the forefront of that paradigm. Much of the criticism came from scholars drawing their inspiration from Marxist-Leninist thought, especially from those who studied the predominantly peasant societies of China, Cuba, and Russia after 1917, but the terms of this criticism did not fully reject structuralist concepts of the past. Two lines of research emerged in the late 1960s and early 1970s that tended to permeate all the disciplines. One was the introduction of class analysis. The modernization paradigm was accused of being ahistorical and overlooking the fact that development was not linear and non-conflictual but characterized by social stratification and conflicts between strata or classes in society. While British anthropologists and American political scientists had been particularly influential until then, it was French anthropologists of a Marxist persuasion that set the tone in undermining structural-functionalism. Georges Balandier was the intellectual mentor for many younger intellectuals such as Marc Auge, Claude Meillassoux, and Emmanuel Terray, who tried to demonstrate that precolonial societies in Africa were not stagnant but constantly undergoing transformation, and had the same self-reproductive features as class societies elsewhere in the world. One question that came to preoccupy this group was the extent to which an "African mode of production" existed. The writings of Cathérine Coquéry-Vidrovitch and Pierre Philippe Rey on this issue were influential in the debates that emerged in English-speaking countries.

The other line of research was in the field of international political economy, drawing from the work of Paul A. Baran and of the Latin American "dependency" scholars such as Andre Gunder Frank and Henrico Cardoso, as well as of Kwame Nkrumah, Ghana's first president. It perceived the dependency of African countries on the economies of the former colonizing powers as the major hurdle to development. While the focus in the modernization theory had been on development, this research focused on underdevelopment, conceived as the inevitable consequence of the export of primary products (such as minerals and agricultural produce), which enriched the industrial countries while reproducing inequalities and stagnation in the African "periphery." This approach had great influence on the production of knowledge in Africa, where the specter of neocolonialism found a quick breeding ground following the disappointments in the first decade of independence. Samir

Amin, an Egyptian economist (based at a United Nations think tank in Dakar, Senegal), Colin Leys, a British political scientist (working in Kenya), and Walter Rodney, a Guyanese economic historian (teaching in Dar es Salaam), were the most influential writers in this genre in the 1970s.

While much of the social science research in the 1960s and 1970s had been driven by the ambition to develop a "grand theory" for the explanation of a wide range of social and political phenomena, the approach that evolved in the 1980s was more responsive to what was increasingly being acknowledged as the great empirical diversity on the African continent. It was difficult, therefore, to pinpoint a single dominant theme that cut across most of the social sciences. One distinct focus during the 1980s that did have followers in several disciplines, however, concerned localization—events happening at the level of individuals, groups, and communities. This "micro" orientation was not totally new, but it began flourishing in the 1980s after research at the macro level reached its limits. It manifested itself in studies on the economic calculus of peasant households (such as those conducted by Goran Hyden and Keith Hart) and in the growing recognition of household economics in the discipline of economics grounded in rational choice theory. The latter presupposes that individuals engage in calculations of costs and benefits to maximize what is perceived as self-interest. This micro orientation provided the basis for rational choice applications in sectoral and macroeconomic behavior as illustrated in the work by Robert H. Bates. It also gave a new boost to anthropologists, who were able to demonstrate how individual behavior cannot be understood in isolation from local systems. Farming systems research, which brought agricultural economists, rural sociologists, and anthropologists together, is one example of this kind of applied research. In political science, this new orientation was becoming evident in more extensive research on peasants and on the informal aspects of politics; for example, the personalized nature of African politics. Another theme that began to receive greater scholarly interest in the 1980s was natural resource management and conservation. This was the first time that geographers could claim they were in the forefront of developing theory and methods. This set of issues cut across disciplinary boundaries and also brought social scientists in closer touch with natural scientists. Research bringing together both categories was becoming quite common, particularly in the

light of the agricultural decline that African countries experienced in the 1980s. Of less significance, but nevertheless important, was the emergence—and greater recognition—in the 1980s of demographic research in Africa. For a long time, demographic studies had been dominated by a small number of British and American scholars, but during the 1980s, as more and more Africans recognized that Africa's rapid population growth and extensive population migrations were serious problems, others, including African social scientists, began to focus on demographics. At least in part related to this kind of research was a growing interest in research by social scientists on public health issues.

Social science research in the 1990s continued along many of the lines started in the 1980s. For example, research on resource conservation was prominent and involved scholars from all disciplines. So were investigations focused on the informal economy. Although gender-based research also began in the 1980s, as far as Africa goes, it was only in the 1990s that it became a prominent part of the social sciences. The most significant new research focus in the 1990s was political reform. Driven by both domestic and international demands, most African governments have introduced reforms aimed at democratizing the political system. Much of this research has been led by political scientists, but it has its adherents also in other disciplines. For example, anthropologists have shared an interest in the development of "civil society," that aspect of social interaction that lies between the state and the individual and that is not focused on acquiring political power at the level of the state. Thus, at the close of the twentieth century the social science research agenda for Africa was varied and rich and generally compatible with research orientations in other regions of the world.

The Training of Social Scientists

In the post–World War II era, the training of U.S. social scientists interested in Africa took place at a number of universities throughout the country but was dominated by those institutions that received federal government funding, notably via the Title VI program of the U.S. Department of Education. The most important of these over the years have been Northwestern University, the University of Wisconsin, Indiana University, Michigan State University, and the University of California at Los Angeles. Somewhere in the range of five thousand

U.S. social scientists were trained at the doctoral level between 1960 and 1995 with anthropology, economics, and political science providing the largest contingents. The number of African Americans trained to teach social science subjects with an African focus has been small but in the 1990s was increasing. The number of graduate students with an interest in African issues continued to be high into the 1990s. It is no coincidence that the membership of the African Studies Association of the United States, where social scientists make up at least half the total, has been growing. In 1995 it was over twenty-five hundred individual members with about 90 percent being U.S.-based faculty and graduate students. With the job market saturated in the latter part of the 1990s, however, one cannot expect such growth to continue.

The African social science community has been trained largely in the United States through funding provided by private foundations, especially the Rockefeller and Ford Foundations, and by the Human Resources Development Program of the U.S. Agency for International Development. A smaller group was trained in the United Kingdom, France, Germany, Switzerland, Scandinavia, and Eastern Europe. Funding for such training was particularly generous in the 1960s and 1970s and it has since dwindled. Thandika Mkandawire, a prominent African social scientist, has identified three generations of African social scientists. The first is the "founding" generation, which was educated during the colonial era, and whose members followed quite closely in the footsteps of their intellectual mentors in the United States and Britain. They were responsible for taking over departments and colleges that had been run by expatriate scholars. It was often their research agendas that influenced incoming African students with an eye on an academic career. The second generation were those social scientists who were selected by the first and typically sent for overseas training in the 1970s while financial assistance was still relatively easy to come by. Upon their return to Africa, however, they typically found that due to higher costs of living, especially during the 1980s, it was difficult to realize one's professional ambition in Africa. Quite a number of the second generation, therefore, have left the social sciences altogether or have taken up jobs as faculty in universities in other countries, including the United States, Canada, Europe, or in international organizations. The third generation consists of those who have been trained in African institutions because they have been un-able to get full funding for graduate education overseas. These scholars have often been loyal to their home institutions in Africa. Because they have had less exposure to life and professional work outside Africa, they have been more adaptable than the second generation to inferior job conditions in African universities; they have also benefited in the 1990s from the modest amounts of aid supplied by national governments and foreign donors. This third group, however, is always on the lookout for opportunities to receive at least sabbatical leaves that allow them to engage in professional development. Such opportunities constitute important alternatives to the short-term consultancy work that often becomes the most important source of income available to supplement their academic salaries.

Social Science Organizations

The New York–based Social Science Research Council (SSRC) has over the years played a leading role in helping to shape the research agenda on area studies, including Africa. In the 1950s, for example, its Committee on Comparative Politics was the body for building theory and also for encouraging funding of research in countries outside the United States. It has continued to be a leader in respect to both these activities. Although its funding resources have always been limited in relation to demand, its fellowships have enjoyed great prestige in the social science community in the United States. The Ford and Rockefeller Foundations have been major funders of the SSRC programs. Another program that has been very important in promoting social science research in Africa is the Fulbright Exchange Program. Since its creation in 1946 it has supported some two thousand graduate students in the social sciences. Although it suffered budget cuts in the mid-1990s its fellowship program for graduate students still remains the single largest U.S. funding source for supporting graduate research in the social sciences outside the country.

The Council for the Development of Economic and Social Research in Africa (CODESRIA) is Africa's own principal research body in the social sciences. It was started in 1973 initially to serve as a coordinating body for directors of social science research centers in Africa. Two years later it adopted a wider mandate and gradually evolved into a pan-African network of social scientists in both English- and French-speaking countries. Its headquarters is in Dakar, Senegal. Through funding from a wide range of international sources,

CODESRIA has been able to encourage and sustain cross-national and interdisciplinary research on such themes as economic and political reforms and gender in development. CODESRIA collaborates closely with similar bodies in other parts of the world. It publishes the quarterly *CODESRIA Bulletin* and a journal titled *Africa Development*. It also manages its own publishing house.

The Organization for Social Science Research in Eastern Africa (OSSREA) is a subregional organization that brings together social scientists from eastern and southern Africa. Started in 1980, it is based in the Ethiopian capital of Addis Ababa. Although it has not been a leader in shaping the intellectual agenda in Africa in the same way as CODESRIA has, it has earned respect among social scientists and funders alike. In the mid-1990s, it was running three separate research competitions catering to a broad range of social scientists in eastern and southern Africa. It publishes its own newsletter and the *Eastern Africa Social Science Review.*

The African Economic Research Consortium (AERC) based in Nairobi came into existence in the latter part of the 1980s and has evolved into a major research and training program for African economists. It is generally regarded as a very successful effort in blending the two and in promoting cooperation among university institutions in various parts of Africa. Its own master's program is run on a regional basis with participating departments providing some courses and AERC providing the rest as students are pulled together for shorter-term intervals by the consortium.

In addition, there are other research bodies around the continent that cater to social scientists, although not exclusively so. One such organization is the West African Research Center in Dakar. There are also a number of private research and consultancy organizations in Africa, most of them national in scope. One organization that has attempted to work on a regional basis is the Southern African Political Economy Series (SAPES), a trust incorporated in Harare, Zimbabwe, with a focus on southern Africa.

Relations Between U.S. and African Social Scientists

Relations between American and African social scientists have always been close but often contentious. Because many African social scientists have been trained in the United States, they are familiar with the intellectual currents shaping the agenda among their American counterparts. The main difference in outlook has been on the question of commitment. Leading American social scientists have typically taken a professionally detached approach to the study of Africa, which has often made them the subject of criticism by their African colleagues. This divergence was particularly pronounced in the 1970s when the continent of Africa was still not fully liberated and many African social scientists embraced a Marxist approach to the study of socioeconomic and political phenomena. Although radicalism among African social scientists has largely subsided, it was an issue as late as the early 1990s, but as the debate between Mahmood Mamdani and Pearl Robinson at that time indicated, the difference between African and American social scientists today follows other lines. Because of the prominence of the issues of democratization in Africa, many controversies stem from interpreting this process and, in particular, the role played by outside agencies that financially support programs in this area. U.S. social scientists have also increasingly seen themselves having a role in explaining Africa to the American public at a time when most of the media coverage from Africa is very one-sidedly focused on the continent's failures.

Although it has become increasingly difficult to obtain funding for training of graduate students from Africa in the United States, and a relatively small number of American social scientists go to teach in Africa under the auspices of the Fulbright Exchange Program, many U.S.-based social scientists have regular contacts with African colleagues through joint research projects. Contacts with scholars in the United States have become important for African social scientists who for budgetary reasons typically have to work under conditions in their home universities that are far from congenial for professional development. Scholars on both sides recognize their interdependence, knowing that the production of knowledge with respect to the social sciences in Africa would be seriously hampered if these ties were broken.

BIBLIOGRAPHY

Bates, Robert H., V. Y. Mudimbe, and Jean O'Barr, eds. *Africa and the Disciplines: The Contributions of Research in Africa to the Social Sciences and Humanities.* Chicago, 1993.

Guyer, Jane. *African Studies in the United States: A Perspective.* Atlanta, Ga., 1996.

Heginbotham, Stanley J. "Rethinking International Scholarship: The Challenge of Transition from the

Cold War Era." *Items* (Social Science Research Council) 48, no. 2/3 (1994): 33–40.

Mamdani, Mahmood. "A Glimpse at African Studies, Made in U.S.A." *CODESRIA Bulletin* 2 (1990): 7–11.

Mkandawire, Thandika. "Problems and Prospects of Social Sciences in Africa." *International Social Science Journal* 45, no. 1 (1993): 129–140.

Robinson, Pearl. "On Paradigms and Political Silence." *CODESRIA Bulletin* 4 (1990): 7.

MICHAEL CHEGE
GORAN HYDEN

See also **Anthropology and the Study of Africa; Political Science and the Study of Africa.**

RESPONSIBILITIES OF AFRICANIST SCHOLARS

Africanists and development practitioners alike tend to perceive sub-Saharan Africa as a conundrum where, for some development workers, every good idea seems to have gone wrong. Representations of African predicaments on the global scene conjure up images of a continent torn apart by civil wars, epidemics, famines, uncontrolled urbanization, and a whole host of other socioeconomic and political pathologies. Intellectual and media constructions of the area suggest scenarios in which the continent might be drifting back to some "dark ages." The question is why several decades of development intervention in sub-Saharan Africa have failed to improve and enhance the quality of life and the life chances of most of the people on the continent. Why has the dominant neoclassical paradigm, based on the modernization theory, failed to produce the much talked about "development" for the continent?

This essay sketches out the different trajectories of development theories and praxis in sub-Saharan Africa. It questions the underlying linear approach inherent in modernization theory and its aspiration for some teleological outcome that is a finished product. It argues that the failure to situate culture and history in the processes of negotiating, accepting, and internalizing foreign notions of development could be responsible for the weakness in establishing development effectiveness. Due to the existence of institutional pluralism, the recurrent dichotomy between "traditional" and "modern" has emerged as a constraint and has been driving the development agenda. Development interventions aim at transforming traditional societies into modern nation-states. The essay notes the weakness of social science analysis and research to serve as a predictive science that informs policy making.

The explanatory power of social sciences has served as an analytical tool for working with such categories as ethnicity, tribalism, corruption, and pluralism. The complexity provided by these categories is sometimes held accountable for the failure of development intervention. The essay situates the responsibility of the African elite in the production of society. It also examines the extent to which civil society has been able to produce a counterdiscourse or a critique of the postcolonial state as the latter articulates its vision of society.

The dominant development paradigm assumes that economic growth is the basis of all development. This paradigm gave new impetus to modernization theories that were premised on the concept of social engineering. The core tenet of the social engineering approach was to formulate development planning in terms of transplants of Western institutions and products to the developing countries. This approach sought to fill the "objects gap" (the lack of modern technological inputs). Under conditions of induced development, the assumption was that the benefits of development would eventually trickle down from the progressive elite to the common people. As a result of oversimplification, it became more a question of identifying the progressive elites to serve as vectors of change. Social research has abundantly demonstrated the inadequacies of the trickle-down approach but has failed to change the trajectory of development intervention in sub-Saharan Africa.

From a historical perspective, the early days of colonial rule in sub-Saharan Africa sought to maintain law and order, finance the colonial enterprise, and pursue the civilizing of the "natives." According to Frederick Lugard, the chief architect of British indirect rule, social research was desirable when it served to resolve pressing concerns of administrators, educators, health and welfare workers, or traders working for the good of Africans. It is not surprising that a key function of research under colonial rule was to provide guidance to administrators for troubleshooting. The development of British structural-functionalism, with its emphasis on situational variations in behavior and processes of social conflict, is a case in point.

The critical factor in this approach was to use the social sciences to facilitate the diffusion of Western technology by overcoming resistance to change arising from traditional values and institutions. In the process, social analysis either became very normative (restatement of customary laws) or pursued village and area studies that had a limited policy formulation role. The anticipated output of these studies was to access and assess the validity of local norms, social structures, and practices.

In summary, early social science research fostered the goals of the colonial enterprise. Local knowledge systems and practices were carefully filtered, using "repugnancy clauses" as gatekeepers. The construction of development discourse has survived essentially as a missionary discourse.

The shift of focus to emphasize poverty reduction in the late 1960s coincided with the rise of neo-Marxist analyses in political economy. In a September 1973 speech, Robert McNamara drew attention to the existence of over 100 million families having tiny landholdings with conditions of cultivation too poor to contribute significantly to production. This "wake-up call" led to some adjustments in the approach to development intervention but no significant change in the underlying assumptions. The basic assumptions still called for the modernization of traditional societies and their incorporation into national and world economies.

The critical shift during this period was the movement away from filling the "objects gap" to one that sought to fill the "policy gap." Failures in development theory and praxis were attributed to weak institutional policies and capacity. Development economics identified market failures and attributed market distortions to state policies. Different scholarly analyses characterized the state as "predatory," "strong," "weak," "soft," or "overdeveloped" and tried to explain the stifling of civil society and markets. The bottom line of this neoliberal approach was to get the state off the back of civil society and to allow the "invisible hand" of the market to allocate scarce resources.

The inadequacies of growth and market models produced inequalities in the distribution of wealth. Social scientists contested the organizing powers of the market and demonstrated the role of culture in the "commodification" of things. When growth models were subjected to critical social analysis, it could easily be demonstrated why the anticipated outcomes could not be achieved due to cultural constructions of these concepts. Arjun Appadurai (ed., *The Social Life of Things: Commodities in Cultural Perspective* [1986]) characterized these cultural processes as the "social life of things." In the same vein, Igor Kopytoff ("The Cultural Biography of Things: Commoditization as Process," in *The Social Life of Things: Commodities in Cultural Perspective*, Appadurai, ed. [1986]) examined the cultural biography of things. The contributions of social research exposed the limits of the totalizing discourse of the market.

Even before these analyses demonstrated the limits of the market, international funding agencies, such as the World Bank, commissioned participatory poverty analyses (qualitative analyses that integrate the perceptions of the poor by different groups in society and what represents poverty in a given cultural context). These analyses mapped out the structural and endemic patterns of resource exclusion that create constraints leading to poverty. Other agencies, such as USAID, devised the New Directions mandate (1973–1975) integrating social analysis in project planning. The new direction sought a "social soundness analysis" of projects, a forerunner of the social assessment advocated by the World Bank. Its goals were

- To assess the relevance of local values, beliefs, and social structures to the technological package under consideration
- To promote cultural integration by fitting innovations into existing social patterns
- To get the impressions villagers and others have of their own circumstances
- To evaluate the impact of programs upon people and their way of life

This interest in social research was driven by the realization that development impact can be internalized if it is grounded in the culture and history of the people. With all these analyses, social research was still relegated to mitigating impacts in project implementation.

To what extent has the African elite contributed to the articulation of a development paradigm that responds to African predicaments? Antonio Gramsci, in *Selections from the Prison Notebooks* (1971), suggested that a viable civil society could emerge only when there are "organic intellectuals" with the capacity to articulate a counterdiscourse to that of the state. Rather than accept the state's vision of society uncritically, the organic intellectuals had the historic role to provide a counterdiscourse to that of the state, serving as a countervailing force to the state's excesses. Consequently, if numerous organizations and groups exist in civil society but lack the capacity to articulate a counterdiscourse to that of the state, that civil society would be considered underdeveloped.

If the organic intellectuals play a critical role in the conception of society, to what extent has the African elite provided an alternative vision to that of the state? A rapid overview of the contribution of Africanist scholars to development theories points to the following trends:

- Most of the critical literature is written by African scholars living in the diaspora or not living in their country of birth.
- Those home-based African scholars who contribute to the ongoing debates on development tend to focus on other countries.
- The few who engage in producing a counterdiscourse to that of the state are either co-opted to become state elite or are silenced. A classic African aphorism says it all: *la bouche qui mange ne parle pas* (the mouth that eats does not speak).

Although African responses to these development paradigms were forcefully stated by scholars such as Samir Amin ("Underdevelopment and Dependence in Black Africa: Origins and Contemporary Forms," *The Journal of Modern African Studies* 10, no. 4 [1972]) and Adebayo Adedeji, their impact on policy formulation in sub-Saharan Africa has been marginal. At the Economic Commission for Africa (ECA), Adebayo Adedeji was the driving force behind the Lagos Plan of Action, which was endorsed by the Organization of African Unity (OAU), yet it was never fully implemented by the member governments. The ECA further proposed an African alternative to the structural adjustment programs that has not been adopted by African policymakers. The agenda is still driven by foreign development assistance. The fact that International Monetary Fund–sponsored structural adjustment programs have not been debated in any of the parliaments in sub-Saharan Africa shows to what extent they have very little social legitimacy or a local constituency for their implementation.

Part of the problem arises from the weakness of civil society in most countries to hold political regimes accountable for the implementation of their development agendas. In some instances, a strong voice has emerged from ecclesiastical society, criticizing the regime in power for having institutionalized the "structures of sin." These counterdiscourses fade away when they are subsumed into ethnic or regional politics. This accounts for the fact that, unlike Latin America, a consistent exposition of the critical tenets of liberation theology has failed to emerge in sub-Saharan Africa.

It is not unusual that the concept of the common good seems to mean different things to public servants. The overriding goal of those seeking public office is to get access to and control over the common good. Jean-François Bayart (*L'État en Afrique:*

La Politique du ventre [1989]) has convincingly demonstrated that public office is perceived through metaphors of "belly politics" or "eating the state." Because the state is seen as a resource base, it is therefore not surprising that the participants in "belly politics" devise strategies that allow them to privatize the common good. In sub-Saharan Africa, the common good is a vanishing resource. The dominant institutional frameworks serve to legitimize the privatization of the common good. Under these predatory structures, the capture of power represents access to the common good. The consolidation of power defines membership in a strategic manner that highlights exclusionary principles weighted in terms of ethnicity and regionalism. Donor-driven reforms of policy frameworks, without the political will to implement a change agenda, do not produce results on the ground. The driving force is to use public office to accumulate resources.

The above analysis demonstrates how several decades of development intervention have failed to reduce poverty in any substantive manner in sub-Saharan Africa. First, the social engineering paradigm of neoclassical theories has not brought about the trickle-down effect of economic growth. Second, a weak civil society in most of sub-Saharan Africa has failed to challenge the policies of the state elite. Third, a weak institutional framework has failed to mold the leaders who are committed to an accountable management of the common good. Under these circumstances, is there a need for new development paradigm?

In the late 1980s, a group of Africans and Africanist scholars set out to search for a new development paradigm. They concluded that a new concept of modernization should be formulated from the vantage point of African predicaments. This yearning to capture the precariousness and instability of the human condition in sub-Saharan Africa is driven by a sense of hopelessness among Africanists and development practitioners. There is a pervasive sense of Africa's irrelevance in the emerging trends and processes of globalization. How can the Africans chart a new pathway that responds to the continent's predicaments? Do we really need a new paradigm?

A change of paradigm, without an enabling environment for development effectiveness, will not automatically put the continent on a trajectory of growth and improved quality of life. The constraints on a conducive environment are overwhelming but surmountable. First, there is need for visionary leadership to refocus institutions to be at the service of the people. Where such strong and committed leadership cannot be developed, development intervention should focus on strengthening existing institutions and developing new ones that are accountable to their users. This second step of setting an appropriate institutional framework should aim at producing a vibrant civil society that ensures the respect of constitutional rights and duties. The guiding principle should be to bring government to the doorsteps of the people. Third, the development community and bilateral donors must allow home-grown institutions and organizations to develop their own culture and legitimacy. Development impact can be sustainable only if it is internalized by the beneficiaries.

In summary, there must be a relocalization of the sources of political power and the mechanisms to ensure accountability. This will create an environment conducive to investment in institutions that will mold future leaders. With a vibrant civil society and strong institutions, a new development paradigm could then be articulated along the following conceptual lines: good governance, inclusive growth, and the sustainable management of the common good. This could be the framework for solving the African development conundrum.

BIBLIOGRAPHY

Adedeji, Adebayo, ed. *Africa Within the World: Beyond Dispossession and Dependence.* London, 1993.

Bates, Robert, V. Y. Mudimbe, and Jean O'Barr, eds. *Africa and the Disciplines: The Contributions of Research in Africa to the Social Sciences and Humanities.* Chicago, 1993.

Bayart, Jean-François. *L'État au Cameroun.* Paris, 1979.

Davidson, Basil. *The Black Man's Burden: Africa and the Curse of the Nation-State.* New York, 1992.

Dilley, Roy, ed. *Contesting Markets: Analyses of Ideology, Discourse, and Practice.* Edinburgh, 1992.

Escobar, Arturo. "Anthropology and the Development Encounter: The Making and Marketing of Development Anthropology." *American Ethnologist* 18, no. 4 (1991): 16–40.

Geschiere, Peter. "Chiefs and Colonial Rule in Cameroon: Inventing Chieftaincy, French and British Style." *Africa* 63, no. 2 (1993): 151–175.

Himmelstrand, Ulf, Kabiru Kinyanjui, and Edward Mburugu. *African Perspectives on Development: Controversies, Dilemmas, and Openings.* New York, 1994.

"Intellectuels africains." *Politique africaine,* no. 51 (1993).

Moore, Sally Falk. *Anthropology and Africa: Changing Perspectives on a Changing Scene.* Charlottesville, Va., 1994.

Robins, E. "The Strategy of Development and the Role of Anthropologist." In *Practicing Development Anthro-*

pology, edited by Edward C. Green. Boulder, Colo., 1986.

Werbner, Richard, "South Central Africa: The Manchester School and After." In *Localizing Strategies: Regional Traditions of Ethnographic Writing.* Edinburgh, 1990.

C. F. FISIY

See also **Anthropology and the Study of Africa; Development; History and the Study of Africa; Political Science and the Study of Africa.**

SCHOLARLY RESOURCES

Virtually all scholarly inquiry by historians into the past of sub-Saharan Africa has taken place since the 1950s. Before this, anthropologists and linguists, and to a lesser degree archaeologists, had touched on the matter incidentally as it happened to affect their own work, but there were few sustained efforts on the part of trained historians to bring the study of Africa into the larger historiographical enterprise. Beginning in the 1950s, however, the approach of independence brought with it the desire to provide the numerous incipient states with pasts that would justify their new status. As a result, historians trained in other fields began to retrain themselves and turn their attention to Africa. Soon they became the first crop of historians specifically imbued with an interest in Africa.

Thus, from the very beginning, in terms of the initial rationale behind the study of the past, Africa has emulated the course of historical study in other times and places. That is, the interest in the past was not entirely disinterestedly intellectual, but was part of a larger and more practical nationalist enterprise. From the very beginning as well, Africanist historians were in a hurry, and the resulting compression of the course of African historical studies into a very short period renders it peculiarly amenable to it being treated as a true microcosm of the ways in which the study of the past are usually organized and pursued.

Not surprisingly, while the body of evidence that has been used to study Africa's history resembles its counterparts in other fields of history, the ways in which its parts have been used have varied according to circumstances. In particular, the relatively late beginning of the study and the fact that both more and less evidence is available than for other areas of the world has created a set of historiographical norms that differ in important ways from those developed elsewhere and earlier.

Written Sources

Nevertheless, as elsewhere, written sources have typically been the predominant form of evidence that has been unearthed and studied. Such evidence for sub-Saharan Africa can be traced as far back as the *Periplus* of the Red Sea, which provided information about large parts of the east coast of Africa in the first century C.E. This early look at the area proved to be an aberration, however, and it was not until several centuries later that the Islamic conquest of northern Africa led to a more sustained interest in areas immediately to the south of the Sahara, the western Sudan.

Several centuries later again, the Europeans, first the Portuguese and then other nations, began to creep down the west coast of Africa and then up the east coast. Almost always their settlements hugged the coasts, but occasionally they spread inland along some rivers. The result was that snatches of information about the surrounding areas were recorded both in chronicles and in local records. Eyewitness accounts of events at these settlements were of course recorded, but regrettably, the former have proved more interesting to historians despite their necessarily hearsay character. Equally unfortunately, very little original material has survived from the Portuguese outposts, where the tenure of Europeans was longest.

Concurrent with these records were the reports of missionaries, who followed the secular authorities and often expanded their interests well beyond those areas accessible to civil administrations. As a consequence, missionary records are of especial importance, but they have yet to be extensively quarried, at least for the period before formal colonial rule, often because they were written in Latin and because access to religious archives tends to be more difficult, but also because of a mistaken impression that the missionaries confined themselves largely to doctrinal matters of only limited appeal.

With the imposition of formal colonial rule, usually late in the nineteenth century—and the exploration that preceded and succeeded it—the amount of written documentation increased manifold, although it often requires deft interpretation because of the persistent but unrecognized ignorance of the colonial authorities about so much in the societies they were attempting to govern. Withal, the body of written evidence for and from this period far surpasses the sum total of all other forms of written materials for previous periods and naturally has been that which historians have most extensively and intensively used, whether they are concerned with the colonial period proper or with its antecedents.

In dealing with this evidence, certain things need to be considered. Up to the late nineteenth century, almost all the available data could be classed as travel accounts, and to a lesser degree that remained true even through the colonial period. As a genre, travel accounts require special handling. They were written to appeal to a particular audience; were often seen through a triumphant Christian and Eurocentric (and, earlier, Islamic) optic, which tended to peculiarize and demean that with which it was not familiar; and competed with the genre of imaginary voyages. Inevitably, such accounts tended to produce information that was at once stereotyped, implausible, and woefully culture bound.

Using these sources critically requires more than separating the unlikely from the likely, or the obviously false from the possibly true. It requires as well a thorough understanding of what concepts of true and false meant at the time such accounts were produced and how this affected their tenor and content. Often, it also requires consulting many versions of the same text as it worked its way from travel notes to typescript to published version. These principles apply to both secular and religious writings, whose distortions were much more similar than different. It also requires other kinds of similarly elusive knowledge—for instance, about the expected audience for these works and the implications of this for their content. Many of them, for instance, were written to raise funds for exploration, conquest, or missionizing—all clear cases where it would have been tempting for authors to gild whatever lilies they were trying to germinate in the minds and purses of their readers. Many also were written in an atmosphere of controversy, as authors and nations competed for priority of discovery.

Another problem, more structural than cultural, that confronts historians is that, until at least the eighteenth century, unacknowledged and wholesale borrowing by one source from earlier ones was regarded not only as acceptable but as an esteemed hallmark of erudition. It often took several decades of using these materials before this antiquated notion became unavoidably apparent to modern historians. Recognizing it means that what was once considered corroborative written testimony is very often no more than the illusion created by this cultural trait manifesting itself over and over again.

Awareness of such characteristics has led to a more sustained interest in critically analyzing these sources rather than simply treating the evidence as unproblematic. But at the same time, this has meant that historians have recognized the need to be less sure about the reliability of their sources.

Archives

African historians have of course availed themselves of the numerous archives concerned with Africa in one degree or another. The variety of these is surprisingly great. Most important are formal governmental archives, whether housed in the former colonial nations or remaining in the former colonies. In addition to these, local and specialized archives—such as ecclesiastical, business, and educational depositories—exist in very large numbers and are beginning to be exploited to a greater degree. To facilitate this, an impressive number of archival guides has been published since the 1950s. An added advantage in using these kinds of materials is that with the passing of time, documents for the entire colonial period have become open in most archives.

Typically, a wide variety of information is to be found in such archival materials, so they have been heavily used by economic, social, and political historians of the colonial period because one of their advantages lies in the fact that they often present data in very raw form, allowing historians to reconfigure them to their own specifications. This is seldom the case for the large body of testimony in the archives on the precolonial past, testimony that was elicited by colonial authorities interested in arranging local administrative structures, who were intent on fitting the material to their own needs. Although the colonial authorities seem not to have realized it in many cases, local informants soon grasped the implications of the colonizers' objectives and often were able to turn the situation to their own advantage by offering precisely what they perceived that their new colonial rulers desired. Those who became most adept at this manipulation gained distinct advantages in the new colonial system, which only encouraged greater use of the practice.

A long-time source of particular importance for African historians is the very extensive body of anthropological or ethnographic literature that began to be formally compiled from the very moment that colonial administrations were in place. Here,

too, the purpose was largely to understand better what were thought to be the norms of the newly colonized societies, in order more effectively to bring them into the new administrative structures. Like archaeology, anthropology during the colonial period operated with certain, now largely outdated, premises in hand, particularly as they related to the origins of African states and other political entities.

This proved to be another case where the Africans who were being subjected to learned scrutiny were not loath to turn such investigation to advantage by learning to provide the same kinds of answers to anthropologists as to the civil authorities, regardless of whether they were true in any objective sense. This set of circumstances has imposed on historians who use these materials the onus of understanding their context and content thoroughly. Often this involves consulting missionary and local administrative materials for balance, as well as making recourse to surviving papers of the anthropologists who published such accounts in order to understand how they often went about their business as government agents rather than as disinterested scholars.

Oral Sources

Historians, not only of Africa but elsewhere, frequently have made use of written accounts without realizing that very often these were merely the last renditions of information that had been transmitted orally from one mouth—and one generation—to the next for unknown periods of time before being committed to writing. Nearly all the sources from early Christianity, early Islam, and the High Middle Ages, as well as from such places as India, Southeast Asia, and pre-Columbian America, fall squarely into this category. In few such cases have historians had the advantage of being able to discern this chain in being, and certainly not in process. One of the critical differentiating characteristics of African historiography has been that the creation and use of various kinds of oral data in Africa are far more susceptible than elsewhere to observation; therefore, its dynamics are more easily understood there.

Intensive collection of oral data by historians began in the late 1950s and peaked in the following two decades. During this time enormous amounts of material were collected in the field by interrogating informants and piecing together whatever information they provided with other oral data, with written records, and with whatever further relevant evidence seemed to exist. This massive collation was seen as—and indeed was—necessary if any substantial knowledge of most parts of Africa before, at the earliest, the mid-nineteenth century was to emerge. Many of the written sources had relied on such testimony, which of course was often noted approvingly by practitioners of oral historiography during these two decades.

Along the way a strong sense of corporate purpose developed among these practitioners and with it a sense of esprit de corps and distinctiveness, which served to encourage many oral historians to confer on the data they collected certain privileges and immunities that they would not have considered suitable for forms of historical evidence which they had not been personally responsible for creating. Therefore, unfortunately, these data have often failed to reach the public domain. The failure to deposit these materials at an early stage can be compared to the actions of archivists who refuse access to the materials under their control or of users of archives who are reluctant to identify their sources adequately. In this case, though, there is the crucial additional disadvantage that these materials were often in formats (e.g., audiotapes) that were too vulnerable to the passage of time to survive and to be made accessible for later use.

The effect is that a significant proportion of the writing on precolonial Africa that has appeared since the 1950s has been based on evidence that is now, and unnecessarily, unavailable. The recent crises in many African archives mean that large bodies of written documentation have been destroyed or scattered. Thus, in a period of less than forty years, an extraordinary amount of evidence has disappeared, which renders some Africanist historical scholarship dangerously exempt from attempts at refutation.

More than any other genre of evidence, oral data require special care in their production and interpretation. This need arises largely from the fact that historians are necessarily active participants in their creation rather than simply acting as interpreters and transmitters of an unchanging written record. The temptations and opportunities to influence unduly the orally derived record as it is being made, combined with the general inaccessibility of the results noted above, have combined to cast into doubt much of this work on grounds that it cannot be tested. On the other hand, the production of a large body of methodological litera-ture in response to the opportunities and challenges provided by this form of research has been one of the principal contributions of Africanist historical scholarship to the larger discipline. A majority of oral methodology research has emanated from Africanists and has been one of the primary ways in which they have influenced the field of history generally.

Archaeology

Archaeology was probably the first historical field in modern times to turn its attention seriously to Africa, since archaeological investigation began well before the end of the nineteenth century. The unfavorable combination of climate and building materials has meant that much less archaeological evidence is available in Africa than in many better-favored areas of the world. Even so, there are many spectacular remains scattered throughout the continent, and some of these, such as Great Zimbabwe in southern Africa and numerous sites in the western Sudan and the interlacustrine area, attracted attention early.

Initially, the interpretation of these sites and others tended to position itself firmly within the era's intellectual trends, with their racial biases. As a consequence of this and the unavailability of epigraphic evidence, the temptation was to impute these sites to various groups of immigrant outsiders. Since then, new techniques, such as radiocarbon dating, and an increasing realization that most of the putative exogenous builders never existed in the first place have transformed these views, so that it is now conventional wisdom that these sites developed locally in response to specific conditions and entirely on the basis of local technologies.

Likewise, the discovery of new sites, less spectacular in some ways but more suggestive in others, such as Igbo-Ukwu and Nok in Nigeria, has forced major reinterpretations of the character, antiquity, and spread of indigenous societies and skills within Africa south of the Sahara. Inevitably, the trend has been to show that more, and more varied and sophisticated, cultures developed earlier, and did so independently rather than as a result of radiating from one of two centers outside tropical Africa—or even within it.

One of the most important of these developments has been the archaeological discovery that iron metallurgy existed in Africa many centuries earlier than once supposed and in a number of local variations, suggesting that, whether or not the notion was invented only once, it was quickly and routinely adapted to local requirements. This discovery, in turn, combined with other evidence, has forced changes in earlier hypotheses as to the timing and directions of the spread of the Bantu languages, and the people speaking them, throughout central, southern, and eastern Africa.

Linguistics

This naturally brings us to consider another category of evidence, that which has developed from the study of the very numerous languages and language families in Africa. Work on this began very early, with the devising of dictionaries as far back as the sixteenth century by missionaries seeking to facilitate the spread of Christian doctrines. By the middle of the nineteenth century, the great Bantu language family had been discerned, if not yet quite delineated, and linguistic study has proceeded apace ever since.

The methodologies of historical linguistics are very specialized, and its principles and arguments are not easily absorbed by those not specially trained. As a result, historians of Africa have found themselves perpetually in thrall to the hypotheses that historical linguists have passed along to them. Sometimes these have been based on too superficial a study of an inadequate sample—at least as determined by later work. As a result, the conclusions of historians about the passages of language, and therefore—or so it is often held—of peoples and cultures, throughout Africa have undergone a surprising number of sea changes in a very short time. Taking into account recent experiences and proceeding more provisionally will mean that the work and conclusions of linguistics will continue to be of special importance in any attempts to discern the broader patterns that characterized Africa before either written or oral—or even archaeological—evidence kicks in.

The work of historians, as well as of linguists, benefits from the production of African-language dictionaries and grammars. Comparing word forms and definitions, for instance, from one ethnic group to another is a useful way to supplement and test other forms of evidence about origins and mutual relationships over time. The propensity to borrow words from other languages, including the languages of the colonizers, also raises interesting questions and provides insights into issues of social and economic relationships both before and during the colonial period.

Photographs and Films

Large collections of photographs relating to Africa taken during the colonial period have long existed, in public and private archives as well as in museums, but only since the 1980s has there been serious scholarly interest in colonial photography. Most of these collections have yet to be organized and studied, but such an effort is at present one of the primary objectives of Africanists in both anthropology and history. Such photographs not only depict the subjects, but also offer important insights on the cultural outlook of the colonial photographers, many of whom were Africans.

In like fashion, films from and about Africa are now being treated as historical sources as well as entertainment. In particular, those films that reach back to the beginning of the twentieth century, when they were produced for ethnographic and propaganda purposes, today are used to understand the cultural norms and activities that they preserved and the preferences of the audiences for which they were intended. Most Africanist films are of more recent vintage, but even these will eventually be used to trace historical aspects of the periods and places involved.

Ancillary Evidence

In other ways Africanist historians have innovatively sought ancillary evidence from disciplines that are seldom consulted by historians in other fields. For instance, both musicological and ethnobotanical evidence has been considered in attempts to understand better the ebb and flow of early African history. This approach has been required by the scantiness of "standard" lines of evidence; nonetheless, experience has shown clearly that, when practiced cautiously, such interdisciplinary work can have the particular value that comes when independent lines of investigation converge.

Conclusion

In less than a lifetime, the scholarly study of African history has progressed from being virtually nonexistent to a discipline supported by a vast and complex panoply of diverse resources. Although most of these existed by the 1950s, many of them, in particular the collections of oral testimony, are largely products of the period beginning then. This range of sources is not peculiarly different from those available in other fields of history, although the balance among them naturally differs because the nature of the evidence for African history makes it unlike that of other cultural areas, just as these areas differ among themselves.

At present there seems to be some inclination to regroup and to consider many of these sources, and their use, anew. Such reassessment is a common practice in the larger field of history; the difference is that there it has taken as long as several centuries, whereas in African history sometimes historians are looking at their own work from the vantage point of their later experience and that of other Africanists, whether historians or not.

BIBLIOGRAPHY

American Historical Association. *Guide to Historical Literature.* Edited by Mary Beth Norton. 3d ed. Vol. 1. New York, 1995.

Fage, J. D. *A Guide to Original Sources for Precolonial Western Africa Published in European Languages.* Rev. ed. Madison, Wis., 1994.

Heintze, Beatrix, and Adam Jones, eds. *European Sources for Sub-Saharan Africa Before 1900: Use and Abuse.* Stuttgart, Germany, 1987.

Henige, David. *Oral Historiography.* London, 1982.

International Council on Archives. *Guide to the Sources of the History of the Nations. B: Africa.* 8 vols. Zug, Switzerland, 1970–1983.

Jewsiewicki, Bogumil, and David S. Newbury, eds. *African Historiographies.* Beverly Hills, Calif., 1986.

Miller, Joseph C., ed. *The African Past Speaks.* Folkestone, U.K., 1980.

Neale, Caroline. *Writing "Independent" History: African Historiography, 1960–1980.* Westport, Conn., 1985.

Robertshaw, Peter, ed. *A History of African Archaeology.* London, 1990.

Shaw, Thurston, et al., eds. *The Archaeology of Africa: Foods, Metals, and Towns.* London, 1993.

Vansina, Jan. *Oral Tradition as History.* Madison, Wis., 1984.

DAVID HENIGE

See also **African Studies; Anthropology and the Study of Africa; Archaeology and Prehistory; Colonialism and Imperialism; History and the Study of Africa; Linguistics and the Study of Africa; Prehistory and the Study of Africa; Travel and Exploration.**

WESTERN RESEARCH AIMS
AND ACHIEVEMENTS

An African proverb says that "the stranger sees what he knows." The history of Western writing about Africa offers a poignant testimony to the truth of this proverb; it raises profound questions about how outsiders do and should go about understanding and dealing with societies they regard as exotic and alien.

The intellectual history of Western contact with Africa thus raises two kinds of questions, one about the sources and shaping of ideas, the other about the standards of validity we apply to such ideas. In what circumstances did the stranger see what he saw, and how far was what he knew relevant to what he saw?

Before the wave of independence in the late 1950s and 1960s, Western imagery of Africa had several common features, regardless of the ideological positions of the writers concerned. One was a tendency to regard African societies as products of their physical environment (including their climate), to a greater extent than would have been permissible in accounts of European societies. Western writers, impressed by the extremes they encountered in the continent, attributed a shaping force to this environment. The effect was to diminish both the creativity and the individuality of African societies; a physical stereotype gave rise to a human stereotype, "the African."

Consistent with this approach was a tendency to depict African societies as essentially passive. Such passivity might be regarded benignly as offering potential for spiritual uplift or other acts of improvement by outsiders, or it might be seen as a source of endless frustration. But in either case, the continent and its peoples were perceived as offering a clean slate.

The coming of independence naturally encouraged a revision of this intellectual legacy. It brought a desire to establish a cultural identity that was both distinctive from and yet comparable to that of the West. Building both upon anthropological work by European (and some American) scholars and upon oral and written sources that, if not new, were newly respected, historians established an African history that was recognizable to Westerners.

In light of the bolder theorizing that has taken hold of history since the late 1970s, some of this work may now seem pedestrian, reading like the orthodox Western narrative histories of kings and conquests. But arguably the very solidity of the work, with its careful use of sources and its circumspect judgments, may have served the cause of African emancipation better than some of the more speculative treatments that followed. Its methodology demanded respect on the part of Western scholars, and its emphasis on politics appealed to the preoccupation of African intellectuals with the meaning and dilemmas of statehood.

A minor mystery of Western research and scholarship in the period since independence concerns the apparent obliviousness of many social scientists to the spirit and implications of the work by historians of Africa. For many economists (including development economists) and political scientists, the notion of Africa as terra incognita still seemed not only credible but exciting. Much of the writing in these disciplines perpetuated, however implicitly, a view of African societies as malleable, as eager recipients of the used intellectual and political machinery of industrialized societies. The crudest simplifications about individuals and entire groups accompanied this approach, depending typically on such arbitrary dichotomies as that between "traditionalists" and "modernizers."

The apparent Afrophilia of most of those concerned did not prevent them from adopting a view that in effect denied the promise of independence, namely, to be different and to be complex and contradictory in one's own way. Afrophilia could also stifle the values and even the powers of observation of outsiders, leading them to see democracy where there was just an ideologically adroit and persuasive leader, and growth where there was just a great deal of emulative investment and a large ministry of planning.

The critics of the modernization school claimed that what Africa needed was an intellectual revolution to give meaning to an independence that sometimes seemed barely more than diplomatic. To them, Africa was a dependency in the broadest cultural as well as political and economic senses, and its liberation had to be a liberation of minds as well as a freeing from poverty. But this approach involved two problems: what would a "liberated" African social science look like, and how, given the all-encompassing character of dependency, could it be possible, both conceptually and politically?

In arguments about the proper priorities of the social sciences lurk some fundamental and perhaps irreconcilable sets of assumptions. On the one hand, there are "universalists," those who believe that the vocation (the values, concepts, and methods) of social inquiry is universal; the strength of this belief seems to correlate with the degree of intellectual self-confidence abroad in a discipline. Economists working in Africa seem, even now, to spend relatively little time worrying about the relevance of the theories they bring to bear on African problems.

On the other hand are the cultural relativists, whose spiritual home is in anthropology and whose working rule is, in the words of Melville J. Herskovits, never "[to] judge the modes of behavior one is describing, or seek to change them"

("Tender- and Tough-Minded Anthropology and the Study of Values in Culture," *Southwestern Journal of Anthropology* 7 [1951]: 24).

Affiliated with them (although much more aggressive) have been intellectual nationalists and socialists (such as the Nigerian Claude Ake), who condemn Western social science as "ethnocentric" and even "imperialist." As with dependency theory, the critique tends to strangle the solution. In anthropological theory "ethnocentrism" is universal, but it may be possible to step outside of inherited prejudices to achieve an appreciation of other cultures. This has, indeed, been the declared educational mission of many Western researchers, though they may have failed to pursue it in relation to their own discipline.

The prevailing critique of ethnocentrism, however, often seems to deny the possibility of such reaching out. It seems to clothe a positively nationalist claim that rejects the validity and the relevance of ideas and values primarily because they are foreign. In a sense, it rejects the "ethnocentrism" of others in order to embrace its own.

Such a position may be intelligible as an expression of the wish to achieve fully the potential of independence and as a reaction against some of the crasser behavior of Western social scientists in Africa, but it has the potential to be stifling and self-consuming. It offers a weapon to shame and silence critics by denouncing them as bearers of foreign concepts and values. Also, since in Africa, as elsewhere, "the nation" encompasses many other, smaller communities, the discrediting of ideas because of the origins of those expressing them can take on its own momentum. As the African political scientist L. Adele Jinadu has put it, "Is an Ewe-speaking political scientist not open to a possible charge of ethnocentrism by his Ashanti colleagues in his interpretation of political processes in Ashanti or even in other parts of Ghana for that matter?" ("Some Reflections on African Political Scientists and African Politics," *West African Journal of Sociology and Political Science* 1 [1978]: 242).

While the arguments briefly described above are as perennial and universal as the nationalism that inspires them, it is worth asking how much impact they have actually had on the research done by both Western and African scholars. Like attending church, they may have a profound, a shallow, or absolutely no impact on the professional lives of individuals.

It is certainly true that there is a pervasive liberal, "anti-ethnocentric" consensus among Western scholars and that "helping Africa" (whether or not Africa is disposed to accept that help) is a very general and public commitment of a kind not so conspicuous among, say, researchers working on Western Europe. The comparison may, indeed, reveal the persistence of the old Western habit of treating "Africa" and "the Africans" in an undifferentiated way and of regarding both as deserving but essentially passive recipients of the good ideas and good works of outsiders.

Indeed, it may be that the human miseries of the continent have worn down both the intellectual protectionism that was so vocally expressed in the 1970s in Africa itself and the inhibitions that outsiders felt about saying what the continent needed, whether in regard to political institutions or economic development. Not the critiquing of African scholars but the daily evidence of poverty and failure has convinced Western researchers that their work should be related to African realities.

BIBLIOGRAPHY

Ake, Claude. *Social Science as Imperialism: A Theory of Political Development*. Ibadan, Nigeria, 1979.

McCall, Daniel F. "American Anthropology and Africa." *African Studies Bulletin* 10 (1967): 20–34.

McKinley, Edward H. *The Lure of Africa: American Interest in Tropical Africa, 1919–1939*. Indianapolis, 1974.

Simpson, George Eaton. *Melville J. Herskovits*. New York, 1973.

Staniland, Martin. *American Intellectuals and African Nationalists, 1955–1970*. New Haven, 1991.

MARTIN STANILAND

See also **Anthropology and the Study of Africa; History and the Study of Africa; Philosophy and the Study of Africa.**

RESETTLEMENT. *See* **Peasants, Peasantries, and Land Settlement.**

RÉUNION

Geography

The island of Réunion, which has a perimeter of 208 kilometers (129 miles), lies 800 kilometers east of Madagascar. Réunion and the islands of Mauritius and Rodrigues to the east comprise the Mascarene Archipelago, a region of great natural beauty.

Volcanic activity in the west-central area ending in the Pliocene epoch (5.3 million to 1.6 million years ago) created three summits above 2,743 meters (9,050 ft.): Piton des Neiges, 3,069 meters

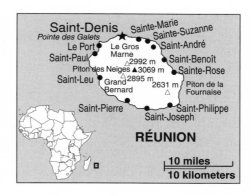

(10,128 ft.); Le Gros Morne, 2,992 meters (9,874 ft.); and Grand Bénard, 2,895 meters (9,554 ft.). The mountains are surrounded by three wide valleys, or cirques, drained by several rivers beginning in narrow gorges. To the southeast, the Piton de la Fournaise crater has been active several times since 1925.

Such topographic variation produces climatic differences and ecological variety. The rainy season lasts from November to April, and the dry season from May to October. The southeast trade winds, however, cause annual rainfall of 4,000 to 7,800 millimeters (160–315 in.) from April to October on the windward side of the island; the north and the west sides receive only 625 millimeters (25 in.) of rainfall in a year. While tropical conditions characterize the island to 760 meters (2,500 ft.), a cool climate exists above 1,500 meters (5,000 ft.). As its name indicates, the Piton des Neiges sees frequent snowfall. Forest originally covered much of the island and is now reduced to 35 percent; eucalyptus and rubber trees have been planted on cleared land.

People

The island was unsettled prior to the seventeenth century. The French flag was raised in 1638 and 1643; by 1664 the French East India Company had initiated a colonization plan. Fifty years later the population of over 1,000 persons was evenly divided between whites (French, Dutch, Italian, and English) and Africans. Soon, slaves were imported from Madagascar, India, and Africa (from both the African coast and the interior). After slavery was abolished in 1848, indentured laborers were brought from India, Malabar, China, Africa, and Annam. Considerable intermarrying caused a mixing of races. In 1996 Réunion had an estimated 679,198 inhabitants. Most of the population is descendant from slaves of African origin and includes Creoles, mulattoes, Chinese, Indians, blacks, and whites. The population is Creole-speaking (with French the official language) and predominantly Roman Catholic.

History

Réunion's political and economic history has been dominated by France. A concerted effort to develop the island began in the early eighteenth century, after B. F. Mahé de Labourdonnais, the governor of the Île de France and Île de Bourbon (Mauritius and Réunion), decided to use Bourbon as a naval base from which to conquer India. However, thereafter he favored Mauritius. Both islands became possessions of the king of France in 1767. The French exercised strong centralized control through an intendant-general based in Mauritius. Following the French Revolution Bourbon's name was changed to Réunion and a colonial assembly created. Measures were enacted but not enforced to grant the inhabitants of Réunion rights of French citizenry.

The nineteenth century began with Napoléon Bonaparte's rule, resulting in the restoration of the royal government system and the abolition of the colonial assembly. Réunion was taken by the British during the Anglo-French War in the Indian Ocean. The year 1811 saw a major slave revolt on Réunion, suppressed by the British; following the Treaty of Paris of 1814, the British returned the island to France. During the centuries of slavery, many runaway slaves led free lives in the mountainous regions while fighting plantation owners. By 1848 the French government had abolished slavery and permitted the colonies to elect deputies to the National Assembly through universal suffrage. Still, the white sugar-plantation owners

View of the Cirque (valley) de Mafate, Réunion. © GERALD CUBITT

dominated, even controlling ex-slaves through a requirement of possession of a *livret de travail* (proof of employment).

Economy

Réunion's economy has been dominated by one export crop, sugarcane, with the bulk of the sugar produced sent to France. Of the arable land surface (26 percent of the total), 70 percent is used for sugarcane cultivation. The crop prospered through the mid-nineteenth century and then met competition in beet sugar grown in France. Seventy-six percent of export earnings came from sugar in 1992. Production averaged 224,000–258,000 tons annually until 1987, dropped to 170,965 tons in 1989, and increased to 226,700 tons in 1992; in 1994–1995 sugar production was 177,355 tons. Although archaic land laws, aging plants, droughts, and tropical storms have hampered the industry's output, production since the 1980s has been undergirded by mechanization. Commerce is dominated by about ten sugar estates controlled by half as many sugar companies; mechanization and rising costs of imported fertilizers have caused bankruptcies among smaller sugar planters. Réunion also grows geranium and vetyver plants, which generate oils used in making perfumes, as well as vanilla; rum and molasses are also exported. Some 10 percent of the population is employed in agricultural labor; one-third that number (twenty thousand persons) find employment in manufacturing (six thousand in sugar processing). Because of its natural beauty, Réunion is a favored tourist site, particularly for the French.

Unemployment and poverty afflict the majority of the population. In 1991 unemployment was 37 percent. Housing conditions are poor, and many children are malnourished. Higher rates of mortality and parasitic infections are found in the lowland regions, where the darker-skinned populations live. Overpopulation has stimulated emigration, particularly to Madagascar and to France. The sugarcane crop encourages seasonal unemployment. Réunion has tried to diversify its economy, with some success in construction.

The French government provides welfare payments (to 75 percent of the population); family and wage support; and financing for housing, health care, and electricity. It controls inflation and covers the huge trade gap (in 1992, exports were only Fr 1.1 million, while imports were Fr 12.7 million). Réunion imports foodstuffs such as meat and rice, manufactured items including motor vehicles, and petroleum products. A five-year regional development plan for Réunion was implemented in 1994. Nearly half of the Fr 10 billion cost is to be met by the European Union.

Government

In the twentieth century, France and Réunion conducted their policy negotiations against the background of an independence movement. The people of Réunion have a heritage of opposition to foreign rule, demonstrated initially in the mountain resistance of runaway slaves. The momentum for self-determination is expressed in the late twentieth century through the Réunion Communist Party. While France does guarantee a market for sugar, many inhabitants of Réunion feel that they do not receive the social and welfare benefits that French citizens in France enjoy and chafe under the rule of a "mother country" primarily interested in the island for its own benefit.

Since 1946 Réunion, with Algeria, French Guiana, and the French West Indies, has been a French overseas department. Since the 1981 election of a Socialist president in France and the 1982 passage of a decentralization law, Réunion has tended to elect to its assembly and the French legislative bodies roughly half conservative seats (or parliamentary deputies) and half Communist, Socialist, and left-allied. Since the 1960s there have been periodic riots and unrest due to unemployment and inflation.

Political issues in the 1980s, sometimes involving demonstrations and strikes, stemmed from Réunion's demands for benefits parallel and equivalent to those received by French citizens in France: social security, an equitable minimum wage, and civil servant's privileges. Violent rioting was inflamed by the denial in 1990 by the French television authority of a license for a new television channel, Télé Free-DOM (a name linking the English word "freedom" with the acronym for Département d'outre-mer, or overseas department), associated with the radio station Radio Free-DOM, favored by Réunion's underprivileged.

Although in 1991 France's minister to overseas departments and territories announced sixty measures to help Réunion, these had little effect on a country suffering from 40 percent unemloyment in 1992. In 1996 Réunion celebrated fifty years as a French department.

Africa South of the Sahara
GEOPOLITICAL

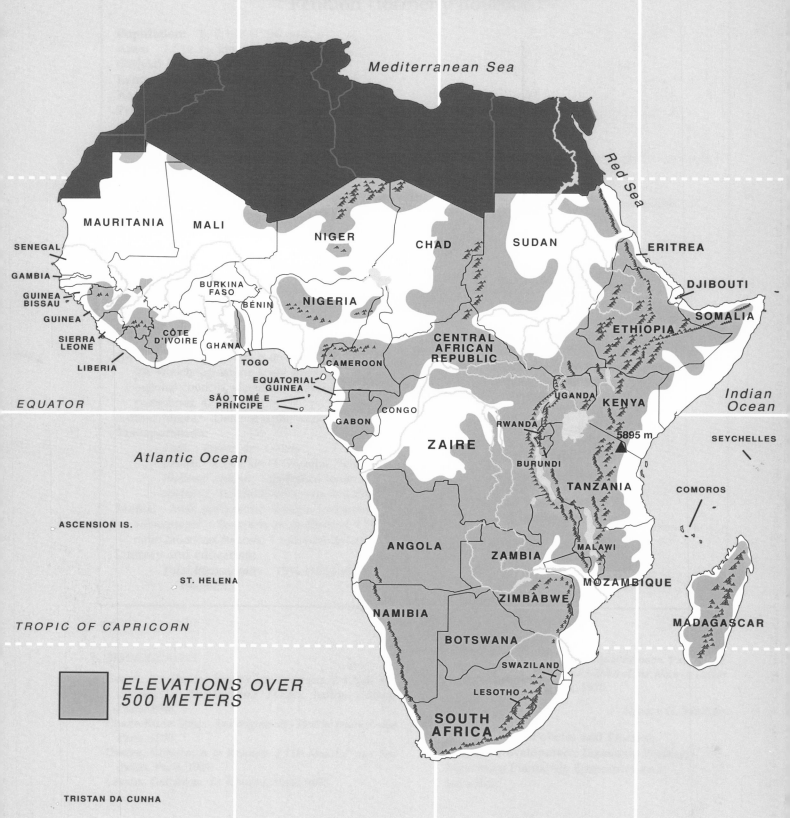

Mediterranean Sea

Red Sea

MAURITANIA   MALI   NIGER   CHAD   SUDAN   ERITREA

SENEGAL   DJIBOUTI

GAMBIA

GUINEA
BISSAU   BURKINA   BÉNIN   NIGERIA
              FASO

GUINEA   CENTRAL   SOMALIA

SIERRA   CÔTE   AFRICAN   ETHIOPIA
LEONE   D'IVOIRE   GHANA   REPUBLIC

LIBERIA   TOGO   CAMEROON

                EQUATORIAL-   UGANDA   KENYA   Indian
                GUINEA   Ocean
        SÃO TOMÉ E
        PRÍNCIPE   CONGO   RWANDA   5895 m   SEYCHELLES
EQUATOR
                          GABON   ZAIRE   BURUNDI

Atlantic Ocean   TANZANIA   COMOROS

ASCENSION IS.

                          ANGOLA   ZAMBIA   MALAWI

ST. HELENA   MOZAMBIQUE   MADAGASCAR

TROPIC OF CAPRICORN   NAMIBIA   ZIMBABWE

                          BOTSWANA   SWAZILAND

                                    LESOTHO

                          SOUTH
                          AFRICA

TRISTAN DA CUNHA

ELEVATIONS OVER
500 METERS

0°   20°   40°